GUSTAV MAHLER

GUSTAV MAHLER

VOLUME 2

VIENNA: THE YEARS OF CHALLENGE
(1897–1904)

HENRY-LOUIS DE LA GRANGE

Oxford   New York

OXFORD UNIVERSITY PRESS

1995

Oxford University Press, Walton Street, Oxford OX2 6DP
Oxford New York Toronto
Delhi Bombay Calcutta Madras Karachi
Kuala Lumpur Singapore Hong Kong Tokyo
Nairobi Dar es Salaam Cape Town
Melbourne Auckland Madrid
and associated companies in
Berlin Ibadan

Oxford is a trade mark of Oxford University Press

Published in the United States
by Oxford University Press Inc., New York
Originally published in 1983 by Librairie Arthème
Fayard, Paris, as Gustav Mahler: Vers la Gloire
1860–1900 and Gustav Mahler: l'âge d'or de Vienne
1900–1907

British Library Cataloguing in Publication Data
Data available

Library of Congress Cataloging in Publication Data
La Grange, Henry-Louis de, 1924–
[Gustav Mahler. English]
Gustav Mahler/Henry-Louis de La Grange,
p. cm.
Rev., enl., and updated translation of the French ed. published in
3 v.: Paris: Fayard, c1979–c1984.
Includes bibliographical references and index.
Contents:—v. 2. Vienna: the years of challenge (1897–1904)
1. Mahler, Gustav, 1860–1911 2. Composers—Austria—Biography.
I. Title.
ML410.M23L3413 1994 780'.92—dc20 [B] 94–18322
ISBN 0–19–315159–6 (v. 2: acid-free paper)

1 3 5 7 9 10 8 6 4 2

Typeset by Best-set Typesetter Ltd., Hong Kong
Printed in the United States of America

PREFACE

The first edition, in English, of Volume i of this book was published in England and the United States in 1973/4. In the twenty years since then, research into Mahler's life and works has continued unabated, significant new material has come to light, and important discoveries have been made by others and by myself. A much improved, corrected, updated, and expanded French version of my first volume was published in 1979. It was followed, in 1983 and 1984, by two other volumes in French, covering the complete span of Mahler's life and career.

Since 1984, I have felt I owed my English-speaking readers a complete, uncut English version of my book. The amount of work involved was considerable. In addition to the translation of the French text, the abundant quotations from original German sources had to be retranslated direct from that language to reduce the risk of error, newly discovered documents had to be incorporated, and due account had to be taken of the many studies and commentaries published in the interim.

The new English edition is to be in four volumes rather than three. Volume i will include the early years; Volume ii and iii the Vienna years; and Volume iv the New York years. Since many Mahlerians still have copies of the earlier English Volume i, my publisher and I decided to start the new edition with Volume ii (the first Vienna volume), then move on to Volumes iii and iv, and to publish the updated and revised Volume i last. The present volume therefore contains, in addition to analyses of Mahler's works composed (or completed) between 1897 and 1904, some of the appendices included in both the original English and French Volume i, i.e. a bibliography of most of the books mentioned or quoted in all the volumes.

In the bibliography, I have decided to include only the most important early articles written on Mahler, as well as all those written since 1984. The others are mentioned and identified in the footnotes in the various volumes, and most of them are summarized in three excellent reference works covering books, newspapers, and magazine articles: Bruno and Eleonore Vondenhoff's *Gustav Mahler Dokumentation*, published in 1978 (supplement in 1983);[1] Simon Michael Namenwirth's huge *Gustav Mahler: A Critical Bibliography* which appeared in 1987;[2] and Susan Filler's *Gustav and Alma Mahler: A Guide to Research* in 1989.[3] Of the recent books and articles, only those concerning the

---

[1] Hans Schneider, Tutzing, 1978 and 1983.
[2] Otto Harassowitz, Wiesbaden, 3 vols., 1987.
[3] Garland, New York and London, 1989.

years 1897 to 1904 of Mahler's life are included in the bibliography of this volume.

Some of my friends and readers have objected to my frequent and sometimes lengthy quotations from the press of Mahler's day. I continue to think I am right to include them. These quotations enable us to listen to contemporary voices giving us their immediate impressions of Mahler's personality and behaviour as conductor and opera-director. They also constitute a record of the reception given by critics and public to performances of Mahler's works. For me they are indispensable as the Greek chorus commenting on the contemporary comedy and tragedy being played before them. And of course those who are impatient to push on with the biographical chronicle can, if they wish, simply skip such passages.

ACKNOWLEDGEMENTS

I must thank the late Alma Mahler for the early interest she took in my work and the many documents she allowed me to examine in her New York house. As to Anna Mahler, her generous help, advice, suggestions, and above all her warm friendship deserve more gratitude that I can ever express in these brief lines.

Countless people have helped me prepare this volume and they all deserve heartfelt thanks. Among them, I must name the late Peter Riethus, for during the early years of my work he traced Mahler's movements around Europe and visited the various cities and countries in which Mahler lived and worked. To Donald Mitchell, I am indebted for his help, advice, and enlightened suggestions.

My thanks should also be extended to the translators with whom I worked since the late 1960s. Of these Johanna Harwood and Meredith Oakes, who translated a large part of this volume, deserve particular mention. Anne Mange performed the heroic task of entering the text into a computer and for this she can never be adequately thanked. Alena Parthonnaud contributed much by keeping my files in order and locating all the documents quoted in my text. Hedda Aflalo and Jutta Périsson also contributed to the enormous task of locating every original document. Patrick Lang was helpful in the insertion of new documents in the 1979–84 text; Marie-Joe Blavette for checking innumerable sources. Karin Sperr's contribution has been invaluable in my Viennese research during the 1960s and 1970s. Bernt Hage did some last-minute research. Edward R. Reilly was extremely helpful in preparing the catalogue of works and identifying the various known manuscripts. Knud Martner read the complete typescript of this volume and was helpful in correcting small errors.

Last but not least I am deeply indebted to my dear friends, Alice Frank and Roy MacDonald Stock, for generous help in bringing this volume to completion. Alice Frank has carefully revised all the translations from original German sources, and Roy MacDonald Stock has been her constant collaborator in this. He has also reread the entire text and made innumerable suggestions for improvements in style and presentation.

My thanks also go to the various libraries who sent me copies of material in their collections, among others the Österreichische Nationalbibliothek and the Stadtbibliothek in Vienna; the Pierpont Morgan Library and the Library of the Performing Arts of New York; the Van Pelt Library in the University of Pennsylvania in Philadelphia; the Jewish National and University Library of Jerusalem; and many others.

CONTENTS

LIST OF ILLUSTRATIONS

PLATES

(between pp. 300–301 and 620–621)

All photographs courtesy of the Bibliothèque musicale Gustav Mahler, Paris, unless otherwise indicated.

FIGURES

INACCESSIBLE SOURCES

The late scholar Hans Moldenhauer owned a highly valuable collection of Mahler documents, poems, autograph scores, letters (including those of Mahler to his wife). Most of them originally belonged to Alma Mahler and were sold after her death. Like the Rosé letters, these precious documents are presently inaccessible to researchers. Some measure of doubt even remains as to the exact contents of the collection.

ABBREVIATIONS

ABB   Anton Bruckner, *Gesammelte Briefe*, ed. Max Auer (Bosse, Regensburg, 1924).

AML   Alma Mahler, *Mein Leben* (Fischer, Frankfurt, 1960); *And the Bridge Is Love*, shortened English version, trans. E. B. Ashton. (Harcourt Brace, New York, 1958).

AMM1   Alma Mahler, *Gustav Mahler: Erinnerungen und Briefe* (Bermann Fischer, Vienna, 1949).

AMM2   Alma Mahler, *Gustav Mahler: Erinnerungen und Briefe* (Propyläen-Ullstein, Frankfurt, 1971).

AMM3   Alma Mahler, *Gustav Mahler: Memories and Letters*, English version, trans. Basil Creighton, ed. Donald Mitchell and Knud Martner (Sphere Books, London, 1990).

BDB   Kurt Blaukopf, *Mahler: Sein Leben, sein Werk und seine Welt in Zeitgenössischen Bildern und Texten* (Universal Edition, Vienna, 1976).

BME   Anna Bahr-Mildenburg, *Erinnerungen* (Wiener Literarische Anstalt, Vienna, 1921).

BMG   Ludwig Karpath, *Begegnung mit dem Genius* (Fiba, Vienna, 1934).

BMS   Paul Bekker, *Gustav Mahlers Symphonien* (Schuster & Loeffler, Berlin, 1921).

BSP   Paul Stefan (ed.), *Gustav Mahler: Ein Bild seiner Persönlichkeit in Widmungen* (Piper, Munich, 1910)

BWB   Bruno Walter, *Briefe 1894–1962* (Fischer, Frankfurt, 1969). Trans. supervised by Lotte Walter Lindt (Knopf, New York, 1959).

BWM   Bruno Walter, *Gustav Mahler* (Reichner, Vienna, 1936).

BWT   Bruno Walter, *Thema und Variationen* (Fischer, Berlin, 1950). *Theme and Variations*, trans. James A. Galston (Knopf, New York, 1946).

DMM1   Donald Mitchell, *Gustav Mahler: The Early Years* (Rockliff, London, 1958). 2nd edn., rev. by Paul Banks and David Matthews (Faber, London, 1980).

DMM2   Donald Mitchell, *Gustav Mahler: The Wunderhorn Years* (Faber, London, 1975).

DMM3   Donald Mitchell, *Gustav Mahler: Songs and Symphonies of Life and Death* (Faber, London 1985).

DNM   Dika Newlin, *Bruckner, Mahler and Schoenberg* (King's Crown, Morningside Heights, New York, 1947).

EDM   Ernst Decsey, *Musik war sein Leben: Lebenserinnerungen* (Deutsch, Vienna, 1962).

EDS   Ernst Decsey, *Stunden mit Mahler* (*Die Musik* (Gustav Mahler-Heft), 10: 18 and 21, Berlin, 1911).

ESM   Erwin Stein, 'Mahler and the Vienna Opera', in Harold Rosenthal (ed.), *The Opera Bedside Book* (Gollancz, London, 1965).

EON   Ernst Otto Nodnagel, *Jenseits von Wagner und Liszt* (Ostpreussische Druckerei, Königsberg, 1902).

EWL   Egon and Emmy Wellesz, *Egon Wellesz, Leben und Werk*, ed. Franz Endler
        (Zsolnay, Vienna, 1981).
FPM   Ferdinand Pfohl, *Gustav Mahler: Eindrücke und Erinnerungen aus den Ham-
        burger Jahren*, ed. Knud Martner (Musikalienhandlung, Hamburg, 1973).
GAB   August Göllerich, *Anton Bruckner: Ein Lebens- und Schaffens-Bild*, ed. and
        completed by Max Auer (9 vols., Bosse, Regensburg, 1936).
GAM   Guido Adler, *Gustav Mahler* (Universal Edition, Vienna, 1st edn., 1911; 2nd
        edn., 1916).
GEM   Gabriel Engel, *Gustav Mahler, Song Symphonist* (Bruckner Society of
        America, New York, 1932).
GWO   Max Graf, *Die Wiener Oper* (Humboldt, Vienna, 1955).
HHS   Hans Heinz Stuckenschmidt, *Schönberg: Leben, Umwelt, Werk* (Atlantis,
        Zurich, 1974).
HFR   Hans Ferdinand Redlich, *Bruckner and Mahler* (Dent, London, 1955).
HMW   Hans Moldenhauer, *Anton von Webern: A Chronicle of his Life and Work*
        (Gollancz, London, 1978).
JFP   Josef Bohuslav Förster, *Der Pilger* (Artia, Prague, 1955).
KIW   Julius Korngold, *Die Korngolds in Wien: Der Musikkritiker und das
        Wunderkind* (Musik & Theater, Zurich, 1991).
KMO   Karl Maria Klob, *Musik und Oper: Kritische Gänge* (Heinrich Kerler, Ulm,
        1953).
LEM   Max Graf, *Legende einer Musikstadt* (Österreichische Buchgemeinschaft,
        Vienna, 1949).
LKR   Liselotte Kitzwegerer, 'Alfred Roller als Bühnenbildner', Ph.D. thesis
        (Vienna, 1959).
LSM   Ludwig Schiedermair, *Gustav Mahler: Eine biographisch-kritische Würdigung*
        (Seemann Nachfolger, Leipzig, n.d. [1901]).
MAB   Max Auer, *Anton Bruckner: Sein Leben und Werk* (Musikwissenschaftlicher
        Verlag, Leipzig, 1941).
MAY   Zoltan Roman, *Gustav Mahler's American Years 1907–11* (Pendragon,
        Stuyvesant, New York, 1989).
MBR1   Gustav Mahler, *Briefe 1879–1911*, ed. Alma Mahler (Zsolnay, Vienna, 1924).
MBR2   Augmented and revised edn. of MBR1, ed. Herta Blaukopf (Zsolnay, Vienna-
        Hamburg, 1982).
MBRS   Gustav Mahler, *Unbekannte Briefe*, ed. Herta Blaukopf (Zsolnay, Vienna,
        1983).
MFM   Friends of Music, *Gustav Mahler: The Composer, the Conductor and the Man*,
        appreciations by distinguished contemporary musicians, publ. on the oc-
        casion of the first performance of Mahler's Eighth Symphony in New York, 9
        Apr. 1916.
MKB   Max Kalbeck, *Johannes Brahms* (8 vols. Deutsche Brahms Gesellschaft,
        Berlin, 1921).
MKW   Max Morold, *Wagners Kampf und Sieg* (2 vols. Amalthea, Zurich, 1930).
MMR   Max Mell, *Alfred Roller* (Wiener Literarische Anstalt, Vienna, 1922).
MSB   Gustav Mahler and Richard Strauss, *Briefwechsel 1888–1911*, ed. Herta
        Blaukopf (Piper Verlag, Munich, 1980).

NBL1 Natalie Bauer-Lechner, *Erinnerungen an Gustav Mahler*, ed. Johann Kilian (Tal, Leipzig, 1923).

NBL2 *Gustav Mahler, Erinnerungen von Natalie Bauer-Lechner*, ed. Herbert Killian, Anmerkungen und Erklärungen von Knud Martner (Wagner, Hamburg, 1984).

OKM Otto Klemperer, *Meine Erinnerungen an Gustav Mahler* (Atlantis, Zurich, 1960).

OR original.

PSE Paul Stefan, *Gustav Mahler's Erbe* (Weber, Munich, 1908).

PSG Paul Stefan, *Das Grab in Wien* (Reiss, Berlin, 1913).

PSM Paul Stefan, *Gustav Mahler* (Piper, Munich, 1st edn., 1910; 3nd edn., 1912).

RBM Alfred Roller, *Die Bildnisse von Gustav Mahler* (Tal, Leipzig, 1922).

RHM Theodor Reik, *The Haunting Melody* (Farrar, Strauss & Young, New York, 1953).

RMA Edward R. Reilly, *Gustav Mahler und Guido Adler: Zur Geschichte einer Freundschaft* (Universal Edition, Vienna, 1978). Engl. version: *Gustav Mahler and Guido Adler: Records of a Friendship* (Cambridge Univ. Press, Cambridge, 1982).

RMH Reeser Eduard, *Gustav Mahler und Holland: Briefe* (Universal Edition, Vienna, 1980).

RSM1 Richard Specht, *Gustav Mahler* (Gosse und Tetzlaff, Berlin, n.d. [1905]).

RSM2 Richard Specht, *Gustav Mahler* (1st edn., illustr., Schuster & Loeffler, Berlin, 1913).

RWM Arnold Schoenberg *et al.*, *Mahler* (Rainer Wunderlich, Leins, Tübingen, 1966).

SBE Richard Strauss, *Briefe an die Eltern* (Atlantis, Zurich, 1954).

SWE Paul Stauber, *Das wahre Erbe Mahlers* (Hubert & Lahme, Vienna, 1909).

SWO Richard Specht, *Das Wiener Operntheater: Erinnerung aus 50 Jahren* (Knepler, Vienna, 1919).

TAM Theodor Wiesengrund Adorno, *Gustav Mahler: Eine musikalische Physiognomik* (Suhrkamp, Frankfurt, 1960).

THE Theodor Helm, *Erinnerungen eines Musikkritikers*, ed. Max Schönherr (Verlag des Herausgebers, Vienna, 1977).

VKM Vladimir Karbusicky, *Gustav Mahler und seine Umwelt* (Wissenschaftliche Buchgesellschaft, Darmstadt, 1978).

WKL Wilhelm Kienzl, *Meine Lebenswanderung: Erlebtes und Erlauschtes* (Engelhorn, Stuttgart, 1926).

WLE Felix Weingartner, *Lebens-Erinnerungen* (2 vols. Orell Füssli, Zurich, 1928–9).

WMW Franz Willnauer, *Gustav Mahler und die Wiener Oper* (Jugend und Volk, Vienna, 1979).

WRE William Ritter, *Études d'Art étranger* (Mercure de France, Paris, 1906).

Additional reference abbreviations for libraries (see also catalogue of works)

HOA Österreichische Nationalbibliothek, Wien, Theatersammlung, Hofoper Archives.

SAG   Straussarchiv, Garmisch.
UPL   Van Pelt Library, Univ. of Pennsylvania, Philadelphia.

Reference abbreviations for unpublished sources

AMS   Alma Mahler, 'Ein Leben mit Gustav Mahler' (Manuscript, BGM).
AMT   Alma Mahler, Tagebuch (Manuscript, UPL).
KMI   Knud Martner, Personal communication to the author.
NBLS   Natalie Bauer-Lechner, *Mahleriana* (partly unpubl. manuscript, BGM).

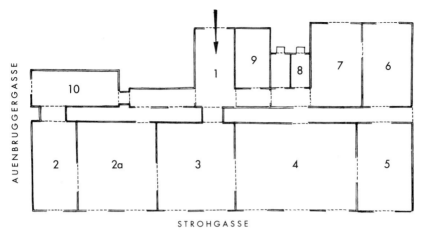

1. Entrance	4. Living room	8. W.C.
2. Mahler's bedroom	5. Alma	9. Bathroom
2a. Mahler's study	6. Children	10. Servant
3. Dining room	7. Kitchen	

Fig. 1. Mahler's apartment, Auenbruggergasse, 2

Fig. 2. Mahler's main itineraries from 1902 to 1907

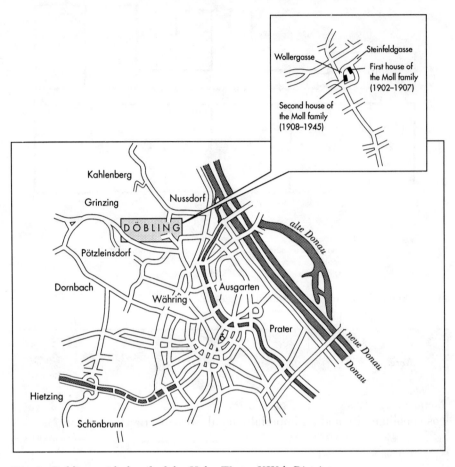

Fig. 3. Döbling, with detail of the Hohe Warte: XIXth District

Vienna and Viennese music—conditions at the Opera

(May–July 1897)

At last I have found a home!

MUCH has been written about Vienna, yet no one has been wholly success-ful in explaining the charm that has endeared the city to so many artists; no one has clearly defined the forces that attracted so many composers and for so long made it the musical capital of Europe. It is the meeting place for north and south, for east and west, for a rich profusion of widely different ethnic groups and influences, all of which have contributed to the unique and vigorous blend of Viennese culture. In 1900 Vienna already had a long history as a cosmopolitan city and an imperial capital, while Germany had only recently shaken off the last vestiges of medieval Kleinstaaterei to achieve unification. Vienna was both loved and hated, but its name was never mentioned without admiration and a touch of envy. Gustav Mahler, a provincial boy from a simple family background, had first encountered this enchanting world at the age of 15 and had never completely recovered from the shock of his discovery. It is easy therefore to imagine his secret pride when, now aged 36, he arrived in 1897 to take up a key position in the capital of Germanic music.

Much of the attraction of Vienna springs from its setting among some of the most beautiful landscapes in the world. Lying just south of the Danube, whose course at this point was diverted in the nineteenth century to protect the city from flooding, Vienna stretches across a plain whose borders rise toward the south and west. The suburbs spread gradually up these gentle slopes, as urban Vienna blends into the foothills of the Wienerwald, thickly covered woodland in which the light green of deciduous trees contrasts with the darker green of conifers. The 'Vienna woods' extend west of the capital as far as the Danube, where the heights of Kahlenberg and Leopoldsberg overlook the river. Beyond the gates of the city, as far as the eye can see, lies a calm, varied, and friendly landscape that, once seen, cannot be forgotten. The villages with their long, low, freshly whitewashed houses, bright roofs, latticed windows, flower-filled gardens, and spreading vines, are reminiscent of eighteenth-century engravings. West of the city, on the slopes of Heiligenstadt, Grinzing, and Nussdorf, the visitor can follow in the footsteps of Schubert and Beethoven, while in the rural creeper-covered taverns he can pause in the shade to taste the new wine, the *Heuriger*. The inhabitants of Vienna go there to escape from the urban bustle and to enjoy the popular orchestras, whose zithers, clarinets, accordions, and violins play the familiar *Schrammelmusik*.[1]

By the turn of the century, Vienna had become an impressive metropolis of two million people, in which the decadence of the empire was hidden beneath a façade of prosperity. During the greater part of the nineteenth century, when Germany was fragmented in a multitude of small states, and had no capital worthy of the name, Vienna was a cosmopolitan European city where Slavs, Germans, Hungarians, Spaniards, Italians, Frenchmen, Flemings, and Jews lived peaceably together. This mixture of nations and races, and the hospitable forum Vienna provided for all sorts of international occasions, gave the city character, atmosphere, and a role as the capital of Central Europe. Vienna was a catalyst, a melting-pot in which the most varied elements, cultures, and geniuses were blended and fused. In the Austrian empire, the industrial revolution had been accompanied by a huge increase in the population—37,700,000 in 1880 to 49,200,000 in 1910—with a corresponding rise in the number of industrial workers—539,000 in 1880 to 2,215,000 in 1902. The numbers of the ruling class and the bourgeoisie had of course also risen substantially and a sociological transformation resulted in a more permissive society, a more luxurious style of living, and a tremendous increase in the size of the musical and artistic public.

Thus, as a prosperous imperial capital, Vienna had long offered artists a field of activity infinitely richer and more varied than any of the German cities; this was why so many German nineteenth-century musicians, among them Beethoven and Brahms, settled there. At that time, life in the hospitable, luxurious, and sensual city was elegant and cultured, while in the German principalities it remained narrow, provincial, and crude. In Vienna, artistic talent was carefully nurtured, along with the arts of knowing how to please and how to converse, good taste, moderation, tolerance, and courtesy. Viennese politeness was legendary. Reference to social and professional rank and status was expressed, even in casual conversation, by forms of address such as *Herr* (or *Frau*) *Doktor*, *Herr* (or *Frau*) *Professor*, *Herr Kammersänger*, *Herr Opernsänger*, *Herr Hofrath*, *Herr Regierungsrath*, frequently interlarded with

[1] Johann Schrammel (1850–93) made his début in 1878, founding the Schrammel Quartet with his brother (a violinist like himself), a guitar player, and a clarinet player. In 1891 the clarinet was replaced by an accordion. The voluptuous, sensual strings of the Schrammel Quartet made it famous. They played in a Viennese restaurant much frequented by the royal family and the aristocracy, and toured the world with a repertoire of marches, waltzes, and popular Viennese songs, some of which Schrammel composed himself. Professional whistlers and yodellers were often soloists with the Schrammel Quartet.

more general courtesy titles like *wohlgeboren, euer Gnaden*, and *gnädige Frau*.[2] None the less, the amiability, permissive morality, and readiness to compromise concealed smouldering passions that could erupt—with fatal consequences, as Austria's readiness to adopt the Nazi ideology was later to prove. But until the turn of the century courtesy reigned supreme and tolerance was considered a moral obligation, even between sworn enemies; they insulted one another in writing but were polite to each other when they met.

One of the most striking aspects of Viennese life was the coffee-house, a centre of communication increasingly taking over from the salons of the aristocracy, a democratic club accessible to all for the modest price of a cup of coffee, where one could spend hours conversing, writing, or playing cards. It was normal practice among the bourgeoisie and government officials to spend part of each day in such an establishment discussing events, exchanging ideas and impressions, and—above all—engaging in intrigue, this being one of the less attractive characteristics of Viennese life. Regular customers had their own tables, their letters were sent direct to the café of their choice, and Viennese and foreign newspapers awaited them punctually. If one wanted to meet a particular journalist, businessman, or musician, it was enough to go on any day at the appropriate hour—usually in the evening—to the café he was known to frequent. Nobody was surprised to receive an important visit in a coffee-house. Some Viennese patronized the same establishment all their lives, and every day the waiters would prepare the same blend of coffee and hand them their messages, their newspapers, their correspondence. Many political decisions, some even of historic importance, were made in such places.

When Mahler reached Vienna, the Emperor Franz Joseph was 67 years old and had reigned for almost fifty years. Although he appears in the works of some chroniclers as a bureaucrat, devoid of humour and relatively narrow-minded, others who knew him personally have described him as a highly intelligent man with a surprisingly fine memory, an acute understanding of the way the Vienna establishment worked, and a sense of duty that kept him working late into the night. His liberal side has been emphasized, as well as his tolerant nature and his hatred of anti-Semitism.[3] In 1867 freedom of religion and conscience (the emancipation of the Jews) had been written into the constitution. Another proof of Franz Joseph's tolerance and open-mindedness was his support of modern trends in art; he subsidized the Secession, and later the Kunstschau. His acute critical judgement was allied to deep Christian faith, and some have seen in him the stabilizing element in an empire whose unity[4] depended, in principle, on a reactionary political philosophy and the

[2] Mr (or Mrs) Doctor; Mr (or Mrs) Chamber Singer (in Vienna, a wife bore the same title as her husband, even if he was a 'Chamber Singer', an honorary title accorded by the Austrian government to the most famous singers at the Opera); Mr (or Mrs) Opera Singer; Mr Court Counsellor; Mr Government Counsellor; Well-born; Your Grace; Gracious Lady.

[3] The Emperor once walked out of a theatre when the audience began chanting an anti-Semitic rhyme.

[4] It should be remembered that Austria-Hungary was at this time a multinational state, and that in 1866

state religion, Catholicism. The fact that the Emperor had none the less appointed a provincial Jew as the head of the most prominent cultural institution of the empire reveals an astonishingly liberal frame of mind. Thanks to the absence of anti-Semitism among the Habsburgs, and in Franz Joseph in particular, a seemingly happy symbiosis existed between the Austrians and the Jews, who played an essential part in the city's life and cultural activities if only because, as true cosmopolitans, they remained aloof from the smouldering quarrels caused by the diversity of nations in the Austrian empire.[5] The Jewish bourgeoisie had taken over a substantial part of the aristocracy's role as patrons of the arts and artists.[6] They had become part of the spirit of Vienna, and at the end of the nineteenth century were to produce a range of creative talent that included Mahler, Schoenberg, Goldmark, Freud, Schnitzler, and Max Reinhardt, as well as a group of innovative writers known as *Jung-Wien*.[7] In a city with such a rare gift for reconciling and uniting the most varied ideological, ethnic, and linguistic groups, the Jews lived and worked in peace, feeling themselves largely free from restraint and prejudice. Nevertheless, it must be said that an undercurrent of anti-Semitism was a permanent feature of Viennese life. Confined to a minority, it could in time of crisis surface and become vociferous in the press.

The exact size of Vienna's Jewish population is hard to ascertain because the more they prospered and became integrated with the Viennese bourgeoisie, the further they tended to move away from religious orthodoxy. Thus many Viennese Jews no longer belonged to the religious national tradition, which the assimilated upper class called 'un pieux souvenir de famille'. However, the difference between those who remained faithful and those who converted was by no means clear-cut. Sigmund Freud once commented that they all shared 'die gleiche seelische Konstruktion' (the same spiritual make-up).[8]

The most influential single factor in forming public opinion was undoubtedly the *Neue Freie Presse*. 'Read everyday by the educated bourgeoisie, high

the population of Austria itself comprised German-speakers (37%), Czechs (24%), Poles (17%), Ruthenians (13%), Slovenes (5%), and Italians (3%).

[5] See Nikolaus Vielmetti, 'Das Judentum im Zeitgenössichen Musikleben', in *Bruckner Symposium 1986: Bruckner, Liszt, Mahler und die Moderne* (Bruckner Institut, Linz, 1989).

[6] In the 18th cent. the Austrian aristocracy played an essential role in this respect. Maria Theresa had been Gluck's patron; Josef II, Mozart's. Ferdinand III, Leopold I, and Charles VI were all composers. Beethoven had several generous aristocratic patrons, but the willingness of the aristocracy to engage in and support cultural activity gradually declined thereafter.

[7] A group of young writers living by their pens, whose modernity, hated by many, was none the less funded, thanks to the liberalism of the Habsburgs, by a number of patrons. The group included writers such as Leopold Andrian, Richard Beer-Hofmann, Hugo von Hofmannsthal, Arthur Schnitzler, Hermann Bahr, and Felix Salten. All of them had had a solid classical education in Vienna's 'humanistische Gymnasien' (grammar schools). They were obsessed with death, symbol of the ephemeral, of evanescence, and decline; they united in rejecting the bourgeois values of the 19th cent., and advocated the frank discussion of social, psychological, and sexual problems. These writers were sometimes referred to as 'impressionists', cultivated 'art for art's sake', and adopted the concept of formal perfection as the supreme goal of literature. This earned them the scorn of Karl Kraus (see below), who published a ferocious attack on them in 1897.

[8] See Vielmetti, 'Das Judentum'.

society, senior civil servants and the leading authorities of the Monarchy':
'without the *Neue Freie Presse*, government in Austria would be impossible' as
a statesman one day remarked.[9] The paper was under Jewish ownership and
management and had for example stoutly defended the cause of Dreyfus. This
infuriated the strident anti-Semitic minority. As a matter of course, the anti-
Semitic press vigorously opposed Mahler's appointment to the Hofoper. Their
opposition abated somewhat in the first period after his appointment but did not
disappear and sometimes took particularly unpleasant forms. The financial
crisis in 1873 had sparked off the first wave of anti-Semitism. A far-reaching
consequence of the stock-market crash was the permeation of anti-Semitism
into Austrian politics. Jews were accused of being responsible for the speculative stock-market activities, even though official investigations proved that
many elements of the population, including some ministers and high aristocracy, had participated in the 'Gründungsfieber' and the attendant scandals. The
'Christlich-Social' party waxed indignant over the large areas of land belonging
to 'cosmopolitan financiers' rather than to 'national families'. When anti-
Semitism was finally organized into a party that became the forerunner of
Nazism, its supporters immediately suggested replacing the Christian calendar
by one that dated from the Battle of the Forest of Teutoburg, where Arminius,
leader of the Germanic tribes, defeated the Romans. The *Deutsche Zeitung* and
the *Deutsches Volksblatt*[10] never stopped attacking Mahler in ways and in terms
that later became typical of Nazi anti-Semitism.[11]

In 1879[12] the Ministerpräsident, Edward Count Taaffe, restricted Jewish
freedom and limited Jewish access to schools and universities. In 1897 one of
the leaders of the anti-Semitic party, Karl Lueger,[13] who was very popular
because of his great talent as a speaker, his striking stature, and his long blond
beard, was elected Mayor (Oberbürgermeister) of Vienna. He continued to
manage the city's affairs right up to the First World War and knew how to
exploit for his own ends the discontent of the embittered middle classes, as did
Hitler later. He can be said to have discovered the political expediency of 'anti-
Semitism'; by offering a scapegoat to the middle classes, he channelled their

[9] *Die Korngolds in Wien* (Musik und Theater, Zurich, 1991), 78 ff. (Hereafter referred to as KIW.)

[10] The *Deutsche Zeitung* sold only 15,000 copies in 1895 but its circulation decreased to 10,000 in 1905.
The pan-Germanic *Deutsches Volksblatt*, violently anti-Dreyfus, was then at the height of its popularity
(30,000 copies in 1900, 35,000 in 1910). Other tendencies represented in the Viennese press of the time
were the *Reichspost* (circulation 6,000 in 1900, 25,000 in 1905), which was Christian-Social; the *Arbeiter-
Zeitung* (24,000 in 1900, 54,000 in 1905), social-democratic; and the *Neue Freie Presse* (55,000 in 1900),
liberal-bourgeois, and with the *Fremden-Blatt* (c.60,000), an organ of the assimilationist Jewish bourgeoisie.
The *NFP* published many young Viennese writers, notably Hofmannsthal and Schnitzler in 1900, Salten in
1906; but it also published many hostile reviews of works by Hauptmann and Hofmannsthal.

[11] As early as 10 Apr. 1897, two days after the announcement of Mahler's appointment, the anti-Semitic
papers attacked the choice of a Jew for Kapellmeister at the Opera, when so many 'young men of talent' could
not find jobs, and Viennese art was already so completely monopolized by Jews.

[12] See above, Vol. i, Chap. 1.

[13] Karl Lueger (1844–1910), a lawyer and ardent anti-Semite, was one of the founders of the Christian
Social Party. He was elected Mayor of Vienna in 1897, after repeated refusals by the Emperor to confirm him
in that post. One of his best-known and oft-quoted remarks was: 'I myself decide who is a Jew and who isn't!'

hatred away from the large landowners and the still feudal aristocracy. None the less, he displayed a certain sense of justice in his handling of the city's affairs and, during his administration, no further restriction of Jewish civic rights took place. According to Stefan Zweig, in spite of the virulence of some extremists, the 'Jewish bourgeoisie', which contributed so much to Viennese culture, led a peaceful, quiet, and usually happy life.[14] As recently as 1899 there had been a notorious murder case which provoked a wave of anti-Semitism. In the town of Polna in Southern Bohemia a shoemaker's apprentice, Leopold Hilsner, was accused of having killed a 19-year-old seamstress in circumstances which pointed to a ritual motivation. A local court sentenced Hilsner to death. At a second trial in 1900 his sentence was commuted to life imprisonment. Coming as it did after the Dreyfus affair, this case was given wide press coverage and Jews throughout Central Europe felt threatened.

In the colourful and varied panorama of Viennese intellectual life the personality of Karl Kraus (1874–1936) stood out like a monolith. The prolific and all-invasive journalist, a brilliant polemicist, did not fit in with any contemporary tendencies or parties, artistic or political. In 1897 he published in the *Wiener Rundschau* a fierce lampoon of *Jung-Wien* writers. In 1899 he founded the satirical review *Die Fackel* (The Torch), soon becoming, and for thirty years remaining, its only contributor and thus gradually compiling a striking chronicle of his times and an eloquent reflection of his acerbic character, contradictory in its intransigence. The anti-Semitic outpourings of Kraus, himself a Jew, typified the strange, tragic phenomenon, quite widespread in his day, of *jüdischer Selbsthass* (Jewish self-hate: the term is Theodor Lessing's). In 1898 he attacked the dawning Zionist movement as 'creating a new ghetto'. He attacked Theodor Herzl's Zionist theories as utopian, and opted for assimilation and against the particularization of Jews. During the Dreyfus case, *Die Fackel* carried on a veritable anti-Dreyfus campaign, mercilessly ridiculing the *Neue Freie Presse* and its defence of Dreyfus. Kraus went so far as to accuse the Jews themselves of being responsible for anti-Semitism. Converted to Catholicism in 1911, he persisted in an increasingly virulent anti-Semitic attitude, despite the rise of Nazism in the 1920s.[15]

Attempts at a defence against anti-Semitism were already being made. The *Österreichische-Israelitische Union* was founded in 1880. This organization, favouring co-operation with the liberals and seeking to establish the identity and recognition of one Jewish nation, can be regarded as one of the earliest sources of the Zionist movement that Theodor Herzl[16] led from 1902, and which

---

[14] Stefan Zweig, *Die Welt von Gestern* (Fischer, Frankfurt, 1970), 17.

[15] cf. Jacques Le Rider, 'Karl Kraus ou l'identité juive déchirée', in François Latraverse and Walter Moser, *Vienne au tournant du siècle* (Albin Michel, Paris, 1988), 103 ff.

[16] Born in Budapest into a rich Jewish family the same year as Mahler (1860), Theodor Herzl belonged to the majority of Viennese Jews whose ideal was assimilation. However, he became the Paris correspondent for the *Neue Freie Presse* and as such reported on Dreyfus's trial and ceremonial degradation in the courtyard of the Invalides. From then on he became obsessed with anti-Semitism and the 'Jewish Question'. Thus he

at that time had the support of between 25 per cent and 45 per cent of the Jewish population.

From the mid-eighteenth century onwards Frederick the Great's combination of diplomacy and military successes began to bring about the decline of Austria as a political power in Europe and the concomitant rise of Prussia to a dominant position among the German states.[17] The Austrian decline was partly concealed by Vienna's prosperity and the brilliance of its culture, particularly in the field of music. By the beginning of the twentieth century, as the political difficulties became insoluble for a government that lacked both efficiency and vitality, Viennese society displayed a curious combination of hedonism and pessimism which gave rise to an amused, blasé, and often morbid scepticism. The Austrian state of mind was well summed up in the witticism that went the rounds at the end of the First World War which solemnly affirmed that the situation for the Germans was 'serious but not desperate' while for the Austrians it was 'desperate but not serious'.

In Vienna, where correct behaviour and good manners were considered essential, to be young was to be suspect. Respectability was epitomized, wrote Zweig, by 'serious, ponderous, slow-moving men': 'My father, my uncle, my professor, the salesmen in the shops . . . and the musicians behind their desks of the Philharmonic were, at forty, portly and "imposing" men.'[18] Beards and grey hair were considered the attributes of dignity, and any manifestation of high spirits was thought unseemly. Bourgeois society above all appreciated moderation and calm, and no one ever gave the impression of being in a hurry. For all posts which called for a sense of responsibility, age was considered one of the essential qualifications. Vienna, unlike Berlin, a newer capital, worshipped its past and treated anything new with prudence and reserve if not hostility. In two short years in Berlin, the Vienna-born Max Reinhardt attained a status that would have taken him at least twenty years to achieve in his native town. So most of the Viennese reacted with a mixture of surprise and indignation to the appointment of a 38-year-old Jew to head their Opera, and this stubborn conservatism was something Mahler always had to contend with.

The essential problem for Viennese creative artists, then, was to reconcile their cosmopolitan tendencies, their easy life, and the destructive cynicism of a people conscious of its political decline, with the passion, stubbornness, and intransigence essential for any important artistic work. The political decline of Vienna and the Austrian empire increased the Viennese taste for culture in general and for music in particular. Since the Austrian monarchy had aban-

---

conceived the idea of a lay Jewish nation built on the model of the modern western states. It was to be a purely political institution for, like many Viennese Jews, Herzl had no strong feeling for the Jewish historical and religious traditions. This is the main reason why he was opposed by many within his own Zionist movement. The rise of anti-Semitism in Austrian politics, after Mayor Lueger's election on 20 Apr. 1897, resulted in the founding of the Zionist weekly paper *Die Welt* which began to appear in June of the same year. During the first Zionist Congress, in Basel in Aug., Herzl was elected president of the Zionist movement.

[17] See Vol. i, Chap. 1.   [18] Zweig, *Die Welt von Gestern*, 11.

doned most of its political ambitions and had lost face on the battlefield, the patriotic pride of the Emperor's subjects took the form of a strong desire for artistic supremacy. Military and political affairs no longer played a preponderant part in the life of either individuals or society. The average Viennese citizen, on opening his paper, would first look not for the account of parliamentary sessions or the reports on world affairs, but for the theatre news. The Chairman of the City Council or the richest banker in the capital might well walk down the street unnoticed, but all the salesgirls and coach-drivers would immediately recognize a famous actor from the Burgtheater or a prima donna from the Opera. In the schools, pupils boasted of such encounters with pride: these well-known personalities were in a sense the collective property of the Viennese, and this fanatical cult of the arts was common to almost all classes of society. The citizens greatly valued concert-halls, theatres, and other places devoted to the arts. When, for example, the Rosé Quartet gave a concert to mark the closing of the Bösendorfer Saal, the members of the audience were still in their seats, sobbing bitterly, an hour after the music had stopped, and some remained even after the lights had been turned out.[19]

Wherever one went in Vienna, people were ready to discuss the Burgtheater, or the Opera. Portraits of leading actors were displayed in all the shop-windows, and the day before an important première at the Opera young college students would play truant and queue for hours to obtain tickets to stand. Stefan Zweig tells us that he showered a boy of humble parentage with presents because, since his uncle was in charge of the lighting at the Opera, he could smuggle Zweig on-stage during rehearsals. There Zweig would 'tremble like Dante rising into the sacred spheres of Paradise'.[20] This Viennese love of spectacle has often been mocked, for it even extended to funerals, marriages, and other manifestations of public life. But such theatre made for amazing quality in operatic and theatrical performance: the audience were so well informed that they noticed every fault, every missed cue, and any cut, however small. Artists were constantly obliged to give of their best; there was no margin for error.

Music and opera had been at the centre of Viennese artistic life for almost two centuries, and the violence of the passions Mahler roused during his years there would have been unthinkable elsewhere. Indeed, music still has real power in Austria, and national vanity is particularly susceptible on this point. The Austrians are justifiably proud of their artists and their musical life. For ten years Mahler's prestige and fame were commensurate with those of the Vienna Opera. Attacked, insulted, incessantly vilified, he was none the less

---

[19] The Viennese infatuation with music and the arts, and with the more popular forms of social activity (dancing the waltz and the polka), might be seen as a form of escapism. Life in the city was not all luxury and brilliant refinement. The nascent social-democratic movement found fertile ground in working-class poverty. Strikes were so frequent that they gave the capital a bad name within the Austro-Hungarian empire.

[20] Zweig, *Die Welt von Gestern*, 42.

one of Austria's national glories, one of the outstanding personalities in the world of European music. Despite the tradition established by Haydn, Mozart, and Beethoven, and although symphonic music became, through them, a specifically Viennese art, opera had reigned supreme in Vienna throughout the nineteenth century. The foremost position in the operatic hierarchy fell to the Kärntnerthortheater, which had been taken over by the Court Opera (Hofoper) at the beginning of the century. German operas naturally occupied an important place in the repertoire with a number of important premières, notably Weber's *Oberon* in 1829, conducted by the Swabian Kapellmeister Conradin Kreutzer, who ran the theatre from 1822 to 1832. But French opera was also well represented early in the century by works of Auber, Boïeldieu, Hérold, and Adam. In 1833 Giacomo Meyerbeer scored a triumph with *Robert le Diable*, thus opening the way for French 'grand opera' in the Austrian capital.

But at the Kärntnerthor, as elsewhere, it was Italian opera that remained supreme. All Rossini's major works reached Vienna before 1825, with the exception of *William Tell*, first performed there in 1830. Bellini made his appearance in 1828 with *Il pirata*, followed by *I Montecchi* (1832) and *La sonnambula* (1835). In 1827 Donizetti was introduced, modestly to be sure, with *L'ajo nell'imbarazzo*. But then came *L'elisir d'amore* (1835), *Lucia* (1837), and *Lucrezia Borgia* (1839). Under the two Italian administrators Balochino and Merelli, half the new productions were Italian, including no fewer than twenty operas by Donizetti who was the star of the day, but works by Saverio Mercadante, Federico Ricci, Pietro Antonio Coppola, Gaetano Rossi were also performed. This double directorate divided its seasons in two, German from July to March, Italian from April to June. Mid-nineteenth-century conventional morality was a powerful force, and in deference to it the German version of *Così fan tutte* from 1840 onwards bore the title *Mädchentreue* (Maidenly Fidelity), with the two girls aware from the start that their lovers were playing a trick on them.

The Prussian Otto Nicolai, engaged at the Kärntnerthor for the 1837–8 season, was quickly promoted to first Kapellmeister of the Hofoper when his opera *Il templario*, sung in German with the title *Der Tempelritter*, received its Viennese première in 1841. His first production, *Fidelio* (with the *Leonore* No. 3 Overture played in the middle of the last act), created a sensation because of the unprecedented dedication he brought to his task. Incensed by the rejection of his own German opera *Die lustigen Weiber von Windsor*, which posterity has recognized as his masterpiece, Nicolai resigned in 1847 and, already unwell, went to Berlin, where he died shortly afterwards.

During the years leading up to the 1848–9 revolution, the 'Vormärz' ('pre-March') period as the Austrians called it, enthusiasm for opera grew to such proportions in Vienna that it spread to other theatres. The Theater an der Wien, the biggest, was run from 1845 by Franz Pokorny, who over three years staged about fifteen major operas by Bellini, Donizetti, Auber, Hérold, and Adam, as well as Weber's *Der Freischütz* and Mozart's *Don Giovanni*. Pokorny's master-stroke, in January 1846, was *Zar und Zimmermann* (The Tsar and the Car-penter), one of the finest works by the Berlin composer Albert Lortzing (1801–51).[21] Lortzing, engaged as Kapellmeister for two years by Pokorny, quickly became disenchanted: 'Musical taste [in Vienna] is the worst possible. . . . There is nothing but Italian music here, or else what resembles it. Even Beethoven is unknown.' Lortzing's own works gradually disappeared from the Viennese repertoire; he encountered serious difficulties with his undisci-plined orchestra; and in 1848 his contract was not renewed. He died in poverty three years later in Berlin.

The failure of this musical and theatrical genius in the Austrian capital was due, in part, to the now fierce competition between the various town theatres. Thus, the Josefstadt theatre put on the first Viennese performances of Meyerbeer's *Les Huguenots* (1839) and several important works by Rossini and Verdi (among them *Nabucco* in 1842). It was there, in 1844, that the Austrian Franz von Suppé conducted the premières of Rossini's *Otello*, Weber's *Preziosa*, Hérold's *Zampa*, and *La Fille du régiment* by Donizetti. Between 1827 and 1841 the Kärntnerthor put on seventeen of Donizetti's operas, most of them favourably received. The composer came to Vienna in March 1842, armed with a letter of introduction from Rossini to Prince Metternich, for the première of a commissioned work, *Linda da Chamonix*. The city gave him a magnificent welcome, and the work was extraordinarily successful. At the end of June, he was appointed Hofkapellmeister and Hofkomponist. The following year his new comic opera, *Don Pasquale*, was much acclaimed. He already appreciated the talents of the young Verdi, and in April 1843 he staged *Nabucco* at the Kärntnerthortheater. On 5 June *Maria di Rohan*, undoubtedly Donizetti's most sombre opera, again aroused passionate enthusiasm at its première: but this turned out to be his last success. His health was deteriorating and his last operas failed in Naples and Paris. Nevertheless, *Dom Sébastien* became one of his best-loved operas in Vienna, with forty-four performances up to the end of the century.

The 1848–9 revolution, unsuccessful though it had been, had a traumatic effect on Viennese life. Nothing in Vienna was the same. The government of Austria, more strongly monarchist than ever, wavered throughout Franz Joseph's interminable reign between liberalism and neo-absolutism. In 1857 the new sovereign, braving the opposition of the army and some of his minis-ters, ordered that the old ramparts around the city be demolished and replaced by a broad boulevard, the Ringstrasse. The following period became known as the 'Ringstrassenzeit', because this necklace of spacious avenues, soon lined with imposing public buildings, gave Vienna an appearance worthy of a mod-ern, imperial capital.

[21] As a composer of German opera, Mahler placed him just below Mozart and Beethoven, and above Weber.

The consequences of the revolution for the Opera were immediate and serious. The two resident directors of the Kärntnerthortheater were dismissed, and the theatre remained dark for most of the two revolutionary years. When it reopened, it was no longer a 'court opera' but simply a 'licensed opera theatre', directly administered by a Civil Servant appointed by the Emperor and coming under the Lord Chamberlain. The first occupant of this post was Julius Cornet, previously director of the Stadt-Theater in Hamburg. He was followed, in 1857, by Karl Eckert, who had been a Kapellmeister since 1854; then, in 1861, came Matteo Salvi, an operatic composer who had been pupil and assistant to Donizetti; and, in 1867, Franz von Dingelstedt, who managed the preparations for the transfer to the new opera-house and left less than a year after the opening.

From 1851 onwards, Italian works came back into the repertoire, one composer, Giuseppe Verdi, being the unquestioned favourite.[22] However, the main post-revolutionary development at the Kärntnerthor was the return of the German repertoire, with a new composer gradually coming to the fore. Richard Wagner had come to Vienna in 1848, having obtained two months' leave from the Intendant at Dresden. At this time his fame was based on his three earliest and much acclaimed works, *Rienzi*, *The Flying Dutchman*, and *Tannhäuser*. Although none of these had yet been performed in Vienna, the newspapers had carried many reports about them. Two years earlier the young Eduard Hanslick, whom history has remembered mainly as Wagner's sworn enemy, had written no less than eleven articles about him in the *Allgemeine Wiener Musikzeitung*, proclaiming him 'the greatest dramatic talent of our day'. Vienna, with its half-million inhabitants, its traditions, its elegance, and its prosperity, seemed the ideal setting for Wagner. In particular, the atmosphere of restlessness that had prevailed there since the March revolution led him to hope that this might be the place where he could realize his dreams of theatrical reform. He met with a great many artists and intellectuals, talked to a number of journalists, and put to the high court officials the idea of creating a national co-operative of Viennese theatres, of which he would naturally be the head. Rumours of these grand plans unfortunately reached Dresden, whose Royal Opera promptly ordered its chief conductor to return to his post. A few months later, after the Saxony revolution of 1849, in which Wagner took part with such enthusiasm that he was exiled to Switzerland, performance of any work of his in Vienna seemed out of the question, and this ban remained in force for some years.

Strange as it may seem, the first Viennese to conduct Wagner's music were the capital's most famous composers of light music, Johann and Josef Strauss, who had long been interested in him and who were bold enough to include symphonic excerpts and overtures from his operas in their orchestra's pro-

---

[22] Works of his premièred at the Kärntnerthor were *Attila* (1851), *Luisa Miller* and *Rigoletto* (1852), *Il trovatore* and *I masnadieri* (1854), *La traviata* (1855), *Giovanna d'Arco* (1857), *Aroldo* (1858), and *Un ballo in maschera* (1864).

grammes. In 1857 Wagner took a mischievous pleasure in humiliating the director of the Court Opera by allowing *Tannhäuser* to be given its first performance at the Josefstadt Theater. Despite the many weaknesses in the performance, the work scored a resounding success, and the Kärntnerthortheater could no longer afford to ignore its composer. Negotiations were set in train and led to the Viennese première of *Lohengrin* on 19 August 1858. Its success was such that it became the sole topic of conversation in Vienna during the weeks that followed, and the authorities were fiercely criticized for having put off the event for so long. *Tannhäuser* and *The Flying Dutchman* were performed the year after, and from then on these three works were permanent features of the Hofoper's repertoire.

Having at last been granted an amnesty by the King of Saxony, Wagner moved to Vienna in 1861. Encouraged by the success of *Lohengrin*, he had decided that the Austrian capital and its court theatre were the ideal place for the world première of his new work, *Tristan und Isolde*, completed two years previously. His enthusiasm for Vienna was short-lived, rehearsals for *Tristan* proving more difficult than expected. A number of journalists conspired against him, and his lavish life-style soon got him into financial difficulties which became more and more pressing, until on 23 March 1864 he was obliged to leave the city, disguised in female dress, in order to escape from his creditors and the threat of imprisonment. Five weeks later, in Zurich, he was visited by an envoy from the young King of Bavaria, and his life took a new and decisive turn. It was thus in Munich, not Vienna, that the world première of *Tristan und Isolde* took place a year later, Vienna having once again lost the opportunity to keep the greatest German composer of the day within its walls.

At that time, all the energies of the court theatre authorities were directed towards the building of a new opera-house, close to the Kärntnerthortheater, but situated on the Ring itself. Work began on the foundations in 1861, the first stone was laid two years later, and construction proceeded in accordance with the designs of two Viennese architects, Eduard van der Null and August Siccard von Siccardsburg. Their project, presented in strictest anonymity, along with thirty-four others, to a selection committee, had been chosen purely on merit. Construction went on for seven years and cost six million gulden (Charles Garnier's Opéra in Paris took eleven years, from 1863 to 1874). Long before it was completed, alarming rumours began circulating in Vienna that the building was beginning to sink into the ground, and that there were structural weaknesses in the design. The architects' names became bywords in the city and everyone began to expect the worst. Van der Null, who had always had depressive tendencies, was so much affected by this campaign of disparagement that he eventually committed suicide a year before the opening. And two months later Siccardsburg also died, probably from the shock caused by the death of his friend and collaborator. These tragic happenings provide yet another instance of the Viennese propensity to believe the worst, for once the building was finished it was found, apart from some minor imperfections inevitable in a project of this scale, to fulfil its functions successfully. The auditorium proved to have one of the best acoustics in Europe, even though it took several months to discover the optimal level for the orchestra pit. Furthermore, it was an attractive building, with its Palladian arcaded façade surmounted by two equestrian statues, its sober lines, and its simple neo-Renaissance decoration.

The 1945 bombardments left only the walls, the main staircase, and the main foyer of the original edifice standing, but at least its façade remains. In Mahler's time, the huge auditorium provided seats for 2,500 people and standing room for 500 more. The elaborate stage machinery, which had recently been electrified, required the attentions of fifty permanent stage-hands and a dozen electricians. For big productions as many as thirty-five additional stage-hands were sometimes employed. The annual subsidy granted by the Emperor rose during the final years of Mahler's tenure to 600,000 kronen, enough to cover the deficit. Many spectators bought annual season tickets for all performances except court galas,[23] but there were also tickets available for half or a quarter of the season, which ran from 1 August[24] to 15 June the following year and comprised more than 300 performances.

The opening gala performance on 25 May 1869 was an event of prime importance in the history of the capital. The Emperor was cheered by an enthusiastic crowd, splendidly dressed with much rustling of silks and clinking of medals, to which further lustre was added by the 4,000 gas-lit pendants and sconces. *Don Giovanni* was performed, with the most brilliant cast then conceivable.[25] Appointed in 1867, Franz Dingelstedt, the last director of the Kärntnerthortheater, became the first director of the new Hofoper, as mentioned earlier. A German with the manners of an aristocrat, a writer, married to a singer, he was a thoroughly experienced professional for whom quality and indeed luxury in production were paramount.

In order to be able to prepare a dozen or so new productions, since none from the former opera-house fitted the dimensions of the new stage, Dingelstedt had the official opening date postponed by several months. Even better, he had the fortunate idea of providing for three different casts to sing each work. Notable among his collaborators was Johann Herbeck, chorus conductor, a teacher at the Conservatory, and a pioneer Wagnerian. It was thanks to him, and his good relationship with Bayreuth, that in February 1870 the Hofoper was able to give the first Viennese performance of *Die Meistersinger*. When Dingelstedt left the Hofoper for the Burgtheater at the end of 1870, Herbeck was naturally asked

---

[23] Thanks to an unusual subscription plan, one could make a down payment in advance and thus have a seat reserved for all performances, subject to confirmation the evening before.

[24] Mahler soon succeeded in having the opening night of the season fixed for a fortnight later, i.e. 15 Aug.

[25] Luise Dustmann (Anna), Maria Wilt (Elvira), Karoline Tellheim (Zerlina), Gustav Walter (Ottavio), Karl Mayerhofer (Masetto), Johann Nepomuk Beck (Don Giovanni), Hans Rokitansky (Leporello), Josef Draxler (Commendatore).

to succeed him and occupied the post for three years. His greatest successes were Verdi's *Aida* in 1874 and Goldmark's *Die Königin von Saba* the following year. Both works were severely criticized by Hanslick, but most of the other critics disagreed with him. In fact the central problem of those years was the economic crisis triggered off by the 1873 stock-exchange crash, which drastically reduced attendances at the Opera, and caused its deficit to grow to such proportions that Herbeck had to resign. The choice, as his successor, of Franz Jauner, whose forte was operetta rather than opera, caused a furore in public opinion and the press. But an experienced manager was just what was needed to surmount the crisis. Jauner quickly pulled off a series of master-strokes, beginning in October 1875 with the Viennese première of *Carmen*, its first performance ever on a large opera stage. Jauner's tenure was also marked by visits from Verdi, who in 1875 conducted *Aida* and the *Requiem*, the appearance of Brahms in person on the podium for the *German Requiem*, and the engagement of Hans Richter, who made his début with a series of *Meistersinger* performances in a virtually uncut version.

After a brief dispute during Herbeck's tenure between Wagner and the Hofoper concerning performance rights, agreement was reached to hold three concerts in the new Musikvereinsaal, the proceeds of which went towards the building of the Bayreuth Theatre. The programmes included the world première of excerpts from *Götterdämmerung*. In 1877, the year in which the first electric lighting was installed in the Hofoper, *Die Walküre* received its first staging there, with sets copied from those in Bayreuth. The *Ring* production was completed two years later, in 1879, with the first performance of *Götterdämmerung*, shortened however by numerous cuts made by Wagner himself. In 1880 Jauner scored one of his greatest artistic successes with a Mozart cycle that included even *Idomeneo* and *La clemenza di Tito*. But the most-performed opera of his tenure was, in fact, Meyerbeer's *Les Huguenots*, a grand opera in the French tradition which went down well with the Viennese public. Nevertheless, all Jauner's flair and skill had not prevented the gradual emptying of the theatre's coffers, and he resigned at the end of 1880.

This time it took six months to find a suitable successor, in the person of the Moravian conductor Wilhelm Jahn. Unlike any of his predecessors, he favoured French and Italian opera, and comedy rather than high drama, thus providing a perfect complement to Richter, to whom he willingly ceded the German, and above all Wagnerian, repertoire. Since these tastes were precisely in line with those of the Viennese, and since Jahn was a likeable bon vivant who liked to please, he quickly became the most popular of all directors and, for this reason, kept his post longer than all the others. It must be said, however, that general circumstances smiled on him: in the two last decades of the century, Austria experienced a period of unprecedented economic growth and the Opera prospered as never before. Jahn, soon given the friendly nickname 'Papa', was not only a talented Kapellmeister, but a great connoisseur of voices, having been a singer himself. He pulled off many contracts that were master-strokes, like the engagement of two German singers, Hermann Winkelmann who was Bayreuth's first Parsifal and Vienna's first Otello, and Theodor Reichmann, first and greatest Amfortas in Bayreuth.

One of the outstanding events of Jahn's tenure was the first performance in 1883, twenty-two years after it was first planned, of *Tristan und Isolde*, conducted by Richter, with Winkelmann, Materna, Reichmann, and Scaria. Several other works introduced by Jahn have retained their place in the international repertoire, notably Ponchielli's *La gioconda* (1884), Verdi's *Otello* (1887) and *Falstaff* (1893), Mascagni's *Cavalleria rusticana* (which achieved a record total of 123 performances in the three years from 1891 onwards), Leoncavallo's *Pagliacci* (1894), Humperdinck's *Hänsel und Gretel* (1894), and Smetana's *The Bartered Bride* (1896). Other first performances included Goldmark's *Heimchen am Herd*, Nessler's *Der Trompeter von Säkkingen*, Wilhelm Kienzl's *Der Evangelimann*, Berlioz's *Béatrice et Bénédict*, Massenet's *Werther*, Liszt's *Die Legende von der heiligen Elisabeth*, and Johann Strauss's *Die Fledermaus* (1894). But none of these could rival in popularity the three operas, *Lohengrin*, *Manon*, and *Cavalleria*.

Of course the Opera was the focus of musical interest in Vienna and had been for two and a half centuries. But there had also been a rich concert life since the start of the nineteenth century. Its beginnings had not been easy, for Vienna was slow in acquiring technical and artistic resources to cope with the huge expansion of the symphonic repertoire then taking place. The Gesellschaft der Musikfreunde, usually known as the Musikverein, founded in 1812, did not find an economically and administratively viable form of activity until three years later, when Gesellschafts-Konzerte in an annual series of four evenings or four matinées were organized, lasting in this form for fifteen years. From 1831, the Gesellschaft's activities reached a new level with the grand opening of a new, purpose-built hall on the Tuchlauben. It was here, in 1839, that Mendelssohn's *Paulus* received its first performance, with Schumann in the audience. However, to gratify public taste, snippets of symphonies were still interspersed with operatic arias and solo virtuoso performances, and serious music lovers began to feel the need for a new music society to organize concerts in Vienna. One of the strangest facts about the Vienna Philharmonic is that there is no official record of the precise date of its foundation. The year usually given is 1842, and indeed this is when Otto Nicolai, whose work with the Imperial Opera I have already mentioned, decided to give two subscription concerts, of which the second, on 27 November, was entitled 'philharmonic' for the first time. It included in its programme Mozart's Symphony in G minor and Beethoven's Fifth. The concern for better quality of performance was at last making itself felt, as is evidenced by the increasing number of rehearsals (thirteen for the third concert of 19 March 1843, at which Beethoven's Ninth Symphony was played).

But Nicolai resigned from his post as director of concerts when his tenure at the Opera ended in 1847 and for the next thirteen years Philharmonic concerts were held only at irregular intervals, while the Gesellschafts-Konzerte continued as before. As the amateur players were progressively replaced by professionals, it was naturally musicians from the Opera who were called in by the Gesellschaft, especially as most of them taught at the Gesellschaft's Conservatory. The result was that the same body of artists ended up providing musicians for two competing music societies. The sensible thing would have been to merge them, redistribute the human resources, combine the financial arrangements, and draw up a common programme. But no such improvements were made until 1860. For the time being, Vienna did not seem to realize that symphonic music had to be put on the same footing as opera. A similar stubbornness in defence of vested interests led to the creation of several competing choirs: the men's choir, the Männergesangverein founded by August Schmidt (1843); the Singverein (1858); the Singakademie and the Akademischer Gesangverein (1858); and five years later the Schubertbund. The best known of these was undoubtedly the Singakademie, which was part of the Musikverein and regularly participated in its concerts. Brahms became its musical director for one season, 1863–4.

The 1848–9 revolution put a stop to all the activities of the Musikverein for three years, the imperial subsidy being withheld until 1851. Later the Gesellschaft resumed its concert activity under a new conductor, Josef Hellmesberger, the Konzertmeister of the Opera orchestra, founder of a famous string quartet, and, for ten years, director of the Conservatory. In 1859 the directorship of the Conservatory was separated from that of the concerts, which were taken over, as was the newly founded Singverein, by Johann Herbeck (1831–77), a 27-year-old Viennese who was one of the most gifted conductors that Austria ever produced and, as seen above, later became the Opera Director. The eleven years of his directorship, up to 1870, were in all respects a golden age for the Gesellschafts-Konzerte. Having created a Gesellschaftsorchester independent of that of the Kärntnerthortheater, which was now refusing to play at the Musikverein's concerts because they competed with those of the Philharmonic, Herbeck made it his job to conduct performances of great masterpieces such as Handel's oratorios, Bach's Passions, and Beethoven's *Missa Solemnis*, the scores of which he committed to memory, something no conductor had ever done before. Nor was he daunted by new music: in 1867 he gave the world première of a Mass (the first) by a provincial organist who had just moved to Vienna, Anton Bruckner.

In 1870, the prestige of the Musikverein was heightened by the opening of a palatial new building designed by Theophil Hansen, and which had taken three years to build, the famous Tuchlauben premises now being far too small. The neo-classical style of the new Musikvereingebäude, characteristic of the Ringstrasse period, combined the severe lines of ancient Greece with the decorative exuberance of the Renaissance. The building possessed a vast and sumptuous auditorium, the 'Goldener Saal', seating 2,000. Its miraculous acoustics have seldom been equalled anywhere in the world, despite all the scientific research done since. After Herbeck's departure and an interim period with Hellmesberger as caretaker, Brahms became head of the Musikverein in 1872. He favoured baroque music (Bach, Handel, Schütz) and little-known classical scores needing a large amount of rehearsal. As previously with the Singakademie, he drew up programmes for the Gesellschafts-Konzerte which were of high quality but did not always attract mass audiences. Furthermore, he was neither a good administrator nor a diplomatic negotiator. He resigned in 1875 and the next two directors of the Gesellschafts-Konzerte did not add to its prestige. Eduard Kremser's greatest feat was to arrange for Liszt in person to conduct the first Viennese performance of his *Graner Mass* in 1875. Wilhelm Gericke followed in his footsteps and programmed Liszt's *Dante Symphony* and the long overdue première of the Berlioz *Requiem*. The Musikverein did not regain its former prestige until 1884, when Hans Richter took over the directorship of the concerts for the next six years. However, in the concluding years of the century, after Richter's resignation, the Musikverein fortunes declined again, with Gericke returning from 1891 to 1895, followed until 1900 by Richard von Perger, a friend of Brahms and a second-rate conductor who later became head of the Conservatory.

Like the Gesellschafts-Konzerte, the Philharmonic concerts were suspended after the 1848–9 revolution until 1853, and there was a further suspension in 1858–9. Between these two blank periods Karl Eckert, director of the Kärntnerthortheater, only conducted six Philharmonic concerts in all. The true beginning of the Philharmonic concerts can thus be established as the day in January 1860 when the members of the Opera orchestra decided to announce a series of four subscription concerts to be held in January, February, and March at the Hofoper.[26] From the beginning, it was decided that the Philharmonic musicians would elect a committee of twelve to administer the orchestra and distribute its profits among the players. Every year, the musicians also elected their conductor. Eckert's departure in September 1860 made it necessary to find a new one. Otto Dessoff, a native of Leipzig and Kapellmeister at the Hofoper, was chosen, and his four concerts attracted such big audiences that a second series was announced at once. From then on, eight concerts were given each year, with a ninth one added twenty years later and called the 'Nicolai-Konzert' in memory of the founder. In 1862 an amendment to the statutes specified that important decisions should be made by means of a secret ballot, a practice still in use today. The development of the orchestra owed a great deal to Dessoff, who retained his post for fifteen years with undiminishing success. His repertoire was mainly classical, but he also produced romantic works

[26] The programme for the first concert, on 15 Jan. 1860, was the Overture to *Anacréon* by Cherubini, the Scherzo from *Roméo et Juliette* by Berlioz, and Beethoven's Seventh Symphony.

(Schumann, Mendelssohn), and premières like the much overdue one of Berlioz's *Symphonie fantastique*, Wagner's *Eine Faust-Ouvertüre*, and, later, works by Brahms and Bruckner. Dessoff also initiated the Novitäten-Konzerte for premières of contemporary music.

At the end of the 1869–70 season, when it was announced that the old Kärntnerthortheater was to be demolished, the Philharmonic found itself without a hall. The new Musikverein building was by then completed, but since it had cost a great deal to build the Gesellschaft could not bring itself to consent to its being used by a rival orchestra. At first a plan to fuse the two orchestras was proposed. But this would have given the Musikverein, owner of the hall, authority over the Philharmonic, which would thus have lost its autonomy. Eventually a compromise formula was reached whereby the committee agreed that it would cease to limit the number of musicians authorized to play in Gesellschafts Konzerte. In exchange, the Philharmonic Orchestra moved into the brand new Musikvereinsaal. For the first Philharmonic concert held there on 13 November 1870, Otto Dessoff conducted the *Freischütz* Overture, Beethoven's Fourth Piano Concerto played by Julius Epstein, and Schumann's Third Symphony. Thus Johann Herbeck, the director of the Opera, found himself in a position of rivalry with his first Kapellmeister, Otto Dessoff, who was also conductor of the Philharmonic. Dessoff finally resigned in 1875, after a last triumph with Beethoven's Ninth Symphony. His successor, Hans Richter, beat all records for directorial longevity, keeping his post from 1875 to 1898 with just one year's break for an extended stay in England. Born in Vienna, Richter was as popular as he was respected for his infallible ear and his memory, his technical proficiency at the podium, his experience as a former orchestra member, and his knowledge of the repertoire. His programmes as a whole remained solidly conservative, and the number of first performances was always limited, though they included works by Brahms and Bruckner. Richter gave the world première of the latter's Fourth Symphony in 1881 and was thus responsible for Bruckner's first Viennese success.

From 1884 Richter, combining the posts of Kapellmeister at the Opera, director of the Philharmonic concerts, and head of the Gesellschafts-Konzerte, controlled all musical activity in the town, and retained absolute power until the end of the century. Although he had won his early fame as a fervent Wagnerian, he not only gave the Viennese première of Brahms's First Symphony but also the world premières of the Second in autumn 1877 and the Third in 1883. He thus managed to remain aloof from contemporary conflicts between the Brahms and Wagner factions.

The rich panorama of Vienna's musical life in those times also included innumerable recitals, chamber concerts, and visits by touring German orchestras. But its crowning glory remained the Hofoper. Ultimate responsibility for its administration, like that of the Burgtheater (the Viennese equivalent of the Comédie-Française), and indeed all imperial institutions and activities in the field of the arts, was in the hands of Prince Rudolf Liechtenstein, the Lord Chamberlain (*Erster Obersthofmeister*), a high court official and administrative dignitary whose knowledge of artistic matters was limited and who did not concern himself with theatre affairs. While he occupied this post, and through-out the whole of Mahler's time there—that is to say, up to 1907—the Opera was in fact administered by Liechtenstein's assistant and future successor, Prince Alfred Montenuovo, a grandson of the Empress Marie Louise and Count Neipperg.[27] It was to him that Mahler had to answer in directing the Hofoper, for, as has already been said, the Emperor almost never interfered. Every inch the elegant aristocrat, with his grey beard and moustache, Montenuovo was well-known for his cold, determined character, his unswerv-ing convictions, his stubbornness, and his unwillingness to forgive anyone against whom he bore a grudge, as he proved much later by his behaviour on the very day of the funeral of his enemy, Crown Prince Franz Ferdinand, after his assassination at Sarajevo. This rather stiff but dignified and exacting bureaucrat admired and respected Mahler, protecting him right to the end from all the intrigues, scandals, and *Affären* the Viennese were able to devise, and even from the Intendant's office itself. He believed both in Mahler's artistic genius and his moral integrity, and only agreed to let him go in 1907 with extreme reluctance.

Prince Montenuovo had his office at the Obersthoftheaterdirektion in the Imperial Palace, and his office manager was Franz Freiherr von Wetschl, whose excessive interference in Opera affairs had been the target of much press criticism towards the end of Jahn's tenure. Wetschl's authority was in fact much diminished by the time Mahler took over. The intermediary post between the Obersthoftheaterdirektion and the artistic direction was held from 1898 on by Freiherr Josef von Bezecny's successor, Baron August von Plappart, the theatre Intendant, whose office was some distance from the Opera, in the Bräunerstrasse. He was concerned almost exclusively with technical and financial matters. Eduard Wlassack was the administration's 'director of the chancellery'. With his friend, the retired opera singer Rosa Papier, he had played a key role in ensuring that Mahler was the successful candidate, and hoped that, with Mahler as his acknowledged protégé, he would be able to keep control of the Opera's affairs. But in fact Mahler did not consider himself responsible to anyone but Prince Montenuovo. A quarrel broke out almost immediately, but then and subsequently Mahler resisted either actively or passively all of Plappart's and Wlassack's efforts to interfere. Wlassack's atti-tude reminded him of 'those princes who elect one of their number Emperor, and then all try to reign together'. He added: 'I am the Emperor, and I am determined to reign.' Wlassack was finally forced to give way, but the struggle was long and bitter, and he became a dangerous enemy thereafter.

---

[27] Montenuovo is the Italian trans. of Neipperg (i.e. Neuberg, 'new mountain').

Although he would later control an army of musicians, technicians, and producers, Mahler, when he arrived at the Hofoper on 27 April 1897, was still only a conductor who had to share performances with the Director Wilhelm Jahn and with several colleagues: Johann Nepomuk Fuchs, the brother of his former harmony professor,[28] Josef Hellmesberger the younger, who was mainly responsible for ballet performances, and, above all, Hans Richter.[29] Richter had conducted the first Bayreuth performances of the *Ring* in the presence of the Master, as well as several first performances in Vienna. His many supporters considered it scandalous that he should not have been appointed as Jahn's successor, though he had no administrative talent or ambition and was already spending a great deal of his time in England. Richter had not been consulted about Mahler's engagement, and did not take kindly to the arrival at the Vienna Opera of a colleague twenty years his junior, who, like himself, specialized in conducting Wagner and who was well-known for his exacting character and his 'modern' ideas. Richter himself embodied tradition, with all the self-indulgence and inflexibility that the term implies.

Foreseeing the problems that this collaboration would entail, Mahler wrote to Richter before leaving Hamburg:

since my earliest youth, you have been my model, and through all the difficulties and troubles of theatrical life I have tried to emulate you. With what rapture did I listen and watch your baton when, as a young man, I attended performances you conducted at the Opera and in the Musikverein hall! Later, when I myself took that frail wooden baton in my hand, the memory of your exploits always guided me. When doubtful about something, I always asked myself: 'What would Hans Richter do?' . . .

Until my dying day, I shall be proud to express my unswerving admiration for you. This is what impels me to write to you today, for, since I have been accorded the honour of working next to you—within your sight, so to speak—I finally have the opportunity of expressing to you all I have felt for so long. I can imagine no greater reward than pleasing you, and should I fail in this, I beg you to give me the benefit of your masterly advice. I am completely at your disposal! It would give me great satisfaction if I could relieve you of any task unworthy of you or that might in any way be disagreeable to you! I beg you to have confidence in me; I will do all I can to deserve it.[30]

The admiration expressed in this letter was more formal than sincere. Mahler usually referred to Richter as 'honest Hans' in his letters, regarding him as

---

[28] Winner of the Beethoven Prize in 1881, when Mahler submitted *Das klagende Lied* (see above, Vol. i, Chap. 5).

[29] Hans Richter, born 4 Apr. 1843, in Györ, Hungary, was the son of a Kapellmeister at the cathedral there and of the singer who sang the role of Venus in the Vienna première of *Tannhäuser*. Having completed his studies at the Vienna Conservatory, he was recommended to Wagner, who summoned him to Lucerne in 1866–7 to copy the score of *Die Meistersinger*. A conductor at the Munich Opera, he also conducted in Paris and Brussels before returning to Lucerne, where he played the trumpet in the first performance of the *Siegfried Idyll* and copied the *Ring* scores. Chief conductor of the Budapest Opera, 1871–5, he was then engaged as a conductor in Vienna. The only conductor in Bayreuth in 1876, he presented Vienna premières of the Wagner dramas. He also directed the Richter Concerts in London.

[30] BMG 66ff. This letter and Richter's reply were publ. for the first time in MKW in 1930.

representing an ossified tradition. However, his intentions were sound enough: he wanted to establish good relations with his celebrated senior. But his attempt was unsuccessful: as a conductor and an interpreter, his personality differed too much from Richter's—so much so that there was nothing he could 'learn' from him. Richter's reply was reserved and even somewhat arrogant. Mahler would find him 'a colleague full of good will', once Richter was 'convinced that Mahler's contribution will be of benefit to the Opera and further our noble art'. In the event Richter was no more capable of appreciating Mahler's conducting that Mahler was capable of appreciating his. The 'generation gap' between them was unbridgeable. But there was never any open clash.

For the time being, however, Mahler's appointment as Opera Director was far from settled, and there remained many difficulties to be overcome: 'It's true I must be prepared to be led a <u>dance</u> but I would like to call the tune <u>myself</u>',[31] he wrote before leaving Hamburg, adding in a later letter: 'What gives me the greatest happiness is not the fact that I have secured a seemingly splendid post, but rather that at last I have found a home, that is if the gods will only guide me! For I must be prepared for a terrible struggle.'[32] On 25 April, the day after he had given his farewell performance in Hamburg, Mahler set off for Vienna, leaving his sister Justi to take care of the removal. On arriving in Vienna he took rooms in the Hotel Bristol close to the Opera[33] and on the same day called upon Bezecny and Wlassack: 'Everything has gone better than I feared', he wrote to Justi. The Viennese were in fact on their best behaviour, and several papers had already sent reporters to interview him. His first meal was a supper party given in his honour by Rosa Papier. Most of his first week in Vienna was spent in official introductions and personal calls. Just like any of the singers newly engaged by the Vienna Opera, Mahler made the round of all the leading critics: he was determined to neglect nothing that might ensure his success.[34] Jahn was still away, but had asked Mahler to come and see him upon his return to Vienna, on 2 May, a Sunday morning. Mahler duly arrived at the director's office, but had to wait until Jahn had finished dealing with a previous visitor, Hans Richter. The old man ultimately received him very pleasantly and introduced him to his nephew, Hubert Wondra, whose official title of Chordirektor actually concealed his true function as 'artistic secretary'.[35] He suggested that Mahler make his début with Mozart's *Don Giovanni*. 'I would have preferred something other than *Don Giovanni* but I could not refuse,' Mahler wrote to Karpath.[36] Later in the week

[31] MBR1, no. 100; MBR2, no. 234 to Fritz Löhr (postmarked Hamburg, 20 Apr. 1897).

[32] MBR1, no. 210; MBR2, no. 238 to Camilla von Stefanovic-Vilovsky, postmarked Hamburg, 25 Apr. 1897.

[33] Letter to Justi of 28 Apr. (RWO). Mahler travelled with a 'childhood friend from Iglau' named Grünfeld. Was this one of the Grünfeld brothers from Prague? Yet Mahler specifically says 'a friend from Iglau'.

[34] BMG 55. Once he became director he had contact with journalists only on very exceptional occasions.

[35] BMG 53 n.

[36] MBR, no. 240, undated (4 May). In a card he sent to Justi the same day, Mahler gives her his Venice

Tannhäuser was suggested, then *Hans Heiling*. In the event, he made his début
with *Lohengrin*.

Since Pollini, the director of the Hamburg Opera, was in Vienna for the
annual meeting of the Deutscher Bühnenverein[37] and staying in Mahler's hotel,
they met in the reception hall. A 'touching meeting!' Mahler wrote ironically to
Mildenburg. The Austrian writer Hermann Bahr happened to be talking to
Pollini when Mahler came in. Bahr never forgot Mahler's entry: 'It was like a
gust of wind forcing a window open, like water bursting from a pipe, . . . like
something elemental.' When Mahler left, a few moments later, 'the wind suddenly dropped, the water was turned off.' 'A strange chap, that conductor, don't
you think?' said Pollini, while Bahr tried to identify the reminiscence that
Mahler's sudden apparition had stirred in his mind. Suddenly he knew; Mahler
had reminded him of Hugo Wolf. The two men were as dissimilar as could be,
but Wolf had often made Bahr think of an animal concealing an enchanted
prince. 'Now here was Mahler, also a maverick and equally untamed. Both
seemed branded with the same mark; perhaps the same curse has been put on
them both. The typical creative musician in each of them was stronger than his
personal characteristics: man and music were inseparable, the man was the
music and the music was the man.'[38]

The next day, Mahler again saw Jahn, who asked him to leave immediately
for Venice, to attend the world première of Leoncavallo's *La Bohème*, which was
programmed at the Hofoper for the following season. Before leaving Vienna,
Mahler had his first meeting with Prince Liechtenstein. The Lord Chamberlain
received him for half an hour with 'extraordinary politeness' and Mahler was
favourably impressed.[39] Jahn was so 'extremely kind'; Richter was beginning to
'be more human', and only Johann Nepomuk Fuchs seemed irreconcilable,
doubtless because 'he lived in the well-founded fear of henceforth having to
limit his gymnastics on the podium'. Physically exhausted from walking up and
down so many stairs, dizzy with the effort of being charming to so many people,
Mahler nevertheless left for Venice on the evening of 4 May in a most cheerful
frame of mind. His career seemed assured, and he would probably be made
director in the autumn. Vienna, with her most enticing smile, had welcomed the
prodigal son's return.

At the Hotel Britannia in Venice, Mahler again met Pollini, and together they
went to the Teatro La Fenice on 6 May, and the San Benedetto Theatre on 7

address as Hotel Britannia. He also confirms that he will make his début with *Don Giovanni*, followed by
Tannhäuser.

[37] Pollini had bought the rights for the performance of Leoncavallo's *Bohème*, which meant that other
German opera-houses were only allowed to produce the opera after the Hamburg Stadt-Theater première,
which took place on 24 Sept. 1897 (KMI).

[38] Bahr read Romain Rolland's novel *Jean Christophe* a few years later, and saw in its hero both the
physical and moral incarnation of Mahler. He also compared Mahler to a Neapolitan musician called Pisani,
described by the novelist Bulwer-Lytton in *Zanoni* (1842). 'Mahler', *Neue Freie Presse* (22 Mar. 1914).

[39] In a note dated 29 Apr., Mahler announces his arrival in Vienna to the Prince and requests him to set
a date for their meeting (PML, Robin Lehmann deposit).

May, to see the two operas based on Murger's *Scènes de la vie de Bohème* which had aroused violent controversy in Italy. The dispute had started one day when Puccini met Leoncavallo by chance in a café and announced that he was at work with his librettist on a 'Bohème'. Leoncavallo furiously reminded him that he himself had considered this subject sometime earlier but had decided to work on it only after hearing that Puccini had refused to consider it. Puccini denied ever having turned it down and concluded indignantly: 'In that case, there will be two *Bohèmes!*' The next day *Il Secolo* announced Leoncavallo's coming opera, and that same evening the *Corriere della Sera* announced Puccini's. Each composer was backed by one of the two main music publishers in Milan, Ricordi and Sonzogno, and Puccini won the first round by finishing his opera well before his rival. His *Bohème* was presented for the first time in Turin on 1 February 1896, whereas Leoncavallo's was only staged a year later in Venice, which was when Mahler saw it.

Before leaving Venice, Mahler sent a card of the Doge's Palace to his sister. He addressed it to 'Giustina Malheurina' and wrote simply: 'I like working at the Vienna Opera much more than at the Hamburg Stadttheater!'[40] As soon as he was back in Vienna, Mahler wrote to Jahn saying that in his opinion Puccini's opera was by far the better of the two. The music was both new and easy to understand, the orchestration 'very effective', the voices admirably treated, the libretto interesting and ably conceived. As for the 'perils inherent in the subject', Mahler thought that a 'certain propriety in the language, combined with the charm of the music, would enable them to be overcome'. Some of the more 'shocking' aspects could in any case be toned down. 'However, I cannot speak in similar terms of Leoncavallo's work', he continued. 'The music is without originality, and poor in inspiration, in spite of all the technical refinements. The text of the first two acts is boring; the third sentimental in the worst sense of the word, and even lewd. Mainly for this last reason I consider its performance in our Royal Theatre to be out of the question', he added.[41] 'Given the sterility of contemporary operatic composition I should like to intercede for the acceptance and presentation of Puccini's opera at the Hofoper, if such performance does not involve insurmountable difficulties.'[42]

Mahler expressed the same opinion three weeks later to the Viennese critic Richard Heuberger, this time even more emphatically: 'Leoncavallo's music and his opera [*Bohème*][43] are like their creator, hollow, pretentious, bombastic and generally tending towards vulgarity. The orchestration is superficial, noisy, and to me literally repulsive. One bar of Puccini is worth more than the whole of Leoncavallo.'[44] Posterity has fully borne out Mahler's assessment.

[40] Ernst Rosé collection, now dispersed.
[41] Nevertheless, Mahler felt that the Puccini libretto weakened towards the end, whereas that of Leoncavallo gathered momentum.
[42] Letter from Mahler to Jahn (HOA, Z.256/1897).
[43] The printed text mentions *Pagliacci* here, but this is probably a misreading of Mahler's handwriting.
[44] Letter to Richard Heuberger, 31 May 1897: *Anbruch* (May 1936), 67.

Leoncavallo's *La Bohème* disappeared from the repertoire (although it has recently had a few revivals), whereas Puccini's is still performed in all the opera-houses in the world. Mahler was particularly eager to intervene because, given the situation at the Hofoper and Jahn's impending departure, he knew that he himself would have to bear the consequences of an unfortunate choice. However, his efforts were in vain, since Jahn was on the best of terms with Leoncavallo and had already committed himself to his opera. Thus the Vienna Opera became one of the very few in the world to perform this *Bohème* ahead of Puccini's.[45]

Having returned to Vienna on 7 May,[46] Mahler began preparations for his début which was scheduled for the 11th. Three days earlier, he attended a performance of *Die Meistersinger* conducted by Richter, whose performance he criticized severely: 'At the beginning I liked it very much', he said to Natalie. 'He conducted the first act like a master, the second like a schoolmaster and the third like a master cobbler.'[47] On the morning of 10 May, Jahn officially presented Mahler to the orchestra as the new conductor who 'has been engaged to help me and take some of the weight off the shoulders of the conductors'.[48] Mahler replied in a speech he had prepared with great care, speaking with assurance despite his nervousness. He said how conscious he was of the honour of working with 'such glorious collaborators'. His diplomacy was received somewhat coolly, however, doubtless because the listeners had already heard of his 'tyranny', and his 'exorbitant demands'.[49] He then started rehearsing *Lohengrin*. Taking the Prelude, he 'discussed each point in detail and turned everything upside down'. For the rest of the opera he had to make do with rehearsing a few isolated passages and correcting some of the soloists.[50] He had expected serious difficulties with the orchestra, but he was delighted with the way they responded: 'In a single rehearsal I accomplished more with them than in years with others. It is true that the auditorium of the Opera idealizes the tone quite incredibly, just as elsewhere defective acoustics give everything an astonishing crudity and grossness.'[51] But most credit must go 'to the Austrian musicians, the élan, the warmth, and the natural gifts of each of them'.

[45] Nevertheless Puccini had won the race for time in Vienna too. His *Bohème* was premièred on 4 Oct. 1897 at the Theater an der Wien, which had always been able to stage works more quickly than the huge Hofoper. Mahler, when he became director, had to honour Jahn's contracts, and reluctantly presented Leoncavallo's *Bohème* the following Feb., after a series of tragi-comic incidents (see below, Chap. 3). Puccini's *Bohème* was not performed at the Hofoper until five years later.

[46] BMG 337.

[47] See Memoirs of Mahler's close friend and confidante, Natalie Bauer-Lechner: NBL1. 77; NBL2. 89. The passage indicates that this performance of *Die Meistersinger* occurred during rehearsals for *The Flying Dutchman* and *The Magic Flute*. The performance on 8 May was the only one given that spring.

[48] Mahler had rehearsed the singers with piano the previous day (KMI).

[49] BMG 54 ff.

[50] In particular the baritone Benedikt Felix, whose errors of rhythm he corrected in the Heerrufer's solo.

[51] Mahler must be thinking of the acoustics of the Stadt-Theater in Hamburg. But according to Mr Berthold Goldschmidt, a well-known conductor and composer who was born in Hamburg and conducted the world première on the BBC of Deryck Cooke's 'performing version' of Mahler's Tenth Symphony, the acoustics there were renowned.

Two days before Mahler's début Viktor von Herzfeld published in the *Neue Musikalische Presse* an enthusiastic article introducing the new Hofoper conductor, and describing him as 'a musician through and through, of impetuous temperament, keen intellect, . . . dramatic to his fingertips'. It was impossible not to admire the way he could simultaneously control both stage and orchestra and his unusual gift of providing pleasure for the eye and the ear simultaneously. In Budapest, Herzfeld recalled, *Die Walküre*, *Lohengrin*, *Don Giovanni*, and *Le nozze di Figaro* had been performed at the Opera with rare perfection by a man who possessed all the qualities of a conductor and a stage director, and who was in addition inspired by an exceptional idealism.

According to the Viennese composer Franz Schmidt, at that time a cellist in the Opera orchestra, the news of Mahler's arrival caused quite a stir:

One fine day, early in 1897, the opera-house was jolted out of its peaceful routine. In the papers for all to read, was the news that Herr Gustav Mahler, Kapellmeister at the Hamburg Theatre, had been engaged as a conductor at the Vienna Opera—As a conductor?   In whose place?—Is one of our Kapellmeisters leaving? The most contradictory rumours flew about. Mahler was coming as fifth Kapellmeister—Nonsense, he was coming as first (supernumerary of course) conductor, on an equal footing with Hans Richter—No, he was coming expressly to relieve the burdens of Director Jahn, who was almost completely blind—No, there was more to it than that: Mahler was going to succeed him as deputy director! But soon all the rumourmongers were shouting in unison: Directorship crisis! Jahn is leaving! Mahler is the future Director! Consternation followed consternation! Mahler was a merciless slave-driver—a brutal tyrant—there would be a complete shake-up—no stone would be left standing—no peace—a reign of terror—you'd better all watch out! And there's even worse to come!

The name Gustav Mahler had a particularly awesome sound in the ears of the orchestral players. It is not surprising therefore that when Jahn introduced him to the orchestra he was very coolly received. Actually things went tolerably well at the beginning; the orchestra, accustomed for years to the same conductor, was at first perceptibly irritated by Mahler's unfamiliarly impulsive conducting, but since he showed patience in dealing with misunderstandings, his relations with the orchestra seemed likely to be less stormy than expected.

Mahler was thoroughly exploited in his months as Kapellmeister. I can clearly remember, for instance, one week in which he conducted *Lohengrin*, *Faust*, *Freischütz* and *L'Africaine* in rapid succession.[52] It was especially interesting to watch him conducting operas in the current repertoire which he had not produced or not rehearsed. Everything came out so very differently, and although his apparent unfamiliarity with the established conducting routine led to some uneasiness and mistakes, he also brought out the inherent, hitherto concealed beauty of many passages. Unsuspected possibilities glimmered in vague outline, promising great events in the near future.

---

[52] Franz Schmidt's memory is exceptionally accurate in this respect, although the 'week' lasted in fact a fortnight. Between 3 and 17 Aug. 1897 Mahler indeed conducted *Faust*, *L'Africaine*, *The Flying Dutchman*, *The Bartered Bride*, *Figaro*, *Le Prophète*, and *Der Freischütz*. In the next week he conducted *Don Giovanni* and a complete *Ring* cycle.

After a few months, the weary Jahn retired from his post and Mahler indeed became director. His directorship broke over the opera-house like an elemental catastrophe. An earthquake of tremendous intensity and duration shook the whole edifice from top to bottom. Everything that was old, outdated, or not in thoroughly good order, inevitably fell away and was lost for ever.

And now began in Vienna one of the greatest musical epochs the city had ever known. Mahler was an absolute monarch who held the whole of musical Vienna in thrall, and with his matchless, intrepid energy he managed, in record time, to regenerate not only the entire artistic workforce but also the Viennese public.[53]

This testimony is particularly striking, coming as it does from a musician who not only failed to warm to Mahler at the time but who later even became his sworn enemy.

Although Mahler's début had been announced only a few days before, the atmosphere in the auditorium was electric on the evening of 11 May 1897. All Mahler's supporters were present: Wlassack in his box, Ludwig Karpath[54] with Rosa Papier in the stalls, Natalie and the Spieglers in the circle—all of them worried and nervous. Apart from them, almost no one in the auditorium knew Mahler. At the end of the Prelude, the 'sublime slowness', the 'nuances and subtle gradations' of his interpretation were striking enough to earn a first round of warm applause, which Mahler acknowledged several times. It was at once clear that the battle had been won. Soloists, chorus, and orchestra surpassed themselves, and during the performance the tense concentration of the performers was matched by the rapt attention of the audience. According to Natalie, the audience applauded each time Mahler's tempos differed from the customary ones; after the Prelude to Act III and at the end of the performance there were great bursts of applause. A crowd of young people, in particular students from the Conservatory, gathered at the stage door to acclaim Mahler. One of them, Josef Reitler, later wrote:

Those who were present at the first performance of *Lohengrin* by Mahler in 1897 never forgot that evening. And this was true of every occasion when Mahler conducted a new production of a well-known work. With all due respect to the mastery of Hans Richter and to his pioneering work for Wagner, it must be said that under Mahler's baton everything was transformed at a stroke and raised to a higher level. . . . We felt ourselves irresistibly raised to a stratosphere of artistry from the heights of which the theatrical events we had experienced hitherto seemed petty and banal.[55]

---

[53] Autograph MS by Franz Schmidt, property of Frau Eva Brandweiner (see Carl Nemeth, *Franz Schmidt: Ein Meister nach Brahms und Bruckner* (Amalthea, Zurich, 1957) 73 ff.).

[54] For the biography of this critic (1866–1936), see above Vol. i, Chap. 13. Karpath's book of memoirs, *Begegnung mit dem Genius* (Fiba, Vienna, 1934 = BMG) is one of the richest sources for Mahler's Vienna years, as are his articles in the *Neues Wiener Tagblatt*. Although he later became an enemy of Mahler's, Karpath had originally taken part in Rosa Papier's and Eduard von Wlassack's canvassing for Mahler's appointment as director (see above Vol. i, Chap. 24, and below, Chap. 12).

[55] Josef Reitler, 'Mahler', unpubl. essay.

The enthusiasm of these young people pleased Mahler even more than the unanimous approval of the critics next day. He remarked later:

They feel what I felt at their age. After longing to hear works that I knew only from score, the performance was almost always a cruel disappointment, because usually only a fraction of what was actually written was brought out. When you finally hear everything, when the effect sometimes even surpasses what you have imagined, then your joy and gratitude toward the man who has made this possible are boundless.[56]

After the performance, Mahler had supper at the Grand Hotel with old friends, among them Albert Spiegler and his wife, and Jakob Grün, who was about to leave his position as Konzertmeister of the orchestra. He questioned Karpath about the reactions of the critics, and in particular of Richard Heuberger[57] of the *Neue Freie Presse* and Max Kalbeck[58] of the *Neues Wiener Tagblatt*. Eduard Hanslick, at 72 still Vienna's most influential critic, wrote occasional *Feuilleton* articles, generally based on serious studies he had made of scores. In the case of Mahler's début, however, he had probably decided to let Heuberger cover the event, if only because it must have been known in Vienna that he had strongly supported the new director's candidature.

Karpath assured Mahler that the praise had indeed been unanimous. The articles in the press the following day proved him right. Ludwig Speidel's particularly pleased Mahler;[59] the critic of the *Fremden-Blatt* began by comparing his conducting to his physical appearance, 'full of energy and delicate understanding', with gestures which assumed a 'spiritual character'. In *Lohengrin*, Speidel continued,

Mahler entered fully into the dreamlike music of the Prelude, and it was only at the climax, with the wind fortissimo, that he suddenly took hold of the entire orchestra; with an abrupt, energetic gesture, he lunged at the trombonists as though with a foil. The effect was magical. . . . He noticed everything. He was in close and constant touch with the chorus, the orchestra and each individual; not one performer missed his smallest gesture. . . . Nothing could show more consideration for the ailing Director of

[56] NBL1. 47; NBL2. 88.

[57] Richard Heuberger (1850–1914), born in Graz, studied as an engineer before devoting himself to music at the age of 26. Director of the Akademischer Gesangverein in Vienna, then leader of the Singakademie in 1878, he was a music critic for the *Wiener Tagblatt*, correspondent for the *Münchner Allgemeine Zeitung*, and finally critic for the *Neue Freie Presse*, 1896–1901. A professor at the Conservatory and leader of the Männergesangverein, he became editor of the *Neue Musikalische Presse* in 1904. He wrote critical and biographical works as well as operas, operettas (notably the successful *Ein Opernball*), and choral works.

[58] Max Kalbeck (1850–1921), born in Breslau, studied law and philosophy and published several books of verse before studying music at the Munich Musikschule. Music critic in Breslau, 1875–80, he became, on Hanslick's recommendation, critic for the *Wiener Allgemeine Zeitung*, then for *Die Presse* in 1883, and the *Montagsrevue* in 1890. He joined the *Neues Wiener Tagblatt* in 1886. He and Hanslick were the principal adversaries of the 'music of the future', i.e. Wagner and Bruckner. The author of several biographies and other books, and trans. of many librettos of operas presented in Vienna, he publ. a 4-vol. biography of Brahms (1904–14). Mahler himself commissioned several opera trans. from him.

[59] Mahler sent his review to Justi with several others. He valued it, because Speidel had the reputation of being very hard to please.

the Opera nor be of more active support for him than the placing of such an artist at his side. Herr Mahler will certainly exert a good artistic influence on the Opera, provided he is given a free hand.

In the *Neues Wiener Tagblatt*, Max Kalbeck, one of the city's most influential critics, at once ranked Mahler among 'the elect'. His conducting dealt a death-blow to 'routine' and suggested that he was 'capable of far more than directing a Wagner opera', perhaps implying that he would be able to direct the entire Hofoper. He had given *Lohengrin* a completely new aspect, and, though certain details had been surprising, the performance as a whole had created a 'highly significant and artistically sympathetic' impression. The Prelude had never been conducted so slowly, but the result had been entirely satisfactory. The vivacity and rhythmic energy of the dialogue, usually dull and long-drawn-out due to the singers' bad habits, 'was a welcome relief', Kalbeck wrote. 'The dramatic crescendo in each scene had been carefully prepared, climaxes were wholly effective', and the audience had accepted Mahler's innovations with surprising willingness.

In the *Wiener Abendpost*, Robert Hirschfeld[60] drew the following portrait of 'the recently appointed and already controversial Kapellmeister', who was 'all life and movement'. Even his profile seemed to 'radiate energy, will-power, and a desire to forge ahead'. Hirschfeld described the light movements of Mahler's baton: 'He not only indicated the rhythms, but he brought each measure to life; and he not only gave signs (*Zeichen*) but signified precisely (*vorzeichnet*) what he wanted.' For the orchestra, Mahler is often 'content to move his torso or significantly turn his head'.

However he never takes his eyes off the singers, imposes his will on everything taking place onstage, guides, enlivens, subdues and blends individual voices into the ensembles. Thus, the vast onstage organism remained in a constant state of tension and animation. . . . He has eyes for everything but the score, which he knows completely. His glance can even penetrate the mass of the chorus, and enter into a visual dialogue with its leaders when necessary. His movements are as clear and distinct as his artistic intentions: not a single finger movement is without meaning; there is no movement that does not have an inner motivation.

The choral performance seemed 'transfigured', though certain piano passages suffered because of the way the chorus at that time was positioned.[61]

---

[60] Robert Hirschfeld (1858–1914) came from a Moravian Jewish family and studied music at the conservatories of Breslau and Vienna. In the latter he also taught musical aesthetics from 1884. In 1885 he publ. a pamphlet criticizing Hanslick. He arranged for stage production Haydn's *Der Apotheker* (*Lo speziale*) and Schubert's *Der vierjährige Posten*, both of which Mahler conducted in Hamburg. He was to become Mahler's most virulent enemy. Two years before his death he took over the direction of the Mozarteum in Salzburg.

[61] Hirschfeld also criticized the behaviour of Winkelmann's admirers, who 'shout their heads off, even when the curtain is up'.

In the *Neue Freie Presse*, the Styrian composer Richard Heuberger[62] had at that time been given to understand that he would take over from Hanslick when Hanslick retired. A lively, witty, and hard-working critic, Heuberger had been a close friend of Brahms, but Hanslick disliked him and considered him unsuitable to succeed him as a critic because he felt his ambition to have his own works performed would bias his judgements.[63] Heuberger joined the other critics in pronouncing the *Lohengrin* performance to be one of the very best ever heard in Vienna:

Mahler is not only an extremely confident and spirited musician, he is an excellent dramatic conductor and has a sense of the theatre: his attention does not stop at the footlights—in fact, it really begins there. He gives *correct* rhythms to the chorus and the soloists, which is most essential to a meaningful interpretation. It is already clear that he prefers the fluid tempos that Richard Wagner loved. He will not tolerate any dragging or distortion. From the orchestra he obtains great restraint in accompaniment, but also great power when it is required for dramatic effect. It was a joy to watch our Philharmonic players attentive to every gesture of their new conductor and to see them convert his clear and eloquent signals into ringing sound.[64]

According to the *Neue Musikalische Presse*, Mahler had gained a hard-earned and total victory, thanks to his 'spiritual power, his exceptional energy', and his 'artistic and human personality':

Just as there are total works of art (*Gesamtkunstwerke*), Mahler is a total conductor (*Gesamtdirigent*). His concern is for the orchestra, the singers and the chorus alike. His glance, his will, his gestures command and unite the ensemble of performers. He thereby achieves not a sum of parts but a unified whole. . . . A small gesture with his head or his left hand, a slight movement of his body, indicates a detail, while a firmer gesture underlines the essential, the principal voice, which must be brought to the fore. Despite his mobility and vivacity, each signal is of such eloquence, each intention so easily grasped, that singers and orchestra follow him easily and joyfully, as if they had been used to him for years.[65]

A 'resolute and a noble' artist, the same anonymous article concluded, Mahler saw his art as a sacred mission. Certain people wished to 'make life difficult' for him at the Opera, but opposition, both secret and open, had ceased after the performance.

The most surprising of all these laudatory articles was undoubtedly that in the anti-Semitic paper, the *Deutsche Zeitung*, whose critic, Theodor Helm, asserted that Mahler was a 'musician of intellect and passion', that he knew the

[62] Heuberger's most ambitious composition was the opera *Das Maifest*, but his most successful works were the ballet *Struwelpeter* and the operetta *Der Opernball*, both performed at the Opera.

[63] See KIW 64 ff.

[64] Cast: Ehrenstein (Elsa), Kaulich (Ortrud), Winkelmann (Lohengrin), Reichmann (Telramund), Grengg (King), Felix (Herald). Heuberger also deplored the disgraceful behaviour of the claque. Mahler was shortly to tackle this problem.

[65] The same writer praised the 'clear and controlled' performance of the Prelude and the 'magic sound' of many passages, such as the Act II choruses and the swan's appearance in Acts I and III.

work 'by heart', that he had put an end to the singers' abuses and made them
keep in time, and that, exactly like Wagner on 2 March 1876, he had conducted
the Prelude 'with unusual slowness, but with the melody rising beautifully from
the various groups of instruments'.[66] 'Everything was admirably precise, meticulously clear, especially the choruses.' Theodor Helm had only one minor
reservation; he claimed that the choruses sang more vigorously under Richter.
His remarks so closely resemble those in an anonymous letter addressed to
Mahler the day after this début that it seems almost certain that Helm was its
author. The writer declared that he had never heard anything like this
Lohengrin since Wagner's death. The tempos, the nuances, and the rhythmic
stress had been those Wagner himself had used. 'This was how the Master
interpreted his work, this was how it was played under his direction; unfortunately since then all has been forgotten.'[67] 'Your conducting is truly Wagnerian,
since you know how to modify the tempo in the spirit of the Master', wrote the
anonymous musician, and concluded his letter with the words: 'since Wagner
and Bülow, no orchestral exploit has been comparable to yours.'[68]

Even Karl Kraus, the terror of the Viennese establishment, warmly welcomed Mahler in a comment in the *Breslauer Zeitung*, though in doing so he
managed, typically, to pour scorn on almost everything and everyone associated
with the Opera at that time. He wrote:

Just recently a Siegfried figure, in the person of a new conductor, has arrived at the
Opera; one can tell from his face that he is determined to get rid of the old, inefficient
management. Herr Mahler's first appearance conducting *Lohengrin* was a success
universally acclaimed in the press. There is a rumour that he will soon be occupying
the Director's chair. Perhaps then the repertoire of the Hofoper will cease to consist
exclusively of *Cavalleria rusticana*, indigenous composers will no longer have their
manuscripts returned unread (they will be returned read), and deserving women
singers will no longer be shown the door without reason. Apparently the new conductor
has given such good proof of his effectiveness that some people are already hard at
work intriguing against him.[69]

Immediately after this début Mahler wrote to Justi, who was still in Hamburg, and sent her the most important press clippings. He was delighted by
their unanimity. 'The anti-Semitic papers are either silent or favourable', he

[66] According to Helm, Mahler had cut the accompaniment added by Richter in order to help the soprano
in the middle of the Act I 'Prayer'.

[67] The slowness of the Prelude, the wonderful softness of the chorus after the hero's farewell to the swan
and in the passage 'Seht, seht, welch seltsam Wunder', the superb crescendo of the Prayer, and many other
moments—all elicited the anonymous writer's enthusiastic admiration, as did the rallentando discreetly
employed by Mahler in the passage 'Rauschen des Festes, seid nun entronnen', in the wedding chorus of Act
III. He reminded Mahler that there had been an elderly cellist in Dresden by the name of Justus Dotzauer
(1783–1860) who had similarly told Wagner that Weber had conducted the opening adagio in the Overture
to *Der Freischütz* as slowly as he.

[68] NBL1. 75 ff.; NBL2. 88.

[69] *Breslauer Zeitung* (16 May 1897): BDB 213. Kraus's famous magazine, *Die Fackel*, had not yet been
founded.

wrote. 'The Opera personnel, members of the orchestra, etc., etc., are quite won over.' He rebuked Justi for complaining that he had not written to her before, saying that he had been so busy that he had hardly had time to breathe. While still looking for a permanent place to live, he had moved into a small furnished flat,[70] after abandoning the idea of renting an apartment in the Brülls' house, 'because of the anti-Semites'. His cook, Elise, had arrived from Hamburg, but had to sleep in the kitchen for the time being. In these first days in Vienna, 'a constant succession of congratulations, visitors, etc.', used up every minute of Mahler's days. But 'thank God, my worries are over! All Vienna welcomes me with real enthusiasm. . . . I am almost certain to be appointed Director soon.'[71] Mahler had even more reason to be pleased during the next few days: Jahn had assigned a number of major works to him, *Die Walküre*, *Siegfried*, *Le nozze di Figaro*, and *The Magic Flute*. This proved that he wished Mahler to be on an equal footing with his colleagues. For *Die Walküre* on 26 May, he was even allowed to rehearse the singers as he pleased. 'Before the holidays, I hope to be firmly entrenched here,' he told Justi. 'Only when you come to live here will you realize how much more humanely I am treated,' he wrote in another letter.

In those early days, Mahler tried to avoid hurting Mildenburg's feelings and to compensate for their separation by writing to her regularly, despite the many other claims on his time. He assured her again that 'sooner or later everything will come right for us'. Mildenburg had received a contract offer from America which he advised her to refuse, for he feared she would be required to sing too much and thought the proposed salary unworthy of her.[72] But the advice Mahler gave Mildenburg frightened Justi, who assumed that her brother had opposed the project so as to invite her to Vienna. Mahler reassured her:

Natalie is being silly and so are you. I never even thought of that. I advised her not to go to America because she could easily lose her voice there. Under no circumstances will she come here. Those are only the schemes of Papier and Natalie, etc. . . . I have had enough of their constant gossiping and now have other things to worry about.

In another letter he added: 'I hope you've recovered from your vertigo (*Drehkrankheit*) (a disease which sheep often suffer from) as I have from my sore throat.' Before leaving Hamburg, Mahler had apparently promised Justi that he would not marry Mildenburg. His exasperation can be sensed beneath the affectionate tone of the letter, and it was with considerable uneasiness that he learnt shortly afterwards that serious consideration was being given to offering Mildenburg an engagement at the Hofoper.

On 19 May, during a short trip to Dresden, where he had gone to attend the première of an opera by Anton Rückauf,[73] *Die Rosenthalerin*, Mahler caught a

---

[70] Universitätstrasse 6, second floor, door 5.

[71] MBR1, no. 161 to Anna von Mildenburg, dated 14 May; MBR2, no. 241.

[72] Besides which, Pollini would demand compensation for breach of contract, for he had told Mahler that he did not intend to let her go for at least a year.

[73] Anton Rückauf (1855–1903), a Czech composer, lived in Vienna, where he had been the permanent

cold. He returned to Vienna still suffering from it, and, as often before, the infection gradually settled in his throat, forcing him to take to his bed for several days. He nevertheless got up to conduct rehearsals of *Die Walküre*, but the performance, scheduled for the 26th, had to be cancelled at the last moment because the Sieglinde, Luise von Ehrenstein, was taken ill. Mahler then devoted his time to preparing two of his other Vienna 'débuts': *The Flying Dutchman* and *The Magic Flute*. While rehearsing the latter he realized that he could not obtain a sufficiently caressing effect from the cellos, for the string section of the orchestra was of Wagnerian dimension. Amid general applause, he summarily reduced the numbers of players by almost half. 'What success!' he said, smiling. 'But, gentlemen, don't imagine that I'm trying to please you! It is my conviction that so large an orchestra can only destroy the delicacy and magic of Mozart's music.'[74]

Mahler started making plans for the following autumn. One of them was a revival of *Der Freischütz*, with new tempos and simplified staging. This project was duly carried out. But this passage in Natalie's memoirs also shows that from the moment he took up his job in Vienna he started dreaming of a complete reform of the operatic stage: 'existing sets and costumes should go to the devil' he said. He planned to guide the public's taste in another direction which had already been adopted in the contemporary spoken theatre, one in which imagination 'must play an essential role'.[75]

During rehearsals of *The Magic Flute* and *Die Walküre*, Mahler's persistent cold had turned into a serious inflammation of the throat. When it seemed that this was subsiding, an abscess developed. Since 21 May[76] he had taken to his bed, getting up only to attend rehearsals. Exhausted and feverish, he almost lost his voice, and until the last moment he was not sure if he would be able to conduct the performance of *The Magic Flute* on 29 May. Natalie, who took excellent care of him in Justi's absence,[77] brought him by carriage to the Opera. As soon as he started to conduct and the music began to take possession of him, he forgot his illness. On the way home, he proudly pointed out to the faithful Natalie that his tempo in the Overture had been almost twice as slow as usual, thanks to which he had been able to accent each quaver in the theme, giving it an altogether different character. He added that the performances he conducted were often shorter than those of other conductors, even though he always gave the melodic elements their full value, without hurrying. The

accompanist of the famous Vienna Opera tenor, Gustav Walter. Brahms frequently advised him. His only opera, *Die Rosenthalerin*, had its first performance in Dresden on 7 May, with some success, but it was never staged in Vienna.

[74] NBL1. 77; NBL2. 89. Later Mahler said that the 'delicate pollen' of Mozart's composition could not survive too large an orchestra.

[75] Mahler added that he wanted to follow the lead already given by the Munich Shakespeare Theatre.

[76] According to a letter to Justi which is easy to date, since it mentions a performance of *Die Walküre*, scheduled for the following day, which had been cancelled due to the illness of Luise von Ehrenstein.

[77] In a letter to Justi, Mahler complained that Natalie 'watches over me like a hawk; if it were up to her, she'd keep me from seeing any woman under fifty'.

difference in a Wagner performance could be as great as half an hour, he said, because 'most conductors don't know how to distinguish the important from the unimportant: they give the same weight to all the passages, instead of just lightly passing over the secondary ones.'[78]

The success of *The Magic Flute* equalled that of *Lohengrin*. In the *Neues Wiener Tagblatt*, Karpath wrote that 'a spirit breathed through the performance, one that has been absent for a long time: the spirit of Mozart'. Mahler was 'as sensitive to Mozart as to Wagner', his style was admirably pure, everyone had been at pains to fall in line with it, and the impression of routine had been banished from the stage. Theodor Helm was equally enthusiastic in the *Deutsche Zeitung*; he reported that at least ten rehearsals had preceded the performance, and that the new conductor had a miraculous influence over the singers' diction and phrasing. The ensemble was admirably 'Mozartian' in style, though 'perhaps over-refined'.[79] In *Die Zeit*, Richard Wallaschek encouraged Mahler's moves towards reform by suggesting the suppression of some of Papageno's spoken replies. These had been retained because of oral stage tradition, but were not to be found in Schikaneder's libretto, and made the character into the grotesque hero of a comic farce, a 'parody of Offenbach'. Whether swayed by the advice of a writer who also taught musicology at the University of Vienna (probably Guido Adler), or by his own personal feelings, Mahler initiated a revision of the libretto which took until the autumn to complete.

The excitement and pleasure of conducting *The Magic Flute* had enabled Mahler to forget the state of his health, but next morning he suddenly felt worse and the doctor found a second abscess forming in his throat.[80] A specialist was summoned, and he decided to lance it immediately. The pain was so great after the operation that Mahler could not eat or even swallow; that evening he received an injection of morphine to relieve the pain. However, after spending three days in bed, he considered himself sufficiently recovered to conduct for a third time on 5 June. This was a performance of *The Flying Dutchman*, and again he managed to impose his personality, despite the insufficient preparation. 'I have succeeded here', he told Natalie,

because of my *Furor*, which in my view is indispensable to any true conductor. It enables him to wrest from even the most mediocre orchestras, choruses, and singers, a performance that corresponds to his own inner image of the work. It is also the reason why I fly into such a rage when they play or sing badly or out of tune. . . . If a woman

[78] NBL1. 80; NBL2. 91.

[79] This is one of the unconvincing reproaches Helm addressed to Mahler to comply with the anti-Semitic views of his paper. Another concerns the Moor (Monostatos) who 'mumbled' his delight at Papageno's bells, thus 'depriving the scene of part of its humour'. Nevertheless, Helm congratulates Mahler for having re-established the Mozartian truth throughout, and particularly for having suppressed the traditional cadence at the end of Pamina's aria. Cast of the 29 May performance: Teleky (Queen of the Night), Forster (Pamina), Mora, Ehrenstein, Kaulich (Three Ladies), Elizza (Papagena), Dippel (Tamino), Felix (Papageno), Reichenberg (Sarastro).   [80] NBL2. 92.

to whom I have been attracted sings a single false note or unmusical phrase, all my affection for her vanishes instantly, even turns to hatred. Conversely, a beautiful voice or some other sign of musical talent has often bewitched me.[81]

After this performance of the early Wagner opera, Theodor Helm, in the *Deutsche Zeitung*, once more expressed unreserved enthusiasm. He compared the 'freshness and decisiveness' of the Overture and of the choral passages with Fuchs's 'superficial and purely conventional' interpretation. The audience moreover, had clearly sensed the difference, for the Overture had been enthusiastically applauded, something that had never happened before. Urged on by an enthusiasm and love for his profession infinitely greater than his predecessor's, Mahler had a positive influence over the soloists. Heuberger admired the firm hand 'that orders and purifies all' and the conductor who penetrates to 'the very heart of the work'. Even the chorus, after a long eclipse, had come out into the light.[82] In his opinion 'the really important new event during the past season goes by the name of "Gustav Mahler"'. Thus, feeling himself unanimously supported by the Viennese press, Mahler could avoid worrying too much about his appointment as director, something which had not been mentioned for some time. Jahn obviously considered him as an indispensable assistant and a means of prolonging his own tenure. If he did not obtain the coveted post of director, Mahler would be content to continue as conductor, provided they gave him a long contract and sufficient remuneration. In the mean time he thought he might be able to take over the direction of the Gesellschafts-Konzerte.

After *The Flying Dutchman*, Mahler was confined to bed for almost a week with a high fever. He emerged from this illness thin and exhausted, weaker than he had ever been. He nevertheless conducted *Lohengrin* on 6 June, and this time Justi, who had joined him in Vienna, was in the audience. But Mahler's doctors feared that the abscesses would recur; one of them warned him of the possibility of chronic 'nasal catarrh' and prescribed daily throat painting, as well as a later operation to remove his tonsils,[83] and several days' complete rest. Mahler finally asked for leave of absence before the end of the season, for the heat in Vienna was becoming harder to bear as the summer approached and he had been advised to rest and convalesce in the mountains. Natalie and Justi had already taken a small house for the summer in Kitzbühel, in Tirol, about 800 metres above sea level. So Justi, Emma, and Elise, the cook, left on 11 June, and Mahler joined them three days later. The Villa Hohenegg was 'the most attractive yet of all our summer places'. The view was superb[84] and the climate excellent. Mahler wrote to Rosa Papier:

[81] NBL1. 79; NBL2. 90. Thus Mahler fell in love successively with Johanna Richter, Betty Frank, Mildenburg, and later, in Vienna, with Selma Kurz and Marie Gutheil-Schoder (probably).

[82] Cast of 5 June performance: Mora (Senta), Schrödter (Erik), Neidl (Holländer), Reichenberg (Daland).

[83] Had Mahler followed this excellent advice, he might have lived longer, for his final illness was due to a rheumatic heart, most likely the consequence of an earlier tonsil infection.

[84] On a card sent by Natalie to Ludwig Karpath on 18 June, Mahler also expresses his enthusiasm this time in a humorous rhyming postscript which also mentions that his throat trouble is now cured (BGM).

We live entirely cut off from the world. Our little house is so isolated and peaceful on the edge of a forest, and surrounded by meadows. Only Johann and Nandl come every day to bring us the mail, spinach, chickens, etc. The marvellous air and the refreshing calm have already made me into half a Hercules (the other half, unhappily, is decidedly absent). We take walks across the hills and in the forests around us, and from time to time we bathe in the nearby Schwarzsee. When it is too hot, we sleep or read. Such is the faithful description of a life pleasanter than I remember ever having experienced before. When, by chance, I have twinges of conscience, I quickly remind myself that I am convalescent; a dignified state that I have only known for the last two weeks; so then I sink back into a *dolce far niente*.[85]

Mahler was already considering building a house and a *Häuschen* in Kitzbühel when three days later an epidemic of scarlet fever broke out in the village. As none of the three family members had ever had this dangerous disease, they decided to abandon this paradise, especially since Mahler was still very weak. So they had to bundle up the scarcely unpacked luggage and look elsewhere for a place to stay. They stopped briefly at Innsbruck[86] before finding in Steinach am Brenner a most attractive house.[87] Unfortunately it had been booked by a Munich family from 1 July onwards, so they spent the last ten days of June there, and Mahler's health gradually improved, thanks to the fresh air and the daily painting of his throat by Justi. Then, all too soon, they had to make way for the Munich family. Moving up toward the Brenner Pass, they found a place to stay in Gries. But the accommodation turned out to be too uncomfortable, and once more they had to leave. This time they went a long way on foot and by bicycle, reaching the Ridnauntal, west of Sterzing,[88] on the southern side of the Alps. At this high altitude, Mahler was delighted to experience both rain and cold, after the exhausting heat of the previous days. Contrary to what one might have expected, all this bustle and being constantly on the move had no ill-effects. It kept him busy and gave him an opportunity to enjoy the mountain air and scenery, something he had not been able to do for several years. It also kept him from pondering too much about his creative work, an obsession that threatened to spoil the idle, sunny holidays whenever he forgot that he was convalescing.

One day, as Mahler and Natalie were bicycling down from Gries to Innsbruck, he began to zigzag erratically across the road. At that point the road ran beside a deep ravine with a mountain stream at the bottom. As they came to a bend, a moment's distraction or a rut in the road made Mahler swerve, and his bicycle ran over the edge of the ravine. He applied his brakes, but it was too late. At the last moment he managed to catch hold of a bush providentially growing on the precipitous slope. Suddenly he was hanging there, his free hand

[85] Letter of June 1897 to Rosa Papier, BMG 72.   [86] At the Reformhotel, Habsburgerhof.

[87] The Villa Zirnheim from which, on 19 June, Mahler wrote a letter of sympathy to his one-time teacher Heinrich Fischer, whose wife had just died (Stadtarchiv Iglau).

[88] Sterzing, in South Tirol, is known in Italy as Vipiteno. In a card to Emil Freund dated 15 July, Mahler calls Ridnaun 'a delightful unspoilt Alpine village'.

still clutching his bicycle, nothing but the raging torrent below. After a few moments he scrambled to safety, unscathed apart from a few scratches on his hands.[89] Mahler's greatest joy was climbing,[90] and once he had scaled a height he hated the thought of having to come down again. 'It's the same when I compose,' he once said to Natalie. 'When I have taken flight (as, for example, in the Finale of the Second), when I have reached a summit, I leave it with great reluctance, and then it is a matter of reaching for another, even higher one, unattainable during the first ascent.'

Every time Mahler found a quiet, picturesque spot on one of his walks, his imagination built a *Häuschen* there, and some distance away, out of earshot, a house. At the end of one excursion he discovered in Vahrn, near Brixen (Bressanone), a villa whose 'Mediterranean gaiety' enchanted him.[91] He decided to finish his vacation there and spent long and unusually idle hours admiring the view. 'It's a magnificent scene, mysterious and promising,' he exclaimed ecstatically, 'like a joyful future stretching out before us. Too beautiful for me to compose anything here!'[92] Nevertheless, after all his long exploratory trips, Vahrn was the place he finally chose for his summer holidays the following year. He rented the Villa Artmann,[93] and there, as fate would have it, he spent what was to prove to be one of the gloomiest and most unproductive summers of his whole life.

[89] NBL2. 93 ff.
[90] On 8 July, the day after his birthday, Mahler climbed the 2,500 metre Amthorspitze.
[91] Mahler and his family were still in Gries on 15 July but had moved to Vahrn by the 23. On 29 July he wrote a card to Justi giving the address 'Villa Mair, Vahrn'.
[92] NBL2. 94.
[93] He later changed his mind and rented less luxurious lodgings for the summer (see below, Chap. 4).

2

Substitute director—opening of the new season— the Opera under Jahn—first reforms

(July–September 1897)

I am knocking my head against the wall, but the wall is giving way . . .

DURING Mahler's summer of convalescence, among the many hopes and fears disturbing his peace of mind, there now arose once more a problem that he thought had been solved by his departure from Hamburg. If he had not yet broken definitively with Anna von Mildenburg, this was probably because he feared some violent reaction on her part and therefore wanted to avoid giving her an unnecessary shock. Now there was a possibility of her being engaged at the Hofoper, thanks once more to the influence of Rosa Papier and her friend Eduard Wlassack. Mahler's first letters to Mildenburg from Vienna were friendly and even somewhat paternal in tone. After refusing the offers from America, she sang that summer in Bayreuth and he often gave her advice. From time to time, in referring to his former post, his letters grew sarcastic:

It seems that my star is in the ascendant again in Hamburg: it appears that Fräulein Sans is now seriously thinking of having me appointed conductor of the Philharmonic. If things go on like this even Marwege[1] may finally consider me a tolerable conductor . . . As for that goose Artner,[2] ignore her. I am delighted that they find so many good things to say about me now. I've heard this from several sources. What a pack of scoundrels! I can't tell you how disgusted I am when I think about them. I beg you, steer clear of them.[3]

Towards the end of June there seems to have been a serious misunderstanding between Mahler and Anna. The immediate occasion of it is not known. Perhaps

---

[1] Marwege, a violinist and member of the Stadt-Theater orchestra in Hamburg, was persistently hostile to Mahler.

[2] Josefine von Artner, a soprano, was a member of the Hamburg Stadt-Theater company.

[3] MBR1, no. 212; MBR2, no. 248, and letter to Mildenburg (ÖNB, Theatersammlung).

she had noticed how the tone of his letters had changed over the previous few months. In any case, Mahler received a telegram from her asking him not to read the registered letter he was about to receive. Meanwhile Rosa Papier had been strongly warning him against renewing their close relationship, and although this intrusion into his private life annoyed him intensely, he knew it was sound advice. On 23 June a further letter from Frau Papier arrived in Steinach, announcing that the plan to engage Mildenburg had become a reality. She would soon be offered a contract. Natalie, who was spending summer with the Mahlers, replied:

Your news about Mildenburg's forthcoming engagement in Vienna burst yesterday evening like a bombshell upon our Tyrolean peace: you cannot imagine what a frightful effect it had, not only upon us women, but almost more on Mahler himself . . . Your kind and well-meant counsel and 'explanations' to Gustav about Mildenburg, which he willingly accepts and understands, coming as they do from you, cannot and will not have the slightest effect on his relationship with her, or rather her enormous power over him and his unresisting and insurmountable weakness where she is concerned. Therein lies, and always lay, the danger: that when he is with her, even with his eyes wide open, he always lets himself get helplessly enmeshed in her net, so much so that no-one (no matter how close to him, no matter how fond he is of them) and least of all he himself, even if he tries with all his strength, can disentangle him. It was because he felt this, and during all those interminable months (from the instant M. came to Hamburg to the moment when, because of her and her alone, he had to leave) learned it by experiences as painful for himself as for others, that there was and is, for him and for all who have anything to do with her, only one solution, and that is separation. If M. really comes to Vienna it will be the worst misfortune that could possibly befall G.—and don't believe, my dear, that I'm exaggerating when I say that. If you had lived through even one day in Hamburg with us you would not only understand our worst fears, you would, in your dear lively way, share them and be greatly alarmed. So if there is anything that can still be done, we implore you in your kindness to avert this disaster that threatens us all![4]

A week later, Mahler himself wrote to Rosa Papier:

Above all I must frankly confess to you that I cannot disagree with our friend Wlassack. It would really be too much to expect the engagement of a talent like M. to be foregone for any kind of personal consideration. Moreover, I could not help smiling over the way our friend expressed himself on the subject, it was all too similar to my own way of thinking; it's little things like that which show the elective affinity between two natures. I think we should let things take their course. Anyway we've a whole year ahead of us; and during that time I shall remove the obstacles between M. and myself that would at the moment make collaboration difficult.—By the way, I must ask you to forgive me for not showing your kind letter to our friend Bauer, as you wished (if I understand you correctly). In this matter she seems to me, contrary to her usual nature, to let her

---

[4] Letter from Natalie to Rosa Papier, 24 June 1897, MS copy found among Ludwig Karpath's papers (BDB 214).

feelings run away with her. I don't know what she wrote to you, but I'm sure she went much too far . . .[5]

These two letters provide vital evidence as to the psychology of Mahler's relationships with both Mildenburg and Natalie. In her letter to Rosa Papier, Natalie certainly exaggerated his weakness. Secretly in love with Mahler for many years, she regarded Mildenburg as a rival to be feared. Above all, she dreaded a repetition of the events she had witnessed in Hamburg, which would effectively put an end to the hopes she still harboured of sharing Mahler's life. Equally clearly, Mildenburg did have a powerful hold over Mahler, and had imprudently created an impossible situation at the Hamburg Stadt-Theater. Moreover, as we shall see later on, Frau Papier herself had no illusions as to the character of her former pupil, and shortly thereafter warned Mahler explicitly and forcefully against renewing the liaison. From this incident and from the various documents still extant, it is possible to draw more general conclusions about Mahler's character, and the weakness that characterized his relations with all the women with whom he fell in love, despite the principles he was on occasion to lay down in this respect.[6] As his dealings with Alma were to demonstrate, this weakness did not necessarily show in his letters, in which he offered much advice and exhortation, and even on occasion made rather serious reproaches.[7] In his daily life he probably behaved quite differently, and this could indicate the need to read between the lines of the letters to the subject of his affections.

Early in July, Mildenburg's engagement at the Hofoper, which until then had seemed uncertain, was confirmed by the administration, and a Vienna paper immediately announced that it was Mahler who had arranged for his 'lady friend' to be offered a place in Vienna. However, it seems doubtful that he had intervened in her favour, as he later asserted. If he did, it is likely that his sole aim was to please Rosa Papier, since Mildenburg was, after all, her best pupil, and the first one to succeed. In a letter written in the middle of July,[8] Mahler advised Mildenburg not to discuss her expectations with anyone. He had told Bezecny and Wlassack how talented she was, and they asked Pollini to free her for the autumn of 1898. In Venice, Pollini had given him to understand that he might consent, because the Emperor of Austria had just awarded him a high imperial decoration. Mahler assured Anna that her success in Bayreuth would 'force your enemies and those who envy you to lay down their arms'; but he had decided all the same to cancel his proposed visit to Bayreuth rather than provoke fresh gossip. Finally, he urged Mildenburg not to drop her negotiations with Berlin, since nothing was as yet decided in Vienna. Once it had been

---

[5] Letter from Mahler to Rosa Papier (BDB 214).

[6] See above, Vol. i, Chap. 20, Mahler's description of the wife he would choose were he ever to marry.

[7] See below, Chap. 12, the long and now famous letter Mahler wrote to Alma at the time of their engagement.

[8] The letter is undated but Mildenburg's appearance as Kundry took place on 19 July (KMI).

officially agreed to give her a contract at the Hofoper, he wrote to her again at the end of July, before leaving the Tyrol.

I have to come straight out and ask you an important question that, despite my desire not to upset you at such an important moment,[9] I cannot put off any longer. I have prepared the ground for you in Vienna to such effect that, with Pollini's consent, they will soon be sending you an offer of engagement. If you accept, it is essential (now that I have a clear picture of conditions here) that we restrict our personal relations to an absolute minimum, in order not to make life for both of us intolerable again.

The entire Opera staff is on the alert because of the gossip from Hamburg, and the news of your engagement will burst like a bombshell. If, therefore, we were to provide the slightest grounds for further gossip, <u>my own position</u> would rapidly become untenable and I'd have to pack my bags again, as I did in Hamburg. You too would suffer once more, even though your job would not be in danger. I must therefore ask you now, dear Anna: do you feel strong enough to work with me here in Vienna and yet avoid all personal contact and preferential treatment, at least for the first year? I trust you realize that this will be just as hard for me as for you and that these words are dictated solely by dire necessity. The stakes are too high, and I dare not, indeed must not, leave either of us with the slightest illusion.

I beg you, my dear Anna, however busy you may be, to give me a brief, but frank and sincere answer! You will soon receive the offer. The difficulties with Pollini will be smoothed and without your having to intervene. But now that the whole matter is almost settled, I am beginning to get cold feet, and I ask myself, as I am asking you, whether we realize what we are taking upon ourselves? Please, answer me at once, for so much depends for me on your reply. I fear we may be imposing an unbearable ordeal upon ourselves and, if you feel that too then I beg you quite simply to refuse the offer and accept the one you will shortly receive from Berlin. Whatever happens, it can only benefit you to have been approached by the Vienna Opera, and that is why I have let matters go this far without discussing it with you. I beg you to answer me quickly and candidly, even if only in a few lines. I'll give you further details as soon as I receive your letter . . .

Mahler's firmness on this occasion was due to the fact that 'the worries and humiliations of the last months in Hamburg are still very fresh in my memory'.[10] Although Mildenburg's answer has not survived, there is no doubt that she accepted Mahler's conditions without admitting to herself that the break between them was final. Later, in fact, she was to complain that he 'had erected an impenetrable wall between them from the very first day she entered his office in Vienna'.[11] The firm letter that Rosa Papier wrote to her in September confirms the unfavourable impression of Anna's character which emerges from the preceding documents:

Mahler has just left me. It has now been decided that you are to sing as a guest in December, with a view to a contract. Mahler said he would write to you today . . . I beg

---

[9] Her first Kundry in *Parsifal*.
[10] Undated letter to Rosa Papier (middle of July).   [11] BMG 75.

you to be reasonable and not to say anything about Mahler having compromised you. It was your fault if he stayed with you until late at night and it was you who chose to advertise the whole affair in your usual way. If you have the courage to do this you must bear the consequences. What is so disastrous? He did not dishonour you, thank God, and for the two of you to marry would be calamitous, absurd, idiotic, sheer folly! Since marriage is out of the question, why continue your liaison? If you were to see one another as often as you did in Hamburg, and if you were to dominate him as you did there, you would both lose your jobs. Don't you realize that the poor man is suffering as a result of his foolishness, don't you understand that, like all men, he is weak?[12]

This letter is again of particular interest because none of Mahler's surviving letters to Anna contain any reproach and there are few contemporary accounts of Anna's character or the nature of their relationship. Now we learn that Anna had come near to blackmailing him by publicizing their liaison. Knowing this makes it easier to understand his attitude. Before closing this important chapter in Mahler's life, it must be added that Mildenburg was rarely indifferent to male admiration. It would perhaps be discourteous to draw up a list of her many 'admirers' for she was as passionate as she was fickle. The list would be a long one and Mahler was undoubtedly right to decide against a marriage which would certainly have ended in disaster.[13]

During his summer of rest and convalescence in the Tyrol, Mahler closely followed what was happening at the Opera. During the first weeks in the country, he studied scores[14] and revised plans for the coming season. But the news from Vienna was not reassuring. A cable from Rosa Papier informed him that 'the Director is staying on', and Mahler immediately wrote to Wlassack for details.[15] The latter replied that 'everything seems to be settled—both Bezecny and Jahn are staying on!' 'No one knows what will happen later on,' Mahler wrote to Mildenburg, 'or when and on what terms my contract will be extended . . . Richter is, and will remain, first conductor. I am anxious to see how things develop. My contract expires in a year's time, and I don't know if or on what terms they will be prepared to renew it.' He nevertheless went out of his way to be diplomatic. 'If things go on like this,' he wrote to Adele Marcus, repeating what he had already said to Mildenburg, 'even Marwege may finally consider me a tolerable conductor . . . What do you think of my "popularity" and the wind blowing in my favour? At present, I have only three enemies in Vienna: Jahn, Richter and Fuchs! Everyone else thinks I'm a charming person and delightful companion! Grrr! . . . What a surprise is in store for them!'[16] On 2 July he wrote to Rosa Papier:

[12] Letter of 24 Sept. 1897, from Rosa Papier to Mildenburg (ÖNB, Theatersammlung).

[13] One of Mildenburg's admirers, the critic Ludwig Karpath, wrote to her on 3 Oct. 1900, reproaching her for being nothing but 'a vain prima donna', interested only in herself and her own comfort. Mahler, he told her, had been right to say that 'one would need the soul of a *valet de chambre* to live with you. . . . And now you complain of your loneliness!' (ÖNB, Theatersammlung.)

[14] HOA contain a letter Mahler wrote to Hofrath Doczi, Johann Strauss's librettist, concerning a revival of *Ritter Pazman*, the Waltz King's only serious opera.

[15] Letter of 19 June (HOA, Z.983/1897).   [16] MBR1, no. 212; MBR2, no. 248.

With determination and calm, both of which I promise you I possess, it is possible to overcome all difficulties . . . I wish things would start moving again. This idleness is getting me down! If only the situation would clarify. If only things would finally come right! If my hands were not tied, I could accomplish so much, but I fear they'll remain tied as long as Wilhelm [Jahn] hangs on to his sinecure.[17]

The next day, without waiting for Frau Papier's reply, Mahler wrote a long letter to Eduard Wlassack:

Dear and venerated Herr Regierungsrath! I hope you will not mind or blame my present idleness, if I permit myself to send you a sign of life. Actually all I want is to have another chat with you. I really miss those brief sessions in the Bräunerstrasse or the Habsburgergasse to which I had grown accustomed. In these quiet days, when I have had much opportunity to think over the recent past, I often felt the need to tell you, my venerated friend (may I be allowed to address you in this way?), how deeply obliged I am to you, and how conscious I am, and always will be, of what you have done for me. I know that you were guided only by your concern for the best interests of the Institute, but I feel that perhaps in the course of events you also came to feel some sympathy with my humble person, and that is what I should now like to thank you for. You have given me more than you can imagine. I have so often wanted to say this to you, but you will understand that shyness has always prevented me from doing so. Now I am putting it in writing, for it is easier to put such things down on paper without blushing. My dearest wish is always to win anew and preserve your confidence and friendship. Only now— having gained some insight into the circumstances—can I really gauge how much energy and personal commitment you must have expended in order to get me accepted. I am firmly convinced that no-one else could have done it. If I now speak of my gratitude it means above all that it will be my sincere endeavour to be a loyal colleague to you, and to share in your troubles and pains. It is a source of satisfaction to me to know that this is exactly what you need, and that it will give the Institute the long-desired impetus.[18]

While his appointment as director remained unconfirmed, it was, of course, in Mahler's interest to court Wlassack's favour. His expressions of devotion and gratitude are here somewhat tainted with obsequiousness towards the man to whom he owed everything and from whom he could expect everything. The rest of the letter consisted mainly of plans for the coming season. Mahler made the following suggestions for revivals: Mozart's *Così fan tutte* which in its 'original version' had just been enormously successful in Munich;[19] Lortzing's *Undine*, much applauded in Berlin;[20] one or several operas by Gluck;[21] *Der Freischütz* conducted by himself, which, with the new cast he was suggesting ('without spending a penny', he added!), would be sure of a resounding success. He also

---

[17] BMG 75.

[18] This long letter (19 pp.) to Wlassack, dated 3 July 1897, formerly belonged to Kammersänger Anton Dermota.

[19] Conducted by Hermann Levi, who was responsible for this 'original version'. Mahler used Levi's score when he revived the work on 4 Oct. 1900.

[20] Despite his admiration for Lortzing, Mahler never revived this work.

[21] Mahler suggested Fuchs as the conductor, with Jahn conducting the first performance only.

proposed a new production of a work by Wagner; Méhul's *Joseph et ses frères*;[22] and possibly the revival of a whole series of operas 'for which the casting is poor, even wrong'.

I could write pages and pages and still not have finished. Naturally this is the way things are in an artistic household which has been run by 'the housekeeper' for years, without 'the lady of the house' taking any interest. But there one has to sit, taking orders from the Herr Professor, one's head swimming with projects and plans like contraband that might be seized at any moment. You will understand with what ill humour and impatience a smuggler like myself remains cooped up in the toll house watching the customs men and the Pharisees take their meal. And now we would have plenty of time to draw up a programme and prepare for its implementation. If only we could sit down and 'go to it'! I have taken far too much of your time, but there was so much I needed to get off my chest.

As it happened, though Mahler was unaware of it, things were rapidly moving in his favour. On 13 July, Intendant Bezecny officially informed the Opera personnel that: 'when the season reopens on 1 August, and for the duration of Director Wilhelm Jahn's leave, that is, for as long as he is unable to direct the affairs of the Opera, his responsibilities will be taken over by Kapellmeister Mahler.'[23] Mahler was then on a long bicycle trip in the Pustertal[24] and therefore did not see a newspaper for several days. Upon his return to Vahrn on 23 July, he got the news of his appointment as deputy director in a letter from Jahn, 'whose shaky signature resembled that of a blind man'. A few hours later another letter came, this time from Wlassack, telling him to go at once to visit Wilhelm Jahn in Trofaiach, Styria, and ask for instructions. Mahler answered immediately: 'Wlassack! Like a thunderbolt, like a bombshell, just when I thought I was further than ever from my goal! I immediately sent you a telegram, both to Vienna and the Semmering, and hope to hear from you soon.' To Rosa Papier, who had also supported him from the outset, Mahler wrote on 26 July:

I was all the more astonished to learn that Wlassack had obtained my appointment as 'deputy', as I'm living in the mountains and never see a newspaper; my friends' congratulations came as something of a surprise, for I had no inkling the Vienna papers had already announced the news. It was a bolt from the blue which, I think, several people may have a hard time getting over.[25]

Mahler was so busy making preparations for a hurried departure that he hardly had time to enjoy the good news. Only a week remained before the reopening

---

[22] Again, despite his fondness for it, Mahler did not revive this opera in Vienna either.

[23] The circular letter was sent from Nauheim, where Bezecny was spending the summer. The same day the Intendant wrote to Jahn to congratulate him on the success of his operation and to break the news: 'It is essential that, in your absence, the direction of the performances should be concentrated in one firm hand.'

[24] This must have been Mahler's first trip to the valley in Südtirol where Toblach is situated. Later on, when he settled in Maiernigg for the summer, he went for bicycle tours there every year.

[25] BMG 77.

of the Opera, and he had visits to make to Jahn and Wlassack and also to
Hanslick in Ischl. As he was boarding the Vienna train at Vahrn, the sight of
some workmen shovelling the last spadefuls of earth on to a grave disturbed
him. 'How long will it be before they'll be throwing it on us?' he asked Natalie.
'That thought should calm us amid all the storms of life; but as long as life holds
us, we must believe in it, we cannot escape it and are completely at the mercy
of the turbulence and raging of the elements.'[26] And indeed the Vienna Opera
was soon to demand all Mahler's energy, causing him momentarily to lose 'his
sense of direction'.

Having left Vahrn on the evening of 26 July, Mahler reached Vienna the next
day and set off again immediately for Baden bei Wien, where he met Wlassack
on the morning of 28 July. At first Wlassack was 'somewhat reserved'. He had
apparently not forgiven Mahler for not rushing to Vienna as soon as he had
heard the news of his appointment. But gradually the atmosphere became
friendlier: 'How was I to know it was so important to him?' Mahler wrote to Rosa
Papier from Vienna on 30 July. 'Surely today is just as good! Anyway he'll be
back tomorrow and we can start working together.' On the advice of both
Wlassack and Richard Heuberger, Hanslick's deputy on the *Neue Freie Presse*,
Mahler then went to Ischl to see Hanslick and thank him for his strong
support.[27] 'I cannot do less,' he wrote to Rosa Papier, 'for everyone says he has
paid me an exceptional honour, and that I would be committing a crime of *lèse-
majesté* if I didn't go.'[28] But his journey to Ischl was fruitless, because Hanslick
was away that day.

On the evening of 28 July, Mahler was received by Jahn in his villa in
Trofaiach in Styria. He spent the whole of the next day there, 'overwhelmed' by
the kindness of the old director, who 'seemed to be afraid of me'. 'If only I knew
whether I should accept his kindness and friendship!' he wrote after this visit.

In any case, I feel it's a good sign that he went to such trouble to be pleasant. He himself
officially announced to me that I must now make my own decisions; however, he then
presented me with the complete program for August (I don't know if he was entitled to
do so). Although I'm not entirely in agreement (it does not suit me at all to have all
those difficult Wagner works in August), I am quite happy to start with it, since I am
still so unfamiliar with personnel questions.[29]

Nevertheless, the visit was an awkward one for Mahler, for he sensed that his
host was completely in the dark regarding the decisions that had been reached
concerning him. 'I must admit that I almost felt guilty at the thought that my
appointment will shorten and embitter the little time that he still has left to
live.'[30] A few days later he said to Karpath:

---

[26] NBL2. 94 ff.

[27] At the end of Aug., Mahler seems to have spent most of his time journeying by rail. On the 27th he
visited Wlassack in Baden and, the following day, Jahn at Trofaiach. On the 29th he was at Ischl, in the
Salzkammergut, where he failed to meet Hanslick and returned that evening to Vienna, where he was met by
Ludwig Karpath at the station (unpubl. telegram to Karpath, Knud Martner collection).

[28] BMG 77.   [29] BMG 79 (letter of 30 July to Rosa Papier).   [30] Ibid.

The poor man doesn't seem to have the slightest suspicion that I shall soon be appointed in his place. I must admit that, from a purely human point of view, I feel terribly sorry for him. But what is the use, for if I do not replace him, someone else will, and I naturally prefer to be the chosen one. Jahn's fate is sealed: when he returns to Vienna early in September, he will be officially asked to submit his resignation.[31]

Mahler returned to Vienna with a sense of triumph and relief, instead of the anxieties he had experienced previously. He first stayed in Pötzleinsdorf,[32] where the Spieglers were on vacation. But the weather was wretched and the local 'society' difficult to bear, so he returned to the city and lived in hotels while waiting for his new apartment. Jahn had 'very kindly' placed an office at his disposal, and there was constant coming and going by Opera employees wishing to consult Mahler about their work. He began to realize that 'the job of deputy director is no bed of roses'.[33] He was literally deluged with difficulties; discipline at the Hofoper was slack at the best of times, but now torrential rains had flooded most of the railway lines round Vienna and many of the Opera's employees were unable to report for duty. *Lohengrin*, announced for the opening performance of the season, on 1 August, almost had to be cancelled, first because of the absence of the singers, then because the baritone Franz Neidl, who was to sing Telramund, fell ill; but at the last minute everything came right. During the performance, according to the *Neue Freie Presse*, Mahler again showed his 'brilliant qualities as a conductor'. He was warmly applauded after the Prelude. The *Fremden-Blatt*, however, noted a 'derailment' in the quintet in the first act,[34] admirably compensated for by the 'superb crescendo' Mahler obtained in the great ensemble that followed. The article attacked the excesses of the 'second chorus', i.e. the claque, which noisily applauded Winkelmann at his first appearance. 'It is only between the acts, i.e. in the intervals, that the receiving half of an artistic performance, i.e. the public, should show its feelings. The acts themselves must be reserved exclusively for the giving half, in other words, the performers.'[35]

Two days later, *William Tell* had to be replaced at the eleventh hour by *Faust*, which Mahler conducted without a single rehearsal. In addition to the administrative tasks that took up so much of his time, he also had to conduct almost every evening in early August, because Fuchs was still on leave and Richter was stranded by the floods at Hainfeld, in Lower Austria. Mahler telegraphed Richter, asking him to come to his aid as quickly as possible, but the older

[31] BMG 57.

[32] Situated in the north-west of central Vienna, Pötzleinsdorf and Währing are today part of the 18th district.

[33] Letter to Justi, 30 July (RWO).

[34] This 'derailment' probably resulted from Mahler's very individual conducting technique, as described above by Franz Schmidt (see Chap. 1). The same critic noted that Wilhelm Hesch was singing the role of the King for the first time; previously it had been taken by Karl Grengg.

[35] Cast of Lohengrin, 1 Aug. 1897: Ehrenstein (Elsa); Kaulich (Ortrud); Winkelmann (Lohengrin); Horwitz (Telramund); Felix (Heerrufer); Hesch (King).

conductor, who thought he detected a shade of reproach in the message, answered that he 'knew his duty' and that his delay was only due to circumstances beyond his control. He finally reached Vienna on 5 or 6 August, and Mahler saw him at once, so as to divide the season's programmes between them. Their meeting was friendlier than Mahler had anticipated, and Richter even agreed to hand over to him the *Ring* cycle productions of *Das Rheingold* and *Die Walküre*, scheduled for late August.[36]

Shortly after returning to Vienna, Mahler had another meeting with Prince Liechtenstein. During their half-hour conversation, the Obersthofmeister confirmed that Jahn would be retired upon his return. In the middle of August, during the rehearsals of the *Ring*, Max Kalbeck, critic of the *Neues Wiener Tagblatt*, wrote from Vienna to his assistant Karpath, giving him news of the Opera, which he said was unrecognizable: work went on there all day long, and 'contrary to past practice, special attention is paid to the classics'. Jahn's return was expected in September, but Kalbeck now considered it impossible for Mahler to relinquish his functions; it would be 'like trying to stop the locomotive of an express train'. In addition, all the Opera personnel were enthusiastically in his favour, especially after a performance of *Le nozze di Figaro* on 14 August.[37]

This performance of Mozart's work delighted not only the audience at the Opera but also Richard Heuberger,[38] assistant critic on the *Neue Freie Presse*:

While it is true that a performance of *Figaro* suffices to transform an ordinary day into a holiday, this is doubly true when the spectator feels protected by the conductor against any musical vagaries. Herr Mahler is such a conductor. He has delved deeply into Mozart's masterpiece, not only in its musical but also in its dramatic aspects, thereby undertaking a renovation still not complete, perhaps, but on which an intelligent and successful start has been made. First and foremost, he has succeeded in obliging the singers to respect the score. In a theatre [a play], no actor, no matter how great or small, could permit himself the slightest modification of our poets' masterpieces, yet, at the opera, this has been a daily occurrence. It is in the most august institutions, employing our greatest singers, that the most serious offences have been committed. How many times have we heard Fräulein X or Herr Y 'improve' Beethoven, Mozart or Wagner?

Now Herr Mahler has resolutely put a stop to all such goings on. With the exception of one passage in the aria 'Deh vieni, non tardar', it all conformed exactly to the score. The sustained tension and vigorous applause of the audience should convince the singers that neither their absurd cadences nor their misplaced 'grace notes' (*Hilfsnoten*)

[36] Eventually Richter let him conduct the other two parts of the cycle as well.

[37] BMG 63. Cast of the 14 Aug. *Le nozze di Figaro*: Forster (Susanna), Sedlmair (Countess), Pohlner (Cherubino), von Thann (Marcellina), Neidl (Figaro), Ritter (Count).

[38] The *Neue Freie Presse* article is unsigned, but Mahler's letter of thanks, quoted below, proves that its author was Heuberger. The chief music critic of this paper was still Hanslick, who also lost no opportunity to defend Mahler. It was probably in this same year that Mahler wrote to the dean of Viennese critics, thanking him 'for having so often and so seriously discussed my work' (letter sold in the 1960s by Heck, the Viennese autograph dealer).

will win them artistic and formal success, but rather their fidelity to the spirit and soul of the work they are interpreting. Our heartfelt thanks to Herr Mahler, for having thus courageously given our excellent artists an unexpected reason for self-confidence.[39]

On the day this article appeared, Mahler wrote to Heuberger thanking him:

My 'renovation', as you call it, would only half succeed if you and the other representatives of public opinion were not with me. What you wrote yesterday, for example, was the first reassurance I have received concerning my performance [of *Figaro*]. I think that henceforth I shall have no more trouble in requiring precision from my artists as the first condition of success. I very much regretted not meeting you last night. There are many details I should have liked to discuss with you.[40]

After a second performance of *Figaro*, Hirschfeld, in the *Wiener Abendpost*, felt that 'Mozart's spirit conducted through the person of Mahler', for

he is able to free the melodic line from the heaviness of material sound so that it rises from the orchestra like perfume from flowers. The delicious ensembles, like the duet preceding the first Finale, floated airily on wings of gossamer. How carefully, how delicately he brought out the nuances in this Finale and the characterization of each individual voice! It would be tempting to point out all the countless refinements, the sparks of intelligence, the skilful improvements to the staging. . . . In the past, *Figaro* has always been a last-minute opera, performed only in case of necessity; this version of Mozart is new to the Hofoper. . . . Mahler has managed to weld the singers, some of whom as individuals may have shortcomings, into an intimate ensemble which makes one forget the dimensions of the hall. He keys everything to Mozart's fortes and pianos in an interpretation which has its own dynamics, its own colour.[41]

Max Graf, writing several years later, when he had become one of Mahler's bitterest critics, recalled what he considered to be the various stages in Mahler's conducting style. In his earlier conducting of *Figaro* in Prague, Mahler was too 'impetuous', whereas in the 1897 performance in Vienna he seemed to 'control both his nerves and the orchestra', and to have become a 'musical thinker'. But in his later years in Vienna, still according to Graf, Mahler had become too 'ecstatic'.[42]

---

[39] Heuberger also congratulated Mahler for having restored to Act II the short Susanna–Cherubino duet and for adding drama to the latter's second aria by making the singer strike a 'delightfully stiff' attitude. The whole performance 'beautifully accompanied by a small orchestra', was the 'most exciting' he had ever heard.

[40] 'Ungedruchte Briefe von Gustav Mahler an Richard Heuberger', *Musikblätter des Anbruch*, 18: 3 (May 1936), 67. In the same letter, Mahler raises the subject of Heuberger's ballet *Struwelpeter*, to be performed at the Hofoper in 1898. Mahler wrote another letter of thanks to Heuberger concerning one of his reviews, after which they exchanged no more letters until 1900. At this time they quarrelled over Mahler's retouched orchestration of Beethoven's Ninth Symphony (see below, Chap. 7).

[41] This was the performance of 27 Sept. The cast was the same as for 14 Aug. with the exception of Michalek (Cherubino) and Hesch (Bartolo). Once again Helm, in the *Deutsche Zeitung*, praised Mahler's conducting, with the sole exception of a ritardando in the Overture. However his paper's anti-Semitic bias made it impossible for Helm to praise Mahler unconditionally.

[42] Graf emphasized the 'naturalness' of the performance of the Act II Finale. As stated above, he later became one of Mahler's persistent critics. In 1907 he praised this 1897 performance at the expense of the new production of the same opera where he criticized Mahler's excessive 'nervous' refinement, subjective style, and muffled sonorities (GWO 82).

During the same month of August Mahler conducted, besides this memorable performance of *Figaro*, *The Flying Dutchman*, *Die lustigen Weiber von Windsor*, *Le Prophète*, *Der Freischütz*, and *Don Giovanni*, and at the same time prepared the complete *Ring* cycle for the end of the month. But it was also necessary to start looking for interesting new works to add to the Opera's repertory. As early as 1895, Natalie had tried to interest him in Hugo Wolf's opera *Der Corregidor*. In his reply at that time, Mahler had asked her to request Wolf to send him a score of his work, 'unless he can or wants to have it produced elsewhere'. 'If it is in my power, I shall see that it is performed, that is to say, assuming I find that it deserves performance. Don't tell him that last part, or else you could simply do it in a slightly vaguer form.'[43] Now, after a long estrangement dating from a quarrel they had fifteen years earlier, Mahler had resumed his friendship and discussed with Wolf the possibility of putting on his opera.[44] During the summer, Mahler was often mentioned in Wolf's correspondence. A letter written to his friend in Graz, Heinrich Potpeschnigg, on 17 May 1897, contained the following passage: 'Yesterday I had a visit from Mahler, the newly engaged conductor, who is very interested in *Der Corregidor* and will do everything he can to get it put on in the coming season.'[45] A few days later, Wolf added that he was going to put the manuscript of his opera at Mahler's disposal.[46] At the beginning of July, Wolf informed Potpeschnigg that in the course of time Mahler had developed into 'quite a decent person'.[47] Later that month he wrote: 'Mahler will come on 1 August, and then we can discuss the performance rights and conditions in detail. You will no doubt have seen in the papers that Mahler has been appointed provisional director. Actually, it is definite that he will be Jahn's successor.'[48]

Wolf also wrote to his friend Hugo Faisst on 10 August:

I shall henceforth be a frequent visitor at the Opera because, since Mahler's appearance on the podium, we can dare once more to enter those 'unheiligen Hallen' . . .[49] Thanks to him—he is temporarily replacing the Director—I can get a box or orchestra stall whenever I want, one advantage being that it does not cost me a penny. They'll be giving *Der Corregidor* at the end of January or February.

Writing to another friend, Oskar Grohe, on 25 August 1897, Wolf said: 'There are many interesting things I'd like to tell you about Mahler, with whom I am

[43] Letter from Mahler to Natalie, 3 Sept. 1895 (NBL2. 38).

[44] In a letter to Wolf's friend Oskar Grohe, Mahler claims that his influence at the Opera is still limited and thus retains for himself the possibility of refusing *Der Corregidor* (letter of 28 June 1897, Hebrew Univ. and National Library, Jerusalem).

[45] Hugo Wolf, *Briefe an Heinrich Potpeschnigg*, ed. H. Nonveiller (Union Deutsche Verlagsgesellschaft, Stuttgart, 1923), 190.

[46] Card to Potpeschnigg of 21 May 1897, Gesellschaft der Musikfreunde, Vienna; letters to Potpeschnigg of 1 July and 11 Aug. 1897 and 4 Feb. 1898, and card from Faisst to Wolf of 9 Aug. 1897 (BGM).

[47] Wolf, *Briefe an Potpeschnigg*, 198, letter of 3 July.

[48] Ibid. 200.

[49] 'Unholy halls', a reference to Sarastro's 'In diesen heilg'n Hallen' (within these sacred halls) in *The Magic Flute*.

on friendly terms again, but I'll follow your example and remain silent.' In a further letter to Potpeschnigg, written on 11 August, Wolf informed him that 'I see a lot of Mahler and we are very friendly, even though he is incredibly busy, standing in for the Director, as you probably already know.'[50] After the performance of *Der Freischütz* on 17 August—'very successful', according to Wolf— the two musicians wound up the evening together at the Spatenbräu restaurant: 'Among other things we spoke of *Der Corregidor* and about the forthcoming performance in Strasbourg. Mahler, when I cornered him about it, thought it could not do any harm if Strasbourg went ahead, since it was still doubtful whether the Vienna Hofoper would perform my work this season.'[51] I shall have more to say below about this renewed friendship between Mahler and Wolf, and the plans for performing *Der Corregidor*, which in fact came to nothing at the time.[52]

Before 24 August, the date set for the beginning of the Wagner cycle, Justi returned to Vienna, where Adele Marcus and her daughter had come to hear Mahler conduct. On 11 August he had already left the furnished rooms in Universitätstrasse and moved into the new apartment, Bartensteingasse 3, where he was to spend more than a year.[53] He enjoyed having a place he could call 'home' again—something he had not been able to do since leaving Hamburg six months before. However, the multiple tasks of administration, reorganization, conducting, and producing took up all his time and energy.[54] When Natalie Bauer-Lechner reached Vienna, she found him deep in the final preparations for the *Ring*,[55] working like a man possessed. He was at the Opera continuously from 9 in the morning to 2 o'clock in the afternoon and, as often as not, had to conduct in the evening. His initial euphoria had already begun to wear off. He even began to find fault with the orchestra, which had pleased him so much at first. Now, for example, he found he could no longer stand the 'eternal portamentos, the swelling of sound in mid-bow', favoured by the string section. The musicians appeared unable to sustain a note without diminishing or swelling it. 'Instead of piano, which should be their usual conversational tone', their habitual level was forte and they would rarely consent to produce a true pianissimo. 'I can't manage to hold them back,' he complained. 'My gestures are not sufficient. If one of the strings has a solo part, the player thinks its purpose is to give him a chance to show off loudly. Even their rhythm is sloppy. But in time I'll change all this.'[56]

---

[50] Wolf, *Briefe an Potpeschnigg*, 201.   [51] Ibid. 202.

[52] See below, Chap. 3.   [53] Until Nov. 1898 (see below).

[54] On 12 Aug. Mahler wrote to Richard Strauss asking his opinion of the tenor who was to sing Loge in *Das Rheingold* and of the 'wooden trumpet' used at the Munich Opera for the 'lustige Weise' in the final act of *Tristan und Isolde* (MSB 51 ff.). That same day he sent the administration a detailed outline of the season's programmes. Before the end of the same month he wrote several letters to the Munich Opera and to its chief conductor Hermann Levi, concerning Levi's new version of Mozart's *Così fan tutte*.

[55] This time the cycle was to be given in four successive performances, with a day's interval between *Die Walküre* and *Siegfried*.

[56] NBL1. 83; NBL2. 97.

On the day of the *Rheingold* première, Mahler was, according to Natalie, as happy and impatient 'as a child on Christmas morning' and could scarcely wait for the evening to arrive. He had obtained permission to have the work performed for the first time without an interval, as Wagner had wished, and even though he had been able to have only one orchestral rehearsal, which he had devoted almost entirely to passages previously cut, he presented the opera in an entirely new light that evening. 'All the performers felt his musical will and were infused with the spirit of the work. Every note and word could be read on his lips; indeed he almost indicated facial expressions and movements to them as he conducted!'[57]

Arnold Rosé, the leader of the orchestra, had assured Mahler that the performance of *Die Walküre* would be more successful than that of *Das Rheingold*, since the musicians knew it better and would be more sure of themselves. But he was proved wrong. 'The dust of negligence and mistakes lies thick over the whole work; much more so than in *Das Rheingold*, which they have played less often, so that the faults are not as deeply ingrained!' Natalie reported that in the last act Mahler gave his cue to the timpanist with whom he had carefully rehearsed a passage involving a long roll; hearing nothing, he glanced angrily in the musician's direction and saw with astonishment that his place was now occupied by someone else: hence the missed entrance. After the performance, Mahler demanded an explanation and was told that, because the timpanist lived in suburban Brunn,[58] he always had to leave the Opera before the end of the evening so as not to miss the last train.[59] Outraged, Mahler sent the man a telegram at midnight, summoning him to his office at 7 o'clock the next morning. He hoped to give him a sleepless night and thus discourage him from repeating the incident. He gave the musician the choice of leaving either the Opera or his home in Brunn, but doubtless finally granted him an allowance to help him to move,[60] for it was then that he learnt that some of the musicians earned no more than 60 gulden a month, a sum on which it was impossible to live in Vienna, even as a bachelor.[61] Mahler decided to obtain a salary increase for them, which would be offset by economies in other fields. In this way, he finally put an end to the system of last-minute replacements in the orchestra.

While staging the last act of *Die Walküre*, Mahler replaced the galloping

[57] NBL1. 83; NBL2. 97. After *Die Walküre*, the Brünnhilde, Sophie Sedlmair, thanked him for having mouthed every syllable of her role to her throughout the performance.

[58] The timpanist, Johann Schnellar, was later to become one of Mahler's favourite members of the Philharmonic Orchestra. Brunn am Gebirge is a small suburb south of Vienna, between Perchtoldsdorf and Mödling.

[59] According to Ernst Decsey, the musician always left at a quarter to 10.

[60] Mahler later complained to Natalie of having had to get up at 6 a.m. so as to reach the Opera ahead of the culprit (NBL1. 85; NBL2. 98). Ernst Decsey, in EDS2. 144, mentions a 'trumpeter', but Natalie's account is more precise and detailed and was written closer to the event.

[61] The musicians' salaries ranged from 660 to 900 gulden per year. They received an additional 'performance allowance' ranging from 120 to 200 gulden a year, which was reduced when they did not play.

horses with projections of flying clouds on a cyclorama, but he was dissatisfied with the Valkyries, who were second-rate soloists or members of the chorus. 'One day, I will only employ first-class singers and then you will see what this scene is really like.' Nevertheless, the *Extrablatt* commented: 'Yesterday for the first time, we heard them sing their ensemble all in tune together and for the first time saw them form beautiful scenic groups in free and lively movement. Also for the first time we were actually able to see the duel between Hunding and Siegfried.'[62] At the end of the cycle—like Brahms many years before, after hearing a performance of *Don Giovanni* in Budapest—Hugo Wolf told Natalie that 'for the first time, I have heard the *Ring* as I have always dreamed of hearing it while reading the score'.[63]

Despite the admiration that he had aroused, Mahler was far from satisfied with the results of his work. 'What a tragedy,' he once said, 'that the greatest composers should have written their works for this pigsty of a theatre, the very nature of which precludes perfection.' None the less, Natalie later recalled how moved she had been by some passages in this production: the 'magic of nature' in the *Siegfried* 'Forest Murmurs', the splendour of Brünnhilde's awakening, and finally the burning passion of the final love-scene, given for the first time uncut. 'It was shameful to cut that,' Mahler exclaimed, 'for it more or less turned Brünnhilde into a harlot who resisted Siegfried's solicitations for only a moment before throwing herself into his arms. The whole transition, in which she tells him everything she is obliged to renounce, and all the intermediate steps that prepare for the great final crescendo, were missing!' The following evening, in *Götterdämmerung*, Mahler restored the essential Brünnhilde–Waltraute scene, but he still had to leave out the Norn scene, since he did not have the necessary singers.[64] However, this performance was again a great success; many enthusiasts called for Mahler to appear at the end of the evening, and a group of young people and Conservatory students gathered to acclaim him as he left the Opera.

The first virtually uncut performance of the *Ring* was to mark the final break between the old and new Wagner conductors. Mahler's tempos, especially at the end of the third act of *Die Walküre*, were often livelier than Richter's. When Max Graf pointed this out, Mahler replied touchily that 'Richter has no idea of the tempos and has certainly forgotten what Wagner's were'. Richter, for his part, told Graf that Mahler's rendering of the 'Magic Fire' (*Feuerzauber*) had impressed him but that Mahler had not succeeded with the apotheosis and transfiguration at the end of the act.[65] These *Ring* evenings, on which Mahler

---

[62] *Illustrirtes Wiener Extrablatt* (27 Aug. 1897), quoted in Robert Werba, 'Marginalien zum Theaterpraktiker Gustav Mahler', in *Gustav Mahler und die Oper*, Symposium Budapest 1989, *Studia Musicologica*, Budapest, 380.

[63] Wolf also praised the performance in a letter written to Oskar Grohe on 1 Sept. 1897: 'We have recently had magnificent performances of the *Ring* under the direction of Mahler, who is creating a sensation here.'

[64] Most of the Opera's best singers were in fact away in Aug., either on holiday or appearing as guest singers abroad.   [65] GWO 86 ff.

had expended so much time and effort, attracted less comment in the press than his earlier performances. After *Die Walküre*, the *Neue Freie Presse* merely stated that Mahler 'conducted with profound seriousness and tremendous enthusiasm', adding that all but one of the passages previously deleted had been restored. In the anti-Semitic *Deutsche Zeitung*, Theodor Helm, whose fairness towards Mahler had probably rendered him suspect, was replaced by his colleague Albert Leitich, who championed Richter. Thus Leitich considered that the effects obtained by Richter in *Das Rheingold* had been 'greater and more profound' than those of Mahler, who 'attenuates certain passages to the work's detriment'.[66] Mahler had certainly been justified in 'restraining the orchestra', but it would have been still better had he lowered the level of the pit.[67] He had 'botched the music and the action' (*versungen und vertan*)[68] in *Die Walküre*. His 'Magic Fire' music had not been nearly as good as Richter's. 'The notes but not the meaning of the music' had been rendered, and the end of the first act had been rushed. *Siegfried* was the best performance of the cycle, except for the 'Forest Murmurs'. The Act III 'Magic Fire' and the final duet, at last performed uncut, had been 'acceptable, because here Mahler followed Richter's tradition'. As for Mahler's *Götterdämmerung*, Leitich considered that it lacked 'the elemental force of destiny'.

The reservations of the anti-Semitic press, long expected by everyone, including Mahler, counted for little amid Vienna's general enthusiasm. There was already much talk of his replacing Jahn. The latter, no doubt having heard of the new conductor's triumphs, returned to Vienna on 1 September, two weeks earlier than planned, though his eyesight had not been much improved by his recent operation.[69] On 10 August, Prince Liechtenstein had instructed Bezecny to persuade Jahn to resign. 'Perhaps this is the final station of the cross before the directorship,' wrote Mahler, who knew of this development.

I have already borne the full weight of the cross, though I haven't as yet had to drudge as I did in Budapest. My position is still uncontested, but once I have my appointment in my pocket, I'll be prepared to resign at any moment. For the time being, of course, I haven't the slightest reason to do so. Even Richter has acknowledged my authority. Ever since I obtained six weeks' leave for him, he considers me a 'suitable representative of directorial dignity'.[70]

[66] However, Leitich approved of the suppression of the interval in *Das Rheingold* and congratulated Mahler for making the Valkyries 'sing and perform together' in the last act of *Die Walküre*. To his mind, the staging and the machinery (e.g. the Rhine in the first scene) badly needed to be 'modernized'.

[67] Cast of *Das Rheingold* on 25 Aug.: Ehrenstein (Freia); Walker (Fricka); Van Dyck (Loge); Ritter (Alberich); Reichmann (Wotan). *Die Walküre* (26 Aug.): Ehrenstein (Sieglinde); Sedlmair (Brünnhilde); Walker (Fricka); Winkelmann (Siegmund); Reichmann (Wotan); Hesch (Hunding). *Siegfried* (28 Aug.): Sedlmair (Brünnhilde); Winkelmann (Siegfried); Schmitt (Mime); Ritter (Alberich); Grengg (Wanderer). *Götterdämmerung* (29 Aug.): Sedlmair (Brühnhilde); Abendroth, Pohlner, Kaulich (Rhinemaidens); Winkelmann (Siegfried); Horwitz (Alberich); Reichenberg (Hagen).

[68] Quotation from *Die Meistersinger* (end of Act I).

[69] Jahn had been almost blind for several months and could no longer read new scores. Instead he learnt them by heart by having them played on the piano by Korrepetitor Raoul Mader (the composer of the ballet *Die Roten Schuhe* and future director of the Budapest Opera).   [70] Letter to Justi of 11 Aug.

Nevertheless Mahler still suffered from doubts and anxiety right up to the moment of his appointment. Hearing of a violent scene between Jahn and Wlassack on the day of their first meeting after Jahn's return, he once more felt remorseful. 'My heart bleeds, I feel terrible about the sick old man,' he said to Karpath. 'But Wlassack tells me we must put an end to it . . . What can we do?' Karpath asked him if Jahn was irrevocably condemned. 'I am absolutely certain of it,' replied Mahler, 'not that I have exerted any pressure, but the administration is determined to bring the thing to a conclusion.'[71] After this conversation Karpath announced briefly in the *Neues Wiener Tagblatt* that Jahn was about to retire because of his failing eyesight. On the same day, Wlassack, realizing that Jahn was determined to hold on to his position, insisted, in the course of a stormy meeting, that he apply for his retirement. Jahn again refused and left Wlassack's office extremely upset. He finally capitulated the next day.

Towards the end of August, Bezecny and Wlassack wrote to the Lord Chamberlain suggesting that, in addition to the award of the imperial medal and the increase in his pension (it had been raised to 6,000 florins) the Emperor should confer on Jahn the title of Hofrath. For his successor, the two officials recommended Mahler and emphasized his recent conversion to catholicism:

Kapellmeister Gustav Mahler, a young Austrian of 37, of the Christian faith, who, in his previous posts as Director of the Royal Budapest Opera and first Kapellmeister at the Hamburg Opera, as well as more recently during his brief spell as deputy conductor here, has given proof of his genius and his efficiency as a musician and man of the theatre. . . . [He had] known how to attract the attention and admiration of the music-loving public and to take by storm, as it were, the affections of the community of artists he leads.

Furthermore, 'the integrity of his character' was well known and the 'artistic direction of the Opera could be safely placed in his hands, with every hope of success'. The financial aspects would be left to the administration.[72] Mahler would receive a salary of 6,000 florins, a 'performance allowance' as conductor of 2,000 florins, and a travel allowance of 2,000 florins.[73] With accommodation allowance of 2,000 florins,[74] his annual salary would amount to 12,000 florins, less than Jahn was receiving by the end of his career.

Knowing that the Emperor would be reluctant to grant Jahn the title of Hofrath, which was given to only the highest officials,[75] Prince Liechtenstein

---

[71] BMG 58.

[72] This clause was to give rise to many problems for Mahler.

[73] A few additional clauses specified the travel expenses to which Mahler would be entitled, as well as the pension increases he would receive periodically: 3,000 florins immediately; 4,000 after ten years of service; 5,000 after fifteen years, and 6,000 after twenty.

[74] The Intendant's office suggested that it should take over the residence previously occupied by the Opera Director.

[75] He conferred it upon Dr Paul Schlenther a few years later, when the latter resigned the directorship of the Burgtheater.

suggested that he merely award him an imperial medal. However, the matter hung fire for a few days, and although the Prince had assured him there was no cause for alarm, Mahler wondered anxiously about the reasons for the delay and feared some eleventh-hour obstacle. Early in October, the Emperor made Jahn a Commander of the Imperial Order of Franz Joseph. The same decree, dated 8 October and signed by the Lord Chamberlain on the 15th, appointed Mahler Director of the Vienna Opera.

Thus, from 8 October 1897, Mahler took over the direction of one of the most renowned musical institutions in the Western world. Considering the fundamental incompatibility between his personality and the free and easy ways of the Viennese, it was not hard to foresee the many serious conflicts that would arise during the next ten years. Vienna was the capital of pleasure, a city that prided itself on not taking anything too seriously, and in which art was considered by some as a leisure pursuit.[76] In no other musical centre of the German-speaking world were people so fond of taking things easily. Mahler, although Viennese by heart and by adoption, was by no means Viennese by temperament. His fanaticism was certain to clash with the deep-rooted Viennese instincts of hedonism, indolence, and devotion to tradition, which were to 'eat into him like acid'. The intensity with which he worked struck the Viennese as strange, to say the least. Neither the orchestra nor the singers, neither the public nor the critics, were given time to breathe. Mahler himself obviously enjoyed this frantic activity; what to another might have seemed like hard labour or torture was to him the liberation of long-repressed energy. No effort that might enable him to realize his dream of scenic perfection and dramatic unity was too great. It was impossible for him to rest or spare himself. He was often exhausted but never relaxed. His inner fire may have frightened some, but it also encouraged and purified those who dared to share his enthusiasm. The strength that enabled him to resist his numerous enemies sprang, above all, from his integrity. As he had previously announced,[77] he was always ready to resign his position as director rather than make artistic concessions. Constantly striving for artistic perfection he drove himself, and others, unsparingly. 'I am up to my eyes in it, as only a theatre director can be. What a terrible, consuming existence!' he wrote to Max Marschalk. 'All my senses and feelings are turned toward the outside. I get farther and farther away from myself. How will it end? I send you greetings! Remember me in the way one usually remembers the dead!'[78]

At the time Mahler took over the direction of the Opera its situation was far from brilliant, largely because of Wilhelm Jahn's long illness. At the beginning, Jahn had been an excellent director and a good conductor, even if, in both

[76] Vienna was one of the last German-speaking cities to stage Wagner's last and greatest works.

[77] The best assessments of Mahler's activity as Opera Director are those of Richard Specht (RSM2 63 ff.) and Paul Stefan (PSM 54 ff. and PSE).

[78] MBR1, no. 196; MBR2, no. 260.

areas, his tastes and aims had always been as different from Mahler's as his physical appearance and his character. At first sight Jahn seemed a typical bourgeois Viennese, comfort-loving, plump, and prosperous, or perhaps a schoolmaster, with a gentle, benevolent face, pointed beard, and big spectacles. The quality of his conducting, however, contradicted this heavy, phlegmatic appearance. He had come to Vienna from Wiesbaden, the most 'French' and 'worldly' of all German towns. What the Viennese considered to be 'French' lightness and delicacy, precision, melodic life, and continuity were his principal qualities as a conductor. Although, as a producer, he lacked the courage to break with the outdated realism of his time, he had never hesitated to devote a great deal of time and effort to the theatrical side of performances. Despite his corpulence, he was always ready in rehearsals to climb out of the pit on to the stage, and adjust the gestures and attitudes of the singers. Nevertheless, he tended to devote more attention to detail than to an overall view, and felt more at home in comic rather than serious opera.[79]

Despite Jahn's preference for French and Italian operas, he had accorded Wagner a large place in the repertoire, always favouring his early works. Yet he had only once given an uncut *Meistersinger*, and usually assigned the later music-dramas like the *Ring* or *Tristan* to Hans Richter, together with the operas of Mozart and Gluck. While sharing Pollini's love of beautiful voices, he also paid great attention to the visual and dramatic elements. Nevertheless, he was an Epicurean, a man incapable of fighting a battle or passionately defending an idea or even of taking a risk, least of all that of being unpopular. Whereas Mahler constantly strove to surpass himself and elevate those around him, Jahn was content to offer refined entertainment to an élite of cultivated aristocrats. A story, true or not, often told about him in Vienna indicates the kind of man he was. He was fond of playing skat (a card game much in favour with Richard Strauss) with the Austrian Minister of War and two singers from the Opera, the baritone Theodor Reichmann and the tenor Fritz Schrödter. It was said that one evening he had made a last-minute change to the advertised programme so that his two partners would be able to complete the game at their leisure.[80]

Jahn's successes as director, producer, and conductor did not include any of the operas Mahler esteemed and admired most. Yet, in each of them, Jahn, within his natural limitations, knew how to attain perfection. Gifted with much common sense, like Pollini, he never lost sight of the box-office takings or the public's taste and did not hesitate to impose enormous cuts in Wagner's operas, which at that time did not always attract full houses. The first Vienna performance of *Tristan und Isolde*, deferred until 1883, with Richter conducting, had

[79] Born in Hof, Moravia, in 1835, Jahn first became a chorister, then a conductor in Budapest from 1854 on. His conducting career took him to Amsterdam, Prague, and Wiesbaden before he became director of the Vienna Opera in 1881.
[80] Leo Slezak, *Mein Lebensmärchen* (Piper, Munich, 1948), 122.

aroused surprise rather than admiration. Thus a great deal remained to be accomplished in this field.

Hans Richter, a legendary figure among conductors, was of course entirely devoted to Wagner and was able to do much to promote his works during Jahn's tenure. Yet he too preferred an easy life and was not prepared to insist when the efforts he made every year to restore at least some of the cuts in Wagner's works came to nothing, though he made up for this in Bayreuth. Jahn took the view that under no circumstances should performances cease to give pleasure. Even in its abridged version, and even with Winkelmann and Materna, *Tristan* usually played to half-full houses and most of the audience left *Die Meistersinger* after the quintet at the beginning of the Act III. Nevertheless, many Viennese felt that to appoint Mahler to a post that was Richter's by right was an ill-considered decision by the Lord Chamberlain, even though everyone knew that Richter had no desire to fill it after his disastrous experiences as director of the Hungarian Opera.[81]

The ensemble of singers formed by Jahn reflected the spirit of his regime, but Mahler gradually made changes in accordance with his own requirements. Some of the survivors from Jahn's and earlier days—the tenor Hermann Winkelmann[82] and the baritone Theodor Reichmann[83]—had retained their popularity, though not perhaps all their former vocal powers. The top gallery at the Vienna Opera still favoured these two old-timers and each of them could rely on his own personal claque. When they appeared together in *Tannhäuser*, the applause turned into a competition between fans who shouted 'Winkel' and those who shouted 'Reich'. Many of the established members of the Opera, in particular the coloratura sopranos Irene Abendroth and Emmy Teleky, the light soprano Ellen Forster, the dramatic soprano Sophie Sedlmair, the American contralto Edyth Walker, the tenor Andreas Dippel,[84] the baritones Josef Ritter and Franz Neidl, and the bass Franz von Reichenberg, had great difficulty in conforming to Mahler's iron discipline. Most of them soon left for other destinations. Two others had already worked with him elsewhere: the baritone Karl Grengg, in London in 1892, and the Czech bass Wilhelm Hesch, in *The*

[81] Both the *Neues Wiener Tagblatt* (14 June 1907), and the *Fremden-Blatt* (4 July) stated that Richter had been offered Jahn's post but had refused it. Apart from the fact that, at that time, he had already been retired by the Vienna Opera, something which would have raised a host of administrative problems, he also felt he was not qualified to manage an opera-house.

[82] Son of a piano manufacturer, Hermann Winkelmann (1849–1912) studied singing in Paris and Hanover. His first engagements were in Altenburg, Darmstadt, and Hamburg. First dramatic tenor at the Vienna Opera, 1883–1906, he created the role of Parsifal in Bayreuth in 1882; in 1883 he became the first Vienna Tristan. By the time Mahler arrived, his voice had become unreliable, his breath short, and his diction distorted. Like many other ageing tenors, he gave a very praiseworthy interpretation of the last act of *Tristan*. He was an intelligent and cultured man and a gifted actor who could take a wide variety of roles.

[83] Theodor Reichmann (1849–1903) studied music and singing in Berlin, Prague, and Milan, then set out upon a brilliant career as a baritone in Magdeburg, Berlin, Rotterdam, Strasbourg, Hamburg, and Munich. His two engagements at the Vienna Opera (1882–9, 1893–1903) were separated by long tours. In Bayreuth in 1882 he created the role of Amfortas in *Parsifal*.

[84] Mahler was to meet Andreas Dippel (1866–1932) again as co-director of the Metropolitan Opera in New York.

Bartered Bride in Hamburg.[85] Both remained at the Vienna Opera, Grengg until 1902 and Hesch until 1908. The lyric tenor Fritz Schrödter had been with the Opera for more than ten years and was exceedingly popular with the public. He stayed on as a member of the Hofoper until 1915, long after his vocal powers had begun to decline.[86]

However, the true stars of the Jahn era were the soprano Marie Renard and the tenor Ernest Van Dyck. The former[87] represented a type much favoured by the Viennese, the 'charming young girl', the lovelorn heroine who was sometimes a countess, sometimes a laundress. She was a true prima donna; she thought only of her pianissimos, her trills, and her roulades, and made little effort to act or to fit in with an ensemble. The Belgian tenor Ernest Van Dyck[88] also became an idol of the Viennese public because of his brilliant voice and outstanding mastery of bel canto. However, even those who admired his exceptional technique and artistry, combining 'Flemish violence' with 'Parisian culture', found him a rather comic figure, with his small round body, tiny head, and round mouth and eyes. His pretentious, stylized acting often made him look ridiculous. Although his Wagner performances were greatly appreciated in Paris, Mahler found them 'perfumed' and 'affected'. His best Wagner role was as Loge in *Das Rheingold*.[89] Both he and Renard constantly relied on their popularity to defy Mahler's authority. After fighting them for two years he got rid of them, and thereafter avoided engaging established stars who were far more concerned with their popularity than with their artistic duties.

Under Jahn's directorship, the smaller roles were often poorly cast. Together with the chorus's lack of discipline, this was one of the main weaknesses of his 'system', for the public applauded individual feats rather than the complete performance. Everyone wanted improvements to be made but no one could suggest how they were to be achieved. In the world of the theatre, artistic success could only be relative and ephemeral. The regular public was reluctant to change its habits, and Vienna as a whole was altogether unprepared for the reforms Mahler had in store. The final years of Jahn's tenure had been particularly disastrous. The initial qualities of his direction had begun to fade. The ensemble of soloists could no longer cover the whole of the repertoire, and new singers constantly had to be brought in from outside. Even the best artists had

---

[85] Wilhelm Hesch had been a member of the Vienna Opera since 1896.

[86] Fritz Schrödter (1855–1924) was a member of the Vienna Opera, 1885–1915.

[87] Marie Renard (1863–1939), whose real name was Marie Pölz, was born into a peasant family in Graz. She made her début there in 1882 as a mezzo-soprano in the role of Azucena in *Il trovatore*. Engaged in Prague and then Berlin, she joined the Vienna Opera in 1888, and left it as a Kammersängerin in 1900 to marry Count Rudolf Kinsky.

[88] Ernest Van Dyck (1861–1923), born in Antwerp, studied singing in Brussels and Paris, where his début with the Lamoureux Orchestra made him a celebrity overnight. For many years he sang the role of Parsifal in Bayreuth. He joined the Vienna Opera in 1888 and left in 1899 to pursue his career in Paris and at the Metropolitan Opera, New York. He later became director of the Théâtre des Champs-Elysées, Paris. In 1914 he gave up singing to become a teacher.

[89] In Paris, in 1909 (or more likely, still, 1907—see below Vol. iv, Chap. 9), Mahler was so incensed by Van Dyck's performance in *Tristan* that he left the box of the Commissioner of Police, his host, without a word of apology (see below, Vol. iii, Chap. 50).

their off moments, all the more noticeable because the chorus was mediocre and the orchestra uneven. Jahn had been especially criticized for having given the job of Chordirektor to his nephew Hubert Wondra and for entrusting him with important administrative duties he was ill-equipped to fulfil. Old-fashioned scenery and the lack of any firm, co-ordinating hand resulted in productions which were increasingly tawdry and fragmented. The casting was often too uneven to attract the public. The stars sometimes feigned illness at the last moment if they considered their stage partners unworthy of them, and they often demanded, and obtained, leave of absence in mid-season. Most of these problems arose because of Jahn's lack of authority, his ill-health, and the incompetence of his subordinates.[90]

Attacks in the press during the last months of Jahn's directorship show how lax it had become. The last singers he engaged,[91] the poor repertoire, his choice of new operas,[92] the last-minute cancellations, and the power he had delegated to his nephew eventually turned most of the critics against him. The *Deutsche Zeitung* was particularly critical of the undue interference in the Opera's affairs exercised by Franz von Wetschl, the administrative treasurer. He may have been a competent financier, but was totally lacking in both artistic and theatrical experience. According to the same article, the staging had become very poor, scarcely worthy of a provincial theatre. August Stoll (an 'incompetent and lazy' producer), Franz Gaul (the designer), and Joseph Hassreiter (the ballet-master) formed 'an iron band that stifled all artistic life at the Hofoper': 'There needs to be a thorough cleansing of the foul and musty atmosphere in which the few people with ability and enterprise can hardly breathe.' Despite their virulent criticism of Jahn, the anti-Semitic press of course disapproved of Mahler's appointment. An article dated 12 September accused him of being 'non-German' and condemned his programme, 'which places German works last', ignoring 'great masterpieces like Wolf's *Der Corregidor* and Cornelius's *Der Cid*'. On the whole, however, these attacks, which everyone had expected, were less violent than might have been feared.

As soon as he was appointed Director, Mahler began to implement the programme of reforms he had prepared during the summer. His first concern was to re-establish discipline. On 10 October he publicly addressed all the

---

[90] *Montags Revue* (4 May 1897). This article, numbered 299/97, is filed in HOA, which shows that the authorities took particular notice of it. It states that 'on paper, the chorus is larger than ever, but in fact, it has never been so mediocre. Also, since many of the choristers' voices are too weak, the Opera is frequently obliged to call in additional singers at the last moment, a costly procedure.' Wondra is accused of favouring certain of the singers by granting them lengthy periods of leave; this had caused deep resentment among the less favoured. Nevertheless, Wondra remained at the Opera throughout Mahler's tenure and became covertly one of his most dangerous enemies.

[91] Three sopranos—Fanny Mora, Emmy Teleky, and Irene Abendroth—as well as Ehrenstein and Elizza, were also under attack from the anti-Semitic press.

[92] In particular André Messager's *Le Chevalier d'Harmenthal* and Albert Kauders's *Walther von der Vogelweide*.

members of the Opera during a rehearsal for the *Magic Flute*, and the following day he issued the following circular:

In order to put an end to the deplorable abuse of the claque, the theatre management took a number of measures that would effectively have stopped this practice, had not some members of the Opera, in the most discreditable manner, secretly sidestepped the regulations on the pretext of defending their own interest. I was happy to learn from my personal conversations with you that you fully agree that the claque must finally be got rid of, since it brings the Opera into discredit and prevents us from attaining our artistic goals. I therefore take the liberty of asking you to give me your word of honour that henceforth you will abstain from any contact with the claque, and will cease all payments and distribution of free tickets, so that we may put an end to a practice that is incompatible with the dignity of our institution. For my part, I promise you that I shall not only do everything in my power to support you in this endeavour, but also, in our common interest, use all the means at my disposal to ensure that our mutual agreement is respected.

'There is a new hope in Vienna. It goes by the name of "Mahler",' wrote Karl Kraus on 24 October. 'Energy and naïvety characterize the Opera's Augean stable sweeper. He recently issued a stringent edict against the claque, requiring not only the singers but also the ballerinas to give their word of honour to shun any contact with hawkers of applause.'[93] Of all the reforms introduced by Mahler, this actually turned out to be one of the most difficult to carry through. Despite his efforts, he never entirely succeeded, even though he went to the length of placing detectives in the gallery to observe the behaviour of the audience. His instructions were followed for some months, but then the singers could stand it no longer and began once again to make secret payments to the claque. The habit does seem to have become more discreet however.[94]

Another drastic reform was to forbid latecomers access to the auditorium during the overtures (except for the boxes and standing area). At the Opera, the overtures were always disturbed by an incessant coming and going.[95] For the Wagner operas, Mahler decided that no one should be allowed in during the whole of the first act.[96] With *Das Rheingold* this was tantamount to preventing latecomers from hearing the opera altogether. Eduard Wlassack asserted that such a measure was inconceivable in Vienna, because these latecomers were often important government officials. But Mahler stuck to his guns. A few incidents gave him the chance to prove his determination. The President of the Länderbank, a certain Herr Palmer who often played whist with the Emperor,

---

[93] *Breslauer Zeitung* (24 Oct.).

[94] See below, Chap. 4, the visit paid in 1898 by the leader of the claque to Reznicek, the composer of *Donna Diana*.

[95] BMG 60 ff.

[96] On 4 Apr. 1900 the *Neue Freie Presse* announced that latecomers would not be admitted during Act I of *Tristan*, *Meistersinger*, or any of the *Ring* dramas. In Wagner's other works, there would be a short pause to admit them after the Overture or Prelude. On 1 Oct. of the same year the same newspaper reported that this same rule would also be applied to Mozart's operas.

occupied a seat on the end of a row and near an exit, which allowed him to come and go without disturbing anyone. He applied directly to Mahler for permission to take his seat after the start of the performance, but Mahler replied that the new rule admitted of no exceptions. One day, while conducting, he saw an usher show a patron to his seat after the curtain had gone up. The next day he sent for the culprit and threatened him with dismissal if such a thing occurred again. To the usher's claim that the latecomer had struck him and opened the door by force, Mahler replied that he doubted a man of the usher's strength would let himself be struck with impunity. Then, leaping from his chair and shaking his fist, he shouted, 'The blow you received was in the shape of a florin slipped into your hand, and if this happens again I'll dismiss you.'

The Viennese press, which for the most part supported Mahler, showed some surprise at his severity, which it considered excessive. On 8 November, a lengthy satirical article entitled 'Regulations for Attendance at the Opera (Measures to be Taken in Connection with the Ordinance against Latecomers)'[97] was published in the *Wiener Sonn- und Montagszeitung*. It started as follows:

1. Each day at 5 pm a cannon will be fired in the Royal Imperial Arsenal, signalling to those wishing to attend the Opera that they should embark on preparations in their homes. On days when performances are scheduled to begin at 6.30, the signal will be given promptly at 4.30.

2. At 6 o'clock, or 5.30 as the case may be, a second shot will alert the opera-goers in outlying suburbs that it is time to embark upon their journey to the Opera house. It has been agreed with Viennese landlords that the caretakers of houses inhabited by the persons wishing to visit the Opera on the relevant days should draw their attention to the 6 o'clock cannon, or the 5.30 cannon as the case may be, and should urge them to leave the house. To this end, all tenants intending to visit the Opera in the evening must inscribe their names on the morning of the relevant day in a visiting book in keeping of the caretaker.

And so on for another thirteen paragraphs, one of them alone consisting of nine subsections!

Some of the members of the imperial court complained to the Emperor, who was astonished at Mahler's intransigence, for he still regarded the theatre as a place of pleasure and entertainment. However, Franz Joseph had appointed Mahler personally and Mahler must be obeyed. From then on, high officials and even members of the imperial family were forbidden to interfere in Opera affairs. Through Prince Liechtenstein, the Emperor instructed Mahler to ignore any suggestions they might make. Henceforth even people of high birth were required to arrive at the Opera on time. With the Emperor behind him, Mahler

[97] 'Regulativ für die Besucher der Hofoper (Vollzugsvorschriften zu dem Erlasse wider das Zuspätkommen).' This document was discovered by Willi Reich among Ludwig Karpath's papers. It is signed 'L. A. Terne', a pseudonym for Robert Hirschfeld and was publ. in the *Festschrift Otto Erich Deutsch zum 80 Geburtstag* (Bärenreiter, Kassel, 1963).

could afford to resist any outside interference. Innumerable anecdotes concerning his inflexible behaviour went the rounds. One of them concerned a singer named Mizzi Günther, who presented herself to him armed with a letter of recommendation from the Crown Prince Franz Ferdinand. Mahler simply tore up the letter and said to her: 'Now, let's hear you sing!'[98]

On another occasion an Austrian singer named Anita Karin,[99] a personal friend of the Archduchess Maria Theresa, complained that Mahler had broken his promise and refused to extend her contract after causing her to turn down another engagement. He 'juggles with our destinies', she said. The story soon reached the ears of the Emperor, who summoned Mahler to his villa in Ischl in midsummer. Mahler was obliged to present himself in full court dress at midday. The Emperor asked him why he did not wish to re-engage Frau Karin. Mahler had hardly finished giving a complicated explanation before Franz Joseph wearily waved his hand and said him: 'That's all right, you know more about it than I do.'[100] On another occasion, when asked by Prince Montenuovo to explain his refusal to engage a singer recommended by the Emperor, Mahler found another way of circumventing the Emperor's instructions: 'Your Highness', he said to the Prince, 'I am fully aware that your wishes and those of His Majesty must be respected at the Opera and that is why I am waiting for a written order to engage the lady.' Once again, the Emperor, having come to respect Mahler's judgement and integrity, made no further attempt to make him reverse his decision.[101] Similarly, there are several instances of Mahler refusing to perform at the Hofoper mediocre works which had been recommended by someone at Court. He thus refused to accommodate his old enemy from Budapest, Count Zichy, who tried by every possible means to have an opera called *Meister Roland* added to the Hofoper repertoire. Mahler also seems to have turned down an even worse opera written by one of the Archdukes.[102]

Having ensured that the people he had to deal with professionally respected him for his integrity and force of character, Mahler saw no need to frequent Viennese society. He was not forgiven for this disdainful attitude, particularly

[98] In 1905 Mizzi Günther created the title-role in Lehár's *The Merry Widow*. On 25 Apr. 1902 the *Neue Freie Presse* reported that Mizzi Günther's *Probesingen* (audition) had been announced, and then immediately cancelled.

[99] Anita Karin's real name was Bertha Anita Krainz (KMI). She had been a member of the Hanover and Berlin operas before Mahler engaged her. Apparently, he did not allow her to sing a single performance (KMI).

[100] See BMG 92 and LEM 142. Karpath is wrong in claiming that Mahler had refused to engage Karin, since she was indeed a member of the Opera, 1 Oct. 1900–30 Sept. 1901. Graf was therefore correct in speaking of her 're-engagement' but wrong in stating that Mahler went from Steinbach to Ischl to see the Emperor, for he had left Steinbach long before, and was now spending his summers in Maiernigg, in Carinthia.

[101] cf. NBL1. 103; NBL2. 117, BMG 63, RSM2. 100, and Edgar Istel, 'Wie Mahler eine Protectionsoper ablehnte', *Münchner Neueste Nachrichten* (23 May 1911). See also below, Vol. iii, Chap. 5, a complete account of this incident, together with the letter Mahler sent to Zichy refusing his work.

[102] The young Archduke Peter Ferdinand fancied himself a composer. According to Max Graf, Mahler refused to perform the work at the Hofoper unless he received the Emperor's express command.

since personal contacts were an essential part of any artistic career in Vienna. Fortunately, he had learnt not to care about gossip. However, while he was deputy director, he heard that there had been disparaging talk about him in the salon of the Countess Anastasia Kielmannsegg, wife of an important official, who entertained the best of the Viennese aristocracy and bourgeoisie. Since his appointment was still pending, Mahler was disturbed by the thought that there might be some intrigue against him. Karpath, thinking to help Mahler, suggested to a soprano named Luise von Ehrenstein that she might make some enquiries of the lady in question, who was an old friend of hers,[103] in order to learn what was going on. Having discovered that the Countess Kielmannsegg felt no animosity toward Mahler and had taken no part in her guests' gossip, Luise rushed to the director's office at the Opera to reassure him personally. This, however, was a great mistake; he was so displeased by the suggestion that he might have solicited such a service from one of his subordinates that he answered her brusquely, showed her unceremoniously to the door, and never forgave her for having put him in such an awkward situation. It was characteristic of Mahler to hate the idea of owing anything to an artist under his authority. Thereafter, according to Karpath, without ever actually being impolite, he was so offhand with Ehrenstein that she soon left the Opera.[104] Mahler later rebuked Karpath too for having interfered in the matter. Once he had been officially appointed he decided not to worry about *Affären* circulating in the Viennese salons. Rumours about him could thus run unchecked, and gave rise to many stories in which he was depicted as a tyrant, a monster, even a devil incarnate, who would listen to no one and was determined to turn everything upside down to suit his own ends.

Within the Opera, Mahler launched a rigorous money-saving programme designed to cut unproductive expenditure. He abolished complimentary tickets and insisted that the newspapers pay for their critics' seats. At the same time, he began to change the repertoire: in his first year of office there were ten times as many Mozart operas, and twenty more Wagner performances than in the previous year. The Opera's daily routine had now greatly changed. Work went on uninterruptedly, the one aim being 'that every performance must conform to the same high standard', whether it be *Cavalleria rusticana* or *Die Meistersinger*.[105] It was a utopian aim for an opera company with such a large repertoire, yet Mahler did his utmost to achieve it. In order to avoid last minute cancellations, he prepared two complete casts for each opera, which meant a considerable amount of extra work in each production. Nevertheless, as in Budapest, he had only one motto: 'work'.

---

[103] Both Luise and her sister, the pianist Gisela von Ehrenstein, had long frequented her salon.

[104] See BMG 113 ff. Ehrenstein resigned in 1899. The reasons for Mahler's lack of consideration toward her were doubtless more artistic than personal. Judging from articles by Leitich and Hirschfeld, Ehrenstein was no great singer.

[105] BMG 88.

'Has Deckner spoken to you about my <u>artistic demands?</u>' he wrote to the baritone Leopold Demuth in December.

He must do so for though I know you were familiar with them in Hamburg, you did not like them. My insistence on them here has benefited everyone and I expect new members to comply with them willingly. Dear Demuth, do you remember all that the notion of 'precision' means for me? Are you both able and willing to submit to my artistic demands, not just passively as in Hamburg where you merely did not offer physical resistance, but <u>actively,</u> by accepting my artistic programme with conviction and enthusiasm? I beg you to give me a <u>frank</u> and clear answer to this question. We must be in complete agreement on this point if we are to sign a contract that could commit us to a lifetime of artistic collaboration.[106]

In November 1897, Mahler wrote in the same vein to Elsa Mackrott, a soprano who had been invited for a few guest performances, and had asked to sing the role of Pamina in *The Magic Flute*, which he had recently restaged. Mahler replied, saying he did not feel that she would have time to learn to 'interpret' this role as he wished during her short stay, and therefore suggested she should choose another part, for he could not let anyone sing in his new productions unless they could conform exactly to his requirements.[107] The following anecdote illustrates Mahler's attention to detail in new productions. While rehearsing the revival of *The Magic Flute*, he made the soprano Elise Elizza repeat the words 'Stirb, Ungeheuer!' (Die, horrid monster) so many times that finally, trembling with rage, she turned and screamed them directly at Mahler himself. Mahler smiled at her and said: 'That would suit you down to the ground, wouldn't it, Fräulein Elizza?' Very soon the legend—which he even encouraged when it suited his purpose—of the tyrannical, ruthless, merciless Mahler spread through Vienna, but the pleasure he gave his audiences and the enthusiastic notices he received in the press were more than sufficient to prevent any hostility from being openly expressed. With a satisfaction tinged perhaps with anxiety, he one day remarked to the Intendant Bezecny: 'I am hitting my head against the wall, but the wall is giving way . . . .'.[108]

---

[106] Letters to Leopold Demuth, 17 Dec. 1897.
[107] Letter to Elsa Mackrott, 14 Nov. 1897 (HOA, Z.605/1897).
[108] PSM 58.

3

Official appointment—first productions—
conflicts with Leoncavallo

(September 1897–February 1898)

A real labour of Sisyphus! A task that will take all my strength ...

WITHOUT waiting for his appointment as director to be officially confirmed, Mahler began a thorough revision of several of the productions in the Opera's repertoire. The first he chose was Lortzing's *Zar und Zimmermann*, of which he was particularly fond and which had not been performed at the Hofoper for almost ten years. It opened to a full house on 11 September and was a great success. The applause was exceptionally warm, and the press enthusiastic. Heuberger praised the purity and quality of the orchestral sound[1] and the improved role of the chorus, which displayed a liveliness and participation in the action never before achieved. What impressed him above all was the way the various elements in the performance had been welded into a unified whole. 'We were expecting a carpenter (*Zimmermann*) and a czar (*Zar*) arrived,' he concluded. The *Neues Wiener Tagblatt* congratulated Mahler both for selecting an unjustly neglected opera and for doing so much to make it a success. It described as exemplary the discreet handling of the accompaniments, and praised Mahler's 'incomparable artistry as a miniaturist, a fine engraver'. This was particularly noticeable in the ensembles, 'which are among the best passages in Lortzing's score'.[2] The *Fremden-Blatt* wrote that Mahler was obviously 'the right man in the right place' and that only people with ulterior motives could fail to be persuaded of that. 'The chorus was so magnificently disciplined that their performance of some passages must be described as virtuoso. In the orchestra, no detail of the master's comic inspiration was

---

[1] He reported that Mahler had placed the violins right around him to improve the sound.

[2] Cast for the performance of 11 Sept.: Forster (Marie); Baier (Widow Browe); Schrödter (Ivanoff); Dippel (Châteauneuf); Reichmann (Zar); Hesch (Van Bett).

missed . . . The ensembles achieved the most gratifying precision, and bore witness to the careful artistry with which this completely revised (*neueinstudiert*) production had been prepared.'

Mahler's first choice of a new work for the Hofoper was surprisingly bold, especially when it is remembered that his official appointment had not yet been confirmed by the Court. *Dalibor*, Smetana's historic and patriotic opera, was regarded by some as a manifesto of Czech nationalism. That the date chosen for the opening night should have been 4 October, the day of the Emperor's nameday celebrations (an annual event), was an additional reason for it to be regarded in some quarters as a provocation. In his *Neues Wiener Tagblatt* review Max Kalbeck noted that Vienna's Czech population made up the majority of the audience; he also noted 'the presence of numerous spectators not usually in the habit of attending opera premières'. A further factor which made the timing of the opening night seem particularly unfortunate was that Präsident Count Badeni had just decreed equality between the Czech and German languages in the law courts and administrations in Bohemia and Moravia. Until then the Czechs within the empire, unlike the Hungarians, had not succeeded in obtaining relatively independent status. Furthermore, the provinces of Bohemia and Moravia were the subject of disputes between Germans and Czechs, since the Czechs had developed faster, economically as well as politically and culturally, than any other non-German-speaking nationality in the empire. For example, Czech cities were linked by rail with Vienna long before similar facilities reached Salzburg or Innsbruck. The new decree had placated the Czechs but greatly angered the German nationalist element in Vienna, leading to a violent demonstration in the streets on 26 November. An anonymous letter of great virulence was addressed to Mahler at the Opera, a month after the première of *Dalibor*, by an angry 'German Austrian': 'So *Dalibor* is back in the repertoire!!—So you insist on fraternizing with the anti-dynastic, inferior Czech nation which has been carrying out acts of violence against the German and Austrian states. Such self-humiliation defies comprehension!'[3]

Smetana was one of Mahler's favourite composers[4] and he succeeded in overcoming all resistance. He prepared the new production with his usual care, exchanging a series of letters and telegrams with František Šubert, the director of the Czech National Theatre in Prague, on the subject of scenery and costumes.[5] He attempted to correct the work's dramatic and musical flaws during rehearsals and made a number of alterations to the score and even to the

---

[3] Anonymous letter dated 7 Nov. 1897 (HOA). *Dalibor* had been performed several times in Vienna in June 1892, at the time of the International Music and Theatre Exhibition 'Ausstellung für Musik und Theaterwesen'.

[4] Mahler had attended a performance of *Dalibor* performed at the National Theatre in Prague during the 1885–6 season and had conducted it at the Hamburg Stadt-Theater in Feb. 1896.

[5] This correspondence is in the National Museum in Prague. Since he was unable to attend the Prague performance on 24 Aug., Mahler sent the stage-director August Stoll and the set-painter Anton Brioschi. He also obtained from the Prague National Theatre models of the sets and sketches for the costumes (HOA 1897).

orchestration. He also dropped the original ending—the victory of the royal troops, followed by a battle scene that ends in Dalibor's death—and added instead some twenty bars of a diminuendo at the end of Milada's funeral chant. The opera thus closed 'on a note of tender emotion' which he considered far more suitable than the bloody battle scene of the original.[6] After rehearsals began, Mahler dropped one of the changes he had planned. At the close of Act II Milada, the heroine, disappears with her torch, leaving the hero alone in the darkness of his prison cell. Dalibor's loneliness is suggested by powerful chords that suddenly break in on the tender melody of the love duet. During rehearsals, Mahler suddenly realized the dramatic effect of these mighty chords which had seemed devoid of musical logic. He considered this to be a typical instance of the difference between 'pure' and dramatic music.[7]

The entire performance of *Dalibor* bore Mahler's imprint: he had supervised and checked every detail, not only of the musical performance, but also of the scenery, costumes, and lighting. Despite the unevenness of the singers bequeathed to him by Jahn, each one fitted in perfectly, the chorus played an active part in the drama, and the orchestra, which had been particularly receptive to his instructions during rehearsals, performed brilliantly. As a result, the opera was a genuine, though quite unexpected, success: thirteen performances were given that season and several more in the next.[8] The critics, however, were rather lukewarm in their praise. Heuberger pointed out the weaknesses of the work, the musical value of which he thought far outweighed its dramatic effectiveness. He admitted that it contained 'real gems', and congratulated Mahler on the improvements he had made in the score.[9] Helm welcomed its inclusion in the repertoire although he thought that it would never become 'a completely coherent, captivating whole, both dramatically and musically', on any German stage, because of the flaws in the libretto and lack of stylistic unity in the score. Hanslick's lengthy review also criticized Smetana's 'insignificant and awkward' libretto[10] but praised his music, the 'excellence' of which was only surpassed by that of his light operas. Nevertheless, *Dalibor* was an 'entirely original' work and a 'welcome addition to the repertoire', though its success stemmed largely from the quality of the performance. Mahler shared with Jahn the exceptional virtue of caring as much about the staging as about the music. He had rehearsed *Dalibor* with 'intelligent insight and minute care' and had brought out all its finer features. Hanslick felt sure that this young,

---

[6] After the 'moving and beautiful' funeral chorus, this 'vulgar spectacle' (Hanslick's words) lasts barely three minutes. In Kalbeck's version, the opera ends with the suicide of the hero.

[7] NBL1. 88; NBL2. 100.

[8] According to Natalie, Mahler kept the cost of this production very low, 3,000 gulden for the staging and scenery and 300 for the costumes. Puccini, who was in Vienna attending performances of his own *Bohème* at the Theater an der Wien, was also present at the première.

[9] Particularly the cutting of the second prison scene (Dalibor's aria while sawing through the bars of his cell) and of the last-act Finale. Heuberger suggested further cuts, especially of certain lengthy interludes.

[10] This libretto, written originally in German by Joseph Wenzig, was trans. into Czech by Erwin Spindler and back into German by Max Kalbeck.

ambitious, and experienced musician would prove to be the right man to 'breathe new life into our Vienna Opera, which has been slumbering wearily for some time'.[11]

Max Kalbeck, who had translated the Czech libretto into German, considered that, while the new version of the final scene, with the hero now being reprieved and the heroine killed, had changed the meaning of the work, its 'splendour nevertheless remains intact'.

The main credit for this must go to Herr Mahler, the Hofoper's new miracle-worker. Only a miracle could have saved the Institute, moribund from top to bottom, from the ruin that threatened it, and we can rejoice that the man capable of performing the miracle has been found. A performance like this heralds the dawn of a new epoch at the Vienna Hofoper; it combined the greatest conceivable individual freedom with the most conscientious and strict technical accuracy, bringing resounding success to all participants without exception . . .

A few years later, when again staging *Dalibor*, Mahler's opinion of the opera was no longer as favourable as it had been in 1897:

You can't imagine how furious I became again today over the flaws in this work. Smetana was a profoundly gifted artist, but he was handicapped by his lack of professional ability and his Czech origins, which cut him off from the rest of European culture. Outside Vienna, this opera is no longer performed, though it contains delightful passages; even here, in my new version, it is difficult to keep it in the repertoire, for the public just will not take to it. Whenever I conduct it, I am constantly exasperated: I would like to make a number of cuts, change the orchestration, sometimes recompose entire passages, for the whole work is clumsy, in spite of its beauty.[12]

On the evening of 9 October, Natalie went to meet Mahler under the arcade of the Opera, after the performance of *Zar und Zimmermann*. While he was still some way off he called out to her: 'My appointment is official!' The next evening there was a performance of *Dalibor*, and he knew that the audience would acclaim him when he appeared in the pit. He dashed to the podium with lightning speed and raised his baton even before sitting down. During the short pause between the end of the overture and the rise of the curtain, he kept his arms raised to prevent any applause, and at the end of the performance, in spite of the frantic clapping and cries of 'Mahler', he declined to appear onstage and take bows with the singers.[13]

Mahler's appointment was greeted with unanimous enthusiasm by the press, though the anti-Semitic papers showed some disapproval by announcing it a

---

[11] Cast of the first performance (4 Oct.): Sedlmair (Milada), Michalek (Jutta), Winkelmann (Dalibor), Dippel (Vitek), Felix (Budivoi), Hesch (Beneš).

[12] NBL1. 173; NBL2. 199. The work remained in the repertoire of the Hofoper until the 1903–4 season, with Winkelmann still in the title-role.

[13] He continued to do this throughout his Viennese career, even after important premières. Arnošt Mahler, in his study, 'Gustav Mahler und seine Heimat', observes that the work lacks a proper overture and has only a brief orchestral introduction. Did Mahler borrow an overture from some other work by Smetana?

day late. Mahler was delighted, above all because his financial future was now secure.[14] Appointed by the Emperor, his engagement would only be terminated by mutual consent, when he would claim his pension. This comforting thought, and the prospect of the operatic work he would be able to accomplish, were marred by only one thought: the many activities that would henceforth fill his life would surely leave him no time to compose. 'You will see', he told Natalie,

I won't be able to stand these horrible conditions, not even until the time when I could ask for my pension with a clear conscience: I wish I could just run away from it now. If only I could prepare as they do in Bayreuth a number of operas (but in my case ten times as many) and bring them to perfection and present them as real festivals, how happy I would be to work at that! But with the situation in our theatre, where there has to be a performance every day, where bad organization and deeply entrenched misman-agement confront me at every step, where, at the very moment of performance, at the height of the battle, I sometimes have to scrap everything and start again from scratch, where I have to be content with a repertoire in which the vulgar jostles with the sublime, where the apathy and stupidity of performers and audience loom over me like insurmountable barriers, then my task becomes a real labour of Sisyphus! A task that will take all my strength, even my life, but that cannot lead either to perfection or success! The worst of it is that, distracted as I am by a thousand different worries, I never have a moment to belong to myself![15]

Mahler could not even bear to talk about the performance of his symphonies. 'For the present, I don't care whether it takes a few years more or less for my works to become known. At the moment I understand myself so little that I often think I'm not the same man as before.'[16] However, this period of pressure and hectic activity also brought moments of intense satisfaction, particularly when he succeeded in a first-rate performance, recognized the progress achieved by the orchestra, and appreciated the efforts the musicians had made to meet his demands. Nor was it unimportant that he could now give free rein to his enthusiastic temperament: he was his own master and the means at his disposal were superior to those in most other European opera-houses. Aston-ished by the admiration and understanding he met at every turn, Mahler sometimes felt he was living in a dream or a fairy-tale. He worked and gave of himself all the more ardently for knowing that the euphoria could not last.

As already mentioned above, one of his tasks as deputy director, and still more as director, was to seek out new works suitable for performance at the Hofoper. Mahler had already begun to receive letters from composers sub-mitting their works in the hope that he would stage them in Vienna. Some of the first to approach him were a composer from Graz whom he had known in Hamburg, Wilhelm Kienzl, who eagerly hoped that his *Don Quixote* would be

[14] In the spring Mahler still seems to have had financial worries, as witness a letter he wrote to Emil Freund asking for a loan of 200 florins (MBR1, no. 233; MBR2, no. 244).

[15] NBL1. 89; NBL2. 102.

[16] Undated letter to Weingartner (Sept.–Oct. 1897) (BGM).

accepted;[17] Wilhelm Bruch, at that time a conductor in Strasbourg;[18] a Czech-born composer called Rudolf Prochaska.[19] Then Josef Förster, his old friend from Hamburg, wrote asking him to come to Prague for the première of his opera *Eva*.[20] None of these approaches led anywhere. However, Mahler had promised Hugo Wolf, his old friend from the Conservatory, that he would stage *Der Corregidor* as soon as he became director in Vienna. Wolf wrote to all his friends to tell them the good news. He was convinced that the performance of his only opera at the Hofoper would bring him the recognition which had for so long evaded him. A master of the Lied, a composer who achieved universality within small forms, he nevertheless shared with many other nineteenth-century composers the ambition of reaching a mass audience with a triumph on stage.[21] Since his expulsion as a rebellious student from the Vienna Conservatory, life had brought him few satisfactions, and few contacts with the public. After his friendship with Mahler had come to an end, an abortive season as a conductor in Salzburg in 1881 had convinced him that the world of the theatre was not for him. He therefore moved back to Vienna where, in 1884, he was, for three years, music critic on the *Wiener Salonblatt*. During this time he had given full rein to the violence of his temperament and prejudices, notably with regard to Brahms who had formerly humiliated and rejected him, and Hanslick, whom he regarded as a sycophant of Brahms, and the chief detractor of Wagner.

From 1887, when he left the *Salonblatt*, Wolf led an altogether solitary life, cut off from the world by his obsession with musical composition and his increasing tendency to quarrel with all and sundry. Financially dependent upon his friends and admirers, Wolf had dreamt during these painful years of writing an opera, the success of which would establish him as a full-time composer. Once again, as in his youth, he began a frantic search for a suitable libretto. He combed the literature of the Western world, reading works by Theodor Körner, Heinrich Heine, Shakespeare, Detlev von Liliencron, Carlo Gozzi, Maurice Maeterlinck, Eugène Scribe, Franz Grillparzer, Gerhart Hauptmann, and Heinrich von Kleist, not to mention a multitude of minor works totally forgotten today. But he could find nothing acceptable, and his

---

[17] Letters from Wilhelm Kienzl to Mahler, 8 and 15 Oct. 1897 (HOA, Z.452/1897). Mahler's replies are dated 11 and 18 Oct. Mahler saw *Don Quixote* in Graz in 1905, and left the theatre in the middle of the performance, thus deeply offending Kienzl.

[18] Letter from Wilhelm Bruch, 14 Oct. 1897, and Mahler's reply of the 18 (HOA, Z.469/1897).

[19] Prochaska submitted his opera *Das Glück* in spring 1898. His letter to Mahler is dated 12 Apr. 1898, and Mahler's reply 13 Apr. (HOA, Z.VI/22/1898).

[20] Letter from Josef Bohuslav Förster dated 12 Dec. 1898 and Mahler's reply on 29 Dec. (HOA, Z.759/1898).

[21] Born in Windischgrätz, in Styria, on 13 Mar. 1860, Hugo Wolf was Mahler's exact contemporary. He died in a Viennese asylum on 22 Feb. 1903. As well as his many volumes of Lieder, for which he remains famous, he composed at least once for orchestra (the symphonic poem *Penthesilea*: 1883–5) and several times for chorus (Lieder for mixed chorus: 1881; *Christnacht*: 1886–9; *Elfenlied*: 1889–91; *Der Feuerreiter*: 1892 and *Dem Vaterland*: 1890–8). For the theatre, apart from *Der Corregidor*, he wrote only incidental music (*Das Fest auf Solhaug*, 1890–1). In his last few months of sanity, he was working on a second opera, *Manuel Venegas*, with libretto by Moritz Hoernes.

frustration grew. It never occurred to him to ask himself why his quest was so difficult. The truth was that he had from the start drastically reduced his chances of success by rejecting in advance whole categories of literature, such as, for example, all tragedies, realistic or naturalistic works, works expressing religious views that were too conventional, practically the entire literary output of the eighteenth century because of what he considered to be its outdated formalism, all subjects based on a mythology of redemption, all historical plays, and all prose dramas. Having tried, like his idol Wagner, to write his own libretto, one day he finally set his heart on a Spanish comic novel, Alarcon's *El sombrero de tres picos* (The Three Cornered Hat). He soon realized that he lacked the necessary literary talent, so he finally accepted an adaptation by Rosa Mayreder, journalist and founder of the Austrian Feminist League. But, as a libretto, Mayreder's adaptation proved to have glaring weaknesses. It was clumsily constructed, the plot was poor, and contained far too many superfluous episodes and unnecessary secondary characters. Wolf spent a whole year, 1895, setting this mediocre libretto to music. Because of his inexperience, the orchestration took him as much time as the composition itself.

Thus Wolf had pinned all his hopes on a Vienna première for *Der Corregidor*. No doubt anxious because a final decision had still not been taken, he decided to call on Mahler at the Hofoper. The probable date of the visit was Saturday, 18 September, three weeks before Mahler's appointment as director was confirmed.[22] Pale, emaciated, eyes staring, Wolf entered Mahler's office, having determined to 'hold a gun to his head'[23] and at last obtain a date for the performance of *Der Corregidor*. In the course of the conversation, he caught sight of a copy of Rubinstein's *The Demon* on the director's desk.[24] He made some disparaging remarks about the work, which Mahler had admired since conducting it in Hamburg. Their talk soon took an unpleasant turn, Mahler standing his ground and contradicting Wolf's arguments with growing vehemence. How dared he speak of the 'weaknesses' of someone else's dramatic work when his own opera had such a weak libretto and a score that was full of unnecessary detail and heavily overorchestrated? It is not difficult to imagine the effect of these harsh words upon Wolf. The argument became so heated that Mahler now had recourse to a procedure worked out in advance for such eventualities. He discreetly rang for the usher, who came in and said: 'The Intendant wishes to see you immediately.' Wolf, rage and bitterness in his heart, left the office without further ado. But the strange logic of his unhinged mind told him that, in failing to appreciate *Der Corregidor*, Mahler had forfeited his title to the directorship of the Opera. He, Wolf, was the rightful incumbent!

[22] See Leopold Spitzer, 'Hugo Wolfs "Manuel Venegas"', *Österreichische Musikzeitschift* (Feb. 1977), 68. According to this article, Wolf's 'struggle with madness' began on 14 Sept. In the days that followed, he worked daily on his new opera, playing sections to members of his circle as he completed them. On Saturday, 18 Sept., he informed two of his friends at lunch that he had just been appointed Opera Director.

[23] See above, Chap. 2, Wolf's letter of 18 Aug. to Heinrich Potpeschnigg.

[24] Rubinstein's *Demon* had its Viennese première under Mahler on 23 Oct. 1899.

He went to Mahler's apartment in the Bartensteingasse, rang the doorbell, and announced to the astounded cook Elise that he was the new director of the Opera.[25] When she slammed the door in his face he hurried off to break the news to his friends. The same Saturday he had lunch with Ferdinand Foll and Edmund Hellmer at the restaurant 'Zum Braunen Hirschen' and 'behaved like a madman, constantly repeating that he was director of the Opera'. The next day he had recovered sufficiently to play the most recently completed fragments of his second opera *Manuel Venegas* for a group of friends in Mödling. But that same afternoon he took from his pocket, 'with an air of diabolical glee', a speech to the staff of the Hofoper announcing Mahler's dismissal. He seemed so totally convinced of what he was saying that his friends realized that he could no longer distinguish between fact and fiction. By Monday morning he was in a violent state, greeting those around him with threats and insults. He had to be physically restrained, and finally it was decided that he should be committed to Dr Svetlin's asylum, some distance from Vienna. In order to persuade him to leave his apartment they told him they were taking him to see Mahler.[26]

During the first few months of his confinement, Wolf was seized with doubts concerning *Manuel Venegas* and started to revise it. He seemed firmly convinced of his own poetic gift, and it was suspected that there was a link between his illness and the poor librettos he had chosen. On 9 October, an article in the *Neues Wiener Tagblatt* broke the distressing news to the Viennese musical world. It disclosed that Wolf had visited the famous tenor Hermann Winkelmann and told him that Mahler's dismissal had just been confirmed to him by Prince Liechtenstein. As the new director, Wolf had offered to renew Winkelmann's contract. After some months of treatment, the doctors decided that Wolf's condition had improved sufficiently for him to be released. Heinrich Potpeschnigg found him a place to stay in the country with the deputy Moritz Staller, in Cilli. But the matter of the première of his opera still preyed on his mind and on 4 February 1898 he wrote to Potpeschnigg: 'I hear from Vienna that Mahler still seems to intend staging *Der Corregidor* in February or March. In this event I should like to draw to your attention the fact that in no case shall I grant performance rights to the Vienna Opera.'[27] On the 22nd, he attended a recital of his Lieder in Vienna, and acknowledged applause for the last time. His tortured mind would allow him no rest. He soon left the pastoral calm of Cilli, and went south to the Adriatic. The Mediterranean sun did not ease his torment and he returned, via Salzburg and Vienna, to Traunkirchen on the Traunsee, in Upper Austria. There, in October 1898, like Schumann half a

[25] Alma Mahler's version of this incident differs from Frank Walker's: she claims that Wolf 'believed himself to be Mahler' and wanted 'to enter his own house'.

[26] See Frank Walker, *Hugo Wolf* (Knopf, New York, 1952), 420; AMM 84; and Ernst Decsey, 'Aus Hugo Wolfs letzten Jahren', *Die Musik*, 1 (Oct. 1901), 139.

[27] Hugo Wolf, *Briefe an Heinrich Potpeschnigg* (Stuttgart, 1912), 218.

century before, he attempted unsuccessfully to drown himself. Finally recognizing his own condition, he was committed at his own request to the asylum he already knew. He died there six years later. Mahler, it seems, spoke to no one about the quarrel he had had with his old friend, and its tragic sequel. However, this should not be taken as proof that he was indifferent to Wolf's misfortunes, for more often than not he was reticent in the face of the most painful events. As we shall see,[28] he finally put on *Der Corregidor* at the Vienna Opera shortly after Wolf's death.

After *Zar und Zimmermann* and *Dalibor*, Mahler restaged *The Magic Flute*, another opera of which he was particularly fond. To enhance its fairy-tale atmosphere, he made all kinds of animals come on stage in the scene in which Tamino plays the flute: a lion was followed by its mate and they lay down peacefully next to each other; a tiger emerged from a thicket; a flock of birds flew in; a hare leapt onto the stage and pricked up its ears ('How I do it is my secret!' Mahler said); a huge serpent coiled itself up in a corner and finally a crocodile climbed out of the Nile.

'You can imagine what a charmingly naive effect is achieved', Mahler said to Natalie,

when Tamino cries out that all creatures come to him except his Pamina. But at the sound of Papageno's chimes the animals quickly take flight. I hope people will understand, and will not consider this a violation of 'classic' Mozart. I express nothing that is not in the text and have simply brought some life to the dreadful boredom of the usual staging.[29]

Mahler made other changes from the traditional staging: the three temples with their inscriptions; the ordeal scene; Tamino's flute and Papageno's glockenspiel placed in the wings rather than in the orchestra; the restoration of the three brass chords at the beginning of the second act, after which the priests entered two by two, holding hands.[30] All the critics mentioned these improvements which they recognized as conforming to Schikaneder's stage directions. The same concern for fidelity led Mahler to have the three genii arrive in aerial chariots covered with roses and drawn by doves. One of the girls complained of dizziness and refused at first to get into the flying machine. Mahler threatened to take the role away from her (she was a mediocre singer in any case) so she promptly overcame her vertigo. From then on the three singers arrived like celestial voyagers, flying down from the upper reaches of the flies.[31] Mahler gave the roles of the Three Ladies to leading members of the ensemble, Sophie Sedlmair, Jenny Pohlner, and Luise Kaulich.[32] Sarastro (Wilhelm

[28] See below, Vol. ii, Chap. 16. *Neue Freie Presse* (19 Oct. 1897) reported that Mahler had attended a meeting of the Hugo Wolf-Verein the day before.   [29] NBL1. 91; NBL2. 102 ff.

[30] In the *Deutsche Zeitung*, Theodor Helm compared the staging of this scene to Bayreuth's entrance of the knights in *Parsifal*.

[31] Josef Scheu, in the *Arbeiter-Zeitung*, accused these three singers of having sung out of tune.

[32] Josef Scheu thought the voices poorly matched, because Pohlner's soprano was weaker than the others. Thus 'triads without a third' were frequently heard.

Hesch replaced Karl Grengg in this role) was not the usual grey-bearded ancient, but a young black-bearded man wearing 'the white tunic of the Nazarene'.[33]

Mahler was also proud of having restored the earthy simplicity of the original text, which had become 'overrefined and insipid'.[34] According to Natalie, 'this new version of *Die Zauberflöte* played with universal success to a packed theatre: the orchestra performed with delicacy in chamber-music style, and the production delighted even the most captious Mozart lovers. Laughter rippled through the theatre when the animals appeared, and Mahler himself often chuckled with childish pleasure during the performance.' He planned further changes for later, such as having the three genii sung by boys and changing the traditional conception of the Queen of the Night, 'who should be a creature of supernatural cast', a 'gigantic goddess-mother capable of carrying all the characters in her nocturnal womb'. For this role he wanted a woman of regal stature, like Mildenburg, who would emerge from the night (and not, as was customary, from a grotto), with her hair blowing free and her black mantle billowing in the wind.[35]

The Vienna critics greeted the new *Magic Flute* with unanimous delight; as enthusiastic as any was Theodor Helm of the anti-Semitic *Deutsche Zeitung*. The only reservation he expressed was the fear that certain details of the staging 'might distract attention from the music'. In his opinion, the almost too faithful restoration of the original text had given the action a logic it had previously lacked. Thanks to the clarity of the singers' diction, the reduced size of the orchestra, and the new cast changes, certain passages 'were transformed'. 'What simple joy and happiness Schikaneder would have felt at seeing this!' he exclaimed after attending another performance.

Heuberger rejoiced that the Hofoper should now be offering a 'new attraction' of the highest quality 'like all those under the new management'. The revised staging had generated a 'healthy excitement'. Each role had been 'thought out anew' and the acting of the singers had been completely transformed: Mahler had demanded and obtained absolute fidelity to the musical text. In the *Neues Wiener Tagblatt* Kalbeck hailed the 'renaissance' brought about by Mahler, who had revealed Mozart's true stature as 'the greatest of musical dramatists'. Once again the new director had 'breathed life into the soul of a masterpiece after careful resurrection of its body', so that, 'astonished and delighted, the listener heard the voice of the original score calling again as

---

[33] *Montagsrevue* (13 Dec. 1897).

[34] The passage 'Kommet, lasst uns auf die Seite geh'n, damit wir, was sie machen sehn?' caused such uproarious laughter at the first rehearsals that Wlassack advised Mahler to cut it, fearing that it would be judged 'too *risqué*'. The phrase 'auf die Seite geh'n' is a German euphemism meaning to go to the toilet.

[35] NBL1. 92; NBL2. 103. Mildenburg's early vocal proficiency in coloratura singing was now a thing of the past and she could never have sung the Queen of the Night. Mahler was thinking only of her physical appearance. Irene Abendroth, who sang the role in this performance, had to transpose her second aria, its tessitura being too high for her.

though from a dream of distant youth, thanks to the extraordinary subtlety of the nuances and the quality of the casting'.[36]

Mahler's reforming zeal began to affect all aspects of the Opera's activities. He was extending the repertoire and giving a larger place to 'quality' operas. Works by Massenet, Mascagni, and Meyerbeer gradually lost their prominence and ballet performances were given on only one night a week. The shortened Wagnerian dramas gradually gave way to uncut performances. Mahler's aim was to build up a 'treasury of exemplary performances' on which he could draw at need and in which 'no jewel would be missing', even 'if it did not appeal to the public': he would merely space out the performances, so as to rekindle the interest of the public and performers. Never in the whole ten years of his tenure was Mahler more universally admired than now. The Emperor himself received him in audience and congratulated him on having mastered the situation in so short a time, and Prince Liechtenstein was equally delighted. His exploits were the talk of the town: even the conservatives conceded that 'something is always happening at the Opera, even if one doesn't always approve'.

During October, Mahler considered adding Méhul's *Joseph et ses frères* to the repertoire and even drew up a cast list,[37] but nothing came of this plan and the opera was never performed at the Hofoper. Instead he staged another opera with which he was familiar: Tchaikovsky's *Eugene Onegin*. This work of a composer already popular in the Vienna concert halls was warmly received. After the première on 19 November Kalbeck, who had translated the libretto into German, pointed out the exceptional nature of the work, which Tchaikovsky had described not as an opera, but as 'lyrical scenes'. Kalbeck felt that the 'conversational' style was 'too rarely interrupted by a passionate outburst'; the orchestra provided only a 'grey and brown sound background' that 'accompanies rather than underlines or comments'. None the less, the composer's dramatic genius was, he thought, beyond question.[38] Hanslick and Heuberger both welcomed the work as an antidote to the 'harsh and violent work of the Italian moderns'. The opera was 'perhaps too delicate for the stage'. Despite its dramatic weakness, *Onegin* deserved a place in the repertoire, because of the composer's 'feeling for form' and 'strength of conviction', and the originality of his inspiration and instrumentation. Thanks to Mahler, who had

---

[36] Kalbeck noted that even the smaller roles had been assigned to first-class singers. Cast of 16 Oct. performance: Abendroth (Queen of the Night); Forster (Pamina); Michalek (Papagena); Sedlmair, Pohlner, Kaulich (Three Ladies); Wallnöfer, Bitschka, and Hartham (Three Genii); Dippel (Tamino); Schrödter (Monostatos); Pacal and Marian (Armed Men); Ritter (Papageno); Neidl (Speaker); Grengg (Sarastro). Marie Renard sang Papagena on 10 Nov. On 9 Dec. Naval sang Tamino, and Max Kalbeck in the *Neues Wiener Tagblatt* approved the idea of making him kneel after his exchange with the priest (*Sprecher*), as if subjugated by the initiate's message. The *Fremden-Blatt* also revealed that Mahler had corrected some changes that had crept into the text over the years, notably in Tamino's first aria and his invocation to the three genii, changes which had spoilt the melodic line.

[37] Hesch (Jacob), Winkelmann (Joseph), Michalek (Benjamin), Reichmann (Siméon), Schrödter (Ruben), Dippel (Nephtali). MS in Mahler's hand (HOA).

[38] Above all, in the ballroom scene and in the final duet.

inspired both the orchestra and the staging, the production had awakened a high degree of 'interest and comprehension'.[39]

On 24 October, Mahler conducted *Tristan und Isolde* for the first time in Vienna, restoring all the passages that had been cut in the past,[40] except for the first part of the love-duet. The performance began at 6.30 and ended much later than usual, but the capacity audience showed no signs of boredom. Wilhelm Kienzl, who had come from Graz to play Mahler the score of his *Don Quixote*, attended the second performance, on 1 November: 'The orchestra (under Mahler's intelligent and vital direction) was splendid beyond description', he wrote in his diary. 'A great delight in itself, but too loud. The big voices of Winkelmann (Tristan) and Frau Sedlmair (a good, worthy Isolde, nothing more) often failed to come through.'[41] Max Kalbeck, a staunch anti-Wagnerian, found Mahler's performance too faithful to Wagner's requirements in the score. His rapid tempos, though strictly correct, had prevented the singers from 'making themselves understood, drowned as they were by the "surging tides" of the orchestra'. After all, 'Wagner himself makes exactness on their part an illusion, for his demands on them are superhuman. . . . Most of the time it doesn't matter whether they sing on pitch or not. . . . The composer's style does not allow for an allegro; he needs six hours where another would be content with half that time.' This article clearly reveals the state of mind still prevailing among the conservative elements in Vienna's musical public.

Although he preferred Richter's 'more powerful' interpretation, Robert Hirschfeld, one of Wagner's staunch Viennese supporters, drew attention to the fact that the public in the boxes had been 'enthralled' and had remained until the last note died away. For the first time the singers on the stage achieved a quality of performance hitherto only provided by the orchestra itself.[42] Mahler was a past master in the art of husbanding his strength and reserving it for climaxes; the result had been irresistible. The staging had also been much improved. In the first act the ship's crew no longer witnessed the lovers' embrace, for the pair were immediately separated by the women and from then on simply held hands and gazed ecstatically at one another. Despite the old-fashioned scenery, the Finales of the other acts were also 'visually beautiful, poetic and full of meaning'. Similar praise is to be found in an article by Helm, who felt that 'the restoration' had much improved the overall effect.[43] 'Wagner's

---

[39] Like Hanslick, Helm discussed at length the weaknesses of the work, whose 'old-fashioned' construction reminded him of the 'early operas, divided into numbers'. Cast of the first performance (19 Nov.): Michalek (Olga), Renard (Tatiana), Schrödter (Lensky), Schittenhelm (Triquet), Ritter (Onegin), Hesch (Gremin).

[40] In the love-duet, Mahler restored at least one of the traditional cuts, the passage where Wagner comments on the meaning of the word *und* (and) (147 ff. in the Breitkopf piano score), but did cut, as usual, 18 pp. earlier in the same duet.   [41] Kienzl's diary, Stadtbibliothek, Vienna.

[42] Hirschfeld is more to be trusted here than Kalbeck, whose preference for Brahms invariably coloured his judgement of Wagner.

[43] Helm noted that certain of Mahler's tempos were slower than Richter's, e.g. in the Prelude; while others, like Isolde's curse, were faster.

all-powerful instrumental language', he concluded, 'has never been rendered more movingly and with such enthusiasm'—a handsome compliment, coming as it did from a confirmed Wagner-supporter who had long considered Richter to be the supreme interpreter and guardian of tradition.[44]

Four days after *Tristan*, Mahler conducted an uncut performance of *Tannhäuser*, with some cast changes, before a large and appreciative audience.[45] Once again Helm praised Mahler's 'energetic conducting', though he did express some reservations concerning tempos.[46] Later on, for *The Flying Dutchman*, Mahler had planned at first to improve the existing staging, but one thing led to another. Everything was altered and improved, the roles recast, the remaining cuts restored, and the sets, the costumes, and the lighting transformed. To do all this and still respect the limitations imposed by time and money, Mahler had to deploy the full measure of his talent as a director. According to Natalie, he proved able to obtain the most astonishing scenic effects with a few decisive adjustments. For Act II he reduced the size of the stage by half,[47] decreased the number of spinning women by two-thirds, and grouped them around the fire. Through the window could be seen the small harbour and the boats at their moorings. Simple dresses replaced the low-cut 'theatrical' peasant gowns. New wigs, 'as natural as possible', had been prepared, but Mahler eliminated half of them at the last minute because they were all identical. The spinners' movements and gestures were carefully rehearsed to make them more realistic and also to underline the women's changing moods: their fear when they think that Senta has gone mad, the sudden outburst of mirth when she begins to stare fixedly at the portrait of the Dutchman. Mahler had taken particular care rehearsing the laughter. To avoid the typical 'opera laugh' he made the singers breathe in on the first 'Ha-ha' and out on the second. At the start of Senta's ballad two of the girls began to laugh, but an older woman checked them. Gradually the song attracted the spinners' attention, and they gathered around Senta, staring at the portrait, which suddenly seemed to come to life. When they realized that she was speaking to it as if it were alive, they became frightened for her and tried to bring her back to her senses.

While Erik was describing his dream to Senta, she remained with her eyes closed, as though hypnotized, leaning on the back of her chair. For Mahler the

---

[44] Cast of the 24 Oct. performance: Sedlmair (Isolde), Kaulich (Brangäne), Winkelmann (Tristan), Neidl (Kurwenal), Grengg (King Mark).

[45] The previous cast was altered by Mahler as follows: Ehrenstein (Elisabeth), Sedlmair (Venus), Michalek (Shepherd), Winkelmann (Tannhäuser), Schrödter (Walter), Reichmann (Wolfram), Grengg (Heinrich), Marian (Bitterolf). On this occasion Helm found it hard to understand why the passage 'Zum Heil den Sündigen' in the second Finale had previously been cut: it now seemed to be the high spot of Tannhäuser's role.

[46] In particular the slowness of the Hymn to Venus and the speed of the Act II March, which he felt exceeded Wagner's intention. (Helm recalled that Wagner, in his short book on orchestral conducting, had complained that this heroic march was too often conducted 'in a clerical tempo'.)

[47] As he had done earlier, for the letter scene in *Eugene Onegin*.

true climax of the opera was Daland's entrance with the Dutchman. The stage direction was then so striking that the entire audience 'froze in terror' at Senta's cry. The two main characters stood motionless, as though rooted to the ground, staring at each other; every eye was drawn to these two people, 'whose feet hardly seemed to touch the ground'. Reichmann's Dutchman, tall, melancholy, and demonic, seemed like a being from another world. During rehearsals Mahler had a hard job to make him stand still. All else having failed, he finally bound the baritone's arms and legs in such a way as to obtain slow, trancelike movements he felt the character demanded—though not without vigorous protest from the singer himself. He also had a line painted on the ground beyond which Reichmann was not allowed to step.[48] His aim, at this crucial moment in the opera was that all action should appear suspended, that the enraptured Dutchman should show no sign of life. Neither of the protagonists were to react in any way to Daland's words as he moved from one to the other. When left alone with Senta, the Dutchman still had to stand motionless. Only at the end of the scene were they to look as though they were about to fall into each other's arms, when Daland reappeared. The effect was thus far more dramatic than when the entire duet is sung with the singers locked in an interminable embrace.

Having lavished so much care on the staging, Mahler flew into a temper during the first performance, when Winkelmann's admirers, among whom was his son, started to applaud him after Erik's exit.

I conduct the whole work, from the very first note, as a colossal build-up to the Dutchman's entrance and those devils ruin it in an instant. They break the spell under which I and the audience had fallen and I have to start all over again. I felt like hitting Winkelmann, who allows, and even encourages, such shameful behaviour.

Later Mahler said that when the curtain fell he rushed backstage and gave the tenor 'the worst dressing-down he ever received'.[49] However, it seems that the 'Hermann-Bündler' in this case had nothing to do with the type of professional claque against which Mahler had already complained. The young students were genuinely inspired by enthusiasm and their friendship for the famous tenor's son. Firmly resolved to teach them a lesson however, Mahler appeared at the artists' entrance as they waited in a crowd for Winkelmann. Surprised, they started cheering Mahler too, but he silenced them with the following words: 'I don't want your applause. You destroy painstakingly prepared works of art and are a disgrace to this house. I got rid of the paid claque that committed such barbarisms for money, and now you come along and do the same thing out of so-called enthusiasm!' Seeing the disappointment on their faces, he added: 'By all means do applaud, but only at the end of an act or when an artist makes an exit, not otherwise.' The students applauded again and

[48] Soon Mahler found to his distress that Reichmann was gradually reverting to all his former bad habits.
[49] NBL1. 95; NBL2. 108.

Mahler, smiling, said: 'Young friends, I'll accept your applause now, because I'm making my exit!'[50]

In the last act Mahler made a special effort to emphasize the contrast between the day-to-day lives of the port's inhabitants and the grim, shadowy existence of the Dutchman's crew. The fishermen and their womenfolk arrived gaily to offer the sailors baskets of food, but a ghostly silence greeted their merry calls. The fisherfolk ended by eating and drinking the contents of the baskets, and the scene closed with a happy dance, again staged with great care by Mahler. As the ship's crew remained silent, the women returned home. The Dutchman witnessed the scene between Erik and Senta, cursed the latter with terrible violence as she clung to his knees, and then tore himself away to give the signal for departure, a strident whistle which awakened the crew from its magic sleep. Will-o'-the-wisps danced above the heads of the phantom sailors, the blood-red sails were unfurled and filled out in the wind, and all the festive lights of the little port suddenly went out. A dark and stormy night fell as the ship left port, and the first flush of redeeming dawn appeared as Senta threw herself into the sea. The shipwrecked vessel sailing up into the sky was also, it seems, 'restaged in a more poetic way' by Mahler.

For this new production, Mahler used one of the earliest versions of the score, though Wagner had subsequently lightened the orchestration, for the Dresden and Zurich performances.[51] When Richter heard of this he made no secret of his disapproval but Mahler replied, 'If Wagner were alive today, he would approve of what I am doing.'[52] Once again, the newspapers reviews were exceptionally favourable. Not one member of the audience arrived late, Kalbeck remarked. Reichmann had 'surpassed himself', and Mahler and the singers had been 'overwhelmed by the applause'. Helm praised the restoration of the cuts[53] and Mahler's conducting, which had been 'full of intelligence and life'.[54]

'I no longer know whether I'm on my head or my heels, and must ask you to be patient for a while', Mahler wrote to a friend at the end of 1897. 'Harassed and exhausted, I come home to eat and snatch some rest, then return to the hurly-burly.'[55] To Behn, who wanted to hear how his composing was getting on, Mahler also confessed that his job 'absorbs all my time and energy'. At the

[50] *Fremden-Blatt* (25 Dec. 1897).

[51] Among the changes, Wagner had scaled down the trombones and percussion for the Dresden performance.

[52] BMG 275. Richter expressed his point of view to Karpath in an interview, *Neues Wiener Tabglatt* (28 Sept. 1902). He also reiterated his admiration for Mahler. Cast of the first night of *The Flying Dutchman*. Sedlmair (Senta), Winkelmann (Erik), Dippel (Steersman), Reichmann (Dutchman).

[53] The opera lasted half an hour longer than usual.

[54] As usual, Helm made one unconvincing criticism: the slowness of the Ballad theme in the Overture.

[55] This letter was written between the first *Dalibor* (4 Oct.) and the first *Eugene Onegin* (19 Nov.) and was probably addressed to the German composer Karl von Kaskel (whose *Sjula* and *Hochzeitsmorgen* Mahler had conducted in Hamburg), for it alludes to an opera called *Die Bettlerin*, and Kaskel had composed an opera of this name (BGM).

Opera, 'everything goes better than I had imagined, and yet worse, for I have not even a moment to think about "work"'.[56] 'The awful treadmill of the Opera is crushing my soul', he wrote in a third letter,[57] and again lamented the fact that he was so cut off from his own compositions. Mahler's life-style was indeed utterly different from that of the typical Viennese citizen: it was entirely work-centred, since he did not frequent any of the salons, and hardly even had time to go to a café. Now and again he would dine with his sisters at the Spatenbräu bar,[58] at the Leidinger restaurant in the Kärntnerstrasse, or, occasionally, after galas or premières, at the Hotel Imperial with people like Hans Kössler and Guido Adler, two old friends who constantly quarrelled on his account, because Kössler reproached Adler for too readily accepting Mahler's 'modern' ideas.[59]

Anna von Mildenburg had finally been invited to sing at the Vienna Opera in December, and on 1 October, Mahler sent her a draft contract that was to be ratified at the end of her guest appearances. But Pollini refused to extend her leave of absence to two weeks instead of one, as Mahler had requested, so Mildenburg finally sang only three guest performances. To avoid too obvious a break, Mahler continued to write her letters containing friendly advice on how to handle the crafty Pollini.[60] Angered by Rosa Papier's reproaches, Mildenburg had accused Mahler of 'indiscretion' regarding their personal affairs.[61] 'What she means by "former rights",' he replied,

I don't understand. And I have never divulged any of our secrets, which concern only ourselves. No doubt she is simply fishing for information and I advise you not to swallow the bait. Following your letter, in which you said that I had treated you badly, I did in fact enlighten her as to the nature of our relationship, as she had completely misinterpreted your remark. But I was not indiscreet! You have nothing to worry about. . . . I am so looking forward to your guest appearances here. You can be certain that I'll do everything I can to help you. Come, then, without bitterness, so that you can grow and prosper here, and won't have to give up my guidance and my personal concern for your artistic well-being. I hope things will go well for you here; after the life of servitude in Hamburg you will find this a new world.[62]

Mildenburg's guest performances started on 8 December with *Die Walküre*, which Richter conducted, and continued with *Lohengrin* on 14 December, and

---

[56] Letter to Behn dated 26 Nov. 1897 (Notar Hertz Collection). In the same letter Mahler assured Behn that 'nothing has changed between us' and invited him to Vienna.

[57] Mahler wrote this to an unknown correspondent (Nicolas Rauch sale, Geneva, 1957), upon whom he feared his works had made a bad impression, which might prejudice their friendship.

[58] At the Philipphof on Lobkowitzplatz (see BMG 176).

[59] BMG 177. Hans Kössler (1853–1926), a composer and organ-player, and one of Brahms's intimates, was also a close friend of Mahler's in Budapest (see above Vol. i, Chap. 15).

[60] Pollini died on 26 Nov. 1897, of an illness from which he had suffered for several years.

[61] See above, Chap. 2, the letter of 24 Sept. Mahler must have revealed to Rosa Papier some of the facts about the liaison to which the letter referred.

[62] Mahler wrote again to Mildenburg a few days later, discussing the dates of her performances. He was prepared to delay her guest appearance, should she not be in good health, until early Dec. In a final, affectionate note he promised to meet her at the station or, if held up at the last moment, to visit her immediately after her arrival.

Fidelio, again conducted by Richter, on 17 December. So the week's leave of absence lasted ten days after all[63] and her performances were very well received. Kalbeck wrote that few débuts had ever been so impatiently awaited, or fulfilled their promise so well. Mildenburg had brought a 'kind of marvellous jubilation' to Brünnhilde's cry, and the audience had immediately burst into applause. The expressive force of her singing and acting had gone from strength to strength. 'It is evident that she has something to say', he wrote, adding that she combined the freshness and vocal powers of youth with all the advantages of a first-rate musical education. In the *Fremden-Blatt*, Ludwig Speidel hailed Mildenburg as a 'born Brünnhilde', possessing all the qualities required for the role even though she was only 24.[64] For several years in Hamburg the young singer had had in Mahler an 'excellent teacher and promoter of vocal talent', who 'had taken a student and moulded her into a professional artist' by giving her an admirable sense of rhythm, an exemplary style, and a diction 'almost worthy of Bayreuth'. Gustav Schönaich, in the *Wiener Allgemeine Zeitung*, praised Mildenburg's dramatic temperament and intelligent acting; her engagement would fill an important gap in the Vienna ensemble, which at the moment possessed only one dramatic soprano.[65] The most successful of Mildenburg's guest appearances was her first Ortrud in *Lohengrin* on 14 December. The freshness and range of her voice, the 'lively energy' of her acting, were again praised, this time by Hirschfeld in the *Abendpost*.[66]

After she left Vienna Mahler sent Mildenburg a note which reflects the state of their relationship:

I understand everything perfectly and only wanted to make the moment of our farewell

[63] It is possible that this prolongation was obtained for medical reasons, for one of Mahler's notes to Mildenburg, apparently dating from this period, mentions a friend of his, Dr Ludwig Boer, the Vienna Opera doctor. (If Mildenburg had already spent some time in Vienna, she would already have met Dr Boer.) Mahler advises her to let him examine her and to sing if he pronounces her fit, so as not to disappoint the public with a last-minute cancellation.

[64] The same article mentions Mildenburg's father who, under the patronym Belschan, had been a well-known and popular captain in the Austrian army, and recalls the scholarship she had received from the Vienna Opera which had covered her Conservatory fees. It had taken all the skill of a Pollini to release her from her obligation to the Hofoper, where she should normally have been engaged upon graduating from the Conservatory.

[65] Schönaich, the most devoted 'Wagnerite' of all the Viennese critics, noted that the 'joyous' interpretation of Brünnhilde's cry was completely new, even contrary to tradition. Gustav Schönaich (1840–1906) was the son of a court official who had been the Austrian Minister of Education, and whose death had left him an orphan at an early age. Frau Schönaich subsequently married a famous doctor, Dr Standhartner, director of the largest hospital in Vienna. She received in her salon the principal artists and greatest musicians of the time. Schönaich studied law at the Univ. of Vienna and for some years held the post of legal consultant to the Bodenkreditanstalt. He was 34 before he became a writer and critic. He first joined the *Wiener Tagblatt*, then *Die Reichswehr*, and finally the *Wiener Allgemeine Zeitung*, of which he was now editor-in-chief. A friend and intimate of Wagner until the latter's death, he remained close to Wagner's family and regularly visited them at Bayreuth, so that he came to be regarded as their semi-official spokesman in Vienna. He was renowned for his wit, culture, and conversational gifts as well as his gourmandise and corpulence. He died of heart disease in 1906.

[66] For this performance Mahler changed the staging of the church scene so that the chorus participated in the action; Hirschfeld thought this a considerable improvement.

easier for you (it was terrible for me, too). There you have the reason for my 'smile', dear Anna, and you must understand it, as I always understand your bad moods, etc. Further, let me tell you once and for all: I shall never 'interpret' anything you do or say, and you can count on my consideration and forbearance. Naturally, should you feel you want to write to me about something, do so without hesitation and straight from the heart. If, however, it is some formal request with which I must deal in my official capacity, then please send me a formal letter that I can put into the files. Let me say again that you have been highly successful and can count on a brilliant future here. Let Hans Sachs look after the rest![67] I hope you know that you can come and live here in all confidence and security. As one of 'my' ensemble, you will be as well looked after as in your father's or your brother's house—or even better![68]

Shortly thereafter, another member of the Hamburg 'ensemble', the baritone Leopold Demuth, was engaged at the Hofoper. The letter Mahler wrote him in December 1897, explaining that he would not allow him to side-step his requirements co cerning 'precision' as he had done in Hamburg, has been quoted above.[69] The baritone's fi st guest appearance occurred on 5 March 1898, in *Ballo in maschera*, a performance in which the beauty and power of his voice earned him immediate success. Only the *Fremde -Blatt* found fault with him for possessing 'the likeable bad

bits of an Italian singer'. Mahler also attempted unsuccessfully to lure W lli Birrenkoven, the Heldentenor, away from Hamburg, offering him in Vienn a position vastly superior to his present one in the 'Theatre Monopol ini'.[70] In March 1898, a Leipzig singer named Paula Dönges gave five gue t performances in Vienna (as Elisabeth, Elsa, Sieglinde, Pamina, Senta). Mahler's correspondence with her shows that he was very keen to engage her at the Hofoper. 'That Director Staegemann should have told you stories abo t the Viennese claque shows scant concern for the truth on his part. Everyone nows that it has <u>ceased</u> to exist since I took over as Director. In the sa e way, anything you might be told about conditions here with the object of issuading you is fiction rather than fact.' 'Artistic conditions in this ins itution are <u>so far above any</u> criticism that after your Leipzig engageme t you will feel as if transported to another world. . . . Vienna is Vienna,

[67] A reference to *Die Meistersinger*, III. ii.

[68] On 20 Dec. Mahler proposed the following conditions for Mildenburg's contract in a letter to the Intendant: a 5-year contract to take effect from 1 June 1898. He had passed on to the administration Mildenburg's letter of 5 Nov. in which she asked for a higher salary than that proposed, 'having received brilliant offers from various theatres, certain of which are offering over 50,000 marks per year'. Mildenburg's contract was signed by her on 7 Mar. 1898 and by Mahler on the 14th (KMI). Her salary in Vienna had finally been set at 14,000 florins per year for the first two years, 15,000 for the third year, 16,000 for the last two. However, Mildenburg fell ill at the end of Mar. 1898, and her début was ultimately postponed until the autumn. Mahler showed great concern, and insisted on Mildenburg's taking sufficient holiday to complete her convalescence (Mahler's letters to Hermann Behn on 4 Apr., 11 Apr., and 18 June 1898).

[69] See above, Chap. 2.

[70] Undated letter from Mahler to Birrenkoven (Joachim Wenzel collection, Hamburg). This and another of Mahler's letters to the tenor were first publ. by Irmgard Scharberth ('Gustav Mahlers Wirken am Hamburger Stadttheater', *Musikforschung*, 22: 4, 455). This first letter can only have been written at the beginning of 1898, for Mahler alludes to the recent guest appearances of Demuth and Mildenburg (see also below, Vol. ii, Chap. 16). Birrenkoven did sing later on at the Hofoper, but only as a guest, in 1904.

ightfully the supreme goal of any artist—even if it were only on account of the public, which will be all you could wish for.' All conditions having been negotiated and a provisional contract signed, the engagement finally failed to materialize, possibly because Dönges's marriage meant that she was unable to free herself from her Leipzig obligations.[71]

In May 1898 the lyric tenor Franz Naval made his début in *The Magic Flute*. 'One can regard him as a true Mozartian singer', wrote Gustav Schönaich on 10 May 1898. 'He displays very sure taste in the cantilena and the recitatives, his portamento is distinguished, and he is totally in control. His soft voice adapts admirably to the requirements of sustained singing. His acting, full of youthful, naïve enthusiasm, deployed a thousand nuances with the greatest of ease. He was an excellent Tamino.' Despite his initial success Naval spent only eighteen months at the Vienna Opera. An experienced singer of great talent rather than a true artist, he could never conform to the daunting standards of a Mahler.

Mahler's new appointment had been widely publicized, so much so that he received at the beginning of November 1897, from an old acquaintance from his Kassel days, the tenor Heuckeshoven, the following letter, which must have appealed to his sense of humour:

Honoured sir, All the papers are full of praise for the energy with which you are re-organizing the Hofoper. It must be a pleasure to sing under your direction, and since your talent for finding new talent has been much admired, I am taking the liberty, fortified by our earlier good relations in Kassel, of asking whether you might not like to discover me for Vienna as well. If your character remains as it was, your career will not have made you too proud and you will read my letter to the end. Since Kassel, my career, though not as brilliant as yours, has nevertheless been brilliant enough. . . . [Here Heuckeshoven lists the theatres in which he has sung and the fees he has received.] I would be a pearl for Vienna. I have a repertoire of one hundred and fifty roles, heroic, lyric and comic almost complete, any of which I can take instantly, without rehearsal; thus Vienna would suffer no longer for lack of a tenor. My voice has developed into a powerful Heldentenor which can fill the biggest theatre and yet has not the slightest defect, a colossal middle range, a brilliant top register, and I can sing French and Italian heroic roles with equal ease, all in the original, although my preference is Wagner. To the lowest note my voice remains clear, melting and powerful.

I have never advertised in newspapers. Nevertheless the producer Überhorst, when he heard me four years ago, wanted to engage me for Dresden; but I did not wish to enter that nest of intrigue. With you it would be different, you have broken with established tradition and give singers the roles which you think would suit them best. Give me a try and engage me for old times' sake, you would risk nothing, and I can propose anything from one to ten guest appearances, after Easter at only 120 florins per performance. You could part company with me after any of the performances and need not ratify my contract until after the tenth. I could sing in the following roles:

[71] Letters from Mahler to Dönges of 20 Nov., undated (Dec. ?), 11, 15, 18, and 28 Dec. 1897; telegrams to Dönges of 30 Nov., 10, 11, and 12 Dec.; letters and telegrams from Dönges to Mahler of 28 Nov., 10, 17, and 21 Dec.; provisional contract 10 Dec.; Intendant's acceptance 28 Dec. 1897 (HOA).

Raoul,[72] Eleazar,[73] Tannhäuser, Trovatore, Radames, Lyonel,[74] Stradella, Pagliacci, Turiddu, Ottavio,[75] Lohengrin, Edgardo,[76] Assad,[77] Fenton,[78] A Masked Ball, Otello, Johann von Leyden,[79] Siegfried, Siegmund, Arnold,[80] Tamino, etc. A real maid-of-all-work. Take the risk, you have nothing to lose . . . I need no rehearsal for any opera, only instructions from the producer and notice of cuts.

My dear old former friend, show the goodness of your heart and make me happy, and I shall be a credit to you. Naturally I should never allow our former friendly relations to compromise the respect due to my master and director, you can rely upon it. . . . I enclose some reviews, respectfully requesting their return, there are hundreds more if you wish . . . P.S. You will surely remember my talent as an actor.[81]

Alas, we have no record of Mahler's reply, if indeed he ever sent one. We can only speculate therefore as to his reaction to the strange mixture of arrogance and humility displayed in Heuckeshoven's letter.

On 31 October Mahler conducted an evening performance of Johann Strauss's *Die Fledermaus* before a full house as a benefit for the theatre's retirement fund, using his best singers. The previous performances of this work at the Opera, in 1894 and 1895, had been matinées. Mahler now made it a part of the Hofoper's repertory with as many as sixteen performances in 1899 and twenty-one in 1900![82] The venerable Waltz King was present on 31 October, and sent Mahler a telegram the next day thanking him for the extreme care he had lavished on his 'old Fledermaus' and praising the performance, which had been 'exemplary, thanks to your brilliant direction'.[83] The press also drew attention to its exceptional quality—some critics even found it 'too subtle'. As 'an accomplished man of the theatre', wrote Heuberger, Mahler had brought out innumerable nuances and hitherto unnoticed humorous orchestral details, while Kalbeck was convinced that Mahler had touched the hearts of many Viennese and won over 'not only the public in general, but also the most demanding musicians': Strauss himself must have found in the score many forgotten qualities that had been buried beneath the dust of routine.[84] Once again Mahler had admirably fulfilled his duty rather than accomplished a labour of love, for he did not share the uncritical enthusiasm of the Viennese for Johann Strauss. Indeed, a few months after Strauss had died, when he was asked to put on his posthumous ballet, *Aschenbrödel*, Mahler stubbornly re-

---

[72] *Les Huguenots.*   [73] *La Juive.*   [74] *Martha.*
[75] *Don Giovanni.*   [76] *Lucia di Lammermoor.*
[77] Goldmark's *Die Königin von Saba.*   [78] *Die Iustigen Weiber von Windsor.*
[79] *Le Prophète.*   [80] *William Tell.*
[81] Letter from Heuckeshoven to Mahler, 31 Oct. 1897 (HOA, Präs. 21 Nov.).
[82] This was the one and only time that Mahler conducted Strauss's most famous operatta (KMI).
[83] Telegram of 2 Nov. (HOA, no. 850).
[84] Leitich criticized Mahler's 'affected tempos' which had 'hampered the beautiful harmonic lines' that Josef Hellmesberger, jun. (the mediocre ballet conductor of the Opera) had brought out so well, 'in the true Viennese manner'. His ire was also roused by Mahler's artificial hesitations, his syncopation in the fourth bar of the famous waltz, and his new and pointless bowings which were 'contrary to the style'. Cast of the 31 Oct. performance: Renard (Rosalinda), Forster (Adele), Abendroth (Orlofsky), Schrödter (Eisenstein), Dippel (Alfred), Felix (Falk), Ritter (Frank), Hesch (Frosch).

fused to include it in the Hofoper repertoire, thus bitterly offending the composer's widow.[85] 'I don't consider waltzes insignificant', he told Natalie Bauer-
Lechner in 1901.

They are characteristic and charming inventions, and I accept them as such. But you
can't call them works of art any more than, for instance, the folksong: 'Ach, wie ist's
möglich denn', however moving that may be. Their asthmatic melodies, always divided
into the same eight-bar periods, and without the slightest attempt at development,
cannot be accepted as 'compositions'. Compare them with Schubert's *Moments Musi-
cals*, for example, works of art with clear line, development and content in every bar.
Strauss is a poor fellow; with all his melodies and 'ideas' going to waste he reminds me
of a man who has to pawn his few possessions in order to keep going, and soon has
nothing left, whereas another (the real composer) can find plenty of notes and small
change in his pockets whenever he needs them.[86]

Although Mahler had lost almost all 'contact with himself', that is to say with
his own compositions, he now had a stroke of luck which ultimately trans-
formed his status as a composer. It came about through the musicologist Guido
Adler, a native of Iglau like himself, and who had been a fellow student at the
University. Adler had gone on to teach musicology at the German University in
Prague, where his reputation as co-editor with Philipp Spitta and Friedrich
Chrysander of the magazine *Vierteljahrschrift für Musikwissenschaft* had led to
his being chosen as head of a new project, the 'Denkmäler der Tonkunst in
Österreich' (Monuments of Music in Austria). The first volumes of this collec-
tion, published *c.*1892 with a subsidy from the Austrian government, contained
the music of three emperors, Ferdinand III, Leopold I, and Joseph I.[87]

The Denkmäler project had brought Guido Adler into contact with many
influential government officials and members of the Austrian aristocracy, and
enabled him to lend effective support to Mahler's application for the post at the
Hofoper. In 1898 Adler was to be appointed Professor at the University of
Vienna, the chair Hanslick had left several years before.[88] Late in 1897, he
obtained from the Society for the Encouragement of German Science, Art, and
Literature in Bohemia[89] a grant of 3,000 gulden for the publication of Mahler's

[85] *Neues Wiener Journal* (28 Mar. 1908). Adele Strauss was soon to be nicknamed 'Die lästige Witwe' (the
irksome widow).

[86] NBL1. 90; NBL2. 134.

[87] Adler edited the catalogue of the big Viennese Theatre and Music Exhibition in 1892 (GAM 22). In
1897 he was instrumental in getting Mahler elected as a member of the committee of the Denkmäler, to which
Bezecny also belonged (see below, Chap. 7).

[88] His first lecture took place on 26 Oct. 1898, in the presence of Bezecny, Lipiner, and Mahler, the
composers Ignaz Brüll, Hermann Grädener, Josef Labor, Anton Rückauf, the musicologist Eusebius
Mandyczewski, and the critics Richard Wallaschek and Robert Hirschfeld: *Neue Musikalische Presse* (30
Oct. 1898).

[89] Gesellschaft zur Förderung deutscher Wissenschaft, Kunst und Literatur in Böhmen. The grant obtained by Adler (6,000 kronen) was paid in two instalments, one half in Jan. 1898 and the other a year later.
Among the 16 composers who received grants from this society were Camillo Horn, Rudolf Prochazka, Emil
Nikolaus von Reznicek, Anton Rückauf, Josef Stransky, and Josef Labor. Mahler received a larger amount
than any of those mentioned (KMI).

First and Third Symphonies, and the orchestral parts of the Second. Mahler hastily supplied a curriculum vitae for the application at the end of 1897.[90] Thus on 21 January 1898, Mahler wrote to Behn asking him to send the plates of the score and the two-piano transcription of the Second Symphony to Eberle. He added:

From now on, naturally, all subventions to Hofmeister must stop. This firm [Waldheim Eberle] does things in style: they have already printed all Bruckner and want to engrave everything of mine, both the piano scores and the orchestral parts. Eberle only do engravings in the style of Röder. They have plenty of capital, and were set up to promote Austrian works. They also find a suitable publisher: my work will probably go to Doblinger. Advertising and distribution will be done on a large scale.[91]

Eventually the task of distributing, publicizing, and copyrighting Mahler's symphonies was entrusted to another Viennese firm, that of Josef Weinberger,[92] which, in December 1897, had published the *Lieder eines fahrenden Gesellen*.[93]

Mahler's relief upon receiving the good news can be imagined. Until then he had constantly worried over his precious manuscripts, since he possessed only the original and one copy of each. He had hardly ever dared to let them out of his possession, which made their chances of becoming known almost non-existent. He well knew that he owed this stroke of luck to his present position: 'It has always been thus', he wrote. 'For he who has, to him shall more be given, and richly given, but whoever has not, from him shall be taken even what he has.' A few weeks later one of Mahler's symphonies was performed for the first time outside Germany. The Belgian composer-conductor Sylvain Dupuis[94] had founded the Nouveaux Concerts in Liège in 1888—an annual series of four

[90] MBR1, no. 233; MBR2, no. 244, to Emil Freund.

[91] A copy of the contract, signed by Mahler on 27 Sept., is among Alma Mahler's papers at the Univ. of Pennsylvania. The terms are that four times a year the publishers will pay Mahler half the revenue from the sale of scores and performance rights, once the costs of printing have been covered.

[92] Josef Weinberger (1855–1928) founded his Viennese publishing firm in 1885. In 1897 he was a founder member of the Gesellschaft der Autoren, Komponisten und Musikverleger (AKM), one of the earliest societies of its kind. He was co-founder of Universal Edition (1901), which he allowed to use his premises until it moved to the Musikvereingebäude in 1914. He published operas by Austrian composers such as Kienzl, Goldmark, and Brüll, and also 8 of Wolf-Ferrari's stage works. A great number of operettas by Eysler, Kalman, Lehàr, Strauss, etc. were included in the Weinberger catalogue.

[93] Letter to Behn of 21 Jan. 1898 (BGM). Mahler wrote to Behn again, a week later, about the reprinting of the Second Symphony (letter of 28 Jan. 1898, Marc Andreae collection, Sorengo, Switzerland). According to Hofmeister's *Musikalisch-literarischer Monatsbericht*, Weinberger publ. the *Lieder eines fahrenden Gesellen* in Dec. 1897 (the contract had been signed at the end of Sept.), the First Symphony in Feb. 1899, and the *Knaben Wunderhorn* in Mar. 1900. Hofmeister brought out the score of the Second Symphony in 1897. The score of the Third Symphony announced in 1899 was not publ. until July 1902, after the first complete performance in Krefeld. In an undated letter to Felix Weingartner (written at the end of 1898), Mahler wrote that the printed scores of both symphonies 'can be made available at any time' (*stehen jeden Moment zu Diensten*) (BGM).

[94] Born in Liège on 9 Oct. 1856, Sylvain Dupuis conducted La Légia, a choral society, from 1886, and founded the Nouveaux Concerts. Conductor, 1900–11, at the Théâtre de la Monnaie in Brussels, he gave many first performances there. Dupuis composed a number of choral and orchestral works, as well as incidental music for plays. He directed the Liège Conservatory 1911–25. He died on 28 Sept. 1931.

evening performances given by some of the best-known soloists and mainly devoted to contemporary works.[95] The courageous Dupuis had invited Strauss the preceding year to conduct one of his symphonic poems and it was probably from him that he heard of the first performance of Mahler's Second Symphony in Berlin two years earlier. Thus he programmed it for 6 March 1898.[96] The work was greeted enthusiastically by public and press. 'This symphony', claimed the *Journal de Liège*, 'affirms a powerful striving for liberation, a will to leave the beaten track and to become ever more free. . . . The initiative lies with those who dare: those who determinedly reach into the unknown and into the heart of all the possibilities yet to be realized, rather than those who glean from fields already harvested.' The bulletin of the Fédération Artistique spoke of 'an energy that is a touch exaggerated. . . . It is difficult if not foolhardy to formulate an opinion about such a considerable work after only one hearing. . . . Thanks to M. Dupuis, revelation has burst upon us of a composer whose name is virtually unknown, and whose gifts and ambitions certainly deserve to emerge from the shadows.' The correspondent of *La Meuse* described his impressions of the five movements in detail. 'At the end of this accomplished performance, the enthusiasm of the audience positively flowed towards those taking part, and Dupuis was acclaimed.' Again, in the *Express*, the composer's powerful drive for independence was recognized: 'Inspired to create on a grand scale, he has dedicated himself to producing a powerful and robust work whose proportions may be exaggerated but whose manner is one of fine intransigence. Instead of addressing seductive smiles to the hearers like certain charming products of the French School, it shakes and subjugates them with a command-ing gesture.'

Dupuis wrote to Mahler to tell him of the success his work had had and to inform him that he planned to give another performance the following year. 'My dear and honoured colleague', Mahler replied on 15 March 1898,

Allow me to express my deep gratitude for the great joy you have given me by taking my work and presenting it in a performance that—according to all the critics—was brilliant. I apologize for not expressing myself in your own beautiful language, which I understand but cannot write.—I scarcely need to tell you how much I should have liked to be present. This is the first time that someone other than myself has cared for one of my spiritual children and has adopted it so completely. It is also the first time that it has won so complete a victory, to judge from the articles I have before me. I owe this to your energy and to your artistic skill, which I can measure more easily than anyone else, since I well know the great difficulties of approach and performance presented by my work.[97]

[95] The list of composers whose works were performed at these concerts includes Brahms, Bruckner, Smetana, Franck, Lalo, Chabrier, Balakirev, Glazounov, Duparc, Chabrier, and Debussy. D'Indy and Strauss had directed festivals of their own works.

[96] The soloists were Marthe Lignière (soprano) and Frieda Lautmann (contralto). The chorus consisted of 'Dames amateurs et de la Société Royale La Légia'. The concert ended with an Aria from Max Bruch's oratorio *Odysseus* (with Lautmann as soloist), followed by Beethoven's *Egmont* Overture.

[97] Mahler further expressed the hope of hearing Dupuis's second performance, should it take place at a

After spending Christmas with his sisters in the Semmering mountains some 60 miles south of Vienna,[98] Mahler returned to confront the New Year, 1898. This would be his first complete year in Vienna, and in the course of it he would finally assert his authority over the Hofoper. His first production was to be the Vienna première of Bizet's *Djamileh*, an opera unknown in Austria but which he had already presented to the Hamburg public. He devoted much energy and enthusiasm to this task for he felt that the 'svelte, aristocratic music' and the 'psychological realism' compensated for the banality of the libretto. To strengthen the dramatic effect he slightly altered the sequence of events[99] and 'took the greatest care with each sound, each word, each movement, even the heroine's dance', performed by Marie Renard.[100] He successfully 'created the magic atmosphere of an Oriental tale' and without undue expense, using bits of scenery borrowed from former productions of other works; nonetheless, the whole performance had an impression of freshness.

Bruno Walter, who had left Breslau for Pressburg at the beginning of the 1897–8 season, had visited Vienna and stayed at Bartensteingasse just before Mahler's appointment.[101] Early in 1897 Mahler had advised Walter to do his military service for a year, during which time he would send him 100 marks a month to help with expenses.[102] This was by any standards an extraordinarily generous offer on Mahler's part for 1,200 marks represented over a month of his Hamburg salary. Walter's appointment in Pressburg meant that he did not take up the offer, but this did not affect Mahler's fatherly interest in him, and he was already planning to engage him at the Vienna Opera. In January 1898, Walter again spent a few days with Mahler to attend the opening night of *Djamileh* on the 22nd. He greatly admired the quality of the musical interpretation, which he later discussed with Mahler during a supper at the Spieglers'. Some of the tempos had surprised him, one passage in particular had been taken very slowly. 'I took that passage faster, even in the final rehearsal,' Mahler told him, 'but it is only in the presence of an audience that I feel quite certain how something should be. To bring out certain things from the orchestra, one can

time when he could get away. Eventually, Dupuis invited him to conduct the performance himself in Jan. 1899 (see below, Chap. 6). (Collection Dupuis, BGM.)

[98] In the postcard he sent to Justi from Semmering on 22 Dec. 1897, Mahler writes that he expects her and Emma to join him.

[99] He also made some changes to the libretto, as is shown by the telegram he sent on 19 Jan. to Simrock, the German publisher of *Djamileh*, asking for his new version to be printed; otherwise the audience would not be able to follow the plot (HOA, autograph telegram of 19 Jan. 1898, and revised version of the text of *Djamileh*).

[100] The dance was usually entrusted to a ballerina rather than to the singer.

[101] See letter from Bruno Walter to his parents, 20 Sept. 1897 (BWB 26). During this stay Walter heard performances of *Zar und Zimmermann*, *Die Walküre*, and *The Flying Dutchman* conducted by Mahler. His season in Pressburg started on 1 Oct. 1897 and ended on 31 Jan. 1898. Thereafter the whole Pressburg Theatre moved to Temesvar. The director, Emanuel Raul, was an old acquaintance of Mahler's since he had formerly headed the Olmütz Theatre in 1883 (KMI).

[102] MBR1, no. 206; MBR2, no. 214. On this occasion Bruno Walter came to show Mahler the piano-duet reduction of the Second Symphony Mahler had commissioned from him (NBL2. 110).

only sketch the beat, or rather what's behind it.'[103] He then reminded Walter
of the maxim quoted countless times by Wagner: 'The essential thing in music
is *clarity.*'

According to Hanslick, *Djamileh* was an opera for the connoisseur rather
than for the general public, but it had received 'a friendly welcome' thanks to
the 'delicate nuances' of its 'exquisite' score, unity of style, 'brilliant technique', 'characteristic touches', 'charming melodies', and 'delightful orchestral
sound'.[104] Helm felt that Bizet had uniquely succeeded in expressing in music
'the delicate poetry of the East'. But the warmest praise of all came from
Kalbeck who had found the 'atmosphere and musical poetry' of the first scene
'unforgettable, magical . . . like the infinite variety of colours and sounds perceived in a dream'. Mahler, he added, was of course largely responsible for this
achievement.[105] In fact, Mahler had every reason to be proud of himself, for
Bizet's little opera was performed eight times during the season. He later told
Natalie that his stage direction, rather than his musical interpretation, was
responsible for the success of the opera. Otherwise he saw no particular reason
why *Djamileh* should be more attractive to the public than *Dalibor* or *Eugene
Onegin.*

Despite the results already attained, he was still not satisfied with the state
of the Opera and the standard of repertoire performances. 'The best way to
teach is by example', was one of his favourite precepts. In Budapest he had
regularly invited guest singers of high repute; he now began to do this in
Vienna. For the first of these 'Ehrengastspiele' (special guest appearances) he
invited the famous *prima donna assoluta* Lilli Lehmann. In January and
February 1898 she appeared successively as Donna Anna, Fidelio, and
Norma,[106] and returned to the Hofoper almost every year until Mahler's departure. For the evening performance of 30 January, *Don Giovanni* was scheduled,
with Richter conducting and Lilli Lehmann as guest artist in the role of Donna
Anna. It looked as though the performance would have to be cancelled because
Fanny Mora, the Donna Elvira, was taken ill at the last moment. To save the
evening, Mahler was obliged to give the role to a singer who had formerly been
at the Dresden Opera, despite Richter's opposition. He was beginning to realize
that getting replacements was one of the thorniest problems for opera in

[103] NBL2. 110. 'Um Gewisses im Orchester herauszubringen, kann man den Takt, oder vielmehr, was ihn
erfüllt, nur malen'.

[104] Hanslick particularly admired the heroine's dance with its choral accompaniment. Kalbeck thought
the work should end with Djamileh's death, and condemned the final love-duet as 'pompous, embarrassing
and superfluous'. Among the work's 'gems' he cited the dance, the Overture, the slaves' March and Haroun's
'Hymn to free love'.

[105] Cast of the first performance (22 Jan. 1898): Renard (Djamileh), Schrödter (Haroun), Schittenhelm
(Splendiano). In the original score, Splendiano was a baritone. Thus the role had been transposed. Heuberger
in the *Wiener Tagblatt* said that the only performer to surpass Renard and Schrödter had been Mahler, on the
podium. The evening also included the performance of a ballet by Josef Bayer, *Rund um Wien.*

[106] The dates of Lehmann's *Gastspiele* were: *Norma* (24 Jan.; 3, 13, and 19 Feb.); *Don Giovanni* (30 Jan.);
Fidelio (9 and 16 Feb.). The production of *Norma* was entirely revised in accordance with Lehmann's wishes.
She gave another five performances at the Hofoper in May.

Austria, since Vienna was the country's only musical centre of importance, whereas Germany had many opera-houses within two hours' travelling distance of each other, making it possible to get last-minute replacements by telephone. Justi and Nina Spiegler were present that evening with Mahler in his box. He listened to every note, and watched everything that happened on the stage: nothing escaped his notice. He was constantly springing to his feet and rushing to the telephone to call the staff backstage: 'What on earth is that costume Dippel (Don Ottavio) is wearing?' he asked the designer Gaul. 'He looks like an undertaker, not a Spanish grandee!' During the ballroom scene, in which the musicians making up the three small orchestras appear onstage in costume, Mahler again hurried to the telephone. 'How can the viola player come on wearing a pince-nez? Let him wear spectacles if he can't see well, but not a pince-nez!' Turning to Nina Spiegler, he added: 'If I let that pass, they would soon come on in *Fidelio* wearing monocles!' A moment later one of the stage musicians played a wrong note: 'Who is that clarinettist on-stage?' he asked, determined to summon the man to his office the next day. In the cemetery scene, he seized the telephone once more: 'Is that supposed to be a marble statue? It looks as though it were made of pasteboard! The singer's make-up is appalling. See that it doesn't happen again!' At the start of the final storm, Mahler complained about the electrician's efforts: 'The lightning is laughable! Has the electrician gone out of his mind?' In the closing scene[107] something happened that almost turned the dramatic ending of the opera into farce. Reichmann wandered around the stage looking for the trapdoor through which he was supposed to disappear, while a stage-hand hesitated to set the collapse of the scenery in motion for fear of hurting him. In desperation, Richter held the final chord, the astonished audience waited, and Mahler, mystified as to what was going on, shouted down the telephone, 'For heaven's sake, isn't that set ever going to fall?'[108]

Many years later, in his memoirs, the Anglo-American stage-director Francis Neilson told the following anecdote which illustrates the lamentable conditions prevailing at the Hofoper at that time. It concerns one of the first performances of *Siegfried* conducted by Mahler in Vienna.

We were walking across the Ringstrasse before the performance when he said to me: 'I do hope the scenery will know you are present and that it will behave with discretion.' Alas, the wretched cloths in the change in the third act went awry and completely spoiled the illusion that Siegfried was climbing up a mountain. Later on, a ragged piece of scenery hung swaying over the head of Siegfried while he gazed upon the sleeping Brünnhilde. When I saw Mahler the next day at lunch, he smiled rather sadly and said, 'It hurts me when anything happens that takes the attention away from the music. Nothing should break the spell.'[109]

[107] The final sextet was cut, according to Mozart's own Vienna version. In this production, the set for the banquet was supposed to collapse and disappear, to be replaced by that of the cemetery.
[108] NBL1. 97; NBL2, 110.
[109] Francis Neilson, *My Life in Two Worlds* (Révisioniste Press, Brooklyn, NY, 1971), i. 226.

the attention away from the music. Nothing should break the spell.'[109] At that time the series of urgently needed reforms planned by the Lord Chamberlain for the higher e helons of the imperial theatres' administration had not yet been carried out, and Intendant Bezecny was still in his post.[110] It was undoubtedly owing to Prince Liechtens ein's insistence that Bezecny finally resigned at the end of January 1898. In a fare ell letter to the members of the Opera, he congratulated himself on having 'had the i ea' of proposing Mahler for director. His successor, Freiherr von Plappart von L enheer, was officially appointed on

February and introduced to the Opera personnel on 20 February. Plappart, addressing the assembled company, congratulated them on having a director 'you can follow with your eyes shut'. One of the journalists invited for the event, who was sitting with his colleagues in the second row of the stalls, overhead Richter, whispering to one of his friends: 'That will give the imbeciles something to write about.' Two hours later a press delegation called on Mahler and demanded that Richter apologize. Mahler replied that he would look into the matter, and with Richter's approval he wrote to Karl Rolleder, publisher of the *Deutsche Zeitung* and doyen and spokesman of journalists, explaining that Richter's remark had not been intended to offend anyone. The matter was duly regarded as settled.[111]

On the occasion of Plappart's appointment, the Dienst-Instruktion dating from 1885 for the Intendant of the Court Theatres[112] was modified, and the Intendant's powers were considerably reduced.[113] Henceforth nearly all important decisions, such as instructions to the directors of the Opera and the Burgtheater, the hiring of artists, and the drawing up of contracts, had to be submitted for approval to the Lord Chamberlain. All negotiations prior to engagements were to be the responsibility of the two directors; the Intendant was to be consulted only after the preliminary guest appearances. Furthermore, four times a year Plappart had to submit to his superior an overall schedule of engagements, a report on the singers and their salaries, and a proposed budget. Henceforth, therefore, real power lay with the Lord Chamberlain's Office. The curtailing of the Intendant's powers was of primary importance to Mahler, since Plappart and his subordinate Wlassack soon became his sworn enemies. Thanks to the new Dienst-Instruktion, he was much less dependent on them than upon their superiors and the Intendant was no longer in a position to block Mahler's initiatives. One of the first conflicts arose over the guest appearance of a celebrated singer. Plappart objected to it, asking Mahler to 'bear in mind the Opera's finances'. Mahler couched his reply in lofty terms: 'Your Excellency, that is not the right approach. An imperial institution such as the

[110] As early as 12 Apr. 1897, the *Neue Freie Presse* had announced Bezecny's resignation and Plappart's appointment, adding that the new Intendant would work much more closely with the Lord Chamberlain.

[111] BMG 101. Karpath received Mahler's autograph letter as a gift from Karl Rolleder, who, being a rabid anti-Semite, did not wish to keep it.

[112] The Dienst-Instruktion (Service Instructions) dating from Nov. 1885 was officially amended in Feb. and May 1898 (HOA, Z.308).

[113] Doubtless because the deficit had increased during the preceding years.

Hofoper should feel honoured to spend money in this way; it could not be put to better use. Nevertheless, I shall do my best to take your request into consideration.'[114] Thus, notwithstanding the change of Intendants, Mahler's authority was increased during his second year as director, in spite of the periodic 'scandals' caused by certain singers. Once, when Mahler had a difference of opinion with the ballet-master, Prince Liechtenstein put it to him in the friendliest possible way that he should not play into the hands of his enemies so readily. Mahler replied that, on the contrary, such storms were necessary from time to time to maintain discipline. 'The establishment of order necessitates the greatest severity', he added. 'Each scandal, then, has a meaning and a beneficial effect: you should summon me only when there are fewer than two "scandals" a week.'[115]

After a *Ring* which Richter and Mahler shared between them,[116] and whose main attraction was that it included Vienna's first complete performance of *Rheingold*, the last weeks of February 1898 were particularly busy at the Opera, for Mahler had inherited from Jahn the thankless task[117] of producing Leoncavallo's *La Bohème*, a work whose dramatic and musical weaknesses he was fully aware of, since he had attended the Venice performance. Leoncavallo, who had heard from Jahn that Mahler disliked this opera, had been exchanging letters with the former Intendant since early September 1897, complaining about the postponement of the first performance, originally planned for 19 November. Mahler had explained the delay: Ernst Van Dyck had invoked a clause in his contract which enabled him to refuse the part of Marcello, and for the moment Vienna had no other singer available for the role. But Leoncavallo was not satisfied with this explanation. He wrote again to the Intendant on 18 September, in comic French, protesting that Van Dyck's refusal did not justify the postponement or, more probably, the cancellation of the première, which was damaging to his reputation:

Ah, I already perceive the changes due to the absence of good Maître Jahn! Nothing like this would ever have happened when he was Director, especially after the problems raised by the *Médicis*.[118] When one has Schrödter available (whom I myself suggested for the role, because I know his voice and his physique would be more suitable), and when one has the nerve to tell me that because Mr Van Dyck does not wish to sing, <u>one can no longer give the opera</u>, it is like saying that the Vienna Opera will be closed when Van Dyck stops singing!! What nonsense! It seems that my enemies

---

[114] The subject of this exchange was probably Lilli Lehmann's guest performance for Jan.–Feb. and May 1898, which thereafter became a yearly event.

[115] NBL1. 103; NBL2. 116.

[116] Mahler conducted *Rheingold* and *Siegfried* (this performance featured Schmedes's Viennese début), and Richter the other two parts of the cycle.

[117] Mahler's letter to Jahn upon returning from Venice, on 8 May 1897, clearly states his preference for Puccini's opera (see above Chap. 1).

[118] Leoncavallo had few scruples when his interests were at stake. Some years earlier, during another trip to Vienna, he had not hesitated to pretend that he was a Jew in order to win the support of the Viennese press, which was mainly in Jewish hands (see BMG 369).

lack inventiveness for their pretexts. And believe me, this is a pretext. As to the value of the work, come here on the 24th or 25th (I will telegraph you the exact date) for the première. Deign to honour the performance with your presence, and you will see the work that Mr Mahler is treating so badly! If you cannot come, send Maître Richter, or someone else in whom you have confidence (but not one of Mr Mahler's friends), and you will learn what my theatrical work is like. I have written to Mr Mahler, asking for Schrödter as tenor, and saying that I do not accept the postponement.

On 18 September Leoncavallo asked Bezecny to 'prevent this infamy' and offered to go to Vienna and plead his cause before Archduke Eugen with whom he had been in touch.[119] But Mahler was not a man to be intimidated by such manœuvres. When Leoncavallo again threatened to 'take the necessary steps if he [Mahler] did not conform to his wishes', he answered that such 'shameful' threats were of slight importance compared to the interests of the Opera. The première had been and would remain scheduled for the end of February. In fact Mahler devoted as much time and care to the work as he would have if it had been a masterpiece. As early as January, he invited the composer to come and be present at all the stage rehearsals.[120]

Leoncavallo reached Vienna in mid-February 1898 and was informed that Van Dyck had decided to 'fall ill', hoping to postpone for three days the first performance, scheduled for 23 February. Having resisted Leoncavallo's intrigues Mahler was determined not to submit to the whims of a singer. Ever since his arrival in Vienna, he had rehearsed two complete casts for each new opera; if Van Dyck would not sing on the première, then Andreas Dippel would take his place. Having earlier insisted that his opera be given with or without Van Dyck, Leoncavallo now decided that Van Dyck was absolutely indispensable to its success. 'Dear Master', he wrote on 17 February, after the penultimate rehearsal,

I am certain that, due to your great artistic conscientiousness and competence, you have already realized, after today's most unfortunate rehearsal, that it is absolutely impossible to give the première next Wednesday! The artists' hesitations and the uncertainty of some members of the orchestra, the lack of ensemble and precision in the chorus, the <u>absolute need</u> to polish the <u>mise en scène</u> further, prompt me to ask you at once to postpone the première until Saturday. . . . I must tell you that <u>I cannot give up</u> Mr Van Dyck in the role of Marcello for the first performance. His collaboration is too essential for such an important première; this point is capital. Moreover you yourself told me three months ago that Mr Van Dyck was <u>indispensable and that without him you would not give my opera!</u>

Leoncavallo concluded his letter with another threat: he hoped he would 'not be obliged to take further steps'.

Mahler wrote back the same day:

[119] Van Dyck himself was in part responsible for Leoncavallo's intervention.
[120] Letter to Leoncavallo of 12 Jan. 1898 (HOA).

Dear Sir, I consider your criticism of the <u>hesitations</u> of the <u>soloists</u> and the <u>orchestra</u> a personal insult. During today's rehearsal, Frau Saville and Herr Felix were in fact uncertain of their roles. You know, however, that neither of them is to sing on the evening of the première! The other soloists can be relied upon, and no one in the world except yourself would dream of doubting the orchestra's ability to perform its task perfectly! Furthermore, my duty to my own reputation is much too important for me to consent to giving a less than satisfactory performance. I only mention this in passing. Let us discuss the matter again after tomorrow's rehearsal, when the première soloists are to sing.

Moreover, whatever date I set for the première, I cannot be sure Mr Van Dyck will be present; I know this from experience. An opera house as important as ours cannot depend upon the caprices or health of a singer. That is why I have prepared two casts, so as not to be embarrassed by possible cancellations. The première must be perfect; on that point we are in agreement. However the decision lies with me alone, and I shall make it tomorrow after the rehearsal. Should you again criticize our work, rather than run the risk of alarming public opinion, I will postpone the première (and entrust it to another conductor).[121] I shall not modify the schedule except in a case of <u>force majeure</u>! <u>Au revoir</u> until tomorrow's rehearsal.

That evening Leoncavallo wrote again just before midnight, pulling in his horns a little: though he claimed the right to 'make a few comments', he nevertheless felt that the most important thing was for Mahler to conduct the première, for he was 'the principal artist, the life and soul of the work'! However, Van Dyck had given him his word of honour he would sing, and in view of this he was sure Mahler would agree to grant him the two extra days of work, since he had not had the stage rehearsals he had asked for. 'You pointed out wittily the other day that I ought to know my Bohème well. May I remind you that I am also <u>the author of my libretto</u> and consequently know what I can ask of my artists.'

The next day, 19 February, Leoncavallo stormed into the opera house, accompanied by a compatriot whose task was to explain to him in Italian what was happening. They took their places in the stalls, ready to watch the rehearsal. As soon as Mahler appeared on the podium, he informed the orchestra and singers of the exchange of letters the previous day ('his tone was agitated', according to Leoncavallo):

Herr Leoncavallo believes that additional rehearsals of his opera are necessary if everything is to go smoothly. I don't agree. I am delighted that he is present now and that his Italian friend can translate everything to him, so that he may know what is being said. I consider his doubts superfluous: an élite of artists are gathered here onstage and in the orchestra pit; they will give his work the best possible performance, certainly better than he could get anywhere else. As director and conductor I can guarantee this and I believe I am qualified to judge. Now that we have double casts, a single singer can no longer make difficulties for me. Ladies and gentlemen, let us

---

[121] The rough draft of this letter is in HOA. At the bottom of the page appears the phrase 'if the première is deferred, Mahler will entrust the baton to one of his colleagues'. Leoncavallo's reply indicates that this phrase was also in the letter he received.

begin the rehearsal and show Herr Leoncavallo what the Vienna Opera is capable of achieving.

Mahler was about to give the signal to begin, when Leoncavallo approached the orchestra pit and, in the midst of general excitement, replied in French. Of course he had the highest regard for the Vienna Opera, 'whose artists are far better suited than anyone else to bear my opera to triumph', but, while considering his work 'with modesty', he none the less thought that he 'could judge the stage production and the voices' and believed it was absolutely imperative that Van Dyck sing the première. Mahler himself had in fact once stated that he would not give the opera without Van Dyck. 'Since Leoncavallo has overcome his scruples and admitted that the Vienna Opera company is capable of performing his opera, I consider the matter closed', Mahler answered, in German. 'Oh no', Leoncavallo shouted, 'permit me to add a few more words.' Mahler, his patience exhausted, said curtly: 'There will be no more talk here. Let us have silence and start to rehearse!' Leoncavallo put on his hat and rushed out of the auditorium.

The rehearsal got under way, but was interrupted in the middle of Act I by the arrival of the stage-director, August Stoll, accompanied by a lawyer. Stoll handed Mahler a letter from Leoncavallo. Mahler refused to accept it, declaring that he had no time to read while conducting, and his heated reply was accompanied by 'such energetic gestures' that the letter was knocked from Stoll's hands. Mahler then went on with the rehearsal, ignoring the lawyer's protest,[122] and at the end of the first act he summed up the morning's proceedings to the singers and the orchestra: 'There's no need to be upset by what has happened, everything has gone perfectly.' Leoncavallo's letter, written in German, accused Mahler of having behaved in a way 'to which I am not accustomed', and once again praised the Viennese artists, whom their director had misinformed regarding the contents of his first letter. He insisted that Van Dyck should sing the première and be given two additional rehearsals.

If you refuse to comply with my wishes, which are artistically justified, and persist in putting on my work in this unprepared, imperfect manner, you will expose my reputation, as well as that of your institution, to a fiasco. Should this be the case, I shall withdraw my opera, protest against its performance, and never again set foot on your stage. The public will then be able to judge how you treat a composer who flatters himself that he has already given to the Vienna Opera a not unsuccessful work.[123]

Leoncavallo may well have had something to do with the letter Mahler received on 20 February, three days before the première, from Frances Saville, who was to sing the role of Mimi with Van Dyck, announcing that if she had not attended the rehearsal that day it was because she had made up her mind not

---

[122] The *Neue Freie Presse* gives the name of the lawyer, Oskar Eirich, Viennese representative of the Parisian Society of Authors, Composers, and Editors.

[123] Leoncavallo is of course referring to *Pagliacci*.

to sing the part, having heard that Frau Forster was to sing it in the première.[124] The next day she informed the press that she would not agree to any extension of her contract and would accordingly be leaving the Hofoper soon. Once again Mahler refused to give in. Thus, and during the two days preceding the première, Leoncavallo aired his grievances to the newspapers, moved heaven and earth to get his own way, and even involved the Italian ambassador, Count Nigra, in the battle. The Lord Chamberlain backed Mahler, however, and advised him to stand firm. Leoncavallo then refused to attend the dress rehearsal on the 21st. This took place at 10.30 in the morning with Dippel in the role of Marcello, and proceeded without incident. Finally realizing that the première would indeed take place as scheduled, Leoncavallo changed his tactics and tried to persuade Van Dyck to sing, even though the tenor had threatened to resign if Mahler performed the opera before his 'complete recovery'.[125] Mahler merely gave Van Dyck an ultimatum: either he must change his mind before noon on the day of the première, or Dippel would sing in his place. On the day of the performance, Van Dyck sent Mahler a doctor's certificate from a certain Professor Chiari, stating that he was suffering from a cough and serious catarrh. But Mahler remained steadfast and did not even bother to reply; at noon he turned the role over to Dippel, and stuck to this decision, despite desperate last-minute appeals by Van Dyck. In the end Leoncavallo attended the première and not only declared himself satisfied but finally admitted that Dippel's personality suited the role of Marcello better than Van Dyck's. The house was full, for the newspapers had given their readers a blow-by-blow account of every phase in the conflict. Mahler rushed to the podium as fast as he could, but was unable to forestall an immediate outburst of thunderous applause. Without turning to acknowledge it, he at once began the Overture. Another burst of applause preceded the beginning of Act II and throughout the performance the keen antagonism between his and Leoncavallo's supporters was obvious.

However, the excellence of the performance failed to convince the Viennese critics that Leoncavallo's *Bohème* was a worthy successor to *I Pagliacci*: Kalbeck called the second act merely a 'useless variation' of the first and considered that the whole opera 'lacked original ideas'. Modern exponents of verismo, he thought, were mistaken in thinking that they could achieve realism

---

[124] Letter from Frances Saville, 20 Jan. 1898 (HOA). Saville had been engaged because of her success in the first Viennese production of Puccini's *La Bohème* at the Theater an der Wien in Oct. 1897. She resigned for the first of several times in Feb. 1898 but stayed at the Hofoper until the end of 1902. According to the 27 Feb. 1902 issue of the French magazine *Le Ménestrel*, it was Mahler who decided to cancel her contract after the première of Leoncavallo's *La Bohème*.

[125] Van Dyck's contract was to terminate in Mar. and had not yet been renewed. As it turned out, he stayed on at the Opera for another year. In his biography, *Ernest van Dijck: Une gloire belge de l'art lyrique* (Librairie Nationale d'Art et d'Histoire, Brussels, 1933), Henri de Curzon states that Van Dyck was quite content to have his contract come to an end in 1898 because he could not get on with the new director. Dr Curzon also claims that Mahler engaged Van Dyck as guest singer 'for an indeterminate period', yet Van Dyck's name does not appear in the list of guest singers at the Vienna Opera after 1900.

without bothering about dramatic construction, which was defective in Leoncavallo's work, since at the end the emphasis suddenly shifted from Musetta to Mimi. 'One cannot celebrate both Shrove Tuesday and Ash Wednesday', Kalbeck concluded. Heuberger criticized the length of the exposition, which was clearly inferior to that in Puccini's *Bohème* (recently presented at the Theater an der Wien). He considered the music of the last two acts clumsy, and the orchestration so heavy that it threatened to drown the singers' voices.[126] Hanslick thought that Puccini had 'more musical talent and feeling for reality', whereas Leoncavallo's painstaking efforts to take the audience along with him into an atmosphere of wild gaiety had failed: 'we cannot be pressured into laughing. . . . The characters onstage constantly voiced the "ha-has" called for by the libretto, but the public did not utter a sound.' The slightest sign of any wit had to be underlined by trombones; a chorus of violins, cellos, and horns had emphasized each line of 'comic dialogue'; the whole effect was one of 'brutal, pretentious hubbub'. Hanslick's conclusion was: 'no creative force, no personality, no sense of beauty—a caricature of Italian music', a criticism no more severe than that of posterity, which, despite a few modern revivals, has all but forgotten Leoncavallo's *Bohème*.[127]

Hanslick's poor opinion of the opera did not prevent him from lavishing high praise on Mahler for the way he had, 'with exemplary self-sacrifice, made every effort to ensure the work's triumph and thus led it to victory'. The opera was in fact successful enough for Mahler later to regret having gone to so much trouble to 'throw dust in the eyes of the Viennese public'. After having worked for almost a year to improve the public's taste and raise the Opera's artistic standards, he had been forced to 'corrupt it against his will', with a magnificent performance of 'rubbish'. He was, however, pleased to have carried the day against Leoncavallo and Van Dyck, something for which he was warmly congratulated by Prince Liechtenstein. Despite his opera's success, Leoncavallo continued to complain[128] (particularly to Karpath) about its 'tepid' reception, which he attributed to Mahler's alterations. He was convinced that Mahler had not done his best and, at the end of March, he appealed to him in all fairness, to continue 'performances embarked upon with such happy success', but to assign the role of Marcello to Schrödter during Dippel's leave of absence. Mahler replied that Schrödter would need two months to learn the part and that Dippel would be back on 10 April. In fact, Leoncavallo's *La Bohème* was dropped after six performances, attendances having declined considerably. But Mahler had carried out his obligations with characteristic integrity, in spite of the mediocre quality of the work and a composer who had done everything in his power to antagonize him.

---

[126] Helm reported that the auditiorium was noticeably emptier during Act IV.

[127] Hanslick even suggested cutting the two middle acts (*Am Ende des Jahrhunderts*, 123 ff.). Cast of the première, 23 Feb.: Forster (Mimi), Renard (Musetta), Dippel (Marcello), Neidl (Rodolfo), Hesch (Schaunard).

[128] See BMG 379, and the *Neue Freie Presse* (19 Oct. 1898). Leoncavallo's letters are in HOA.

4

First Philharmonic Concerts—first battles at the Opera—the *Ring* and *Der Freischütz* (March–December 1898)

I can make the whole Opera dance on the tip of
one finger, so I derive no satisfaction from it.

L ATE in 1897, as we have seen, Guido Adler obtained a grant from the Gesellschaft zur Förderung deutscher Wissenschaft, Kunst, und Literatur in Böhmen (Society for the Encouragement of German Science, Art, and Literature in Bohemia) for the publication of Mahler's symphonies. In applying for it he submitted an official report to the Society, and also a detailed account (*Referat*) of Mahler's life and career, with special reference to performances and publications of his works.[1] 'I personally value him greatly—as a good friend and as an artist. He always keeps the artistic ideal in view,' Adler added as a postscript: 'Mahler and Strauss are in the first rank and also, to speak frankly, in the vanguard of the most modern movement in music.' Adler analysed the Symphonies and their general structure enthusiastically, wisely making a few reservations about the 'unerhörten Kakophonien' (preposterous cacophonies) of the third movement of the Third Symphony,[2] where, he admitted, Mahler 'frequently transgresses the conventional limits assigned to pure beauty in our time'. He went on to ask whether posterity might not judge otherwise.[3] It was

---

[1] See above, Chap. 3. The report and the *Referat* are among Adler's papers at the Univ. of Georgia (RAM 27 ff.) Among Mahler's early works, Adler mentions: Lieder and chamber works, the opera *Die Argonauten* (from before 1880); *Rübezahl*, a Märchenspiel on a text written by the composer; the *Lieder eines fahrenden Gesellen*; the *Humoresken*; and of course Symphonies Nos. 1, 2, and 3, following a number of 'early symphonic sketches'.

[2] A single page of notes on this symphony, written on the official notepaper of the Vienna Opera, and included in Adler's papers, suggests that he discussed the work with Mahler himself before writing the report. Adler's papers also contain a draft of a brief review, probably intended for one of the Prague newspapers.

[3] Alma Mahler, when mentioning Adler in her memoirs, depicts him as a pedantic musicologist, a notorious conservative, which is far from the truth. With Felix Mottl, he had founded the Akademischer

thus thanks to the generous intervention of Guido Adler that Mahler's symphonies began to reach a broad public. Previously only the score of the Second had been published, by Hofmeister in Leipzig at the end of 1897. Mahler wrote to Adler expressing his pleasure and gratitude. He even offered to travel to the Bohemian capital with the contralto Edyth Walker to perform the solo from the Second and some of his Lieder before the Prague Gesellschaft's committee.[4]

At this time the possibility of Mahler conducting one of his Symphonies with the German Philharmonic in Prague was already being discussed. Angelo Neumann, on being consulted, was enthusiastic. Although he had summarily dismissed Mahler from the German Theatre in Prague in 1888,[5] he had continued to admire and respect him. After all it was he, more than anyone, who had discovered Mahler and given him a chance to make himself known. The First Symphony, the only one not requiring a choir, was chosen, and the date was fixed for 3 March 1898. Neumann asked Franz Schalk, first Kapellmeister of the German Opera, to conduct all the rehearsals, for Mahler's schedule in Vienna meant that he could only be present at the last one. Franz Schalk[6] was three years younger than Mahler, who had known him at the Conservatory. He was the younger brother of Josef Schalk, Bruckner's best-known disciple, and had himself been a pupil of Bruckner.[7] Before going to Prague, Mahler wrote to Schalk in his most characteristic style:

A fifth trumpet for the final movement would be fantastic, if you can find one. Ditto a second harp. When I say mutes, I mean that the horns should insert sordines. The term 'gestopft' means to mute by using the hand. I beg you, dear Schalk, use only the largest

Wagnerverein; he championed Mahler the composer in 1897, and later Schoenberg and his Vereinigung in 1904.

[4] RAM 29. The American contralto Edyth Walker had been a member of the Vienna Opera since 1895. Mahler's letter is not dated but it was most likely written in Dec. 1897, just before he received the grant for the publication of his symphonies. In 1903 Mahler was accused by Edyth Walker's admirers of having so persistently 'persecuted her' for a long time that she had no choice but to resign.

[5] See Vol. i, Chap. 10.

[6] Franz Schalk (Vienna 27 May 1863; Edlach 3 Sept. 1931) was the son of a Linz tradesman who moved to Vienna in 1857 and died of a heart attack at the age of 35. The eldest son, Josef Schalk (1857–1901) had almost finished his studies at the Conservatory (where he became a disciple of Bruckner and friend of Hugo Wolf, and later a piano teacher) when Franz began to display musical gifts. At the Vienna Conservatory Franz studied with Josef Hellmesberger (violin) and Julius Epstein (piano). He also became a pupil (for counterpoint and composition) of Bruckner, who exerted a decisive influence on him. Later Bruckner entrusted the Schalk brothers with the task of transcribing his symphonies for the piano. They were also responsible for the first publ. versions, revised and abridged. After brief periods as a conductor, in Czernowitz and Reichenberg, Schalk's career as a theatrical Kapellmeister really began in Graz in 1890. He also conducted concerts there until 1895, and put on unabridged performances of Wagner's operas in the theatre and Bruckner's symphonies in concerts. In 1895 Angelo Neumann offered him an engagement with the German Opera in Prague, where he also conducted the Philharmonic Concerts. He replaced Weingartner at the Berlin Opera, 1898–1901, and conducted Wagner seasons in London and New York. Josef's illness induced him to accept Mahler's offer to return to Vienna and replace Hans Richter at the Opera. Schalk succeeded Ferdinand Löwe in 1904 as director of the Gesellschafts-Konzerte and was later appointed director of the Staatsoper, first with Richard Strauss (1918–24) and then alone (1924–8).

[7] See above, Vol. i, Chap. 4.

of <u>string</u> sections—but no second-rate players . . . I am frightfully pressed and look forward to getting to know you better during my stay in Prague. Please take care of the score—It's my <u>only</u> copy! Perhaps you might drop me another line on how the rehearsals are progressing . . . The entire <u>first movement</u> (excepting the great build-up) should be played with the <u>utmost</u> tenderness. And the final movement with the utmost strength. A reinforcement of the <u>horn section</u> at the end is most desirable! Play the <u>third movement humorously</u> (but in an eerie way). Play the trio from the Scherzo very calmly and tenderly. The introduction to the first movement is <u>not</u> music but the <u>sound of nature</u>![8]

Two days before the concert, Mahler wrote to František Šubert, director of the Czech Theatre, thanking him for putting some of his players at Neumann's disposal for the performance.[9] Later Schalk wrote a reminiscence[10] which mentioned the considerable number of rehearsals, both general and sectional, needed to overcome the difficulties of the work. He gave the following account of Mahler's stay:

I fetched him from the Blauer Stern early in the morning for the rehearsal. He was already sitting in the hotel's little coffee house, laconic and withdrawn, his gaze and his facial expression very serious. We set off for the rehearsal straight away. The orchestra, in imposing strength, was already assembled on the stage of the Deutsches Theater, and greeted its former conductor very warmly. Mahler, with touching indulgence, ignored a few small (and also larger) weaknesses. He was obviously very happy that in general the work and its meaning came through. He did not drag the rehearsal out, but brought it to a close by expressing his satisfaction, delightedly acknowledged by all. The performance succeeded beyond all expectation. Mahler was enthusiastically and endlessly applauded. There was not the slightest shadow of opposition. Once again the Prague public confirmed its reputation, acquired and celebrated at the time of Berlioz, Liszt and Wagner, as a forward-looking audience *par excellence*.

The Prague press reports point out that each movement of the Symphony was vigorously applauded. During the final ovation, Mahler was presented with a palm and laurel crown on stage.[11] After the concert there was a sumptuous banquet organized by Neumann with his usual lordly generosity. It was attended by all the important people of the city, without distinction of nationality, among them the director of the Conservatory, Ludwig Slansky (Mahler's old rival at the German Theatre), Guido Adler, Siegfried Lipiner, the

---

[8] Undated letter to Franz Schalk (ÖNB). MBRS 159; English version, Gollancz, 155.

[9] Letter to František Šubert, Narodni Muzeum, Prague.

[10] This article was publ. in the *Prager Tagblatt* and reproduced in the *Neues Wiener Tagblatt* (undated press cutting, Eleonore Vondenhoff collection).

[11] The fourth and final subscription concert began at 7.30. Franz Schalk conducted the second part of the programme: (1) Beethoven, *An die Hoffnung*; (2) Berlioz, *La Damnation de Faust*: Minuet and Danse des Sylphides; (3) Heinrich Hermann, Lied, 'Drei Wanderer'; Schumann, Lied, 'Mit Myrthen und Rosen'; Schubert, Lied, 'Sei mir gegrüsst'; (4) Beethoven, Overture Leonora No. 3. The vocal works were sung by Karl Scheidemantel, of the Dresden Opera. The German Theatre's orchestra of 57 players was augmented for the occasion with 25 players from the Czech Theatre and the whole concert was a benefit for the German Opera orchestra and chorus pension fund. The First Symphony was in four movements as we know it today, the Andante having been dropped in a previous revision.

members of the Opera and the Theatre, leading journalists, and a number of high officials.[12] An actor by the name of Richard Tauber[13] made a speech in Mahler's honour. But the high point of the evening was the appearance in person of the director of the German Opera, Angelo Neumann, with a large envelope in his hand. In a breathless hush which revealed the curiosity of his audience, he began to read very slowly, 'with appropriate pathos', a letter written him in 1885 by a certain young conductor at the Kassel Opera. People soon guessed that it was the letter by Mahler quoted above.[14] Despite all the festivities accompanying it, the event received relatively little coverage in Prague's German newspapers. The *Prager Abendblatt* only published a preview article that spoke of the 'fiery Magyar wines'(!)[15] and Slav motifs of the third movement. The *Bohemia* gave the only full account of the concert itself and also mentioned the battles that had raged around the work. Even Mahler's enemies, it said, must recognize the 'abundant imagination' and 'passionate exaltation' of a composer who 'cares little about the possibilities of performance and the chances of success with the general public'. Nor could these enemies deny the captivating beauty of certain details and the 'startling new effects of instrumentation'. Mahler undoubtedly belonged to the 'modern school of out-door painting', but he had not yet freed himself from 'the style of his master, Bruckner'. The article also deserves merit for praising the parodic Funeral March, though it regretted that the Finale failed to provide either 'any clear-cut impression or any true artistic enjoyment'.

On the same evening as this Prague concert, Ferdinand Löwe, another of Bruckner's pupils, conducted the Munich Kaim Orchestra in the Vienna première of the Andante from the Second Symphony. The short movement was, as usual, well received. Helm found it difficult to judge the whole symphony from this short, 'melodious and ably orchestrated' extract, but considered its 'studied naïveté' and 'reminiscences' unattractive. Heuberger, on the other hand, praised its 'charming sound' and its resemblance to a 'graceful ländler'.[16]

---

[12] On this occasion Mahler made the acquaintance of the Czech conductor Josef Stransky who in 1911 was to replace him at the head of the New York Philharmonic. Stransky wrote him a long and 'enthusiastic' letter the day after the concert, and Mahler thanked him warmly, saying he had 'long doubted that he would live to see the day when his music would find an echo in a few men's hearts'. Mozart had been the 'singer of love', he, Mahler hoped he might claim to be called the 'singer of nature' (*New York Herald Tribune*, 22 Mar. 1931).

[13] Born in Vienna in 1861, Anton Richard Tauber was a member of the German Theatre in Prague, 1892–1900. He became superintendent of the Chernowitz theatre in 1912. The son he adopted in 1913 became the famous tenor Richard Tauber. After the Prague concert, the tenor Gustav Löwe reminded Mahler that he had sung in *Der Trompeter von Säkkingen* under his direction. Arias from operas and Lieder were also performed, after which a group of society ladies sang Tyrolian duets.

[14] See above, Vol. i, Chap. 9.

[15] Misinformed about the date of composition, the writer thought the work was 'a reminiscence of the time Mahler spent conducting in Budapest'.

[16] The concert programme also included the Overture to Cornelius's *Der Barbier von Bagdad*; Beethoven's Violin Concerto (soloist Rettig, concert-master of the orchestra); Brahms's *Variations on a Theme by Haydn*; and Beethoven's Fifth Symphony. Ferdinand Löwe (1865–1925) was born in Vienna, studied at the Conservatory there, mainly under Anton Bruckner, and later became professor of choral singing. In 1897 he was appointed conductor of the Kaim Orchestra in Munich (Mahler was also considered for this post) and at the

Kalbeck felt a 'clear influence' of Beethoven and Brahms in this piece, which he found 'harmonious, melodious, lilting and dancelike; it does honour to the composer's talent and confirms his technical mastery'. The day before the Vienna concert, another short Mahler movement, the *Blumenstück* from the Third Symphony, was conducted in a Museum Concert in Frankfurt by Josef Grossmann.[17] It seemed that for the moment all the public wanted to hear of Mahler were these brief symphonic fragments. The success of the First Symphony in Prague was therefore a pleasant surprise which must have consoled him for many disappointments, and reminded him that even if, for the present, he had no time to think of composing, he was none the less the author of three major symphonies that the world was bound to discover one day.

The *Illustrirtes Wiener Extrablatt* of 1 April informed its readers of 'rumours' concerning a crisis at the Opera, and announced that Mahler was to take several days' leave. The Opera was closed as usual for Easter week, and he left for Abbazia, a resort on the Adriatic coast, where from then on he spent a short Easter holiday every year. On this occasion, he much needed a short rest from work, since he was soon to undergo an operation for haemorrhoids. He was back in Vienna on Easter Sunday (10 April),[18] conducting *Lohengrin*. Three days later he went with Wlassack to Budapest, where he attended a performance of the ballet *Die Rothen Schuhe*, by Raoul Mader, a former Korrepetitor at the Hofoper, who was no doubt hoping that Mahler would put the work on in Vienna.[19] He also revisited the Hungarian Opera after six years of absence and was received by the director. On his return to Vienna, Bruno Walter came to spend ten days with him at the Bartensteingasse and Mahler played the revised score of *Das klagende Lied* to him for the first time.[20] Walter, deeply impressed, urged him to have the work published. Mahler accordingly completed the last and definitive version of the score the following spring.

The only important operatic event in the spring of 1898 was a new production of *Aida* which opened on 29 April, and was greeted with the same unanimous enthusiasm as Mahler's earlier *Neueinstudierungen*. Though he had

same time director of the Wiener Singakademie; he conducted the Konzertverein Orchestra from 1900 to 1904. From 1908 until 1914 he was director of the Munich Konzertverein, then of the Vienna Musikakademie. He collaborated with Franz Schalk on the first publ. version of Bruckner's Fourth Symphony. Löwe alone was responsible for the 1st edn. of Bruckner's Ninth Symphony in 1903, also with many cuts. After leaving the Kaim Orchestra, he was engaged for a year by the Vienna Opera. (See above, Vol. i, Chap. 24, the letter that Mahler wrote about Löwe to Richard Heuberger.)

[17] Programme of the concert given on 2 Mar. at the Frankfurt Opera: Beethoven, Fifth Symphony; *Fidelio*: Leonore's aria (Frau Diosy-Handel); Mahler, 'Blumenstück' (second movement from the Third Symphony); Liszt, *Hungarian Rhapsody No. 1*, for orchestra; Brahms, Schubert, and Goldmark: Lieder (with piano accompaniment: same soloist); Weber, Overture *Euryanthe*.

[18] In a letter addressed to Hermann Behn on 4 Apr. 1898 (numbered by the addressee no. 25), Mahler says he is about to leave for Abbazia.

[19] Mahler gave his consent. The date of this performance in Budapest was 13 Apr.

[20] NBL2. 117. It was in Apr. 1898 that Mahler reported to Natalie (with many inaccuracies) the story of *Das klagende Lied* and the Beethoven Prize (see Vol. i, Chap. 5). Mahler revised the score for the last time in spring 1899. The piano score was publ. in 1900 by Weinberger.

reservations about some of the tempos,[21] Helm was full of admiration for Mahler's magnificent achievement. He praised the marvellous pianissimos in the Prelude and the clarity and grandiose effect of the second Finale, which had been much applauded. Heuberger also admired the 'magnificent development' of the triumphal procession for which Mahler used 'a slow, majestic tempo', as also in the priest's chorus and the women's chorus in Act II. The whole interpretation showed genius, he felt, and the liveliness and eloquence of the orchestra had greatly contributed to the dramatic action.[22] In May, Lilli Lehmann made her second visit of the year, appearing not only in *Norma* (revived for her in February), and *Fidelio* (two performances), but also as Isolde, and Brünnhilde in *Götterdämmerung*, her favourite Wagnerian roles.[23]

During the early months of 1898 Mahler's popularity in Vienna steadily increased, while his superiors became ever more convinced of his efficiency as director. Nevertheless he began to realize the drawbacks of his post and the amount of time and effort the administration of the Hofoper required. He told Natalie and Justi:

You cannot imagine how bored I am already with running this Opera, in spite of all the work it involves! Perhaps it's because nothing presents me with the slightest difficulty. I can make the whole Opera dance on the tip of one finger. So I derive no satisfaction from it, unlike the intense joy I experience when I am composing. I feel at present like a travelling salesman who, while going about his own business must, as a sideline, also work for others; only in my case, the sideline has become my main job, so that I no longer have the opportunity and time for the supreme task with which the Lord has entrusted me . . . I find it repugnant to live in the midst of all this splendour. How people admire me and grovel to me! How I'd love to tell them how miserably small I feel, and that, in my job here, I want nothing but to do my duty![24]

One might ascribe Mahler's discouragement to a temporary accumulation of frustrations. Such outbursts frequently occurred during his Vienna tenure, and yet he was to stay on at the Hofoper until 1907. However, a new fact has recently emerged which casts a different light on the matter. In the spring of 1898 he received an offer from America which he took very seriously, as witness the following letter to the Berlin soprano Lilli Lehmann:

[21] As compared with Verdi's interpretation when he conducted the opera in Vienna in June 1875. According to Helm, it should never be forgotten that *Aida* is the work of a 'warm-blooded Mediterranean'. *Aida* is the only Italian opera Mahler conducted repeatedly himself in Vienna.

[22] Cast for the performance on 29 Apr.: Sedlmair (Aida), Walker (Amneris), Winkelmann (Radames), Reichmann (Amonasro).

[23] HOA possess three autograph telegrams from Mahler to Lilli Lehmann. They all concern her *Gastspiel* in May (2 May and two telegrams of 10 May 1898, HOA, Z.227/1898). Performance dates: *Götterdämmerung* (17 May); *Fidelio* (9 and 26 May); *Tristan* (22 May); and *Norma* (27 May). Olive Fremstad, who became famous in the USA as a Wagnerian singer and later was Mahler's own Isolde at the Metropolitan Opera in 1908–9, sang Brangäne on 22 May. The conductor was Mahler, who hardly ever yielded the baton to anyone else for this work.

[24] NBL1. 102; NBL2. 116.

Dear friend, I have just received an offer to go to New York as conductor of 50 concerts per season and director of the 'National Conservatory of Music of America'—7 months each year.

I have been asked to name my own financial <u>terms</u>.

Please, dear friend, send me a telegram immediately telling me how much I should ask for—since I don't know how things are in America. I am afraid of getting it wrong. I am asked to state the sum in Reichsmarks.

As I gather from your letter, I have you to thank for this offer.—It was so <u>nice</u> of you to have thought of me and I am so grateful that I can hardly find words in a mere letter to express my feelings.

I must also ask you to say nothing of this <u>to any living soul</u> for the moment, since for me <u>everything</u> depends on <u>no-one</u> knowing anything <u>at this end</u>.

Please, dear friend, let me know by telegram how much in Reichmarks I should ask for this double activity. As director of the Conservatory I would not have to teach, only direct and [?] approximately seven hours a week.

And Mahler adds, in a postscript: 'Please answer me <u>quickly</u>. Would it perhaps be better if I asked the New Yorkers themselves to make a proposal? Please do not say a word to my sister about this letter.'[25] Mahler's apparent willingness to accept the American offer cannot be ascribed merely to his early dissatisfaction with the conditions prevailing at the Opera and in Vienna in general. It must be remembered that the salary offered him in New York would undoubtedly have been considerably higher than the one he received at the Hofoper. Furthermore, his New York duties would have occupied only seven months of each year. Thus he could have devoted four or five months to composition. This was in fact the main reason why, in 1907, he decided to leave the Vienna Opera and accept the offer he then received from the Metropolitan Opera.

Thus, after the first thrill of triumph which had accompanied his appointment, Mahler, for whom the exercise of power quickly lost its attraction, was beginning to realize how painful it was to have to forgo creative work. His ill-health also influenced his mood, and he thought of the operation he was shortly to undergo. Moreover, some of his reforms were taking longer to carry out than he had foreseen. Reichmann, Winkelmann, Van Dyck, and Renard were not

[25] Undated letter to Lilli Lehmann (MBRS, 106). Zoltan Roman shows that the letter Mahler received in 1907 from a Berlin impresario, also active in New York, Charles Löwenstein, makes it possible to date the letter to Lehmann precisely. It starts thus: 'I hope you will recall our correspondence of some years ago when I approached you to assume the leadership of my former grand subscription concerts here, from which you were prevented by the illness and death of your conductor Herr Dr Fuchs.' Roman rightly points out that, since Anton Seidl had died suddenly on 28 Mar. 1898, at a time when the plans for a permanent orchestra in New York had been finalized, since the National Conservatory had been without a permanent director after Dvořák's departure in 1895, and since Löwenstein mentions Lehmann as having suggested Mahler's name, this letter was undoubtedly written in spring 1898. Lilli Lehmann had sung at the Hofoper, 24 Jan.–16 Feb., and she was about to return there (for performances planned from 17 to 29 May). This would explain why Mahler expects to see her shortly. As to Justi, she might have planned to visit Lehmann in Berlin on her way to or from Hamburg, where Mahler's furniture had most likely been stored until he found a suitable apartment in Vienna. The project for a permanent orchestra in New York came to nothing, until the Philharmonic was finally reorganized on a permanent basis—for Mahler in 1909. Emil Paur directed the National Conservatory from 1899 until 1902 (see MAY 2 ff.).

prepared to surrender overnight to a presumptuous younger man:[26] they paid
lip-service to his orders, while secretly taking every opportunity of challenging
his authority. There was a world of difference between the easygoing comfort
of the opera life that had previously been the rule and the incessant work that
was now expected from everyone, especially since the stars felt that in the
past the public had been more than satisfied with their performances. Mahler's
main preoccupation during the early months of 1898 was to discover new
artists who could adapt themselves more easily to his methods. Fortunately,
some of the singers of the Jahn regime were intelligent and adaptable enough
to understand him and adjust their performances in accordance with his
wishes, however successful they might have been in the past. One such case
was Reichmann, a man of exceptional kindness and integrity. He had an
extraordinarily expressive voice, even though it had lost much of its former
carrying power, but his musicality and sense of rhythm were often at fault as I
have already noted. Mahler found his acting mannered and blamed him for the
way in which he angled for the limelight and held his high notes to draw
applause.[27] At first their relationship was stormy. After long years of Richter's
quiet authority, Reichmann found it hard to adjust to the presence at the Opera
of a 'nervous', 'tyrannical' revolutionary who disturbed and altered everything
to suit his 'whims'. He found Mahler's behaviour and manner infuriating and
once even swore he would 'throttle him'. He particularly objected to his efforts
to outlaw the claque and was the only one honest enough openly to admit it. 'I
can't sing without applause', he said, 'a cold house strangles my voice! . . . A
director who forbids the stimulating claque knows nothing of the temperament
of an artist.'[28]

During a performance of *Tannhäuser* at the end of 1898, some members of
the audience tried to applaud Reichmann's second act aria, while others, who
were aware of the new ruling, whistled as the applause started. The baritone
took this as a personal insult, threw down his lyre, and sang the rest of the act
'with studied indifference'. The same thing happened again in the last act and
this time he not only threw his instrument down noisily, but shouted 'unrepeat-
able' insults at the hecklers.[29] Another anecdote, told by Bruno Walter, demonstrates the baritone's narcissistic character. During the second act of *The
Flying Dutchman* Reichmann was supposed to stand still, but he kept moving
about. Mahler upbraided him: 'Herr Reichmann, you are a great artist, but you
don't know how to stand still.' Whereupon Reichmann said to Hesch (playing
Daland): 'Did you hear? He said I'm a great artist.'

However, Mahler went out of his way to show the ageing singer the greatest

---

[26] Marie Renard and Ernest Van Dyck both resigned in 1900.

[27] Reichmann had other faults, which were due to his age, though they were amply compensated by his
artistry: he frequently sang out of tune and sometimes missed his high notes.

[28] *Fremden-Blatt* (23 May 1903), 11.

[29] These incidents occurred during a Christmas performance in 1898, with Josef Hellmesberger, jun.,
conducting. *Deutsche Zeitung* (28 Dec.).

possible esteem and admiration. Here, for example, is the letter he wrote to him on 26 May 1898, granting the leave Reichmann had requested to sing in another theatre: 'I agree to your request with pleasure, wishing to demonstrate not only, once again, my readiness to be of service to such an outstanding artist, but also my continuing willingness to grant leave to members of the company as far as possible in accordance with their wishes.'[30] In the same letter, however, he warned Reichmann never to count on having leave 'guaranteed by contract (*kontraktlich festgesetzten Urlaube*), which was and would remain contrary to the principles of his policy as director. How many battles he fought on exactly this point! Fortunately his superiors fully supported him, so he always had his way. This same Reichmann, one of the most celebrated Hans Sachses in the history of *Die Meistersinger*,[31] altered many aspects of his well-known performance under Mahler's influence. Mahler made him work at every detail and attempted to force him to respect the note values printed in the score. In the Act II *Schusterlied*, for instance, Reichmann never knew exactly when to strike the hammer blows and had to rely on a prompter in the wings to give him his cues. His diary records his exasperation, but also later his gratitude when, thanks to his work with Mahler, he achieved one of the greatest successes of his career.[32]

If an artist like Reichmann was able to see in Mahler someone who was inexorably driven by a high aesthetic purpose, there were others who considered him nothing but a tyrant—an implacable despot. Richard Specht's description of Mahler as an opera director is one of the most thorough and no doubt also one of the most accurate. He recalls Mahler's Draconian measures to discourage temperamental displays by star singers. He would engage minor singers for important parts; thanks to him they would enjoy a moment of glory, only to accuse him later of having ruined their careers when they were no longer the centre of attraction. In Vienna, more even than in Hamburg, he imposed a new concept of work which included training in musical expression, gesture and posture, acting, and diction. Whenever he had a moment he would hurry to the rooms in which the soloists and chorus were rehearsing. If the coaches failed to satisfy him, he would interrupt to demonstrate what he wanted. As he could hardly treat conductors in the same way, he often summoned the singers to his office after rehearsals, to work on the passages that had displeased him.[33] Mahler was not only a musician, but a man of the theatre and he expected every performance to be a dramatical and musical rebirth of the work in question. He considered the appearance, personality, and dramatic ability of the singers as much as their voices when he was distributing parts. This caused him at times to make mistakes and entrust

---

[30] Autograph draft of a letter from Mahler to Reichmann (HOA, 26 May 1898).

[31] See Erwin Stein, 'Mahler and the Vienna Opera', in Harold Rosenthal, ed., *The Opera Bedside Book* (Gollancz, London, 1965).

[32] See below, Chap. 6.   [33] NBL2. 114.

dramatic parts to lyric tenors, heroic roles to Italian tenors, and even bass parts to baritones.[34]

As in Hamburg, Mahler's temper sometimes got out of hand. When his face was distorted by rage it took on the 'demoniacal' expression often referred to by his enemies. His usually calm brown eyes would seem to flash green fire. His full, almost feminine lips would be contorted into a malevolent smile, with the right-hand corner of his mouth drawn down into such a menacing expression that the offender 'in the dock' was too frightened to move. It was not only recalcitrance or disobedience that aroused his anger, but mediocrity, incompetence, or simply lack of self-confidence. Artists were often unable to forgive him for the way in which he had humiliated them. This could lead to unpleasant repercussions, for the singers in Vienna had powers of retaliation that were non-existent elsewhere; most of them had contacts with journalists who asked for nothing better than to be told of an *Affäre* or 'scandal'. Mahler's demands and his perfectionist ideals meant nothing to most of the singers. They thought only of their careers; he, on the other hand, regarded them as instruments to be used in the service of a cause, and he discarded anything that hindered the realization of his ideals. He was thus accused of 'ruining voices', of wounding sensibilities to the quick, of 'exhausting his collaborators', and of 'working them till they dropped'. Among the difficulties frequently encountered by Mahler was the wounded pride of singers who regarded themselves as stars (which they often were not) and were then offered tiny roles like the Valkyries, the Three Genii in *The Magic Flute*, or the vocal quartet introducing Wolfram's solo in the second act of *Tannhäuser*.

In 1898 the battles with singers had already begun and they were to continue to the end of Mahler's term. A dispute developed in January with the tenor Andreas Dippel, due to a misunderstanding about leave of absence. The letters exchanged grew more and more acrimonious. Dippel maintained that the conditions of his new contract were not in conformity with the promises made to him verbally by Mahler and Wlassack in November. Mahler stood firm, knowing that he and the management were in accord, and eventually Dippel handed in his resignation, which Mahler was unable to accept until the end of the season.[35] In August, the American contralto Edyth Walker wrote to Mahler complaining that she had been deprived at the last moment of the role of Ortrud in *Lohengrin* and threatening to resign if such humiliating treatment continued. Receiving no reply, she wrote again three days later, recalling that it was not only the role of Ortrud that had been taken away from her, but also those of the Page in *Les Huguenots* and Adriano in *Rienzi*. Such 'insults' had induced her to demand the termination of her contract, especially since she had consistently

---

[34] He gave the part of Kaspar in *Der Freischütz* to Josef Ritter, a baritone, a choice that was condemned by all the critics except Kalbeck (see below).

[35] Letters from Dippel to Mahler of 14, 19, 22 Jan. and 4, 7, and 12 Feb.; letters from Mahler to Dippel of 5 and 8 Feb.; draft contract of 16 Jan.; and doctor's certificate of 13 Feb. 1898 (HOA).

been refused permission to sing elsewhere on the grounds that she was indispensable to Vienna.[36] In the event Edyth Walker remained at the Hofoper until 1903, but she was continually in conflict with Mahler for a variety of reasons. They were artistically and personally incompatible with each other, but because she was extremely popular with the public, Mahler was obliged to put up with her.

However, pending Walker's eventual departure, he began to look for other contraltos. In August he engaged one without any preliminary *Gastspiel*. This was the Viennese Ottilie Fellwock, a former pupil of the famous Pauline Lucca, but she seems not to have satisfied anyone, for she stayed at the Hofoper for only one year.[37] Another, Karoline Kusmitsch, remained until 1902 without achieving any notable success. But there was a soprano among the new members of the Opera who was to be better appreciated both by the public and by Mahler himself. She was Rita Michalek, a lyric-coloratura soprano, who was engaged on 1 September 1897[38] and stayed until 1910, although her corpulence and the premature decline of her vocal powers began to affect her career from 1905 onwards. She must have had a particularly pure and silvery tone, for in 1901 Mahler used her for the first performance of his Fourth Symphony in Munich, and later in Vienna. It has sometimes been alleged that Mahler's interest in her was more than artistic, but there is no convincing evidence to prove or disprove the rumour.

While Mahler never hesitated to make great demands upon singers and upon all who worked with him, he never forgot that anything he could do to improve their material circumstances would make it easier for them to meet those demands. In April 1898, in particular, he increased the number of rehearsals, but also increased the salaries of the chorus, while seizing the opportunity to forbid any substitution among them.[39] He also saw that something had to be done to improve conditions among the stage-hands. Just as he was beginning to realize the immensity of his reforming task and how lengthy the process would be, the anti-Semitic press launched a series of bitter attacks against him. In April, the *Illustrirtes Wiener Extrablatt* spoke of a crisis at the Opera, while the satirical paper *Kikeriki* published an article entitled 'Get Rid of Mahler, the Executioner of Art', in which he was accused of leading the Opera to ruin. Placed at its head thanks to 'the intrigues of an old singer and her lover', he was torturing his subordinates, tyrannizing the public, removing Italian opera from the repertory, dismissing and disgracing well-known singers, etc. But for the time being these criticisms carried little weight in the face of his overwhelming

---

[36] Letters from Edyth Walker, 13, 16, and 17 Aug. 1898 (HOA, Z.501/1898).

[37] It was Ottilie Fellwock who later sang the contralto solo in the Third Symphony in Prague, on 25 Feb. 1904 (see below, Chap. 16).

[38] A letter of 29 Sept. 1897, signed by Mahler, must have been written to Rita Michalek. It concerns three of the roles that she sang in the first weeks of her engagement: *La Fille du régiment*, Siebel in *Margarethe* (*Faust*), and *The Bartered Bride* (BGM).

[39] *Neue Freie Presse* (9 May 1898).

success. The record of his first year at the Opera was impressive indeed, Wagner taking first place with sixty-two performances of nine works, twenty-two more than the year before. In an article published at the end of the season, Richard Heuberger[40] voiced his satisfaction not only with the number of Wagnerian performances but also with the fact that these uncut versions had played to full houses. Furthermore, no conductor's repertoire was fixed in advance and they enjoyed great freedom of choice. Richter had not been obliged to conduct more frequently than he wished and thus had not, as in previous years, shown signs of exhaustion due to overwork.[41] The idea that Mahler and Richter should take it in turns to conduct certain works had been a great success, as it had aroused healthy controversy among the public. Gluck and Weber were in temporary eclipse, but *Zar und Zimmermann* and the *Magic Flute* had been performed frequently and were always well received.[42] Thus Heuberger concluded that things had definitely improved at the Hofoper.[43]

In poor health for some time, Mahler had to take a leave of absence from the Opera on 5 June to enter the Rudolphinerhaus clinic in Döbling for a haemorrhoid operation to stop the bleeding from which he had been suffering for most of the season. He stayed there a week and then left in mid-June to convalesce in Vahrn where he had booked a villa. Natalie's manuscript, which has been carefully censored by another hand, refers to 'sickening private circumstances' (*widrige private Verhältnisse*) in Mahler's personal life, which prevented him from enjoying nature and freedom that summer; but he himself was to affirm the following year that his troubles had been purely physical.[44] Although Natalie herself came to Vahrn around 11 July and bombarded Mahler as usual with suggestions and advice, her diaries contain little information about their activities that summer.[45] On 14 July she took all the occupants of the Villa Artmann[46] in search of a path that she had known as a child and that

---

[40] *Neue Musikalische Presse* (19 June 1898).

[41] During the 1897–8 season, Mahler conducted 111 performances, Richter 39, and Fuchs 57.

[42] The most frequently performed works during this season were: *Lohengrin, Dalibor, Pagliacci*, and *Onegin* (12); *Hänsel und Gretel* and *Cavalleria* (10); *Faust* and *Zar und Zimmermann* (10); *Walküre, Djamileh, Evangelimann, The Flying Dutchman, Heimchen* (8); *Figaro, The Bartered Bride*, and *Magic Flute* (7). Specht compared the length of the Wagner performances under Mahler (uncut) and Jahn. The starting and finishing times of Jahn's evening performances follow, with Mahler's times in parentheses: *Lohengrin* and *Tannhäuser*, 7–10.26 p.m. (7–11); *Götterdämmerung*, 7–10.30 (7–11.50); *Tristan*, 7–10.52 (7–11.30). Richard Specht, *Das Wiener Operntheater: Erinnerung aus 50 Jahren* (Knepler, Vienna, 1919), 56.

[43] He believed that Mahler had been right to cut the number of evenings devoted to Meyerbeer down to 7. Among the works newly added to the repertory, he found only Leoncavallo's *La Bohème* unworthy of the Vienna Opera.

[44] NBL2. 119. (See below.)

[45] Natalie stayed on in Vahrn after Mahler's return to Vienna and wrote him long letters full of every kind of suggestions: to bathe, to go cycling, and to breathe country air.

[46] Another source mentions 'Villa Kaley'. On 2 Dec. 1897 Justi wrote to Frau Artmann, the mother of the owner of the villa, cancelling the booking for the summer of 1898 and requesting a return of the deposit of 50 florins (BGM). This still leaves open the possibility that Mahler changed his mind and rented the Villa Artmann after all.

led into the mountains as far as the Schalderertal. From the first summit they had a magnificent view of Vahrn, Brixen, the monastery of Neustift, and the castle of Bodeneck, right across to the snow-capped crest of the Brenner and the rugged peaks of the Dolomites in the distance. Mahler, it seems, was so enthusiastic that he decided to take the same walk almost every day. Indeed, about ten years later, on holiday in Toblach, he sometimes returned to Vahrn, visiting the house of the rector of the Vienna Technische Hochschule, Emil Artmann, where a group of highly placed people including the Austro-Hungarian Foreign Minister, von Kallay, and the Intendant of Court Music in Munich, Karl von Perfall, were staying.[47]

The summer of 1898, however, was spoilt for him by a protracted period of pain, the aftermath of his operation.[48] According to Natalie, he endured it 'heroically'. 'My pains have still not ceased,' Mahler wrote to Behn on 30 July. 'It seems to be a tedious business. Naturally I haven't worked much under the circumstances, though I've set some more things from *Des Knaben Wunderhorn*.'[49] In another letter, this time to Bruno Walter, Mahler complains that 'My summer has been completely ruined by the wretched operation. I am in pain most of the day.'[50] An incident reported by Natalie provides additional evidence of his irritability that summer. One evening at Vahrn he happened to read in a Berlin paper that a professor in a German university had refused to teach medicine to women students. He flew into a rage at the idea and exclaimed: 'This dyed-in-the-wool German (*dieser Teutsche*) is certainly an ox; his ideal woman is and must always remain a cow.' As hinted in his letter to Behn, Mahler did at last resume at Vahrn his creative activity. He informed Natalie that he had completed 'three new songs' from the *Wunderhorn*, 'just to prove I can still do it'. The autograph scores of 'Lied des Verfolgten im Turm' and 'Wo die schönen Trompeten blasen' are indeed dated July 1898. According to Natalie, Mahler said that one of these Lieder, which he considered to be 'the best', expressed 'the violent contrariness and fury that, for various reasons, are my constant mood this summer'.[51] The third was either 'Revelge' or 'Der Tamboursg'sell', the other two songs that he later composed on texts from

[47] *Dolomiten* (Bozen (Bolzano), 29 July 1986). Ernest Parschalk's article states that Mahler stayed at the Villa Artmann together with the Austrian Minister of Foreign Affairs, Benjamin von Kallay. In a personal letter, Dr Parschalk informed me that the local newspaper also mentioned Mahler's presence (unfortunately at an unknown date) in the Villa Planatsch, a new house which included two different apartments, together with that of Karl von Perfall, Generalintendant in Munich. During the same summer (presumably of 1898), Arnold Rosé gave a concert with his Quartet in the nearby Gasthof Waldsacker.

[48] Writing to Nina Spiegler from Vahrn on 1 Aug., Mahler, reporting on his health, told her that he was in pain every morning from 9.30 to about 2 p.m. and then from 3 to 4 p.m.

[49] Letter to Behn (numbered 41 by the addressee), PML (see MBRS 31).

[50] Unpubl. letter to Bruno Walter, LPA.

[51] The song alluded to by Mahler as 'furious' is in all likelihood 'Lied des Verfolgten im Turm'. He gave the MSS to Nina Spiegler the following year and wrote on the first page in dedication: 'Born in pain, I hope the child doesn't show any signs of it' ('Das war unter Schmerzen geboren; hoffentlich sieht man's dem Kinde nicht an'). It seems he was annoyed with Natalie for thinking that he was referring to mental anguish when he had meant physical suffering, so before 'Schmerzen' he inserted the word 'hinterweltlichen' (in the nether regions). (NBLS, May 1899.)

the *Wunderhorn* in 1899 and 1901, and which would thus have been sketched in 1898.

Back in Vienna on 2 August[52] Mahler presumably met Bruno Walter, for the young man was eager to show him the definitive version of the piano duet transcriptions of the first two symphonies which Mahler had commissioned from him and which were soon to be published. At this time, Walter had just obtained a post at the Riga Theatre in Estonia. For unknown reasons but which seem to have been linked to the arrival of his sisters in Vienna on 3 August, Mahler did not want Walter to visit him later than 2 August, and eventually suggested that the visit should take place during the three days he would be alone before Justi and Emma's return. Some time before, probably in Hamburg, there had apparently been a romance between Emma and Bruno Walter, but he was a year younger than she, which at the time probably counted as a major obstacle to their marriage.[53] Now Emma was engaged to the cellist Eduard Rosé, the elder brother of the Philharmonic's Konzertmeister, Mahler's fellow student at the Vienna Conservatory, who had been on the friendliest of terms with the family and had spent part of the summer with them at Vahrn. During the holiday that Mahler spent in Vahrn, Arnold was present and the future brothers-in-law played music together. It was at this time that Mahler discovered Brahms's Sonatas for clarinet and piano, which he played with Rosé in transcription, deciding that he had previously been far too superficial in his judgement of them.[54] Eduard Rosé was four years older than Arnold. In 1882 he had founded the famous Rosé Quartet with his younger brother (then only 19!). But no doubt it was the meteoric rise of Arnold, Konzertmeister of the Philharmonic at the age of 17,[55] that prompted his less brilliant elder brother to emigrate. Shortly after their marriage, which took place in Vienna on 25 August,[56] Eduard and Emma left for Boston where he had been engaged as cellist by the Boston Symphony Orchestra.[57] Alma Mahler much later claimed that Eduard's marriage to Emma had been arranged by Justine and Arnold who, according to her, had already embarked on the intimate relationship which was to lead to their marriage in 1902.[58] But as usual Alma's testimony regarding her sister-in-law always needs to be treated with caution. Whatever the truth of the matter, Eduard certainly got no advantage from the

---

[52] Letter to Nina Spiegler (quoted above).

[53] 'Justi has explained why a visit in August does not seem desirable.' Emma had probably not yet left for the USA with her husband and Justi found it advisable not to let her meet Bruno Walter again. Mahler's second letter adds: 'My sister will arrive on Wednesday (3 Aug.) and this means, however distressing it may be, that for certain reasons you should no longer be in Vienna by then!' (undated letter from Mahler to Bruno Walter, LPA).

[54] NBL2. 139 (see below, Chap. 6).			[55] He remained in this post for 57 years (1881–1938).

[56] The witnesses for the marriage were Mahler and the impresario Alexander Rosé.

[57] Eduard Rosé was born on 24 Mar. 1859 in Jassy (Iasi, now in Romania). He remained only two years in the USA, Emma having failed to adapt to her new country. Rudolf Krzyzanowski subsequently engaged him as Konzertmeister and cello soloist at the Weimar Theatre. He also taught at the Weimar Conservatory.

[58] While Justi and Arnold may have been attracted to each other, it is unlikely that their liaison had begun by then.

marriage, Mahler having roundly declared that he could never engage his brother-in-law at the Vienna Opera.[59]

The autumn of 1898 was also marked by the preparations Mahler and Justi made for their move in November from the Bartensteingasse lodgings to a large apartment on the third floor of a handsome and comfortable block of flats that had recently been built according to plans by Otto Wagner,[60] a short distance from what is now the Konzerthaus and ten minutes' walk from the Opera. The entrance was in the narrow Auenbruggergasse, but the principal façade looked onto the Schwarzenbergplatz and the Rennweg, leading to the Belvedere.[61]

During August, the first month of the new season, Mahler left most of the conducting to Richter and Hellmesberger, reserving for himself only *Lohengrin* on the 15th (and 30th) and *The Magic Flute* on the 28th. On the 26th Richter, who was not feeling well, relinquished his baton, and Mahler thus fulfilled one of his dreams, to conduct a Viennese performance of *Die Meistersinger*,[62] with most of the cuts restored, before a house that was packed in spite of the humid summer heat. Strangely enough, the anti-Semitic *Deutsche Zeitung* was the only paper to report this event; Albert Leitich admired Mahler's energetic rendering of the two Finales and the 'dreamy poetry' of the Prelude to Act III. According to him, the slow tempos brought out the strength and brilliance of the opera. However, the principal task of those first weeks was to renovate the old production of the *Ring*, whose opening night was delayed for ten days by the assassination of the Empress Elisabeth in Geneva on 10 September. Mahler's enthusiasm for the project was all the greater since he now had two first-rate Wagnerian singers: Anna von Mildenburg, who had just arrived in Vienna on a permanent engagement, and the Danish tenor Erik Schmedes.[63] The latter was fond of telling the following story about his first trip to Vienna and his audition with Mahler. He had been a baritone at the Dresden Opera for three years when

[59] This information was provided by the late Ernst Rosé, son of Emma and Eduard Rosé.

[60] One of the most eminent members of the Secession (see above, Vol. i, Chap. 24, and below, Chap. 13). The address of the Mahlers' apartment was Auenbruggergasse 2, Staircase 2, Door 28 (information obtained from the present tenant, Mr Bernt Hage).

[61] Police records indicate that Mahler moved into Auenbruggergasse on 19 Nov. 1898. He left the flat on 7 Oct. 1909, before returning to the USA. On his later, brief visits to Vienna he stayed with his parents-in-law in the Hohe Warte. (See *Nachrichten zur Mahler-Forschung*, 5, Internationale Gustav Mahler Gesellschaft, Vienna, Mar. 1991.) On 15 Nov. 1898, Mahler wrote to the Intendant asking to have his direct telephone connection to the Opera transferred from the Bartensteingasse to the Auenbruggergasse apartment.

[62] A letter from Richter dated 27 Aug. thanks Mahler for having granted him leave of absence because of pain in his arms; this had been his only reason for giving up *Die Meistersinger*. Cast for the performance of 26 Aug.: Forster (Eva), Spielmann (David), Winkelmann (Walther), Reichmann (Sachs), Reichenberg (Pogner), Horwitz (Kothner).

[63] Erik Schmedes (1868–1931) was born in Gentofte, near Copenhagen and grew up in a family of musicians and singers. He studied in Berlin and Vienna as a baritone and sang in Wiesbaden, Nuremberg, and eventually Hamburg. On Pollini's advice, he became a tenor, at first singing lyric parts. Mahler engaged him as a Heldentenor in 1898 and his first appearance on the Viennese stage was as a guest singer in *Siegfried* on 11 Feb. His contract came into force on 1 June and he stayed with the Hofoper until 1924.

one day, out of simple curiosity, he had sung one single tenor phrase from *Les Huguenots* on the stage. Ernst von Schuch, chancing to hear him, immediately advised him to take up his studies again and become a tenor. Meanwhile Pollini, having been told what was happening, arrived on the scene. He advised Schmedes to study with a certain teacher in Dresden. And then a few days later, Schmedes received a telegram from Mahler advising him of Pollini's death and asking him to come immediately to Vienna for an audition.

At this time Schmedes's tenor repertory was still very limited. In the train on the way to Vienna, he was feverishly studying the Grail narration from *Lohengrin* which he was to sing for his audition. He happened to raise his eyes from the score and saw in the corridor a superb creature, elegantly dressed, who seemed not at all unfriendly, for she returned his gaze and was soon engaged in animated conversation with him. What was more, she agreed to meet him two days later by the Schiller monument in Vienna. The next day, Erik Schmedes was walking timidly into Mahler's office at the Opera, when he almost collided with a tall young woman who was just coming out. The brevity of their exchange, 'Oh!' and 'Ah!', betrayed a mixture of recognition and surprise, but alas a certain disappointment. For of course this was the young woman from the train, Anna von Mildenburg. Later the great tenor, when asked what happened next, always replied rather sadly: 'Nothing at all, the magic was gone! For ten years we performed together all the lovers in all the great operas, but offstage our relationship remained purely professional!'[64] A few months after this first encounter with Mildenburg, Schmedes became a member of the Opera and one of Mahler's favourite singers. For the moment, he was singing his first complete *Ring* in Vienna. Mahler, despite the severe pains which continued to plague him,[65] spent all his waking moments thinking up improvements 'like a crazy gambler who passed his days and nights mulling over the cards and calculating the odds'.[66] He recast the parts many times in his head and endlessly reconsidered every problem in the hope of finding another detail that could be improved. Prior to the cycle a new production of *Götterdämmerung* was put on 4 September 'with a new (excellent) cast'[67] and the *Neue Freie Presse* praised the singers' 'Sprechgesangton', much preferable to the usual frantic shrieking.

In *Das Rheingold* on 20 September, Mahler gave the role of Fricka to Sedlmair, Froh to Schmedes, and Donner to Demuth. All of them far surpassed their predecessors in these roles, largely because they had 'not learned bad habits from earlier productions'. Mahler admired Josef Ritter's Alberich so

[64] Dagmar Schmedes, 'Das Rendez-vous fand nicht statt', *Salzburger Nachrichten* (29 May 1976).

[65] In a letter to Albert Spiegler dated 27 Aug., Mahler informed him that his pains were 'getting no better' and that they moved him to 'rage at the powers of the nether world'.

[66] NBL2. 121.

[67] In an undated letter to Guido Adler (RAM 29), Mahler announces his intention of staging for the first time Reznicek's *Donna Diana*, a work 'that attracts by its great freshness'. The contract with Reznicek's publisher was signed on 16 Apr. 1898 (KMI).

much that 'although he had almost lost his voice he would be worth his salary even if he only sang four times a year!' Grengg and Reichenberg, as the two giants, were another improvement on the previous cast, thanks to their 'Cyclopean strength', their 'rugged appearance', and their perfect diction. The Magic Thunder Storm was a success, thanks to Demuth's powerful baritone, but Mahler still found the reaction of the gods at the moment of Fasolt's murder far from convincing. Although *Das Rheingold* was less popular than the three other parts of the *Ring* cycle, it played to a full house on the first night. The *Neue Freie Presse* praised most of Mahler's changes and especially that of the main set. Only part of Valhalla was now visible,[68] the rest being left to that essential collaborator in any theatrical performance, the imagination of the audience. Mahler was also praised for casting important singers in secondary parts and for infusing 'a little Mahlerian nervousness' (*Mahlersche Nervosität*) into each dwarf in the Nibelheim episode.[69]

In *Die Walküre*, Sofie Sedlmair was cast as Sieglinde for the first time, and Natalie wrote that she had brought a 'magical tenderness' to the part.[70] As Brünnhilde, Mildenburg was a 'true goddess'. Mahler was delighted with her performance, which he had built up from scratch, but he found Reichmann, whose interpretation he had tried in vain to improve, a 'languid and feeble' Wotan. The orchestra was just as unsatisfactory as it had been in *Das Rheingold*. 'Too much negligence and error, accumulated here over the years, lie like a curse upon the orchestra in the same way as the dragon Fafner lies upon the gold.'[71] In *Siegfried*, a newly engaged tenor, Julius Spielmann, who was an intelligent and gifted artist, nevertheless introduced some 'unforgivable clowning' to the role of Mime:

'He cuts his own throat,' said Mahler, 'and I'm going to fire him immediately. He's already ruined by the sloppy habits of the theatre routine. The worst thing about his performance is his Jewish jargon. No doubt, with Mime, Wagner intended to ridicule the Jews (with all the traits he bestowed on them—excessive humility and greed—the jargon is textually and musically so cleverly suggested) but for God's sake, it must not be exaggerated and overdone, as Spielmann does it, and in Vienna at that, at the "K.K. Hofoper". This is sheer folly, a welcome scandal for the Viennese. I know of only one

[68] The new Valhalla, designed by Anton Brioschi, was much appreciated by the anonymous critic of the *Neue Musikalische Presse* (25 Sept. 1898), which pictured it on the first page of his review.

[69] Cast of the 20 Sept. performance: Sedlmair (Fricka), Michalek, Kusmitsch, and Kaulich (Rhine-maidens), Schmedes (Froh), Van Dyck (Loge), Ritter (Alberich), Reichmann (Wotan), Demuth (Donner), Grengg and Reichenberg (Giants).

[70] NBL2. 122. Mahler never shared Natalie's enthusiasm for Sophie Sedlmair, who was a member of the Hofoper until 1907 but was generally used as an understudy or replacement.

[71] Cast of *Die Walküre* on 22 Sept.: Sedlmair (Sieglinde), Mildenburg (Brünnhilde), Reichmann (Wotan). After an earlier performance of 6 May, Theodor Helm wrote in the *Deutsche Zeitung* that Mahler's *Walküre* had 'less style' than Richter's and that his 'nervous haste' destroyed 'the highly poetic atmosphere'. Although some passages were 'nobly and expressively interpreted', Helm felt it would have been better to 'follow Richter's example', in particular 'his admirable broadening of the tempo in the closing phrases'.

Mime,' he concluded, 'and that is myself . . . you wouldn't believe what there is in that part nor what I could make of it.'[72]

Mahler found Schmedes's Siegfried particularly unsatisfactory. Although the tenor's heroic appearance and personality were perfectly suited to the part, his acting was 'no longer as natural and modest (*schlicht*) as before', while his musical interpretation was 'more inaccurate and careless'. Mahler was so angry with him that he didn't look at him once during the performance and wouldn't speak to him afterwards. He refused to take him to supper, and scolded him severely the following day. Demuth, on the other hand, delighted him as Wanderer, because 'his somewhat indolent temperament was well suited to the calm and disillusioned God'. Mildenburg was the only singer who finally satisfied him entirely that evening, for 'the divine expression' that she brought to the Valkyrie's awakening of love and life was the crowning glory of the opera.[73]

In *Götterdämmerung*, Mahler conducted the Norn scene for the first time in Vienna. According to Natalie, he conveyed its 'mystic significance' so power-fully to eye and ear that 'it made you shudder and at the same time feel elated and carried away'. Thanks to Mildenburg, the Waltraute scene, which had previously been cut, was the success of the evening. Schmedes had corrected his recent faults, and the two of them 'seemed to dominate the drama like a pair of demigods'. With the very modest means at his disposal, Mahler had eradi-cated all the earlier absurdities in the staging and created an atmosphere heavy with foreboding. In the final tableau he cut out the vision of the doomed gods and suggested the burning of Valhalla by an effect resembling an aurora borealis. It was the first step toward a reform particularly dear to his heart—the abolition of realism. The chorus and orchestra seemed transformed, revitalized, compared with the previous year. In this final phase of the cycle even the orchestra pleased him, particularly in the Funeral March. He was delighted at having obtained this improvement fairly easily, particularly after his intermi-nable but inconclusive struggles of the year before.

According to Heuberger,[74] 'an unprecedented suspense' held the audience spellbound during the whole performance of *Götterdämmerung* from 7 p.m. until 11.45. Again, Heuberger praised the singers' new conversational style, a *Sprechgesang* infinitely preferable to the shrill cries of earlier performances. Reichenberg, in particular, distinguished himself by lowering the volume of his

[72] NBL1. 122. Albert Kauders (1854–1912), writing in the *Neues Wiener Tagblatt*, described Spielmann's Mime as 'the caricature of a caricature'. He also criticized the slowness of some of Mahler's tempos. Spielmann had been a member of the Hofoper since 1 Aug., but Mahler did indeed dismiss him at the beginning of the following year, although the tenor demanded 'to be released of his contract' immediately after the *Siegfried* performance because of Mahler's censorious remarks.

[73] Cast of the performance on 23 Sept.: Mildenburg (Brünnhilde), Schmedes (Siegfried), Spielmann (Mime), Demuth (Wanderer).

[74] This article, like his previous ones, was unsigned, but Heuberger was definitely the author, for Hanslick now wrote rarely, and almost always signed his reports.

voice for the first time, while Mildenburg's vocal splendour and dramatic fire brought back 'the era of the Opera's glory'. The orchestra's performance was admirable, the effect of the increased number of rehearsals 'unmistakable', and Mahler could only be criticized for a few moments of excessive haste, notably the Funeral March and the final scene. Vienna 'has rarely seen such a performance, and this evening the Hofoper was transformed into a Festspielhaus'.[75]

After some hesitation Mahler suppressed the rope in the Norn scene, using a real rope for rehearsals and then removing it at the last moment. So the Norns only mimed the throwing of the rope into the air and catching it, and the fact that there was no rope was hardly noticed. He nevertheless received a letter of protest from Cosima Wagner, to which he replied that he had taken this step 'at the dictates of his conscience as an artist and man of the theatre'. Gustav Schönaich, who dined frequently with Mahler and Natalie, brought the matter up again on behalf of the Wagner family. 'Spare yourself this trouble, I beg you!' replied Mahler.

You must concede that I too understand something of these problems and don't let myself get carried away by my own ideas—I abandon nineteen out of twenty of them every day. At Bayreuth, I have never yet seen this scene done successfully; it was managed so badly, the last time [I was there], that the Norns dropped the rope and had to stoop down to pick it up. If they can't manage it in Bayreuth, where no pains are spared over rehearsals, it seems clear that it is impossible. . . . I am certain that Wagner would have been much more tolerant than his descendants, and would have agreed with my choice of the lesser of two evils.[76]

The *Ring* brought Mahler into conflict with the Intendant over the electricians' and stage-hands' wages. Their work had been especially arduous and, because of the long rehearsals, most of them had not been able to get home to eat; Mahler felt that, as their pay was very low,[77] they should be given a bonus of two florins each to encourage their enthusiasm and goodwill.[78] But Intendant Plappart wrote to him on 26 September, refusing this request, acknowledging that 'the production has been unusually successful'. He maintained that such special payments 'are only justified in the case of spectacular ballets, which make much greater demands on the technical staff'. Mahler finally paid the 94 gulden out of his own pocket, though he pretended to his friends that he had won his point.[79] He considered that the wages and conditions of the stage-

[75] Cast of the performance on 25 Sept. 1898: Mildenburg (Brünnhilde), Walker (Waltraute), Schmedes (Siegfried), Demuth (Gunther), Reichenberg (Hagen).

[76] NBL1. 108; NBL2. 125. This incident did not affect Mahler's relations with the Wagner family. Cosima Wagner wrote him in early summer to say she would be delighted to attend the performance of *Rienzi* that he was planning for the following winter. In any case she was far too diplomatic to quarrel with the director of the Vienna Opera at a time when she was trying to establish her son Siegfried's operas.

[77] Between 35 and 50 florins a month for a job with no fixed hours.

[78] Letter from Mahler to the Intendant (22 Sept., HOA, no. 547/1898).

[79] NBL2. 123. That same day, Mahler told Natalie that he often 'readily paid out small sums' and that after each rehearsal he bought sausages and beer for the children playing the dwarfs of Nibelheim, which cost him about 9 gulden each time.

hands and technicians should be looked into immediately, with a view to making improvements. He was ashamed that he had done nothing about these unfortunate men sooner; in fact he hardly knew them and only saw them coming on stage from time to time like 'avenging angels'.[80]

It was during the summer of 1898 that the decisive moves were made which resulted in Mahler's succeeding Richter as head of the Philharmonic Concerts.[81] The annual meeting during which the committee members were elected and the conductor chosen took place on 10 May 1898 for the 1898–9 season. At that time, Richter had been unanimously confirmed in his position. Strange as it may seem, it was not Richter but Mahler who presided at the next session of the committee on 28 August. It seems that negotiations with him had been entered into behind Richter's back, and that Mahler's engagement for the following season had been decided in advance, without Richter's knowledge. The committee met on 22 September, for the last time under Richter's presidency. 'After opening the meeting, Herr Hofkapellmeister Richter announced that owing to a torn ligament in his right arm he would be unable to conduct the Philharmonic concerts in the coming season. . . . This announcement was noted with profound regret.' Richter recommended that either Mahler or Ferdinand Löwe should succeed him, and it was then officially decided that Mahler should be approached. On 23 September, Richter submitted his resignation in writing and on the evening of the same day an official delegation came from the orchestra to ask Mahler to direct the concerts. The next day, at a hastily convened 'extraordinary general meeting', a good many of the members were amazed to discover that their former head had resigned. Nevertheless, 'Herr Hofopern-Direktor Mahler having declared himself willing to assume direction of the Philharmonic Concerts, Herr Direktor Mahler was elected Conductor of the Philharmonic concerts by acclamation.'

We can only speculate as to the exact sequence of events between May and August 1898 that led to the change-over. Mahler must certainly have had unofficial meetings with various members of the committee. That this committee should have readily and unanimously accepted Richter's resignation and Mahler's engagement is hard to understand, however, for as we shall see from the events that followed, many of its members were by no means unconditional supporters of the director of the Opera. It is clear, in any case, that the pains in Richter's arm were not the real reason for his resignation.[82] It seems more likely that, having become aware of the contacts between Mahler and the

---

[80] After a long struggle and after first raising the orchestra members' salaries, he obtained a general salary increase for the technical staff around 1900.

[81] In connection with what follows, see Clemens Hellsberg's study 'Gustav Mahler und die Wiener Philharmoniker', *Musikblätter der Wiener Philharmoniker*, 40: 198 ff., which makes use for the first time of the minutes of the Philharmonic's meetings, thus correcting numerous second-hand sources.

[82] In an article on the first Philharmonic concert in November, Hanslick suggested that Richter's ills were not perhaps as serious as he claimed, since they did not prevent him from conducting a considerable number of operas and concerts, particularly in England.

committee, he chose the most honourable, peaceable, and discreet solution: that of leaving the Philharmonic and the Austrian capital forever.[83]

Mahler, on the other hand, had the wind in his sails; everyone was talking about him; both press and public eagerly awaited the programme for the new season. Although the thought of the extra work entailed by his new position might have made him hesitate for a moment, he was seeing one of his life's dearest dreams come true. Not only did this new heaven-sent honour make him undisputed king of music in Vienna;[84] it also gave him the satisfaction of having at his disposal an orchestra which he could mould as he wished, both at the Opera and now in the symphonic repertory. The Philharmonic subscription concerts took place every second Sunday at 12.30. There were eight in the series, plus a few special concerts—the Nicolai concert, a yearly benefit for the Opera pension fund, and the separate Gesellschafts-Konzerte which depended for their musicians on members of the Philharmonic. The psychological climate of this new collaboration between Mahler and the orchestra was clear from the first rehearsal. In the welcoming speech to Mahler, Joseph Helmsky, the first horn player, spoke mainly of the loss that the orchestra had suffered by Richter's departure. Mahler in his reply had to do the same:

First I must express my regret at losing a colleague as valuable as Hans Richter. I didn't take seriously his decision to leave the Philharmonic concerts, in which he achieved so many well-deserved triumphs. I therefore hesitated until the last moment before responding to your appeal, and accepted only when I realized that the circumstances that led to Richter's decision were irreversible. Now that I find myself at the head of your admirable association, I would like to express the joy I feel at the idea of making music with you outside the theatre.

Richter's relationship with the Philharmonic had been one based on mutual affection and esteem, whereas they had now contracted with Mahler a marriage of convenience. For most of the orchestra, the comforts of an equable, peaceable coexistence counted for more than 'artistic truth'. Richter's placid and debonair character, and his easygoing attitude had suited them perfectly. 'He sometimes suffered from an excess of confidence, in both his talent and his craft,' wrote Kalbeck of Richter, 'but he was never guilty of bad taste or complacency.[85] Neither was his conducting ever personal or subjective. A profound but instinctive musicality guided his gestures and his interpretations,' whereas with Mahler, all spiritual, moral, and artistic problems were

[83] According to Clemens Hellsberg, the dubious events of this summer might help to explain the subsequent tension in Mahler's relations with the orchestra. Most of the papers regarded Richter's decision as temporary and recalled his temporary resignation from the Philharmonic during the 1882–3 season.

[84] Predictably, the *Deutsche Zeitung* regretted the Philharmonic's choice and Richter's departure, which it hoped would not be permanent. Mahler was the first 'non-German' conductor of the orchestra and could not be expected to defend German music properly. (!) The 'Jewish press' was accused of speaking of Richter as though he were 'dead or finished'.

[85] In a farewell article, written on the occasion of Mahler's first concert, Kalbeck wrote of Richter: 'He didn't always want to do what he could, but he could always do what he wanted.' *Neues Wiener Tagblatt* (7 Nov. 1898).

inextricably bound up with the problems of his profession. His 'modern' approach was as much that of a philosopher or a writer as that of a musician. He demanded far more in rehearsal than Richter. He caused shock and surprise when he insisted on getting to the heart of things, and took nothing for granted. Long experience had convinced him that tradition was not an absolute value. The previous February, for instance, he had given Natalie some striking examples of tempo errors in Mozart, Wagner, and *Fidelio*. Sometimes the choice of a tempo should depend upon an 'unconscious reminiscence' on the part of a composer. One day, when Gustav Schönaich criticized him for too rapid a tempo in the Prelude to the third act of *Lohengrin*, claiming that Wagner himself had conducted it more slowly, Mahler replied that, in his opinion, the piece in question was a reminiscence from Beethoven and that, when composers introduced such 'unconscious recollections' into their work, the 'copy' almost never altered the tempo of the 'original'.[86]

Ex. 1

In Mahler's opinion bad singers and players could distort a work beyond all recognition. 'The worst of it is,' he added,

> that this kind of superficial performance can become the tradition. Then, when someone comes along who wants to blow the pale embers of the work into a living flame, he is accused of being a heretic and an innovator. That is what happened to Wagner. Except here at the Opera, where I am understood and approved, I am heaped with invective and obloquy wherever I conduct.[87]

It was a fact that the modern trend of Mahler's interpretations had displeased and shocked the public and the critics everywhere, and his anxiety on this subject was particularly justified in Vienna, where the tradition of the Philharmonic Orchestra was staunchly conservative. Even Brahms, a conservative composer who was Viennese by adoption, had not been performed by the Philharmonic as often as by German orchestras. The routine that Richter had established was only rarely disturbed by guest appearances of conductors like Bülow, Strauss, Nikisch, or Weingartner.

Two days before the first concert a group of musicians[88] showed their hostility in the particularly unpleasant form of an anonymous article in the *Deutsche*

[86] NBLS. 29 May 1899.

[87] NBL1. 99; NBL2. 112. Mahler also thought that the sense of tempo and phrasing had been lost and that conducting had been reduced to beating time. Only operatic music had been spared to some extent, because the words and actions facilitated its comprehension. 'Orchestral music, on the other hand gives full rein to stupidity and ignorance, or, at best, subjectivity.'

[88] According to NBL1. 110 and NBL2. 127, it was 'a desperate attempt by a few members of the singers and musicians at the Opera to get rid of Mahler'.

Zeitung entitled 'The Jewish Regime at the Vienna Opera'.[89] Theodor Helm had warned Mahler about it but was unable to prevent its appearance. The author claimed that he was 'not concerned about Mahler's results[90] but about the methods by which they were obtained', and 'If we view matters from this angle, his work appears in quite a different light.' Though the uncut productions were a happy innovation, Mahler distracted the orchestra and the singers by his exaggerated gestures on the podium, which were responsible for 'many wrong notes': absolute disaster would occur if musicians were to place all their confidence in his baton.

What Herr Mahler sometimes does cannot be called conducting. It is more like the gesticulations of a dervish and, when the Kapellmeister has St. Vitus's dance, it's really very difficult to keep time. His left hand often doesn't know what the right one is doing; this may be all very well for 'charity', but it's extremely harmful when conducting an orchestra . . .[91] Often his left hand marks the 'Bohemian circle' with convulsive jerks, scrapes for hidden treasures, shudders and shakes, clutches, searches, smothers, battles through the waves, strangles infants, moulds, slaps; in a word it is often in a state of delirium tremens, but it does not conduct. . . .[92] Mahler's conducting is affected; it is meant to impress the public but not at all intended for the performers, whom it confuses, rather than helps. . . . Mahler wants to leave the stamp of his personality everywhere and the result is frequently a caricature.[93]

All men of taste, musicians or laymen, know very well what Mahler is aiming at and find it offensive. Nevertheless, his pretensions grow with his success. In the orchestra, there are some lackeys who want to earn the good graces of their all-powerful chief at all costs. With or without previous prompting, one of the members even proposed that Mahler's great Symphony for chorus and orchestra be given at a Philharmonic concert! But the orchestra rebelled; in view of the colossal efforts the musicians are obliged to make to fulfil their Director's demands at the Opera alone, they preferred to perform a symphony by little Beethoven rather than one by the great Mahler.

The article ended with a bitter attack on Arnold Rosé,[94] who had become 'head of all the Kapellmeister'. The anonymous author also accused Mahler of trying to 'improve Beethoven'[95] on the grounds that Beethoven 'had not succeeded in carrying out all his intentions'. He goes on:

---

[89] The initials E. Th. appear at the bottom of the article.

[90] The author acknowledged 'Mahler's great success as Director of the Opera'.

[91] Most present-day conductors consider the independence of their hands as an essential feature of modern technique.

[92] This malicious description does not have the effect the author intended, for it gives a striking and by no means unfavourable impression of Mahler conducting.

[93] The recent *Freischütz* had revealed 'an absolutely new and unusual conception for musicians impregnated with the spirit of Weber . . . and this at a time when a certain stability had just been reached in the interpretation of his work'. Mahler had 'turned it into a caricature, changing for example, the last allegro into an allegretto! Atrocious!' This same tempo aroused Kalbeck's admiration (see below).

[94] The 'talented brother-in-law' was contrasted with his 'untalented' brother, 'who is in America'.

[95] Mahler had among other things contemplated an orchestral performance of Beethoven's Quartet in C sharp minor, op. 131 (NBL1. 111; NBL2. 125).

Beethoven's talent for orchestration must have been very imperfect for he failed to use an E flat clarinet in the Coriolan Overture.[96] How lucky your are, Beethoven, to have found an epigone to immortalize your work; without him, Coriolan would have been eternally deprived of the E flat clarinet. . . . If Herr Mahler wants to make corrections he should tackle the works of Mendelssohn and Rubinstein, though the Jews would probably not stand for that. But let him leave our Beethoven in peace, he impresses and pleases us, even without an E flat clarinet and without Mahler! . . . Yes, Herr Mahler has E flat clarinets on the brain. Not content with adding one to the *Eroica*, he has also reinforced the trombones and double basses, and it is even being said that he will send his brother-in-law to Jericho to rediscover Joshua's trumpet, because Aryan trumpets are not loud enough for him. Perhaps he will find a means of obtaining the trumpets of Israel for the Opera, the self-same trumpets that the entire Jewish press have been blasting in praise of 'Herr Direktor', and then perhaps, the walls will come tumbling down. The orchestra is preparing to hold the forthcoming rehearsals of the *Eroica* on the Steinfeld,[97] so that Mahler can employ the field artillery with some guns to reinforce the kettledrums.

From the same source, we learn that Mahler had apparently acquired the nickname of 'Duty Sergeant' (*Kaporal von Tag*) due to his tone of voice when addressing the members of the orchestra.

Nobody, from the most insignificant employee and stagehand right up to—but excluding—his brother-in-law, is completely free from the feeling of anti-Semitism toward the Director; even the Jewish members of the Orchestra, except of course for the talented brother-in-law, have become anti-Semites. They are willing enough to work . . . but no one will stand for the militaristic tone of his commands. They did their duty well enough under Richter and Jahn, and are ready to continue, but they have the right to be treated as artists and civilized human beings, not browbeaten into submission. Resistance is smouldering, even the most cowardly and submissive musicians will finally join the majority, and one of these days Mahler will find himself without an orchestra. Then we'll see how, with only his brother-in-law to help, he will manage to put on *Tristan*. He will have no choice but to engage the Prelouver Stadtkapelle . . . or he could perform *Tristan* with a harmonica and his two brothers-in-law (the gifted one as well as the American). The ensemble would be marvellous, provided he adds an E flat clarinet!

If they fail to say amen to all the dictates of Mahler's caprices and whims, the older members of the orchestra can expect to be treated like the menials. The number of musicians who have been pensioned off places a heavy strain on the Opera pension fund and puts its future at risk. The chorus alone has found the decisive tone and manner needed to combat this Jewish audacity. They have committed themselves upon their honour to deal jointly and as one man with the Duty Sergeant, and have obliged him to capitulate. Musicians should insist on being treated, not only as human beings,

---

[96] One of Mahler's most 'scandalous changes' had been to use an E flat clarinet for Beethoven's 'Eroica' Symphony and Coriolàn. This instrument had previously been confined to military music and Berlioz's *Symphonie fantastique*. According to Helm, Mahler bowed to pressure and suppressed the clarinet before the concert.

[97] Steinfeld was a military training area well-known to the Viennese.

but also as artists. Their unity would force Mahler to change his attitude, because it is conceivable to have the Opera without Mahler, but not without the orchestra.

This article, whose alleged purpose is to protect the purity of German music from degradation by a tyrannical conductor, is in fact a prize example of the virulence of anti-Semitism in the Vienna of 1898. It was written while rehearsals for the first Philharmonic Concert were going on, and the details of orchestral 'retouching' were supplied by a member of the orchestra who also sent, to the Intendant and to various newspapers, anonymous letters signed: 'A musician who wants to hear the authentic, unadulterated Beethoven.' In a letter to the Intendant dated 23 November, Mahler wrote that it was inadmissible for a member of his orchestra thus to conspire against him. Having obtained the original of one of the letters, he had it analysed by a graphologist, who had 'confirmed his suspicions and identified the writer'.[98] Nevertheless he decided not to inflict any sanctions;[99] he only wanted to know who he was, because this sort of attack 'turns against its author anyway and discredits him'. Mahler's integrity made his position invulnerable and in any case the article's savage anti-Semitism robbed the other criticisms it contained of any power to convince.

The first concert took place on 6 November. Mahler conducted the Coriolan Overture, Mozart's Symphony in G minor, and Beethoven's 'Eroica' Symphony. When he appeared on the platform the public gave him a cool reception, showing that they missed Richter.[100]

In the *Neues Wiener Tagblatt*, Max Kalbeck drew a striking portrait of Mahler on the podium:

Instead of the blond giant who had faced the orchestra, solid and calm, firm as a rock, a slender, nervous, incredibly supple silhouette sprang onto the rostrum. We were already acquainted with that silhouette's almost diabolical powers of suggestion and we now realized that his spell would be as powerful in the concert hall as it was in the theatre. The mood of the audience gradually grew warmer and there was loud applause after the closing strains of the 'Eroica' brought the concert to an end. Mahler conducted everything from memory; his calm and the economy of his gestures were remarkable. He was able to work out every tiny detail in rehearsal. There was never time to achieve this perfection at the Opera where he had often been obliged to improvise and bring out new subtleties during the performance itself.

Mahler considered the Coriolan Overture to be one of the most concentrated and densely packed of Beethoven's works, and also one of the most neglected. He identified with it more than with any other piece of music because of its 'ever-growing intensity of expression, in which harshness and violence alter-

---

[98] Mahler got the Opera to pay one graphologist, Professor Skallipitzky, but he had to pay a second expert out of his own pocket (see below, Chap. 5).

[99] Letter to the Intendant, 9 Dec.

[100] The correspondent of the *Neue Zeitschrift für Musik* described the musicians' attitude to Mahler as one of 'glacial silence'.

nate with tenderness and expressiveness'. For him 'the whole destiny of
Coriolanus' was embodied in the first five chords.[101] The last work Richter had
conducted at the Philharmonic, a few months before, had been the 'Eroica', and
Mahler, in choosing it for his opening concert, no doubt wished to show his
determination to impose new conceptions. As at the Opera, where he had
closed the auditorium to latecomers, he now discouraged hungry music lovers
from leaving for lunch after the Scherzo by looking round at them angrily. 'From
the impetuous unisono and the pizzicati, right through to the end, the Finale
was one of the great moments of the concert,' wrote Natalie. A few months
earlier Mahler had spoken to her of his ideas concerning this movement. The
pizzicato bass motif was not in fact the main theme and should not be played
too fast, because in that passage, really, 'Beethoven is trying, thoughtfully,
humorously, to walk, and gradually succeeds in doing so'. Accordingly, the last
notes, like an answer to his efforts, should be a little faster. Against this
background, which accompanies and guides the whole movement, the themes
unfold, singing and ringing, and must on no account be played too fast.[102]

Hanslick's review, in the *Neue Freie Presse* the next day, proved that Mahler's
admirers were not recruited exclusively from the ranks of the young revolution-
aries. Although he regretted Richter's departure, Hanslick thought that the
'Philharmonic could not have found a more highly esteemed or better conductor than Mahler', and noted that 'this conviction seems to be shared by the
public, since the entire series was sold out immediately after the first provisional announcement of Mahler's appointment'. There could be no doubt, he
thought, that this magnificent 'vote of confidence' was 'more than justified by
Mahler's performance'. During three long rehearsals he had made the orchestra
go over works 'which, for years now, our excellent musicians have mastered so
completely both in their heads and with their fingers, that they could almost
play them in their sleep'. But Mahler wanted them played 'awake' and indeed
with complete commitment and awareness. That was why each of these masterpieces had seemed new. 'This is not the proper place,' Hanslick went on,

to enumerate the new musical details that sparkled like diamonds, without detracting
from the unity of form and mood. Mahler's principal aim is to tune each piece to a
dominating idea and preserve its character and style. This is clearest in the Mozart
Symphony, which some people might have liked to hear performed with stronger
accents and more glowing colours. Nevertheless, it was thus and not otherwise that
Mahler wished to underline the character of this luminous, immaculate music, coming
as it did between Beethoven's two volcanoes. The Coriolan Overture and the 'Eroica'
produced an indescribable impression. Seldom before have we heard this music

[101] According to Mahler, 'they should not be played (though they always are) as five equal beats, but
should be interpreted expressively, as an ascension to a climax that then ebbs away on the two final chords'.
He criticized those who interpreted the passage as 'graceful': the semiquavers in the violins, he claimed,
should not be played with bravura but 'strongly, like growling thunder' (NBL1. 109; NBL2. 126).

[102] NBL1. 99; NBL2. 112. (Feb. 1898.) On the same day, Mahler spoke feelingly of the Symphony's second
movement, which evoked 'the hero's funeral procession in all its power and tragedy'.

performed with such clarity and transparency in the most delicate of textures and with such overwhelming overall grandeur and power. The public, used to the best, gave free rein to its enthusiasm after each movement of the 'Eroica', and never tired of calling back the man in command time and time again. All's well that starts well!

Though Hanslick accepted and approved the 'novelty' of Mahler's interpretations, his colleagues were more reserved. Kalbeck found the contrast between the two themes in Coriolan over-emphasized and thought that, as a whole, it lacked 'sombre pride and angry grandeur'. On the other hand, Mahler had approached the 'personal, subjective and passionate' Mozart symphony 'thinking he could convey the classic spirit with coldness in the guise of objectivity'.[103] He had accelerated and slowed the tempo too freely but had failed to bring out the nuances. In the 'Eroica', he had shown 'strategic vision', and his imperious and calm approach had mastered and clarified the most complex polyphony.[104] Kalbeck concluded by comparing Mahler with Bülow: 'May he acquire all that unforgettable master's qualities and avoid his faults.'

The Viennese musicologist, Robert Werba, has pointed out that the G minor Symphony was the only one by Mozart programmed in this first series of Philharmonic concerts, and that Mahler conducted only one other Mozart symphony in the following season. Werba collected all the reviews of these two performances, and they tell us a great deal about what people thought of Mozart at that time.[105] For Gustav Schönaich, Mahler's conducting of the Symphony No. 40 was 'beyond all praise'. 'Never had one been more blissfully aware of the winged, light genius of this masterpiece. A spirit of grace and delicacy breathed through the performance.' Other critics' opinions concerning the tempos diverged considerably. Helm described that of the first movement as 'traditional', whereas the *Neuigkeit Weltblatt* and the *Reichswehr* remarked on his exaggerated slowness. For Hirschfeld, 'Mahler, without slipping into the excesses of the hysterical *neudeutsch* school, gave the melody a flowing, individual line not closely tied to the beat but free, like song.' That alone was enough to make Mahler's modifications of the tempo acceptable.

The *Arbeiter-Zeitung* compared Mahler's measured gestures on the concert platform with his restless movements at the Opera, 'where sometimes he seems not to have enough hands for all the directions he wants to give'. While conducting at the concert his left hand hardly ever moved, except here and there to trace a motif.[106] In the *Abendpost*, Hirschfeld pointed out the difference between dramatic and symphonic conducting, and admitted that Mahler had proved his familiarity with the symphonic repertory. This 'strange, elegant, almost indifferent' reading had brought Mozart closer to Haydn than to

---

[103] Kalbeck claimed that the first theme had lacked 'colour and expression', suggesting a 'hired dancer' rather than a 'sorrowing Grace'. It seemed to be characteristic of Mahler to 'concentrate all feeling into secondary themes, the main theme being despatched as briefly and severely as possible'.

[104] In Kalbeck's view, this clarity in the first movement was due to the moderate tempo.

[105] Robert Werba, 'Mahlers Mozartbild', *Mitteilungsblatt der Mozartgemeinde Wien*, Oct. 1977.

[106] Ibid.

Beethoven.[107] Mahler's tempo modifications (*Wandlungen des Tempo*) 'annoy our old folk', because they involved 'taking certain liberties with the melody', but they had done no harm to Mozart. The performance of Coriolan was 'animated, dramatic', its driving vigour 'unaffected by the highlighting of beautiful details'. However, Mahler's interpretation of the symphony was 'a protest against its title—"Eroica"', because Beethoven's pathos which Richter had so often evoked, was missing. However clear, however interesting this performance had been, however noble and powerful the Funeral March, Mahler had failed 'to plumb the innermost depths of feeling'.[108] Once again Helm's article revealed the conflict between his personal feelings and the policy of his newspaper. He bravely declared that the instrumental 'retouching' had been almost imperceptible, and had not deserved so much unfavourable publicity. Although Mahler's conducting had grown calmer, he had not attained 'the imposing, magisterial dignity of Hans Richter'. As with Bülow, Mahler's concern was mainly for 'interesting and surprising detail',[109] Coriolan had been 'truly dramatic' in spite of the slow tempo.[110] The 'strangely expressionless' opening of the 'Eroica' had come as a surprise. Later the magnificent crescendos were 'due in the first place to our Philharmonic which received the lion's share of the applause'.[111] For Helm, the dramatic rendering of the Funeral March was the climax of the concert. Some time later, in the *Musikalisches Wochenblatt* where he was more at liberty to express his true opinion, the same critic praised the freedom of Mahler's conducting, which was so different from the 'metronomic rigour' of the classical conductors, and revealed him as a fervent adept of Wagner's doctrines.[112]

At the second concert on 20 November, the programme consisted of Weber's *Oberon* Overture, Schubert's 'Unfinished' Symphony, and Berlioz's *Symphonie fantastique*. Weber's overture, 'all sparkle and fire', was loudly applauded, but Mahler's interpretation of Schubert, in spite of its 'divine tenderness' and exemplary orchestral legato, was less warmly received. Theodor Helm even judged it to be 'somewhat unnatural'. This might have been the consequence of Mahler's reaction against the 'exaggerated sentimentality dear to the Viennese, their constant tendency to pull out all the stops (*ewiges Loslegen*), which completely falsified not only the spirit but the structure of a work'.[113] More than

---

[107] However, he was delighted by the colour and phrasing in the Andante.

[108] Yet Hirschfeld praised the 'powerful build-up' of the Variations in the Finale, which, he felt, largely justified the audience's acclaim.

[109] As in Hamburg, this 'concentration on detail' found many detractors among the critics. The *Neue Zeitschrift* correspondent, for instance, felt that the general effect had been compromised.

[110] Helm judged the tempo in the second movement of the Mozart Symphony to be 'faster and more changeable' than was usual.

[111] The Viennese public, it seems, had not yet abandoned the barbarous custom of applauding between the movements.

[112] Helm approved the slowness of the Trio of the 'Eroica', which allowed the horns to play their part correctly.

[113] NBL2. 127.

sixty years after its first Viennese performance the Austrian public was still uneasy about the *Fantastique*. Some of the audience left the hall after the third and fourth movements, thereby infuriating Mahler, because 'though this work is not perhaps of the highest artistic achievement', it contained, in his opinion, such 'spirit and originality (*Geist und Eigenart*) that it fully deserves a hearing, especially when given a performance such as might never be heard again'. He was even more infuriated by the attitude of the critics: 'There is always something new to be learned from conducting a work like this, yet critics have the effrontery to condemn it out of hand after hearing it only once.'[114]

'Mahler led his troops even more independently than the first time,' wrote Kalbeck, 'and was even more successful in convincing the public of his Philharmonic mission. . . . He controls himself and therefore he controls others. Whenever he errs it is by conviction rather than through weakness.' He seemed at the head of his orchestra 'as blissful as a violinist who finally has a Stradivarius in his hands', while others in his place might have lost their head. His musical development brought him closer to the romantic than to the classical school, and 'Wagner would not have conducted the *Unfinished Symphony* and the *Oberon* Overture any differently.'[115] He was a conductor who could not identify himself with the purely musical aspect of a work except through the medium of its poetical contents. He imagined a 'hidden programme' and under his baton the two works were transformed into 'colourful pictures' and 'dreams of magic light'. The *Symphonie fantastique*, which was 'impossible to understand without a programme' and 'all the more laughable the more the composer tries to be serious', aroused the conservative Kalbeck's ire. Having come to 'the end of his musical gifts', Berlioz had, 'in one rash leap, taken himself outside the confines of music', and others who did not even have his spirit and temperament had 'gone leaping after him'. Such short-sightedness was to be expected from Vienna's music critics, for the Austrian capital was—and has remained—one of the most conservative cities in the whole musical world. Hanslick even argued that Mahler should have had the courage to cut the whole of Berlioz's Finale, even though, as a 'conscientious and impulsive' conductor, he 'brought it back to life with a blend of understanding and genius which made it interesting and effective, if not beautiful.'[116]

[114] Ibid. Mahler wrote to Adler on 7 Nov. 1898, asking if he could lend him a score of the *Fantastique*, or if not, if he could obtain him another one (RAM 30). See DMM2. 333 ff. on the close relationship between the music of Berlioz and Mahler. Mitchell reveals a striking resemblance between a theme from the Overture to *Benvenuto Cellini* and a theme that occurs in the Finale of Mahler's Second. See also Henry-Louis de La Grange, 'Berlioz und Mahler: Vom musikalischen Roman zum Sphärengesang', in *Festschrift Constantin Floros* (Breitkopf, Wiesbaden, 1990), 87 ff.

[115] Despite this, the *Deutsche Zeitung* criticized the slowness of the Overture's initial adagio, the frequent changes of tempo in the subsequent allegro and the whole of the *Unfinished*, whose unity and charm were destroyed in a plethora of nuances.

[116] The famous critic recalled a Vienna performance of the *Fantastique* conducted by Berlioz in 1846, all of whose rehearsals he had attended. The composer had conducted the first Allegro slower than Mahler, and *Un bal* faster.

Finally, in the *Musikalisches Wochenblatt*, Helm had reservations about Mahler's tempos in the *Unfinished*, but could not conceive of anything more 'fascinating' than his interpretation of the *Fantastique*.

From experience Mahler had developed a personal and unconventional attitude with regard to concert programmes. Whenever they included a long, serious piece, he preferred to place it at the start of the evening, so that the audience could concentrate better. Thus he began the third Philharmonic concert of 4 December with Brahms's Second Symphony, followed by Dvořák's new symphonic poem, *Heldenlied* (Hero's Song), which was still in manuscript form;[117] the 'Variations on the Austrian Anthem' from Haydn's 'Emperor' Quartet,[118] and Mendelssohn's Overture to *A Midsummer Night's Dream*. Dvořák attended the concert and acknowledged the applause which followed the première of his work. The next day, Hanslick, lauded its instrumentation and the composer's 'contrapuntal skill'. He then went on to praise Mahler's Brahms performance which had been full of 'care and love'.[119] He had thus shown his affection for the music of a composer who had 'for years, though in vain, recommended him for Vienna'. Theodor Helm in the *Deutsche Zeitung* claimed that Weingartner's interpretation, three years earlier, of the Second Symphony had been more 'poetic'. However, Mahler had surpassed all his colleagues in the Finale, in which he had proved that it was possible to conduct 'with calm and energy at the same time'.[120] Hirschfeld, on the contrary, thought that Brahms's work had 'never received a more poetic interpretation'. In following Brahms's markings ('moderato', 'tranquillo') to the letter Mahler had created a 'purer, more personal, more introspective atmosphere' than Weingartner had done.[121] Kalbeck, Brahms's biographer and friend, waxed ecstatic about the 'marvellous clarity, devoid of any trace of pedantry', of this interpretation, in which Mahler 'has respected the composer's slightest indications and has known how to transmit them easily and subtly to the performers'.[122] In the last concert of the year, given on 18 December, Mahler conducted the first Vienna performance of Bizet's symphonic suite *Roma*, followed by the *Siegfried Idyll*

[117] Anti-Czech as well as anti-Semitic, the *Deutsche Zeitung* remarked that, in spite of tepid applause, Dvořák appeared immediately to thank the orchestra and the audience. He later reappeared twice more, thus no doubt giving the Vienna correspondent of the Czech newspaper *Národní Listy* occasion to 'cable to his paper the news of the national hero's great triumph'. Three letters from Mahler to Dvořák, dated 3 and 5 Oct. and 17 Nov. (Prague, Anton Dvořák Bequest), led up to this performance of *Heldenlied*. Mahler asked for a recent, unperformed orchestral work and Dvořák sent both *Die Waldtaube* (Holoubek) and *Heldenlied* (Píseň Bohatýrská) (letter from Dvořák to Mahler, RWO).

[118] To celebrate the 50th anniversary of the Kaiser's coronation.

[119] In the same article Hanslick also extolled Brahms's 'personal orchestral colour', though this is far from being one of the most original aspects of his orchestral music.

[120] According to Helm, the Finale had never been so well conducted nor so well received, in Vienna. However, he reproached Mahler for announcing his programmes only one week in advance.

[121] Hirschfeld also defended Dvořák's work against the indifference of the public and the hostility of his colleagues.

[122] Kalbeck nevertheless disapproved of Mahler's interpretation of the first movement, 'too fast and too pathetic in tone', but noted that the last three movements had 'enraptured the general public and connoisseurs alike'.

and Beethoven's Eighth Symphony. Hirschfeld praised 'the charm, tenderness and delicacy' of *Roma*, the 'warm and penetrating' interpretation of Wagner's little *Idyll*, and the 'profound seriousness and true artistic feeling' that had revealed many aspects of the Eighth Symphony 'hidden in earlier performances'.[123] Helm, a convinced Wagnerian if ever there was one, wrote that Mahler had 'laid bare his heart' in his 'noble and deeply felt' interpretation of the *Siegfried Idyll*, while the anonymous Viennese correspondent of the Leipzig magazine *Neue Zeitschrift für Musik* took the opposite view: Mahler had 'dissected' the piece and given the public an 'anatomical plate' of the young Siegfried. Even the Beethoven performance had managed to achieve 'the very opposite of the composer's intentions. Thus the only surprise of the concert was the public's patience.'

Mahler's activities at the Opera, from then on, fell into four different categories of event which have been carefully defined and differentiated by Franz Willnauer in his book *Mahler und die Wiener Oper*.[124] Besides the normal revivals, with a minimum of preparation except for changes in cast (*Wiederaufnahmen*), the *Neueinstudierungen* were prepared with a large number of rehearsals, with piano and with orchestra. So, of course, were the new productions (*Neuinszenierungen*) and even more the premières of new works (*Erstaufführungen*). For the Emperor's name-day, 4 October, at the beginning of the 1898–9 season, Mahler had prepared a *Neueinstudierung* of Boieldieu's *La Dame blanche*, which had long been absent from the repertoire. According to Hanslick, the effort was necessary, for the style of romantic opera had been lost since the musicians and singers had been contaminated by 'highly dramatic and declamatory music'.[125] Mahler's masterly conducting had restored to Boieldieu's music its true worth. The same care and enthusiasm had been devoted to the staging as with the *Ring*. Hirschfeld praised the 'pure, joyous expression' that Mahler had achieved through 'the enchantment of sustained mezza-voce'; although essentially a man of modern outlook, Mahler did try to apply that modernity to old music; nor did he impose that music on our sensibilities 'but gently led us back towards it'. Few people realized what a great achievement that was.[126] Kalbeck applauded a new and 'valiant artistic deed', thanks to which this eternally youthful 'Lady' had, like *Der Freischütz* and *The Barber of Seville*, preserved her 'popular national character' and had been 'reborn in all her pristine clarity'. He criticized only the large size of the stage and the auditorium, which did the work a disservice by favouring the singers at the expense of the orchestra.

[123] The *Neues Wiener Tagblatt's* anonymous critic particularly applauded the varied and moderate tempos, especially in the Finale of the Beethoven Symphony.

[124] WMW 75 and 208 ff.   [125] A transparent allusion to Wagnerian drama.

[126] Cast of the first performance on 4 Oct.: Michalek (Margarete), Sedlmair (Anna), Naval (Georges Brown), Spielmann (Dickson), Grengg (Gaveston). Kalbeck called Naval and Sedlmair 'ideal heroes' for this opera. Mahler, in his opinion, had been right to restore the orchestral balance of Boieldieu's time by reducing the string section.

Gustav Mahler

The preparations for the revival of *Der Freischütz*, on 21 October, demanded an even greater effort from Mahler, for this was to be one of the first important steps in his theatrical reform. He spent no less than an hour and a half rehearsing the Overture alone, to the growing exasperation of the musicians.[127] The original production contained many ludicrous details. Hanslick listed some examples from the Wolfsschlucht scene: Samiel's red tights; the noisy waterfall that drowned both orchestra and singers; the devils waltzing in the background; the 'terrifying' creatures crawling around the fire; the riders in the 'infernal hunt' descending on horseback from the wings and dashing to and fro on the stage, brandishing beneath the actors' noses primitive fireworks which were meant to emit a 'chaos of smoke and sparks'. At a time when realism even to the point of absurdity was still the predominant fashion in the theatre, Mahler discarded all such cardboard and papier-mâché stage props and suggested ghostly happenings by a mere interplay of light and shade. In his production the Wolfsschlucht became a narrow ravine framed by two huge rocks. Simple clouds of smoke and flickering will-o'-the-wisps took the place of the cyclorama projection—the black boar and the flaming wheels of the fantastic hunt. There were those who felt a certain nostalgia for these familiar phenomena.

As soon as he had reached Vienna, even before his appointment to the Opera, Mahler had expressed revolutionary views about the performance of *Der Freischütz*. 'You ought some time to hear Weber's *Freischütz* conducted by me,' he had told Natalie,

you wouldn't know it was the same piece, simply because I take completely different tempi—the right ones, in other words!—so that things can be heard that never normally are . . . The second Finale is always played fast and loud for instance—while I have it slow and quiet, a magnificent effect. The music should rise softly to heaven like the whispered confession of guilt. Then comes the prayer, played with tremendous force: a wonderful contrast which otherwise gets lost. The interpretation of Weber always gives rise to serious misunderstandings. . . . If I become Director, I shall restage *Freischütz*, and you will be amazed! Not a single one of the soloists will keep his role, because when casting one must consider the man as a whole, not only his voice. If I don't have the right singer for each part, I will cast the whole thing with guest artists rather than use someone unsuitable.[128]

A year later, in October 1898, Mahler kept his word. He presented the opera in its original form, three acts instead of four, for the first time in Vienna. The final trio of the Wolfsschlucht scene was played in front of the curtain. It was followed by a short pause which allowed the change of scenery to be completed.

---

[127] According to Helm, Mahler conducted the Overture 'in the manner of Wagner and Bülow', with the introduction very slow and soft and the numerous stirring changes of tempo in the Allegro. Hirschfeld considered Mahler to be 'Wagner's chief heir', because of the way he contrasted slow and fast tempos, creating a strong tension from the very first bars.

[128] NBL1. 77; NBL2. 89.

Mahler hesitated for a long time before casting Kaspar, as he considered neither of the Opera's basses was completely suitable; Reichenberg was too debonair, and Hesch ridiculous because of his Czech accent. In the end Mahler chose a baritone, Josef Ritter,[129] who managed, thanks to his intelligence and artistry and in spite of his vocal deficiencies, to bring out the demonic nature of the character. His aria had, of course, to be transposed, but apart from Kalbeck, most of the Viennese critics were not disturbed by this daring innovation.

Hanslick, though he found the ideas behind the new production excellent, for the previous one had been grotesque, nevertheless considered that the staging of the Wolfsschlucht episode was too bleak and bare.[130] Hirschfeld blamed Mahler for trying to impose 'dramatic logic' on the opera, for depriving it of its 'childlike magic', its make-believe ghosts, its good old Singspiel naïveté, and for turning it into a 'music-drama—an opera for the educated'.[131] Like his colleagues, Kalbeck criticized the bareness of the sets, but unlike Hirschfeld, he praised Mahler for trying to give back to the work 'its simplicity and legendary character' by stripping it of the refinements and splendours of *opera seria*.[132]

Besides putting on three new *Neueinstudierungen*, Mahler spent much time improving the ones he could not restage completely. On 29 October he gave Vienna its first uncut performance of *Tristan*.[133] It was very well received, though the theatre was not full. Fortunately, just over two months later, on 7 January, the opera's fiftieth performance in Vienna played to a full house. Henceforth Mahler stopped presenting separate parts of the *Ring* and gave instead the complete uncut cycle several times a year.[134] On 5 November, after a performance of *Don Giovanni*, the second conducted by Mahler in Vienna, Kalbeck noted that in spite of 'some mistakes and inadequacies, the masterful touch of the new conductor was noticeable, even after only one rehearsal. . . .

[129] Born in 1859 in Salzburg, Josef Ritter started his theatrical career in Munich. There followed an engagement by Pollini in Hamburg. He joined the Vienna Opera in 1889, where he was highly successful in most of the big baritone roles: Don Giovanni, Pizarro, Rigoletto, Alberich, etc. Unfortunately his voice tired early and from 1901 he could no longer manage the leading roles. Nevertheless Mahler kept him on at the Opera until 1905, considering him still indispensable for certain parts. In 1907 Ritter became afflicted with religious mania, and ended his days in an asylum.

[130] According to Helm (*Musikalisches Wochenblatt* (1899), 101), Mahler was later forced to replace some of the 'apparitions' he had cut. Cast of the first performance on 21 Oct.: Michalek (Ännchen), Forster (Agathe), Schrödter (Max), Spielmann (Kilian), Ritter (Kaspar), Neidl (Fürst), Hesch (Eremit).

[131] Hirschfeld also praised Mahler's 'magnificent artistic work', his suppression of meaningless appoggiaturas, the 'nobility of the phrasing' and the 'tender mezza voce effects'.

[132] Kalbeck considered the 'marvellously staged' Finale in the last act the crowning moment of the performance. Schrödter and Forster sang 'in a much more natural and feeling manner than before'.

[133] The performance lasted from 7 to 11.30 p.m. Cast: Sedlmair (Isolde), Winkelmann (Tristan).

[134] Four complete cycles in the 1898–9 season. Mahler had ordered a new red velvet curtain, which opened in the centre, as in Bayreuth, to enable the singers to take their bows. In the *Wochenblatt*, Helm reported that the Intendant had refused to bring forward the starting time, but that although *Götterdämmerung* on 1 Jan. had lasted from 7 p.m. to 11.45, not a single person had left before the final chord.

How much deep-rooted prejudice and inherited error still have to be swept away!' he added. 'The will to clean things up is there and also the strength to carry it through.' Anything was better than the 'routine of sleek smoothness that characterized *Don Giovanni* in the past'.[135]

There was only one important première in view at the start of the season, *Donna Diana*, a comic opera by the Viennese composer Emil Nikolaus von Reznicek.[136] The summer before, Reznicek had been spending his holidays at Etretat, on the coast of Normandy, when Mahler had summoned him to Vienna by telegram and spent long hours with him at the Bartensteingasse or out walking, discussing the work and its production. At that time Reznicek held the post of conductor of the Mannheim Theatre orchestra and Mahler mentioned the possibility of an engagement in Vienna, though he warned him that, if this materialized, he would insist on having his say, even for operas entirely under Reznicek's responsibility. One day the two musicians took a cab together outside the Opera and Mahler told his companion that the cab driver took every opportunity of showing his dislike, although he always tipped him generously. Reznicek was astonished, as he had not observed the slightest sign of hostility, but Mahler stuck to his story. Perhaps the enmity with which he had been surrounded, and, above all, the press's growing hostility, was beginning to have an effect on his character. I shall return to this subject later.

By August Mahler had informed Reznicek of the date of the projected première and invited him to attend the rehearsals. He even suggested that he come earlier in order to discuss the casting and production. In addition, he asked Reznicek to make a certain number of changes in his score to reinforce the musical and dramatic effect. Some time before the rehearsals, he wrote to him from Vienna, proposing a slight change to the last scene:[137] 'I beg you, my friend, compose these four lines as effectively as possible and send them to me as soon as you can. There's no other way of doing it! And it would be a great mistake not to. Forgive my haste! And let me have the pleasure of an affirmative reply by return mail.' A few days later, Mahler wrote again:

Dear friend! Thank you with all my heart for the now magnificently realized passage.— We're right in the middle of things. On the 16 we have the first *Sitzprobe* [a rehearsal in which all singers sit with their scores, while the orchestra performs the music] and on the 17 the rehearsals with the cast on stage begin. Altogether we have scheduled:

    135 Cast for the performance of 4 Nov.: Mildenburg (Donna Anna), Demuth (Don Giovanni).

    136 Emil Nikolaus von Reznicek was born in Vienna on 4 May 1860. He studied law before taking up music on the advice of Busoni and Weingartner. After studying under Reinecke at the Leipzig Conservatory, he embarked in 1883 on a career as an opera conductor. He took the libretto of *Donna Diana*, his fourth opera, from a Spanish play by Augustin Moreto called *El desden con el desden*, which had been successfully produced at the Vienna Burgtheater. His opera was first performed in Prague on 16 Dec. 1894 and had considerable success in Germany. Knud Martner has drawn my attention to the unreliability of some of Reznicek's reminiscences. In his *Anbruch* article (see below), he does not mention any visits to Mahler's apartment.

    137 The lines Mahler wanted altered start with 'So lass mich denn . . .'. This letter now belongs to Dr Gian Andrea Nogler, Zurich (MBRS 138).

3 *Sitzproben*, 6 stage rehearsals, 6 full orchestral rehearsals, and 2 dress rehearsals with full lighting. The casting has turned out very well. I'm looking forward to a performance that will be to some extent worthy of your delightful work. . . . When can you come?[138]

This letter gives further proof of the attention Mahler paid to detail while preparing a Vienna Opera première.[139] A few days later, after rehearsals had begun, he wrote a final note to Reznicek: 'We all have one great wish—could you have yet another go at the enclosed? Dormitasti, bonus Homerus! More impulsion and melody! Not recitative, but musical peaks! Dear Reznicek! Do it quickly and send it straight away!'[140]

On arriving in Vienna, Reznicek was both bewildered and delighted by all the pains taken to satisfy him. Mahler continually turned to him to ask his opinion. Later in his career, the author of *Donna Diana* acknowledged that never again had he found a conductor so scrupulous, nor heard one of his works so perfectly performed and conducted. On his own admission, the performance was infinitely superior to any he could have prepared himself. Before the dress rehearsal, Mahler revealed once again the extent of his theatrical experience. He warned Reznicek that the invited audience was always cool and advised him to go and congratulate the prima donna, Marie Renard, as soon as the curtain fell. Just as Reznicek was carrying out this advice, he heard Mahler whisper in his ear: 'More, more compliments!' During the dress rehearsal, applause began to break out after the orchestral interlude. Mahler turned round and with a furious gesture silenced it at once. He later explained to Reznicek how he had thus done him great service: 'The Interlude is followed by Floretta's Lied. Once the rule against applauding had been broken, they would also have clapped this piece and then Perin's Lied; as a result the heroine's great aria would have fallen flat, because of its place at the end of the act and because of its serious character. And if this had happened, the prima donna would probably have cancelled tomorrow night.'[141]

The day before the opening, Reznicek was astonished to receive a visit from the old leader of the claque, which Mahler had claimed to have eliminated for ever. He repeated what he had been told to the old man, who smiled and replied: 'Yes, it's true, Mr Mahler doesn't know what's necessary in the theatre. All the same, he can't do anything without me, and the Herr Director will leave one day, but I'll still be here!' Despite all Mahler's efforts, *Donna Diana* achieved only moderate success. Hirschfeld criticized Reznicek's score for 'passivity', 'reserve', and lack of character and originality. According to him, it

---

[138] Undated letter to Reznicek, *c.* Nov. 1898). See Max Chop, *E. N. von Reznicek: Sein Leben und sein Werk* (Universal Edition, Vienna, n.d.), 47 (MBRS 140).

[139] The most telling example of this aspect of Mahler's professional conscientiousness is the letter he wrote in May 1898 to the Berlin librettist Julius Wolff, explaining the weaknesses of his poem *Renata*. See below, Vol. iii, Chap. 5.

[140] Undated letter to Reznicek, *c.* Oct. 1898 (Bruno Walter collection, LPA; MBRS 139).

[141] *Musikblätter des Anbruch* (Mahler issue), 2: 7 (Apr. 1920), 298.

'trailed behind the action' to which it 'bore no relation anyway'. Mahler had played the 'leading role' in the work, lending it unity through his magnificent performance. In the *Fremden-Blatt*, Speidel condemned Reznicek's 'continual *parlando*', his long 'musical conversation': 'Reznicek is not on the friendliest footing with song. . . . In this work, . . . there dwells an outstanding virtuoso of the orchestra. . . . His melodic invention is not up to his technique and sense of colour. From the point of view of melody the first act is bleak and desolate.' Kalbeck blamed the failure chiefly on the libretto. However, the musical style and the vocal writing also displeased him. Helm, in the *Musikalisches Wochenblatt*, described *Donna Diana* as a 'perpetuum mobile in 3/16 time', while Hanslick regretted the stilted vocal declamation and the poverty of Reznicek's libretto, thanks to which 'only the orchestra and the ballet dancers have rewarding tasks to perform in *Donna Diana*'. The orchestration showed 'a virtuosity that was marvellous and at the same time exasperating', but it continually smothered the voices, so that the ear never had a moment's rest. In this case the Viennese critics' verdict coincides with that of posterity. Only a few orchestral pieces from *Donna Diana* have survived in the German symphonic repertoire; the rest of the work has sunk into oblivion.[142] For once, Mahler's own judgement was more favourable than that of the public and the critics.

Mahler was faced with a particularly thorny problem at the Vienna Opera owing to Johann Nepomuk Fuchs's imminent departure and the reduced activity of Richter, whose departure could also be predicted. He immediately thought of replacing one of them with Bruno Walter, who was now conducting at the Riga Theatre. In October 1898, Walter received the following letter from Mahler:

This to ask you if you are able and willing to accept my offer of an appointment at the Vienna Court Opera. If so, I would send you a contract to become operative from the termination of your present one in Riga; we would then see how to get you out as soon as possible. I'd like it best if you could start with us next autumn, as soon as you are free.[143]

Walter later admitted that he felt unsure of himself at that time. He 'needed more self-confidence before being once more exposed to Mahler's powerful influence'. Thus his reply was hesitant and embarrassed. Mahler, who had expected him to accept immediately, was disappointed. 'What are all these evasions in your letter,' he wrote.

[142] *Donna Diana* was performed five times in 1898 and twice the following year. Cast for the première of 9 Dec.: Renard (Diana), Michalek (Floretta), Naval (Cesar), Demuth (Perin). Renard and Naval were later replaced by Mildenburg and Schmedes, both of whom Helm found too heroic for their roles, suggesting that Van Dyck or Schrödter would have been far better suited in the part of Cesar. This he cited as a typical example of Mahler's 'arbitrary casting'.

[143] MBR1, no. 244; MBR2, no. 264, dated 28 Oct. 1898.

When I make an offer, I know what I'm doing. I need an aide-de-camp with a field marshal's baton in his knapsack (at present I am conducting everything and I'm exhausted). What does it matter to you or to the public to know whom you will succeed? Furthermore, you won't be any more accomplished in two or even ten years' time. If one amounts to anything at all, one is always learning. You yourself could not tell me where, today, you could learn more than you could here with me. So have the courage to accept and, for the rest, rely on me and on your own ambitions. I am very anxious to have you before 1900, since I shall be dead by then if things go on like this! Let me ask you again to explain yourself by return of post, and without evasions! You will receive a starting salary of five thousand florins.[144]

A letter Walter wrote to his parents in November shows that he was still uncertain about his future at this juncture. 'Because of my hesitations and deliberations there is a slight coolness between Mahler and me (that is to say, on his side); I've been waiting for the last eight days for his final decision.'[145] In fact Walter, having thought of Munich, Berlin, and Dresden as possibilities, was now almost certain of obtaining a post at the Mannheim Theatre, if Mahler would consent to recommend him warmly to the Intendant.[146] Mahler eventually understood that this offer from Mannheim had been the main reason for Walter's hesitation. He wrote to him in December:

The situation is not yet ripe. I have to say to you, though, that your behaviour in this business has created many problems for me. More trust in me on your side would have spared me this. I shall be able to take the decision at the end of the year. Until then, be patient, without in any way considering yourself bound. I have recommended you very warmly to Mannheim.[147]

Walter for his part resented Mahler's failure to reply to the long letter he had written, and the fact that he engaged another conductor in his place.[148] 'It will certainly lead to a complete break between Mahler and me!' Walter wrote to his parents. Fortunately the break did not take place, partly because Mahler had not engaged another conductor, and principally because Richter finally decided to postpone his departure from Vienna. Fuchs did not leave the Opera until the following year, and Ferdinand Löwe, who had been engaged on 1 October, shared the work with him during Richter's absence. The problem thus remained unsolved for more than a year. 'You have misinterpreted my silence completely,' Mahler wrote to Walter several months later, at the beginning of 1899.

---

[144] MBR1, no. 245; MBR2, no. 265.   [145] BWB 30, dated 18 Nov. 1898.

[146] Unpubl. letter to Bruno Walter, Nov. 1898 (LPA).

[147] Undated letter from Mahler to Bruno Walter (Nov.–Dec. 1898), LPA. Bruno Walter's letters to his parents (BWB 38) show that Mahler's telegrams were probably lost.

[148] This was Karl Gille (1861–1917), who had replaced Mahler at the Stadt-Theater in Hamburg, and whom Walter wrongly imagined to have been engaged in his place (Bruno Walter, BWB 32, letter of 30 Jan. 1898).

As you well know, I was always the laziest of correspondents but, nowadays, every line is a sacrifice for me! I forgave you a long time ago, if there was anything to forgive. Now I never give the matter a thought. In any case, the position here has changed and for the time being nothing is available. So let's forget about it and remain friends![149]

Walter thus pursued his apprenticeship far away from Vienna and from Mahler. Two years later, when he felt strong enough not to be consumed by the Mahlerian fire, he accepted the new offer which came to him from Vienna. This engagement proved to be of great consequence not only for Bruno Walter himself, but also for the Vienna Opera.

[149] MBR1, no. 246; MBR2, no. 266.

5

New anti-Semitic campaign—second Philharmonic season—the Second Symphony in Liège and Vienna (January–May 1899)

> In this morass there is no honourable
> way I can keep my head above water.

THE anti-Semitism so violently expressed on the occasion of the first Philharmonic Concert reappeared early in 1899, in the guise of one of those 'scandals' of which the Viennese were so fond. Following the assassination of the Empress Elisabeth in September 1898, the Court had been in mourning. The city authorities accordingly decided that the big charity ball held each year at the Rathaus should be replaced by a special Philharmonic Concert, scheduled for 1 February. Oberbürgermeister Lueger and his city council further decided to invite an 'Aryan', Felix Mottl, to conduct it, regardless of the fact that Mahler was the conductor of the Philharmonic Concerts and was thus being publicly slighted.

At that time, however, Mahler still had numerous supporters among the Philharmonic players. On 31 December the orchestra committee sent a letter to the Oberbürgermeister invoking a clause in the Philharmonic's new regulations stipulating that the orchestra could be conducted only by its titular chief. They therefore requested that Mahler be invited to conduct. Mahler scrupulously refrained from making any comments or otherwise influencing the players' decision.[1] But the anti-Semitic press nevertheless asserted that he had threatened to resign and thus 'compelled and coerced' the orchestra into taking this action. The director's behaviour was all the more scandalous, they said, because the concert was for charity and Mottl, although his career had taken him

---

[1] Things were no longer the same by Sept. 1900, when in a 'director's circular' to the members of the orchestra he reminded them of the contents of statute 31: 'No member is permitted . . . to take part in public performances . . . for which an entrance fee is collected from the listeners without written permission from the director.'

away to Karlsruhe, was a Viennese musician who had risen from the ranks of the orchestra itself. Anyone else—someone like Richter, for example—would have had the grace to stand down in such a situation. Mahler, however, had proved that he was incapable of a generous gesture, so anxious was he to monopolize the musical life of Vienna. If he was as great as his supporters claimed, why did he fear Mottl's competition? Feelings of solidarity and loyalty should have inspired his course of action, instead of which he had let himself be guided by his Jewish hatred for non-Jews, thus revealing his true character.[2] The Philharmonic had often invited 'guest' conductors such as Siegfried Wagner and Humperdinck, but apparently it could no longer be conducted by anybody else, because the present conductor was a Jew.[3] On 10 January the Oberbürgermeister announced in the press that he would not accept Mahler as conductor for the concert, as this would be tantamount to giving him 'the city's official blessing'. Thus the whole project was finally abandoned.

The fifth Philharmonic Concert, on 15 January, promised to be particularly stormy. Not only was it expected that the audience would demonstrate over the affair of the charity concert, but Mahler had also conceived the daring idea of including in the programme Beethoven's Quartet in F minor, Op. 95, played by the whole string section of the orchestra. Hanslick reported that Mahler had given the following justification:

Chamber music by definition is intended for performance in a domestic setting. It is really only enjoyed by the performers. Once it is transferred to the concert hall, the intimacy is lost; but more still is lost: in a large space the four parts are weakened and do not reach the listener with the strength intended by the composer. I give them this strength by reinforcing each part. Don't we do the same in the orchestral movements of Haydn and in the Mozart overtures? Does this alter the character of those works? Certainly not. The sound volume of a work must be adapted to the dimensions of the hall in which it is to be given. In a small theatre I would give the *Nibelungen* with a reduced orchestra, just as in an enormous theatre I would reinforce it.[4]

Beethoven's last Quartets, which 'in their very conception have a different dimension . . .', Mahler told Natalie,

simply <u>demand</u> a string orchestra. As an example, I would choose the greatest and the most difficult, the Quartet in C sharp minor, and I shall reproduce Wagner's text for it as proof that these works can only be played in this manner. For the musicians, this

---

[2] Karpath claims that Theodor Helm had been literally obliged to attack Mahler, despite the respect he felt for him, and that sometime later, and to redeem himself, he sent Mahler one of his books with this inscription: 'To the faithful upholder of the Wagner and Mozart traditions, to the unsurpassed interpreter of *Tristan*.' (BMG 172 ff.).

[3] *Deutsche Zeitung* devoted no fewer than five articles to this 'scandal'. The issue of 11 Jan. announced that the Oberbürgermeister had finally decided to cancel the concert; that of 17 Jan. stigmatized 'Jewish tyranny' and the 'lies of the Jewish press'. It also underlined the fact that Mahler was not the head of the orchestra, but only of the Philharmonic Concerts.

[4] Quoted by Hanslick in the *Neue Freie Presse* (17 Jan. 1899).

naturally poses new and much more subtle technical and interpretation problems than the most difficult symphonies, but it will greatly benefit them and me, and it is the only way for me to get the very best out of them. The style for this type of work has yet to be created. Not a note of the composition is to be changed. At first I had thought of adding double basses, but had to drop the idea, so utterly solid and inviolable is the construction. You will see what an unsuspected effect the result will have.[5]

Before the concert started, Mahler said to Hanslick in ominous tones: 'Today I am fully prepared for a fight; you'll see that all the Philistines will rise up as one man against this performance of the Quartet instead of being curious and pleased at hearing it like this for once.'[6] In fact, Mahler's enemies were indeed in a strong position and did not hesitate to take advantage of it. Right from the start of the concert some of the audience booed, others applauded, thus demonstrating Vienna's mixed reaction to the affair of the charity concert.[7] According to Natalie, the short, vehement first movement of the Quartet passed 'like a tempest', while in the expressive passages Mahler obtained a 'discreet piano' and 'a magical sound which could not have been bettered by a single string instrument'. However, 'the Lilliputians in the concert hall refused to accept this offering from two giants, one dead and one alive'.[8] The end of the first movement was greeted with deathly silence. At the end of the second, applause broke out, mixed with some vigorous boos from, among others, two young men seated in the front row. Mahler sent one of the orchestral musicians to ask them to leave the hall, otherwise he would have the whole row cleared. They stopped booing, but sent back a message that, despite their admiration for him, they could not accept this orchestral rendering of the Quartet. After the Finale, the audience's reaction was very cool, and this still further increased Mahler's anger.

Schumann's First Symphony, on the other hand, was warmly applauded. Mahler had painstakingly annotated and revised the orchestral parts, suppressing 'everything the composer had put in that could not be played'. The opening trumpets, 'seeming capable of toppling the walls of Jericho', resounded out with incomparable strength and radiance but without violence or harshness. Mahler explained to Natalie that he had obtained this effect 'because I always make the top part the loudest: otherwise it is often drowned if the instrumentation or performance is at fault. For when the middle parts dominate, the sonority is vulgar (*ordinär*).'[9] A year before, he had said:

[5] NBL1. 107 ff.; NBL2. 125. Hanslick's article gives the impression that Mahler 'did occasionally strengthen the cellos with double basses'. Ed. by David Matthews, the score has been publ. recently (Josef Weinberger, London, 1990). The double basses are indeed used to double the cellos, but only in very few passages in the score.

[6] NBL1. 111; NBL2. 128.

[7] *Deutsche Zeitung* reported that Mahler was hissed as he entered, and that the hissing was immediately followed by applause.

[8] NBL2. 128.

[9] NBL1. 112; NBL2. 129. Mahler also mentioned at this time how important it was for the string instruments to be perfectly tuned.

When making music the main thing, which is so often sinned against, is that the lower parts should never be louder than the top one, for then the melody, the clarity and the musical logic are all destroyed. The lower human voice and the deeper instruments are naturally louder. Thus, nine times out of ten the accompaniment drowns the melodic line.[10]

According to Natalie, he had taken even more trouble than usual with this Schumann symphony, so often badly played, and had painstakingly eliminated one by one the errors of previous performances. The concert concluded with Tchaikovsky's noisy '1812' Overture, a first performance in Vienna, which was warmly applauded.

Lunching with Rosé and Natalie after the concert, Mahler enthused about Schumann's 'marvellous' symphonies. He could not understand why Wagner had underestimated, and indeed condemned them. 'Perhaps he had heard a bad, "incomprehensible" performance that gave him the wrong impression. In any case, he has caused a lot of harm by prejudicing most of his followers who even today are stupid enough to look down their noses at Schumann and make fun of him.' Arnold Rosé mentioned that various critics had plied him with questions about Mahler's rendering of the Beethoven quartet. Mahler replied that, even if it was only out of stubbornness, he intended to carry on with the venture and to put Beethoven's Quartet in C sharp minor[11] on the programme for the final Philharmonic Concert.

Hanslick was the only critic to declare that he was not prepared to 'refuse for pedantic reasons a new impression, an unusual pleasure'.[12] In his view, the experiment could be considered largely successful, thanks to the splendid orchestra. Mahler had in fact made no changes to the score. Other works such as the Schubert and Mendelssohn Octets demanded the same sort of strengthening, but these were still exceptions which were not likely to become the rule. In the *Deutsche Zeitung*, Helm deserved even more credit for achieving a certain objectivity. But he still considered that the experiment was ill-advised, because the 'chaste', intimate character of the quartet had been lost.[13] Kalbeck also condemned Mahler's 'arbitrary act'. He considered that a string quartet was a coming together of four individual personalities, of four voices, and that it was unnatural to multiply the number of performers, especially since the orchestral conductor's role in all this was to be nothing more than the 'fifth wheel of the carriage'. Instead of the 'delicate polyphony of four good "friends" . . . there was only an army marching in step'. The instruments playing the middle parts had been drowned throughout, and the overall effect was regrettably uniform and monotonous. Fortunately the Schumann symphony,

---

[10] NBL2. 114.

[11] According to Theodor Helm, it was Arnold Rosé who had influenced Mahler in his choice of the Quartet in F minor rather than the one in C sharp minor.

[12] *Neue Freie Presse* (17 Jan. 1899).

[13] The same thing had been tried before, Helm stated, by Habeneck, with the Paris Conservatoire orchestra, and by Liszt, who had orchestrated Beethoven's 'Archduke' Trio.

interpreted 'with genius', had made amends for the 'sin against Beethoven'. Hirschfeld, in similar terms, condemned the uniformity and lack of harmonic balance in the 'transcription', and criticized the 'absence of all emotion'. He, too, was dazzled by the interpretation of the Schumann symphony, but, like most of his colleagues, he considered the din made in Tchaikovsky's '1812' Overture to be 'antimusical'.

Two days later, at the Opera, Mahler conducted the first important première of the new year: Karl Goldmark's *Die Kriegsgefangene* (The Captive Maiden),[14] an opera based—like Gluck's two *Iphigénies*, Berlioz's *Les Troyens*, August Bungert's *Die Homerische Welt*, and Chabrier's *Briséis*—on the *Iliad*. The action takes place in Achilles' tent, and centres around the burial of Patroclus and Achilles' anger with Briseis, a slave captured during the Trojan War, because she wishes to give Hector an honourable burial. During a lengthy scene with Priam, Achilles finally consents to the burial of Hector, and the work ends with a long love-duet with Briseis. Hanslick severely criticized the weakness of this static libretto and condemned Goldmark's 'Wagnerian' style, his 'tiresome and boring' music, and his 'long, monotonous declamations, sustained by constant orchestral polyphony'.[15] The warmth of the reception given to the opera had been entirely due to Mahler's magnificent performance and the excellent cast.[16] Kalbeck was as non-committal as possible about an opera he clearly disliked: he found its good qualities 'not very obvious', praised the 'perfect' orchestral performance, and noted that the response of the audience, initially cool, had grown progressively warmer. But the *Allgemeine Zeitung*[17] wrote that the Viennese public had been disappointed with this new opera by the composer of *Die Königin von Saba*, and had found it lacking in depth, sensitivity, and power. After six performances *Die Kriegsgefangene* was dropped from the repertoire. As usual, the production had been of the highest quality, though Mahler himself had not much enjoyed his task. In fact he never had a high opinion of Goldmark either as a man or as a composer. '*Das Heimchen am Herd* first opened my eyes to the banality of his music, its weakness and its sentimentality', he had said a year before.

Merlin also deeply disappointed me[18] and I never liked the overture to *Sakuntala*. The only exception is *Die Königin von Saba*, for I must admit that the first two acts enchant

[14] The title of the work was originally *Briseis*, but Goldmark changed it when he heard of Chabrier's opera of that name. Mahler wrote to Goldmark concerning this first performance shortly after his appointment in 1897. The composer said how delighted he would be to have a work of his put on again in Vienna and Mahler replied that his plan was to prepare a new production *of Die Königin von Saba* or *Merlin*. At this time *Die Kriegsgefangene* was nearing completion and the two musicians corresponded further in summer 1898 to work out the casting and date for the first night, and also to discuss some alterations to the libretto (letters to Goldmark, undated (1897?), and July 1898, BGM).

[15] Hanslick had always criticized Wagner's 'pullulating orchestra' that encouraged 'mere vocal declamation'.

[16] Cast of the 17 Jan. première: Renard (Briseis), Walker (Thetis), Pacal (Automedon), Reichmann (Achilles), Neidl (Agamemnon), Hesch (Priam).   [17] 27 Jan. 1899, 63.

[18] He must have studied this score with particular care, for the libretto was by his friend Siegfried Lipiner.

me, especially the scene in the temple. The music of the Ark of the Convenant is really grandiose, there is something of the spirit of the Old Testament in its power and splendour. The rest of Goldmark's music is superficial and its witty orchestration and instrumentation does not save it. Brahms was of the same opinion. Indeed, one evening in Hamburg, when we were returning together from a performance of the Overture to *Sakuntala*, he was even harsher (than I was) in his judgment. That day he was so annoyed and irritated with Goldmark and his music that at the time I thought he was going too far![19]

Mahler's position at the Opera, and the fact that his scores were now available from a publisher, greatly helped his career as a composer, but though he was performed more frequently, his works were rarely well received. In December, Ernst von Schuch gave the first Dresden performance of the First Symphony[20] in the presence of the King of Saxony. It was received with weak applause and vigorous boos and the next day was torn to pieces by the press. In the *Dresdner Zeitung*, Albert Fuchs considered it 'the dullest work that the new epoch has so far produced in the realm of symphonic composition'. He deplored the 'apathetic calm' of the first movement and its lack of inspiration, as well as the banality of the Trio and 'Frère Jacques'.[21] Only the melancholy theme of the second Trio in the Funeral March had given momentary pleasure, but the 'kettledrum orgies', the 'Wagnerian reminiscences', and the 'final Chorale à la Rubinstein' were not enough to make the Finale interesting. This critic found it regrettable to use orchestral forces of such quality for so thankless a task.

In the *Dresdner Nachrichten*, Hermann Starcke was equally censorious. In his opinion, Schuch had obviously wanted to make a friendly gesture toward the director of the Hofoper, but he should in fact have 'refused the Symphony', because it was intolerable to have to listen to such a lengthy piece, such a 'conglomeration of nervous impressions', as part of a Königliche Kapelle concert. Mahler had 'desperately tried to write something other than a classical symphony' and had frantically strained after originality. The first movement, a 'botanical entertainment', contained 'all the pastoral devices known to music', while the 'agitation' and 'vulgarity' of the Finale had 'disturbed and embarrassed' the listeners. This Symphony was nothing but 'tilting at windmills'. The 'lowering of its coffin' had been greeted with 'much booing and hissing'. Finally, the magazine *Neue Musikalische Presse*[22] considered that the inner movements

[19] NBLS, Feb. 1898.

[20] The rest of the programme of this third Königliche Kapelle concert, which took place at the Dresden Opera on 16 Dec. 1898, consisted of an aria from Paisiello's *Prosperina* (soloist Nina Faliero); the *Suite miniature* by César Cui; the 'Chanson sarrasine' by Victorin de Joncières; Saint-Saëns's 'Chanson florentine' (both sung by Nina Faliero); and Beethoven's Leonora Overture No. 3. Later, in 1905, Nina Faliero-Dalcroze gave the first Paris performance of three of the *Lieder eines fahrenden Gesellen* at the Concerts Lamoureux.

[21] The *Dresdner Zeitung* tried to define the atmosphere of this Funeral March, by quoting the text not of the last of the *Lieder eines fahrenden Gesellen*, the theme of which is used for the Trio, but the third, 'Ich hab' ein glühend Messer'.

[22] Yet, in its issue of 1 Feb. 1899, coinciding with the publication of the score, this magazine carried a favourable account of the work, signed by Hans Geissler.

'had shown the composer's talents to best advantage' with themes that were 'attractive and easy to understand'. Unfortunately neither the first movement nor the Finale had proved convincing, at least as a whole, because of the disproportion 'between form and content'. As for the orchestration, it was 'fastidious, but often precious as well'.

In Liège, on the other hand, Sylvain Dupuis's performance of the Second Symphony had been so well received the year before that Mahler had agreed to conduct another, for he wished to 'make the acquaintance of the first town to welcome one of my spiritual children'.[23] The day after the première of *Die Kriegsgefangene*, he thus left for Liège. He arrived there on the morning of 19 January, feeling rested and ready for anything. Dupuis and his wife—'a pleasant young couple'—went to great trouble to make him comfortable, so much so that he was finally embarrassed by their efforts and decided to accept no further invitations of this sort when on tour, except from very close friends, for he found that excessive consideration and attention were tiring when he was trying to concentrate on the work in hand. The town of Liège did not impress Mahler, and neither did Sylvain Dupuis's orchestra, which he thought 'mediocre and rough (*ruppig*)'. However, he realized that compared with the Vienna orchestra, no matter what might be said about it, every other orchestra in the world must seem poor. He also found that the additional instruments needed for the performance had not arrived—the bass tubas, contrabassoons, and five-stringed double basses. He made a final effort to obtain them, and when this failed, he had to alter the orchestration of some passages at the last moment.[24] Luckily the chorus master was competent and obviously full of good intentions, but the sopranos and contraltos still infuriated Mahler by singing off-key. He swore to himself a hundred times not to become involved in adventures of this sort again, for 'the misery of life such as I have described it in the first movements is never-ending here'. Despite all this, and although the soloists were 'very French',[25] the concert promised to be successful.

On Sunday afternoon, 22 January, at 3.30, the third of the Liège season of Nouveaux Concerts duly began. The Second Symphony took up the whole of the first half of the programme.[26] The second half, conducted by Sylvain Dupuis,

---

[23] In his letter of 27 Oct., Sylvain Dupuis reminds Mahler of the concert the previous year. 'I am writing today to ask not only if you would like to attend the repeat of your Symphony, but also whether you would like to conduct it yourself, along with the other pieces included in the programme of the concert. . . . I should be glad of the chance to become personally acquainted with you.' In another letter, dated 9 Jan. 1899, Dupuis invites Mahler to come and stay with him in Liège and suggests a full rehearsal on Friday, 20 Jan., at 1 p.m. The whole correspondence between Mahler and Sylvain Dupuis is now in BGM. In a letter dated 29 Oct. Mahler asks his Belgian colleague to place his symphony at the start of the concert because it needs an audience with 'freshness of spirit'. He agrees to come without remuneration and to pay his own travelling expenses.

[24] NBLS, Apr. 1899. Mahler added that he was also short of a harp.

[25] Undated letter to Justi (21 Jan.) (RWO).

[26] The soloists in the Second Symphony were Marthe Lignière (soprano), who had sung the preceding year, and Mme Caro-Lucas (contralto). The chorus was that of La Légia, of which Dupuis was the appointed conductor.

included Saint-Saëns's *Danse macabre* and two pieces for piano and orchestra played by Busoni, Weber's *Konzertstück* and Liszt's Second Concerto. Despite the less than first-rate quality of the performance, Mahler's work made a deep impression. 'Aware of the importance of the event' wrote the *Gazette de Liège* the next day, 'the public listened with close attention that turned to growing enthusiasm'. 'The matinée performance had been an unqualified success': Mahler was called six times to acknowledge the applause and was presented with a 'monumental wreath of real laurel leaves, sent from Vienna by his admirers'. This symphony, the 'most masterly work of its kind since Mendelssohn', was 'a composition of genius that does honour to the German school'. 'In this colossal and sublime work', the critic added, 'the music sweeps irresistibly over us like an autumn gale.' It was impossible not to be 'electrified by the Allegro maestoso', won over by the good humour of the Scherzo and the emotion of the Andante,[27] or 'filled with admiration for the gigantic Finale'. Having exhausted his epithets, the critic finally exclaimed: 'Masterpiece, masterpiece, masterpiece!' Mahler's splendid conducting had been 'original and impulsive', underlining the 'flexibility of the beat, accentuating the rhythm, and giving the greatest importance to tone'.[28]

The anonymous critic of the *Journal de Liège* considered that

Mahler's Symphony, despite its grand design, is to a certain extent the work of a sceptic. This vast poem of life exalts fatality and the inexorable grip of Destiny far more than singing our sublimated sufferings and joys. . . . One feels oneself engaged in a sort of flirtation with a joy which is lacking abandonment or confidence. . . . The work seems to be analysing itself. . . . This life is no longer simply lived, it spills over from among the alchemies of scepticism and disillusionment.

A strange prediction of what Mahler's music means to us today, written over sixty years before Adorno! The *Journal* found Mahler's conducting 'surprising in its clarity, conciseness, delivering all details with almost mathematical exactitude yet deploying such grandeur despite its wonderful composure!' Another paper, the *Express*, drew a vivid picture of Mahler on the podium: 'A turbulent, writhing conductor, beating desperately with his arms, starting back, his eyes full of life behind the glasses of a pince-nez perched crookedly on his nose, the physiognomy of a dyspeptic, a gnome rearing out of a magic box. . . . M. Mahler's Symphony is a sort of Symphony of Suffering through which we approach God and Eternal Life.' After describing each movement in turn, the *Express* concludes with a panegyric about the chorus's work:

Care with the dynamics, respect for the composer's intentions, perfect homogeneity, rigorous precision, . . . everything combined to throw into striking relief the vast dimensions of the Finale of this Symphony, certainly one of the most curious of the last

---

[27] In this respect, the Liège critic lacked insight, for the Scherzo is sardonic rather than good-humoured, and the Andante graceful rather than emotional.

[28] The anonymous writer's remarks concerning Busoni's performance are unusually enlightened.

few years from the point of view of polyphony and counterpoint, and definitely also one of the most original in terms of the descriptive power of a modern orchestra in the hands of a harmonist fully armed for battle . . .

The same critic quoted some of the remarks Mahler made in the course of an interview before the concert: he declared himself 'really touched by the quality and conviction of the singers. . . . In Germany we have few such conscientious performers, and I beg you to believe that I was astonished by the effects that can be achieved with singers like your fellow-citizens!' *La Meuse* confirmed that 'Mahler showed his gratitude to all, and considering how strict he is, the satisfaction expressed by him in the most flattering terms constitutes, for the initiator Sylvain Dupuis and his zealous collaborators, an unforgettable mark of approval.'

The only dissenting voice in this chorus of praise was that of the correspondent of the *Journal de Bruxelles*, who wrote that: 'This uneven work, performed yesterday, was very beautiful in parts, weak in others. One is too aware of effort, of the desire to be original, and we seek in vain for a sequence or a governing idea in this series of movements so abruptly juxtaposed.' Nevertheless, Mahler went home with excellent memories of his trip to Belgium: 'I received your kind letter after my return from Liège, where my Second Symphony (C minor), which you know from Berlin, was given its second performance to almost frantic applause,' he wrote to Annie Sommerfeld-Mincieux in Hamburg.[29] In June he sent the score of the First Symphony to Liège with the following French dedication: 'A mon bon et cher ami, M. Sylvain Dupuis, en souvenir des belles journées. Gustav Mahler.'[30]

Back in Vienna, Mahler started rehearsing the sixth Philharmonic Concert (29 January), with a programme comprised of the first Vienna performance of Liszt's seventh symphonic poem *Festklänge*, Mendelssohn's Hebridean Overture, a 'Rigaudon' from Rameau's *Dardanus*, and the première of Hermann Götz's Symphony in F major.[31] Hanslick, always an enemy of the so-called *neudeutsch* school, deplored the *Festklänge*'s melodic poverty and its plethora of 'Turkish music'. Its success in the concert was, in his opinion, due entirely to the high quality of the performance. As for Götz's symphony, Hanslick could hear nothing in it beyond the work of 'an experienced Kapellmeister' totally

---

[29] In the same letter (MBRS 129), Mahler enthusiastically approved Frau Sommerfeld's idea of having one of his works performed in Paris by the Lamoureux Orchestra, and offered to conduct it himself. Concerning Annie Sommerfeld, see above Vol. i, Chap. 21. Mahler must have taken the train immediately after the Liège concert, for he stopped in Munich the next day, on his way back, to attend a performance of Siegfried Wagner's *Der Bärenhäuter*, the première of which he was about to conduct in Vienna.

[30] BGM. Sylvain Dupuis's enthusiasm for Mahler's music was confirmed three years later when he conducted the Second Symphony twice in Brussels, on 13 and 14 Apr. 1902, in the Théâtre de la Monnaie (see below).

[31] Hermann Götz (1840–76), organist and composer, born in Königsberg, studied in Berlin under Hans von Bülow. A prolific composer of instrumental and orchestral music, he taught in Switzerland for some time and died at the early age of 36 after having added to the modern German repertoire one of its finest operas, *Der Widerspenstigen Zähmung* (The Taming of the Shrew).

lacking in originality. The critic of the *Neues Wiener Tagblatt* took the same line and decided that it would have been better to leave the *Festklänge* unknown rather than to 'reveal all its poverty'. In his opinion, Mahler had 'destroyed' Mendelssohn's overture by an 'excess of delicacy' and 'countless changes of tempo'.

In the middle of February, Mahler agreed to stand in for Strauss as conductor at a concert of contemporary music (Novitäten Konzert) put on by the Society of Authors, Composers, and Music Publishers and given by the Opera orchestra. Usually, composers conducted their pieces themselves at these concerts but it was under Mahler's baton that Vienna heard the first performance of the two Preludes to the first and third acts of Strauss's *Guntram*.[32] Engelbert Humperdinck, who had attended the première of Mahler's Second Symphony in Berlin, was present to conduct his *Maurische Rhapsodie* and Wilhelm Kienzl two Interludes from his opera *Don Quixote*. Mahler's relation with the Graz composer had always been somewhat strained, yet this time they went together for walks in the countryside around Vienna.[33] Kienzl relates in his diary that the hall was absolutely full for the Novitäten Konzert, and that Cosima Wagner was present with her daughters to witness the triumph of her son Siegfried, whose Overture to *Der Barenhäuter* was also on the programme and frantically applauded.[34] Afterwards a banquet was given at the Meissl und Schaden Restaurant for the three composers present, and Mahler felt obliged to attend for diplomatic reasons, despite his dislike of formal banqueting of this kind.

A week later, the penultimate subscription concert gave Mahler an opportunity of realizing an old plan—that of conducting a Bruckner symphony with the Philharmonic. After considerable thought, he chose the Sixth, no doubt because it had never been performed in its entirety.[35] It was followed by three numbers from Beethoven's *Egmont* music, and Schubert's *Rosamunde* Overture. Placed at the beginning of the programme, Bruckner's work was very well received, but some Bruckner supporters blamed Mahler for the many cuts (in

[32] This 'Novitäten Konzert' took place at 12.30 on Sunday, 19 Feb. 1899, in the Grosser Musikvereinssaal. First Siegfried Wagner conducted the Overture to *Der Bärenhäuter*; then Humperdinck performed his own *Maurische Rhapsodie*, and Wilhelm Kienzl the interludes from the first and third acts of his opera *Don Quixote*; the extracts from *Guntram* followed.

[33] Wilhelm Kienzl's diary (Stadtbibliothek, Vienna) informs us (3 Oct.) that it was intended originally to include works by Saint-Saëns and Goldmark in the programme. It seems that at this time Mahler promised Kienzl that he would go to Prague or Berlin for one of the first performances of *Don Quixote*.

[34] According to Kienzl, Otto Böhler's and Oscar Garvens's well-known caricatures and silhouettes of Mahler were sketched during this concert. However, the English conductor and composer Berthold Goldschmidt is convinced that Böhler's famous silhouettes depict Mahler conducting at the Opera. Here is a passage from the letter he wrote to me on the subject: 'Mahler is *seated* on the podium, using gestures characteristic of an opera performance directed towards the stage with the brass on the right, casting a stern glance at the audience, a flash on his spectacles before the curtain goes up, while imposing a pianissimo upon the first and second violins to left and right (perhaps it is the beginning of the Overture to *Figaro*), all of this seen, it is clear, from a darkened auditorium, not a concert hall.' (Nov. 1975.)

[35] Sixteen years earlier Jahn had given the first, incomplete performance, consisting of the two middle movements—all that the composer heard before his death. In 1899, the work had not yet been publ. and Mahler conducted it from a MS.

particular the third thematic group) and for altering the original orchestration.[36] A convinced Brucknerian, Helm[37] condemned this 'revision'; Schönaich on the other hand approved of it, claiming that it had increased the 'logic' of Bruckner's thought. For Heuberger, Bruckner was 'at once under- and over-estimated'. The work contained 'moments of genius' but it was the trumpets and trombones, rather than the musical thought, that 'vanquished all resistance' in the listener, who was thus 'bludgeoned into submission rather than persuaded'. Two other newspapers, the *Neues Wiener Journal* and the *Deutsches Volksblatt*, defended Bruckner, expressing astonishment that the shortest of his symphonies should have had to wait so long for its first performance, whereas his two subsequent ones had already been performed. The *Volksblatt* emphasized the audacity and originality of the Sixth (*Sechste*) which the composer himself considered the boldest (*keckste*) of all his symphonies. Most critics agreed that the performance had been admirable, and Kauders even claimed that its success was mainly due to Mahler's 'burning artistic conviction', his understanding, and his 'power of suggestion', which had triumphed over 'prejudice and polemics'. As for the rest of the programme, Hanslick waxed indignant at the introduction of a second piccolo into the final Allegro of the *Egmont* Overture, but conceded that the crescendos had been 'stupefying' and the performance a triumph. Kauders, too, mentioned the audience's 'boundless enthusiasm' after the *Egmont* Overture.[38]

A few days later Mahler left for Frankfurt am Main, where he had been invited to conduct his First Symphony at the final subscription concert on 8 March.[39] This time the orchestra was better than the one in Liège and the musicians 'increasingly enthusiastic as they got to know the work'.[40] Mahler was 'more encouraged by this growing admiration of professionals than worried by the lukewarm reactions of the laymen'.[41] When he came on to the podium the whole orchestra applauded with an enthusiasm which contrasted strangely, according to the *Allgemeine Zeitung*, with the 'bitter disappointment' shown by the audience. 'Astonished silence, and polite, rather than enthusiastic, applause', was how Mahler described it. He added that he took only two curtain calls. According to the *Frankfurter Zeitung*, he should not have refused to supply his listeners with programme notes. His work showed 'vivacity of feeling' rather than 'originality and inventive force', despite his determination

[36] GAB IV. i. 660.

[37] In the *Musikalisches Wochenblatt*, Helm wrote of the considerable success of this 'sensational première'. In the *Deutsche Zeitung* he severely criticized the cuts, which he found unjustified, especially in the first movement.

[38] The soloist in the *Egmont* songs, 'Die Trommel gerühret' and 'Freudvoll und Leidvoll', was Marcella Pregi.

[39] The First Symphony formed the first part of the concert. It was preceded by Beethoven's Coriolan Overture conducted by Ludwig Rottenberg and followed by an aria from Haydn's *Die Schöpfung*, 'Auf starkem Fittige', sung by Hedwig Schacko (whom Mahler invited to sing as a guest at the Hofoper), and Beethoven's Eighth Symphony, again under the baton of the local conductor, Rottenberg.

[40] NBL2. 129.   [41] NBLS.

to produce 'something new at any price'. Also, he too often gave way 'to his taste for over-refined, baroque instrumentation'. The *Allgemeine Musik-Zeitung* contrasted his technical and intellectual genius with 'his weak inventiveness and his hollow, puffed-up workmanship'.

After his return to Vienna, Mahler was forced, for purely diplomatic reasons, to conduct *La risurrezione di Lazzaro*, an oratorio by a young priest, Don Lorenzo Perosi,[42] who had just been named director of music at the Sistine Chapel. Despite his music's lack of character, Perosi was considered by some to be a 'new Palestrina'; he was frequently invited to conduct his music all over Europe and, thanks to loud publicity carefully promoted by the Catholic Church, was hailed as a renovator of religious music. *La risurrezione di Lazzaro* had been heard in Vienna for the first time in 1898, conducted by the composer. Now, due to the influence of some strongly Catholic members of the Imperial Court, such as the Archduchess Josefa, two more benefit performances had been organized for 13 and 14 March 1899, with soloists brought in for the most part from Italy. Once more Mahler devoted himself wholeheartedly to a thankless task. According to Robert Hirschfeld, he managed to 'bathe the work in a gentle, noble light', to surround it with a 'halo'. Hanslick, feeling that his age entitled him to speak the truth, deplored the score's lack of invention and lyricism. Only a really devout believer, he said, could escape from deadly boredom when listening to it. Heuberger, less courageous, spoke only of the 'admirable' performance, while Kalbeck considered that Perosi had an 'unexceptional, attractive talent that lacked personality'. Theodor Helm expressed disappointment at the 'operatic' style of the arias and the 'absence of style' of the rest.[43]

On 19 March, less than a week after the Perosi oratorio, in the midst of a particularly busy concert season, Mahler conducted the eighth and final Philharmonic Concert, a Beethoven festival that included the Overture to *Fidelio*, the Fifth Piano Concerto (with Busoni as soloist), and the Seventh Symphony. In Hamburg he had anticipated that, if he were to try to impose his conceptions of Beethoven upon the Vienna Philharmonic 'as trained by Richter', he would encounter insurmountable difficulties. His stormy, dynamic,

---

[42] Lorenzo Perosi (1872–1956) had attended the Conservatories of Rome and Milan and completed his studies in Germany. Choirmaster of St Mark's, Venice (1894), ordained priest (1895), he had just embarked on a career as conductor of his own oratorios, composed to Latin texts. At 26, he had already composed three: *La transfigurazione del Nostro Signore Gesù Cristo*, *La risurrezione di Lazzaro*, and *La risurrezione di Cristo*. His main skill lay in 'bringing back to life the austere melodic formulas of Palestrina and Bach by investing them with all the attractive assets of the modern orchestra'. Perosi's career was interrupted several times, starting in 1915, because of nervous breakdowns of increasing intensity. At the turn of the century, his oratorios had an extraordinary international success. Although his style appears today naïve and eclectic, Romain Rolland wrote enthusiastically in his praise: see *Musiciens d'aujourd'hui* (Hachette, Paris, 1928), 168 ff.

[43] Soloists at the performances of 13 and 14 Mar. (Musikvereinsaal): Amelia Fusco (Martha), Lotte von Bärensfeld (Mary), Guido Vaccari (Evangelist), Silla Carobbi (Christ), Emil Vaupel (Servant). The *Neue Freie Presse* thought them all mediocre, except for the baritone. The 300-voice choir was drawn from various choral societies. The orchestra was that of the Hofoper.

impassioned 'modern' interpretations, did in fact scandalize the Viennese, though not as much as his retouching of the orchestration. But for the moment he was still *persona grata* and in the event this Beethoven concert proved to be one of the rare occasions when he received almost unanimous praise. To his mind, the reason that the Seventh was one of the least popular of Beethoven's symphonies was because 'it suffers even more than the others from bad performances', especially the Finale whose many surprising features called for 'a free and animated interpretation that holds back here, forges ahead there and broadly lingers elsewhere'. The Finale should have 'a dionysian effect' on the audience. To Natalie he said:

You should have heard the force I unleashed there, but it did not sound out of proportion, as the principal theme stayed predominant, and every passage, line and ornament came through as clear and bright as could be. In order to obtain this result, each musician must give all he has, indeed he must give even more than he has, he must surpass himself, as I told them recently. And I force them to do this because each one of them believes that I will throw myself at him and tear him to shreds if he does not do what I want. When they strain with all their might in this way, the impossible can be achieved.[44]

According to the reviews, Mahler's conducting and Busoni's solo playing in the E flat concerto 'had equal claim to greatness', giving an impression of partnership without one discordant note. Nevertheless, Richter accosted Busoni in London some time later and said that he had heard that 'Mahler had given him a lesson' during the rehearsal. 'It's the limit!' he added. 'He cannot bear soloists because he lacks technique and is unable to conduct from the score, which a conductor should be able to do as easily as a pianist sight reads.'[45] But Richter was then about to leave Vienna, and it was with growing exasperation that he viewed Mahler's success and increasing popularity as a virtuoso director who often conducted from memory. During his fifteen years of constant work in theatres, Mahler had acquired extensive experience, and nobody could accuse him of 'lack of technique'. Busoni had known Mahler since his Leipzig days. They had played together in a Hamburg concert in 1894; then again in Liège, only a month before the Vienna concert. Their relationship had always been cordial. Busoni's comment, in the letter to his wife telling her the story, that Richter 'got this off his chest', clearly indicates that he did not agree with him. Another anecdote concerning Busoni's Vienna stay is related by Otto Klemperer. Arriving in Vienna on the morning of the first rehearsal, it seems that the pianist found an urgent message from Mahler waiting at his hotel: he wanted to see him at once at the Opera. Busoni hurried there without even taking the time to shave or to have breakfast. After a long wait, he was astonished to see Mahler burst from his office and run over to him,

[44] NBL1. 113; NBL2. 130.
[45] *Busoni, Briefe an seine Frau*, ed. Friedrich Schnapp (Rotapfel, Erknboch, 1935), 25 (22 June 1899).

holding out his hand: 'You agree, don't you, my dear Busoni, the Finale must not be too fast!' After a quick 'Goodbye' he disappeared again, but not before whistling for him the main theme of the movement.[46] Mahler clearly feared that the famous pianist's virtuosity might induce him to hasten the tempo. The fact that he could treat Busoni in such an unceremonious manner seems to imply that they were on excellent terms with each other.

The critics, then, were virtually unanimous in their praise of this Beethoven concert. Admittedly Helm, in his review in the *Deutsche Zeitung*, allowed himself to suppose that, 'doubtless due to lack of inclination and time', Mahler had on this occasion not prepared a new work. In his view, Richter's Beethoven performances had been far superior. But Hirschfeld, the same Hirschfeld who was soon to give Houston Chamberlain such an unfavourable description of Mahler,[47] found his Beethoven interpretation 'unsurpassable'.[48] Mahler, he wrote, was spiritually 'in close and firm contact' with the composer. The joint exploit of artistic perfection achieved by conductor, orchestra, and soloist had created 'the true Beethoven atmosphere'. According to Kalbeck, 'everyone surpassed himself in paying worthy homage to the genius of Beethoven', while 'the most flattering of ovations' had brought to an end both the concert and the season, which had been 'a succession of brilliant victories' for Mahler.

At the Nicolai Concert on 9 April, Mahler, waiving his royalties, had decided to conduct the Vienna première of his own Second Symphony. This project promptly stirred up a great deal of excitement in the ranks of the orchestra. Two cellists named Theobald Kretzschmann and Josef Sulzer spread a rumour that the work had been badly received everywhere, and at their instigation another article appeared in the *Deutsche Zeitung*, in which it was alleged that Mahler had made a 'mistake in orchestration that one learns to avoid during one's first year at the Conservatory', that he had reduced the sum that would accrue to the Philharmonic pension fund by insisting on hiring supplementary musicians, and that he had 'persecuted' the first trumpeter throughout the winter[49] and then replaced him by another musician whom he had already insulted during a rehearsal.[50] Mahler did not reply to this article, despite the disgust he felt at the ingratitude of those for whom the previous year he had obtained salary increases totalling 30,000 florins[51] at the Opera, not to mention the substantial amounts that he had earned for them by attracting full houses to the

---

[46] OKM 19.

[47] See below the letter sent by Houston Chamberlain to his future mother-in-law, Cosima Wagner, after a rehearsal of *Der Bärenhäuter*.

[48] However, Hirschfeld questioned some of Mahler's tempos, in particular the slowness of the Trio.

[49] This must have been Franz Ginzl, who left the orchestra on 31 Mar. 1898.

[50] The article in the *Deutsche Zeitung* (8 Apr. 1899) adds that Mahler 'might have preferred to throw at him the music stand that he had just had built at the orchestra's expense during his trip to Frankfurt'.

[51] This claim by Mahler is confirmed by an official document (HOA, General Intendanz No. 544; Mar.–May 1898). Agreed on 24 May, a 20% increase in the salary of the singers and orchestral musicians was accompanied by an equivalent increase in their pensions.

Philharmonic Concerts throughout the year. The increase in the box-office receipts had greatly exceeded the cost of the first performance of his Second Symphony,[52] but the cabal that had been formed inside the orchestra hoped to bring about his departure or at least the cancellation of the project. During the first rehearsal, which Justi and Natalie discreetly watched from a box, the musicians were, as always, suspicious, even hostile, for the work was 'entirely strange' to them. But, with a few exceptions, they were gradually won over. Orchestral parts probably used in these rehearsals have been found in the Philharmonic's archives: they include humorous notes added by the musicians, who sought relief in this way from the strict control that Mahler exercised. Thus, at the very beginning, where the score specifies: *Mit durchaus ernstem und feierlichem Ausdruck* (with thoroughly grave and solemn expression), some wits added *im Gesicht* (on the face); the *Grosser Appell* became *der grosse Rappel* (the great lunacy); etc.[53]

Mahler conducted these rehearsals with 'lightning speed and intensity'. He 'stamped his feet when he was not satisfied, slashed the air with his baton whenever he heard a wrong note, shouted and raged when a musician would not admit to a mistake he had made, but calmed down as soon as he confessed to it'. As always, he rehearsed the various instrumental groups separately in awkward passages and paid special attention to the percussion section, which had some particularly difficult passages to play. He kept insisting that the kettledrummer play faster and louder, even when it was pointed out that the drumskin might split, as had happened in Berlin. But Mahler continued to ask for more sound, until eventually one of the drumsticks broke. In his exasperation at constantly being asked to play louder, the drummer finally struck with all his strength and then asked derisively, 'Is that loud enough?' 'Even louder!' Mahler shouted. The unfortunate player hammered more violently still on the drum, his face screwed up with effort, as though to say 'The devil himself could do no better.' Then Mahler shouted, 'Bravo! Very good! And now still louder!'[54] In the course of four rehearsals held within one week, Mahler achieved excellent results by training the musicians thoroughly and teaching them to understand exactly what he wanted. However, he complained bitterly about the Singverein, whose standard had declined since it had been taken over by second-rate conductors like Wilhelm Gericke and Richard von Perger.[55] When unaccompanied, the singers, despite their willingness and enthusiasm, went

[52] BMG 174. At first Mahler had thought of paying out of his own pocket for the additional musicians needed for the Second Symphony, particularly the four double bass players who had to be added to the ten Philharmonic musicians. Ludwig Karpath and other friends dissuaded him, telling him that the anti-Semitic press would take advantage of such an action to assert that he had paid the orchestra to perform his symphony, whereas in reality the orchestral committee had asked him for this first performance.

[53] Cf. Kurt and Herta Blaukopf, *Die Wiener Philharmoniker* (Zsolnay, Vienna, 1986), 228.

[54] NBL1. 114; NBL2. 131. This episode which Natalie reports, was told—in almost identical terms—in the article (quoted above) that the *Deutsche Zeitung* publ. during the rehearsals.

[55] Mahler asked Perger before the concert for a rehearsal with the chorus alone (catalogue of Heck, Viennese autograph dealer).

out of tune. One of the singers, Victor Junk, described in his memoirs how Mahler walked along the rows of the chorus, listening to each singer's intonation, and even making some of them sing alone; half of them immediately left.[56] In spite of all the attention to detail that Mahler brought to these rehearsals, the result was inferior to that achieved in Berlin.

On 9 April 1899 Natalie, who had missed the Berlin première in 1895, heard for the first time the Second in its orchestral version. It seemed to her that the sonority of the orchestra had 'expanded'—up, down, and indeed in all directions, thanks to the new instruments Mahler had employed. Yet they were so well adapted to the composition, so completely 'determined' by it, that the listener was aware of the enhanced effect but not of the means by which it was produced. Despite the deeply conservative attitude of the Viennese, Mahler's personality aroused such interest that the hall was filled to capacity for the concert.[57] At the end of the first movement there was already some lively and almost unanimous applause, but the second, as usual, won enthusiastic approval. The cellos, carefully rehearsed by Mahler, interpreted their lovely counter-melody 'with quiet control, neither dragging nor lacking restraint'.[58] The audience was disconcerted by the 'frightening humour' of the Scherzo and surprised by its brusque conclusion so that it was followed by 'deathly silence, and finally some timid applause'.[59]

Sung 'simply and movingly' by Marcella Pregi, who, Mahler thought, 'would never be surpassed',[60] 'Urlicht' (the fifth movement) was so loudly applauded that Mahler decided to repeat it, not so much to please the public as to respect his own indications regarding the uninterrupted transition to the last movement. In the Finale, the small group of brass instruments placed in the wings was less effective than it had been in Berlin, mainly because of the hall's acoustics. At the end the Musikverein's wheezy organ was incapable of suggesting 'an ascension to the upper regions, far above the crumbling walls of the terrestrial dome'. Most of the listeners were awed by the elemental power of this movement, and Mahler's enemies 'did not express their disapproval as noisily and angrily' as before, his position now being more firmly assured. The applause turned into jubilation and after the concert a long ovation brought him forward many times to acknowledge the applause, and this continued 'right out

[56] See Elisabeth Walmlek-Junk, *Hans Pfitzner und Wien* (Schneider, Tutzing, 1986), 218 ff.
[57] According to the *Neue Musikalische Presse*, Mahler conducted with particularly 'calm and precise' movements.
[58] This refers to the long cello counter-melody beginning at the seventh bar after the no. 5 in the score. The excessive sentimentality displayed by some modern conductors in this movement thus stands condemned by Mahler himself.
[59] Five months later, after hearing an eight-hand piano performance of the Second, Mahler observed that 'the most beautiful passage' in the Scherzo, the quiet central theme, the only contrast in this 'restless brazier' of a movement, disappears completely: he had not been able to bring himself to reintroduce it in another key. That would have been contrary to its nature: like the aloe, it could only flower once (NBL2. 149).
[60] As a gesture of gratitude to her, Mahler wrote the opening bars of the alto part—'O Röschen rot'—in a note containing the following words: 'Don't forget, dear lady, your Gustav Mahler who much reveres you. In memory of 9 April!' The soprano soloist engaged for the concert was Lotte von Bärensfeld.

to the foyer, the stairs and the street'.[61] Mahler was delighted by this somewhat unexpected triumph, not only because he had at last resumed contact with his own work, but also because in his heart of hearts he had dreamt of succeeding as a composer in Vienna ever since he was 19, when he had completed *Das klagende Lied*. The same evening he discussed his work at length with Natalie, but the next morning he had a rude awakening when he read the first reviews, most of them unfavourable.[62]

In the *Deutsche Zeitung*, Maximilian Muntz wrote that Mahler and 'his clique', had gone beyond all limits. Not content with having 'pushed his Symphony forward, as previously described', he had planned and 'ensured its outward success at the performance'. Dubious procedures of this kind were the only possible explanation as to why such a plethora of 'purely superficial' effects and the 'ear-tickling middle movements' could be applauded with such wild enthusiasm by an 'almost exclusively Jewish audience' in a manner which 'defied all the rules of decency'. A public that, out of laziness and prejudice, shunned Liszt, Bruckner, and Richard Strauss, adolescents who had clamoured for 'their Mahler' at the tops of their voices, could not genuinely have detected the slightest trace of music in such cacophonies. Amid this 'shameless enthusiasm on the part of young Israel', boos from those who had been justly indignant over this scandalous success and the insignificance of the music had 'clearly revealed that Mahler's star has begun to wane'. Returning to the attack the next day, Muntz wrote that he would resist the temptation to employ against Mahler 'all the insults and outrages that his clique have proffered against Bruckner, Liszt and Strauss',[63] although they would all be justified, particularly their reproach of 'pompous impotence'. 'Could anybody', he asked, 'discern in all this hubbub a work of art, to say nothing of a symphony?' He called the two middle movements 'banal musical buffooneries' that 'tickled the ear' and 'soothed the auditory nerve'. The whole composition was 'a slap in the face to the fundamental rules of a work of art'. It revealed 'the composer's intention to create a great work, his consciousness of his own inability to carry it out, and his desire to hide this inability with clever tricks'. The 'contrast between the huge means employed and the puniness of the ideas', the 'calculated and deliberate deceiving of the listener', the 'pompous sham, comparable to that of Meyerbeer', the 'total absence of original ideas and motives', the 'shameless pillage of the most diverse musical sources, Weber, Bruckner, Wagner and Volkmann',[64] the 'purely analytical thematic working-out', the 'purely physical

---

[61] Helm was in Italy at the time of the concert, and his *Musikalisches Wochenblatt* article reflects only what he was told upon his return. The success had been 'enormous' but the critics' verdicts 'totally divergent'.

[62] NBL2. 133.

[63] One could hardly describe Mahler himself as having 'insulted' these three composers, since that same season he had conducted Bruckner's Sixth, Liszt's *Festklänge*, and Strauss's *Guntram* Preludes.

[64] The son of a Jewish cantor, (Friedrich) Robert Volkmann (1815–83), was a prolific composer. He was much influenced by Schumann and Mendelssohn, both of whom he met in Leipzig, where he studied composition for five years. Later he settled in Budapest, where he taught at the National Music Academy. The

overexcitation of the auditory nerve', the 'megalomania and self-adoration':
these, according to Muntz, were the crimes committed by Mahler, who was the
very 'incarnation of Jewish musical decadence, ignoring all measure, all regard, all restraint in the pursuit of his goal'. His behaviour towards the orchestra clearly demonstrated that he considered it a horse he was 'ready to ride to
a standstill in order to reach his personal ends'.

One of Mahler's most virulent opponents, the anonymous correspondent of
the *Neue Zeitschrift für Musik*, claimed that he had 'no talent whatsoever as a
composer'. Consequently, Mahler did not attempt to write music and was
content to create 'sound effects'. Concerning the sensitive issue of 'programme
music', the same critic added ironically: 'as those who think they know what
Mahler's purposes are inform us, his tone pictures concern problems which
cannot be understood by ordinary mental processes (*ausserhalb dem Bereiche
der Erkenntnissfähigkeit*). Thus we too cannot be expected to make any judgement as to whether the music accurately portrays what it is supposed to
describe.'

Predictably the liberal *Neue Freie Presse* took quite another view. Nevertheless, its anonymous critic[65] also castigated Mahler on many counts. The Second
Symphony was likened to an 'imaginary play', a musical play full of reminiscences, since the Andante evoked the serenades of Robert Fuchs (one of
Mahler's teachers)[66] and the Scherzo recalled Bizet, Wagner, and Berlioz. As to
the great paroxysms of the Finale, they 'lost all concept of harmony and
counterpoint'. The same effect could have been obtained 'without a score if all
the musicians had been simultaneously permitted to rage at will and fortissimo
on their instruments'. Nevertheless, the general effect had been 'favourable,
even overpowering'. Mahler was undeniably a very talented composer, with a
lively imagination and a strong and well-defined personality, even if his work
was not entirely 'well-rounded or above criticism in all its parts'. He deserved
all the public's attention, and his success had been considerable, despite a
'factious opposition'. In the *Neues Wiener Tagblatt*, Karpath expressed unreserved praise. He found the work fascinating from the first note to the last, and
called it a true symphony, conceived along polyphonic lines; its orchestration
was magical and it was directly descended from Beethoven, Schubert, and
Wagner. Mahler was an artist of genius, who must continue composing at all
costs. It would not be long before people began to admire what at present
astonished them.

After this third performance, Mahler expressed his regret at a serious defect
in the work which had not hitherto struck him: the excessive contrast between
the dramatic ending of the first movement and the dancing rhythm of the
Andante. The cause of this was that he had conceived the two movements

bulk of his output is instrumental. Liszt accepted the dedication of his Piano Trio which was also admired
by Bülow and Wagner. His works closely adhere to classical models but his thematic material is often banal.

[65] Almost certainly Richard Heuberger.   [66] See Vol. i, Chap. 3.

separately in Leipzig, not intending to string them together in the same symphony: it would probably have been better to start the Andante with the cantabile cello melody, but by now he was no longer close enough to his work to be able to carry out such a change. Five months later he heard a private performance of a two-piano eight-hand transcription of the Second Symphony, played by four excellent musicians who were all enthusiastic about the work, which they had heard Mahler conduct. Once again, this caused him to make a few disillusioned remarks: tempos, phrasing, expression all seemed to him so wrong that the result was chaos: and all this was conducted and rehearsed by someone who believed he was 'in the tradition'.[67] 'At least this shows us what traditions are: they don't exist! Everything is left to individual initiative and unless a genius revives them, they are lost. Now I fully understand why Brahms allowed people to play his works whichever way they liked. He knew it was useless to say anything. His attitude springs from bitter experience and resignation.'[68] It was probably on this occasion that Natalie sent Mahler the anonymous postcard, dated 5 October, with the following text: 'Greetings, Gustav, the one and only! Whoever today is not carried away by the C-minor is a scoundrel or an ass, or both. Long live Gustav, the divine! A fervent admirer.'[69]

Even before the press started to disparage Mahler's symphony and its composer, he himself had been disappointed at the reaction of most the 'professionals' in the hall, some of whom were his friends. Eusebius Mandyczewski,[70] the musicologist, said for instance that the work showed talent but lacked 'unity in the developments and true thematic progression'. 'As though it were possible to form the slightest judgement on a single hearing,' said an exasperated Mahler. 'These gentlemen always attribute their disappointment to the work and its author, without realizing that their own limited capacity of judgement and understanding might be at fault.' After having condemned the symphony roundly, the Viennese critics he met in cafés and restaurants were constantly trying to talk to him and seemed to enjoy his company more than ever, while he, on the other hand, enjoyed theirs less than ever. One day he gave vent to his exasperation to Natalie, claiming that he had told some of them that, for his Third Symphony, in order to obtain a mournful, hollow sound, he would have human skulls (those of critics, of course) knocked against each other. 'To obtain the particularly high notes required for this work, he would satisfy his own bloodthirsty instincts by having some musicians slaughtered before the concert (to punish them for their carelessness) and would use their skins for the

---

[67] This would seem to have been Bruno Walter, yet the letter he wrote to his parents on 23 Nov. 1899 proves that he did not visit Vienna in Nov. (BWB 37). Heinrich von Bocklet's arrangement for two pianos, eight hands, was only publ. by Universal Edition in 1914. Thus the performance Mahler attended on 12 Nov. 1899 must have been played from MS.

[68] NBL1. 132; NBL2. 149.　　　[69] PML.

[70] Eusebius Mandyczewski (1857–1929) was a friend of Brahms, editor of the complete works of Haydn and Schubert, a professor at the Vienna Conservatory, head librarian of the Musikverein, and occasionally a composer.

drums—unless the critics would offer him their own, which would be every bit as good as oxhides.'[71]

Mahler's feelings towards Vienna critics can be readily understood when one reads the vitriolic review published in *Die Reichswehr* by Hans Liebstöckl, undoubtedly Vienna's most gifted pamphleteer. Although he and Liebstöckl disagreed about Mahler, Julius Korngold paid tribute in his Memoirs to his young colleague's wit, irony, and the fact that he was unaffected by considerations of fashion.[72] Wagner was so much of a religion for Liebstöckl that he was more than reserved towards his successors, including Richard Strauss.

On 10 April, Liebstöckl sharpened his claws in a short summary describing Mahler's symphony as 'four-dimensional music', with the sound reaching the listener 'from left and right, above and below'. The work was full of 'infernal noises' rather than 'melodic invention' and he planned to return to the subject soon. Sure enough, two days later, the same newspaper published the following masterpiece of irony, under the same signature:

The symphony is sick and will probably die; not because Herr Felix Weingarttner recently gave us such a favourable bulletin concerning its health—Herr Weingartner is inclined to take responsibility for things he cannot talk about—but because of conductors who compose. No matter that, as the symphony withers people are transplanting it to the tropical regions of the Opera house; what grows in its place will simply no longer be called a symphony; even today, as the shroud is slipped on, one hears the shame-faced description 'symphonic poem', and bids it a happy putrefaction. Hans Richter and Ferdinand Löwe have kept well away from the dangerous temptation to ease the symphony's demise in this way. They do not compose at all. Löwe once frankly admitted that he had tried but had soon found he had nothing special to say. Courageous self-awareness that does this artist credit. Herr Mahler's temperament is less attuned to such fine inner promptings. This cannot be altered; the two-child family unfortunately does not apply to symphonic composers, so Mahler's Second Symphony will acquire more brothers and sisters until they number nine, or ten, or twelve, since even in Beethoven's times, to quote a minor example, it was sometimes customary to stop at nine. Admittedly no one knows whether the ideas that come to him, or may come to him, will stretch to nine symphonies, for nine symphonies demand a great deal of time, and one hopes to be safely in the land of eternal glory before sundown. For young composers seeking sudden fame it is probably advisable, therefore, to start straight away with their 'Ninth' and then to stop with their second, if there are enough ideas and enough time. Gustav Mahler, after his First Symphony, immediately opted for his—ninth. It is self-evident that such a ninth must set out in search of a problem, that it must, with increasing clamour, raise a problem concerning life or humanity, which—even through music—cannot be solved, but which allows you to behave as if it had been. Everything in it must aim straight for immortality. An orchestra of 130 was assembled, a mixed chorus bespoken, things got quite lively below the podium and

[71] NBL2. 133.

[72] Hans Liebstöckl (1872–1908) reviewed concerts and operas for *Die Reichswehr* and the *Illustrirtes Wiener Extrablatt* throughout Mahler's directorship. He died of heart-disease shortly after Mahler left Vienna.

soon even the quiet corridors of the Musikvereinssaal echoed with 'voices calling in the wilderness' and were shaken by the blare of the Last Trump . . .

The following description of each movement does not have the same verve. Liebstöckl's list of Mahler's reminiscences resembles those of his colleagues: Beethoven, Schubert, and Weber; *Parsifal*, *Lohengrin*, the *Ring*; and even Tchaikovsky and Dvořák. But he continues in better vein:

The fourth movement brings us Mahler the philosopher, who has steeped himself in *Des Knaben Wunderhorn*. At this point Marcella Pregi sang a melody derived from Mozart on the innocent plaint of the 'Röschen roth'. It was the best part of the whole thing. But now, while the child awaits the 'tiny light' that God is supposed to give him, the Last Judgment breaks upon us, in 'Scherzo tempo'. What follows is music of the fourth dimension. It is impossible to describe what happens. No two bars come from the same place, the 'voice in the wilderness' is heard from the corridor, against the background of a choral march, the poor sinners' teeth chatter in tremolando while they chromatically pour out their tortured hearts, until at last a long procession marches by with a resurrected piccolo at its head. The hubbub is repeated several times: there is thunder and lightning, one hears moaning and cries for help, and fractured triplets whimper. Then finally in the 'Last Trump' a canary breaks triumphantly through all the cacophony, while the choir, amid a truly hellish dim, tries to make us understand that it embodies the idea of resurrection. The Last Judgment concludes with a fortissimo involving the whole orchestra 'in a supreme deployment of force'. I cannot help it, despite the great applause of a public which formerly so strongly voiced its dislike of Richard Strauss's incomparable *Also sprach Zarathustra*, all this theatrical noise strikes me as high school student stuff. . . . A bold orchestral leap beyond the stars to— a heap of burnt-out cinders.

Throughout this busy and varied concert season, Mahler's work at the Opera did not slacken. In February there were first performances of two early works: Haydn's *Der Apotheker* (*Lo Speziale*) and Lortzing's *Die Opernprobe* (The Opera Rehearsal). Haydn's little comedy, borrowed from a Goldoni play, had been translated and 'adapted' by the critic Robert Hirschfeld[73] and had already been conducted by Mahler in Hamburg. Again he accompanied the recitatives himself on the piano and replaced the lost Overture[74] with the 'London' Symphony (No. 104), which, according to Hanslick, he performed 'in an unforgettable manner, perhaps never equalled anywhere in the world'. The story of the old apothecary Sempronio, infatuated with his pretty niece, whom he loses to a young suitor after being tricked many times, was in the standard *commedia dell'arte* tradition. Hanslick praised the imagination displayed in Haydn's ensembles and called the whole revival a delight, thanks to the perfect direction and casting.[75] Helm, on the other hand, found this little opera 'too pure and

---

[73] It had already been given in the Vienna Carltheater in 1895 as a benefit performance.

[74] It has since been recovered.

[75] According to Hanslick, 18th-cent. style had 'become foreign' to singers. Hesch, with his Czech accent that was such a problem in serious roles, had brought a 'delicious savour' to the principal role. Cast of the 10 Feb. première: *Der Apotheker*: Michalek (Griletta), Pohlner (Volpino), Schrödter (Mengone), Hesch

too light' for a vast opera-house, but Hirschfeld congratulated Mahler on devoting all his art and all his efforts to 'helping us to enjoy and appreciate Haydn's work'. The accompaniment to the recitatives was 'airy and free' and the whole performance had been characterized by a freshness, a vivacity, an improvisatory style perfectly suited to an *opera buffa*.

Die Opernprobe, based on an old French play by Philippe Poisson[76] called *L'Impromptu de Champagne*, was the swan-song of Albert Lortzing, the German opera composer who died at 50 in poverty, after being vastly underrated in Vienna where he conducted during the last years of his life.[77] Hanslick praised the exquisite freshness of the work while admitting that it was not on a level with *Der Waffenschmied* or *Zar und Zimmermann*. The composer's libretto, like all those by Lortzing, was delightful, and this was one of the all-too-rare German comic operas worthy of revival. Hirschfeld marvelled at Mahler's 'matchless sense of style', which had been true to the score's real values, while avoiding two hidden dangers, an 'excess of old-fashioned stiffness' and an over-sophisticated modern attitude.

The only important première in the 1898–9 season was a work by a new operatic composer who bore a great name, since he was none other than the only son of the composer of the *Ring*. Richard Wagner had encouraged Siegfried to take up architecture, but the boy, who was only 14 when his father died, had later studied music under such celebrated teachers as Richter and Humperdinck and had finally decided to write operas. His first, *Der Bärenhäuter* (The Sluggard), performed in Munich on 22 January 1899, had been favourably received, something which it would be unfair to attribute entirely to its composer's name. In a libretto, written by himself ('there are obligations one cannot escape when one bears the name of Wagner', Hanslick remarked ironically), Siegfried relates the adventures of a young soldier named Hans Kraft, who descends into hell and is employed there to heat up Satan's cauldrons. He is saved by St Peter, who wins his soul at dice. The devil takes his revenge by turning the soldier into a dirty, lice-ridden vagabond who is redeemed in the last act by the love of a young girl. The Wagnerian influence is easy to detect: the idea of redemption by love, the legendary subject borrowed from the world of the sagas, the journey into hell, and so on. Siegfried Wagner, having studied music rather too late, lacked both technical skill and originality, but he made a wise choice in turning to folklore

(Sempronio). *Die Opernprobe*: Michalek (Louise), Baier (Countess), Forster (Hannchen), Naval (Adolf), Demuth (Johann), Felix (Christopher), Hesch (Count). *Der Apotheker* was performed six times, *Die Opernprobe* eleven times. The *Neue Freie Presse* of 14 Feb. noted that Mahler had used a 'pianino' (probably an upright) to accompany the recitatives.

[76] Philippe Poisson (1662–1743) was an actor at the Théâtre-Français. *L'Impromptu de Champagne* dates from 1733.

[77] At that time a composer's rights were so badly protected that even the most famous musicians could not manage to live on them. Hence, the tremendous difficulties Wagner had to face in his early years, and Weber throughout his life.

for his inspiration, in order to escape, as much as possible, the influence of his great father.

The *Bärenhäuter*'s success, both with the Viennese public and the critics, can be measured by the fact that it was performed eighteen times in 1898 alone. Mahler was fully aware of the work's weaknesses and deserves all the more credit for having staged it and produced it with his usual scrupulous care.[78] In his opinion,

the quality of the work was insufficient to interest the intelligentsia; neither was it likely to appeal to the general public, who were impressed by Mascagni and Leoncavallo. . . . The first act is so superior to the others that it hardly seemed to have been written by the same man. The melodies have no sooner begun than they are over, but the opera as a whole had a certain charm and an incontestable gracefulness that might be due to the fact that Siegfried was born on Sunday, a lucky omen.

Mahler had made a number of cuts in the score[79] and considered that these were largely responsible for the success of his Vienna production, since everywhere else the work had been a failure or near failure. Cosima Wagner, who now spent more time furthering her son's opera than those of her late husband, wrote to Mahler to protest at these 'inadmissible' cuts, and Mahler, according to Natalie, felt a mixture of utter amazement and exasperation when he realized 'that she apparently rated her son's works as high as those of Richard Wagner.

He did not give way, however, but expressed his opinions to Siegfried with complete frankness, telling him that the last act was 'rubbish' (*Schund*) and that only a 'base flatterer' could have said otherwise. No one could ignore the fact that he was completely opposed to cuts since he had replaced all those formerly made in the works of Richard Wagner!

Thus Mahler's conversation with Siegfried ended on a somewhat sour note.[80]

The conflict concerning Mahler's cuts has left a trace in the form of a letter written to Frau Cosima by Houston Chamberlain and dated 4 March, the day after Siegfried's arrival in Vienna. Despite his fatigue, Siegfried had been carried off by Mahler to a first rehearsal of *Der Bärenhäuter*. 'Nevertheless', wrote Chamberlain,

he found in this rehearsal—alongside many annoyances, probably inevitable—much to delight him, especially Schmedes; and was very pleased at the excellent preparation of the singers. Any perceptive and disinterested person could foresee the many sharp disappointments that Mahler himself was bound to cause him—the so-called 'qualities'

[78] After the eleventh performance (12 May), before a full house, Mahler enumerated to Natalie the faults of Siegfried's opera. In one of the two surviving copies of her MS this passage has been crossed out to make it illegible.

[79] Before the première there was a misunderstanding between Mahler and Julius Knise, the Bayreuth producer who had come to assist with the Viennese production. Knise spoke of 'Gruppieren' (grouping) which Mahler misheard as 'Coupüren' (cuts), proceeding to explain to him why these were indispensable.

[80] Three works are listed as having been revived in Apr. and May, none of them conducted by Mahler. They were Donizetti's *La Fille du régiment*, Maillard's *Les Dragons de Villars*, and Verdi's *Rigoletto*.

of such people consist almost entirely in the negation of the inadequacies of others; they have no resources of their own—but I think that Siegfried, backed by his singers and armed with his quiet, commanding obstinacy, will defeat his impulsive, spineless opponent all along the line. The slight clouds that now and then shadowed his magnificent forehead in the early part of the evening were soon completely dispersed. Dr Hirschfeld (an extremely sympathetic person, author of the beautiful, unique article in *Die Waage* . . .) explained to us very clearly the way Mahler everywhere and at all times negates; it is, so to speak, his only mode of expression; but then, by way of double negation, one sometimes gets an affirmation. We parted, not late, cheerful and confident.[81]

An astonishing document, it reveals a great deal about attitudes in the Bayreuth inner circle sixteen years after Wagner's death. Mahler, as a Jew, was 'spineless' and capable only of negation, even when affirming! It is also interesting to note that Hirschfeld's hostility toward Mahler, which was soon to become blatant, was already apparent in his private conversation.

The truth is, however, that Mahler had made the cuts in the score of *Der Bärenhäuter* solely to strengthen its dramatic effect. Firmly convinced of her son's great talent and faithful to the family's anti-Semitic tradition, Frau Cosima at once spread a completely different version of the affair, according to which Mahler had simply failed to understand the essence of the work he had agreed to conduct. On 12 March 1899 she wrote to one of her friends:[82]

My son is at present in Vienna, to direct the *Bärenhäuter*, and has written to tell me how kind all the Opera staff have been to him. The director, Mahler, was very helpful and has done all in his power to rehearse and produce the work, but has decided, for some mysterious reason—or perhaps one which it is only too easy to explain—to make some quite incomprehensible cuts; for example, all of Luisel's prayer, which must be considered as the heart of the work, as well as all other parts where there is an atmosphere of 'communion': In front of everyone, my son asked him calmly: 'Is it all the religious part which you dislike?' But showing great composure, he has managed to get the most important passage replaced. The incident is all the more interesting since I am just reading a book: Chamberlain's *XIXth century*,[83] in which the author explains that what

[81] *Cosima Wagner und Houston Chamberlain, Im Briefwechsel 1888–1908*, ed. Paul Pretzsch (Reclam, Leipzig, 1934), 555. In HOA, there is an autograph telegram from Mahler to Siegfried Wagner, dated 28 Feb., asking him to arrive on 4 Mar. at the latest to take over the rehearsals during his four days' absence in Frankfurt (HOA, Z. 85/1899). Houston Chamberlain (1855–1927), son of an English general, was born in Portsmouth but brought up in Switzerland. After publishing many articles celebrating Wagner (and his biography of 1896), he took German nationality and became anti-Semitic, germanophile, and a supporter of German unification. In 1899 he had just published his most famous book, *Grundlagen des XIX Jahrhunderts* (Foundations of the 19th Century), a synthesis of the racist theories of Gobineau and Wagner, curiously dedicated to a Jewish scholar, Julius von Wiesner. In this work, Chamberlain spoke of the threat that the 'ethnic chaos' of racial mixing represented to civilization. He later wrote studies of Kant (1905) and Goethe (1912). His friend Karl Kraus benevolently described him as a 'Kulturforscher', and in 1901–2 published two of his articles in *Die Fackel*. In 1908 he married Eva, daughter of Cosima and Richard Wagner. Much later, Adolf Hitler regarded him as 'the ideal Englishman'.
[82] *Briefwechsel zwischen Cosima Wagner und Fürst Ernst zu Hohenlohe-Langenburg* (Gotha, Stuttgart, 1937), 183.
[83] Houston Chamberlain's *magnum opus* (see n. 81).

distinguishes the Semites from the Germans is that the latter have a strong penchant for religion, which the Semites lack completely . . .

Be that as it may, and despite the 'narrow limits' imposed by his 'Semitic' nature, Mahler's position in the world of music was too important for Frau Cosima seriously to think of quarrelling with him. The consequences for the career of her much-loved son might have been unfortunate, so the bridges between Bayreuth and the Hofoper were never burnt. Mahler, for his part, did his best to support a work that owed the only true success it ever experienced to his enthusiasm and professional conscientiousness. In December 1899, he even invited Siegfried to Vienna to conduct it himself.[84]

After the first performance of *Der Bärenhäuter*, Hanslick expressed sympathy with Siegfried for being Wagner's son, but admitted that he had been agreeably surprised by the opera, particularly the second act. In the first and the last, it seemed to him that the young composer had been too willing to imitate his father's style.[85] Karpath, like Hanslick, judged that Mahler's direction had been largely responsible for the success.[86] Heuberger wrote at some length extolling the merits of a composer who, in his eyes, was not an imitator but a well-defined personality, a poet, a 'naïve Siegfried personality' with an authentic talent that lacked only maturity and greater care in the choice of his materials. He noted the various influences in the score, Weber, Lortzing, Nicolai, Humperdinck, and considered that the music lacked a character of its own,[87] yet he found it 'expressive', 'dramatic', often 'witty', and at times even 'ardent'. Siegfried had successfully revived the simple, fresh emotion of 'fairy tales' along with 'utterly authentic German humour'. Only Theodor Helm could find no merit whatsoever in Siegfried's opera, which he thought displayed neither talent nor technique. Thus he attributed its success to the public's curiosity about him.

One April evening, a few days after the performance of his Second Symphony, Mahler felt feverish, and awoke the next morning with influenza and had

---

[84] A few months later, probably in connection with this occasion, Mahler sent Siegfried a cordial letter, declaring himself 'as angry as you are'. This 'high-handed action of bureaucracy' would show 'what I, the Director, have to suffer here . . . Don't let it, I beg of you, spoil this splendid evening'. He concluded: 'Remember, my dear friend, that all Vienna, and especially all of us here at the Opera, are thinking of you today with affection and gratitude . . .' (Wahnfried Archives, Bayreuth). No doubt the Opera administration had decided to cancel a performance or perhaps to lower the conductor-composer's fee. HOA also contains an autograph telegram from Mahler, dated 2 Dec., offering Siegfried four rehearsals before the performance he was to conduct, plus a two-hour orchestral rehearsal. Yet Siegfried, in a short letter sent on 12 Nov., had not asked for a rehearsal, but merely for 'practice for some of the choral passages' (HOA, Z.595/1899).

[85] He particularly regretted the length of the work, in which Siegfried had wrongly tried at any price to avoid the 'operatic' genre with its separation between sections. In Hanslick's opinion, this convention had nothing fundamentally wrong with it, and 'the old name of opera has never harmed good music, while the proud title "*Musikdrama*" has never redeemed what is bad'.

[86] Cast of the 27 Mar. première: Michalek (Luise), Schmedes (Hans Kraft), Hesch (Devil). *Der Bärenhäuter* was revived at the Rudolfstadt (Thuringia) Festival in July 1992, for the first time since 1953.

[87] Karpath suggested further cuts which would enhance some fine passages like that at the end of Act II and the recognition scene in the third, after which the inspiration weakened.

to remain in bed all day. A doctor was sent for, who forbade him to conduct *Der Bärenhäuter*[88] that night. Mahler spent the whole day dozing, which was so unlike him that the whole family became worried. In the evening Justi was chatting with Natalie in the next room when he called to them to say that he no longer had a temperature and was hungry. They kept him company till midnight and then left him with some food beside his bed. This rapid recovery was considered by the family as further proof of Mahler's solid constitution. He caused great astonishment at the Opera the next day when he arrived in excellent health, although the newspapers were already full of news about his illness.

The number of Wagner performances at the Opera was slightly reduced in the 1898–9 season (fifty-five in all, as against sixty-two the previous season), but most were given absolutely uncut. Mozart was performed fifteen times, Weber ten times with *Der Freischütz*. The other most-performed works were *Pagliacci* (15); *Cavalleria rusticana* and *Der Bärenhäuter* (13); *Faust* (12); *Die Opernprobe, Carmen,* and *La Dame blanche* (10); Kienzl's *Der Evangelimann* (8); *Hänsel und Gretel* and *Donna Diana* (7); *Der Apotheker, Djamileh,* and *Onegin* (6).

As soon as the Philharmonic season came to an end, Mahler began to set aside some time each day to revise the scores of the Third Symphony and *Das klagende Lied*, which were about to be published. During his previous revision of the cantata in Hamburg in 1893, he had done away with the off-stage orchestra in the second half, hoping to make the piece 'easier to perform'. Now, he realized that this change had been prejudicial to the music, and he restored his original version.[89] Before the scores were published, Mahler would have liked to run through them at least once with an orchestra. Once, many years earlier, Bruckner had said to Hermann Behn 'Now I'll have no further need of the Schalks',[90] and Mahler would have liked to feel the same about the Philharmonic. But a 'trial' performance would have been of great help to him in checking his orchestration. Unfortunately, the hostility and passive resistance of some of the musicians made this impossible. Mahler felt sad and bitter that he could not request such a small service from the colleagues on whom he spent so much of his energy and attention.[91]

On 9 May a serious accident occurred during the dress rehearsal of the *Neueinstudierung* of Daniel Auber's *Fra Diavolo*. Franz Neidl, the baritone, had forgotten that a cut had been made in the dialogue preceding the second

[88] This was the performance of 17 Apr.

[89] NBL1. 106; NBL2. 124. Mahler also complained of having 'lost the original version'. Perhaps this referred to the first score, now in the library at Yale Univ., which had already been put aside by Justi (unless he found it later and presented it to her).

[90] NBLS, 4 May 1899. See Vol. i, Chap. 4.

[91] The hostility of the Philharmonic musicians continued to grow. Over a quarter of them voted against Mahler at the time of his re-election in Aug. A new anti-Semitic campaign was to be unleashed later in the year by the *Deutsche Zeitung*, which stressed his 'tyranny' and his 'brutality'.

act Finale, and advanced too far downstage: he was struck by the iron curtain as it was being lowered. He reeled under the blow and fell unconscious. Dr Ludwig Boer, the Opera doctor, was immediately summoned, and Mahler suspended the rehearsal. He felt both alarmed and somehow guilty, as though 'he himself had brought about the accident'. During the preceding scene, Rita Michalek, the young soprano, had had to undress, at least symbolically, and some of the musicians in the pit had stood up in order to get a better view of her. Mahler, exasperated, had ordered them to pay attention to their scores and from then on had conducted in a fury, without once glancing towards the stage, while wondering how he could avoid performing this 'none the less exquisite and in no sense frivolous' opera. This was when the accident had occurred, and he feared that he had caused it by his 'angry conducting'. Neidl was at once carried to his dressing-room, where he remained unconscious for some time. Mahler stayed by his side, refusing to go home until the doctor had reassured him regarding the baritone's condition.[92]

Six years later Neidl, now retired, sued the Vienna Opera for damages. During the inquiry that followed the accident things had taken an acrimonious turn. The baritone claimed that Mahler was mainly responsible for the accident and for his 'cerebral haemorrhage', since he had ordered the curtain down too soon. Neidl said that his career had been interrupted by the accident and his subsequent nervous breakdown. He claimed damages of 50,000 kronen, and told the court that Mahler had admitted responsibility by giving him 8,000 kronen for his medical expenses. Called as a witness, Mahler then declared that payment had been a simple 'act of humanity'. He had been able to establish beyond doubt that Neidl had crossed both the limiting lines drawn onstage[93]—crossing even the first of these was strictly forbidden and would in any case have entailed disciplinary action. The baritone had never shown the kind of fiery temperament which could result in his crossing the line by mistake, it therefore seemed more likely that he had attempted to show off in order to obtain the renewal of his contract. In fact Neidl had been neither cut nor bruised, but had only suffered from 'nervous shock'. As to the curtain, it was the baritone himself who gave the signal for it to be lowered, with a prearranged stage gesture. Neidl's responsibility having thus been proved, he did not win his case,[94] but many of Mahler's enemies considered this as yet another proof of his 'cruelty',[95] ignoring the fact that it was obviously his duty to defend his institution against fraudulent claims.

[92] Neidl's accident brought about two immediate changes in the schedule, one of which was the postponement of the revival of *Fra Diavolo* until the autumn.

[93] The first is called the 'artist's line' and the second the 'police limit'. One step further and Neidl would have found himself in front of the curtain, facing the laughter of the audience.

[94] *Neue Freie Presse* and *Neues Wiener Journal* (Jan. 1905).

[95] Paul Stauber accused Mahler of having worn out Neidl by totally inhuman treatment, of having ruined his voice by giving him roles that were too dramatic, and of having prevented him from being paid damages by giving evidence against him (SWE 16).

Regardless of the efforts Mahler made to reorganize the Opera, the critics were as usual finding fault with his policies. At the time of the première of the Second Symphony in April, the anonymous correspondent of the most famous German musical periodical, the *Neue Zeitschrift für Musik*, made fun of his attempts to find new conductors to share his burdens. He ended up by having to conduct all the premières himself. Furthermore, since he was overworked, he did not have the necessary time to search for new works, and merely revived old ones instead. The few premières had been disappointing and the new works ill-chosen, both from the musical and the dramatic point of view. Mahler was apparently prejudiced against the works of the *neudeutsch* school. He was also guilty of errors in casting, of having destroyed the natural balance between orchestra and chorus, of errors of judgement in the engagement of singers (*Fehlverplichtungen*), and in the choice of guest artists. The anonymous critic seemed blissfully unconscious of the problems which face any opera director, for whom it is often impossible to predict whether a new work or a new singer will be a success or not.[96]

Such articles probably did not particularly upset Mahler or influence him in any respect for he was by now well inured to them. Nevertheless, he was sometimes discouraged with the Opera routine. After attending a miserable performance of *Le Prophète* conducted by Fuchs on 7 May 1899, a depressed Mahler was again plagued with doubts about his work at the Opera. He said to Natalie:

I feel like a procurer who has to supply the public with a prostitute to suit its every whim and fancy. If she does not please and finds no taker, I am not earning my keep and must cast desperately around for another one to put up for sale. It is the most despicable profession imaginable. If the performance or the set is bad, I am answerable, and on such nights I feel as if I have done something wrong.[97]

The friends he met at a café after the performance put all the blame for *Le Prophète*'s lack of success on to Meyerbeer, whom they utterly condemned, but Mahler defended the composer, arguing that while he, Mahler, had boundless love and whole-hearted admiration for Wagner, that did not mean that he could no longer appreciate other composers who were 'smaller, less gifted and less productive; that would be like throwing the baby out with the bath water'. About the same time, a performance at the Burgtheater[98] caused Mahler to compare the purity of the spoken theatre with his own 'inartistic activity' at the Opera. 'You'll see,' he said, 'one fine day I'll suddenly pack up and leave. In this morass there is no honourable way I can keep my head above water.' Some weeks earlier he had told Reznicek: 'My position could change from one day to

---

[96] See Helmut Kirchmeyer, 'Mahler Berichterstattung der "Neuen Zeitschrift für Musik" zwischen 1889 and 1911', in M. T. Vogt (ed.), *Das Gustav-Mahler-Fest Hamburg, 1989* (Bärenreiter, Kassel, 1991). The unfavourable review of Mahler's policies as Opera Director was accompanied by a violent castigation of the Second Symphony.

[97] NBLS.   [98] NBLS, 25 May, performance of Pedro Calderon's *El Alcalde de Zalamea*.

the next, for I am quite determined to hand in my resignation if necessary! Even if they throw me out, I will have done them good!'[99] This pessimism sprang partly from the long months of overwork and from the many truly 'inartistic' aspects of his position as director. But, as we shall see, it was also the result of the merciless battle he was then fighting against the Opera and officialdom.

[99] *Musikblätter des Anbruchs* (Mahler issue) (Universal Edition, Vienna, 1930), 298.

6

War with the administration—difficulties with the singers—Alt-Aussee, the Fourth Symphony

(May–December 1899)

Just a test, to find out whether the source has dried up completely.

A S we have seen, Hofrath Wlassack, the Kanzleidirektor and a key figure in the Hofoper administration,[1] could fairly claim to have played an important part in securing Mahler's appointment. But he quickly realized that his 'protégé' was an 'ungrateful wretch'. Intendant Plappart had also become Mahler's sworn enemy, and as soon as he was appointed lost no opportunity to let Mahler feel the weight of administrative authority. Hardly a day passed without some fresh interference, a demand for an explanation, or a complaint about an alleged breach of procedure. When, in the autumn of 1898, Mahler drew up the annual list of contract singers, giving both their current and their proposed new salaries, the sum total of his recommended increases came to 60,000 florins.[2] Not only were his proposals rejected, but Plappart put forward a counter-proposal for a further saving on this item[3] by dismissing several of the older singers. He also urged the need for the strictest economy in general, since under Mahler all Hofoper budget items were already overspent. True, performances at the Hofoper had drawn larger audiences than in previous years and

---

[1] Eduard von Wlassack made most of the important decisions for his superior, Intendant Plappart, as did Prince Montenuovo for Prince Liechtenstein. Rosa Papier seems to have shared Wlassack's feelings about Mahler's ingratitude, to judge from the following paragraph in a letter to Mildenburg written on 4 Jan. 1903: 'It would be small-minded to insist that Mahler show some gratitude for my having so enthusiastically helped him to become Opera Director. But it is really very rude of him to dare to treat me as if I didn't exist, just because he no longer needs me; he does not even show me the common politeness due to any woman. At one time he spent hours in my waiting room, but now that he is married, he never comes to see me; he hasn't even introduced his wife to me, etc. You yourself wrote to me from Hamburg: "He would walk over dead bodies", and you were right.'

[2] 25,000 florins more for the men, 35,000 more for the women.

[3] 24,000 florins (HOA, no. 308/X/1898 and 33.363/484).

receipts had increased, but this was a small matter compared with the size of the overall deficit, which had to be reduced at all costs.

In December, the Intendant sent Mahler a formal reminder that he had repeatedly asked him to prepare a Dienst-Instruktion (a set of rules for the management of the Opera) similar to the one drawn up by the director of the Burgtheater. Mahler complied, and naturally included in it the powers already attributed to himself in the official decree appointing him. But Plappart promptly proposed changes: in particular he wanted to compel Mahler to draw up a general programme for the season in advance, and to obtain his (Plappart's) prior agreement in writing for all decisions. Mahler insisted on the right to make decisions on his own 'in cases of emergency',[4] though he was prepared to ask for the Intendant's approval afterwards and as a matter of form. He also wanted the right to choose for himself the new works to be added to the repertoire in the course of the season. Mahler won this first round, for the changes proposed by the Intendant do not appear in the final version of Mahler's Dienst-Instruktion. This preliminary clash was of great importance because most of the disagreements that flared up later stemmed from it. Shortly afterwards Plappart expressed his lack of confidence in Mahler's handling of the finances in an official letter to the Lord Chamberlain, which was delivered together with a second, confidential letter,[5] in which he recommended the appointment of an official who would be responsible for supervising expenditures and financial projects for all new productions. This last suggestion seemed 'vague and not very effective' to Prince Liechtenstein, who feared that it would be 'open to various interpretations', and Mahler prevailed again, for his Dienst-Instruktion, signed by the interested parties on 10 February, did not limit his previous powers.[6]

No sooner had that trial of strength ended than another began. This time it concerned two of Mahler's 'victims', the stage-manager Albert Stritt and the soprano Frances Saville, both protégés of the Intendant. The former, hired in 1898, claimed that he had received from Mahler 'an assurance that for the duration of his one-year contract he would continue to supervise the staging of operas on which he had worked'. Returning from a leave of absence in January, he had learnt from one of the Opera attendants that 'he had been relieved of his duties'.[7] Stritt maintained that he had done nothing to deserve this 'disgrace' but felt that he could not continue to accept a salary for doing nothing. He therefore protested strongly to the Intendant, reminding him that initially Mahler had been satisfied with his work. Subsequently Mahler had asserted

[4] He wished to have the right, under the heading 'daily expenses', to make small payments to employees for particular work done. That he was never to be officially entitled to use Opera funds in this way was an important point in his long letter to the Lord Chamberlain quoted below.

[5] The official letter, unlike the confidential one, was meant to be passed on to Mahler.

[6] HOA, no. 1560/1898 (12, 15, 25 Oct.) and nos. 1873, 2241, and 381/1899.

[7] Stritt claimed he had been denied access to the stage, but Mahler, writing to the Lord Chamberlain, asserted that he had given no such order.

that he 'simply needed an overseer, not a creative artist, as stage-manager'. At the end of February, Mahler received a curt note from the Intendant demanding an 'immediate' explanation. As exasperated 'as if they had dictated a tempo' to him for an opera, he replied just as curtly that he had been compelled to 'give up using Stritt as stage-manager, the latter having proved himself incapable of carrying out his wishes'.[8] Mahler particularly resented this official interference because he had already discussed the matter with the Intendant. Stritt, on the other hand, had been seen several times in Plappart's office where he had obviously been invited to formulate his complaints officially.

On 28 February Mahler justified his decision to the Intendant at greater length. A singer could quickly be appraised by the conductor and the public, but it took longer to judge the more complex activities of a stage-manager. When a candidate seemed to have the required qualifications but was working elsewhere, the only solution was to offer him a temporary contract, observe him at work, and let him go if he proved unsuitable. Mahler himself had had to carry out many duties which he would normally have expected Stritt to do, and 'it is not really possible to have a clear idea of what that involves unless one has had to do it'.[9]

It is the right and duty of a Director to decide how the human resources put at his disposal are to be used. Even the ill-intentioned, if they respect the truth, cannot claim that in matters relating to this institution my actions have been guided by other than objective considerations; furthermore, it should be obvious by now that I have the knowledge required to judge artists and performances. These facts impel me to point out that complaints like Herr Stritt's should be rejected from the outset. To compel me to interrupt important work to attend 'immediately'[10] to incidents of this kind, is to hamper me in the execution of my duties, and thus to harm the Imperial and Royal Opera. Surely it cannot be the intention of the administration to add to my many and often unavoidable troubles and distractions, and compel me to waste on trivial matters a large proportion of time, energy, and strength, all of which are entirely absorbed, often to the furthest limits of my physical endurance, with grave and serious problems.

Mahler could hardly have been more explicit in telling the Intendant to mind his own business, and stop wasting his time. As for the American soprano Frances Saville, whether Mahler had conceived for her one of those 'infatuations' of which he was often accused, or whether he had engaged her reluctantly, as Karpath alleged,[11] she had won the public's favour and, feeling that she was poorly treated by the director, she had defied his authority on several occasions. Mahler had then expressed his displeasure by reducing her performances to a minimum, which drove the young prima donna to seek guest

---

[8] HOA, Z.156/1899 and Z.331, 14 and 24 Feb. 1899.   [9] HOA, Z.156/1899.

[10] 'Schleunigst': here Mahler is quoting the word used by the Intendant in his note.

[11] The Prince of Wales was said to have personally recommended this young singer (BMG 379–80). She made her Vienna début at the Theater an der Wien on 5 Oct. 1897 in Puccini's *La Bohème*. Mahler had already quarrelled with her during rehearsals of Leoncavallo's *La Bohème*, when she had refused to sing the role of Mimi at the première because her partner in the first cast, Ernest van Dyck, had cried off.

engagements elsewhere to make up for the financial loss that she was suffering in Vienna.[12] Mahler complained that Plappart had extended her leave without consulting him: it must be the director's responsibility to decide both the dates of the singers' leaves of absence and their schedule of performances, as well as the payment of indemnities.[13] Two days later the Intendant defended himself in an angry letter to the Lord Chamberlain. Mahler had complained that he couldn't find roles that suited Saville, and the extension of her leave had made no difference to the repertoire. Furthermore, Mahler had refused to concern himself with the Stritt affair and treated it as an 'insignificant matter'. Both the tone and content of Mahler's letter were 'unacceptable' and contrary to Opera procedure. In another—unofficial—letter Plappart refuted Mahler[14] point by point, accusing him of losing interest in his protégés, of getting rid of them by humiliating them in every conceivable way, and of wasting money with his changes of mind.

In Stritt's case the whole dispute concerned an indemnity of 500 gulden which the Intendant had granted without Mahler's knowledge. Mahler had criticized Plappart for not consulting him and thereby wasting money.[15] The Lord Chamberlain decided that Mahler had been wrong about Stritt and right about Saville, and informed the Intendant in an unofficial letter that, in his opinion, 'by studying in advance the interests of the singer and the Opera', he could easily have foreseen and avoided this 'discord'. In an official letter, however, destined to be read by Mahler, Liechtenstein agreed that the tone and content of Mahler's letter were 'contrary to procedure'. He also accused him of inconsistency: by protesting about the indemnity granted to Stritt, Mahler was defending his alleged rights in claiming that the Intendant had not acted in the best interests of the Opera, whereas, by no longer using Saville, it was he who was open to this charge. The appropriate procedure in this case apparently did not apply to himself: despite Mahler's 'artistic ambitions and the success he had achieved', Liechtenstein felt he must insist that Mahler respect procedure in the future, because 'only those who know how to obey can govern properly'.

Stung to the quick by this criticism and unaware that the Lord Chamberlain considered him in the right regarding Saville, Mahler, with the help of his old friend Siegfried Lipiner, drew up a long report[16] in which he 'defended his honour', gave his version of the facts, and tried to show how the administration

---

[12] She was to receive her full salary of 900 gulden during this time.

[13] Mahler's letter dated 27 Mar., written 26 Mar. (HOA, no. 233/1899).

[14] Plappart explained that he had granted leave to Saville because she had 'already cost the Opera dear'. In her engagement from 8 Dec. 1897 and 7 Dec. 1898, i.e. during one year, she had been paid a high salary but had sung only 20 performances instead of the 64 envisaged in her contract.

[15] As Stritt had found a post in Strasbourg, Mahler felt that it should have been possible to cancel his contract by mutual agreement and without indemnity. It was essential in this case to make a distinction between the terms *Übersiedlungsbeitrag* (contribution to moving expenses), which Mahler would have proposed, and *Abfertigung* (indemnity) which the Intendant was free to grant without consultation.

[16] Dated 24 Apr. 1899 (HOA, Z.568.111/1899).

had constantly placed all sorts of obstacles in his path. He admitted being wrong in the case of Stritt, but pointed out that he had informed the Intendant verbally of his intentions and that the latter had encouraged Stritt, who had said repeatedly 'we'll see who is the stronger, Mahler or I'. The 'urgent' note from the Intendant had exasperated him because the members of the Opera would now be encouraged to defy the director with the Intendant's blessing. Any trace of discipline would thus disappear. In the Stritt affair, he had realized that Plappart was trying to force his hand, but he had none the less preferred not to keep a collaborator whose work would ultimately 'damage the opera'. In the future he himself must be allowed to *propose* any measures that concerned the personnel. The Intendant had usurped his rights in this respect, as well as concealing his intentions from Mahler. Since he was the director and because of his long theatrical experience, it was imperative that, in a case of this kind, he should have the 'second-last word, the final one being that of the General-Intendant'.[17] The Intendant had rebuked him for the tone of his letter, but the truth of the matter was that he (Mahler) had no time to seek out paraphrases or conventional formulas. His 'dry statement of facts' (*herbe Sachlichkeit*) was in no sense a lack of respect but the way he felt he should express himself under the circumstances. After the Saville affair, any singer might decide to follow her lead and oppose the director. Each day new incidents proved to him that he, and he alone, was capable of making decisions concerning the repertoire and the singers.

Mahler then recalled the many reforms that he had tried to impose in the interests of the Opera, and for which he needed the Lord Chamberlain's support. There were many interlocking cogs in the immense and complex theatrical machine, and seemingly isolated circumstances were in fact inter-related. One ill-considered action could be the cause of many more, and therefore no detail could be overlooked. The public, the artists, and indeed the director were human beings, and it was impossible to predict what their reactions would be. Mahler gave concrete examples to support this assertion. For instance, before his arrival, the regulation stipulating that singers who had cancelled their appearances would not receive a 'performance allowance' had not been consistently applied. This had encouraged pretended illnesses and cancellations and had caused the Opera a considerable financial loss. Each singer thought himself an 'exception' to the rule; each one was secretly jealous of—or hated—his neighbour, either believing himself unjustly treated or spe-cially protected; there was resentment against the director, and defiance, thus producing more cancellations—in other words, demoralization. Mahler, on the other hand, had insisted on the strict and unqualified observance of this rule. It had to apply to everyone or else it would be useless.

To alleviate these 'sanctions', Mahler had tried to take into consideration

[17] This was a veiled but justified criticism of the Intendant. All the newspaper articles of the time state that Plappart 'had no theatrical experience'.

proven illnesses and accidents and to soften the blow by letting the artist in question sing oftener. One of the women singers, furious at losing her 'performance allowance' for the second time, had recently complained to the Intendant, who had advised her to 'write him a little letter'. Fortunately, she had not dared to do so but had reported Plappart's words to Mahler. He wondered if the Intendant understood the possible consequence of his act. It could have led indirectly to another singer reporting sick the very next day, to the serious detriment of the Opera. Then, in the most interesting part of his letter, Mahler draws up a long list of the obstacles that the Intendant had put in his path. When he had suggested putting on Weber's *Oberon*, Plappart had curtly replied that he 'was not in favour of it'. When he spoke of *Rienzi*, which he thought could be a great success if it were completely restaged, he received a similar reply.[18] Whenever he wished to persist, must Mahler then expect further difficulties and find ways of overcoming them? While working on a new production, he sometimes needed additional expenditure. To get what he wanted, must he resort to stratagems, and invent artistic reasons he didn't really believe in to make his arguments more persuasive? Such special pleading would tax the abilities even of a clever lawyer, and was not something Mahler could bring himself to engage in. One of the particularities of a theatre director's job was that, unlike an administrator, he could not write reports on the most important aspects of his activity: his profession required him to work as an individual, with personal ideas, feelings, and convictions. Since he alone was responsible for everything that took place inside the theatre, he should at least have the rights attached to such a responsibility. When, for example, he felt completely convinced that sham stage furniture would damage the general effect of a production, and when he was refused the additional credits made necessary by such a decision, how could he persuade his superiors that he was right? When the Intendant told him that 'settings that have been considered usable for years cannot suddenly be judged unusable', what could he do, since this was a question of artistic judgement? All improvements could be vetoed if one thought that what was good enough in the past would be good enough in the future.

In opera, success did not depend on music alone. The charm of a setting, its novelty, the harmony and vivacity of a tableau, a judicious collaboration between action and music, all had tangible effects on box-office receipts. By being obstructive, the administration could achieve small economies in the short term, but in the long run this could cause the Opera incalculable damage, as seemingly small details could contribute to the theatrical effectiveness of a work. Mahler instanced the *Djamileh* production in which the gilt trellis cut off one side of the stage and created an air of intimacy, and the carpet which was unrolled in front of the heroine for her dance; in the *Dalibor* production, the

---

[18] *Rienzi* was finally restaged in Jan. 1902.

barrier that prevented the chorus from swarming over the stage and focused the audience's attention on the central action. Such seemingly unimportant details could make all the difference to the success of a performance. It was sometimes only during final rehearsals, when he saw the work as a whole, that Mahler would become aware of the need for small additional expenditures of this kind, and to be met with refusals, necessitating a further round of demands, had a paralysing effect. On the eve of the revival of *Der Freischütz*, he had noticed that Agathe's and Aennchen's costumes were ridiculous—the first was a dress buttoned up to the chin, and the second a fashionable gown. Pressed for time, and having received no answer to a request addressed to the administration, he had ordered two new costumes without realizing the indignation that this decision would arouse.[19] Yet surely this had been the right thing to do, even if he had gone about it in the wrong way? Furthermore, the previous November, after the scurrilous article in the *Deutsche Zeitung*, he had paid an expert graphologist out of his own pocket in order to unmask the culprit. When a second opinion was considered necessary, he had asked the Intendant to refund him the expert's fee of 40 gulden, since the matter was official. The Intendant's agreement had once more been accompanied by severe criticism.[20] After several such incidents he could not help wondering whether the Opera's interests would not be better served if the administration stopped placing obstacles in his path and obliging him constantly to interrupt his work in order to concern himself with trivia. The time and energy of its director were part of the Opera's capital. Should they be wasted on such footling questions?

Although in Budapest he had already shown his dislike of useless expenditure, he nevertheless thought it indispensable to reward suitably exceptional efforts made by the Opera's technical staff. The simultaneous productions of *Der Apotheker* and *Die Opernprobe* had cost the Opera almost nothing[21] but had required extensive preparation. Was he not right to recompense the stage-hands? After the *Ring*, for which they had worked exceptionally hard, the administration had thanked him for the success of the performances by refusing to pay for the men's midday meals (the total sum involved was 94 gulden), though the performance and even the singers' safety depended upon the stage-hands. The *Ring* cycle was unique, and he had been told that there was no precedent for the men's claims. Yet, during rehearsals of the ballet *Tanzmärchen*, 400 gulden in 'meal allowances' had been paid to the technical personnel. Eventually he had paid the men out of his own pocket for the *Ring*.

In the realm of stage décor Mahler believed that he had already shown how much he disliked any kind of extravagance. He was in fact deeply opposed to it, but felt that he must take into consideration the taste of the public, unless

---

[19] Mahler is careful to note in this respect that, 'resolutely opposed as always to needless expenditure', he had reduced to 45 gulden the costumier's original estimate of 130.

[20] See Chap. 4 and Mahler's letter to the Intendant of 23 Nov. 1898.   [21] Exactly 58 gulden.

there were artistic reasons for not doing so. He had been refused 10,000 gulden to present Giordano's *Andrea Chénier*, though this amount would have been easily recovered by the opera's certain success.[22] Mahler did not envisage building extravagant sets, he only wished to recreate the historic atmosphere, and that inevitably cost money. In any case, that outlay would have been more wisely spent than the 7,500 gulden allotted in 1896 to Messager's *Le Chevalier d'Harmental*. However, thanks to savings made at the start of the season, 20,000 gulden out of the Opera's 24,000 gulden subsidy remained to be used in the autumn.[23]

Once again, Mahler demanded to be given a say in the preparation of the preliminary budget, as he alone knew all the practical details of running the theatre. Surely the administration could make an effort to back him up in his work, since coping with 'the pride, vanity, and laziness of individual singers' took up a great deal of his time—time that should have been fully devoted to rehearsals, preparing new works for performance, working out stage-settings, and searching for possible new productions. One moment he would be interrupted by a singer determined to have a new costume, the next by another complaining of having been 'driven almost crazy' by the casual comment of a critic. Then someone else would threaten to leave the Opera on the pretext that her rival had been given the best roles or because there had been an unexpected cancellation possibly requiring changes in the repertoire. All this was of course part of the daily battle fought by opera-house directors, but the Intendant appeared to forget that, when he needlessly placed further responsibilities on Mahler's shoulders.

Although the Lord Chamberlain's reply is not in the Opera archives, it is clear from subsequent events that Mahler won the argument.[24] A further incident in March also provided Mahler with a splendid opportunity to put Plappart in the wrong. On the occasion of the première of *Der Bärenhäuter* on 27 March, many people queued at the box-office from 6 o'clock in the morning, only to be told at half past 12 that the box-office would not open for this performance, as all tickets were being taken and distributed by the management. There were 'agitated scenes' in the disappointed crowd, and a delegation of 'people of the highest social standing' had called on the director to complain about 'the

[22] The administration also regarded as too high the sum of 700 gulden claimed by the publisher Sonzogno for renting orchestral parts for this production. This surprised Mahler, because most of the other recent productions had cost more. Three figures he furnished in this regard are: 1,800 gulden for Smetana's *Tajemství* (The Secret), 1,800 gulden for *Hubička* (The Kiss, by the same composer), 2,000 gulden for Leoncavallo's *I Medici*. It is strange that Mahler should have mentioned the last-named opera since it was never performed at the Hofoper.

[23] Mahler then detailed the net cost of each of the year's new productions: 736 gulden (*Die Kriegsgefangene*), 58 gulden (*Der Apotheker* and *Die Opernprobe*), and 3,727 gulden (*Der Bärenhäuter*), a total of 4,521 gulden.

[24] When Weingartner was appointed to replace Mahler in 1907, he found the 1898 Dienst-Instruktion 'an old and outdated' document. Wetschl advised him 'to let sleeping dogs lie' because it had never been applied.

cavalier treatment meted out to Opera patrons by the Intendant's Office'. Would opera lovers henceforth be obliged to buy their tickets direct from the Intendant? Such a situation could obviously not continue without doing serious harm to the Opera.[25]

In Mahler's life the clash with Plappart was but another episode in the long series which had begun in Prague with Neumann, and continued in Leipzig and Hamburg with Staegemann and Pollini. But now in Vienna Mahler had won his spurs. He was clearly the right man in the right place and the Imperial Court would support him through thick and thin. The Intendant's bias against him was so obvious that the Lord Chamberlain must have become aware of it and he realized that he had to choose between Mahler and Plappart. For the time being, Prince Liechtenstein was probably content to urge the director to be patient. Subsequently, he discussed matters with him more frequently in order to minimize future disagreements.[26]

In the midst of these frustrating squabbles Mahler thought longingly of nature and the peace and quiet of the countryside in the summer months when he would take up his composing—the only activity that gave him unalloyed pleasure. For this purpose he rented a large house in Laussa, near Losenstein in Upper Austria, but before taking refuge there he had to go to Prague. After Mahler's success there the previous year, Neumann had invited him to his first annual May Festival, where he was to conclude a series of performances of Wagner's works with a performance of Beethoven's Ninth Symphony on 4 June 1899.[27] Before leaving for Prague, Mahler decided to make new markings in the score and searched for clean orchestral parts. He discovered to his amazement that Richter had failed to enter most of Wagner's alterations into the Philharmonic score. As he was planning to conduct the work in Vienna the following season, he set about modifying the orchestral parts, though doubtless because of the scandal it had provoked in Hamburg he abandoned his boldest innovation, the placing of part of the wind section backstage for the march episode in the Finale.[28] The Czech conductor, Josef Stransky, later recalled a remark made to him by the famous and redoubted director of the Court Opera. Mahler confided to his younger colleague that he still trembled as he went up the stairs to the office of Angelo Neumann, 'the man of the grand posture' (*Der Mann der grossen Pose*), just as he had at the age of 24, the first time he visited him as a young conductor.

Magnus Dawison (or Davidsohn), who sang the bass-baritone part in the

---

[25] Autograph draft of a letter from Mahler to the Intendant, 28 Mar. 1899 (HOA, Z.242/1899).

[26] During his holidays, Mahler received a further 'call to order' from the Intendant concerning leave granted to a singer.

[27] The Symphony was to be preceded, as thirteen years before, by excerpts from *Parsifal*. The Prelude was to be conducted by Stransky, the Good Friday music by Josef Manas, and the Transformation music by Desider Markus. Soloists for the Ninth Symphony: M. Ruzek, sop.; M. Claus, al.; E. Guszalewicz, ten.; M. Dawison, bs. The chorus was made up of members of the Deutscher Singverein, of the Deutscher Männergesangverein and of the Sangverein 'Tauwitz'.

[28] See Vol. i, Chap. 20.

Beethoven symphony, wrote an account of his first meeting with Mahler. According to him, it was at a rehearsal of *Lohengrin* which Mahler had agreed to
conduct at the Neues Deutsches Theater two days before the concert.[29]
Dawison, then in his early twenties, recruited to opera from synagogue cantor
training by Angelo Neumann barely twelve months before, had been given the
part of King Heinrich. He described how during the performance Mahler made
the wind instruments sound like a gigantic organ, which nevertheless accompanied the singers with great delicacy! The next morning he attended the
rehearsal of the Ninth. In the afternoon, walking in the street near the theatre,
he heard someone behind him call out: 'Heil König Heinrich!' Thinking it was
a fellow-singer pulling his leg, he turned round and found himself face-to-face
with Mahler. The great man was friendly and relaxed, asked him about himself,
and then invited him into the Blauer Stern Hotel, where he was staying, for a
cup of coffee and a chat. Over coffee Mahler reminisced about Prague, which
he had known since his earliest youth as the capital of the country in which he
had been born. Dawison told Mahler of his musical studies, and his early
ambition to become a synagogue cantor like his ancestors. Mahler, with an
impatient frown, commented: 'But then you would have been lost to the world
of art!' Dawison was reflecting that Mahler, a Jew after all, could rarely have
been in a synagogue, when suddenly Mahler asked him to come into the hotel
music-room and sing him something in Hebrew.

I complied, with joy in my heart. I first sang him a composition by one of our synagogue
authors. Mahler thought it had too little musical content. Then I asked him if I might
now improvise on the basis of words of prayer. He agreed. I quickly ran up and down
the scale, and then began to sing. I sang with all my heart and soul, I put in all the
Jewish *Weltschmerz*, but also all the meaning of the words. The master listened. And as
I came to the end, the old Day of Reconciliation prayer: 'Do not forsake us when our
strength falters', he whispered in a dry voice: 'Yes, that is religious! That's how I heard
it as a child, sung by the old prayer-leader in the village synagogue.' He sat silent for
a while, lost in thought. Suddenly he sat down at the piano and began to play. To
improvise. I heard phrase for phrase the melody I had used, and which I could not have
repeated since I had only improvised it. It had become something quite different. He
clothed the heavy minor mode in other, wonderfully blossoming harmonies. And I sat
spellbound, thinking only how much our religious worship would have gained if only
he, the great man, had not turned away from it and from all that he regarded as a
frustrating burden. And yet it is not a burden, but precisely what gives content and
value to Jewish life! It was as if he was still struggling to get over a violent emotional

[29] The records show that the *Lohengrin* performance took place on 14 May 1899 and not two or three days
before the Ninth Symphony performance. It was conducted by Leo Blech but Mahler might possibly have
been there, since it has been confirmed that he was certainly in Prague on the 15th to attend a performance
of Zdeněk Fibich's *Šárka*. This performance ultimately took place on the 16th. It had been inserted in the
National Opera's programme at the composer's request because he wanted Mahler to see it. But, if Dawison's
memory lets him down as regards the date and the occasion of his meeting with Mahler, the rest of the story
rings true.

shock. Our conversation was at an end. He shook me warmly by the hand, and said simply: 'I shan't forget you.'[30]

Magnus Dawison's unique testimony seems to prove that Mahler, despite his conversion and his loss of contact with the faith of his youth, had by no means forgotten his experiences in the Iglau synagogue. On 2 June, with Beethoven's 'Hymn to Joy', he turned to another kind of faith, one which, in his adult years, had become closer to his heart, that of the brotherhood of all mankind. When he arrived for the first rehearsal, Mahler sent all the musicians home, except for the cellos and basses, with whom he proceeded to rehearse for three hours the long recitative which opens the Finale.[31] The Czech chorus, whose women's section particularly pleased Mahler, worked under him with admirable zeal and proved itself superior to its Viennese counterpart. Unfortunately, the orchestra lacked 'precision and experience', and, despite all his efforts, he could not elicit a performance of the hoped-for quality.

Nevertheless, the Neues Deutsches Theater must have had a festive look when Mahler made his entry. The orchestra pit had been covered over and transformed into a veritable flower garden in the middle of which the larger-than-life and laurel-wreathed bust of Wagner stood out. At the back of the stage, on a high pedestal, stood the bust of Beethoven. The packed hall applauded rapturously at the end of the evening. Mahler was particularly pleased with the praise from the critic Richard Batka, a fervent admirer of Richard Strauss, who now took up Mahler's cause and promised to see that the Second Symphony was performed in Prague.[32] The reviews disappointingly do not discuss Mahler's interpretation of the Ninth Symphony; most of the articles merely list important people in the audience and describe the banquet following the concert, which Mahler did not attend, since he had to leave at once for Vienna.

On 7 June, before going on vacation, Mahler attended the funeral of Johann Strauss, who had died three days earlier. Studying the faces around him during the ceremony and the funeral procession, he reflected bitterly that they expressed nothing but indifference and stupidity; not one of them appeared to be really moved or concerned. Some were thinking of their own affairs, other were

[30] See *Zeitung des Centralvereins deutscher Staatsbürger jüdischen Glaubens*, 14 (1935), 2. Magnus Dawison (or Davidsohn) was born in 1877 in Beuthen, Oberschlesien, and later became cantor in a Berlin synagogue. I am indebted to Dr Bernd Sponheuer for calling this article to my attention.

[31] Josef Stransky's article, 'Begegnungen mit Gustav Mahler', was publ. in the Berlin magazine *Signale für die Musikalische Welt* (19 July 1911), 1027, and the *New York Herald Tribune* (22 Mar. 1931). Seated in Neumann's box for the first half of the programme, Mahler heard Stransky conduct the Prelude to *Parsifal*, and, to mark the occasion, presented him with the dedicated score of his First Symphony. Stransky also mentions the performance of Fibich's opera *Šárka* which Mahler attended in May at the National Theatre (see n. 29). According to Stransky, Mahler went with him after the performance to Café Continental where they had a long talk. They were watched by the well-known Czech painter and engraver Emil Orlik. He eventually produced a sketch on a postcard which delighted Mahler so much that he sent it to his sister Justi, and later on invited the painter to visit him in Vienna.

[32] The Second Symphony was in fact performed in Prague twice in succession in Dec. 1903, conducted by Oscar Nedbal.

discussing copyright or the dead man's will. At the church, the pastor, a Protestant minister named Zimmermann, made an unctuous speech that totally failed to create the appropriate atmosphere, and the Männergesangverein added to Mahler's uneasiness with an a cappella chorale which finished a tone and a half lower than it had begun.

With a feeling of great relief, Mahler left Vienna a few days later with Justi and Natalie for Laussa, a small village off the beaten track, south of Steyr and Linz,[33] where he counted on finding the peace and quiet for which he longed. Scarcely had they arrived with their bags, trunks, books, music, food, clothing, and even Mahler's hired piano, when they discovered to their horror that the ground floor of the house containing all the comfortable rooms was locked, the owners having reserved it for themselves. Only a small, uncomfortable, poorly furnished apartment was left for them above. There was no question of staying in Laussa under such conditions, and all three set out with their belongings in search of another summer retreat—at a time when most of them had long since been booked. Mahler was longing to get to work, and he sent off frantic telegrams in all directions. Ten days passed in this wearying search. As always when he was not working, Mahler relaxed in spite of everything, and little by little his feeling of tension subsided.

In Alt-Aussee, a small watering place in the Salzkammergut known for its saline baths, the travellers thought that they had finally found a haven of tranquillity, and the Villa Kerry (mistakenly called Seri in Natalie's *Mahleriana*), situated a half-hour's walk above the town, seemed perfectly suited to Mahler's needs. Unhappily, he soon found out that from it he could hear the municipal orchestra, which gave daily concerts, on a bandstand in the centre of the thermal establishment, to the people taking the cure. In despair, he complained bitterly of 'his mood being completely shattered' and feared 'that these six weeks, the only ones I have in the whole year', would be lost. 'I can't even just enjoy myself like anyone else', he continued,

or wait calmly for the holy spirit to visit me, for the end of vacation is always hanging over my head like the sword of Damocles. It is torture for me to do something when I'm not completely in the mood and when I feel that the result will not be entirely right. What a poor devil the composer is! A scholar or poet can prepare himself by studies, the painter by the contemplation of nature and, thus inspired, put themselves in the proper frame of mind, whereas I have nothing but this sheet of blank paper before me and I must be able to smell [lifting it to his nose in exasperation] what is going to be on it.[34]

The weather was cold and rainy, as it often is in the Salzkammergut.[35] But gradually Mahler emerged from his depression and began to think about a new composition. As usual, he chose to work in a small, poorly furnished room, well

---

[33] Not far from Bad Hall where Mahler had had his first engagement as conductor.
[34] NBL2. 135.
[35] Writing to Selma Kurz on 5 July, Mahler said he was so cold he could barely hold his pen (BGM).

away from the others, under the eaves. There, late one evening, he talked with
Natalie, who asked him if he intended to finish the Lied he had sketched out
the year before in Vahrn, and not touched since. He shook his head gloomily,
saying that the sketch had not been carried far enough: 'The life of a baby born
in the sixth or maybe even the fifth month can perhaps be saved,' he said, 'but
not that of an embryo, which needs a longer period in the protective maternal
womb in order to reach maturity.'[36] Scarcely had he delivered himself of this
pessimistic prognosis than the effects of a laxative he had taken that morning
caused him to break off the conversation and retire. A little while later he
returned, as cheerful 'as the *Malade imaginaire*', bringing with him the complete sketch of 'Revelge', a new Wunderhorn Lied that he had just jotted down
in his notebook. Later on, it amused Mahler to remind his friends of the
confined quarters in which he had composed this Lied, which he considered
the most beautiful and the most successful of his *Humoresken*, perhaps even
'the most important of all his Lieder'.[37]

It was then that Mahler spoke to Natalie of Carl Loewe, author of the well-
known *Balladen*:

He would understand my *Humoresken*, for he was really a precursor in this form of
composition. But he did not fully exploit its potential and uses a piano, whereas an
orchestra is absolutely essential for a broad composition which explores the subject to
its uttermost depths. Nor did he manage to cut himself free from the conventional form.
Each of his stanzas is identical in every detail with the preceding one, whereas for me
it is an essential principle in composition that the music must keep moving forward
with the content of the poem (*durchkomponieren*). Also, the vigour and variety of
his inventiveness and technique are not all they might be. In my work you will never
find repetition in the music when the verses themselves change, precisely because
music must obey the law of change without end, development without end, just as
the world, even in one and the same place, is forever changing, forever new. But of
course, this development must also be a forward movement, otherwise it is not worth
bothering with.[38]

Loewe, however, was not the only composer whose Lieder Mahler had studied
before composing his own. In Hamburg, he had been encouraged by his former
friend, the critic Ferdinand Pfohl, a great admirer of Robert Franz, to play the
latter's Lieder on the piano. Together one day they went through a volume of

[36] NBLS. Mahler probably used this sketch for 'Der Tamboursg'sell' in 1901.

[37] The problem of dating the two late *Wunderhorn-Lieder*, and in particular of identifying which Lied it was
that had remained unfinished in Vahrn the previous summer, is obscured rather than clarified by these
reported comments of Mahler. His remark about the unfinished state of the sketch was made *before* 'Revelge'
was composed, and the possibility remains that that was the Lied sketched out in 1898. Another remark, that
he had for a long time been determined to set that particular poem to music, but had failed to find the
necessary inspiration, seems to preclude the possibility that he had already sketched out the music for it. In
that case, and if Mahler did not destroy his sketch, the unfinished 1898 Lied could only be the
'Tamboursg'sell'. However, statements made by Mahler in 1901 seem to rule that out as well (see below,
Chap. 10).

[38] NBL1. 119; NBL2. 136.

about thirty, Mahler picking out several that he liked.[39] Here and there he criticized the 'agitated motion' and 'tragic character' of the accompaniments, which he regarded as 'exaggerations of musical expression'.[40] Pfohl realized on this occasion that Mahler had 'no deep contact' with Franz's music, although he found his use of the *Volkslied* in the 'art' Lied exemplary.[41]

During the rest of June 1899, Mahler continued to work in spite of 'odious interruptions and the hubbub of the band, which plays serenades, funeral marches and wedding marches every day from eleven o'clock, and on Sunday from eight in the morning'. His room was very cold and damp and it never stopped raining, but in spite of it all he orchestrated 'Revelge', constantly fearful of interruptions that might delay even this almost mechanical task. For many years he had wanted to set this poem to music, but the inspiration had not come until that famous evening.[42] The first movement of the Third Symphony now seemed to have been only a 'simple rhythmic study' for this Lied, which he could never have composed without it. It was comparable to 'the cross-section of a tree that carries on a small surface the traces of its entire life and development'.

You will be amazed at the eerie, mystical content of this poem which consists of a series of sketches but is never the less intensely vivid: the drummer at the head of his troops passes his beloved's house, then falls on the battle-field and they are beaten by the enemy . . . He calls on his comrades not to leave him lying there wounded, but no one hears him because they are all falling down around him 'like mown grass'. He then gets to his feet and, 'so as not to lose himself', starts beating the drum again and leads his side to victory; the soldiers then march back through the streets of the town, and their skeletons stand 'like tombstones' before the beloved's windows. . . . About this poem Goethe wrote: 'Beyond price for anyone who has sufficient imagination to piece the story together (*nachzufolgen*)!'[43]

The wintry spell of weather continued until 8 July. Although the house was heated every day, Mahler felt cold. This interfered with his work, and he lost the healthy look he had acquired during his walks in the first week of his vacation. He nevertheless completed the orchestration of 'Revelge' down to the smallest detail, instead of waiting as usual until he returned to Vienna. On 7 July, his birthday, he played his new song to Justi, Natalie, and Arnold Rosé, who, moved and deeply impressed, at once understood the greatness of its 'naïve simplicity' and 'artistic perfection'. Once again a poem from the

---

[39] In particular 'Gute Nacht', on a poem by Eichendorff, which echoed 'the melancholy of a Schubert Lied', and two *Volkslieder*, 'Mei Mutter mag mi nit' and 'Das traurige Mädchen' ('Ich weiss ja, warum ich so traurig bin'), and above all 'Lieber Schatz, sei wieder gut'.

[40] Especially in 'Wenn ich ein Immlein war', 'Mädchen mit dem roten Mündchen', and 'Aus meinen grossen Schmerzen'.

[41] FPM 56.   [42] NBLS, 2 July 1899.

[43] Excerpt from a letter from Natalie to Nina Spiegler (10 July 1899) quoted in NBLS. These remarks help to explain the space and breadth, the 'symphonic' character, of this Lied, unparalleled in Mahler's work until *Das Lied von der Erde*.

Wunderhorn had enabled Mahler to 'create a world', whereas a more perfect text would only have limited him.

Despite his worries and the endless interruptions, Mahler devoted some of his time to friends like Arnold Rosé, Siegfried Lipiner, and Ludwig Rottenberg (the Frankfurt conductor), who came to visit him. He also delved into his favourite authors. He read Goethe's correspondence with Schiller, his *Conversations with Eckermann*, his writing on aesthetics,[44] and *Wahlverwandtschaften* (Elective Affinities), as well as *The Bacchae* of Euripides and Paul Sabatier's *Saint François d'Assise*. He found time too to devour *Adam*, Siegfried Lipiner's new verse play, 'with delight and the deepest admiration'.[45] He also dipped into a small volume of Schubert's works which Dr Stöger[46] had sent him, sometimes even during the evening meal.[47] He sight-read works by Handel and Bach and, with his future brother-in-law, Arnold Rosé, played transcriptions of Brahms's Clarinet Quintet and Clarinet Sonatas, which he had discovered with delight the year before. Remembering how he had 'changed his mind'[48] about the Brahms pieces, he felt he could no longer be indignant at the foolishness and lack of judgement of the musical public, since even professionals were capable of such mistakes. Although his vacation was almost over, Mahler seemed at ease and happy, for the household was peaceful, 'partly due to the absence of Emma', whose 'disturbing presence' had sometimes weighed on him, at least according to Natalie.[49] Emma was in fact spending her holiday in Europe, in Pörtschach on the Wörthersee, as can be seen from a card that Mahler, Natalie, Justi, and Arnold sent her from Alt-Aussee.[50] She was about to leave for the United States, where her husband, Eduard, had been engaged as a cellist by the Boston Symphony Orchestra. Shortly after he returned to Vienna, in October, Mahler wrote to Franz Kneisel, the concert-master of the orchestra, asking for his 'support and indulgence' for his brother-in-law.[51]

Excursions into the town of Alt-Aussee itself nevertheless tried Mahler's patience. He kept running into acquaintances there; even worse, strangers would recognize him, follow him, call to him, or stare at him open-mouthed, 'as though he were an outlaw'. He did not feel safe even in the villa, where he

[44] 'One volume of the *Schriften zur Kunst*', Natalie specified, but there is no work of this title in Goethe's writings.

[45] NBLS.

[46] A friend or acquaintance not elsewhere mentioned either in Natalie's *Mahleriana* or in Mahler's correspondence.

[47] Mahler would have liked to see the whole literature of music available in miniature scores that he could carry with him on vacation. The Eulenburg miniature score series was soon to fulfil his wishes.

[48] He had 'discovered' and played them with Arnold Rosé in Vahrn during the summer of 1898.

[49] We have seen that Emma married Eduard Rosé the previous year. The 'lack of harmony' had probably come from her difficulty in adapting to the family atmosphere, and in being continually dominated by Mahler and Justi, as is proved by, among other things, the letters they sent her, which are often about Emma's behaviour and difficult character (formerly in the Ernst Rosé collection which was sold at Sotheby's in 1984).

[50] Postcard of 11 July 1899 (BGM).

[51] Letter from Mahler to Kneisel dated 1 Oct. 1899 (BGM). Mahler reminds the violinist of their meeting, some years before, in Ischl, where Kneisel had been visiting Brahms. Later on, in New York, Kneisel was to become a member of Mahler's circle of friends (see below, Vol. iv, Chap. 6).

received anonymous cards and letters, often from female admirers who wanted an autograph or a picture of him, and there were sometimes shouts of 'Long live Mahler!' from tourists in carriages or on bicycles. Sometimes while out walking he would hear whispers of 'It's Mahler!'—to which he sometimes replied crossly, 'I suppose you want an autograph?' 'All that I ask,' he would groan, 'is that they don't start looking at me through opera-glasses.' With each day that passed he became more anxious to avoid all contact with such idlers, who struck him as simply bored and empty-headed.

As in previous summers, Mahler went for long walks. On 22 July, after climbing the Pfeiferalm by a track that provided beautiful views, he began thinking aloud to Natalie, as he often did. 'Music should always express yearning, a yearning beyond the things of this world. Even as a child, it was something mysterious and exalting for me; though at that time my fancy also added trifles that were not there at all.' Inevitably he returned to his chief preoccupation, the interruption of his creative work. 'During these three summers, I have felt like a swimmer who takes a few strokes just to convince himself that he still knows how to swim; or who tests the water to find out whether the source has dried up completely: there is a trickle in mine, but not more.'[52] And in fact Mahler had no intention of undertaking any other important work after finishing 'Revelge'. He corrected the proofs of the Third Symphony and *Das klagende Lied*, and was pleased by the excellence of Josef von Wöss's[53] piano transcription of the latter work, which he was delighted to find 'clear and easy to play and yet so complete'.[54] He went over the second and third movements of the Third Symphony with Arnold Rosé in order to mark the bowings, which he did not want to leave to the musicians. To achieve perfect unity, he insisted that the phrasing marks must be identical in all the parts. In rereading this work everything seemed so strange and new that he himself was astonished, particularly by the Scherzo, 'the most farcical and at the same time the most tragic piece that ever existed, as only music can transport us with one magic shift from the one to the other'. 'It is as if all nature is making faces and sticking out its tongue; but it also contains such gruesome, panicky humour that it inspires horror rather than laughter.' The next passage (The Night) comes 'like the awakening from a nightmare', or 'the gentle dawn of self-awareness'.[55]

Around mid-July, after these various tasks were finished, the inhabitants of the Villa Kerry noticed that Mahler's absences were becoming more frequent and protracted. They soon guessed that, despite all he had said, he had begun working again, but this time he was composing more than a Lied. Unfortunately only ten days of vacation remained, but, determined to accomplish the imposs-

[52] NBL1. 119 ff.; NBL2. 136.

[53] Josef Venantius von Wöss (1863–1943), son of an army officer, studied music at the Vienna Conservatory. Piano teacher in Moravia, then harmony teacher in Vienna, and a fairly prolific composer, he made piano transcriptions of Mahler's Symphonies Nos. 3, 4, 8, and 9.

[54] Letter to Josef von Wöss (summer 1899), Internationale Mahler Gesellschaft, Vienna.

[55] NBL1. 118; NBL2. 135.

ible, he went on working despite all obstacles, and began to take walks on his own or drop behind his companions to jot down a melodic idea, something 'he had not done since *Das klagende Lied*'.[56] Even during these walks he could not escape the *Kuhgäste*,[57] the idiotic tourists who made him long for a solitary *Häuschen*. He even came to envy Beethoven's deafness, despite the great pain and sorrow that it had caused him:[58] at least it had had the merit of isolating Beethoven from the 'empty' and destructive restlessness of the world and of locking him up forever in his own creation. Fearing that he might forget what had come into his mind, he took to carrying a notebook around with him, for otherwise

> If when I'm out I think of something in my composition that I want to alter, and imagine that I shall write it in when I return—when I get home, it's gone, I no longer have any idea what it was! And it's the same with everything else. If I read something or experience something, and then want to tell someone about it—it's no good, I no longer know anything about it. I'm like someone with too good a digestion: whatever he eats is immediately assimilated into his body or discarded, according to whether he can absorb it or not, but it no longer exists as what it was.[59]

On 21 July Siegfried Lipiner visited Alt-Aussee to read his 'symphonic drama' *Hippolytos*. Mahler had already read it and spent the afternoon working, leaving Lipiner, Justi, Natalie, and Arnold Rosé as audience. The 'fount' of his imagination was flowing freely again, so much so that he even began to wonder where all the musical material was coming from. Composition appeared to be 'a building, in which one is always constructing a new edifice with the same blocks. From childhood, the only time one gathers and assimilates, the blocks are all there, waiting to be used'.[60] Mahler's chief anxiety was that the vacation time left to him was getting shorter and shorter. Later he recalled the dreadful anguish of those last days in Alt-Aussee, when he set to work each morning, his project rising before his eyes like a tower that he had scarcely begun to build, while he asked himself: 'Will I be able to retain it and make it my own during the few remaining days? How long till that damned band starts up again?'[61] This idea threw him into such agitation and anguish that he began to suffer from attacks of dizziness. A few days before his departure he, Justi, and Rosé

---

[56] Besides being disturbed by the local band, Mahler was often bothered by the yodeling of merry groups of mountaineers, who were encouraged and wildly applauded by the tourists; he was convinced that 'these people would surely not otherwise dream of pointlessly screaming like this after a day's hard work'.

[57] A pun on *Kurgäste* (cure guests) and *Kuh* (cow).

[58] On 5 May 1899, Mahler, who was reading one of his favourite books, Ludwig Nohl's biography from contemporaries' testimonies, spoke of Beethoven's deafness, his isolation and loneliness (*Isolierung und Einsamkeit*), which had been the source of some of the most colossal and beautiful musical creations in the world. He compared it with the life of Christ and the Stations of Cross, except that Beethoven's suffering had lasted 'not for thirty days [sic], but for many years' (NBLS).

[59] NBL2. 138.   [60] NBL1. 120; NBL2. 138.

[61] NBL1. 125; NBL2. 138. This conversation with Natalie took place when she returned to Vienna from the Wörthersee in Sept. 1899. By this time Mahler had bought his plot of land in Maiernigg and had commissioned the *Häuschen*.

climbed the Sattel, a small mountain from which they intended to make their way down to Alt-Aussee. As he was walking peacefully behind his companions down a rather steep path they suddenly seemed to step into empty space. For the first time in his life, he had such an attack of giddiness that he almost fainted. Justi saw that he was deathly pale, ran to take his arm, and made the company go back the way they had come. As the inevitable day of departure drew nearer, the psychosomatic symptoms intensified so much that he had to stop working:

I have never had trouble finishing an entirely sketched composition, but my imagination often deserts me during the first draft. This time, however, ideas poured out so abundantly that I scarcely knew how to catch them all and was almost at a loss to fit everything in. And what a frightful 'wrong note' the holidays ended on, leaving me haunted by the fear that this terrible feeling of dizziness will take hold of me whenever I want to work again. Now I am going to have a *Häuschen*, and peace, and all that does me good, but the Creator will be absent!

And yet the astonishing fact is that this composition which so tormented Mahler has such an atmosphere of well-being, naïveté, and love of life, and that in the midst of a creative output predominantly tragic in mood, the Fourth Symphony is so delightfully carefree, a sort of lyrical intermezzo among his other powerful, tragic symphonies.

At the end of July, Mahler left with Natalie and Rosé for Ischl, where he was to visit Prince Liechtenstein and meet Lipiner, whom he then accompanied to Sankt Wolfgang, near Salzburg. The two friends spent the 30 July together there, happy and relaxed, talking about old days, and Mahler related amusing episodes about his life in Hamburg and Budapest.[62] Two days later he had to return to Vienna, where new conflicts with the Intendant awaited him. In Alt-Aussee on 13 July he had received an extremely unpleasant letter from Plappart, accusing him of having behaved in an 'incredible' manner in 'flagrant contradiction' of the principles he should observe, by granting the bass Wilhelm Hesch a prolongation of his leave of absence.[63] This letter was doubtless the reason for Mahler's visit, on the way home, to Prince Liechtenstein, who must have agreed to his answering these charges in a letter that gave vent to his indignation. In it he reminded the Intendant that he had entreated Hesch never to fail him at the last minute as the other Opera basses[64] often did, and that by co-operating Hesch had overworked himself; his doctor had certified that he could not resume work without gravely endangering his health. Mahler had therefore promised him that at the beginning of August he would be granted leave to take a cure at Karlsbad. It also seemed to Mahler an excellent occasion to present a new bass named Moritz Frauscher without causing

---

[62] NBL1. 121; NBL2. 140. Among others, the incident at the Stadtwäldchen Café (see Vol. i, Chap. 23).

[63] During his leave, Hesch was paid his full salary, which had just been significantly increased (HOA, 13 July, Z.413/1899).

[64] Grengg and Reichenberg.

unnecessary rivalry. The Intendant had never before blamed him for granting leave for rest or convalescence, because he knew that Mahler had always been very strict. Questions of humanity apart, the interests of the Opera required the singers to be in good health and to perform under the best possible conditions. Furthermore, this convalescence would give Hesch an opportunity to recover from a recent personal sorrow, his wife's death.[65] In conclusion, Mahler again demanded full authority in all matters concerning Opera personnel, since he did his best to avoid making administrative mistakes, adding that 'a theatre cannot be run as strictly as a business office'.[66] Although he never gave leave to singers solely to permit them to accept guest appearances elsewhere,[67] he would continue to grant leave for health reasons, and he had given the administration sufficient proof of his firmness in this matter.

Upon his return on 1 August,[68] Mahler was confronted with one of those problems he knew were 'inherent in a director's work'. The tenor Fritz Schrödter refused to learn the role of Eisenstein in *Die Fledermaus*, alleging that it was beneath his dignity.[69] Mahler's reply was the following:

An operetta is simply a small and lighthearted opera and many classical works are given this title. The fact that recently compositions without musical value have been called operettas makes no difference. Johann Strauss's work surpasses them in every way, notably in its excellent musical diction, and that is why the administration has not hesitated to include it in the Opera repertoire. You yourself, dear Herr Schrödter, have often sung works that are far below the level of *Die Fledermaus*—Am Wörther See, for example. . . . I very much regret that I cannot accede to your wish to be withdrawn from the role of Eisenstein or to be paid a bonus for singing it. However, in view of the fact that quite exceptional use is to be made of your artistic powers during the coming season, I shall gladly try to give the role of Eisenstein to another member of the company on some occasions, so that you can alternate. I should also like to point out that the matter has already been laid before the General-Intendanz and that an appeal in that quarter will not meet with success . . .

In a note dated 21 September, the Intendant reproached Mahler for allowing 'a bad habit to take root' by permitting Selma Kurz to repeat the last stanza of the Schmink-Arie in *Mignon*,[70] and by again giving way to the audience the next day by encoring the duet sung by Hesch and Schrödter in *The Bartered Bride*.[71] This time, Mahler's reply was heavily ironic:

I must call your attention to the fact that it is absolutely impossible to ask, from the podium, during a performance, for the authorities' consent to an encore. A work of art

---

[65] Hesch had begun to experience the first symptoms of the cancer that eventually proved fatal, and was shortly to have the first of several operations.

[66] This was a quotation from his long letter to Prince Liechtenstein written in Apr.

[67] Mahler no doubt refers to the type of leave granted by the Intendant to Frances Saville in Mar.

[68] Among the reasons for his immediate return, Mahler mentions Fuchs's illness.

[69] Performance of 7 Aug.

[70] This is how the 'Styrienne' is referred to in German-speaking countries. Johann Ress, Selma Kurz's singing teacher, wrote cadenzas for this aria which subsequently became notorious for their difficulty.

[71] This occurred during a performance conducted by Mahler on 21 Sept. (HOA, no. 1521 ex 1899).

depends, and always will depend, upon the inspiration of the moment; under no circumstances can it be subject to any control other than the good taste and good will of the performers. Of course, in keeping with my obligations and past practice, I will not permit a repetition of this kind of thing. May I point out, however, that under conditions such as prevailed during the last two performances, when I was confronted with a spontaneous demand by the audience, it is almost a physical impossibility to resist this demand. Furthermore, I should like to remind you that there are several precedents for this . . . when the administration did not seem to find it necessary to hold the Director accountable.

In August, Mahler took advantage of a relatively leisurely start to the season to go and breathe some mountain air. Feeling the oppressive heat of the capital, he went to the Semmering and spent two days on the Hochschneeberg before rainy weather cut short his stay. He had planned to go to Dresden at the end of the month to see Rubinstein's *The Demon*, which he was soon to conduct at the Hofoper, but he gave up this journey because Fuchs was ill and on leave until the end of September. Thus Mahler himself had to conduct a great many more performances than planned,[72] and he sent Reichmann and Stoll to Dresden in his place. At the end of the month he nevertheless managed to join Justi and Natalie in Maiernigg, on the Wörthersee in Carinthia. The recent Laussa adventure and the disastrous Alt-Aussee summer had convinced him that calm and seclusion were indispensable to his creative activities. He had considered renting a house on a long-term basis, or building one in Carinthia or southern Tyrol,[73] where the climate is much better than in the Salzkammergut. Justi and Natalie therefore set off from Alt-Aussee on an exploratory bicycle trip to go house-hunting. On 18 August, by now thoroughly disheartened, they arrived at Maria Wörth on the Wörthersee.[74] There, boarding the little steamer for Maria Loretto, at the eastern tip of the lake, they met Anna von Mildenburg, who was a native of those parts and who offered to accompany them on their search. She persuaded them to go with her to Maiernigg, a small place on the south (less frequented) shore of the lake. There she introduced them to an amateur architect, Alfred Theuer, who was spending the summer with his family at Villa Schwarzenfels, a house he had built for himself on a rocky promontory overlooking the lake. Theuer suggested finding a villa large enough to put up the whole family, which they would rent for the following summer pending the construction of the Mahler Villa, for which he could draw up the plans and supervise the building. Natalie and Justi began visiting sites along the lake and comparing their relative advantages in terms of isolation, peace, and quiet. Summoned by telegram, Mahler was invited by Theuer to stay with them at

[72] Autograph telegram to Ernst von Schuch of 27 Aug. 1899 (HOA, Z.467/1899) and undated letter to an unknown recipient (PML). In this letter, Mahler says he cannot be counted on for Aug. or Sept. and cannot even promise to be free by Apr. Johann Nepomuk Fuchs died on 5 Oct.

[73] Letter to Justi, Aug. 1899.

[74] This large Carinthian lake, with its particularly mild climate, is Austria's equivalent of the Mediterranean.

Schwarzenfels and join in the search. For several days they prospected in vain, and Mahler was already picturing himself back in Vienna without having made a decision, when at last he found what he wanted, a wooded plot of land on the shores of the lake, far from any other habitation, and which included, at some distance from the site for the house itself, where the ground rose up to the fringe of a real primeval forest, the ideal place for a *Häuschen* that would be completely isolated from the outside world. Before even knowing if the land was for sale, they started drafting and discussing plans, and Mahler gave Theuer his instructions. The architect promised to remain in Maiernigg until the end of October to make sure that the *Häuschen* would be ready for the following year.

Eight letters from Mahler to Alfred Theuer are extant: they discuss the choice of the site and the final plans for the villa.[75] The large plot of land Mahler had chosen was next to Theuer's own property and belonged to a certain Fürst Orsini und Rosenberg, to whom an initial offer of 3,000 florins was made. 'We have grown so accustomed to our plans for the future', Mahler wrote, 'that we would be grievously disappointed if an insurmountable difficulty arose at this stage!' He eventually agreed to a price of 4,000 florins, on condition that the cost of installing the water supply was included.[76] It was then (at the beginning of September) that he definitively accepted Theuer's plans. He was eager to buy or rent the wooded hill (*Kogel*) behind the site of the future house, and would have a fence put up at his own expense to prevent anyone disturbing him while he worked. The two plans (for the residence and the *Häuschen*) were to be ready by the time he arrived in Maiernigg on 10 September. Work could start immediately, but Mahler was already worrying about being disturbed the following summer by sounds of hammering and sawing that might be audible from the *Häuschen*.

He was overwhelmed by the beauty of the Wörthersee when he returned on 10 September to sign the deed of purchase and the architect's contract. The little church of Maria Wörth was mirrored in the lake at the end of its narrow peninsula, around which small sailing boats drifted like white swans. Mahler decided that only the landscape of Lago Maggiore could compare with the one that now lay before him. He bustled to and fro, inspecting the ground and discussing every detail of the house. All the necessary decisions had been taken by the time he returned to Vienna, and for the following summer he rented the Villa Antonia, a twenty-minute walk from the site of the *Häuschen*. Now he could look forward to his next vacation with confidence. Here, in this tranquil spot, nothing would prevent him from finishing his Fourth Symphony.

Despite his conflicts with the Intendant and the singers, Mahler was happy in his work at the Opera that autumn, for he now knew better how to cope with

---

[75] Six of these letters are in ÖNB, and two others in the collection of G. A. Nogler in Zurich. Seven of them were written between 27 Aug. and 7 or 8 Sept. 1899.

[76] The exact price was 3,755 gulden. The plot of land (c.2,700 m²) was further enlarged, during the summer of 1901, when Mahler bought a further 1,200 m² (KMI).

the Intendant, and his reforms were beginning to make themselves felt. The ensemble had never been better: he had just engaged the excellent mezzo-soprano Laura Hilgermann, whose personality was admirably suited to 'naïve and sentimental roles'.[77] On 3 September, Selma Kurz, a lyric-coloratura soprano only 24 years old, won considerable praise as a guest singer in *Mignon*.[78] Born in Bielitz (Biala), Galicia in 1874, she was of modest origins; the family of eleven children was supported by her mother, her father having been blinded in an accident. A Jewish cantor discovered her vocal talent and sent her to Vienna to study singing. A number of patrons financed her studies with the famous Johann Ress, a patient, careful, and experienced teacher, who became her spiritual mentor and paternal friend. Pollini had heard Kurz in a public audition in Vienna but had not succeeded in engaging her before his death in 1897 (although a *Personen-Verzeichnis* from the Hamburg Opera lists her in 1896 as a member for the forthcoming season). She then sang for the Intendant of the Frankfurt Opera, Emil Claar, who immediately offered her an engagement. Mahler had probably heard of her through Max Kalbeck who, after the recital she gave at the Bösendorfersaal before leaving for Frankfurt, asked in an article in the *Neues Wiener Tagblatt* 'if it were wise to let her leave her native Austria'. In Frankfurt, where she first appeared, in September 1896, as Elisabeth in *Tannhäuser* and in *Carmen*, *Faust*, and *Djamileh*, her success was immediate and Ludwig Rottenberg recommended her to Mahler. Nevertheless she continued her studies in Vienna with Ress and with Marie Schröder-Hanfstängel. Much later her friend, the journalist Julius Stern, left an account of her first audition at the Hofoper. In spring 1898 the young singer arrived there with Johann Ress and her accompanist, Marie Brossement. Aware that she was facing a decisive test in front of an intractable director known for his high standards, Kurz's nerves were at breaking point. The three were taken into the red room normally used for the auditions. Mahler rushed in without any greeting, saying simply: 'If you please'. Selma Kurz began with Elisabeth's first aria from *Tannhäuser* and continued with arias from *Carmen* and *Faust*. Mahler listened with extreme concentration, not saying a word. Suddenly he went to the piano and took over the accompaniment, asking her to sing many other arias, of increasingly difficulty. Finally he stood up, saying: 'That's enough! Let's go back to my office now to talk about your roles and salary . . .'.[79] Indeed,

---

[77] Daughter of a Viennese schoolteacher, Laura Hilgermann (1859–1947) had studied music in Vienna. She made her stage début in Prague in 1885 while Mahler was there, and was engaged by him in Budapest in 1890. Later she toured with Grieg, singing his Lieder, and taught singing at the Budapest Conservatory.

[78] It was Mahler who later directed Kurz towards the lyric-coloratura repertoire, having tried with little success to have her sing dramatic roles. On 4 Sept. 1910, she married Vienna's most famous gynaecologist, Professor Halban. Her daughter, Desi Halban von Saher, showed great kindness in making available to me, at the time of the first English publication of my Vol. i, the letters her mother received from Mahler (now in BGM, together with most of Selma Kurz's papers). Her career continued under Mahler's successors in Vienna and brought her international fame both in the Opera and on the concert stage. She died in 1933.

[79] See articles by Maria Brossement, *Neues Wiener Tagblatt* (12 May 1931) and Julius Stern, *Wiener Volkszeitung* (21 Apr. and 14 July 1929).

he was so impressed, and even moved, that he immediately offered Kurz a contract with a salary of 5,000 gulden a month. On 31 May 1898, he wrote to Emil Claar in Frankfurt:

I have engaged Fräulein Kurz for the coming season at the Vienna Hofoper. I believe I can offer her good and suitable emplacement. She still has weaknesses, and is only a beginner, but against this she has charm and all the attraction of youth, which weighs with us as we are not exactly spoilt in this respect. Her repertoire is, as far as I can see, very limited, and she seems to me not sufficiently mature for it. For this reason I hope that it will not be too difficult for you to release her to us straight away, for this would not pose any great problems for you but would be of great service to our Institute.[80]

According to Selma Kurz herself, Emil Claar was furious at the idea of her leaving his theatre, and in fact delayed her departure as much as possible by a protracted refusal to speak to her and by putting all sorts of obstacles in her way. However, it is clear from Kurz's letters to her confidante and protectress Hermine Baum that she herself was prey to misgivings concerning conditions of work in Vienna and Mahler's alleged unreliability. When he conducted his First Symphony in Frankfurt in March 1899 he met the young singer again[81] and showed a solicitude that did not go unnoticed. 'He devoted almost all his time to me,' Selma Kurz wrote to Hermine Baum,

much to the envy of the other members, because the whole company was excited about his presence and every member was hoping for a possible engagement. I sang for him a few times. . . . The next day we had lunch together at the Frankfurter Hof and he was *so* nice! Then, the weather being magnificent, we went and walked in the woods and he talked about lots of things. First he spoke about Elisabeth (in *Tannhäuser*) and told me what was good and what was bad. He told me how hard they are intriguing against me in Vienna.[82]

After this first meeting, Mahler wrote to the young girl regularly, advising her which roles to study and working out plans to release her from her obligations in Frankfurt. He asked her to 'be good enough to send me a line from time to time about your studies and your life in general'.

Kurz's début in Vienna was further delayed by a diagnosis of serious anaemia in spring 1899, followed by a rest cure taking up part of July and August. After briefly considering *Faust*, Mahler suggested *Mignon* for her début, 'as many things in it pleased him'. It was therefore in *Mignon* that the young singer made her first appearance at the Hofoper on 3 September 1899:

Already in the first act I had a great success. But what happened in the third act after I finished the Mirror[83] song is impossible for me to describe. All the opera habitués said

[80] Letter of 31 May 1898 (HOA). Mahler telegraphed Kurz on 20 June asking her to free herself as soon as possible (HOA, Z.393/1898, autograph telegram of 20 June).

[81] See above, Vol. i, Chap. 20.

[82] Letter to Hermine Baum dated 11 Mar. 1899 (Kurz-Halban Collection, BGM).

[83] This refers once again to the 'Styrienne' in Act II, earlier called by the Intendant the 'Schmink-Arie', which we already know was encored that night (see above). It may seem surprising that Selma Kurz made her

that they had never witnessed anything like it. It was forbidden to repeat a *Gesangstück* but that evening it was absolutely forced upon Mahler and he could not help himself. He had to take up his baton and give a sign for repeat. The next day he was summoned to Prince Montenuovo [the Lord Chamberlain] and had to explain and excuse his action. From then on however I always had to repeat this aria. My next part was Margarete in *Faust*.[84] To me and to those present that evening will remain truly unforgettable. . . . When I left the stage I heard confused murmuring from the audience. I could not understand what had happened. In my dressing room I started to cry bitterly. I thought I had sung so badly and that I was a failure. There was a knock on my door and Mahler breathlessly stormed in with the words, 'Mädel! Sie sind gemacht!' [Girl, you're made!].[85]

At this time Mahler was often heard to exclaim, 'I'll make another Patti of her!' And indeed Selma Kurz became a star whose fame added to the prestige of the Vienna Opera.

That autumn Mahler at last got the Lord Chamberlain's office to consent to a reduction in the length of the season, which henceforth would begin on 15 August instead of 1 August. The main reasons for this change were no doubt to ease the burden on the singers and to avoid playing to half-empty houses while most of the Viennese were still on holiday. But for Mahler himself the change had the considerable advantage of increasing his vacation time by a fortnight, so that the period at his disposal for composing would from now on be at least six weeks.[86]

The first two events of the new season could be regarded as concessions made to public taste. On 18 April the previous season, Donizetti's *La Fille du régiment* had been highly successful, with a guest singer named Hedwig Schacko[87] greatly praised by the critics. Mahler therefore decided to present

début in a mezzo role and then immediately afterward sang the soprano role of Marguerite. However, her fabulous career was based not only on the agility of her voice but also on its unusually broad range. Although she became a coloratura soprano, she always kept, in the low register, the timbre of the mezzo she had been at the beginning.

[84] The performance of 30 Sept. Mahler granted Kurz two weeks' rest after she had rehearsed and performed this taxing role (letter to Hermine Baum of 19 Sept. 1899, Kurz-Halban collection, BGM).

[85] Desi Halban, 'My Mother Selma Kurz', *Recorded Sound* (London, Jan. 1973).

[86] That year Mahler also tried to persuade the members of the orchestra to wear evening clothes during the performances and thus give the auditorium a 'festive' appearance. But the idea met with stubborn resistance and had to be abandoned.

[87] The previous Mar., Hedwig Schacko had sung some solos with Rottenberg as conductor, during the concert in which Mahler had conducted his First Symphony. Her guest appearances, 18–27 Apr. 1899, also included *Figaro* (Susanna: the 27th), *La Fille du régiment* (the 18th), *La Poupée de Nuremberg* (the 24th). She had already won considerable success at the Hofoper as Gretel (*Hänsel und Gretel*) in 1895. According to her daughter, Marie Schacko Abravanel, Mahler offered Schacko an engagement in 1899 but she could not bring herself to accept it because of Viennese 'intrigues'. In a letter to an unknown recipient she complains, the day after the performance of 18 Apr., about the conflicts with her colleagues: 'In all the time I've been working in the theatre, I've never known backstage politics like *this*!—I hope I have a protector in the person of Director Mahler, in any case he treats me with great respect and has even said in my presence that he esteems me as much in human terms and for my character as he does artistically. . . . Anyway I'm going to have a serious talk with him about the circumstances I uncovered yesterday which have made me furious and miserable.' (BGM) *Fremden-Blatt* (19 Apr.) observed that Schacko would be a 'fortunate acquisition' for

the opera again in September with a company member, Margarete Michalek. Heuberger felt she was not up to the part and, although Mahler took great pains over this revival, the hall was not full. Donizetti's short and lovely *opera buffa* Hanslick found soothing to the nerves after the 'dramatic and musical poison' of 'verismo'. According to Hirschfeld, the new version had been carefully attuned to 'the strengths and weaknesses of Michalek'; the sound of the orchestra was finely disciplined, but the enthusiastic applause of the audience had been intended mainly for the singers,[88] since the score itself, although illuminated by Mahler's interpretation, 'had obvious weaknesses'. Some time later, the revival of Auber's *Fra Diavolo*, which had been postponed because of Neidl's accident, finally took place on 29 September. According to Hirschfeld, it was a unqualified success, thanks to 'the universality of Mahler's genius', which could deal equally well with 'the anguish of the Norn scene, the pure gold of *Die Zauberflöte*, the ardour of the Italians, and the grace of the French'. He found the casting as well as the freshness and charm of the musical performance irreproachable. Karpath compared this 'miraculous renaissance' of *Fra Diavolo* to that of *Zar und Zimmermann* in 1897; Mahler 'knows how to extract what is still fresh from yellowing pages, awaken the slumbering, make the threadbare shine anew.'[89]

To help solve the increased workload caused by Fuchs's illness and Richter's absence, Mahler had hired, the previous spring, one of Bruckner's former disciples, Ferdinand Löwe, who had been successful as director of the Kaim Orchestra. Löwe had no theatrical experience, but his début in *Hänsel und Gretel* had shown great promise after only two rehearsals. Some days later Mahler entrusted *Lohengrin* to him, this time without any rehearsals, and the result was not good.[90] Löwe 'is not familiar with the tempos of the singers or the orchestra' and could not even pretend to hold them together. It was therefore decided to grant him an indemnity of 5,000 gulden and the title of *Hofopernkapellmeister*,[91] provided he agreed not to conduct there any more. Mahler was thus once more confronted with a huge burden of work, for Richter had asked for his annual leave to conduct in England. Hellmesberger was also on leave, Fuchs had still not recovered and the Chordirektor Karl Luze had a limited repertoire. Mahler invited three guest conductors to share the load: Paul Prill, who had been one of his assistants in Hamburg and who was now

Vienna because of the 'velvety softness' of her voice and her remarkable gifts as an actress. Her daughter also informed me that she used to possess several letters from Mahler, but that these were lost during the war.

[88] Cast of the performance of 6 Sept.: Michalek (Marie), Baier (Marquise), Schrödter (Tonio), Frauscher (Sulpice), Schmitt (Hortensio). The previous Apr., Naval and Reichenberg had sung the principal roles with Hedwig Schacko.

[89] Cast of the first performance, on 29 Sept.: Michalek (Zerline), Walker (Pamela), Schrödter (Fra Diavolo), Pacal (Lorenzo), Neidl (Lord Koolbaum), Stoll and Hesch (Bandits).

[90] Löwe conducted *Lohengrin* on 27 Nov. and 27 Dec. 1898.

[91] The affair was reported in the *Musikalisches Wochenblatt* by Theodor Helm, who accused Mahler of another momentary infatuation. Löwe's debut in *Hänsel* was on 28 Oct. 1898, and the first unfortunate *Lohengrin* on 1 Nov.

in Nuremberg, Josef Göllrich from Düsseldorf, and Ludwig Rottenberg from Frankfurt,[92] but their performances failed to convince either Mahler or the public.

Mahler had met Rottenberg the previous March in Frankfurt, where they had both conducted at the same concert, and they had met again in Alt-Aussee. Mahler assigned *Don Giovanni* (17 October), *Der Freischütz* (22 October), and *Tristan* (24 October) to him. Justi, having attended some of Rottenberg's rehearsals, wrote to her sister Emma that the orchestra 'receives him with great warmth. I am very pleased about his engagement, at least he's someone who won't intrigue'.[93] Nevertheless Mahler had to admit that while Rottenberg had conducted these operas 'conscientiously and with precision, better than all the others', he had not brought out 'the true living spirit of the work, as I feel it so clearly and deeply in my own soul'. 'I must get used to this,' he said. 'A work remains

a book with seven seals, hermetically closed until the day a creator arrives to open it. How it hurts to see works buried alive this way, and how frightening is the growing isolation of which I become more and more conscious. It would be best to cut oneself off from the world, for any hope of being understood is vain. I am filled with distaste, not only for opera, but I would even like to give up the concerts. The only thing that I will not and cannot give up is my creative work. But it is not for the outside world that I persevere; it will be the last to understand and accept it. I have barred my own way too thoroughly for that: I create for myself alone.'[94]

Once again, with characteristic inconsistency, Mahler's repudiated 'the world', and in particular the Vienna Opera, but at the same time was feverishly active within its walls. The lack of conductors remained a major problem, especially since Fuchs had died on 4 October. Another candidate was Leo Blech, a pupil of Humperdinck with whom Mahler had been corresponding before their first meeting in Frankfurt. Blech's letters had expressed great admiration and devotion for Mahler, who finally decided against engaging him, however, for fear that he would be accused of filling the opera with Jews. After so many failures, the wisest choice seemed to be Franz Schalk, whom Mahler had met at the Conservatory and whose talents had impressed him the previous year in Prague.[95] Schalk never became close to him, either as a man or a musician, but his Viennese origin and training spoke strongly in his favour. In November Schalk agreed to replace Fuchs if he were offered at least the same

---

[92] Born in Czernowitz (Bukovina), Ludwig Rottenberg (1864–1932) had been a private pupil of Robert Fuchs and Eusebius Mandyczewski in Vienna. He began his career as an accompanist for recitals and was appointed director of the Orchesterverein of the Gesellschaft der Musikfreunde in 1884. First Kapellmeister at the Stadtheater in Brünn (1891–2), he was recommended by Brahms and Bülow to the Frankfurt Opera in 1893, and was active there until 1926. He also composed some 30 Lieder, piano and chamber music, and an opera. He was the father-in-law of Paul Hindemith.

[93] Letter from Justi to Emma of 25 Oct. 1899 (Ernst Rosé Collection sold at Sotheby's, New York, on 12 Dec. 1984).

[94] NBL1. 129ff.; NBL2. 146.   [95] See above, Chap. 4.

salary as he was receiving at the Berlin Opera, which he wanted to leave so as to be closer to his elder brother, who was seriously ill in Vienna. He appeared as guest conductor at the Hofoper early in 1900, and was engaged on 1 September.[96] On 9 October, for the revival of *Lucia di Lammermoor*, Mahler entrusted the conductor's baton to Karl Luze, a former member of the Opera chorus who had become Korrepetitor, then Chordirigent. He did not do the job very well, apparently, and Mahler's enemies, notably the correspondent of the *Neue Zeitschrift für Musik*, waxed indignant over Luze's 'incompetence', the poor casting,[97] and the fact that Saville, who was outstanding in the title role, had been granted leave of absence during the winter months—a new whim of Mahler's to be added to a series of 'falls from grace' experienced by Van Dyck, Dippel, and, most recently, Luise von Ehrenstein.[98]

After *Dalibor* and *The Bartered Bride*,[99] Mahler seriously considered putting on another Smetana opera. He started corresponding again with František Šubert, director of the Czech Theatre in Prague, this time on the subject of *Libuše*, which he eventually rejected. He then considered Dvořák's most famous opera *Rusalka*. The Czech composer travelled to Vienna the following year to sign a contract with the Opera, only to learn that he was being offered a mere 5 per cent of the takings, whereas in Prague he had always been paid 10 per cent. In vain Mahler explained to him that this was the rule in Vienna and that he would still receive a far greater total amount, given that the receipts from ticket sales were bound to be more than twice those in Prague: the old master refused to give way and *Rusalka* was never given at the Hofoper.[100] Mahler's next choice was Rubinstein's *The Demon*, which he had conducted in Hamburg, and which two years earlier had been the subject of his quarrel with Hugo Wolf. Despite its dramatic flaws, the work still had a special appeal for him and he personally rehearsed and conducted its first Vienna performance on 23 October. In the story, adapted from Lermontov, a young woman struggles with the devil, who, out of love for her, arranges her fiancé's death. In the last act the tempter appears in the convent where the heroine has taken refuge but fails to win her soul.

Rehearsals for *The Demon* seem to have been particularly lively, for the

---

[96] Schalk made his début as a guest conductor in *Lohengrin* on 8 Feb. 1900.

[97] The anonymous critic found the range of the role of Edgar too high for Schrödter's voice and judged the tenor Arthur Preuss, whom Mahler had just engaged, scarcely worthy of a provincial theatre. Cast of the 9 Oct. performance: Saville (Lucia), Schrödter (Edgar), Demuth (Ashton), Frauscher (Raymond), Preuss (Arturo).

[98] Luise von Ehrenstein's last performance on the Viennese stage was in 1899, in one of her best parts, the title-role in Liszt's *Die Legende von der heiligen Elisabeth*, which was given each year on 19 Nov., the anniversary of the death of the Empress Elisabeth.

[99] The première of Smetana's most famous opera had taken place at the Hofoper on 4 Oct. 1896, six months before Mahler's appointment. But it was he who contrived to keep it in the repertoire, with performances every year until he left Vienna.

[100] Arnošt Mahler, 'Gustav Mahler und seine Heimat', unpubl. MS. The writer states that the casting had already been decided, with Mahler's agreement. It would have included Marie Gutheil-Schoder, Leo Slezak, and Wilhelm Hesch, which means that the première would have taken place in 1900 or 1901.

press carried various stories about them. Mahler, as usual, prepared two different casts. The role of Prince Sinodar, the heroine's fiancé, was to be sung at the première by Franz Naval and at the second performance by the Bohemian tenor Franz Pacal. During the funeral procession, the dead prince was to be carried right to the front of the stage. The dancers carrying the coffin made no objection to Naval, who was light and slim. But Pacal weighed more than 100 kilos. The exhausted dancers nearly went on strike, and the day after the performance sent a delegation to Mahler asking either for a bonus payment such as the Burgtheater gave in similar cases or that the live tenor be replaced by a papier-mâché corpse. The *Fremden-Blatt* informed its readers that Mahler would never agree to such a substitution, but did not relate whether he finally paid the bonus.[101] The same paper later described another incident that took place during one of the early rehearsals of Rubinstein's opera. Mahler was rehearsing an ensemble with an upright piano when a clothes-moth from the carpet alighted on his shirt. Edyth Walker was about to kill it when Mahler stopped her:

What makes you think it doesn't have the right to eat my clothing? No doubt you think that clothes are there to keep us warm, but the clothes-moth is just as sure they are for food, and I think it has a right to its opinion. As for me, I don't have the right to kill it because it exists in a different world. Even when I'm conducting, if a fly lands on my score it always sets me thinking. I start wondering what has brought it there and what it can be feeling. I leave it to enjoy itself, and take care not to kill it as I turn the pages.

At the end of the rehearsal, two of the singers, thinking they would take advantage of Mahler's mood, asked him to reconsider the case of an Opera employee who was to be pensioned off. 'Ladies,' he said, 'do you think *I* like causing pain? The man is incapable of carrying out his responsibilities, and there's nothing I can do about it. I can't even concentrate on conducting so long as he is there.'[102]

Mahler's principal task, during the rehearsals for *The Demon*, was to teach Theodor Reichmann a new role to add to the list of diabolical characters which had become his speciality.[103] As before, he recognized and admired the baritone's artistry, but he could not forgive his carelessness as to rhythm and intonation, his vanity, his old-fashioned acting style, and his conventional gestures onstage. The title-role in *The Demon* was the only one he had ever worked right through with Mahler, who proved in rehearsal to be extremely demanding. In the second act there is a wedding scene where the Demon is supposed to appear before the guests and servants, unseen by anyone except the heroine whose fiancé is soon to die on his way to the church. Mahler had the idea of having the evil spirit start addressing Tamara not from the stage but from the prompter's box.

[101] *Fremden-Blatt* (22 Oct. 1899).   [102] Ibid. (21 May 1911).
[103] Among others, Marschner's *Vampyr* and *Hans Heiling*, and Wagner's *Flying Dutchman*.

'You mean symbolically, Herr Direktor,' replied the bewildered baritone. 'You want my voice to sound as if it were coming from the prompter's box.' 'No, my dear Reichmann,' said Mahler, 'I mean physically, that is to say, before the second act begins you climb down into the prompter's box and then sing from there towards the stage. Think of the effect it will have on the house when the audience suddenly hears a ghostly voice sounding from a completely new, unexpected direction! People will really think it is a summons from beyond . . . Just do as I say, dear Reichmann, and try it.' 'But my dear Direktor,' answered the singer in well-modulated, piteous tones, 'You're saying that not only do I have to spend practically the whole opera in a trap, but now I have to go down into Fröhlich's chamber [Fröhlich was the prompter] and sing down there.'[104]

Eventually Mahler abandoned this idea and decided to create an impression of the supernatural by draping a veil of gauze around the singer, to whom the idea of being heard without being seen was simply intolerable. Furthermore, Mahler insisted that Reichmann should exercise the ultimate degree of self-restraint, making him remain motionless most of the time, and suppressing all his usual grand gestures. The great baritone accepted this during rehearsals, but in the third performance, on 29 October, he again ignored Mahler's instructions, and fled to his dressing-room as soon as the curtain fell to escape the inevitable scene. Mahler expressed his strong displeasure to Karl Luze, who passed on the message only too well. Thus, on 1 November, Mahler received a letter written by Reichmann in language that was characteristically bizarre, with chaotic punctuation that betrayed the writer's distress. He began by defending himself, claiming never to have wished to show any ill-will, and to have tried to follow all Mahler's advice to the letter during rehearsals and the first two performances. 'When I perceived that my health and my voice were in danger,' he went on,

then I had to free myself from your tyrannical yoke and follow my own feelings. Your haste, your continual urging and gesticulating from the podium, might put off a person far calmer and less artistically engaged than myself. On the night, it is the artist who has to stick his neck out and you are asking too much in insisting that he do only what you want. I have proved that I am a person in my own right and that you must place a certain amount of faith in me. I am always grateful to an artist like yourself for good advice, but I shall not allow myself to be tyrannized by anyone. I wanted to make an exception with you, but I find it is impossible. Incidentally, all my colleagues are of the same opinion that, with all due respect, you push your demands too far, and I was often the only one to stand up for you, saying again and again he means well, 'he is a great artist.'

What you ask is not possible. Namely, to do only what you want in tempo, gesture and expression. I have been in the theatre for 30 years, so I, too, can have my ideas about certain things. You have completely misunderstood the role of the Demon, and deprived it of all its mystery. The success on Sunday was much greater than before. But the main thing is that my nerves will not stand up to such bullying. You threaten to take

Hans Sachs away from me, all right, do it if you wish, even though this is such a well established role that you and I would have no quarrels about it. I have sung this role under great conductors, always to mutual satisfaction! You say you are afraid you would get angry again, but I don't mind if once again you intend to grind me down with your world-famous despotism. . . . Do you really think you could boycott me! No, certainly not! It is not nice of you to blow up the whole thing in this way and you are certainly wrong if you think that your opinion is the only right one. I have too big a name as an artist for anyone to be able to harm me, and I shall leave no stone unturned to protect myself from your persecutions. Thank God I have friends enough here among the public, and I do not think they would allow a Reichmann to be sacrificed to your whims.

To conclude, I should like to say that I don't understand how you can go to the extreme of such deadly hate and spite just because for once I dared to be myself. It is not gentlemanly. And what is not gentlemanly will never win through.[105]

In his reply, Mahler apologized for being brief, for 'I have no time, and besides, my explanations would be of no use.' 'Nothing I said should have permitted Luze to draw the conclusions he did.' The misunderstanding would never have occurred if Reichmann had replied to the message Mahler sent him through Hubert Wondra, and if he had come in person to set matters straight, rather than refusing everything and invoking a paragraph of his contract. If the baritone had heard words passed on and distorted by an intermediary, he had only himself to blame. There was in any case no question of 'boycotting' him, or of 'pursuing him with deadly hatred', or even of depriving him of the role of Sachs which was one of his best, and 'one of the glories of the German stage'. As director of the Opera, Mahler would do his best to see that Reichmann continued to be happy. He would be anxious to 'retain, support and encourage one of our, in all respects, outstanding members'.

The Demon, over which Mahler took such trouble, and which provoked so many incidents, was almost unanimously rejected by the Viennese critics. Hanslick called the whole opera an interminable duet.[106] Despite the many cuts[107] Mahler had made to tighten up and strengthen the action,[108] Theodor Helm wondered why he had bothered to revive such an old work (first performed in 1875) after Rubinstein's many theatrical failures. According to

[105] Theodor Reichmann's letter and Mahler's answer, both dated 1 Nov. 1899 (HOA).

[106] Although Anton Rubinstein himself had visited Vienna to conduct the first performance of some of his operas, according to Hanslick he was never successful at the Hofoper.

[107] In particular he cut the Finale of Act II, where Tamara's father was seen setting off to war against the Tartars. The act now ended in Tamara's convent, with the preceding chorus.

[108] Hanslick praised Mildenburg's performance to the skies, including her runs trills and chromatic scales, poured out with sovereign ease, even in the top register. This proves that she had so far lost little of her early vocal agility. Justi, who attended the première, wrote in her letter to Emma of 25 Oct. 1899 that 'Mildenburg was in her old form again'. Later she added that 'Gustav has not been lucky with *The Demon*, I think next week will be the last performance. Mildenburg was magnificent, almost like in her best Hamburg period.' (Letter of 5 Nov., Ernst Rosé Collection.) As for Reichmann, Hanslick judged that he had added a new and magnificent creation to the sombre roles he favoured. Cast for the first performance on 23 Oct.: Mildenburg (Tamara), Kaulich (Nurse), Walker (Angel), Naval (Sinodar), Pacal (Messager), Reichmann (Demon), Grengg (Gudal), Hesch (Servant, then Guardian of the Convent). *The Demon* was performed only five times at the Hofoper. It was never revived.

Helm, the audience was left uncertain as to whether the hero was a ghost or a real person. The music didn't clarify things, because Rubinstein was unable to characterize his dramatis personae or suggest an atmosphere of evil. The work oscillated constantly between oratorio and opera, and the melodic invention was not strong enough to hold the interest. Mahler had laboured over the production, galvanizing all the forces at his command, 'as if he were dealing with a superb tragedy rather than a stillborn drama'. Why had he not chosen 'a great German work' instead? Schönaich, in the *Allgemeine Zeitung*, praised the high quality of the production. For Hirschfeld, who deplored the 'old-fashioned romanticism' of the libretto, the hero was 'an underworld neurotic', and Rubinstein's music an 'oriental bazaar of beautiful musical passages' that bore no relationship to the libretto situations.

Four days after the première of *The Demon*, Mahler decided because of the opera's lukewarm reception to cut a few musical numbers, particularly in the overlong second act. But he also decided to alter some details in the staging. To achieve this, he called a rehearsal which lasted several hours, just as the members of the cast were hoping to be allowed to recover from their exertions in preparing the première. To stimulate them, he improvised a short speech in which he reminded them of Frederick the Great of Prussia 'who knew better than anyone how to restore the morale of his troops, particularly after a battle which they believed they had lost, and lead them on to a great victory'. 'The performance we offered of *The Demon*', Mahler said, 'was appreciated (*anerkannt*)—I would almost say more than it deserved—by the public and the critics, and as far as we are concerned we could be satisfied with that. But we must aim higher than personal satisfaction. We have to see that the work itself carries the day and achieves victory.' Mahler then alluded to similar cases, like that of *Fidelio* and *Die Meistersinger*, which were not successful right away. Apparently Mahler's words achieved their object, for the singers began again to rehearse with zeal and enthusiasm. It seems that that evening the work was warmly applauded.[109]

Mahler, as we have seen, had denied planning to 'take Hans Sachs away' from Reichmann. One month later, in the new production of *Die Meistersinger* on 26 November, the role was performed by the baritone's younger rival Leopold Demuth. Yet Mahler's intention was certainly not to vex Reichmann, but rather to allow Demuth, who had sung the role in Bayreuth the previous summer, to take it up again from time to time. Obviously no one at the Hofoper could claim exclusive rights to a particular part. Reichmann must have yielded to these solid arguments, since the Opera archives contain no further exchange of letters on the subject. Despite the difficulty he had had in working with him on *The Demon*, Mahler wanted to rework Sachs with him completely for further performances, this time no doubt to dispel his anxieties. Reichmann's difficulty

---

[109] *Neue Freie Presse* (28 Oct. 1899).

in conforming to Mahler's redoubtable discipline is mentioned again and again in his private diary, which was later discovered by chance by the writer Felix Salten. In a naïve, almost childish hand Reichmann covers page after page with expressions of rage, furious interjections, threats against Mahler, all interspersed with exclamation marks that show the extent of his agitation: Mahler is a tyrant who is about to desecrate *Die Meistersinger*. Instead of having mercy he 'tries by force to violate my true nature', to 'attack the very roots of my art'. He 'understands nothing of my natural gifts', he attempts 'to obtain from me the most obscure and laborious effects'. The whole early part of the diary is filled with similar expressions; Mahler is referred to as a 'little Jewish Kobold' who shamelessly forces him to start again from scratch, who dares to drill him like a beginner, him, the famous Kammersänger. In any case, he will not accept such treatment any longer, but 'at the first opportunity, I'll take him by the throat'. The day Reichmann finally sang Hans Sachs, however, he was acclaimed as never before and the explosions of anger in his diary change to a hymn of delight and gratitude:

Thanks be to God and . . . to Mahler! . . . It is true, he drove me crazy, it is true he was often lacking in respect towards me, but all is forgiven and forgotten, for he has forced me to surpass myself. Never, but never, have I sung the role better: I didn't believe it possible that I could be so effective, never have I been so acclaimed! Yes, I must kneel at Mahler's feet, and apologize in front of everyone![110]

The performance of *Die Meistersinger* on 26 November was to be given complete, with no cuts whatsoever,[111] for the first time in Vienna, and Mahler devoted almost all of the previous month to it. To Natalie, he noted with relief that 'my fear that I might weary of this work after hearing it too often has fortunately proved groundless'. He had not conducted it for two years, which was in fact sufficient 'to make it as—indeed even more meaningful to me than before'. 'I tell you, what a work this is!' he concluded, 'If German art were to disappear completely, one could reconstruct it from *Die Meistersinger*. Everything else seems empty and superfluous in comparison.'[112] During the final week Mahler conducted three orchestral rehearsals and three complete stage rehearsals. Although the performance lasted almost five hours, including the

---

[110] Felix Salten, *Gestalten und Erscheinungen* (Fischer, Berlin, 1913), 127; RSM2. 76, and Ludwig Karpath, *Lachender Musiker* (Knorr & Hirth, Munich, 1929), 95.

[111] Hans Geissler wrote in the *Neue Musikalische Presse* that Richter had already restored some of the cuts. The following episodes were reinstated by Mahler: in Act II, the second stanza of Sach's Lied and that of Beckmesser's Serenade; in the last act, the Lieder sung by Beckmesser and Walther, as well as Sachs's monologue, 'Hat man mit dem Schuhwerk nicht seine Not'; the comic intermezzo accompanying Beckmesser's appearance, and, at the end of the last act, part of the scene with Sachs and the chorus. The restored passages, about 100 pp. in the score, only added 20 minutes in all to the performance.

[112] NBL2. 144. Mahler always showed great enthusiasm when he brought out a *Neuinszenierung* of this kind. He would forget all the others and find the one in hand superior to everything that had gone before. Despite all his enthusiasm in 1899, he soon stopped conducting *Die Meistersinger*, which disappeared for ever from his own repertoire (not of course from the Vienna Opera's) after this revival.

intermissions,[113] the theatre was full and not a single member of the audience arrived late or left before the final chord was played. In record time Mahler had renewed and transformed the whole opera: he even reduced the stage area for Sachs's workshop, despite the opposition of the Intendant, who felt that no changes were necessary in so 'popular' an opera. Before the curtain rose the audience was as expectant 'as for a première', according to the *Neues Wiener Tagblatt*. Loud applause followed the Prelude although there was also some booing from a group of young anti-Semites in the balcony who were doubtless angry that Reichmann had been replaced by Demuth, a Jew. The other members of the audience then redoubled their applause, so that after five minutes the tumult threatened to ruin the atmosphere. Mahler cut the applause short by starting the first act, but the same thing happened before Act III. In this case he had to wait, so as not to spoil the quiet and lovely Prelude, until the opposing sides had ceased their confrontation. Each time he raised his baton, the noise increased. Resigned, he finally sat down and leaned forward, as though the whole thing had nothing to do with him, as if he 'calmly offered his back to an inevitable downpour'. Among the particularly successful moments of this performance, Natalie singles out Walther's reply, 'Fanget an',[114] in the first act, which seemed 'the divine birth of creative genius' and received vigorous applause, and the Finale of the second act which 'was perfection and clarity itself, compared with the noisy confusion of previous performances'. Selma Kurz was an exquisite Eva, fresh and youthful,[115] and Sachs's 'Wahn' monologue, sung in a simple yet moving way by Demuth, made a deep impression. Only Benedikt Felix's Beckmesser was a great disappointment to Mahler, presumably because he made it too much of a caricature. About that, as about the character of Mime, Mahler felt that he himself 'was the only person capable of playing the role well'. As he left the Opera after the performance, a young admirer who had been waiting outside the door ran towards him and astonished him by impulsively kissing his hand.[116]

The following day's reviews were for once as enthusiastic as the audience had been. According to the *Neues Wiener Tagblatt*, the whole work had been not only revived 'but brought to life as its composer had intended and wished'. Mahler had restored its comic tone; he had clarified the 'richly woven polyphony' and emphasized the relationship between the various motifs; he had created new ties between the stage and the orchestra, which had carried out all

[113] *Neues Wiener Tagblatt* states that the performance lasted from 18.35 to 23.30. The interval after Act II was about 20 minutes.

[114] Schott's pocket score, 322.

[115] This was Mahler's opinion, coloured perhaps by his personal feelings, because most critics did not share his admiration for the new Eva, except however for Ludwig Rottenberg, who wrote a letter of congratulation and encouragement to Kurz from Frankfurt. 'It was *very nice* of you to think of me a little that evening; but also you know how much I enjoyed working on the role of Eva with you. I can well imagine how fresh and young this "Evchen" must have been, in looks as well as in voice!' (letter to Selma Kurz of 1 Dec. 1899, Kurz-Halban collection, BGM.)

[116] Cast of the performance of 26 Nov. 1899: Kurz (Eva), Schrödter (David), Winkelmann (Walther), Demuth (Sachs), Felix (Beckmesser), Rellé (Magdalene), Frauscher (Pogner), Stehmann (Kothner).

his intentions perfectly. Winkelmann and Schrödter had been outstanding as Walther and David; the orchestra and chorus had surpassed themselves; and the audience's enthusiasm had taken on 'a Mediterranean quality'. Strangely enough, only the *Neue Freie Presse* was not convinced of the wisdom of replacing the cuts[117] and thought that excessive zeal had been expended on this revival with the result that the artists had shown 'constraint'.[118] Mahler's tempos had been 'inhumanly strict',[119] forcing the singers to carry on 'a sort of conversation'. The critic admitted, however, that the rest of the performance had been exemplary, particularly the orchestra, the chorus, and the staging. He added a special word of praise for the animated and natural movements of the crowd.[120]

Ludwig Speidel used the word 'superhuman' to describe Mahler's ability to get the most out of the means at his disposal: even in Bayreuth a performance of comparable quality had never been heard; such 'perfect harmony between stage and orchestra, between eye and ear', right up to the tremendous second act Finale, in which the singers and everyone in the crowd seemed to have been individually rehearsed. Everything was lively, harmonious, and effective. The chorus seemed to be singing an entirely new score, and the soloists (even those who, like Winkelmann and Schrödter, had sung their parts a hundred times) appeared to have come fresh to their roles. Hirschfeld reviewed the performance at great length and found it 'worthy of Bayreuth': for the first time in Vienna, *Die Meistersinger* had been treated as the light, fast-flowing comedy it really was; the dialogues had been speeded up; instead of a trailing encumbrance the orchestra had become a moving force—it had never drowned the singers, so that each word and all the most subtle relationships between the motifs could be easily perceived. The first dialogue between Walther and Eva had seemed like an easygoing, rapid improvisation, 'suitable to a first meeting'. In the ensemble of the apprentices each singer had expressed by his gestures a character of his own. During Walther's first song, the growing agitation of the mastersingers had been magnificently portrayed, 'each voice within the group preserving its own character and full value'. 'Even Bayreuth cannot surpass [the performance of] this ensemble. To attribute it merely to good staging would be quite inappropriate, for it is the result of an overall artistic conception fully realized in all its components parts.'[121]

[117] It claimed that all that had been restored was 'repetition and passages detrimental to the dramatic effect'.

[118] The Act I chorale had been too perfectly performed, since it is supposedly sung by a church choir.

[119] Although the Prelude had been played too fast, many passages had been deprived of their gaiety by being taken too slow, for instance the chorus of apprentices, the chorus at the beginning of Act II (*Johannistag*), and Sachs's two monologues.

[120] The critic approved the reduction in the size of the stage for Sachs's workshop, but questioned the décor in Act II, where the shoemaker's house concealed the action from part of the audience. It rated Demuth's performance lower than Reichmann's, despite his splendid voice, but admired the speed with which Selma Kurz had mastered all the dramatic and musical subtleties of Eva.

[121] Hirschfeld also praised the chorus, especially for the way it 'had participated in the action' in the last scene. He liked the use of a metal harp brought in from Bayreuth for Beckmesser's accompaniment. He had reservations only about some of the 'pedal points' introduced by Mahler and about some details of the

Even the anti-Semitic press was unable to find much wrong with the new
Meistersinger, and yet on 19 November, a week before the première, the
Deutsche Zeitung had attacked Mahler as fiercely as before. An anonymous
author, pretending of course to be 'unprejudiced', denounced the 'incredible
brutalities' the members of the Philharmonic Orchestra had to endure, and the
'violence' done to works in the classical repertoire. Despite the orchestra's
'unequalled hatred' for him, Mahler had succeeded in getting himself elected
as its director,[122] thanks to his 'well-organized clique'. He kept his position at
the Opera only because of the 'systematic adulation' of the Jewish press. But
his latest ventures had gone too far, and their results had done 'incalculable
harm to the Opera'. In the beginning Mahler's role had been easy, because
reforms had been essential after the complete stagnation of Jahn's regime:
Mahler would not have kept his post for more than six weeks if he had not
carried them out. Yet he had not presented a single new work of quality, not
even that masterpiece by the greatest living German composer, *Der
Corregidor*.[123] So far he had concentrated chiefly on 'unscrupulous exploitation'
of the Wagnerian dramas, so that his famous 'undeniable successes' were in
fact no more than could have been expected. No one escaped his 'brutal
tyranny'; 'he wounds, offends, humiliates, and drives the best singers from the
Opera, thereby threatening it with ruin.' For several months, for instance,
Mahler had prevented Ellen Forster from singing and had assigned all her roles
to Rita Michalek, his current 'favourite'. For some time past he had deprived
Marie Renard of her best roles, by withdrawing *Manon*, *Werther*, and *Mignon*
from the repertoire.[124] As for Winkelmann, he had just humiliated him by
reducing his salary in his new contract; he had done the same thing to Neidl,
who, hearing the news before he had recovered from his accident in May, had
had a 'nervous breakdown'. This intolerable tyranny was not confined to the
singers. Josef Hellmesberger, junior, conductor of the ballet, had just learnt
that his new contract contained an 'incredible' clause, namely that he 'would no
longer be allowed to conduct operas', he who had saved so many performances
by replacing an indisposed conductor at the last moment.[125] Every day, singers
such as Schrödter, Sedlmair, and Felix had to put up with Mahler's bad temper
and serve as his whipping boys. Two members of the orchestra had just been
dismissed by Mahler for having 'once played wrong notes' and for 'conspiring
against him'. Wishing to remain 'objective', the anonymous author refrained

staging, among them the 'radiant sun' in Sachs's workshop during the big Act III monologue. Demuth's Sachs
he found slightly monotonous compared with Reichmann's, while Kurz's Eva struck him as too passive and
Felix's Beckmesser 'too serious'.

[122] Judging from his letter to Justi at the end of Aug., Mahler had seriously considered giving up his
Philharmonic activity.

[123] Mahler produced Wolf's opera in 1904, with little success (see below, Chap. 16).

[124] Mahler did not think much of these three French operas.

[125] Hellmesberger was undoubtedly the least talented of the well-known Viennese conductors. His
limitations became apparent to all in 1901, when he took over the Philharmonic Concerts from Mahler (see
below, Chap. 10).

from listing Mahler's numerous other misdeeds, for instance 'how one gets appointed Director of the Vienna Opera'. He only wanted to show that Mahler was doing serious harm to the musical life of Vienna.

It was against this background of hateful personal attacks, persistently fostered by the anti-Semitic press, that Mahler was to launch his second season of Philharmonic Concerts, during which he would provoke an even greater measure of hostile criticism by breaking with some of the most hallowed of Viennese musical traditions.

7

Fresh anti-Semitic attacks—Richter's departure—Beethoven's Ninth Symphony—Hirschfeld's declaration of war

(December 1899–April 1900)

If people want to censure me, they should do it 'hat in hand'.

FROM the beginning of 1899 the atmosphere within the Vienna Philharmonic deteriorated, powerful opposition to Mahler having arisen following the events of the previous summer. The warring factions now brought their quarrel into the open, publishing articles for or against the director of the Opera in various Viennese papers. At the annual general meeting of 30 May, Mahler's opponents moved that the election of the chief conductor be deferred,[1] and that Hans Richter be approached to see if he was prepared to resume direction of the concerts. This attachment to Richter was after all quite understandable. As Franz Heinrich, a second violinist who later became the secretary and manager of the orchestra, put it: 'two-thirds of the orchestra owe their musical education to him. . . . Richter is like a father to us, and it is permissible to state that love for a father will always outweigh the love we might feel for a relative, even one who, like Director Mahler, has become very dear to us'.[2] The double motion was accepted by 54 votes to 41. This victory for the opposition turned, however, to a crushing defeat since—improbable as it may seem—no one had made sure in advance that Richter would ultimately consent. The maestro's laconic reply arrived from Bayreuth on 1 August: 'Honoured sirs! To your obliging and to me very flattering request I must reply that it is impossible for me to assume direction of the Philharmonic Concerts in

---

[1] Apparently the interim president of the committee, Roman Kukula, a convinced Mahler partisan, was forced to resign at the beginning of the meeting.

[2] Minutes of the Philharmonic, GZ. 60/99, as quoted by C. Hellsberg, *Gustav Mahler und die Wiener Philharmoniker*, op. cit., 219.

the 1899/1900 season, since I shall be away from Vienna . . . for two periods of six weeks'. It was now necessary to wait until the end of the holidays before an 'extraordinary general meeting' could be called on 24 August, in the course of which Mahler's supporters clearly declared themselves: 61 musicians out of the 84 present voted for Mahler. Theobald Kretschmann, Mahler's old enemy, went so far as to propose the election of Josef Hellmesberger, junior.[3] Kretschmann was no doubt the musician who, on the day of the election, distributed leaflets thanking Mahler for having stood in for Richter and congratulating the latter on his recovery from the 'affliction of the hand' which had prevented him from conducting concerts. The implication of this document was that Richter should once again be invited to head the concerts, or that anyway a conductor other than Mahler should be elected.[4] When Mahler found that he had not been chosen unanimously, he at first wanted to stand down, insisting that 'as director, I must be above parties, and cannot head an organization divided into factions'.[5] The committee, caught in an embarrassing situation, engaged in feverish activity over the next few days. It met on 28 August and then on 4, 5, 9, 10, and 16 September to discuss various possible solutions. Mahler was by now deeply offended and reluctant to accept the post. Three successive delegations were sent to him to persuade him, but without success. Already, several papers began to express anxiety about the future of the orchestra, left in the hands of 'guest conductors'. Many journalists felt that the orchestra was wrong to resent the work Mahler demanded of them. As one put it, 'a certain conductor put forward by the minority might indeed make life easier for the orchestra by cutting down on first performances and rehearsals, yet the public would be the loser'.[6]

According to the 9 September issue of the *Neue Freie Presse*, Mahler sought nothing less than an overwhelming vote of confidence; should he turn down the second offer about to be made, then Mottl would be elected instead, or, at best, the orchestra would have to make do with guest conductors. At a meeting on 16 September, 90 out of 96 musicians voted by a show of hands for Mahler. Moreover, the committee set out to counteract by every possible means the 'agitation by a few isolated players against the conductor, which spoils the climate for artistic endeavour'.[7] That same day, it was announced that Mahler was willing to continue as conductor and that he would take the orchestra to

[3] The orchestra consisted of 110 members. Of the other votes cast 19 were for Hellmesberger, 1 was for Mottl, and 3 were invalidated. The cellist Moritz Weippert had suggested a simple show of hands in Mahler's favour, whereupon Kretschmann had immediately proposed Hellmesberger.

[4] The first page of this document was reproduced in the catalogue of an exhibition put on by the Vienna Philharmonic. The document is held in their archives.

[5] *Neue Freie Presse* (10 Sept. 1899).

[6] Taken from an article in the *Neue Freie Presse* at the time of the first Philharmonic Concert. (Its prediction came true two years later, when Hellmesberger took over the Philharmonic.) Mahler wrote to Justi at the end of Aug. that he would probably not accept the post.

[7] According to Clemens Hellsberg, 'the Director's extreme reaction—after all he had made six delegations of the Philharmonic orchestra eat humble pie!—was degrading for both sides.'

Paris the following June.[8] Indeed the Philharmonic needed Mahler[9] more than
ever, for the Philharmonic Concerts were to be faced for the first time with
serious competition in the form of the Concertverein (or Konzertverein) Orchestra. This had just been formed under the direction of Ferdinand Löwe who, as
we have seen, had left the Opera with substantial compensation for the breach
of his contract. Henceforth the Concertverein was to organize every year
several series of subscription concerts, the first one taking place on 30 October
1900.[10] Critics immediately welcomed the fact that Vienna was now endowed
with 'something other cities already possess: an orchestra entirely independent
of the theatre'. Although Löwe several times included works by Mahler in his
programmes, Mahler never ceased to regard him as a second-rate conductor,
and rarely attended any of his concerts.

The 5 November programme of the season's first Philharmonic Concert
began, as did that of the Concertverein's, with Weber's *Euryanthe* Overture. It
was followed by Mozart's 'Jupiter' Symphony and Beethoven's Fifth Symphony.
While rehearsing the Beethoven, Mahler was tormented by doubts about the
interpretation of the opening bars, the famous 'knocks of Destiny'. He recalled
that, in Hamburg, critics had reproached him for unduly lengthening the
fermatas. He was convinced that their duration should be in direct proportion to that of the bar,[11] but admitted he had never been clear as to exactly
what Beethoven intended.[12] It was unlikely that a musician of Beethoven's
stature could have made a mistake, since everything in his work was 'clarity,
luminosity, and utter awareness' (*höchstes Bewusstein*),[13] and every marking 'a
revelation'. Nevertheless, whenever he attended a performance of the Fifth
Symphony, Mahler noted the imprecise rendering of the three introductory
'knocks'; sometimes there seemed to be four notes, and sometimes five. He felt
the problem to be almost insoluble for a conductor who had not completely
solved the problem of the upbeat. 'If Beethoven had emphasized each of these
"knocks" with the kettledrums, the rigorous tempo would have been easier to
maintain, because the orchestra would be obliged to play in perfect unison,'[14]
he concluded.

[8] Five weeks later, all tickets for the scheduled concerts were already sold out, and a 2nd series was being
contemplated, which shows what an attraction Mahler's name then was to the public (cf. letters from Justine
to Emma Rosé of 25 Oct. and 5 Nov. 1899, former collection of Ernst Rosé). In the event, only the first
concert (5 Nov.) and the Nicolai Concert at the end of the season (see below, n. 20) were 'repeated'.

[9] One of the reasons for the tense relations between Mahler and the orchestra may have been the fact that
he, unlike his predecessors, was never president or even a member of the orchestra's committee. From 30
May 1899 the former function was assumed by the bass-player Franz Simandl; all important documents bear
his signature along with Mahler's (cf. H. and K. Blaukopf, *Die Wiener Philharmoniker* (Zsolnay, Vienna,
1986), 177).

[10] Programme of the Concertverein's first concert, given at 5.30 p.m. at the Musikvereinssaal: Weber,
Euryanthe Overture; Mozart, 'Jupiter' Symphony; Wagner, *Eine Faust-Ouvertüre*; Schubert, C major
Symphony.

[11] That is to say, equalling two or four bars in 2/4 or 4/4 tempo.

[12] The score shows a whole bar held before the second fermata, but this same bar does not appear after the
first 'knock'.

[13] NBL1. 130; NBL2. 147.   [14] NBL2. 147.

The rehearsals of the Fifth Symphony did not increase his popularity with the orchestra. He was frustrated by the musicians' 'style and bad phrasing' and, despite all his good intentions, lost his temper, shouting, 'Gentlemen, this must not be washed down the drain (*heruntergespült*)!'[15] A few moments later, angered by a bad phrasing, he almost demolished the podium by stamping his feet and broke his baton when stopping the orchestra.

Mahler was convinced that Beethoven's powerful first movement must express an 'urgent and stormy restlessness'. The first notes should sound like 'a violent assault, stemmed by a giant's fist in the fermatas'. He considered that the famous sentence attributed to Beethoven—'Destiny knocking at the door'—was a pale and inadequate description of the movement's meaning. For him the first notes cried out 'Beethoven here!' When the musicians started to get angry and resented his insistence, he snapped: 'Gentlemen, if you will save your rage for the performance, we shall at least play the beginning correctly.'[16] In the second movement, Mahler attempted to lighten the theme, bringing out its grace and elegance.[17] To Natalie he explained that

the most powerful (*kräftigste*) artist is also invariably the most delicate; this is as true of Beethoven as of others: naturally, because the intensity of the whole man, the depth of his feeling and perception, extends in all directions. Of all Beethoven's symphonies, only the First, Second and Fourth are still well performed by contemporary conductors and orchestras, all the others are lost in their hands. Only Wagner was faithful to Beethoven's spirit, and today I am. One could say that he discovered all Beethoven's symphonies. If I succeed, it's because I frighten each musician into abandoning his little ego and soaring above himself.[18]

When conducting Beethoven's Ninth Symphony in Prague the year before, Mahler had been overjoyed when Richard Batka, in the *Prager Tagblatt*, had compared his interpretation with Wagner's, showing, by reference to contemporary reports, the degree to which Mahler's renditions and even his instrumental changes had resembled his predecessor's:

Our aims were always identical and almost always achieved in the same way. Sometimes, we achieved the same result by completely different methods, but our intentions never conflicted. There are great violinists and great singers, in short, great interpreters, but there are not many great conductors, even fewer than there are good composers. Indeed, only those who themselves create can interpret faithfully, and usually they lack the necessary conducting experience; fortunately for them, most of them do not exercise this profession!

---

[15] Literally 'flushed down the drain'. A pun on *heruntergespielt* (badly played).

[16] AMM1. 126; AMM2. 127.

[17] He asked the violas to play the first semiquavers of the bar downbow, instead of clumsily emphasizing it, and to give precise values to the dotted notes.

[18] NBL. 130; NBL2. 148. This passage from Natalie's MS shows that the accusations of tyranny brought against Mahler were to some extent justified.

Mahler's interpretation of Beethoven's Fifth created a sensation, for he again changed the instrumentation, particularly of a passage in the Finale. The news had been carefully spread by his enemies in the orchestra.[19] According to Ludwig Karpath, the public waited impatiently for the 'scandalous' passage and was disappointed to discover that the modification was almost unnoticeable. Some of the critics cried sacrilege, but others (the *Neue Freie Presse*, for example) merely emphasized the concert's extraordinary success. So many people had been turned away for lack of seats that the committee decided to give a second performance three days later.[20] Mahler's conception of Beethoven, his changes in the instrumentation, and his tempos were sharply criticized and at times approved by the Viennese press. Robert Hirschfeld hailed Mahler's version of the Fifth Symphony as 'moving by its very novelty', for the conductor saw in Beethoven not the ultimate perfection of classical development, but a 'mighty prophet of the new style in music'.[21] At this time, Hirschfeld was prepared to accept most of the instrumental retouching,[22] except for the audacious doubling of the bassoons in the Finale, which he regarded as 'intolerable and contrary to the nature of Beethoven's music'. Schönaich was also opposed to this[23] and certain other 'surprising and unusual' features, such as the fast pace of the first movement[24] and the slowness of the next two.[25] He conceded that the 'triumphal jubilation' of the Finale, with its 'noble pride and blinding brilliance', was 'eminently typical of Beethoven'. In another article in the *Wiener Tagblatt*, the same critic, in a more liberal mood, declared that it was ridiculous to be put off by new tempos, even if they were contrary to tradition, and to refuse to recognize Mahler's feeling for Beethoven's 'grand style'. His powerful accentuation, his imposing crescendos, and the radiance of the final hymn of victory indeed revealed 'a magnificently talented conductor, who is entirely familiar with the work'.

The Philharmonic had not played Mozart's 'Jupiter' Symphony for ten years.

[19] In the Finale, just before the presto coda, Beethoven assigns the theme (G, C, G, E, D, C, G) first to the bassoons, then the horns. Mahler had the horns enter with the bassoons. In the first movement, he entrusted the famous solo to two oboes playing in unison. According to Karpath, the orchestra musicians had once again pointed out the changes to the critics before the concert (BMG 131).

[20] This 2nd concert took place on 8 Nov. at 7.30.

[21] He wrote that Mahler had built the entire first movement out of the opening notes, which had not been played evenly, but like 'a chaos of strokes producing a shuddering vibration from the violins'. Throughout the movement he had maintained a 'frightening dramatic tension', which abated only in the last bars. The tempo for the Andante con moto had been very slow, perhaps too much so, but this same slow pace had shrouded the Scherzo in an aura of inexpressible mystery, a telling preparation for the triumphal explosion of the Finale.

[22] Particularly the use of a piccolo in the Finale. However, he objected to the muting of the horns at the beginning of the Scherzo and the doubling of the bassoons by the horns in the Finale: although he had tried to subdue their tone, Mahler had in fact altered their actual sound (see above). Schönaich, on the other hand, claimed that such doubling was 'accepted by all the famous conductors in Germany'.

[23] According to Karpath, Schönaich always opposed Mahler's instrumental changes because he was afraid that Vienna would regard him as a 'desecrator of Beethoven'.

[24] Wagner and Bülow had played it slower, he claimed.

[25] In his view, the slow tempo of the Scherzo had had 'particularly curious' results in the famous double-bass passage in the Trio.

Hirschfeld thought Mahler's interpretation of it as 'incontestable and irreproachable' as his interpretation of *The Magic Flute* and *Le nozze di Figaro*. 'In works in which there is no conflict, but only absolute perfection', Mahler ceased to express his own personality and revealed instead a Mozart 'pure and unadulterated, bathed in gentle light and devoid of any modernism'. The performance of the Finale's complex polyphony had been exemplary with its free and effortless pursuit of Mozart's airy grace, 'the last word in the art of conducting and of orchestral technique'. It was impossible to lay down fixed rules for 'this impressionistic style of conducting', with its spontaneous changes of colours and shading of rhythmic inflections and restraint. Nor could one fully identify oneself with Mahler's very personal interpretations, but merely 'try to get attuned to them'. The orchestra had responded magnificently to every impulse, and the violins, in particular, had played 'not as an ensemble, but as one man'.

On the subject of the 'Jupiter' Symphony an anonymous review in *Die Waage* rejoiced that the current generation had found a 'new Mozart' to delight in. Mahler knew, 'better than anyone, how to render the style and spirit of Mozart, his power, his grace, his delicate colours, his golden sheen'. Richard Robert, in the *Illustrirtes Wiener Extrablatt*, seconded Schönaich (*Allgemeine Zeitung*) in his dislike of the placing of Beethoven's Fifth Symphony in the same programme, as it had destroyed the effect of the Mozart and made it seem like 'child's-play'. Schönaich thought that Mahler's gifts as a Mozart conductor had never shown to better advantage: 'Like an absolutely perfect crystal, this wonderful work shone with all the colours of the spectrum.' Mahler never failed to bring out the delicacy and grace of rococo art, not in deference to some 'historic fad' but by revealing 'its true soul'. Every movement had been enthusiastically received. Even Hans Puchstein, in the anti-Semitic *Deutsches Volksblatt*, recognized that the performance of the double fugue in the Finale had been, quite simply, masterly. After making fun of the 'snobs' who had subscribed to the concerts of the Philharmonic even before the programmes had been announced, Helm praised the 'high degree of virtuosity' of the performances, although Mahler's interpretations were 'as personal as usual',[26] which showed that he had paid not the slightest attention to all the criticism expressed the previous year.

The second concert, on 19 November, included only two works: Beethoven's Second Symphony and the first of Strauss's symphonic poems, *Aus Italien*.[27] In view of their personal and professional relationship, as well as the high quality of the music, Mahler was bound to conduct performances of one of Strauss's works, yet it is somewhat surprising that he should have chosen the weakest of

---

[26] He singled out the rapid tempo of the first movement of the Fifth Symphony, the 'celestial passage' in the Andante to which Mahler, taking it with excessive slowness, had given 'a sentimental and Mendelssohnian flavour', and the instrumental changes in the Finale.

[27] Mahler had then written to Strauss expressing his admiration and asking him to send more of his scores.

his symphonic poems. However, he himself explained that he had heard *Aus Italien* in Budapest ten years before and that the theme of the Finale had immediately caught his attention, so much so that he had regarded it as proof of Strauss's genius. He later discovered that the melody was that of a well-known song, 'Funiculi, funiculà'.

Had the author of the melody been born a German in the land of symphonic music, he might have been a great musician.[28] Don't imagine that a really important artistic thought falls into your lap by chance. Inventiveness is above all a sign of divine favour. If something like that could happen to you as to a gambler winning a big prize in a lottery, all you would have to do is to keep on at it and one day something really important might come out of it. But [in composition] going on trying is in vain; if the gods have not put the ticket with the right number in your cradle, blind chance will never make you a present of it.[29]

During the rehearsals for the same concert, Mahler addressed his musicians as follows when they came to the Finale of Beethoven's Second Symphony:

Take a good look at this passage; where do you find any of the 'monumental calm', or any of the verve (*Schwung*) that you are usually asked to apply to Beethoven's music, often in the wrong place? Here, you will find only grace and humour, there, reserve and tenderness. But suddenly one comes across an ardent passage, an unparalleled crescendo or a tremendous élan, which must be approached in quite a different spirit: you must then sweep the audience off its feet by the sheer intensity, warmth and grandeur of your playing.[30]

Here Mahler felt that he had explained an essential aspect of his approach to interpretation and that he had been well understood.

The first Viennese performance of Strauss's *Aus Italien* did not improve Hanslick's opinion of the composer. While admiring its instrumentation and some of its melodic ideas, he discerned in it 'nothing new, nothing significant', nothing that 'leaves a lasting impression'. The piece, in his view, failed to render the atmosphere of Italy, and the manner in which 'Funiculi, funiculà' was introduced into the Finale seemed to him entirely gratuitous. Though an artist and composer 'full of temperament and poetic ideas and clever in the choice of his effects', Strauss was not in his view a great creative artist (*schaffender Künstler*), and the public's applause had been addressed mainly to the quality of the performance. Another enemy of the *neudeutsch* tendency, Max Kalbeck couldn't hear anything in *Aus Italien* except 'Strauss's disappointment on seeing the Italian landscapes he had heard so much about'. At the tomb of Cecilia Metella he had thought only of the Wälsungen, and had

---

[28] Clearly, Mahler did not know that the composer of 'Funiculi, funiculà' was Luigi Denza (1846–1922) and that he was still alive at the time.

[29] NBL1. 126; NBL2. 144.

[30] Ibid. Mahler's striving for contrasts of atmosphere within a work, charm versus emotion or gentleness versus violence, differed radically from Richter's more 'architectural' performances and was one of the essential characteristics of his conducting, as stressed by many of his contemporaries.

expressed his feelings in 'weak, commonplace melodies' showing 'poverty-stricken and hard-pressed' invention and quite inadequate creative powers. The 'concentration of ideas and of form indispensable to symphonic music' was altogether lacking, so that the work revealed only the talent and cleverness of the composer. The very considerable success of the performance could only be attributed to the quality of the orchestra and to Mahler himself, with his 'gift of identifying with the composers he interprets'.

Once more dipping his pen in vitriol, Hirschfeld commiserated with 'this unfortunate young man striding with such refined sensibilities and such strangely excited nerves through the peaceful campagna romana'. To him, Strauss's 'combinatory art' and 'prickly counterpoint' suggested a forest of cactus rather than the famous landscapes to which the composer remained totally foreign. Theodor Helm was the only critic to defend Strauss, noting that the two latter movements had been 'irresistibly effective' with the audience, thanks in part to Mahler's 'energetic and intelligent' conducting.[31]

The third concert, on 8 December, included Brahms's Third Symphony, a work for which Mahler had the greatest enthusiasm. True, its orchestration lacked brilliance and the conductor longed to retouch it but dared not, lest he shock the critics. Doubtless it was out of sheer 'anti-Wagnerism' that Brahms had deprived himself of 'such a wealth of modern orchestral means', which he had nevertheless used in his chamber music. In order to strengthen the violins, Mahler thought of making the second violins play in unison with the first in the most important passages. In his view Brahms's music had only one limitation, that of 'never bursting its bonds and soaring above life and sorrow on this earth to freer and brighter worlds. Brahms treats everything in a profound, fervent and personal manner, but he always remains a prisoner of this earthly life, never lifting his eyes to the highest summits; it is for this reason that his works will never achieve the greatest, the ultimate effect'.[32] Yet at other times Mahler would acknowledge the greatness of Brahms's music, although he was very conscious of the abyss that separated the two of them as creators. 'I was again dumbfounded,' he said the following winter, while studying the score of another of Brahms's symphonies,[33]

to see what a puritan Brahms is. Everything resembling ornamentation, embellishment or fantasy is strictly excluded from his works, leaving nothing but a hard and austere play of sounds, albeit very brilliant and ingenious. From this, which seems to be all that matters to him, speaks a great artist and a great man. I've often wondered whether my style and mode of musical expression, which differ so radically from his, are perhaps nothing more than (Catholic) mystical humbug.[34]

[31] He criticized Mahler for having destroyed the atmosphere by over-emphasizing Beethoven's accents in the Larghetto of the Second Symphony (presumably referring to the passage which starts at the 32nd bar of the movement).   [32] NBL1. 134; NBL2. 150.

[33] NBLS, 14 Nov. 1900. The MS mentions the 'Symphony in B flat'. Does this perhaps mean the second, in D?

[34] The word 'Catholic' is crossed out in NBLS, the MS copy of Natalie's *Mahleriana* (BGM).

Mahler's interpretation of Brahms was almost unanimously acclaimed by
the Viennese critics. Hirschfeld praised it to the skies, with one exception, the
third movement, in which he found the tempo too slow and 'contrary to the
vivacity and grace sought by the composer'.

After Dvořák had turned down his offer to produce *Rusalka*, Mahler was
anxious to perform one of his new orchestral works at the Philharmonic. He had
received several scores which were still unperformed in Vienna and finally
accepted the symphonic poem, Op. 110, *Die Waldtaube* (The Wood Pigeon),
although with some reluctance, it seems.[35] 'This sort of concoction,' he said to
Natalie,

gives people a bad opinion of 'programme music'. They don't see the difference
between such works and others that have nothing in common with them, beyond being
based on a text and having titles or some definite subject matter, such as Beethoven's
Ninth or his 'Pastoral' Symphony, or even my own Third Symphony if I had left in the
titles.

Conducting *Die Weihe des Hauses* after *Die Waldtaube*, Mahler felt like the
'giant Antaeus finding the ground under his feet again':

Here I have no doubts about the interpretation, whereas with the others I find myself
groping and searching and wondering whether I'm being faithful to their intentions.
With Beethoven and Wagner, I feel sure of myself: there's only one way to play their
works. They're like lofty mountains towering above the vanity and futility of this world
and in this way they surpass all others. However, we should not scorn the others who
have also created beauty in their own way.[36]

Hanslick's verdict on *Die Waldtaube* was the same as Mahler's. Although the
work suggested a 'strong and individual nature' and contained passages of
'charming grace and naïvety', the music was like 'a lovely prisoner fettered
between two guards and held to a prescribed path'. The changes in atmosphere
and the sequence of the different episodes had no musical justification, and the
listener was allowed no freedom. Compositional procedures of this kind should
really be confined to opera. Schönaich considered that the 'programme' of *Die
Waldtaube* was only superficially connected with the perfectly 'honourable'
music of Dvořák, who had strayed into a blind alley. The procedure of musical
description, borrowed from Liszt, seemed equally 'frightening' and 'irrational'
to Hirschfeld, in whose eyes Dvořák's 'powerful harmonic and melodic invention' and 'masterly technique' had been deployed completely in vain. As we
have seen, the same critic had nothing but praise for the performance of
Brahms's Third Symphony.[37]

[35] NBL1. 134; NBL2. 150. Dvořák had sent this score to Mahler the previous year, along with *Heldenlied*,
Op. 111. On 23 Sept. 1899 Mahler wrote to say that if 'you really have no new work for me, I will conduct
Die Waldtaube' (Prague, Anton Dvořák Bequest).

[36] NBL1. 134; NBL2. 150.

[37] Hirschfeld questioned only the tempo of the third movement, whose slowness was 'contrary to the
vivacity and grace intended by the composer'.

Mahler quite deliberately took the risk of finally alienating all the conservatives in Vienna by playing Beethoven's 'Pastoral' Symphony at the last Philharmonic Concert of the year, on 17 December. It was with this work that he had caused a scandal in Hamburg some years earlier. Of all Beethoven's works this was undoubtedly one of his favourites. In order to understand it, he told Natalie, 'one must have a <u>feeling for nature</u>, which most people (conductors) lack, incredible as it may seem'. From the very start of the piece,

one must realise how naïvely Beethoven had conceived the title 'awakening of happy feelings on arrival in the country', what he felt when breathing fresh air, or seeing the sun and the open sky or when he was surrounded by forests and meadows. In particular, no one seems able to render the Scene by the brook, which is taken either too fast (in four beats), or too slowly (in twelve beats). The former is usually the case, because of Beethoven's joke at the end of it: surprised by the rain, the nature lovers run for shelter and the tempo accelerates.[38] This is why these idiots play the whole movement too fast, whereas, as an effective contrast to this acceleration, most of it should flow as tranquilly as the stream itself, in keeping with the uniform and continuous flow of the accompaniment, which must be monotonous in the extreme.[39] Against this monotonous accompaniment stands out music of such beauty and spontaneity that only those totally lacking in humour and sensitivity could find it boring . . . Even Bülow, who far outshone all other conductors in intelligence, failed to render it correctly.

The cause of Bülow's failure in interpreting the 'Pastoral' was that he had no feeling for nature, as Frau von Bülow had told Mahler.[40] In fact, Mahler was convinced that people had mistaken the meaning of 'molto moto', which he thought was intended to be 'molto moderato'.[41] 'Until a creative musician feels the musical and artistic need for this tempo,' said Mahler, 'and can justify it to his orchestra's satisfaction, this absurd indication will continue to be followed to the letter.' Only two passages—two bars of the slow movement and four of the Finale—seemed to Mahler to express Beethoven's 'subjective feeling' and

[38] Natalie must be referring here to the third movement rather than the second.

[39] NBL1. 100; NBL2. 151. As in Hamburg, the moderate tempo of this movement surprised the critics, but Mahler had decided that the marking 'molto moto' was in fact a misreading. Just as Beethoven often replaced 'allegro' by *all°*, 'moto' was in his opinion an abbreviation of 'moderato'. This explanation had been suggested to him by the cellist Josef Sulzer, who had also explained that 'moto' should have been 'mosso' in correct Italian and that the marking appeared nowhere else in Beethoven. Josef Sulzer recalled in his memoirs that both Richter and Dessoff had used a tempo far slower than their contemporaries in the 'brook' scene. He claimed that it was Dessoff who had first decided that 'molto moto' (very fast) should be read as 'molto moderato': J. Sulzer, *Ernstes und Heiteres aus den Erinnerungen eines Wiener Philharmonikers* (Eisenstein, Leipzig, 1910). The only critic who showed understanding for Mahler's moderate tempo was Hirschfeld, who was aware of Sulzer's suggestion.

[40] NBL1. 100; NBL2. 114 ff.

[41] NBL1. 134; NBL2. 150. This supposition seemed perfectly reasonable since 'molto moto' is grammatically impossible and abbreviations of the type *moᵗ°* for *moderato* were common in the 18th and early 19th cents. None the less, the autograph MS kept in the Beethovenhaus in Bonn clearly shows that 'moto' is not an abbreviation of 'moderato', but an expression of Beethoven's intention of making the tempo fluid. Beethoven has crossed out the added words 'quasi allegretto', probably because of the risk that conductors would hurry the tempo too much. He must therefore have meant 'Andante con moto' or 'Andante molto mosso' (cf. *Nachrichten zu Mahler-Forschung*, Internationale Mahler Gesellschaft, no. 19 (Mar. 1988), 17).

'passionate emotion'.[42] Elsewhere, nature spoke for itself; therefore, the conducting of the whole piece should emphasize, and be constructed around, these two passages.

Before the 'Pastoral' Symphony, Mahler conducted Spohr's overture to *Jessonda*,[43] after which the guest violinist Marie Soldat-Roeger, who led the string quartet of which Natalie Bauer-Lechner was a member, played the Brahms Violin Concerto. Her teacher, the famous Joseph Joachim, who was in Vienna with his quartet, asked Mahler's permission to attend the final rehearsal in order to hear his former pupil. At first Mahler hesitated, for he had never forgiven Joachim for taking sides with Brahms against Wagner's music, but Natalie persuaded him to let Joachim attend by reminding him of the latter's encouragement of young performers and composers. In fact, he gave in readily after hearing a private recital by the Joachim Quartet in the house of Karl Wittgenstein, the famous businessman and music lover who had been a close friend of Brahms.[44] This concert had so delighted him that, at the rehearsal, he asked the orchestra to rise in the violinist's honour and made him a short and exceedingly warm speech of welcome.

Mahler was still *persona grata* in Vienna, and his revolutionary conception of the 'Pastoral' Symphony was better received than it had been in Hamburg. Even Theodor Helm reluctantly confessed how much he had enjoyed the performance. He was pleased to note that Mahler had emphasized the thunderstorm passage in which, 'precisely as that divine music requires, the heavens broke with an almighty crash'. He found the 'Scene by the Brook' 'marvellously phrased', despite the rather too slow tempo.[45] Hirschfeld called Mahler's interpretation 'a true miracle of sound'. The conductor was not content merely to conduct, he 'shapes and models, makes everything germinate and flower as if it was being created anew under our very eyes' and transported the audience 'on paths of poetry through every mood'. Despite its slow tempo, the Andante had never been so enchanting, nor the birdsong so natural.

It was no longer an 'artifice' which Beethoven had appended to the movement, but, with its dreamlike tranquillity and veiled sounds, a touching, dim echo from the innermost depths of a man who could no longer be reached by external sounds, like a faint recall of lost happiness that had come from hearing the simplest voices of nature. You could

[42] NBLS.

[43] A number of critics declared this work not worth reviving. Helm was particularly impressed by the performance of the Brahms Concerto.

[44] Karl Wittgenstein was the father of Ludwig Wittgenstein, the great philosopher and of the pianist Paul Wittgenstein who lost his right arm in the First World War and commissioned concertos for the left hand from Ravel, Prokofiev, and Richard Strauss. Mahler was *not* a regular visitor at the Wittgensteins' house, as claimed by S. Toulmin and A. Janik in their book, *Wittgenstein's Vienna* (Simon & Schuster, New York, 1973). This mistake arose from a printer's error (*Mahler*, instead of *Maler* = painter) in the German edn. (Fischer, Berlin, 1950) of Bruno Walter's book, *Thema und Variationen*, as has been demonstrated by Dr Herta Blaukopf (cf. *Nachrichten zu Mahler-Forschung*, ibid., no. 23 (Mar. 1990), 15).

[45] He made the same criticism of the tempo in the Scherzo.

no longer smile at the 'birdsong fun' (*Vogelspass*); instead there were tears, and one's heart seemed to stand still . . .[46]

Schönaich also considered that the slow pace at which Mahler took the middle movements of the 'Pastoral' was justified by the effect he obtained.[47] Most of the critics had nothing but praise for the performance of the Brahms Concerto by Marie Soldat-Roeger who, according to Hanslick, 'harmoniously blended energy and sweetness'.

Exhausted by a particularly busy opening to the opera season and by the Philharmonic Concerts,[48] Mahler spent the last few days of the year and New Year's Day in the country with Justi and Natalie at Rodaun, a little village a few kilometres to the south-west of Vienna, on the road to Mödling. At first glance the place so enchanted him that he decided in future to spend all his free time there. However, the very evening of his arrival, he realized that the little inn where he was staying was somewhat noisy. He wanted to leave immediately, and Justi and Natalie had a hard time persuading him to remain overnight. That same evening, he met with Josef Stritzko, the director of the Waldheim-Eberle firm which printed his works, and had a long talk with him about the 'Denkmäler der Tonkunst in Österreich' (Monuments of Musical Composition in Austria) then in process of publication under the direction of Guido Adler. Mahler told him bluntly that the collection contained only 'mediocrities of the last century' and that it was a pity to spend so much money publishing them.[49] He himself was a member of the committee that selected the works to be published and he had attended one of its first meetings with Baron Bezecny, Wilhelm Ritter von Hartel, and Guido Adler. However, the lengthy discussion of points that could have been dealt with in a few words had made him so impatient that he had pleaded a rehearsal as an excuse to walk out in the middle of the meeting, vowing to himself that he would never attend another.

As the year, and with it the nineteenth century, drew to a close, an event occurred which had nothing to do with music and attracted little notice at the time, but ultimately proved to be of great significance in shaping our views on the way the human mind works. In November 1899 the Viennese neurologist Sigmund Freud published a book entitled *Die Traumdeutung*.[50] Only 600 copies were printed, and it took several years to sell them. Max Burckhard,[51] the former director of the Burgtheater, wrote lengthy articles in two successive

---

[46] Hirschfeld's eulogy is all the more interesting in that he was soon to switch from great enthusiasm to the most virulent denigration of Mahler's interpretations.

[47] He also observed that the Scherzo was a peasant rondo.

[48] Justi had got him into the habit of taking a walk in the Prater each afternoon, thanks to which she claimed he was 'in much better form than usual this year' (letter from Justine to Emma Rosé of 25 Oct. 1899, former Ernst Rosé collection).

[49] Edward Reilly observes that, of the 13 vols. publ. by 1900, only 3 contained works from the 18th cent. He suggests that Mahler was appointed to the committee in 1898, replacing Brahms; however Mahler's name is not mentioned in the archives of the Denkmäler (RAM 31).

[50] Franz Deuticke, Leipzig and Vienna, 4 Nov. 1899.

[51] Max Burckhard was a close friend of Carl and Anna Moll and one of Alma Schindler's first admirers.

issues of *Die Zeit*, ridiculing the author in every possible way. He went so far as to describe Freud's fundamental theory, that dreams can be interpreted as revelations of our subconscious, as a 'clever prank'. But neither Burckhard's articles nor any subsequent criticism was able to prevent the subversive ferment of Freudian thinking from gradually gaining ground, until today it is generally recognized as having brought about one of the greatest revolutions of the twentieth century.

For Mahler, the year 1900 brought not only his fortieth birthday but also his breakthrough at the Opera. Richter's departure and that of Jahn's main star singers, Marie Renard and Ernest Van Dyck, marked the end of the 'old regime' and enabled him firmly to establish his own methods. Lilli Lehmann's protracted guest appearance in December—it lasted a whole week and gave the members of the Opera what Mahler called their annual 'singing lesson'—was part of the new approach.[52] Despite its success, Mahler again laid himself open to criticism for the considerable expense to the Opera that such a *Gastspiel* represented. However, he continued to make Lehmann's visits an annual event.

On 6 January a new press campaign was launched against him by the *Deutsches Volksblatt*. Not content with casting aspersions on Mahler's character, questioning his competence as a conductor, condemning the way he ran the Opera and his 'betrayal' of the classical masters, the anti-Semitic newspaper also challenged his integrity, in an article written purportedly in Budapest under the pseudonym Bela Inden:[53]

The recent news that the present director of the Hofoper is about to be offered a new contract[54] extending over several years has caused a certain amount of astonishment among art lovers here, since, considering the said gentleman's past exploits, with which everyone in Budapest is familiar, one would have expected precisely the opposite to happen. Herr Mahler must be an exceedingly lucky person, for the circumstances surrounding his departure from the Royal Hungarian Opera were such that people in the know doubted that he would succeed in getting himself re-employed as a conductor by even a modest provincial theatre. It was not his musical talents that were at issue, but matters which have to be judged by standards of ordinary decency. That Herr Mahler all too frequently blew his own trumpet in order to take the credit for the merits of others was pardonable in view of his notorious vanity; that he set up a pasha's regime and obliged every male and female member of the Budapest Opera to pay homage to him in one way or another could be overlooked on account of the loose morals of Hungarian society; that he was presumptuous could be attributed to his Semitic origins; and that he even had himself baptized in order to advance his career was also understandable because of his race. However, ugly rumours concerning his traffic in percentages, author's royalties and commissions were never denied and eventually led to, let us say, his resignation.

---

[52] Telegram from Mahler to Lilli Lehmann, 22 Nov. 1899 (HOA). Lilli Lehmann sang *Norma* (16 and 23 Dec.), *Fidelio* (the 18th), and *Don Giovanni* (the 21th).

[53] Dated 3 Jan.

[54] In fact Mahler had never signed a contract, since he had been appointed by the Emperor.

When he left the Royal Hungarian Opera to reappear as a star at the foremost artistic institution of the Empire, Hungarians merely smiled pityingly at the thought that a man who had retired so dishonourably from an official Court position in Budapest should subsequently be called to an office in the imperial city, which put him in direct contact with the highest authorities. Although it seemed unlikely, we could only suppose that the Court officials and the administration of the Imperial Opera were not informed in detail of Herr Mahler's activities in Budapest. We presumed, however, that they would soon be apprised of the facts and predicted that the gentleman in question would therefore not occupy his present position for long. . . . Thanks mainly to the influence of a certain nobleman[55] who wished to spare him, the circumstances of his dismissal have so far been hushed up. Nevertheless, there are still innumerable witnesses of his 'exploits' in the Hungarian capital who, if it were necessary, could reveal the truth about a man who has attained such giddy heights solely because he has powerful protectors. If the rumour that he is to be kept on as director of the Vienna Opera (where he has already done so much harm) should prove true, then many hitherto sealed mouths will doubtless soon open. For any cultivated person, however chauvinistic he may be, considers art an international sanctuary, the guardianship of which should be entrusted only to hands that are clean, and sanctified by true genius.

This time Mahler's enemies had gone too far. The calumny was all the more odious for being vague and insidious—quite apart from being totally unfounded. However, the *Deutsches Volksblatt*[56] was an important newspaper, the mouthpiece of the Vienna municipality, Mahler feared therefore that some people might believe its slanderous allegations. He went to see Prince Montenuovo to ask him whether it would be advisable to publish a denial. Aristocrat that he was, Montenuovo forbade him to enter into any sort of discussion with his slanderers. Not at all reassured, Mahler went to see the critic Ludwig Karpath, who still had numerous contacts in Budapest, and eventually asked him to mention the matter to Count Apponyi who knew perfectly well that none of the allegations were founded. The Count also refused to intervene or issue any sort of denial.[57] A surprised and saddened Mahler concluded that this must be due to his own refusal to present Ödön Mihalovich's operas in Vienna. However, letters of support addressed to the authorities of the Vienna Opera by his friends in Budapest, and even by the former administrator of the Budapest Opera, Franz Beniczky, amply proved the absurdity of the *Volksblatt's* accusations.

---

[55] Undoubtedly Count Apponyi.

[56] Both the *Deutsche Zeitung* and the *Deutsches Volksblatt* were organs of the anti-Semitic Christian Democratic Party, of which Mayor Lueger was the leader.

[57] Learning that Count Apponyi was in Vienna, Karpath went to catch him at the end of the session held by the Magyar delegation at the Hungarian Palace in the Bankgasse. But the Count brushed him off with 'I haven't a moment to spare and won't raise a finger for Mahler'. Later on, however, he wrote a eulogy of Mahler's activities in Budapest in his memoirs. In 1930, in the hope of clearing up the whole affair, Karpath wrote to the director of the Budapest Opera, Desider Vidor, who was writing a history of the establishment. Vidor answered that he had never come across anything in the course of his work to justify the *Volksblatt's* accusations: 'There is absolutely no question of Mahler ever having profited financially from his directorship of the Budapest Opera, especially since he never had anything to do with its financial management.' It is not possible at present to check the research carried out by Vidor.

Four days after the *Volksblatt* article, the *Deutsche Zeitung* also set out to prove that Mahler was leading the Opera down the road to ruin. Despite the obvious harm it was suffering under his directorship, the Lord Chamberlain seemed inclined to close his eyes, instead of 'removing this harmful man' and putting an end to his activities. The only reason why the whole city of Vienna had not yet turned against him was because it remained ignorant of many of the transgressions he had committed at the Opera, and also because the press had adopted a shamefully partisan attitude toward him.

Despite the wishes of all impartial people in Vienna, despite the warnings of all the musicians concerned (some of them world-renowned), despite the many serious accusations brought by an oppressed, disconcerted and discontented personnel, despite the undeniable failures manifest in a deplorable repertoire and an even more deplorable box-office record, and, finally, despite the extraordinary rumours concerning his resignation from the Budapest Opera, Gustav Mahler is kept on solely by the two Obersthofmeister, and in the first place by Prince Liechtenstein.

The same paper attacked the Obersthofmeister who was to blame for this disgraceful state of affairs, since he had chosen as Intendant a mere civil servant who knew nothing about the theatre and could be of no help in important matters. 'This fault on the part of the Obersthofmeister is the more regrettable as the discipline throughout the Opera is deteriorating dangerously because of it; the Obersthofmeister regards Mahler's stern discipline as a virtue, without realizing that, imposed by this parvenu, it degenerates into injustice, brutality and tyranny . . .'. Since the Intendant was incapable of performing his duties, the Obersthofmeister had become the director's immediate superior; and Prince Liechtenstein, who was formerly Master of the Horse, knew less than nothing about running a theatre and was quite unaware of the measures that should be taken against 'the Mahler misdeeds'. Instead of always going to Mahler for information, he should have occasionally consulted reliable people. He thus bore the full responsibility for the decline of the Opera. About Mahler there was nothing further to be said, but Prince Liechtenstein should make some enquiries and then act quickly, before it was too late!

Throughout the first months of 1900 the two anti-Semitic papers persisted in their attacks. At Marie Renard's farewell performance, on 29 January, he was 'the only person at the Opera who did not join the demonstration, quite simply because he is the cause of this irreplaceable artist's departure'. During the applause[58] he 'stood in the front of his box for a few moments, looking pale and drawn' and biting his lips with ill-disguised agitation as he contemplated

---

[58] Marie Renard was only 37 and still at the height of her powers. She was leaving to marry Count Kinsky and had chosen as her farewell the role of *Carmen*, in which she had made her début in Vienna on 18 Aug. 1887. She took more than 15 curtain-calls at the end of Act I and nearly 40 at the end of the opera, before taking leave of the public with a short speech improvised amid a sea of flowers and laurel wreaths. The final ovation lasted almost 45 minutes. According to Helm's *Musikalisches Wochenblatt* articles, she took 130 curtain-calls.

Renard's triumph. Unfortunately, he had already left by the time somebody in the audience shouted out: 'Away with Mahler, let us keep Renard.' Ten days later the *Deutsches Volksblatt*[59] announced another 'misdeed'. Mahler was supposed to have stuck his tongue out at Demuth, because the latter had accelerated the tempo during a performance of *Die Meistersinger*.[60] Frau Forster, who was singing Eva, had been so taken aback that she had almost sung off-beat. 'Even servants would not be allowed to behave in this vulgar manner' concluded the anonymous author.[61] In the middle of February, the *Deutsche Zeitung* wrote of an 'uneven and disorderly' performance of *Zar und Zimmermann*, in which Naval had been replaced at the last minute (on 9 February) by August Stoll, a singer 'recently relegated to the background because of his incompetence'.[62] The Emperor had left the hall after the second act, but had returned two days later for a performance of *Fra Diavolo*, which Mahler had only decided to conduct himself at the last moment upon hearing that His Majesty would be present. His 'nervous and spasmodic vibrations' had caused such confusion that he had been forced to stop the singers in the middle of an ensemble and make them begin it again, a very rare occurrence at the Opera. The impression Mahler had made on the Emperor at these two performances could not have been 'altogether favourable'. On 22 February the *Deutsche Zeitung* attributed to Mahler some disagreeable remarks about the members of the Opera and their behaviour towards him: 'People who spend the whole night drinking and . . . and then can't sing the next day have no professional integrity,' he was supposed to have said in front of witnesses. This was taken to be a reference to the supper held by Marie Renard after her farewell, a supper to which Mahler had 'for obvious reasons' not been invited, and the day after which one of the singers who had attended had been taken ill. Remarks like this 'showed a man in his true colours', the article concluded.[63]

If the anti-Semitic press considered such minor incidents justification for attacking Mahler. Richter's departure was to provide them with far better opportunity. Having signed a new five-year contract with the Opera, which doubled his salary,[64] Richter wrote a formal letter to the director of the Opera on 28 February to ask that his contract be annulled, because 'my health and, above all, my nerves make it impossible for me to carry out my duties in the manner expected of me'. In recent years the mere business of conducting an entire performance had required every ounce of energy he possessed. He had

[59] The passage was reproduced from the *Neues Wiener Journal*.   [60] On 2 Feb.

[61] The *Deutsche Zeitung* explains that Demuth was hastening the tempo and Mahler signalled this to him with his tongue instead of his hands which were then fully occupied. Thanks to this unusual signal 'singer and conductor were quickly back in unison'.

[62] Stoll was also assistant producer at the Vienna Opera.

[63] In Mar., *Deutsche Zeitung* again attacked Mahler, this time because he had pensioned off a dancer, Frau Rathner, sacking her 'with his usual brutality' and thus showing his hatred for ballet and his ignorance, common to all Jews, of good manners.

[64] From 6,000 to 12,000 gulden.

been conducting in the theatre since 1859, and at the Vienna Opera since 1868.[65] In a personal letter written three days earlier to Mahler, Richter had spoken of these years as 'war years' which had 'counted double' because of the great number of premières he had led.

My life in the theatre has been one long struggle against incomprehension, baseness and incompetence, all too rarely compensated by the joy of achieving artistic success or of having had devoted and selfless collaborators. Even when, by chance, I experienced such unmitigated joy, it has invariably been short-lived, for the Viennese press has never lost time in poisoning it with its spiteful and offensive criticisms. It is not my intention to rake up old grievances; I merely wished to explain why I am fed up with the theatre!

As a reward for his services, Richter asked only that he be released from his obligations, which he nevertheless agreed to fulfil until the end of May. He also sent Mahler a personal letter in which he stressed 'the excessive nervous tension of life in the theatre, tension that is becoming dangerous both for me and for my family'. He frankly admitted to having signed the new contract only because he knew of 'no better way of finding a suitable job elsewhere'. No one could consider him capable of facing another five years of theatrical activity, since he now hated the theatre and in future wanted to conduct only concerts. Mahler would surely understand his position and, 'out of the kindness of his heart', release him from a post 'for which I am no longer strong enough and in which I no longer take any pleasure'.[66]

These letters placed Mahler in an extremely awkward position. In order to persuade Richter to remain, he had gone to a great deal of trouble to have his salary raised from 6,000 to 12,000 gulden, only to learn that he had signed the contract solely for the purpose of being in a favourable position to discuss terms with the Hallé Concert Society, which eventually offered him five times the salary he was getting in Vienna. Mahler knew that the newspapers would blame him for Richter's departure. 'I do not deny that I did oust him,' he told Karpath later. 'It was not out of ill-will, but simply because of my success. I would never have been able to undermine his position if he had spent all his time in Vienna and taken the trouble to interpret Wagner to perfection.'[67] Realizing that there was nothing he could do to prevent Richter from leaving, he asked Karpath to draw up a statement for the *Wiener Abendpost* mentioning Richter's two letters and his appeal to Mahler's 'kindness of heart'.[68] Some time later he sent Richter a letter saying that he would agree to cancel his contract, since he realized that

[65] Of the 32 years, Richter in fact had 28 to his credit, since he had been away from Vienna during several seasons.

[66] BMG 158 ff.

[67] Since Richter was Siegfried Wagner's godfather, Mahler had tried, in vain, to get him to conduct the first performance of *Der Bärenhäuter*. He was nevertheless accused of robbing his illustrious senior of 'the joy of guiding Richard Wagner's son's first steps in the theatre'.

[68] The statement was published on 3 Mar. With Schalk's help, Karpath copied out the two letters himself (BMG 158 ff.).

it would be pointless to try to keep him against his will. Expressing his 'surprise and indeed dismay', he wrote:

You told me, when you signed the contract, that you looked forward to continuing your artistic activity with me and said that you would devote yourself entirely to furthering the interests of our institution. Having received such an assurance from you, your present decision was the last thing I expected. Not only will it be difficult for me to find a suitable person to replace you, but my own work load will be considerably increased.

He ended his letter by extending his 'warmest and most sincere thanks' and saying that he would always remember Richter with emotion and gratitude.[69]

Despite his well-intentioned efforts,[70] Mahler had in fact rendered Richter's position at the Vienna Opera untenable. By his determined reforms, his demands for hitherto unheard-of fidelity and precision in performance, and his introduction of uncut presentations of Wagner[71] (which earned him the reputation of being Wagner's 'saviour'), he had drawn all the public's attention to himself. There was simply not enough room for two artists of such stature working side by side in the same theatre. Furthermore, Richter deeply resented the Viennese press's attitude, which seemed to have forgotten his own glorious past and extolled Mahler as 'the man of the day'.

As expected, the *Deutsches Volksblatt* described Richter's departure as 'the latest of the Mahler epoch' and accused the young director of having 'disgusted and ousted a brilliant and therefore dangerous rival'. After replacing Marie Renard with a Jewess, Selma Kurz, he was now replacing Richter by Franz Schalk, of Jewish extraction.[72] And the only reason he got away with it was because the Emperor had appointed as Obersthofmeister a Master of the Horse who knew more about equines than art. The *Deutsche Zeitung* accused Mahler of having 'rid' himself, by his innumerable underhanded provocations, of 'the most celebrated Kapellmeister of the day', thereby depriving Viennese musical life of its leader; and all because he was jealous of his art, his authority, and his very presence. 'The manner in which Richter was made to come to dislike his work in Vienna constitutes one of the ugliest chapters in Viennese musical

---

[69] HOA, Praes. 19 Mar. 1900.

[70] Some of Mahler's innovations, in particular his instrumental changes in *Tannhäuser*, had angered Richter, who had pronounced them 'contrary to the spirit of the work' (MKW ii. 253). On 24 Feb. 1902 he wrote a letter to Karpath, publ. on 28 Sept. 1902 in the *Neues Wiener Tagblatt*. In it he paid tribute to Mahler's 'extraordinary abilities' and prodigious zeal. There was no one, apart from Mottl, so well-qualified to direct the Vienna Opera. He and Mahler had always had 'an excellent relationship'. He found it ridiculous that anyone should denigrate him. For his part, he questioned only Mahler's 'improvements' to masterpieces like *Tannhäuser* or *The Flying Dutchman*. Mahler had 'ample talent without committing such crimes as these, which seem intended only as self-advertisement at any price'.

[71] Many years ago the London autograph firm Otto Haas sold a letter written by Mahler to Richter, doubtless before the latter left Vienna. In cordial, even friendly terms, Mahler asks for his advice on two Wagnerian singers and pleads in favour of certain of the Opera musicians: 'It would be exceedingly unkind of me not to take into account the justified claims of these men who have carried out their tasks enthusiastically and spent the best years of their lives in our institution. I feel sure you will agree with me.'

[72] This statement is incorrect. Schalk does not figure in any of the lists of 'non-Aryans' published by the Nazi authorities, whose research in such matters was always very thorough.

history.' Out of sheer duplicity Mahler had extolled him, but it should be remembered how, on Mahler's arrival, and after only a few performances, the Jewish press had praised him to high heaven, as though in the past everything had been mediocre and insignificant until the coming of the Messiah.[73] The supreme authority at the Opera would one day have to answer to the Viennese public 'for the loss suffered by the Hofoper'.

On 18 March the *Deutsche Zeitung* published an 'Open Letter to Gustav Mahler', in which an anonymous journalist attacked Mahler's administration and, above all, his repertoire. He claimed that he had at first been delighted to see him throw off the inertia of the Jahn era and breathe new life into Mozart, Auber, and Boieldieu. However, instead of Handel and Gluck, Berlioz's operas, Cornelius's *Der Barbier von Bagdad*, or Wolf's *Der Corregidor*, Vienna had been offered no more than a few Jewish works like *The Demon* and *Die Kriegsgefangene*, or such mediocrities as Siegfried Wagner's *Der Bärenhäuter* and Reznicek's *Donna Diana*. As conductor of the Philharmonic, Mahler had not only neglected Liszt and Bruckner, he had massacred them. As for Beethoven's Ninth, he had merely used it to show off![74]

And do you know why, Herr Mahler? Because the man is too great for you; because taste, routine and a sense of history are not sufficient for such tasks . . . and you were bound to fail when confronted with the 'really great'. We suspected as much when we heard you conduct Wagner; your performances of Beethoven and Bruckner have entirely confirmed our suspicions.

'Anyone else would have been dismissed', the anonymous author continued, but his 'insolence and childish ambition' had obviously gone to his head. He had endeavoured to command attention as a creator, but the sound and fury of his 'great symphonies' had merely revealed his inner emptiness. Disregarding one of his own rules, he had used the Philharmonic Concerts to his advantage, promoting his own orchestral Lieder which he called *Volkslieder*.[75] 'Forgive, O hallowed German people, this insult he is thereby inflicting upon you!'

'Like a satrap' he had installed himself in Vienna's musical life. He hated and feared those whose importance he could not deny and, by force or cunning, removed those who did not please him. His ruthlessness, which had been accepted initially because he appeared to be dedicated to a 'sacred cause', turned out to be merely despicable, since it served his own 'unsacred person'. By throwing out Marie Renard, Hans Richter, and Ferdinand Löwe, he had deprived the Opera of a wealth of talent. Richter publicly admitted that he was fed up with being thwarted and crossed at every turn. Mahler had finally cast

[73] *Neue Freie Presse* carried a long tribute to Richter signed by Richard Heuberger. It gave his life story and recalled his many feigned resignations, the most famous of which occurred at the end of a particularly successful performance of Beethoven's Ninth Symphony, with Richter yielding to the audience's enthusiastic applause and consenting to stay. Heuberger took leave of this 'powerful artist' with respect and admiration.
[74] The writer is alluding to the performance Mahler conducted at the Nicolai Concert on 18 Feb. 1900.
[75] On 14 Jan. 1900, Selma Kurz sang five Lieder by Mahler at a Philharmonic Concert (see below).

aside his sheep's clothing and shown his true face, which was frightening. Typically, as a tyrant, he distrusted every single major artist. Was he not planning to take over the whole Opera and fill all the posts with his own creatures, as he was attempting to do at the Philharmonic? Was he not intending to create a conductorship for Marie Gutheil-Schoder's[76] husband and relegate the younger Hellmesberger to the Burgtheater? 'Since we can expect nothing more from you, we have quite simply decided to turn our backs on you. However, there still remains a faint ray of hope, which you yourself, by your very excesses, have kept alive: we all know that the folly and tyranny of dictators lead, if not to their death, at least to their downfall.' Thus ended another collector's item in the long list of scurrilous attacks. One can only wonder whether any other city in the world has ever heaped such base insults and injury on its great men.

Fortunately, Mahler's devotion to art, combined with practical good sense, stimulated his energies, and gave him the strength to cope with a workload that left him little time for despondency. The year 1900 was one of the busiest of his career. One of the first events at the Opera was all the more exceptional for being unplanned. This was a single performance on 19 January by the famous Australian soprano Nellie Melba. Later she wrote in her memoirs how at the beginning of the month she had given two concerts with the 'orchestra of the Musikvereinssaal'[77] and how Prince Liechtenstein had called on her on the Emperor's behalf, asking her to sing a special performance of Verdi's *La traviata*, followed by the Mad Scene from *Lucia di Lammermoor*. Melba at once apologized for not being able to sing in German, but was assured that she could choose whatever language she wished. A date was fixed, initially 18 January but eventually the 19, immediately after the concerts she was about to give in Budapest. She was offered a fee of 1,000 kronen, with subscriptions suspended and all seats costing double their usual price. In a letter dated 17 January, the great singer asked Mahler to pay her entire fee into the Opera's pension fund.[78]

The day before the performance, Melba arrived in Vienna, too late for any kind of rehearsal. All that was possible was a meeting with Hans Richter, who was to conduct, to discuss tempos. Richter having assured her that he knew she would sing Verdi, not 'Melba-Verdi', the singer made no difficulties about accepting his suggestions. The performance, in the presence of the Emperor 'incognito' in his box with three of the archdukes, started at 7 p.m. precisely. The hall was packed to the doors, and the ladies of the aristocracy, sumptuously dressed, wore their most precious jewels. Despite all this, the applause decidedly lacked warmth, although the first-act aria was encored. Only the last act produced a real ovation, which further increased after the famous crescendo trill on B flat in Donizetti's Mad Scene, a trill that 'the whole house seemed to

---

[76] The new soprano Mahler had just engaged at the Opera.　　[77] On 8 and 15 Jan.

[78] HOA, G.Z.39/1900; letters from Mahler and the Intendant, 10 Jan.; a note from the Intendant on the 14th; Melba's letter of the 17th.

have been waiting for'.[79] During an intermission, Mahler appeared in person to present Melba with a laurel crown. As might have been expected, the response of the press was guarded. The *Neue Freie Presse* conceded that she was

a virtuoso of the voice, princess of coloratura, queen of trills. Those prepared to content themselves with rather inexpressive textbook singing, flashing roulades, brilliant staccati, get their money's worth as Melba, dressed up as Traviata or Lucia, displays her art and artifice. Those seeking more go away empty. Melba's soul speaks neither in her singing nor in her rather primitive acting. The audience, filling every seat in our opera house despite the 'Patti-prices', remained fairly cool.

Despite this, and doubtless to thank the diva for her generosity in respect of the Opera's pension fund, the Emperor awarded her the coveted title of *Kammersängerin*.[80] For Mahler, the evening had been only 'moderately agreeable'. Referring to the great singer's rather cold, instrument-like perfection, he said, 'I'd rather listen to a clarinet!'[81]

Three days after this memorable *Gastspiel*, Mahler conducted the Opera's first première of 1900. It was *Es war einmal* (Once upon a Time), the second opera by Alexander (von) Zemlinsky.[82] Zemlinsky was then only 29 years old but he was already considered one of the brightest hopes of the young generation of composers. Admitted in 1884, at the age of 12, to the Vienna Conservatory, he had remained there for thirteen years, studying piano (with Wilhelm Rausch and Anton Door) and composition (with Johann Nepomuk Fuchs), and also harmony and counterpoint (with Robert Fuchs). A brilliantly gifted pupil, he had earned a considerable number of awards and prizes. His first published composition, a cycle of waltzes named *Ländliche Tänze*, Op. 1, had appeared in 1892, and the same year two of his orchestral works were performed in the presence of Brahms, to whom the young composer was introduced.[83] In 1896 two new chamber works by Zemlinsky[84] made such an impression on Brahms

---

[79] *Neues Wiener Tagblatt* (19 Jan. 1900).

[80] Melba describes in her memoirs how the Emperor received her at 11 a.m., the day after her performance of *Traviata*. It seems he told her that, thanks to her, he had made his first visit to the theatre since the death of the Empress 16 months before. Cast for the performance on 19 Jan.: Melba (Violetta), Naval (Alfredo), Neidl (Germont).

[81] NBLS.

[82] Zemlinsky's father, Adolf, called himself for unknown reasons von Zemlinsky but his son dropped the 'von' as soon as he had made a name for himself as a composer. The family was of Viennese origin and, according to Alfred Clayton, Adolf's forefathers did not come from Moravia as is often stated but from Slovakia. His wife, born Clara Semo, was a Sephardic Jewess for whom Adolf converted to Judaism and he later became the secretary of the Turkish Israelite Community in Vienna. Adolf also wrote several novels and, from 1893 on, edited the satirical magazine *Wiener Punsch* (see Otto Biba, *Alexander Zemlinsky: Bin ich kein Wiener?* Catalogue of the exhibition commemorating the 50th anniversary of the composer's death, Archiv der Gesellschaft der Musikfreunde, Vienna, 1992, and Alfred Clayton, 'Was man über Alexander Zemlinsky wissen sollte', in programme of Philharmonic Concert, Vienna, 23 May 1992).

[83] The first movement of a Symphony in D minor (1892) and a Suite for Orchestra (1895) were performed on 18 May at the Grosse Musikvereinsaal. The only other work by a living composer on the programme was Brahms's *Akademische Festouvertüre*.

[84] A Suite for Violin and Piano was performed by Rudolf Fitzner and Zemlinsky himself during a concert of the Fitzner Quartet, together with Brahms's Third Quartet. Later on, a String Quintet by Zemlinsky was played by the Hellmesberger Quartet.

that he invited the young man to his house and gave him some advice. He also recommended that he take part in a composition contest he had initiated for a chamber work with solo wind instrument. Zemlinsky accordingly composed his very Brahmsian Trio, Op. 3, for piano, clarinet, and cello, and was awarded third prize. Brahms recommended it to his publisher, Simrock, who accepted it.

In the mean time, the young man had met Arnold Schoenberg. In 1895 he took over the leadership of the Polyhymnia Orchestra, a semi-professional group of Conservatory graduates and undergraduates in which Schoenberg was one of the cellists. In the following year, 1897, Zemlinsky won the Musikverein's Beethoven prize for his Symphony in B flat[85] and Simrock published his First Quartet, Op. 4. He was also appointed vice-president of the Tonkünstler Verein, which Brahms had long supported and whose president was Brahms's friend Richard Heuberger. Thus, the young man was already a well-known and recognized figure among the younger generation of Viennese composers.

Not only had Zemlinsky earned himself a reputation as a composer of instrumental music, but, in 1896, he had also won the coveted Bavarian Luitpold-Prize for his first opera, *Sarema*, which was subsequently performed in Munich with Milka Ternina in the title-role. It is not surprising, therefore, that Mahler agreed to perform his second opera. *Es war einmal* was based on a Danish play by Holger Drachmann, itself inspired by a well-known folk-tale.[86] It reminded Mahler of his own early *Rübezahl*, except that he found it 'terribly simplified and flat'. Nevertheless, six weeks after receiving the score, he invited Zemlinsky to come and play it to him on the piano.[87] He was immediately struck both by the young man's 'incredible technique' and by the lack of originality of his music, which was 'so full of resemblances and plagiarisms' that 'Zemlinsky must have a very bad memory to have failed to avoid them'.[88] Despite this, he decided to stage the work and managed to overcome all resistance to the project. The story is that of a cold princess wooed by a young prince disguised as a gypsy. In exchange for a kiss, he presents her with wonderful gifts, which cause her to be disowned by her father, the King. She then marries the young man, who succeeds in transforming her into a warm and loving human being. With the help of Lipiner, Zemlinsky slightly abridged and

[85] The rules of the 1897 contest required that a symphony be submitted anonymously, with only an epigram as title. The first prize was shared by two composers, Zemlinsky and Robert Gound. Their two symphonies were premièred together on 5 Mar. 1899, at the Musikvereinsaal, by the Tonkünstler Orchestra (made up in the main of Philharmonic musicians).

[86] In 1887, the Danish poet Holger Drachmann had turned a Scandinavian folk-tale into a play, for which a Danish composer, Peter Erasmus Lange-Müller, had provided incidental music. Maximilian Singer, Zemlinsky's librettist, based his text on the German trans. of Holger Drachmann's play, which had been performed in Vienna in 1894 with incidental music by Max Weinzierl (KMI).

[87] See *Neue Freie Presse* (29 Apr. 1917): 'Aus der Mahler Zeit Zemlinskys'.

[88] NBLS. This remark shows that, despite the accusations so frequently levelled at him, Mahler had never knowingly been guilty of plagiarism and believed every composer should avoid over-obvious 'reminiscences'.

modified the libretto,[89] and the first performance, as with all the others prepared by Mahler, was superb. It was performed twelve times during the season
and was thus remarkably successful, so much so that Mahler was delighted to
have discovered a new creative talent.

Hanslick, in his review of the opera, deplored the influence of Wagner on
young composers, who 'elaborate modest themes to excess'. While praising
Zemlinsky's talent and sound technique, he nevertheless found his music 'too
artificial and too subtle' for the simplicity of the libretto, the vocal parts too
declamatory and not sufficiently melodious, and the orchestration too sumptuous. In a more indulgent mood, Heuberger paid tribute to Zemlinsky's 'theatrical talent' and, while criticizing his lack of creativity, admired his musical,
dramatic, and orchestral virtuosity and gift for 'illustration'. The only thing
wrong with his music, Heuberger felt, was that it illustrated 'the visible rather
than the invisible and described actions rather than feelings'. The anti-Semitic
press, as well as the Viennese correspondent of the *Neue Zeitschift*,[90] used *Es
war einmal* as a new excuse to attack Mahler, declaring that he was interested
in Zemlinsky only because of his Slavic name, since the composer had neither
creative talent nor dramatic gifts, but merely a feeling for orchestration.

During the first half of February, Mahler put on a partially renewed and
recast revival of *Tristan und Isolde*. Performed on the day of the seventeenth
anniversary of Wagner's death, it met with tremendous success. Winkelmann
was in particularly good voice and Mildenburg was making her first appearance
in Vienna as Isolde, one of the roles with which she was to be most closely
associated. The *Deutsches Volksblatt* praised her 'brilliant strength, fiery
temperament, exceptional intelligence and noble and powerful voice', and
compared her favourably with Amalie Materna and Lilli Lehmann, the two
greatest interpreters of the part. Some slight signs of vocal fatigue, due to her
long rehearsals with Mahler, passed almost unnoticed. The paper acknowledged that, of all Wagner's works, *Tristan* was the most suited to Mahler's
'non-German' temperament, whereas the 'typically German' quality of *Die
Meistersinger* and the *Ring* remained alien to him.[91]

The *Neue Freie Presse* also praised Mildenburg's 'burning, passionate interpretation'. Hirschfeld was one of the few critics to dislike her Isolde, which he

[89] Heuberger congratulated Zemlinsky on having accepted these changes and understood their useful-
ness. ÖNB (Musiksammlung) possesses a MS score with corrections and additions in Mahler's hand. This
amended version was used for the 1990 recording of *Es war einmal*.

[90] According to the Leipzig magazine, the first act of *Es war einmal* was nothing but an 'elaboration of the
flower girls' theme from *Parsifal* and was only applauded by the composer's friends. Cast of the first
performance, on 22 Jan.: Reichenberg (King), Kurz (Princess), Schmedes (Prince), Hesch (Kaspar), Pacal
(Pretender), Pohlner. The work was last performed in Mannheim and Prague in 1912, before being reintro-
duced in Kiel in 1990-1: cf. *Frankfurter Allgemeine Zeitung* (20 Mar. 1990). A complete recording has
recently been issued.

[91] According to the *Fremden-Blatt*, Mildenburg had also been studying the part with Cosima Wagner. At
the opening performance, Mahler was greeted with a storm of mixed applause and catcalls, the latter
doubtless due to Richter's departure. Cast of the performance of 13 Feb. 1900: Mildenburg (Isolde), Edyth
Walker (Brangäne), Winkelmann (Tristan), Grengg (Marke), Demuth (Kurwenal).

called a 'fury of gigantic stature and strength, frightening to see', with her 'ample garment blowing about her in wild baroque curves, every fold raging, all bonds and bands appearing to burst with hatred. Admittedly this was a fury of convenience, for it is of course easier to rage than to develop psychologically.' Her 'talent for adaptation' took the place of 'soul, individuality, authenticity'. Thus Winkelmann had been the 'only true sustaining force of the performance', along with Mahler, who with 'very slight, almost imperceptible movements' had exercised 'the free, poetic power of burning interpretative genius'.

The *Fremden-Blatt* criticized Mildenburg for her heroism and lack of femininity, her subdivision of the musical phrases and her 'dramatic ecstasy', which it claimed lacked authenticity. Kalbeck, for his part, saw her as a 'goddess of fate and a prophetess rather than a woman in love', but he praised the grandeur and nobility as well as the accuracy of her singing. Shortly after this *Tristan* revival, the composer Wilhelm Kienzl, on a visit to Vienna, heard one of the last performances of *Meistersinger* to be conducted by Mahler himself and wrote in his diary:

I have never heard such polyphonic clarity in the Prelude, everything original yet never studied. The first act was wonderfully successful, the second very good too. On the other hand in the third, where the wit, feeling and substance of German humour are uppermost, Mahler failed in various ways. He just slowed everything down, which achieves nothing. However, the production was splendid and the orchestra sounded divine.[92]

After *Eugene Onegin*, Mahler decided to put on another Tchaikovsky work, which he had already conducted in Hamburg, *Yolanta*, a one-act opera, his last, based on a play by the Danish author, Henrik Hertz, *King René's Daughter*. According to Hanslick, the heroine of the story, a blind princess whose sight is restored by love, was 'more a musical soul than a dramatic character', and this 'pale blue' idyll was eminently suited to what Albert Kauders called 'Tchaikovsky's feminine musical soul'. Mahler prepared the performance with his usual meticulous attention to detail. To teach Selma Kurz, who sang the princess, how to move like a blind person, he blindfolded her during rehearsals. The première had to be put off because Naval fell ill and when it did take place, on 22 March, he had a relapse and lost his voice at the crucial moment of his duet with the heroine. Only the presence of mind of another tenor, Franz Pacal, who was singing a small part, saved the day.[93] Nevertheless, because of the change of tenor, the curtain had to be lowered before the final scene, thus marring the success of the première. Despite Mahler's conducting, the audience showed 'more interest than enthusiasm'.

[92] Kienzl's diary, Stadtbibliothek, Vienna. Cast of the performance on 29 Apr.: Kurz (Eva), Rellé (Magdalena), Winkelmann (Walther), Felix (Beckmesser), Reichmann (Sachs), Reichenberg (Pogner).
[93] According to Helm, Franz Pacal sang most of the part standing behind Naval, who merely struck the attitudes and went through the motions. The *Fremden-Blatt* claimed that the audience had laughed and that Pacal had later been reprimanded.

'The refined product of a great artist rather than a masterpiece or an effective stage piece,' said Hanslick, who (because of a few 'frankly trite' scenes) found Tchaikovsky's last opera inferior to *Eugene Onegin*. Alfred Kauders was alone in thinking that the modern opera repertory included few works of such engaging melodiousness, such harmonious form, such rich themes, and such general charm as *Yolanta*, which he felt should remain in the repertoire as 'the testament of a great and noble artist'.[94]

Since Hellmesberger was unwell part of the time, Richter was on tour, and Schalk had not yet arrived,[95] Mahler was again obliged to conduct an exceptionally large number of performances in the first months of 1900. He described this frenzy of activity, which consumed most of his time and energy, as 'shameful prostitution', and the Opera as 'a blast furnace that reduces the noblest material to slag', adding that rehearsals of the Philharmonic Concerts constituted his 'only moments of happiness'.[96] The first of these concerts took place on 14 January, when Mahler conducted the first performance in Vienna of a selection of his own orchestral Lieder. He had debated the choice at length with his family, with the Spieglers, with Lipiner, and with Arnold Rosé, for they all had their favourites. He finally chose the second and fourth songs from the *Lieder eines fahrenden Gesellen* and three songs from *Des Knaben Wunderhorn*: 'Das irdische Leben', 'Wo die schönen Trompeten blasen', and 'Wer hat dies Liedlein erdacht'. Since Michalek was ill,[97] he decided to try out a relative newcomer at the Opera, Selma Kurz. According to Natalie, he gave Kurz the Lieder without telling her who had composed them, and she was so enthusiastic that he asked her to perform them in place of Michalek. She sang them by heart and Mahler was amazed at the quality of her voice, which he found even better adapted to concert singing than to the stage, particularly 'the incomparable softness (*Weichheit*)' of her attack, her legato, and the vocal control of her piano.[98]

The tone of these remarks, as recorded by Natalie, reveals an enthusiasm that reached beyond the limits of art. Mahler himself had often admitted that he was unable to hear a beautiful female voice without falling slightly in love with

[94] Cast of the performance of 22 Mar. 1900: Kurz (Yolanta), Rellé (Martha), Pohlner (Brigitta), Kusmitsch (Laura), Naval (Vaudemont), Pacal (Almerich), Demuth (Robert), Neidl (Ebn Jahia), Hesch (King). The evening also included Delibes's ballet *Sylvia*.

[95] On 22 Mar. Mahler wrote to the Intendant asking that Schalk's salary be paid from 20 Mar., since he had made himself available to the Opera where Mahler urgently needed an assistant conductor. He added that Schalk's contract would only become effective on 1 Sept. and that he would have to be granted a few days' leave to go to Berlin. In an autograph telegram of 28 Feb. to the assistant Intendant of the Berlin Opera, Henry Pierson, Mahler asked if it might be possible to release Schalk straightaway, for this would be of the greatest service to the Vienna Opera (HOA, Z.62/1900).

[96] NBLS. Mahler again complained of his workload at the Hofoper in these terms after a performance of Molière's *Le Misanthrope* at the Burgtheater.

[97] She had a bad cold, according to Natalie.

[98] In an official letter dated the day of the concert, Mahler and Franz Simandl, president of the Philharmonic committee, thank Selma Kurz for appearing in the fifth subscription concert, which implies that she probably received no fee.

the singer. Selma Kurz had a warm and supple voice, which she used with consummate art; moreover, she was young and very beautiful and Mahler fell for this combination of charms. Among the letters and notes he sent the young singer there are some which, while seemingly insignificant, prove the interest Mahler took in her career, as formerly with Mildenburg; for instance this one, hastily written in pencil: 'Excellent. It is a great success, and also the critics will not be able to pull it down. It gives me great pleasure.' He must have asked Lilli Lehmann to come and hear his protégée, for he writes: 'I have just spoken to Lilli Lehmann. She was truly enthusiastic. Will tell you more about it tomorrow. This I do not write as consolation but as the truth. <u>My word of honour.</u>'[99]

The tone has already changed in the letters and notes that follow. In March 1900, during rehearsals for *Yolanta*, Mahler took Selma Kurz to see a new friend, the 'painter in embroidery' Henrietta Mankiewicz, to be made up.[100] A note dating from the same period asks her to come to his office so they can arrange a rendezvous. In other notes, Mahler gently chides her for 'running away after the rehearsal' before he could speak to her, or alludes to *Tannhäuser* for which Kurz was studying the part of Elisabeth. Subsequently—and he is by now addressing her in the familiar 'Du' form—he tells her that he is coming to see her for two hours one afternoon, asks whether she is tired after the journey she has made, and goes on: 'I am still very happy, and want very much to see you. Could we meet for a moment this evening?' Clearly Mahler and Selma are falling in love. Subsequent letters which seem to date from May 1900[101] show that they are still seeing each other in secret between rehearsals, often at the Opera itself.

One evening Mahler asked Selma to come to a performance of *The Magic Flute* that he was to conduct[102] and to meet him afterwards. There are two more substantial letters that must also date from this time. One reads:

Dear Selma, You can imagine how agitated I was by your letter. I wanted so much to talk to you today, but it's *Rheingold* this evening! One thing is clear! What happened so quickly was the thing that is always bound to happen under such circumstances and that I had already predicted: we came into conflict because of the unnatural restraint we have to show when we are in the presence of others—or even when we're alone, if we're not sure of being undisturbed. This caused you to . . . people are continually

---

[99] This card was most likely written during Lilli Lehmann's guest performance in Vienna in Dec. Lehmann could have heard the second performance of *Meistersinger* on 25 Dec.

[100] The première of Tchaikovsky's opera was on 22 Mar. Selma Kurz's daughter, Desi Halban, relates that, during the rehearsals for *Yolanta*, her mother experienced difficulty in making a crescendo on high G. Her teacher, called in for the occasion, recommended special exercises that enabled her to overcome this technical problem.

[101] The first long letter and one of the short notes refer to a performance of *Rheingold*, probably the one on 5 May 1900.

[102] This must have been the performance of 20 May, the only one Mahler conducted during the first six months of 1900. It is interesting to note that in 1901 he invited his fiancée, Alma Schindler, to a performance of the *Flute* that he was conducting at the Opera.

coming into my office and interrupting me to distraction! I can't go on with this letter but must get some sign of life to you as quickly as possible. My dear Selma, believe me—I love you! Yet feel that you are right about many things. I can't answer it all in this haste. I have to talk to you! But when? Could I come to you tomorrow morning at home? Yes? If that is all right with you, I could send you a message this evening saying when! If you don't reply I shall come. But better still: write me a word. What you call my <u>moods</u>, which are such a fundamental part of my nature, you cannot yet understand because you are too young. Because of that you often <u>mis</u>understand. But it's not that I don't love you, or love you less! Please believe me—I was thunderstruck when I read that! Many greetings from <u>your</u> Gustav.

Plainly this liaison, like others Mahler had, had its crises. As with Mildenburg, a major cause of misunderstandings was the fact that the lovers, working in the same theatre, were forced to hide their feelings. In a subsequent letter, Mahler wrote:

My dearest Selma, After a sleepless night I'm tormented by the thought that things were probably no better with you. I can't bear it unless you let me know how you are. What was it yesterday that upset you so much? I kept turning it over in my mind during the night, and finally decided that perhaps the absent-minded way I received you last night was the (in the circumstances unnoticed) starting point of your displeasure. Selma, for the love of heaven, it <u>can't</u> go on like this. <u>Believe</u> in my love, that it is something <u>unique</u> in my life and will remain so! Always remember that we are at the beginning of a long road that we should travel fresh and <u>unwearied</u>. We must help each other, we are both impulsive people and therefore risk continual <u>misunderstandings</u> amid perpetual assurances of understanding! Let us live on together and <u>love</u> each other without hindrance, refusing to let <u>others</u> . . . shake our happy certainty. What are those bugbears on the horizon you are being warned against? Have these people the slightest idea of what I am like? What experience have they of me? How could they understand something that they only know by hearsay? And you draw conclusions on the basis of these vague shadows, and think you see me in my true light when I am lit by these 'guttering candles!' Yes I am a complicated person, often a puzzle to myself, but that should be all the more reason not to label me with an 'on dit', and then to hang your little head that I love so much, if at first sight some of the things they say appear to be true.[103] Look at me yourself, my love—but don't <u>test</u> me, live and love! Only love sees the truth! Please, my beloved Selma, write me just <u>one word</u>, how you are, whether you love me, and whether you trust me! I'm writing in haste, in response to an impulse that suddenly seized me and all but dragged me out of the house! See! That's how I want it always to be, and so should you! To speak at once, to talk! Holding nothing back, for things that are held back grow terribly until they cut off all air and light. If only I could see you and speak with you today for only <u>one</u> moment! My darling, my love, I embrace you and kiss you. Write me a word, the porter (whom I've chosen for safety's sake) will bring it to me in my office. <u>Ever</u>, Gustav . . . Don't make me wait!

This letter is a moving testimony to the difficulties of the hole-and-corner relationship they were obliged to have with each other. Music had brought them

103 The meaning of this sentence is not absolutely clear in the original because of an illegible word.

together, but music also held them apart: they both had their careers to think of! In her short biography of her mother, based on personal recollections and first-hand accounts, Desi Halban von Saher tells us what Selma Kurz herself had to say on the subject: she and Mahler were indeed very much in love, and spoke of marriage, but soon realized that they did not really suit each other. Besides, it was forbidden for the Director of the Vienna Opera to be married to a member of the company, and the young woman was firmly resolved not to give up her career.

A note that must definitely have been written after the two letters above shows that their relations had already cooled. Memories of Hamburg and Mildenburg had made Mahler more cautious than before, especially in a city where the papers were always on the look-out for the latest scandal. Mahler's last private letter to Selma Kurz dates from the beginning of the following summer:

Dearest Selma, My silence is for a very specific reason: I am working, and have to cut myself off from the outside world. Don't you remember that I told you that in advance? So please be nice and send me a postcard now and then, for I want to know how things are with you! It's very important for you to rest during the holidays because you will be at full stretch next season. On no account work on anything but Sieglinde. I too am not terribly well, for my old problem has started up again and is giving me a great deal of bother. Paris was frightfully exhausting[104] and evidently did me a lot of harm. Did you feel well in Marienbad . . . ? I am returning to Vienna around the middle of August, I am already looking forward to seeing you and am most anxious to know what 'state' your voice will be in . . . Isn't three hours' practice a day rather excessive? Stop singing at the slightest sign of fatigue.[105]

The tone here is already quite different, and it is clear that all ties of an intimate, romantic nature have been broken off. In the meantime, in any case, another important event had taken place which had apparently had important consequences in Mahler's private life: the engagement at the Hofoper of Marie Gutheil-Schoder, who by no means possessed the velvet timbre and flawless technique of Selma Kurz, but who suited his artistic requirements exactly.[106] Thus the liaison with Kurz had been as brief as it was passionate. At the beginning, the young singer's greatest attraction had been her miraculous voice, which on 14 January 1900 brought some of Mahler's orchestral Lieder to a Viennese audience, with resounding success not only for the soloist but also the composer. The last song, 'Wer hat dies Liedlein erdacht', suited Kurz's virtuoso technique to perfection, and was immediately encored. Natalie concluded, too hastily alas, that the time had come when the public 'no longer distrusted Mahler's works'. The next day, upon reading the newspapers, Mahler

---

[104] Mahler had conducted several concerts there in June with the Philharmonic Orchestra during the International Exhibition (see below).

[105] The 18 letters and notes that Mahler wrote to Selma Kurz are now in BGM (Kurz-Halban collection).

[106] See below, Chap. 8.

and his friends realized that they had been mistaken. Curiously enough, Max Kalbeck, always the archconservative among the Viennese critics, was the only one who recognized the 'intensely personal' beauty of the songs, with which Mahler had created 'a new musical form', the orchestral Lied. 'Far more than merely interesting or experimental', these pieces were 'the precious achievements of a fertile imagination, masterpieces, models of their kind'. Mahler had 'entered into the soul' of the popular Lied and 'assimilated its secrets'. Thanks to his exceptionally discreet use of the orchestra, 'these songs, true children of nature, display their exquisite orchestral raiment with such modesty and spontaneity that one would think they had been born in it'.[107] Mahler responded to Kalbeck's unexpected praise by writing a letter on the spur of the moment:

I cannot refrain from telling you how happy your charming words about my Lieder have made me. Please believe me when I say that it is not because you praise me so much! I have become relatively hardened to 'censorship'. But what you wrote surprises and delights me. Surprises, because at last someone has said what I had already given up hope of ever hearing, i.e. the things that matter to me; delights, because it is you who say it. So please forgive the incursion and the scrawl.[108]

As was to be expected, the anti-Semitic papers savagely attacked Mahler. The *Deutsches Volksblatt* acknowledged that his orchestration was excellent, but declared that it was no great merit in someone of his profession. On the other hand, it questioned his 'musical illustration' and 'declamatory style'[109] and was indignant that these Lieder were praised and applauded whereas Richard Strauss's were so frequently condemned.[110] In the *Deutsche Zeitung*, Theodor Helm noted that Mahler had 'broken his own rules' by introducing a soloist at the Philharmonic, and this merely for his own glory, although he had not yet conducted a single work by either Bruckner or Liszt during the season. His Lieder were 'subtly orchestrated in the manner of the Secession, yet their melodic invention was anything but original', and they did not begin to take the place of an important orchestral work. Helm also denounced Mahler's 'errors of diction' and his laborious 'striving for a naïve and popular tone'. Helm's *Wochenblatt* is as usual less harsh: he pointed out, but this time without condemning it, the contrast between the 'popular' style of the Lieder and the subtlety of their orchestration. The *Neue musikalische Presse* accused Mahler of 'composing only with his intellect', while the most important German music

[107] Kalbeck praised the Funeral March episode in the last of the *Gesellen-Lieder* and, in *Das irdische Leben*, 'the monotonous throbbing of the accompaniment' to illustrate hunger. Only one aspect of the cycle bothered him: its conclusion in a key other than that in which it began.

[108] Bayrische Staatsbibliothek, Munich, Signatur: Kalbeckiana.

[109] Paradoxically, the anonymous reviewer found that the passage 'nimmer, nimmer mehr' in the second song conveyed no feeling of sorrow whatsoever, whereas the music accompanying the words 'alles wieder gut' in the last was 'almost a groan'. Moreover, this song and 'Wo die schönen Trompeten blasen' were 'mannered and affected'.

[110] According to Helm, Mahler's success was far greater than that of other 'daring Secessionists' such as Strauss. The opinions expressed in the *Volksblatt* and the *Deutsche Zeitung* are very similar, and once again Helm was doubtless the anonymous author (H.) of the first.

journal, the *Neue Zeitschrift*, found the four Lieder formless, 'unsingable', and totally lacking in any sort of charm. However, since the anonymous reviewer asserted that they had been sung by Rita Michalek, it seems more than likely that he had not actually attended the concert.

Hanslick, always irreproachably courteous towards Mahler, showed some embarrassment. The conductor of the Philharmonic had undoubtedly proved his modesty by so long withholding from the Viennese public 'works that have achieved great success elsewhere'. The composer of these Lieder was against the traditional and customary, he was 'what the French would call a "chercheur", without attributing any pejorative sense to the word'. His songs were a sort of cross between Lieder, arias, and dramatic scenes, and Hanslick (quite rightly) considered that the only genuine precedents that could be found for them were Berlioz's great orchestral songs. Although a 'modern', Mahler had endeavoured to 'run to the other extreme' by adopting the naïveté, sentimentality, and simple, concise, and somewhat clumsy language of the *Volkslied*. Unfortunately the texts were not at all his genre and simply did not lend themselves to an accompaniment that, with all its exuberance and sudden modulations, was far too rich and too subtle for them. However, he had carried off the 'daring undertaking' with 'great sensitivity and masterly technique', and the future might well belong to the musical 'Secession' represented by Mahler, Strauss, and Wolf.[111] While paying tribute to Mahler's 'stupendous technical skill', Hirschfeld objected to the orchestra's trespassing on the domain of the Lied. To him, the striving to find exactly the right tone and colour for every word, which led to constant changes of atmosphere, was another 'manifestation of modern individualism'. Mahler's music, he said, was very personal and enthralled both one's intellect and one's emotions. However, there were moments when the shifting and complex voices of the orchestra tended to submerge the song and one heard the incidental rather than the essential.[112]

In *Die Zeit* an anonymous critic wrote that, while using 'all the resources of the modern orchestra', Mahler had not offered enough in the way of 'specific musical inventiveness'. According to the *Arbeiter-Zeitung*, Mahler's 'colouristic refinement' made demands which only very few orchestras could satisfy. Unfortunately the content was anything but modern. Mahler imitated the 'naïvety and clumsiness' of popular tradition (*Volkston*). Modern elements such as the occasional dissonance or bold modulation were 'added extraneously'.

There is a glaring disproportion between what is to be expressed and the means used to express it. Like a genre picture on a huge canvas, or a sturdy peasant child dressed

---

[111] For Selma Kurz, Hanslick had nothing but praise: her voice was pleasant, she showed complete mastery of the words and sounds and sang with warmth and spontaneous feeling. Hirschfeld, on the other hand, felt she had sung 'disjointedly, with no sense of continuity, and her diction was careless, passive and dull'. Helm also raised certain objections to her diction.

[112] Hirschfeld was none the less perceptive enough to point out the relationship between Mahler's music and that of Berlioz, with whose *Carnaval romain* the concert ended.

up to enhance its beauty in elaborate clothes of silk and gold. The simple songs seemed, for all the composer's virtuoso orchestral technique, overloaded, the voice demoted to a secondary position. . . . These were orchestral pieces with the voice explaining the 'programme'.

Once again, the majority of the critics had thus sided against Mahler, condemning the apparent contrast between the simplicity of a folk-song and the complexity of the orchestration,

as though a folk song could have nothing profound to express, as though it were not possible to say everything in a few simple words, merely by suggestion and allusion, as though, in its endeavour to convey the hidden meaning in such a text, the music didn't need to be far richer than that accompanying the fully elaborated text of any art song![113]

According to Natalie, Mahler said he was more surprised by Kalbeck's praise than by the critical comments written by Heuberger, for 'the latter composed bad operettas and resented Mahler's refusal to perform them'. However, when Gustav Schönaich wrote that nothing remained in these compositions either of 'Knaben' or of 'Wunderhorn', Mahler was hurt, since Schönaich had always professed to admire him whole-heartedly and had, so to speak, been raised and educated (*heranwuchs*) in Bayreuth.[114]

Mahler had begun the concert with Schumann's Fourth Symphony. Its 'Beethovenian' beauty filled him with admiration, and he had spent long hours revising its orchestration in order to bring out what the work endeavoured to express and in the way the composer imagined it. Since at least some of the critics wrote that for the first time Schumann had seemed to them a good orchestrator, he felt that he had been successful.[115] Hirschfeld said that Mahler had 'illuminated every detail of the work and expressed the quintessence of the romantic spirit'.[116] In Mahler's hands, he added, the Philharmonic had become 'an instrument that responded to the merest touch, a keyboard with an un-limited range of orchestral colours, which obeyed the slightest indication of his will'. According to the *Arbeiter-Zeitung*, which had been so critical of Mahler's Lieder, 'the Schumann Symphony made an impression that was all the stronger because, in accordance with the composer's intentions, the work was performed without a break, so that latecomers had to wait outside the doors and were unable to disturb the listeners' concentration by taking their seats between the movements.' Only the anti-Semitic papers expressed their usual reservations. The *Deutsche Zeitung* attacked the tempos in the Schumann, while the *Deutsches Volksblatt* preferred Richter's 'more inspiring and enthusiastic' inter-pretation of Berlioz's *Carnaval romain*. After the concert, Natalie irritated Mahler by saying she had found the Berlioz Overture 'too superficial and

[113] NBLS, Jan. 1900.   [114] Ibid.
[115] *Deutsche Zeitung* disapproved of several features in Mahler's interpretation of this work, particularly the slow tempo of the first Allegro and its acceleration at the beginning of the development.
[116] Hirschfeld particularly admired the way in which he managed the transitions between the first two and the last two movements.

decorative' after his Lieder. He curtly assured her that 'no work, no matter how great or beautiful, can detract from a work that follows. On the contrary, it can only heighten its effect, assuming it has some sort of content and quality.'

A month after the first Viennese performance of Mahler's Lieder, Selma Kurz sang three others with piano accompaniment during a concert by the Rosé Quartet in the main auditorium of the Musikverein: 'Erinnerung', 'Hans und Grete', and 'Scheiden und Meiden'. The audience was so enthusiastic that it encored the last two, and Kalbeck's critique once again contained high praise. Unlike his colleagues, he felt that the 'popular' style came entirely naturally to Mahler, as much from the musical as from the literary point of view.[117]

In the sixth Philharmonic Concert on 28 January, Mahler included Bruckner's Romantic Symphony, Mendelssohn's Overture *Meeresstille und glückliche Fahrt*, and Wagner's *Kaisermarch*.[118] Although he had made some cuts in the second and fourth movements of Bruckner's symphony, he wondered at the last moment whether he had been right to include it in the programme, which in principle should only offer masterpieces. 'One cannot really expect the public to listen to these scraps of music and glaring absurdities,' he said 'even if they are frequently surrounded by sublime ideas and themes.'[119] This 'revised and corrected' version of a Bruckner symphony was bound to shock the Brucknerians. Theodor Helm accused Mahler of 'wilfully rearranging tempos and dynamics', 'exaggerating the accents', and, worst of all, 'tearing the poetic and musical form of the work to shreds' with his cuts: the symphony had always been given in its entirety before.[120] The next work on the programme, the Mendelssohn Overture, had seemed 'rather pale', while the Wagner March,[121] played too fast, had made little impact. This was hardly surprising, as 'one could hardly expect Mahler to possess the true German spirit'. Kalbeck, on the

[117] The rest of the concert on 9 Feb. comprised a Piano Quartet by Bernhard Scholz (director of the Frankfurt Conservatory); Brahms's songs 'Feldeinsamkeit' and 'Ständchen', accompanied, like the two Mahler Lieder, by Ferdinand Foll (Korrepetitor at the Opera); and finally the Beethoven Septet. On 15 Feb. Eugen Gura, a baritone with the Munich Opera, included three Lieder by Mahler in a recital at the Kleiner Musikvereinssaal: 'Wo die schönen Trompeten blasen', the last of the *Lieder eines fahrenden Gesellen* and one of the last *Wunderhorn-Lieder* with piano, 'Selbstgefühl'. Eugen Gura (1842–1906), born in Bohemia, studied painting concurrently with courses in music at the Munich Conservatory, and was engaged by the Munich Opera in 1865. After singing in Breslau, Leipzig, and Hamburg, and then again in Munich, he abandoned opera in 1896 and became very popular as a recitalist, singing mainly Löwe and Wolf, whose Lieder he was one of the first singers to perform regularly.

[118] Once again, the unusual order of Mahler's programmes can be explained by his desire to play the longest and most difficult work while the audience was still fresh enough to listen to it. In this way, he also hoped to stop the Viennese public from leaving before the Finales of the symphonies, which it was apt to do, even with Brahms. The *Neue Zeitschrift* correspondent reproached Mahler for having conducted the *Kaisermarsch* in honour of Kaiser Wilhelm II's birthday, whereas he had discontinued the custom of giving a new opera each year on Franz Joseph's birthday.

[119] NBLS.

[120] Helm acknowledged, however, that many sections had been 'magnificently played', in particular the Scherzo. He rejected Mahler's 'furious haste' in the return in the major mode of the subsidiary theme in the Finale, where Bruckner's marking was 'etwas beleben' (a little faster); and also disapproved of the slow tempo of the Trio. On the other hand, the same Trio had been played too fast in Richter's performance in the presence of the composer in 1896.

[121] The Philharmonic had played this work under Wagner's direction on 1 and 14 Mar. 1875.

other hand, called Mahler's interpretation of Bruckner's Fourth a true rebirth: for the first time Bruckner, 'strange magician, so strong in his faith, so weak in thought, bewitched the general public'. Superb themes were clumsily built into a 'schematic, arbitrary, baroque' structure, and if listeners had not tired of the composer's 'incalculable, crazy and desperate flights of fancy' it was thanks to the orchestra and above all to Mahler, who had abridged the work and given his performance 'the strangely fascinating character of a free improvisation'. Hirschfeld entirely shared this point of view. Mahler had 'demonstrated how deeply he penetrated the works of his master', who was never before so warmly applauded. Although Bruckner's musical concept was 'far removed from classical form', Mahler had rendered his themes and his 'sound mystique' comprehensible and accessible. Furthermore, he had revealed Bruckner's 'musical logic' by bringing out this or that motif, rhythmic figure, or sound effect, even in transitional passages, thus allowing 'the spirit of the work to transcend details of form'. By omitting certain 'peculiar caesuras' so as not to 'tear the fabric' he had served the work with love and comprehension, whereas others battled 'for the letter of the law, and against Bruckner'.[122] However, he had not succeeded in rescuing the *Meeresstille* Overture. Despite the 'mystic slowness' of the opening Adagio, all that was revealed was a 'strip of water with a cramped horizon'. Mahler thought otherwise: he had enjoyed rehearsing this Overture and admired Mendelssohn's 'splendid colours and orchestral mastery': if he had composed nothing but this Overture, the *Hebrides*, and the Fourth Symphony, he would in Mahler's estimation still remain one of the greatest composers of all time.[123] The Nicolai Concert, given each year as a benefit for the Philharmonic pension fund, was expected to present a substantial work for chorus and orchestra. After presenting his own Second Symphony the previous year, Mahler had decided to conduct, on 18 February 1900, Beethoven's Ninth.

In Hamburg, he had undertaken bold experiments, such as placing the winds backstage for the 'Alla marcia' episode in the Finale, though he had abandoned the idea before the performance. Nevertheless he had added his own orchestral rearrangements to those of Wagner. Despite this, rehearsals for once proceeded harmoniously. Mahler was delighted with the Singakademie and wrote to its conductor, his old friend the poet-musician Richard von Kralik, to congratulate him and thank him for 'the devotion and warm understanding of the Singakademie, who played a major part in enabling us to communicate the enthusiasm that fired us to the thousands who were listening'. He hoped their collaboration would continue, now that 'a link has been established of the finest companionship, that of common devotion to great, true art'. The hall was packed for the concert and Mahler's success surpassed any he had ever achieved in Vienna. The final ovation went on for a long time and even the chorus

[122] Hirschfeld particularly admired the 'mysterious veil' Mahler had drawn over the Scherzo.
[123] NBLS.

joined in. Moreover, the tickets had sold out so rapidly that the concert had to be repeated the following Thursday.[124] Having been informed of the originality of some of Mahler's tempos, Prince Liechtenstein said to him afterwards: 'A very beautiful performance, Herr Mahler, quite magnificent, and what a success! However, I have heard other tempos!' Mahler replied, calmly: 'Oh really, so Your Highness has heard this work before?'[125]

No doubt exasperated by the unprecedented success of this concert, the Viennese reviewers, who had so far maintained a relatively courteous tone even in their harshest pronouncements, abandoned all restraint. Kalbeck alone defended Mahler and his 'version' in moderate but authoritative terms. For him the event had been not just a concert but a 'celebration in music', such as the creator of the Ninth had envisioned when he had 'sung for humanity' his song of songs. The hall had been 'a temple, the massed audience a flock of the devout, the performance a sacred ceremony'. Never before, even in the most successful performances, had each movement reached the listener in such an intense and personal way. While Mahler, a passionate admirer of Beethoven familiar with every detail of the score, 'could rely on his emotions or compassion which measures Beethoven's melody by his own heartbeat', 'he [nevertheless] possessed all the experience necessary to support his judgement with historical consideration'. Neither his emotions nor his intellect were infallible, of course, but when they erred it was 'always in the service of truth'. Should every alteration, however small, be treated as a crime of *lèse-majesté* against a score that remained (without a Prince Charming to waken it) as good as dead?[126] After all, the fidelity of a musical performance was 'a question of confidence'. When a conductor delivered such a clear, expressive and convincing image of a work of this stature, without losing a single detail, when he was able so boldly to recreate the immense pyramid of the Finale with not a single stone out of place, he deserved the confidence of the public, even if it did not always share his views.

But the majority of the critics disagreed. For Schönaich, Mahler should never have allowed himself liberties that even Wagner had not taken. These criticisms were mild compared to those of Heuberger in the *Neue Freie Presse*. For him, the 'dreadful practice of "painting over" (*übermahlen*)[127] the works of classic masters' was 'erroneous' and 'barbaric'. Not only the sound but also the meaning of certain passages in the Ninth had been altered, in defiance of the composer's explicit intentions. Even if Beethoven had not always attained his

---

[124] 22 Feb.   [125] LEM 144.

[126] According to Kalbeck, Mahler was able, thanks to his slow tempo in the Scherzo, to restore the balance between strings and woodwinds. This tempo also destroyed the somewhat comic effect of their duets (bassoon-clarinet and oboe-flute) and rendered the kettledrums more thunderous. Wagner had already introduced some necessary modifications, such as adding horns in the D major return of the second theme of the Scherzo. Only two features bothered Kalbeck in Mahler's version: the kettledrum roll in the last fortissimo of the main theme and the omission of the opening eight bars in the return of the Scherzo.

[127] Heuberger, like many of his contemporaries, punned on 'Mahler' and 'Maler' (a painter).

goal, which in any case was not true, Wagner's modifications were quite sufficient. While reaffirming his admiration for Mahler's work in the theatre, Heuberger wanted to 'cry Halt!' because changing the orchestration of the Ninth Symphony was just as criminal as remodelling Michelangelo's *Moses*.[128]

Coming from a critic who, since 1897, had always defended him, this violent rebuff cut Mahler to the quick. A few days later, when Heuberger asked him for a copy of his score of the Ninth so that he could see the changes for himself, Mahler replied:

My score will remain in my hands, and I don't believe it would be of any use to you if my performance was not either. However I am very willing to go through this score with you, or anybody else, and show you my approach to Beethoven's notation, if you are prepared to take the trouble to come and see me for that purpose. But I would have to have an assurance from you that you were truly concerned to learn from me about my intentions, and not just to obtain material for more controversy, which I don't have time for, even if I had the inclination for that sort of thing. An artist convinces by his deeds. In this case, however, I have had to speak out in order to contradict unfounded assumptions which I would have seemed to accept if I had left them unchallenged.[129]

Hirschfeld, a brilliant polemicist if ever there was one, seized the occasion to embark on a long series of bitter attacks which only ceased when Mahler left Vienna, seven years later. Here are the salient passages of his article, published in the *Abendpost* immediately after the performance of the Ninth:

Each note is lit up, the darkest pathways are illuminated, nothing is lost; the voices that murmur in the shadows are exposed to the glare of the sun, airy lines are weighed down, every nervous fibre of the melody is detached and isolated from the sound fabric as if with a scalpel. Great surges of sound or subtle nuances draw attention to every minute detail in the melos; a ritardando or an accelerando alerts the audience to what is coming, for fear it should miss anything. This Ninth Symphony is a triumph of lucidity. . . . With it, Mahler has asserted himself as a modernist, at least in so far as this modern age drives towards science. . . . Instead of silencing him, the grandeur of the Ninth Symphony has aroused his intellect . . . and he has scaled its heights with clever interpretations and pretty details.

Hirschfeld went on to give examples: the horn diminuendo in the D major melody of the Trio in the Scherzo was superb, but was not in Beethoven's score. 'The playing of the big melody in the Finale where it appeared in the basses was admirable but as always, the simplest approach would have been the best. . . . The sublime scorned details, and an aesthete had remarked quite rightly that the pyramids of Egypt lost their grandeur once the steps leading to the top became visible.' Mahler aspired to beauty, clarity, purity, but he did not attain grandeur. Everywhere this was lacking, for he wanted to 'interpret' the work,

---

[128] Furthermore, in Heuberger's opinion, almost all Mahler's tempos had been too slow, and he had been obliged to speed them up later on in the movements.

[129] Robert Hernried, 'Ungedruckte Briefe von Gustav Mahler', *Musikblätter des Anbruch*, 18 (1936), 3, 65 ff.

instead of believing in it and following his faith, like Richter, without trying to 'understand'. The pathos of the 'Eroica', the Funeral March from *Götterdämmerung*, the Ninth, all were alien to him, for nerves could play no part in the great overwhelming peace of deep-felt emotion, and intelligence even less.[130] While admitting that the performance itself had been irreproachable and that Mahler had shown the greatest mastery in the big choral and orchestral masses, Hirschfeld went so far as to contest even Wagner's instrumental modifications. 'If all that the "public" does not pick up is to be re-orchestrated', he went on, then 'no line of any score would remain intact. . . . Where should we be if we agreed with Mahler that the letter of the score is meaningless and that interpretation is all?' Like Hirschfeld, the anti-Semitic papers left no hyperbole unused in their condemnation of Mahler. In the *Deutsche Zeitung* Helm claimed that the Ninth had been literally disfigured[131] to the point of being unrecognizable, and nostalgically recalled the 'simple, noble, grand' style of Richter.[132] For the *Deutsches Volksblatt* too, the 'Old God' had accomplished miracles of which the 'new idol' was incapable.[133] Mahler should content himself with writing 'superhuman symphonies' and not meddle idly with those of Beethoven.[134]

Sensing serious opposition within the orchestra during rehearsals of the Ninth, Mahler realized that this was not unconnected with the press attacks. With the help of his friend Lipiner, he therefore wrote the following text, to be given out in the hall with the programme at the second performance the following Thursday:

In as much as certain published utterances might have spread the belief among a portion of the public that the conductor of today's performance might have undertaken arbitrary alterations of details in Beethoven's works, and in particular in his Ninth Symphony, it seems imperative not to withhold a few explanatory observations on this subject.

Owing to an ear complaint which ultimately left him totally deaf, Beethoven lost his indispensable and intimate contact with reality and the world of physical sound at the

---

[130] Hirschfeld complained of Mahler's tendency to neglect certain lesser passages and over-emphasize others (a principle that Mahler had consciously developed and often applied). He said that undercurrents (*Unterströmungen*) had impeded the flow of the first movement, that the Scherzo lacked vigour (*Wucht*), which even a Beethoven pianissimo should possess, and that, because of the cuts, the Trio had assumed too much importance. He claimed that 'the tyranny of the modern conductor casts sacrilegious doubts upon Beethoven's sense of form'.

[131] Notably by the doubling of the woodwinds and horns in the second part of the Scherzo, and the noisy trumpets in the sombre and powerful conclusion to the first movement. Three days later, Helm added (like Kalbeck) to his list of grievances the dropping of eight bars from the repeat of the first part of the Scherzo.

[132] In his 4 Apr. 1897 performance.

[133] It claimed that Richter had brought a greater intimacy and warmth to the Adagio.

[134] The similarity of the terms and opinions expressed here and in the *Deutsche Zeitung* leaves no doubt that Theodor Helm was the author of both articles. The soloists in the concerts of 18 and 22 Feb. were Marie Katzmayr (s), Leonore Rellé (ms), Franz Pacal (t), Wilhelm Hesch (bs). On 22 Feb., in the evening performance, the Ninth Symphony was preceded by the Overture *Die Weihe des Hauses*. The Singakademie and the Schubertbund both participated in this performance.

very stage of his creative activity in which the prodigious increase in his powers of imagination impelled him to discover new means of expression and to achieve a hitherto unprecedentedly vigorous mode of orchestration. Equally well known is the fact that the limitations of the brass instruments of his time quite simply rendered them incapable of producing certain sequences of notes required for the development of a melody. Since then the imperfections of these instruments have been corrected and it would therefore seem almost criminal not to use them so as to perform Beethoven's works as perfectly as possible.

Richard Wagner, who throughout his life fought passionately, both in word and in deed, to rescue the interpretation of Beethoven's works from a neglect that was becoming intolerable, explained in his *Concerning the Execution of the Ninth Symphony* how this symphony should be performed in order to conform as nearly as possible to the intention of its creator. And all conductors since then have followed the same path. Because of his deep conviction, confirmed by his experience with this work, the conductor of today's concert has followed precisely the same course, without, as far as the essential is concerned, trespassing beyond the limits set by Wagner.

There can, of course, be no question of any instrumental modifications, alterations or even 'improvement' of Beethoven's work. The long-observed custom of multiplying the strings has resulted—and, indeed, for many years past—in an increase in the number of wind instruments; but this was merely to amplify the sound of these instruments and not at all to give them a new orchestral role. On the contrary, their number was increased for the sole purpose of amplifying the sound. On this point, as on every other concerning the interpretation of the work, both in its entirety and in detail, the conductor can demonstrate, score in hand (and the more one goes into details, the more convincingly), that, far from following any arbitrary purpose, but also without allowing himself to be led astray by 'tradition', he was constantly and solely concerned with carrying out Beethoven's wishes even in seemingly insignificant details, and with ensuring that nothing the master intended should be sacrificed or drowned in a general confusion of sound.

Far from calming the tempest or winning over his enemies, Mahler's text merely poured oil on the flames and the press reacted even more violently than it had four days earlier. In the *Neue Freie Presse*, Heuberger recalled how Hans von Bülow had been in the habit of making controversial speeches at the beginning of his concerts. While 'refusing to discuss with Mahler the validity or non-validity of his Beethoven interpretation', he considered it necessary to protest against the distribution of pamphlets before a concert. Otherwise the habit might spread. People came to a concert to hear music, not to read writings on aesthetics. Kauders, in the *Neues Wiener Journal*, also compared Mahler with Bülow, calling him a 'high priest of art' and a member of the *ecclesia militans*, and defended him against charges of having 're-orchestrated' or 'improved' the work. But he thought that he and all people should know that the inner ear of a composer was more infallible than his physical ear and that Beethoven had created some of his greatest masterpieces when he was completely deaf.

Helm, in almost identical terms, rejected Mahler's attitude as well as his efforts to justify himself. As for Hirschfeld, using the pseudonym 'King-fu' he published a long satirical article in his deadliest ironical vein in the *Sonn- und Montags-Zeitung*:[135]

Herr Direktor Mahler has . . . written a speech and distributed it to the assembled public. We now possess one of his writings, no doubt the beginning of his collected works; a decree, a summons, formally dated and signed Gustav Mahler. Its style and tone are a happy mixture of official gravity and benevolence. The occasion, a perform- ance of the Ninth Symphony conducted by Gustav Mahler, was unquestionably greater than the shadow it has cast. We censured it, not so much for the instrumental tricks in which Herr Mahler indulged yet again, but because the powerful work did not produce the powerful effect expected. Others were more severe: they took note of and debited him with each new trumpet, each new horn. This was too much for Herr Mahler: he had to refute the 'published utterances'. At the second performance of the symphony, a leaflet containing the latest decree was pressed into the hand of every concertgoer. Surprised, we took our seats: we read and read. Mark Twain used such writings more cleverly. One recalls his defence of an article he had written in an agricultural journal, where he defended what he had done by simply restating what he had done. Gustav Mahler was doing the same, but he meant it seriously.

Beethoven was stone deaf. Herr Mahler sorely bewails that fact, but one would think that, precisely because of his deafness, the great man would incline to dense rather than sparse orchestration. Herr Mahler denies this and maintains that we should compensate for the imperfection of the instruments of Beethoven's time. He then sets out to prove that he undertook no instrumental modifications, but that they were both necessary and inevitable! Herr Mahler is not obliged to be acquainted with the laws of logic and is therefore not obliged to apply them. Herr Mahler is not obliged to write intelligible German, but neither is he obliged to demonstrate this fact to the public . . .[136]

Thus Lipiner's clumsily worded arguments served Mahler's cause no better than the famous retouches to the orchestration it had set out to justify. No other event in Mahler's Viennese career had provoked such fierce controversy. As for Hirschfeld, his attacks now became the rule and no longer the exception. Mahler found this hard to take. Though reluctant to admit it, he would have been grateful for the support of such a talented journalist. 'Hirschfeld's attacks are so absurd', he said to Karpath, 'that they no longer interest me. It's his tone that I find outrageous. If people want to censure me, they should do it "hat in hand". He adds nothing to his reputation by treating me so rudely. In any case, he can do his worst; I shall go my own sweet way and stick to my guns.'[137] The motives for Hirschfeld's persistent antagonism and injustice have often been

---

[135] KMI.
[136] BMG 137. In the *Wiener Abendpost* (23 Feb.) Hirschfeld refuted point by point Mahler's justification and accused him of 'making music perversely', of boasting, and of 'violently attacking the critics'. He none the less claimed to admire Mahler 'more than those who applaud him'.
[137] BMG 138.

questioned. We have seen him in 1899 describing Mahler as a spirit of negation to Houston Chamberlain.[138] Nevertheless he was one of the most gifted of Viennese critics as regards liveliness of mind and style. Paul Stefan, in his early Mahler biography and other writings, was of the opinion that Hirschfeld never forgave Mahler for the failure of Mozart's opera fragment *Zaide*, which he had edited and completed; but that was not performed until 1902, whereas his hostility dates from two years earlier.[139] It seems more likely, as Karpath suggested, that he would have liked to be on good personal terms with Mahler and was offended that the latter held him at arm's length. As a matter of fact, when he first took on the directorship of the Vienna Opera, Mahler had rather enjoyed Hirschfeld's company and his lively wit. One note at least, written in Vienna,[140] shows their relations to have been friendly at the beginning of Mahler's tenure in Vienna: 'You can be certain that what you write makes me very happy. Where you are concerned, and contrary to my custom, I can't completely hide my personal feelings. Which at least proves my esteem. I am very pleased that we shall meet on ground where our paths converge.' Later on, however, when Hirschfeld began to attack every move he made, Mahler began to regard him as a vain, intolerant, irascible, and embittered man, 'exasperated by [other people's] success' and 'jealously and malevolently opposed to anything young and new'. Undoubtedly Mahler's enemies had found in Hirschfeld a leader and a highly eloquent spokesman, who would stop at nothing in his campaign of systematic denigration.

[138]   See above, Chap. 5.

[139]   A pamphlet by Paul Stauber, *Das wahre Erbe Mahlers*, while much too virulent to be always convincing, nevertheless proves Stefan wrong on this particular point (SWE).

[140]   Another letter, written from Hamburg, proves that Mahler had made Hirschfeld's acquaintance before coming to Vienna (see above, Vol. i, Chap. 21). Mahler's letters to Hirschfeld belong to Mrs Joyce Hirschfeld-Hammerschlag of Belfast.

8

Venice—Paris—Maiernigg—completion of the Fourth Symphony—Gutheil-Schoder joins the Hofoper

(April–August 1900)

> I ask nothing of fate except a quiet little spot and a few weeks
> every year in which I can be entirely my own master.

AFTER the uproar over the Ninth Symphony, the last two Philharmonic Concerts took place in an atmosphere of relative calm. The seventh concert, on 18 March, began with Haydn's E flat major 'Drumroll' Symphony (No. 103). This and Weber's *Konzertstück* (Liszt's version), with Ferruccio Busoni as piano soloist,[1] were acclaimed as 'outstanding successes' by the *Neue Freie Presse*. The other items in the programme were Liszt's *Mephisto Waltz*, one of the Philharmonic's old favourites, and Karl Goldmark's concert overture *Im Frühling*. According to Richard Robert, the orchestra had never played better, although certain details in Haydn's symphony, and in particular the overemotional interpretation of the introduction, had been alien to his style.[2]

During rehearsals for the last concert, on 1 April, Mahler was very pleased that he had included Brahms's *Variations on a Theme of Haydn* in the programme, since the composer showed an 'unparalleled musical mastery' in the piece:

He [Brahms] takes the seed from its pod and nurses it through all the stages of development to its highest degree of perfection. In fact, he has no rivals in this field,

---

[1] A letter in Mahler's own hand to Emil Gutmann urges him to allow Busoni to take part in this Philharmonic Concert, no soloist being programmed for the eighth. Mahler assures the impresario that the public attendance at the recitals which the famous virtuoso was to give in Vienna at that time would not be adversely affected by his appearance with the orchestra (Bayrische Staatsbibliothek, Munich).

[2] Richard Robert was one of those who contested the brevity of Mahler's appoggiatura in the second theme of the initial Allegro (in bar 4). He also criticized Busoni for playing Liszt's version of Weber's *Konzertstück* rather than the original.

not even Beethoven, whose Variations, albeit admirable, are of a totally different nature. His inventiveness makes him soar into other distant realms and he does not keep so closely to the details of the theme. The Andante of my own Second Symphony and the *Blumenstück* from the Third are also variations, but they are just as far removed as Beethoven's from Brahms's rigorous elaboration of the same theme. Rather than a continuous development of the same sequence of notes,[3] mine are decorative variations, arabesques and garlands woven around the theme. Brahms's variations are like an enchanted stream, with banks so sure that not a drop gets lost, even at the sharpest bends. On the other hand, Schubert's way of composing (his Symphony in C Major is also in the programme) is utterly different. His music is like a rushing river flowing freely and indomitably, so abundant that without needing to contain it you can drink freely wherever you put your lips to the water.[4]

Despite the enthusiasm with which it had been rehearsed, the concert received a mediocre press. Even Kalbeck was hostile: 'our dull and cloudy spring weather pervaded the hall; the nightingales in Schubert's symphony remained silent, the anemones and violets in Brahms's Variations hung their heads and the radiant sun in the Leonore Overture never emerged from the clouds.' Kalbeck thought that the applause, especially after the Scherzo in the Schubert symphony, had been conventional and polite rather than enthusiastic. Mahler had again overstepped the bounds of the permissible.

Were it not for the fact that one must make allowances for human failings, we would find it incomprehensible that so intelligent, so sensitive an artist could be moved by his rigorous idealism to avoid making even the slightest concession to the routine he so abominates; he prefers the strange and unusual to the immediate and obvious. He thinks he will save himself from misunderstandings by emphasizing every point on which he differs from general opinion, and in the end he breaks up the work of art into a number of salient points. Must we remind him that too many dynamics are just as objectionable as none at all, for they leave nothing to the listener's imagination and either exasperate or bore him. The interpreter destroys all artistic enjoyment by drawing attention to himself rather than to the work he is interpreting. Doubtless nothing could be more painful to Herr Mahler than to be taken for a vain virtuoso; yet he lavished more intellect on the C major Symphony than is to be found in the whole of Schubert.

The anonymous critic of the *Wiener Sonn- und Montags Zeitung* (no doubt Hirschfeld) criticized Mahler's 'mannered pianissimos', while Helm, in the

---

[3] NBL2. 153. Three months later, in his Fourth Symphony, Mahler completed the only genuine Variations he ever composed. He had most likely sketched the slow movement at Aussee (see below).

[4] Mahler also drew Natalie's attention to the fact that the score of this Symphony, unlike that of the 'Unfinished', had no dynamic markings, so that the conductors simply had to invent their own for performance purposes. A score of Schubert's C major Symphony with Mahler's markings is now owned by the Bayrische Staatsbibliothek in Munich (Mus. MSS No. 7000). (See Peter Andraschke, 'Die Retouchen Gustav Mahlers an die 7. Symphonie von Franz Schubert', *Archiv für Musikwissenschaft*, 32: 2 (1975), 106 ff., and below, Vol. iv, appendix 1.) Peter Andraschke catalogues the main alterations: two additional trumpets, new dynamic markings, voices doubled at the octave, deletion of certain instrumental passages, bowings for the strings, pauses introduced here and there, and added accents.

Deutsche Zeitung, considered that the *Leonore* Overture, despite its frequent performances in the theatre, was cleverly chosen as the closing apotheosis of the Philharmonic season,[5] though the way it had been performed had been anything but exemplary. He congratulated Mahler for making no cuts in the Schubert, but went on to criticize his non-observance of the repeat of the second part of the Scherzo and to reject his 'contortion' of certain tempos, particularly in the Andante.[6] As for the Brahms, that had been put in the wrong place in the programme, for an audience 'electrified by the irresistible rhythms of the Schubert Finale' was in no mood to appreciate the 'interwoven counterpoint' of the Variations. The *Deutsches Volksblatt* claimed that Mahler had not equalled Richter in the Schubert symphony.[7] Later, in the Brahms Variations, the sound had seemed 'hard and dry'. Despite the virtuosity of the players, the audience had been mystified by the 'ritardandos and other extravagances' in the *Leonore* Overture. Hans Geissler, in the *Neue Musikalische Presse*, deplored the fact that none of the classic masters, even Schubert, could escape Mahler's habit of altering every score he conducted.[8]

After the final concert, Hirschfeld pronounced a less negative verdict than one might have expected on the season as a whole:

Mahler's interpretations are very meaningful (*sinnig*) and very personal (*eigen*), but also exceedingly wayward (*eigensinnig*). Controversial details aside it is above all the wealth of stimulating ideas that will be remembered. With his infectious enthusiasm, he inspires orchestra and audience, and rouses the tired spirit from its lethargy. With such a conductor, one does not merely hear the music, one is privileged to share in his innermost feelings. Even those who would resist such delight are carried away by Mahler. Thus their leader constantly spurs the musicians of the Philharmonic onto further glories . . .

In the *Wochenblatt*, Helm complained of Mahler's tendency to sacrifice the whole for the details, his excessive preoccupation with problems of accentuation, and the fact that he was apt to turn andantes into adagios and allegros into prestos and to underline with sforzandos certain details that could more easily have been emphasized in some other way. One listened to his interpretations with the greatest interest, but not without a secret fear of being suddenly 'upset, even offended, by some arbitrary modification of a traditional interpretation'. Moreover, it was deplorable that he did not prepare his programmes in advance so as to form an ensemble or a cycle and that 'he always gave himself

---

[5] Like the London critics ten years before, he questioned the choice of a moderate tempo for the beginning of the Allegro in this Overture.

[6] He also objected to the introduction of a piccolo in the scoring.

[7] After a 'dull and empty' opening Andante, the Allegro had been 'far too vigorous'. Only the last two movements had been 'superb', especially the long decrescendo in the Finale. Hirschfeld criticized the whole performance for its 'lack of naturalness and simplicity'.

[8] The *Neue Zeitschrift* correspondent, who had from the beginning been hostile to Mahler in every respect, accused him of having 'destroyed and vulgarized' this great symphony by his excessive use of the trumpets and his ill-conceived doublings such as horns with trumpets, or trombones and flutes with piccolos.

the leading part'.[9] In spite of the critics' hostility, the Philharmonic Concerts had attracted larger audiences than ever before, and the box-office receipts exceeded those of any previous season. Accordingly, an announcement appeared in the *Neue Zeitschrift*[10] to the effect that on 30 May 1900 Mahler had been unanimously re-elected director of the orchestra for the following year.

At the end of the concert season, while Mahler was spending his Easter holidays in Venice, Richard Strauss conducted a Philharmonic Concert in Berlin at which the soprano Emilie Herzog[11] sang three of Mahler's *Wunderhorn-Lieder*.[12] Mahler had probably suggested this performance himself, because Weinberger had just published a version for voice and piano of the twelve orchestral Lieder in this collection.[13] The performance had more success than the premières Mahler had conducted in Berlin in the 1890s. The public encored 'Rheinlegendchen', but the critics had their usual reservations. Otto Lessmann in the *Allgemeine Musik-Zeitung* felt that the Lieder did not fit in with the rest of the concert and that, without 'their elegantly elaborated instrumental adornment', they would lose much of their charm. As usual, it was their folk-music aspect (*Volkstümlichkeit*) that aroused disapproval. According to the *Vossische Zeitung*, their character was neither clear nor pure, and sometimes bordered on vulgarity; the *Berliner Börsenzeitung* called it 'contrived simplicity' and condemned the contrast between 'the style of the texts and the refinement of the orchestration'; while the *Berliner Börsen Courier* wrote that Mahler had 'done better', and that, despite 'his enchanting orchestration', his efforts to adopt a 'popular' style were in vain.[14]

'Your Lieder, which Frau Herzog sang splendidly,' Strauss wrote to Mahler in April,

delighted both me and the public. Needless to say, as far as our lofty critics were concerned, they could not be taken seriously, for any work that isn't tinged with a certain dose of boredom 'lacks style' in a concert. That reminds me, has your Third Symphony been published yet? I'd like to conduct your *Was die Blumen erzählen* in Paris next winter! . . . by way of an introduction . . .

[9] Helm again criticized Mahler for favouring Czech works and for his famous alterations which had given rise to the term: *Übermalung*, a pun on Mahler's name and *übermalen* = to paint over (a picture).

[10] Quoted in the *Neues Wiener Tagblatt*. In fact 86 musicians out of 89 voted for Mahler.

[11] Emilie Herzog (1859–1923), a lyric soprano of Russian origin, sang at the Munich Opera and the Berlin Opera and made a name for herself as a Mozart singer. A number of her recordings survive.

[12] Strauss mentions this concert in a letter written to his parents in Charlottenburg on 5 Apr.

[13] See DMM2. 249 ff. Since the first publication of his Vol. ii, Donald Mitchell has corrected the date when Weinberger brought out the *Wunderhorn-Lieder*: 1900, not 1899. The 2 original vols. contained the ten Lieder themselves, and also piano reductions by Mahler himself of 'Urlicht' (the fourth movement of the Second Symphony) and 'Es sungen drei Engel' (the fifth movement of the Third). Weinberger subsequently issued the orchestral scores one by one, except for 'Es sungen', which was announced but never appeared and is only available on hire.

[14] The programme for the Philharmonic Concert of 9 Apr. 1900, the Wagner-Verein's third, conducted by Richard Strauss, was as follows: Berlioz, *5 Mai*; Beethoven, Ninth Symphony; Berlioz, *Rob Roy*; Mahler, *Drei Lieder* ('Verlor'ne Mühe'; 'Wo die schönen Trompeten blasen'; 'Rheinlegendchen') (Emilie Herzog); Wagner, *Kaisermarsch*.

'It goes without saying,' he added in a postscript 'that I only presented your Lieder so as to be sure that you'd accept my ballet!' Strauss was referring to an earlier passage in the same letter in which he asked Mahler to conduct at the Vienna Opera the ballet he was composing, a somewhat daring work that 'differs from the customary hopping-about'.[15] He demanded 'a brief Yes or No: in the latter case without the usual phrases and excuses I know so well!' Shocked by Strauss's somewhat tactless humour, Mahler wrote back saying he would accept the ballet straight away, provided Strauss sent him the scenario by return of post so that he could draw up a rough estimate for the décor and costumes. 'But why the devil did you have to add such a postscript?' he went on.

You must indeed have had some pretty bad experiences to try on the *Manus lavat*[16] game with me, even as a joke. Believe me, I'm happy whenever I can pay your work the homage it deserves. Naturally, I have to proceed with caution in my efforts to educate the Viennese, after the decades of stupidities they have had dinned into them. That I am not vain, and am used to doing without the outward pleasures of authorship, you must have noticed. I ask nothing of fate except a quiet little spot and a few weeks every year in which I can be entirely my own master and, if I am lucky, at least one good performance, so that I can for once hear what I have done. My warmest thanks for performing my trifles. I have read the scribblers, and come to my own conclusions.[17] Always the same old song. You will not take it amiss if I ask you not to play just one movement from a symphony. It would be too misunderstood. But I'll be very glad to send you the Third Symphony! (not so that you perform it, for I know that that would give rise to great difficulties—it lasts two hours.)

On the evening of 7 April, Mahler and Natalie boarded the train for Venice. Justi was to join them there with Selma Kurz, with whom he was evidently still emotionally involved. The holiday began most unpromisingly, for the incessant rain had caused a landslide in the mountains and their train was held up. When the passengers were told they would have to wait several hours for another train to arrive from the opposite direction, Mahler returned to his berth and slept peacefully while his fellow travellers fidgeted restlessly and bumped into one another in the dark. And when everyone was finally asked to change trains, bag and baggage, in the pouring rain, he roared with laughter at the sight of a canary being laboriously carried in its cage, along with a thousand other pieces of luggage: the bird could have flown over the landslide with the greatest of ease! Having missed their connection and lost half a day, the travellers stopped

[15] RWO. Strauss was shortly to devote himself mainly to opera, and this turning point in his career caused him to leave a lot of works half-finished. The ballet referred to here is *Kythere*, for which Strauss himself had put together the underlying story. The score remained unfinished, the composer having decided that the story had too much material in it, enough for three evenings. However, Strauss reused certain themes in *Ariadne* and *Josefslegende*: cf. *Richard Strauss-Jahrbuch*, 1959/60 (Boosey & Hawkes, Bonn, 1960) and *Briefwechsel Strauss/Schuh* (Atlantis, Zurich, 1969).

[16] *Manus manum lavat*, meaning 'one hand washes the other', i.e. 'one good turn deserves another'.

[17] A reference to the articles in the Berlin press.

at Klagenfurt, capital of Carinthia, a short distance away from the Wörthersee. Here, Mahler was beginning to feel on home ground, knowing that the house and the *Häuschen* were being built nearby. At the Kaiser von Österreich Hotel, where he met some old acquaintances, he made an effort to be friendly and considerate to all, in order to build up 'the best possible reputation for myself as a homeowner' and also in the hope that 'here, people will be kind and trustful and treat me like a human being rather than the bad character the Viennese critics consider me to be'.

When the train reached the Alpine passes the incessant rain turned to snow. Mahler sat chatting with Natalie in their compartment and laughing over some silly statement which Guido Adler had recently made. Partly for fun and partly out of irritation, he had nicknamed him 'Science' (*Wissenschaft*), an epithet that the musicologist good-humouredly accepted. Adler considered art and science to be one, like a Janus column with two faces, while for Mahler they were irreconcilable and incompatible.

What a lot of nonsense he's started proclaiming again about 'heresies' (*Irrlehren*) in Wagner's writings and the 'abolition' of the chorus in his works. Had he felt the desire or the need to do so, Wagner would have been quite capable of using the chorus to the utmost effect. And then, his naïve conception of the nature of Mozart's polyphonic composition: he says he envies him his ability to hear and retain each voice separately and at the same time as all the others, even in the most complex polyphony. That, however, is an impossibility, a complete fallacy. I'm convinced that even the greatest musical genius is incapable of composing in that way. One simply can't hear each voice separately for more than a moment, any more than one can follow a precise point in the ocean, for one's eye rapidly becomes distracted and ends up by seeing nothing but the mass of water. The rainbow, with its billions of constantly changing drops, provides an even better example. One can only see the magnificent whole, without being able to distinguish a single one of its components or even separate colours, so blurred are the borders. Besides, could anything be more pointless than this endeavour to analyse and break up something which forms and is conceived as a perfect whole? It would harm rather than help the understanding of the work. In trying to grasp and define it, you virtually dismember and destroy it.[18] What counts is that it should give the impression of an indivisible and unfathomable whole, divine, inexhaustible, infinite. Waves, rainbows and polyphonic compositions should all be approached in the same way. Any attempt to explain this impression scientifically seems hardly worthwhile compared with the full, artistic, godlike experience of what has been created and what should be heard as a whole.

Adler, in his folly or ignorance, fancies that when Mozart, as the legend has it, was obliged to compose the overture to *Don Giovanni* in one night and had no time to jot it down in score form, he wrote each part separately while constantly hearing the whole in his mind's ear, a feat that would call for quasi-supernatural powers of imagination. For such people, all great artists, once they are dead, are magicians and no amount of

[18] NBLS. This assertion is particularly noteworthy, since, as we have seen, Mahler was frequently accused of being an 'analytic' conductor and of over-emphasizing details.

explaining on the part of a musician more intelligent than they will be of any use. My efforts met with a sceptical smile. I told him that, if Mozart really composed that Overture in one night, he doubtless went about it in the same way as I did when I had to compose a scherzo in one night for an exam at the Conservatory. Since I hadn't the time to write a complete score, I spread out the sheets for the various parts in front of me and wrote out the scherzo, but not, as our Guido imagines, writing the complete parts one after another, for that would have been impossible.[19]

Often in the course of the previous years we have seen Mahler thus pointing out some real or imagined flaw in the theories of some of his most faithful friends. In Adler's case it would be unfair to conclude that the musicologist was just another narrow-minded pedant, out of touch with reality. Not only was he fully conscious of Mahler's genius, not only had he always admired him and defended even his boldest initiatives, but four years later he vigorously supported Schoenberg and his friends, being the first to present in a newspaper article the newly founded 'Vereinigung der schaffenden Tonkünstler Wiens' to the Viennese public. Evidently, Mahler could not bear to be contradicted: he invariably dug his heels in and became impervious to argument if someone advanced an opinion contrary to his.

After a journey enlivened by discourse of this sort, Mahler and Natalie reached Venice late the following night under a cloud-laden sky. The next morning however they were greeted by brilliant sunshine. Because of the nocturnal hubbub in the streets of the old city, Mahler had changed rooms three times and still not found one that was quiet enough for him to get some sleep. The day after their arrival, he and Natalie went for a long walk along the embankment opposite the Giudecca, a neighbourhood entirely free of the tourists who infested the centre of the city. Mahler decided to go there every day, and it was during one of these walks that an incident occurred that particularly amused him in view of a similar misadventure he had recently had in Vienna. Being suddenly taken short, he had looked around for some place to relieve himself and had managed to find a toilet in the courtyard of a private house. However, the caretaker saw him leave and rushed out in fury to protest and shout insults down the street after him. Mahler could not help wondering whether she would have preferred him to use the street! Walking along the Giudecca Canal, he was again taken short and, with Natalie acting as interpreter, asked a beggar where he could find a toilet. The beggar, with a broad grin, led him to a private residence, where he was most courteously received by the lady of the house and ceremoniously installed in her elegant drawing-room—with a chamber pot! Exceedingly embarrassed, he asked whether there was not a more private place, but upon his hostess's assurance that he would not be disturbed, he did what he had to do, sitting awkwardly amid the baskets of oranges and vases of flowers adorning her

[19] Ibid., Apr. 1900.

drawing-room. When he took his leave, the charming lady presented him with a bunch of violets.

According to Natalie, it was on this trip that, for the first time in his life, Mahler took an interest in the visual arts and diligently visited all the monuments of Venetian painting and architecture. She felt that his former indifference was due solely to a lack in his education and that the discovery of these arts would enrich his own work. Mahler himself had long been resigned to this trait in his nature. 'To me, such theorizing is as pointless as that of people who wonder what sort of a life they would have led if they'd married someone else. The children of the union exist. One loves them and can't imagine them as being any different from what they are. Therefore there's no point in discussing the matter any further.'[20] Lipiner had attempted to educate him three years before by giving him a collection of photographs, engravings, and coloured reproductions, together with copious explanations. Mahler had taken no interest in these lessons, maintaining that his lack of visual curiosity was common to all musicians and that visual beauty, particularly in nature, merely made him more introspective. While he was busy transforming everything into sound, any external object that attracted his attention also distracted it, and, for that very reason, he scorned elegant and even comfortable furnishings, contenting himself, as at Steinbach, with a table, a chair, a piano, and a few prints stuck on the wall. Later on that winter he conceded that Lipiner had picked a particularly inopportune moment, when he had been unusually busy at the Opera. However, someone else had recently been trying to open his eyes.

A few months before his trip to Venice, Mahler had made the acquaintance of an artist named Henriette Mankiewicz, who, stricken with a chronic disease that rendered her virtually an invalid, bore her sufferings 'with angelic fortitude'. He often went to see her, and the two of them frequently discussed the stage sets at the Opera as well as painting in general. The letters he wrote show how close Mahler felt to this new friend of his. On 17 March 1900, in particular, he wrote:

I feel that you, too, have need of a word of friendship and affection. So I shall tell you straight away that I am extremely fond of you and that I consider you, in every sense of the word, as belonging to me, since we all belong to those who belong to us. In my thoughts I want you never to be separated from the circle of those who belong in my life. If only your health would be restored! This is a far more selfish wish than you can imagine![21]

[20] NBLS.

[21] Letters to Henriette Mankiewicz of 17 May and June 1900 (LCW). In Natalie's eye the feeling for nature and the sense of colour displayed by Henriette Mankiewicz in her embroidered panels defined her as an artist rather than a decorator. *Neues Wiener Tagblatt* (24 June 1900) noted that the artist received a gold medal at the International Exhibition in Paris. Mahler and Justi sent her a postcard of the Doges' Palace in Venice with a fragment of home-made doggerel: 'Here neither horse nor carriage can be found, | But it's just the place to get around | For the really discerning travelling man; | Greetings from the Barbarian! (*Aus der Stadt ohne Wagen und Pferd | In der man doch am wohlsten fährt | Wenn man Talent hat, wohl zu fahren | Sei gegrüsst von dem Barbaren*).

Mahler asked Henriette to give some singers at the Opera advice about their dress and general appearance. He sent Selma Kurz to her, and wrote to her of Mildenburg: 'She has learned a <u>great deal</u> from you. Now it's always a pleasure to look at her. She even attracts people who remain tied to an ideal of barmaid beauty. It seems to me that the essential thing you were able to teach her was: to see for herself and discover for herself.' In Paris the following summer, Mahler, who had sworn not to go near the International Exhibition, paid a visit to the Austrian pavilion to see Henriette Mankiewicz's embroidered panels:

As soon as I arrived, I made a pilgrimage amid all sorts of difficulties to No. 1222. There, intoxicated with colours and impressions, I stood amazed in my ignorance at such a wealth of colour being painted on to cloth with needle and thread. . . . I have just read about your gold medal in the papers and was delighted![22]

Soon, Henriette also became friends with Natalie,[23] who copied out for her the first books of her *Mahleriana* to 'help her understand' their mutual friend Gustav.[24]

Upon his return from Venice, Mahler's time was more than ever taken up by his activities at the Opera, where he still had little or no help. By this time Richter had departed, while Schalk had still not obtained leave from the Berlin Opera. Thus Mahler was himself obliged to conduct the two complete *Ring* cycles given before and after the Easter holidays.[25] Some of the critics objected to the length of these complete performances, which ended so late that public transport had ceased to run. They also criticized his attempts to simplify and stylize the staging. The *Neue Musikalische Presse* felt that he was demanding too much of the audience when he expected it to imagine the rainbow bridge leading to Valhalla at the end of *Das Rheingold*.[26] On the other hand,

his conducting constantly created new miracles of sound and shading. Such delicacy in the pianissimos, such exuberance in the fortissimos, such utter harmony between stage

[22] Letter to Henriette Mankiewicz, June 1900 (LCW).

[23] When Mahler first met Henriette Mankiewicz, Natalie Bauer-Lechner was touring France with her quartet.

[24] BGM.

[25] Since the first of these cycles was given during the final rehearsals of Tchaikovsky's *Yolanta*, Mahler must indeed have been stretched to the limit during that week. He conducted the complete and unabridged *Ring* cycle five times during the season, each time to a full house.

[26] According to the *Musikalische Presse*, Mildenburg had been an ideal Brünnhilde and Schmedes a superb Loge. Wotan had been sung by two different baritones, Demuth having fallen ill after *Das Rheingold* and only recovered in time for *Siegfried*. Cast of *Das Rheingold* (20 Mar.): Ritter (Alberich), Stehmann (Donner), Demuth (Wotan), Grengg (Fasolt), Reichenberg (Fafner), Korb, Kusmitch, Rellé (Rhine maidens), Forster (Freia), Sedlmair (Fricka), Walker (Erda), Schmedes (Loge), Schittenhelm (Mime). *Die Walküre* (21 Mar.): Hilgermann (Sieglinde), Mildenburg (Brünnhilde), Walker (Fricka and Rossweise), Winkelmann (Siegmund), Reichmann (Wotan), Reichenberg (Hunding). *Siegfried* (23 Mar.): Korb (Forest Bird), Mildenburg (Brünnhilde), Walker (Erda), Schmedes (Siegfried), Lieban (Mime), Ritter (Alberich), Demuth (Wotan), Winkelmann (Froh) Reichenberg (Fafner). Later in the season, Mildenburg was occasionally replaced by Sedlmair, Stehmann by Demuth, and Reichenberg by Hesch. *Götterdämmerung* (26 Mar.): Kusmitch (Gutrune), Mildenburg (Brünnhilde), Walker (Waltraute), Schmedes (Siegfried), Reichenberg (Hagen). After *Das Rheingold*, Hirschfeld noted some of the inadequacies in the sets and machinery.

and orchestra! Each instrument spoke, each phrase had plastic beauty, each drum-beat significance. Moreover, the immense crescendo, which mounted steadily from the beginning of Act III of *Gotterdämmerung* and reached its climax with the death of Siegfried, was sublime.[27]

At the end of March, Mahler invited Wilhelm Kienzl, to conduct the fiftieth performance of his only popular work, *Der Evangelimann*. After an exchange of letters and telegrams,[28] the performance finally took place on 30 April, in the presence of the Emperor. Shortly afterwards, Lilli Lehmann returned to the Opera for a series of guest performances. The prima donna's ingenuous vanity is touchingly expressed in some of the letters she wrote to Mahler beforehand,[29] such as that dated 6 March: 'I sang *Norma* for the third time yesterday, and <u>very well</u>', or that of 13 March: 'You can hardly imagine the stupendous reception I was given here [in Paris]; not only was I recalled three times after the aria from *Armida*, but I also had to repeat the Schubert Lieder . . . and took four curtain calls after the final scene of *Götterdämmerung*. It was truly magnificent . . .'; or again, on 6 April: 'I've just sung Valentine [in *Les Huguenots*] in Wiesbaden <u>very well</u>!' and in a postscript added the same day: 'This time you must make me an honorary member of the Opera (*Ehrenmitglied*). I've been waiting for that for so long'.[30]

For a short season of Italian opera in May, Mahler had engaged a troupe from Italy with two star singers, the soprano Gemma Bellincioni and the tenor Fernando de Lucia, who were old acquaintances from Hamburg days. The chief attraction of this season was the Vienna première of Umberto Giordano's *Fedora*, conducted by Schalk who had just arrived from Berlin. Giordano had been invited to attend the rehearsals, during which Mahler had long talks with him, particularly about Verdi, whom Mahler greatly admired. Giordano told him that the old maestro hated having people talk to him about his own music, but was always happy to discuss other people's and especially that of Puccini and Giordano himself.[31] Verdi had devoted the greater part of his savings to building a home for aged musicians, and planned to open it with a performance of his new opera, *King Lear*.[32] He continued to compose every day from 7 in the

[27] According to the same source, hisses were mingled with the applause, and came no doubt from Richter partisans. The writer congratulates Mahler on having had the courage to avoid all cuts and to make latecomers wait until the ends of the acts. In the second cycle, Helm criticized only certain details of casting, and noted that some guest singers had been successful. Julius Lieban had been a more realistic and tragic Mime than any of his predecessors in Vienna, and Otto Briesemeister had far surpassed Schmedes as Loge.

[28] HOA, telegrams from Mahler to Kienzl, 29 and 30 Mar., and letter, 3 Apr. (Z.252/1900). Letters from Kienzl, 31 Mar., 9 and 16 Apr.

[29] Letters to Lilli Lehmann: Staatsarchiv, Vienna, and Staatsarchiv, Berlin. RWO includes a letter from Lilli Lehmann dated 16 Nov. 1899.

[30] Lilli Lehmann's series of guest appearances included six performances: *Le nozze di Figaro* (23 Apr.), *Aida* (26 Apr.), *Fidelio* (28 Apr.), *Don Giovanni* (1 May), and *Norma* (24 Apr. and 3 May). The soprano warmly recommended both Charpentier's *Louise* and Erlanger's *Le Juif polonais* to Mahler, who gave the first opera in Vienna in 1903 and the second three years later.

[31] Giordano added that Verdi had no interest either in Mascagni or in Leoncavallo.

[32] Boito worked for some time on a libretto, based on the Shakespeare play, but Verdi felt he was too old to compose another opera.

morning until 11 at night, for he felt that a composer should constantly exercise his pen, even if he later scrapped what he had written.

At that time Mahler was particularly interested in Verdi. Not only did he admire his music, but also his seriousness, his austerity, and modesty: 'Throwing in the ideas as they occur to him, stringing them together and passing straight on to the next, he takes hold of them, puts them into a logical sequence and then elaborates them again until they reach their final form. Only then do they become music.' In Mahler's opinion, this facile and abundant invention often concealed the poverty and shortcomings of the creative musician. This applied to most opera composers, including Lortzing and Weber. 'On the other hand, what an immense difference, what depth and perfection in Beethoven's and Wagner's music!' Mozart belonged to the same class. 'A genius of the highest order, a renovator of music and opera of greatest style. The abundance of his invention is combined with sublime beauty of form and with the ultimate fulfilment and deepening (*Vertiefung*) of those forms.'[33]

Giordano's vivacity and 'sunny charm' enchanted Mahler, and *Fedora* increased his admiration for his talent, which he compared to that of the young Verdi. When he finally decided that the music of *Fedora* 'doesn't mean that much to me' and handed the performance over to Schalk, Giordano was bitterly disappointed, since Schalk lacked Mahler's 'temperament'.[34] For Justi, Natalie, and the Spieglers, *Fedora* provided yet another example of the degree to which Mahler's judgement as an interpreter could blunt his critical faculties. He himself acknowledged this but felt that it was due neither to weakness nor bias, but to the leniency of an interpreter and theatre director who sought to re-create a work, to experience it in his imagination and identify himself with it as though it were his own. He readily admitted, however, that, were he a critic and obliged to judge 'from the stalls', his opinion might well be different. 'But I don't have to do that, thank God!'[35] Subsequently both the public and the press judged *Fedora* much more severely than Mahler. Although the hall was packed on the opening night, only the second act was unanimously well received. The work's success, such as it was, was attributed to the presence of the composer, who was very popular in Vienna, and to the prestige of the prima donna. Heuberger and Helm detected an 'obvious Wagnerian influence' in the opera. They regretted the fact that, apart from a few 'set pieces', the music was mainly 'utilitarian' and that, despite the eloquence and expressivity of the musical language, the invention was not rich. Furthermore, Frau Bellincioni, known as 'the Duse of Italian opera', was not in good voice that night and had been obliged to try and compensate for her weaknesses by the realism and intensity of her acting.[36]

---

[33] NBL1. 128; NBL2. 146. The following year Natalie also put on record Mahler's admiration for Verdi as an orchestrator (see below Chap. 11).

[34] On 15 May, Giordano had heard him conduct *The Flying Dutchman*.

[35] NBLS, 16 May 1900.

[36] According to the *Neue Zeitschrift*, Bellincioni had great difficulty with the Act I cabaletta of *La traviata*.

Mahler derived real pleasure from his contact with the Italians, but was none the less struck by their absence of what he regarded as 'humour': 'They are themselves sunshine and happiness, direct representatives of the joy of living, laughter itself, and have no need to laugh at this world.' Although he well understood and savoured their good qualities, he also became aware of their unreliability. Their season, comprising three performances of *Fedora* followed by *La traviata* and *Rigoletto*, should in fact have contained more works, but it turned out that some of the singers had not learnt their roles, while others had to leave Vienna to fulfil engagements abroad. Some had been prepared to tell lies in order to obtain higher fees, so the end of the Italian season brought financial recriminations. Thus it was without regret that Mahler took leave of these Mediterraneans whom he had welcomed so enthusiastically. The Italian visit ended with a deficit, for ticket prices had been doubled for the occasion at a time when, with the season nearing its end, public interest in the theatre was flagging.

During the month of May, Mahler immersed himself in Tolstoy's *Resurrection*. The work upset him so much that he became depressed and irritable, because 'I'm quite unable to reconcile the meaning of my own life with the truth as revealed by this book, which has caused the scales to fall from my eyes.' At this time he was awarded the Order of King Alexander of Serbia, but refused to carry out the formalities necessary for acceptance of the honour, so that when the list of those decorated was published, his name was missing.[37] Attending a performance of Molière's *Le Misanthrope* at the Burgtheater, he complained of the rapidity with which the actors spoke the opening scenes, drawing Natalie's and Nanna Spiegler's attention to the way he himself, when conducting, never failed to outline each new element clearly and firmly, so that the listener would recognize it when it reappeared later. On the other hand, when it recurred, it could be taken more quickly and lightly. To illustrate his point, he took Nanna's opera-glasses and swivelled them round at great speed, to prove that it was impossible to identify a fast-moving object. He went on to observe that the most persistent sources of the resistance he had encountered in his first years had by now been overcome. At which one of his listeners exclaimed:

'And isn't it remarkable that the one who's so good at giving orders and exacting compliance is the most recalcitrant and disobedient of them all!' 'You think I don't obey? But you're wrong,' he replied. 'If I don't obey you, it's because there's nothing you can give me orders about. But you'll hardly find anyone more obedient than I when it really matters. What is it but obedience, when I go into a work down to the last detail and have no peace or rest until it's there just as its creator wanted it and dreamt of it. And if it doesn't work out, I can't sleep at night, plagued and tormented by some crotchet that wasn't correct!'[38]

---

[37] NBL2. 154. Mahler had already received several decorations, but he always refused to wear them and, on his departure from the Vienna Opera, left them behind in his desk drawer.

[38] Ibid.

The most important event of the end of the season was a new production of *Carmen*, with Marie Gutheil-Schoder, a guest singer new to Vienna, in the title-role.[39] Gutheil-Schoder was a first-rate dramatic talent and, in Mahler's own words, a 'musical genius'. Born of poor parents in Weimar, she had studied under Virginia Naumann-Gungl, a friend of Mahler's in his younger days in Kassel,[40] though he considered her unique attributes as an artist to have been largely self-taught. Mahler became interested in her from hearsay[41] after a guest appearance she made in Berlin. She was then plodding away for a salary of 5,000 marks a year at the Weimar Opera, but, in the few letters they exchanged, Mahler immediately recognized a genuine character. He therefore invited her to the Vienna Opera, where she made her début on 19 February 1900 in *Pagliacci*. Gutheil-Schoder recalls that first evening in her memoirs. Mahler visited her in her dressing-room before the performance and strongly protested at the red wig in which she proposed to sing Nedda. She cut him short, telling him to wait and see whether it would work. Later on, she decided that it was the ingenuousness of this reaction which had enabled her to establish harmonious relations with the imperious genius who was to fascinate her for the next seven years.

The *Deutsches Volksblatt* immediately spoke of Gutheil-Schoder as a possible successor to Marie Renard, but the anonymous critic advised against engaging this 'remarkable actress' because of 'her extremely ordinary voice and by no means outstanding vocal talents'. What Vienna needed was an 'exceptional singer', not a 'decadent actress'.[42] Heuberger, on the other hand, hailed this young 'guest' as 'one of the most interesting discoveries of recent years'. Despite the harshness of her voice, her acting talent was worthy of the stage, for she knew how to create a character by her least gesture and movement. She sang the 'Ballatella' lying on her back, and entirely altered her interpretation for the *commedia dell'arte* of the second act, while emphasizing each appearance of the real person behind the 'part' with a subtlety extremely rare at the Opera. Speidel, too, greeted the new Nedda as an artist who was 'authentic, interesting and original in virtually every movement and vocal phrase', singing 'not with her voice but with her nerves' and 'entering into reality' with devas-

[39] Marie Gutheil-Schoder was born in Weimar on 17 Feb. 1874, and studied at the local Conservatory. In 1891, she was engaged by the Baron von Bronsart, Intendant of the Weimar Opera, where she sang notably under the baton of Richard Strauss. Until 1926 she remained one of the most popular members of the Vienna Opera, where she was later active as a stage director. Her first husband, the violinist Gustav Gutheil, conducted in Strasbourg and Weimar, and later went to Vienna, where he directed the popular concerts of the Concertverein. Marie Gutheil-Schoder subsequently married a Viennese photographer, Franz Setzer, and died on 19 Oct. 1935.
[40] See Marie Gutheil-Schoder, 'Weimar', *Fremden-Blatt* (15 Apr. 1906).
[41] Gemma Bellincioni, who had sung *Cavalleria rusticana* with her in Weimar, had drawn Mahler's attention to Gutheil-Schoder. According to Max Graf, Mahler read of her in an article signed Franz Servaes in *Die Zeit*, reviewing a performance of *Carmen* in Weimar (GWO 140).
[42] Continuing in the same vein, the paper accused Schalk of having performed such acrobatics in the pit that 'it could have been Mahler we were watching' and wondered whether 'Gutheil-Schoder and Schalk are not of the same race as the director?' In Schalk's case the supposition was unfounded.

tating effect at the end of the work. Karpath praised the truth and humanity of her interpretation, while Helm claimed that the role had never been played in Vienna so naturally and convincingly. Schönaich admired the way she epitomized, with her 'frizzy, unkempt hair', a ragged 'strolling player'. Most critics nevertheless pointed out that her voice was small and of unremarkable timbre.[43]

Two days later, after Maillart's *Les Dragons de Villars*, the second opera in which Gutheil-Schoder sang, Hirschfeld wondered whether, with her 'lack of vocal grace and mellowness', she would ever be able to make a name for herself in a city that particularly loved vocal beauty. The new soprano's guest appearances covered less than a week. On 24 February she scored a unanimous success in *Carmen*, a part that, according to Helm, 'seemed written for her', such was her capacity to identify herself with the character and 'suddenly switch from mirth to raging passion and from bitter contempt to total indifference'. Her performance was questionable only in passages in which she was required merely to sing 'calmly but lyrically', for in these she was distinctly inferior to Marie Renard, who had preceded her in this sensational part.[44]

Gutheil-Schoder's success in Vienna was such that it attracted the attention of several impresarios, and as a result Mahler had to offer her a substantial salary[45] in order to keep her. Having engaged her, he decided to revive *Carmen*, since he had long been looking for a singer capable of both singing and acting this title-role. He replaced the spoken dialogue with recitative,[46] assigned the children's chorus in Act I to real children, and directed the choruses of soldiers and cigarette girls to perfection. He made the singers of the quintet sit around a table rather than stand near the footlights and had the setting of the smugglers' den entirely remodelled in the third act. In short, he meticulously revised every dramatic and musical aspect of the production. His admiration for Gutheil-Schoder grew with each of her expressive words, gestures, and notes, and with each eloquent motion of her flexible body. She brought so much personality to her part that there was practically nothing he had to teach her. The slightest indication, the briefest word sufficed to make her understand and even surpass his wishes:

It's always in women that I find the best and the greatest. Schoder and Mildenburg tower above all the others, proving that there's no cause for despair and that character

[43] Cast for the performance of 19 Feb.: Gutheil-Schoder (Nedda), Schrödter (Canio), Demuth (Tonio).

[44] It is obvious that Helm greatly admired Gutheil-Schoder from the start and made these reservations solely in order to conform to the anti-Semitic line of his paper.

[45] 16,000 gulden a year. On 28 Feb. Mahler telegraphed her: 'Contract accepted. Hope you will be here this autumn. Congratulations.' (Autograph telegram, HOA.)

[46] These recitatives were composed by Ernst Guiraud, a close friend of Bizet, for the Viennese première on 23 Oct. 1875; but Jauner, director at the time, used only some of them, keeping the spoken dialogue in a number of scenes. It was not until 26 May 1900 that Mahler used all the recitatives for the first time in Vienna; cf. Edgar Istel, *Bizet und 'Carmen': Der Künstler und sein Werk* (Engelhorns, Stuttgart, 1927), 102.

and talent still exist on the stage alongside all the affectation, grease paint and dishonesty. . . . Gutheil-Schoder is another example of the enigma of personality, which is the sum of all that one is. With her mediocre voice and its even disagreeable middle register, she might appear totally insignificant. Yet each sound she utters has 'soul' (*Seele*), each gesture and attitude is a revelation of the character she's playing. She understands its very essence and brings out all its traits as only a creative genius can do.[47]

To Mahler, the great moments in opera could never be exclusively vocal. They occurred when a singer succeeded in 're-creating a role, in breathing life into it. Where that is the case, it doesn't matter if there's an occasional rough spot'.[48] This conception of opera was neither new nor peculiar to Gutheil-Schoder. Wilhelmine Schröder-Devrient won Wagner's heart at a time when audiences raved only about vocal feats, trills, ornaments, and roulades. All the great opera composers had looked for expression of feeling, stage presence, and identification with character in their interpreters, though they rarely got what they wanted. In preferring Gutheil-Schoder and Mildenburg to Selma Kurz or Marie Renard, Mahler was adhering to a tradition that extended from Monteverdi to Wagner and that differentiated operatic from concert music. The young singer he had just engaged was not only an artist in the full sense of the word, but was full of ardour and zeal; she had the rare capacity of adapting to a variety of genres and styles and gave first priority to expression, even in virtuoso passages. She rapidly became an eminent interpreter of Mozart, proving a memorable Pamina, Elvira, Susanna, and Cherubino, each of which roles she characterized with consummate skill, changing even the colour of her voice to suit the role and the situation. Later her outstanding abilities as an actress were to make her a fabulous Elektra, and her musicianship the ideal soloist for Schönberg's *Erwartung* and Second Quartet. To those who heard her sing the title-roles in *Carmen* and Gluck's *Iphigénie en Tauride*, or Frau Fluth in *Die lustigen Weiber von Windsor*, she remained unforgettable. Though instinct or intuition may have played a larger part in her interpretation than was usually supposed, she had immediately recognized the limitations of her voice and sought, and achieved, a thrilling unity of music, gesture, and text. At first, the novelty of her art disconcerted the public and aroused violent hostility on the part of certain critics. Nevertheless, Mahler came to regard her as an indispensable collaborator, for she conformed exactly to his theatrical and musical requirements.

After the *Neueinstudierung of Carmen*, Heuberger congratulated Mahler on having engaged Gutheil-Schoder, for though she might make mistakes as a 'repertory singer', she possessed gifts which were 'supremely unusual, captivating and brilliant'. The anonymous critic of the *Extrablatt* described her as 'a living paradox, a great singer with a small voice', who in *Carmen* 'turned into

[47] NBL1. 135; NBL2. 155.   [48] NBL2. 155.

a slender, supple, lively and passionate Spanish gypsy'.[49] Karpath found her voice improved since her earlier appearances and congratulated her on having 'thrown new light on certain aspects of the part'.[50] Later, however, many critics were to denounce Gutheil-Schoder's vocal limitations, particularly when Mahler cast her in parts for which she did not really possess the required voice or personality. Max Graf, the *Neues Wiener Journal* music critic, remembered seeing Mahler seated one day in the Imperial Café, a huge pile of newspapers on the table in front of him, distressed by the realization that not one Vienna critic had found anything to admire in her performance as Eva in *Die Meistersinger*.[51]

Reviewing *Carmen*, Kalbeck agreed with Karpath that the new prima donna had improved vocally.[52] She was no longer forcing her voice, and was preserving it for dramatic climaxes. In addition Mahler had rightly emphasized the popular aspect of the work, its dances, marches, and also certain arias, for it was from these that Bizet's opera took its character. No one since Pauline Lucca had been able to impart such passion to the role, and performances had been languishing in routine and mediocrity. Gutheil-Schoder was a true, authentic Carmen:

The instinct of an inspired singer, and the sensitivity of a conducting genius, have rescued a neglected opera from the atrophy that threatened it; they breathed new life into all its parts, and restored it to the important place in the repertoire that it deserves. . . . The hand of the dramaturge who wields the baton is everywhere at work, bringing life and order, movement and clarity to the forces, without in any way jeopardising the musical form. . . .[53] For the first time, Vienna saw Bizet's work as Nietzsche had imagined it!

The schedule of performances in the 1899–1900 season showed a slight increase in the number of Wagner performances[54] (59 as compared to 55 the previous year) and a slight drop in performances of Mozart[55] (13 as compared to 15). The other works most performed were *Die Fledermaus* (20 performances), *Cavalleria rusticana* (14), *Es war einmal* (11) *Faust* and *Mignon* (10), *Carmen* (9), *Fra Diavolo* and *Yolanta* (8), *Der Evangelimann* (7), *Aida* and *Manon* (6). Mahler, having the previous year obtained an increase in salary for

---

[49] This critic claimed, nevertheless, that her voice had weakened in the last act.

[50] Cast of the performance of 26 May 1900: Michalek (Micaela), Gutheil-Schoder (Carmen), Pohlner (Mercédès), Kusmitch (Frasquita), Naval (José), Neidl (Escamillo), Frauscher (Zuniga).

[51] GWO 80.

[52] He thought the progress she had made showed 'brilliant' intelligence. She had simplified her stage presentation and was able to conserve her vocal resources for moments of dramatic intensity.

[53] Kalbeck admired above all the freedom of execution in the ensembles like the Quintet and the Card Scene, which seemed like 'lively, spontaneous conversations'. Mahler had also brought to life the 'street festival' of the last act and the unleashed passions of the crowd, thus illuminating and intensifying the final catastrophe.

[54] The most frequently performed work was *Tannhäuser* (12 performances). Then came *Lohengrin* (10), *Die Meistersinger* and *The Flying Dutchman* (7), *the Ring*, always given as a complete cycle (5), and *Tristan* (3).

[55] *Don Giovanni* (7), *The Marriage of Figaro* (4), *The Magic Flute* (2).

the chorus and orchestra, this time achieved the same for the stage-hands, whose pay and working conditions he had for some time been trying to improve. He also obtained the dismissal of the chief stage designer, Franz Gaul, whose influence he had gradually managed to undermine. Gaul had held this position since 1867, and his predilection for ballet had contributed not a little to their strained relations, given that Mahler considered this art form to be no more than light entertainment for the wealthy. Mahler finally persuaded the administration not to renew his contract, and Gaul was retired and replaced by Heinrich Lefler, a far more gifted painter who, without breaking with Vienna's all-powerful traditionalism, was in close contact with several members of the modern school.[56]

As conductor of the Philharmonic Concerts, Mahler set out for Paris early in June 1900. The International Exhibition, with its provincial villages, its bold, brand-new glass and steel buildings, the Grand and Petit Palais, the new Alexandre-III bridge, the innumerable white pavilions that made the city look like a gigantic spa, and countless other attractions, drew a constant flow of visitors from all parts of the world. To add three concerts by the Vienna Philharmonic Orchestra, which had never previously travelled abroad,[57] to the long programme of official festivities was proof of courage rather than wisdom. The visit was patronized and encouraged by Princess Pauline Metternich-Sandor, whose husband had been Austrian ambassador in Paris under Napoleon III and who had already been instrumental in bringing about the première of *Tannhäuser* at the Paris Opéra in 1861. According to the *Neue Freie Presse*, quoted in *Die Fackel*, the well-meaning princess made a fool of herself by asserting in an interview with a Paris paper on 15 June that Mahler had played the double bass in an orchestra conducted by Wagner, causing the master to declare: 'At last I can hear that the double bass has strings!'

At an early stage Guido Adler's help was enlisted, no doubt by Mahler, to help organize the Paris concerts. Among his papers is a letter from an anonymous French correspondent recommending a concert agent called François Benkey,[58] and also a letter from Romain Rolland dated 2 February, suggesting that Mahler write to the Commission des Auditions Musicales if the orchestra's visit was to be official. In that case the concerts would take place in 'the big hall of the Trocadéro, which unfortunately has mediocre acoustics?' If, on the other hand, the visit was unofficial, Rolland recommended an agent by the name of Demets and the Nouveau Théâtre in the rue Blanche, which had the disadvan-

---

[56] The article, publ. on 5 Apr. 1900 in *Illustrirtes Wiener Extrablatt*, mentioned both Lefler and Kolo Moser as possible successors to Gaul, but it was still too early for the Vienna Opera to engage a member of the scandalous Secession to which Moser belonged, together with Alfred Roller, who succeeded Lefler in 1903. Gaul died in July 1906.

[57] It had given only four concerts outside Vienna: one in Salzburg for the Mozart centenary, another in Brünn (Brno) with Richter, and the other two in Graz and Budapest. The Männergesangverein on the other hand had made numerous tours financed by a special fund maintained by private donations.

[58] RAM 33.

tage of being small. 'There is no doubt', he added, 'that concerts by the Vienna orchestra would be of great interest to us, especially at a time when Paris is really curious to hear German conductors. In any case, if things do not go ahead now, M. Mahler should visit next winter. I am sure he would be a success.' In fact the visit was official, but not all the concerts took place in the Trocadéro, some being given in the Théâtre du Châtelet.

The preparations were carried out with an enthusiasm and an attention to detail that today seem surprising, even touching, now that most major orchestras go on tour as a matter of course. All the musicians of the Philharmonic committed themselves in writing to participate in this 'patriotic enterprise'. In organizing the trip, the Philharmonic committee counted on a *succès d'estime*, and thought it had provided for all possible emergencies by establishing a guarantee fund of 20,000 kronen, underwritten by a few wealthy Viennese citizens, to cover the musicians' travel and living expenses. Mahler seems to have opposed the project at first, on the grounds that the heat of June and the atmosphere of an international exhibition would make it impossible to engage in serious music.[59] Later on, as the end of an exhausting season approached, he yearned for the peace and quiet of the just completed *Häuschen* and his misgivings grew. However, when he realized that the musicians were disappointed at his lack of enthusiasm, he finally agreed to go.[60] He therefore attended several meetings of the committee and participated in discussions about the technical details. A month before the visit was due to start several players had second thoughts and wanted to withdraw in spite of their pledge in writing. Mahler had to intervene personally at the general meeting of 12 May 1900 in order to persuade them to go. Strangely enough, Arnold Rosé, Mahler's future brother-in-law, seems to have been among the opponents of the project. The minutes of the meeting make amusing reading:

The programmes drawn up by Director Mahler would each take no more than two hours and consisted almost entirely of works taken from last winter's repertoire, with the object of avoiding numerous rehearsals. (Deafening applause.) Hereupon Konzertmeister Rosé took the floor and said that the public in Paris was unrewarding, the hotel would be full of bed-bugs, everything very expensive, etc. Herr Heinrich expressed his astonishment, since the Paris trip had originally been the idea of his brother, Alexander Rosé, and Konzertmeister Rosé had been one of the first to sign the paper. After which, Director Mahler exhorted all the gentlemen to take part in the trip.—Adopted.[61]

[59] RAM 33, and Romain Rolland's letter to Guido Adler of 17 Feb. (Univ. of Georgia, Guido Adler papers). Rolland also wrote to Adler about a conference of the International Society for Comparative History in which they were both to take part.

[60] Only the correspondent of the *Neue Zeitschrift* asserted that Mahler had 'prompted' his musicians to undertake this tour, but his constant disparagement of Mahler renders the statement totally unreliable. Several Viennese journalists went to Paris with the orchestra to write about the journey and the concerts.

[61] Minutes of the Philharmonic Orchestra, G.Z.29/900, taken from Hellsberg, *Gustav Mahler und die Wiener Philharmoniker*, 221.

In the wake of this sudden but welcome resumption of consensus Mahler was given a resounding vote of confidence a few days later, at the annual election of the conductor for the 1900–1 season, winning 86 votes out of 89.

The orchestra set out from Vienna on the evening of 15 June. Thanks to Princess Metternich,[62] Mahler was graciously welcomed by the Austro-Hungarian ambassador, Count Wolkenstein, and stayed at the Embassy. Hardly had he stepped off the train when he saw huge posters announcing concerts 'under the direction of M. Gustav Malheur [*sic*], Director of the Imperial and Royal Court Opera'.[63] 'That's a fine start!' he complained. To his relief, he discovered that the programmes had not yet been printed, so that there was still time to correct the spelling. Other things, however, inspired him with more serious misgivings. The preparation and publicity for the concerts had been practically non-existent. Barely a week before the first concert the press devoted a number of front-page articles to the subject, hailing the three orchestral concerts and the two benefit concerts by the Männergesangverein as 'major artistic manifestations which will occupy a significant place in the musical annals of 1900'.[64] Thereafter only one short article appeared in *Le Figaro*,[65] whereas a thoroughgoing publicity campaign would have been necessary to attract adequate audiences to five concerts in one week in big halls such as the Châtelet and, above all, the huge Trocadéro auditorium. At the last moment, a large number of free tickets had to be handed out to members of the Austrian colony, but many seats remained empty notwithstanding.

Mahler set out to discover Paris, which made a great impression on him; he wrote to Justi that 'the difference between this city and Vienna is as great as that between Vienna and Iglau.' His apartment at the Embassy was quiet and isolated, and there he met Viennese acquaintances, such as Count and Countess Kielmannsegg. During the first days of his stay he took long walks through the outskirts of Paris with an Austrian friend named Mandl[66] or Arnold Rosé, and made excursions to Saint-Germain and Versailles, from where he went on a long walk across fields and woods to Marly. He devoted his first evenings to visiting the Exhibition, which he praised to Justi with his usual brevity by saying that 'its illuminations evoke the Arabian Nights'.[67]

[62] She had gone to stay with her friend Countess de Pourtalès in Paris three weeks before, in order to publicize the concerts.

[63] BMG 151. Fortunately for his peace of mind, Mahler could not have known that, 80 years later, his name would so often be spelt 'Malher' in France!

[64] *Le Figaro* (16 June 1900).

[65] This article was reproduced in *Neues Wiener Tagblatt* (12 June). The same paper tells how Princess Metternich was obliged to pay innumerable visits to important members of Parisian society, to newspaper editors, and to members of the Société de charité maternelle, for whose benefit the Männergesangverein was giving a concert.

[66] This was probably the composer Richard Mandl (1859–1918), born in Prosnitz (Moravia), who studied at the Vienna Conservatory and later became a pupil of Léo Delibes in Paris. He returned to Vienna in 1900 and wrote a symphonic poem entitled *Grisélidis* and a number of symphonies and chamber works in a style which was an original combination of French and German influences.

[67] Letter to Justi (RWO).

The first concert took place (at 2.30) on the broiling hot afternoon of 18 June in the Théâtre du Châtelet. The meagre audience included such celebrities as the Minister of National Education, the writers Anatole France and Catulle Mendès, Calmette, the editor-in-chief of *Le Figaro*, the composers Saint-Saëns and Alfred Bruneau, Countess de Pourtalès, the singer Victor Maurel,[68] the parliamentarian Jules Roche, the industrialist Krupp, Georges Clemenceau and his brother-in-law, Jacques Maire, as well as Colonel Picquart, the hero of the Dreyfus affair and a great music lover, who was later to become one of Mahler's close friends. The fact that the hall was half-empty was not considered cause for undue alarm: since it was felt not only that the French wanted to be certain before attending a concert that the event would be worthwhile, but also that the press notices would attract larger crowds to the still to come concerts.

The afternoon was a tremendous success. An atmosphere of euphoria reigned in the hall, in which most of the Paris Austrian colony had gathered. The Viennese correspondents wrote that the Prelude to *Die Meistersinger* had been extremely impressive because of the exceptional sonority of the orchestra, the brilliance of the strings, and the power of the brasses, whereas Mozart's Symphony in G minor had in contrast been 'as simple and transparent as only Mahler could make it'. In the *Leonore* Overture No. 3, the pianissimo of the first theme of the Allegro had had a phantasmagorical effect as it gradually mounted in a crescendo to a grandiose forte. The audience had been enraptured and had applauded wildly. The tension had increased during the second half of the concert, made up of the Overture to *Oberon* and Beethoven's Fifth Symphony. Mahler's 'version' of the Beethoven had been received with some surprise, but its sheer force had overcome all hesitations and the whole concert had ended in a veritable triumph for the conductor. Throughout the afternoon, the attentiveness of the audience was such that Mahler felt confident that the Trocadéro concerts would attract a considerably larger public.

The articles in the French press are highly interesting. For the first time, foreign ears had heard and judged both the Philharmonic and Mahler's interpretations of the classical repertoire.[69] The most picturesque, if not the most enlightened, commentary, was that published in *Comœdia* by 'l'Ouvreuse', alias Willy, husband of Colette, the famous novelist:[70]

Yesterday at the Châtelet the Vienna Philharmonic Society (of which all the artists, according to the programme, are members of the Imperial and Royal Court Opera),

[68] He played the principal role in the première of Camille Erlanger's *Le Juif polonais*. Mahler saw him in this part at the Opéra-Comique during his stay in Paris.

[69] Mahler had only once conducted outside the German-speaking area, in Liège in 1899. But then he was performing one of his own works, the Second Symphony.

[70] Willy, pseudonym of Henry Gauthier-Villars (1859–1931). Helped by a team of ghost writers, including Vincent d'Indy and Pierre de Bréville, who provided him with technical information, he first contributed to several periodicals, then to the *Echo de Paris*, whose circulation increased because of his articles, and then to *Comœdia*. He was one of the first Parisian critics to support Wagner and later Debussy. His articles, written in a light-hearted and satirical style, full of word plays, were lengthy and intended for a broad public. They were later publ. in 11 successive vols. from 1890 to 1905.

gave its first concert. Large audience, enthusiastic reception, very finished perform-ance. Rather too finished: by his abuse of dynamics, his strenuous cultivation of contrasts and his exaggerated polish, a conductor as meticulous as M. Mahler ends up by upsetting his audience which, bewildered by this excess of arabesques, loses track of the general outline of the work thus messed about; certainly the Mozart Symphony in G minor would have been better without so much clever fussing over trifles. But let us acknowledge a skilfully achieved build-up in the Leonore Overture, and even a degree of lift-off in that passage—you know the one I mean—in the *Oberon* Overture.

In another article, Willy conceded that Mahler had displayed 'stunning skill at dynamic progressions, amazing brio' in the *Leonore* and *Oberon* Overtures. But he considered him 'too dextrous' and found, in the Beethoven symphony ('where I was charmed by the violins'), 'too much cleverness, too many gim-micks'. The Andante, 'less slow than at the Conservatoire, drifted along ravish-ingly'. In the Scherzo, 'despite a certain dryness', the famous build-up to the Finale was superb, although the horns, 'disguised as trombones',[71] had seemed less assured than their French counterparts.

The other Paris critics were more serious and discerning. Pierre Lalo,[72] in *Le Temps*, emphasized 'the qualities of this orchestra', which clearly distinguished it from most French orchestras. He particularly praised the strings, for 'the precision and vigour of their attack, their velvety richness, their powerful or delicate sound and their consummate virtuosity', which was far superior to anything that Paris had ever heard. He preferred the French woodwinds to the 'heavier and harsher Viennese instruments', but admired the excellence of the brass. The performance as a whole he regarded as 'enviable', giving 'an im-pression of exact discipline, obedient zeal and sustained concentration not always seen in French orchestras'. As far as Mahler's interpretations were concerned, Pierre Lalo found his *Meistersinger* Prelude[73] very different from Richter's and declared that he had 'some difficulty in discerning the advan-tages of the change'. For Weber, he preferred Nikisch's chivalrous impetuosity and romantic passion to Mahler's 'somewhat over-abundant nuances and dy-namics'. Mahler's Beethoven he found 'highly unusual, highly personal and also highly debatable'.[74] He preferred Richter's 'sovereign simplicity'. His

---

[71] Willy was apparently missing the nasal sonority of French horn-playing, which is unsuitable for the German repertory.

[72] Pierre Lalo (1866–1943), son of the composer of the *Symphonie espagnole*, had a long career as music critic for the *Journal des Débats*, the *Revue de Paris*, and *Le Temps*, and also the *Courrier musical* and *Comœdia*. He also wrote several works of criticism and musicology.

[73] According to Gustave Robert, *La Musique à Paris 1898–1900* (Delagrave, Paris, 1901), 308, the tempo of this Prelude was slightly faster than usual, the 'banner' theme lacked breadth, and the big run preceding it was 'rather dry', the violins playing at the heel of the bow and covering only about a finger-length with each stroke. The superimposition of the three motifs was 'perfectly clear' but this very clarity produced a performance that was at times 'rather dull'.

[74] The tempos greatly surprised him, especially the slowness of the opening theme. Yet it had been this very slowness ('which is becoming more and more customary in Germany') that had given the piece 'all its meaning and tragic power'. Nevertheless, the Scherzo had seemed 'excessively dragged out' and the Finale,

conclusion was that the defects of German conductors were the opposite of those of their French colleagues: 'whereas we give no thought to the scores of the masters, our neighbours give them far too much. They discover some intention in every note, emphasize every detail and end up by overcomplicating the structure and destroying the plan of a composition . . .'.

It is quite revealing that the French critics, while making numerous comments on Mahler's tempos, which they were convinced were arbitrary choices on his part, his subjective ritardandos, his unjustified pauses, his excessive dynamics, and his other extravagances, did not say a word about the changes in orchestration that he had made to Beethoven's Fifth Symphony, whereas in Germany these liberties had 'provoked violent controversies linked to the jealousy with which the integrity of the musical heritage was guarded. One is strongly tempted to conclude that there was, if not a lack of familiarity among French musicians concerning the German repertoire, at least a certain indifference.'[75]

Like Lalo, Gaston Salvayre, in *Gil Blas*,[76] regretted Richter's absence, while acknowledging the great skill of M. Charles (*sic*) Mahler. The Mozart symphony had 'lacked gaiety' while that of Beethoven had 'contained many tempo changes not marked in the score'. Only the two Overtures had fully pleased him. Alfred Bruneau wrote admiringly in *Le Figaro* of the Philharmonic's discipline and its 'extraordinary' precision, all the more so because its conductor used, in interpreting the works presented, 'the most vivid imagination, and infinite freedom'. 'In these works,' he continued, 'M. G. Mahler varies the tempo according to his own inspiration. . . . In these works he indicates with sober gestures the grand outline, the principal sections, without ever beating time in the usual sense of the term. The ensemble thus obtained is truly miraculous.'[77] Beethoven's Fifth had been played with an 'immense, majestic slowness', a slowness 'common in Germany', that attained 'real eloquence'. After an 'exquisite' performance of the Mozart symphony,[78] the Leonore Overture No. 3, 'the major work of the programme, both aroused and deserved the

with its 'constant changes' of tempo, had 'sacrificed some of its unity and grandeur to these convulsions'. Robert, *La Musique*, pointed out the 'precision' of the double basses in the Trio. Lalo regretted that Mahler, 'one of the most distinguished composers of the German school', had not included one of his own works in the programme.

[75] See Yves Simon, 'Les Premières Tribulations de Mahler en France', in *Gustav Mahler—un homme, une œuvre, une époque* (Catalogue de l'exposition du Musée d'Art Moderne, Paris 1985), 162 ff.

[76] Gaston Salvayre (1847–1916), composer and music critic. A native of Toulouse, he studied under Antoine Marmontel and Ambroise Thomas at the Paris Conservatory. Prix de Rome, he composed music mainly for the stage, both operas and ballets.

[77] Bruneau was very surprised by the interpretation of the opening theme in the Mozart symphony, 'reduced through short bow strokes and subtle dynamics to the minute proportions of old-fashioned miniatures, fragile and faded'.

[78] Salvayre also questioned Mahler's Mozart interpretation and his tempos, while the critic of *L'Echo de Paris* objected, like many Viennese critics, to 'over-detailed' preparation and an 'excess of perfection' which obscured the main outlines of the music. Robert (*La Musique*) pointed out that the Mozart had 'lacked breadth' and had shown too much emphasis on detail. He found the crotchets in the Finale too detached.

greatest and most whole-hearted admiration; its poetry, its vehemence, its sovereign splendour were expressed in an entirely novel and absolutely superb manner and the whole constituted a genuine revelation'. Like Lalo and Salvayre, Alfred Bruneau, the composer whose operas Mahler had conducted some years before in Hamburg,[79] wrote that the work that had without doubt provoked the greatest admiration was the *Leonore* Overture.

In an interview published on 21 June in *Le Soir*, Mahler tactfully said that his Parisian success had delighted him and that he was himself passionately fond of French music ancient and modern.[80] The following day *Le Soir* published an article by its critic, B. de Lomagne,[81] who said he was an 'unconditional admirer' of the Philharmonic's performances, which were 'masterly, flawless, absolutely remarkable for their smoothness, their homogeneity, their disciplined power and the delicacy and subtlety of their gradations'. Oscar Berggruen, in *Le Ménestrel*, admired Mahler's programme, 'thought up with infinite subtlety so as to bring out all the qualities of the orchestra'. In the Prelude to *Die Meistersinger*, he had revealed 'its firm structure, despite the rich and sparkling colours woven into the polyphonic texture of the piece, which is as amusing and glittering as an old gold-threaded Flemish tapestry'. From then on the orchestra 'had won its battle, as had its conductor, whose gestures are totally and forcefully sober and who rarely uses his left hand, which rests on his hip, practically all the time'. The public had been disconcerted, according to the same critic, by Mahler's slow tempo and pianissimo in the opening passages of the Leonore Overture No. 3. But then 'his brio and fire worked wonders where the score demanded it'. In the Mozart symphony, 'the gourmets were enraptured by the delicious languor of the strings', while the 'grandiose, Promethean cast' of Beethoven's C minor Symphony had been superbly rendered. 'The audience admired the beauty and power of the renderings', he concluded, 'and the unity and coalescence of the orchestra, though

[79] See Vol. i. On 24 June 1900 Alfred Bruneau sent Mahler a copy of his article with the following note: 'I enclose my article, happy to have been able publicly to express my great admiration for you and your magnificent orchestra.' The rest of the letter was about Bruneau's new opera, which he hoped Mahler would put on at the Vienna Opera.

[80] In an interview on 19 June in *Le Gaulois*, Mahler gave the names of the French composers most frequently played in Vienna. The same paper described the stream of admirers who went to congratulate Malher (*sic*) backstage after the first concert, among whom was the 'talented pianist' Madame Roger Miclos, who said she had been 'moved to tears'.

[81] B. de Lomagne, *nom de plume* of both Albert Soubies (1846–1918) and Charles Malherbe (1853–1911). Albert Soubies studied under Marie Gabriel Savard, François Guilmant, and François Bazin at the Paris Conservatory. He became chief editor of the *Almanach des spectacles* and of a History of Music consisting of several small vols. each devoted to one country or region. With Charles Malherbe he also wrote a *Précis d'histoire de l'Opéra-Comique*, a volume of *Mélanges sur Richard Wagner*, and another on *L'Œuvre dramatique de Wagner*. From 1876 onwards he wrote regularly as music critic in *Le Soir*, and from 1885 onwards in the *Revue d'art dramatique*, the *Ménestrel*, and the *Guide musical*. Charles Malherbe, composer and musicologist, contributed to various journals and reviews, including the *Ménestrel* and the *Guide musical*. From 1899 to his death he held the post of librarian at the Paris Opéra. He was the author of a biography of Daniel François Auber, and also collaborated in the publication of the complete works of Rameau and Berlioz.

each phrase stood out clearly, and whole-heartedly accepted some tempos that differed from Conservatoire traditions.'

Thus in general the reactions of both the public and the press were favourable. The following evening, again at the Châtelet, the Männergesangverein gave a choral concert under the baton of Richard von Perger, with the famous tenor Hermann Winkelmann as soloist. The auditorium was much fuller than that on the previous day.[82] The second half of the concert was to have opened with Mahler conducting the Overture to *Der Freischütz*. The audience were waiting for him to appear when the president of the Männergesangverein, Franz Schneiderhan, came out to announce in French that Mahler was indisposed and had begged to be excused for a while, during which Perger would conduct Wagner's *Das Liebesmahl der Apostel*. Overcome either by exhaustion or by the heat, Mahler had in fact collapsed on reaching the theatre[83] and had to lie down on the caretaker's bed for about twenty minutes to recover. After the *Liebesmahl*, Schneiderhan addressed a few words of thanks to the audience and, just as people were beginning to think that Mahler would be replaced by his brother-in-law, Arnold Rosé, he appeared, looking very pale, and was greeted by thunderous applause. At the end of the *Freischütz* Overture, which, according to Willy,[84] was 'brilliantly played', he was again rapturously applauded.

His time before concerts completely taken up by rehearsals. Mahler saw little of Paris itself and its monuments—he did not even get to the Louvre—but in any case the hectic atmosphere of the Exhibition spoiled the city's charm for him: 'All this wild uproar all around me,' he wrote to Nanna Spiegler,

—how incredibly inappropriate to be playing music for the French at this time, with the World Exhibition going on—is so distasteful that I cannot even enjoy this beautiful Paris. I simply can't tell you how utterly everything is empty speechifying, posturing lies! . . . There is really only one word for it all: Ugh! For the first few days (before the first concert) it was not so bad. I went for walks in the countryside outside Paris—it is really so lovely and full of memories of the various Louis and Napoleons that nowhere else perhaps does one feel so strongly the transitory nature of things. But now there is a concert every day, and I can no longer get out of town. So far I have kept aloof from official welcomes, banquets, etc., and hope to do so until I leave! Actually all that seems to be what counts most! I assure you, dear friends, it could all be done without

[82] On the morning of this concert, the Männergesangverein gave a short concert at the Austrian Embassy, in the presence of the President of the Republic, Emile Loubet, Minister Alexander Millerand, and the Prefect of Police. The programme for the Châtelet concert of 19 June was as follows: Herbeck, *Werners Lied*; Brahms, *Wiegenlied*; Schubert, *Gondelfahrt*; Schumann, *Ritornelli*; Kremser, *Vieux chœur hollandais*; Wagner, *Lohengrin*, 'Grail Song'; Kremser, *An die Madonna* (soloist: Hermann Winkelmann); Weber, *Der Freischütz* Overture. The Paris press informed its readers that Massenet and Saint-Saëns attended this concert, which drew an audience of 2,800 and brought in 20,000 francs. According to Ludwig Karpath, the whole sum was donated to the Société maternelle.

[83] According to Karpath, who sent a daily report to the *Neues Wiener Tagblatt*, Mahler had been suffering from a violent migraine for two days and on arriving backstage had almost fainted into the arms of Arnold Rosé.

[84] L'Ouvreuse (Willy), in *La Ronde des blanches*, 104.

any music-making, and <u>la gloire</u> would not suffer in the least. I positively feel like laughing when I take up my baton. Oh! Oh! Oh! . . . On Sunday morning, I hope, I shall be bathing in the Wörthersee. Heaven knows when I shall get rid of this sense of disgust! I feel as if I had prostituted myself![85]

Before the final concert, Mahler had to attend a banquet given by the President of the Republic in honour of the Viennese musicians at the Hotel Continental. But at least during his visit to Paris he made two new friends: Colonel Picquart and Paul Clemenceau, younger brother of the 'Tiger'. Both spoke perfect German. Paul Clemenceau's wife was Austrian by birth, daughter of Moritz Szeps, a noted Viennese journalist. As for Picquart, Mahler immediately appreciated his 'strong personality, integrity, exceptional class'. Although at the time Charpentier's *Louise* was the biggest operatic hit in Paris and everybody was rushing to see it, Mahler refused to do so, since he had already studied its score.[86] But he did go to the Opéra Comique to hear Erlanger's *Le Juif polonais*, which Lilli Lehmann had recently brought to his attention.[87]

For the concert given by the Männergesangverein, the committee had to resort to distributing a large number of complimentary tickets. Even for the final concerts, which were to take place in the immense auditorium of the Trocadéro,[88] the sale of tickets was negligible, and things began to look serious. The guarantee fund was almost exhausted, and there was not going to be enough money left to pay for the return journey of the orchestra. Mahler and Arnold Rosé discussed matters with Ludwig Karpath one evening at the Café Poucet. In the middle of the conversation, Mahler suddenly blurted out in a loud voice, 'And I tell you, German art is the only art!', thereby attracting the indignant attention of other customers sitting nearby. The musicians were beginning to be anxious and to criticize the members of the committee who had talked them into this venture. Some of them had already unsuccessfully appealed to Princess Metternich for help. Eventually Mahler asked her to approach Baron Albert Rothschild, the financier, who was in Paris at the time. This she refused to do, since she was obliged to ask him for money each year for her good works and did not wish to run the risk of a rebuff. So, on the day of the final concert, Mahler himself went to see Baron Rothschild, who immediately offered to advance him the 4,000 kronen he contributed annually to the Philharmonic Orchestra. Mahler was forced to tell him that what they needed was at least 20,000 francs[89] in order to be able to pay their journey home. Rothschild was a cold man who had little interest in music and felt he

[85] Letter to Nanna Spiegler of 20 June 1900 (PML).

[86] Karpath provides this information, thereby proving that a score could indeed remain a 'dead letter', even for someone like Mahler, who was to produce *Louise* in Vienna in 1903, and who developed a real enthusiasm, at least in the beginning, for Charpentier's 'Roman musical'.

[87] BMG 153 and AMM 132. According to Karpath, who accompanied him, it immediately aroused his interest. Alma's claim that this was because of Erlanger's use of the sleigh-bells, which reminded him of those in his own Fourth Symphony, is more than dubious.

[88] It had 4,500 seats.   [89] The franc and the krone were more or less at parity.

had done his patriotic duty with his annual donation to the orchestra. He asked who on earth had encouraged the musicians to undertake so foolhardy a venture. Mahler merely pointed out that if Baron Albert found it impossible to pay the sum, he would be obliged to pay it himself, which would mean sacrificing his entire savings. Rothschild eventually promised that his secretary would deliver the sum at the Trocadéro that afternoon. While the musicians were tuning up before the concert, the secretary of the committee, Franz Simandl, came to tell them that, thanks to Mahler's intervention, Baron Rothschild had put up the money for their return journey. They all cheered Mahler and invited him to dine with them that evening.

Meanwhile, the enthusiastic reports in the French press had borne fruit and there were larger audiences at the final concerts. A Parisian impresario even offered the committee an advance of 20,000 francs for five more concerts. The Viennese, however, decided to refuse, since they felt they had enough, both of the bustle of the Exhibition and of the dreadful auditorium of the Trocadéro, with its grubby flags, its pseudo-oriental decoration, and its abominable acoustics. Mahler had tried to improve things by rearranging the seating of the orchestra; even so, most of the nuances and subtleties of his interpretations were lost because the strings were almost inaudible and the brass was disproportionately loud. The programme of the concert of 20 June consisted of Beethoven's Egmont Overture, the Prelude and *Liebestod* from *Tristan und Isolde*, and a Beethoven Romance, played by Arnold Rosé; it concluded with Berlioz's *Symphonie fantastique* as a tribute to France. The overture was warmly applauded, and the excerpts from *Tristan* were given an enthusiastic hearing. As for the *Symphonie fantastique*, despite the fact that it was an old war-horse of Parisian orchestras, Mahler's interpretation of it was considered 'brilliant', and he was called back to the podium no less than twelve times by an ecstatic audience, while someone presented him with a laurel wreath on behalf of the Société Maternelle for whose benefit he had conducted the evening before. Each time he was called back he turned to the players and bowed to show his appreciation. 'Never has an orchestra been so applauded in Paris,' claimed the *Neue Freie Presse* the next day.

For its final concert the following day, the Philharmonic treated the Parisians to two Viennese works they had not yet heard, Karl Goldmark's Overture *Im Frühling* ('In Spring') and the Scherzo from Bruckner's 'Romantic' Symphony. Oscar Berggruen, in *Le Ménestrel*, contrived an unusual description of Bruckner's style, which he said combined 'the joyful serenity of Haydn with all the orchestral refinements of Berlioz and Wagner'. Besides these two pieces, the programme included Beethoven's 'Eroica' Symphony, Schubert's 'Unfinished', and the Overture to *Tannhäuser*, which the audience applauded with shouts of 'Hurrah for the orchestra! Hurrah for Mahler! *Au revoir!*'[90] Berggruen

---

[90] Before leaving the podium Mahler made a short farewell speech in which he expressed the orchestra's thanks to Princess Metternich.

deplored the fact that the wretched acoustics had not only prevented the ten double basses from 'delivering their beautiful phrases with the desired intensity' at the beginning of the 'Unfinished' Symphony,[91] but, in the Overture to *Tannhäuser*, had rendered the characteristic motif on the violins practically inaudible above the pilgrims' theme played by the brass.

Although it had drawn an audience of about 4,000 people, including such musicians as Henri de Curzon, Emile Palhadilhe, Camille Saint-Saëns, and Gustave Charpentier, and almost all the best seats had been sold, this third and last orchestral concert was virtually ignored by the press. Willy again accused Mahler of being 'too slick' and too cold, and of having 'conducted Wagner as though he had never heard his prodigious predecessor, Hans Richter'. 'And why illuminate things that belong in the shadows? I heard one lady enthusing: "How well he brought out the second-violin figurations that everyone normally leaves buried!" Madame, would you then also enthuse if he brought out the cords on his underpants?' The Prelude to *Tristan* distressed Willy 'because of a certain inexplicable and to be quite honest, even rather unintelligent coldness here and there, alternating with superbly rendered passages. . . . As for the *Eroica*, thus chopped up, no, no! . . . True, there was a large audience in the hall, but Beethoven was absent.' In Willy's opinion, it was too easy 'to have eight horns blow certain themes written for one or two'. Instead of sounding 'a gay sylvan fanfare, the Trio of the Scherzo snivelled gloomily'. Willy did admit, however, that his disappointment had been largely due to the appalling acoustics of the Trocadéro, for 'even God's musicians, the angels, archangels *ac beata seraphim*, would be incapable of producing any effect there'. He concluded with a final tribute to the 'Kapellmeister, who sometimes beats time, frequently beats the dynamic, but never beats about the bush'.[92]

According to Gustave Robert, who was soon to publish a collection of articles about the musical activities of those years, Mahler's 'conducting technique resembled Richter's more than that of Mottl, Weingartner, Strauss, or Nikisch'. He concluded that there was an 'Austrian tradition' closer to the French than the German one. Perhaps Mahler showed exaggerated concern with details, perhaps one could wish for 'more abandon, more life'. But Robert emphasized the standards of the orchestra, its sincerity, the way Mahler 'forgot himself' and 'thought only of the composer' without ever seeking to impose a personal interpretation. It is worth comparing this fresh and unprejudiced view with those of the numerous critics who had accused Mahler of 'wanting to be new at any price'. 'We are left with the impression of having heard performances full of taste, even nobility,' concluded Robert, 'that do great honour to the players and their conductors.'[93]

---

[91] Karpath made the same criticism in the *Neues Wiener Tagblatt* (22 June).

[92] An untranslatable French pun: 'qui bat parfois la mesure, souvent la nuance et jamais la campagne'; *battre la campagne* means 'to let one's mind wander'.

[93] *La Musique*. Robert's view was that the Viennese strings, despite their technical mastery, lacked the

At Karpath's suggestion, Catulle Mendès,[94] one of the leading Paris critics of the time, summed up his impression of the concerts in the following letter to the editor in chief of the *Neues Wiener Tagblatt*, published on 22 June.

With its strikingly perfect discipline and its rare, alternately powerful or delicate, sonorous opulence, M. Mahler's orchestra won us over immediately. The strings vibrate in glorious unison, whether their tones be strident or languishing; the woodwinds, of which there seem to me to be a greater number than in most orchestras, achieve exceptional accuracy in their plaintive tone, as though only one man graded their sonority, while the brasses, when required to do so, burst forth in magnificent thunder. As to the spirit in which the works were performed, and which was that of the 'Kapellmeister', many people found it truly inspiring, whereas others were surprised, particularly in Mozart's Symphony in G minor, by certain *rallentandi*, a somewhat excessively subtle gradation and the too harsh contrast between *pianissimi* and *fortissimi*. It is certain that in recent times a number of conductors—among them some of the most skilled and celebrated—have, in their eagerness to be different from their colleagues, sought to present 'personal' interpretations even of works of genius. Should we blame them? I believe that we can see, in the originality they strive for, not the desire to be taken as special so much as their laudable desire to penetrate more deeply into masterworks; they are like servers at the altar who, in their burning piety, observe a cult in all its details, even where these verge on superstition. There is no one to equal Gustav Mahler in the simplicity of his deportment and the sobriety of his gestures, which can suddenly become magnificently impetuous. Everything about him reveals a headstrong and highly strung personality, while his approach to a work and manner of conducting are at once stately and intimate. His interpretation of the Overture to *Die Meistersinger* showed fine feeling, both for the structure of the principal themes and by the way he emphasized them (even Richter could not have done better); that of *Der Freischütz* was infinitely poetic and that of *Oberon* ineffably delicate, light and, one might almost say, fairylike.[95]

A few days later Karl Kraus, in his most biting style, published the following account of the orchestra's trip to Paris:

The effusive columns to which we have been treated in connection with the 'Paris Tour' of our Opera Orchestra and the Männergesangsverein are nothing compared with the humble notice put out, as ticket-seller, by the Princess Metternich. It even tells us the names of all the ladies who took boxes. It is to be hoped we shall also receive an

---

'broad sound' of French strings. He may have been misled by the acoustics of the Trocadéro. The first movement of the 'Eroica', and its Scherzo, seemed to him slower than usual. He thought that Mahler took the B flat motif in the opening Allegro too slowly (this probably refers to the second theme) and played the staccato bars that followed rather dryly (probably the beginning of the development).

[94] Catulle Mendès (1841–1909), writer, drama and music critic, native of Bordeaux. In 1861 he founded the *Revue fantaisiste* to defend modern art. As critic on the *Journal* from 1895 onwards he ardently supported Wagner's music, and instituted in 1898 a new series of chamber-music concerts, the 'Jeudis populaires'. Husband of Judith Gauthier (author of historical tales, plays, novels and novelettes), he also wrote many opera librettos for Chabrier (*Gwendoline*), Messager (*Isoline*), Erlanger (*Fils de l'étoile*), Debussy (*Rodrigue et Chimène*). His poems were also put to music by several composers, including Bizet, Chabrier, Fauré, Messager, Saint-Saëns, Pierné, and Roussel.

[95] Letter dated 19 June. This is a trans. of the German text, published in the *Neues Wiener Tagblatt* (22 June), which was of course itself a trans. from the French.

account of the ecstatic terms in which the ladies Mandl, Porges, Ephrussi, Burger, Back, Brandeis,[96] and other representatives of the French nobility expressed themselves concerning Herr Mahler's appearance. Telegraphed reports of how the mens' choir was obliged to change trains—'and the Philharmonic players, too, had to change three times'—have led to heart-rending scenes here. But we were somewhat relieved by the intelligence that Herr Dr Marmorek, of the 'Paris Writers', Herr Blowitz and 'the art-loving Colonel Picquart' had attended the concert. The latter 'came in civilian clothes and listened to the productions of the Viennese artists with rapt attention'. Obviously those brass bands have given him an interest in other musical instruments. Furthermore: the Philharmonic played the third Leonore Overture. And, after all, the *Neue Freie Presse* had demanded some time ago that 'a new Beethoven' immortalize Picquart's glorious deeds. Picquart must have wanted to check for himself that the old Beethoven would do for now—for which he did not even need the brass . . . A drop of gall in the cup that runneth over: 'The hall was'—quoting the *Neues Wiener Tagblatt* word for word—'only half sold out'.[97]

Judging by the following letter which he sent to his friend Henriette Mankiewicz as soon as he reached Maiernigg, Mahler's view of the journey to Paris was not much different from that of Karl Kraus:

Paris was for me, as I expected, a big desert. The concerts, which have left a bad taste in my mouth, I'll tell you about when I see you. Any music-making which requires deep inner concentration was out of place in that turmoil. As you can imagine, we, miserable musicians, wandered around there like larks in a crowd of sparrows. Even the most thick-skinned among the Philharmonic were aware of this contradiction. Ultimately everything was painted over in big brush-strokes of publicity, and splodged out in all directions by obliging hacks as a pioneering journey for 'German' or even 'Viennese' art. We were ashamed and left depressed. That the tragedy should not lack its comic episode was ensured by the Silenus of our Bacchic train: the 'Männergesangverein' in black jackets and white ties, hurling their glee club choruses from full throats and full bellies to the four winds as they left Paris. Enthroned above everybody was the biggest loudmouth of all, Princess Pauline, 'la gloire' dripping red from her lips into the sweat of her face.[98] It was a great moment to hear her lecture a circle of reporters from *Le Figaro*, *Le Temps* and other papers about the finer points of the Vienna Philharmonic's conception of Beethoven; a wild waterspout of words, and Paris society holding its dishes carefully underneath so as not to miss a single drop.[99]

All things considered, the four concerts gave Mahler precious little satisfaction. Although the takings of the last one amounted to 12,000 francs, which fortunately reduced the deficit, he came away with the impression that Paris, like Vienna, considered his interpretations of Beethoven 'anticlassical', which in the main was true. Principally because of the Catulle Mendès letter,[100] once

---

[96] Most of the names Kraus quotes are of bourgeois Jewish families, generally of Austrian origin. Given his anti-Semitic tendencies, it is obvious that the phrase 'representatives of the French nobility' is ironic.

[97] *Die Fackel* (June 1900) 29. One is reminded here of Kraus's hostility to the Dreyfusard cause, as defended by the *Neue Freie Presse*, and of his anti-Semitic feelings in general.

[98] Later Mahler was to speak to his wife with disgust of the 'red lips' of Princess Metternich.

[99] Letter to Henriette Mankiewicz, June 1900, LCW.   [100] See above.

in Maiernigg he again commented bitterly on the subject in the presence of Natalie, noting that his interpretations of classical works shocked both public and musicians. 'For them to think it "classic", a work has to be stiff and all of a piece like a sausage. Or, to use another metaphor, it seems to me as if they were to look at a face and complain that's it's broken up by the mouth, nose and eyes, and would be more beautiful without them!' On another occasion he said:

My interpretation of works other than the most modern, such as of Beethoven's C minor or Mozart's G minor Symphonies, is as alien to people as my own works. I realised this again in Paris. They keep on talking about 'subtle nuances' and 'arbitrary alterations' because the difference between the real work, in the way I present it, and the cold and empty performance to which they're accustomed, is like the difference between a tree covered in fragrant leaves and the bare branches of a tree in winter.[101]

Mahler deplored the fact that the French press had said so little about the concerts and that what it did say was thoroughly superficial.[102] He and his musicians had not felt at home amid the tumult of the Exhibition, but they had at least been gratified by 'the enthusiasm of the true friends of art'. On the eve of their departure from Paris, Mahler had dined with the musicians of the orchestra at the Buffet Rapp, where they were all staying. They cheered him loudly on his arrival, and the evening constituted one of the few relaxed and pleasant moments of his three years' work with them, and also one of the rare satisfactions of the trip, which had won him nothing but the hearts and admiration of a few French music lovers. The members of the orchestra, on returning to Vienna, found one of their dearest wishes gratified: as recompense for their Paris performances, the Emperor granted them the title of 'k. u. k. Hofmusiker' (Royal and Imperial Court Musician), which every member would henceforth be entitled to use after only ten years of service. The following February, His Majesty even deigned 'benevolently to allow the expression of his supreme gratitude to be communicated to the honourable Philharmonic Society'.[103]

Mahler, having thus sacrificed ten days of his impatiently awaited and hard-won holidays in the Paris furnace,[104] joyfully and eagerly set out for home and something he had had to do without for four years: a *Häuschen* isolated in the woods, in which he hoped he would at last be able to finish his Fourth Symphony. He reached Maiernigg on 23 June and immediately dashed off to the *Häuschen*, which was some twenty minutes on foot from the Villa Antonia, which he had rented for the summer. He threaded his way along a narrow footpath that twisted and turned through 'all the marvels and terrors of the

---

[101] NBLS.

[102] In an interview with Karpath for the *Neues Wiener Tagblatt*, Mahler added that the Viennese papers would certainly have made greater efforts to bring such an important event to the public's notice, but that the Paris critics had none the less saved what could be saved of the unfortunate tour.

[103] See Hellsberg, *Mahler*, 247.

[104] The following year, Mahler refused to conduct the Philharmonic at the Salzburg Festival, 'for I need my holidays to rest' (HOA, Z.282/1901: letter from Intendant Plappart to Mahler, 22 Mar. 1901; a draft reply is handwritten at the top of the letter).

forest' and, as he closed behind him the *Häuschen's* two latticed doors that had been discreetly placed at the rear to discourage visitors, he finally savoured 'peace, security and Dionysiac wonder'. Here he would even be able to work with the window open and breathe the pure forest air, instead of having to keep doors and windows tightly closed against the noise, as he had had to do in Steinbach. The sensation of peace and quiet was so intense that he at once decided to have his breakfast brought there every day, rain or shine, and brushed aside all Justi's objections about the difficulty of reaching the place. However, after the commotion of the Paris trip and the strain of the previous season, he found it difficult to settle down to creative work.[105] He could not forget the forebodings which had tormented him the previous autumn, when he had feared that by the time he had a *Häuschen* he might no longer be capable of composing. However, this period of composer's block—something he had experienced on other occasions[106]—was probably largely due to physical exhaustion and also to the fact that he was trying to pick up the threads of a half-finished work traumatically interrupted the previous summer, rather than starting something new. One of his letters to Henriette Mankiewicz shows how he was dreading the prospect of being unable to resume composing:

I can see from your letters to me and to others that you are worried about me; I am always amazed how accurate your intuition is where I am concerned. You are quite right! I'm going into this summer shaking like a leaf. Do you know about vertigo on the edge of the void? Woe is me if it gets hold of me this summer! I had a foretaste of it last summer, and feel it is the only thing I could not bear.[107]

However, after about ten days, Natalie and Justi, noticing that he lapsed more often into silence and remained in his *Häuschen* for up to eight or ten hours at a stretch, concluded that he had begun composing again. This was indeed the case and, although 7 July marked his fortieth birthday, he decided to put off celebrating it for a month in the hope that by then his work would be nearing completion. On 14 July he wrote to Nanna Spiegler:[108] 'I was completely immersed in the Fourth, looking neither to the right nor to the left'. Returning from Klagenfurt with Natalie one day, he sadly reflected that Mozart and Schubert were dead at his age.

How much they had composed, and how much time I've lost! Until I went to Steinbach, I didn't know how to provide myself, during the little time at my disposal, with the peace and solitude I need. And to think that I almost gave up composing for that reason! Now, during these few short weeks, I have to work every moment of the day, even when I'm weary and out of sorts, merely in order to get things finished. This is very strenuous for me and can't do my work any good![109]

---

[105] Two letters from Selma Kurz to Hermine Baum (22 June and 17 July 1900) show us that Mahler's Paris illness was not without consequences: his internal bleeding (Selma speaks of his 'old trouble') started again and became more serious (BGM, Fonds Desi Halban).

[106] See n. 131 for the psychological conclusion that Theodor Reik drew from this period of composer's block and from the terms in which Mahler confided his anguish to Natalie.

[107] LCW.   [108] Postcard of 14 July (PML, Lehmann deposit).   [109] NBLS.

All the same, Mahler occasionally found time for an excursion, such as that of 12 July, when he bicycled to Viktring. Along the way, he carefully steered his bicycle round a cockchafer he saw crawling over the road. 'I am becoming increasingly aware of the fact that even the cockchafer is an individual whose life must be respected,' he said, 'just as we and our existence certainly depend on countless occasions on the forbearance of higher forms of life (as for example our Earth, which is surely one such higher being).'[110] During his holiday he also read through the whole of Schubert's chamber music and at times judged it severely.

At most four out of twelve [works] are good; likewise, only eighty of his eight hundred Lieder are really beautiful, which admittedly is quite enough. But it would have been better if he had not composed all the trivial stuff which might almost make one doubt his talent, however enthusiastic one might be about his other works! This stems from the fact that his technical ability falls a long way short of his sensitivity and inventiveness. How facile his approach to composition is! Six sequences in a row and then another in a different key. No development (*Verarbeitung*), no artistically perfected shaping of his initial theme. Instead, he simply repeats himself, so that one could cut out half of it without damaging the whole.[111]

Still on the subject of Schubert's music, Mahler went on to formulate a basic principle of composition which is of great significance in view of the evolution of his own compositional technique towards what Adorno called the 'non-reversibility' (*Nicht-Umkehrbarkeit*) of time:

Every repetition is in itself a lie. Like life, a work of art must continuously develop (*sich weiter entwickeln*). If it does not it becomes untruth and pretence. For Schubert's melody, like that of Beethoven and Wagner, is already <u>eternal</u> melody; that is why he should not employ the formalism that constituted the perfectly genuine basis of Mozart's and Haydn's works in their day.

'Now I can understand why, shortly before his death, Schubert wanted to take up counterpoint; he realized what he lacked . . .'. On this occasion Mahler admitted that he too, much to his regret, lacked a thorough grounding in counterpoint. His intelligence usually helped him to overcome this lacuna, but the effort required was quite disproportionate.[112]

Besides going over Schubert, Mahler began to re-read E. T. A. Hoffmann, who, in his opinion, 'wrote more intelligently about music than anyone else'

[110] Twenty years after the letter to Steiner and eight years before *Das Lied von der Erde*, Mahler once more refers to the Earth as a pagan divinity.

[111] NBL1. 138; NBL2. 158. In fact Schubert wrote not 800, but just over 600 Lieder, The remark about repetitions is significant, as exact thematic repetitions are extremely rare in Mahler's music. On the other hand, his work contains many repeats which are not identical but near enough to create the effect of repetition upon the listener (cf. *Nachrichten zur Mahler-Forschung*, no. 19, IMG).

[112] NBL1. 138; NBL2. 159. See also the passage quoted above (Chap. 6) on the same subject (NBL1. 119; NBL2. 136). Mahler thus implicitly confirms that his teachers at the Vienna Conservatory considered his contrapuntal gifts good enough to allow a less thorough study of this discipline. It is somewhat surprising, however, that he should have been granted the Conservatory diploma without having to satisfy the examiners in this discipline.

and exactly in the right words, beautifully expressed. On the other hand, he considered Hoffmann's music more or less negligible, including his opera *Undine*, which he found clumsy and amateurish; one could see what he had intended and one was bound to admire the quality of his imagination, but his technique was definitely too coarse. Mahler on the other hand felt incapable of expressing his feelings in poetry, because his literary ability fell so far short of his musical skill.

Mahler had brought to Maiernigg the score of a symphony by Hans Rott, an old friend from his Conservatory days, in order to study it with a view to eventual performance in the Philharmonic Concerts. 'What music lost in him is immeasurable,' he said to Natalie.

Already in this First Symphony, which he wrote at the age of twenty and which makes of him—it's not too much to say—the founder of the modern symphony as I understand it, his genius soars to such heights. At the same time he wasn't yet altogether able to achieve what he wanted. It's as if someone had gone all out to break the high jump record and failed by a centimetre to clear the bar. But I know <u>what</u> he was aiming at. He is so much akin to what is most particular about me, that we seem to me like two fruits from the same tree, growing from the same soil, nourished by the same air. I could have benefited greatly from him, and perhaps between us we could have virtually covered the whole range of the new musical era that was then opening up.[113]

During that same summer, Mahler received from his friend Siegfried Lipiner the manuscript of his latest play, *Hippolytos*. The previous year in Aussee, he had been given another play recently finished by Lipiner, *Adam*, at first intended to serve as prologue to a vast trilogy, *Christus*, whose three main sections, *Maria Magdalena*, *Judas Ischariot*, and *Paulus in Rom*, were never completed. As usual with Lipiner, *Adam* presented the confrontation between two protagonists embodying two main ideas: Cain, the man of instinct (*Triebmensch*) and Abel, the man of reason (*Vernunftsmensch*). Cain is a tortured being full of doubt, aspiring to knowledge among endless torments, doomed never to realize himself either subconsciously, or through knowledge, or even through nature, which he has come to hate. Abel, on the other hand, lives in harmony with nature, having discovered what it is that unites instinct and reason and is in fact the way to God. This is the reason why his brother kills him. After the murder, Cain is not punished but returned to nature. His punishment is losing the love of Eve, his mother, and being eternally deprived, along with his descendants, of all hope of revelation (*Erkenntnis*). Eve alone escapes the duality of instinct and reason. Not only is she the mother of the human race but, like Erda, she knows the future and holds all the keys to the tragic dilemma of the human condition. Thus the play is really a long philosophical discourse on the causes and effects of Abel's murder by

---

[113] NBL1. 157; NBL2. 157. Hans Rott's Symphony in E major was given its première by the Cincinnati Philharmonia Orchestra on 4 Mar. 1989.

Cain.[114] Mahler's enthusiasm for Lipiner had continued undiminished since his student days and he wrote to him immediately:

This is a truly Dionysiac work! Believe me, no one else alive today, except me, will understand it. There is some affinity with it, to my mind, in Euripides' *Bacchae*. Only Euripides always talks too much about these things without naming them. <u>What</u> ever is it that delivers all living creatures into the power of Dionysus? Wine intoxicates, intensifying the drinker's condition. But <u>what</u> is wine?—No visual representation has ever yet succeeded in capturing what flows spontaneously from music, from every note. <u>This</u> music lives and breathes throughout your play. It is really unique.—Instead of telling of wine or describing its effects, it <u>is</u> wine, it <u>is</u> Dionysus! It seems to me, incidentally, that what Dionysus personified to the ancients was simply <u>instinct</u>, in the grandiose mystical sense in which you have interpreted it. There, too, those possessed by it are driven forth to become one with the animals.[115]

Now Mahler eagerly plunged into Lipiner's *Hippolytos*. Once again there were two characters representing two opposing forces, based on Nietzsche's distinction between the Apollonian and the Dionysiac. Phaedra represented the life force (*Lebensdrang*), and Hippolytos the repose of the soul (*Seelenstille*). At the end of the play the two principles were united, when Phaedra's 'fire' entered the soul of Hippolytos, who fell incestuously in love with his stepmother. Once again this was a long philosophical poem rather than a play, for there was practically no action, only versified dialogue spoken by characters much too abstract to come to life; and once again, Lipiner's verbal gifts failed to disguise his basic lack of originality. Nevertheless, Mahler was won over as before, even if, this time, he ventured a few timid criticisms:

Just one thing I must tell you: on my first reading of the second act I was rather disconcerted by the reasons given for Phaedra's death. It struck me as a weakening of the naïve myth, rather the way I always feel it is weakened in Grillparzer's *Argonauts*. It seemed to me that this 'toning down' of the apparently brutal solution was sentimental (in Schiller's sense of the word). But then I resorted to your proven method—approaching a work of art with a completely <u>blank</u> mind—and read it a second time without preconceptions, whereupon I instantly understood what you meant. In fact, now I could hardly imagine any other solution.—Well, so there is a question I have been able to answer for myself.

One thing about your essential nature has again become crystal clear to me: a new, deep connection between your creativeness and the musical side of your being. I am coming to understand more and more of your semi-humorous complaints that the gods did not endow you with the gift of music. My dear Siegfried: you do make music! No one will ever be able to understand you better than a musician and, I may specifically add: than <u>myself</u>. It sometimes seems to me quite a joke how closely my 'music' is related to yours . . .

---

[114] Hartmut von Hartungen, 'Der Dichter Siegfried Lipiner', thesis, Ludwig-Maximilians Universität, Munich, 1932. *Adam*, publ. in Stuttgart in 1913, was performed in Dresden in Nov. 1915.

[115] MBR1, no. 260; MBR2, no. 269.

Mahler goes on to criticize, with the greatest tact, one of the characters in his friend's play, a high priest functioning as a confidant in the manner of classical tragedy, his only task being to listen and to make generalized responses. Then he tries to persuade Lipiner to finish his trilogy by simply not thinking beyond the next scene, just as it is better not to keep trying to see the top of a mountain the moment one has begun to climb it.

It has happened to me that I have suddenly realized that a last movement was <u>beyond the limits of the work</u>. What I mean might be explained in a metaphor: one often stands in a big hall with a mirror at the end of it, and one is entirely mistaken about the form; it is only when one comes to the borderline that one realizes that one has been tricked by the mirror and therefore has been aiming for the wrong thing. I don't know whether I have made myself clear.[116]

In the autumn Mahler again wrote to Lipiner about *Hippolytos*, which he had reread at leisure:

I think I have now grasped the conflict that prevails in earthly life between maidenly and womanly love (Artemis-Aphrodite), which also manifests itself in young men. In your *Hippolytos* it is the other way round,—Phaedra, the woman, is purified by Hippolytos's reluctance and it is wonderful to feel that this sublimity is the insoluble contradiction in life as a whole, one that takes on its most decisive and most fateful form only in the lives of lovers. That is why the lovers have to die, not in atonement for their tragic guilt, but because a wonderful, mystical connection between love and death brings everything to fruition and completion in them.—What is peculiar, something I have found in no other poet, is how in your works concepts merge into each other—the strange relatedness, indeed unity, of all life and creation suddenly becoming clear as it does only in music.—If I should not have understood aright, do please enlighten me.—Such a great work is of course not simply wound around the spool of some kind of 'idea', and its essence can no more be expressed by it than the essence of the universe.[117]

Whatever Lipiner's limitations as a poet, we cannot but be grateful to him for having provoked in Mahler a degree of literary fervour rarely seen in a musician, and for having led him to express some of his own key ideas concerning artistic creation. In this connection, Mahler that summer had one of the most curious experiences of his career as a composer. When he finally resumed working on the Fourth Symphony, he discovered that a 'second self' had been active during the long sleep of his conscious 'self', and he continued and brought to maturity the work apparently broken off by his return to the Opera. He was amazed to discover that the Fourth Symphony was far nearer completion than when he had stopped working on it the previous year at Aussee, even though he had never had it consciously in mind:

On the contrary, I tried to avoid thinking about it, because of the pain and frustration this would cause me. But probably my real 'self', rejecting the unreal life (*Scheinleben*)

[116] MBR1, no. 262; MBR2, no. 278.   [117] MBR1, no. 264; MBR2, no. 280.

I am leading, said: 'All this is rubbish, I refuse to be affected by it' and brought me to the innermost recesses of my soul. To itself, to its—that is, to my—purer, loftier life. Most people never discover this 'second self' because they flee from it, and kill it by social contacts. They don't realize that their salvation lies in solitude, in which it instantly appears and, unnoticed, goes to work.[118]

Despite its total isolation, the *Häuschen* still on occasions failed to provide Mahler with the calm he dreamt of. He put up scarecrows and detonated blank cartridges in vain—the birds continued their endless twittering, and the following year it was found that they had been nesting in the roof. Moreover, Alfred Theuer's dogs barked, and the barrel organs and military bands on the other side of the lake bothered him. Now and again, as at Steinbach, the summer visitors paid wandering musicians to go and disturb him, for they had discovered his phobia about noise. His idiosyncrasy and 'semi-madness' became the joke of the neighbourhood. 'Nowadays the creative artist is like a fly which has arrived when summer is over; that's why his wings droop so sadly,' he complained, deploring the barbarity of the human environment from which he could not escape, because most of his fellow men had no idea what it meant to respect personal freedom, 'preoccupied as they are with satisfying their immediate, childish whims, like pulling up flowers and continually slaughtering animals'. Mahler even began to 'envy the deaf and the blind who are shut off from this miserable world, and to understand why a musician might even deliberately deprive himself of hearing, just as Democritus had blinded himself'.[119]

In spite of everything, things went much more smoothly than he had expected, as witness his earlier remarks to Natalie about the Fourth Symphony, of which, he told her, he had composed 'about half of each movement' the year before:

You can imagine what I felt like when I had to interrupt my work and leave Aussee, for I was sure it would be quite impossible to take it up again. And indeed it has meant a gigantic effort. I made a bundle of all the sketches, which are undecipherable to anyone but me, put it in the bottom drawer of my desk and haven't been able to think of it since without experiencing the most excruciating anguish.[120]

The Fourth Symphony was to be in G major and was to last forty-five minutes, no longer, that is, than just the first movement of the Third.[121] 'Originally I had

---

[118] NBL1. 141; NBL2. 161. Although he probably had not yet heard of Freud's work or writings, Mahler here anticipated one of Freud's principal discoveries, the subconscious. In the same conversation he speaks of a similar episode in his creative life when he was writing 'Hans und Grethe' in Leipzig. He wrote the music for the second verse. Later the same night, he had woken with a start with the first and the third complete in his head. Surprising as it may seem, he is very much mistaken here, for the song in question was written in Vienna in 1880, under the title 'Maitanz im Grünen' (see above, Vol. i, App. 1). Yet it seems that the Lied referred to by Natalie as 'Ringelreih'n' must be 'Hans und Grethe', for the words in question occur in the opening refrain, and nowhere else in Mahler's Lieder.

[119] NBL1. 138; NBL2. 159.   [120] NBL1. 146; NBL2. 164.

[121] Actually the Fourth Symphony lasts almost an hour, and the first movement of the Third rarely more than 35 minutes.

conceived it as "a Symphonic Humoresque" but it later developed into a symphony of normal length, while in former times, when I thought I was writing an ordinary symphony, it turned out to be three times as long, as in my Second and Third'. 'Das himmlische Leben', the Lied originally intended for his Third Symphony, was to form its Finale, and he already thought of it as the 'tapering spire of the edifice'.[122]

What I had in mind was extremely hard to achieve; imagine the uniform blue of the sky which is much more difficult to render than all its changing and contrasting hues. Well, that's the general atmosphere of the piece. Occasionally, however, it darkens and becomes phantasmagorical and terrifying: but it is not that it becomes overcast, for the sun continues to shine in its eternal blue, only to us it suddenly seems horrific, just as, on the most beautiful day in a sunlit forest, one can be seized with panic and terror. The Scherzo, mysterious, intricate and sinister, will make your hair stand on end, but it will be followed by the Adagio, which puts everything right again and shows that no harm was intended.

He added that not only had the Scherzo recalled something he had written earlier, the Scherzo of the Second Symphony, but that he had 'introduced new elements into the old framework.'[123] Only later did Mahler realize the wealth of substance in 'Das himmlische Leben', this Lied having engendered 'no fewer than five movements in the Third and the Fourth': 'One doesn't realize what can lie in an—at first sight—insignificant little thing. . . . Looking at the smallest inner circle doesn't tell you how far the concentric circles radiating out from such a circle will eventually spread, the formula πr^2 holding for the biggest as for the tiniest.'[124]

Despite its uniformity the work was tremendously lively from beginning to end. In fact, Mahler thought he had never before made quite as much use of polyphony. 'The thousand little pieces of mosaic that make up the picture are shaken up and it becomes unrecognizable, as in a kaleidoscope, as though a rainbow suddenly disintegrated into millions of dancing drops so that the whole edifice seems to rock and dissolve'. This was especially true of the Andante, which he regarded as the best movement and in which he had composed his 'first real and fully developed variations. . . . A divinely joyful and profoundly sad melody pervades it throughout, so that you'll at once laugh and cry'. Initially, Mahler called this Andante 'The smile of St Ursula' for it 'bore her features'.[125] But in composing it he also saw, as in his childhood, his mother's infinitely sad face, as though she were laughing through her tears, 'for she too, in spite of her immense sufferings, always lovingly resolved and pardoned all things'. Contrary to what he had done with his Third Symphony, Mahler would

---

[122] The Lied had of course been originally conceived and composed as a separate entity. *Verjüngende Spitze*—the image is that of a church spire that forms the light and airy summit of the edifice.

[123] NBL1. 143; NBL2. 163.   [124] NBL2. 172, Nov. 1900.

[125] NBL1. 144; NBL2. 163. St Ursula is one of the saints in the poem 'Das himmlische Leben'. Mahler was completely ignorant of her legend, 'otherwise he could not have depicted her with such beauty and precision'.

not hear of giving any titles to his new work, even though he had 'devised some marvellous ones', for he had no wish to 'divulge them to stupid critics and audiences who would again misunderstand and distort them in the worst possible way'.

In the slow movement, which he called alternately Andante and Adagio, he felt he had achieved 'the most complex mixtures of colours ever produced'. The decrescendo at the end, 'music of the spheres' (*sphärisch*), had an 'almost religious and Catholic atmosphere. . . . Neither in this movement nor anywhere else in the symphony, in keeping with its subject, will there be a single fortissimo, and those who accuse me of always having recourse to grandiose means will be astonished: in the entire Fourth, there are no trombones.' In fact, he would have liked to use them for a few bars at the end of the Adagio, but decided it was not worthwhile introducing them for such a short passage.[126]

Originality, either in style or in instrumentation, mattered less than ever to Mahler, and if he did sometimes achieve it, it was never deliberate. 'At one time I liked all that was striking in my works,' he had declared the previous summer to Natalie,

everything that broke away, even if only in appearance, from the usual. In the same way, a young man eagerly draws attention to himself by the way he dresses, while later on he is only too glad not to be different from others, since deep inside he is so utterly different, anyway. Today I am quite satisfied to pour the content (of my work) into traditional moulds, and I carefully avoid any unnecessary innovation. At one time I used to force myself to end in A flat minor a piece that began in D. Today, on the other hand, I go to a great deal of trouble to end in the original key.[127]

Going over his first movement again, Mahler noticed too late two reminiscences that he had inadvertently allowed to creep in, the first from one of Brahms's symphonies, and which Brahms himself had 'purloined from Weber', and the second from one of Beethoven's Piano Concertos.[128] Despite its apparent unconventionality this movement was constructed 'in strict accordance with the academic rules of form'. Moreover, the entire work was 'artistically the most polished' he had yet composed. Altogether he felt that he had at last reached the peak of his skill and would henceforth be able to compose from strength. During a bicycle ride with Natalie, he again talked about the first movement, which 'begins as if it didn't know how to count up to three, but then

[126] NBL1. 143; NBL2. 163.

[127] NBL1. 120; NBL2. 138. That same day Mahler also mentioned how difficult it had been to end his First Symphony in D, while his first theme had really been in A. 'It would have been quite different,' he added, 'if I had guided the conclusion toward this key.'

[128] This passage and another concerning Zemlinsky and *Es war einmal* (see above, Chap. 7) prove that Mahler sometimes borrowed deliberately, but at times had to be on his guard against doing so unconsciously. On this particular subject, see Henry-Louis de La Grange, 'Music on Music in Mahler: Reminiscences, Allusions and Quotations', unpubl. article. Also Miriam K. Whaples, 'Mahler and Schubert's A minor Sonata D.784', *Music and Letters*, 65: 3 (July 1984), 255 ff. and Rosamund McGuinness, 'Mahler und Brahms', *Neue Zeitschrift für Music*, 3 (1977), 215 ff.

suddenly starts to multiply on a grand scale and ends up by calculating in dizzying millions'. He called the short fanfare of the development a 'little summons' (*kleiner Appell*), in contrast to the 'great summons' in the Finale of the Second Symphony. 'Just when the confusion is at its height and the erstwhile disciplined troops are stampeding, a command from the general instantly causes them to rally round the standard.'[129]

Mahler realized that his Fourth Symphony was closely related to his first three, that it rounded them off, and that the four together formed a veritable tetralogy. The affinity between the Fourth and Third was particularly marked, since the two had themes in common, an occurrence so odd and unusual that he himself was disturbed by it. Marvelling at the world of sound in which he was now living more happily than ever, he told Natalie:

Music is vastly superior to poetry; it can express everything. Thanks to a modulation or an interrupted cadence, it can communicate directly and in universal terms what the other arts are forced to describe or circumscribe. Our modern Impressionist poets would love to do this; express moods and feelings, but, apart from the fact that they're bunglers, they cannot possibly do it with words.[130]

As July slipped by, Mahler derived increasing pleasure from the climate, atmosphere, and scenery of Maiernigg. The house was steadily taking shape down by the lake, and he had been making secret wagers as to which would be completed first, it or the Symphony. At the beginning of the summer, he had despairingly noted the rapidity with which the work on the house was progressing, but he had soon caught up with it, and the Symphony was now nearing completion, whereas the house would not be ready until the end of the summer.[131] For the first time, he had not worn himself out by 'ceaseless struggle agaist hostile forces which absorbed more nervous energy than he could put into his work', nor had he ever enjoyed composing as much as he did there.

His many walks through the 'mysterious labyrinths of the forest bordering the lake, which lure one into the unknown', were his only moments of rest and relaxation while composing that summer. He was delighted with the diversity of the scenery and of walks in the surroundings of Maiernigg, particularly since he had been afraid of being bored there. There were few good roads, but numerous footpaths, unknown to the Maiernigg 'Kuhgäste',[132] along which one could wander without meeting a soul. 'He walks for hours in these mountains

---

[129] NBL1. 145; NBL2. 164.   [130] NBL2. 161.

[131] Theodor Reik, the psychoanalyst, compares this 'obsession' with something Mahler had said the year before: 'The day my house is ready, inspiration will fail me and I won't be able to work any more'. According to Reik, such obsessions have hidden meaning: the building of the house and its completion represented a reward for the completion of the Symphony, and Mahler perhaps felt guilty for having ordered the house before he had finished his work. In other respects, the house symbolized woman, and the obsession about a completed house in which it would be impossible to work revealed, Reik says, an impotence complex that relates to Mahler's latent desire to marry. Mahler frequently identified creative fecundity with physical fecundity (RHM 320).

[132] The pun he had used the previous year at Alt-Aussee. *Kurgäste* means guests taking the cure; *Kuh* of course means cow.

and forests without meeting a living soul, as if this God-given world was part of Gustav's private property,' wrote Natalie to Lipiner on 26 July.[133] He often went down to the lake to inspect the work on his house and would stand watching the workmen or suggesting improvements. Nevertheless, he continued to be haunted by the fear that his holiday would come to an end before he had finished his work, and began to inveigh against the 'damned Opera' and the slavery that he loathed with every fibre of his being, especially when he thought of it at Maiernigg, in the 'pure kingdom of his own activity'. 'It's not just the pressure to finish the piece, whatever the cost,' wrote Natalie,

it's the thought of what is being lost—and cannot be recovered—as he goes along. For he says himself that, when he is working, ideas come pouring in, and he could spend the whole year capturing and collecting them all. As it is, he has to throw away everything that doesn't fit in with the piece he's working on. It's awful to think of it![134]

In between the various stages of composition, he undertook a few lengthier excursions. On 15 July he left for a tour on his own of the valley of Ampezzo, precisely in order to get away from his work and to be able 'to judge it from a distance'. On the way he was stopped by the police, who, seeing him with a two-day beard, an open shirt, no jacket, no braces, and no belt, mistook him for a vagrant. He returned, sunburnt, on 19 July and gleefully recounted the incident. He had walked and bicycled for four days without saying a word to a soul. Several Viennese had recognized him but had fortunately not dared to speak to him, for 'I looked so furious whenever someone came up to me that they went away immediately and left me in peace.'[135]

Speaking of nature Mahler said it astonished him that

people always regard it as something superficial. This is true of its external aspects, but those who have not trembled in the face of its eternal and divine mystery cannot begin to understand it. We can only guess but not grasp or penetrate it. In fact there's a story in the Edda which offers a good example of what I mean; the one in which the giants pour the sea into the drinking horn of the biggest drinker of them all, who has boasted that he can drain any amount. He drinks and drinks until he's exhausted, but it doesn't get any less. Then he realizes he's been tricked and throws his horn away. The sea is of course infinite and every work of art must contain a trace of this infinity if it's to be an image of nature.

'What moves us in a work of art', he had said a little earlier, 'is precisely its mysterious and unfathomable elements. Any work of art that can be taken in at a glance loses its magic and its power of attraction, just as the most beautiful of parks, once you know all its paths, must seem boring so that you no longer feel like walking in it.'[136]

A few days after his return from Ampezzo, Mahler told his family:

---

[133] A section of this letter is quoted in NBLS, 26 July 1900.
[134] Ibid., letter from Natalie to Siegfried and Clementine Lipiner.
[135] Ibid.   [136] NBL1. 140; NBL2. 160.

Today something strange happened to me. Under the compelling logic of a passage that I had to change, everything that followed it became so topsy-turvy that I suddenly realized to my astonishment that I was in a completely different world. It was as if you thought you were going for a walk in flowery Elysian fields, and found yourself surrounded by the nocturnal blood-curdling horrors of Tartarus. Faces and emanations of such secret worlds, which I myself find horrifying, often occur in my works. This time, it is the forest with its wonders and horrors that has inspired me and insinuated itself into my symphony. I'm coming increasingly to realize that you don't compose, you <u>are</u> composed (*man wird komponiert*).[137]

Towards the end of July, when his Symphony was almost finished, Mahler remembered how, only a month before, he had laboured anxiously, fearing all the while that his work would reflect his mental distress, yet in the end he had never, since Steinbach days, worked with so much joy and exhilaration. Perhaps after all, he reflected, it was not necessary that a work 'should gush forth spontaneously from one's mood like a stream of lava'. Perhaps a sure technique, 'that true art which is always at the disposal of him who possesses it and which overcomes all difficulties, including his own discomfort', was enough.[138] When, on 5 August, he announced the completion of his Symphony, he as usual did so sadly, for he suddenly felt 'empty and depressed because life has lost all its meaning'. Happy, none the less, at what he had achieved, he remained for some time absorbed in thoughts of his new work. 'This summer was so lovely,' he wrote to Nanna Spiegler on his return to Vienna,

that I feel really armed for the winter. If in future I can guarantee myself inner and outer peace for the summer, then some kind of human existence becomes possible for me here in Vienna as well. . . . This winter I shall produce a fair copy of my work, and that will give my life a point of rest among all the turmoil, just the thing I have lacked over the last few years. One feels so godforsaken when one has to live without a sanctuary. I in particular am joyless and have to wear a mask that must sometimes seem to you to be grinning strangely. Especially last winter, when I had to abandon my work, the one I have just finished, at its most delicate, even embryonic stage, and had given it up altogether, I couldn't believe that one could ever pick up such tenuous threads again. But it's peculiar, as soon as I am in the midst of nature and by myself, everything that is base and trivial vanishes without trace. On such days <u>nothing scares me</u>; and this helps me again and again.

[137] NBL1. 140; NBL2. 161. In his article, 'Der Wissenschaftliche Kontext der musikalischen Gedankenwelt Gustav Mahlers: Wien um 1900' (Bruckner Symposium, Linz, 1986), Moritz Csáky has pointed out an interesting similarity between this well-known phrase of Mahler's and some passages from the writings of Hofmannsthal. The most striking one is from the latter's *Gespräch über Geschichte* (1903): 'We do not possess our own selves; we are breathed upon from outside, long-drawn breaths out of us and then back in to us. . . . Where do they [the animals, i.e. the symbols] get their strength? How could he [the man] die in the animal [symbol]? Because we and the world are not different things. . . . in our body the whole universe is closely compressed.' (Hofmannsthal, *Gesammelte Werke*, i. 497 ff.). Csáky also compares Mahler's 1900 statement to a passage from a much quoted letter written by him to Bruno Walter in 1909: 'What <u>thinks</u> in us? and what <u>does</u> in us?' ('Was denket in uns? und was tut in uns?') (MBR, no. 381; MBR, no. 404).

[138] NBL1. 146; NBL2. 164.

'It is so profoundly different from my other symphonies,' he continued, speaking of the Fourth

but this <u>has</u> to be; it would be impossible for me to repeat a particular state—and just as life goes on, so I tread new paths in each new work. That is why in the beginning it's so difficult for me to get down to work. Any kind of routine that you have acquired is of no use. You have to learn everything afresh to suit the new work. So you remain for ever a <u>beginner</u>. It used to worry me and fill me with doubts about myself. But since I've come to understand it, it stands as a guarantee for the authenticity and lasting quality of my works. So for the first time I can look at the future without the worst kind of doubts, though I would not dare to be confident. It is and remains a gift from God, which, like any gift of love, cannot be deserved or asked for.[139]

At the end of the summer Hubert Wondra, one of the chief administrators at the Vienna Opera, arrived to discuss the repertoire of the coming season, and they took long walks together. One day, on the path leading to Klagenfurt, the sound of a barrel organ, which delighted Wondra, upset Mahler considerably. However, when a second barrel organ struck up and threatened to drown out the first, he began to enjoy himself, whereas Wondra became exasperated at this 'caterwauling'. A military band soon joined in the fun, whereat Wondra covered up his ears in despair and fury while Mahler stood listening in ecstasy, as though rooted to the spot. Recounting this incident to Arnold Rosé, Mahler added that his reaction should not surprise anyone who liked his symphonies. Thereafter, he often returned to the same spot to hear distant melodies, military bands, and male choruses mingle with the noise of merry-go-rounds, shooting booths, and puppet-shows, which came across the lake with prodigious clarity. 'Can you hear it? There's polyphony for you!' he exclaimed, as he evoked childhood memories of the forest of Iglau.[140] 'Just like this, the themes should come from different directions, and their rhythms and melodies should be just as dissimilar (the rest is merely writing in several parts and disguised homophony). But the artist adapts, orders, and unites them into a harmonious whole.'

Before returning to Vienna, Mahler freed himself from his companions and on 10 August set out, map in hand, to bicycle to Velden, which he reached after making a considerable detour as far as the Loiblpass in the Karawanken, which separates Carinthia from Slovenia.[141] Having started out on the wrong road, he realized, just as he thought he was about to reach his goal, that he still had almost a thousand metres to climb before reaching the road down to Velden on the other side of the pass. Worn out, he paid a young boy a florin to push his bicycle to the top of the pass while he took a short cut. Just before reaching the top, he took the wrong way again and, rather than retrace his steps, scrambled

---

[139] Letter to Nanna Spiegler, 18 Aug. 1900 (PML).   [140] NBL1. 147; NBL2. 165.

[141] On 2 Aug., Mahler wrote to Guido Adler telling him that he was intending to make this trip and would therefore probably not see him in Maiernigg. He gave as his address the Pension Saxonia, in Innichen, near Toblach, in Südtirol (Univ. of Georgia Library).

up a rocky slope on all fours and landed in a culvert, fortunately dry, whose smooth and almost vertical brick walls offered no hold. In the end, he discovered a section of the wall that had begun to crumble and, grabbing hold of some ferns which he feared might give way under his weight, he painfully hoisted himself up onto the road. When the boy, who had been waiting a long time for him, saw him appear from the wrong direction, soaked in sweat and with his hands and feet torn by the rocks and brambles, he stared in amazement as if he had seen a ghost. And in fact it took over a week for the cuts and scratches to heal.

Such excursions worried Justi, not only because of her brother's imprudence and absent-mindedness, but also because he always lost practically everything he took with him. On this occasion it was his bicycle bag containing his linen and all his belongings.[142] Yet these solitary expeditions were a source of infinite pleasure and relaxation to a composer trammelled with the obligations of an official position and soon to face another season as exhausting as the previous one. In Maiernigg Mahler had found his promised land, his retreat, a place of fulfilment for body and mind. The forests, the lake, and the mountains offered him not only his favourite scenery but also the opportunity to practise the sports he preferred: walking, cycling, swimming, rowing, and climbing. Brought up in the harsher climes of central Europe, he found the Mediterranean mildness of Carinthia a perpetual caress. In his solitary hiding-place in the heart of the forest he could at last be in contact with the vital forces he needed to nourish his work and which he claimed entirely dictated it. Within easy reach, the apocalyptic chaos of the Dolomites acted for him as a sort of mental space which stimulated his imagination and inspired him with a profound desire to emulate nature by the colossal scale of the works he composed. Several times he made a pilgrimage to the Misurina lake, to escape the torment of a creative block and consult the oracle of the earth goddess. The composer had found his roots. Here, he would find the inspiration to pour out most of his future works (Symphonies Nos. 5, 6, 7, and 8, and the *Rückert-Lieder*). Maiernigg was indeed the turning point in his creative life.

What was more, the house to which he had given so much care was nearly completed: a family house for a man without a wife. Was it a sign? It seemed that his amorous adventures were dwindling of their own accord. Here, too, everything seemed to point to a landfall: fourteen months later he finally met the love of his life, Alma—for whom, without knowing it, he had built the house at Maiernigg and who would spend six high summers of companionship and work with him there. Mahler was just 40, the age when people seek stability.

The man had changed, the musician too. A generation of works had come to an end with the 'Wunderhorn-Symphonien'. Now Mahler's symphonies turned away from popular sources, from the use of choirs and even from the solo voice.

---

[142] NBL2. 165.

His art was progressively breaking free from a figurative aesthetic in favour of abstract values: perfection of form, density of writing. His maturity was expressed in distance, in height, in liberation from contingencies. But this took him away from his public before he had really conquered it. He was to have his first real success in two years' time, with the first complete performance of the Third Symphony, the score of which he had completed as early as 1896. But in 1902 he was finishing the Fifth Symphony, which was much less successful. For the present Mahler was preparing for combat, cost what it might. He drew his strength from himself alone, in the certainty of his genius and the truth of his message.

At the Vienna Opera, we have seen that he had succeeded in eliminating the last traces of the old regime. His hands were now free and he could erect his own interpretative structure. Men and procedures had been bent to his reformist will. He was returning as absolute master to a theatre where all was open to him: the choice of programmes, the organization of work, the recruitment of artists, the risks of musical performance, and even those of stage production. Here, too, he now had at his disposal all the elements he needed to achieve consistently high standards and thus rediscover the meaning of opera by breathing new life into it. In a sense, the turn of the century was also the turning point in Mahler's life, work and career. Mahler belonged to a new world. In audacity and prophetic power he was akin to Kafka, Freud, Schoenberg, Klimt, and the Secession artists. But what really distinguished him was his acute awareness of renewal; the limpid and sharp quality of his thought; the solidity of his reasoning and his unshakeable confidence in the truth of the future. We shall soon see that he made the mistake of being right too soon. But today we know that he was right to hope.

9

Quarrel with the Bühnenverein—triumph of the Second Symphony in Munich—Failure of the First in Vienna—beginning of the third season of the Philharmonic

(August–December 1900)

> The underlying spirit . . . can only reveal
> itself through clearly heard forms.

THE manuscript of the Adagio in the Fourth Symphony ends with the words: 'The third movement, and with it the whole symphony, completed on Sunday 6 August, at Maiernigg.'[1] Since 6 August 1900 was a Monday, it is most likely that Mahler really completed his *Partiturentwurf* (first full orchestra score) on Sunday 5 August. He put some finishing touches to the orchestration and copied the score, as he usually did, during the winter. It would have been natural for him to have experienced a sense of emptiness now that the burst of creative activity was over, but he was happy and relieved at having found his bearings as a symphonist after four years of silence. His painter friend, Henriette Mankiewicz, was among the first to hear the news:

I'm sure you'll forgive my silence—I've been up to my neck in finishing my new work, and couldn't allow myself to look to right or left. Now it is finished and I'm quite alone and having a most enjoyable rest; and am thinking of your friendship. I think some of your beautiful pictures have worked themselves into my music, and you have given me enormous pleasure.[2]

---

[1] BGM.

[2] This letter to Henriette Mankiewicz (LCW), is dated '12 August': the year is almost certainly 1900. In it Mahler alludes to his friend's paintings, as he does in another letter of 3 Sept. of that year. If the letter of '12 Aug.' had been written in 1902, when his next symphony, the Fifth, was completed, Mahler would certainly have mentioned Alma, whom he had married some months earlier.

Be happy for me—everything half-done is <u>behind me</u> [*alles Halbe ist <u>hinter mir</u>*]. If only
I could learn from my mistakes! Unfortunately I don't have this capacity but must
console myself with another gift of the gods: the urge and the ability to grow healthy,
and to open the windows wide and let out the stale air. . . . All your flowers are in my
new symphony! When I received them it was as if they had grown out of my work.[3]

Thanks to the extra two weeks' holiday he had obtained for the whole staff of the
Opera, he only returned to Vienna on 15 August, leaving Natalie and Justi to
supervise the work on the house for another six weeks. 'I am still drawing
strength from the magnificent summer, and can't tell you how happy I feel in my
new role as villa-proprietor, nor with what joyful hopes, even confidence, I face
the future.'[4]

   During the first weeks of the season, he devoted all his energies to a new
production of Mozart's *Così fan tutte*, which he had been contemplating for
three years.[5] Mozart's last Da Ponte opera was still not fully accepted. It had
practically disappeared from the repertoire during the nineteenth century,
because Lorenzo da Ponte's cynical and frivolous humour had shocked the
moralistic bourgeois sentiments of the romantic era. It was nine years since
the Vienna Opera had performed it. Before that, there had been a series
of 'versions', revised and edited to eliminate the obvious 'faults' of the original text: 'improbability', 'frivolity', and 'vapidity'.[6] Even in Paris, in 1863,
Barbier and Carré, librettists for Gounod's *Faust*, had adapted *Così* to
a libretto of their own, taken from Shakespeare's *Love's Labour's Lost*. In
Ludwig Schneider's version, performed in Vienna in 1872 under the title
Weibertreue ('Female Constancy')—of all things!—the heroines, warned by
Despina of the deception as soon as the fiancés had departed, play-acted
throughout all subsequent events, only pretending to let themselves be seduced
by the young 'Turks'. In a production in Stuttgart in 1858, the laws of morality
were met in a slightly different way, by having the girls courted by their own
fiancés.

   A revival in Vienna in 1880, directed by Franz Jauner, with spoken dialogue
replacing the recitatives, found more success with the public than with the
critics. At that time Hanslick pontificated that no performance, no matter how
perfect, could save the work from the 'foolishness' and improbability of its
libretto: 'It cannot be denied that this mindless text, whose characters are
incapable of inspiring sympathy, paralysed Mozart's creative imagination
and forced him into an insipid formalism.' Despite such reservations, *Così*

---

   [3] Letter of 3 Sept. 1900 (LCW).

   [4] Letter to Alfred Theuer. Catalogue of Nebehay, the Vienna autograph dealer, 1974.

   [5] In 1897 Mahler had corresponded with Hermann Levi, who had conducted the première of *Parsifal* and
was then conductor at the Munich Opera, about Levi's new version of *Così fan tutte*.

   [6] Robert Werba has listed the 19 different titles under which the work was given between 1791 and 1863
(*Zeitschrift der Mozart-Gemeinde Wien* (May 1978), 11: 'Mahlers Mozart-Bild: Così fan Tutte'). The *coup de
grâce* was administered in Dresden, in 1909, when the tenor Karl Scheidemantel completely suppressed Da
Ponte's libretto, replacing it with another taken from a Calderón play, *Dame Kobold*.

continued to be performed at the Hofoper with sets by Johann Kautsky and costumes by Franz Gaul, but rarely more than once a year, and only until 1891.

Mahler himself certainly discussed the problem of the libretto of *Così*, but what he said has not been recorded. That he remained attached to Mozart's original version is shown by his desire, many times expressed, to respect its every detail. In 1900 his original intention was to mount a 'Mozart cycle' with a revival of *Così* as its first event. In the end he gave up this idea, probably for financial reasons, but not before preparing a real 'Mozart stage' of restricted dimensions, permitting rapid scene changes.[7] Having opted for Levi's new version, Mahler corresponded with him on the subject of scene changes. Levi advised him to revive a baroque procedure and have the sets brought in from the wings, but Mahler finally decided on a revolving stage. One had been constructed by Karl Lautenschläger at the Munich Theatre for plays by Goethe and Shakespeare, and then transferred to the Munich Opera specifically for *Così*. Mahler went there in September, and must have been satisfied with this solution, for he immediately adopted it for Vienna.[8] Levi's German version had the great advantages of using his own translation,[9] which was of a high literary standard, and of restoring the *recitativo secco*, which Mahler was to accompany himself at the keyboard.[10] In order to speed up the action somewhat, most of Levi's cuts were retained.[11] At the beginning of the second act, which in the original starts with a recitative, Mahler added, by way of overture, the Finale of the *Divertimento*, K.287 and, for the scene changes, he composed some instrumental interludes on themes taken from the work itself.[12]

Anton Brioschi, official designer of the Vienna Opera since 1886, was commissioned to paint new sets, but the costumes were entrusted to Heinrich Lefler, the new *Leiter des Ausstattungswesens* (head of design) recently ap-

[7] *Neue Musik-Zeitung* (Oct.) announced that the rest of the cycle would be given from May 1901, but Mahler must have lacked the necessary funds or decided that his Viennese singers did not yet constitute the 'ensemble' necessary for Mozart. The cycle was finally performed in 1906, with new stage sets by Roller, in celebration of the 150th anniversary of Mozart's birth.

[8] It was a big circular platform, 15 m. in diameter, made up of 30 wooden sections. It could be installed on a stage without any previous modifications in little more than an hour.

[9] The score publ. by Breitkopf (no. 1666) ascribes to Levi the revision of an old trans. by Eduard Devrient and C. Niese, as well as the authorship of a partly new trans.

[10] Hermann Levi had advised Mahler to do this in 1897, not knowing that his younger colleague had already done so in Prague, Budapest, and Hamburg.

[11] These included numerous passages of recitative: two alternative cuts (one long, one short) in Ferrando's aria 'Ah! lo veggio' (no. 24 in the score) of which Levi preferred the longer because 'the aria is fairly insignificant musically, but very difficult to sing': a cut in Guglielmo's aria (no. 26: 'Donne mie, la fate a tanti'), which Levi considered 'very entertaining and musically successful with its bassoon accompaniment' but which 'greatly slowed down the action'; and Dorabella's entire aria (no. 28: 'E amor un ladroncello') 'for the same reason'. Levi added that he had the duo with chorus 'Secondate, aurette amiche' (no. 21) performed behind the scenes, while the two heroines emerged from the house and moved upstage, with the two fiancés disembarking during the choral refrain. The first three bars of the following recitative were cut, so that it now started with the two girls' reply, 'Cos'è tal mascherata?' Finally, Levi could not bring himself to cut Ferrando's aria (no. 17: 'Un aura amorosa'), despite the fact that Mozart had added it as an afterthought, to please a singer. Here he had made only one change: Guglielmo and Alfonso exited before the aria so as not to be left standing throughout (letter from Hermann Levi to Mahler, 1 Nov. 1897, HOA, Z.351/1897).

[12] Wagner did the same thing in his version of Gluck's *Iphigénie en Aulide*.

pointed by Mahler. As usual, rehearsals were lively, and the papers eagerly reported Mahler's verbal sallies and his confrontations with certain singers. Frances Saville, the American soprano, who had quarrelled fiercely with Mahler the year before, was singing Fiordiligi while Dorabella was sung by Laura Hilgermann, whose supple, warm voice with its big range was ideally suited to the role. The Despina was one of the most humorous and subtle creations of Marie Gutheil-Schoder, who enjoyed a veritable triumph, despite the number of critics who continued to object to her 'dry' voice. The male singers included Franz Naval, a tenor with perfect voice control;[13] the sumptuous baritone Leopold Demuth whom Mahler had brought from Hamburg; and the Czech bass Wilhelm Hesch, also an experienced Mozart singer with, according to Hanslick, 'a discreet sense of comedy' despite the dramatic size of his voice. This casting was retained virtually intact throughout the season. Max Kalbeck acknowledged that he had never heard a 'Mozart ensemble' of such quality in his life. As for Hanslick, he thought the singers seemed 'made for each other'. But he nevertheless condemned the work once again, considering that Mozart had failed in his attempt to superimpose 'a musical garden on Da Ponte's poetic desert'[14] and describing the text as 'superficial, without heart or mind' and 'self-consciously vulgar'. He considered that the revolving stage had enabled the action to move smoothly forward and had given it 'a unity impossible to achieve by any other means'.[15] Further, Mahler had at last brought to the recitatives, translated into German, the lightness and speed they required. Marie Gutheil-Schoder[16] in particular had surpassed herself in this respect.

Max Kalbeck expressed further reservations about the libretto of *Così*, but his conclusion was more positive than that of his distinguished colleagues:

This idealized opera silences all the criticisms one might make of it on a moral or aesthetic level, if you envisage the whole as a play of sound, a play of imagination, delighting in the most exquisite combinations and, with enchanting grace and spontaneity, determining the artistic forms and creating a stage event so apparently simple and natural that it could have been invented by a child. The new production, rehearsed

[13] Hans Puchstein in the *Deutsche Zeitung* claimed, however, that his voice had recently lost 'a great deal of its volume and velvet'. The same critic found Gutheil-Schoder's portrayal 'anti-natural', 'affected', and 'intolerable', and alleged that the 'Jewish gesticulations' of her hands were sufficient in themselves to prove that those who claimed she was of 'Aryan' origin were wrong.

[14] Hanslick still found the score of *Così* inferior to those of *Figaro* and *Don Giovanni*, for despite its 'unsurpassable' ensembles it 'lacked contrast'. Furthermore, Act II did not maintain the same high standard of the first. In Kalbeck's opinion, too, *Così* continued to be performed solely out of respect for the composer of *The Magic Flute*, *Figaro*, and *Don Giovanni*, and despite the 'lack of dramatic invention' in this 'brutal farce'. Its music remained 'impersonal and abstract' and did not characterize the protagonists, who for this reason seemed to 'move in a vacuum'.

[15] According to Karl Maria Klob, the revolving stage nevertheless had a major disadvantage: the singers could no longer be seen from the fourth gallery when they moved upstage. The same author claims that the curtains, coming down lower than usual, harmed the acoustics (KMO 81).

[16] Hanslick, who was hearing Gutheil-Schoder for the first time that night, wrote that her Despina had 'exquisite grace and extreme skill', despite a certain overactivity. Helm, on the other hand, found her inferior to Marie Renard in the same role.

and conducted by Gustav Mahler, obliges us to look at the work from this angle, whereas before we had never been particularly impressed by it. This performance never referred to tradition, neither superficially nor in depth. The unexpected result was that it showed that tradition has been falsified, mistaken . . .

In the *Arbeiter-Zeitung*, the Socialist Party newspaper, Josef Scheu congratulated Mahler above all on having conducted piano and pianissimo, but found the perpetual *mezza* voce of the singers slightly wearisome. Theodor Helm described the work as 'stillborn', inferior to Mozart's other operas, but he praised Mahler for having re-established the tone of *comédie rococo*[17] and *opera buffa*, and for showing a desire for 'fidelity to the text' which was infinitely preferable to the 'liberties' he took with Beethoven.

Wallaschek also belittled the work, quoting Wagner's words that it was 'fortunate that Mozart did not write his best music for this text, otherwise we would have to put up with the idiotic, even baneful story more often'. Only Mahler's hard work and intelligence had mitigated the glaring faults of the libretto. Hirschfeld, finally, rejoiced at having seen all the energies and capabilities at the Hofoper focused on 'a single result, with a seriousness very rare in the world of theatre, usually given over to tinsel and sham':

In Mahler's interpretation, the strictest artistic conscience fashioned the airiest orchestral figurations, the subtlest nuances, the exquisite grace of the gestures in sound. The *recitativo secco* could not have been performed in a suppler, finer, wittier manner by German singers. Mahler succeeded in imparting to his faithful ensemble not only the style of former days, but also a feeling for the very typically Italian *recitativo secco* to the point where they appeared to be drawing on many years of experience. Thus Gustav Mahler has not only revealed a work, but allowed us with deep emotion to gain insight into the soul of Mozart, a soul that suffered greatly but brought gaiety and joy to the world.

It is strange to note that on this occasion it was the most persistently hostile of Mahler's critics who best understood and appreciated his work. Unfortunately, despite the interest and curiosity aroused by the revolving stage, the Viennese public was still not ready to adopt *Così*, and it was dropped after seven performances, not to be seen again until 1905. In those four years when *Così* was absent from the repertoire, the three operas of Mozart's maturity, *Don Giovanni*, *The Magic Flute*, and *Figaro*, were regularly performed, but in productions which Mahler had so far been unable to revise thoroughly. The *Flute* in particular became one of his specialities. The cast of the new 1897 production gradually changed. On 27 August 1899, for instance, Mahler conducted it (after Beethoven's *Egmont* Overture) to celebrate the 150th anniversary of Goethe's birth. According to Liebstöckl, Ellen Forster was, as before, an uninspired Pamina, 'inevitably wearisome'. Franz Naval, on the other hand

---

[17] However, he disapproved of the reinstatement of the *recitativo secco*, which he found monotonous because of its keyboard accompaniment.

showed himself as Tamino to be 'a thoroughbred Mozartian', while Hesch remained a 'captivating' Sarastro and Frauscher a perfect Speaker. Liebstöckl wrote that Demuth had performed Papageno with 'a most effective dry humour' and that Arthur Preuss, as Monostatos, had given his role exceptional profile. Only Elise Elizza, the Queen of the Night, failed to please the critic of *Die Reichswehr*. He claimed that Mahler had given her the role in compensation for the many occasions when she had sung tiny parts like the First Genie in the same work, the leader of the chorus in *Figaro*, or the Shepherd in *Tannhäuser*. He considered that her 'ample soubrette voice' and 'pleasant timbre' were far too 'distinguished' to be given over to acrobatics: 'She bravely warbles and coos as required, but the effort is always visible'.[18]

Fifteen months later, Mahler again conducted *The Magic Flute*. This time Lefler had designed some costumes which Hirschfeld liked: 'Herr Lefler deserves thanks for the queen's hairstyle, which blends in a symbolic and fantastic way into the shadows of night, and for the artistically inspired costumes of the Three Ladies. Shall we soon see similar changes to the Three Genii and to the dance in the temple, which calls for a stylized conception?'[19] Gustav Schönaich found the casting perfect, particularly Gutheil-Schoder, who was making her début as Pamina:

Her appearance recalls an antique figure painted by Raphael. Her singing and acting go together, intermingled in chaste sweetness. All was artistically felt and interpreted, yet without a shadow of exaggeration in the subtleties of the dynamics. To give just one example: when Sarastro, appearing unexpectedly, terrorizes Papageno and Pamina who are attempting to escape, Papageno asks, 'But what shall we tell him?' and Pamina replies, 'The truth, even if a crime!' The established custom has been that Pamina declaimed these words in accents of heroic determination. With Frau Schoder, on the contrary, there is an inimitable mixture of embarrassment and slight, affectionate reproach aimed at Papageno, as if the very idea of telling anything other than the truth were being suggested to her for the first time in her life. A stroke of genius, not isolated either, and for me, at least, a handsome recompense for the lack of softness in the middle register of her voice.[20]

So it seems that the Viennese press was far from unanimously hostile to the new soprano. We shall soon see, however, what torrents of fury were unleashed when Mahler tried to cast her in other roles which perhaps suited her less well. For Gutheil-Schoder's début in the *Flute*, Hesch and Naval successfully repeated the roles they had sung before, while the baritone Hans Geissler, a 'guest' in the role of Papageno, was only moderately acclaimed. Hans Breuer, the new Monostatos, 'lacked temperament', but the casting of the secondary roles tells us again how exacting Mahler was: the Three Ladies were Mildenburg, Hilgermann, and Walker, while Elizza, Von Thann, and Kusmitsch sang the Three Genies. At that time the Opera did not seem to possess the fireproof

---

[18] *Reichswehr* (28 Aug. 1899).   [19] *Abendpost* (26 Nov. 1900).
[20] *Wiener Allgemeine Zeitung* (27 Nov. 1900).

virtuoso needed for the role of Queen of the Night and Frances Saville had great difficulty in reaching Mozart's dizzy heights. What was more, her staccato lacked precision.[21]

A year later, the ensemble for *The Magic Flute* was at last enriched by an ideal Queen of the Night, Selma Kurz,[22] who by now bore comparison with 'the most famous virtuoso singers'. Tamino, the brilliant and generous tenor Leo Slezak, just engaged by Mahler,[23] produced 'uninterrupted floods of youthful, sumptuous sound'. Unfortunately the audience was, according to Liebstöckl, 'unfair to the great art of Gutheil-Schoder'. 'Sympathy and antipathy are bad counsellors', he wrote. 'They always end by putting mediocrity on the throne.' Mahler himself was opposed by a section of the audience that day: 'It is quite out of place to hiss him on the rostrum', wrote Liebstöckl, 'while his friends applaud him. How long will these childish vendettas last? In these lean musical times, an artist like him has the right to be treated with more consideration!'[24]

The only 'novelty' presented at the end of the year 1900 was the Austrian composer Joseph Reiter's[25] one-act opera *Der Bundschuh* (The Sandal), which had its Hofoper première on 14 November. Composer of numerous choral works, Reiter had made his theatre début with this 'national' opera, which was first performed at Troppau in 1894. It was presumably out of diplomatic necessity and as a concession to the German Nationalist Party that Mahler put it on in Vienna.[26] Max Morold's libretto dealt with a particularly 'German' episode of the sixteenth-century Peasants' War, the love affair of a young Lutheran peasant, Hans Fuchs, and a young chatelaine, Ehrengard, and their deaths as a result of the struggle between their respective classes. Although Reiter's music could not overcome the flimsiness of the libretto,[27] Mahler, as always, threw himself heart and soul into the undertaking. He even wrote a letter to Morold during the final rehearsals,[28] drawing his attention to the musical and stage directions that were incompatible with dramatic verisimilitude. He also suggested making a few slight changes in the text: for instance, 'Wehrlos Weib' (defenceless woman) instead of 'Zartes Weib' (tender woman), since it would be more in keeping with Mildenburg's 'powerful physique' and with the fact that, at this juncture in the action, the heroine, Ehrengard, was enthroned in a judge's chair under a lime-tree. He ended with the words:

[21] Ibid.   [22] Kurz made her début in this role on 3 Nov. 1901.

[23] See below, Chap. 10.   [24] *Reichswehr* (4 Nov. 1901).

[25] Joseph Reiter (1862–1939), born in Braunau am Inn, the son of an organist, studied at Linz. He taught at the Volkschule in Hietzing, was a choirmaster in Vienna, 1886–1907, later director of the Mozarteum in Salzburg, and still later conductor at the Hofburgtheater. As well as chamber music and numerous choral works, Reiter composed four operas, of which *Der Bundschuh* was the first. A 'Reiterbund' had been founded to promote his works.

[26] According to Karl Maurice Klob, Reiter was much influenced by Wilhelm Kienzl. Apart from a few Lieder, the entire opera was written in Wagnerian *Sprechgesang* (KMO 89).

[27] Mahler wrote to Mildenburg in 1900: 'I hope you're relieved to see what a bootee this "sandal" is!'

[28] MS letter from Mahler, Stadtbibliothek, Vienna, no. 74932.

'I trust that I have convinced you as to these points; however, out of respect for the author's wishes, I am prepared to bow to your will if you insist.' *Der Bundschuh* was not a great success and ran to only five performances. However, there is no doubt that the production was first-rate, as both the composer and the librettist wrote to Mahler the day after the première to express their delight and their gratitude for 'the perfection of every touch and every dramatic and musical detail, as well as the excellence of the casting down to the smallest roles'.

The critics showed no mercy. Kalbeck called the opera 'a belated offshoot of the sanguinary tradition of Italian drama'. Despite the 'intensely patriotic spirit' manifest in the subject and its treatment, he found its dramatic qualities meagre, its orchestration heavy, and the composer's predilection for 'folklorism' excessive. Helm, perhaps because of the political tendencies of his paper, was somewhat less harsh. He thought the new opera 'interesting' despite the lack of originality of the score, which was heavily influenced both by Wagner and Italian verismo. A few weeks later, in the *Wochenblatt*, he acknowledged that Reiter was only an 'embryonic talent', and that the success of *Der Bundschuh* had been 'due, above all, to the magnificent performance'.[29] This was the general verdict of the press, and that notably of the most eminent of the 'infernal judges', Eduard Hanslick, in whose eyes Reiter was simply an 'explosive dilettante' devoid of melodic imagination, and far too subject to the influence of Wagner.[30]

Throughout Mahler's tenure at the Vienna Opera, the choice of new works, and in particular the decisions he often had to make to turn down composers of talent, remained one of the least pleasant sides of his duties as director. In 1899, straight after the warmly received première of *Donna Diana*, he had asked Nikolaus von Reznicek to send him his next work. In September 1900 he received the first two acts of a 'Volksoper' (popular opera), *Till Eulenspiegel*, which Reznicek very much wanted premièred at the Vienna Opera, having even worked out the 'ideal' casting: Gutheil-Schoder, Schrödter, Hesch, and Grengg. Mahler replied to him in unvarnished terms, explaining that he found the libretto 'much too insipid' and the humour 'forced' and that he did not think that even 'fresh and lively' music could possibly save it. He could not under any circumstances give the work its première in Vienna, but would as usual be prepared to revise his judgement after a performance elsewhere. 'I am terribly sorry,' he concluded, 'but I have to be honest.'[31]

[29] Helm detected and censored 'wrong notes' and 'grotesque and bizarre' patches in Reiter's score.

[30] Hanslick makes ironic mention of Reiter's popularity with choral societies and a small group of admirers. Cast for the première of 13 Nov.: Mildenburg (Ehrengard), Sedlmair (Ulrike), Walker, Schmedes (Hans), Breuer (Schneider), Grengg (Weber), Stehmann (Hartmann). The first performance was followed by a ballet, *Coppélia* by Léo Delibes; the second, on 16 Nov., by *Sylvia*, the third (19 Nov.) by *Die Roten Schuhe*, and that of the 22nd by *Pagliacci* and another ballet, *Harlekin als Elektriker*. On 6 Dec. the programme was completed by *Cavalleria rusticana* and *Harlekin* and conducted in its entirety by Franz Schalk.

[31] Letter from Reznicek to Mahler of 12 Sept., and reply of the 24th (HOA, Z.VI.1901). *Till Eulenspiegel* was first performed in Breslau in 1902.

In the autumn of 1900 Mahler had urgently to solve a major problem that had been hanging over him for several years, that of finding an assistant conductor who could take over some of his responsibilities. True, Franz Schalk had replaced Richter[32] in May and, even though Mahler did not consider him to be a musician of great depth, he could confidently let him look after part of the repertory. But Fuchs had still not been replaced. Thus Mahler's burden of work was still far too heavy. In September, Leo Blech, with whom he had been negotiating for a year, wrote to him that, as far as he was concerned, nothing in the world would prevent him from responding to his appeal. Thus he would do his best to free himself from his five-year contract with Neumann at the Prague Opera. Considering the latter's high regard for Mahler, he felt sure he would succeed. Blech went on to complain of the all too numerous 'deficiencies' he saw around him[33] and which 'drain the energies that I would prefer to devote to more noble ends. . . . Every artistic success is a bitter struggle from which I almost always emerge victorious, but it's a Pyrrhic victory,' he added. It was a letter that so closely resembled those Mahler himself had written when he was young that it could not fail to move him.

Blech had been warmly recommended to Mahler by Humperdinck, but Neumann proved intractable. So Mahler again offered the post to Bruno Walter:

Will you now come sans façon? Will you and can you become and be to me what I need? Without standing on ceremony—all from the point of view of the brilliant future that opens up before you here—if so, accept, and the thing is settled. As a starting salary you would have 5000 florins, which would in time increase considerably. Please reply at once![34]

In fact, negotiations between Mahler and his former assistant from Hamburg had never been broken off, as is proved by the young conductor's letters to his family, as well as by the various letters Mahler wrote him, of which some remain unpublished. In November 1899, Mahler had tried to recruit him for the Hofoper, but now discussions between Walter and the Berlin Opera were already too advanced and he could not free himself.[35] A last-minute hitch in Berlin raised Mahler's hopes for a few days. 'It distresses me', wrote Walter to his mother,

to disappoint him a second time with a refusal. . . . Don't you think the warmth of his note is touching? Since the issue is negative, I've promised him I'll do every-thing possible to extricate myself from Berlin. . . . It deeply upset me to have to deprive him of the great joy that the prospect of my arrival in Vienna would have caused him . . .[36]

---

[32] In a letter written to Schalk at the beginning of Aug. 1900, Mahler informs him that the first performance he is to conduct after the holidays will be *Aida* on 11 Aug. (cf. MBRS 165).

[33] 'Das Unzulängliche, das in vielen Dingen hier Ereignis ist.' A paraphrase of the last lines of Goethe's *Faust*: 'Das Unzulängliche, hier wird's Ereignis'.

[34] MBR1, no. 248; MBR2, no. 273.   [35] BWB 37.

[36] Letter of 23 Nov. 1899 to Johanna Schlesinger.

In June 1900 Walter came to Vienna for a few days to talk with Mahler, who offered him Richter's post with a starting salary of 6,000 gulden.[37] At this time he was still uncertain of being able to terminate his Berlin contract. Despite this, Mahler was sufficiently committed to this plan to write him the following letter in the spring of 1901:

You can put your mind completely at rest and wait as long as the gentlemen choose to make you. I have already broken off all negotiations in respect of the Kapellmeister and am in absolutely no hurry, even if it takes months! So once more, don't worry. I regard our plan as definitive. You should begin your activity only when the Emperor's permission is given.—Have a good rest—take a cold water cure if possible. Everything in Vienna will stay as it is until you arrive; which means I shall manage as before with Schalk and Hellmesberger. One thing I must ask you, though it may seem funny. Shave off your beard before you come to Vienna. I have important reasons for this that I shall explain in person when I have a chance.[38]

Did Mahler still consider, as before, that a conductor needed his eyes, his mouth, and his whole face to exercise the necessary authority over the players, and that he should therefore not have a beard? In any case he seems to have been more than ever determined to engage his former Hamburg assistant. He had already sent him a contract form stipulating that his engagement, and his salary, would take effect from 1 July, even if he was not yet free by that date. 'Mahler has behaved in an admirable, moving manner, like the truest and finest friend,' Walter wrote to his parents. 'Without the assurance he has given me, my situation would have been unbearable and the cure I am taking would have been impossible. . . . Mahler's assurance that he will have me and no one else, and will wait as long as it takes, allows me to take the strongest possible line (with regard to the Berlin Opera).'[39] If Mahler was so eager to see Bruno Walter arrive, it was probably because all his other efforts, except for the engagement of Franz Schalk, had ended in defeat. At the beginning of 1901 he had considered another candidate, Franz Mikorey,[40] who held a post at the Elberfeld Theatre. Mahler offered him a trial contract to be confirmed if he were sufficiently successful as a 'guest'. Mikorey made his début at the Hofoper on 7 May in *Le Prophète*, but made no great impression on the public or the press. This fresh set-back finally convinced Mahler that he must wait for Bruno Walter. Free at last, Walter made his début at the Hofoper in September 1901.

For some time there had been rumours in Vienna about the probable resignation of Intendant Plappart, whose position at the Opera had been consider-

---

[37] Mahler had promised to augment the 5,000 gulden mentioned in the letter quoted above after a few weeks.

[38] Unpubl. letter, undated, LPA.   [39] BWB 43. Letter of 15 Aug. 1901.

[40] Born in Munich, Franz Mikorey (1873–1947), was the son of a famous tenor at the Bavarian Opera. He studied conducting with Hermann Levi and composition with Ludwig Thuille and Heinrich von Herzogenberg. After a succession of appointments in Prague, Regensburg, and Elberfeld, he became conductor at the Dessau Theatre, then director of the Helsinki Opera (1919) and, in 1924, of the Braunschweig Opera. He wrote three operas and several symphonic works.

ably weakened by his confrontation with Mahler in 1899. The *Neues Wiener Tagblatt* of 9 November 1900 stated that the matter had been raised twice before. However, it was a fact that the real power now lay with Prince Montenuovo who was virtually running the Opera, the role of the Intendant thus being reduced to a minimum. Mahler was of course very glad to have won his case, all the more so since, in the autumn of 1900, he once again became involved in a quarrel. This arose in fact out of a much bigger conflict between the directors of the Vienna and Munich Operas and the Deutscher Bühnenverein (Association of German Theatres), whose president was none other than Count Hochberg, composer of the memorable *Wärwolf*.[41]

Shortly before, the Intendant of the Munich theatres had complained to the Bühnenverein about offers made to Munich actors by Paul Schlenther, the director of the Burgtheater in Vienna. A few months later, Mahler had made an offer to a singer at the Munich Opera, Josef Geis, and had even sent him a contract, which was 'to become effective upon the arrival of the singer at the Vienna Opera, in the event that he has legally succeeded in freeing himself from his present obligations'. However, one of the fundamental rules of the Deutscher Bühnenverein stipulated that its agents and impresarios would automatically be excluded from the Verein if they endeavoured, with tempting offers, to entice singers from another member theatre. As a result of Mahler's offer the Munich Intendant, Ernst von Possart, had to raise Geis's salary in order to keep him, and had complained about it to Hochberg. The latter had in turn written to Prince Montenuovo to denounce this procedure and demand that the Vienna Opera apologize to the Munich Opera. Hochberg's letter had hardly reached Vienna before a Munich paper reported that, while in Munich to conduct his Second Symphony, Mahler had made similar offers to several other singers at the Opera.[42] Possart had run into him in the foyer of the Munich Opera and had informed him of his intention to submit the case to the Bühnenverein.[43] Mahler had retorted that if the Bühnenverein censured him, he and Schlenther, his colleague at the Burgtheater, would quit the association and thus be free to engage whomsoever they pleased.

Obviously, such a decision was quite outside Mahler's competence, and Plappart consequently demanded an explanation. Mahler replied with a long letter stating that he had sent Geis the draft contract because the latter had not only expressed his desire to be engaged in Vienna, but had also felt certain he would obtain a formal release from his Munich contract. However, Geis was so dishonest as to use the offer as a means of putting pressure on Possart, who had promptly confiscated the contract offer and sent it to Count Hochberg, a

---

[41] See Vol. i, Chap. 20.

[42] This article was repr. in *Neue Freie Presse* (7 Nov. 1900). Among the singers Mahler had thus 'enticed', the paper named two who were relatively unknown, Elise Feinhals and a Frl. Klopfer, and the celebrated Olive Fremstad, who was to be Mahler's Isolde at the Metropolitan Opera in New York in 1908. Mahler conducted his Second Symphony in Munich on 20 Oct.

[43] This time, in early Sept. 1900, Mahler was in Munich to see *Così fan tutte*.

proceeding which had 'dumbfounded' Mahler. As to his encounter with Possart, he added, it had indeed taken place at the end of October. Knowing nothing of the Bühnenverein's regulations he was unaware of having committed the slightest infraction, especially as the draft stipulated as a preliminary condition the 'legal' annulment of the singer's Munich contract. Besides, rival theatres constantly tried to lure members of the Vienna Opera by far less fair means. When he had said that it might eventually be a good thing if the Vienna Opera left the Bühnenverein, Possart had replied that he had on occasion thought of doing so himself. Both had been expressing purely personal opinions, and he failed to understand why this private conversation had been reported in a newspaper.[44] Obliged to support his director, Plappart put it to Hochberg that the rule in question was designed to protect the little theatres rather than the royal theatres, but that he would nevertheless instruct his two directors to see to it that such an incident did not recur.[45] He subsequently sent both Mahler and Schlenther a stiff note reminding them of the numerous complaints recently lodged by the Bühnenverein and demanding that they henceforth refrain from offering contracts without his agreement.[46] Once more, the censure was clear, even though the infraction had been purely formal.[47] Hochberg continued to press for compensation from the Hofoper, but this was refused.

Now that he was free in Vienna to control every theatrical and musical detail of the performances, and was no longer opposed by stars who considered they had the right to resist him, Mahler could pursue and even extend his reforms. He coached the new singers in order to break them of the habit of overgesticulating and thus reducing the significance and expressiveness of their acting.

When a character says 'you', he uses his arm and finger to point dramatically to the character he's addressing, and when he speaks of his 'heart', he places his hand over it. The women constantly raise their hand to their faces, it makes you feel sick! To put a stop to this, I forbid them to use their arms during rehearsals; only when they have learned to give full expression to the dramatic and musical content of their parts without gesticulating do I allow them to use their arms and hands. At the same time, I make them study the musical substance of their parts meticulously and to the last detail; once they are utterly conversant with them and begin, as it were, to live them, I ask them to re-create the role themselves with the maximum artistic freedom. The

[44] In fact, Mahler undoubtedly realized that, furious at having had to increase Geis's salary, Possart had deliberately done him an ill turn.

[45] Implicitly blaming Possart, Plappart in his second letter used Mahler's argument about the private nature of the discussion between the director of the Vienna Opera and the Munich Intendant. Hochberg's reply indicated that he had only reacted so strongly because he believed the Hofoper was genuinely quitting the Bühnenverein, to found an Austrian association which might or might not be affiliated to his own.

[46] He specified, however, that he was not referring to 'preliminary discussions' but to definite offers, for which the rules required them to obtain beforehand the written permission of the Intendant.

[47] The contents and tone of this letter show that Mahler had won his case in his clash with the Intendant two years earlier. Indeed, but for this, his 'breach of discipline' would have been taken much more seriously.

final result is never as slovenly or as careless from a rhythmic point of view as if I had not trained them properly from the beginning.[48]

Mahler had persuaded the stage-director August Stoll,[49] who taught at the Conservatory, to make his students play their roles initially with their arms tied together. To him this was essential, since 'natural' gestures were always ridiculous. No singer, even if thoroughly versed in his part, was capable of finding the correct gesture by himself.

Unless every motion is stylized and translated into art, unless every step and expression is sublimated, the whole performance becomes puerile. You can see a mile away that this is Mr Smith and nobody else. Considering that everything, even the cobbler's trade, has to be painstakingly learned, why should an actor be capable of creating a musical and dramatic role spontaneously and without any guidance? No, like all other techniques it requires thorough study and hard work.[50]

As an example, Mahler cited Mildenburg, who had been so awkward and clumsy to begin with and then blossomed into the 'most admirable and truly classic' of actresses. She was often compared to Eleonora Duse, her regal bearing, noble femininity, and imposing proportions creating a stir at her every entrance. Moreover, her musical talents matched her dramatic qualities. According to Schoenberg's pupil Erwin Stein,[51] her voice was, at that time, one of the most magnificent one could hear anywhere and her range such that she could sing either soprano or mezzo roles such as Ortrud or Amneris.[52] Her top notes were already beginning to be less smooth, but she managed to fill every word with drama and significance. As Brünnhilde, her face reflected all the shades of emotion inherent in that role, particularly in the great final scene with Wotan. Her contemporaries described her in *Fidelio* as 'animated at the outset by unshakable determination' and then, after Florestan's release, 'tender and devout in the face of her own destiny', but always convincing in all her attitudes and expressions. She had come to sense Mahler's every wish so absolutely that she hardly needed to look at him during performances, a fact that particularly pleased him, for he felt that the conductor's baton was there to guide only 'beginners, or people devoid of musical sense', whereas the true actor-singer, so essential for Wagner roles, should sense his wishes without having to look at him. 'There must be a common will, a perfect accord on the spiritual sense of the work, leading to a secret but profound understanding that alone can accomplish the composer's intention.' Mildenburg described how Mahler, if he wanted her to look at him at a particular moment, would warn her before the performance. 'It was generally in ensembles, or in places where we singers

---

[48] NBL1. 154; NBL2. 180.

[49] August Stoll (1854–1918), a baritone and later stage-director, had joined the Hofoper in 1884.

[50] NBL1. 154 and NBL2. 180.

[51] See Harold Rosenthal (ed.), *The Opera Bedbook* (Gollancz, London, 1965).

[52] Unfortunately, her voice soon began to show signs of fatigue, and she often sparked off crises for Mahler by cancelling at the last moment.

perhaps could not hear the orchestra properly, for example in the second act of *Tristan* where the two protagonists sing sitting on a bench.'[53]

Within the 'ensemble' of singers he was gradually building up at the Hofoper, Mahler tried to convert the jealousy so prevalent at the Opera into healthy rivalry. When, on his advice, Selma Kurz was learning the role of Sieglinde, he asked Mildenburg not only to coach her, but also to sing the entire role for her as he had taught it to her years before. Each gesture and each movement she showed to Kurz was so entrancing that he himself was moved. 'She now is', he told his close friends,

what I imagined she'd become when she arrived in Hamburg, as a beginner barely out of the Conservatory. However imperfect she may have been then, her dramatic and musical genius already illuminated everything she did. When she appeared before Siegmund in the *Todesverkündigung*, she was so simple yet so majestic, her tone so deeply moving—something I had never heard or seen before.[54]

Gutheil-Schoder, after an initial period of resistance due to her exceedingly forceful personality and innate talent,[55] adopted Mahler's ideas, realizing how much she could learn from him. She was so gifted that Mahler only had to give her a hint or show her something once for her to take advantage of it instantly. We have seen that she was far from having the unanimous approval of the Viennese press and public. A year after her arrival in Vienna, Max Graf was still able to ask, in an article in the magazine *Bühne und Welt*, whether she would ever be totally accepted in Vienna, this sensual and quasi-Mediterranean metropolis, where voices were appreciated above all for their sensuous beauty. Yet the art of a Gutheil-Schoder was 'so special and unique' that it was easy to understand how she could 'fascinate a temperament so constantly in motion as Gustav Mahler's'. 'This exceptional singer is a modern phenomenon, mixing inspiration and technique, passion and intellect in a remarkable way. It is always interesting to see how her lively intelligence truly infuses her passions and how her inner flame kindles her intelligence.'

According to Max Graf, the young singer's extraordinary capacity for identifying with her roles was bound to appeal to Mahler because

he does not allow artistic tasks to suit the individual nature of the singers, but asks his singers to adapt to the most varied requirements, continually broadening and working on their individuality. . . . A gifted and inspired artist gains by this. He has breathing space, room to develop, as well as being spurred on to further achievements by the lively enthusiasm of the Director of the Opera.

Nevertheless, Graf added, although Gutheil-Schoder's work showed a wealth of soul and intelligence, her small, not very sensuous voice was basically better suited to soubrette and operetta roles than to grand opera. This very limitation was what goaded her ever further, making her interpretation of each character

---

[53] BME 31.   [54] NBL1. 148; NBL2. 167.   [55] Ibid.

quite different from that of any other singer. Graf claimed that character parts (*Chargenrolle*) were what suited her best. He noted that, for example, she lacked the vocal sweetness and smoothness necessary for Pamina. Instead, she made of her a 'fairytale princess, pale and dreamy, with long blond hair and black eyes, vivid and languorous, as if cut out from a painting'. Thus, one was 'seized, captivated by this exotic creation'. Despina became a ladies' maid of 'venomous insight, a sharp and caustic tongue, rapid movements, quick, nervous gesticulations, a Paris chambermaid of 1900, not Mozart's little Despina'. The ear lost its power, said the critic, and the mind was 'so stimulated that the total effect is overwhelming'.[56] 'Recently', Graf continued,

Mahler had made a particularly bold experiment, casting Gutheil-Schoder as Eva in *Die Meistersinger*. She had been torn to pieces by the Viennese press. What did Mahler do? He immediately announced a second performance with the same singer. And then, when there had been hissing mixed with the applause at the curtain calls, he had forbidden all the performers to take their bows, and the stage had remained empty.

Indeed, after the first performance of *Die Meistersinger* featuring Mahler's 'favourite' artist, on 11 November 1900,[57] the press was full of the 'scandal'. The *Fremden-Blatt* even reported that Mahler had wanted a police superintendent to be stationed in the gallery in order to identify and eject those who hissed. The character (Eva) emerged as a 'nervous lover inspired by the Secession' (*Fremden-Blatt*) whose 'expressions, gestures and movements transformed love into a pathological sexual problem', and who 'vibrated to her fingertips with morbid sensuality' (*Wiener Abendpost*). The *Abendpost* critic also claimed that this Eva loved Stolzing

feverishly, as if the score of *Die Meistersinger* had been written by Krafft-Ebbing. If this is to be our Eva, Stolzing would be the great Pan, Hans Sachs a bearded centaur and David a young deer. Pending such a transformation, Frau Gutheil-Schoder should be more moderate, rather than crushing beneath the dominance of a 'Super Eva' the excellent team we possess for *Die Meistersinger*. For what possible reason has the interest of one of the most respected masterworks of the German stage been reduced to that of a character study (*Modellstudie*)? Even Director Mahler seems to have been afflicted by the new Eva's Bacchic agitation, the whole performance taking on an air of neurosis.[58]

Yet of all the members of the Opera, Gutheil-Schoder was Mahler's most faithful, conscientious and talented collaborator, the one who best succeeded in adopting in depth his ideas on the theatre:

In singing, everything depends on diction. Interpretation, even from the musical point of view, ought always to be built on words. No matter how beautifully a phrase is sung,

[56] *Bühne und Welt*, 3 (1901), 381, 'Marie Gutheil-Schoder'.

[57] Cast for this performance: Reichmann (Sachs), Hesch (Pogner), Felix (Beckmesser), Winkelmann (Walther), Schrödter (David), Gutheil-Schoder (Eva), Hilgermann (Magdalena).

[58] *Wiener Abendpost* and *Fremden-Blatt* (12 Nov. 1900).

if the singer fails to bring out the full meaning of its words, it will not produce the desired effect, even though the audience might not always recognize the cause of its disappointment. If, for instance, instead of singing *Mutter*, a singer follows the music and breaks up the word into *Mu-tter*, its dramatic effect will be lost; just as if, instead of 'Trutz' (short and sharp), he sings 'Tru-tz', the sense and expression are gone, even though his voice might be divine. Short vowels should always remain as short as the corresponding notes; otherwise the word and its sound, which should be as inseparable as the body and the soul, become disunited. The ideal song must be based on the words; the sound virtually makes itself, if you speak the words with their full meaning and sharply accentuated. . . . The most important thing in a singer is his 'r'; if he can get that right, strange as it may seem, he can't be entirely bad.[59]

While filling the Opera with exceptionally talented and willing artists like Mildenburg and Gutheil-Schoder, Mahler continued to have difficulties with others who resisted him because they considered themselves stars. One day he rushed backstage between the second and third acts of *Lohengrin*,[60] once again to tell Reichmann that 'your rhythm is impossible', but the baritone, unperturbed, replied: 'nobody cares about your rhythm! . . . My fans are only interested in my voice!' Van Dyck having left the Opera in the autumn of 1900, some months after Marie Renard, Mahler found himself at loggerheads with the tenor Franz Naval, who had taken over some of Van Dyck's roles and who also had the 'star' mentality.[61] Naval finally handed in his resignation, which Mahler, in order not to appear to be giving in to him, accepted, though with regret. According to Karpath, Naval left numerous admirers in Vienna, and his departure was considered fresh proof of Mahler's 'tyranny'. With the new singers he had engaged, Mahler was demanding to the point of checking even their personal habits and way of life. For instance, he discovered that the Opera's Heldentenor, Erik Schmedes, often sat up drinking and smoking in a certain café until late at night. Mahler was particularly worried to find him there smoking a cigar although he was supposed to sing Siegfried the next day. All other arguments having failed, Mahler asked Schmedes to imagine how disappointed his admirers, who had come to hear him in one of his best roles would be only to find him replaced by Leo Slezak, the young Moravian tenor who had just made a sensational début at the Hofoper.[62] Without more ado Schmedes took the cigar from his mouth, got up, and left the café with a broad smile on his face. The next day, with characteristic naïvety, he took care to give of his best.[63] Later Mahler had to find other tricks to prevent him from putting his voice in danger, especially when Schmedes started to go on long horse rides in the Prater and frequently caught cold. In 1901 Mahler suggested that in *Rienzi* he should ride on to the stage on his own horse. Terrified by the noise of the

[59] NBL2. 167.
[60] Reichmann was singing the role of Telramund. The anecdote was later told by Erik Schmedes.
[61] Mahler had engaged both Naval and Saville after the first Theater an der Wien performance of Puccini's *La Bohème* in 1897 (BMG 380). Naval made his Viennese Hofoper début in 1898.
[62] See below, Chap. 10.   [63] GWO 80 and LEM 313.

orchestra, the horse almost charged the walk-ons and provoked a panic. This narrow escape apparently persuaded Schmedes to abandon equestrianism as a sport too perilous for a singer.[64]

During the 1900–1 season, Mahler made efforts to recruit a number of new singers, but none of them materialized. Among the women, Kathi Bettaque, a former member of his Hamburg Stadt-Theater ensemble, and later a member of the Munich Opera, was not even invited to the Hofoper despite an exchange of letters and telegrams, probably because she asked too high a fee.[65] Some singers were eliminated after auditions, while others, like the contralto Ottilie Metzger, were invited but not engaged.[66] The greatest failure of the season seems to have been the baritone Theodor Bertram, another member of Mahler's company at the Hamburg Stadt-Theater. Invited to the Hofoper in May 1900, he was immediately engaged, but for what must be one of the shortest periods in the Opera's history: eighteen days![67]

Another abortive attempt to recruit new talent led to a final break between Mahler and Ferdinand Pfohl. In February 1901 the Hamburg critic wrote to Mahler to recommend a young dramatic soprano, Katharina Rösing, a member of the Düsseldorf Theatre and incidentally his sister-in-law, who was coming to Vienna for an audition. Unfortunately the audition took place while Mahler was recovering from the serious haemorrhage that interrupted his work in February–March 1901. She sang for one of the Korrepetitors of the Opera, who advised against her engagement. The following June, the young soprano wrote to Mahler expressing her resentment, and refusing to make a further trip to Vienna lest she be disappointed once again! Pfohl added a few lines in his own hand, 'regretting the turn events had taken'.[68] Strangely, Ferdinand Pfohl's memoirs mention an almost identical incident, but attribute it to Hermann Behn. Pfohl alleges that Behn sent a young singer to Mahler, recommending her warmly. Mahler is said to have received her with great coolness and to have told her, on learning that she was from North Germany, that he had a strong antipathy to people from that region. Such behaviour seems totally foreign to Mahler's character as we know it, and the story is probably a complete fabrication. Pfohl claims that Mahler's rudeness cut Behn to the quick, and that Behn even refused to have anything more to do with Mahler. Yet Mahler's affectionate reunion with his old friend and patron on the occasion of the première of the Fifth Symphony in Hamburg shows that they had never seriously quarrelled. It is true, however, that the Katharina Rösing incident put an

---

[64] Unfortunately, as will be seen below, Schmedes replaced his famous horse, first by a bicycle, then a motorcycle, and finally an open car.

[65] HOA, no. 154, ZL.177/1901. Letter of 17 Feb. 1901.

[66] HOA, Z.251/1901. Letters of 26 Mar. and 23 Apr. 1901. In 1910, Ottilie Metzger took part in the première of the Eighth Symphony in Munich.

[67] HOA, no. 155. Autograph letters and telegrams from Mahler, 28 Mar. and 16 May 1900. Mahler offered Bertram an annual salary of 20,000 kronen. His engagement lasted from 1 to 19 Sept. 1900.

[68] HOA, Z.195/1901, letters of 16 Feb. from Ferdinand Pfohl and 12 June from Katharina Rösing. The singer asks for her February travel expenses.

end to relations between Mahler and Ferdinand Pfohl, who stubbornly refused to meet him again in 1905.[69]

After a long period during which he had prepared and conducted all the important performances almost single-handed, Mahler entrusted the baton to Franz Schalk for the first time on 26 October for a revival of Verdi's *Il trovatore* in which he had endeavoured to 'purge [the production] of routine and apathy'. The expectancy of the audience that evening was such that several critics compared the atmosphere with that of a première. Moreover, Mahler had indulged in a particularly bold experiment by assigning the role of Leonora to Selma Kurz, whose voice was generally found inadequate for the part.[70] Heuberger wrote that it was 'unfair to put Frl. Kurz in such a risky situation'. Despite some very good passages, she was not a great success.

Ten days earlier, on 15 October, accompanied by Justi and Natalie, Mahler took the train for Munich,[71] where the newly founded Hugo Wolf-Verein[72] had decided to include his Second Symphony in its inaugural concert. He was so delighted at this fresh opportunity to conduct and hear his own work that he spared no financial sacrifice to ensure a first-rate performance and threw himself heart and soul into preparing it. He was apprehensive of the reactions of a press and public that had never heard any of his works before. At the last moment, the Intendant of the Munich Opera, Ernst von Possart, 'jealous of the Vienna Opera's success under his direction',[73] tried to thwart him by refusing to allow one of his sopranos to take part in the concert, although she had sung all the rehearsals. Moreover, after the penultimate rehearsal, Mahler had to dismiss another soprano whose voice was inadequate. Luckily, however, the wife of the conductor of the Verein, Agnes Stavenhagen, offered to replace her and, after rehearsing the part once with Mahler at the piano, sang it to perfection. It was unfortunate that the contralto soloist, Elise Feinhals, lacked emotional intensity. 'For this part,' Mahler said, 'I need the voice and naïve expression of a child, since I myself, when I heard the tinkling of a small bell,

[69] See below, Vol. iii, Chap. 2.

[70] Cast of *Il trovatore*: Kurz (Leonora), Walker (Azucena), Schrödter (Manrico), Demuth (Conte di Luna).

[71] For this reason Mahler handed over the fourth performance of *Così fan tutte* to Schalk. He asked Max Graf to telegraph a report to him immediately afterwards.

[72] According to the *Allgemeine Musik-Zeitung* (2 Nov. 1900), during a general assembly on 23 Oct., 'exclusive propaganda' for Wolf's music was deemed henceforth unnecessary and the Verein decided to change its name to Münchner Gesellschaft für moderne Tonkunst (Munich Society for Modern Music). Among the members of the Verein, whose president was the conductor and Liszt pupil Bernhard Stavenhagen, were the composer Hermann Bischoff and two critics, Arthur Seidl and Ludwig Schiedermair, both authors of early monographs on Mahler.

[73] NBL2. 168. It seems that Possart also resented Mahler's having 'borrowed' the idea of the revolving stage for *Così* from the Munich Opera. That the misunderstanding between Mahler and Possart was short-lived is proved by a series of letters of 1903, preserved in the HOA, about the engagement of the latter's daughter at the Vienna Opera. Possart begged Mahler to give Poppi (von Possart) a one-year contract and have her make her début under his direction. Mahler was obliged to refuse the request, because 'I would never obtain the consent of my superiors' to an engagement without a 'preliminary invitation'. (HOA, June–July 1903, Z.2635.)

1. Mahler (1898)

2. Mahler and his sister Justine (1899)

3. Mahler and his brother-in-law, the violinist Arnold Rosé (1899)

4. Natalie Bauer-Lechner (after 1897)

5. Bertha Zuckerkandl

6. Siegried Lipiner

7. The young Bruno Walter, Mahler's assistant at the Hofoper

8. Alma Schindler, aged 16

9. Alma Schindler, aged 18

10. Mahler and Alma at
    Basel (1903)

11. The Mahler villa, Maiernigg am Wörthersee

12. Alma and Putzi at Maiernigg (probably 1904)

13. Alma at Maiernigg (1903)

14. The Componierhäuschen, Maiernigg am Wörthersee

15. Auenbruggergasse, 2, Vienna; Mahler's apartment was on the top floor, facing the Strohgasse (© Claudius Lang)

16. The new Secession exhibition hall, 1898 (architect: Josef Maria Olbrich) (Bildarchiv des Österreichischen Nationalbiblioteks)

17. Planning the Beethoven exhibition at the Secession, 1902. From left to right: Anton Stark, Gustav Klimt (in chair), Kolo Moser, Adolf Boehm, Maximilian Lenz (lying down), Ernst Stöhr (in hat), Wilh. List, Emil Orlik (sitting), Maximilian Kurzweil, Leopold Stolba, Carl Moll (reclining), Rudolf Bacher (photograph by Moriz Nähr; Bildarchiv des Österreichischen Nationalbiblioteks)

18. Max Klinger, *Beethovendenkmal*, with Roller's fresco *Die sinkende Nacht* in the background; Secession exhibition 1902 (Bildarchiv des Österreichischen Nationalbibliotheks)

19. Beethoven hitting Mahler; cartoon from *Kikeriki*, 24 April 1902, on the occasion of the Beethoven exhibition at the Secession. The caption reads: Beethoven: 'At last I've got you! Just wait, you botcher of my symphonies!'

20. Gustav Klimt, 'Die wohlberüstete Stärke', detail of the *Beethovenfries* (1902)

21. Carl Moll, *The Hohe Warte under snow* (woodcut)

22. The Vienna Hofoper at the turn of the century: inside the auditorium

23. The Vienna Hofoper: the main staircase

24. Exterior of the Hofoper in Mahler's time

25. Marie Renard as Manon, Ernest Van Dyck as Des Grieux

26. Mahler conducting at the Hofoper (silhouette by Otto Böhler)

27. Sketch of Mahler conducting
    by Emil Orlik (6 March 1902)
    (Bildarchiv des Österreich-
    ischen Nationalbibliotheks)

28. Etching of Mahler by Emil
    Orlik (1902)

29. Eduard Wlassack, senior administrator at the Hofoper

30. Rosa Papier, contralto and singing teacher. She and Wlassack used their influence to have Mahler appointed at the Hofoper

31. Hans Richter, principal
    conductor at the Hofoper from
    1875 to 1900

32. Eduard Hanslick, the doyen
    of Vienna's music critics

33. Hans Richter (silhouette by
    Hans Schliessmann)

34. Wilhelm Jahn, Mahler's predecessor as
    Director of the Hofoper (silhouette by
    Hans Schliessmann)

35. Mahler (silhouette by
    Hans Schliessmann)

36. Franz Schalk (silhouette by
    Hans Schliessmann)

K. K. Hof- Operntheater.

Dinstag den 11. Mai 1897.

119. Vorstellung im Jahres-Abonnement.

Lohengrin.

Romantische Oper in 3 Akten von Richard Wagner.

Heinrich der Vogler, deutscher König	Hr. Grengg.
Lohengrin	Hr. Winkelmann.
Elsa von Brabant	Fr. Ehrenstein.
Herzog Gottfried, ihr Bruder	Frl. Berger.
Friedrich von Telramund, brabantischer Graf	Hr. Reichmann.
Ortrud, seine Gemalin	Fr. Kaulich.
Der Heerrufer des Königs	Hr. Felix.
	Hr. Schmitt.
Vier brabantische Edle	Hr. Schittenhelm.
	Hr. Frei.
	Hr. Marian.

Sächsische und thüringische Grafen und Edle.
Brabantische Grafen und Edle, Edelfrauen, Edelknaben.
Mannen, Frauen, Knechte.

Ort der Handlung: Antwerpen. — Zeit: Die erste Hälfte des zehnten Jahrhunderts.
Die neue Dekoration im 2. Akt von Anton Brioschi jun., k. k. Hoftheatermaler.
Kostüme nach Zeichnungen von Fr. Gaul.

Kassa-Eröffnung gegen halb 7 Uhr. Anfang 7 Uhr. Ende gegen halb 11 Uhr.

Mittwoch	den 12. Die Jüdin.		Samstag	den 15. Hans Heiling.
Donnerstag	den 13. Das Heimchen am Herd.		Sonntag	den 16. Die Afrikanerin.
Freitag	den 14. Die lustigen Weiber von Windsor.			

Falls eine angekündigte Vorstellung abgeändert werden sollte, kann von den für dieselbe gelösten Karten auch zur Ersatz-vorstellung Gebrauch gemacht, oder der dafür entrichtete Betrag, jedoch spätestens am Tage der Vorstellung bis halb 7 Uhr Abends (resp. eine halbe Stunde vor dem für Beginn der Vorstellung angesetzten Zeitpunkt) bei sonstigem Verlust des Anspruches an der Kassa zurückverlangt werden.

Preise der Plätze:

Eine Loge Parterre oder I. Galerie	fl. 25.—	Ein Sitz Parterre 2.—4. Reihe	fl. 3.—
Eine Loge II. Galerie	fl. 15.—	Ein Sitz III. Galerie 1. Reihe	fl. 2.75
Eine Loge III. Galerie	fl. 10.—	Ein Sitz III. Galerie 2. Reihe	fl. 2.25
Ein Logensitz Parterre oder I. Galerie	fl. 6.—	Ein Sitz III. Galerie 3.—4. Reihe	fl. 1.25
Ein Logensitz II. Galerie	fl. 4.—	Ein Sitz IV. Galerie 1. Reihe, Mitte	fl 2.—
Ein Logensitz III. Galerie	fl. 3.—	Ein Sitz IV. Galerie 1. Reihe, Seite	fl. 1.50
Ein Sitz Parquet 4. Reihe	fl. 6.—	Ein Sitz IV. Galerie 2. und 3. Reihe	fl 1.50
Ein Sitz Parquet 2.—5. Reihe	fl. 4.50	Ein Sitz IV. Galerie 4.—6. Reihe	fl. 1.25
Ein Sitz Parquet 6.—9. Reihe	fl. 4.—	Eintritt in das Parterre (nur Herren gestattet)	fl. 1.—
Ein Sitz Parquet 10.—13. Reihe	fl. 3.50	Eintritt in die III. Galerie	fl. —.80
Ein Sitz Parterre 1. Reihe	fl. 3.50	Eintritt in die IV. Galerie	fl. —.60

Zu jeder im Repertoire angekündigten Vorstellung erfolgt Tags vorher bis 1 Uhr Nach-mittags die Ausgabe der Stammsitze; um 2 Uhr Nachmittags (Tags vorher) beginnt der allgemeine Verkauf von Logen und Sitzen.

37. Poster announcing the performance of *Lohengrin* with which
Mahler made his debut at the Hofoper (11 May 1897)

38. Franz Schalk, Mahler's assistant at the Hofoper

39. Gustave Charpentier

40. The Hofoper Ensemble (c. 1901)

imagined the soul to be in heaven where it will have to start afresh, in a state of chrysalis, as a small child.'[74]

The Munich chorus also caused Mahler problems. Although inferior to those in Berlin, the female voices were none the less better than in Vienna, and the choristers plunged enthusiastically into the task. The tenors were too few and changed at each rehearsal. At the dress rehearsal they sang one of the passages a cappella so badly that Mahler interrupted with a despairing 'Oh! This will never do!' For a moment he considered cancelling the whole concert so as not to compromise his work, but presently announced, calmly and confidently, that he had thought of a solution to the problem and would tell them about it after the rehearsal. He had in fact decided to have the passage in question played by the clarinets, which, being near the tenors, would help them to sing in tune. Nevertheless, it was a makeshift solution to which he resorted with great reluctance. He made the tenors rehearse for another three and a half hours the following morning and was obliged to pay out of his own pocket for both this extra rehearsal and the one he had previously demanded for the Scherzo. Since the Munich orchestra was no match for the Vienna Philharmonic, he foresaw a performance inferior to that of the previous year, but looked forward confidently to the Finale, which, in Vienna, had been spoilt by the mediocrity of the chorus and the asthmatic sound of the Musikverein organ. 'The statue may lack a "little toe" or the "tip of a thumb" this time, but not, as in Vienna, its head.' One of the Munich orchestra's drawbacks was its shortage of strings, only twelve each of first and second violins, whereas Mahler dreamt of having his symphony performed by thirty violins, eighteen cellos, and sixteen double-basses: 'When that happens, people will be amazed to see how much it magnifies the effect!'

For once Mahler's anxieties were unfounded, for Munich was immensely impressed by the Second Symphony. The public had been looking forward to the concert as a major event in contemporary music.[75] At the dress rehearsal on Friday morning, and even more so the evening of the concert, the celebrated director of the Vienna Opera was greeted with warm applause. The audience included such well-known musicians as Felix Weingartner, Eugen d'Albert, and the Intendant-General of Bavarian theatres, Baron von Perfall. According to Natalie, the audience found the first movement disconcerting, but their appreciation was aroused by the second. Enthusiasm increased throughout the remaining movements, which Mahler conducted without a pause and, at the moment of the 'bird of death', one could have heard a pin drop in the hall. The chorus remained seated when they began to sing[76] as directed by Mahler in the score, and the audience seemed to quiver with emotion.

[74] This is an allusion to a passage in the last scene of *Faust, Part II*, which Mahler was to set to music in his Eighth Symphony.

[75] See the article by Paula Reber, Munich correspondent of the *Neue Zeitschrift für Musik*.

[76] NBL2. 170. They rose only for the last verse.

The Finale was of exceptional amplitude. 'Only then did I realize' Mahler said later,

what enormous waves of sound are unleashed, and how they would shatter the audience if the crescendo were not so gradual, rising up again and again, and if it were not inwardly so justified that the ear actually comes to expect it as a supreme satisfaction. If one were to tell the audience that the worst explosions in the first movement were childsplay in comparison to that of the Finale, they would fear for their eardrums! ... Only the man who organizes and constructs such a work can fully appreciate the importance of wise moderation. Imagine what effects I could have produced if I had let the chorus and organ come in earlier! But I preferred to keep them for the climax and do without the earlier effect.

The *Bayrische Kurier* report took the sudden dead silence that ensued after the last note as abundant proof of the audience's state of emotion; it was immediately succeeded by 'unparalleled jubilation', and it seemed to Natalie as though the ovation would never end. A large number of people crowded around the podium, while others waved their handkerchiefs from their seats. Surrounded by a group of friends at the Park Hotel after the concert, Mahler, happy and relaxed, held forth at length on the subject of programme music, and recalled the misunderstandings that his own programmes had caused. Would not his letter to the critic Arthur Seidl, written in 1897 and now published by Seidl in the *Allgemeine Zeitung*,[77] revive them? Would he not be regarded as an advocate of programme music, when in fact he was opposed to it and considered it

one of the biggest musical and artistic errors? Those who are capable of writing it are not artists. It's a different matter when a master's work becomes so alive and lucid that one can't help reading some action or event into it; or when a composer tries, after the event, as I've always done, to explain his work to himself by some mental picture; or indeed when his message takes on a sublimity and form such that he can no longer be content with mere sound and seeks a higher means of expression by resorting to the human voice and the poetic word, as Beethoven did in his Ninth and I did in my own Symphony in C Minor. This has nothing to do with that trivial, erroneous process of giving a name to a specific happening and illustrating it programmatically step by step.[78]

Mahler had refused to allow the old programme of his Second Symphony to be distributed for the Munich concert, even though the text had already been printed. 'Music must speak for itself. The most sublime and universal message it is meant to convey is contained in the words of the conclusion. The deeper meaning of a work, its message, will only emerge gradually, more often than not after the composer's death. . . . The most important thing is to take it as music,

---

[77] MBR1, no. 209; MBR2, no. 216 of 17 Feb. 1897. Mahler expatiates on his Second Symphony, its programme, and the inspiration of its Finale, as well as on what he owes to Strauss's success (see Vol. i, Chap. 23). Seidl's article was a preview, published the day before the concert.

[78] NBL2. 170 ff.

solely as music!' In the end, he regretted having exaggerated his admiration for Strauss in his letter to Seidl. 'There', he said to Natalie, 'you see the price one pays when one is not completely sincere and makes the slightest concession out of friendship! They've taken me at my word and now consider me an advocate of Strauss and of programme music, which I ought to fight fiercely and openly.'[79]

After the Munich concert Guido Adler recalled the strangely contrasting reactions, at the Berlin première in 1895,[80] of three prominent figures, Richard Strauss, Karl Muck, and Wilhelm Kienzl, to a passage in the first movement. Strauss had exclaimed that it had given him an idea, which, Mahler commented, Strauss had made use of in his latest works, though with a difference. Whereas Strauss used 'cacophony' unnecessarily and merely for the 'fun of offending', his own use of it was justified by the strict laws of polyphony. 'Indeed, I try more and more to avoid harshness and even to remove it subsequently, where possible, as in the passage in question [in the Second Symphony] whereas Strauss contrives gratuitous dissonances, solely to provoke and attract attention.' After this third hearing of his big symphony Mahler again had doubts about the strong contrast between the end of the first and the beginning of the second movement. He had thought of remedying this by placing the Scherzo after the first movement, but then the moods of the Andante and the following 'Urlicht' would not have been sufficiently contrasted, since their keys were too closely related. When composing the Third and Fourth Symphonies, he had overcome this difficulty by planning and sketching the sequence both of the movements and their keys.[81]

For the first time in Mahler's career, the critics did not immediately spoil the pleasure he had derived from the audience's rapturous reaction. Even the article in the *Allgemeine Zeitung*, which was one of the least enthusiastic, acknowledged that the Second Symphony was a 'very competent and undeniably interesting' work and compared it to Strauss's symphonic poem *Also sprach Zarathustra*, pointing out that it too portrayed 'the human being grappling with the concept of immortality', leading us through contrasting regions of 'earthly suffering, joy and passion'. The two subtitles of the Finale, 'Der Rufer in der Wüste' (The Call in the Desert) and 'Der grosse Appell' (The Great Summons), proved that this was a programme symphony and belonged to the school of Bruckner. Its religious atmosphere, choruses, and the prominent role given to the brass instruments likewise confirmed this, even though Mahler's aims were totally different. However, despite his profound knowledge of all the 'secrets of musical technique' and superior mastery of form, he lacked

[79] See Vol. i, Chap. 23. Mahler's opinion of Strauss changed completely when he heard *Salome* (see below, Vol. iii, Chap. 4).

[80] See Vol. i, Chap. 20.

[81] Several versions of the Third Symphony's overall plan have survived (see above, Vol. i, App. 1). Mahler stated at this time that he had dropped the Andante of the First Symphony for the same reason, though he clearly had other, more serious reasons.

Bruckner's 'noble faculty for transforming themes and rendering them expressive'. The critic nevertheless admired the first movement, 'constructed with grammatical clarity', which, with 'two somewhat meagre themes', expressed the very depths of sorrow; the transparency of the Andante with its 'cries of despair within a stylized waltz'; the 'berliozissimo' Scherzo; the simple and profoundly touching pathos of 'Urlicht'; and then, the Finale, which he had found captivating in spite of its slightly 'affected' ending. 'Shattered, flabbergasted and enraptured', the audience had responded with endlessly renewed applause.

Of the Munich dailies, *Der Sammler* deplored the excessive publicity surrounding Mahler, since it aroused the 'distrust of thoughtful people'. By defining his music as 'lived' rather than 'composed', all other 'mere composers' were implicitly condemned. Incomprehensible without a programme, the Second Symphony showed more striving for grandeur than 'demonic creative urge'. The first movement stood out above all the others, and particularly above the Andante, which lacked melodic distinction, and the Scherzo, which was 'unimaginative and trivial' and full of 'musical and instrumental tricks of doubtful effect'. But this hostile reaction turned out to be the exception. The *Bayrische Kurier* reported that Mahler's 'sweeping victory' had 'established the Wolf-Verein'. The anonymous critic preferred the first and final movements to those in between, which contained 'too much witty piquancy (*Pikanterien*) and flirtation with quite impossible cacophonies and dissonances'. None the less, this same critic did Mahler the uncommon honour of praising 'the rare originality' of his thematic imagination and instrumentation, and also congratulated him on never being boring and on keeping the audience on tenterhooks thanks to his matchless subtlety. Even Strauss, he said, could not make the public hold its breath to this degree. And yet the great symphonic poems of Strauss had prepared the way for Mahler, who obviously had carefully studied the works of Berlioz, Liszt, Bruckner, and Wagner. More specifically, the critic admired the magnificent pathos of the first movement and the Viennese charm and originality of the second, while pronouncing the 'Urlicht' 'a gem of poetry, of lyric and religious feeling'. As for the lofty and introspective Finale, and especially the intervention of the chorus, which was 'unique in modern music', it showed Mahler to be a 'symphonic dramatist'.

A month later, Rudolf Louis, one of the most distinguished Munich critics, discussed the triumphal success of the concert in the review *Kunstwart*. A convinced anti-Semite, German nationalist, and friend of Hans Pfitzner, he held that Mahler did not possess a 'powerful and personal' imagination, but was an eclectic whose themes were almost all borrowed. True, his dynamic and fiery temperament rendered his musical language captivating and compelled the audience, at least during the performance, to 'surrender unconditionally to the composer'. Subsequently, upon recovering its judgement, it was left with the embarrassing impression of having been fooled and 'overwhelmed rather than convinced'. Nevertheless, Mahler was neither a poseur nor a charlatan, and there could be no doubt as to the seriousness of his intentions. As a craftsman, Strauss was his only peer. With almost unparalleled audacity, he disregarded all the traditional rules of music, but for all that there was something disturbing and 'unattractive' about his work. To a certain extent, it lacked true elevation; he described immortality without suggesting the beyond, the world-to-come of Christian theology, that is the negation of time, for he had 'no sense of eternity'. While refusing to admit to any anti-Semitic tendencies, Louis regarded this as a 'specifically Jewish' element in Mahler's work, which he was therefore unable to accept whole-heartedly.[82]

Other critics tried to view the 'Mahler problem' from a more detached point of view. The Munich journalist Arthur Seidl, in a number of articles, some of them published in anti-Semitic magazines, discerned two principal streams in German music, one from the north and the other from the south. Thus he contrasted Bach with Handel, Beethoven with Cherubini, Schumann with Mendelssohn, Wagner with Liszt, Brahms with Bruckner, Strauss with Mahler, and poked fun at the 'astonishment of the musical astronomers at the sudden appearance of this bright new star in the artistic sky'. With a moderation and lucidity rare in those days, Seidl considered that 'it is not possible to accuse Mahler of having attempted to write tone poetry before he had mastered musical syntax', and that 'it is too soon to pass a final judgment without examining at the same time recent technical developments and new forms of expressing modern ideas.'[83]

On the whole, the reactions of the Munich press had been exceptionally favourable, and those of the German magazines and periodicals even more so, their enthusiastic accounts spreading the news of Mahler's triumph everywhere. According to Paula Reber, the Munich correspondent of the *Neue Zeitschrift für Musik*, no one meeting Mahler for even five minutes could deny the 'religious seriousness' with which he regarded his art, even if, in the opening of the Second Symphony, he had perpetrated a 'good bad joke', a mixture of Richard and Siegfried Wagner with a few bars of a funeral march by Chopin and Beethoven thrown in. Nevertheless, Mahler had shown that he knew the meaning of the term 'allegro maestoso'. The other movements were excellent, notably the Finale, whose 'absolutely enthralling, indescribable, supernatural, lofty and powerful beauty' was impossible to imagine without having heard it. The Hugo Wolf-Verein could not have made a happier choice.

The *Musikalisches Wochenblatt* regarded Mahler above all as a disciple of Bruckner, but gifted with such a powerful imagination that he could in no way be regarded as an imitator. The anonymous correspondent began by praising

---

[82] Louis obviously subscribed to the fable, all too prevalent at his time, of Jewish 'materialism'. In his *Die deutsche Musik der Gegenwart* (1909) he again succumbed to the temptation of treating Mahler's 'case' from the point of view of his Jewishness, claiming that he 'speaks musical German with the accent, the cadence and above all the gestures of the excessively oriental Jew' (see Vol. iii, Chap. 7).

[83] Arthur Seidl, *Moderner Geist in der deutschen Tonkunst* (Bosse, Regensburg, 1912), 62.

the calm and the authority of his conducting: 'One listens motionless, wonderstruck as a master reveals his innermost self through his art'. Karl Pottgiesser, in the *Allgemeine Musik-Zeitung*, agreed with a review Rudolf Louis had published in the same paper two years earlier, after studying the score of the symphony.[84] He had expressed admiration for the composer's technical mastery and the boldness of his harmony and counterpoint, but thought it lacked the 'power of conviction of true genius'. Nevertheless, Pottgiesser found the effect 'fascinating', though at times 'somewhat superficial'. In the first movement, he said, Mahler made up with rhythmic interest and 'tragic power' what was lacking in melodic originality.[85] Finally, the *Neue Musik-Zeitung* applauded 'one of the season's most outstanding events' and claimed that this 'colossus in sound' showed everything of which 'modern orchestral art and technique' were capable, with 'heaps of crowded dissonances' but also 'titanic power'. This critic found, however, like most of his colleagues, that the 'superb technique' outstripped the 'originality of invention'.

Thus, for once, Mahler had no reason to complain of either the public or the critics. 'Those gentlemen are already changing their tune',[86] he wrote to Justi, who was staying with Emma in Weimar. 'Here in Vienna everybody talks about my success. I will send you the Munich articles as soon as I have got them all.' He also told his sister that Munich had decided to give his Second Symphony again, two weeks later, under the baton of Bernard Stavenhagen.[87] But he had already learnt to be cautious about the undertakings of this conductor who, despite his reputation as a former Liszt pupil, seems to have been a mediocre interpreter, at least with orchestras and with new music. At the beginning of November, the Munich composer Ludwig Thuille, whose best-known stage work, *Lobetanz*, Mahler was soon to put on in Vienna, confirmed his worst fears:

Although no doubt you have been fully informed of the 'Musical Academy's' performance of your mighty C minor Symphony, I must warmly and sincerely congratulate you on the brilliant success that this unique work obtained, even with the usually rather cool Odeon audience. The success was even more remarkable in that the performance was greatly inferior to the one you conducted, much more so than expected, for almost all the tempos were wrong. The first movement was reasonably correct but without any grandeur. The two middle movements were too fast (the semiquaver triplets in the second movement were completely blurred). Almost everything was missing from the third movement, sometimes even the correct notes. The 'Urlicht' was beautiful, for

---

[84] No. 25/26, 1898.

[85] Programme of the concert of 20 Oct., which took place at the Kaimsaal: Berlioz's Rob Roy Overture and Richard Strauss's *Hymnus*, Op. 33 No. 3, for voice and orchestra (soloist Elise Feinhals). This first half of the concert was conducted by Siegmund von Hausegger; the second half consisted entirely of Mahler's Second Symphony. The chorus was made up of members of the Porges'schen Chorverein and the Lehrergesangverein.

[86] Letter to Justi of 24 Oct. 1900 (RWO).

[87] Letter of 25 Oct. (RWO). The symphony was played again on 8 Nov. at the Allerheiligen Konzert of the Münchner Musikalische Akademie and conducted by Stavenhagen, to whom Mahler afterwards sent a telegram of thanks and congratulations.

although Frl. Ritter does not have a lovely voice like Frau Feinhals, she put her whole soul into it. Relatively speaking, the best of all the movements was the tremendous last movement, which anyway—assuming the chorus does the half of what it should— moved me profoundly: I know little modern music to which even we professionals listen with bated breath from beginning to end. I don't know if I should admire or envy you for having given the world so powerful a work.[88]

Thuille was of course grateful to Mahler for putting his opera, *Lobetanz*, on the *Spielplan* of the Hofoper, and his letter must be viewed against the background of his gratitude, but the admiration expressed in it seems genuine enough. So Mahler had some justification for speaking of a radical change in the attitude of professionals and public towards him. At last he was being thought of as an important personality in contemporary music. Besides, echoes of his resounding success in Munich spread quickly. In Berlin, the choral conductor Siegfried Ochs asked if Mahler could come at the end of the year to conduct his work a second time, but Mahler replied that he would not be able to do so, since December was already too taken up with a Philharmonic Concert and the première of *Lobetanz* (which was eventually postponed to the beginning of the following year). The Berlin performance finally took place, with Mahler conducting, the following autumn.[89]

If Mahler had hoped for a general change of attitude on the part of the critics, however, he was to be bitterly disappointed, and this only a month later, when his First Symphony was performed in Vienna at the second Philharmonic Concert on 18 November. After some hesitation because of the strict rules of the Philharmonic, Mahler allowed Justi and Natalie to attend the rehearsals for this concert, which was to begin with Beethoven's Overture to *Die Geschöpfe des Prometheus* and Schumann's Overture to *Manfred*. He had carefully revised the orchestration of the latter, for 'Schumann's indications are, as almost always, contrary to his intentions'. Natalie expressed surprise that he had put two such masterpieces on the programme with his First, but he retorted that 'the best cannot harm the good, but only enhance it and prepare its way in beauty'.[90] Regrettably, the Viennese public thought otherwise, since, from the opening bars of the First Symphony (the strange A pedal), a mixture of uneasiness and irritation made itself felt in the hall. A number of people, and especially those in the pit and the boxes who attended concerts only because it was the thing to do, began to laugh, cough, or clear their throats, in the face of 'this weird and incomprehensible music'. On the other hand, a lot of young people, students or pupils of the Conservatory, followed the performance with great interest and,

[88] Letter to Mahler from Ludwig Thuille, 7 Nov. 1900, former Ernst Rosé collection. Thuille also writes of the forthcoming première of *Lobetanz*.

[89] Card from Mahler to Siegfried Ochs, Staatliches Institut für Musikforschung, Preussischer Kulturbesitz, Berlin. Mahler suggested that Ochs come to Vienna so that he could explain his intentions to him.

[90] NBL2. 176 ff.

from the end of the first movement, their enthusiasm clashed with the disapproval of the rest of the audience.[91]

As usual, the second movement was warmly applauded, but the Funeral March dumbfounded the audience and provoked derisive laughter. Only the absence of a pause between the last two movements prevented them from leaving, and the stormy Finale forced them to be quiet. At the end of the performance there was an 'uncanny silence', after which came the first timid 'Bravo!', which was greeted by violent hissing followed by hesitant, and then stormy applause. Whereupon, just as in Weimar six years before, pandemonium broke loose. Mahler had fled at the first catcall, but returned only to thank his young admirers, who continued to acclaim him, unmoved by the disapproval of the 'reasonable' members of the audience. For Mahler's friends the concert was torture, Natalie reports, because 'we heard it with the audience's ears. All the pleasure we had derived from it during the rehearsals was gone; we dreaded all the passages in which we foresaw that the unusual treatment of the instruments would arouse the audience's indignation and longed only for the moment it would all be over and done with.'[92] From the end of the introduction, Mahler himself had sensed the hostility and, anxious to get through the Symphony as quickly as possible, had accelerated most of the tempos. Once his 'martyrdom' was over, he went home with some friends but, contrary to what they expected, did not seem in the least downhearted. 'After this,' he exclaimed, 'there's no danger that I shall compose to order or seek to curry favour with the public. The First Symphony is and always will be my child of sorrow!'

The Viennese critics reacted even more negatively than they had to the Second Symphony. 'One of us must be crazy, and it isn't me!' Hanslick's article began. With an objectivity that does him credit he admits having asked himself at the end of the performance whether it was not, after all, he who was crazy; but he continued to feel that the First Symphony was 'alien to music'. Admittedly, he said, a more thorough knowledge of the score might perhaps have helped him to a better understanding of its significance, but only on condition that a programme had been available to explain the connecting links between its different movements. What was the meaning of the sudden irruption of the 'end of the world' Finale, of the Funeral March in the form of a students' round? In his perplexity, he was obliged to confine himself to admiring Mahler's 'innumerable witty details and stupendous orchestral technique'. Theodor Helm,[93] in the *Deutsche Zeitung*, quoted the programme Mahler had published

[91] According to an article in *Wiener Allgemeine Zeitung* (20 Nov.) the commotion had begun even before the concert. Following orders received the police had refused to allow some of the young people who had been queuing for standing room to install themselves, as they usually did, on the stage behind the orchestra, so that many of them had had to remain outside.

[92] NBL2. 177.

[93] Theodor Otto Helm (1843–1920), son of a leading Viennese doctor, was orphaned at the age of 2. Studying law, and at the same time music under the aegis of Bruckner, he held an administrative post before

in Weimar in 1894 and recalled that this 'crude din, interpreted in Weimar as deliberate parody of the excesses of the new German school, had been indignantly rejected'. Contrary to a well-established custom, Mahler had forbidden the publication of even a thematic analysis in Vienna, doubtless fearing that his 'quotations' from Beethoven, Wagner, and Bruckner, Mendelssohn, Weber, etc., might thus be revealed.[94] This hypermodern work jumped, without any sort of transition, from pastoral innocence to savage bedlam. The audience, caught between Mahler's 'clique' of young admirers and his enemies, did not know what to think. Quite a few of them probably laughed uproariously at the 'grotesque cacophonies and explosions' of the Finale—unless they actually had earache as a result. With or without a programme, the Symphony was both a 'stylistic absurdity' and a 'total failure', and Mahler should never have been allowed to inflict it on the Philharmonic Orchestra and audience while Vienna continued to be deprived of so many estimable works.

Even Gustav Schönaich, who until then had shown considerable fairness in his assessment of Mahler, and had found his Second Symphony 'pleasing and intensely personal', could perceive no links between the movements of the First and declared the 'tone structure' completely irrational. 'Is it a weasel, a cloud or a camel?' he asked, paraphrasing Shakespeare.[95] The 'auditory pleasures' had irritated him as much as the dissonances, for all had seemed equally unmotivated. Mahler had been a master of orchestration sixteen years before, but his personality had still not asserted itself. Recalling that Wagner had feared that Berlioz would end up being 'buried beneath his own orchestral machinery', Schönaich remarked that Mahler had also succumbed to the hazardous joys of using a hitherto unprecedented orchestral language, and that, without fully realizing it, he attached more importance to 'the glittering outer garment of the thought than to the thought itself'. Moreover, his humour merely grated, for 'Callot's manner' was unsuited to music. It was impossible to discern the slightest link between the catastrophic fourth movement and the rest. Mahler should never have risked his reputation as a composer by performing such a work.

As in Weimar, where blows had been exchanged in the streets after the concert, and where the 'irony' of the First Symphony had been all the worse

starting his career as a music journalist in 1867, when he replaced his brother-in-law as music critic of the *Fremden-Blatt*. He became a correspondent for *Neue Musikalische Presse*, *Musikalisches Wochenblatt*, and several other journals. At one time Hanslick thought of choosing him as his successor at the *Neue Freie Presse*, but in 1884 Helm joined the new *Deutsche Zeitung*. Editor for several years of the music magazine founded by the firm of Bösendorfer, he became a Bruckner specialist, though he also wrote many articles about Brahms. He taught Musical Aesthetics at the Conservatory, and in 1907 became editor-in-chief of the magazine created by amalgamating the *Leipziger Wochenschrift*, the *Neue Zeitschrift für Musik*, and the *Musikalisches Wochenblatt*. He published numerous studies of Beethoven, Mozart, and Bruckner. His memoirs, *Fünfzig Jahre Wiener Musikleben: Erinnerungen eines Musikkritikers*, were publ. in 101 successive issues of the magazine *Der Merker* (1915–20). In 1977 they were brought out in 1 vol. by Max Schönherr (see Bibliography).

[94] However, wrote Helm, one could easily find them in the score, since it had already been publ.
[95] *Hamlet*, III ii. 390–400.

received since the heading 'Titan'[96] had led people to expect a heroic work, there was a complete misunderstanding. Robert Hirschfeld,[97] in the *Wiener Abendpost*, affected to believe that Mahler had not intended anyone to take him seriously. In his opinion, it was quite normal that such a versatile artist should have wanted to compose a 'satire on the symphony', parodying 'inspiration' and making fun of those who 'fill up reams of music paper until the spark of inspiration begins to burn'. He had therefore lined up a host of reminiscences. In his third movement, he had ridiculed heroic funeral marches. In such a context, one could not take anything seriously, even the beautiful melody of the Finale. With its 'formless' themes, the first movement had 'no organic development', and even the crescendos were quite unwarranted; the whole was arranged like a 'shop-window', with burlesque counterpoints added to totally unrelated themes and countermelodies.[98] In the Finale, with its clamour of vulgar themes, Hirschfeld saw only a 'satire on the overwhelming conceit of powerful modern geniuses'. Even Mahler's orchestration was a caricature, for it aspired only to having the instruments play in an unnatural manner and in unaccustomed registers. The harmonics of the Introduction suggested no more than the creaking of a door, and could hardly have constituted a more effective mockery of the 'modern search for originality'. Although certain passages of the symphony were 'marvellous and intoxicating', the piece as a whole proved that the 'physical or material' aspect of a work and a composer's craftsmanship were of little importance in comparison with the content of the music.

While Hirschfeld pretended to believe that Mahler was joking, Max Kalbeck[99] credited him with the noblest of intentions. Mahler's sarcasm seemed to him to be of a 'tragic nature', because there could be no doubt about his sincerity. In his article 'Gustav Mahler's Sinfonia Ironica', he points out that even if the work had been a total failure, the regenerator of the Vienna Opera

---

[96] Josef Bohuslav Förster, 'Gustav Mahler in Hamburg', *Prager Presse*, 8 (21 May 1922). Förster observes that no one had previously composed an entire movement in parody style. It is true that even Berlioz in the *Symphonie fantastique* treats only one theme, or at most one episode, in this style.

[97] Robert Hirschfeld (1858–1914) was born in Moravia to a rabbinical family. He began his student years in Breslau and completed them in Vienna, attending both the Conservatory and the Univ. With a doctorate in music, he was appointed Professor of Aesthetics at the Conservatory in 1884. In 1896 he replaced Hans Paumgartner (Rosa Papier's husband) on the *Wiener Zeitung* (founded in 1813) and from then wrote regular 'feuilletons' in the evening edn. of the paper, the *Wiener Abendpost*. Giving up his chair at the Conservatory in 1899, he devoted himself entirely to music criticism and to organizing concerts of early music. In 1913 he became director of the Salzburg Mozarteum, and began a long collaboration with Richard von Perger on a history of the Gesellschaft der Musikfreunde which was not published until 1912. He made versions of three operas, Schubert's *Der vierjährige Posten*, Mozart's *Zaide*, and Haydn's *Lo speziale* (*Der Apotheker*).

[98] Hirschfeld also jeered at Mahler's use of the omnipresent 'fourth' motif, intended to suggest the cuckoo, while the real bird 'sings only minor thirds'.

[99] See above, Chap. 1, Max Kalbeck's biography. The newspaper whose music coverage he shared with Ludwig Karpath, *Neues Wiener Tagblatt* (founded in 1867), was, like *Neue Freie Presse*, democratic and liberal. Kalbeck, like Hanslick, tended to the conservative, even reactionary. He admired Mahler as a conductor and administrator far more than as a composer, and had always been more or less hostile to Wagner and Bruckner.

deserved more respect than the public had shown him.[100] Kalbeck was greatly impressed with certain aspects but did not consider it to be 'a chef-d'œuvre of absolute music'. Clearly, his symphony had not stood the test of appearing without a commentary or a programme. Despite the beauty of certain details, it was the work of a young man still imbued with the extravaganzas of Berlioz and Liszt, by no means a 'masterpiece of pure music'. In Kalbeck's opinion, only two genres were open to symphonic music, the idyllic and the heroic, perfectly represented in Beethoven's 'Pastoral' and 'Eroica' Symphonies. Mahler had endeavoured to unite them with the help of an element alien to pure music, namely irony. This element, however, had no place in music, except in combination with the word, for 'the noblest of the arts', that of sound, cannot 'say the opposite of that which it means'. The 'corrosive harshness of irony' sufficed to explain the fragmentary character of the first and last movements of the First Symphony, for Mahler had not managed to protect its broad and stately form from this rupture. Drawn from Callot and Hoffmann, he went on, Mahler's tragi-comic effects were incomprehensible without a programme. Moreover, his fertile imagination had led him to create innumerable small motifs that might have formed the substance of a new Scherzo or Adagio. Far from being worthless, the first movement and the Finale contained many excellent ideas. However, the composer's efforts to depict the crises and convulsions of the human soul were merely an indiscretion of youth, just as his fondness for popular songs partially explained the lack of thematic development indispensable to any symphony worth the name. As for his orchestration, it was incomparable and deserved a thorough study. The Symphony was a veritable summary of the laws of instrumentation, its effects having been prepared with supreme skill 'for the greater enjoyment and, also, terror of the audience'.[101] It is strange to see an intelligent and lucid critic here discovering, one by one, some of the 'clues' to Mahler's music, without in any way understanding its essential nature, bound, as he is, by a servile attachment to the past and to 'laws' which great artists owe it to themselves to transcend.

The idea of irony dominated all accounts of the Viennese première of the First Symphony. Even Karl Kraus made it the leitmotif of one of his more sarcastic paragraphs:

Last Sunday, at the performance of Gustav Mahler's 'Sinfonia ironica' (in D major), Mahler-friends and Mahler-foes fought a furious battle. A music-lover has told me how it began. The third movement of the symphony wantonly parodies a funeral march. Adepts of music understood the parody and began to laugh. Thereupon, tremendous annoyance among Herr Mahler's friends, who were of the opinion that it was not proper

---

[100] But Mahler need not feel offended, Kalbeck added, for Brahms's Fourth Symphony had been no better received.

[101] As with Bruckner, Kalbeck preferred the inner movements to the others. He thought however, that the 'Bacchic' Scherzo, alluding to the *Freischütz* waltz, might be 'even more enchanting' in the theatre, as a ballet, than in the concert hall. As for the Funeral March, the parodic melody in thirds of the first Trio moved him so much that he was inclined to forget that it was parodic.

to laugh at a funeral march. The Mahler-friends therefore tried to hiss the laughers into silence. This, however, was too much for the Mahler-foes. Wanting to show that they refused to accept Herr Mahler's funeral march as serious music, they also laughed to deride Herr Mahler. Mockers and admirers of the composer fought bravely on. But the music-lovers who had been the first to laugh did not laugh long. In the noise of battle the amusing sounds from the orchestra could no longer be heard.[102]

The *Neue Musik-Zeitung* described the 'scandal' of the First in the most contemptuous manner, though without the bite of Karl Kraus:

If this difficult, complicated work is to be taken as a parody, the joke is too long and laborious. What is Berlioz, what is Richard Strauss, compared with Gustav Mahler? Timid beginners, not of the right stuff. Above the wild waves of strange, disorientating, utterly new sound mixtures, above the hellish noises—each instrument being required to do what it is least capable of—rise melodic passages that are sweetly attractive, and well-known themes, a waltz from *Der Freischütz*, the round *Frère Jacques*. Gustav Mahler's contrapuntal art is quite astounding, and how furiously he misuses it! Different at any price. The cuckoo is not permitted to call in minor thirds. It is condemned to fourths. The whole score is filled with fourths, and for 50 bars all the strings, with cellos and basses, divided, incidentally, into three parts, hold . . . a wretched harmonic on A. The horns are expressly required to stand up to produce the loudest possible sound, 'Bell in the air', says the score. The strings on the violins are played *col legno*. Not a single instrument sounds as it actually should . . .

The Viennese critics had never before shown such unanimity in their condemnation of Mahler. That evening he dined at Henriette Mankiewicz's with Justi, Natalie, and Rosé and, when asked to sign an autograph fan, scribbled the words: 'Der ausgepfiffene Gustav Mahler' (Gustav Mahler—the man they booed off). Earlier that evening he had attended Liszt's *Die Legende von der heiligen Elisabeth*,[103] whose 'religious tranquillity' had seemed like a 'balm and a veritable blessing' after his own thorny and impassioned work.[104] But the charm of Liszt's *Elisabeth* did not soothe Mahler for long, and he vented his resentment against Vienna, which had once more received his music so badly. He would really have liked to escape from it for a while. He felt particularly bitter about the attitude of the members of the orchestra, who, better than anyone else, would have been able to understand his work. But they had deserted him and indeed rejoiced at the fiasco: at the end of the Symphony the musicians had simply left the stage, smiling contemptuously without waiting for him, while in Berlin and elsewhere they had always stood by him and his work, applauding with their bows.

---

[102] *Die Fackel* (Nov. 1900).

[103] It was performed each year at the Hofoper on the anniversary of Empress Elisabeth's assassination. The title-role on 19 Nov. was sung by the Munich soprano Agnes Stavenhagen, who had just participated in the Munich performance of Mahler's Second Symphony (NBLS).

[104] 'This work needs the support of the stage,' he said of the Liszt oratorio to Natalie a year later (NBL1. 175; NBL2. 201, 19 Nov. 1901).

A few days later, at the first rehearsal of the next concert, Mahler, without intending to do so, unburdened himself in an improvised speech: 'I did not face the orchestra like a man offended and wounded in his pride, but like a general abandoned and sacrificed by his soldiers,' he later told Natalie. No artistic collaboration was possible, he had said, unless the air was cleared between the leader and his troops. That was why he was greatly concerned about their relationship, which could only be based on mutual affection or break down altogether. He had often shown his devotion to them, not only as their conductor but also as a man and as their friend, and he had proved it by intervening on their behalf and looking after their interests. They, on the other hand, did not like him and intrigued and rebelled against him whenever they could. If he had believed they would go along with him artistically, he had been disillusioned again and again. The behaviour of the audience after the performance of his First Symphony had again shaken their confidence in him. He was the last to be surprised or angry, he continued, when people failed to enjoy one of his works at first hearing. They had let themselves be influenced by the audience, and this he had found all the more regrettable since it was only during the first rehearsal that they had found the work shocking and bewildering. Thereafter, they had come to understand it, and eventually even acknowledged that they had been utterly carried away by it. But they had forgotten all that the moment they saw the audience and the critics turn against him.

He knew perfectly well, as everybody did, that 'You, Herr Kretschmann,'[105] (the cellist opened his eyes wide with astonishment at being thus addressed personally)

have asked, at a recent session of the Philharmonic committee, who had given Herr Mahler the right to include his symphony in the programme. The answer, which I've no desire to hide from you, is that I and I alone *assumed* the right. For there is a right I reserve to myself in all circumstances: the right to draw up programmes alone and exactly as I wish. If that's not compatible with the democratic constitution of your association, which I find extremely congenial in other respects, tell me so frankly and I shall resign at once.[106]

Behind the stunned and leaden silence in which his speech was received, Mahler sensed the musicians' suppressed irritation. He began to rehearse, thinking of his own Lied, 'Des Antonius von Padua Fischpredigt'. No doubt he cursed himself afterwards for having thus futilely unburdened his heart to men who feared but did not like him, and who would later be only too ready to forget all that they owed him.

The first Philharmonic Concert of the 1900–1 season had taken place on 4 November, two weeks before the Vienna premiere of his First Symphony. Mahler had begun it with Berlioz's Rob Roy Overture, an early work and new to Vienna.

---

[105] This was the cellist Theobald Kretschmann, Mahler's sworn enemy and the author of several volumes of memoirs (*Tempi passati*, etc.).

[106] NBLS, Nov. 1900.

Helm had called it an 'interesting curiosity', Hanslick 'the barren and clumsy work of a dilettante', and Kalbeck had felt that Berlioz would have done better to destroy it. Once again, the highlight of the concert was Beethoven's 'Eroica' Symphony. This time Mahler decided to make an example of those Viennese who wanted to leave for lunch at the beginning of the Finale by lengthening the fermata which precedes the main theme. His furious glances, and the mutterings of the rest of the audience, forced those who had stood up to sit down again. Once again Helm complained about some of his tempos, in particular the slowness of the Scherzo and Trio, and about the 'instrumental retouching and the excessive reinforcement of the brass in the Finale'.[107] As for Wagner's *Eine Faust-Ouvertüre* which completed the programme, Kalbeck considered that Mahler had done his best to lend interest to a work which had none, except for historical reasons. Hirschfeld, deliberately ambiguous, declared that Mahler had magnificently realized his 'heroic fantasies' (*Eroica Phantasien*). As far as the *Neue Musikalische Presse* was concerned, Mahler had 'translated the Beethoven symphonies into Turkish', the changes he had introduced being 'more terrifying than impressive'.[108]

Faithful once again to the land of his youth, Bohemia, Mahler included in the programme of the third Philharmonic Concert two works by Smetana, *Vltava* and the Prelude to *Libuše*. He thought it a pity that the opera was not up to the standard of its Prelude, and resolved to revise it some day, as he had *Dalibor*, so that it would be able to hold the stage.[109] Unlike Mahler, Kalbeck felt that the Prelude to *Libuše* cut a sorry figure at the concert and contained 'too much din and not enough symphonic development', an opinion that Hanslick shared. *Vltava*, on the other hand, won everyone's approval. Hanslick found Smetana's talent not only 'genuine and brilliant' in this piece, but also entirely original, despite the influence of Liszt; while Kalbeck praised the warmth of the melodies and the beauty of the music. Although the critics' hostility usually left him cold, after the concert Mahler was upset that his rendering of the second *Leonore* Overture[110] and of Beethoven in general[111] had again provoked their anger. The previous neglect of this Overture seemed to him to be thoroughly unjust, and he had devoted 'as much time to it as I do to a whole Beethoven symphony, until it was what I wanted it to be and what it is'. Hanslick

---

[107] According to Hans Geissler, correspondent of *Neue Musikalische Presse*, Mahler repeatedly made them play with their bells in the air.

[108] For Hans Geissler, the performance of the first two movements of the 'Eroica' was 'one of Mahler's most accomplished feats', but the slowness of the Scherzo seemed 'unforgivable'.

[109] In a letter of 13 Sept. 1899, to František Adolf Šubert, the director of the Czech Theatre in Prague, Mahler wrote that he intended to put on three Russian operas at the Hofoper: Dargomizhsky's *Rusalka*, Glinka's *Ruslan and Ludmilla*, and Rimsky-Korsakov's *May Night*. On 7 May of that year he had already sent Šubert a telegram concerning *Libuše* since he had hoped to be able to attend a performance of it at the Prague Opera.

[110] The second item on the programme, 2 Dec. 1900, between Bach's Concerto in D minor and Franck's *Variations symphoniques*. The concert ended with Smetana's two works.

[111] Kalbeck was alone in claiming that, in this overture, Mahler had 'taken the orchestra into a long and marvellous dramatic recitation that kept the audience spellbound'.

reproached him with his 'inaudible pianissimos' and 'long oratorical pauses',[112] which he considered too subtle.

Natalie wrote that Mahler had been criticized for

a performance that was too fussy (*tüftelig*) and laborious (*peinlich*) (which implied that it was petty (*kleinlich*)). As a result 'grand outline' and 'free impetus' had suffered (for these great minds!). Hanslick could not understand why it is necessary to hear all these details and finer points—and it is a leading critic and music journalist who dared to write that! As if here, as in all art or science, awareness, clarity and lucidity were not indispensable! The underlying spirit, which can only reveal itself through clearly heard forms, must obviously remain forever hidden from them. And so must all that is spiritual, incommensurable, in the interpreter, the re-creator himself—particularly a great one. In him they will see only intelligence and clarity, nothing else, never his genius![113]

An unusual feature of the third concert was the presence of a soloist, the pianist Carl Friedberg,[114] who played Bach's Concerto in D Minor and the Vienna première of César Franck's *Variations symphoniques*. Kalbeck summarily dismissed Bach's concerto 'as an arrangement of a lost violin concerto' and said that he supposed the soloist 'bore this cross in order to obtain forgiveness for his sins as a virtuoso as well as for those of other pianists',[115] a judgement that, coming from the pen of so conservative a critic, was somewhat surprising, to say the least. Franck's *Variations symphoniques* were given a good reception. Helm considered them 'very interesting' and, like Hanslick, preferred them to *Les Béatitudes*. He later called them not only 'extremely interesting and ambitious', but also 'beautifully written and orchestrated'. Kalbeck admired the 'piquant, never importunate' orchestration and the 'tender, affectionate' treatment of the piano.

To commemorate the 130th anniversary of Beethoven's birth, Mahler, on 16 December, conducted a Beethoven Festival concert that included the Coriolan Overture and the First and Fourth Symphonies. During the rehearsals he was entranced with the beauty of the First Symphony, in which he saw a 'supremely accomplished Haydn', and envied Beethoven for having been able thus to adopt a style familiar to his contemporaries, to whom 'his future, fully formed personality would have seemed incomprehensible and mad, as indeed it did when he produced his Fourth Symphony'.[116] Kalbeck was completely won over

[112] The quotation from Hanslick figures in NBLS, and its accuracy shows that Mahler read criticisms far more attentively than he would usually admit.

[113] NBLS, Nov. 1900.

[114] Carl Friedberg (1872–1955), born in Bingen am Rhein, a pupil of Clara Schumann at the Frankfurt Hochschule and Heidelberg Univ., had begun his career as a piano virtuoso before the turn of the century. He taught at the Frankfurt (1893–1904) and Cologne Conservatory (1904–14) and spent several years in the USA. Thereafter, he became assistant conductor to Eugène Ysaÿe in Brussels, returning to the USA in 1923 to teach at the New York Institute of Musical Art and at the Juilliard School. Elly Ney and Percy Grainger were among his pupils. He later formed a trio with Karl Flesch and Hugo Becker.

[115] In Hanslick's opinion, the work had been badly served by an overlarge string orchestra.

[116] NBL1. 152; NBL2. 178ff.

by the performance of Coriolan: Mahler had 'brought out the contrasts sharply and convincingly, and stirred the heart with the tragic greatness of the hero, who died fighting gods and men'.[117] Kalbeck also acknowledged that where Mahler departed from tradition, he did so deliberately, and that in general he showed a more scrupulous respect for the composer's markings than most other conductors, even underlining them so that they would not escape the notice of the players.

Towards the end of 1900, Mahler's health began to give cause for alarm. The nervous energy he expended on operas and concerts brought back his headaches and stomach-aches and caused a recurrence of his 'subterranean troubles'. Although these danger signals should have made him wary, he insisted upon conducting the entire *Ring* cycle himself before Christmas. This was a great success, all the more remarkable because of the inauspicious moment at which it was given—the beginning of the holidays, when, as a rule, the Viennese public had neither the money nor the time to attend. Afterwards, instead of taking a few days' holiday to recover his health, he busied himself with putting the finishing touches to his Fourth Symphony, which he wanted to hand over to his publisher Doblinger at the beginning of the new year. He therefore gave up the excursions he had planned, but was soon to regret having overtaxed his reserves of energy.

[117] Kalbeck questioned the 'staccato' style of the introduction to the Finale of the First Symphony, resulting from Mahler's 'insertion of short breaths between the different fragments of the theme'. He also objected to the fast tempo in the Finale of the Fourth. This had made it impossible for the bassoons to play the principal theme at the restatement, and he wondered whether Mahler had sought to create a comic effect in the belief that was Beethoveen's intention. *Neue Zeitschrift* criticized the slowness of the Andante and the speed of the Finale in the First Symphony.

10

Première of *Das Klagende Lied*—illness and operation—resignation from the Philharmonic— the Fifth Symphony and the Rückert-Lieder

(January–August 1901)

> It's not just a question of scaling an unknown peak,
> but of plotting, step by step, a path up to it.

DURING the Christmas holidays, Mahler worked two hours every morning and evening to revise the score of the Fourth Symphony, which Doblinger planned to publish, together with 'Revelge', before the première in Munich in November. He told Natalie that he had, with great difficulty, restored the original version of the Scherzo, i.e. as he had drafted it eighteen months earlier at Alt-Aussee. At that time it had been much longer and had ended in a tarantella. 'Again and again I realize,' he said, 'that the first intention, the first draft is the only right and usable one.' As he went through his work he was struck by the relatively modest means he had used in the Fourth as compared with his previous symphonies, and he likened the sound of the Scherzo to 'spider's webs, or one of those woollen shawls so delicately worked that you can fold them into a nutshell, or if you unfold them they stretch endlessly and show the most wonderful design knitted with thread as fine as hair'.[1] He made some changes to the violin solo, and decided that the violin should be tuned a whole tone higher than usual, so that 'it will have a harsh and shrill sound, as though Death were playing it'. He also altered 'the disposition of the various instrumental voices', for during the interval between Aussee and Maiernigg everything had grown and swollen 'like ganglions on a limb'.[2] 'Could you believe', he said to Natalie the following year, 'I had far more trouble orchestrating the theme of the first movement, which is of childish simplicity and utterly instinc-

---

[1] NBL1. 153; NBL2. 179.
[2] Ibid. The AFC (see Catalogue) of the Scherzo was completed on 5 Jan. 1901.

tive, than if it had been the most complex polyphony. In fact it's strange; I have
never been able to think of music otherwise than in terms of polyphony.' With
the apparent inconsistency that was typical of him, he concluded: 'Nevertheless, in this passage I probably miss counterpoint—orthodox counterpoint (*der
reiner Satz*) which, for any pupil who has practised it, would automatically take
over.' He also emphasized the 'unassuming' entrance of the theme, describing
it as being 'like dewdrops lying on a flower before sunrise, which burst into a
thousand lights and colours with the first ray of sunshine and sparkle in a sea
of radiance'.[3]

At the Opera, Mahler continued his renovation of the Wagner productions.
After the complete *Ring* of 1898,[4] the uncut *Tristan* of 29 October 1898[5] was
followed by an uncut *Lohengrin* on 27 December 1900. On this occasion,
some critics again found his veneration for Wagner excessive, but the public
applauded enthusiastically, the work still being one of the most popular
of Wagner's operas. Before the new production of *Tannhäuser*, which was
to take place in May, Mahler decided to revive Wagner's first operatic success,
Rienzi. First performed at the Hofoper in 1871, the work had not been
seen there since 1891. As usual, Mahler threw himself into his task, working
as though he were reviving one of the greatest works in the repertory.
Indeed, he felt that *Rienzi* had been unjustly neglected and that, 'if you
look at it as grand opera, the genre to which it belongs, it's hard to imagine
anything more effective. What [dramatic] power it has!'[6] Wagner himself,
conscious that *Rienzi* was too long, had made a shorter version for the Bayreuth
festival, but Mahler, after studying this, decided that it was 'inadequate,
. . . contrary to the musical sense', and prepared a version of his own, reducing
the length to three and a half hours, which he found quite sufficient for
the substance.

While hoping that the new production of *Rienzi* would be successful, he had
few illusions on the subject: 'Certain works badly performed always draw a
crowd, whereas others, which are unquestionably masterpieces, fail to attract
the public even when staged to perfection.' Carried away by his enthusiasm for
this labour of re-creation, he dumbfounded one of the Viennese critics by
asking 'whether he didn't agree that *Rienzi* was Wagner's most beautiful opera

³ NBL1. 154; NBL2. 179.

⁴ The complete cycle continued to be given at regular intervals through 1900–1 and the following seasons,
with occasional changes in the casting. In *Rheingold*, Mayr and Frauscher replaced Grengg and Reichenberg
as the two giants, and Förster-Lauterer took over from Forster as Freia. Kurz replaced Hilgermann as
Sieglinde, while Fricka in *Walküre* passed to Hilgermann from Walker. Sedlmair and Mildenburg alternated
as Brünnhilde in *Siegfried* (where Schmedes retained the title-role), while Weidemann followed Demuth as
Der Wanderer. In *Götterdämmerung*, Schmedes and Winkelmann shared Siegfried, Förster-Lauterer took
over Gutrune from Gutheil-Schoder, Mayr replaced Frauscher and Grengg as Hagen, and Weidemann
followed Demuth (Gunther).

⁵ See above, Chap. 4. Pending the new staging of Feb. 1903, the work was regularly performed as it was
on 5 Jan. 1901, with the following cast, subject to a few variations: Winkelmann (Tristan), Frauscher (Marke),
Mildenburg (Isolde), Stehmann (Kurwenal), Pacal (Melot), Hilgermann (Brangäne).

⁶ NBLS, Jan. 1901.

and the greatest musical drama ever composed'.[7] The unidentified critic may have been Schönaich for, according to Max Graf, he had long since noticed this peculiar trait in Mahler's character: 'I'll tell you what your enthusiasm reminds me of,' he said to Mahler one day in the Café Impérial, *'foie gras'*. Mahler asked him what he meant, and Schönaich replied, 'Because geese are force-fed until they develop a liver disease which produces the succulent foie gras. You, when you prepare a new production, stuff yourself with enthusiasm and this results in a marvellous performance.' Thereafter, when staging an opera that required a great deal of effort, Mahler would often announce, 'the foie gras will soon be ready', and later on, when the critics began to attack each of his innovations, *'die Herren Vorgesetzten* once again consider it a liver disease. . . . But we think the foie gras will be excellent!'[8]

Casting *Rienzi* presented knotty problems, in particular because of the high tessitura of the two principal roles. To facilitate the task of the two leads, Winkelmann[9] and Mildenburg, Mahler gave some of their high notes to the tenor Franz Pacal and the soprano Elise Elizza, whom he hid among the choristers. At the same time, he prepared alternative casts so that the opera would have a longer run.[10] Only one story of the rehearsal has come down to us (apart from Mahler's Machiavellian suggestion to Schmedes that he go on stage mounted on his own horse, thus causing panic in the chorus).[11] Hermann Riedel, a trumpeter engaged by the Hofoper in 1894 as a 'stage musician' (*Bühnenmusiker*), was given the task, in the first act, of playing the sustained A which was to be the Roman people's signal for revolt. Mahler asked the *Bühnen* (stage) Kapellmeister Anton Wunderer to have the trumpeter hold the note as long as his breath would permit, swelling it before letting it die away. The fateful moment arrived. There was silence on the stage, and in the wings the trumpet began its A. After half a minute, the note still not having increased in volume, Mahler called to Wunderer: 'What's happened to the crescendo?'—'It's coming, Herr Direktor, please be patient.' Another quarter of a minute, then a half, and still there was no crescendo. Finally, after about a minute, the sound of the instrument rose imperceptibly to a mezzo forte, to a forte, then to a superb fortissimo, before dying away little by little to a barely audible pianissimo. 'Not bad,' said Mahler, 'not bad, but that wasn't one trumpeter, one man can't breathe that long, it was three or four of them behind the scenes taking turns!' When Wunderer assured him that it had been Riedel on his own, Mahler, refusing to believe it, asked the trumpeter to repeat his exploit on stage, in his presence. So the trumpeter, who had formerly been with the Royal and Imperial Military band, stood in front of the prompter's box and played his A again, in

[7] See EDS2. 147. In GWO 79, Max Graf asserts that it was he who was asked this extraordinary question.

[8] Max Graf, *Neues Wiener Journal* (26 June 1921) and GWO 79. Mahler often referred to the critics as 'Die Herren Vorgesetzten' (the bosses).

[9] Schmedes replaced him on the opening night.

[10] NBLS.   [11] See above, Chap. 9.

the presence of the stupefied singers, chorus, and orchestra. Mahler, who timed the note and found that Riedel had held it for two minutes, presented him with a silver coin from his pocket and ordered him to be present every time *Rienzi* was performed.[12]

A few days before the première, which was to take place on 21 January, Mahler had to stay in bed with an acute inflammation of the throat and a high temperature and, with great reluctance, had to entrust the final rehearsals to one of his assistants. From his sickbed, he demanded detailed progress reports by telephone and continued to dispense orders and instructions. On the day of the première, although his tonsils were still swollen, he insisted upon conducting the performance himself in spite of Justi's and Natalie's protests. The entire day was fraught with difficulties of every description. It had initially been intended that Erik Schmedes should sing the première of the new production and Hermann Winkelmann the second performance. But this had angered the *Hermann-Bündler* (Winkelmann fans), who had threatened to demonstrate if their hero was not given the première. Schmedes had therefore agreed with Mahler that he would take the second performance. But now Winkelmann, who had sung at the dress rehearsal, fell ill towards the end of the morning. People searched everywhere for Schmedes to tell him he would have to take the role, but failed to find him. He later recalled how he had been taking a Turkish bath that morning when he had suddenly heard a great noise in the reception office: it was Mahler who had finally found out where he was and had come to break the news to him. The unfortunate Schmedes, very distressed, reminded Mahler of a threatening letter he had received, but Mahler was adamant, refusing to postpone the première. Early in the afternoon he declared that he had caught cold coming out of the steam-bath and would not be able to sing. In fact it was a case of stage fright, and Schmedes burst into tears when Mahler insisted he must sing. Mahler learnt of this while taking a short rest in the middle of his exhausting day. He immediately wrote Schmedes a long letter which had the desired effect,[13] for finally he sang, 'and sang very well'. Two letters in the Opera archives support Natalie's account of these events. In the first, the tenor announces that he is 'terribly agitated' and fears that 'the state of my voice will not permit me to sing tonight'. The second, written by his wife Marie, is doubtless a reply to Mahler's letter. She informs him that Schmedes had gone to bed to calm himself, and that despite everything he would sing, 'to help the Herr Direktor out of the difficulty he is in'.[14]

Hardly had this problem been overcome when another one arose. This time it was Mildenburg who, on the morning of the première, developed a fever that

---

[12] See *Wiener Monatshefte* (Jan. 1958), 15: 'Der lange Atem: Eine heitere Erinnerung', by Rudolf von Eichtal.

[13] Mahler's letters to Schmedes have apparently disappeared. The tenor's daughter, Dagmar, believed they had been sold or lost by his second wife.

[14] HOA, Präs, 22 Jan. 1901.

may also have been no more than a fit of nerves; fortunately, she recovered at the last moment, but Jenny Pohlner had to take over the part of the Messenger of Peace from Michalek, who dropped out at the very last moment. Although the task of preparing an alternative cast had demanded a considerable amount of extra effort and filled the rehearsal rooms from morning to evening during the final weeks, Mahler thought that the quality of the result had made it worthwhile. His influence was manifest throughout the performance; the singers and the chorus acted 'with complete naturalness', and Brioschi's costumes and sets, for which Mahler had had an uphill struggle to obtain the necessary funds, contributed to the success of the evening, which was assured from the end of the Overture. Schmedes, not fully recovered from his attack of stage fright, did not sing full voice during the first two acts, but let himself go in the final one, realizing that the threatened 'scandal' had not taken place and that he was already being vigorously applauded.[15] Far from rejoicing at such a revival, the majority of the critics devoted the greater part of their articles to enumerating the weakness in this 'early work',[16] weakness which Wagner himself had recognized and which, they said, made the opera unworthy of so much effort. Some objected to the restoration of the cuts, others to the casting of certain parts. Schmedes was particularly badly treated.

'As if that bunch of idiots knew the first thing about it', exclaimed Mahler

and could presume to quote (and in fact misquote) what Wagner said on this subject at a time when his genius had developed towards further and higher spheres. It is as if a lofty, creative, fulfilled spirit, about to shuffle off its mortal coil, had referred to it as 'a corpse', and then a few wretched little human lice, who are nothing and have done nothing, come along and dare to use his own words against him![17]

Thus Mahler reaffirmed his admiration for a work that, despite its inadequacies and imperfections, heralded Wagner's future greatness. Moreover, he was confident that the derogatory comments of the press would do it no harm, and he was right, for *Rienzi* was performed eight times in 1901 and several times each season up until 1918.

Indeed, the Viennese press was almost unanimously opposed to the revival. Hanslick wondered why Mahler had gone to so much trouble, considering that the 1871 and 1872 productions had shown that '*Rienzi* was of no more than biographical interest'. No opera director alive would have agreed to give it if he had not known its composer's name. Everything in it was contrary to Wagner's mature style and the interminable score only deafened and exhausted the

---

[15] 'Die Dinge der Vergangenheit, Lebenserinnerungen von Kammersänger Erik Schmedes', ed. H. Hergeth, *Sonntags-Beilage* of the *Neues Wiener Tagblatt*, 5 (21 June 1931).

[16] Hanslick claimed that the score of *Rienzi* represented the triumph of 'melodic song' furnished with a noisy, symmetrical orchestral accompaniment; of 'modulation without mystery'; and of traditional form. He regarded it as the collective work of Spontini, Donizetti, Meyerbeer, Weber, and Marschner, rather than of Wagner.

[17] NBLS, Jan. 1901.

listeners.[18] The composer's victory lay only in the apathy and discomfiture of the audience, dismayed by all this banality, now clamorous, now sentimental.[19] Mahler had been the life and soul of the performance, sparing no pains to ensure its success, and the gigantic efforts had 'seemed to multiply his strength tenfold. . . . If Wagner had attended his performance,' Hanslick concluded, 'how he would have rejoiced . . . no, how irritated he would have been, he who strove for thirty years to live down *Rienzi*'.

Helm, in a long article in the *Musikalisches Wochenblatt*, condemned the negative attitude of Hanslick, who had been seen leaving his box at the end of the second act and who had 'plagiarized himself' by repeating word for word his review of 1871. He had proved once and for all the 'frivolity' of his judgement. Helm congratulated Mahler on having restored many items from the original version, and in particular the funeral chorus of the Roman nobles, which had 'intensified and deepened the dramatic significance of the work'. In the *Deutsche Zeitung*, shortly after the première, the same critic nevertheless recognized that, despite its moments of beauty the score was 'pompous', full of hollow and vulgar passages, and that the performance had perhaps been too complete. But Helm's objective and moderate comments were not echoed by any of the other Viennese critics. Kalbeck, like Hanslick, considered that, in *Rienzi*, Wagner had wanted to surpass Meyerbeer, his rival of the time, but had failed even to equal him. There were too many gaps and too few new works in the Vienna Opera's repertoire for so much money and effort to have been devoted to an exhumation of this sort, even if the public, which always loved a spectacle,[20] had greeted it warmly. Hirschfeld approved the restoration of passages previously cut, and felt that this had improved the work. But Mahler's conducting did not convince him: certainly he had 'commanded his artistic troops with genius', but his phrasing and tempos had 'lacked naturalness'.[21]

A few days after the première of *Rienzi*, Mahler heard news of an event that must genuinely have affected him. This was the death, on 27 January, of a composer for whom he had many times expressed an almost affectionate veneration, though they had never been in direct contact: Giuseppe Verdi.[22] At the end of April, two performances of the Requiem were conducted ('somewhat complacently', thought Theodor Helm) in honour of his memory by Pietro Mascagni, with the great hall of the Musikverein draped in black for the occasion. Part of the profit was donated to the foundation Verdi had provided for in his will. Mahler probably attended one of the performances. He invited

---

[18] According to Hanslick, no important item was missing from Mahler's version, except perhaps a women's pantomime scene (in the Finale of Act II).

[19] Of the cast, Hanslick praised Schmedes and Mildenburg highly, but found Walker 'correct, but cold' in the role of Adriano.

[20] Kalbeck claimed there had been as many as 400 people on the stage.

[21] The first performance, on 21 Jan., a benefit for the Opera pension fund, took place with the following cast: Pohlner (Messenger), Mildenburg (Irene), Walker (Adriano), Schmedes (Rienzi), Neidl (Orsini), Breuer (Baroncelli), Felix (Cecco) Hesch (Cardinal), Reichenberg (Colonna).

[22] See above, Chap. 8, an account of Mahler's conversation with Umberto Giordano about Verdi in 1900.

Mascagni to conduct a performance of *Cavalleria rusticana* at the Opera, although he had not retained the fervent admiration he had once felt for its composer.[23]

A few lines in Natalie's notebooks show that, despite his constantly over-burdened schedule as conductor and administrator, Mahler had not lost his interest in chamber music, which in Hamburg had been one of his favourite entertainments. At the beginning of January he attended a rehearsal of the Soldat-Roeger Quartet, of which Natalie was a member. Beethoven's Trio in E flat, Op. 70 No. 2,[24] and Brahms's A minor Quartet were on the programme. For the first movement of the latter, Mahler recommended a 'broad, comfortable tempo, like the outline of Brahms himself'. Once again he was delighted to hear 'chamber music' in the intimate framework for which it was intended. He claimed that 'chamber music concerts in [large] halls are a decadent practice of our times, and I never enjoy them in the slightest'.[25]

At the beginning of 1901, Mahler eagerly resumed his work with the Vienna Philharmonic. On 13 January, in the first concert of the year, he conducted Mendelssohn's Scottish Symphony. Hanslick found his performance 'exquisite',[26] while Helm considered it inferior to Richter's.[27] The chief event of this concert was the first Viennese performance of Tchaikovsky's *Manfred*,[28] which Mahler rehearsed with the greatest care, going so far as to note metronome markings, and their changes within the movements, on the score.[29] Although today the issue of programme music no longer seems of vital importance, the music critics of Mahler's time were obsessed by it. Hanslick claimed that Tchaikovsky's other symphonic works captivated listeners thanks to the 'musical charm and simplicity of feeling' which disguised their weaknesses. The score of *Manfred*, on the other hand, seemed to him 'nebulous, unhealthy, psychologically overexcited'. The composer, in his desire to describe the struggles and afflictions of his hero, wound up 'making the listener even more unhappy than he himself was'. Admittedly the 'Spirit of the Mountains'[30] had been well received by the public, but the final 'Infernal Bacchanale' had terminated the concert in 'the height of bad taste'. Even if the work was

---

[23] The performance took place on 1 May (THE 298).

[24] In this Trio, played by the violinist Marie Soldat, the pianist Marie Baumayer, and the cellist Lucy Herbert-Campbell, Mahler recommended that the Introduction be performed as calmly as possible, 'without a trace of expression' in the first bar, the expression appearing only with the trills.

[25] NBLS, 6 Jan. 1901.

[26] However, Hanslick found the tempo of the Introduction 'a little too moderate'. Josef Reitler, then 18 years old, recalls that he was struck by the violence of Mahler's sforzatos in the symphony's Adagio, generally played 'so sentimentally'. 'It was as if the ray of a giant spotlight had sprung up in the hall.' ('Ein jugendlicher Mahler-Enthusiast', unpubl. MS, p. 3. See below, Vol. iii, Chap. 6).

[27] Helm accused Mahler of having failed to respect Mendelssohn's indications that there should be no pauses between the movements.

[28] At the last moment Mahler dropped Weber's Chinese Overture, *Turandot*, from the programme, since it would have made the concert unduly long. He included it on a later occasion.

[29] Max Graf observed that he saw this score in Mahler's office at the Opera (GWO 84).

[30] Mahler had suppressed the headings on the score.

'brilliantly orchestrated', he concluded, one found oneself wondering, as with Berlioz, 'what it is that is being orchestrated'.

Helm, after criticizing the length of a programme composed of two symphonies, judged that the performance of *Manfred*, inspired by Mahler's 'fiery spirit', had been a 'minor miracle'. But the work was none the less 'programme music, ultramodern, revelling in dissonance and in gloom'. Hirschfeld, like him, considered that only the impetuous performance had lent a semblance of strength and depth to Tchaikovsky's symphonic poem, whose subject-matter eclipsed its form and made it 'monstrous and weakly constructed'. Finally, according to the *Neues Wiener Tagblatt*, Mahler had, by juxtaposing Mendelssohn and Tchaikovsky, shown 'the superiority of the symphonist's art to that of the symphonic poet'. Unfortunately, this lesson had been paid for by 'an hour of torture to the nerves'. The work was 'monstrous, incomprehensible with or without a programme, a compilation of insignificant phrases, badly constructed, boneless, trailing like worms'.

Though still not fully recovered from his tonsilitis, Mahler conducted Beethoven's Ninth Symphony, for the third time in Vienna, at the Nicolai Concert of 27 January. The public having once again fought for tickets, both the final rehearsal and the concert itself were played to full houses. As before, the atmosphere was electric throughout the performance, which was greeted with storms of applause.[31] For all that, the critics declared that they could not reverse their earlier verdict: Mahler had not conducted Beethoven, but rather 'his own version' of Beethoven, a version 'lacking calm and majesty'.[32] For Hirschfeld, this interpretation of the Ninth was no more than a 'curiosity'; with every performance it seemed to 'move further away from Beethoven and nearer to Mahler'. Its 'very nature' did not permit a 'balanced judgement'. Nor was there any point in trying to fit Mahler's complicated ways of thinking into any critical system. Even if he wanted to do things differently, he would not be able to. His analytical approach, which concentrated on individual elements of a work of art instead of combining them, could not relate to the greatness of the Ninth any more than to the pathos of the 'Eroica'. Kalbeck found the 'coarseness, harshness and inequalities' in Mahler's interpretation more glaring than ever and felt that they had 'chilled' the audience. Mahler would have done better to give up his 'version', but unfortunately he was one of those unquiet spirits who were always seeking to outdo themselves.[33] As in the previous year, Heuberger accused Mahler of conducting an 'arrangement' of Beethoven, even though he had not put his own name beside the composer's on the programme. Such a powerful poem gained nothing from being touched up, since by altering

[31] Nevertheless, the anonymous correspondent of the *Neue Zeitschrift* asserted that 'by altering the performance of the work in a manner alien to that of the composer', Mahler had left the public 'cold and hostile'.

[32] This is Mahler's own summing up of the critics' comments.

[33] Kalbeck thought that the tempo of the first movement should have been 'more majestic'. In the second movement, he found the main Adagio too slow, whereas the Andante episode had been too fast.

the colouring of a work one inevitably modified its essence. He felt that the applause had been noticeably cool after the early movements. Yet Heuberger and Kalbeck both conceded that technically the performance had been almost unsurpassable. Kalbeck declared, however, that the Finale had by no means achieved its usual dithyrambic effect, despite the exploits of all the performers.[34]

Thus, Mahler's 'version' was once more condemned as scandalous. During rehearsals for one of the three performances of the Ninth that he conducted in Vienna, Mahler remarked to the assembled musicians: 'Of course I don't improve or correct Beethoven, I simply double important passages, as does my friend Rosenthal.' One of the players reported this remark to the Philharmonic's former conductor, Hans Richter, now the revered director of the Manchester Concerts Association. When they next met, Richter accused Moriz Rosenthal, the great Viennese pianist, of not showing respect for Beethoven's scores. Rosenthal, in his reminiscences about Mahler, explains how the misunderstanding came about. Once, in Hamburg, he and Mahler had dined together at the Burgomaster's residence and afterwards the pianist had played Beethoven's Sonata Opus 111 and some Liszt pieces for the guests. As he finished, Mahler came up to him and whispered: 'I'm sorry you had to play for these coffee-bags [*Cafésäcke*] . . .'. He then raised his voice and complimented him on his playing of the Variations in the Beethoven Sonata, adding that, if he had had Rosenthal's technique, in his place he would have played all the thematic passages in the first movement in octaves, for such doublings 'simply clarify the composer's intentions'. Rosenthal had not the slightest intention of doing anything of the kind, but the idea that he might not take the advice into account never entered Mahler's mind; hence the remark he subsequently made in front of the orchestra and the scandalized reaction of Hans Richter, in whose eyes Mahler was an incorrigible 'corrector' of Beethoven's works.[35]

Of all the criticisms levelled at him, none hurt Mahler so much as the accusation that he lacked calm and could not do justice to Beethoven's grandeur:

Their verdict is based above all on the structure of the Adagio. Yet they haven't the slightest idea of what it means to build up an Adagio with such calm and unity! To

[34] Soloists for the concert of 27 Jan.: Elise Elizza, Karoline Kusmitsch, Franz Naval, Moritz Frauscher. Members of the Schubertbund chorus joined the Singakademie. The general rehearsal took place two days ealier at 3.00 p.m. with a different group of soloists: Hilgermann, Winkelmann, and Hesch (besides Elizza).

[35] Moriz Rosenthal, *Mahleriana*, quoted by Hans and Rosaleen Moldenhauer, 'Gustav Mahler und Moriz Rosenthal', in the magazine *Das Orchester* (Mainz, May 1982), 431. Moriz Rosenthal (1862–1946), born in Lemberg (Lvov), was the son of a professor at the Conservatory, and studied there from an early age with Karol Mikuli, himself a pupil of Chopin. When his family moved to Vienna in 1875, Rosenthal entered the Conservatory, studying with Julius Epstein and Rafaël Joseffy. He studied with Liszt in Weimar and Rome (1876–8). Later, he dropped music for a while and studied philosophy at the Vienna Univ. He became one of the greatest virtuosi of his time, making numerous visits to the USA, where he settled in 1938. According to his memoirs, Rosenthal met Mahler in 1888 through Julius Epstein, who had invited his former pupil to play his First Symphony for him and a few guests.

conduct it, even to wield the baton, you need a stillness in the hand, as if you were describing large circles with a spoon brimful of water without spilling a single drop.[36]

After being challenged as an interpreter, Mahler was to come under fire as a composer two weeks later. The Viennese publisher Josef Weinberger had just published the 'child of sorrow' he had composed in his twentieth year, *Das klagende Lied*, and this was to be given its first performance on 17 February 1901, at a 'special concert' of the Wiener Singakademie. Since the work presented considerable difficulties, Mahler having composed it at a time 'when I naïvely thought that the whole world would accept it and play it immediately', it required numerous rehearsals, the final one taking place before public and press on the afternoon of 16 February.[37] The Singakademie was far from being a good chorus, and Mahler had to contend not only with the technical difficulties inherent in the music, but also with the laziness and virulent anti-Semitism of its members and particularly the men, many of whom arrived late, in ones and twos, for the first rehearsal. He began to wonder whether he would not have done better to produce the work with the Opera chorus, but he was finally won over by the zeal and musical talent of the women singers, thanks to whom the rehearsals became a source of both human and artistic pleasure, and by the fact that almost all the singers turned up on time for the second rehearsal and did their very best to please him.

Mahler was struck by the surprising originality of this youthful work, which 'sprang from his brain as complete and fully armed as Minerva from the head of Zeus'; 'in my innocence,' he said to Natalie, 'I was bolder—in the use of an offstage orchestra, and in everything else specifically "Mahlerian"—than I have ever been since.'[38] The memory of the difficulties and torments he had suffered as a composer at the age of 20 led him to take a pessimistic view of Vienna's musical life. The city was sadly lacking in concert halls and music schools, and this could only be put right by subsidies and intervention by the public authorities. Owing to the high price of tickets, the few concerts given catered for no more than about 10,000 relatively well-off people, and the creation of a new orchestra,[39] which would provide music for other classes of society, was therefore a cause for rejoicing. The Opera was an exception, since it was already publicly funded and administered. There all works of any consequence were almost certain to be performed at least a dozen times, whereas the composers of music for the concert hall had the greatest difficulty in obtaining so much as a hearing. 'Even the most famous and best-loved classics are heard at most once a year.'[40]

---

[36] NBL2. 182.

[37] Alma Mahler owned a copy of a letter written by Mahler to the critic Max Kalbeck, inviting him to his rehearsal (BGM).

[38] NBL2. 182 ff. and NBLS, Feb. 1901.

[39] The Konzertverein, founded in 1900, to which Mahler later entrusted the Vienna première of his Sixth Symphony.

[40] NBLS, Jan. 1901.

Justi and Natalie persuaded Mahler to let them attend the first rehearsals with orchestra of *Das klagende Lied*. Hidden on the balcony of the Musikverein, they listened, utterly delighted, to Gustav's youthful masterpiece. As usual, he was very particular about certain things, and 'poor Wunderer' in particular had to repeat a very difficult passage six times over, 'with angelic patience'.[41] Mahler asked Franz Schalk and Bruno Walter to sit in one of the furthest boxes so that they could check the sound balance: 'Herr Schalk, is it too weak here?' or 'Herr Walter, is the trumpet clear enough?' He was to make a habit of doing this at all subsequent rehearsals of premières. Even with such a large chorus, Mahler's unerring ear was able to discern any false note within the mass of sound. 'Gentlemen,' he called, 'someone is singing a C sharp!' Leaving the podium, he went and stood by the tenors and had the passage repeated. The wrong note must have been graven on the memory of the singer, for he sang it again, and Mahler smiled with satisfaction at having discovered him. As always, the performance was first-rate. The hall was almost sold out for both the final rehearsal and the concert and each was a tremendous success. Mahler was called back repeatedly to take bows with the soloists.[42]

As might have been expected, the critics took the opportunity of venting their sarcasm on this 'eccentric work of youth', the prize-winner undoubtedly being Hans Liebstöckl, able polemicist and music critic of *Die Reichswehr*:

As a composer, Herr Mahler has just had an experience vouchsafed to very few. He has the power to put his creations into the best conceivable hands: he can entrust his symphonies to the best orchestra in the world, the Philharmonic, his songs to the most celebrated singers, and his instructions to one of the finest conductors: Gustav Mahler ... *Das klagende Lied* quickly obtained a majority vote from the audience. Herr Mahler, the conductor and composer, was stormily applauded. One section of the audience not belonging to the Mahler faction, remained cool. They were unable to applaud the conductor without having the composer acknowledge their plaudits ...

The day after the concert, Robert Hirschfeld wrote ecstatically of the quality of the performance, and in particular the excellence of the chorus, but only to complain that 'such trouble is never taken over a performance of Bach'. He also suggested that Vienna risked becoming a city of 'musical eccentricities'. But these brief comments were only a foretaste of what was to come. Five days later, Hirschfeld devoted one of his longest articles ever to *Das klagende Lied*, which seemed to him full of subversive tendencies:

[41] Maria Komorn, 'Gustav Mahler und die Jugend', *Neues Wiener Journal* (31 Aug. 1930). She describes a rehearsal of *Das klagende Lied* which she links with the first performance in 1901. Actually it was probably for the second, in 1902, for Bruno Walter is mentioned as being present and he did not begin work in Vienna until Sept. 1901. There were several musicians by the name of Wunderer in the Vienna Philharmonic. The one mentioned here is probably the oboist Alexander Wunderer (a member 1900–37), or else the hornplayer Anton Wunderer, mentioned above in connection with the rehearsals for *Rienzi*.

[42] Exceptionally, the final rehearsal on 16 Jan. was a paying event. The late Ernst Rosé, Mahler's nephew, owned a handwritten letter by Princess Pauline Metternich-Sandor, expressing to the director her 'lively enthusiasm for your superb work' which she had applauded 'until my gloves were in rags'.

How could so young a man carry in his head such a world of discordant sounds and strange nuances? . . . To have his revenge on his music teachers (and their disciplines), this hothead wanted to assuage his longing for impossible counterpoints, give vent to an imagination bursting with bombastic sounds. No amount of orchestral din was loud enough for him, he could think no musical thought through, obsessed as he was with the instrumental effects that swarmed through his head, demanding to be used at all costs, no matter what the context. The slightest untried device for obtaining orchestral colour sent him into raptures, his thoughts were all of whether to have sponge or wooden sticks for the percussion; a pizzicato chord, pitched in a desperately high register that hurt the ear seemed to him a revelation; his most fervent wish was for things that would surprise and shock. At twenty, one wants to surpass all known models, the storms of spring create havoc in the mind, immaturity is mistaken for the highest wisdom, ugliness of sound for a canon of beauty, the devious for the direct, folly for courage, the reverse for the obverse.

If Mahler had chosen the 'popular' style, it was because it was 'the style furthest removed from his youthful, precious and overheated mind.' The length of the work, its subject, the division of the episodes, the splitting up of the narration between different voices, its 'harmonic overanimation', the use of the orchestra offstage, the 'effects that become an end in themselves', its operatic style, its affected simplicity, the dissonances caused by the intermittent superimposing of the chorus on the orchestra and the great melodic leaps in the vocal parts: all these 'abnormalities' Hirschfeld condemned as 'indefensible':

Today, Mahler conducts his youthful follies but no longer composes them. Since his nineteenth year he has had experience and contact with masterpieces and knows the value of a judicious economy of means. He knows that each art form has its own laws, which were not laid down arbitrarily but developed naturally, and that the ultimate consequence of this development is called style. In art, there is only one crime, but it is a capital one, the crime against style . . .

For Hirschfeld, the choral writing of *Das klagende Lied* was a 'crime against the nature of the human voice':

Today, Herr Direktor Mahler himself smiles at the dilettantism of his early vocal writing. Youth lacks maturity, and aesthetic maturity always comes later than intellectual maturity. Yet there are people who do not recognize this elementary truth, and who have complete confidence in themselves: blinded by self-glorification and self-adoration, they will never reach aesthetic maturity but continue, throughout their lives, to create curiosities and anomalies. . . . Gustav Mahler is well aware of the dangers of such individualism, which refuses to recognize the concepts of style, development and the attainment of perfection; he knows that, in art as in life, it is the feelings of society in general rather than those of one individual which determine the laws and the rules. A man who clings to his own ideas in the centre of the vicious circle of his abnormalities doubtless reasons as follows: 'I do not acknowledge the criticism of those whom I displease. Do as I do: we live for ourselves, let us not bother about others. I am proud of having a head that is different from those of the others, the rest of the common herd. They cannot understand that my head is turned towards the future, and that it is beautiful. And I pity all those who have different heads and are incapable of recognizing the beauty of mine!'

It would be a waste of time to take the trouble to refute such arguments. Gustav Mahler composed *Das klagende Lied* when he was nineteen; today, he would not dare to uphold its merits before the majority of reasonable people. But I understand why he performed it. He wants to prove that, at nineteen, he had more orchestral effects in his head than most musicians of that age. As I have already said, the demonstration has cost a lot of money; and it has succeeded.

How was it possible that a critic could be so blinded by prejudice? Obviously, twenty years after it had been composed, Mahler's 'child of sorrow' had lost none of its power to shock, even to outrage conservatives. Max Kalbeck's *Neues Wiener Tagblatt* article also bears witness to this fact. His opinion was almost identical with Hirschfeld's, although more mildly expressed. He particularly objected to the 'sharp contrast between form and content, subject matter and presentation . . . Who has ever seen a nightingale two metres tall?' Mahler had sought to 'make a songbird out of an ostrich'. His work resembled neither an oratorio nor a symphonic poem. Or perhaps, in the final analysis, it was

a symphonic poem with a programme set to music. . . . In any kind of programme music, the musical component, to begin with, pretends to be the handmaiden of poetry. . . . In Mahler's symphonic poem, too . . . the orchestra appears at first to introduce, accompany and sustain the singing, but the instruments soon adopt a threatening attitude toward the human voice and its uncertainties. They reveal their true intentions and force it to go along with them. The voice realizes all too late that it has fallen into the hands of thieves and murderers. Subjected to the most frightful tortures, it is obliged to surrender all it possesses to satisfy the insatiable greed of its tormentors and is finally left half dead by the wayside.

Not content with this elaborate metaphor, Kalbeck went on to argue forcefully against the complexity of means used by Mahler to deal with such a meagre narrative. The solo voices alone he compared to an 'orchestra' that 'modifies, colours, completes and reinforces the instrumental mass'. Mahler had chosen them above all for reasons of instrumental sound quality:

His sole aim is to paint with sound, he is concerned only with the surface of things, and never penetrates to their essence. Everything human is foreign to him. The text, despite its pretentiousness and affectation, touches our feelings far more than the music. Such a situation would be comic if it were not so tragic. Wherefore all the noise? The effect of *Das klagende Lied* upon the crowd can in no way be purely artistic. . . . The healthy ear resists the tempter, whether he be called Liszt, Berlioz, Strauss or Mahler.

Furthermore, according to Kalbeck, Mahler's prodigious technique was bound to interest musicians, but also to arouse concern because it contained 'the germs of a disease that could be fatal for the art of music'. Fortunately, Mahler had done better since: 'We hope and wish that the spark of truth shining in the midst of his youthful errors may one day become a brilliant flame that, for him and for others, will light the way to the desired goal.'

According to Heuberger, who was gradually taking over from Hanslick on the *Neue Freie Presse*, *Das klagende Lied* contained only 'a few rare moments of touching and authentic music, some remarkable and vividly defined moods, . . . original but terribly laboured harmonies, and orchestral experiments that reveal an unquiet spirit', a true 'cult of the ugly'. Mahler, above all a man of the theatre, 'obtained anti-musical effects by anti-musical means'. If there were automatic penalties in music, as sometimes in law, this composer would incur them. He had 'created a flood of ugliness, . . . atrociously mangled the human voice and unnaturally dislocated melody, rhythm and harmony'. The two acts—the first a sort of symphonic cantata, the second an 'opera without costumes'—hung together very badly. Only the orchestra came off well, for the orchestration showed more sophistication than that of Strauss, Berlioz, and Wagner put together.

In the *Deutsche Zeitung*, always ready to denounce some dark plot hatched by the Jews and the powers of finance in the capital, Theodor Helm revealed the close relations between Mahler, 'his brother-in-law, the impresario and music merchant Alexander Rosé', and Friedrich Ehrbar, the director of the Singakademie.[43] They alone had made the performance of *Das klagende Lied* possible. Moreover, he said, since the work had been announced with much fanfare and well in advance as 'sensational', since it had required a veritable army of performers, since the composer had conducted it in person, it had attracted his 'faithful' followers, and could hardly have failed to rouse the interest and enthusiasm of the public, even if it had been twice as lamentable (*kläglich*).[44] Despite a few 'interesting' passages, it could not 'satisfy' anyone, owing to the disproportion between its subject and its means, its arbitrary use of solo voices, and the difficulty of its vocal writing. Mildenburg's soprano part was 'particularly inhuman and hard on the voice', and she had merited the tremendous applause she was given. The work possessed no originality whatsoever, for it recalled the 'ancient synagogal chants', Mahler's childhood memories, interspersed with reminiscences of Wagner and Bruckner.[45] In Helm's eyes the presence of an offstage orchestra had confused the listener and

---

[43] Son of a well-known Viennese piano manufacturer, Friedrich Ehrbar had just taken over the directorship of the Singakademie, which, founded in 1888 to perform the a cappella works of the old Italian composers, had since run into difficulties. To restore it to its former glory, Ehrbar himself had invested large sums of money in the enterprise. The concert of 17 Feb. brought in a considerable sum, despite the fact that it had meant enlisting and paying 500 performers, including not only the extra musicians but also the Schubertbund, to reinforce the rather weak male contingent of the Singverein. The repeat performance planned for Mar. was postponed until the following year, Mahler having fallen ill shortly before it.

[44] Helm makes a pun about the 'Klagende Lied' (Song of lamentation) being doubly 'kläglich' (lamentable).

[45] According to Helm, 'the typically Mahlerian theme of 'Der Spielmann' was merely an old-fashioned gavotte, and the piece as a whole constantly changed style'. It showed mainly 'just how thoroughly young Mahler had studied Wagner's scores'.

seemed 'positively vulgar', and *Das klagende Lied* was altogether 'an insignificant trifle' compared with Wagner's *Eine Faust-Ouvertüre*, which had preceded it.[46] It must be added that the critics' disapproval had not the slightest effect on the behaviour of the public: Mahler felt so confident that he and Ehrbar planned a repeat performance of the work in March with the same performers.

The sixth Philharmonic Concert, on 24 February, went off relatively smoothly. For the third time since his appointment as titular head, Mahler conducted a Bruckner symphony. This time it was the Fifth, which the Philharmonic had not performed before. Vienna's many Bruckner supporters, far from welcoming the performance, found it particularly offensive. Their spokesman, Helm, accused Mahler of an 'outrageous lack of regard' for his former master and of having 'with an impious hand, smashed the magnificent whole into unconnected fragments, leaving only its torso intact'.[47] It is true that Mahler had this time made far more significant cuts[48] than in the two symphonies he had previously conducted, thus revealing the profound ambiguity of his feelings about Bruckner's music.

He had already shown this ambiguity in 1898, when he refused to subscribe to a collection proposed by friends and admirers of Bruckner to erect a statue in his memory. Word of his refusal had been spread by musicians glad of the chance to do him harm. He explained his position at the Philharmonic rehearsal:

The fact that I did not respond to this appeal . . . should not be taken to mean that I am against Bruckner. On the contrary, I am one of the most enthusiastic admirers, both of the man and his works. However, I disliked the idea of seeing my name alongside those of people who never concerned themselves with him in his lifetime and who gave anything but wholehearted support to him and his works. I have tried to raise a

[46] Soloists for the first performance on 17 Feb. 1901: Elizza and Mildenburg (sopranos), Walker (contralto), Schrödter (tenor). *Das klagende Lied* was preceded only by the Wagner overture. The concert took place at 12.30. The orchestra was the Vienna Philharmonic with 'additional wind-instruments'. The general rehearsal was held on the previous day.

[47] The complete list of the crimes of which Helm accused Mahler reads as follows: cutting about 200 bars in the first two movements, inverting certain elements in the first, cutting the third theme and the characteristic unison passage that follows it, inserting transitions of his own invention; cutting the restatement of the great 4/4 melody, the most beautiful passage in the Adagio according to Helm, so that the final crescendo of the principal theme had come far too soon; finally, accelerating several tempos and particularly that of the Scherzo, in which, disregarding the indications in the score, Mahler had failed to slow down for the second theme. Helm indignantly recalled the unabridged performances Löwe had conducted in Vienna, on 1 Mar. 1898 and 15 Apr. 1899. The world première had been given by the Kaim Orchestra (THE 275) conducted by Franz Schalk, in Graz on 8 Apr. 1894.

[48] To be precise, 160 bars from the first movement, 94 from the second, and 69 from the fourth. On the other hand Mahler had added to the recapitulation of the principal theme in the first movement several bars borrowed from the exposition. He changed many of the tempos and dynamic markings, and here and there the orchestration. At the beginning of the third group of themes, which he cut, he wrote in the Doblinger score he used for the Vienna performance: 'Sehr schade! Aber es muss sein!' (A pity! But it has to be!) See Ernst Hilmar: '"Schade, aber es muss(te) sein": Zu Gustav Mahlers Strichen und Retouchen insbesondere am Beispiel der V. Symphonie Anton Bruckners', *Bruckner Studien* (1975), 187.

monument to Bruckner in my own way, and have made it a point of honour to interest myself in his works and to play them with all possible veneration.[49]

In Vienna, where the musical world was always on the look-out for a new 'scandal', Mahler's 'ingratitude' towards his former mentor must have fuelled a good deal of gossip. It is true that he had earlier conducted the Philharmonic in an abridged version of the Sixth Symphony[50] and, in 1900, he had made many small cuts in the Fourth, especially in the second movement and the Finale. Before the concert of 27 February 1901, Mahler spoke about Bruckner with the brutal frankness characteristic of him when he was with close friends: by shortening the first movement, he had sought 'merely to eliminate what is empty and irrelevant'. The symphony as a whole caused him more pain than pleasure. Many splendid passages and themes 'of Beethovenian grandeur', were not carried through, developed, and integrated into the whole. The general effect was that of 'a mishmash' devoid of any logical structure, 'a sort of fabric that someone has woven with old bits of thread chosen at random and coarsely knotted, without bothering about whether or not they blend in and without noticing that they destroy the unity and beauty of the ensemble'.[51] While he liked the Scherzo, and above all the Trio, 'with its marvellous original, "typically Viennese" melody', he added:

You'll see! There's nothing to be done for Bruckner without a scalpel. As he is at present he will never really take his place in the repertoire. I've done my best to make him live. Possibly the three symphonies I've done here with the Philharmonic will be the ones most often performed, but with all the cuts I've made.[52]

These remarks, which reflect the mature Mahler's considered judgement concerning Bruckner's music, may be compared with two other passages in Natalie's unpublished manuscript. One day in January 1900, when she was passing the monument to Bruckner in the Stadtpark in Vienna, Natalie witnessed the following scene which she later described to Mahler. Two small boys, upon seeing this tiny bust dwarfed between the two immense figures crowning it with laurels, had exclaimed: 'The little fellow is too small for all that fuss!'—a remark that had neatly summed up both the disproportion inherent in his work and Mahler's true opinion.[53] A year later, after having re-read Bruckner's First Symphony, his unfavourable opinion was reinforced:

It has left me with the worst possible impression! Without any transition, the most magnificent rubs shoulders with the most mediocre. After a superb beginning, a whole lot of confused and disordered nonsense, as clumsy from a contrapuntal as from a musical point of view, follows by way of development. At the end of this desert (*Wüste*),

[49] *Fremden-Blatt* (23 Feb. 1899), quoted in GAB 29.
[50] Theodor Helm had then warned his readers in *Deutsche Zeitung* of the absence of numerous passages, of 6 or 7 bars here, or 20 there.
[51] NBLS, Feb. 1901.   [52] Ibid.
[53] 'Der Mann is z'klan für die G'schicht' (NBLS, Jan. 1900). The words are Natalie's, but it is clear from the context that Mahler shared her opinion.

the beautiful theme returns (unchanged!), followed anew by the most appalling wilderness (*ärgste Wüstenei*). The conclusion is grandiose but bears no relation, either profound or superficial, to the rest.[54]

Given these severe views, it is no surprise that Mahler treated Bruckner's Fifth in a 'sacrilegious' way. The score at his disposal, newly published by Doblinger, and already considerably retouched and abridged by Franz Schalk, had been conducted in its entirety in 1898 and 1899 by Ferdinand Löwe. Now Max Vancsa, in the *Neue Musikalische Presse*, reproached Mahler with 'passing himself off as a pupil and disciple of Bruckner, when his whole decadent and excitable personality remains fundamentally detached from the naïve creativity of a genius like Anton Bruckner (or indeed like Beethoven), who simply followed his abundant inspiration rather than producing intellectually contrived compositions'. Theodor Helm accused Mahler of having 'torn to shreds' the first movement of the Fifth Symphony and, in so doing, having justified those who complained of the master's 'lack of logic and clarity'.[55] Helm berated Mahler for having 'violated' Bruckner's tempos by accelerating them beyond all reason in order to reach the Finale, the only movement he had conducted with 'unparalleled power, dash, virtuosity, beauty of sound and intelligence'. Whereas the 'snobs' among the Philharmonic public had perhaps applauded more warmly the work thus abridged, he added, 'the connoisseurs were filled with boundless fury and bitterness at such a shameful mutilation of the first half of an immortal creation.'[56] Beside this 'colossal Symphony', the two other pieces on the programme, Weber's little Chinese Overture, *Turandot*[57] and Dvořák's Serenade, Opus 44, for wind instruments (receiving its first Viennese performance) had seemed, according to Helm, very lightweight,[58] an opinion not shared by Mahler himself, who had derived great pleasure from conducting Dvořák's little masterpiece: 'Several people sit down and engage in the loveliest music-making, with more in it than in many big orchestral works. It shows how enjoyable and genuinely musical Dvořák's talent is, when confined to a small frame. But when he tries to be big, he becomes empty and pompous.'[59] Unlike Helm, Hirschfeld found the Serenade indescribably 'charming'. Although in principle opposed to all abridgement, he made an exception in the case of

[54] NBLS, 29 Sept. 1901. In summer 1904, Mahler re-read Bruckner's scores, and again judged them harshly (see below, Chap. 16).

[55] Like many other critics, the Viennese correspondent of the *Neue Zeitschrift* thought Bruckner incapable of coping with large musical structures and added that, because of his lack of any 'sense of form', his music was made up of a succession of 'little phrases'.

[56] Theodor Helm notes in his memoirs that Ferdinand Löwe conducted an uncut performance at the Konzertverein several months later, on 12 Dec. 1901.

[57] Mahler probably chose this Overture, based on an 'authentic' Chinese theme noted by Jean-Jacques Rousseau, because of its piquant orchestration, but Helm saw it as merely a 'witty curiosity'.

[58] Helm was indignant that the audience should have been 'so naïve and puerile' as to encore the Trio of this Serenade, before the repeat of the Minuet. Kalbeck judged that the listeners had given the work a triumphal welcome because in it Dvořák showed no ambition other than to 'make music'.

[59] NBLS, Feb. 1901.

Bruckner, who made a practice of 'piling block upon block, with new ideas in between'. Kalbeck whole-heartedly agreed because, to his mind, Bruckner wrote down anything that crossed his mind, so that his scores often resembled a collage of sketch-books. Bruckner would have been far greater if he had practised 'order, clarity and economy', and Mahler had done him a service by making cuts and putting on such a brilliant performance.

When the sixth Philharmonic Concert was over, Mahler had no idea that he would never conduct another, at least as titular conductor. For some time his relatives and friends had noticed that he looked ill, his features drawn, but had not dared to mention it. They were accustomed to see him constantly pushing himself to the limit and not taking any rest. A serious bout of influenza at the end of January should have served as a warning. On 24 February, after conducting the sixth Philharmonic Concert at 12.30, he was again on the podium, at the Opera, in the evening, for the 110th anniversary performance of *The Magic Flute*. A pretty young Viennese girl in the audience, who was later to play a major part in his life, looked at 'that Lucifer-like face, those pale cheeks, those eyes like burning coals', and declared to her companions, 'with deep compassion', that 'this man can't go on like that.'[60] And indeed, that same night, Mahler suffered a sudden and violent haemorrhage. As he had experienced these before, he ignored it for some time before calling Justi, who was horrified to find him lying in a pool of blood.[61] She telephoned immediately to Mahler's physician (Dr Singer),[62] but the iced water baths he prescribed did not help, and they were obliged to call in a surgeon, Dr Julius Hochenegg,[63] whom they had difficulty in contacting. He immediately saw the gravity of the situation and said that 'had he come half an hour later, it would have been too late'. He managed to staunch the haemorrhage, which had been caused by a haemorrhoid located high up in the intestinal tract.

The following morning, Mahler awoke feeling extremely weak, but very much alive and aware that he had had a narrow escape, as witness the remarks he made to Natalie:

You know, last night I nearly passed away. When I saw the faces of the two doctors (Singer and Hochenegg), I thought my last hour had come. While they were putting in the tube, which was frightfully painful but quick, they kept checking my pulse and my heart. Fortunately it was solidly installed in my breast and determined not to give up so soon. . . . While I was hovering on the border between life and death, I wondered whether it would not be better to have done with it at once, since everyone must come

---

[60] AMM 23. Alma Mahler mistakenly claims that it was a performance of *Die Meistersinger*.

[61] In a letter to Richard Strauss (MSB 58ff.), Mahler claims to have lost $2\frac{1}{2}$ litres of blood during the haemorrhage.

[62] Two Dr Singers were listed in the medical directory. Gustav Singer (1867–1944), a specialist in intestinal troubles at the Wiener Allgemeines Krankenhaus, seems the more likely of the two to have treated Mahler.

[63] Professor Julius von Hochenegg (1859–1940), the director of Sanatorium Löw at the time of Mahler's operation, was a celebrated surgeon who had studied under Theodor Billroth.

to that in the end. Besides, the prospect of dying did not frighten me in the least, provided my affairs are in order, and to return to life seemed almost a nuisance.

With his customary resilience he soon realized that his fears had been somewhat exaggerated. However, he was informed that, after a few days' rest, he would have to undergo an operation (his third for the same complaint) to avoid a relapse.[64]

The same day, Mahler had the score of his Fourth Symphony brought to him in bed, the copyist having just finished the first two movements. He noticed that the Scherzo had been labelled as the third movement, and was horrified to think that 'if I had died last night, the entire structure and significance of the work would have been destroyed by putting the movements in the wrong order, since the Adagio is essential as the basis of, and transition to, the Finale. With the second movement placed third, the whole thing would have made no sense.' Another passage, where he had written a second version alongside the first with the intention of choosing between the two later on, also upset him.

Had they been printed one after the other, the result would have been awful; for if someone who understood (e.g. Walter) had left out the pointless repetition, they would not have believed him; the army of Philistines and brainless simpletons, who somehow imagine that music is their property, would have pounced on him with screams of indignation because he, the novice, who had the cheek to be still alive, had dared to correct a 'classic' work. For, after my death, . . . all those who at present would dearly like to lynch me, will call me 'a classic', 'an immortal', 'their master'.

He even drafted the obituary notice that would doubtless appear in the newspaper: 'Gustav Mahler had finally met the fate he deserved for his many misdeeds'.

Mahler recovered so rapidly that Hochenegg, the surgeon, decided to operate on him a week later. The Emperor made a personal appeal to Hochenegg to spare no effort in looking after the director of the Opera and to ensure his speedy recovery and return to work. This pleased Mahler greatly, despite his scorn for honours and decorations. He was also delighted by the warm concern shown by Prince Montenuovo, who called on him several times and told him not to worry. He assured him, jokingly, that he would not allow the Intendant to make a mess of things in Mahler's absence, but that he, Montenuovo, would deal and discuss everything directly with Mahler's subordinates. To please him, he also speeded up an order increasing Mahler's salary, and sent it to him on the eve of his operation.[65] He was henceforth to receive 7,000 instead of 6,000 florins per year, plus a further 11,000 instead of 6,000 in various allowances,[66]

[64] Justi wrote to Berliner on 2 Mar. giving him news of her brother and telling him that Mahler would have to be re-examined and possibly operated on the following Monday (BGM).

[65] NBLS, Mar. 1901. On 3 Mar., Mahler received the news that the decree, dated 2 Mar., had been signed.

[66] The 11,000 florins comprised an additional emolument (*Functionszulage*) of 5,000 florins (including an allowance for his rent), a 'fixed allowance' payable, like the rest of his income, in monthly instalments, of 3,000 florins, and an annual 'carriage allowance' of 3,000 florins (HOA, letter of 2 Mar. 1901, signed by

the increase to apply from the beginning of the year. The pension to which he would be entitled after ten years of service was also to be increased.[67] The news came as a relief to Mahler, who had already begun to worry about the cost of his illness.

Expertly performed on 4 March by Hochenegg, assisted by Mahler's friend Dr Ludwig Boer, the operation dispelled all anxiety for Mahler's health, but, since the deterioration of the lining of the intestinal tract was even worse than he had feared, Hochenegg prescribed a long period of convalescence. Mahler was moved to a nursing home on the outskirts of Vienna and given strict orders not to work more than a few hours a day. One evening, when Natalie went to see him to relieve his loneliness, the conversation turned towards music and Beethoven's Quartets, which Mahler considered 'far more polyphonic than his symphonies. This was of course natural given the absence of the accompaniment and padding of the orchestration.' He added that his own 'Fourth Symphony had been constructed like a quartet, except that there were as many as six to ten separate voices'. Nevertheless he greatly feared that people would not see the wood for the trees and that this eminently cheerful work, which was easier to play and shorter than its the earlier ones, would fall flat.

Three years earlier, before he began work on the Fourth Symphony, Mahler had said something which sheds some light on the predominant role of polyphony in his later symphonies:

At its highest level music becomes again, as at the lowest, homophonic. The master of polyphony, who is exclusively polyphonic, is Bach. The founder and creator of modern polyphony is Beethoven. . . . Wagner used genuine polyphony only in *Tristan* and *Die Meistersinger*, . . . for the themes of the *Ring*, for instance, are built almost entirely on chords. . . . In true polyphony, the various themes run independently alongside each other each with its own beginning and conclusion as differentiated as possible from the others, thereby allowing the listener to follow each theme individually.[68]

During those long, peaceful hours at the Sanatorium Löw, he plunged once more into the volumes of the Bachgesellschaft and made the following comments to Natalie:

Bach often reminds me of those stone effigies lying with folded hands on top of their tombs, and which always move me because they suggest the continuation of life beyond the limits of existence. They seem to be fervently desiring the survival of the soul, and

---

Plappart). The Emperor's decree is dated 22 Feb. and was therefore promulgated before Mahler's illness.

[67] Mahler was still to be entitled to a pension of 3,000 florins a year after ten years of service, but the amount of the pension was thereafter to increase by 1,000 florins every year instead of every five years (see Chap. 2). The decree also stipulated that he would be retired only if he were incapable of pursuing his activities or dismissed by the Lord Chamberlain.

[68] NBL1. 104; NBL2. 117. The previous summer, in Maiernigg, he had expressed a strikingly original conception of polyphony while listening with Wondra to the noises coming across the Wörthersee (see above, Chap. 8 and NBL1. 147; NBL2. 167).

to believe in it now more than they did during their lifetime. Bach, too, has something so petrified about him that only a small minority are capable of making him come alive. This is because of all those bad performances of his works in which nothing conjures up the great cantor playing to himself on the harpsichord. Instead of the true Bach, his interpreters give the public nothing but a wretched skeleton. The chords that were intended to give this marvellous fullness of body are simply left out, as though Bach had provided a figured bass without rhyme or reason. And yet it must be played, and what a magnificent roar those rising and falling chords produce.[69] This is how you should perform the Violin Sonatas, which it's quite absurd to expect one little violinist to play, and also all the Cantatas, and you would be amazed at the sound they would produce.[70]

He said that one day he had played through Bach's cantata 'Ich sündiger Mensch wer wird mich erlösen',[71] which to him was 'one of the most beautiful and perhaps even *the* most beautiful of his works', and one that opened up the widest perspectives. He marvelled at 'this miraculous freedom of Bach's, which probably no other musician has ever attained and which is based on his unparalleled skill and command of technique. In Bach,' he exclaimed, 'all the vital cells of music are united as the world is in God; there has never been any polyphony greater than this!'[72] And yet, when Bach died, everyone had mourned the 'excellent organist' without ever mentioning the composer![73] Two years before, he had said he wanted to give the *St Matthew Passion* as a benefit performance for the Opera's pension fund. He would enhance its polyphony by placing an orchestra and a chorus on each side of the stage:

I would place a third chorus, to represent the congregation of the faithful, the people, somewhere else and, in addition, a boys' chorus as high up as possible, around the organ, so that their voices would seem to come from heaven. You would see what an effect it would have, sharing out questions and answers, instead of having it all run together higgledy-piggledy, as they usually do it nowadays.[74]

---

[69] Made up of movements taken from two orchestral suites, the Bach Suite that Mahler was to conduct and publish in New York includes a carefully noted realization of the figured bass 'for organ and clavicembalo'. In it he specified that it was 'to be regarded as a rough draft, with the richest possible harmonies in the tuttis and delicate nuances in the *piano* (soft) passages'. The organ plays only in the Overture (see below, Vol. iiii, App. 1).

[70] Throughout his life Mahler had a pronounced dislike for violin recitals. For instance, at Alt-Aussee in summer 1899 (NBLS) he said: 'As a solo instrument, the violin stands out above all for the insignificance of its literature, which, with a few exceptions, consists of nothing but "dances on a tightrope" and is devoid of art.'

[71] The cantata to which Mahler was referring was either 'Ich elender Mensch' (no. 48) or 'Ich armer Mensch, ich Sündenknecht' (no. 55).

[72] NBL1. 157; NBL2. 184.   [73] NBLS, Mar. 1901.

[74] NBL1. 112; NBL2. 130. In this, as in many other instances, Mahler proved to be a forerunner. His preoccupation with 'stereophony', i.e. the idea of separating different orchestral and choral groups in space, originated during the Renaissance and baroque period and it was taken up again many years after Mahler's death, in the 1950s and 1960s. Mahler bases the whole conception of the Eighth Symphony on a 'stereophonic' placing of the two main choruses. It is most unfortunate that present-day performances should so rarely attempt to reproduce his own deployment of forces for the first performance.

But for that I would need a different hall from that of the Musikverein, perhaps a huge drill hall like the one in Münden near Kassel,[75] where I conducted *Paulus* with choruses from all the neighbouring towns.

During Mahler's convalescence, the Opera continued to run 'like clockwork'. From his bed he supervised the rehearsals of Ludwig Thuille's *Lobetanz*, the première of which was conducted by Franz Schalk on 18 March. Naturally it lacked the refinement and clarity that Mahler alone could have conferred upon the staging and the music. For this reason, perhaps, it was not particularly successful. Helm considered the work 'pleasantly poetic', despite the heterogeneous style, the halting inspiration, and the 'thinness' of the plot. Only the third act received warm applause. Schönaich, like Helm, attributed most of the work's success to the performance,[76] while Kauders acknowledged 'the charm of certain numbers' but regretted the unoriginality of the whole. The *Deutsches Volksblatt* took advantage of the limited success of *Lobetanz*, which was dropped from the repertory after only six performances, to attack Mahler's administration in general. Hans Puchstein had listened to the first performances under Jahn in the last years of his direction, and concluded that they had pleased the public more than Mahler's.[77] Only the partisans of the current director, in their 'blindness', could deny the evidence. Mahler had different views of course and blamed this relative failure largely on his own absence. 'It's as if you put too much water into the lemonade, you can't drink it, it is so boring and insipid, I would have added a touch more lemon, and perhaps made it tastier.'[78]

On 20 March Mahler and Justi set off by train for Abbazia,[79] where he had spent his Easter holidays in 1898, since the Opera was always closed during Holy Week. This year he had rented a four-room apartment on the top floor of the Villa Jeannette for more than two weeks since he had left Vienna ten days early. As usual, he picked an attic room for himself, with a view over the whole countryside. Arnold Rosé joined the household on his return from a tour of Italy with his quartet, and the ever-faithful Natalie arrived on 30 March. They spent their evenings on the vast terrace-roof of the villa, which overlooked the island-studded sea. Mahler 'was in such good humour that nothing bothered him'. He devoted several hours a day to completing the revision of his Fourth Symphony, recopying the Adagio and reorchestrating the Finale, in which he had decided to use the full orchestra instead of the reduced forces he had chosen for the

[75] Mahler must have meant the drill hall of the infantry regiment of Kassel, where the 1885 performance took place, and not the smaller hall in Münden, where he rehearsed the choruses.
[76] Especially on the part of Gutheil-Schoder.
[77] Puchstein was unfair enough to include *Dalibor*, one of Mahler's greatest personal successes, in Jahn's list of premières, on the grounds that the opening night had been just before the latter's departure.
[78] Cast of the first performance (18 Mar.): Gutheil-Schoder (Princess), Pohlner (First Young Girl), von Thann (spoken part), Naval (Lobetanz), Preuss (Student), Frauscher (King), Stehmann, Ritter, and Grengg (spoken parts).
[79] Now called Opatija in Croatia, a famous beach on the Istrian peninsula, near Trieste.

Lied. 'I'm living here, as it were, in the atmosphere of my Fourth,' he wrote to Guido Adler. 'I'm preparing it for publication and expect to have it ready tomorrow or the day after . . .'. With its mixture of 'malice, profound mysticism and delicious absurdities', the text of the Finale, which he had set to music nine years before in Hamburg, continued to delight him. 'Everything is turned upside down, causality simply has no meaning! As if suddenly you were looking at the other side of the moon,' he said of it one evening as he watched the moon rise behind the mountains and bathe the sea and the coast in a flood of silvery light. He mused on the endless succession of problems which he encountered every time he was composing a new work:

It's not just a question of scaling an unknown peak, but of plotting, step by step, a path up to it. But the audience and the 'judges' come rushing in and start snuffling around with noses too short to reach beyond the nearest bush. They maybe find a turd, but they never behold the divine freedom and beauty of nature. Then they criticize furiously, nothing satisfies them, everything must be different and done differently, whereas previously it would not even have occurred to them that such a path was possible. Indeed, they even blame us for the fact that nature is thus and not otherwise.[00]

Although he could now rejoice at the idea of having his scores in print, Mahler was no longer impatient for them to be played. Probably because opportunities were becoming more numerous, his attitude began to change. A first sign of this development is the reply he gave (no doubt upon his return from Abbazia) to a friend who urged him to make some effort to get his works known and performed: 'They will do all that is necessary themselves now or later on. Must one be present, when one becomes immortal?'[81] Nevertheless, he was now anxious to make up for lost time, and devoted much thought to the rules and techniques of composition. The concept of polyphony was beginning to obsess him and he could no longer whole-heartedly admire any music which was not truly polyphonic, like that of Tchaikovsky, for instance, about which his judgement was particularly harsh. 'Colour, too, should be something more than what he gives us,' he said to Guido Adler who had praised Tchaikovsky's rich orchestral palette in the *Symphonie pathétique*.[82]

That's just humbug (*Geflunker*), sand in the eyes. When you take a closer look, very little remains. Those arpeggios through all the heights and depths, those meaningless sequences of chords, can't disguise the emptiness and lack of inspiration. If you take a coloured dot and swing it round an axis, it looks like a shimmering circle.

[80] NBL2. 185.

[81] NBL2. 186. This undated passage is missing in NBLS and comes immediately after Natalie's account (printed in NBL1. 158; NBL2. 186) of a discussion with Guido Adler on Tchaikovsky's *Pathétique* which appears in NBLS, dated 18 Apr.

[82] Ibid. The work had been conducted in Vienna by Nikisch with the Berlin Philharmonic Orchestra. The Viennese impresario had had the original idea of giving the audience a choice of three symphonies, Beethoven's Fifth, Brahms's First, or the *Pathétique*. The last had obtained the most votes (THE 297). Franz Schalk also included Tchaikovsky's Sixth in the programme of the last Philharmonic Concert of the season (24 Mar.), which he conducted in Mahler's stead.

But when it comes to rest it's just the same old dot again, and even the cat won't play with it.[83]

During his peaceful days of convalescence at Abbazia, Mahler devoted more time than usual to walking and to conversation. During a walk along the beach in the moonlight, he told Natalie of a dream he had had when he was 8 years old, and which later seemed to him to be a premonition of his vagabond existence:

My mother, my brother Ernst and I were standing one evening by the window of the sitting room, when my mother cried: 'God, what is happening!' The sky filled with yellow smoke, the stars began to move, and flew together or engulfed each other, as if it were the end of the world. Suddenly I was in the market place below. The fiery vapour followed me, and as I looked back I saw coming out of it a huge figure—the eternal Jew. His cloak, blown by the wind, stood up like a giant hump between his shoulders; his right arm rested on a tall staff that bore a golden cross. I fled before him in terror, but in a few strides he caught up with me and tried to force me to take his staff (a symbol of his endless wandering). I woke with a scream of terror.[84]

The same evening, he recalled an equally distressing dream he had in July 1891, when he had gone to Gastein to visit Pollini, and Natalie had joined him there. He had found himself amid a throng of people in a vast and brilliantly lit hall just at the moment when the last guest arrived, a very tall man of somewhat stiff bearing, immaculately dressed and with the air of a bon vivant. But he knew: this was death. He tried to get away from the mysterious guest, to reach the end of the room. The man, whom nobody seemed to recognize, followed him, as though drawn to him by some magnetic power, to the furthest corner of the room, behind a curtain. There the stranger seized his arm in an iron grip and said: 'You must come with me!' He struggled desperately to tear himself away, and eventually freed himself.[85]

Upon arriving in Abbazia on 30 March, Natalie had found Gustav 'rested, with all his strength and good humour restored'. He was

In such good spirits that nothing could spoil his mood. But he would not have been able to endure such a long stay without having brought his Fourth Symphony, on which he worked several hours a day. It was our staple topic of conversation during the walks

---

[83] NBL1. 158; NBL2. 186, dated 18 Apr. 1901 in NBLS. Considering his low estimate of the *Symphonie pathétique* as a work of art, it was an irony of fate that Mahler had later to conduct it more often than any other work in New York.

[84] NBL2. 185. The task of deciphering the true meaning of this dream should be left to specialists, psychiatrists and others. But the presence of Ernst is significant (he was still alive, for Mahler said he had had this dream at the age of 8) and so is that of Marie Mahler. The wandering Jew also appears in the famous letter to Josef Steiner (MBR1, no. 1; MBR2, no. 5). This passage was probably inspired by the dream in question (see above, Vol. i, Chap. 5), and in a childhood dream Mahler described in 1904 to Alma and her friend Erica Tietze-Conrat (so similar that it was probably the same dream retold in different terms). The juxtaposition of the staff, symbol of the wandering Jew, and the gold cross, shows how closely linked were the two religions, Judaism and Christianity, in Mahler even as a child.

[85] See above, Vol. i, Chap. 16. Mahler might have remembered this dream at this particular time because he was recovering from an illness that had brought him close to death.

which we took, two by two (Justi and Rosé, Gustav and I) according to outward physical strength and inward preference—that is, they on a flat path along the sea, and we up into the mountains.[86]

This simple sentence in Natalie's unpublished manuscript reveals a secret she later tried to hide. She had by no means lost hope, quite the contrary, that her long friendship and passionate interest would culminate in marriage, and it is obvious that Mahler's behaviour towards her was, for the moment, far from discouraging. Admittedly some contemporary witnesses who did not like Natalie, Emma Adler in particular, picture her as a 'calculating flirt' who 'changed lovers like clothes', but the wife of Victor Adler, a leading figure in the Austrian socialist movement, resented the way Natalie had infatuated her brother-in-law, Siegmund Adler. She was probably biased, therefore. It is clear that Natalie was passionately in love at least twice: with Siegfried Lipiner, recognized by Emma Adler as having treated Natalie, his most fervent admirer, very shabbily, and then with Mahler, for whom her intense feeling can be glimpsed on a number of occasions in her memoirs. Although she sometimes irritated him, he nevertheless appreciated her enthusiasm, her musicianship, her modest and self-effacing attitude as a witness of his life and work, her intelligence, and her musical gifts. Unfortunately for her, Mahler was soon to uncover a family intrigue with disconcerting ramifications: he found out the real nature of the relationship between Justi and Arnold Rosé[87] and the 'pact' concluded between the two women. Natalie, it seems, had threatened to tell Mahler everything if Justi refused to encourage and facilitate her intimate walks with him. This makes it easier to understand Natalie's bitter disappointment when she learnt of Mahler's engagement eight months later. The original version of Alma Mahler's memoirs contains a cruel anecdote concerning Natalie, the details of which, however, are unreliable, for Alma always resented anyone who had played an important part in Mahler's life before she entered it. Yet there is a ring of truth about it. According to her, at the end of the summer of 1901, after Mahler's return to Vienna, Natalie stayed on at Maiernigg with Justi to tidy up the house, but had actually arranged to have an urgent telegram[88] sent to her from Vienna in order to have an excuse for joining him. Back in the capital, she implored him to marry her and even tried to embrace him, but he repulsed her with these cruel words: 'I can't love you, I can only love a beautiful woman', to which she had replied, 'But I *am* beautiful. Ask Henriette Mankiewicz!' Still according to Alma's memoirs, Natalie gave up all hope after this rebuff.

The holiday in Abbazia did Mahler a world of good:

[86] NBLS, Apr. 1901

[87] According to Alma Mahler, Mahler never forgave his sister for her 'betrayal', but this statement is somewhat doubtful, for Mahler's letters to Justi reveal no trace of even a passing estrangement between brother and sister.

[88] AMS. The rest of the story is told in the next chapter.

My health is improving hourly. . . . I'm so busy eating, sleeping and going for walks that I've hardly a minute to spare. I'm extremely well, and a completely 'different person'. I'll soon be coming to eat a huge supper with you. N.B. I eat everything only lots of it![89]

I've finally realized that the hidden cause of all my ills was the thing the doctors have just discovered. But for my haemorrhage, they might never have discovered it. . . . As for Vienna, these last weeks have taught me a lesson and I hope I shall never again allow myself to be overwhelmed by such a whirlwind of inferior work. In future I shall be the pilot and leave the oars to others. Though I shall have to train some better sailors.[90]

Despite the radical improvement in his general health, Mahler continued to suffer each morning from pains caused by his operation, and sometimes these lasted until 3 in the afternoon. This worried him, especially when he realized that he would soon have to begin conducting again, and he could find no way of relieving the pain when it became too acute.[91] He had suffered in a similar way in July 1889, at the time of his previous operation, and had only found relief through massage after his return to Budapest. This time the pains seem to have subsided, for Mahler makes no further allusion to them in his correspondence. He put on 6 kilos in weight during his two-week stay in Abbazia.

Two Philharmonic Concerts had taken place after the operation, but in his absence the first one was conducted by Josef Hellmesberger, junior, on 10 March and the second by Franz Schalk. Both were rapturously applauded. Most critics reviewed them favourably, with words that were so many 'poisoned arrows'[92] directed at Mahler: 'Not since Richter's departure had such solid conducting in the good old "classic" style been heard as Hellmesberger's (the most insignificant time-beater that ever was)', Natalie writes,[93] undoubtedly reflecting Mahler's opinion. 'And there was nothing "schalkhaft" (mischievous) about Schalk.' She goes on quoting the Viennese reviewers:

'All was serious and worthy, as befitted the great works and their masters [another dig at Mahler]. Thus did a lofty artistic Areopagus smile in satisfaction as sweet mediocrity returned to the holy halls (*heiligen Hallen*).'[94] For Gustav, all this—which he read with some anger—made it easier for him to give up the direction of the concerts, and he declined in advance, 'for health reasons', an invitation to stand for re-election for the coming winter. Still it is dreadfully sad that again he should have to give up the

---

[89] Letter to Nana Spiegler quoted above.

[90] Undated letter to Guido Adler (late Mar., RAM 35).

[91] Undated letter (of 1 or 2 Apr.) to Dr Josef Winter, the surgeon Mahler had known in his youth in the German nationalist circle of Richard von Kralik (see above, Vol. i, Chap. 4, etc.). Mahler informs him that so far he has not taken morphine, and reveals that he suffered in the same way after the operation he underwent in Munich in July 1889 (see above, Vol. i, Chap. 14). At that time he had found in Budapest a masseur who, by applying a special technique, was able to empty his rectum completely, so that after a week the pains ceased. Unfortunately he never again found another masseur able to do this. Much later, in June 1910, Josef Winter, Edler von Wigmar (1857–1916), took Mahler on a long car-drive, in search for the plot of land or the house Mahler was planning to buy (AMM1. 452; AMM2. 360; see below Vol. iv, Chap. 8).

[92] NBLS, Apr. 1901.   [93] Ibid.

[94] Quotation from *The Magic Flute*.

concerts (and keep the Opera) for this undiluted artistic activity gave him great pleasure and filled a need—indeed, he felt it to be a purification process after the much hated, anti-artistic bustle at the Opera.[95]

A glance at the contemporary press makes it easy to understand Mahler's bitterness. Hirschfeld rejoiced above all that Hellmesberger was 'without wilfulness', a virtue that he felt made up for the 'lack of individuality':

To be sure, he does not present all of Beethoven, but neither does he try to present anything other or more than Beethoven. The audience would rather complete the picture in its imagination than have to remove extraneous elements from it. A portrait from which a few of the sitter's features are missing will always seem a better likeness and more successful than even the cleverest of images or reproductions containing the slightest foreign element. I am both willing and able to hear more than is offered me with my inner ear, but I cannot, even with the utmost good will, cut out anything that I actually hear. . . . An atmosphere of profound peace pervaded the hall, every personal element, in so far as it did not come from Beethoven, seemed to have been erased, and we all experienced perfect happiness, as though we had left our nerves behind in the cloakroom.

Max Graf, in the *Neues Wiener Journal*, was delighted to rediscover 'good old musical blood' and a tradition and soundness of craftsmanship in Hellmesberger that fully made up for his 'lack of initiative'. The enthusiasm of the audience, too often 'overstimulated, blasé and numbed' had rewarded this conductor for the modesty of his aspirations.[96] In the same way, Helm exulted at having rediscovered a conductor 'who does not impose his own personality at the expense of the work' and was not possessed of 'the demon of wanting to do everything better than it had been done in the past'. The correspondent of the *Neue Zeitschrift für Musik* dwelt on the interminable applause of an audience 'delighted finally to hear Beethoven's works performed as he had intended them to be'.[97]

These articles clearly reveal the orchestra's hostile feeling towards Mahler, for the friendly relationship which had been generated by the visit to Paris in the preceding summer had been short-lived. At the beginning of the season, the director of the Opera sent out a 'circular' henceforth requiring the members of the orchestra, in accordance with the existing statutes, to obtain written permission before taking part in public performances outside the

[95] NBLS, Apr. 1901. See above, Vol. i, Chap. 19, where Mahler expresses similar sentiments in Hamburg.

[96] In the book he wrote in his old age about the Vienna Opera (GWO), Max Graf made no reference whatever to the countless articles in which he had relentlessly attacked Mahler, who was thus correct in predicting that his worst enemies in the press, even those who called him 'a rogue and villain' in his lifetime, would honour him after his death as a 'classic' and an 'immortal'.

[97] Though he belonged to an anti-Semitic paper, Helm was alone in admitting, in the *Wochenblatt*, that the subscriptions had fallen off as soon as it had become known that the Philharmonic Concerts would be conducted by Josef Hellmesberger, jun. But he added that the latter had been applauded from the beginning of his first concert in the new season by an 'Aryan German' audience. Unlike Mahler, he had had the good idea of publishing the programmes of the entire eight concerts in advance. Mahler had drawn up his programmes 'to suit his personal convenience, and in a manner that was arbitrary rather than artistic'.

Opera.[98] Although Mahler was only enforcing a rule that already existed, this letter was greeted with indignation, since from now on even the Philharmonic Concerts would be subject to this condition. The uproar was such that he had to attend the committee meeting of 25 September 1900 to calm troubled spirits by declaring that the circular did not refer either to the Philharmonic Concerts or to the Gesellschafts-Konzerte, and that it was simply a formality. Nevertheless the ill-feeling remained, and even increased at the rehearsals and performance of Mahler's First Symphony in November and the *Klagende Lied* in February. After January's Nicolai Conzert, he had already hinted to a delegation from the orchestra that he would probably be obliged to relinquish his position as director of the concerts for reasons of health. Things came to a head again in March, when he refused the orchestra permission to take part in two concerts for the Schubertbund, a men's chorus, justifying his refusal on by quoting the famous circular.[99]

A few days before Mahler's return from Abbazia to Vienna, an anonymous article in *Die Reichswehr*, probably from the lively pen of Hans Liebstöckl, gave what may well have been an accurate picture of the situation:

In Philharmonic circles the movement of opposition to Director Mahler grows ever stronger. The nervous temperament of this conductor, his excessive zeal in the organization of rehearsals, and in particular his weakness in letting himself be influenced by his 'confidants', are losing him the sympathy of many [musicians] who, until now, out of conviction or self-interest, have been his supporters. Energetic efforts are being made to find a new candidate for this prestigious post. The affair is being handled in strict secrecy, to avoid conflict. It is known that the election will be held in September. Perhaps Director Mahler, now aware of the planned campaign against him, will in the meantime be able to give assurances which would calm down the situation.[100]

Indignant at this paragraph, the critic Ludwig Karpath immediately sent it to Justi in Abbazia, advising her not to show it to Mahler. 'I've told my brother nothing about it,' she replied,

and he reads no papers here, so he will not find out, nor does it matter what the *Reichswehr* writes, the important thing is that my brother will certainly no longer conduct the Philharmonic concerts because he is simply not strong enough. He will conduct no Wagner this season, the first time he conducts will be the first act of *Die Königin von Saba* at the 'théâtre paré' gala,[101] but please do not breathe a word of this. In this way he will be able to avoid any excitement caused by ovations, and he has wanted for a long time to revive *Die Königin von S.* in Vienna.[102]

---

[98] This 'circular' letter was dated 19 Sept. 1900.
[99] See Clemens Hellsberg, *Gustav Mahler und die Wiener Philharmoniker*, 247 ff.
[100] *Die Reichswehr* (2 Apr. 1901).
[101] Actually Mahler conducted *Così fan tutte* on 12 Apr. He then conducted the first performance of the *Neueinstudierung* of *Tannhäuser* on 11 May, and the second on 2 June, which shows that by then he was well enough to tackle Wagner.
[102] Letter to Karpath from Justi, dated 5 Apr. Estate of Ludwig Karpath.

The critics showed the same barbed enthusiasm two weeks later on 24 March,[103] after the final concert of the season conducted by Schalk, which included Tchaikovsky's *Pathétique*. 'The best part of it all,' wrote Max Graf, 'is that, for the first time since Richter's departure, people were delighted to hear a conductor who, in all objectivity, gave free rein to the innate genius of the orchestra.' It would have been difficult indeed to find a more malicious way of putting it!

Returning from Abbazia, Mahler undoubtedly felt considerable bitterness at seeing these two Viennese conductors, neither of whom was outstanding, praised at his expense. At all events, Natalie tells us, the critics' ingratitude strengthened his resolve not to stand again for the conductorship of the Philharmonic. Thus, when a delegation of the orchestra, headed by the horn-player Emil Wipperich, came to ask him not to withdraw, he replied that he would stand again only if he were unanimously re-elected, knowing full well that no conductor, not even Richter, had ever secured such a vote.[104] But Mahler's mind was made up and he therefore wrote the following letter to the committee:

Dear Sirs, I sincerely regret to have to inform you that, owing to my ill health and the exhausting work imposed by my position, I no longer feel able to conduct the Philharmonic concerts. I ask you to convey this decision, with the expression of my profound regret, to the honourable members of your corporation and to assure them of my sincere gratitude to them for the confidence they have hitherto shown me. I need hardly add that, in future as in the past, one of my most cherished duties will be to encourage and assist the Philharmonic and its conductor in every way possible and on occasion, if my strength permits, to conduct the orchestra myself.[105]

Relieved at being able to choose a conductor of their liking, the musicians promptly elected the least talented of them all, Josef Hellmesberger, junior.[106] It is worth retracing the life of this typically Viennese musician, for it reveals a great deal about the musical ways of the Austrian capital. His grandfather was Georg Hellmesberger, a famous violinist who had participated in the première of Beethoven's Ninth Symphony and had been one of the founders of

---

[103] Helm congratulated Schalk on giving the première of a symphony by Hermann Grädener, which, it seems, Mahler had refused, although it had been accepted by Richter.

[104] BMG 168–9 and Richard von Perger, *Fünfzig Jahre Wiener Philharmoniker* (Fromme, Vienna, 1910), 42.

[105] Mahler's decision was evidently not made public immediately, for *Neue Freie Presse* (14 May 1901) announced that the Philharmonic committee had just approached him again and that he had replied that 'his doctor had categorically forbidden him to resume the direction of the concerts'. According to Hellsberg, *Mahler*, Mahler had announced unofficially to the committee on 27 Jan. 1901 his intention of retiring.

[106] Born 9 Apr. 1855, Josef (Pepi) Hellmesberger, jun. had joined the Vienna Opera as a violinist in 1884. In 1886 he became Konzertmeister, and in 1900 Kapellmeister. He conducted the Philharmonic, 1901–3, and was forced to leave Vienna after being beaten up in the street by the father of a young ballerina he had seduced. He became a conductor at the Stuttgart Opera, and died in Vienna on 25 Apr. 1907. His election was achieved, rather oddly, in several stages; on 13 May 1901 the members were asked to decide between a Viennese conductor, a foreign conductor, or several foreign conductors. After a heated debate, in the course of which it emerged that Mahler had unofficially recommended Schuch to succeed him, 51 out of 81 members voted for a Viennese conductor. On 28 May Hellmesberger was finally elected with 63 votes out of 90.

the 'Viennese school for violin' and the Philharmonic Orchestra. His father was Josef Hellmesberger senior, formerly Konzertmeister of the Philharmonic, founder of the famous Quartet and director of the Conservatory while Mahler was studying there, and his mother was a well-known Viennese actress. Josef junior showed from earliest infancy an exceptional talent for the violin, a talent discovered and developed by his father, who had taught Josef Joachim, the Schrammel brothers, and a whole generation of Viennese violinists. Young Hellmesberger's name had been at first linked with that of Johann Strauss because of a concert given in 1867. In the middle of a Strauss programme which included the première of the *Blue Danube*, young Pepi, in a wig and rococo costume, had then made his first public appearance at the head of an instrumental Sextet playing Mozart's *Musical Joke*. At 15, 'Kronprinz (Crown Prince) Pepi' became second violinist in his father's Quartet. At 18 he became a *cause célèbre* in Vienna when his father approached the Emperor in an attempt to have him excused from military service. The Emperor peremptorily refused, remarking that 'even Crown Prince Rudolph had not been able to get out of it'. No matter! With rare energy and adaptability, Pepi used his military service to further his musical career. He became solo violinist and second kapellmeister of his regimental band, and from then on showed a liking and a marked talent for light music, combined with the ability to compose by the yard vaudeville trifles in 3/4 time, apparently without effort. His enjoyable spell of military service once completed, Pepi returned to his place in the Quartet, and to the ranks of the violins in the Hofkapelle and the Opera, and at the same time became a teacher at the Conservatory, which was still directed by his father. In 1879 he made his début as an operetta composer with *Anno 1815*, which was followed by many other works in the same genre. All were performed, some with great success, either in the Carl-Theater or in the café of Anton Ronacher in the Prater.

All his life Pepi was able to switch without effort from light to serious music, playing the violin at the Opera or in the Philharmonic, or stepping in to replace the Kapellmeister of the 'Banda' of the Franz Ferdinand Regiment in the cafés and pleasure gardens of the capital. In 1881 he was appointed vice-Kapellmeister at the Ring-Theater, the Viennese equivalent of the Paris Opéra-Comique. His career almost came to an abrupt end as a result of the 1881 fire, which broke out just as he was about to conduct the second German-language performance of Offenbach's *Les Contes d'Hoffmann*. He and his father, who was in the audience, were lucky to escape with their lives: the toll of fatalities caused by the fire amounted to nearly 400. Undaunted by this interruption to his career, Pepi went back to conducting his former regimental band in Vienna's parks and places of entertainment, for which he composed a Pot-pourri on themes from the *Les Contes d'Hoffmann*. He also had no scruples about conducting operettas at the Carl-Theater, an activity which some people found incompatible with the dignity of a court musician. Nevertheless, Pepi's enforced concentration on the lighter side of music was evidently not held against him, for he was soon appointed ballet conductor at the Hofoper and became a Konzertmeister of the orchestra. This new development led to the writing of some of his famous ballets: *Harlekin als Elektriker* (Harlequin as Electrician, 1884), *Die verwandelte Katze* (The Transformed Cat, 1887), and *Die Perle von Iberien* (The Pearl of Iberia, 1902). It need hardly be said that, after Mahler's appointment in 1897, the daily life and meteoric career of 'Kronprinz Pepi' lost some of their glitter, for his exceptional gift of improvisation, which enabled him to conduct any opera, even one by Wagner, without any rehearsal, was now regarded as a vice rather than a virtue.[107]

The nature of the highly successful career of this gifted but superficial musician, remarkable above all for his versatility, partly explains the cruel shock it must have been to Mahler to see him appointed in his place as chief conductor of the Philharmonic Orchestra. Hellmesberger himself was dumbfounded by this unexpected honour and presumably even more so by the laurel wreath presented to him after the first concert of the 1901–2 season. Even he realized that he had neither the personality nor the stature to attract the public, and, in fact, attendances soon began to decline, as did the artistic level of the concerts. Under Mahler, applications for subscriptions had increased so much that the committee had been able to raise the price of tickets, and as a result the musicians' individual incomes, which had come to about 300 florins per concert in Richter's time, rose to 350. Under Hellmesberger, this fell back to 300 again and then dwindled to no more than 200 during his second and last season.[108] Although their financial loss was thus quite substantial, most of the musicians were glad to see Mahler go, since their complaints against him at the Opera grew with every day that passed.[109] However, Hellmesberger, no doubt anxious to preserve good relations with Mahler, invited him to conduct the first Viennese performance of his Fourth Symphony at one of the subscription concerts.

Most of the musicians had never accepted Mahler's 'scandalous' initiatives and his lack of respect for their sacrosanct 'tradition'. In his memoirs, the cellist Theobald Kretschmann clearly expressed the general opinion of the orchestra's musicians:

Mahler ceaselessly tried to innovate by bringing a new clarity into his performances, but all too often he disturbed (*störte*) the overall sweep of the work by introducing too many analytical refinements. Unfortunately, in his enthusiasm and eagerness he went

---

[107] Jodak Freyenfels, 'Mahler und der fesche Pepi: Eine Konfrontation und ihre Elemente', *Neue Zeitschrift für Musik*, 132 (1971), 4, 78.

[108] See *Neue Freie Presse* (10 Oct. 1903).

[109] Mahler was to conduct the Philharmonic on four more occasions, namely the Vienna première of his Fourth Symphony, on 12 Jan. 1902, that of his Third Symphony, given at a 'special concert' on 14 Dec. 1904, of his Fifth at a Gesellschafts-Konzert on 7 Dec. 1905, and finally at his farewell concert to Vienna, the Gesellschafts-Konzert of 26 Nov. 1907, at which he conducted his Second Symphony. In 1907 he entrusted the first performance of his Sixth Symphony to the Konzertverein orchestra.

so far as to alter the instrumentation; he himself even claimed to be a symphonist. Only time will tell whether all this has done art a service. Opinions differed considerably on the subject.[110]

Kretschmann also reproached Mahler for his 'delight in shocking people by doing just the opposite of what all the other conductors did', particularly with Wagner, whose tradition was authentically represented only by Richter. Had not one of his Vienna friends exclaimed, after hearing Mahler conduct at the opera: 'I no longer recognize our *Meistersinger*! O holy Hans Richter!'[111] According to Kretschmann, Hellmesberger had immediately won over the orchestra and confirmed his 'early exploits' by conducting Beethoven's Ninth Symphony 'entirely in the spirit of Richter'. However, in his criticism of Mahler, Kretschmann did not go as far as the confirmed anti-Semites of the orchestra, who accused him of interpreting the repertoire works with 'cold intelligence' and 'rabbinical logic', rather than genuine emotion. 'Consequently, even when, transcending details, he tried to interpret the work as a whole, he did so in an arbitrary and not an organic manner, thus disfiguring the most sublime German masterpieces.'[112] Thus Kretschmann, like the majority of the Philharmonic musicians, was not sorry to see Mahler go.

In his description of the first Philharmonic concert conducted by Hellmesberger after Mahler's departure, Paul Stefan has adequately expressed the general feeling of relief experienced by the Viennese establishment.

He was acclaimed. He was seen as a liberator, just as, seven years later, Weingartner was seen as the liberator of the Hofoper. Mahler, the forceful, was gone, and now began an unexciting time very much to the taste of good society, a tame and lukewarm jumble without will or strength. And the conductor was presented with a laurel wreath by the city of Vienna. The scion of an old Viennese family had replaced the uncomfortable Jew. That this had been Mahler, and that the new conductor was just the opposite, what did it matter to them? He was one of theirs.[113]

In spite of the furious hostility of the players, Mahler, thanks to his conducting technique and his previously unheard-of demands in matters of sound and precision, had a decisive influence on the style and tradition of the orchestra which lasted long after his departure. There can be no doubt that he was deeply hurt and disappointed by the attitude of the musicians. He felt that he had done

---

[110] Theobald Kretschmann, *Tempi passati: Aus den Erinnerungen eines Musikanten*, 2 vols. (Prohaska, Vienna, 1910), ii. 166. Kretschmann recalls the 'scandal' of the 60-string performance of Beethoven's Quartet in F minor and reproaches Mahler for his 'sacrilegious attitude' toward composers like Beethoven and Schumann, his preference for the 'extreme registers' of the bass tuba and the E flat clarinet, and finally (and most vehemently) for his tempos in *Die Walküre*. 'When he conducted it, everything was "dragging and disjointed" (*verschleppt und zerrissen*). The "Magic Fire" of the third act, on the other hand, was far too hurried and completely lacked grandeur and solemnity (*Weihe*). Its performance even became technically impossible.'

[111] Ibid. 160.

[112] Karl Blessinger, *Mendelssohn, Meyerbeer, Mahler: Drei Kapitel Judentum in der Musik als Schlüssel zur Musikgeschichte des 19. Jahrhunderts* (Hahnefeld, Berlin, 1939), 81.

[113] PSG 16.

far more for their standing and material well-being than his predecessors; besides getting them a rise in salary at the Opera, he had succeeded, after the Paris concerts in 1900, in having them named Hofmusiker, a title by which they set great store. Having thus abandoned all musical activity in Vienna other than the Opera, he was to devote himself to the latter with renewed energy. It seems that he recovered completely from his haemorrhage and his operation, though for some time after his return from Abbazia he had to walk with two sticks.[114]

As in the past, many of Mahler's problems as director of the Opera were due to the jealousy and rivalry among his 'ensemble' of singers. Two years earlier, he had had a hard time smoothing the ruffled feathers of Reichmann.[115] Again, on 28 January 1901, the baritone wrote to express his 'amazement and indignation' at finding his name 'struck off the programme' of *Meistersinger* the following Saturday:

You have assured me, both orally and in writing, that my incarnation of Hans Sachs was one of the most accomplished on the German stage and now, for no reason at all, you refuse to give this part to me??? I greatly admire your art and have made every effort not to upset you and to be at your disposal at all times, so as not to add to the difficulties you have to contend with. Yet you reward me with this uncalled-for slight, as if it was impossible for you to live in peace with me, as though you wished to prove to me that I am nothing but a poor devil of a subordinate who does not deserve any consideration! No, if this is how you treat me, I shall move heaven and earth to leave you and to resign from an institution that shows so little respect and gratitude.

The fact was that Reichmann was obsessed with jealousy for his younger rival, Leopold Demuth, who, though both theatrically and artistically his inferior, still had all the vocal freshness and ease in the high register which Reichmann had lost. Mahler answered him on the spur of the moment:

I have just received your letter (at home and in the middle of my lunch, for which I well deserve an hour of leisure and peace). I have already told you how much I admire your interpretation of Hans Sachs. I now tell you so again and shall go on telling you so as often as you wish. However, I have never told you that I would grant you the monopoly of either this or any other part, nor shall I ever do so for, in an institution like the Vienna Opera, so important a part cannot belong to any one person. I have decided to assign it to Herr Demuth this time, after a long interval, in order that he should not forget it and also in order to be able, in case of emergency (which, please God, will not arise), to count on him to replace you.

Moreover, it just so happens that *Der fliegende Holländer* is coming up and that this is another of your most masterly interpretations. Today, you will sing Wolfram and I therefore see no reason why you should feel sorry for yourself. I feel obliged to tell you quite frankly and in all friendship that I consider this pettifoggery unworthy both of you and of me. If anyone has reason to complain of me and my attitude, it is not you. I have never at any time been lacking in respect or regard for you and you should not degrade

[114] AMS.   [115] See above, Chap. 6.

yourself by constantly complaining, like a mere beginner, because someone else has sung one of your parts.

Our artistic relations are based on mutual esteem and, at least as far as I am concerned, on friendship. You should not therefore give way to passing ill-humour and (forgive me the harsh words) entirely misplaced self-esteem, and again and again destroy our good relations by your exorbitant demands. Do remember that you and I are here to serve the Opera, the Opera is not, as you sometimes seem to think, here to serve us. Please consider it a mark of respect for so valuable a member of this same Opera as you are that I am answering your letter so patiently and at such length, but do not bend the bow too far! You have already suffered unfortunate consequences of so doing and I would be very sorry to see a man whom I sincerely respect, both as a human being and an artist, re-embark upon such a disastrous course. I am in considerable pain and you have very thoughtlessly deprived me today of the little time I had to rest. I do not think it was very fair of you. Your faithful admirer, Gustav Mahler.[116]

Another exchange of letters reveals the wealth of patience Mahler had to expend on him. Reichmann wrote to him asking for a short leave of absence on the grounds that the day before, despite a stomach upset, he had sung the role of the Dutchman through to the end because he knew Demuth was not ready to replace him and he did not want to embarrass Mahler.

This is the result of your predilection for this gentleman[117] [who is to be] in the new productions of *Don Giovanni* and *Le nozze di Figaro*, as well as in a performance, to be given in the presence of the Emperor, of *Die Königin von Saba*, and now in an unabridged production of *Tannhäuser*. Do you want to drive me from the Opera altogether? I have sung Wolfram unabridged in Bayreuth, Berlin and Munich. I hope that you will now prove to me that I still find some favour in your eyes, otherwise I shall be deeply hurt, since my admiration and respect for your art are boundless.[118]

Ten days later Reichmann expressed his despair at having to renounce singing Sachs because he had lost his voice

as a result of singing Telramund before I had completely recovered from an attack of catarrh: . . . I am distraught beyond words, for I am not, thank God, prone to such accidents. If I do not completely recover, I shall request a fortnight's leave to convalesce in the South. As you have often intervened on our behalf I would ask you to see to it that my pay is not reduced. I repeat: this would not have happened had I not sung Telramund. My nerves are strained to breaking point and my life is that of a martyr.

And yet the following day he declared that he had fully recovered and ten days later he again wrote to Mahler imploring him not to send him on holiday but to let him sing the final *Meistersinger* of the season.

Do curb your enthusiasm for certain persons![119] You can be enchanted by them without being unjust to me, for there is no reason why you should thus prematurely take some of my roles away from me and assign them to others. Wait till my vocal powers are

---

diminished. While I am still in full possession of my voice, I shall not let anyone oust me. . . . No, Herr Direktor, you cannot indulge your inclination towards another person at my expense. You should not undermine my splendid position and degrade me. I cannot and will not surrender anything that is due to me. How seldom have you let me sing in recent times! You promised me the Templar![120] Nothing, nothing.[121]

Ludwig Karpath tells a famous story about Reichmann. Apparently he became so exasperated at Mahler's 'favouritism' that he finally wrote and told him that he refused ever to sing under his baton again! He doubtless imagined that Mahler would let one of his assistants conduct the performances in which he was singing, but Mahler, with good-humoured sarcasm, replied that, 'in future, he would automatically exempt him from singing any of the works he was conducting'. Since Mahler's repertoire included most of the operas in which the baritone achieved his greatest successes, Reichmann had to give in.[122] Until his death in 1903, he was a member of the Vienna Opera, a specialist in 'dark' characters such as Hans Heiling, the Flying Dutchman, Wotan, but also a memorable Wolfram and an unforgettable Sachs.[123]

A few months later, the plague of jealousy between singers again struck the Opera. Its victim this time was the Wagnerian tenor, Erik Schmedes, for whom the competition of his young colleague, Leo Slezak, had become unbearable.[124] Slezak had auditioned for Mahler in 1898, when he belonged to the Brünn (Brno) Opera, but had since then been engaged in Berlin for three years. On the day of the audition, when he sang the first solo from *Lohengrin*, a voice interrupted him from the shadows of the stalls: 'I warn you, if you drag it, you can go to the devil!'[125] Slezak must in fact have had a tendency to slow down, for later Mahler often scolded him about matters of rhythm and tempo. However, his voice had such freshness and brilliance that Mahler wanted to engage him on the spot, though at first he was unsuccessful.[126] Finally Slezak made his début as a guest at the Vienna Opera on 23 January 1901,[127] in *William Tell*, and was an immediate sensation. The audience at the Hofoper was dazzled by

[120] In Marschner's *Der Templer und die Jüdin*.
[121] Letter from Reichmann, 29 May 1901 (HOA).
[122] Ludwig Karpath, *Lachende Musiker* (Knorr & Hirth, Munich, 1929), 95.
[123] Born in 1850, Theodor Reichmann died on 22 May 1903. According to Theodor Helm, he always gave his worst performance in the role of Don Giovanni (THE 317).
[124] Born in Schönberg, Moravia, Leo Slezak (1873–1946) studied as an engineer before becoming a singer. He made his début in Brno in 1896, in *Lohengrin*, and was subsequently engaged by the Berlin Opera. He was a member of the Vienna Opera until 1912, and again 1917–34. In 1907 he studied for some time in Paris with Jean de Reszke. After Mahler's death, he had a triumphant career, appearing on all the world's important stages, especially in the USA.
[125] Leo Slezak, 'Gustav Mahler', *Moderne Welt*, 3: 7 (1922–3), 17. The story of this audition, which was also the first encounter between Slezak and Mahler, is told with a lightly satirical tone which lends it great charm. It is no doubt true to life.
[126] See below.
[127] That evening Slezak and the soprano had a difference of opinion. The latter wished to incorporate a cadenza into their duet, a kind of 'exotic *Kakezerei*' that she would perform while he held one note and 'served only to supply a musical background'. Slezak refused, declaring himself incapable of learning anything new only two days before his first 'guest' performance.

his youthful voice, whose suppleness and breadth enabled him to take light parts as well as dramatic tenor roles.[128] Two days later, Mahler received the following letter from Schmedes:

In recent times many things have happened that make it very difficult for me to continue working at the Opera with pleasure and satisfaction. Nastiness on the part of the press and from many other quarters that suddenly run me down and deprive me of all desire to go on working here, all this has made me deeply unhappy, and I very much fear that, unless things change, my voice and my personality will suffer very much in the long run. Therefore I find myself obliged to ask you to let me go.

I am the sort of person who thrives only in pleasant and friendly surroundings; inner sorrow, agitation and annoyance are extremely harmful to me, and have disastrous effects on my artistic activity in general! I can give my best only in the kind of conditions that prevailed during the first two years of my engagement. Only they can ensure my inner equilibrium and allow the talent that God gave me to reach full maturity. You, too, used to behave differently, how often did you say, 'Schmedes alone saved the performance for me!' You spoke to me after every act, spurred me on and gave me such joy and encouragement that I performed with self-confidence. Now you hardly say anything, and that depresses and affects me profoundly. In one word, dear Herr Director, all this makes me so deeply unhappy that eventually my work here will not be much good. Having always been told that I was among the best, I now feel the opposite, and it is too much; I cannot endure it. Since I am so depressed and find so little happiness here, I might earn honours and money elsewhere if you were to allow me to accept some important, flattering and advantageous offers as for instance to sing Siegfried in Paris. Once again you have refused, though it would have made me very happy and brought in some money, both of which I need. You told me recently that a change in my contract, that is to say a financial improvement, is not to be expected. All this makes me so unhappy, so bitter, so sick, that I cannot hear it any longer. Seeing that under the circumstances I cannot make my fortune here, I must seek it elsewhere, and I ask you therefore to give serious consideration to my request.[129]

Moving though this letter is in its frankness and simplicity, it must have tried Mahler's patience sorely. In his reply, which has not survived,[130] he must have tried to ease the pain inflicted by Slezak's success on Schmedes's self-esteem, and no doubt convinced him that any change in his (Mahler's) attitude was purely imaginary. The archives of the Opera do not contain any further letter from the Danish tenor until the summer. In August, however, Schmedes again sought permission to sing, the following April, in the first Paris performance of *Götterdämmerung*, conducted by Alfred Cortot with a 'first-rate cast'. A simple 'no' was scribbled by Mahler on the original of this second letter. He con-

---

[128] Slezak was a particular favourite of the public as Stolzing in *Meistersinger*. When Mahler offered him an engagement in 1898, he asked journalists to keep silent until the tenor was free. Unfortunately Ludwig Karpath, not wanting to be 'led by the nose' by Mahler, revealed the planned engagement in a *Neues Wiener Tagblatt* article. It duly fell through (BMG 395). Mahler persuaded the Emperor to award a decoration to the director of the Berlin Opera to free Slezak a few months before the end of his contract.

[129] Letter of 25 Jan. 1901 (HOA).

[130] As mentioned above, Mahler's letters to Schmedes have disappeared.

sidered it his duty to prevent the members of the Vienna Opera from tiring their voices singing abroad, while in Vienna they so often asked for leave of absence to recover from the strain of the season.

Some time later, Slezak's consistent and outstanding success again began to depress Schmedes, especially since early in the autumn he was forced by a severe bout of influenza to take to his bed, leaving the field clear for his young rival. In a letter of 5 November, he complains of Slezak being given heroic roles like Tannhäuser, while he had expected him to be kept for the lighter roles.

My young colleague Herr Slezak sings so many roles and gets so many things, while I am given nothing. I know this is due to the fact that I cannot be relied on as much as had been hoped; that is regrettable and I am the first to suffer from this. . . . I hope, Herr Direktor, you will treat me more kindly again; as I said to you before, I am capable of doing anything, as long as you look after me and are kind to me.[131]

Such documents show what an enormous expenditure of patience and tact Mahler often had to make in order to keep the vast machinery of the Opera turning over smoothly. Another 'problem' singer was the tenor Franz Pacal, who, having received a very advantageous offer from the Frankfurt Opera the year before, had agreed to remain in Vienna only on the strength of certain promises Mahler had made. Later on he said that the director had not only denied having made them, declaring he had no recollection of them, but had also added: 'If you dare speak to me like that, I shall have nothing more to do with you.' Pacal thereupon wrote to the Intendant and the Lord Chamberlain complaining that Mahler had 'ruined my career' by describing him to the whole Opera as a 'man without talent' who 'should be kicked out of the theatre'.

The most noteworthy event in the closing weeks of the 1900–1 Hofoper season was a *Neueinstudierung* (not a *Neuinszenierung*) of *Tannhäuser*, which opened on 11 May 1901. Mahler restored all the passages previously cut, using as basis the original (Dresden) version of the score, more perhaps from necessity than conviction, since his negotiations with C. F. Peters, publishers of the Paris version, had come to nothing.[132] Unfortunately, the Intendant's office this

---

[131] HOA. Although relations between Mahler and Schmedes soon became cordial again, Mahler soon found himself in conflict with Slezak, who quickly became a star, was fêted by the public, and began to receive invitations from everywhere. In Feb. 1901, Mahler had to forbid him to extend his stay in Breslau, where he was singing *Tannhäuser* and had been subsequently asked to take part in a concert (letter from Slezak of 21 Feb., HOA). This was the beginning of a long series of confrontations with the young tenor: he never whole-heartedly accepted the rules of the Vienna Opera, according to which leave to sing abroad was only exceptionally granted.

[132] Gustav Schönaich relates that the firm demanded a copyright fee, whereas Helm attributed Mahler's decision not to give the Paris version to his dislike of ballet. Certain of Mahler's 'improvements' were not appreciated by the Viennese Wagnerites, and particularly Richter, who, in a letter to Karpath (24 Feb. 1902), publ. in *Neues Wiener Tagblatt* (28 Sept.), summed up the 'crimes' he had committed in *The Flying Dutchman* (see Chap. 3) and *Tannhäuser*. In the latter opera, Richter said, the wind instruments symbolized the serious, virtuous, and religious elements, while the violins personified sensuality. Thus, in the Prelude to Act II, the pure joy of Elisabeth (oboes) contrasted with the ironic laughter of Venus (violins). Yet, at the end of the final act, Mahler had omitted the woodwinds in the Pilgrims' Chorus when the flowering staff is brought in! He was far too talented, Richter said, to perpetrate such atrocities and should know better than to give the impression that he was 'trying to be different at all costs'.

time imposed strict economy. This in no way diminished Mahler's zeal and enthusiasm, or his customary meticulousness in rehearsals. A much later article of reminiscences tells how Mahler had obtained permission from Prince Montenuovo to use, for the Landgraf's entrance in the first act, the entire pack of dogs from the imperial hunting lodge at Göding, about seventy pedigree dogs, controlled by hunt officials and youthful helpers. He held a special two-hour rehearsal for them, to ensure in particular that the dogs would bark during their entry with the Landgraf[133] and subsequently keep silent so as not to interrupt the music. Mahler became very fond of the dogs, and at each performance brought them special titbits to eat. In this same scene, it was customary practice to bring on some docile but dispirited horses which the Landgraf, Walther, Wolfram, and their acolytes would mount as they left the Wartburg. Mahler objected to the choice of such plebeian hacks. Since the characters were nobles, he wanted them to have horses to match. Surely in the Opera, as in the army, fine people should have fine horses? Again, it seems, he got his way with the Lord Chamberlain.[134]

The critics did not fail to notice the inadequacies of the *Tannhäuser* sets and costumes. Schönaich deplored, above all, the 'impossible garments' of the aristocratic guests of the Wartburg, which he found painfully shabby in comparison to the magnificent costumes worn by the royal retinue when it made its entry in Goldmark's *Die Königin von Saba* in the new version that had recently been put on. Nevertheless, he acknowledged the merits of several of the changes Mahler had made, especially those of the Venusberg scene and the closing scene, which had previously been neglected. The entire performance had revealed the hand of Gustav Mahler, particularly the 'miraculous' precision of every semiquaver; however, Schönaich disapproved of certain of the 'dragged-out and distorted' tempos, which were contrary to the composer's metronomic indications and out of keeping with his style.[135] Even though

---

[133] *Fremden-Blatt* (12 May 1901) confirms, in its column 'Aus der Theaterwelt', that Mahler gave over an entire rehearsal to the dogs, adding that he tried in vain to make them bark fortissimo when the Landgraf sounded his horn. Apparently, 12 horns were used in this scene.

[134] The same article of reminiscences, publ. much later for another revival of *Tannhäuser*, relates that on one occasion Mahler, wanting to congratulate Mildenburg at the end of the opera for her performance as Elisabeth, rushed on to the stage, to the bier where she was still lying after the funeral procession in the Finale, only to find a nameless ballerina replacing her. As it happens, however, the role of Elisabeth was sung in this production by Selma Kurz, while Mildenburg sang Venus, so the anecdote should be taken with a grain of salt, unless Mahler's congratulations were in fact intended for Kurz (Julius Stern, *Wiener Theaterwoche*: undated press cutting, Vondenhoff collection). The article probably appeared in the *Wiener Volkszeitung*, for which Stern was writing at the time. It dates from 1919–26, when *Tannhäuser* was revived, and Franz Schalk and Richard Strauss were co-directors of the Vienna Opera.

[135] Schönaich admitted that Wagner had declared he would 'definitely give up this type of indication', for every time he heard a tempo that was inexact or contrary to his intentions in either *The Flying Dutchman* or *Tannhäuser*, it almost always turned out to be 'that of the metronome'. However, some of the slow tempos and 'distortions' introduced by Mahler, seemed to Schönaich foreign to the spirit of the Master, who had conducted the work himself in Vienna in 1875. Transformed into an Adagio, the Landgraf's monologue ('Noch bleibe denn . . .') had lost all its effect, the singer having been 'imprisoned' in the walls. In the official address that followed, the contrasts between 'fury' and 'excessive gentleness' had been 'exaggerated, and contrary to reason' and the 'rigid precision of the rendition had been unsuited to the lyric and poetic

Wagner had fought hard for slow tempos, he had never advocated such excesses, which 'turn reason into folly and blessings into curses'. Besides, the conductor's 'tyrannical' baton had caused difficulties for the singers at certain points in the work. As to Selma Kurz, her personality was utterly unsuited to the part of Elisabeth. Her gestures and expressions seemed far too 'calculated', and 'calculated by whom?', the critic wondered.

The theatre columnist of the *Fremden-Blatt* made fun of the concern with detail that Mahler had shown during rehearsals, especially in the Venusberg scene and the scene with the dogs. However, the music critic of the same paper acknowledged that the musical interpretation as a whole was imbued with Wagner's spirit, even if at times it seemed untrue to it. Kauders pronounced it a 'miracle of the art of interpretation', and full of 'delicate shadings of expression, and surprising, novel and subtle dynamic nuances', while Heuberger detected Mahler's influence in every last detail of the score, the singing and the acting, the movements of the crowd, and the 'grandiose style' of the whole performance. With this new light cast upon it, the opera seemed completely fresh. This same 'freshness', however, appeared to Hirschfeld to be entirely artificial. The *Abendpost* critic accused Mahler of performing the Overture 'bar by bar'. No doubt he had discovered 'new philosophical reasons' for having 'dulled, held back, and weakened' so many passages, but ultimately this had led him to 'devote all the power of his genius to a lost cause'. In the *Arbeiter Zeitung*, Joseph Scheu[136] admitted that the applause had been particularly enthusiastic, especially after the Overture and after the first act, but claimed that 'in the long run the numerous deliberate, calculated and contrived touches, the overall plan of the principal tempi, and the too-frequent, mannered deadening of the natural sound of the voices, became tiring'. Theodor Helm questioned not only the casting[137] but also the restoration of all the

passages', for it had made them sound 'more like outbursts of anger'. As far as the restoration of the former cuts was concerned, Schönaich was happy to hear the Finale of Act II and Elisabeth's prayer in their entirety, but not the duet of the two heroes, which he considered one of the weakest and most outmoded passages of Wagner's music. Mahler had also restored the middle verse of Tannhäuser's Hymn to Venus. In Kalbeck's view, none of the passages thus salvaged was worth the honour.

[136] According to Scheu, the Finale of Act II had not yet been performed in its original form, despite the restoration of all the cuts. Joseph Scheu (1841–1904), studied horn and composition at the Vienna Conservatory. Composer of the Hymn of the Social Democratic Movement, the *Lied der Arbeit* (Song of Work), he founded in 1872 the Wiener Musikverband (Vienna Musical Association) and in 1878 the Arbeitersängerbund (Workers' Choral Association). Throughout his life he did his best to popularize classical music, but as a man of culture and a professional musician, he did not hesitate to use learned allusions or technical terms, so that his writings were addressed more to the élite than to the masses. Although Mahler was still on good terms with Victor Adler, a friend from his student days and leading figure of the Social Democratic Movement of which the *Arbeiter Zeitung* (founded in 1895) was the principal organ, Scheu was one of the few journalists to have criticized Mahler from the beginning, as a performer for his 'lack of respect for the classics', and as a man for his 'tyrannical' personality (see Elisabeth Désirée Schuschitz, 'Die Wiener Musikkritik in der Ära Gustav Mahler, 1897–1907', thesis, Vienna, 1978). On his death in 1904, Scheu was replaced by David Joseph Bach, a close friend of Schoenberg and Webern, and a great admirer of Mahler.

[137] In his view, the cast was not of sufficiently high quality to bring the weaker passages to life. Selma Kurz sang a 'snivelling, sentimental Elisabeth, devoid of nobility', Winkelmann was not in good voice on the first night, and Mildenburg lacked seductiveness as Venus.

previously cut passages, for he felt that the Dresden version contained too much that was redundant and dreary. Besides, he wrote, Mahler had frequently erred in his choice of tempos, in particular with the 'unbearable slowness' of the Hymn to Venus and several other passages in the first act,[138] where he was all the more to blame since Wagner had often complained that his music was conducted too slowly. Helm nevertheless conceded that the beauty and power of the crescendos often made up for such extravagances.[139]

Two events of lesser importance completed the season at the Opera. One was a splendid revival of Karl Goldmark's most famous opera, *Die Königin von Saba*, the only work of his for which Mahler had a certain admiration.[140] The anti-Semitic press accused Mahler of having spent 10,000 kronen on its sumptuous scenery and costumes, but, as always, he had endeavoured to impose unity on the various elements of the production. With the composer's consent, he had made some cuts, including the storm in the last act.[141] The *Neueinstudierung* was a great success, but the *Deutsche Zeitung* characteristically accused Mahler of devoting too much time and energy to an inferior work by a Jew who was nothing but a poor imitator of Wagner and Meyerbeer, while neglecting such German composers as Weber, Cornelius, and Hugo Wolf.[142] Never, Leitich wrote, had the weaknesses of Goldmark's opera been so glaringly exposed, despite Mahler's 'improvements' and the lavishness of the production. Finally, to satisfy the taste of the general public, Mahler put on a *Neueinstudierung* of Flotow's *Martha*,[143] one of the most popular operas of the German repertoire which he himself had frequently conducted in his youth. He took this opportunity to introduce a young conductor who was, like himself, of Jewish Czech origin, Gustav Brecher.[144] A protégé of Richard Strauss, who had

[138] Especially 'gegrüsst sei uns'. Helm mentioned the ovation that had greeted the Overture, but preferred Nikisch's performance.

[139] Cast of the performance of 12 May 1901: Kurz (Elisabeth), Mildenburg (Venus), Kusmitsch (Shepherd), Winkelmann (Tannhäuser), Preuss (Walther), Demuth (Wolfram), Frauscher (Landgraf).

[140] Cast of the first performance (20 Apr. 1901): Mildenburg (Queen of Sheba), Schrödter (Assad), Demuth (Solomon), Hesch (High Priest).

[141] See above, Chap 5. Mahler's opinion of Goldmark and his best-known opera.

[142] Mahler, however, had no personal feeling whatsoever for Goldmark, who had refused to intervene on his behalf when he was hoping to be appointed to the Vienna Opera. A letter Goldmark wrote him in May 1900, in reply to a telegram of good wishes on his 70th birthday, shows that their relations were far from cordial: 'Although I am frequently too loquacious in my operas, forgive me for being brief today', he began, doubtless alluding to Mahler's low opinion of his works, and concluded in the deliberately ambiguous tone that characterizes the whole letter: 'You know very well what I think of the genius Gustav Mahler' (RWO). In 1902 Mahler refused to mount Goldmark's latest opera, *Götz von Berlichingen*, which was not performed in Vienna until 1910.

[143] Cast of the performance of 4 May 1901: Saville (Martha), Hilgermann (Nancy), Naval (Lionel), Felix (Lord Tristan), Hesch (Plunkett).

[144] Gustav Brecher (1878–1940) was born in Teplitz and studied at the Leipzig Conservatory. While still a schoolboy, he composed a symphonic poem, *Rosmersholm*. He was discovered by Richard Strauss who launched him on a career in opera. Later on, he made his theatrical début in Leipzig. Mahler got him a job at the Olmütz Theater, where he himself had conducted. Brecher subsequently pursued his career in Hamburg, Cologne, Frankfurt am Main, Leipzig, and Berlin. He is mentioned in a letter Strauss addressed to Mahler on 28 Jan. 1901 (see below Chap. 11), 'I wrote today to Gustav Brecher. He will approach you shortly. Make him welcome! He is a talented and cultivated man who, I am sure, will do you good service.'

warmly recommended him, he was not successful in Vienna. The anti-Semitic press claimed he had not managed 'to give the requisite precision to the ensembles'. Only the *Neue Freie Presse* found them 'faultless'. For once, Mahler agreed with his adversaries. In a letter to Strauss written in August, he called Brecher a 'charming and likable boy' but felt that he had 'far too little routine and experience' for the Vienna Opera, and promised to find him a temporary job in the provinces for a couple of seasons.[145] Brecher's failure convinced Mahler that he must write once again to his favourite and most zealous disciple, Bruno Walter, to offer him a post as conductor, and the problem which for two years had caused him so many headaches was at last resolved.

The schedule of the 1900–1 season shows a large increase in Wagner performances (70, as against 59 the previous year), with six complete *Ring* cycles and a chronological sequence of his main works, from *Rienzi* to *Götterdämmerung*. The number of Mozart performances was also higher: 21 as compared with 13 the previous year. The most performed works were *Fledermaus* (17), *Carmen* and *Tannhäuser* (14), *Il trovatore* (13), *Lohengrin* (12), *Faust* and *Mignon* (11), *Pagliacci* and *Die Königin von Saba* (10), *Aida*, *Die Meistersinger*, and *Manon* (9), *Cosi* (8), *Siegfried* and *The Flying Dutchman* (7). Thus Mahler had finally succeeded in significantly reducing the proportion of light works and of Italian and French operas in favour of major German works. Franz Willnauer, who divides the years of Mahler's directorship into three periods, observes that, in the early years, he was constantly on the podium (almost as much as in Hamburg), learning for himself the qualities and faults of the Viennese ensemble.[146] From 1900 on, his efforts were directed less to presenting works in an exemplary manner than to extending the repertoire and forging a cohesive team with the new singers he was to engage or with those at his disposal. Some productions had aged: but he let them be until such time as he had the funds to revise them completely. When that happened, he fully recast them and started rehearsing the musical interpretation from scratch. After 1900 Mahler also conducted far less frequently himself[147] and tried all sorts of experiments in casting. Examining the Hofoper *Spielplan*, Franz

---

[145] Brecher's failure at the Vienna Opera is all the more mystifying since he subsequently had a brilliant career as a conductor, notably in performing the works of Richard Strauss (see Vol. iii, Chap. 8). It was he who encouraged Peters Edition to publish Mahler's Fifth Symphony (see below, Chap. 15). According to Otto Klemperer, he was particularly gifted for the theatre. He later married one of the daughters of the director of the big German electricity company AEG (Allgemeine Electrizitäts-Gesellschaft), where Arnold Berliner held an important post, and was one of the Jews who, in their firm conviction of belonging to the German nation, refused to leave when the Nazis came to power. After losing everything he possessed, Brecher and his wife escaped to Lisbon in 1940; not having received their American visas, they had to return to Belgium. A fisherman at Ostend promised to take them in his boat to England, but they were never seen again (Peter Heyworth, *Conversations with Klemperer* (Gollancz, London, 1973), 39).

[146] WMW 75 and 208 ff.

[147] During his first season, Mahler conducted 111 performances of 23 operas; in 1898–9, 99 performances (14 operas); and in 1899–1900, 97 performances of 28 operas. In 1900–1, he conducted 53 performances of 19 operas (but it must be recalled that his schedule was disrupted by illness); in the following season, 36 performances of 11 operas; in 1902–3, 53 performances of 12 operas; in 1903–4, 38 performances of 11 operas. For the financial results of each season, soloists's salaries, and ticket prices, see Vol. iii, App.

Willnauer also identifies the period after 1900 as that in which the Vienna Opera became a genuine 'repertory theatre', though of limited scope. Between 1900 and 1904, the accent was to be on 'events' prepared with meticulous care, rather than on current repertoire and exploits by individual singers. It was at this time that the press began to blame Mahler for devoting all his energy to a few exceptional performances and letting the quality of the rest deteriorate.

With the Opera season behind him, Mahler was at last able to look forward to a quiet summer in his new house at Maiernigg. It had been nearing completion when he left there at the end of the previous summer. During the winter, he had constantly urged Alfred Theuer, his architect, to do everything possible to finish the job before his return to Carinthia. Having obtained permission from the court officials, no doubt because of his health, to leave Vienna early, he took the train to Klagenfurt on 5 June. Justi had gone ahead to put everything in order at the 'Villa Mahler' and make it look 'lived in'. Ideally situated between the forest and the lake, the house stands today exactly as Mahler built it. A solid rather than elegant building, old-fashioned in style at a time when Austria had assumed a leading role in modern art and architecture, it is a tall, comfortable, well-built house, something between a lake-side villa and a mountain chalet, suggesting solidity and prosperity. It stood on ground that sloped steeply down to the lake. A footbridge led straight into the main living area, the ground floor, from which a stair descended to the basement and the lake shore. From every window, there was a panoramic view over the Wörthersee, Justi's room and the main living-room opening on to a loggia, the roof of which served as veranda for the dining-room and guest room on the first floor. On the second floor, Mahler's quarters included a small dressing-room and a washroom. The bedroom opened on to a balcony. It was furnished with a huge table so that it could also be used as a study. Standing outside and looking out over the Wörthersee on the day he arrived, he exclaimed, 'It's too beautiful, one shouldn't allow oneself such a thing.' In the innermost recesses of his puritanical soul, he felt as though, after having so long forsworn luxury, pleasures, and everything that could contribute to making his life more enjoyable, he had arrived there by some strange irony of fate. He often smiled to himself during the summer as he pondered the novelty, so utterly unexpected, of his life as a house-owner.

The day of his arrival, 5 June, Justi wrote to Henriette Mankiewicz, who had sent her friends a porcelain service for the villa:

I'm in such a whirl over my new condition as 'villa-proprietress' that so far I've hardly been able to sleep at night. Gustav is beside himself with happiness over the house, on the whole it has turned out much better than we expected as far as the situation is concerned. We would have liked it inwardly and outwardly not quite so ordinary, but these are things that can easily be changed in the autumn. Gustav's room is wonderful, and he feels very well in it . . .[148]

[148] Letter from Justine Mahler to Henriette Manckiewicz, 5 June [1901], LCW.

However, the things that pleased Mahler most were the garden and a piece of forest land he owned and through which he had had stepped paths built, together with a 'shore walk' on the embankment below the house that became his favourite place for strolling after dinner. During one of his first exploratory walks, he was delighted to discover a spring close by his property which would supply the house with drinking water. He hastened to buy the additional piece of land, had the flow of water measured, and took a passionate interest in the tapping process, which required the digging of several channels.[149] On the lake-shore Mahler had a small boat-house built to hold two boats and, on either side of it, two bathing huts with flat roofs for sunbathing. He went there daily, for he had become one of the first advocates of the 'new method' of alternate swimming and sunbathing. He also got into the habit of plunging into the lake first thing every morning.

The *Häuschen* was linked to the house by a steep path that became dangerously slippery when it rained (and it rained a great deal during the first two weeks in Maiernigg).[150] From the moment he arrived, Mahler took refuge there for several hours each day, but complained of his usual difficulties in resuming his composing. In the meantime, he prepared himself by reading books and music. An article by Hermann Kretzschmar[151] he happened to read in a magazine particularly interested him, because it provided scientific justification for the principles of the interpretation of early music which he himself had arrived at by instinct, 'like a diviner surveying a terrain with his rod for running water', whereas to arrive at the same result, science needs a barometer and a hygrometer—or indeed a pig that finds moisture because there are truffles there'.[152]

From his Fourth Symphony onwards, polyphony played an ever-increasing part in Mahler's music. Thus Natalie's observation that he regularly received and carefully studied the volumes of the Bachgesellschaft is of the utmost significance. Not only the polyphonic works but the harmonizations of chorales fascinated him: 'Bach was not concerned with the novelty of the themes,' he said, 'but primarily with their treatment, their development and the hundreds of possibilities of transforming them, just as the Greeks always used the same subjects in their tragedies and comedies, but each time gave them different forms.'[153] Bach's place in musical history seemed to him to be unchallenged. 'His miraculous polyphony was unparalleled in his time and will remain so for *all* time', he exclaimed after reading the Third Motet.

[149] NBL1. 160; NBL2. 187.

[150] In Sept. 1900 Natalie, who had stayed on alone at Maiernigg, had written Mahler several letters informing him of the progress of the building and telling him about her difficulties in finding a direct route between the new house and the *Häuschen*.

[151] Hermann Kretzschmar (1848–1924) studied at the Conservatories of Leipzig and Dresden, had a brief career as a conductor and then taught history of music at the Univ. of Leipzig, where he directed both the Bachgesellschaft and the chorus of the Riedelverein. He wrote many books and articles and, together with Hugo Riemann, was regarded as the most eminent German musicologist of his time.

[152] NBL1. 160; NBL2. 188.   [153] NBL1. 161; NBL2. 189.

The way the eight voices are led along in a polyphony which he alone masters is unbelievable! I am only slowly learning to read them (they're impossible to play on the piano), but I'd love to perform them someday and I must do so. The world would be amazed. I can't tell you how much Bach teaches me (but then, of course, I'm nothing but a child sitting at his feet), for my method of composing is innately 'Bachic!'[154] If only I had the time to devote myself entirely to the teachings of the greatest of all masters! Just think what it would do for me, I can hardly grasp it myself! However, it's to him that I shall devote my time, when at long last I belong entirely to myself.[155]

Mahler promised himself that, when that time came, he would read numerous scores by the masters, and above all those he did not yet know. Why, he wondered, were there so many complete editions of classic writers, but not of classic composers whom every musician ought to know? Even among Beethoven's works there were still some, such as the First Mass, which he himself did not know. In his view, reading scores was a must for every musician. While talking to Natalie a few weeks previously about a blind musician,[156] he had agreed that a man deprived of his sight could be predestined to become a musician, but

only if he could absorb existing compositions in the same way as one who sees; for hearing scores played on the piano or in bad performances can never replace the reading of a score for somebody who wants to create. And how could he compose without writing down the possible versions and modifications? Nobody can do it for him; indeed, the presence of a stranger would be death to his creative activity. If I lost my hearing I think I could go on composing; but if I lost my sight it would be the end of my creative work; at most I could be useful as a teacher.[157]

During the peaceful summer of 1901, Mahler also re-read the songs of Schumann, 'one of the greatest composers of this kind of music, ranking alongside Schubert', a musician who

surpassed all others in his mastery of the perfectly enclosed form of the Lied; his subject always lies within limits of the Lied so that he never includes anything that takes him beyond. Contained sensibility, true lyricism and deep melancholy lie in his songs, of which the less famous ones, not sung all the time like *Frauen-Liebe und -Leben*, are my favourites.[158]

In his youth, reading scores of the greatest masters had depressed him, for in his egoism he had thought, 'You, you'll never be able to do anything like that! Now things are reversed, anything less good or weak depresses me as much as

[154] The pun on Bach and Bacchus (who appears in the first movement of the Third Symphony) is typical of Mahler.
[155] NBL1. 161ff. NBL2. 189. Mahler's own Bachgesellschaft volumes were sold in London, at an auction held in 1992 by Sotheby's.
[156] NBLS, Mar. 1901. The musician's name was Rudolf Braun (1869–1925) and he was then quite well-known. Mahler had given three of his pantomimes at the Hofoper.
[157] It is surprising not to find Mahler alluding here to Beethoven, whom he idolized and repeatedly gave as an example.
[158] NBL1. 161; NBL2. 188ff.

if I myself had composed something bad or inadequate.' And he added the deservedly famous remark: 'A work whose limits can be seen smells of mortality, which I cannot tolerate in art.'[159] Early in the summer Mahler also played chamber music on the top floor of the house with Natalie and Rosé, he himself being obliged to use the mediocre piano he had hired in Klagenfurt. The two violinists played for him the Violin-Duos by Spohr, whose elegance and skilful instrumental writing he admired, and then he and Rosé played transcriptions of Brahm's Clarinet Sonatas, which they had gone through in Vahrn two years before. This time Mahler wondered how he could have had such a poor impression of them initially. 'Everything needs to be approached in the right mood (*Stimmung*),' Mahler said, 'otherwise it loses its effect.'[160]

After one of these musical evenings, Mahler and Natalie, still full of the music they had played, went for a walk along the lake shore and the new pathway to the spring whose clear water so delighted him, and he again went into ecstasies over the beauty of the place: 'You see,' he said, 'once again it turns out to be true: what you desire in your youth you get in abundance in old age. Would you ever have believed that we would be able to call so heavenly a place "ours"?'[161] 'Happy as children,' Natalie writes, they went up to the house, 'from the darkness of the garden up to Gustav's brilliantly lit room.' Then, from the balcony, they looked at the sky, and at the myriad stars reflected in the still waters of the lake. The better to enjoy the sight, they put the lights out and talked for a long time in the dark. Hardly had they parted to go to bed when Mahler heard a feeble cry like a groan coming from the shore. He dashed out on to the balcony, shouting, 'Who's there?' but, hearing nothing more, he went back to bed. A few minutes later, wailings and gurglings sent him flying barefoot down the stairs and out to the lake. In the water close by the little landing stage, he made out a man who ('through drunkenness or with bad intentions', writes Natalie) had fallen into the water and seemed about to drown. With great difficulty—for the stranger clung to him and nearly pulled him under—he got him out, laid him down, unconscious, on the bank, and then ran to call the others. They all bustled about reviving him, comforting him, feeding him. He recovered and left in due course, provided with dry clothes, without telling them his name.[162]

From 5 June, the very beginning of his holiday, Mahler started composing Lieder. The first sketch of 'Ich atmet' einen Lindenduft' is dated 9 June. 'Blicke mir nicht', based on another Rückert poem, is dated 14 June. Others followed: the last of the *Wunderhorn-Lieder*, 'Der Tamboursg'sell', was finished in piano score on 12 July. 'Ich bin der Welt abhanden gekommen', another *Rückert-Lied*,

[159] NBL1. 163; NBL2. 190.   [160] NBL2. 191.

[161] The possessive 'ours' which appears in Natalie's text could really have been used by Mahler in the sense of the 'family' of which she had obviously become a member. But it is also a fact that her relationship with Mahler was closer and warmer than ever before.

[162] NBL2. 192. *Neue Freie Presse* (31 July 1901) related that Mahler had seen a man about to drown near a sailing-boat and had brought him ashore semi-conscious. This might be a distortion of the same incident.

concluded that summer's rich harvest of songs on 16 August. Yet, during the first weeks at Maiernigg, Mahler could not settle down to more intensive work. No doubt feeling discouraged, he decided to allow himself two weeks of complete rest in July. However, no sooner had he resolved to do this, than he plunged into what his friends assumed to be a symphony. Such was the intensity of his creative impulse that even the noise of hammering and sawing that reached him from the villa did not disturb him. Even walking and admiring the beauties of nature did not interrupt his work: he carried with him everywhere a small notebook to jot down the ideas as they came into his head. Why, he lamented, had he not done so much earlier? If the abundant flow of inspiration were one day to run dry, he would be able to draw on what he had stored up over the years. 'What a waste of superhuman effort and strength', he exclaimed,

to have to create everything on the spur of the moment, with no store or collection (in the literal sense of the word) to draw on. If, on the other hand, I had let nothing go to waste during the summer but had collected everything and stored it up, I would only have to stretch out my hand in order to find what I need. This is how Beethoven, towards the end of his life, unearthed and used themes he had noted down years before.[163]

In August, Mahler brought up the subject of these notebooks again, stating that he on no account wanted them to survive his death:

I will destroy everything that is not finished, for such fragments only lead to misunderstandings. What have they discovered from Beethoven's notebooks? That he apparently worked on several different projects at once because they found sketches for them in the same notebook? Not at all! He had never ceased to have all sorts of ideas which he jotted down and kept for future use at a suitable opportunity. Or they talk about the 'progress accomplished' in the final versions, but no one knows what his first inspiration might have become in his hands.[164]

Although Mahler still kept silent as to the nature of his activity, none of his family doubted that it was a major project he was working on. In early August, during another walk with Natalie, he began to speak of Brahms, of Steinbach, and of Ischl.

They were the most blissful days of my life, those of my honeymoon with my muse! Since then it has become a real marriage. We have one child after another, as though that were quite normal, and it hardly even occurs to us to thank one another for this happiness. . . . My present creative work is that of an adult, a man of ripe experience. Although I no longer attain my former heights of enthusiasm, I am now in full command of my powers and my technique, I feel that I am master of my means of expression and capable of carrying out anything I put my hand to.[165]

During this first holiday as a 'property-owner', Mahler had to deal with the

[163] NBL1. 162; NBL2. 189 ff.   [164] NBLS, Aug. 1901.   [165] NBL2. 192, 4 Aug. 1901.

current problems of the Hofoper just as he had done in previous summers. Przistaupinsky, his secretary, came and stayed for a few days in Krumpendorf, on the other side of the lake, visiting him almost every day to discuss questions with him. Przistaupinsky's letters to Ferdinand Graf and Carl Sageder, his assistants who were still in Vienna, speak of 'the Herr Director's good health and good humour'.[166] As happened every summer, some of the singers were trying to get their leave extended. Mahler had to refuse such an extension to Mildenburg, reminding her that she had to sing Irene in *Rienzi* on 1 September.[167] Fritz Schrödter waxed indignant at being granted leave as if it were a favour, when he had a contractual right to it. In a letter remarkable for its pugnacity and impertinence, he went so far as to threaten legal proceedings against the Opera if this were refused him![168]

At the end of July 1901, Mahler received from Richard Heuberger, whom he had known ever since his Budapest days, a letter of surprising length and insistence. The previous year the critic of the *Neue Freie Presse* had attacked Mahler violently on the occasion of the famous Philharmonic performance of Beethoven's Ninth. Now Heuberger, as a composer of operettas, urged the director of the Opera, who three years before had included his ballet *Der Struwelpeter*[169] in the repertoire, to consider his operetta *Ein Opernball* (An Opera Ball). The arguments he put forward did not do him credit, as the following résumé shows: the work in question was 'generally considered' to be superior to all others in the genre: it was so popular with the Viennese public that it would be sold out the day the performance was announced; only Mahler's well-known care and expertise could help to overcome the exceptional difficulties of the score and ensure an altogether faithful performance: the composer would gladly rehearse the singers himself, help with the production, and even conduct it—indeed he was very anxious to do so! Heuberger suggested which singers should be chosen, and added:

Make this sacrifice for me and look at the score of the *Opernball*, so that you can see I'm offering you something good, not something risky.... I won't pester you any further, but only ask you to think the matter over and bring to it that love which you would never deny to anything good, whatever the genre. From this beginning there might emerge a repertoire piece that could stand beside *Die Fledermaus*.[170]

Mahler's reply, which shows what dignity he could summon up on such occasions, deserves to be quoted in full:

---

[166] Letters of 19, 23, and 26 July from Przistaupinsky to Ferdinand Graf, of 15 July to Carl Sageder, of 29 July from Mahler to Carl Sageder, and of 6 Aug. from Przistaupinsky to the same (HOA, no. 156/1901).

[167] Undated letter to Mildenburg (ÖNB, Theatersammlung). The previous Dec., Mahler had had to refuse Mildenburg time off to sing in Bayreuth, 'because the doctors require that she take at last two or three months' holiday a year, this being indispensable for her recuperation' (HOA, autograph telegram of 12 Dec. from Mahler to Cosima Wagner).

[168] Letter from Schrödter to Mahler of 14 and 26 June 1901, and Mahler's replies of 23 June and 6 July 1901 (HOA, no. 160; Z.VIII.109/1901). Mahler eventually granted Schrödter an extra week's leave.

[169] The première took place on 8 Jan. 1898. The work was given thirteen times that year but never revived.

[170] Letter from Heuberger to Mahler, 21 July 1901 (HOA, Z.514/1901).

At the moment it is not possible for me to reply fully to your kind letter. You perhaps are not aware that my 'time' during holidays is short, and that I have to be miserly with every minute. But I do ask you to consider me completely at your disposal once I am back in Vienna and have resumed my duties; even if I seem to be under pressure. I suggest that you send me the score of your *Opernball*, which unfortunately I do not know, so that I can have it in my hands in <u>Vienna</u> at the end of August; I shall be back myself at about that time. You can rest assured of my sincere efforts to do what is best for you and your work. I shall be delighted if I am able to share the opinions you pass on to me of the work and its virtues.[171]

Unfortunately, the judgement Mahler subsequently formed on *Ein Opernball* forced him to disappoint its composer, whose operetta was never performed at the Hofoper. It is generally admitted that Heuberger's frustration increased the number of unfavourable reviews of Mahler's productions he published in the *Neue Freie Presse*.

At the beginning of August, Justi and Rosé left Maiernigg with Albine Adler[172] and Dr Ludwig Boer, the physician of the Vienna Opera, for Heiligenblut, where Justi was to take a cure prescribed for her after an operation she had undergone the previous year. Left alone with Natalie for a few days, Mahler revelled in the complete peace and quiet 'that he so badly needs and is so seldom granted, however forcefully and stubbornly he keeps on asking for it'. Here Natalie adds a somewhat enigmatic comment about the 'complexities of the very affectionate, but never simple and smooth-running relationship of the brother and sister'. It was probably no accident that this family life, in which Justi played the role of wife, was soon to come to an abrupt end.

From time to time, the peaceful isolation of the Villa Mahler was disturbed by intruders. On 25 July a boat approached the house and, amid catcalls, shouts, and the noise of clashing oars, a whole group of young people carried on a quasi-confidential conversation: 'Do tell me what you've got against Mahler. What's he done to you . . .', 'He wrote a bad Symphony (the First), and the *Klagende Lied*'—and the uproar continued louder than ever. The following day, he was gazing at the lake from his balcony, when some young girls spied him from a motorboat and began to shriek, 'Mahler! Look there! Bravo! Bravo!' He beat a hasty retreat into his room, for such an ovation was just as distressing

[171] This reply is dated by Mahler himself, in Maiernigg, 23 July 1891!. The postmark, clearly legible on the envelope, gives the real date: 24 July 1901. The text was publ. in Robert Henried's article (*Musikblätter des Anbruch*, 18 (May 1936). See Vol. i, Chap. 5, and Vol. ii, Chap. 1). A copy of Mahler's reply is in the Opera archives (HOA, Z.514/1901). At the beginning of Sept. Mahler received a letter from another composer, Alfred Ottokar Lorenz (1868–1939), Kapellmeister in Koburg-Gotha, reminding him that he had sent him a number of scores through Natalie. Mahler's reply is a polite refusal: he has examined Lorenz's works 'with great interest' because they reveal 'an exceptionally gifted musician'. 'I shall remember them if the circumstances arise', he adds (letter from Lorenz to Mahler, 31 Aug. 1901, and reply of 12 Sept. HOA, Z.604/1901).

[172] A childhood friend of the Mahlers, from Iglau.

to him as the shouts of the day before, but he could not help smiling to himself as he thought of the contrast between the two scenes.[173]

Throughout the summer, Mahler seemed calm and relaxed. As usual, he made a few excursions, but they were less successful than those of the previous year, for the weather was poor. One day, he raced up to the Drei Bärenhütte in pelting rain and came back soaked and with his shoes full of water.[174] However, despite such mishaps and the frequent disturbances, he remained unusually serene. Whereas the previous year he had continually waged war on birds, and especially on those nesting in the roof of his *Häuschen*, he was now on excellent terms with them and enjoyed listening to them. He called them 'the first composers' and sometimes had the feeling he would be quite unable to equal them. 'Already as a child,' he said, 'I used to listen to these songs that start off like conscious melody and rhythm and then degenerate into inarticulate chirping, as though some four-footed creature suddenly sat up on its hind legs and then fell back into its natural position.'[175] It was a contradiction typical of Mahler that he could wage war on animals that disturbed his work, then turn and look at them with naïve romantic wonder. Two years earlier, on a visit to Sankt Wolfgang[176] near Salzburg, he had been amused by a small dachshund, which was enjoying his caresses, but suddenly became fascinated by the smell of cooking and forgot him completely. The immediate, total, and absolute truthfulness of animals, for whom life is always in the present, never failed to delight and stimulate him, for it was the complete opposite of human behaviour.

During the signally sterile summer of 1897, he had talked about nature's influence on his work and quoted as examples the squawking of hens, peacocks, and crows, as well as the noise of waterfalls, the ringing of bells, and even 'the melodious creaking of a door'. At Steinach am Brenner, the strangely modulated cawing of a crow had made him 'desperately sad', whereas at Steinbach am Attersee, two years earlier, these same cries had made such an impression on him that he had introduced them into the Finale of the Second Symphony.[177] 'It's in nature', he explained,

that we find our primeval themes and rhythms. . . . Man, and particularly the artist, derives his forms and subject matter from the world around him, to which he naturally lends a totally different and much wider meaning, either because he is in a state of blissful harmony with nature or because he is in painful or negative and hostile conflict with her or is trying to cope with her with humour or irony. Such are the sources, in the

---

[173] NBL1. 164; NBL2. 191.

[174] Letter of 20 Aug. to Nanna Spiegler (PML, Robin Lehmann deposit). On 26 June he had sent her a postcard of Pörtschach am Wörthersee via Natalie.

[175] NBL1. 160; NBL2. 188.   [176] NBL2. 139, end of July 1899.

[177] Mahler nevertheless observed that, when he introduced birdsong into his music, he did not imitate reality, but stylized it. For example, in his First Symphony he had used a fourth to suggest the cuckoo, not a third as in nature. He had never concerned himself with whether this conformed with reality, yet everyone had recognized this 'voice of spring' in the first movement.

narrowest sense of the word, of an artist's style: noble and sublime: sentimental and tragic; or satirical and humorous.[178]

However, the Mahler of 1897 was still immersed in the universe of the *Wunderhorn* and the Third Symphony, obsessed by its beauty and moved by its tragic dissonances. The Mahler of 1901, on the other hand, could listen to the birds with pleasure and serenity and, during these exceptionally happy days, ideas for his new symphony flowed abundantly. He finally broached the subject with Natalie at the beginning of August, when he was in the middle of the Scherzo: 'Both the construction and the ordering of the details and relation-ships (*Verhältnisse*) demand great artistic mastery because this apparent con-fusion must, as in a Gothic cathedral, be resolved into supreme order and harmony.' On 5 August he again talked to his faithful friend about this particu-lar movement, feeling that it was perhaps the grandest he had ever composed.

You wouldn't believe the trouble it's giving me, the obstacles and thorns it's strewing in my way, largely because of the simplicity of its themes, which are almost all based on tonic and dominant chords. No one else would dare do such a thing today. The progression of the chords presents formidable difficulties, above all on account of my principle that nothing should be repeated but everything should develop from within itself. The individual voices are so difficult to play that only soloists will be able to manage them. Thanks to my thorough knowledge of the orchestra and the instruments, the boldest passages and melodic movements (*Passagen und Bewegungen*) poured easily from my pen.[179]

Having borrowed a theme by Thomas Koschat, 'An dem blauen See', in the second movement,[180] Mahler was thankful to have taken it from this mediocre composer rather than from Beethoven, who 'was able to develop all of his themes himself'.[181]

He had already begun to realize that his Scherzo was entirely different from anything he had composed before:

It is so thoroughly kneaded that there is not a single grain in it which isn't blended and transformed. Each note is full of vitality and everything in it revolves as though in a whirlwind or the tail of a comet. Neither romantic nor mystical elements belong in it, it's merely the expression of an unparalleled power, that of man in the full light of day who has reached the climax of his life. The entire work will be orchestrated in the same vein, no harps or English horns.[182] The human voice has absolutely no place in it. It

---

[178] NBL1. 81; NBL2. 95. This conversation was noted by Natalie at Ridnaun, near Sterzing and the Brenner pass, on 12 July 1897. Mahler's statement provides an explanation of the 'mixture of styles' for which the critics continually attacked him. It is therefore of cardinal importance to the understanding of his music.

[179] NBL1. 164; NBL2. 192 ff. Later, however, the orchestration of the Fifth Symphony underwent several radical revisions. Of all Mahler's works, it was one of the most troublesome in this respect.

[180] Mahler calls it the 'second movement', but the preceding passage clearly refers to the 'third movement' of the Symphony. Doubtless he had not yet split the first movement in two.

[181] Thomas Koschat (1845–1914), a Carinthian composer, was the author of numerous folkloric waltzes for male chorus on texts in the Carinthian dialect. His 'Liederspiel', *Am Wörthersee*, had just been given at the Vienna Opera. I have been unable to identify the theme Mahler 'borrowed' in Koschat's score.

[182] Nevertheless these two instruments are used in the final orchestration.

doesn't need words for everything is expressed in terms of pure music. It will be a proper Symphony in four movements,[183] each one of them independent, complete in itself, and linked to the others solely by affinity of mood.[184]

As mentioned earlier, while working on his Scherzo, Mahler also composed several Lieder which he orchestrated as he went along. On 10 August he invited Natalie to the *Häuschen* so that he could play them to her. Only 'Der Tamboursg'sell' was based on a poem from the *Wunderhorn*, and the musical idea for it had come to him one day as he was leaving the table. He had hastily jotted down the first notes of the melody in the dim light of the hall, then and gone and settled near the spring where he had quickly completed it. Only then did he realize with surprise that what he had written was not a symphonic motif but that of a Lied. Recalling the opening words of 'Der Tamboursg'sell', he realized that they fitted the music so perfectly that the latter seemed to have been created for them. At the *Häuschen* he compared the whole text with the music and found that not one word or one note was missing and that the two matched each other from start to finish.[185]

Looking at Mahler's output in the summer of 1901, one is first struck by its extraordinary abundance. It is a veritable creative explosion: eight orchestral Lieder and (probably) three symphonic movements,[186] not counting the sketches Mahler must have made for the following movements if he kept to his usual practice. But the most striking aspect of all this is the character of the works themselves which, created at a time of great calm, serenity even, and in the comfort of a brand-new house, are nearly all funereal or at least mournful. Natalie's unpublished manuscript, of which I published large extracts as early as 1973, offers a very plausible explanation of this curious phenomenon, in that it describes Mahler's haemorrhage, and mentions the remarks he made immediately afterwards, as well as the doctors' fears, of which he was fully aware. Fortunately there exists another account of Mahler's state of mind after his haemorrhage, in an article published eleven years later by Bruno Walter:

When, around 1900,[187] not long before I moved to Vienna, I came from Berlin to visit Mahler, I found him just recovered from a severe illness. He was older, milder and gentler, and a profound and grave peace seemed to have pervaded his being. Years later I told him how deeply this change had moved me. 'Yes, I did learn something then,' he

[183] Apparently Mahler had not yet decided to divide the first movement into Funeral March and Allegro.
[184] Obviously, Mahler had not yet conceived the complex thematic relationships linking the March and its following Allegro; this Allegro and the Finale; the Scherzo and the Finale; and the Adagietto and the Finale.
[185] NBL1. 166; NBL2. 193. An almost identical incident occurred while he was composing his Eighth Symphony (see Vol. iii, Chap. 6). Mahler's statement confirms a passage in Natalie's *Mahleriana* where he declares that, for him, 'melody always proceeds from the text, which in a sense creates its own melody; never the reverse'.
[186] Unfortunately neither Natalie nor Alma are very informative about the composition of the Fifth. Natalie unequivocally states that the Scherzo dates from 1901, but gives no firm assurance as to whether the double first movement was composed the same summer. No doubt remains, however, as to the date of composition of the Finale: 1902 (see below, Chap. 14).
[187] This is plainly a slip of memory. Bruno Walter moved to Vienna in autumn 1901.

replied, 'but it is the kind of thing one can't talk about.' I realized that he had felt that death was close to him, and looking back, I thought I could see that even then he had been illuminated by a ray of that wonderful evening light in which he saw the world in his last years. You seemed, I said, referring to this impression, 'to feel so secure in a beatific vision of the world, that I could only look at you with envy; for I, on the other hand, was feeling the full unhappiness of my uncertain attitude towards the world. Experience and reflection pitilessly presented me with the blackest, most hopeless view of the world; longing, intuition and the revelations music brought me were the only things that calmed and consoled me, and seemed to hint that there was a wonderful sense behind it all.' 'My dear friend,' Mahler replied, 'I did possess certainty, but I lost it again; and I'll find it again tomorrow and will lose it again the next day'.[188]

That Mahler, after his haemorrhage, was obsessed by the idea of death is also shown by the following passage from a letter he wrote to Bruno Walter eight years later: 'I can't help thinking very often of Lipiner. Why don't you ever write anything about him? I should like to know whether he still thinks the same way about death as he did eight years ago, when he told me about his very peculiar views (at my somewhat importunate request—I was just convalescent after haemorrhage).'[189]

Irrefutable evidence of the profound change in Mahler's personality from 1901 onwards is, in fact, the music he composed that summer. Not only is the character and indeed the essence of the music often new; the style itself, sober and unadorned, reveals an artist who is already exploring another world. Much of the music—the three *Kindertotenlieder*, 'Der Tamboursg'sell', 'Um Mitternacht', and the first two movements of the Fifth Symphony—is imbued with gloom or even despair. Admittedly two of the *Rückert-Lieder*, 'Ich atmet' einen linden Duft' and 'Ich bin der Welt', are serene in mood, but they are the meditations of a man who is already looking beyond immediate cares and sorrows of the world and who yearns for peace.

The first day he played 'Der Tamboursg'sell' and the *Kindertotenlieder*[190] to Natalie, Mahler exclaimed: 'it hurt me to write them and I grieve for the world which will one day have to hear them, they are so sad.'[191] The powerful major

---

[188] Bruno Walter, 'Mahlers Weg: Ein Erinnerungsblatt', *Der Merker*, 3: 5 (Mar. 1912), 166.

[189] MBR1, no. 381; MBR2, no. 404 to Bruno Walter, undated (Feb.–Mar. 1909).

[190] In the first MSS, Mahler always uses Rückert's antiquated spelling: *Kindertodtenlieder*.

[191] NBL1. 166; NBL2. 193 ff. Natalie does not indicate how many of the *Kindertotenlieder* were composed during that summer. However, before he returned to Vienna, Mahler gave her, as a token of their friendship, the MSS of *seven* Lieder which included three *Kindertotenlieder*. (An examination of the two MSS in the PML seems to indicate that they were Nos. 1, 3, and 4.) See below, Appendix 1 and also Christopher O. Lewis, 'On the Chronology of the Kindertotenlieder', *Revue Mahler Review*, 1 (1987), BGM, Paris. In AMM, Alma Mahler asserts that *three* others were composed in 1904, whereas only two date from that year. AML re-establishes the truth as stated by Natalie. A careful reading of the *Mahleriana* shows that, during that summer, Mahler composed eight, not seven, Lieder. 'Ich bin der Welt' is not mentioned in the paragraph entitled *Seven Lieder*, but has another paragraph to itself in a different place (NBL1. 166; NBL2. 194). Natalie claims that, on 10 Aug., Mahler played her six *Rückert-Lieder* (3 *Kindertotenlieder* and 3 other songs) plus 'Der Tamboursg'sell'. 'Ich bin der Welt' was not quite finished at this time since the MS is dated 16 Aug. and it is common knowledge that Mahler disliked playing his works to anyone before they were finished. Theodor Reik analyses the creative process that gave rise to *Kindertotenlieder* in the following way. He suggests that Mahler

tutti concluding 'Um Mitternacht'[192] reminded Natalie of the end of the Second Symphony, while the text of 'Blicke mir nicht in die Lieder' seemed to her 'so typical of him that he could have written it himself'. However, he thought that it was the least important of the Lieder he had composed during the summer, and that, for that very reason, it would undoubtedly be 'the most successful'. During his last few days in Maiernigg, Mahler completed, on 16 August, another *Rückert-Lied* he had started at the beginning of the holidays and then dropped for his symphony. This was 'Ich bin der Welt abhanden gekommen'. 'It's myself,' he said to Natalie, as he stressed its intimate and personal nature and tried to define its mood of complete but restrained fulfilment: 'it's the feeling that fills us right up to our lips but does not pass them.' On the other hand, 'Ich atmet' described 'the way one feels in the presence of a beloved being of whom one is completely sure without a single word needing to be spoken'.[193]

Thus of all Mahler's summer holidays, none was as productive as that of 1901, when he completed eight Lieder that are reckoned among his greatest achievements in this field, and two movements of the Fifth Symphony. His first stay in his new house had completely dispelled his chronic anxieties about any possible creative impotence. It was with the usual gloom at the prospect of having to wait another whole year before resuming his work that he left to return to Vienna.[194] 'All things considered, I can be quite satisfied with what I've accomplished this summer,' he wrote to Nanna Spiegler just before leaving Maiernigg.[195]

Of course, it's the same old story, too much haste and too little time! And I always have to leave when I'm right in the middle of something. But with time I have come to feel more resigned to it, for I have finally come to realize that a creator can interrupt his labour without injuring his child and resume it at an opportune moment, somewhat like hens, who sit conscientiously on their eggs and then suddenly go off and feed.

had been toying with the idea of getting married for over a year and that this had revived the memory of certain of his parents' anxieties. Moreover, according to Reik, he must have known that one of Rückert's 'dead children' was called Ernst. Thus, while composing the *Kindertotenlieder*, he 'identified himself with his father by putting himself into the frame of mind of a man who had lost a son named Ernst.' This, according to Reik, would explain his intense emotion and the 'compulsion' to set the poems to music. A number of people have pointed out the striking thematic similarity between the first of the *Kindertotenlieder* and the Funeral March of the Fifth Symphony (bars 313–15). On the composition of the *Kindertotenlieder*, see Edward F. Kravitt, 'Mahler's Dirges for his own Death', 24 Feb. 1901, in *Musical Quarterly*, 64 (July 1978): 3. In particular, Edward Kravitt draws a parallel between the poem 'Um Mitternacht' ('I heard the beating of my heart') and the suffering that Mahler himself experienced when, in the middle of the night, he came close to dying.

[192] In the MS of 'Um Mitternacht' with piano accompaniment, from the collection of William Ritter, Mahler wrote 'composed in 1899 or 1900' (BGM). However, Natalie was always accurate and scrupulous and we can be sure it was Mahler who was mistaken in this case.

[193] NBL1. 166; NBL2. 194.

[194] MBR1, no. 322; MBR2, no. 296, to Henriette Mankiewicz, written the day Mahler left Maiernigg, 23 or 24 Aug.

[195] Letter of 20 Aug. 1901 (PML, Robin Lehmann deposit).

Although the most important problem of Mahler's creative life, that of the interruptions necessitated by his activity as a conductor and administrator, thus seemed to have been solved, he nevertheless had no illusions as to either the fate of his works or their reception by the public:

I've read almost nothing this summer because I've been too busy with my work. The situation hasn't changed for ten years now and there'll soon be no other solution left to me than to follow Quintus Fixlein's example and write my library myself. As a result, somebody will one day put up a plaque on my Häuschen in the forest, 'G.M., a man of great fame in his time, sat here every morning'. Please do not make a mistake and put up the plaque on the little hut next door, where such a token of respect would doubtless be more appropriate but quite incomprehensible to anyone but Natalie and myself . . .'[196] What a good thing it is for mothers that they do not have to interrupt the process of giving birth—for the babies too, perhaps.[197]

[196] NBLS. Mahler often joked with friends about the amount of time he spent in the lavatory. As seen above, it was there, in Alt-Aussee, that he sketched a whole Lied, 'Revelge' (see above, Chap. 6).

[197] Undated letter to Henriette Mankiewicz, 23 or 24 Aug. 1901.

11

Correspondence with Strauss—arrival of Bruno Walter—*Die lustigen Weiber von Windsor* and *Les Contes d'Hoffmann*—première of the Fourth Symphony

(September–December 1901)

The only right way is to see everything afresh and create it anew.

SINCE the performance of the First Symphony at the Weimar Festival in 1894,[1] Mahler had been in touch with Strauss mostly by mail. Meanwhile, the young lion of German music had risen to the height of fame. This was the time of his last great symphonic poems, *Also sprach Zarathustra* (1896), *Don Quixote* (1897), and *Ein Heldenleben* (1898), which had caused a furore at each new hearing and had confirmed Strauss as head of the *neudeutsch* school and the greatest German composer since Wagner. As a conductor he was perhaps less of a celebrity than Mahler but he had nevertheless occupied a number of important posts: at the Weimar Opera (1889–91 and 1893–4), then in Munich (1894–8), and finally as first Kapellmeister at the Berlin Opera. Nor had he stopped conducting concerts. As we have seen, he had performed three of Mahler's *Wunderhorn-Lieder* in spring 1900. The Weimar fiasco did not seem to have lessened his interest in Mahler's symphonies either, for he had recommended the Second to the Liège conductor Sylvain Dupuis.[2] During the summer of 1900, he wrote to Mahler:

How are you? Don't you compose at all any more? It would be a thousand pities if you devoted your entire artistic energy, for which I certainly have the greatest admiration, to the thankless position of theatre director! The theatre can never be made into an

[1] See above, Vol. i, Chap. 19.
[2] The granddaughter of Sylvain Dupuis, Mme Jacqueline Roskam, brought to my attention the fact that Strauss conducted a concert in Liège on 13 Dec. 1896 and that that was probably when he recommended Mahler's Second Symphony for performance in Liège.

'artistic institution'. Is your Third Symphony printed yet? If, perhaps, you have an extra score, you will certainly have no more diligent and appreciative reader than your always devoted Rich. Strauss.[3]

Strauss's Berlin appointment did not have the same negative effect on his creative life as Mahler's all-absorbing activity at the Vienna Opera. On the contrary, after a few months he found enough time and energy to spare to enter on a new stage in his career as a composer. It seems that after the première of *Ein Heldenleben* on 3 May 1899 he must have realized that he had exhausted the possibilities of illustrative music. His restless genius now turned towards the stage, which remained, at the end of the nineteenth century, the crowning glory in a composer's career. In summer 1900 Strauss had written to Mahler: 'After you so kindly held out the prospect of the performance of my ballet in Vienna, I immediately rejected the plan of the whole ballet *Kometentanz* and began to compose a ballet in three acts, the first sketch of which is now almost finished.'[4] This was *Kythere*, which likewise remained, as we have seen, unfinished. Strauss spent the rest of 1900 composing *Feuersnot*, a half-symbolic, half-humorous opera on a text specially written by the Munich poet Ernst von Wolzogen. In January 1901, during a tour with the Kaim Orchestra, Strauss came to Vienna to conduct a concert of his own works. Mahler enjoyed the charm of the Lieder, sung by Pauline Strauss, and the humour of *Till Eulenspiegel* far more than *Ein Heldenleben* which, in his view, 'oscillated between the abstruse and the banal'. Strauss and his wife dined with Mahler, who found him 'modest, likeable, not particularly profound (*bedeutend*), but hard-working and decent (*tüchtig und ehrlich*)'.[5] Strauss played passages from his new opera at the piano, and Mahler, liking its humour and the sense of proportion which he felt had been lacking in previous works, decided at once to put it on at the Hofoper.

Two months later he wrote to Strauss concerning *Feuersnot*:

I'm very sorry indeed that you won't let Vienna give the première of your opera, even though I don't crave 'first performances' since I'm not too concerned about what *die Herren Journalisten* consider an 'event' in our institution. If I like a work, I accept it and give it as soon as possible. As far as your opera is concerned, however, the situation is slightly different, for it must be given a model performance. We, and I say this without boasting, can produce it with more care and attention than anyone else and, most important, we can take our time over it. I must therefore, thinking primarily of what is best for your work, refuse any sort of 'race against other theatres' unless, having

[3] Letter of 18 Aug. 1900: MSB (Erweiterte Neuausgabe, Piper, Munich, 1988), 228.

[4] See above, Chap. 8. In autumn 1900, Hofmannsthal also submitted to Strauss a synopsis for a three-act ballet, *Der Triumph der Zeit*. Strauss hesitated for a time and then rejected it. Hofmannsthal next offered it to Zemlinsky who set to work on it immediately (see below, Chap. 12 and Chap. 16).

[5] NBLS, Jan. 1901. Mahler had invited Strauss to conduct the performance of *Heldenleben* at the Vienna Philharmonic (see MSB 56, Sept.–Oct. 1900). Strauss wrote to his parents on 14 Oct. that he had had to decline the invitation because he was committed to the impresario Albert Gutmann to conduct this work on 23 Jan. (SBE 56).

duly considered the matter, you still insist upon a time limit, in which case I'll do everything I can to satisfy you. (Between you and me, this latter consideration seems to me to be by far the most important and I therefore trust you'll permit me to join with you in this aim.)[6]

The two musicians exchanged numerous letters during the summer of 1901 because the Viennese censor had raised objections to *Feuersnot*, and Mahler was therefore unable to fix a date for its première. Not having heard from Vienna or the censor, he wrote to inform Strauss of this obstacle before leaving Maiernigg: 'Our very moral Intendant, who manages to be on just as good terms with the graces and the Nine Muses as with our patron saints, is plotting to prevent the performance; all my arguments are in vain, and every time I appeal to "common sense" I get nowhere.' As soon as he was back in Vienna, Mahler set himself to overcoming the censor's resistance, and soon succeeded in doing so.[7]

At the same time, Strauss continued to do his best to promote Mahler's works. On 14 March he conducted the *Lieder eines fahrenden Gesellen* in Prague with the baritone Erich Hunold.[8] In January 1901, Mahler had finally sent him the score of his Third Symphony (completed six years before but never performed in its entirety), to which, according to Natalie, he had added the ambiguous inscription: 'Mein lieber Strauss, was nimmst Du Dir daraus?'[9] On 28 January he received the following reply from his colleague:

Have received the Third! Many thanks! I must unfortunately postpone studying what seems, again, to be a very interesting creation for quieter times than the present, when I have to conduct daily (including standing in for Muck, who is ill). That I, as an old connoisseur of scores, look forward tremendously to your Symphony, I need not assure you.[10]

In June 1901, during the 37th Festival of the Allgemeiner Deutscher Musikverein, in Heidelberg, Strauss was elected president of the society.

[6] This letter, which belongs to the Amsterdam composer and musicologist Marius Flothuis, must have been written in Mar. 1901, because Mahler mentions his haemorrhage in Feb. (MSB 58 ff.). *Feuersnot* had its world première in Dresden on 21 Nov. 1901.

[7] Mahler wrote to Strauss at the beginning of Dec. to let him know that the censor had at last withdrawn his objections (MSB, 71 ff.).

[8] Since this fourth and last Philharmonic Concert would otherwise have consisted entirely of Strauss's own works, he did Mahler the honour of including his Lieder cycle in the programme, which then consisted of the Prelude to Act II of *Guntram*, three Lieder with orchestral accompaniment ('Meinem Kinde', 'Muttertändelei', and 'Wiegenlied'), sung by Pauline de Ahna Strauss, and, as the highlight of the concert, the symphonic poem *Also sprach Zarathustra*. Mahler's second Lied was encored. The newspaper *Bohemia* said that, because of their laboured naïveté, the texts of the *Wunderhorn-Lieder* were less interesting than 'the musical construction and spicy orchestration' Mahler had given them.

[9] NBLS stresses the fact that this inscription had 'several meanings', doubtless including both 'What do you make of this?' and 'How much of this will you swallow?' Mahler and Strauss remained on 'Sie' terms all their lives, thus the quotation is probably not literal. Mahler was not wrong in thinking that Strauss would have reservations about parts of the Third (see below, Chap. 13). Strauss nevertheless persuaded the committee of the Allgemeiner Deutscher Musikverein to give it its first complete performance the following year.

[10] Letter from Strauss to Mahler, 28 Jan. 1901 (MSB 68, formerly in Ernst Rosé collection, Washington).

Thanks to this new position his support of Mahler was to become much more effective. Indeed, the première of the complete Third Symphony was finally to be the main event of the 1902 Festival of the Verein. For the moment Strauss was still intending to conduct it in one of the six Novitäten Konzerte he had scheduled in Berlin for the following winter.[11] However, when Max von Schillings told him that the Fourth Symphony required only modest orchestral resources, he wrote to Mahler on 3 July to suggest that he give that instead, since he was neither sure that he would have sufficient time to rehearse the Third nor that the stage of the Krolloper, where the concerts were to take place, was big enough to hold such a large number of performers.[12] Mahler replied that, 'the Fourth has already been published,' and added:

I haven't yet completed the orchestration and besides I don't want to give the Berlin public, which doesn't know me and has been prejudiced against me by a short-sighted press, the première of a new work that, because it's the first that is more or less easy to perform, might, if it were received in a kindly and unbiased fashion, win for me the only reward I expect for my creative activity, that of being heard and understood.[13] What is more, I have in any case promised its première to Munich, where the Kaim Orchestra and the Odeon are having such a tug-of-war over it that I'm finding it hard to choose between them. So for the moment, dear Strauss, I'd rather you didn't include the Fourth in your projects.

He also stipulated that, if the Third was performed, both the orchestra and the acoustics should be first-rate and, since the Symphony lasted two hours, it should be the only work on the programme. He apologized for 'being so difficult in return for all your kindness', but nevertheless pleaded in favour of either the Third or, if Strauss had a good chorus at his disposal, *Das klagende Lied*.

In this letter, written in midsummer, Mahler again mentioned the fuss the Viennese censorship was making about *Feuersnot*. Strauss's answer deals mainly with his plans for a performance of the Third: 'What a pig-headed fellow you are! But never mind! It's just part of your charm!' He then confirmed a plan he had already suggested to Mahler: he could give the Third, in accordance with his conditions, not in Berlin, but the following year in the contemporary music festival of the Allgemeiner Deutscher Musikverein, where he was all-powerful. He had not considered performing the Fourth Symphony 'for the glory of a first performance', but merely in case he were unable to give the Third in accordance with Mahler's stipulations. As far as the Berlin concert on 18 November was concerned, he would attempt to attract the public by playing Liszt's symphonic poem *Tasso* and the Love Scene from *Feuersnot*, before the Third Symphony, adding that he preferred not to attempt *Das klagende Lied*, since he was not sure enough of his chorus.[14]

[11] Undated letter from Strauss to Mahler, June 1901 (RWO, MSB 226 ff.). With very few exceptions, all of Mahler's letters to Strauss are in SAG.

[12] This letter, written at Interlaken, was auctioned by Stargardt at Marburg in Nov. 1965 (no. 1077).

[13] The German sentence is very long, and it is quoted here as it appeared in the original text.

[14] Letter from Strauss to Mahler, 11 July 1901 (RWO, MSB 226).

Once again, Mahler raised objections. Strauss's programme was unthinkable, he wrote, for there would have to be two intermissions including the required ten-minute intermission after the first movement of the Third, with the result that the concert would last over three hours and the audience would be worn out by the two new works. He asked Strauss to give either some Lieder or, if the concert were to take place in the Philharmonic Hall,[15] which had an excellent organ, the Second Symphony rather than the Third. He said he would also agree to a performance of his Fourth Symphony provided it took place after that in Munich, failing which he suggested the First, unless Strauss regarded as an insurmountable obstacle the fact that it had been a complete flop in Berlin a few years earlier.[16] Strauss's patience was obviously inexhaustible, for he eventually included the Fourth Symphony in the programme of a concert which would take place after the Munich première,[17] and postponed the performance of the Third until the following Allgemeiner Deutscher Musikverein festival to be held at Krefeld[18] in the Rhineland in 1902.

Considering the way press and public usually received Mahler's works, it is quite surprising to find the musical directors of the time competing with each other for the honour of giving the first performance of the Fourth. Some time later, Strauss was to write to Richard Sternfeld, director of another Berlin concert association, asking him not to invite Mahler to conduct his new symphony:

You know that I can only give new works. . . . Mahler's Fourth is my principal attraction (*Hauptzugstück*). . . . Your concerts are not, like mine, made up exclusively of first performances. Why don't you invite Mahler to conduct his First or Second Symphony in December? It would not hurt the Berlin public to hear these difficult works again. Unfortunately I cannot relinquish the Fourth: this is not a personal decision; I am speaking for our whole organization. So why don't you perform the Second, or the excellent *Klagende Lied*.[19]

Even the Vienna Philharmonic sent several delegations to Mahler, asking him to entrust them with the first performance of the Fourth. He told them to take the matter up directly with Weingartner, to whom he had promised the world première in Munich.[20]

[15] It eventually took place at the Krolloper, also called the Neues Königliches Opernhaus.

[16] See above, Vol. i, Chap. 22.

[17] Postcard of 17 Aug. 1901 (RWO, MSB 69 ff.). The performance eventually took place on 16 Dec., probably because the Munich première had been postponed.

[18] Shortly after he became president of the Allgemeiner Deutscher Musikverein, Strauss mentioned his plan for the performance of Mahler's Third in an undated letter written to Mahler on Musikverein notepaper (RWO, MSB 61). This would be the first complete performance of the work, and would be conducted by Mahler himself.

[19] Letter to Richard Sternfeld (1858–1926), professor of musical history at the Univ. of Berlin, composer, critic, and author of many books: cf. Franz Grasberger (ed.), *Die Welt um Richard Strauss in Briefen* (Schneider, Tutzing, 1969), 139.

[20] Undated letter to Weingartner, c.May 1901 (BGM). In it Mahler states that the score will be published in Oct.

Shortly afterwards, Mahler wrote to Weingartner:

May I ask you a direct question, and beg you to give me a frank answer? Do you have any objection to my conducting the first performance myself? I hope you understand why I am asking this? You know that there is no one in the world to whom I would entrust my work with more pleasure and confidence than yourself! But the fact that I have never heard this work, that I am anxious about the rehearsals because of the unusual orchestration, and that I am not sure if I have really succeeded in expressing what I intended, makes me wish to be on the podium for the first performance, for I am the only one who knows my score by heart. . . . I am not used to listening from the hall and making sudden changes. Up to now, I have always been able to go over my scores at least once with my own orchestra, and this gave me a certain sense of security. I have almost always had to make essential changes [during rehearsal].[21]

Again no doubt for reasons of health, Mahler succeeded in prolonging his summer holiday until 26 August, roughly a fortnight after the beginning of the new season at the Opera,[22] leaving Maiernigg on a gloriously moonlit but bitterly cold night. Natalie accompanied him to the station in Klagenfurt, and they had to huddle up close to one another in the car in order to keep warm. 'As a mark of our perfect harmony that summer', Mahler gave her, before he left, the autographs of his most recent Lieder.[23] Natalie's *Mahleriana* show that she herself was back in Vienna three days later, and it was doubtless then that the harrowing scene described by Alma Mahler in *Ein Leben mit Mahler* occurred, when Natalie tried to persuade Mahler to marry her.[24]

No sooner had Mahler returned to Vienna than he plunged once more into Opera affairs. During the first week or so he lunched every day at the Imperial Hotel with Arnold Rosé and Dr Boer and took walks, as always in autumn, in the Wienerwald.[25] A delegation from the Philharmonic,[26] headed by Franz Simandl, called on him, doubtless in a last attempt to persuade him to resume conducting the concerts, for, in a letter to Justi, he referred to 'poor Hellmesberger, who is still waiting for an official honour'.[27] On 29 August he attended a performance of *Faust*, with Katharina Fleischer-Edel of the Ham-

[21] Undated letter to Weingartner, c.May 1901 (BGM).
[22] Undated Letter to Strauss, end of Aug. 1901 (MSB 70 ff.) and letter from Mahler to Justi, 27 Aug. (RWO).
[23] 'Seven' Lieder, she confirms, for 'Ich bin der Welt' was definitely not included (see above, Chap. 10).
[24] See above, Chap. 10.
[25] On 7 Sept. he went to Heiligenstadt with his friend Fritz Löhr (letter to Justi, RWO).
[26] Mahler sometimes referred to the Philharmonic players as 'die Viehharmoniker' (*Vieh* meaning *cattle*) (letter to Justi, 27 Aug., RWO).
[27] On 28 May 1901, Josef Hellmesberger, jun., was elected conductor of the Philharmonic Orchestra. But the decision was still not definitive, hence Simandl's visit to Mahler, with another proposal from the committee. In autumn 1901, votes were taken at two general meetings. The first was to decide whether the orchestra would be conducted by one or several Viennese conductors, or one or several non-Viennese conductors. The result of the vote was 51 to 82 for one Viennese conductor. The second elected Hellmesberger, jun., by a majority of 63 out of 90 votes.

burg Stadt-Theater as Marguerite.[28] Once again this work[29] filled him with 'utter disgust', a feeling which, after a whole summer devoted to composition, everything to do with the Hofoper inspired in him.

I can no longer feel the same involvement with this quagmire, for inwardly I've lost touch with it; I'm above it and it's become completely alien to me. My world is elsewhere and this one has ceased to concern me. But I sympathize with Wagner's fury, carrying out his supreme task in the theatre, and having to plough up the ground and change the soil before he could build his work on it.[30]

After a performance of *The Flying Dutchman*, on 4 September, Mahler again returned from the Opera discouraged and told Natalie that, although he had made quite a hit with the audience, Theodor Bertram, newly engaged on the basis of their long collaboration in Hamburg, had been thoroughly disappointing in the title-role.[31] He had not been any more successful than his predecessors at 'giving the impression of centuries-old suffering'. Schalk, moreover, had not helped matters with his 'restless tempos'. In this opera, the tempos should, on the contrary, be infinitely smooth, 'like the long waves of the ever-rolling sea and the long shadows cast by this elemental work'. Mahler confessed, however, that he himself would have had difficulty in making Wagner's intentions clear and in rendering the eternal Wanderer's 'petrified calm' without a singer who possessed the necessary grandeur and power.

A few years ago, when we prepared that revival, I was able to get something of it into Reichmann, with indescribable difficulty: not through painstaking explanation, talk and demonstration, none of that worked; but because I had the idea of tying up his arms and legs for his scene with Senta in Act 2. And when he was allowed—very sparingly— to move, I had a line marked on the stage that he wasn't allowed to cross. In that way, he retained some of the stillness that I wanted. But now he's forgotten it all.[32]

Mahler certainly admired Bertram in many respects for, in a letter written to Strauss in August,[33] he spoke highly of his acting and even more highly of his voice, whose 'high register is as beautiful as its low'. However, the baritone

---

[28] Katharina Fleischer-Edel (1875–1928), dramatic soprano born in Mühlheim, in the Ruhr, had studied at the Cologne and Dresden Conservatories. She had been a member of the Dresden Opera, 1894–7, before she was engaged by Pollini at the Hamburg Stadt-Theater.

[29] This letter to Justi, dated 5 Sept., formerly belonged to David Stivender of New York. The baritone Theodor Bertram, whom Mahler had known well at the Hamburg Stadt-Theater, was also a guest performer that night, in the role of Mephisto.

[30] NBLS.

[31] Yet, in summer 1901, Theodor Bertram had made a tremendous hit as Wotan at Bayreuth. He had appeared as a guest in Vienna the preceding spring, singing the Count in *Le nozze di Figaro* (23 May) and Mephisto in *Faust* (25 May) and he had immediately been engaged. Although his Don Giovanni (31 May) had been disappointing, he apparently had 'a voice like a trumpet', which he too frequently forced and, according to Max Graf, was 'too realistic' as the Dutchman (*Die Musik*, 1: 3 (Nov. 1901), 260).

[32] NBLS. See above, Vol. i, Chap. 7. It is clear that Mahler, obsessed as ever with the myth of the Wandering Jew, is here identifying the Dutchman with it.

[33] He suggested him for the leading role in *Feuersnot* in preference to Demuth, who, despite his vocal superiority, 'hasn't a particle of genius'.

must have got wind of Mahler's reservations about his Dutchman, for a letter he wrote him on 6 September betrays his wounded pride. It starts with a refusal to sing a role in *Lohengrin* that he considers 'secondary and unworthy of my reputation'[34] and continues:

Would you kindly let me know in advance the days of the month on which my presence will not be required, so that I can at least arrange to earn elsewhere the money I need to feed my family. . . . Should it be impossible for you to give me leave to do this, I shall be obliged, much to my regret, to hand in my resignation. When I signed my contract, you treated me, even in artistic matters, in a entirely different manner, but now you criticize and challenge me in every respect, notably for the quality of my voice, which, only yesterday, you judged so superb. As I have already told you, I only signed the contract in order to be able to work with a person of superior talents who would understand me; being in Vienna adds no particular lustre to my name.

Bertram was obviously deeply offended, but Mahler just as obviously could not allow him to 'earn money elsewhere'. He therefore accepted his resignation. Bertram's engagement had lasted only nineteen days, probably the Vienna Opera's shortest ever.[35]

On 5 September, the day Mahler conducted for the second time in the new season, in *Tannhäuser*, he wrote to Justi describing his first days back in Vienna. They had been entirely taken up with administrative tasks. Anna von Mildenburg had just returned from her holiday. Arriving in Vienna, Mahler found three letters from her, 'obviously dictated by Lipiner', who, now that she was having an affair with him, influenced her strongly. 'I pretty much had it out with her, and asked her most decidedly not to use an intermediary any more, if she wanted something from me. But I imagine the correspondence with Lipiner will continue. I shall remain cool.'[36]

After the performance of *Tannhäuser*, Mahler complained of the orchestra. It seemed to have gone downhill since he had stopped conducting it so frequently, and traces of the sloppiness he had worked so hard to eliminate were beginning to reappear. 'What a labour of Sisyphus one carries on in this infamous place where one can't achieve anything wholly beautiful or absolutely pure,' he complained. A few days later, steeped in the 'sacred bath' of nature in the Wienerwald, he added:

And it's for that that I wear myself to the bone, to that that I'm obliged to devote all my time and my entire being! 'What's Hecuba to him, or he to Hecuba?'[37] Could anything be more repulsive than the incredible vanity and emptiness of theatrical life in which no one thinks of anything but his or her interests and not a soul considers for one second either the work of art or its creator!

[34] Probably the Heerrufer (Herald), not Telramund.
[35] From 1 to 19 Sept. *Neue Freie Presse* (19 Sept. 1901) announced that Mahler had 'granted' Theodor Bertram permission to terminate his contract and offered him financial assistance. He had a tragic end: in 1907 he hanged himself, in the toilets of the Bayreuth railway station.
[36] Letter quoted at n. 29, former property of David Stivender.
[37] A line from Shakespeare's *Hamlet*.

Vienna was hardly better than Hamburg, where 'I used to go and hide in a box room so as not to hear or see anything and weep bitter tears during the intervals.'[38]

As a compensation for these disappointments, two happy events occurred in the new season. At the end of August Mahler was visited by two very good friends from Hamburg, the composer Josef Bohuslav Förster and his wife, Bertha Förster-Lauterer, who hoped he would engage her at the Hofoper. He found her 'just as good as before as far as her voice is concerned', whereas, in Hamburg she 'was not in full possession of her means'. Thus he invited her to sing the title-role in *Mignon* and Sieglinde in *Die Walküre* in October.[39] Delighted to see her again, Mahler once more spoke to Natalie about the importance of the text in opera and

the difference between intelligent and unintelligent singers. The former manage to communicate the substance and soul of their part by building on the sound of the words, whereas the latter don't articulate, and the text loses it meaning and significance. They treat it as though it were unable to share, either inwardly or superficially, in the melody. . . . Such artists can, at a pinch, make good violinists, but they'll never be either good singers or good actors.[40]

An even greater pleasure for Mahler was the arrival of his closest associate in Hamburg and his favourite disciple, Bruno Walter. The 24-year-old conductor was thrilled with both Vienna and the Opera, especially after hearing his master and friend conduct *Tristan und Isolde* on 19 September. 'To hear this work conducted by Mahler is more than one can bear,' he exclaimed. 'I always have the feeling I might die in the middle of *Tristan* if I were to listen intently every second, and I sometimes wonder if that isn't what one <u>should</u> do.'[41] With his youthful enthusiasm and exceptional talent, Bruno Walter was in an ideal position to profit from Mahler's example and indirect teaching. A few days after his arrival, he made his début at the Opera with *Aida* on 27 September. Mahler followed the performance from his box. He was so happy with it that he frequently expressed his approval aloud: 'every tempo and every musical

[38] NBLS.

[39] Letter to Justi dated 27 Aug., quoted above (RWO). Förster had announced in a letter of 25 July that he would come to Vienna at the end of Aug., on his way to Hamburg whither he was returning to teach at the Conservatory (HOA, no. 156, Z.501/1901). After *Die Meistersinger*, Helm wrote enthusiastically about Förster-Lauterer, while regretting that her voice had 'lost some of its freshness'. Graf also complained of her 'excess of vocal maturity', though expressing the liveliest admiration for the new soprano's artistic qualities (*Die Musik*, 1: 3 (Nov. 1901), 261). During her Gastspiel, Förster-Lauterer was a sensation as Sieglinde on 11 Sept. Engaged from 1 Oct., she sang in succession *Der Wildschütz*, *Mignon*, Sulamith in *Die Königin von Saba*, and Eva in *Die Meistersinger*.

[40] NBLS.

[41] NBLS. Bruno Walter added that he was deeply impressed by Mildenburg's performance, and by the progress she had made since the Hamburg years. Concerning the *Tristan* of 19 Sept., Walter wrote to his parents: 'It was an unattainable ideal, grandeur worthy of antiquity and quintessential simplicity (*Einfachheit im Wesen*)' (BWB 44, letter dated 29 Sept. 1901). Lipiner came to supper with Mahler afterwards and, 'although the writer had resolved to hold his tongue', Walter notes that he fascinated his listeners, 'speaking of Goethe and the last act of *Faust Part II* with real depth and wisdom'.

intonation filled me with serene satisfaction'. Immediately he looked forward to being able to entrust the most difficult works to the young man with complete confidence, whereas, when his other assistants conducted, he was 'in constant agony, musically seasick'.[42] According to Ludwig Karpath, Mahler had hesitated a great deal before engaging Walter, not because of his youth, but because he was Jewish, although a Protestant convert. When Engelbert Humperdinck had recommended his pupil, Leo Blech, Mahler had refused him for this very reason: 'Even if, as you say, he has been baptised, it is impossible. I have been too, which doesn't prevent the anti-Semites from regarding me as Jewish. There can't be more than one Jew at the Hofoper.'[43] Karpath claims that Mahler overcame his anxiety in Bruno Walter's case only after he (Karpath) had tentatively tested the matter out with the Lord Chamberlain.

Unfortunately, Mahler's enthusiasm was not shared by the Vienna critics who were only too happy to find an excuse to renew their attacks and lost no time in detecting signs of a 'slavish imitation' of Mahler in Walter. Furthermore, 'the Vienna Opera is not a school for budding conductors'. In the *Deutsche Zeitung*, Theodor Helm called him 'an executor of Mahler's intentions' and accused him of imitating 'even his hand movements and the nervous contractions at the corners of his mouth'. While acknowledging his control of both stage and orchestra, Max Graf also condemned Walter's 'servile imitation' of Mahler, from his 'slight, angular gestures, looks of ecstasy and nervous agitation to his sword thrusts aimed at the instruments', and pronounced him nothing but a bundle of 'affectation, fabrication and inauthenticity'.[44]

Here is Bruno Walter's account to his parents of his début in Vienna:

Aida was absolutely excellent; Mahler and all his circle congratulated me very warmly; Mahler said I had become 'quite a fellow'. The orchestra performed beautifully; they responded enthusiastically to my every movement, and crowded around me at the end of each act saying nice things. What the public thought I couldn't tell; *Aida* has no Overture, and the plentiful applause during the opera might equally well have been addressed to the singers. I'm sending you some reviews, they are all of the same type, unpleasant, irrelevant, stupid, or rather laughable. Mahler tells me that nothing matters less than what the press says here; they are a bunch of idiots, yapping like dogs at every new face, growling for a while and then a few years later one is 'our Walter'; I am not much disturbed by the behaviour of the press, Mahler's satisfaction, the acceptance of the singers and—most important—the wonderful behaviour of the orchestra are quite enough for me. That last point is very significant for me, on account of the Philharmonic concerts. Mahler has declined to continue as head. They don't much like Schalk; faute de mieux they have Hellmesberger, a priceless time-thumper.[45]

[42] NBL1. 168; NBL2. 196.

[43] BMG 179. Karpath states that he was present at this discussion. He explains that, during the early years, Mahler took great care not to favour Walter above Schalk, who had seniority. Thus Walter did not really make his mark in Vienna until after Mahler's departure.

[44] See Die *Musik*, 1: 3, 261. Cast of the first performance conducted by Bruno Walter in Vienna on 27 Sept. 1901: Mildenburg (Aida), Walker (Amneris), Slezak (Radames), Reichmann (Amonasro), Grengg (Ramfis).

[45] Letter quoted in n. 41 (BWB 44).

Two months later the critics' fury had still not abated, but the young conductor was undismayed:

The press is almost unanimously hostile, the anti-Semitic papers frankly hateful (thank God they don't read them in Germany), some are trying to kill me with silence. . . . I can do without success with public and press; I am young, and can afford to wait for fame and great triumphs, especially as I already had a generous taste of those in Riga. Now what I want to do is learn, and develop as far as possible. I am conducting a great deal. . . . Until now, whenever Mahler put on a fully worked out revival, he saw all its extraordinary greatness disappear as soon as, overburdened with work, he handed it over to Hellmesberger or Schalk. Now it is my task to keep these productions at their high level; a hard and worthy occupation. While I hope in this way to become a really great conductor here, I also have enough leisure time to work for myself.[46]

Walter concluded by painting a very grim picture to his parents of the anti-Semitism of the Viennese press, which continually spoke of 'Jewish rogues', 'Jewish vulgarity', or 'more Jewish filth'. 'You can't imagine what these papers are like. If I didn't resent handing over 5 Kreuzer to that rabble, I'd half like to send you a paper for your amusement!'

Despite the critics' disapproval, Mahler stuck to his guns and assigned Walter such operas as *L'Africaine*, *Tannhäuser*, and *The Flying Dutchman*, which soon became exclusively his province when Mahler did not conduct them himself, and eventually even *Die Meistersinger*, *Fidelio*, and *The Magic Flute*. Later on he engaged an Italian conductor for the Italian operas, but in the meantime entrusted most of them too to Walter. However, before finally achieving his first undisputed success the following year, Walter was obliged to fight a grim battle. After a performance of *Tannhäuser*, the critics unanimously condemned his holding so important a post. For the first time in his life, he was insulted, humiliated, and declared 'incapable of conducting even a military band'. In despair, he went to see Mahler, who described to him in detail the complexities and intrigues of Vienna's artistic life, stressing the pleasure the Viennese papers took in dragging artists in the mud and explaining that, since they had not managed to find anything with which to reproach him for several months, the arrival of a young conductor known to be his protégé had provided them with an opportunity that was too good to be missed.[47]

In addition to the increasingly frequent and violent attacks of the press, Walter became aware of distinct hostility on the part of the Opera singers and musicians and finally began to have doubts about his conducting technique, in which he thought he perceived serious flaws. He therefore considered leaving Vienna at the end of the season for Cologne, where he had been offered the position of first conductor on very favourable terms.[48] He had recently got

[46] BWB 46, letter of 20 Nov. 1901.   [47] BWT 222.
[48] The following passage from a letter Mahler wrote to Weingartner proves that Bruno Walter indeed had such intentions: 'Schlesinger is still talking of leaving! It's not impossible that he may go when his temporary contract ends. But nothing can be settled before the summer.' (Undated letter, Jan.–Feb. 1902, BGM.).

married, and his wife decided to go and consult Mahler without telling her husband. Mahler said he was afraid Walter had lost the battle and could no longer be a success in Vienna. Regretfully, therefore, he recommended his accepting the position in Cologne, but emphasized that Walter was in no way responsible for his failure. Encouraged by this answer, the young conductor decided to continue the struggle and, 'above all, to regain his self-confidence'. Aware that his beat lacked precision, he applied himself to improving it by keeping a constant watch on himself and exercising all his self-critical faculties. He thus won 'the essential battle, that against his own uncertainty'.[49]

Richard Specht, the critic who later became one of Mahler's first biographers, confirms that Bruno Walter was still immature at this time and too frequently imitated Mahler both on and off the podium. Like him, he walked with a jerky stride, like him he shouted, laid down the law, preached, and stormed, instead of just speaking normally, like him he bit his lips and chewed his nails. He went into contortions on the podium, he expressed and lived the music with his body, and his conducting was agitated, uneven, nervous, and impulsive. He made a cult of stormy vehemence, fervour, and passion, and tended to over-emphasize odd episodes and secondary passages. In time, however, he calmed down, his technique matured, and the real Walter, who was more easygoing and romantic, less harsh and eloquent than Mahler, finally came to the fore and asserted his innate sense of drama, his zeal and enthusiasm, and his love of beautiful orchestral sound and ability to obtain it. Whatever his faults may have been at the time, Mahler far preferred Walter's expressive intensity to Schalk's prosaic style. With his broad tempos and the veil that seemed to settle over the orchestra when he conducted, Schalk gave the impression of being so preoccupied with the letter of the score that he did not always notice the weaknesses and deficiencies in the performance. He was not without a sense of beauty and he abhorred sentimentality as much as coarseness, but he lived in a sort of ivory tower. Taste rather than fervour dominated both his life and his art, so that he never saw eye to eye with Mahler, whom he only really came to understand and appreciate after his death. Mahler did his best never to favour Walter at Schalk's expense and never to forget the latter's seniority, but could not restrain himself so far as to conceal his preference.[50]

After one of his evening performances during this disastrous first season in Vienna, Walter had the pleasant surprise of receiving a note in a familiar hand which read: 'Bravo! Calm, precise! Orchestra very expressive. Beautiful and well-controlled tempos. Mahler.'[51] This warm praise from so venerated a source

---

[49] Also see George H. Pollock, 'On Freud's Psychotherapy of Bruno Walter', *Annual of Psychoanalysis*, 3 (New York, 1975): 294.

[50] Between Sept. 1901 and Dec. 1907, i.e. during Mahler's tenure at the Opera, Walter conducted almost 500 performances. According to Alma, in 1907 Mahler subjected Schalk to a crushing humiliation in front of the orchestra (see below, Vol. iii, Chap. 15).

[51] LPA.

was worth more to him than a wealth of critical acclaim. None the less, the young conductor, aware that only time could soften the memory of these attacks, which had come near to destroying his self-confidence, turned, at least provisionally, to a new field of activity, playing chamber-music recitals with Arnold Rosé in the Bösendorfersaal. In this new guise he was greeted by public and press with unexpected warmth, so much so that these concerts became one of Vienna's musical institutions, taking place regularly for the next fifteen years.

Mahler was not mistaken when he explained to his favourite disciple that the hostile criticism he had encountered was part of the general campaign against himself (Mahler), and that his enemies would not scruple to use any stick which came to hand to beat him. Yet, for the moment, the quality of his work and the success of all his enterprises had made him a difficult target to attack directly. That year, however, he acquired a new and redoubtable enemy in the person of Karl Kraus. In autumn 1901, probably at the instigation of one of the anti-Semitic critics,[52] Kraus wrote the following article in *Die Fackel*:

News of the serious artistic decline of our Hofoperntheater is at last beginning to find its way into the columns of the liberal press. Since artistic defects have found material expression in the form of a deficit in the Opera's pension fund, they can now be recognized by that kind of journalism which can only think of the qualitative in quantitative terms, i.e. how much does it cost, and where is the money to come from. So far, liberal critics have reported as little of Herr Mahler's squandering of artistic resources as they have of the pathetic state of decay in which seventy operas in the repertoire have been allowed to moulder while the other twenty were being lavishly tarted up. But now that the pension fund is no longer solvent, even the *Neue Freie Presse* cautiously hints that over the last three years the personnel of the Opera has been subject to bad husbandry, and can only explain the sudden rise in the number of pensioners by suggesting that 'genuine illness is partly to blame'. How great must be Herr Mahler's guilt, readers will say to themselves, if it is pointed out, even in the newspaper that not long ago publicly gave its music critic advice he had already been following for a year in secret, not to waste his talents on operetta—which since the collapse of the Theater an der Wien brings in so little profit—but to write a comic opera, whose destiny he could safely entrust to the Director of the Opera—so often reviewed by him—and to his colleagues in the press.[53]

And yet of all grounds on which to attack Herr Mahler, the crisis in the Opera's pension fund is the least sound. There is nothing wrong with Mahler's pensioning off invalid or nearly invalid artists; what is wrong is that he makes artists at their peak into invalids before their time. But our liberal journalists need a scapegoat; and they have

---

[52] As we have seen, although a Jew himself, Karl Kraus was violently opposed to the 'Jewish press', above all the *Neue Freie Presse*.

[53] Kraus is here indulging in sheer gratuitous malice. Not only had the articles of Richard Heuberger (clearly the target, since he wrote operettas) been frequently hostile to Mahler, particularly with reference to his 'versions' of Beethoven's symphonies, but Mahler had also just refused to put on his operetta *Ein Opernball* (see above, Chap. 10). If he did in fact advise the critic to write a comic opera, it was never performed at the Hofoper.

turned upon Hofrath Wetschl[54] as 'standing nearest' to the Director of the Opera. Upon whom might they not turn if given the chance, full of anxiety as they are that they themselves might be caught out?[55]

The same criticism has been levelled at many operatic reformers before and since Mahler, who have had the courage to retire singers and musicians not giving satisfaction, thus subjecting pension funds to additional burdens they cannot bear. It is unlikely that the 'changes of mood' with which Mahler was taxed when he fired certain singers after only a few months actually cost the Opera much. Surely it was unjust to criticize him for retiring artists solely in order to raise the artistic level of his 'ensemble' and his orchestra.

Walter was not the only one to be the target for an outcry in the press at the beginning of the new season, for early in September Mahler took it into his head to assign the role of Venus in *Tannhäuser* to Marie Gutheil-Schoder.[56] Hirschfeld seized this opportunity to attack his entire management policy. Feigning to admire the 'reassuring soundness' of Mahler's artistic ideas, he deplored the fact that 'his mischievous spirit so frequently causes him to leave the straight and narrow path and forsake the realm of art'. 'His quirks and shortcomings,' he said, 'should have been kept out of public life and would have been if he had had a variety of interests on which to exercise his *daemon*, but he unfortunately has only one, art, with the result that his personal feelings constantly intruded on it.' He always let himself be guided by his personal likes and dislikes, and the more one criticized his protégés, the more he upheld them. Thus the favours heaped first on Julius Spielmann and then on Rita Michalek had been stepped up in the face of the critics' protests. He seemed impelled to choose tempos because they were different from those of other conductors, whereas his natural tendency would probably have been the right one. The Opera was not a testing ground, nor a school for young conductors. Mahler knew this perfectly well, yet he was continually bringing in débutant conductors, doubtless in the hope of finding more docile ones.[57]

Thus, claimed Hirschfeld, Mahler was turning the Hofoper into a testing ground, a laboratory. There, great singers were sometimes allotted small parts and vice versa,[58] and certain performances stood out one evening because of some new detail, only for that detail to be discarded the following day.

Strange objects lie abandoned in the corners of this laboratory: cast off tempos, dust-ridden favourites and moth-eaten ensembles whose holes have to be patched up by people like Pacal and Elizza. Only Mahler's masterly hand can lend a semblance of order and harmony to all these conflicting elements which include the good and the

[54] Franz von Wetschl was the general treasurer of Vienna's two Court Theatres.

[55] *Die Fackel*, 3 (Oct. 1901), 22.

[56] In a letter to Justi (RWO), Mahler himself described her interpretation as 'grossartig' (superb).

[57] Hirschfeld's targets here are Gustav Brecher and Bruno Walter.

[58] 'One day, a horn is pressed into the service of the Landgrave of Thuringia, the next day it is a pack of hunting dogs and then, at the next performance, a poor old horse dragged out of well-earned retirement.' Hirschfeld is alluding to the *Neueinstudierung* of *Tannhäuser* the previous May.

mediocre, the splendid and the outmoded. He takes especial pride in his unceasing experiments, whereas other people aspire to continuity and stability. His latest experiment has been Gutheil-Schoder, whose very presence constitutes a permanent challenge to the wishes of the public and of friends of art. With her, Mahler has realized the impossible: our Despina, our Cherubino has been introduced into Wagner's Hörselberg as Venus. One fine day, however, Frau Gutheil-Schoder will come in an eighth note too late and immediately fall into dire disgrace with the Director, a mishap that will finally enable her to mature calmly and steadily in accordance with her true nature. For the time being, she continues to enjoy his dangerous favour and is therefore obliged constantly to jump from one role to another and attempt the impossible.

While acknowledging the young singer's musical instinct and her artistic intelligence, Hirschfeld none the less pointed out the limitations of her 'brittle' (*spröde*) voice and said that she had neither the vocal volume for nor the vaguest affinity with the role of Venus, for it was hard to imagine that personage as 'a calm and calculating intelligence', that is to say, a complete contradiction to the 'pleasures of the Venusberg'.

Out of love for his Goddess of Pure Reason, Mahler toned down her music, and even reduced the Venusberg music in the Prelude to an academic discourse. Frau Gutheil-Schoder asked her questions uncertainly and prepared her movements and poses with the thoughtful care of a window dresser. Despite an etiolated and enfeebled orchestra, she produced cramped sound rather than song. She fought not with Tannhäuser but with her part, so that the hero could not but regard the episode as a passing fancy and joyfully return to the warmth of human passion. Thus both the music and the basic meaning of the drama were totally distorted and perverted. The aesthetic restraint of the Venusberg music may be original and the notion of a chaste Venusberg is doubtless a modern interpretation evolved during a nebulous philosophical discussion around a café table, but we protest against this violation of Wagner's intentions. . . . Since Gustav Mahler makes bold to be so personal and so arbitrary, we must simply close our eyes to the brilliant artist we so admire, and point out his deplorable obstinacy, obstinacy that is detrimental to the development of the very Hofoper which had begun to flourish again under his direction.

The casting of *Tannhäuser* also angered Theodor Helm, a Wagnerite of the old school, who declared he had attended a 'parody of the Venusberg scene':

Gutheil-Schoder sang Venus, or rather uttered a series of piercing, meaningless and totally incoherent sounds instead of words, as though strangling with asthma. Still less did she portray Venus: we saw a small, thin figure, obviously female, dressed in a pink tunic, who waved her skinny arms and rapacious fingers dangerously around Tannhäuser's face, so that he involuntarily shielded himself from this living spectre . . . Such was Gutheil-Schoder's Venus, a figure out of Holbein's *Dance of Death*, a Dutch vision of St Anthony rather than the goddess of love . . .

Helm felt it his duty 'stoutly to defend a great work of art from such blasphemy and such an insult', adding that Gutheil-Schoder had been ill-advised to subject her voice to such 'tortures' and Mahler equally ill-advised to abuse Wagner as he did Beethoven, by altering his orchestration.[59]

In the autumn of the previous year, Mahler had intended to restage one of the most popular masterpieces of the German Singspiel, but had come up against the opposition of the Intendant, who found his planned production of Nicolai's *Die lustigen Weiber von Windsor* 'too expensive'. Mahler, taking up some of the arguments he had used eighteen months before in his long letter to the Lord Chamberlain, explained that he would only justify his requests on aesthetic and subjective grounds and was therefore unable to furnish more precise arguments. It would not be a question of renewing all the costumes but only of refurbishing those of the chorus, above all for the fairyland of the last act, when the chorus had to be on stage with the ballet. It would be impossible to paint new scenery on the old canvases because the Opera no longer possessed any that were clean enough, and, try as he might, the painter would not be able to recondition them in time. Not only could the estimate not be lowered, but any delay would have adverse effects on the Opera's finances by increasing the projected expenditure.[60]

Despite these unanswerable arguments, the Intendant must have held out, for Mahler had to wait a whole year before giving *Die lustigen Weiber*, the *Neueinstudierung* of which was finally presented on 4 October 1901, in honour of the Emperor's name-day. According to Natalie, Mahler thouroughly enjoyed

the charming work which he prized very highly from the musical point of view and whose text, an excellent rendering of the gaiety of the Shakespearian original, provided the most wonderful background. He guided and acted out every word, every note and every movement so that the performers enjoyed themselves even more than the public could possibly enjoy the performance.[61]

As always, he expended as much time and care on it as he would have devoted to a serious opera. Marie Gutheil-Schoder, the Frau Fluth in this production, tells in her memoirs of a small, but striking detail in this new production. During the second act which takes place in Frau Fluth's room, she pretends to cry because her husband is jealous and has just made a scene. He then goes up to her and says, 'I have learned from a letter that Sir John Falstaff was with you!' Whereupon, instead of letting her leap up immediately in amazement and protest, Mahler made her remain motionless for a whole bar, which not only created considerable suspense but also heightened the comic effect of her subsequent shriek. As usual, Mahler restored the full text of the opera and cut out all the interpolations. To her dying day, Gutheil-Schoder cherished the memory of those rehearsals, while Mahler in return was constantly enchanted by her 'genius' and the eagerness with which she carried out his slightest wish.

[59] Helm proceeded to quote Richter's comments on the orchestration of *Tannhäuser* and his criticisms of Mahler's retouchings, from the letter he wrote to Karpath (see above, Chap. 10).

[60] Letter from Mahler to the Intendant's office, 25 Nov. 1900 (HOA, Z.1862).

[61] NBL2. 197 and NBLS.

To him such artists were 'compensation for the stupidity, resistance and the lack of talent I have hitherto encountered'. The revolving stage from *Così fan tutte*, brought back for this production, seemed to him to serve the work and its 'Shakespearian fantasy' admirably.[62]

The revival of *Die lustigen Weiber* was greeted with enthusiasm by the audiences, an enthusiasm shared, for once, by the majority of the critics. Kalbeck pronounced the performance 'full of genius'. It had brought back for Nicolai's admirers all the modest grace of his music, and done full justice to his inexhaustible comic invention, his 'musical witticisms' and his perfect technique, a product of the best schools. Mahler had discovered 'the opera's tender soul' in the Nocturne in the third act and emphasized the fantastic element, thanks largely to the revolving stage, which set the work in a sort of dreamland. Whether or not one shared his conceptions, one would be hard put to it to imagine a more enjoyable and riveting night at the theatre. Everyone had fallen under the sway of this 'modern magician' and the performers had succeeded in maintaining the illusion, especially Gutheil-Schoder, the 'fairy of this poetic and musical dream'.

Equally enthusiastic, Heuberger claimed that until now the *Lustigen Weiber* had almost always been 'massacred' in Vienna, and that Mahler had been right to expend so much effort on Nicolai's masterpiece. Indeed, this revised production was far more interesting than many 'premières'. As always, the director had gone to even more trouble than all his collaborators put together, had rethought the work from start to finish, and had brought out the dramatic significance of each note. A new work had been heard, previously unknown, imbued with the modern spirit, yet containing many traditional elements like the coloratura passages which, far from seeming outdated, had played their part in the dramatic effect. Gutheil-Schoder, 'an artist and a virtuoso in both singing and acting', was one of the few singers to possess 'a genuine sense of humour', which she combined with 'the noblest and most sublime stage art'. Heuberger even went so far as to suggest that the recently invented device of the 'cinematographe' should be used to record her performance for posterity,[63] though it would have been even better if certain details had been somewhat simplified.

Hirschfeld, while recognizing that Mahler had devoted all 'the power of his genius' to this production, regretted that he had not chosen Verdi's *Falstaff* rather than *Die lustigen Weiber*. Incapable as ever of unreserved admiration, he accused the director of the Opera of 'underlining every witticism in red pencil, as if the score were a tourist map'. In his opinion, the unassuming Nicolai would not himself have been 'so presumptuous, so demanding, so preoccupied

---

[62] Helm, on the other hand, found it quite pointless for this work, and even damaging to the ballet in Act III.

[63] The 'cinematographe' had been invented by the Lumière brothers and first demonstrated in Paris in 1895.

with the infallible effect of every semiquaver'. But if the 'prodigiously witty' musical performance and the lively and charming stage production perhaps merited admiration, Gutheil-Schoder had merely 'trumpeted Nicolaian parodies' in the audience's ears, very nearly piercing them with her shrieks. Striving at all costs for comic effects, she 'tied herself into knots with reptilian movements and grimaces which were supposed to be funny'. Theodor Helm did not share Hirschfeld's prejudices. Thus he acknowledged that, although some of her effects were exaggerated, Gutheil-Schoder's general performance had been excellent, while her vocal art was 'progressing'. In his view, however, Mahler 'in his quest for precision and refinement'[64] had lost the spirit of the work.

A month later, Gutheil-Schoder starred in another important new production, that of Offenbach's *Les Contes d'Hoffmann*, which had not been performed in Vienna since the fire at the Ringtheater on 8 December 1881, when several hundred people had perished.[65] With this opera, Mahler hoped to achieve a financial success comparable to that of *Cavalleria rusticana* and *Pagliacci* and thus be able to restage works dearer to him by Mozart and Wagner. While not indifferent to Offenbach's music, since he had conducted his operettas at the start of his career, what appealed to him most about *Les Contes* was that it recaptured some of the romantic genius of an author who had so moved and influenced him in his youth. A piano reduction of the work, annotated by the Hofoper's inspector Franz Skofitz, reveals some of the changes Mahler made to the score. There are cuts, extra bars, and interventions, showing once again that Mahler took great liberties with scores when he considered it necessary for practical dramaturgical reasons.[66] Since he planned for a large number of performances, he simultaneously rehearsed alternate casts, a procedure that presented serious problems,[67] mainly because he had insisted that the singers attend all the rehearsals, including those in which they were not taking part, so that they would become familiar with the staging. For

[64] He thought that some of the tempos should have been more animated and energetic. Cast of the performance of 4 Oct. 1901: Michalek (Anna), Gutheil-Schoder (Frau Fluth), Hilgermann (Frau Reich), Naval (Fenton), Breuer (Spärlich), Demuth (Fluth), Ritter (Cajus), Frauscher (Reich), Grengg (Falstaff).

[65] Located on the Schottenring, the Ringtheater, which had opened its doors on 17 Jan. 1874, burnt down at around 7.30 p.m. on 8 Dec. 1881, just before the second performance of *Les Contes d'Hoffmann*. Bruckner was terrified because the window of the room where he kept all the MSS of his unpubl. symphonies gave on to the theatre. Rebuilt and transformed, the Ringtheater reopened in 1898 in another part of the city as the Kaiser Jubiläumstheater (today's Volksoper).

[66] Here are the details of these changes: 13 extra bars in the Prelude (no. 1); the music for the entr'acte of Act I is replaced by the entr'acte from Act III (no. 24); in the finale to Act I (no. 12), the chorus accompanying Olympia's coloratura is dispensed with; the *Canzone* (no. 15) in Act II is replaced by a passage from Act I (no. 8). Skofitz also notes the durations of the three acts at the two dress rehearsals and at the première of 11 Nov. when they were noticeably shorter (cf. K. Blaukopf, 'The Tales of Hoffmann under Mahler', *Nachrichten zu Mahler Forschung*, 23 (Mar. 1990), 5).

[67] Cast of the first performance on 11 Nov. 1901: Gutheil-Schoder (Olympia, Giulietta, Antonia), Kusmitsch (Niklaus), Hilgermann (mother's voice), Schrödter (Hoffmann), Schittenhelm (Spalanzani), Pacal (Nathanaël), Breuer (Andreas, Cochenille, Pitinacchio), Neidl (Schlemihl), Ritter (Lindorf, Coppelius, Dapertutto, Dr Miracle), Frauscher (Krespel), Marian (Luther), Stehmann (Hermann). In the second cast, the minor roles were sung by the same people, but Saville and Kurz alternated with Gutheil-Schoder, Naval with Schrödter, and Ritter with Hesch.

example, Franz Naval wrote to excuse himself for not having attended one in which his rival, Fritz Schrödter, was taking part.

I am not exaggerating when I say that it is torture to me to listen to him, for nothing could be more painful than two artists comparing themselves with one another during their respective performances. Every artist, you will grant as much, must create in isolation, without seeing or hearing how another develops the same theme for fear of involuntarily adopting certain gestures of his interpretation and being accused of plagiarism, which is to be avoided at all costs. On the other hand, an artist obviously benefits greatly from the advice of a genuine master and I mean, in this case, yours. However, such a master never makes the same suggestions to two different artists, for their personalities are not the same and each must be guided in accordance with his own.[68]

Speaking of the solitude indispensable to every artist, of his rights in society, and above all of the different advice a great director would give to different artists in the same role, Naval probably did not realize how close the ideas he was expressing were to Mahler's own. So close, indeed, that it seems likely he won his point: the absence of a reply to this letter in the Opera archives suggests that he was not penalized for 'insubordination'.

Three days before the opening night, at the dress rehearsal, which now took place not in public, but before a group of trusted guests,[69] Mahler still stopped the orchestra half a dozen times, notably the violins in the 'very simple G major waltz'[70] so that the rubato would be exactly as he wanted it.[71] Again, his preparation was meticulous, and the première played to a packed house, was rapturously applauded. The next day, Kalbeck declared that he had been at one of the Hofoper's most brilliant opening nights.[72] Hanslick wrote at length about the work and its performance, and observed that this was the first time an opera had been performed two nights running with different casts.[73] As Hoffmann, he found Schrödter 'too passionate and realistic', while Naval had captured the romantic character of a young Werther. Since the triple role of the heroine required 'more intelligence than feeling, and more art than voice' he had found Gutheil-Schoder dazzling, far better even than Frances Saville. The sumptuous décor for the Venice act had contributed a great deal to the success of a work which, despite patches of tedium and obscurity in the libretto, was of great interest.

Hirschfeld, in a long feuilleton which for once was exceptionally favourable, attributed Mahler's liking for Hoffmann to his taste for irony, and linked this to

[68] Letter of 9 Oct. 1901 (HOA).

[69] The Vienna Stadtbibliothek contains a MS letter from Mahler to the *Fremden-Blatt* critic Ludwig Speidel, inviting him to the dress rehearsal of *Les Contes d'Hoffmann*, on Friday, 8 Nov. at 10.30 a.m. It will 'not be open to the public' for he has 'long since abandoned that practice' (IN 175.937).

[70] This was the Finale of Act II (no. 12 in the Choudens score) in the version used at the time.

[71] *Neue Freie Presse* (11 Nov. 1901).

[72] The audience even encored the Intermezzo preceding Act III, i.e. the reprise of the famous Barcarolle.

[73] Hanslick recalled that, 37 years before, the Hofoper had unsuccessfully mounted *Die Rheinnixen*, a romantic opera by Offenbach whose 'elves' chorus' had become the Barcarolle in *Les Contes d'Hoffmann*.

his predilection for 'improving immortal works'. Thanks to countless rehearsals he had created for Offenbach's opera special lighting effects, and a dynamic, an expression, and a tone that were all absolutely individual and characteristic. Even Gutheil-Schoder seemed to him to have 'adapted marvellously to Hoffmannesque irony'. Theodor Helm praised the opera's 'charming lyricism' and subsequently emphasized its huge financial success in the *Musikalisches Wochenblatt*. Indeed, *Les Contes d'Hoffmann* was performed sixteen times between 11 November and the end of the year, thirty times in 1902, and remained in the repertory for twenty-five years. Mahler ultimately came to regret its popularity, complaining that he was tired of having to conduct it so frequently.[74]

Nevertheless, this triumph encouraged him to think of new projects. One day he began to reflect on the operatic repertoire as a whole. Of all the German operatic composers, Mozart was, in his view, the most 'certain of his goal in all that he undertook'. If he were compelled to choose a third composer to put alongside Mozart and Wagner, it would not be Weber, because he had died too young and his last two works, *Euryanthe* and *Oberon* were unfortunately not accomplished masterpieces. If one took account of not only music but also text and action, then Lortzing was probably the third star in the galaxy of German operatic composers, despite the fact that he too had died young and had not been able to put in enough work on his operas.[75] *Zar und Zimmermann* and *Wildschütz* placed him, with Mozart and Wagner, among the greatest talents. As usual, Mahler set *Fidelio* in a class apart, and even perhaps above all other operas, for 'in each of the fields in which he exerted himself, Beethoven always succeeded in creating something outstanding'.

With the arrival of Bruno Walter, Mahler had not only acquired a conductor worthy of his confidence and anxious to comply with his wishes, but also renewed contact with a staunch and faithful friend, one of those he most liked to talk with. Over dinner one evening in late September, he discussed the problems of conducting and interpretation with Walter and Lipiner:

I've come to the conclusion that the markings in a score usually exceed the composer's intentions. The forte is too loud, the piano too soft, the largo too slow, the presto too fast and the crescendos, diminuendos and accelerandos exaggerated. As for me, how sober and restrained my conducting has become compared to what it once was! When one sees the extent to which everything is exaggerated and deformed in one's own music, one begins to realize what others suffer. In fact, one is almost tempted not to give any indications of tempo, nuance or expression but to let each interpreter express one's work in accordance with his own personal conception of it.

Playing the four-hand arrangement of his recently completed Fourth Symphony

[74] NBL1. 175; NBL2. 200 ff.
[75] NBL1. 174; NBL2. 199 ff. Although still virtually unknown outside Germany, Lortzing was in fact a composer of very considerable calibre, who wrote his own excellent librettos.

with Joseph von Wöss,[76] he let him take the initiative just to see what he would make of the dynamics; when Wöss mistakenly over-emphasized one of them, he simply erased it from the score.[77]

A few days later Walter, visiting Mahler, argued that there were certain passages in the symphonic repertory that seemed to him to present no problem of interpretation because 'they can only be thus and not otherwise'. Mahler advised him to beware of opinions and prejudices of this sort, founded 'sometimes on chance and sometimes on early impressions or tenacious memories'. 'The only right way is to see everything afresh and create it anew,'[78] he concluded. It was with this in mind that he had once told Ludwig Rottenberg,[79] who was visiting him in Alt-Aussee:

One should know a work by heart before learning it by heart. You know what I mean: one must have a grasp of its form and content before learning the notes. One can thus give a far clearer and more spontaneous picture of the whole. In my experience, this way of proceeding revealed to me the spirit of a work and I was only then able to determine its form (*es nun erst richtig aufzubauen vermochte*).[80]

Early in October, Mahler was discussing Beethoven's *Missa Solemnis* with Lipiner, Walter, and Natalie:

Probably you have never heard it, for the academic performances it gets are intolerable, and if any work needs to be very freely interpreted, that one does. I'd love to be able to give it just once, but it would be impossible in Vienna, where, shame to say, a [suitable] chorus does not exist, for one would need a gigantic mass of singers, a veritable sea of voices.

Lipiner having asked if it was really true that Beethoven's vocal writing was poor, he replied:

If the singers lack enthusiasm, yes, but if the conductor succeeds in communicating a bit of the divine spark to them, the result is phenomenal. Witness the passage *Ahnest Du den Schöpfer, Welt?* from the Ninth Symphony. You remember how jubilant it sounded when I conducted it, yet it's usually atrociously tortured because the singers want to spare themselves instead of giving everything they've got to it. It's the same thing with the *Missa Solemnis*. I didn't understand it myself to begin with, the Credo least of all; because the tempo indicated was presto, I played it too fast (this will always be the case). But one day I forgot the indication and played it to myself in accordance

[76] Joseph von Wöss (Vol. i, Chap. 6) had become one of Vienna's most valued transcribers and proof correctors. I owe the supplementary information that follows to the late Hans Heinsheimer, long-time collaborator of Universal Edition, and later of Schirmer music. Wöss had two operas of his own performed, *Lenzlüge* (Spring Lies: Elberfeld, 1905) and *Flaviennes Abenteuer* (Flavienne's Adventure: Breslau, 1910). He also wrote a Sakuntala Overture and a Piano Sextet. 'He was very calm and quiet. . . . Like Mahler, he had been a pupil of Krenn, and he became one of the masters of his art, which consisted of preparing music manuscripts for printing, an art often underestimated because little known.' Mahler, in an undated card to Joseph von Wöss, compliments him on a piano reduction that is 'exceptionally successful and astonishingly clear' (BGM).

[77] NBL1. 168 and NBLS.   [78] NBLS.
[79] Rottenberg's visit to Alt-Aussee took place in summer 1899.   [80] NBL2. 139.

with the meaning of the work as a whole[81] and, for the first time, saw it before me as it ought to be. What is strange is the way Beethoven declaimed the Credo with a kind of rage: 'I believe because it's absurd to believe,' whereas Bach put those words to music quite differently, with confidence and piety.[82]

For Mahler, the big event of the autumn was to be the first performance of his Fourth Symphony, which was to take place in Munich on 25 November. For him it was important because no new symphonic work of his had been performed since the première of his Second Symphony in 1895. The Munich première was to be followed by several other performances, for Weingartner had included the new work in the programme of the Kaim Orchestra's tour, and Strauss had invited Mahler to conduct it himself in Berlin.[83] Before handing over the final version of the score to his publisher, Mahler wanted to check his orchestration. He therefore arranged a reading rehearsal with the Philharmonic on 12 October, which also served as a first rehearsal for the Vienna première they were to give in January.[84] From the opening bar, the session promised to be difficult, for the novelty and complexity of the work considerably upset the musicians. Mahler immediately sensed their hostility by their behaviour and the looks on their faces. 'And it's on this dead rubble' he exclaimed, 'that I must build a whole flourishing world!'[85]

The violins, and later the cellos, were 'too ponderous (*massig*) and loud in the lovely cantabile themes', whereas the 'dithyrambic crescendo of the same theme at the end could not be strong and jubilant enough for him'. This initial theme, which the audience would undoubtedly find 'too simple and old-fashioned', gradually turned into 'six or seven different themes, all of them elaborated in the development'. For Mahler, indeed, to deserve the name of 'symphony' a musical work had to contain this 'richness of substance', this 'authentically organic development':

It must have something cosmic and inexhaustible like the world and life itself in order to be worthy of the name. Its structure should be such that nothing inorganic, no chance patching or mending, disrupts it.[86] The gaiety of the first movements is that of a strange higher world that tends to bewilder and terrify us. In the last movement, a child explains the meaning of it all, for he still belongs to this world of chrysalids, which is nevertheless at a higher level than ours.[87]

---

[81] NBL2. 139. This passage might lead one to believe that Mahler had conducted the *Missa Solemnis*. However, this is not so and he undoubtedly made the 'mistakes' he mentions while reading it at the piano.

[82] NBLS.

[83] Mahler had also been corresponding since summer 1899 with Jules Sachs's Berlin Concert Bureau, which had invited him to come and conduct one of his works in the German capital, but the project never materialized (see Mahler's letter of summer 1899, Stargardt catalogue, Oct. 1989, no. 549).

[84] The Philharmonic Orchestra had agreed to rehearse and perform Mahler's new symphony as a means of relieving the tension left behind by his resignation and the choice of Hellmesberger to replace him.

[85] NBL2. 197 ff.

[86] It was precisely these patchings and mendings that Mahler censured in Bruckner's symphonies. This 'organic unity', even in the most complex developments, is an all-important feature of his own mature works.

[87] A further reference to the well-known line from *Faust, Part II*.

During the rehearsal Mahler asked the first violinist to tune his instrument one tone higher than usual for the Scherzo and to accentuate the harsh and strident sound thus obtained. He even considered[88] assigning this part to a viola and having the concert-master play it. Moreover, because the strings, and particularly the cellos, over-emphasized them, he erased certain crescendo and diminuendo indications from the beginning of the Adagio. 'Orchestration is in no way aimed at creating sound effects, but rather at clearly expressing what one has to say. In this respect, no one has taught me more than Verdi, who opened up an entirely new road.'[89] He cut a few notes from the Variations because they not only thickened the sound and blurred the outline but also seemed unnecessary, the harmony being quite adequately suggested by the part-writing, 'which, like the work of a miniaturist, consists in the meeting and touching of interwoven lines'.

In the hope of avoiding possible exaggerations, Mahler had become more wary than ever in his choice of indications of tempo. Instead of ritardando, he wrote simply *nicht eilen* ('do not hurry') and, conversely, for a slight increase of speed, *nicht schleppen* ('do not drag'). 'Such are the tricks one needs to use with musicians,' he remarked.[90] Correcting the score of the Fourth Symphony one evening ten days later, he discovered a faulty chord progression. 'There was something coarse about this passage, which bothered me every time I heard it, but I didn't realize what it was. When you find something like that in your score, it's like a member of the aristocracy suddenly discovering a swineherd in his family tree.' In this connection, he and Walter discussed the 'hidden octaves' Walter said he had discovered in the part-writing, for instance, in Bach's and Schumann's music. 'It's only in Beethoven,' Mahler said, 'that I've never found any. The others have the excuse that they wrote such a lot. When one composes only one work each year, they really shouldn't occur.'[91]

Though full of gaiety and sunlight, the Fourth Symphony had cost Mahler more toil and anguish than the two huge symphonies that had preceded it. He privately hoped that its modest dimensions and clarity of style would at last win him the approval of both public and players. Indeed, it was because he had achieved his first outstanding success in Munich the year before that he had decided to give this première to the Kaim Orchestra. He had prepared for it at

[88] Natalie says that 'he decided' (*beschloss*), but the score itself proves that he later gave up this idea (NBL1. 171; NBL2. 198).

[89] This statement will not surprise those who have studied the orchestration—both original and remarkably effective—of *Otello, Falstaff*, and the Requiem.

[90] Hence the unusual indications in Mahler's scores. In late 1900 he had already complained to Natalie about the way in which his indications were misconstrued. For instance, the Scherzo of his Second Symphony was played too slowly, like an étude, because he had noted 'mit ruhiger, fliessender Bewegung' (with calm, flowing motion). It was for the same reason that he had done away with such indications as 'mit innigster Empfindung' (with intense feeling) at the beginning of the Adagio of his Third Symphony. He used laughingly to recall the indication 'mit teuflischer Wildheit' (with devilish fury) he had inscribed above the second movement of *Das klagende Lied* when he was 20.

[91] NBL1. 172; NBL2. 199 (21 Oct. 1901).

length in an exchange of letters with the orchestra's principal conductor, Felix Weingartner,[92] whom he had already asked that summer to let him conduct the world première himself. Weingartner had intended to include a Brahms symphony in the same programme, but Mahler no doubt made him change his mind, by begging him to replace it by works that were easier to understand and perform. Not only were four full rehearsals scarcely enough for him to rehearse the Fourth, but he wanted the public to be fresh and receptive when they heard it. He was also against another vocal work preceding his symphony, for he wanted the appearance of the soprano to come as a complete surprise before the Finale. 'These are of course all secondary considerations, only valid for the first performance. I have every confidence in you and your artistic judgement for all the others.'[93]

The Munich concert was first planned for 18 November, but at the end of October Mahler sent Weingartner a telegram asking him to postpone it for a week, because of 'insurmountable difficulties'.[94] In fact the first performance of *Les Contes d'Hoffmann* was scheduled for 11 November, and Mahler anticipated having to conduct the work several times in the following week in order to take advantage of its sure success. On 20 November Mahler left Vienna by the night train with Natalie and Justi. The following morning, during the first rehearsal in Munich, he realized that he had taken on a Herculean task, one which he compared to that of 'a sculptor setting out to make a statue from a coarse block of stone', for the musicians, though full of enthusiasm, were young and inexperienced. Moreover, their lack of polish made him more than ever aware of the subtle orchestration and technical difficulties of the work, especially after the happy-go-lucky Second, which they had managed fairly easily the year before. Unfortunately, the best member of the orchestra, the first cellist, had to leave Munich on the day of the concert because his father had died,[95] and Mahler soon realized that neither the performance as a whole nor the quality of the sound that he had worked so hard over, mixing the timbres and using certain instruments in unusual ways, would fully satisfy him.[96]

As always upon his arrival in another city, he made several courtesy calls in between rehearsals. Coming home one day, a friend of his, the critic Arthur

---

[92] Weingartner, who was co-director with Siegmund von Hausegger of the Kaim Orchestra, was then considered a member of the 'modern' school.

[93] Undated letter to Weingartner, Sept.–Oct. 1901 (BGM). Mahler added that Rita Michalek would accept any 'reasonable' fee offered by Kaim. She would participate 'out of enthusiasm' and had even agreed not to sing another solo. Finally, the young soprano received only 'travelling expenses' amounting to 200 florins. Mahler's requests were not granted, for Weingartner placed his *Wallfahrt nach Kevlaar*, for alto voice and orchestra in the programme before the Fourth.

[94] Telegrams from Mahler to Weingartner, 31 Oct. and 1 Nov. (BGM).

[95] This reminded Mahler of the evening when he had had to conduct a performance in Budapest immediately after being informed of his mother's death.

[96] NBL1. 176; NBL2. 201ff. In a letter written in Oct. Mahler asked Weingartner for at least 14 first violins, 12 second violins, 8 violas, as many cellos, and at least 6 double-basses for the first performance, begging him to 'understand the anxiety of a creator who, for the first time, launches his work into the world' (BMG).

Seidl, found his cook greatly perturbed. In her lively Bavarian dialect she told him that a fierce-looking gentleman dressed all in black had arrived at the house and was in Herr Seidl's room. 'Very strange the man is, and he scared me as much as if it had been a thief or a murderer trying to get into the bedroom at any price. He's in there right now at the table writing something down . . .'. The strange gentleman was of course Mahler who, thinking he had mistaken the time, was writing to Seidl to ask for another appointment.[97]

With the Fourth Symphony, which was shorter than its predecessors and required no more than a normal-sized orchestra, Mahler obviously hoped to be more readily understood. Before him, Wagner, with *Tristan und Isolde*, had originally meant to compose an 'Italianate', and therefore more 'popular', opera than the *Ring* but had ended up asserting his own musical personality yet more strongly. In just the same way, Mahler had expressed himself more personally than ever in the new symphony. Indeed, his almost neo-classical 'simplicity' was to disconcert the public far more even than the 'gigantic dimensions and epic style of his previous works. William Ritter, a young French-Swiss musician[98] living in Munich, who had never heard any of Mahler's works but was intrigued by what he had heard about his Second Symphony, attended the final rehearsal, and wrote the following account of it:

Weingartner was rehearsing his part of the concert when Mahler and his friends, among them Klaus Pringsheim,[99] came in and sat down in the front row of the red plush stalls. A thin little man with spectacles, swarthy, frizzy-haired, sallow complexion, with a very pointed head, dressed all in black, in a frock coat: looked like a clergyman, very absorbed. Weingartner finished and went off. Mahler strode quickly up to the podium and immediately inspired us with confidence. Great calm, absolute simplicity, the man was sure of himself and totally without charlatanism. One couldn't have said as much of Weingartner at that time. No reaction from the orchestra, but they seemed to have that passive look musicians put on when they don't intend to commit themselves: 'We'll play what's put before us but we won't answer for it.' And Weingartner had prudently slipped away . . . Something was up . . . We felt it at once . . . This symphony obviously spelt danger.

It began . . . We understood at once . . . It was quite extraordinary . . . A tinkling bell . . . of a horse or a mule, that was it . . . Emma Bovary would have thought at once of a steep path in the Sierra . . . *tras los montes*. A tinkling bell accompanied by two

[97] Arthur Seidl, *Aufsätze, Studien und Skizzen* (Bosse, Regensburg, 1926), ii. 309.

[98] William Ritter (1863–1955), Swiss writer, painter, and art critic. After studying in his home town of Neuchâtel, in Dôle, and finally at the Univ. of Vienna, Ritter travelled widely, dividing his interests between music and the fine arts. He crossed Europe several times as far as Romania, in search of new methods of expression and national traditions. He became a specialist on Czech art, thanks to the influence of his collaborator and friend Janko Cadra. He settled in Munich (1900–14), where he was French tutor to Prince Ruprecht of Bavaria. He wrote numerous articles for music and art reviews, and counted many famous painters and composers among his friends. Publications include *Études d'art étranger* (Mercure de France, Paris, 1906) and the first French biography of Smetana (Alcan, Paris, 1908). After 1914 he settled in Switzerland, where he continued to paint and write articles until his death.

[99] Klaus Pringsheim, son of a rich Munich bourgeois family, chose a career in music. His sister, Katia, was soon to marry Thomas Mann (see below, Vol. iii, Chap. 2).

flutes staccato, while a clarinet in A slowly tried out a reverential figure . . . And straight away the first theme . . . But such that since Haydn—but with what additional seasoning—no symphony had served up anything so graceful, so enticing, so melodious and so prolonged . . . It was at once childish and, would you believe it, not half cheeky . . . and, above all, nothing less than innocent . . . Just like in the theatre when the ingénue is played by the most dissolute member of the troupe. We're at once bewitched and flabbergasted, won over and horrified. Besides, we were the kind of audience who were still not too accustomed to hearing muted horns. But now the orchestra began its buffoonery, emitting sounds that came as a surprise even after Strauss's *Till Eulenspiegel* and Dukas' *Apprenti Sorcier*. We didn't know what to think. 'What shocking music!' muttered somebody near me . . . Finally the first movement came to an end. We had never been so embarrassed—obviously we weren't going to admit we might have liked it! Was that really serious music? And the audience, which was fairly large, seemed just as disconcerted. I was sitting next to the poet Wolfskehl, a friend of Stefan George. Modernist though he was, he seemed just as dumbfounded as we were, he agreed with us: 'Nothing but Viennese corruption, carnival, *G'schnas*,[100] just the stuff for Ronacher's [the big Viennese cabaret-theatre].' The second movement seemed more serious, but so sinister after the festive rough-and-tumble and humour of the first! Then came the third, a heart-rending funeral march soon mixed up with a sort of gaiety, and we couldn't make head or tail of it. And suddenly, as rondo finale, the extraordinary, inexplicable soprano song about the angels' kitchen, from *Des Knaben Wunderhorn*. What did it all add up to? And where had we got to from the majestic world of great music ranging from Bach's Passions to the austere, Promethean and magnificent symphonies of the Beethovens, Brahmses and Bruckners? It was as though we'd gone from Bayreuth to the *Überbrettl* [a variety theatre in Berlin].

And the audience around us was just as bewildered as we were! But being German and not thinking for a moment that the Kaim Orchestra and a director of the Vienna Opera would make fun of them, they were reacting less than we were . . . Wit, we decided! Jewish wit which had invaded the domain of the symphony and was, as elsewhere, acting as a corrosive, if the shade of Mendelssohn will pardon us for saying so!

And in the evening [at the première itself], having had the afternoon to think over our impressions, we booed our heads off, as they boo only in Paris or in Italy! Which, as always happens, served merely to give renewed strength to the partisans who opposed us at all costs. The audience, moreover, had been pretty much hand-picked . . . All of Munich's Jewry was there . . . Hearing us booing in this way, a woman fixed us with a venomous snake-like stare—I can still see her eyes—and heaped insults upon us . . . The following day, the Vienna papers announced that the applause for this première of the Fourth in Munich had been *stürmisch* (tumultuous). But Mahler, as far as we were concerned, was henceforth . . . a sort of Raskol of German musical orthodoxy.[101]

William Ritter's colourful style vividly recreates the atmosphere in the hall and the reactions of the audience to this 'scandalous' work. He left the rehearsal 'disgusted, declaring to all and sundry that I would never have believed

---

[100] *G'schnas*: carnival or masquerade in Viennese slang and, by extension, a work of no value.
[101] 'Souvenirs sur Gustav Mahler', *Schweizerische Musikzeitung*, 101: 1 (Feb. 1961), 30 ff.

anyone capable of writing such shocking music', and feeling that he had been 'revelling in an undeniable way in a sort of musical Black Mass' and that, indeed, Satan and all his rites and works had 'never chosen a better home in an orchestra'. In a more sober style, Natalie also describes the amazement at the simplicity of the first theme on the part of an audience expecting something 'earth-shattering' from Mahler. Thereafter, unable to follow the complexity of events in the development, the audience went from astonishment to consternation and, at the end of the movement, a great many boos were to be heard amid the applause. The Scherzo baffled it still more, so that Mahler's young admirers were no longer able to drown out the booing. Fortunately, however, Rita Michalek, the attractive young singer who had been engaged at the Hofoper four years earlier, saved the day. Her almost childlike freshness was perfectly suited to the final Lied and her very youth and charm calmed 'the flood of opposition and exasperation' and 'poured oil on the troubled waters'.[102]

Fully aware of the audience's mood, Mahler let Michalek take several bows before reappearing himself. He then sent her into the wings and fulfilled his obligation 'in a manner more furious than friendly'. After the final rehearsal several of the musicians had told him 'that they hadn't been able to make head or tail of the work but would do their best to change their minds the following day'. However, when not a single one of them, except for Weingartner, came to say 'anything sensible that might please him', he realized that the Fourth had lost him most of the admirers that the Second had won for him the year before.

Ritter also describes the storm raised in the peaceful Bavarian capital by 'this symphony, generally taken to be humorous and paradoxical', which he had found 'infernal':

The first movement could be Daniel in the lions' den, Orpheus slaughtered by the Maenads, genius delivered to the beasts! It's nothing but acrobatics and the performance of a lady in tights in a menagerie. 'It's a menagerie' was the first impression and the cry of dismay of one of us upon hearing these comic sounds that are tried out and do their level best one after the other in this first movement, a movement ideally pretty, fresh and graceful in its piano version, which lulls any suspicion that prodigious and clownish things might be going on in the orchestra. It's the continual head down, legs up of Salome's dance in the porch of Rouen Cathedral. And one can imagine the astonishment with which old Haydn, himself a lover of jokes and musical 'quips', would have listened to this fearsome revival of the *Toy Symphony*[103] in which he imitated the

---

[102] NBL2. 202. Rita Michalek had graduated from the Vienna Conservatory in June 1897. She was immediately engaged by Jahn and became a member of the Vienna Opera on 1 Sept. 1897. *Neue Freie Presse* describes the audience as divided between two parties, those in the stalls remaining aloof while those in the cheap seats, and notably in the standing area, overflowed with enthusiasm. The concert programme of 25 Nov. consisted of a little Mozart Symphony in G major, 'composed when he was thirteen years old' (doubtless K.74 or K.129), a work for contralto and orchestra by Weingartner, *Wallfahrt nach Kevlaar*, Mahler's symphony, a group of Lieder (Brahms's 'Immer leise', Schumann's 'Waldesgespräch', Reisenauer's 'Der Ritter', and Cornelius's 'Wiegenlied'), sung, like the *Wallfahrt*, by Therese Behr and accompanied at the piano by Weingartner, and Beethoven's Egmont Overture.

[103] The Toy Symphony is now known to have been composed not by Haydn but by Leopold Mozart.

squawking of fowl and the squeals of animals . . . The plain fact is—and it was as typical as our regrettable booing (in Munich!)—that, throughout the performance, one row of people after another got the giggles. At a certain moment, a voice shouted out 'grossartig' (magnificent) and the owner of it burst out laughing. An absolutely delicious waltz melody, though played very simply by an ordinary violin, appears amid the croaking swamps—the symphony opens with what sounds like a series of croaks by toads—and itself turns into a nasal parody, submitting to the influence of its environment!

The same William Ritter truculently enumerates Mahler's surprising 'sound effects', the muted trumpets, harp harmonics, and 'dividing up' of the instruments, as well as the constant changes of tempo, and describes his indignation at the third movement, which 'at one moment is dying so gently of consumption, and the next is working itself up into paroxysms of frenzy'. As to Michalek's entry after the Adagio, 'It was not oil poured on troubled waters but fuel added to the fire . . . With the most complete lack of chivalry, we became enraged at this "expedient to silence us" and our animosity redoubled. . . . It would be impossible', Ritter continues,

to convey the sensation of madness (there's no other word for it) that such a symphony can arouse! It's no consolation to me to think that the feeling of revulsion that rose in my soul upon hearing this work was shared by a good half of the calm and serious Germany that applauds absolutely safe, not to say totally reliable musicians. . . .[104] What blinded my friends and me was everything about it that seemed to us to be merely vulgar self-advertisement; the way in which it constantly appealed to the lowest instincts of the crowd and so expertly caressed and aroused the sensuality latent in each one of us, inciting it to indulge itself; it was the breeze of contagious madness that made one shriek with laughter; the constant overloading and perversion of an alluring melody with every possible large or small sound effect; the way it swung from the sublime to the ridiculous, in an apparent effort to please everyone from the aristocrat down to the peasant; the way in which its Jewish and Nietzschean spirit defied our Christian spirit with its sacrilegious buffoonery and the fact that it exasperated our loyalty to the past by crushing all our artistic principles to a pulp.

As far as these young music lovers were concerned, Ritter went on, Mahler had 'multiplied a hundredfold the sarcasm of Heine and his caricaturish parody of the greatest and most sacred things in the most idolized art' and had introduced 'jugglers into the temple and the circus into the cathedral', with the result that they had 'perceived nothing of the symphony except the desperate sublimity of the beginning of the third movement', which they had considered yet another 'profanation' upon seeing it 'revert to delirium'. Taking 'the boards for the show, and the painted clowns of the parade and the backdrop coarsely daubed with wild beasts for the drama', they had regarded Mahler as 'one of the most dangerous adversaries of our aesthetic faith and our national aesthetics'. Soon, however, they had been forced to recognize 'the musical giant

[104] WRE 280.

behind the grimaces and the thoroughbred horse beneath the grotesque trappings'.[105]

Ritter's verbal extravaganzas give a clear picture of the Munich public's reactions to the 'scandal' of the Fourth Symphony. As far as Ritter himself was concerned, the impression Mahler's music had made on him was too strong to be entirely negative: he 'couldn't sleep any more' because of it; he and his friends were 'indelibly marked' by it.

Obviously the road to Damascus, with the thunderbolt and the dazzling light, had worked faster. But here revelation followed reflection. And this reflection, permanently with us, could not have been simpler or more down-to-earth: You rebel against this music. You reject it with all your wisdom, all your experience and all your convictions . . . but you're fighting against your own pleasure . . . you're trying to be virtuous . . . But deep down . . . there's nothing you like better. You're defeated. Whether you will or no, you admire it! It was bound to happen that you, an anti-Semite, should be bowled over by admiration for something Jewish![106]

More deeply disturbed than he would admit even to himself, Ritter wrote Mahler a letter whose frankness pleased the composer, for he sent him the still-unpublished proofs of the orchestral score and the arrangement for piano four hands of the Fourth Symphony almost by return post.[107] And the young people who had so booed its première began to 'feel their way' cautiously towards the disparaged work and ended up by 'conceding its mastery and veiling their faces'.

The Munich journalists, however, were not disposed to show the same broadmindedness, and lost no time in reflecting the general disappointment. The following day only the *Allgemeine-Zeitung* showed some degree of moderation, declaring that the boos had not drowned out the applause and that the work was 'not readily accessible and, in any case, impossible to judge after only one hearing'. The first movement, it said, recalled the Andante of the Second Symphony:

Mellifluous, exquisitely transparent and felicitously modelled themes with pleasant rhythms that Mahler, with admirable contrapuntal skill, weaves into a filigree of the highest quality. The individual instruments are almost constantly treated as soloists, chamber music on a grand scale and sometimes even relaxed drawing-room music. Meanwhile, amusing but subtle and technically ultra-refined chatter on the part of the orchestra, which babbles, cackles, squeaks, burlesques, roars and creaks in every corner; an endeavour to translate into music and cacophony St Anthony as painted by Breughel or Callot. The second movement is too much like the first and therein lies its weakness. A contrast, a change of mood, is needed. It also contains musical jokes of doubtful taste. A horde of goblins roams around tormenting the audience, and while they don't actually slap their faces they pierce or tickle their ears, pull their hair and

---

[105] WRE 272. [106] *Schweizerische Musikzeitung*, article quoted in n. 100, 31.
[107] Letter from Mahler to Ritter of 31 Dec. 1901, MBRS 145. Mahler also asks the young critic to send him the articles he has written.

repeatedly hit them on the nose. And then, quite suddenly, an exquisite melody reappears, a melody brimming with charm and roguishness, a genuine melody, healthy, well modelled, radiating Viennese gaiety and spirit, a cross between a Ländler and a sentimental and parodic couplet. . . . The theme of the slow movement is long drawn-out and has little or no character, while its development contains totally vacuous passages . . . As for the *Volkstümlichkeit* of the Finale, it is highly questionable and totally inappropriate as a last movement of a Symphony . . .

Finally this critic referred to the passages of caricature in *Die Meistersinger*, such as Walter's 'Diese Meister' or Beckmesser's appearance on the platform in the last act:

The grotesquely comic means something in the theatre but, in a symphony, it must at least be justified by a precise programme, if it is not to degenerate into a hodgepodge of dissonances and instrumental jokes devoid of artistic maturity. In my view, the musical and spiritual content of the work is insignificant in comparison with its pretensions, which test both the patience of the audience and the quality of the orchestra. It assumes the most imposing symphonic airs but the audience does not know whether it should take the composer seriously or whether he just wants to dazzle it with the fireworks of his irony and his skill as a sensation-monger. This sort of thing trespasses against the holy spirit of music, a veracious spirit that, even in humour, tolerates no inauthenticity.

After recalling the numerous controversies stirred up by Mahler and his symphonies, the anonymous critic of the *Münchener Zeitung* launched into a lengthy analysis of his own disappointment. Although he had not been entirely convinced of the genuineness of the artistic emotions expressed in the Second Symphony, mainly because of the vastness of the means employed and its supreme technical refinement, he could not understand why Mahler had now presented such a totally different work, whose content was 'neither sufficiently clear nor sufficiently important to hold the audience's interest'; such a 'succession of disjointed and heterogeneous atmospheres and expressions mixed with instrumental quirks and affectations'. Was Mahler merely indulging in tasteless jokes at the expense of his audience? Was he being satirically 'Viennese'? Mahler was now 'opposed in principle to programmes', yet only a programme could possibly have 'made the work's images and points of departure comprehensible to the listener'. As it was, the Fourth repeatedly touched on the dubious genre which, as the saying went, was 'the only one not permissible'. The third movement, the most successful one of the four, strayed and was lost among endless melodic developments. 'Whether the whole was intended as satire or just as a bad joke, it should in the one case have been shorter, in the other, more trenchant'. As for the Finale, 'strangest of all symphonic endings', it had been 'enjoyed as a song, certainly not as a Finale'.

The *Bayrische Kurier*[108] also failed to understand why the 'brilliant'

---

[108] The author of this review probably also wrote the one in the *Allgemeine Musik-Zeitung*, for the opinions expressed are almost identical.

composer of the Second Symphony had produced a work such as this. People had looked forward to something 'powerful and transcendental', or at least to 'dazzling effects and tragic pathos', and instead he had come up with this 'tame Humoresque loaded with orchestral mannerisms and of a protean style that ranges between Mozart, Richard Strauss and Koschat'. This 'restless and nervous' work, full of 'incredible cacophony', had remained incomprehensible; it conjured up visions of 'a man so haunted by painful and disagreeable hallucinations that he cannot sleep'. Only the last two movements had aroused a certain amount of interest.

Likewise, *Der Sammler*'s anonymous reviewer found Mahler's 'simplicity verging on affectation' and made fun of his 'clownish pranks' and 'cats' chorus'. An article in the *Kleine Journal* similarly objected to the 'decadent nervousness' of the work, its lack of stylistic unity, and its 'many reminiscences' of Wagner and popular gypsy music. In this critic's view, Mahler was 'making a mistake in using only superlatives and in constantly maintaining his expression at a paroxysmal level of intensity. . . . Despite the complexity, the refinement of the counterpoint and harmony, the 'almost hysterical instrumental transparency', there was 'a desperate lack of profundity and power'. Nevertheless, the critic concluded, the Finale was 'quite simply a work of genius': 'All honour to the young people who had the courage to express their opinion in defiance of the indignant majority.'

Mahler's only genuine defender was the critic of the *Münchener Post*, who proclaimed the new work a 'great step forward on the road to artistic clarity', the expression of a genuine and powerful personality that succeeded in 'gilding the miseries of life with Dionysiac gaiety'. It was 'a treasury of striking (*sinnfällige*), original (*urwüchsige*) and joyfully welling melodies', and its 'polyphonic experiments, sometimes going to the brink of sheer cacophony', could be understood without real discomfort. Even the 'acerbity' of the language and the passages that were 'grotesque' in no way repelled this writer, who felt that Weingartner deserved to be thanked by true friends of art for the 'broadmindedness' he had shown in introducing this remarkable work. Unfortunately, such approval was exceptional, not only in the Munich press but also in the music periodicals, which all condemned the Fourth Symphony. Karl Potgiesser, in the *Allgemeine Musik-Zeitung*, declared it vastly inferior to the Second, in spite of its interesting and occasionally even fascinating orchestration. It was incomprehensible without a programme, and unlikely to satisfy anyone with its totally unoriginal themes. When the voice had made its entry, the stupefied listeners had had the impression of witnessing 'the silting up of the river of music'. According to Theodor Kroyer, in *Die Musik*, 'the bad seed perceptible in parts of the Second Symphony had become immense spiky thistles in the Fourth'.[109] Its 'false images' had neither originality nor personal

---

[109] *Die Musik*, 1: 6 (Dec. 1901), 549. Founded in 1901 by the composer-conductor Bernhard Schuster (1870–1934) and published bi-monthly by the Leipzig firm Schuster & Loeffler, *Die Musik* soon assumed a

inspiration, not one genuine emotion or true colour. It was nothing but 'technique, calculation, vanity, a morbid and insipid supermusic, a shapeless stylistic monstrosity that collapses under a surfeit of witty details.' Finally, the *Neue Musikalische Presse*[110] stressed the curiosity that the work had aroused after the triumphant success of the Second, a curiosity equalled only by most of the listeners' disappointment when confronted with this strange amalgam of 'eccentricities', 'affected simplicity and extreme sophistication', 'elements borrowed from Viennese popular music and from heterogeneous passing styles', 'instrumental sallies', and 'mixed colours'. It was impossible to extrapolate from all this the slightest meaning, the slightest overall impression. One began to wonder if Mahler was not simply making fun of his audience, since he even refused them the explanation and 'programme' they so sorely needed. Perhaps he was doing to the Viennese what Strauss had done to the citizens of Munich in *Feuersnot*. As long as the key to these puzzles was missing, there was nothing to do but admit one's disappointment.

Thus, the critics were unanimous in condemning the Fourth Symphony on the grounds of style, form, and content. Only a select few attempted to rise above the mêlée and to understand Mahler's unique position in the context of his time. The Leipzig critic Arthur Seidl confirms[111] that most musicians in Munich were expecting another Second Symphony and did not even go to the trouble of studying the score or trying to make something of the work. He himself had changed his opinion between the rehearsals and the concert, although, in the absence of any written commentary, everyone had found it incomprehensible. 'One ends up wondering,' wrote Seidl,

whether texts and 'programmes' have not made audiences so deaf they can no longer react spontaneously or make an effort to understand a work. . . . Mahler is a real 'God Seeker.' His most secret inner being contemplates the immensity of nature with a really religious fervour; he is inexorably drawn toward the enigma of existence. I thus disagree entirely with the widespread opinion that, as a musician, he is content to exercise his biting irony and his misplaced scepticism at the expense of celestial joys . . . (I wish to God that others had the same serious, almost sacred approach to their work!) . . . The truth is quite different: it is the critics who consider him with an ironic eye and find only affectation in his music; it is they who are stubborn and who cannot find the key to his naïve and childlike fairy-tale world!

leading role among the German musical magazines, particularly in the promotion of contemporary music. In 1901 it boasted of 160 collaborators and 120 correspondents. Each issue comprised about 70 pp., and a large number of illustrations and documents. Indexes were published every three months.

[110] *Neue Musik-Zeitung's* review, signed A.H., was almost identical in content and therefore undoubtedly by the same writer. He was the critic and conductor Arthur Hahn (1858–1913), well-known for his articles on Strauss. Siegfried Schmalzriedt, in his catalogue of reviews by another critic, August Halm, wrongly credits him with this review—*Von Form und Sinn* (Breitkopf & Härtel, Wiesbaden, 1978). The error was discovered by Rudolph Stephan, *Musikforschung*, 32 (1979), 163.

[111] His account of the Munich concert was reproduced in 1926 in *Aufsätze*, i. 291. See above Vol. i, Chap. 23 for Arthur Seidl's biography.

Although mistaken in supposing that the famous 'reminiscences' from Haydn, Mozart, Schubert, Bruckner, etc., are 'deliberate and intentional', Seidl proves in this article that he was one of the few receptive minds who considered Mahler as something more than a charlatan and a symbol of the musical decadence of his time.

The Jewish composer Ernest Bloch, who was ill in Munich at the time of the first performance of the Fourth Symphony, related how, the following day, one of his friends burst into his bedroom to speak of the 'musical Voltaire', the 'sceptic', the 'ironist', whose 'icy sarcasm' had pierced him through.[112] But, of all Mahler's contemporaries, it was William Ritter who best defined the sources and nature of his music and expressed the strange, simultaneous terror and fascination experienced by many of Mahler's most staunch supporters:

From Nietzsche he has acquired an impassioned and sarcastic vehemence that encourages him to risk all in order to assert his passions, his enthusiasms, his monumental, sidesplitting humour, and no doubt his utter contempt for humanity. What he has to say comes from Nietzsche; the art of saying it, from Bruckner; and the way he says it, from Vienna and his race.

Perhaps this Jewish heritage is in fact responsible for his nervous predisposition toward an often epileptical musical form of expression, and for his stubborn clinging to his own prejudices whether ridiculous or sublime; for his indomitable urge to impose, at any price, his most exorbitant demands, as well as his desire for beauty; his need to prove the opposition wrong by any means, to force hate to disgorge admiration, and for the power with which he exploits luxury, opulence and the odd and unexpected to the full; then there is his harmonious orderliness and infallible balance in composition, which conjures up the perfect balance of a *credit* and *debit* account, and evokes expert banking operations; and finally there is that very special note of concupiscence, whose affiliations with the *Song of Songs* are evident and which has somehow come down to him via the banks of the blue Danube. It is indeed Vienna that he has to thank for such a plethora of fresh and youthful riches; the guileless sensuality of the melodic lines which even the king of the waltz himself, Johann Strauss, only possessed to a lesser degree; the continual musical curtsies, the melodic spasms, the dancing, swooning rhythms, the languishing inflections of desire, which give his work so disquieting and troubled a character (morally, for the physical limpidity is absolute). This strange, solemn and yet fun-loving city has certainly also influenced him by its secessionist aberration and the extreme bad taste fomented by its carnival of many peoples: and he also owes to it—to his old Austrian background—some adorably old-fashioned and sentimental touches. Finally, in these composite surroundings, where East meets West and North meets South, where Slavism overlaps Germanism and Italianism with Magyarism, the whole fermented by a Jewish yeast, it is easy to imagine what eccentricities can cross the mind of a musician of genius rising to the challenge of knowing that the gayest Opera house in Europe depends on him.[113]

Ritter goes on to describe certain of the public's reactions to Mahler's Vienna themes:

[112] *Le Courrier musical* (1 July 1904).   [113] WRE 249.

And when some of them appear, moist and persuasive, tantalizing and seductive, then you should see the lewd glances in the concert hall, the salacious dribble at the corners of the mouths of some of the old men, and above all the ugly, whoring laughs of certain respectable women! And the glances are first exchanged and then averted! It would be enough to put one off Mahler for life if the antidote did not immediately appear in the form of the dismay of both fools and cods, the turkey-cock anger of the critics and the modest blushes of the hypocrites. Mr Mahler has all the attributes required to write the symphony-ballet and the symphony-panorama of our dreams.[114]

Ritter's obsessional preoccupation with the Viennese sources of Mahler's art prevented him perhaps from understanding how much more important his works were as promises for the future than as insults to the past. And yet the subconscious and almost surrealist approach of the young Neuchâtel art critic gave him a much deeper understanding of Mahler than did the sterile didacticism of most music professionals of the time.

Weingartner had consented to let Mahler conduct the world première of the Fourth Symphony, but he himself conducted it on the Kaim Orchestra's tour, which took in Nuremberg, Darmstadt, Frankfurt am Main, Karlsruhe, and Stuttgart. Except in Stuttgart, public and press were unanimously uncomprehending, exasperated, and disdainful. In Darmstadt, two days after the Munich première, the audience was wholly baffled. Applause after the first and second movements was practically drowned out by energetic boos and hisses. Only the Adagio and the Finale were somewhat better received. The critic of the *Darmstädter Zeitung* acknowledged that Mahler possessed 'dramatic genius, and a virtuoso's mastery of orchestration', and even 'inventive originality, and a genuine sense of beauty'. But it seemed to him that in this work Mahler had flung together, as if at random, all imaginable sounds, beautiful and ugly. Like Richard Strauss, he wrote 'interesting and witty' music which set the intelligence to work in a way that was 'sometimes agreeable, sometimes not'. 'In general, he spares us the trouble of letting the music penetrate through our ears to our hearts.'[115] The anonymous Darmstadt correspondent of the Viennese *Neue Freie Presse* dwelt on the work's originality, and the fantastic skill of its orchestration. A sense of 'fresh, abundant, pulsating life' emerged from it, so that 'despite the strangeness of its content' it had been 'very well received' by the public. The *Darmstädter Tagblatt*, on the other hand, inveighed against this 'musical enigma': its 'grotesque character', its 'naïvety', its 'folksiness', and its 'risky transitions and harmonies mixed with baroque clichés'. Apart from his 'astonishing technical ability', Mahler seemed to possess above all an 'undeniable comic gift'.

In Nuremberg, the day after the Munich première, the reception was even colder. According to the *Generalanzeiger*, only the erroneous report of success

---

[114] WRE 254.

[115] The author of this review was probably also that of the brief account in *Die Musik*, identified as Otto Waldästl, and speaks in almost identical terms of the Fourth's 'musical enigmas'.

in Munich prompted the applause of 'a few gregarious people who have no opinions of their own'. The only praiseworthy thing about this pure *Kapellmeistermusik* was its orchestration. The first movement was a hotchpotch of a hackneyed sentimental ditty, interlaced with 'some classical embellishments' and 'strange Secessionist contortions', and 'an outmoded and droning type of Turkish music' mixed with 'Scottish bagpipe squeals' and a pot-pourri of 'Gypsy, Russian, Bohemian and Hungarian' melodies; in short, a 'thoroughly international piece'. The return of the German melody would have been a consolation if it had not been previously 'translated into so many different languages' and preceded by such 'musical vaudeville'. After having committed such 'fearful musical crimes' in the Scherzo, with his 'international yodellings', Mahler had proceeded to 'murmur sweet nothings' (*Dideldumdel*) in the Adagio. And the interminable final Lied adorned with serious melismata that had followed this 'third act of a comedy rather than a symphony' had conjured up a 'young girl wearing her grandmother's pleated bonnet'. After the frills and furbelows of this 'Vaudeville-Symphony', the pure music of Brahms had finally afforded the audience unadulterated enjoyment.

The following day, Henriette Mankiewicz attended the concert in Frankfurt, where the public's reaction was such that she preferred to say nothing to Mahler about it but spoke only to Natalie.[116] The majority of the audience seemed to think the whole thing was 'a joke or a scandalous hoax'. The *Musikalisches Wochenblatt* correspondent compared the 'angry and violent' hissing to 'the sound of an autumn wind blowing through the dead leaves and twigs of a forest'. The *Frankfurter Zeitung* had prepared the ground by publishing a review of the Munich performance which called the symphony an 'immense disappointment', accused Mahler of having sought 'cacophony at any price', alleged that he had reached 'a dead end in his symphonic development', and had allowed 'his melodic spring to dry up'. The anonymous reviewer also reproached him with propounding disconcerting and even insoluble riddles by juxtaposing a burlesque and caricatural style with the folkloric simplicity of Schubert and Viennese songs:

Worldly tumult smothers the melody of the heart, the coarse noises of this lower world drown out the serene beauty and destroy the contemplative dreaming of the idealistic artist. Unless he is able to save his soul from despair by escaping into romantic fantasies of a blissful and sparkling paradise, the creator's childlike innocence will inevitably turn into a grimace of disgust and tedium.

Mahler had modelled himself as much on Callot and Hoffmann as on Berlioz and Liszt, the same review concluded, and had composed 'programme music without a programme, literary music that satisfies none of the basic requirements of music, namely, feeling, imagination, atmosphere'.

[116] NBL2. 203.

Two days later, the same paper's own music critic took the same view after the Frankfurt performance. He said that the approving smiles of the many people in the audience who had enjoyed the popular Viennese melodies had rapidly frozen on their faces at the sound of the atrociously and deliberately false notes and 'ear-torturing effects', which exceeded anything of this kind anyone had ever heard. The composer's talent was manifest solely in the orchestration and the whole work had worn the audience down. According to *Die Musik*, the Frankfurt public had condemned it utterly on account of its 'ill-fermented ideological content, its reckless and cacophonous developments and its, as always, wilful incomprehension of Beethoven's Ninth'.[117] As for the *Musikalisches Wochenblatt*, it claimed that the public's negative reactions were fully justified for it had realized it was being made fun of; the work was incomprehensible and the music 'insipid, humourless, tiresome, painful and built on vulgar themes that, thanks to all sorts of expedients, just went on and on'.[118]

At Karlsruhe, third stop on the tour, Weingartner began the concert with Berlioz's King Lear Overture in an almost empty hall. He then had someone announce that he was not feeling well and needed a short rest. When he returned to the podium half an hour later, he conducted only the Finale of Mahler's Fourth Symphony. In its review, *Die Musik* intimated that his courage had failed him at the prospect of conducting the whole work. Adam Heid, in the *Badische Landeszeitung*, surmised that the many performances of this 'cacophonous Fourth have overstrained his nerves' and added that, despite its 'affected simplicity', the piece was 'complicated and incomprehensible'. The *Karlsruher Zeitung* criticized the choice of text[119] but praised the 'pleasant and well-trained' voice of Rita Michalek.

The only town in which the symphony was given a favourable reception was Stuttgart, where the *Schwäbischer Merkur* classed Mahler 'above composers of simple talent' and claimed that, although his aims were not clear, he was one of the 'new stars that are steadily rising and in no danger of falling back into the night'. In spite of its oddities, the work gave an impression of unity. Rather than the musical 'thunder and lightning' that everyone expected, it was a touching

---

[117] It has to be said that the resemblance between Mahler's Fourth and Beethoven's Ninth is far-fetched. It must have been the use of the voice in the Finale (or the Adagio with its Variations on two themes) that prompted this very strange comparison.

[118] This same critic claimed that Weingartner's reputation had been badly damaged by this enterprise and that he had only given the work 'out of friendship for a highly placed musician', while the Nuremberg correspondent of *Die Musik* stated that Mahler planned to reward Weingartner by giving the latter's *Oreste* in Vienna.

[119] The programmes of the concerts were as follows. Nuremberg (26 Nov.): Berlioz, *King Lear* Overture; Mahler, Fourth Symphony; Brahms, Fourth Symphony; Beethoven, *Egmont* Overture. Darmstadt (27 Nov.): Mahler, Fourth Symphony; Brahms, Fourth Symphony; Beethoven, *Egmont* Overture. Frankfurt (28 Nov.): Mahler, Fourth Symphony; Brahms, Fourth Symphony; Berlioz, *King Lear* Overture. Karlsruhe (29 Nov.): Berlioz, *King Lear* Overture; Mahler, Finale of the Fourth Symphony; Beethoven, First Symphony and *Leonore* Overture No. 3. Stuttgart (30 Nov.): Mahler, Fourth Symphony; Brahms, Fourth Symphony; Beethoven, *Leonore* Overture No. 3.

idyll, a 'wreath of good-humoured melodies and folk dances'. The critic of the *Neues Tagblatt*, on the other hand, condemned the symphony in the usual way for its 'vulgar passages, its sentimentality and its affectation'. He hoped he would 'never again encounter this Mahlerian tone painting, either on earth or in heaven'.

Altogether this disastrous tour had only served to weaken Mahler's already insecure reputation as a composer. On the last day of the four, 30 November, Felix Weingartner wrote to him from Stuttgart seeking his pardon for the previous day's concert, when he had played only the Finale of the Symphony:

Yesterday in Karlsruhe I suffered a misfortune which unfortunately also affected your symphony. Probably because of a previous personal upset, I had an attack of vertigo that started during the first item on the programme, the Lear Overture of Berlioz, and led to vomiting and other such pleasant things. To cut a long story short, the concert was interrupted for about 50 minutes. Afterwards I was so done up that I didn't trust myself to conduct your work, which requires the greatest degree of alertness on the part of the conductor, especially as the lighting in the hall was bad and everything was still dancing before my eyes. For the sake both of your work and of Fräulein Michalek, it was announced that the last movement of your symphony would be played as a single piece, and that's what we did. Afterwards I conducted the First Symphony and Leonora of Beethoven, two pieces that, if I can't exactly conduct them in my sleep, I can at least conduct without a score, which, considering the state I was in, was easier than trying with difficulty to decipher a score. I am truly sorry, but it was better than conducting badly, or having to stop in the middle of the work.

Today I am still very unwell, but I am having a complete rest and feel hopeful that I shall be at my post tonight. As I telegraphed you, the symphony had a great success in Nuremberg, only weakening after the second movement. The public didn't know what to make of it. In Darmstadt, for some inexplicable reason, there was a certain amount of opposition after the Adagio, whereas the first movement—as everywhere—made a strong impression, and the last had a good, undisputed success.

In Frankfurt, inflammatory articles from Munich were published in the papers and Wertheim, our noble impresario, told me that after the second movement, which was particularly attacked, there was to be organized opposition. He faithfully assured me that for his part he had also seen to a claque. But both you and I well know what such manœuvres are worth.

Therefore I reflected on another means of meeting the opposition, namely by cutting or omitting the second movement. Naturally I soon rejected that. Instead I warned the orchestra in advance, and when I noticed a certain amount of unrest at the end of the second movement I raised my left hand—and carried straight on with the Adagio. Those who wanted to hiss did so, of course, after the third movement, but by then the applause was so strong and lasting that the opposition was stifled. The last movement was unanimously applauded. My method was not very nice, but I know you will understand that one stoops to these things when a work is not going to be allowed a fair hearing. It was a matter of countering a great wrong with a little one. Tonight after the second movement I shall simply stop. If they want to hiss, they can. But I'm convinced they won't be coming with that in mind. Unfortunately it will be impossible to repeat the symphony at the next Kaim Konzert. A important Munich institution of leading importance cannot ignore Rheinberger's death,[120] and I shall have to do something of his, just as I performed something of Taubert's in Berlin when he departed this life.[121] As Burmester[122] is playing the Tchaikovsky Concerto, there will not be time for a long symphony, and I am going to do Haydn's *Military*. The question is, would repeating it so soon be any use. The opposition might well be even stronger as a result of the wonderfully sympathetic attitude of the 'bosses' (*Vorgesetzten*), especially as until now I have never repeated a new work. It is easy to confuse personal gratification with the objective service one wants to render to the work. Nevertheless I would certainly have done it if Rheinberger had not 'voted against it' it by dying.

I am very much looking forward to having your work unfurl before me again today. But now I know it thoroughly, and believe that the performances would meet with your approval, especially since I am calmer than when I conducted it in front of you for the first time. Fräulein Michalek, whom I've only got to know quite superficially, I'm afraid, as we have both had to nurse ourselves and haven't been able to spend much time together, has done her part very charmingly and with great success.

I'm sending the parts and the bells to Strauss tonight. I shall be heartily glad, dear friend, if your memories of our time together in Munich are as happy as mine, and in this hope I greet you as your affectionate and long-devoted, Felix Weingartner.[123]

The least that can be said is that the conductor of the Kaim Orchestra does not distinguish himself here by his courage or sincerity. His protestations of friendship and loyalty are too numerous and insistent not to reveal the embarrassment which the failure of the work, and the public's furious demonstrations, had caused him. Mahler did not need to be unusually perspicacious to see that his colleague was only seeking to go back on his promises so as to avoid confronting the public once again with such a provocative work. Weingartner himself retained traumatic memories of the tour, and never conducted a note of Mahler again. Moreover, his personal relations with Mahler were badly affected. Weingartner must have complained of receiving no reply to the above letter, for in spring 1902 Mahler wrote to him: 'If I remember rightly, do I really owe you a letter? You promised me a report on your activities, but alas, I never received it. . . . You cannot imagine the nervous and tense atmosphere in which I live! I don't even have time to think of myself, let alone my friends!'[124] It is quite obvious that Mahler, offended by his colleague's letter, had firmly resolved not to maintain the friendly links of the past. They did not communicate again until 1907, when Weingartner took over from Mahler at the Vienna Opera.[125]

Needless to say, Mahler was cut to the quick by the insults of the Munich

---

[120] The composer Joseph Gabriel Rheinberger (1839–1901), who had taught organ, piano, and composition at the Munich Conservatory, had died on 25 Nov.

[121] (Carl Gottfried) Wilhelm Taubert (1811–91), a Berlin composer and pianist, Hofkapellmeister 1845–70.

[122] Willy Burmester (1869–1933), a famous Berlin violinist, pupil of Joseph Joachim.

[123] Letter from Weingartner to Mahler, dated 30 Nov. 1901, former Ernst Rosé collection, Washington.

[124] Undated letter from Mahler to Weingartner (Mar. or Apr. 1902), BGM.

[125] See below Vol. iii, Chap. 10.

critics who had 'beaten the Fourth to death in the name of the Second' and refused to admit that he had any imagination or originality. He declared them 'corrupted by programme music' and 'incapable of appreciating any work from a purely musical point of view'. He felt that it had all begun with Liszt and Berlioz, 'who at least had talent and who, with their "programmes", arrived at new means of expression . . . Since they've now become universally accepted, what further purpose do such crutches serve?'[126]

Two weeks after the Munich concert Mahler, who had read the papers and grasped the full extent of his failure, set out with a heavy heart for Berlin,[127] where the critics had always been particularly hard on him. The concert at which Strauss had invited him to conduct the Fourth Symphony was one of the series given by the Tonkünstler Orchestra and was to take place at the Krolloper. Together with the orchestral material for the symphony, Mahler had sent Strauss a letter[128] telling him that he would only arrive in time for the last three rehearsals, since he had not yet decided whether or not he would in fact conduct it himself. The young Czech soprano Emmy Destinn was apparently supposed to sing the Finale,[129] and Mahler wrote to her advising her not to adopt the 'parodic tone' that the text seemed at first sight to suggest, but 'the simplest and most modest tone possible'.[130] However, either because she was not free on the appointed day or because Mahler's music did not appeal to her, Destinn did not participate in the Berlin première.[131] Her place was taken by Thila Plaichinger,[132] with whom Mahler declared himself pleased, at least during rehearsals.[133]

On his way to Berlin, Mahler spent 10 December in Dresden, rehearsing the two ladies engaged to sing in his Second Symphony under Ernst von Schuch's baton, and was so reassured by the latter's enthusiasm that he conceived high hopes for the success of this concert on 20 December. He was equally re-assured after the first Berlin rehearsal of the Fourth Symphony the following morning, so that he and Strauss agreed that he would conduct the première

---

[126]   NBL1. 178; NBL2. 203.

[127]   Shortly before Mahler left for Berlin, Ignaz Paderewski had given two concerts with orchestra in Vienna. He asked Mahler to conduct them, but Mahler had to refuse as he was busy at the Opera on those nights and was thus deprived of the pleasure of hearing Paderewski play (cf. Mahler's undated letter to the Viennese concert agent Albert Gutmann, undated, BGM).

[128]   This letter is now in the Gemeente Museum in The Hague. Mahler also informs Strauss that *Feuersnot* had finally been passed by the Viennese censorship (MSB 71 ff.).

[129]   In this letter Mahler tells Strauss that the sleigh-bells required for the performance will be sent directly to Berlin by Weingartner (MSB 73).

[130]   This letter forms part of the Emmy Destinn bequest, which is preserved in the Prague Museum (Theatrical Section, 1884/26).

[131]   Mahler encountered her again at the Metropolitan Opera, New York (see below Vol. iv, Chap. 4).

[132]   The Viennese soprano Thila Plaichinger (1868–1939) was a pupil of Josef Gänsbacher and Luise Dustmann. Pollini engaged her for the Hamburg Stadt-Theater in 1893. Later she became the leading dramatic soprano at Strasbourg (1894–1901) and at the Berlin Opera (1901–14), where she was the first Berlin Elektra and a famous Brünnhilde and Isolde. She appeared in Beecham's 1910 season as Elektra, Elisabeth, and Isolde.

[133]   Undated letter to Justi, 11 Dec. 1901 (RWO).

himself. In the afternoon of the same day, he set out to meet his old friend, Rudolf Krzyzanowski, now conductor of the Weimar Opera. His aim was to put in a good word for his brother-in-law, the cellist Eduard Rosé, Emma's husband. After a two-year stay in Boston, the Rosés had returned to Europe in summer 1900 and Eduard had been engaged as first cellist at the Weimar Theatre in September of that year.[134] During their walk together to the Belvedere, Krzyzanowski proved as 'kind and trusting as always' and promised to hasten Eduard's appointment. Having found, moreover, that the 'friendliest of relations' had been established between Emma and the Krzyzanowski family, Mahler left Weimar again with that load off his mind.[135]

During his stay in Berlin, Mahler renewed contact with Arnold Berliner, one of his oldest, most faithful, and devoted friends. Their relations had been less close since Mahler had moved to Vienna, but a letter he had written to Berliner three months earlier shows that, for him at any rate their friendship was by no means a thing of the past:

I was delighted with your letter. It gives me a welcome opportunity to say that my feelings towards you have not changed and that I recall our old relationship with undiminished affection. I have always seen the cause of our separation as simply—the separation itself. I can really remember no other cause. . . . My life being what it is, I cannot maintain relations with close friends over long distances; I simply haven't enough time. . . . I hope to come to Berlin in the course of this winter. Then I shall certainly look you up, and I am convinced we shall find each other unchanged.[136]

The final rehearsals of the Fourth Symphony took place in an excellent atmosphere. Mahler was more delighted with the attitude of the Tonkünstler Orchestra than with its professional abilities.[137] The concert of 16 December, the third in the series of Novitäten Konzerte conducted by Strauss at the

[134] The post of solo cellist at Weimar having become vacant in spring 1900, Mahler had recommended his brother-in-law to Krzyzanowski and to Vignau, the Intendant of the theatre. Eduard was then living in the USA, which made his engagement difficult as he should have been present in person for a *Probevorspiel*. Vignau nevertheless finally agreed to engage him solely on Mahler's recommendation. This departure from practice shows how much weight the word of the Vienna Opera Director carried in European musical circles. Eduard's contract stipulated an annual fixed salary of 3,100 marks, to which were added a post at the Conservatory and leaves of absence for solo activities: a considerable improvement on his previous appointments. Furthermore, Rosé could obtain life tenure after a trial period of 6 months; it was to facilitate the granting of this that Mahler visited Krzyzanowski. (See letters from Krzyzanowski to Mahler of spring 1900; letters from Vignau to Mahler of 4 and 7 June; letters from Justine to Emma Rosé of 22 June and 18 July 1900, in former Ernst Rosé collection.) Mahler's letter to Justi of 12 Dec. (RWO) reveals that Eduard Rosé had had trouble with the violinist Alfred Krasselt (1872–1908), founder of a string quartet bearing his own name, whose brother Mahler had just engaged as a cellist in Vienna (this was Rudolf Krasselt, 1879–1954, later conductor at the Deutsches Opernhaus in Berlin). Ernest Rosé's collection included the autograph draft of a letter to Rudolf Krasselt, which Mahler wrote for his brother-in-law Arnold Rosé. In it, Rosé accuses the cellist of having behaved 'like a bad colleague' towards his brother in Weimar, and of having 'forged new weapons' against him. 'In these circumstances', he declares that he can no longer engage him in his own string quartet in Vienna as planned. He wants to let him know this immediately, in case this decision caused him to change his plans (and no doubt give up his engagement at the Vienna Opera).
[135] Letters to Justi of 11 and 12 Dec. (RWO).
[136] MBR1, no. 279; MBR2, no. 298, dated 29 Aug. 1901 (BGM).
[137] He described the musicians in a letter to Anna von Mildenburg as 'very rough' (*sehr ruppig*).

Krolloper at 8 o'clock, began with Liszt's symphonic poem *Les Préludes*, which was followed by the Fourth Symphony conducted by Mahler himself. Three of Friedrich Rösch's *Mörike-Lieder*[138] with orchestral accompaniment and the Love Scene from *Feuersnot* completed the programme. The audience's disappointment with the first movements of the symphony was even more virulently displayed than in Munich and, although the Adagio was a great success, the Finale, in which the soprano proved unequal to her task, raised a storm of boos that mingled with and finally drowned out the applause. Mahler drew the conclusion that Berlin's musical circles were as hostile to him as ever, and the reviews proved him right the following day.

Indeed, the Berlin press took a malicious delight in tearing the new work to shreds. The *Börsenzeitung* branded Mahler a 'member of the extreme left' and an 'ultra' of the neudeutsch school and said that, compared to the 'bombastic pathos' of the gigantic and pretentious Second Symphony, the new work was

an idyll about Arcadian shepherds or a musical illustration of Watteauesque rococo . . . In this work, Herr Mahler has tried to be as simple and naïve as possible. The trouble is that one cannot believe in this naïveté because it does not match his face. . . . It smacks of a raillery, a deliberate fraud perpetrated at the expense of the audience, and only the dazzling orchestration and the use of all the newest techniques remind one that this is a contemporary work. Does Herr Mahler aim to be the composer of tomorrow? Perhaps this sweet and simple style, this conscious leaning (*Anlehnen*) toward the old and the very old, this formlessness and these gigantic false endings (*Trugschlüsse*) are signs of ultranovelty and hypermodernism.

With its 'affected and vulgar' simplicity, the same newspaper added, the Finale was nothing but a caricature of the Finale of Beethoven's Ninth Symphony. In it, Herr Mahler proved 'incapable of giving adequate musical expression to the wonderful, naïve poetry of such a folksong'.[139]

Leopold Schmidt,[140] in the *Berliner Tageblatt*, declared that he could give no more than his own personal impressions of this 'Second [*sic*] Symphony', which, like all the new works presented at the Strauss concert, had been applauded indiscriminately by a group of 'radical progressives'. The themes of the first movement, playing on the old Viennese 'Gemütlichkeit', recalled Lanner and Koschat, but soon the contradictory style used in the development repelled the listener.

The colours become garish and are strangely mixed, a restless mind toys with material that is alien to its soul. When the folk themes return they border on the trivial. One begins to see that the composer really has nothing to say to us, that he cannot find a

---

[138] 'Bekenntnis', 'Wie wundersam', and 'Lied vom Winde'. Born in Meiningen in 1862, Friedrich Rösch conducted the Berlin Akademischer Gesangverein for which he composed numerous works. Together with Strauss and Hans Sommer, he had founded the Genossenschaft Deutscher Tonsetzer, which Mahler was soon to join. He died in 1925.

[139] This critic went on to praise *Feuersnot* in rather unconvincing terms.

[140] See below, Vol. iii, Chap. 4, the biography of this critic.

way out of his initial ideas, that a rhythm, once it has seized him, controls him like an idée fixe.

The Scherzo contained 'thoughts strung along in a row', while the Adagio, which started with 'a very pretty notion' nevertheless wound up on a 'Viennese dance floor'. With its 'odd humour', the Finale outshone the other movements, but its relationship to them remained mysterious. Mahler's technique was no doubt fabulous, but 'it is devoutly to be hoped that the time when people were more interested in *how* a work was composed than in what it expressed is definitively over'.

The *Vossische Zeitung* regretted finding no trace in the Fourth Symphony of the 'striving for power and the struggle with his genius' that had marked the Second. Unsatisfactory either as pure music or as 'programme music', short on inspiration, and weak in construction, the work wore down the audience with its excessive length and insoluble riddles. The paper wondered how a 'clever' musician like Mahler could have failed to perceive the absence of style in this interminable symphony, in this 'idyll that bores and anaesthetizes with its lack of contrast'. It consisted of nothing but 'witty and artful details without any genuine melody or any climax in the crescendos'. The *Börsenzeitung*, too, failed to understand the 'childlike' character of the themes in the first movement. In the absence of an explanatory programme, it could find no link between the 'seriousness' of the Adagio and the 'naïvety' of the rest of the work.

Ferocious as these articles were, none were quite so bitingly sarcastic as that signed by Carl Krebs[141] and published in *Der Tag*:

Gustav Mahler's so-called Symphony No. 4, which Richard Strauss presented at his third subscription concert, is nothing but a silly joke in poor taste, a really silly joke. I imagine the conception and execution of this pasticcio were as follows: Herr Mahler finally discovered that he lacked the essential faculties for composing, since, at best, his musical invention produced only reminiscences of peasant songs, Viennese dances or Hungarian ditties. Having realized this, he decided to abandon composition but, before taking leave of it, he wanted to wreak vengeance on his contemporaries by making fools of them. Thus he said to himself: 'I'll see just how much the public can be made to swallow without perceiving that it's being ridiculed.' So he took the ingredients at his disposal, a little 'Viennesishness', a little 'Hungarianishness' and a lot of boredom, and wrote four movements, the third of which has something almost heroic about it, so unbelievable, so monumental and boundless as the desert is the emptiness that pervades it. He then treated himself to another good joke; rightly surmising that all the boredom he had concocted would send his audience to sleep, he proceeded to have the entire orchestra shriek fortissimo in order to terrify and startle even the most inveterate sleepers out of their trance. Yes, that is Herr Mahler! On to

[141] Carl Krebs (1857–1937), born in Hanseberg, near Königsberg (Neumark), first studied natural science, and then music at the Hochschule für Musik in Berlin and with Philip Spitta at the Univ. A lecturer in music history at the Hochschule, he wrote numerous articles for the *Vossische Zeitung*, *Moderne Kunst*, and *Deutsche Rundschau*, keeping a connection with *Der Tag* until 1931. He left several musicological works and a book about conducting: *Meister des Taktstocks* (Schuster & Loeffler, Berlin, 1919).

this bric-a-brac he glued a few instrumental effects, such as a squealing flute, a howling trumpet and a clinking harp, to hold the whole thing together, and finally forced a soprano voice to sing an old street refrain in the Hungarian pot-pourri of the last movement. Thereupon he examined his opus, found that it served his purpose perfectly and handed it over to Richard Strauss. The latter also looked it over and said: 'Ah! What a marvellous joke, we'll make real fools of the public with this!' And indeed, the public noticed absolutely nothing, it applauded very prettily and so much so that it silenced the few people who, since they are not altogether lacking in artistic receptivity, had hooted. Dear Public, you truly deserve 'composers' like Gustav Mahler . . .[142]

Even Oskar Eichberg, who had been one of Mahler's friends and supporters when he was making his début in Berlin, wondered if the composer of the Fourth Symphony had not set out deliberately to flout the public with themes that were 'really only fit for children's songs' and contrasted oddly with the subtlety of the orchestral trimmings. However, he preferred to reserve judgement concerning the work as a whole, of which he had sincerely admired only the orchestration.

In the various German and Austrian monthlies, the verdict of the anonymous reviewers was just as unfavourable. One of them declared that even the 'glorious and solemn' Adagio ended in a farce and added that 'if such is the future of the symphony, then this is the end of all musical logic'.[143] Others made unfavourable comparisons between the Second Symphony and the 'oddities, curiosities, absurdities and eccentricities of the Fourth', which, chameleon-like, 'constantly switches, too rapidly and without transition, from beautiful to ugly, from genuine to artificial and from naïve to sophisticated'.[144] In the face of such incomprehension among the professionals, Mahler's only consolation was the enthusiasm shown by Strauss, who had attended all the rehearsals and become 'more and more' interested in the work. After hearing the Adagio, he had said that he himself would have been 'quite incapable of writing such a piece', and, pointing to a particularly dissonant passage in the Scherzo, had laughingly remarked, 'There you've depicted a meeting with your critics.' That evening he also remarked: 'I've studied the score of your Second Symphony very thoroughly and benefited from certain of the lessons it contains.'[145]

Although this latest meeting of Mahler and Strauss in December 1901 was friendlier than usual, the views they exchanged were as far apart as ever. Strauss probably found the Fourth Symphony inferior to the Second, while Mahler, unaware that Strauss was soon to become one of the greatest opera composers of all time, still regarded him as a *neudeutsch* composer of symphonic poems of a specifically illustrative kind. 'I talked very seriously with

[142] The entire article is quoted by Seidl, *Aufsätze*, i. 296.
[143] *Allgemeine Musik-Zeitung.*   [144] *Musikalisches Wochenblatt.*
[145] NBL1. 178; NBL2. 203. Strauss subsequently sent Mahler signed copies of all his scores in token of his admiration.

him in Berlin, and tried to point out that he had come to a dead end,' Mahler
wrote after their meeting. 'Unfortunately he couldn't quite follow me. He's a
very dear fellow and I'm touched by the way he behaves toward me, yet I can't
be anything to him because I already see beyond him, while he sees only the
pedestal as far as I'm concerned . . .'.[146] Their two points of view, two tempera-
ments, and two aesthetics pursued their separate ways in a conversation that
lasted late into the night.

On his way back from Berlin, Mahler stopped a second time in Dresden, a
city where, thanks to Schuch's open-mindedness and courage, a lot of modern
music was being played. At the request of the King of Saxony, Mahler had
drawn up a 'programme' for the Second Symphony, a programme 'intended to
be read by someone rather naïve and superficial'.[147] Whereas the First Symphony had caused amazement in Dresden, the Second was warmly applauded
by an audience that tried to force Mahler to take a bow, while he, 'hidden in
an orchestra seat, was happy as a faun not to be recognized'.[148] Unfortunately,
the press had its usual reservations. Heinrich Platvecker[149] declared in the
Dresdner Zeitung that, for want of a thematic analysis, he was unable to make
head or tail of these tedious outpourings of questionable inspiration. In his
opinion, Strauss in *Tod und Verklärung* and Berlioz in the *Symphonie
fantastique* had dealt with a similar subject, but their works showed them to be
far more original musical personalities. In Mahler's symphony, the features of
Berlioz, Bruckner, Liszt, and Schubert showed through. Despite the beauty of
certain details,

the whole is unfortunately marred by dissonances constantly shifting like the patterns
in a kaleidoscope, by 'noises' and by its interminable length. The 'overachievement'
and 'glorification in technical powers' were already familiar to those who had heard the
First Symphony, but here they were much worse. Mahler would create something of
lasting worth if he could concentrate his material. His Symphony is at least half an hour
too long.

Hermann Starcke of the *Dresdner Nachrichten* claimed that the work had
been received with 'profound indifference' in Dresden and that the applause
had been intended solely for the performers. Nor was this to be wondered at, for
the symphony consisted of nothing but 'a play of characterless, aimless and

[146] AMM1. 275: AMM2. 251.
[147] Mahler sent Justi this programme during the Berlin rehearsals. It was published in *Dresdner
Nachrichten* (20 Dec.), with the following introduction: 'At the very special request of the direction, Gustav
Mahler, who is averse to all explanations and all programs of any kind or description, has written the
following general comments in order to make the world of emotions expressed in his work more accessible
to the audience at the première.' This programme is quoted in toto in Alma Mahler's *Erinnerungen* (AMM1.
267 ff.; AMM2. 245 ff.; see above Vol. i, App. 1).
[148] The Dresden concert of 20 Dec. consisted of Mahler's Second Symphony, the Overture to Cherubini's
Anacréon, Sarastro's two arias from *The Magic Flute*, an aria from Verdi's *Simone Boccanegra*, and a song by
Rotole (?), *La mia bandiera*, all of which were sung by the Italian bass Vittorio Arimondi. The soloists in
Mahler's symphony were Erika Wedekind and Johanna von Chavanne.
[149] See below, Vol. iii, Chap. 9, the biography of this critic.

shapeless sounds, an endless conglomeration of odds and ends culled from here and there, sham sentiments'. Driven by the urge to 'create something exceptional', Mahler had produced only music that was 'neither new nor interesting, without appeal to the ear or to the emotions': music that deserved the title 'music of boredom' and that showed 'no regard for the unfortunate listeners who, with tortured minds and ears, could only follow its chaos by exerting their last ounce of physical strength'. It was like 'a hermaphrodite trying to stand for a whole race'. The *Musikalisches Wochenblatt* likewise dwelt on the length and 'absence of style' of the work, in which nothing touched the soul, and the listener was, 'so to speak, belaboured with pathos'. It was mostly just 'huge phrases without any conviction, without any eternal idea to enlighten the heart'. Symptomatic of 'the incredible confusion and virtuosic decadence' of modern music, it belonged in the 'abnormal babies department of an anatomical museum of music'.

This time, music critics all over Germany seemed to have agreed among themselves that Mahler's music hardly deserved a hearing. Even in Graz, in Austria, where people had expected a 'superhuman' symphony like the Second, the First, under the baton of the local conductor, Martin Spörr, had struck them as no more than a poor joke, too caricatural and eclectic to be of interest. Here again, most of the listeners were perplexed by what they heard, and the light applause that followed the first movements had changed to energetic booing by the time the last note of the Finale had been played.[150] In Brussels, where the heroic Sylvain Dupuis now directed operas and concerts at the Théâtre de la Monnaie, the Second Symphony was to be favourably received in Spring 1902. However, the press was again reserved. The correspondent of the French *Guide musical*, N. Liez, found the symphony lacking 'in reserve and precision': 'one searches in vain for a guiding idea and the absence of logic of the development aggravates this defect. The themes, more often than not devoid of personality, follow on thick and fast and it is hard to understand what the soloists and chorus are doing in the last movements.' 'The work would gain by being cut', this critic wrote, for its length (and the reminiscences it contained) were responsible for the public's lack of understanding and acceptance.[151]

Back in Vienna from Berlin, Mahler must have wondered whether it was worth his while, from now on, to travel and conduct his music, since he invariably met with nothing but hostility and incomprehension. His disappointment was all the greater because of the high hopes he had entertained for the Fourth. The only bright spot in this dark year of his career as composer seems to have been the publication in Leipzig of the first monograph about him.[152] It

---

[150] Wilhelm Kienzl, *Im Konzert* (Allgemeiner Verein für deutsche Literatur, Berlin, 1908), 49.

[151] The third of the 'Concerts populaires' took place on 13 Apr. at the Théâtre de la Monnaie, and was repeated the next day. Both soloists (C. Friché and G. Bastien) and chorus were member of the Theatre ensembles.

[152] See below Vol. iii, Chap. 1. Ludwig Schiedermair's monograph was publ. without date at the end of 1901, in Leipzig, by Hermann Seemann, in the collection *Moderne Musiker*.

contained only thirty-seven pages, signed by the Munich critic Ludwig Schiedermair. Its content was thin, but for Mahler the fact that it had been published had a symbolic significance. Henceforth, the hostility of the critics and the incomprehension of the majority of listeners could not prevent him from occupying a place among German composers. The Fourth's failure had cruelly dashed his hopes. Fortunately, however, his personal life was about to enter upon a new stage, and a major event was to take his mind off the animosity and contempt that he encountered on all sides each time he presented a new work.

12

Alma Schindler—Mahler in love—engagement
(December 1901–January 1902)

> ... one voice that drowns out everything else and
> that will never again fall silent in my heart ...

T HE stormy concerts in Munich and Berlin made Mahler more aware than
ever of his loneliness and isolation as a composer and of the obstacles
he still had to surmount in order to be heard and understood. The fact that
people had applauded his Second Symphony and booed his Fourth—which he
had thought was more readily understandable—meant little as far as he was
concerned, except to show the narrow-mindedness of a public corrupted by
'programme music':

If, one day, one of my works should finally come to be understood (for the last fifteen
years I've been fighting against shallowness and incomprehension and experiencing all
the hardships and misery of a pioneer), and particularly in Vienna, where, after all,
people have an instinctive conception of my personality, this should no more bother you
or shake your confidence in my work than does their incomprehension or hostility. The
important thing is never to let oneself be guided by the opinion of one's contemporaries
and, in both one's life and one's work, to continue steadfastly on one's way without
letting oneself be either defeated by failure or diverted by applause. The fact is that I
think some of the seeds I've sown are now beginning to come up. I'm deeply happy that
it should be happening just now and that you, my dearest beloved, will not have to
suffer all the thorns, though I shall never spare you them when it's a question of
remaining true to myself—and, from now on, to you too, for you and I will henceforth
be one. We will help and encourage one another to remain constantly and proudly
indifferent to all outside things, for that is the high honour to which we aspire.[1]

Thus Mahler, as a human being if not as a composer, no longer felt alone. For
the first time in months[2] a note of loving tenderness appears in his letters. To

---

[1] AMM1. 272; AMM2. 249, undated letter (16 Dec. 1902).

[2] He may have written letters of an intimate nature to Rita Michalek and Marie Gutheil-Schoder, with

whom was this declaration of intimate complicity addressed? It had all begun the year before in Paris, where he had met Sophie Szeps,[3] a young Viennese woman married to the French engineer Paul Clemenceau. They had become good friends, and she had asked him to visit, as soon as he got back to Vienna, her sister Berta Zuckerkandl, herself the wife of a well-known Viennese professor of anatomy, and who entertained intellectuals and artists in her salon every Sunday. Born in 1864, Berta had not only received an exceptional education, but at 17 had become private secretary to her father, who was keenly interested in world politics, a man of great culture with important connections in the artistic world, professing francophile views rare in the Austrian empire at the time. Berta herself was a friend of the architect Otto Wagner, and of Gustav Klimt and Georges Clemenceau. She married young, in 1886, and had one son, Fritz, born in 1893.[4] Mahler had taken an immediate liking to the Zuckerkandls and accepted an invitation to dine with them on 7 November 1901,[5] in order to see Sophie Clemenceau, then on a visit to Vienna and staying with her sister.[6] He sat beside her at table. Opposite them were Gustav Klimt[7] and the ex-director of the Burgtheater, Max Burckhard,[8] and, between them, a fair-haired girl whose good looks, but also her 'caustic (*herb*) and abrupt' conversational sallies, had attracted his attention earlier in the evening. She was carrying on an animated conversation, punctuated by peals of laughter, with her two neighbours,[9] and Mahler, becoming more and more intrigued, finally asked: 'May others join in the fun?' He had hardly made the request when another guest arrived and apologized for his late arrival by saying that he had just come from a concert by the great Czech violinist Jan Kubelik.[10] Mahler

each of whom he appears to have been emotionally entangled for some time. But if such letters ever existed they have not come to light.

[3] Sophie Clemenceau and Berta Zuckerkandl were the daughters of Moritz Szeps, a liberal and 'progressive' journalist, close friend of Crown Prince Rudolph and founder of the *Wiener Tagblatt* and later of the *Neues Wiener Tagblatt*. One day Georg von Schönerer (see above, Vol. i, Chap. 5), leader of the *Deutschnational* wing of the Austrian Socialist Party, raided the editor's office of this 'Jewish rag' with a group of rowdies. As a result, he was imprisoned, and deprived of citizen's rights for five years.

[4] She joined the editorial staff of the *Neues Wiener Journal* in 1924, and became 'the most important foreign affairs commentator in Austria'. After the First World War she founded the Salzburg Festival along with Hofmannsthal, Strauss, and Reinhardt. See Célia Bertin, *La Femme à Vienne au temps de Freud* (Stock, Paris, 1989), 173.

[5] The date of this first meeting can easily be deduced, for Alma Mahler tells of the late arrival of a guest who had just come from 'a Jan Kubelik concert', and it was on the evening of 7 Nov. that the great violinist was the soloist with the Konzertverein Orchestra conducted by Alexander Zemlinsky.

[6] The Zuckerkandls, like the Molls, lived in the 19th district of Vienna, in the Alserbachstrasse.

[7] See below, Chap. 13, the biography of Klimt, the initiator, sometime president, and always spiritual leader of the Secession.

[8] Max Burckhard (1854–1912), author and drama critic, director of the Burgtheater, 1890–7, after which he held an important office in the magistracy. According to Carl Moll's memoirs, Alfred Roller was also present that evening. Anna Moll was ill and had stayed at home.

[9] According to Alma's diaries (AMT), however, she hardly exchanged two words with Klimt that evening.

[10] Jan Kubelik (1880–1940), son of a Czech gardener and born in Michle, near Prague, studied at the Conservatory there. From 1898, he toured in Austria-Hungary, Romania, Italy, France, England, and Russia, where he was applauded by the Tsar and Empress in person. His fame was such that a wealthy Viennese patron gave him a historic violin, a Guarnerius. Kubelik married the daughter of a Hungarian aristocratic

was delighted to hear the girl remark that she was not interested in concerts by virtuosi.

The conversation then turned to the decadence of Vienna's artistic life and of the Viennese ballet in particular. Mahler told how an archduke had written urging him to engage a singer who was young and pretty, but quite without talent. When the somewhat abashed Lord Chamberlain had come to ask him for his reply, he had said merely, 'Tell His Highness that I threw his letter into the waste paper basket.' Burckhard remarked that the fact that the archduke had not pressed the matter showed how much things had changed in the last ten years in Vienna. When he had been director of the Burgtheater an archduchess had insisted that a play be banned because it featured an unmarried woman who had had an illegitimate child. 'Why,' said the girl, 'did the public accept such a thing? Why didn't it demand the dismissal of a director who allowed himself to be treated like that?' 'Only youth could ask such a question,' Mahler replied, 'it hasn't yet learned about cowardice and compromise.' Thereupon he relapsed into his customary silence and turned his attention to choosing an apple for his dessert.[11]

After dinner, the guests split into groups and Mahler contrived to remain near the girl, who was now discussing physical beauty and its many criteria. Mahler said that Socrates' head was beautiful. The girl said that she thought Alexander Zemlinsky was handsome too, because of the intelligence that shone in his eyes, even though he was reputed to be one of the ugliest men in Vienna. Mahler shrugged his shoulders, and said he thought that was going a bit too far. A few moments later, Frau Zuckerkandl heard voices raised in anger and came over to the group. Alma Schindler, flushed with anger, eyes blazing, was confronting Mahler, who, equally furious, was hopping madly about, sometimes halting abruptly, like a wading bird, one leg raised. They were quarrelling about a ballet by Zemlinsky entitled *Das goldene Herz* (The Golden Heart).[12]

'You have no right to keep a score that's been submitted to you lying around for a whole year,' Alma was saying, 'especially when it comes from a real musician like Zemlinsky. You should have given him an answer, even if it was only "no".' 'But the ballet is quite worthless,' Mahler complained. 'No one will be able to make sense of it. How can you,

family and their son became the famous conductor Rafael Kubelik. In 1901 Jan Kubelik had just returned from a triumphal tour of the USA. He sometimes gave 9 or 10 recitals a season in Vienna. They were nearly always sold out, even in the large Musikvereinsaal, and their success had become almost legendary (THE 287 and 301).

[11] This part of the conversation is related in Berta Zuckerkandl's *Österreich Intim* (Propyläen, Ullstein, Frankfurt, 1970), 42. It should be noted that Berta tends to embroider her accounts.

[12] As we have seen above (Chap. 11), Strauss, after hesitating for some time, had refused Hofmannsthal's synopsis in 1900. The name of Act I of *Der Triumph der Zeit* was in fact *Das gläserne Herz* (The Glass Heart). In the first months of 1901, Zemlinsky had composed Act I in *Particell* and the second in full score. Hugo von Hofmannsthal wrote to him on 18 Sept. 1901, concerning *Der Triumph der Zeit*, whose libretto 'has been with Mahler for some weeks' (see below, Chap. 16). Zemlinsky conducted an orchestral Suite (in three movements) of the ballet on 18 Feb. 1903, in a concert given by the Concertverein under Ferdinand Löwe. ('Hugo von Hofmannsthal', *Frankfurter Allgemeine Zeitung* (2 Feb. 1974), 28)

who are interested in music and who are, I believe, studying it, possibly defend such trash?' 'In the first place, it's not trash and you've probably not even taken the trouble to have a good look at it. And secondly, even if it is bad music, that's no excuse for not being polite!'

Mahler bit his lip, but then held out his hand saying, 'Let's make peace! I don't promise to put on the ballet, of course, but I like the way you support your music teacher so courageously and express your opinion so frankly. I do promise therefore to send for Zemlinsky not later than tomorrow.' Alma then asked if he would like her to explain the complex symbolism of Zemlinsky's ballet (the libretto was by Hofmannsthal).[13] 'I can't wait to hear your explanation,' he replied. Stung by the sarcasm in his voice, she insisted that he first explain the plot of *Die Braut von Korea* (The Korean Bride), a particularly absurd ballet by Josef Bayer, which was then featuring prominently in the Opera's repertoire.[14] Delighted by this counter-attack, he smiled broadly, and began enquiring about her studies. He asked her to show him some of her works one day, and even tried to get her to fix a date.

Meanwhile, the guests had begun to leave. Alma and Mahler were standing alone, surrounded, as she wrote later, 'by that void created around themselves by two people who have found one another'. She promised she would come and see him as soon as she had 'something good' to show him. He smiled, almost as if to say: 'Then I shall have to wait a long time.' Alma now began to feel ashamed she had so lost her temper with someone she sincerely admired, and turned away. But Sophie Clemenceau and Berta Zuckerkandl came up, and Mahler invited them to come—with Alma—to his dress rehearsal of the *Les Contes d'Hoffmann* the following morning. 'It's a work of which I'm very fond,' he explained. 'All through his life, Offenbach longed to outgrow operetta and compose an opera. He succeeded in doing so only in his old age, when he was at death's door. Such is the fate of every one of us: only when dying do we achieve perfection.' Preparing to go, he assured Frau Zuckerkandl that for the first time in his life he had enjoyed dining out. Alma also came to take leave of her hosts. She had still not finally accepted Mahler's invitation. Hearing that she lived at the Hohe Warte,[15] he offered to walk her home, but she declined because it was so late. He tried once more to make her promise to come and see him at the Opera. 'Yes, yes, provided I've done some good work,' she replied. 'Word of honour?' ('Ein Mann, ein Wort?') he called after her.[16]

---

[13] The complete MS score of the *Tanzpoem Der Triumph der Zeit* survives in the Zemlinsky collection in LCW. The ballet was recently performed in Zurich (19 Jan. 1992) and Hamburg (June 1992).

[14] *Die Braut von Korea* had its first performance in May 1897, conducted by the composer Josef Bayer. Mahler dropped it from the repertory in 1901, after 38 performances.

[15] The Hohe Warte is a hill on the outskirts of Vienna, near Grinzing, where modern villas were then being built, mainly by artists. Since Alma had attended the Zuckerkandl party with her stepfather, Carl Moll, it seems unlikely that Mahler could in fact have offered to take her home.

[16] After Mahler had left, Alma again apologized for having lost her temper, but Berta only smiled slyly. She later claimed that, since Klimt had been in love with Alma when she was 16 and Burckhard was in love with her at the time, she had jokingly remarked to the young girl, 'This evening, I invited your past (pointing to

The above account of their first meeting demonstrates clearly the powerful attraction Alma Schindler, for all her 22 years, had immediately exerted on the distinguished Opera Director. Mahler was a man of alert and penetrating intellect, a musician by instinct, by training, and by profession, but he remained marked by the provincial bourgeois origins that had long kept him apart from Viennese society and artistic circles. He had immersed himself in music, but had also read widely and deeply. These two passions had provided an escape from the mediocrity of his early life. But he had never felt entirely at home in the world of the visual arts, as Alma had been since childhood. She had been born in Vienna, her father and later her stepfather were painters, and all the Muses seemed to have gathered around her cradle. Her father, Emil Jakob Schindler, was to become the most celebrated landscape painter of the Austrian empire.[17] Her great-uncle, Alexander Schindler, owner of Leopoldskron Castle, near Salzburg, had written novels under the aristocratic *nom de plume* of Julius von der Traun, and had also played an important role as a liberal member of parliament. In 1873 Emil Jakob had been profoundly impressed by an exhibition in Vienna of painters of the École de Barbizon; seven years later, he decided to go and work in Paris, where he met another Viennese painter, the famous medievalist Hans Makart. Subsequently, Makart lent Schindler his studio in the Gusshausstrasse in Vienna for an entire winter. He passed on to him his taste for luxury and his romantic nostalgia for the past. Alma relates how the two artists took to giving 'Renaissance parties' together, in which the guests were sumptuously dressed, Liszt played the piano under garlands of roses, and velvet-clad pages served a profusion of fine wines.

In 1878, Schindler was awarded the Karl-Ludwig Medal for one of his pictures, *Mondaufgang im Prater*. The same year, in Vienna, he became acquainted with Anna Bergen, a young singer whose father, the owner of a small brewery in Hamburg, had sent her to Vienna to complete her musical studies.[18] Schindler himself was a good amateur singer. Thus he and Anna took part in a private performance of Peter Winter's operetta *Lenardo und Blandine*.[19] Anna had already made her stage début, under Felix Mottl, and

Klimt), your present (pointing to Burckhard), and, who knows, perhaps your future (Mahler)!'(*Österreich intim*, 43)

[17] Born in Vienna on 27 Apr. 1842, Schindler studied at the Akademie under the aegis of Albert Zimmermann and Rudolf Jettel. He devoted himself from his earliest youth to landscape painting, and five of his larger canvases now hang in Vienna's Museum of Natural History. He won several prizes, was made an honorary member of the Vienna Akademie in 1888 and later of the Munich Akademie. He is today considered to be one of the few late 19th-cent. Austrian painters of international stature.

[18] Claus Jacob Ary Bergen (1 Dec. 1817–21 Nov. 1891) had nine children of whom Anna was the second. Anna's mother (Metta Margaretha Bergen, née Roggenkamp) was born on 28 Aug. 1826 and died on 14 June 1902. Anna Bergen is recorded in the *Deutscher Bühnen Almanach* as a member of the Burgtheater for the 1878–9 season. On 19 Oct. 1878 she sang one of the leading parts in Josef Forster's comic opera *Die Wallfahrt der Königin* (KMI).

[19] Knud Martner suggests that the operetta was probably *Operette für Liedertafeln*, by Franz Mögele, which had had its first performance at the Künstlerhaus on 17 Jan. 1876 and was probably revived there at a later date.

had been engaged at the Leipzig Theatre. But love triumphed. She decided to abandon her career and marry, on 4 February 1879, the young painter whose talent and good looks had enchanted her. For two years the young couple lived in poverty that sometimes became extreme. The smallness of their means was equalled only by the extravagance of Emil's tastes. There was a story that one day the only pair of shoes he possessed were so worn he could no longer go out in them. Not having the money to buy new ones, the young man hit on an ingenious way of solving the problem: he hired a carriage, with driver, for a month, without thought of the expense. He did not doubt for a moment that one day he would be famous, and would have plenty of money.[20]

In those years Schindler devoted himself entirely to his painting, but he was still unknown and hard up for money. A year after the wedding, he moved with his wife and child to Bad Goisern, near Ischl, where they lived for three years. In 1881 Schindler received the Reichel-Kunstpreis of 1,500 florins for one of his landscapes and took as a pupil a young and highly talented artist, Carl Moll, who was later to marry his widow. That year, success finally arrived, in the form of two rich patrons who decided to buy all his pictures. By 1885, Emil Jakob had already made enough money to rent from Prince Karl Liechtenstein a small Renaissance castle, called Plankenberg, in Upper Austria not far from Vienna. He moved there with his family, and in this romantic home, surrounded by woods and complete with legendary ghost, he gave brilliant parties and sometimes musical evenings.[21] It was here, in surroundings as idyllic and poetic as her father's romantic landscapes, that Alma spent her childhood.[22]

The portrait she has left us of her father is flattering in the extreme. She talks of his handsome looks, his 'inborn aristocratic nature', his close friendship with Archduke Johannes Orth, his brilliant conversation, his passion for music, his fine tenor voice, and moving renderings of Schumann's Lieder. From her earliest childhood, Alma had spent hours listening to him and watching him paint. She was only just 8 when he told her the story of Goethe's *Faust* and gave her the book, urging her to read it and keep it carefully, for 'it's the most beautiful book in the world'. Schindler soon became one of the most highly esteemed painters in Vienna. He was awarded many prizes, the Kaiser himself buying some of his pictures. He lived in grand style with his family, and young Alma grew up surrounded by luxury, art, and artists. Many of her 'flower dreams' (*Blüten-Träume*)[23] and fantasies later came true. She pictured herself

---

[20] Anecdote told to the author by Mahler's daughter, Anna.

[21] See Carl Moll, *Emil Jakob Schindler* (Österreichische Staatsdruckerei, Vienna, 1930), 40.

[22] The description of Alma's childhood and adolescence comes from AML.

[23] 'Blüten-Träume' is a term of special significance, certainly used by Alma herself, as proved by Theodor Pollak's use of it in his letter quoted below, dated 27 Aug. 1901. Later, when Mahler found Alma in tears one day, obviously tormented by regrets and longings, he asked her if perhaps her sadness came from the fact that her 'Blüten-Träume' had not come true. The term was used by Goethe in his poem *Prometheus*: 'Wähntest du etwa, | Ich sollte das Leben hassen, | In Wüsten fliehen, | Weil nicht alle | Blütenträume reiften?'

entertaining famous men[24] in vast Italian gardens, dressed in long velvet robes and floating around in gondolas.

Anna Schindler tried to exercise a moderating influence over her daughter, but only succeeded in inspiring Alma with profound contempt for her. Moreover, according to Alma, her parents often had violent quarrels, but these merely reinforced Alma's love for her father. In 1887, when she was 8 years old, her parents took her with them on a tour lasting several months through Dalmatia, the Crown Prince having commissioned Schindler to do a series of drawings and water-colours of the principal towns on the coast.[25] The tour ended with a long stay on Corfu, which Alma never forgot, for it was there that she began seriously to study music and composition.

In 1892, the year of the cholera epidemic in Hamburg, Schindler was seized by violent intestinal pains just as the family was about to leave for Sylt off the North Sea coast. Carl Moll went on ahead with Anna and the children. Schindler joined them after stopping in Munich and Leipzig. The doctors had made a mistake in their diagnosis, and the journey, undertaken when his condition was acute, proved fatal. He died in Sylt on 9 August, of an intestinal blockage, and Anna Schindler had to break the news to her two daughters.[26] Alma, who was not yet 13, immediately realized that she had lost not only her father but also her 'guiding star', whom she had always done everything she could to please and whose look of understanding had been the only thing that satisfied 'all my vanity and ambition'. After Schindler's death, his family returned to Vienna from Mondsee, in the Salzkammergut, where they had settled after leaving Plankenberg.[27]

Alma had by now become an avid reader of books. According to her memoirs, written much later, her mother took very little notice of her. Feeling 'completely cut off inwardly' from her immediate surroundings, Alma also began to study counterpoint with a blind organist, Joseph Labor. Just as Mahler had done in his youth, she devoured reams of musical scores. She discovered Wagner, and developed such a passion for his music that she irreparably ruined the pretty voice with which nature had endowed her by singing all the Wagne-

[24] A large number of famous men did in fact become her intimate friends, and she devoted the greater part of her long life to four of them: Mahler, the architect Walter Gropius, the painter Oskar Kokoschka, and the writer Franz Werfel.

[25] They were to illustrate a book series being brought out by a group of Viennese financiers, *Die Österreichische Monarchie im Wort und Bild* (24 vols., 1886–1902).

[26] Margarethe Julie (Grete) Schindler (16 Aug. 1880–194?), two years younger than Alma, was not Schindler's daughter. Her real father was the painter Julius Victor Berger, one of Gustav Klimt's teachers. He is mentioned in an early TS of Alma's memoirs (UPL). On 4 Sept. 1900, in Bad Goisern, Grete married Wilhelm Legler, a pupil of Moll, and had a son, Wilhelm Carl Emil, an architect (1902–60). Legler divorced Grete in 1917. After several attempts at suicide, she was committed to an asylum. On 5 Oct. 1940 she was reported as living in Gross Schweidnitz (Silesia) in a camp or hospital where the Nazis interned and probably exterminated the mentally deranged. Schindler's *Nachlass*—in all 250 paintings and 77 water-colours and drawings—were sold at an auction arranged by Carl Moll on 5–7 Dec. 1892 (KMI)

[27] For some months the Moll–Schindler family lived in the Theresianum 6, in the same house as Nina Hofmann, and in which Otto Mahler committed suicide in 1895 (KMI).

rian roles one after the other. As a consequence of measles she was also slightly deaf, a defect which worsened in her adolescence. But she hid this handicap, which did not affect her musical sense, and the look of concentrated attention on her face during conversation simply 'made her seem enormously interested in what one was saying to her'.[28] Eager to increase her knowledge, she looked about her for men who could give her guidance. Each stage in her intellectual development took place under the aegis of a new mentor who fell in love with her. Max Burckhard, the director of the Burgtheater,[29] a generous and cultivated man who first revealed Ibsen and Hauptmann to the Viennese theatregoers, sent her two huge linen baskets containing a virtual library of classics as a Christmas present. At 17, she was still 'completely unawakened', but her curiosity was already aroused by Burckhard's 'forceful virility'. However, when later he began to woo her more ardently she was 'quite unmoved' and had no difficulty in repelling his advances. He was nevertheless a powerful influence, leading her notably to discover Nietzsche, whose influence over her became considerable at this impressionable stage of her life.

Alma was 16 when, on 3 November 1895, her mother, after three years of widowhood, married Carl Moll,[30] Schindler's principal disciple, a handsome man with a patriarchal beard whose face, Alma said, resembled that of a medieval wood-carving of St Joseph. According to her, however, this remarriage had only increased her scorn for her mother. She contemptuously describes Moll as an 'eternal student', an artist who threw away the little talent nature had given him by continually changing schools. She could not understand how her mother, after having had as husband a 'complete clock', could now marry a mere 'pendulum'. According to her, moreover, Moll's efforts to educate his stepdaughter aroused 'nothing but hatred on my part'.[31] In reaction to the academism of Viennese art, Moll and some of his friends had recently formed the 'Secession', a movement composed of painters, sculptors, and architects who met regularly at his house. The leader, or at any rate the dominant personality of the group, Gustav Klimt[32] had in turn undertaken to educate Alma in the visual arts. However, he too fell in love with her. In 1899 he had been invited to join the Molls on the last part of their Italian trip in the spring.

---

[28] See Bertin, *La Femme à Vienne*, 193.

[29] He left this post in 1897, just when Mahler was being appointed.

[30] A daughter Maria, Alma's half-sister, was born of this second marriage on 9 Aug. 1899. (She was thus three years older than Alma's first child by Mahler.)

[31] See Chap. 13. Moll was in fact a painter of great talent despite his limited output. His pictures in the Museum der Stadt Wien and the Oberes Belvedere have withstood the test of time. They show not only technical mastery, but a very subtle sense of colour, and a style that, although intimate and realistic, has exceptional poetry and charm. When writing the final version of AML Alma had good reason to be angry with him, for after the Anschluss he fell under the influence of his daughter Maria Eberstaller, a confirmed Nazi. According to Anna Mahler's later testimony, Alma was on excellent terms with Moll until the 1920s. Then she began to lose faith in him, when Moll purchased in Italy some Donatello statues that turned out to be fakes. On the evening of the historic dinner party the Zuckerkandls, who regarded Alma as 'the daughter of the house', introduced her to Mahler as 'Fräulein Moll', a mistake which she very firmly corrected.

[32] It will be recalled that, at the dinner, Alma was seated between Gustav Klimt and Max Burckhard.

This time, however, the very violence of Klimt's passion awoke a response in Alma. Anna Moll, who happened to learn from her daughter's diary that Klimt had kissed her, put an immediate stop to the nascent idyll, something for which Alma never forgave her.[33]

To console herself, Alma immersed herself once more in her musical studies. She also decided to take lessons in sculpture. She went each day to the Prater to work with a well-known sculptor, Edmund Hellmer.[34] At the same time she continued to study composition, not now with the blind organist Joseph Labor but, from the summer of 1900 on, with Alexander Zemlinsky, whom she had met at a party on 26 February 1900.[35] Often during these lessons, master and pupil would spend hours playing through scores (in particular that of *Tristan und Isolde*). Alma describes him as a 'frightful gnome . . . small, chinless, toothless . . . and unwashed'. She nevertheless became irresistibly attracted to him, too. Indeed, by her own admission, 'the hideous Turkish drawing-room' of the friends with whom she was then living in Vienna almost 'became the scene of my fall', and only her 'old-fashioned upbringing' and her 'mother's daily sermons' prevented her from giving herself to him.

A letter from Theobald Pollak[36] to Alma, written in August 1901 and quoted in her diary, gives quite a full picture of the girl's life in the months preceding her marriage. She was reading Stendhal and looking forward to reading Gorky. She detested Schiller, whom she nicknamed 'der Moraltrompeter' (the trumpeter of morals), but was by now steeped in Nietzsche and his thinking. At this time, she had just attended a Mozart Festival concert with Burckhard in Salzburg, and she was on the point of becoming an 'aunt', as her sister Grete, married the previous year, was expecting a baby.[37] She had often talked with Pollak, her confidant, about having one herself, and was dreading her forthcoming move to the Hohe Warte, fearing that she would be too far from Vienna to go so often to concerts and the Opera, or be visited by her friends. It seems she was then working on an opera or a symphonic work based on a Hoffmann novel, *Die Bergwerke zu Falun* (The Mines of Falun).

Zemlinsky had told Alma of Mahler's superhuman efforts on behalf of his second opera, *Es war einmal*, including his painstaking revision of both text and music. On that occasion she and Zemlinsky had spontaneously raised their glasses 'to the man of whom only good can be spoken'.[38] Vienna was then

[33] See below, Chap. 16, the moving letter Klimt wrote in May 1899 to Carl Moll, who had accused him of trying to seduce his stepdaughter.

[34] BWT 229. Walter recalls going with Mahler to fetch her one day from the studio of Edmund Hellmer, who was also Hugo Wolf's friend and biographer.

[35] See above, Chap. 7, Zemlinsky's biography.

[36] He was an old friend of Emil Jakob Schindler, who through his contacts in the administration had obtained for him a post at the Austrian Ministry of Transport (see Vol. iii, Chap. 9). The letter was transcribed by Alma into her diary (UPL).

[37] Alma's other sister, Maria Moll, had been born in 1899, and was thus only one year older than her nephew, Grete Legler's son.

[38] AML 29.

buzzing with slanderous rumours of Mahler's exploits as a Don Juan and of the favours he bestowed on the female singers with whom he became enamoured. Perhaps this added to the strange fascination[39] Alma felt for Mahler as a conductor, for her view of him as a composer was quite different. The previous year she had heard the First Symphony and had left the hall 'full of anger and bitterness'. And yet, 'I cannot lie,' she wrote. 'He had always possessed for me a secret and powerful attraction, which I now concealed.'[40] 'For six months now, I've been doing my best not to meet him,' she told the Zuckerkandls when they ran into her on the Ring in the autumn of 1901 and invited her to dine at their house with him. This in spite of the fact that Justi had telephoned them that very day to ask that no other guests be invited, since Mahler could not bear strangers. A week later, Berta Zuckerkandl, who must have guessed what her refusal concealed, invited Alma again. Mahler had excused himself at the last moment the week before but had promised to come this time in order to see Sophie Clemenceau again. The fact that two of Alma's best friends, Klimt and Burckhard, were also going to be present, finally persuaded her to accept the invitation.

Alma returned home after the party in a thoroughly bad mood. She felt she had not been herself and had 'created misunderstandings'. Because of her 'shyness', she either said nothing, or suddenly blurted out all she thought 'in such a way that I appear to be brazen and forward'. But it was precisely this that had captivated Mahler and several others before him. He, on the other hand, had been very dogmatic that evening, she thought. He had prefaced all his remarks with 'Yes, but let me tell you . . . !' as though he had been addressing a public meeting. Alma presumed that this dictatorial manner must be due to the loneliness of a man who was accustomed to wielding absolute power over others. But she was fascinated in spite of herself. 'I must confess I liked him enormously,' she wrote in her diary. 'To be sure, he's very keyed up. He was like a bull in a china shop. He's pure oxygen: you get burnt if you go too close . . .'.[41]

The morning after the party, Berta Zuckerkandl and Sophie Clemenceau took Alma to the Opera, where they found Mahler impatiently waiting for them outside his office. He helped the young girl off with her coat, which he kept on his arm, but quite forgot to render the same service to the two ladies. Then, with an awkward gesture, he invited them all into his office, where the two sisters

---

[39] Interesting light is thrown on this fascination by a postcard sent to Alma from Alt-Aussee on 5 July 1899 and addressed, 'Frl. Alma Schindler, H.6, Stammbach bei Goisern'. The address is probably in Justi's hand, but on the other side it reads: 'Sole genuine signature, protected by law: Gustav Mahler. Beware of imitations!' Justi must have served as intermediary in obtaining this signature for the young woman, overcome with admiration for the conductor. (This card was part of the collection of Frau Ida Wagner, who was Alma's housekeeper and nurse in her final years and who died in Vienna some years ago.) On 29 Dec. 1901, after the announcement of Alma's engagement, the Vienna *Fremden-Blatt* wrote about an excursion which Mahler and Justi made to the Hallstättersee, a short distance from Alt-Aussee, in summer 1899. Alma was introduced there to Mahler by 'a singing teacher from the Vienna Conservatory', no doubt Gustav Geiringer who was present when Alma met Ludwig Karpath in Nov. 1901 (KMI).

[40] AMS.   [41] AMT.

engaged him in conversation while Alma, 'incapable of making small talk', leafed through a pile of scores on the piano. Mahler kept covertly glancing at her, but she, 'with the typical unconcern of youth', was not impressed by show or position. She was as yet unaware of the only thing that might have made her feel humble—'his inner stature'. Nevertheless, a first inkling of 'a new and perplexing respect for the outstanding man he was' began to come over her. Finally, he called over to her: 'Fräulein Schindler, did you sleep well?' 'Very well indeed. Why shouldn't I have?' 'I didn't sleep a wink all night!' That said, he accompanied the three of them into the auditorium. On taking leave of them he reminded Alma of her promise to come and see him. The dress rehearsal of *Les Contes d'Hoffmann* got smoothly under way. Mahler interrupted it only once at the beginning of the second act, when Gutheil-Schoder (as Giulietta) came on stage in a gown split at the side up to the waist. Shocked at this 'indecency' he sent her off at once to have it sewn up. While this was being done he could be heard muttering to himself about the 'shamelessness' of the singer who could dare 'to appear on stage improperly dressed'. Alma understood then that 'the theatre was something sacred for him'.

The next morning Alma was still in bed when the following anonymous poem was brought to her:

> Das kam so über Nacht!
> Hätt' ich's doch nicht gedacht
> Dass Contrapunkt und Formenlehre
> Mich noch einmal das Herz beschwere
>
> So über eine Nacht
> Gewann es Übermacht!
> Und alle Stimmen führen nur
> Mehr homophon zu einer Spur!
>
> Das kam so über Nacht
> —Ich habe sie durchwacht—
> Dass ich, wenn's klopft, im Augenblick
> Die Augen nach der Türe schickt'!
>
> Ich hör's: ein Mann—ein Wort!
> Es tönt mir immerfort—
> Ein Canon jeder Art:
> Ich blick' zur Tür—und wart'!
>
> It happened overnight.
> I never would have thought
> That counterpoint and theory of form
> Would trouble my heart again
>
> So all night long
> The rising chorus filled my mind,
> 'Til all the voices merged
> To sing the self-same tune.

It happened overnight,
I stayed wide awake,
So that, when the knock came,
My eyes would at once turn to the door.

Now I hear it: word of honour!
Ever and again it sings in my ears—
A canon of some sort:
I watch the door—and wait.[42]

The author of the poem had deliberately given himself away by his transparent allusions, and in her book Alma claims that she saw through them at once. She nevertheless showed the poem to her mother, who, 'convinced that a man like Mahler would never send poems to unknown young girls', concluded that the whole thing was a hoax. Thus Alma herself remained in doubt. However, thanks to Burckhard, she was not unaware that she had made quite an impression on Mahler. The two men had left the Zuckerkandls' house together, and Mahler had declared: 'That girl is intelligent and interesting. I didn't like her at first. She seemed to be just a doll. After all, it's not every day one meets a pretty young girl who's actually busying herself with something serious',[43] after which he plied Burckhard with further questions, which the latter refused to answer, saying merely that, 'Those who are acquainted with Fräulein Schindler know who she is. The others should mind their own business.'

Alma now found Mahler constantly in her thoughts, and felt very guilty about it. The entries in her diary at this time show that her relationship with Zemlinsky had reached an advanced stage, much more advanced than she was later to admit in her two books. She was, or at any rate thought she was, deeply in love with him and even wanted to have a child by him. Of the letters Zemlinsky wrote her, more than a hundred have survived,[44] and about forty of these are extremely passionate in tone and content. They show that Alma encouraged his love, even though in the early stages she said that she wished to remain free and would not consider marriage. She then seems to have driven the unfortunate composer to distraction with her sudden changes of mood, moments of almost tender affection alternating with sudden fits of coldness. Zemlinsky was quite humble in the early letters: 'I love you, but you're too beautiful for me. Men like me may deserve such happiness, but they never get

---

[42] AMM1. 25; AMM2. 40. Although in AMM Alma claims she received the poem on 9 Nov., it is first mentioned in AMT on 19 Nov., and again on the following day.

[43] Despite Alma's statement in AMM, it is clear from Alma's entry in AMT for 8 Nov. that she knew about Mahler's conversation with Burckhard.

[44] In the Alma Mahler archive (UPL), there are typed copies of 107 letters, and original MSS of two others. With them is an extract from Alma's diary, dated 20, 21, 22, 23, 24, and 25 Mar. 1901, and later given the title 'The Tragedy of the Ugly Man'. Most of the letters are undated: 52 of them date from 1901, and precede the break resulting from Alma's engagement to Mahler; 28 were written between 1904 and 1910, during Mahler's lifetime (two of them are actually addressed to him); 27 others (and a MS) were written after Mahler's death (1912 to 1926).

it.'[45] After an exchange of kisses, his professions of love become more intense. In the middle of March he begins to complain:

You're really very strange: sometimes, especially in letters, enchantingly lovable, and then cold, blasé and indifferent. But not at all complicated; don't think that! Quite transparent to an interested observer. Do you know how, incidentally? Look how your compositions start—warm, feminine, deeply felt—and then come the odds and ends, runs, passages without style. Olbrich[46] would have a song of yours sung by one of Barnum's circus company, in the traditional black coat and clown's bonnet.[47]

Sometimes Zemlinsky, overcome with emotion, abases himself: 'I want to kneel to you, kiss your dress, worship you like something sacred.' But he was not Alma's only suitor. Her diary records, on 23 March, a visit from a young man called Felix Muhr, desperate to marry her. This she could not seriously contemplate, for she 'felt nothing for him', although he was 'charming, distinguished and cultivated'.[48] 'It's frightful! The people I love have at the most respect for me, while the people I don't care about love me.' The same day the 'Secretary of the Secession'[49] also called to ask her to marry him. She turned him down flat: 'Second proposal this week,' she wrote, 'like in a sixpenny novel'!

A few days later, Zemlinsky writes again: 'One thought obsesses me: you must belong to me completely, completely! Come to me, don't leave me, prove that you love me as much as you've shown recently. Prove that you couldn't, that you wouldn't, love another more than me! I can't understand how you yourself can believe that your love might fade during the summer!' The young musician tries to persuade his beloved that she should not marry just for wealth,[50] and writes two crucial pages:

Your letter has stirred up something in me that I have kept in check for a long time, although I've often felt the urge to have it out with you. My love, you never miss an opportunity to emphasize how ridiculously little I am and have, how much there is that makes me unsuitable for you. Again and again I've heard from you what people have said to you: I am frightfully ugly, I have no money, perhaps no talent either, and also I'm dreadfully stupid! My pride is finally beginning to rebel! Don't be angry—I must get it all off my chest. You've always been the one with something to give! All right—anyway, for the last four weeks I have not been behaving as myself! But I've always been the one with something to give, always, always!!! I have nothing, I'm not handsome, I'm

---

[45] Undated letter (probably from the beginning of 1901).

[46] A celebrated Secession architect, designer of the building constructed in 1898 for the group's exhibitions.

[47] A copy of this letter is included in AMT, and this enables it to be dated 19 Mar. 1901.

[48] 'Perhaps we would be happy together, but I can't imagine it,' she continues. 'It would be a marriage of convenience in the best sense of the word, for I don't care about his money. But my work! He would permit me everything. The greatest freedom. He would not be jealous. . . . Marriage, a thought I can't think through. To give my body to a man I don't love. Or never give it, never? Always half? Only half?'

[49] In Dec. 1901 the Secretary of the Secession was François Hancke.

[50] Alma told him of Muhr's proposal, and he momentarily disappointed her by advising her (doubtless ironically) to accept.

supposed, beggar that I am, to be grateful that you love me—a little. It's extremely unnatural, directly contrary to nature in fact—and presumptuous—to think that I could belong to you!! Well, why? I can't for the life of me see why? Your mama, whom I otherwise much admire, doesn't ask: Does he love you?, but, Has he got any money? She would be perfectly prepared to accept my ugliness as part of the deal. My love! Do you have so much to give, so infinitely much, that others must be beggars in comparison?! Love for love, that's all I know. I can't and won't be put in an inferior position. All my pride is now up in arms. I am, after all, just a little bit of a somebody—and possibly worth the whole of that bunch of artists, those poseurs, libertarians, that you go around with and esteem so much. I've achieved something, and have the power to achieve a thousand times more. . . . You are very beautiful, and I know how much I prize your beauty. But later? In twenty years??? With your own particular brand of cruelty you don't spare me the slightest detail. Dr Muhr with his pots of money! To which I reply: Herr Zemlinsky with his talent! So there!

The next day another letter from Alma provoked the following indignant reply:

Your last letter! All the sweet things that one could read into it, if one wanted to, don't really come from your heart. The thought uppermost in your mind at the moment is: 'I am absolutely not the woman for him!' Inwardly or outwardly. Why this obsession? You've certainly had time enough to get to know me! I was for ever hearing, and now am for ever reading: 'You are ugly, too small,' and God knows what other nonsense! You can't tell me often enough what a great sacrifice you will be making! I don't want that! I absolutely can't stand it. It brings right out into the open the unfeminine side of you. Your chief desire is to shine, and for that, more than anything, you need money, and then a 'comparably handsome' man! Love is scarcely necessary for that. But love is all I have. Therefore, I don't suit you. That is the substance of your last two letters. I get the point. I shall not stand in your way. And when I really think about it—can you give me what I want from a woman? Beauty soon fades, and after all one finally gets accustomed to it. Besides, beautiful women are for making love to, not marrying. Isn't that so? I need so much love, so much blind faith and devotion. . . . I love you far more passionately than I have been able to show you. But I have to be the master, not the slave!! I can only be the master! I can humble myself before my own love, but not if it's demanded of me. Above all I can't endure knowing that you think you're the one with more to give! And it isn't true!! I always give more, because inwardly I am richer! . . . So, I'm frightfully ugly? Very well, so be it! I thank God that I am. And I thank God there have been so many girls who have seen through my ugliness to my soul without ever mentioning it to me, so that I could know that I am nonetheless a man, who can't be lightly dismissed because of that, and who is worth something for himself all the same.

It is worth quoting these letters at length because of what they reveal of Alma's character. When she married Mahler she also regarded herself as having made an exceptional sacrifice, and frequently reminded him of the fact. The only difference, at least in the beginning, was that because of his position, and the authority he possessed as a great artist, she dared not do it quite so frankly. In the following months, Zemlinsky's infatuation continued to grow. The two young people corresponded throughout the summer, unknown to Carl and Anna Moll. Sometimes the young musician's letters were those of a music teacher giving a correspondence course in composition. He and Alma often discussed what they had both been reading: Nietzsche, Bierbaum, Keller, Edgar Allan Poe, Ibsen, Mirbeau. Sometimes Zemlinsky again became reproachful: 'Your last-but-one letter upset me terribly. That cold superior tone, certain observations that I'll come back to, all that seemed to me to indicate weariness, certainly not love . . .'. But whether that was true or not, as soon as Alma sensed a coldness on his part, or considered that his silence suggested he was moving away from her, she grew jealous. Then she would even complain about the amount of time he had devoted to one of his pupils. Here we see another essential aspect of her character, the jealousy that was always ready to break out in any sphere, not only that of love.

When the summer was over, the two lovers met again in Vienna. In the last of their letters of that year still extant, written probably in October, they already speak of the moment when their union is to be consummated, of 'burning embraces', but Alex again complains of Alma's underlying 'coldness'. Living together is discussed. Alma declares: 'I want to be the mother of your children' and Zemlinsky replies:

If only you were really sincere in saying that! You weren't! Your whole letter in all its warmth was—cold! Why otherwise did you write: 'I am unhappy'? Why? For what reason? I know why: all your attitudes, your infinite vanity, your pleasure-seeking, all of that prevents you from being happy about us! . . . You tell me I must believe you love me, yet so often you provide me with proof to the contrary!

In the last letter from 1901 still extant Alex asks the girl, as a 'proof of love', for an hour spent together, alone, not in her parents' presence. Unfortunately, the letters concerning the break have not survived[51] and it is only through reading Alma's diary that one can guess what they must have contained. An agonizing choice, which is reflected in her diary, confronted Alma:

Whether, if he doesn't give himself to me completely, my nerves would go to pieces: or whether, if he were to give himself completely, consequences would follow? Both are equally dangerous! And I long so madly for his embraces. The touch of his hand deep inside me.—I shall never forget it—such a glow—and such a blissful feeling swept through me—Yes, one can be completely happy—perfect happiness does exist. In the arms of my beloved I have come to know that—one little [nuance][52] more and I would have been a god—And once again, everything about him is sacred to me, I want to kneel down in front of him and kiss his naked belly (*offenen Schoss*)—kiss everything, everything! Amen!

[51] Alma destroyed them, probably because she feared that the reproaches they contained would show her in too harsh a light.

[52] The word 'nuance' is almost illegible, but seems to be the only one appropriate to the meaning of the sentence.

On 11 November, as seen above, Alma attended the première of *Les Contes d'Hoffmann*, and her diary shows that Mahler was increasingly in her mind. On the 18th she went to the Opera again, with her mother this time, to hear Gluck's *Orfeo ed Euridice*[53]. Her thoughts wandered, and she looked up to the director's box. At first, Mahler did not recognize her, but then 'he started to flirt with me in a way I would never have believed of so deadly serious a man'. During the interval she and her mother were walking in the foyer when he suddenly appeared in front of them. After Alma had introduced him to her mother, he invited them into his office for a cup of tea. Having taken an instant liking to Frau Moll,[54] he was at his most 'affable and charming' with her. Alma, doubt-less somewhat jealous, went over to the piano. Mahler was due to leave for Munich two days later to conduct the première of his Fourth Symphony, but he accepted Frau Moll's invitation to visit them at the Hohe Warte as soon as he got back, and took his big engagement book from the drawer to arrange the date. Alma promised to change the time of her counterpoint lesson on the agreed day. As she and her mother were leaving, she asked him jokingly if he would consider taking her on at the Opera as a conductor. He replied that he would, adding that he was sure that her conducting would please him. 'Your judgment would not be objective,' she said. 'No judgment is ever objective' he replied. That evening, they parted like a pair of lovers, 'convinced that some-thing important and wonderful had entered our lives'.[55]

After the performance, Alma and her mother joined Burckhard and Moll in a restaurant for supper, and Moll, on being told about their encounter, up-braided his wife for having allowed her daughter to enter the office of that notorious 'womaniser'.[56] From then on, according to Alma, he did his best to break up her budding affair by pointing out the disadvantages of marrying a man like Mahler: his age, his debts, his ill health, his 'precarious' position at the Opera. 'He's not good-looking, and his music is apparently not worth much,' he concluded. Burckhard, his jealousy aroused, asked Alma what her answer would be if Mahler asked her to marry him. 'I would accept,' she replied at once. Whereupon Burckhard, good Nietzschean and convinced racist that he was, exclaimed:

But it would be a sin for so good-looking a girl of such good family as you to spoil it all by marrying that rachitic, degenerate Jew.[57] Think of your children—it would be a sin!

---

[53] The performance, conducted by Bruno Walter, was followed by the ballet *Coppélia* conducted by Josef Bayer.

[54] In Alma Mahler's *Erinnerungen*, one senses the annoyance this reciprocal affection caused her, probably because of her profound hostility towards her mother.

[55] AMM1. 27; AMM2. 42.

[56] AMS explains that Mahler was said to be exploiting his position as director in order to seduce all young female members of the Opera.

[57] In AMM, Frau Mahler tries to minimize the anti-Semitism of Burckhard's remarks. The two original MSS have *verderben* or *verschweindeln* (instead of *verdunkeln*) and *degenerierten rachitischen Juden* instead of *degenerierten älteren Mann*.

Besides which, fire and water can, at a pinch, get along together, but not fire and fire. You would be the one to suffer, not him, and you deserve better than that.

But Alma was by no means convinced. She did her best to hide the excitement and interest aroused in her by this conversation. She waited impatiently for Mahler to return, and confided to her diary on 20 November: 'I ought to be ashamed of myself—but Mahler's image lives within me. I'll tear out this poisonous weed—in another's place. My poor, poor Alex! If only the poem were from him, if only. I could hate myself!' Two days later she wrote:

So far away from my Gustav, so infinitely far.—I've sent Alex a fateful letter. What will come of it? He'll write me a sarcastic and really angry letter and never come back again. Oh, what I'm losing! Such a marvellous teacher! I've certainly miscalculated this time. Whatever happens, I must bear the consequences! It's entirely my fault, yet it was so beautiful! And Gustav—such a woman chaser [*so eine Flatterseele*]. He's had affairs with everyone—Mildenburg, Michalek, Kurz etc., all of them . . .[58]

One day after he returned from Munich, on 27 November, Mahler conducted *Les Contes d'Hoffmann*. But Alma occupied his heart and mind. On Thursday 28 November,[59] she was working out figured basses with Robert Gound, when the maid burst in, breathless, and blurted out: 'Gustav Mahler is downstairs!'[60] A few moments later, he entered her room for the first time. Since the Molls had only just moved to the Hohe Warte,[61] Alma's books were still all piled on the floor, and he started to go through them, commenting on each one. Coming upon the complete works of Nietzsche, he put on a shocked expression and curtly told her to throw them in the fire then and there. She refused. 'If they are really so detestable,' she said, 'you should find it easy to convince me of it. In the meantime, you would surely agree that it would be more reasonable for me to leave Nietzsche on my shelves, and not read him, than to burn him and keep on longing to read him afterwards.' He was annoyed at that, but soon recovered and suggested that they take a walk. As they were going downstairs, they met Frau Moll, who invited him to stay for dinner, adding, 'We're having *Paprikahändl*[62] and . . . Burckhard.' 'I don't much care for either,' he said drily, but accepted all the same, adding that he would first have to walk down to the post office in Döbling to telephone home.[63]

---

[58] Alma's diary, 22 Nov.

[59] Alma is mistaken when in her diary she gives the 27th as the date of Mahler's first visit. She mentions having attended a concert on the 26th which in fact took place on the 27th, as recorded in the programme. Furthermore, Mahler was conducting *Les Contes d'Hoffmann* at the Opera on the 27th (KMI).

[60] 'And that was the end of counterpoint forever and a day', Alma writes in AMM. Yet AMT shows that she continued to take lessons in counterpoint with Gound into the New Year.

[61] The Molls moved into their brand-new house designed by Josef Hoffmann, 8 Steinfeldgasse, on 1 Oct. 1901. Previously they had lived close to the centre of Vienna, in the Theresianumgasse.

[62] Chicken with cream and paprika.

[63] Some details here are taken from Carl Moll's memoirs (BGM). The Molls had not had the telephone installed at the Hohe Warte in 1901 (KMI).

'Side by side, at once close and yet strangers,' Mahler and Alma, their feet crunching on the fresh snow, set out for Döbling.[64] His shoelaces kept coming undone, and Alma was touched by the childish awkwardness with which he invariably chose the highest and most uncomfortable places on which to rest his foot while he did them up again. Upon reaching Döbling, he realized he had forgotten his home telephone number and had to call the Opera.[65] When he finally got through to Justi, he told her, without further explanation, that he would not be home for dinner, something, Alma notes, that had never occurred in all the nine years he and his sister had lived together.

In silence, they slowly went back up the hill to the Hohe Warte. Suddenly Mahler said: 'It's not easy to marry a man like me! I must be entirely free. I can't allow myself to be hampered by any material responsibilities. I could lose my job at the Opera from one day to the next.' The realization that he was thus 'dictating his will and rule of life' to her, without so much as asking her opinion, almost took Alma's breath away. However, his statement of his need for freedom as an artist seemed self-evident to her. She was the daughter of an artist, she had always lived among artists. So she understood and shared his views in that regard. They walked on in silence, admiring the reflection of the street lamps on the snow. Mahler seemed pleased and reassured. When they got back to the house, he went up to Alma's room with her and kissed her for the first time.[66] Thereupon, he began to talk about their getting married as soon as possible 'as though it were a simple and obvious thing, as though it had all been settled by the few words he'd uttered along the way—so why wait?'

When they went down to dinner half an hour later, Burckhard and a young architect who had also fallen under Alma's spell[67] had already arrived. Mahler enchanted everyone with his wit and charm. He strongly defended Schiller against Alma's indifference and Burckhard's dislike, quoting a large number of his poems by heart. His defence was so convincing that, 'after allowing him to kiss me without really wanting him to and after letting him fix the date for our marriage', she no longer doubted that 'both these decisions are right and for the best and I can no longer live without him . . . He's the only man who can give meaning to my life, for he stands head and shoulders above all the other men I've known.'

The following morning, Mahler sent her his Lieder. She and Zemlinsky went through them, 'he with intense scorn, I coldly. Indeed, they're not him—such contrived naïveté and simplicity from the most complicated of persons. I'd so much like to tell him so, but am afraid of offending him'. Not daring to admit that she found them 'inauthentic', she finally wrote:

---

[64] According to Moll's memoirs, he and Kolo Moser walked, conversing, a little way behind.

[65] Mahler's private number was apparently not in the telephone book (KMI).

[66] According to AMT, it was only on 1 Dec., when Mahler paid his second visit to the Hohe Warte, that he kissed Alma for the first time.

[67] This might have been Felix Muhr who appears for the last time in AMT on 9 Dec. (KMI).

Dear Herr Direktor, Many many thanks! I don't want to write anything about the Lieder—there are things I want to say, and things I want to ask. How I look forward to Monday! I'd very much like you to read what Maeterlinck wrote on 'Silence'—I was so strongly reminded of it during our first beautiful walk together. It was singularly beautiful and glorious. You'll have gradually to get used to my handwriting—so this must suffice as a beginning. I clasp your hand warmly and send you my kindest regards—until Monday! Alma Schindler.[68]

In the letter accompanying his Lieder, Mahler had written: 'Yesterday was very pleasant and happy, despite all the uneasiness; I felt it on my way home, after L[69] had left me and I was alone. All the love and loveliness continued to reverberate softly within me, even in my dreams.'[70] But Alma was in torment. A terrible struggle was going on in her mind: 'Alex was here and rather angry about Mahler—but otherwise as sweet as ever. I had the feeling that I belong to him . . . Conflicting emotions inside me. Alex versus Mahler—I have complete confidence in Mahler.'[71] Two days later,[72] after another visit by Mahler to the Hohe Warte, she wrote:

He told me that he loves me—we kissed—he played his things for me—my senses remain numb . . . his caresses are sweet and nice. If only I knew—him or him—I must gradually wean Alex away from me. I'm overwhelmed with remorse; if only all that hadn't happened—I would have become engaged today. But I couldn't return his caresses—someone stood between us . . . I told him so without mentioning the name— I had to tell him! . . . Had he but come three years earlier. A mouth undefiled! . . . I'm in a terrible dilemma.

The following day she wrote:

I keep saying softly to myself my 'beloved' and each time I add 'Alex'! Can I really love Mahler as much as he deserves and it lies within my power to love someone. Will I ever understand his art—and he mine!? With Alex—this mutual understanding. Mahler only said, 'That must be taken seriously. It's something I hadn't expected!' How shall I tell Alex that!? I am on 'Du' terms with Mahler—he told me how much he loves me and I wasn't able to say anything in return. Do I really love him? I've no idea— sometimes I think quite simply 'no'. So many things about him annoy me: his smell— the way he sings—something in the way he speaks! And physical longing? how passionately I burned with longing for Alex—at first . . . Every minute—every second—and now—yes, I desire, but no longer with the same passion! Perhaps I can't love that way a second time. He [Mahler] is a stranger to me, our tastes run in different directions . . . He said to me, 'Alma, think it over very carefully—if at that moment I disappointed you, say so. Today, I can still get over it—although it will be hard—but in four months' time, it may no longer be possible'.

And I don't know what's going on inside me—whether I love him or whether I don't love him—whether it's the director—the superb conductor—or the man . . . if, when I

---

[68] Alma copied this letter into her diary. After Mahler's death, she destroyed all her letters to him.

[69] 'L' was surely the painter Wilhelm Legler (1875–1951), who had married Alma's sister Grete (see above, n. 26).

[70] AMM1. 255; AMM2. 235.   [71] Thur. 28 and Sat. 30 Nov.   [72] Mon. 2 Dec.

stop thinking about the one, something remains for the other. And his music, which I find so utterly foreign to me? To put it plainly, I don't believe in him as a composer! And I am supposed to bind my life to the man . . . The fact is he was nearer to me from afar than he is at close quarters. I'm terribly afraid . . . And if I now say 'no'—a dream of many years gone up in smoke! We kissed but without coming really close. Although his hands are expressive, I don't love them as much as Alex's. Habit can do a lot of things—and so can time . . . but patience is not my Mahler's forte. What am I to do? And supposing Alex becomes great and mighty? . . . I've written to him—I've no idea what's going on inside me—This morning, I played some of the first act![73] It's so near to my heart! There's one thing that tortures me: whether or not Mahler will encourage me to work—whether or not he'll support my art—whether he'll love it as Alex does— for *he* loves it for itself.

On Tuesday, 3 December, Mahler sent Alma tickets for *Les Contes d'Hoffmann*, which he was to conduct that evening, and also wrote that he would be leaving for Berlin on the following Monday.

Since I'll have to stay away for about ten days, I'm very miserable and fear I fought my fight against the clay household gods[74] quite in vain yesterday. Only the wounds I received in the process will remain. However, neither was it at all nice of you to resign yourself patiently and submissively to fate and just let me remain in exile for a whole week. Hero was quite different: she said 'come tomorrow'. So I shall not swim across the Hellespont but like a modern Leander, steam by fast train and sleeper via Berlin to Döbling and arrive in a completely 'decadent' state after all the strain and sleepless nights. . . . The vanquished victor, Pyrrhus.[75]

At the end of each act of *Les Contes d'Hoffmann*, Mahler turned around to throw a loving glance at Alma. 'If only he were Alex,' she noted in her diary that night. 'Oh, if only I'd already told Alex—I'm constantly thinking of the other one, Mahler [probably a slip of the pen for the young architect] sat in our row—oh God! If he doesn't come to us again before he leaves, I'll go to him.' The following day, Mahler wrote her another letter in which he talked about Hoffmann, one of his favourite authors, and Offenbach's opera, which he loved,

although Hoffmann's 'spirit is all but gone from it and only the phlegm remains'. . . . It's only with the greatest inner repugnance that I manage to get to the end of the first two acts. But yesterday it was a pleasure—because it was for you! The third act is more felicitous; at least it contains the material with which one can, by using one's own inventive powers, recreate the demoniac traits of the original! . . . In these few days, it's already become such a pleasant habit to chat with you—to fight for my cause or even to hold my tongue, that I cherish and express but one fervent wish before I leave: that you be and remain a loving comrade (*Kamerad*) to me and that you make a small effort

---

[73] This probably refers to *Es war einmal*, the score of which Zemlinsky had sent to Alma, or else *Der Triumph der Zeit* (see above, n. 12), on which he had been working all summer. The score was completed on 25 Dec. 1901. Zemlinsky conducted the première of a Suite based on the ballet on 18 Feb. 1903.

[74] Mahler was probably referring to Alma's books, possibly also to her friends.

[75] AMM1. 255; AMM2. 236.

so that I may be the same to you. Remember our beloved Evchen and Hans Sachs! Good-bye![76]

'I keep thinking of him more and more,' Alma wrote in her diary after reading this letter.

His dear, dear smile, I've actually kissed this man, and what is more, he's kissed me. I'm beginning to think that I really do love him. Alex is like a lead weight. I really do want him [Mahler] now. I think about him all the time—His dear, dear eyes—If only Alex—if only he had already been told—that will be frightful. If only I see Mahler before he leaves! . . . Evening, this letter—I could cry! I have the feeling that I've lost him—and I was already thinking he was mine—A marvellous stroke of luck! I feel utterly miserable. I must see him—before he leaves—I've got to see him. He doesn't want me, he's abandoning me—that last sentence, that terrible last sentence! I realize now how much I love him—I suddenly feel so empty. I must go to him tomorrow. My longing knows no bounds. Evchen and Hans Sachs—an empty subterfuge—it's just not possible![77]

That last sentence in Mahler's letter continued to haunt and torment her throughout the following day: 'Evchen and Hans Sachs, I was not prepared for that.' On Saturday, he could resist no longer and went to see her:

We kissed each other countless times. I have a warm feeling when he holds me in his arms. If only he goes on loving me like that. But he's a man of changing moods, frightfully temperamental. He tried to convert me to his way of thinking. I shan't see him for the next 10 days—he leaves for Berlin on Monday. I don't know what else to write. But my heart is for him and against Alex. I've never watched the hands of the clock so closely as today. I wasn't able to do any work at all, for sheer longing. The thought of Tuesday makes me tremble. My poor Alex. I'm convinced he knows everything, feels everything . . . I keep seeing Gustav's eyes before me—so kind and so dear to me—and ceaselessly questioning—and his beautiful hands somewhat spoiled because he bites his nails. He'll write to me from Berlin. I've never in my life met anyone who was more foreign to me than he—so foreign and yet so close! I really can't explain it—perhaps it's precisely that that attracts me to him. But he must leave me the way I am—I'm already conscious of the changes that are coming over me because of him. He takes a lot from me but he gives a lot. If things go on like that, he'll make another, a new person of me. A better person? I don't know, I don't know anything—my future is more than ever just one big question mark. It's all in his hands now. He told me everything today, all his sins and I some of mine. He guessed Alexeus's name and was appalled—he couldn't understand it. That's enough for today—and without a glance into the

---

[76] AMM1. 256; AMM2. 237. Letter of 5 Dec. already quoted in Chap. 11. At this time, according to Knud Martner (AMM3. 397), Carl Moll was about to make a trip to Berlin and Mahler had probably tried to persuade Alma to travel with him, but neither she nor the family found this advisable. Thus Moll alone attended the Berlin performance of the Fourth Symphony.

[77] Knud Martner has noted that Mahler's reference to 'Evchen and Hans Sachs' was crucial in his relationship to Alma. AMT shows that she had been hitherto rather lukewarm towards Mahler but now found herself passionately in love with him. It is obvious from Mahler's letter written on 5 Dec. that he did come on Sat. 7 Dec. and that he and Alma were secretly engaged on that day, exactly one month after they first met. In the interim they had only met privately on two occasions (AMM3. 397).

mysterious 'tomorrow'. At least we had today and that was beautiful, really beautiful. He's the purest person I've ever met—because the (thank God) few experiences Mahler has had were ordinary run-of-the-mill affairs.

On Sunday, 8 December, the day after they had been secretly engaged, Mahler sent Alma the score of *Das klagende Lied* together with the following letter: 'Here is a "Tale" from the days of my youth! You gave me real joy yesterday. You both listened to me and answered me so sweetly. Alas, such an afternoon is dreadfully short and the coda in the evening is almost sad.' He was going to conduct *The Magic Flute* for her that evening:

Today brings me the evening during which we shall be together and united in the deepest sense of the word. I'll think of you through every bar and conduct just for you. It will be like yesterday at the piano when I talked to you so frankly and straight from my heart. But the days to follow! That's when I'll be going through everything in my mind, the least of your words, the least of your expressions.[78] Every so often, I'll pause, and have that suspicious look that so frequently surprises you. It isn't <u>suspicion</u>, in the usual sense of the word, but a questioning, to you and to the future. My dearest, <u>learn to answer</u>! It's very difficult. You have to have examined yourself and know yourself well. But <u>questioning</u> is still more difficult! This can be learned only through the fullest and most intimate relationship with the other person. My dearest, my love, learn to <u>question</u>! You seemed to me yesterday to be so different and so much more mature. I sense that these last few days have opened up and revealed a host of things to you. What will it be like when I come again? I'll then ask you again: <u>Do you love me</u>? <u>More than yesterday</u>? Did you know me and do you recognize me? Now, Addio, my love, my comrade![79]

Late at night, having received that letter, Alma wrote in her diary:

I feel as though all were chaos inside me—everything's crashing down and something new is springing. A new vision of the world, a new belief. Oh—if only his love holds firm—he is in a position to give infinitely much. I'm quite incapable of doing any work—I don't know why. Alex had already given me everything—I already had a lot myself and had picked up a lot. Now I'll have to discard a lot to make room for new things, better things. At midday today he sent me *Das klagende Lied*. Today wonderful. Melodics of an inspired life[80] but the structure good and effective. I can imagine that it is deeply moving in several places.

During the 'heavenly' (*himmlisch*) performance of *The Magic Flute* that Mahler privately dedicated to her on the evening of 8 December, Alma recognized for the first time the

genuine grandeur and beauty of this work. Then I looked at Gustav and couldn't help smiling like one transfigured. At the end of both acts, and particularly after the last, he

---

[78] This passage was omitted in AMM.

[79] Letter of 8 Dec. (AMM1. 258; AMM2. 238). A few sentences are missing in the publ. version.

[80] 'Melodik ein beselten Leben' probably intended to be 'Melodik eines beseelten Lebens'—the grammar and syntax of Alma's diary jottings often leave much to be desired, a result no doubt of her unorthodox early education.

gave me a tender loving look—a thread was spun from him to me. Later on, we drove past him—he was walking with his sister and Lechner-Bauer [*sic*] and didn't see me. My wonderful Gustav. Think, think of me!

The following morning, Alma was finally sure she was in love. 'I . . . pace up and down in my room, now over to his photograph, now back again to his last letter.' In the afternoon, Mahler sent her a box of chocolates and still another letter:

How happy I'd be to receive a line from you upon my arrival at the Palace Hotel in Berlin. It would be like a little bit of home in that strange lodging, for, from now on, home is the place where I know you are. The least sign of your precious life will make me forget for a few moments the pain of being parted from you. Write to me about *Die Zauberflöte*, too, I can well imagine that a thing like that is not yet within your grasp, since you're still too much all of that yourself. This was also long the case with me as far as the works you call 'naïve' are concerned. Nevertheless, everything you tell me about yourself is adorable and precious to me, even the most trivial things. Please don't go to any trouble over your letters: just put down the words that come into your head. Always imagine, when you're writing to me, that I'm sitting beside you and that you're chatting about everything under the sun. I'd always like to know all about your life— in detail! Just one thing, my Alma: please write legibly!⁸¹

Before his departure, Mahler had told Justi everything and they had talked 'until late in the night'. 'She understands everything and will be a faithful friend to us,' he wrote to Alma, asking her to give him an exact account of the meeting he had arranged between them.⁸² According to Alma, however, he had said nothing to Justi at first, 'for fear of the dire effects of her jealousy'. One day, as he and Justi were walking on the Ring together, they had met Carl Moll, whom he had introduced to her. Justi had exclaimed, 'What a nice chap, that Moll,' and Mahler had rashly replied, 'Yes, but wait till you meet her mother!'⁸³ In fact, Justi had already begun to suspect that a feminine attachment might lie behind her brother's frequent absences, but now the truth was out.⁸⁴ As we shall see, however, Alma Mahler's assertions, and especially those concerning her sister-in-law, are highly unreliable. 'It's too cruel that I have to go away again

⁸¹ This letter was probably written in Vienna, at the railway station, just before Mahler boarded the train for Dresden (AMM3. 398). Alma omitted this sentence from the printed text, like all Mahler's allusions to her illegible writing.

⁸² Letter quoted above, 9 Dec.

⁸³ Bruno Walter's letter to his parents, quoted later, contains an almost identical account of this incident, which can definitely not have taken place, as Walter claims, just before the press announcement of Mahler's engagement. Mahler's letter to Alma makes it clear that he spoke to his sister *before* leaving for Berlin.

⁸⁴ According to Alma, Justi did not know the truth when she joined her brother in Dresden and could not understand why Mahler asked her things like: 'Can an elderly man marry a young girl? . . . Has he the right?' and: 'Has autumn the right to enchain the spring?' In point of fact, Mahler had spoken to Justi on 8 Dec. If he had not done so before, it was hardly out of fear of her jealousy but rather because he himself was not sure of Alma's feelings (AMM3. 365). According to AMT, Justi met Alma on 14 Dec., i.e. before she went to Dresden. As for the questions, which Mahler was asking himself as much as his sister, they appear in the letter (quoted below) he wrote to Justi from Berlin.

at this precise moment,' Mahler complained in his last letter written before leaving Vienna.

I'm so unhappy about it and yet it's almost like the voice of the Master, the Teacher (I'm using these words in order not to say 'God', since we haven't discussed that subject fully enough and I couldn't bear a meaningless phrase to come between us). It cries: 'Be courageous, be forbearing, be patient!' You see, my dearest, we shall need this throughout our lives, and even when this Teacher appears in storms, he must always remain intelligible to us. Oh God, there's so much noise going on around me, I can't write any more! I can't even hear my own thoughts any more—only the <u>one voice</u> that drowns out everything else and that will never again fall silent in my heart, a voice that repeats one phrase, one tune: 'I love you, my Alma!'[85]

No sooner had he arrived in Berlin[86] than he sat down to write to Alma again.

I'm conducting my symphony myself. Oh, if only you could be here! However, whereas others have to guess my life from my music, you, you, my Alma, starting from your knowledge of me, from the all-embracing present, and made perceptive by love, will learn everything about me—you will become me and I you. Astronomers are obliged to identify stars by their rays (and still grope around in darkness because their procedure—it's called spectral analysis—enables them to discover only earth-related substances: the original stuff of which the star is made remains forever inscrutable)—but what could the rays mean to him who inhabits the star itself. True, the comparison is not entirely apt, but it does most nearly convey what I feel at this moment and what makes me so calm and so happy.

What will it be like once you share everything with me and I everything with you—when this violent and urgent desire mixed with so much fear and anxiety is assuaged and we, even when parted, know everything about one another and are able to love and pervade one another without misgivings! (Not that I'd give up anything that comes to me on account of you, not even the apprehension and the pain—don't misunderstand what I've just said.) I must be off now to the rehearsal. If notes and sound waves had as much force as my longing for you, you would hear them ringing all this afternoon. To you, for you—everything that in me lives! My beloved Alma!—Your G.[87]

After Mahler's departure Alma in turn felt calmer and more self-confident. 'I feel I'm becoming a better person—he's uplifting me. My longing for him will not die away.' Nevertheless, the very day Mahler left, she received a 'handsome, rich, cultured and musical' young man[88] who had long been courting her. They played several piano duets together and he finally asked her again what her 'intentions' were concerning him. 'I couldn't do otherwise than tell him the truth—hard as it was for me,' she wrote in her diary that evening.

---

[85] AMM1. 260; AMM2. 239.

[86] Mahler had spent the day of 10 Dec. in Dresden, rehearsing the Second Symphony (AMM3. 398).

[87] Undated letter (11 Dec. 1901, AMM1. 261; AMM2. 240).

[88] Strange as it may seem, Alma several times refers to him as 'Mahler.' Perhaps it was Felix Muhr, mentioned in Alma's diary in the entry of 23 Mar., where a letter he has sent, proposing marriage, is extensively quoted.

He stood before me pale and trembling and said: 'Fräulein, if you say "no" I shall kill myself.' I was filled with pity. I like him so much—as a friend—and am convinced I'm not mistaken???—Shall I take him—as a friend?!! But there are things that are beyond our control. My love and longing for you are boundless, Gustav, my dearest, my beloved . . . I desire only one thing, I dream of only one thing, to belong to you alone.

Doubtless out of jealousy, the young man proceeded to tell Alma that a doctor friend of his had said that 'Gustav has an incurable disease, his strength is visibly diminishing'. Thus she adds in her diary: 'Oh God, I'll take care of him as if he were my child—he musn't be destroyed because of me. I'll curb my desire and my passion—my strength and youth shall make him well again, my beloved master . . . So much has happened within me in this past fortnight!!! I've become so old!'[89]

Alma finally met Justi at the Zuckerkandls' two days after Mahler's departure: 'There's one thing I like very much about her—I recognize him in her . . . I'm going to see her on Saturday.' Justi in turn wrote Mahler a letter full of 'warmth and gaiety', mostly about Alma. 'How nice it would be if everything— for you and for me—turns out the way it appears to be going at the moment!' he replied.[90] 'I beg of you really truly to love Alma, it would make me twice as happy again. Yet she's still so young and my courage keeps faltering when I think of the difference in our ages. If you can, keep calm and consider, or at least help me to think it over. It's no small matter and the wish must not be father to the thought.'[91]

Mahler was clearly by no means unaware that there was a problematical side to his projected marriage. He begged Justi to help Alma to understand 'how I live and what I'm like'. He even invited his sister to join him in Dresden. The trip would be his birthday present to her, she would be able to hear his Second Symphony and the two of them would discuss their future. He was worried about Alma's first letter, which he found a little 'childish'.[92]

I still have to be very careful. The dear girl is in a terrible whirl at the moment. She's in a completely unaccustomed situation, and I must absolutely keep my eyes open for us both. She will have to mature a lot, as I have just clearly understood, before on my side I could envisage a decision so heavy with consequences. You, in any case, are absolutely free to act and, whatever happens, we shall always keep close. I want to see you happy and shall help you in anything where you need to think clearly or be reassured.[93]

Three days later he wrote to Justi that a further letter from Alma had

---

[89] AMT 9 and 10 Dec.
[90] This clearly refers both to Justi's marriage with Rosé and to his own.
[91] Undated letter, 11 Dec. (RWO).
[92] This was probably the letter where Alma described the 'handsome, cultivated, musical' young man who was prepared to kill himself for her sake.
[93] Undated letter, 12 Dec. (BGM).

removed all my doubts about her warmth of heart and her essential honesty . . . There's only one thing that worries me: whether a man who will soon be old has the right to bind so much youth and freshness to his overripeness, to chain spring to autumn, missing out summer?[94] I know I have much to give, but the rights of youth cannot be bought at any price. If Beethoven, Wagner and Goethe were to come back to life today, she would kneel down and worship them with youthful passion—but flowers only bud and blossom in spring—that's the big question for me. For a while, of course, everything would be alright. But what will happen when my fruitful autumn gives way to winter? Do you see what I mean?[95]

During Mahler's absence, Alma and Justi became friends. Alma duly went to the Auenbruggergasse on 14 December and saw Mahler's room, his bed, his desk, and his books. Justi went out of her way to be 'kind and nice'. During the visit, a letter arrived for Justi in which Mahler had enclosed, for Alma, the programme of the Second Symphony.[96] Alma 'saw in Justi the features of her brother; when she spoke, it was like him speaking'. But her diary reveals that she was secretly worried:

She watches me, Argus-eyed, my words and movements and feelings, and immediately passes on her anxieties to Gustav.[97]

There are several things about her that annoy me. If she continues to watch me with such inquisitiveness, things could become dangerous for me. If, for instance, she should discover that I'm heartless and loveless—things which I only whisper to my diary—that I'm incapable of any warm feelings, that it's all nothing but calculation, cold, clear-headed calculation.[98] For he's a sick man and could lose his job from one day to the next; he's Jewish, not young, and deeply in debt as a composer. So where's the calculation? Is it just stupidity then? No, there's something that draws me to him, no doubt about it! But if Justi conspires against me and he falls out of love with me, I won't die. I love him and I shall stick with him! . . . I'm terribly uneasy. I have a nasty feeling Justi is poisoning his love for me. I can't explain it, but I'm worried.

But Justi was not the only one to have suspicions about Alma. Despite her youth, the young girl had already acquired a considerable reputation as a flirt. She was thought to be frivolous and capricious, and she took an obvious pleasure in seeing men succumb to her attractions. Mahler was well aware of this, and in any case she had not really attempted to conceal this aspect of her personality from him. Indeed, in one of her letters, she had told him about the musical young man who had threatened to commit suicide for love of her,[99] and he had scolded her by return of post:

[94] These 'enigmatic' phrases, which are in fact perfectly clear, are the same as the ones which, according to Alma, Mahler put to Justi in Dresden.
[95] Undated letter, 15 Dec. (RWO).
[96] This programme was written especially for King Albert of Saxony. Alma copied the entire text in her diary.
[97] Alma's diary, 18 Dec.   [98] 'All untrue', Alma notes in the margin.
[99] As we have seen, this was probably Felix Muhr.

So a handsome, young, rich, cultured and musical gentleman gave you such a difficult afternoon? Almschi, Almschi, do stop and think it over again! God knows what an exchange you're making. I don't possess half these fine qualities! He stood before you pale and trembling—and is even prepared to kill himself! I would never do that! How I'd like to ruffle your darling mop of hair! Anyway, you know I'd like it better if it were not so immaculately curled! If only I weren't constantly surrounded by a whole escort of people here, who don't leave me alone for one second! I have so much to say to you.

Earlier in the same letter Mahler had written:

Oh, Almschi (is that how it's spelled?) if you would only write more clearly! Believe me, I'd gladly spend hours deciphering these precious hieroglyphs, but the thing that torments me is that the immediacy of the message is lost when, instead of feeling as if I were listening to your voice and feeling you near me, I'm constantly interrupted and sorely frustrated by having to stop every second to unravel and decipher. Besides, it frequently happens that there are several words I simply can't make out despite all my efforts. My beloved girl, do take the trouble to write clearly! Separate the letters, and make the consonants clear![100]

In another letter written shortly after, Mahler talked about his attitude to worldly success as a composer.

I now find myself (especially lately, since my thoughts have become bound up with you) prey to a thoroughly vulgar, indeed, for people of my sort, almost unworthy ambition! I now want successes, recognition and whatever else all these insignificant and, in the true sense of the word, meaningless things are called! I want to win honour for you! Don't misunderstand what I mean by ambition! I've had ambition for years, but not in the sense of wanting the honour my neighbours and contemporaries can bestow on me. But to be understood and appreciated by my equals, even if I were fated not to find such people in my lifetime (and, indeed, they are only to be found beyond time and space), I have always striven for that, and from now on that will be my highest aim in life. And in that you will have to help me, my beloved. And, you know, to gain this reward, this crown of laurels, one must forgo the acclaim of the crowd, and indeed that of the great and the good (who aren't always able to follow either). How gladly I've borne the slaps of the Philistines and the scorn and hatred of the ignorant (*Unmündigen*) up to now! Oh yes, I'm, unfortunately, all too well aware that the little respect I have won is perhaps due only to a misunderstanding, or at best a vague intuition of something higher but inaccessible. Needless to say, I'm not referring to my activities as a 'director' or a conductor, for these are, after all, and in the fullest sense of the words, only abilities and merits of an inferior kind. Please send me your answer to this question: Do you understand me, are you willing to go along with me. Alma! Would you be able to bear with me all the adversity, the external trappings of shame, and joyfully take up such a cross? . . .

---

[100] AMM1. 262; AMM2. 241. This letter from Berlin, dated 'Thursday, 14 Dec.' was doubtless written on the 12th. In her book, Alma omitted the whole of the first part, quoted above, as she did most references to her private life and her handwriting.

... 'I no longer imagined it possible that one day I should experience such happiness, to be loved as I love,' continued Mahler two days later.

Every time a woman has crossed my path, I've had painfully to recognize once more how wide the gulf is between dreams of happiness and inadequate reality. I blamed myself for it and became completely resigned to it. Young though you are, Alma, you yourself know how it has been with you and will be able to understand my feelings when, with all the impulse of my heart and my being, I now not only feel, but may also say, with supreme tenderness and bliss, that I'm in love for the first time! I still can't rid myself of the fear and dread that so beautiful and sweet a dream may vanish, and can hardly wait for the moment when I shall inhale from your mouth and your life's breath the certainty and fullest awareness that my ship of life has come through the storms of the high seas and is now safe in its home port. I realize that we first came truly close to one another the last time we were together and that, although apparently separated, we've now become truly united for the first time.[101]

Just as everything that I am is henceforth yours, so I encompass all that is you with my whole soul. Oh God, today, from sheer longing and worry for you, my life, I'm holding forth like Walther von Stolzing and forgetting the other half, poor Hans Sachs, who, after all, is far more deserving of your love. See! My love! I'm sometimes almost sad that one cannot deserve or earn the highest thing, it has to come as a gift.[102] You've given me so much, my Alma! You've so sweetly declared what you'd like to be to me. When I think of what I want and ought to be to you, I'm almost awe-struck. I've so deep and strong an awareness of my duties—which are also my supreme happiness—that I wouldn't dare make you any vows or promises for fear of tempting fate! And I think that you feel it as I do myself; what inspires us and unites us is a power outside us and over us; quietly to venerate it will be our religion! If, at such a moment, I pronounce the name of God to you, you will understand, through the almighty passion of your and my love, that this power takes us both in its embrace and make us into one! ...

What I find so infinitely sweet about you is that you're so genuine, so unpretentious. I can't imagine you saying something you don't really mean. That is, in fact, the one sin against the Holy Ghost. It amounts to a lie, because one is deceiving oneself! Do you remember our first conversation in the presence of Burckhard? Everything I said was directed solely to you that evening. God already wanted us to become one—only we didn't know it—but I had already received the baptism of fire! Oh, Alma, my dearest, my dearly beloved, I'd like to go on talking to you like this about my innermost self and can't get around to telling you what's going on around me! Yet that, too, I must do! We must indeed share everything.[103]

After the final rehearsal of the Fourth Symphony on 15 December, Mahler wrote again to his fiancée in the lounge of his hotel, amid the 'hurry and scurry of the waiters and guests'. He expressed his admiration for Friedrich Hölderlin, 'one of my favourites both as a poet and as a human being. Indeed he is one of the truly great...', and complained once more about their separation. 'Heavens! When I imagine myself back in that room, under that roof, I become

[101] AMM1. 264; AMM2. 242.   [102] The last clause has been omitted in Alma's book.
[103] AMM1. 266; AMM2. 244.

so impatient and wild that I could get up and leave straightaway!'[104] Mahler's reply to her letter about the 'pale young man' upset Alma, for she sensed the reproach behind the teasing. 'How profoundly you pleased and encouraged me!' he wrote on 16 December.

How vividly I realize that love has made you perceptive and that 'everything became clear to you!' From the tone of my letter, you recognized, with incredible sensitivity, that your letter, to which this was the reply, had—how should I put it—somewhat disturbed me. Perhaps I hadn't read it properly. But there's one thing you've misunderstood: I have never in the slightest considered that you are faced with a <u>choice</u>. And that passage that begins 'Almschi, Almschi!'—I remember it perfectly—was meant in a bantering tone that you don't yet know in me. If I had been speaking to you, I would have laughed and pinched your ear. I was only teasing. You see, my beloved girl, I was so longing for a few words from you at that moment, and then along came this enumeration of the young man's accomplishments and, above all, I couldn't understand how such a thing could matter so much to you. As though you were frittering your heart away! At that moment, the difference in our ages, which (since we began corresponding) I'd not felt anymore and was immensely happy that I hadn't, suddenly weighed on me anew. However, I made every effort to get over it <u>immediately</u>. And this, my Alma, must be our strenuous endeavour, throughout our lives, never to let <u>susceptibility</u> get the better of us. But I had to be frank and write it out of my soul. . . .[105] Soon we'll come face to face at last and learn to know one another. . . . Before, it was all really only a sort of 'conversation' between us—the social barriers, etc., were removed by this letter in which, for the first time, my beloved, you struck the note that will determine our lives and our love . . .[106]

Before returning to Vienna, Mahler asked Alma to tell her mother 'everything':

As you know, I wanted to talk to her myself to begin with—but that was when I (and above all you) was still undecided.—At that time, it would have been more of a consultation with her, since she knows you so well. But now that everything's already so definite and indissoluble between us, I wouldn't know what to say to her other than 'Give me what belongs to me. Allow me to breathe and to live'—for your love has become as much a condition of my existence as the beating of my pulse and my heart. And it seems to me to be ever more significant and fundamental to our whole future that, precisely during our 'high time' (*hohe Zeit*) (which is in fact the true <u>wedding</u> (*Hochzeit*), where souls intermingle after having 'recognized' one another) we have been not physically but only spiritually united and have grown together so closely. We could not in many months have told one another so much nor have understood all this so fully

---

[104] AMM2. 271; AMM1. 248.

[105] Unpubl. opening lines of a letter of 16 Dec. (dated 17th in AMM), AMM1. 272; AMM2. 249.

[106] AMM1. 271; AMM2. 248. In her anxiety to hide her uneasiness, Alma probably misunderstood what Mahler wrote concerning success. In the passage quoted at the beginning of this chapter, he advises her not to underestimate success. Two pages of this same letter, written on the morning of 16 Dec., have been inverted. The unpubl. first part of it directly precedes the passage beginning 'Schütte das Kind' (AMM1. 272) and ending 'der wir geizen'. The passage 'Eigentlich kommt es mir' (AMM1. 271; AMM2. 249) is both preceded and followed by a few more unpubl. lines, then comes the passage 'Ich bitte dich auch', which is in turn followed by the last paragraph of AMM1. 271 (AMM2. 248), which ends on p. 272.

as we have in these two (interminably long) weeks. I'm so blissfully aware that, in this short time, we've ripened under a sun more powerful than that radiant star above, for the latter requires an entire summer, whereas our whole beings have blossomed in two weeks. This would certainly not have been so if I hadn't had to go away at the very moment when, in the literal sense of the words, you opened up and gave yourself to me. . . . My—I'm having trouble finding words. They're all so hollow, because they've been worn out by apathy and faintheartedness. You know, my only treasure, what it means when I say 'My dearest beloved! My Alma!' May you be blessed and preserved for me! Oh that I may become a blessing to your life since that, from now on, is the earthly kingdom in which I take root and hope to grow.[107]

Three days before his return, Mahler wrote from Dresden to tell his fiancée about his visit to Strauss.[108] He enclosed another copy of the programme of the Second Symphony, explaining that it was 'intended only for more superficial and unintelligent people', and bitterly lamenting the fact that she could not hear the Second Symphony before the Fourth, which would be 'completely alien' to her on account of its 'humour' and 'naïveté'. Once again, he told her that she had become the focal point of his whole existence and that he was constantly thinking of 'the details of our future life'.[109]

Left to her own devices during Mahler's absence, Alma had by no means given up making conquests. This is what she wrote in her diary one evening, after going to a performance of *Die Meistersinger*:[110]

Across the aisle, but in the same row, sat young Dr. Adler, whom I find exceedingly attractive, and I more than flirted with him. We ended by smiling at one another. I suddenly noticed to my horror that Mahler[111] was sitting next to him and had probably been watching the whole manœuvre. I was ashamed, quite simply ashamed. Then I noticed that M. was looking away, so I quickly glanced in Adler's direction and we gazed longingly at one another—he's got long, beautiful hands—not caring about who might be watching us. There's something extraordinarily sensual in such exchanges of glances and the man's very handsome, with black night eyes and . . . in short, a face that I find attractive. It has class, which is more than one can say for the good Mahler.[112] But of course I remain faithful to Gustav in my thoughts. These brazen glances didn't come from the heart.

That same day, Alma had finally resolved to 'make a clean breast of it' to Zemlinsky:

I've written to Alex; he'll be furious and never forgive me. I wrote: 'Alex! You're staying away because you know everything. You know about all that's happened. You know

---

[107] AMM1. 271; AMM2. 248.   [108] See Chap. 11.

[109] AMM1. 274; AMM2. 251. Letter of 18 (not 19) Dec.

[110] 12 Dec. No mistake is possible because this was the only performance of *Die Meistersinger* given in Vienna during Mahler's absence. According to Alma's diary, the principals were Gutheil-Schoder, Hilgermann, Winkelmann, Schrödter, and Hesch.

[111] Here again, Alma refers to her pale, rich young suitor (probably Felix Muhr) as 'Mahler'. But no confusion is possible, as the real Mahler was in Berlin.

[112] 'Mahler'. Probably the young man already mentioned.

even unimaginable thoughts. These last weeks have been torture for me. You know how much I loved you. You filled my life entirely. This love has ended as suddenly as it began, it's been supplanted—and now I'm in love again with renewed intensity! I'd like to go down on my knees to beg your forgiveness for the pain that I've caused you. There are things that are beyond our power to control—perhaps you can explain them. You who know me much better than I know myself. I shall never forget the blissful hours I have had thanks to you—don't you forget them either. If you're the man I think you are, you'll come on Monday, give me your hand and the first kiss of friendship. Be nice, Alex, we can mean so much to each other, if you're willing, and remain faithful friends forever. But above all, please answer me at once and say exactly what you feel—Mama won't read the letter. Forgive me, I don't know what's going on in me any more. Your Alma.'[113]

'My poor Alex,' she wrote in her diary four days later,

he's terribly angry, refuses to write and quite rightly hates me. I could weep at the thought of the pain I'm causing him—the poor, poor fellow! I loved him so much. Afternoon—I'd just got up, because I'm, inexplicably, so exhausted, when I suddenly had a premonition that something was about to happen. I went to the door and . . . Alex was coming up the stairs—I was speechless. He came into the room, paler than usual and rather quiet. I went to him, drew his head onto my breast and kissed his hair—I felt so strange. Only then did we sit down beside each other—we, who had wrestled with one another in the fiercest frenzies of passion—to talk about what was on our minds; he was a bit sarcastic, as usual, but otherwise kind, touchingly kind. My eyes were filled with tears the whole time, but my senses were silent. A beautiful, beautiful feeling was buried today. Gustav, you'll have to do a lot to make up for it. Although it was I who told him that I didn't love him anymore and he should really have been the one to feel humiliated, it was I who felt that very strongly . . . He seemed so dignified and so pure, so vastly superior to me! Had he but uttered an angry or accusing word, I would never have felt this way. I revere you, Alex, as much as it is possible to revere anyone . . .[114]

Later that day she wrote: 'My poor Alex, his face betrayed his suffering. You noble, noble person! . . . I'm physically ill from all the emotional turmoil of the last weeks.' The following day, she received another letter from Mahler, which strengthened her decision.

He's a dear, dear man. What a joy it is to think of him. How kindly and lovingly he writes. And Alex?—if only I knew how he was feeling—poor fellow. But one thing was curious: I was and remained quite calm yesterday, I looked at him and suddenly realized with a shudder how ugly he is, how strongly he smells, etc.—midsummer night's dream![115]—things that I hadn't noticed at all before. It's strange, all the same. Could there really be something from outside that comes over people? There seems to be. Sometimes I have the impression that there is. I shall never forget these last weeks.

---

[113] Alma copied this letter into AMT.   [114] AMT, 16 Dec.
[115] Here Alma refers to the episode where the fairy Titania, under the influence of a love potion, passionately kisses Bottom the weaver, who is disguised as an ass.

Mahler had been surprised and shocked by several things Alma had written in her letters. They seemed to indicate misunderstandings so serious that he felt they had to be cleared up immediately. One day, for instance, she excused herself for writing 'more briefly than usual', explaining that she was expecting Zemlinsky, who 'knows everything and yet still continues to give me lessons', thus showing 'fortitude and magnanimity' in the way in which he was overcoming his grief. In another letter she told Mahler about an afternoon she had spent with Justi 'without talking lovingly' about him. She even described a conversation with Burckhard, in which he had said that two people with personalities (*Individualitäten*) as strong as hers and Mahler's could never be happy together, for one of them would eventually have to 'be the loser'.[116]

These things exasperated Mahler. Feeling that nothing should be left in doubt, he wrote a last letter to Alma just before leaving Dresden.

Hotel Bellevue, Dresden
[Thursday 19 December 1901][117]
My dearest Almschi!
It's with a somewhat heavy heart that I'm writing to you today, my beloved Alma, for I know I must hurt you and yet I can't do otherwise. I've got to tell you the feelings that your letter of yesterday aroused in me, for they're so basic to our relationship that they must be clarified and thoroughly discussed once and for all if we're to be happy together.

Admittedly, I only read between the lines (for once again, my Almschi, it was only with the greatest difficulty that I managed to read the lines themselves). There seems to me to be a glaring contradiction between this letter and those which I've been receiving from you since the evening of *Die Zauberflöte*. You wrote then: 'I want to become the sort of person you <u>wish</u> and <u>need</u>!' These words made me immensely happy and blissfully confident. Now, perhaps without realizing it, you take them back. Let me begin by going through your letter point by point. First, your conversation with Burckhard—what do you understand by personality (*Individualität*)?[118] Do you consider yourself a personality? You remember I once told you that every human being has something indefinably personal that cannot be attributed to either heredity or environment. It's this that somehow makes a person peculiarly what he or she is and, in this sense, every human being is an individual (*Individuum*). But what you and Burckhard mean is something quite different. A human being can only acquire the sort of personality you mean after a long experience of struggle and suffering and thanks to an inherent and powerfully developed disposition. Such a personality is very rare. Besides, you couldn't possibly already be the sort of person who's found a rational ground for her existence within herself and who, in all circumstances, maintains and develops her own individual and immutable nature and preserves it from all that's alien and negative, for everything in you is as yet unformed, unspoken and undeveloped. Although you're an adorable, infinitely adorable and enchanting girl with an upright soul,

---

[116] 'Must I be the loser?' she had written in her diary that day. 'I can't and won't. And yet I feel I'm on a lower level and it wouldn't hurt me to be pulled up a bit.' (Alma's diary, 15 Dec.)

[117] Like most of Mahler's letters, this one was undated.

[118] Mahler used the word 'Individualität' for 'personality' throughout the letter.

and a richly talented, frank and already self-assured person, you're still not a personality. What you are to me, Alma, what you could perhaps be or become—the dearest and most sublime object of my life, the loyal and courageous companion who understands and advances me, my stronghold invulnerable to enemies from both within and without, my peace, my heaven, in which I can constantly immerse myself, find myself again and rebuild myself—is so unutterably exalted and beautiful, so much and so great, in a word, my wife. But even this will not make you a personality in the sense in which the word is applied to those supreme beings who not only shape their own existence but also that of humanity and who alone deserve to be called personalities. I can tell you one thing, however, and that is that in order to be or to become such a personality, it's no use whatsoever just to desire or to wish it. Goldmark once told me with pride that he deliberately avoided listening to, or looking at, any new music in order not to lose his personality. And that to me, my little Alma, was proof of his total lack of personality! It's just as though one were to avoid eating beef at all costs in order not to turn into a bull. You must realize, my Alma, that everything you absorb can only be nourishment to you and will determine your inner growth either favorably or unfavorably. The important thing is that this nourishment should agree with you, be beneficial to you and that your organism should be able to digest it. Not one of the Burckhards, Zemlinskys, etc., is a personality. Each one of them has his own peculiarity—such as an eccentric address, illegible handwriting, etc.—which, because inwardly lacking self-confidence, he defends, by constantly remaining on his guard against his 'nourishment' for fear of becoming unoriginal. A true personality, on the other hand, is like a robust organism that, with unconscious sureness, seeks out and digests the nourishment appropriate to it and vigorously rejects what is unsuitable. Happy he whose early development is not impeded or even completely upset by harmful things. Perhaps an initially healthy organism lays the foundation for its own subsequent weakness and sickliness by being fed on unsuitable and noxious things.

Now, after this somewhat lengthy introduction, I finally come to you! My Alma, look! Your entire youth, and therefore your entire life, has been constantly threatened, escorted, directed (while you always thought you were independent) and abused by these highly confused companions who spend their time groping around in the dark and on false trails, drowning out their inner beings with loud shouting and continually mistaking the shell for the nut. They've constantly flattered you, not because you enriched their lives with your own but because you exchanged big-sounding words with them (genuine opposition makes them uncomfortable, for they only like grandiloquent words—I'm referring more to people like Burckhard than to Zemlinsky, whom I don't know but imagine to be rather better, although he's undoubtedly confused and insecure too), because you all intoxicate each other with verbosity (you think yourselves 'enlightened', but you merely drew your curtains so that you could worship your beloved gaslight as though it were the sun) and because you're beautiful and attractive to men who, without realizing it, instinctively pay homage to charm. Just imagine if you were ugly, my Alma. You've become (and however harsh I sound you'll nevertheless forgive me because of my real and already inexhaustible love for you) vain about the things these people think they see in you and wish to see in you (i.e., you would really like to be what you appear to them to be) but which, thank God, and as you yourself said in your sweet letter, is only the superficial part of you. Since these people also flatter each other all the time and instinctively oppose a superior being because he disconcerts them and makes demands on them that they cannot live up to, they find you, on account of your charms, an exceptionally attractive and, due to your lack of pertinent argument, a most <u>comfortable</u> opponent. Thus all of you have spent your time running around in circles and presuming to settle the affairs of humanity between you—'<u>What you can't touch is utterly remote from you</u>.'[119] And the <u>arrogance</u> that invariably characterizes such people, who regard their own insignificant and exceedingly limited thought processes as the sole task of intellectuals—of that arrogance even you, my Almschi, are not free. Some of your remarks (and I've no intention of taking you to task for them, for I know full well that they're only a façon de parler—even though that, too, comes from an acquired way of thinking) such as that 'we don't <u>agree</u> on several things, ideas, etc.' prove it, as do many others! My little Alma, we must agree in <u>our love</u> and in our hearts! But in our ideas? My Alma! What are your ideas? Schopenhauer's chapter on women, the whole deceitful and viciously shameless immorality of Nietzsche's superiority of an élite, the turbid meanderings of Maeterlinck's drunken mind, Bierbaum and company's public house humour, etc., etc.? These, <u>thank God</u>, are not your ideas but theirs! That this wonderful and supremely incomprehensible world is nothing more than the humorless joke of some thoroughly musty and obtuse 'natural force', totally unconscious of either itself or us (and therefore not even on a level with man, for whom all of you have so little regard), a bubble that will one day burst; that this miraculous heart that so inexplicably fills me with bliss or grief is only a lump of flesh with two valves, my brain merely a mass of very cleverly 'twisted' jelly interwoven with fibres and filaments filled with blood, etc., etc. is certainly not your idea but that of everybody who, in truth, comes by it very easily now that the great scientists (exclusively great men who, moreover, didn't regard life as a mathematical exercise) have discovered it, thanks to the labours they <u>performed</u> so diligently, <u>silently</u> and without bragging.

So here am I, poor fellow, who couldn't sleep at night for joy at having found her, her who, <u>from the start</u>, was intimately at one with him in everything, who, as a woman, belonged wholly to him and had become an integral part of him; who had even written to him that she felt she could do nothing better than embrace and enter into his world; who, through her faith in him, no longer searches but has become convinced that his creed is hers, because she loves him, etc., etc.

Again I wonder what this obsession is that has fixed itself in that little head I love so indescribably dearly, that you must be and remain yourself—and what will become of this obsession when once our passion is sated (and that will be very soon) and we have to begin, not merely residing, but living together and loving one another in companionship? This brings me to the point that is the real heart and core of all my anxieties, fears and misgivings, the real reason why every detail that points to it has acquired such significance: you write '<u>to you and of my music</u>—<u>Forgive me, but we must take that into account too</u>!' In this matter, my Alma, it's absolutely imperative that we understand one another clearly at <u>once</u>, before we see each other again! Unfortunately, I have to begin with you and am, indeed, in the strange position of having, in a sense to set <u>my</u> music against yours, of having to put it into the proper perspective and defend it against you, who don't really know it and in any case don't yet understand it. You won't think me vain, will you, Alma? Believe me, this is the first time in my life that I'm talking about it to someone who doesn't have the right approach to it. Would it be

---

[119] *Faust, Part II*, i. 4918.

possible for you, from now on, to regard <u>my</u> music as <u>yours</u>? I prefer not to discuss 'your' music in detail just now—I'll revert to it later. In general, however—how do you picture the married life of a husband and wife who are both composers? Have you any idea how ridiculous and, in time, how degrading for both of us such a peculiarly competitive relationship would inevitably become? What will happen if, just when you're 'in the mood', you're obliged to attend to the house or to something I might happen to need, since, as you wrote, you ought to relieve me of the menial details of life? Don't misunderstand me and start imagining that I hold the bourgeois view of the relationship between husband and wife, which regards the latter as a sort of plaything for her husband and, at the same time, as his housekeeper. Surely you would never suspect me of feeling and thinking that way, would you? But one thing is certain and that is that you must become 'what I need' if we are to be happy together, i.e., my wife, not my colleague. Would it mean the destruction of your life and would you feel you were having to forgo an indispensable highlight of your existence if you were to give up <u>your</u> music entirely in order to possess and also to be mine instead?

This point <u>must</u> be settled between us before we can even contemplate a union for life. For instance, what do you mean by 'I haven't done any work since! . . . Now I'm going to get down to work', etc., etc.—What sort of work? Composing? For your own pleasure or in order to enrich humanity's heritage? You write 'I feel that I now have nothing better to do than to submerge myself in you, I play your songs, read your letters, etc.' I understood and imbibed this like a promise of eternal bliss. But the fact that, precisely during this period (which I've called our true 'Hoch Zeit') (high time), your conscience should be bothering you because you're not working on theory or counterpoint, is incomprehensible to me! As I've already said, I'm not talking about your compositions, which in any case I don't know yet, but only about the nature of your relationship to me, which must perforce shape our future. I must go now—to work (you see, I <u>really</u> must, for a whole company of 300 people is waiting for me). I'll continue this letter—perhaps the most important I'll ever have to write to you—this afternoon.

There, the rehearsal's over and here I am again, pretty tired and also really rather depressed. I have read through what I wrote this morning, but it was written in such haste, since it must be in your hands tomorrow, that I fear it's become quite illegible; so don't fling my own reproaches back at me, for it's only due to the haste that my profession imposes on me. You, however, have only <u>one</u> profession from now on: <u>to make me happy</u>. Do you understand what I mean, Alma? I'm quite aware that you must be happy with me in order to be able to make me happy, but the roles in this play, which could as easily turn out to be a comedy as a tragedy (and either would be wrong), must be correctly assigned. The role of 'composer', the 'worker's' role, falls to me—yours is that of the loving companion and understanding partner! Are you satisfied with it? I'm asking a great deal, a very great deal—and I can and may do so because I know what I have to give and will give in exchange.

I simply cannot understand the heartless way in which you treat Zemlinsky. Were you in love with him? Then how can you now demand that he play the unhappy role of continuing to be your teacher? You consider it manly and noble of him that, with suffering written on his face, he sits facing you, meek and silent and, as it were, 'obeys orders'?! You were in love with him and can endure this? And what sort of a face should I put on if I were sitting there too—and you ought to be thinking of me as sitting there too! Is your life not subject to other forces of nature now—hasn't its course been altered too much for you to be willing and able gradually to resume your former activities, theory (nature of the violin? was what I read but couldn't understand), Philharmonic concerts conducted by Hellmesberger (!) etc.? How were you able to 'make conversation' with my sister whose heart was wide open to you and who was only too anxious to give you the whole of it? Could you really spend a whole afternoon with her without talking lovingly of me and about me? Almschi, Almschi—it's all quite incomprehensible to me! What sort of conventions are these that can still come between us—what fourth instance is still imminent?! What's all this about 'stubborness', about 'pride'? Towards me who trustingly gave my whole heart and, from the first moment, dedicated my whole life to you—(though I also know certain pretty, rich, cultivated, young, etc., girls and women). I beg you, Almschi, read my letter carefully. There must never be any question of a passing flirtation between us. Before we talk to each other again, things must be absolutely clear between us. You've got to know <u>what</u> I desire and expect from you, what I can offer you and what <u>you must be to me</u>. You must 'renounce' (as you write) all <u>superficiality</u>, all <u>convention</u>, all vanity and delusion (as far as personality and work are concerned). You must give yourself to me <u>unconditionally</u>, shape your future life, in every detail, entirely in accordance with my needs and desire nothing in return save my <u>love</u>! What this last is, Alma, I can't tell you—I've talked of it too much already. I can tell you one thing more, however: I could sacrifice both my life and my happiness for the one I loved as I would love you if you were to become my wife.

I had to unburden myself in this unrestrained and almost (it must seem immodest to you) immoderate manner today. And, Alma, I must have your answer to this letter before I come to see you on Saturday. You will have these lines by tomorrow, Friday, so you can and, if you're what I hope you are, indeed will <u>have to answer</u> me immediately and get your letter to me by Saturday afternoon. Better still, I'll send a servant to pick it up at your house on Saturday morning. Almschi, beloved, be strict with yourself— and (sweet and beautiful though I otherwise find it) don't be swayed by your love for me. Imagine that you're writing to a stranger who has to report to me. Tell me everything you have to tell me quite ruthlessly and bear in mind that to part now would be infinitely preferable to a continued self-deception for, as I know myself, that would end in a disaster for both of us.

What a terrible moment I'm preparing for you—I do realize it, Alma—but you will appreciate that I myself am suffering just as much, even though this is poor consolation. Although I'm aware that you don't yet know Him I pray God that He may guide your hand, my beloved, so that it may write the truth and not be moved by infatuation— for this is a crucial moment that will decide the fate of two lives for eternity! God bless you, my dearest, my love, whatever you may have to tell me. I won't write tomorrow but will wait for your letter on Saturday and, as I've said, I'll send a servant to get it, so have it ready.

A thousand loving kisses, my Alma, and I beg you: be truthful!
Your Gustav.[120]

---

[120] The original of this letter, which Alma always claimed in my presence to have destroyed, is now in the Moldenhauer Archive, Spokane, Washington, USA. A copy has also survived in one of the typed MSS of *Ein Leben mit Gustav Mahler*. It was first publ. in the first version of my biography (Doubleday, New York, 1973). Like all passages from Alma's diaries and letter in this chapter, it was trans. for this vol. by Roy MacDonald Stock.

One wonders what to make of such a letter, which points up Mahler's self-centredness as much as his love for Alma. In his desire for total honesty, he goes straight to the point and cares little about hurting his fiancée's feelings. For instance, he doesn't hesitate to write: 'Just imagine if you were ugly', thereby implying that 'people find you witty only because you're beautiful'. Though passionately in love and therefore weak and vulnerable, Mahler nevertheless attempts to remain lucid and is constantly questioning himself, fearful of his infatuation. His criticisms of Alma are strikingly similar to those made by Zemlinsky.[121] In fact it would be hard to imagine a woman less likely to bow to his demands than Alma. Flirtatious and selfish, capricious and vain, she was nevertheless momentarily swept away by the force of his personality and the intensity of his genius. After receiving his letter, she wrote in her diary:

Friday, 20 December. Shopping with Else in an open cab. Back home to this letter. My heart stood still—Give up my music—relinquish the one thing I've lived for until now? My first thought was to call the whole thing off . . . But then I burst into tears because I realized that I love him. Half fainting, I dressed and, still crying, went by cab to the *Siegfried* performance! I told Pollak and he was furious—he'd never have believed it possible. I feel as though my heart had been torn from my breast by an icy hand. Mama and I talked about him until deep into the night. She read the letter—! I was so distraught. I find it so inconsiderate and clumsy of him—it could have come out by itself—very gently—but this way it will forever remain a thorn in my side . . .

Saturday, 21 December. I forced myself to sleep soundly the whole night, read through his letter first thing this morning and suddenly felt warm all over. How would it be if, out of love for him, I were to give up—that which has been! I must now admit that hardly any music interests me apart from his. Yes, he's right—I must live entirely for him, in order that he may be happy. I now feel in a strange way that I deeply and truly love him. For how long? I don't know, but that's already a great deal—a great deal. I long for him more than I can say.

By advising her daughter to break with Mahler, it seems that Anna Moll in fact helped her to decide to give in, since Alma had consulted her mother only in order to test her loyalty. After she had written to Mahler to give him the required promise, Alma's heart 'trembled in expectation' throughout the morning. While she was out on an errand in Döbling, she ran into Mahler's servant, who was on his way to pick up her answer and bring her another letter, which, in her excitement, she read on the spot.

A thousand heartfelt regards from the same air you breathe, my homeland! I'd hardly entered my room (how lovely that you already know it!) before I saw the sweet and familiar lines from your hand and, not without emotion, read the tender words that must have been written before my letter of yesterday. That has weighed heavily on my soul these past two days, as I thought of the first impression I must have made on you. I hope for you as well as for myself that you read only my love and loyalty in it and appreciated

---

[121] In the letter quoted above.

their strength and depth. You understood, didn't you, how hard and implacably truthful I can be in love. Everything must be clear between us before we embrace one another—for this afternoon I'll no longer have the composure or self-control to tell you and ask you about all that must be decided. Never have I more ardently desired or more fearfully awaited a letter from you than the one my servant will shortly bring me. What will you say to me! But don't misunderstand me, the thing that really matters is not what you say, but what you are! The passion that has now quite literally enslaved us must for the moment be kept under control (and this can be done only if we're not together— that's precisely why I've been writing while there is still time), so that we may with inward reassurance and loving confidence be able to tie the knot that must bind us together indissolubly until our last breath.[122]

After receiving Alma's letter, which was the greatest proof of love she could possibly have given him, Mahler went to the Hohe Warte that afternoon looking calmer and more confident. For the time being, the clouds were dispersed.[123] A few days after his return, he brought his fiancée the score of the Fourth Symphony. She did not understand it at all, and with excessive candour declared: 'For that kind of thing I prefer Haydn!' He smiled, and predicted that she would think differently one day. While they were playing passages from the work together at the piano, Alma dropped a note and Mahler said: 'I'll make you a present of the semiquaver, even a quaver, or a crotchet, or even—all of it—or me!' Afterwards they went down to Frau Moll, and Mahler said, 'Mama, we've finished playing but I still need your daughter's hand.'[124]

'How lovely it was yesterday!' Alma wrote in her diary the following day.

My longing for him is indescribable. Everything about him is dear and familiar to me, his breath so pure . . . I feel that I could live for him . . . If—then we'd get married in spring—that's what I've been thinking . . . Oh!—To have a child by him if only he's strong enough. He so desperately hopes for that. Nothing, nothing, nothing—other than to belong to him.

She went to see Justi in the afternoon and she and Mahler kissed each other when his sister was out of the room and held hands in the cab on the way back to the Hohe Warte. Carl Moll had had a 'kind and serious' talk with Alma that same morning:

He remonstrated with me. He's right. On the one hand, he felt he could be glad because he thinks that Gustav can't last much longer . . .[125] but he thinks differently as far as I'm concerned. I have no heart?! ['too much', she added later in the margin] yet I have such a warm feeling for him. And I also have the feeling that he uplifts me, whereas my being

---

[122] AMM1. 276; AMM2. 253.

[123] In fact Alma never completely gave up composing. But she later maintained that the wound inflicted by Mahler's ban long continued to fester and never completely healed.

[124] According to AMT, this episode occurred on 4 Jan. 1902. A similar one is recorded in AMT on 7 Dec. 1901 (the title of the work they played together is not disclosed), but at this time Mahler had not yet formally asked Anna Moll for Alma's hand (AMM3. 365).

[125] The sentence is unfinished. The conversation with Moll took place on 22 Dec. According to Mahler's letter, written in Berlin on 15 Dec., Moll had attended the performance of the Fourth Symphony there.

with Burckhard encourages my flippancy. I feel ashamed of my obscenity (*Zoten*) when Gustav's listening—and also can hardly say all I'm thinking. Is one happier with a frivolous and unscrupulous life, or when one has woven oneself such a beautiful and sublime conception of the world? Freer in the first case—happier??? One becomes a better and more noble person. Again, is that not an obstacle on the way to freedom? Yes, yes, a thousand times yes, and I say unto you, be hard! He's right: we're suited to each other like fire and water—both mentally and physically! Yes, certainly! But must one of us be the loser? Couldn't two radically different views with the help of love be made into one beautiful one? I know everything—he's a sick man, my poor darling, he weighs 63 kilos—far too little—I'll look after him as though he were a child. I love him with infinite affection. It's sweet that he can't pronounce his R's and curious that he would like me to be called Marie[126] because he loves the strong R in the middle of the name—curious and . . . ! I'm so afraid that he'll fall ill; I don't know how to explain it— I can just see him lying in a pool of blood.

Alma here reveals her hidden motivation. She loves Mahler not only because he is, as she herself puts it, 'great and important', but also because he appears to her to be weak and defenceless, and because she hopes, thanks to him, to escape from herself and her preoccupation with smutty stories (Zoten).

On 23 December, Mahler went with Justi to the Hohe Warte, and he and Alma became officially engaged in the presence of Carl and Anna Moll. 'From now on,' Alma wrote,

he alone must fill my heart, he alone. From now on I will never even look at any other man. Everything to him, my husband! We're already so united that we can hardly get any closer. Whereas I was madly, passionately in love with Alex Z., I'm now filled with the most sacred feelings. I once told Z. I wanted to become the mother of his children, but I wasn't really sincere. I thought then that I was incapable of feeling anything so deep and so beautiful—today, I didn't say it but I feel it. When we sit pressed up against one another like that, it's though he were my body—not the slightest bit strange—so unimaginably precious to me . . .[127]

She still lived in 'fear of the gods who can't tolerate any pure joy', but she was prepared to give up everything for Mahler, since 'I already belong to him to him and to Justi whom I love because she's his flesh and blood. Justi told Mama that Gustav had said: ". . . Isn't it a crime for me, Autumn, to chain Spring to my side? She will have to forgo Summer." No, my Gustav, no!' Mahler now took to going to the Hohe Warte almost every day, often staying until late at night. And sometimes, when he missed the last tramcar, he cheerfully walked all the way home, right across the city. One day, he and Alma discussed religion. The daughter of free thinkers, she violently opposed Christian beliefs. He was indignant at her lack of faith and 'found myself in the curious position of a Jew upholding Christ to a Gentile'.

---

[126] Freud remarked that Mahler's habit of calling his wife by his mother's Christian name was a symptom of 'Mutterbindung'.

[127] AMT, 23 Dec. 1901.

One evening, at a dinner party, Alma met the critic Ludwig Karpath. She listened to him discussing Mahler with the composer Adalbert von Goldschmidt.[128] Furious at having had the score of his latest work returned to him by the Director of the Opera, Goldschmidt violently attacked Mahler: 'He's not even a man, he's a gnome and his music's not music'. Karpath warmly defended Mahler, declaring that he was 'in a position to know, since it was thanks to me that the Hofoper engaged him!' The following day, Mahler asked Alma about the party and she, 'knowing nothing about Karpath except that he was Goldmark's nephew', told Mahler what he had said. Mahler was furious.[129]

In his memoirs, Hanslick's successor on the *Neue Freie Presse*, Julius Korngold, has painted a portrait of his colleague Ludwig Karpath which is not altogether flattering. According to him, Karpath lacked systematic musical education and had long since concluded that his only chance of holding his own among his better qualified colleagues was to establish close relationships with influential people. He could be kind and helpful as long as his vanity wasn't at stake. He had undoubtedly hoped that Mahler would be grateful for the help he had provided at the time of his appointment. It seems he had a particular gift for ingratiating himself with important personages and had no doubt hoped to become Mahler's confidant and adviser, something he succeeded in doing later on with several other famous musicians, such as Felix Mottl, Richard Strauss, Felix Weingartner, Franz Schalk, and Bruno Walter. He made himself indispensable by acting as intermediary between artists and the high-ranking officials with whom he was on the best of terms. Karpath's special talents eventually earned him the position of chairman of the Vienna Music Critics' Association and the titles of Hofrat and Professor, 'in recognition of his "profound knowledge"', as his sycophantic supporters, in their equally profound ignorance, felt immediately obliged to proclaim'.[130]

A few days after Alma had told Mahler of Karpath's remark, Karpath came to see Mahler to ask him to write an article about the Opera's forthcoming projects for the Christmas issue of his paper. Mahler refused, saying he had 'neither the time nor the inclination to write articles.' But just as Karpath was leaving, he called him back: 'Wait, there's something I have to say to you!' He

---

[128] There is a slight discrepancy between Alma's account and that of Karpath, who does not mention Goldschmidt. Adalbert von Goldschmidt (1832–1906), a Viennese composer, wrote several operas on texts he wrote himself: *Helianthus*, performed in Leipzig in 1881; *Gäa*, a huge dramatic trilogy which remains unperformed and unpubl.; *Die fromme Helene*; and an oratorio *Die sieben Todsünden*, which had a short-lived success in Berlin. The incident took place on 19 Nov. 1901, according to AMT.

[129] Reading Alma's memoirs, we find that indiscretions of this kind in her past were by no means unusual. In 1900 her stepfather had told her of the intrigues within the Austrian section of the International Exhibition in Paris. She had reported this conversation to Karl Kraus, who publ. in *Die Fackel* an article which infuriated Carl Moll and created needless ill-feeling. The same thing happened later, when Alma informed Kraus about Julius Epstein's machinations at the Conservatory, or at least passed on what she knew of them from Zemlinsky. Kraus wrote a biting account of them, with consequences that can be imagined (AML 24). In 1906, indiscreet talk by Alma gave rise to a temporary quarrel between Bruno Walter and Pfitzner, one of his closest friends (see below, Vol. iii, Chap. 3).

[130] KIW 70 ff.

then reproached him with having publicly defended the contralto Edyth Walker, 'who's no longer suited to my ensemble'. Karpath replied that his opinion was shared by the majority of the Viennese public, whereat Mahler sat bolt upright in his chair and exclaimed, 'I think I know better than you and your colleagues whether or not I can use a singer! As a result of your attacks, the prince has forced me to re-engage her.[131] I take that as a personal offence!' And then, raising his voice: 'Don't forget the respect you owe me as Director of the Opera—and I'm not talking about myself as a composer. For a while, I thought you understood my work, but I see now that I was wrong. Anyhow, I couldn't care less what you and your colleagues write about me as a composer, but,' he added, rising and shaking his fist at Karpath, 'if you try to undermine my authority as Director of the Opera, I'll show you!' Then, abruptly, he sat down again, asked Karpath to do likewise, and finally came to the point. He accused the critic of having lied by declaring in public that he Mahler owed his position as director of the Opera to him. Karpath admitted to having touched on the subject two days earlier but said that it had been in private, with a young girl he had met at the house of the singing teacher, Gustav Gciringer. Moreover, he had merely said that he had been not 'uninvolved' (*unbeteiligt*) in Mahler's appointment. The young girl had plied him with numerous questions, but the conversation had gone no further. Mahler then calmed down and explained with a smile that the conversation had been reported to him quite differently. Karpath was upset that he, a 'fanatic of the truth',[132] should have been thus misrepresented, but before they parted Mahler assured him that he bore him no grudge.[133] The incident at least served to open Alma's eyes to her fiancé's touchiness, and perhaps alerted Mahler to one of her most alarming character-istics, which was always to set her friends and acquaintances against each other by repeating, more or less faithfully, things they had said about each other.

When Mahler went to the Hohe Warte on the day before Christmas, he found his fiancée excitedly making all sorts of preparations that seemed to him somewhat 'excessive' and 'superficial', but he nevertheless stayed a long time with her. 'We felt our blood racing, listened to our hearts beating and were happy . . . I wish I already belonged to him,' she noted. Burckhard, Kolo Moser,

---

[131] Edyth Walker's contract, dated 24 Jan. 1902 and signed by the singer and by Mahler, was sold by Stargardt in Mar. 1988 (catal. 641, no. 914). Her last performance at the Opera was on 22 Sept. 1903.

[132] BMG 104 ff. If one reads *Begegnung mit dem Genius* and compares Karpath's writings with those of other contemporary witnesses, one is indeed impressed with the strict impartiality and fairness of his reporting.

[133] At the end of Dec., when Mahler's engagement was announced, Karpath finally understood what had happened, and wrote to Alma deploring her lack of discretion. She claims that this incident was the cause of a quarrel between Mahler and Karpath, but the quarrel in fact took place three years later, after the first Viennese performance of the *Wunderhorn-Lieder* (see below, Vol. iii, Chap. 2). The disagreement of 1905 did not in any case lead to a complete break with Karpath, who came and interviewed the director of the Opera at the time of his resignation. On the other hand, Mahler resented to the end of his days the article Karpath wrote for the *Münchner Neueste Nachrichten* a few days before his departure for the USA (see below, Vol. iii, Chap. 10).

and Zemlinsky dined at the Hohe Warte that evening; Mahler went home to be with Justi, but had a letter delivered to his fiancée:

The first Christmas Eve on which I send you my good wishes, and also the last, for from now on, my beloved girl, we shall spend it together. What will it be like, Alma, when soon, I hope, united, we shall no longer have need of any go-between?! When I sit here in my room, I can already picture you reigning by my side. My—our happiness seems like a fruit that—having ripened quickly in the warm sun of a love that is perhaps untried but nevertheless happy and confident in the future—will fall from the tree straight into our laps. This day, which united us and all men, even before we knew about one another, in joyful and childlike faith, should always remain a symbol to us so that, even though united and happy in our love, we may leave room in our hearts for the rest of mankind—because an immense and superhuman love, which we can only call divine, has bound us together with a bond that links us indissolubly to all living beings.

On this day, which belongs to children, in whom the seeds of both earthly and divine love take root according to where the Sower casts them, I bless you, my dearest Life. May my life become a blessing to yours, so that, above and beyond our earthly love and through its essence, which must be sacred, you may come to know the divine love, and be able 'silently to revere the unfathomable'! (Essentially, what it all comes down to is that we can never be completely happy so long as there are others who are unhappy). You must understand, my Alma, that I'm unable to say anything else to you today—perhaps nothing will enable you to appreciate the boundlessness and sanctity of my love for you more fully than the fact that—now that I'm so close to the fulfilment of my highest wish and am so intensely happy—I would like to transport us both beyond ourselves into those regions where we shall experience a breath of the eternal and divine—It's <u>thus</u> that I'd like to be yours and you must be mine![134]

On Christmas afternoon, Mahler invited Alma to the Auenbruggergasse. 'I sat on his lap the whole time—I love him so unutterably. We kissed each other so much. He had to conduct *Tannhäuser*. I stayed behind with Justi. I like her.' That day, when he came back from the Opera, Mahler took from his portfolio a sheet of paper, folded in four, saying: 'Today I stole for you.' 'It was,' writes Alma,

the inner title page of *Tannhäuser*. At the bottom right hand corner was written 'On 7 February 1847 I conducted the 13th performance from this score. Richard Wagner.' While conducting *Tannhäuser* that evening Mahler had been upset, as often before, at the thought of this sacred page being turned by any and every Kapellmeister, getting worn and dirty, so he got the idea of removing it. I was fantastically happy. Mahler felt he had rescued it, for the Kapellmeisters thumbed it over carelessly, and Wagner's words were actually almost unrecognizable beneath the dirt and grease of conductors' fingers. We smoothed out the sheet and had it framed. In all innocence I hung it on the wall of our music room.

[134] AMM1. 277; AMM2. 254.

Unfortunately Arnold Rosé spotted it there a few days later and, declaring that 'the whole Opera had been looking for it', took away the precious page.[135]

On 27 December, as the result of someone's indiscretion, the news of Mahler's engagement burst on Vienna like a bombshell. The *Neue Freie Presse* was the first to publish the news in the evening edition, and all the other papers repeated it the next morning. They went into raptures about Alma's youth, beauty, and musical talents, and she received a shower of letters, bouquets, and telegrams. The following evening she went to dinner at the Auenbruggergasse, hoping to calm Mahler, who was exasperated by all the publicity. 'Drank "brotherhood" toast of friendship with Arnold Rosé, but otherwise spent most of the time alone with Gustav in his room. We stood for a long time in a dark corridor and were happy. My one and only wish is to make him happy. He deserves to be.'[136] On the evening of 29 December, Mahler conducted Nicolai's *Die lustigen Weiber* and, for the first time, Alma sat in his box. However, she was so embarrassed by all the opera-glasses trained on her that she did not hear a note of the music and finally moved to the back of the box, where Mildenburg wearing her most ingratiating smile came to congratulate her. Mahler received more prolonged applause than usual and had to take several curtain-calls at the end of the performance. After supper at Hartmann's Restaurant with the Molls, Justi, and Arnold Rosé, he and Alma went for a walk together and decided to get married in the middle of February.

Mahler had told the news to a few close friends before it was announced in the press. To Guido Adler he wrote:

I am engaged! It's still a secret, and I'm only telling those closest to me. My bride's name is Alma Schindler. If you know her, you know everything. If not, I should have to overstep the boundaries of art once more to depict her in words. Forgive me if I don't know what else to say to you today, and please continue to give me your precious friendship in my 'new life'.[137]

After the news had appeared in the press, Mahler wrote thanking Countess Wydenbruck for her congratulations, but regretted seeing 'such an entirely personal matter dragged into the public eye'.[138] A letter from Bruno Walter to his parents describes Mahler's state of mind at that time, and the worries of his friends:

Well, children, what do you think of Mahler's engagement? A surprise, no? Justi's engagement to our Konzertmeister Rosé is an old story; those two would have re-

---

[135] AMM1. 102; AMM2. 106. Alma does not date this episode, but it could only have happened on 25 Dec. 1901, because Mahler did not conduct *Tannhäuser* after that date. The *Tannhäuser* score is now in the ÖNB (Mus. Hs. 3254/1–3). Traces where the page has been folded in four are clearly visible, while Wagner's surname is almost illegible (AMM3. 375).

[136] AMT, 28 Dec.   [137] RAM 36.

[138] BGM. Mahler also sent a card to Prince Montenuovo, laconically announcing the news (Kurt Blaukopf, *Gustav Mahler oder der Zeitgenosse der Zukunft* (Molden, Vienna, 1969), 197).

nounced wedlock if Mahler had not also got engaged; Justi would otherwise not have left her brother alone. His engagement has surprised everyone; even the Lipiners and Spieglers learned of it through the papers; and we too of course. Even Justi heard of it by chance just two days before,[139] when she and Mahler met his future father-in-law in the street and afterwards, when she expressed surprise at his intimacy with that gentleman, Mahler replied: 'Well, perhaps I should tell you that I'm engaged to his daughter.' His bride, Alma Schindler, daughter of the late distinguished landscape painter Schindler (her mother remarried with the painter Moll, so the father-in-law is really her stepfather), is 22 years old, tall and slim and a dazzling beauty, the most beautiful girl in Vienna, from a good family and very rich. Nonetheless we, his friends, are very worried about this thing; he is 41 and she 22, she is a celebrated beauty, accustomed to a glittering life in society, while he is so unworldly and fond of solitude; and there are plenty of other problems one could mention; he himself feels very awkward and embarrassed about being a bridegroom, and is furious if one congratu-lates him. . . . He greeted me with the words: 'What do you think, the papers have got me engaged! That's to say, it's true, I am actually engaged; but please don't congratulate me, or—just congratulate me very quickly—and now let's not talk about it any more.' A funny sort of bridegroom, eh? But they are said to be very much in love.[140]

According to Alma, Mahler had never had any sexual experiences (or so, at any rate, he had apparently told her) and viewed the approach of the moment when their union would be consummated with apprehension. She says that she failed to understand his fears; in her diary she repeatedly refers to the strain that incomplete sexual encounters were putting on both of them.

30 December. Rendez-vous with Gustav . . . We halfway united today . . . He let me feel his strength, his life—and that with such a pure and sacred sensation that I would never have imagined possible . . . He must be suffering terribly. I can guess his torment by my own . . . No one knows how unspeakably intense is my desire. And yet—I can't imagine giving myself to him before the time is ripe. The feeling of wrongdoing and shame would debase the whole gloriously sacred mystery . . . we could hardly tear ourselves away from one another. Why these frightful conventions? Why can't I just move in with him?—Without the blessing. Oh! We're consumed with desire, it's sapping all our strength. He bared his chest and I put my hand on his heart—I feel as though his body were mine . . . I had my hair loose—he likes it that way . . . Oh, to have a child by him! His mind, my looks. If only I were already his!'

On the afternoon of New Year's Day, the two of them were alone in Mahler's room, and, after an exchange of caresses, the supreme moment seemed to have come when

suddenly he lost all his strength and lay limp on my breast, almost crying with shame. I comforted him, even though I was desperately miserable myself. We went home depressed and shattered. He became somewhat more cheerful, but I was suddenly overcome and couldn't help crying—sobbing my heart out—on his chest. . . . I can't

[139] Because Justi knew of her brother's engagement since 9 Dec., the meeting with Moll on the Ring obviously took place before that date.
[140] BWB 52.

describe how frustrating I found the whole thing. First the turmoil deep inside me, then the goal so near—and no satisfaction. And then his self-reproaches, his frightful self-reproaches! My beloved.

However, the single phrase 'Bliss upon bliss' (*Wonne über Wonne*) she recorded for 4 January[141] would seem to indicate that the first obstacles had been overcome. A few days later, Alma noted that 'My poor Gustav is undergoing medical treatment—an inflamed swelling—ice packs, hip-baths, etc., etc.— Was it due to my prolonged resistance? How he must suffer!' Nevertheless, she soon became pregnant. According to her memoirs, this pregnancy before their marriage was a source of 'dreadful torment' to both of them. They had perforce to acknowledge 'the profound truth underlying the laws of bourgeois morality'.

In the meantime, the two families were getting acquainted. On 29 December, Alma sat in the directorial box with her mother and Justi for a performance of *Die lustigen Weiber*. Arnold joined them later for dinner at the Hartmann Restaurant and the date of the two marriages was then decided upon. Two days later, Carl and Anna Moll invited Mahler, Justi, and Arnold for an evening at the Hohe Warte. Since Mahler and Alma had arranged their wedding for mid-February, it was decided that Arnold and Justi would also get married on the same day; Alma could thus move immediately into Justi's room. Over the years, her feelings for her sister-in-law gradually changed from friendliness and affection to hatred.[142] Her memoirs, written many years later, reveal this animosity, which renders many of her assertions doubtful. As noted earlier, if she is to be believed, Mahler's anger when he discovered the intimate relationship between his sister and Arnold Rosé was such that he did not speak to her for several weeks.[143] However, none of Mahler's letters to Justi which have survived confirm this; on the contrary, they contain frequent references to Rosé and even suggest that Mahler was well aware of his sister's feelings toward him. In December, he had written to her from Berlin: 'If only the situation, for you and for me, would take the turn it seems for the moment to be taking!' So he was already thinking of their double marriage. Having overcome her initial distrust, Justi, for her part, became very fond of Alma and did her best to allay her brother's qualms. If Mahler and his sister did have any rows on the subject of Rosé, they took place before he met Alma, for his letters to Justi in 1901 show nothing but affection. Besides, for several years now Mahler had been very close to his future brother-in-law.

As for Mahler's friends and acquaintances, we have already seen that it was with some concern that they viewed his forthcoming marriage to so lovely and lively a young girl who, moreover, moved in a social circle entirely different

[141] In fact, 2 Jan.
[142] Anna Mahler told me in personal conversation that Justi, a warm and passionate woman, though not always good at expressing herself, had a great liking for her sister-in-law for several years, a feeling that was at first completely reciprocated.
[143] According to Alma, Mahler's 'fury' at his sister's 'betrayal' contributed to his own decision to marry, but the lack of any further evidence casts doubt on this assertion.

from their own. Everything about her shocked and irritated them, she later reported: her clothes, her hair-style, her behaviour in public, and the freedom of her language. She for her part made no secret of her scorn for them; she thought they were provincial, narrow-minded, and petty, and objected to the fact that they seemed to treat Mahler as though he were their property.[144] She felt that they were liabilities whom 'Mahler has been dragging behind him like shackles round his feet ever since his youth'.

However, both parties merely eyed each other somewhat suspiciously until they were officially introduced at a dinner that Mahler gave at the Auenbruggergasse on 5 January.[145] He had invited Lipiner and his wife Clementine (sister of Albert Spiegler), Nanna Spiegler (Lipiner's previous wife) and her husband Albert, Mildenburg, Kolo Moser, the Molls, Justi, and Arnold Rosé. Alma later recalled the 'bogus formality' of the party, at which, feeling she was being inspected with all too obvious hostility, she did her best to shock and offend everybody. She had sourly remarked, even before the party, that 'I get no pleasure from being in the company of old ladies'. Throughout the evening, she spoke to no one but her mother and her fiancé and, on the rare occasions when she joined in general conversation, it was either to be rude or to shock with unorthodox opinions. On the subject of the courts and magistrates, she referred to the judges as 'powdered old crones'; of Plato's *Symposium*, she said that it had 'tickled her pink', and about a painting by Guido Reni, of which Lipiner was particularly fond, she asked with calculated ingenuousness, 'What on earth does it represent?' The last straw came when Mildenburg asked her what she thought of Mahler's music and she replied, 'I know very little of it and the little I do know I don't like.' The whole company gaped in consternation. Frau Moll blushed with shame, and only Mahler burst out laughing. In fact, he appeared to take great delight in his fiancée's caustic remarks and kept having long whispered conversations with her, to the exclusion of the rest of the guests. However, sensing the consternation this last sally had caused, he found some trifling excuse to take Alma off to his room. 'It was ghastly in there,' he said. 'We'll be better off alone here for a while.' She complained of the 'examination' to which she was being subjected, and in particular of Lipiner's attitude, his 'superior' tone, and his way of addressing her as 'Mädchen'. She considered him to be 'the most sterile person I've ever met.' How dared he insist that she admire Plato and Guido Reni, who were of no interest to her whatsoever? The absence of the betrothed couple having become somewhat prolonged, Justi went along to remonstrate with them, but in vain. She tried again some fifteen minutes later. When they did finally return to the drawing-room, Mahler made Alma sit between himself and Anna Moll on

---

[144] Alma speaks of 'an old lawyer, dull and obtrusive' who is obviously Emil Freund, Mahler's counsellor until the end of his life. Another former friend she particularly disliked was Fritz Löhr.

[145] Once again Alma's dates do not correspond to the actual weekdays. Thus the dinner party took place either on Fri. 3 Jan. or Sun. 5 Jan.

the sofa, and there, apart from exchanging a few absent-minded words with Mildenburg, she steadfastly continued to ignore the rest of the guests.

They voiced their indignation the following day, in a letter from Lipiner to which Mahler replied, attempting to minimize the incident. Alma, he said, was young, shy, and embarrassed by these strangers whose distrustful looks and obvious misgivings had driven her to distraction. They should be more tolerant and forgive her because of her youth and inexperience. Far from being pacified, however, Lipiner wrote a second letter, which has been preserved in one of Alma's manuscripts and which clearly reveals just how badly Mahler and Alma had behaved. He reproached Mahler for his 'contempt for his fellow-men' (*Menschenverachtung*), his 'profound, lasting and everlasting coldness', and the self-centredness that made him underestimate the wounds he inflicted on the grounds that he himself had already forgotten them. 'At heart,' Lipiner continued, 'you don't consider anyone a person; we're all just <u>objects</u> to you. For no reason at all, you throw people away—you usually pick them up again—but not always—and everything's supposed to be all right again. You make no exceptions for anyone . . .'. As for Alma, Lipiner had 'finished' with her from the evening of the party. Perhaps 'she <u>alone</u>' would satisfy Gustav's requirements. In that case, he could live with her in splendid isolation, undisturbed by 'troublesome, useless people'. Rather than a 'shy and timid young girl', she was all 'unnaturalness, superficiality and heartlessness (*Lieblosigkeit*)', and her behaviour could not have been more affected (*unwahr*) and foolish (*unklug*). Moreover, her remarks were those of an 'unpleasantly impudent, opinionated and hypercritical' creature who, 'from the start, is loath to associate with people to whom she's obliged to show <u>respect</u>, who, straight away, finds it disagreeable that people "judge" her—and who expresses her annoyance in ugly and extravagant language'. Lipiner wondered whether Alma really had 'a deep relationship' with Gustav, and whether Gustav was not allowing himself to be deceived by excuses that did not come directly from her but that he himself had senselessly provoked her to utter.[146]

A break between Mahler and his friends thus seemed inevitable. Alma affirms that they 'swore to ruin me and launched a violent campaign against me'. According to her, moreover, Mildenburg, who had become Lipiner's mistress, was only pretending to be resigned to Mahler's indifference and his firm resolve never to renew his affair with her. Since her arrival in Vienna, their relations had frequently been strained, and he had undoubtedly had to exercise a great deal of self-control on numerous occasions, for example, in the letter he wrote to her shortly before his engagement to Alma was announced.

My very dear Anna, how could you do such a thing to me and run away like that? Were you offended with me? I had something very urgent to write and was sure <u>you'd</u> wait for me! I did so want to have a chat with you. You will come back *soon*, won't you?

[146] AMS contains a copy of this letter and also of another and probably subsequent letter. Bruno Walter possessed another copy of it.

I'll come and see you soon, not just for a quarter of an hour but for a whole afternoon . . . You hope the new events won't cast any shadow over my world. That is all in God's hands, but there's one thing I hope and am sure of, since I know you so well: they won't and must not cast any over your world. In any case, all that is in God's hands, but also in *ours*, for we already know each other in God. Your Gustav.

Alma recounts that, after the official announcement of the engagement, Mildenburg called on Mahler in his office, made a scene, and even pretended to faint, but Mahler, who was well acquainted with her theatrical tricks, 'asked her to walk out into the street with him, where she had to control herself'. She then apparently tried to persuade him to get back to addressing her with the familiar *Du*, but he replied that he would have to consult his fiancée about it. Changing her tactics, she pretended to be interested in Alma, with the result that Mahler promised that he would bring Alma to see her. Like many other men in his situation, he began by lying to his fiancée, claiming that he had never actually had an affair with Mildenburg.[147] Be that as it may, he did indeed take his fiancée one afternoon to Hietzing, where the famous singer occupied a 'gloomy hotel room'. Mildenburg installed Alma in a corner with a score and then made some feeble excuse to drag Mahler off into another room, where their conversation rapidly turned into a heated argument. Meanwhile, Alma studied the 'atrocious' engravings by Franz Strassen illustrating the piano score of *Tristan und Isolde*.[148] She and Mahler then proceeded to quarrel about them on the way home because he admired them, but as Alma puts it, 'the quarrel had nothing to do with either Strassen or his insignificant engravings'. In point of fact, two conflicting influences were at war within Mahler; that of his friends, Lipiner in particular, and that of Alma, daughter and stepdaughter of painters, who 'refused to put up with their contempt and arrogance'. They had thought they could 'use me and my twenty years as a docile instrument to prolong and consolidate their power over Mahler', she wrote. When they realized they had been mistaken, they did their utmost to prove to him her lack of maturity in every possible way.

However, it seems that Mahler must have felt some remorse after that difficult evening when Alma gave free rein to her impudence and contrariness. Between the final rehearsal and the Viennese première of the Fourth Symphony he wrote to Nanna Spiegler:

Tremendously glad you like it so much. You can imagine how much I too felt the need

---

[147] However, according to AMS, Alma had been informed by Mahler of his earlier affair. Furthermore he told her Justi in Hamburg had done everything she could to put an end to it before 'that snake smothered him'. The most painful moment was just before he left for Vienna, when Anna was more in love with him than ever, whereas he had cooled off. After performances she would pursue him through the dark lanes near the theatre, throw herself at his feet, and burst into tears at the slightest excuse. She also disgusted him by parading in front of him completely naked. Still according to Alma's account, Mildenburg was the main reason for his leaving Hamburg. He even had to forbid her to set foot in his house. Mildenburg's final trick was to feign illness and summon a Dominican priest to marry them.

[148] The vocal score of *Tristan*, illustrated by Franz Strassen, had just been publ. by Breitkopf und Härtel.

to talk to you about it. But 'I can't lend words so much importance'[149]—as Siegfried does—the main thing is, the work is there and it's been granted to me to come close to you through it, since you like it and were able to follow it. Incidentally, you'll enjoy it even more tomorrow. Its delicate working doesn't stand up well to an empty echoing hall. Also the interruptions were disturbing but, alas, necessary.[150]

Alma maintains that Mahler's friends made their final attempt to discredit her in January, on the occasion of the second performance of *Das klagende Lied*, which Mahler was conducting, by telling him that she had 'flirted' with other people in the hall all through the first half of the concert.[151] On the same occasion, Mildenburg, though prostrate on her dressing-room sofa after feigning another swoon, made the 'sacrifice' of singing the 'formidable' soprano part, and Mahler's friends hastened to magnify her heroism and the sufferings she had endured. Consequently, he was 'cold and reserved' toward his fiancée after the concert, but a long talk soon cleared up the misunderstanding between them, and, writes Alma, Justi then realized that 'we had found one another for good'. The following passage from a letter Hermann Behn wrote to his former mistress Mildenburg on 26 November 1902, typifies the attitude of Mahler's friends towards his marriage: 'I simply can't make head nor tail of Gustav's marriage! Why did he get married and why did he marry that woman?'[152] Having heard that Alma did not like her husband's music, he added: 'That, at least, is what I am told . . . Is it true? It would be really tragic!'[153]

As a direct result of this new development in Mahler's life, Natalie Bauer-Lechner's manuscript ends abruptly in January 1902,[154] just at the time of the Vienna première of the Fourth Symphony. Its concluding sentence, concerning her feelings about Mahler's marriage, speaks for itself: 'Mahler became engaged to Alma Schindler six weeks ago. If I were to discuss this event, I would find myself in the position of a doctor obliged to treat his nearest and dearest in a life or death situation. Whether these pages are brought to a conclusion must rest with the Supreme and Eternal Master!' The dignity of this conclusion does Natalie credit and demonstrates her strength of character. If she was able

---

[149] Quotation from the Lipiner letter summarized above.

[150] Undated letter to Nanna Spiegler (11 Jan.), PML.

[151] Alma denies that she was flirting: she was merely nodding across to an old friend, the chairman of the Gesellschaft der Musikfreunde, 'pleased as she was to recognise a friendly face in the hall where she knew all eyes were on her' (see below, Chap. 13).

[152] In the same letter, Behn complains that Mahler had completely forgotten him since their last meeting at Lipiner's in Nov. 1899. He had also heard that Mahler was complaining of his (Behn's) transcription of the Second Symphony, whereas he had told him personally, when making him a present of the original MS of the work, that it was 'a model of transcription for the piano'. In fact Mahler was never really satisfied with the transcription, as Natalie recorded, and he was often irritated by the importance Behn attached to it. All the same, Behn and he met again with real pleasure, fully reciprocated, when he conducted in Hamburg in Mar. 1905 and again in 1908.

[153] Another letter written by Behn to Mildenburg two years later, shows that relations between her and Mahler had 'calmed down', and were now on an artistic rather than personal level. In the same note, Behn criticizes Mahler for turning his back on Lipiner.

[154] Just before the end, there is an entry, dated 15 Nov. (after Mahler's first meeting with Alma), describing a long walk along the Danube with Mahler and Lipiner, during which the two men discussed Plato.

so calmly to rise above this painful experience it was thanks to her natural stability, and to her independence, her habit of relying only upon herself. She found support in her love of nature and of work, attributes which she and Mahler had in common. Like him, she liked to get up very early in order to write, feeling that 'he who has salvaged his little bit of freedom and activity in the morning cannot be affected even by the worst, if the day lays on his head his fragmented, confused life'.[155] If, like others whose love is not requited, she could at times be importunate, she was none the less the most faithful and devoted of friends, and the most precious witness and chronicler. Her ideal in writing was 'not only to leave out all subjectivity in information and presentation but also to record of my own life's content and that of others only that which is of general and objective interest, that which, if I may say so, is typical, generally true, and generally instructive, and to eliminate and stand aloof once and for all from the purely personal'. In this she saw a 'justice and humaneness' which for her was a compensation for 'the mightily emotional creative power of genius with its biases, its impetuosity, and its passion'.[156] In regard to her relation with and interest in Mahler, Natalie's following self-evaluation is also worth noting:

I have rarely had lasting power or influence over people, in spite of my ardent love and strongest interest for them, and a total abandonment and spending of myself where I loved most deeply. Perhaps I was too loving and understanding and demanded nothing for myself. Thus I have experienced that colder, unstable, and tyrannical natures gained far more power and influence with others than I. It may also be due to my calm and even temper which lacked the demonic [and] breathtaking; because a great and moody friend once told me: with me one always knew where one was and how one stood, and did not have to woo always anew as with others, which livened and nurtured the fantasy [of men].

Due to Natalie's reticence, it may never be possible to establish the true nature and intensity of her relationship with Mahler.[157]

There have been many conjectures, in particular, about the fate of the letters Mahler wrote to Natalie over the years. A passage in the *Fragmente* seems to suggest that Gustav burnt them, probably at the time of his engagement. This would mean that she had returned them to him sometime after their break.[158] In any case, it is highly significant that Natalie was not present at the dinner Mahler arranged at his house for Alma to meet his friends, whether because she was not invited or because she refused to meet the scatter-brain that Mahler had preferred to her. In the years that followed, Mahler's alienation from her seems to have been complete. In any case the few letters Natalie wrote to Mildenburg and which have been preserved never mention him

---

[155] Frank Loschnigg, 'The Cultural Education of Gustav Mahler' (Ph.D. thesis, Univ. of Wisconsin-Madison, 1976), 412–14. I have retained the author's trans. of Natalie's original.

[156] Ibid.   [157] Ibid. 415.

[158] *Fragmente* (Rudolf Lechner und Sohn, Vienna, 1907), 162.

again.[159] Deprived of one of the reasons for her existence—the diary in which she had meticulously noted Mahler's every word—she continued her activities with the Soldat-Roeger Quartet, but spent her last years alone and in abject poverty. A hitherto unknown passage in Alma's *Ein Leben mit Gustav Mahler* claims that, soon after Gustav's marriage, Natalie took another lover, a painter, with whom she hastened to 'flaunt her liaison'. Mahler perhaps showed that he had cared for her more than he had owned by remarking later (with some measure of cruelty) that 'she could at least have waited until the year of mourning was over'.

According to Emma Adler, whose unpublished memoirs have already been quoted more than once, Natalie was able to provide for herself so long as she was able to give concerts and teach. Eventually, however, as the result of a serious illness, she had to give up all professional activity. A generous woman friend took her in to live with her for a while, but Natalie was too proud to accept such a dependent relationship for long. She went first to a home for the elderly, and then, suffering from a mental disorder, to a lunatic asylum. One day many years later Emma Adler decided to go and visit the home where Natalie had stayed before she was committed. She found a tiny, damp, miserable room, with wallpaper hanging off the walls and rickety furniture, lit only by an old bedside lamp with a torn shade. Although she had never liked this woman whom she had always regarded as a calculating flirt (*kalte Kokette*), Victor Adler's wife felt sad that day, remembering the luxurious life Natalie had led when married to Alexander Bauer, and thinking of her lonely death far from all those she had loved—Mahler, Lipiner, her husband, and his daughter: all of whom, incidentally, had died before she did.[160]

Natalie passed away on 8 May 1921, almost exactly ten years after the man she had so passionately admired and loved. The drastically abridged version of her *Mahleriana*, edited by her nephew Johann Kilian,[161] was published by Tal Verlag in 1923. A very substantial manuscript in a copyist's hand with autograph corrections, now at the Bibliothèque Musicale Gustav Mahler in Paris, fills many bound copybooks. There are numerous corrections in Natalie's own writing. Unfortunately the diary seems to have passed through various hands after the death of its author. Many pages are missing, thus depriving us no doubt of a wealth of further information about the psychological atmosphere and the crisis and conflicts which took place in Mahler's family and circle of friends.

Why was it that Mahler, instead of enjoying his engagement as a happy and

---

[159] In a letter Natalie wrote to Mildenburg on 4 Nov. 1921 she asked the latter to save her old clothes for her.

[160] Emma Adler, 'Tagebuch', 1115, Verein für Geschichte der Arbeiterbewegung, Vienna.

[161] Johann Killian (1879–1959) was the husband of Friederike Lechner (1885–1952), Natalie's niece and universal heir. Johann Killian's son, Herbert, publ. a new edn. of Natalie's *Erinnerungen* in 1984 (NBL2) using one of his aunt's original MSS. Of two incomplete copies in BGM, one was made for Henriette Manckiewicz. Both contain a great number of unpubl. passages.

enriching experience, went through a period which Alma described as 'filled with anxiety and torment'? She ascribes this solely to his lack of sexual experience, but it seems more likely that he was apprehensive of taking on responsibility for so young and lovely a creature. So many things separated him from Alma, not only age, but social milieu, and also the weight of the past which he carried on his shoulders: 'You're lucky, you were born to "joy and plenty" and can trip lightly through life, no dark past clings to you, no family dependents. I've had to plod laboriously my whole life with lumps of clay on my boots.'[162] Later Alma tried to explain to Arthur Schnitzler, the great Viennese novelist, why she and Gustav had found the period of their engagement such a trial. As long as she and Mahler had been seeing each other in secret, she said, communication had been easy. But after their engagement had been announced she had begun to find it hard to understand him: 'For hours I would walk beside him in the Belvedere Gardens, and when he asked why I didn't say anything I would finally confess: "You've been talking Chinese to me. I haven't understood a word".' Suddenly the engaged couple realized with dismay how far apart they were in many fields. Alma, nourished since her earliest days on a diet of philosophers like Nietzsche and Schopenhauer, found herself 'incapable of sharing Gustav's admiration for Dostoyevsky'.[163]

As for Mahler, he was acutely aware that in marrying him Alma was expressing only one side of her nature, as is shown by the long letter he wrote her in December 1901. It was then that she wrote in her diary:

Which is the real me? Won't I make him and myself unhappy if I lie—but am I lying? This deep feeling of happiness when he smiles at me—is that also a lie? No, no. I must drive out the other me, the one which has dominated up to now—that one must stand down. I must do everything I can to become a human being, let everything possible happen to me.[164]

Two weeks later she noted:

For a while, I've been genuinely happy, that's why I've not written anything these last few days—but things are different now. He wants me to be different, totally different; I want it too—I can manage it so long as I'm with him—but when I'm alone my second self, vain and bad, comes back and demands to be let out. And I go along with it. My eyes radiate frivolity, my lips lie—lie unceasingly—and he feels it, knows it. It's only now that it's dawned on me! I must go up to him. Yesterday afternoon . . . he begged me to say something and I couldn't find a single warm word, not one. I wept—that was how it ended.[165]

That night she wrote:

Spent the evening with Pollak. We talked a lot about Gustav. I got some of my resentment off my chest. Everything that was raging inside me had to come out. If we

---

[162] AMM1. 21; AMM2. 37.   [163] AML 182.
[164] AMT, 31 Dec.   [165] AMT, 16 Jan.

get that far and I do become his, then I must get a move on now already to ensure that I get the place that's due to me—artistically, that is. . . .[166] He thinks nothing of my art but highly of his own, while I think nothing of his but highly of mine!—that's the way it is!

On 6 January,[167] however, she wrote: 'He sent me his Fifth [Fourth] Symphony yesterday. We played it through together today; I found it thrilling and liked it enormously.' But on 16 January she added:

Now he's continually talking about protecting his art. I can't do that. With Zemlinsky, it would even have been all right because I appreciate his art with him—he's a wonderful gifted fellow. But Gustav is so poor, so frightfully poor. If he only knew how poor he is, he would hide his face in shame. And I'll always have to lie . . . to lie constantly, throughout my life—with him, that's just possible—but with Justi, that female! I have the feeling she's checking up on me the whole time . . . But I must be free, completely free![168]

These lines, scribbled in barely coherent desperation in her diary, show that Alma, at least, was aware of the dangers to which their coming marriage was about to expose two people so singularly unsuited to share a life together: Mahler, the man of genius, ardent, overflowing with love but authoritarian and demanding, a prisoner of himself and his ideals, a devotee of the absolute and hence incapable of either understanding or allowing for human failings, was confronted by a woman who was tossed this way and that by the violent and often conflicting impulses of her capricious temperament, a coquette, conceited, flighty, and frivolous certainly, but also attractive, witty, spontaneous, profoundly musical—a woman simultaneously capable of great generosity and the most sordid meanness, of the most absolute honesty and the most devious duplicity. The whole drama was to unfold not only between her and Mahler but even more between the many conflicting facets of her own character. Would she be able to hold in check those inclinations and desires which, as she well knew, her life with Mahler could not possibly satisfy? The frankness and lucidity she shows in laying bare the most intimate aspects of her nature in her diary do her credit. While she often preferred, in her two books, to embellish certain truths for posterity, she was at least absolutely honest with herself. Moreover, all those who knew her and who have read the original versions of her various writings know that, when she put pen to paper, she could often be her own worst enemy.

---

[166] 'So muss ich mich schon jetzt gehörig rühren, um mir den Platz zu sichern, der mir gebührt. Nämlich künstlerisch.' Alma's writing often being almost illegible, the word *gebührt* is almost impossible to make out.

[167] 'Sat. 6 Jan.' is another example of the frequent inaccuracies which were to be found in the dating of entries in Alma's memoirs. 6 Jan. 1902 was a Mon.; the Sat. in question must have been 4 Jan. Also it was not the Fifth Symphony that Mahler sent Alma (this work was not finished until the following summer), but the Fourth, which had just been printed (KMI). The following note was attached: 'Just arrived here! Take it, the first!'

[168] This is the last of Alma's MS diary pages preserved in UPL. The extracts quoted in the next chapters survive only in a typed and incomplete copy.

She was certainly not unaware of the risks she was taking by marrying a man of such stature.

In spite of the sufferings and conflicts their union was to engender, Alma transformed and enriched Mahler's life and gave him a new incentive to live, to strive, and, of course, to create. Dignity, moderation, conventions, and objectivity mattered little to her. But she had the presence and majesty of a goddess and men longed to lay offerings at her feet. She was to be Mahler's goal, his 'safe anchorage', his essential reason for living. Of course he too had guessed and anticipated the potential difficulties and conflicts, but he confronted them steadfastly, trusting in the vital force of his love and the unique qualities of the splendid creature fate had placed in his path.

13

Strauss and *Feuersnot*—the Fourth Symphony in
Vienna—marriage and journey to Russia—Beethoven
Exhibition at the Secession—première of the Third
Symphony—the Krefeld triumph

(January–June 1902)

My time will come when his is past.

EARLY in 1902, in the midst of all the joys and worries of his engagement
to Alma, Mahler had another fierce battle to fight: the Viennese première
of the Fourth Symphony.[1] Happily, Alma was now constantly by his side,
attending all rehearsals. She became familiar with every detail of the work,
though without understanding its overall structure and significance. During a
walk along the banks of the Danube, Mahler tried to explain his symphony
to her by comparing it to 'a primitive painting on a gold background', but she
was baffled by its naïvety and intentional archaisms (*Antikisieren*) which she
considered 'childish'. Because of a recent conflict between Mahler and the
orchestra concerning the new musicians he had engaged for the Opera,[2]
the atmosphere at rehearsals was extremely tense. Mahler raged and stamped
his feet, finding fault with one player after another. The musicians showed their
resentment, played reluctantly, and even threatened to walk out of rehearsals.
Alma did her best to calm him down.

On 12 January, as always when Mahler conducted one of his own works,
the Grosser Musikvereinsaal was packed at 12.30 for the fifth Philharmonic
Concert. His betrothal was by now public knowledge and Alma was 'feeling

---

[1] At the first Philharmonic Concert of 1902, Mahler's symphony (with Rita Michalek as soprano soloist),
was preceded by Beethoven's *König Stefan* Overture, conducted by Hellmesberger. According to the anti-
Semitic *Deutsche Zeitung* (10 Sept. 1902), the orchestra committee hoped this performance would appease
Mahler, who was still smarting from the two recent conflicts with the musicians.
[2] See below for details of this serious *Affäre*.

wretched', aware that everyone was staring at her. Her embarrassment was such that she could hear 'the blood coursing in my ears'. Prolonged cheering welcomed Mahler back onto the podium after nearly eleven months' absence. However, the hostility of the majority of the audience soon became even more obvious than in Munich or Berlin, and 'from the start sarcastic smiles and remarks' made it clear that many people were there only to demonstrate against Mahler. A few boos were heard between the movements, the applause was sparse, and, according to Natalie Bauer-Lechner, at the end of the concert 'several people in the audience cried "Shame"', declaring that they had been made fun of and that it was shocking there had not been more booing'. Not far from Bruno Walter, two young men vociferously proclaimed their disapproval of this 'horrible, unmusical music', and Walter shouted back that 'Mahler and his immortal work will still be alive long after you are dead and buried'. A few days later Mahler admitted his own deep discouragement: 'No one knows yet what to make of it, or whether it should be taken by mouth or absorbed *per anum!*'[3] Undeterred, however, he repeated his new work eight days later at a 'special' evening concert with the Singakademie choir. A second Viennese performance of the First Symphony had originally been announced but instead Mahler decided to perform the Fourth again, hoping no doubt that a second hearing might earn him a few enlightened admirers. The following item on the programme was *Das klagende Lied* (also a second performance). This was the occasion on which Mahler's friends accused Alma of having spent the evening 'flirting' in the auditorium, while Mildenburg, on stage, 'sacrificed herself for him at the risk of losing her voice'.[4]

Like their colleagues in Berlin and Munich, the Viennese critics were almost unanimous in their condemnation of the 'contrived naïvetés' of the Fourth Symphony and its numerous 'quotations'. Even Albert Kauders, whose article in the *Fremden-Blatt* was comparatively moderate, regarded it as nothing but

---

[3] NBL1. 179; NBL2. 204, almost the last lines in Natalie's *Mahleriana*.

[4] Mahler wrote two letters concerning this second performance of *Das klagende Lied*. One, dated 21 Jan., to Friedrich Ehrbar, the director of the Singakademie, thanking him for his 'immense sympathy and most energetic and successful collaboration' during the previous day's concert (Stadtbibliothek, Vienna). The other, before the concert, was to a singer (probably Edyth Walker). A year earlier, he had considered dividing the contralto part of the *Klagende Lied* between Walker and Hermine Kittel, an alto who had just joined the Hofoper (see below, Chap. 14) in order to differentiate the voice of the narrator from the *Knabenstimme* (child's voice). Walker had doubtless considered this episode too short to justify her participation in the concert, for Mahler reminds her in this letter that Mildenburg had agreed to sing only the third stanza of the soprano part, and begs her not to be 'petty', but to 'help a composer in difficulty' by 'accepting a solo part which may not be very important from the point of view of length, but which demands the highest artistry' (BGM). *Das klagende Lied* was performed on 20 Jan. by Elizza (soprano), Mildenburg (soprano), Walker (contralto), Kittel (contralto), Schmedes (tenor) (Schrödter had been previously announced as tenor soloist). The orchestra was made up of 'members of the Vienna Opera', plus a group of extra winds and the Singakademie choir. Alma Mahler, in AMM, confuses the concert of 12 Jan. in which the Fourth Symphony was preceded merely by Beethoven's *König Stefan* Overture, and that of 20 Jan. which included the second performance of *Das klagende Lied*. The score of the symphony was published by Doblinger in Sept. 1902. Mr James Fuld's collection in New York contains a copy of the original edn. with the following dedication by Mahler to Nanna Spiegler: 'Dear Nanna, here are some of my new finger exercises, just published. You have permission to botch them (*daneben zu greifen*) as much as you like!'

affectation. Taking his cue from Haydn rather than Bruckner, Mahler had nevertheless 'played the devil and given his hyper-modern work an odour of brimstone'. The werewolf 'comes strolling along in sheep's clothing', but 'his air of innocence is progressively distorted into an infernal grimace'. Moreover, the heaven of the Finale was more like hell, since 'so many pagans and Moslems prowl about in it'.[5] Kauders found the contrasts of the work 'arbitrary' and its ugliness unacceptable. According to the *Illustrirtes Wiener Extrablatt*, the Fourth was incomprehensible without a 'programme' and unredeemed by either its 'virtuoso' refinements or its sound effects.

Similarly Kalbeck condemned the thematic material of the work as being hardly adequate for a 'pantomime ballet':

The *Episoden*, interruptions, digressions, explosions and evolutions (*Evolutionen*) disturb and distract the listener... Amor, disguised as a boy, drives a carriage with tinkling bells which is preceded by the graceful swaying figure of an exquisite dancer. She is familiar to us, as if we had met her a hundred years ago, in the days of Weber and Cherubini ... In due course she is joined by another girl, a 'child of the people' simple and naive. The journey now runs into difficulties, the initial harmony is broken by ear-splitting dissonances and the whole degenerates into a terrible battle between folksong and art song (*Volks- und Kunstgesang*).

Had Mahler intended to compose a musical illustration of a particular poetical thought process, one of the forced marriages between two different kinds of artistic expression that had become so popular since Liszt and Berlioz? Kalbeck was by no means convinced. If anything, Mahler had produced programme music in spite of himself. The tender and skilful Adagio was as far removed from the rest of the work as 'Heaven from Hell in a medieval mystery play', and the Scherzo plunged the audience 'into the circle of the Inferno reserved for Bohemian musicians'. However the audience was not deterred by the eccentricities of 'a clever-clever composer', but it left the hall puzzled by an unsolved and perhaps insoluble enigma.

Theodor Helm was also left wondering:

This Fourth Symphony by our hyper-secessionist and gifted Opera Director is a most curious thing! Apparently he has made it his business this time to work with the most simple, ... old-fashioned, even childlike melodies possible.... And why all of this? In order.... to depict a kind of celebration in the hereafter which is vividly portrayed as the fabled land of milk and honey in which there is feasting and drinking, while eleven thousand maidens perform a dance.... I regret to have to say, however, that I lack any feeling for this kind of grotesque musical humour. I therefore find it impossible to take Mahler's Fourth Symphony seriously...[6]

---

[5] Both Kauders and Helm mention a resemblance of the second stanza of *Das klagende Lied* to *Parsifal* which seems far from obvious today. Furthermore, the première of *Parsifal* (1882) took place nearly two years after Mahler completed his score (1880).

[6] See *Musikalisches Wochenblatt*, 33: 5 (Jan. 1902), 69.

Helm also found the work's numerous 'reminiscences' too obvious. The mixture of shrill cacophonies and popular Viennese music made one wonder whether Mahler was making fun of the public, and provided the wrong environment for the grave, nobly conceived Adagio, one of the most beautiful passages written in recent times.

Hans Liebstöckl's review shows that the key to the fairy-tale world of the Fourth Symphony was as far from his grasp as that to the metaphysical conflict of the Second. The witty and clever critic of *Die Reichswehr* admitted to having found 'delicious passages' here and there in the new work. He compared Mahler with Strauss, his more famous contemporary, in the following terms: 'Richard is more the philosopher, Gustav more the man of the theatre. Both have an extraordinary capacity for orchestration, both are great lovers of refinement. Richard is, however, more "will and idea",[7] Gustav more a medieval dreamer, a pre-raphaelite, ready at any moment to blow into the *Knaben Wunderhorn* and enter Paradise.' The same critic emphasized, not without perspicacity, the 'dry glow' of this 'medieval' music, 'its fondness for sharp lines, its deliberate harmonic poverty, its noisy simplicity, its virtuosity in the striking of attitudes, its visionary imagination . . . and its tortured inventiveness, its quest for redemption . . . and its contempt for form.' But his conclusions were more commonplace: 'The music Mahler writes is not good music . . .There are too many purposes and intentions, too much artifice and extravagance . . . It is chance music, a glittering arrangement of hollow nutshells.' If Liebstöckl had been able to foresee the brilliant future of 'chance' in the music of the second half of the twentieth century, he would probably have used a different term to characterize Mahler's music. For Mahler's name would probably be the last one to occur to anybody looking for a precursor to John Cage.

Heuberger found Mahler's intentions equally obscure, since he had refused to clarify them with a programme. In this 'pastoral symphony', Mahler had chosen to follow the most difficult path of all, that of naïveté and gaiety. Haydn whom he had obviously chosen as his patron saint, would never have dreamt of 'using the same language as his great-grandfather'. Thus disguised, Mahler had composed a few 'pleasant and charming' passages devoid of masks and wigs, particularly in the Adagio. But the 'unsingable' Finale seemed to evoke an unhappy soul tormented by hell-fire rather than an angel. After discussing the symphony in more general terms as the most serious of all musical forms, Hirschfeld also blamed Mahler for not divulging his programme and thus practising 'symphonic perplexity' (*Verblüffung*). He betrayed symphonic form in many different ways: with tinkling bells, glorified Ländler, idealized shouts of joy (*Juchzern*), and yodels in canon.[8] All this affected folksiness (*Volkstümlichkeit*), Hirschfeld wrote, conjures up visions of 'Papa Haydn ratt-

---

[7] An allusion to Schopenhauer's *magnum opus*.

[8] He particularly condemns all the 'literature' accompanying the first bars, i.e. the score's numerous dynamic markings and tempo indications.

ling past in a motor car enveloped in a cloud of gasoline fumes'. 'This "dispersed" music is the very opposite of symphonic art,' he observed.

Max Graf,[9] the youngest of the Viennese critics, reacted as negatively as his older colleagues. As he saw it, 'this symphony has to be read from back to front like a Hebrew bible'. Everything shocked him, from the conclusion in E major and its 'bizarre, ugly, shrill and tortured sounds' to the 'arbitrary, medieval declamation and poverty of ideas in the Finale'.[10] The story of Max Graf's earlier relationship with Mahler and his music is worth relating in some detail. Graf, a staunch conservative despite his youth, although unstable and vacillating in his judgements, was at first a fervent admirer of Mahler, even to the point of asking him in 1899 whether he could dedicate a book of essays called *Wagnerprobleme* to him. At this time Mahler replied:

If you think I may not agree with some of your essays, it seems to me that (however much I appreciate the honour of standing godfather to one of your children), my name ought not to appear on the title page. I confidently leave the resolution of this delicate problem to you, for you may well have more experience than I of literary protocol. For my part, I frankly admit that, just as I do not consider myself as belonging to any 'party', so I acknowledge at all times the freedom of the individual to think and believe what he or she is able and/or wants to believe. Why should one not have the right to invite even one's enemies to dinner? At least, you will understand what I mean by that. In the present case, though, I wonder if it won't create misunderstandings among both young and old. It is simply a question of 'knowing what is customary'. If you feel that the 'godfather' should be of one 'mind' with the child, I think it would be better to leave out my name. If this is not the case, then I shall duly appreciate the honour. Yours most sincerely, Gustav Mahler. P.S. When all's said and done, I'm not of the opposite opinion, since I've long permitted myself the luxury of having no opinion whatsoever on such complicated matters.[11]

In *Wagnerprobleme*, Graf set out to compare Mahler as a conductor with Richter. His preference for the latter was obvious, but he considered that the two conductors complemented each other, and that 'Mahler's gifts begin where

[9] Founded in 1893, the *Neues Wiener Journal*, did not enjoy a very favourable reputation in Vienna. The arts page consisted mainly of an anonymous diary made up of snippets of theatrical gossip. The paper was considered to have a mainly female readership and to be more a means of satisfying their curiosity than furthering the cause of art. Albert Kauders was succeeded, in 1901, by the young Max Graf. Born in 1873 in Prague, Graf had taken a doctorate in law at the same time as studying music with Hanslick and Bruckner. Joining the staff of the *Allgemeine Zeitung* in 1900, he later became a lecturer in history of music and musical aesthetics at the Conservatory and at the Univ. of Vienna. He worked for the *Neue Freie Presse*, then for *Die Zeit*, and became a Vienna correspondent for the *Prager Tagblatt*. Emigrating to the USA in 1938, he wrote for various American papers and magazines. In 1947 he returned to Vienna and became music critic of *Die Weltpresse*, continuing until 1957. Graf, who died in 1958, wrote several books on musical life in Vienna (see Bibliography). In autumn 1906, he was replaced on the *Neues Wiener Journal* by Heinrich Reinhardt, who became one of the leaders of the anti-Mahler campaign in 1907. However the paper's other critic, Elsa Bienenfeld, had been a Schoenberg pupil, and she remained a faithful supporter of Mahler to the end.

[10] Like Helm, Graf mentioned a similarity between the opening theme and Julius Stern's waltz 'Das ist halt weanerisch'.

[11] GWO 88.

Richter's end'. Shortly after the publication of his book he apparently heard he had incurred the displeasure of Mahler, who, in his eyes, had the 'weakness' of failing to admire his famous colleague. Three years later, in 1902, Graf published the article summarized above on the Fourth Symphony, and another, in the magazine *Die Waage*, in which he drew attention to Mahler's little-known 'childish' aspect, for instance the fun he got out of certain passages of *The Magic Flute* and *Così fan tutte*. It was precisely this side of his character that he was revealing in the Fourth Symphony, which was thus undoubtedly the most authentic work he had written. From then on, Graf's praises slide insidiously into denigration: Mahler 'does not look for ingenious modulatory detours, like a true musician', he 'flings open the door and jumps into the new tonality': 'What a lack of musical discretion, or facility' he adds. 'If one wants to treat the first movement as pure music, then one has to admit that these themes are not themes, this construction is not construction and these harmonies are not harmonies. If what I continually learn from the Symphonies of Haydn, Mozart and Beethoven is the truth, then the Mahlerian kind of musical fairytale is unspeakably childish.'

Having thus fired two broadsides at the Fourth Symphony, Graf felt impelled to visit its creator to explain his feelings to him. Mahler very quickly interrupted his explanation to say, in a peremptory fashion, that 'he had obviously understood nothing about the work'. Caught on the raw, Graf retorted that when he had previously defended the Second Symphony, Mahler did not think so badly of him. 'Yes I did,' said Mahler calmly, without a trace of sarcasm. 'I assure you that I've never altered my opinion: you understood me as little then as you do now!' Needless to say, Graf was thenceforth to swell the already crowded ranks of Mahler's enemies. Much later, in his memoirs, which contain a very subjective and inaccurate version of this incident,[12] Graf declared that Mahler, who had up to that time been 'disarmingly friendly', 'gay and communicative', became 'petty, vain and egocentric' in his dealings with him.[13]

This incident typifies Mahler's attitude towards the *Herren Vorgesetzten*. After an important première he generally wanted to know what they had said during the interval, but he had almost no regular contact with them. Ludwig Karpath was one exception. His memoirs recall a few of his meetings with Mahler during the early years of his directorship. One day, for example, he met him towards midday on the Ring and they started to discuss Opera affairs. They failed to agree, and Mahler said to him several times: 'Don't say that, you're

---

[12] The incident has been reported by several authors, notably Richard Specht, 'Mahler's Feinde', *Musikblätter des Anbruch*, 2: 7–8 (1920), 82, and Ernst Decsey, *Die Spieldose* (Tal, Leipzig, 1922), 134. Max Graf tells it in quite a different fashion. After reading his article on the Fourth Symphony Mahler is supposed to have said: 'I don't understand how a man who understood the Second so well can so fail to understand the Fourth.' This version is unreliable, if only because Graf's memoirs make no mention of his violent and persistent attacks against Mahle: GWO 91 and *Erlebnisse mit Gustav Mahler*, 1 and 2, *Neues Wiener Journal* (19 and 26 June 1921).

[13] Max Graf, *Jede Stunde war erfüllt* (Forum, Vienna, 1957), 24.

taking a big risk!' Finally, Karpath asked what the risk was and Mahler, laughing, said that he had been intending to invite him to lunch and that *Marillenknödel*[14] were on the menu. 'Now,' he continued, 'I won't invite you and you won't get any!' When Karpath replied that it wasn't one of his favourite dishes, he received the reply: 'How can a Viennese not be interested in Marillenknödel? I find that so incredible that I'm going to take you home anyway to eat this wonderful dessert. My sister Justi has got the authentic recipe, and we'll soon see whether you can remain indifferent!' Karpath, himself a highly accomplished cook, acknowledges that Mahler at any rate succeeded in convincing him of the excellence of the recipe.

On another occasion the two of them were again on the Ring, discussing a symphony of Mahler's which 'had just had a success in Germany'. They started talking about music in general, and were so absorbed that Mahler completely forgot that Karpath was again expected to lunch. As it happened, Karpath had once more irritated him by contradicting him. At half past 2 the critic gently reminded him of the lunch invitation, whereupon Mahler took him by the arm, warning him that it would be an improvised meal. According to Karpath, the meal was calm and the antagonists finally parted company 'well pleased with each other'. 'On such occasions,' adds Karpath, 'you realized that Mahler actually liked you.'[15]

But these were only episodic encounters. The only time Mahler had any really close contact with a Viennese critic was with Julius Korngold, who strongly defended him during the last years of his tenure. With another critic, Max Kalbeck, his relationship was more professional than friendly. A native of Breslau, Kalbeck, a tall man with a shock of blond hair protruding from under his slouch-hat, was even more of an anti-Wagnerian than Hanslick. His life-work was of course the large four-volume Brahms biography which he only completed in 1914. Kalbeck could on occasions be childishly naïve and idealistic. But he had a lively pen and an ironic turn of phrase. Hanslick said of him that 'he had a sword crossed with a lyre on his coat of arms'. One of Kalbeck's *bêtes noires* was Theodor Reichmann, of whom he once wrote: 'Reichmann sang this role as if he had a murder on his conscience, and indeed he murdered the role.'[16] Kalbeck was a gifted writer and poet. He translated many librettos for operas and, in 1905, Mahler was to entrust him with the task of providing new translations of *Don Giovanni* and *Figaro* for the coming Mozart year.

Mahler often read the papers. Both Natalie and Richard Specht say that he always claimed that he was never upset by hostile criticism, which, as we have seen, was by no means always true. When talking to the critics, he sometimes liked to tease them. He knew very well that the 'stubbornness' they accused

---

[14] This had been Mahler's favourite dessert since Prague: apricot dumplings in a potato pastry (see Vol. iii, App., for the recipe).
[15] BMG 177.   [16] KIW 74 ff.

him of was simply his need to follow his own path, without worrying about the
opinion of the public or the 'connoisseurs'. Besides, even if the conservative
old guard was firmly resolved to deny him the slightest creative talent, there
were fortunately some young musicians in Vienna who perceived his music
very differently: such as the tall, shy adolescent who made his way backstage
after a concert and begged him, in a voice trembling with emotion, to let him
have the baton he had used to conduct the performance. The young musician—
his name was Alban Berg—kept the baton all his life as a treasured souvenir
of an event which he would never forget.[17] Two days after the première of the
Fourth Symphony there appeared in the *Wiener Morgenzeitung* a witty parody
of the Finale, written by Heinrich Reinhardt, a critic and also a composer of
operettas. The text, ridiculing the work and the concert, faithfully reproduces
the rhythm and rhymes of the *Wunderhorn-Lied*, an achievement which adds
particular savour to the irresistible attack.

The Viennese première of the Fourth Symphony had at least one fortunate
consequence. For the first time, an important publishing house, Doblinger,
decided to include a new Mahler work in its catalogue without the financial
participation of a sponsor as had been necessary with the preceding symphonies. Waldheim-Eberle remained the owners of the performance rights.
However, the score was published for once before the première and the parts
soon after, while a piano four-hands arrangement by Josef Venantius von Wöss
was quickly put on sale.[18] Admittedly, Doblinger was not as important a
publishing house as Peters or Schott. Its beginnings had been modest, to say
the least. In 1876 Bernhard Herzmansky had bought a small business founded
by Ludwig Doblinger in 1856. His son, also named Bernhard, soon expanded
the firm and started publishing music, at first operettas and piano exercises
for beginners. In 1901, the year before the Viennese première of the Fourth
Symphony, an important change took place. Two operettas in the Doblinger
catalogue, Heinrich Reinhardt's *Das süsse Mädel* and Carl Michael Ziehrer's
Die Landstreicher, proved enormously successful, establishing the firm as the
principal publisher of Viennese operettas. A few years later, it was to make
large profits, with world-wide successes like Franz Lehar's *Merry Widow* (1905)
and Oscar Straus's *Waltz Dream* (1907). Herzmansky's sudden prosperity resulted in a change in his policies as a publisher. He decided to include in
his catalogue a number of contemporary composers: in particular, works by
Ernö von Dohnanyi and Alexander von Zemlinsky, as well as Mahler's new
symphony.[19]

[17] Maria Komorn, 'Gustav Mahler und die Jugend: Erlebnisse aus meiner Kindheit', *Neues Wiener Journal* (31 Aug. 1930).
[18] See below, the biography of Josef von Wöss.
[19] In 1903 Herzmansky launched a still more ambitious project, the publ. of Bruckner's Fifth Symphony and that of his two Masses, ed. in collaboration with Universal Edition. In 1909 Herzmansky finally handed over all his Mahler rights (and the Bruckner ones) to Universal Edition, which at the same time purchased those of the earlier symphonies from Waldheim Eberle and thus became Mahler's principal publisher.

Preparations for the Fourth Symphony première only kept Mahler away a few days from the Hofoper, where rehearsals for *Feuersnot*, Richard Strauss's new opera, were to absorb all his time and energy for several weeks. Departing from the obvious Wagnerian influence on *Guntram*, Strauss had turned towards a lighter vein and collaborated in a libretto, which was written in the Bavarian dialect by Ernst von Wolzogen,[20] the creator of the famous Berlin Überbrettl cabaret. *Feuersnot* abounded in scabrous details, for Strauss had decided to get even with Munich (his native city) and its Philistine inhabitants and to take revenge for the treatment meted out to him and 'his master Richard Wagner'. With the help of his librettist, he satirized the bourgeois mentality of the Bavarians and their contempt for art. The hero of *Feuersnot*, Kunrad, is a dreamer, a poet, an artist, and an idealist. On St John's Eve he has dared publicly to kiss Diemut, the burgomeister's daughter, with whom he has suddenly fallen in love. Both overjoyed and vexed, she decides to punish him. She offers to hoist him up to her room in the basket used to deliver her groceries and then leaves him stranded half-way up in the basket, exposed to the gibes of passers-by. But Kunrad is something of a magician. Recalling the vexations suffered by his master Reichhart (Wagner),[21] he puts out at a stroke all the fires and lights of the town, before launching into a diatribe against his fellow-citizens, followed by a hymn of praise to the irresistible force of love. The terrified populace begs Diemut to put an end to the joke. She eventually hauls Kunrad the rest of the way up and, as the lights gradually come on again, a big orchestral episode, at the time occasionally referred to as 'symphonic variations on a wedding night procured by force', depicts their amorous sport. A love-duet by the young couple rises into the summer night, mingled with a wedding hymn by the chorus.

Despite its *risqué* subject-matter, the work had been successful at its Dresden première on 21 November 1901. In Vienna, the 'scandalous' nature of the text, which had so delighted Strauss, raised grave difficulties with the censor, who reminded Mahler that the Hofoper was an apanage of the Imperial Court. The same difficulties were soon to arise in Berlin, where Strauss was principal conductor at the Opera. The German Imperial Court was even more puritanical than the Austrian, and the censor hesitated for a long time, and only gave way because the work had gained a *succès d'estime* in Vienna. Even then, it was programmed right at the end of the season, in the hope that it might then slip off the bill unnoticed by the public.

[20] Ernst von Wolzogen (1855–1934) was the son of Baron von Wolzogen, the Intendant of the Schwerin Opera, and the stepbrother of Hans von Wolzogen, the well-known friend and supporter of Wagner. A writer and novelist, he founded in 1901 the Überbrettl, a sort of avant-garde cabaret which strove to reflect current ideas and sentiments. Although short-lived, the Überbrettl was extremely influential. The playwright Frank Wedekind and the Viennese composer Oscar Straus both contributed to its success and Schoenberg was employed there for several months.
[21] The allusion gains in piquancy from the fact that Strauss's father, the hornplayer Franz Strauss, was one of Wagner's most tenacious enemies.

In Vienna, difficulties with the censor were at last smoothed out by a few changes in the text, and Mahler worked out the casting in a long exchange of letters with Strauss.[22] On 5 January, Strauss wrote expressing his desire to conduct the première on the 29th, because he had Viennese engagements for the 30th and 31st;[23] and he made some performance suggestions.[24] The same letter alluded ironically to the way the Berlin press greeted Mahler's Fourth Symphony:

What did you think of the Berlin critics' St Vitus dance over your Fourth? I must say, it far surpassed even my worst expectations. Congratulations, and also from my wife, on your engagement: anyway it will put you in your best mood for the *Feuersnot* rehearsals, so I can congratulate myself as well. Although I do not yet know her, best wishes to the lovely bride, and all the best to you, Your ever faithful Richard Strauss.[25]

A few days later, Mahler finally confirmed the date of the Viennese première, 29 January, the dress rehearsal taking place on the 27th. He advised Strauss not to conduct, for one rehearsal would not be enough to accustom the performers to a new conductor. Could he not arrive a week before the première?[26] Strauss obviously stuck to his decision to conduct himself, for Mahler tells him in the next letter that everything will be ready and that all he will need to do, when he arrives, is to walk up to the podium. All that matters to him is that the best interests of the work should be served: 'I have lovingly prepared everything, neglecting none of your instructions,' he adds. 'It's all there, down to the smallest detail . . .'.

Arriving in Vienna on Saturday 26 January, Strauss was amazed by the quality of the performance and immediately decided to yield the baton to Mahler for the première.[27] He changed nothing but a few small production details.[28] The dress rehearsal was a great success in almost every respect, and Strauss wrote to his father about it. He thought that only Mahler's 'frightful

[22] For the principal role, Mahler preferred Bertram to Demuth who, despite his 'very beautiful voice, hasn't the spark of genius'. (Demuth did sing Kunrad in Jan. 1902, since Bertram had already left Vienna.) For the female lead, Mahler considered both Gutheil-Schoder and Kurz, but decided that the latter, despite her 'marvellous voice', was not a good enough actress (letter to Strauss, mid-July 1901, MSB2. 230, 67 ff.). Rita Michalek finally sang the première. Strauss feared that Kunrad's tessitura would be too high for Bertram. 'Besides, B., as his Sachs in Berlin convinced me, has through years of guest appearances become so sloppy rhythmically that I would not like to entrust my melodies to him.—My dear friend Schoder is quite impossible! In this little part no acting is needed. The opera is played almost entirely in the dark; one needs only a <u>very</u> beautiful voice with [a] light, radiant high register, and little Schoder has neither at her disposal. Thus I urgently plead for Demuth and Kurz!' (cf. letters from Strauss to Mahler of 14 June, undated letter (end of July) and letter from Mahler to Strauss, 11 July 1901, MSB2).
[23] Strauss made two appearances in Vienna as an accompanist. On 30 Jan. he played the piano part in his 'melodrama for speaker and piano' *Enoch Arden*, the words being spoken by Ernst von Possart, director of the Munich Opera, and on 31 Jan. he accompanied his wife in a recital of his Lieder.
[24] He suggests the use of a few chorus members in unison with the heroine in several passages where her voice might be drowned.
[25] HOA, letter of 5 Jan. 1902 (Präs. 7 Mar.).
[26] MSB 76.   [27] Contrary to Alma's claim.
[28] He wanted the lights to be dimmed more rapidly as Kunrad was pronouncing his curse (cf. Helm's article in the *Wochenblatt*).

nervousness' had slightly affected the playing, but described 'the admirable Viennese orchestra' in ecstatic terms: for sheer beauty of sound it was without doubt the best in Europe. The sets and costumes were superb and the performance first-rate, especially that of the two principals, Demuth and Michalek. He had nothing but praise for Mahler's 'kindness' and for the superhuman efforts that he, and indeed the entire company, had made.[29]

Strauss's joy and astonishment can be better understood when it is remembered that his well-known pragmatism often inclined him to accept as inevitable the imperfections inherent in any theatrical production, something the perfectionist Mahler was much more reluctant to do. It was at this time that the two musicians established the relationship, part trust and part mistrust, part admiration and part incomprehension, part professional esteem and part personal incompatibility, which lasted through all their dealings with each other during Mahler's Vienna years. It would be difficult to imagine two more different personalities, in temperament, artistic aims, and even physical appearance: Strauss a blond giant with broad shoulders, a full, gentle face, flowing moustache, and an air of good humour; Mahler, a dark, sharp-featured 'gnome' with an obstinate mouth, thin lips, and flashing eyes; Strauss, the famous child of fortune, firmly but comfortably convinced of his artistic superiority, a bon vivant, even an epicure, admired and celebrated as a composer since the age of 12, and displaying in all things, in his art as in his sense of reality, a disarming ease; Mahler whose victories had been won only through blood, sweat, and tears, handicapped from childhood by his race, his modest origins, and his family, who had battled all his life to defend the highest ethical and artistic values, and to master his own inner conflicts; Mahler, the self-made man, bleeding and bruised, the eternal *Unzeitgemässe* (stranger to his time),[30] a man for whom art was a cause to defend and a mission to accomplish. Strauss, on the other hand, the born musician, the eminent professional, adapted easily to the demands of his time (*Zeitgemässe*); meticulous, but confident of his gifts; the creator and conductor laden with honours, fêted by the whole of Germany as 'Richard the Second', in other words, as the greatest composer since Wagner. For him, music had never involved any particular effort, still less a battle.

From 1902 the Mahler–Strauss dialogue which had begun fifteen years earlier was enriched by two female voices, those of Alma and Pauline. New dissonances were thus to bring a new and sometimes even grotesque note into the lively exchanges of views between the husbands. The character of Pauline Strauss and her relationship with her husband can only be explained by casting a brief look back at the young soprano who, at 27, had followed Strauss from

---

[29] Strauss also wrote to his father that Siegfried Wagner, who had come to Vienna to conduct a Nicolai Konzert, had attended this final rehearsal and complimented him at length (SBE 251).

[30] According to Richard Specht, Mahler often spoke of himself as an 'Unzeitgemässe' (a man out of his time: the word was used by Nietzsche in his *Unzeitgemässe Betrachtungen*), as opposed to Strauss, 'the great *Zeitgemässe*'.

Munich to the Weimar Opera, where she soon earned herself quite a reputation, for her unpredictable rages even more than for her professional qualities. The story of her engagement to Strauss was known throughout Germany. One day she flounced out of a rehearsal-room after throwing her score at the Herr Kapellmeister's face. A delegation from the orchestra subsequently called on Strauss, innocent victim of this public outrage, to assure him that 'henceforth the orchestra will refuse to participate in any performance involving this young artist'. To their astonishment he replied: 'But she's my fiancée!'[31] Their personal relationship during their engagement and throughout their married life never ceased to be stormy. At one point they even separated for more than a year. Pauline's volcanic temperament continued to erupt at regular intervals. She was to make it her duty to bring her husband to heel, to organize his life, to make him compose each day at an appointed time. She did not fail, when the opportunity arose, to criticize him bitterly for the 'difficulty' of his music, which she thought the public would never be able to understand.

Since she was born the daughter of a provincial general, Pauline was firmly convinced of her social superiority and she often reminded her husband of the *mésalliance* she had made. In her heart of hearts, she knew that Strauss needed her and valued in her above all the woman of order, the accomplished house-keeper, the guardian of the hearth, even the tigress she sometimes became. He freely acknowledged that he 'needed all that'. Alma, on the other hand, Viennese, schooled in the social graces, even if that meant being sometimes thoroughly insincere, could only disapprove of Pauline's brutal frankness. Her account of what happened the evening of the première of *Feuersnot* reveals surprise and shock bordering on outrage.[32] Pauline sat in Mahler's box and Alma, who was next to her, was startled to hear her mutter under her breath: 'How could anyone like such mediocrity? Mahler is fooling himself, he's only pretending he likes it! He must know perfectly well that it's all stolen from Wagner and Maxi and others!' On asking timidly who 'Maxi' was, Alma was amazed to discover that Panline was referring to Max von Schillings, a composer 'who far surpassed Strauss'![33] She took care not to reply, for she had already sensed that even the slightest agreement on her part might provoke Pauline to take the opposite point of view and contradict her own words. Strauss took nearly a dozen curtain-calls although some booing was audible

---

[31] Alma's memoirs provide a rather different version of this scene (AML 122) but Strauss himself was later to reminisce that it had taken place during a rehearsal for the last scene of his opera *Guntram*, in which Pauline de Ahna was the female lead. He had had several times to interrupt the tenor, who did not know his part very well, when Pauline, furious, shouted at him: 'Why not correct me?' Upon her future husband's declaring that he was satisfied with her and could therefore not correct her, she threw the score at him and left the room (see Willi Schuh, *Richard Strauss: Jugend und frühe Meisterjahre. Lebenschronik 1864–1898* (Atlantis, Zurich, 1976), 354).

[32] In her memoirs, she nevertheless admits to having appreciated Pauline's 'frankness' and also her 'musicality' (AML 122).

[33] See below, Chap. 15. *Feuersnot* contains a quotation from *Das Nachtlager von Granada* by Konradin Kreutzer, as *Salome* contains one from *The Barber of Seville*.

among the cheers from the gallery. When Strauss asked his wife backstage what she thought of his new success, she went at him like a wildcat: 'You thief! How dare you show your face to me? I'm not coming with you, you disgust me!' Astonished and exasperated, Mahler hustled the two of them into a rehearsal room where the sound of angry voices was clearly audible through the door. He waited outside for them to fight it out. But he finally lost patience and shouted that he and Alma were leaving. The door was flung open and Strauss tottered out, while Pauline, as angry as ever, shrieked after him: 'You go, I'm going back to the hotel and going to stay on my own tonight!' Strauss timidly asked if he might at least take her to the hotel: 'Only if you stay ten paces behind me,' she said, and the pair set off with the composer trailing behind his wife 'like a faithful dog'. When he eventually joined Mahler and Alma at the restaurant, he apologized: 'My wife can be a bit rough, but you know—it's what I need!' Throughout supper Strauss's conversation disturbed and depressed Mahler even more than the previous scenes: 'like a travelling salesman' (*Musterkartenagent*), Strauss could speak of nothing but his royalties and took out a pencil to calculate them. Franz Schalk, who was also present, whispered to Alma: 'The sad thing is that he's not even joking, on the contrary, he's in deadly earnest.'

'The entire evening was unsatisfactory,' Mahler wrote to his fiancée a few days later.

The atmosphere Strauss creates is so disillusioning that one literally becomes a stranger to oneself. If these are the fruits of the tree, how can one love the tree? You were right on target with your remarks about him. And I am proud of you for having so spontaneously found the right words. Surely it's preferable to eat the bread of poverty and walk in the light rather than lose oneself in everything mean and base! The time will come when people will see the wheat separated from the chaff—and my time will come when his is past. Would that I might live it at your side! But I hope that you, my Lux, will see it and remember the days when you recognized the sun through the haze—just as that day you know at the Stadtpark when it seemed to everyone just an ugly red spot.[34]

Alma must have scolded him for his taciturnity at the restaurant that evening, for he adds:

What could I possibly contribute to this coffee-house talk, at a moment so sublime as that of a performance which, after all, releases my creative energy too and ought to free one from everyday cares, instead of dragging one down into the mire in a conversation about royalties and capital (the everlasting dreams of Strauss's imagination, which are almost inseparable from his enthusiasm).[35]

Despite this 'final dissonance' (of which Strauss was certainly unaware for

---

[34] AMM1. 280; AMM2. 255. This is the source of Mahler's oft-quoted phrase 'My time will come', but the second part of the sentence 'when his is past' is always left out.

[35] AMM1. 281; AMM2. 256.

that kind of talk was so natural to him that he seems never to have sensed—
or at least cared about—Mahler's disapproval) the rehearsals and première of
Feuersnot left Strauss with good memories only:

I can't imagine a better moment than when you're conducting the second performance
of *Feuersnot* to thank you once again from the bottom of my heart for the unsurpassable
beauty of the performance you created of my work last week. I hope you will do it often
again. In my mind I am still luxuriating in the bewitching orchestral sound,
the wonderful designs produced by the genius of Brioschi and Lefler, the splendid
poetry in sound with which the beautiful voices of the soloists and chorus delighted
my ear . . .

Strauss's enthusiastic comments are far removed from the measured, courteous
tone usually adopted on such occasions. Strauss goes on to ask Mahler to pass
on his thanks to Stoll, the producer, Luze, the chorus conductor, and the
lighting technicians. He looks forward to hearing the opera again if it is still
running when he next arrives in Vienna on 21 March.[36]

Feuersnot, like Mahler's symphonies, aroused the Viennese critics more to
indignation than admiration. They particularly disapproved of its frivolous
libretto and the way he compared himself and his 'daring' to Wagner. Even
Theodor Helm, who, at least in the *Deutsche Zeitung*, always favoured 'German'
works, criticized the 'very curious form of the libretto . . . which seems . . . an
impudent attempt to transfer the Überbrettl style to the Wagnerian stage'.
Strauss, he said, was at once too brazen in his subject-matter and too intellectual in his music. The only interesting thing about the opera, as far as he was
concerned, was the orchestration. Even such charming numbers as the trio of
young girls rapidly degenerated into 'tortured harmonies, modulations and
other far-fetched complexities'. In Max Kalbeck's opinion, *Feuersnot* was a
work 'as ambiguous as its title', which ominously combined 'amorous ardour
and lack of fire'. Its jokes were 'indecent in the extreme' and the innumerable
plagiarisms in the score attained 'the heights of bad taste'. In short, Kalbeck
found nothing to admire in this 'clever orchestral babble and uproar' other than
Strauss's 'technical mastery'.

A staunch enemy of Wagnerian music-drama, and even more so of Wagner's
imitators who 'resort to copying what is unimportant', Hanslick condemned
Strauss's post-Wagnerian aesthetics and, above all, his orchestral love scene,
which he pronounced 'obscene'. Despite its 'dazzling technique', the whole
work exuded nothing but 'excruciating boredom'. 'If, now and again, a pleasing
little melody emerges, after two or three bars it is mercilessly rejected and
drowned in a sea of modulations and orchestral combinations . . .' The folk-
tunes quoted in the ensembles are ruined by 'venomous harmonies and grim-
acing rhythms'. *Feuersnot* was doomed to oblivion, devoid as it was of true
melody, and 'the song of the soul' (*die singende Seele*). The 'tyranny of the

[36] Letter of 4 Feb. 1902 (HOA, Präs. 6 Feb.), MSB 77.

orchestra' jeopardized 'the principles of drama' and for this reason Strauss could not be considered a 'born theatre composer'. Hirschfeld wrote in similar terms of Strauss's 'dislocation of natural forms and natural feelings', his 'deliberate deviation from the right note', his 'irrational' and 'artificial' art. His orchestration was so complex that 'one longs for a natural sound'. Hirschfeld did concede, however, that Mahler had miraculously subjugated this 'jumble of disconnected sounds', and playing on the German word for score, *Partitur*, complimented him on his skilful rendering of this 'Partitur made up entirely of particles'.[37]

While *Feuersnot*, Strauss's second venture into the operatic scene, is certainly not one of his best operas, the Viennese critics were of course quite wrong to say that he had no talent for the stage. Their damning reviews nevertheless had the usual adverse effects on the size of audiences. In a letter he wrote to Strauss in February, Mahler had to admit that the Viennese 'have been swayed by the press'.[38] Although a fourth performance was scheduled for the evening of Shrove Monday when, as he pointed out to Strauss, the Opera usually played to a full house, he had to cancel it because too few tickets had been sold. He nevertheless promised Strauss that he would not give up and that he would conduct *Feuersnot* again, probably on 4 April, with a new ballet, or in the autumn with another one-act opera.[39]

It drives me to despair that one must thus submit to the judgment of a narrow-minded and cowardly Areopagus from which there is no appeal. I was not without hope on the night of the première but, alas, I am unable to tell you anything more, dear friend, about the fate of your child (of <u>my</u> child of sorrow). I hope to have better news for you in April.

Strauss must have reacted strongly to this bad news, for in Mahler's next letter he asked Strauss not to question his goodwill, but to understand that it was impossible for him to give an opera that the public wouldn't come to see: the Intendant would immediately veto it and the theatre would be completely empty by the fifth performance. Experience had taught him that there was nothing to be done in a case like this. However, since Strauss wanted him to, he would try to give *Feuersnot* again with some 'popular' work like *Cavalleria rusticana* or *Hänsel und Gretel*—not, however, with *Pagliacci*, for Demuth could not sing two roles in one evening. Nevertheless, he feared that juxtaposition with such works would be prejudicial to *Feuersnot* and that the Intendant might refuse permission even to announce them together.[40] At the end of

---

[37] Cast of the Vienna première on 29 Jan. 1902: Michalek (Diemut), Elizza, von Thann, and Kittel (Elsbeth, Margret, and Wigelis), Breuer (Bailliff), Schittenhelm (Tulbeck), Demuth (Kunrad), Felix, Marian, Grengg (Bürgomeister), Frauscher, Stehmann, Kaulich, Kusmitsch. Strauss's opera was followed by *Rouge et noir*, a ballet by Josef Bayer and a mediocre score, according to Hanslick. The following season, Ritter replaced Grengg, Pacal took over from Schittenhelm, and Pohlner took over from Kusmitsch.

[38] A letter to Strauss dated 18 Feb. gives the figures for the receipts from the first performances: (1) 3,100 florins, (2) 1,600 florins, (3) 1,300 florins, (4) 900 florins. This last performance was the one that was cancelled (MSB 78 ff.).

[39] Letter to Strauss, 18 Feb. (MSB 78 ff.).   [40] MSB 80.

February, he again wrote to Strauss on the day of the première of *Der dot Mon*, which he hoped to schedule with *Feuersnot* in March. He even thought of inviting him to conduct the opera himself, but this plan fell through too when *Der dot Mon* also failed. *Feuersnot* was nevertheless performed again on a number of occasions, coupled with various ballets.[41]

The day after the première of *Feuersnot*, Mahler left under doctor's orders for the Semmering for a few days' rest, intended to alleviate his circulatory troubles.[42] His marriage was set for late February or March, and as he watched the snow fall on the Semmering, he dreamt of their future happiness and of Russia, for he was to leave with Alma immediately after the wedding for a series of concerts there. Meanwhile, at the Opera, February was marked by two events. The first was a *Neueinstudierung* of Boieldieu's *La Dame blanche*, a work still very popular in Vienna,[43] with a new cast. Hanslick declared that Mahler brought so much freshness, life, and polish to the performance that the opera 'seemed to have been written yesterday'. Karpath shared his enthusiasm, admiring in particular the way Mahler had modernized the staging so economically and yet managed to preserve all its original sparkle.[44] The second event was the world première at the end of February of *Der dot Mon*. This one-act opera by the Styrian composer Josef Forster,[45] was, in contrast, an almost complete failure. The libretto was based on a farce written in 1533 by Hans Sachs, the Renaissance poet-musician and shoemaker immortalized in *Die Meistersinger*. 'Der dot Mon'—the dead man—only pretends to be dead in order to test his wife, who immediately proclaims her intention of burying him quickly and remarrying at once. However, the dead man's 'resurrection' fails to work, since his cunning wife declares that she saw through his trick immediately and deliberately set out to make a fool of him.

Forster was neither a 'modern' nor a 'revolutionary' in the world of music. On the contrary, the score was composed in the 'old German' tradition and even included a few genuine sixteenth-century melodies. Many critics reproached him for the 'eclecticism' of his style.[46] Theodor Helm complained about the noisy orchestration and Gutheil-Schoder's heavy-handed interpretation.[47]

[41] On 14 Mar., with Bayer's *Rund um Wien*, and in Apr. with Josef Hellmesberger's *Die Perle von Iberien*. In all, *Feuersnot* was performed 9 times in 1902, twice in 1904, and once in June 1905.

[42] AMM1. 281; AMM2. 256. Alma was supposed to join him there and he duly went to meet her at the station on 2 Feb. but she never appeared.

[43] Mahler had revived it three years earlier.

[44] Cast of the performance of 15 Feb. 1902: Michalek (Jenny), Gutheil-Schoder (Anna), Hilgermann (Margarete), Naval (George Brown), Breuer (Dickson), Frauscher (Gaveston).

[45] Josef Forster should not be confused with Mahler's Czech friend Josef Bohuslav Förster, husband of the soprano Berta Förster-Lauterer. The composer of two ballets, Forster had some years before won first prize with his one-act *Die Rose von Pontevedra* in a competition organized by Prince Ernst of Coburg-Gotha. No fewer than 120 works had been submitted.

[46] Critics discerned the influence of Wagner (especially *Meistersinger*), Humperdinck, Nicolai, and Ambroise Thomas.

[47] As always, Gutheil-Schoder's performance gave rise to contradictory reactions. Helm found it overdone, Hirschfeld deemed it totally devoid of naturalness, while Graf preferred Marie Renard's conventional acting. Only Hanslick pronounced it 'masterly'.

Hanslick, on the other hand, defended Forster's music, calling it 'pink-cheeked, . . . bright, warm, translucent, . . . an antidote to the dangerous tendencies of such moderns as Strauss'. He even went so far as to predict a brilliant future for *Der dot Mon*, which, after eleven performances, of which Mahler conducted only the first three, sank into oblivion in 1903. Hirschfeld, on the other hand, thought that Forster had been too ambitious in choosing this subject, for he had been unable to retain the flavour of the original text. The music, he declared, was totally irrelevant to the text and 'plods along from one eight-bar phrase to the next, mixing styles, manners and ideas of every hue but completely lacking any personal colour'. As for Max Graf, while criticizing Forster's clumsiness and heterogeneous style, he nevertheless maintained that it was one of the best new operas Vienna had heard for many years.[48]

Ever since his engagement Mahler had had nagging doubts about the possible consequences of his marriage, and also felt guilty about his fiancée's pregnancy, which Alma did her best to conceal, despite frequent bouts of sickness. The date of the ceremony had to be postponed several times because Justi wanted her marriage to Arnold Rosé to coincide with her brother's, after which she would move out of the Auenbruggergasse apartment. It seems that Arnold could not obtain the necessary papers from Jassy, his birthplace in Romania.[49] Relations with Gustav's old friends were virtually at an end. From this point on, Natalie and Lipiner were completely set aside, and only Guido Adler continued to make frequent visits to the Auenbruggergasse.[50] Others, like the Spieglers, kept their distance. In fact they failed to understand that Alma's 'scandalous' attitude, her independence and unpredictability, fascinated Mahler perhaps even more than her beauty, probably because he had until that time been too much in the company of blind devotees and courtiers. Even Emil Freund, Mahler's childhood friend and his lawyer, considered the future of the marriage to be very uncertain, and advised Mahler to become a Protestant convert in order to facilitate any eventual divorce.[51] Alma's own friends, like Berta Zuckerkandl, were secretly worried because they had long been aware of her dominating, 'over-possessive' nature.[52]

The wedding date was finally fixed for 9 March. To avoid any inopportune publicity, it was decided that the ceremony would take place in the strictest privacy in the sacristy of the majestic Karlskirche, a masterpiece of Viennese

---

[48] Cast of the 28 Feb. première: Gutheil-Schoder (The Woman), Hilgermann (The Female Neighbour), Breuer (The Male Neighbour), Stehmann (The Man). *Der dot Mon* was followed by a revival of Forster's ballet *Der Spielmann*.

[49] AMS.

[50] On the day before the performance of *Klagende Lied* on 20 Jan. Mahler wrote to Adler apologizing for having missed a rendezvous. After a particularly long and exhausting rehearsal of *Feuersnot* he had lain down for what was intended to be a short nap after lunch and had not woken again until 5.30 p.m. He invites Adler to supper the following day, after the concert, at the Leidinger Restaurant (RAM 38).

[51] According to Frau Löwenbach, wife of a lawyer in Prague, whose family was intimate with Freund's.

[52] Zuckerkandl, *Österreich Intim*, 62.

baroque.[53] A rumour having spread that it would take place at 5.30, a large crowd, mostly women, gathered inside the church. It was then announced that the ceremony had already been held in the sacristy at 1.30. Alma came by cab with her mother and Justine, while Mahler walked through the pouring rain with his two witnesses, Carl Moll and Arnold Rosé. Everyone was dressed informally; Mahler wore a grey suit, a black overcoat, and a soft-felt hat. When the time came to kneel, he misjudged the position of his prie-dieu and fell on his knees to the floor. Because he was so short, he had to stand up again before he could kneel down properly, much to the sympathetic amusement of the officiating priest.[54]

A few days later, Karl Kraus[55] joked in *Die Fackel* about the 'strict privacy' so loudly proclaimed by the *Neue Freie Presse* (always the main target of his attacks on the Viennese press). If he is to be believed, the privacy was only relative:

'The wedding of Direktor Mahler took place in the strictest secrecy'. At least that is the claim in the columns of our daily newspapers. But they have not omitted the fact that 'Herr Mahler wore a dark grey suit, a black coat, a broad-brimmed black felt hat and galoshes' (special details courtesy of the *NFP*). Apart from the mother of the bride, the two witnesses—Rosé the concertmaster, and Carl Moll the painter—and the sacristan, no-one attended the ceremony. Did Herr Rosé, Herr Moll, or possibly the sacristan himself furnish the reports? Only the *Montagsrevue* seems to have sent its own trusted representative. He tells us that 'The church was packed with distinguished people, mostly recruited from the world of the arts. The entire company of the Opera, and its orchestra, and representatives from the *Obersthofmeisteramt*, the Intendant's office and so forth were present'. So there seem to be differences of opinion. That's what happens when the papers are not promptly informed, when Direktor Mahler's wedding, like the suicide of the Knight von Holzingen, takes place 'in strictest privacy'.

Nevertheless, the papers do record that there was no official message of congratulation to the newly-weds after the ceremony, and that the witnesses were charged with passing on the best wishes of the Opera personnel.[56] Alma later recalled the wedding meal that the two families took together. The atmos-

---

[53] According to *Neue Freie Presse*, the wedding had originally been set for 8 Mar. but was subsequently put off until the following day because 'Alma would not be of age until the 9th' (a surprising statement in view of the fact that Alma was 22) and because 'that date had been engraved on the ring'. The parish register carries another wrong date, 9 Feb. but that is definitely an error by the priest.

[54] According to the *Wiener Theater Almanach* and the church register (BDB 208), the name of the officiating priest was Josef Pfob.

[55] Karl Kraus had founded *Die Fackel* in 1899 (see Chap. 1). Several of his friends, notably Detlev von Liliencron, Peter Altenberg, and Frank Wedekind, collaborated on it until 1911. He later became the sole contributor. Kraus's articles had secured him a number of mortal enemies in Vienna, notably Hermann Bahr, whom he libelled in the most shameless manner and who won the case he brought against Kraus (see AML 182 and Chap. 12, Kraus using Alma's indiscretion to gather secrets on which he based some of his most biting epigrams).

[56] They had offered to send Mahler the Opera chorus to sing a nuptial serenade, but he had declined this honour. The two weddings were announced on the same very plain card, bearing only the four names and the date.

phere was calm, there were even periods of silence. Then she and Gustav returned to their respective apartments to finish packing before leaving for St Petersburg that evening. Justi and Arnold were married the next day, 10 March.[57] Their new apartment, 8 Salesianergasse, was only a short walk from the Auenbruggergasse.

Once on the train bound for Russia, Mahler began to relax and Alma breathed a sigh of relief at no longer having to hide her pregnancy. According to her, all went well until the stifling heat of the carriage brought on one of Mahler's violent migraines.[58] Alma, more and more worried, watched as he paced up and down the corridor like one possessed, 'his face white as chalk' and his teeth clenched. At every station he got out and, to the amazement of the Russians muffled in their furs, strode up and down the platform, hatless, coatless, and gloveless in a temperature of −30 degrees centigrade.[59] He arrived in St Petersburg with chilblains, a fever, a sore throat, and an incessant cough, exhausted from not having slept for two whole days and nights. He was therefore delighted to find his cousin Gustav Frank,[60] who held an important official post as head of the state press, waiting for them on the platform. One of the couple's first visits was to the Hermitage museum, where Mahler, delighted and much more receptive of the visual arts because of his new painter friends, conceived a deep and lasting admiration for Rembrandt.[61] Alma was happy to be so far away from Vienna, and in a letter to his sister Mahler wrote: 'I can give you the best possible news concerning Alma. You'll be happy to see that she has blossomed in every way.'[62] He himself had recovered from his various ailments, and both marriage and Russia suited him perfectly. They were invited out almost every day and Mahler had high hopes for the concerts, since the orchestra had great style, was 'excellent, very obedient', besides being full of enthusiasm and respect for himself. He and Alma had hoped to attend the Opera, but the theatres were closed for Lent and they saw only a benefit performance of *Eugene Onegin*—which was, however, admirably produced.

Mahler greatly appreciated the company of Frank, his wife, and four children, who 'remind me of the Hermann family', and felt completely at home in their house. Under his cousin's guidance, he and Alma set out to explore St Petersburg, and were much taken with its palaces and avenues, its elegance, gaiety, and luxury. They went for sleigh-rides on the frozen Neva and were

[57] At the Evangelical church on the Dorotheergasse, no. 18. It seems highly unlikely that Mahler failed to attend his sister's wedding, so he and Alma must have left for Russia on the evening of 10 Mar. or the morning of 11 Mar. (KMI).

[58] Considering the doubts and misgivings to which Alma says Mahler had been prey throughout their engagement, it seems possible that the various ailments he suffered in the train and in St Petersburg were partly psychosomatic.

[59] Alma is probably exaggerating the low temperature for Mahler wrote to Justi shortly afterwards: 'It is <u>not</u> cold here. We manage very well with our (winter) clothing.' (KMI).

[60] Anna Hermann, Marie Mahler's younger sister, had married Ignaz Frank. Their son was Gustav Frank, with whom Mahler had shared a room in Vienna in his youth.

[61] Letter to Justi, c.14 Mar. (RWO).   [62] Letter to Justi, 18 Mar. (RWO).

astounded to see trams running across the ice. Blissfully unaware that no Russian would dream of riding in an open vehicle in the wintertime, Mahler hired a small troika and took Alma out for drives. Both of them were greatly intrigued by Russian displays of piety, particularly one evening when, in the Arctic cold, they visited Kazan Cathedral and their coachman, totally ignoring them, threw himself flat on his face in the snow to pray. By the time he finished his prayers and returned to the horses, his two passengers were frozen stiff. Five years earlier, Mahler had had little or no contact with Moscow society, but now that he was Director of the Vienna Opera a number of aristocratic families in St Petersburg vied for the honour of entertaining him. One evening he and Alma were invited to dine with a cabinet minister called Saburoff, but were so bored that they left the party as soon as they could without giving offence. After the final rehearsal for the first concert, Mahler proudly wrote to Justi that 'the Grand Duchess Constantine came up and spoke to me in the friendliest way' and that he and Alma had dined the evening before with a member of the Imperial family, the Duke of Mecklenburg, who kept his own string quartet and had spoken enthusiastically about the Rosé Quartet. Mahler hoped to arrange for the Quartet to tour Russia. Unfortunately, most conversations were in French, a language in which Mahler was not very proficient. He was particularly hampered one evening when the elderly Julia Abbaza, a well-known but somewhat hysterical figure in St Petersburg society who made a point of meeting every important musical visitor, questioned him about eternal life and the survival of the soul in the light of the Second Symphony and its 'programme'.[63] On the other hand, whenever he tried to talk to the Russians about his favourite author, Dostoevsky, he was surprised to meet with only reticence or disdain.

Just as in 1897, Mahler's visit ended considerably less happily than it began. He grew tired of Russian food and Russian life, and both he and Alma eventually caught cold during a sleigh-ride. He began to cough again and was reduced to whispering during rehearsals. These began at 9.00 a.m., so that he was now unable to go on excursions or accept any invitations except from the Franks. He conducted the first concert with a splitting headache, and though he was vigorously applauded, he was already homesick and looked forward eagerly to returning to Vienna, with 2,800 florins in his pocket to help to pay off his debts.[64]

Mahler's three concerts took place in the vast, superb, sparkling white hall of the 'Assembly of the Nobles' (now the auditorium of the St Petersburg Philharmonic). On 17 March at 9 p.m. Mahler conducted Mozart's Symphony in

[63] AMS. On Julia Fiodorovna Abbaza, see below Vol. iii, Chap. 10.

[64] The affectionate letters Mahler wrote to Justi at this time show that their relationship had lost nothing of its warmth. The last one mentions Schoenberg's *Verklärte Nacht*, the première of which, given in Vienna on 18 Mar. by the Rosé Quartet, together with Grädener's Quartet Op. 33 and Brahms's Quintet No. 1, was a great success. Justi had told Mahler about it in one of her letters and he replied that he regretted not having heard it, for, judging from her description, it would have been of 'great interest to me' (RWO).

G minor and Beethoven's 'Eroica' Symphony as he had done at his first concert in Vienna in 1898; then, instead of the Coriolan Overture, the Prelude and 'Liebestod' from *Tristan*. Both audience and orchestra hailed the performance with an ovation. Alma, seated backstage, was able to observe Mahler's parted lips and ecstatic expression; she thought his face 'divinely beautiful' when he conducted. Once again she felt the full importance of the mission entrusted to her husband and inwardly vowed to 'live for him and do my utmost to remove all obstacles from his path'. At the end of the 'Eroica' Symphony, she happened to overhear two members of the audience speaking French. They agreed that 'Mahler's tempos differ radically from traditional ones, but his interpretation is as beautiful as it is novel.' She could not help admiring their lack of prejudice, particularly compared to the Viennese, who invariably questioned any new and original interpretation. However, Mahler's concerts do not seem to have aroused a great deal of interest in the higher spheres of the Russian musical establishment. In his *Souvenirs of N. A. Rimsky-Korsakov*, Vasilii Iastriebtsev refers to him very briefly. He mentions that on 5 March, when having cocoa with the famous Russian composer, they talked about Mahler, who they thought was 'very good indeed in Beethoven, though somewhat static and mannered'.[65] Before Mahler's arrival, the *Russkaya Muzykalnaya Gazeta* commented briefly on Mahler's programme and career. Subsequently it published an article by Max Graf in which he referred to Mahler as a 'modern' interpreter, heir to Wagner, and a man for whom 'tradition, style and classicism are only empty words'. Curiously enough, the magazine did not mention Mahler's previous visit to Russia in 1897.

Judging by the brevity of the various reviews of Mahler's concerts, music criticism in St Petersburg was still in its infancy. The article in the *San-Petersburgkye Vedomosti* (which was reprinted in the *Neues Wiener Journal*) mentions only the first concert. Mahler is depicted as 'an austere, bespectacled little man who resembles a clergyman. . . . All his strength seems to be concentrated in his piercing, irresistible eyes, which literally hypnotize the musicians'. 'His gestures are extremely simple. . . . He does not, like some other famous conductors, distract the musicians' attention with eccentric gestures. He sometimes leaves the orchestra completely to itself before then marking, suddenly and with extreme determination, some characteristic point.' The same critic praised his eminently Viennese interpretation of a Mozart symphony, the way he emphasized the middle voices, the whole thing 'living, new and original'; and also the 'hidden passion' which suffused the *Tristan* extracts.

---

[65] Vasilii Vasilévitch Iastriebtsev, *Souvenirs of N. A. Rimsky-Korsakov* (Leningrad, 1960; Columbia University, New York, 1985), 236. On the following page, Rimsky-Korsakov is reported to have attended the rehearsal of Mahler's second concert and to have judged that 'like most contemporary conductors, he mutilated Beethoven's *Egmont*'. At the first concert, Olympia Boronat sang Rosina's aria from the *Barber of Seville* and the bell aria from *Lakmé*. The American pianist Ernest Schelling then played the Piano Concerto in F minor by Chopin, and as an encore the *Grand Polonaise* in A-flat major. Both artists were accompanied—rather indifferently, according to the press—by a conductor called Nicolay Kroichevsky.

But the image he gave of the 'Eroica' seemed to this critic inferior to Richter's, which was 'more balanced and less nervous'. In Mahler, St Petersburg had discovered 'a phenomenal conductor, and the most modest of men, who refused to present any of his own works, but interpreted the German classics in all their historical veracity, and modern works with great intensity of feeling'. According to the same newspaper, the public gave Mahler only a moderately enthusiastic reception when he made his entrance, but he immediately proved himself an 'eminent' conductor and was warmly applauded after the 'Eroica'.

In the *Birzhevye Vedomosti*, Nikolas Soloviev,[66] one of the capital's foremost critics, compared Mahler to a 'high priest performing a sacred and divine rite' and praised his capacity to draw out from the orchestra 'an endless variety of nuances'. He termed him 'an enemy of superficial effect,' an 'austere' artist 'but devoid of any pedantic dryness'. A brief and superficial article in *Novoye Vremya* describes Mahler as 'a straightforward conductor, very experienced and of refined taste'. 'His utterance can be compared with that of a great orator: the different parts are admirably articulated and punctuated, the principal idea is clearly brought out, more than it would be with grandiloquent effects'. But the anonymous critic seems to have been still more impressed with the talent of the pianist, Ernest Schelling, and by the famous artistry of Olympia Boronat, a coloratura soprano who, in his opinion, might thenceforth rival Patti, Sembrich, and Barrientos; Mahler was said to be about to invite her to the Vienna Opera.

Only the weekly *Russkaya Muzykalnaya Gazeta* published a detailed criticism of this first concert. The anonymous critic described Mahler as 'a profoundly serious artist with clearly defined objectives, and he knows how to attain them with exemplary sureness, clarity and precision'. His interpretation was as intelligent as it was sensitive, without achieving Nikisch's intensity of passion; nevertheless the economy and precision of his gestures produced a high degree of creative tension among the orchestra. The performance was absolutely transparent, with not a single note lost, light and shade masterfully distributed, and detail constantly subordinated to the continuity and unity of the whole.[67] The noble simplicity of the Funeral March and the absence of superficial effects in the Scherzo of the 'Eroica' showed that Mahler strove wherever possible to emphasize the expressive content of a work. His interpretation of Mozart's symphony had been 'vivacious, honest, powerful, dynamic and devoid of the slightest hint of routine or excessive and sugary refinement', indeed a revelation of the master's true face. 'Just as a metaphysician transcends outward appearances, so Mahler makes a few photophonic [*sic*] gener-

[66] Nikolay Feopemptovitch Soloviev (1846–1916), writer, critic, collector of folk-songs, and composer, had studied medicine before entering the St Petersburg Conservatory, where he was a pupil of Nikolay Zaremba. After orchestrating Alexander Serov's posthumous opera, *Vrazh'ya sila* (Hostile Power), he taught at the Conservatory and was a critic for a few 'national' newspapers and reviews such as the *Novoye Vremya* and *Birzhevye Vedomosti* becoming known for his reactionary views and his nimble pen. As a composer, he produced quite a large number of rather mediocre works, operas in particular.

[67] According to this critic, Mahler accompanied each crescendo by a ritardando.

alizations. He follows only the musical thought without concerning himself with historical images or associations which, although superficially linked to the music, have no fundamental importance'. As far as the *Tristan* excerpts were concerned, this critic remarked that, whereas Richter made them sombre and awe-inspiring, a 'Triumph of Death', and Nikisch brought to them a feverish ecstasy, Mahler's slow tempo produced instead a 'languid, perverse and poisonous' effect. And no matter how impressive the unity and beauty of such an interpretation might be, Richter's was 'more imposing, more tragic and more profound'.

The programme of the second concert on 23 March included Tchaikovsky's Manfred Symphony, Beethoven's Egmont Overture, and Wagner's *Eine Faust-Overtüre*. Between the Overtures, Mahler accompanied one of Liszt's last pupils, Emil Sauer, who performed his own Piano Concerto in E minor.[68] The *Novoye Vremya* critic thought that the concert had been a 'considerable but not outstanding' success. Mahler knew how to 'emphasize the characteristic touches of each composer' and had surpassed himself in the Wagner overture thanks to 'the beauty of his nuances' and 'the flights of his imagination'. However, the same critic disliked Mahler's slow tempos in *Manfred* and disapproved of the cuts he made in the score.[69] On the other hand, in the *Birzhevye Vedomosti*, Nicolay Soloviev found Mahler's performance 'sensational thanks to its melodic expression and its extraordinarily subtle and varied shading'. He also praised his sober restraint in *Egmont*.[70] As for the *Muzykalnaya Gazeta*, it declared that Mahler had brought to *Manfred* certain qualities lacking in Tchaikovsky's score, such as unity and concentration, and that although his interpretation had all the requisite dash and fire, he had been well advised to tone down the symphony's contrasts and its 'frenzied and somewhat theatrically passionate outbursts'.[71] Finally the *San-Petersburgkye Vedomosti* deplored, in Mahler's conducting, a 'mania for holding back the tempo', which was entirely misplaced in *Manfred*, 'whose highly strung musical text cannot endure this constraint'. He conducted the work 'like a symphony, without any regard for the programme', which is no surprise, given Mahler's professed contempt for 'programme music' as a genre.

The third and last concert, on 29 March, consisted of shorter works. At the last moment, Bruckner's Fourth Symphony was replaced by Haydn's 'Drumroll' Symphony in E flat (No. 103)—because he had been warned that Bruckner would not meet the public's taste, the *Gazéta* claimed—followed by the Overture to Der *Freischütz*, the Funeral March from *Götterdämmerung* (which replaced the Coriolan Overture); then came Tchaikovsky's Violin Concerto

---

[68] The famous pianist played a Chopin waltz and one of his own Études as encores.

[69] He was also amazed that, in the 'Pastoral', Mahler had replaced the church bell by an orchestral bell.

[70] Like the *Gazeta*'s critic, Soloviev particularly admired Mahler's slow tempo in the *Egmont* coda, which conferred on the episode admirable power and solemnity.

[71] For the same reason, even the *Birzhevye Vedomosti* found his interpretation 'lifeless rather than inspiring'.

(played by the Russian virtuoso Alexander Petchnikoff)[72] and finally the Prelude to *Die Meistersinger*. This time, a few critics expressed reservations. All agreed that the Funeral March was the highlight of the evening, but the *Birzhevye Vedomosti* remarked that Wagner's works were 'so eloquent in themselves' that one could only wonder to what extent their success should be attributed to the conductor! Nikolay Soloviev had not the slightest doubt about this performance, 'so sublime' and 'so imbued with the spirit of the work' that it was encored.[73] However, the *Novoye Vremya* considered the 'new works' in the programme of 29 March simply 'outworn and outmoded' and ascribed Mahler's success to the unusually large orchestra (102 musicians).[74] Most of the critics considered Haydn's Symphony in E flat one of this master's weakest works. Like his colleagues, the anonymous critic of the *San-Petersburgkye Vedomosti* considered that it was to Wagner that Mahler brought 'something extraordinary' and observed that the Funeral March from *Götterdämmerung* had been frantically applauded, as had the Overture to *Der Freischütz*, though in the latter 'the rallentandos were not justified by any indication in the score'.

Once again, it was the *Muzykalnaya Gazeta* which made the most perceptive comments on this last concert, praising the 'vivacity, simplicity and unity' of Mahler's Haydn interpretation. Unlike Nikisch, 'who identifies himself with the drama of the symphony's hero', Mahler is predominantly serious, simple, and profound in his approach, though 'somewhat ascetic, and more controlled than emotional'. As a theatre conductor, Mahler does not identify himself completely with the music but 'follows its action like the chorus in a tragedy or bows to it like a high priest before an altar'. Thus, although a few Russian concert-goers both understood and admired Mahler, it is obvious that he had once again disconcerted many more for whom Nikisch remained the German conductor *par excellence*. Moreover, it seems that there was no great tradition of conducting in Russia, as there was in Germany, and with a few exceptions all the best conductors were foreigners. In order to appreciate a conducting style as original and exceptional as Mahler's, however, it was necessary to compare it with that of his contemporaries, with the traditions from which it sprang and yet so considerably differed. N. V. Kasanli, a Russian critic reporting for the German magazine *Die Musik*, defined Mahler as a musician 'who places the work above his own personality and tries to convey the ideas of its composer rather than to attract attention by excessive gesticulation'. This was faint praise in comparison to the adulation the Russians lavished on Nikisch at that time.[75]

---

[72] As encores, Alexander Abramovich Petchnikoff (1873–1949) and a pianist called Dulov played the *Havanaise* by Saint-Saëns and two pieces by César Cui, one of them named *Cavatina*.

[73] Soloviev reported that Mahler conducted the Wagner works without a score. The *Muzykalnaya Gazeta* regretted that the strings, reduced in number, had been drowned out by the brass.

[74] This critic condemned some of Mahler's slow tempos, particularly in the Allegro of the *Freischütz* Overture and the Andante of the Haydn Symphony.

[75] Kasanli praised Mahler's 'incomparable virtuosity' and, contrary to most contemporary critics, claimed that he 'avoided tempo changes' (*Die Musik*, 1: 15–16 (May 1902), 1517).

Mahler and Alma left St Peterburg immediately after the final concert. They wanted to stop in Warsaw on their way home. Unfortunately, however, Mahler's fees had been paid by cheque, and they realized in the train that all they had in cash was 5 roubles. At Warsaw station they found a hotel carriage which at least got them half-way across the city. As it was still Lent,[76] all the shops were shut and the streets barely lit. The carriage finally stopped in front of a cheerfully lit hotel. Fearing that 5 roubles wouldn't buy them dinner there, they told the doorman they would come back later and wandered off aimlessly through the dark and empty streets. Before long they were accosted by a 'nocturnal character' in a frock-coat who whispered to the foreigners that he could guide them to the city's forbidden pleasures. They quickened their pace, turned down a bleak side street, managed to find a carriage, and drove back to the station, which by this time seemed bright and friendly, compared with the rest of the town. There they waited for their train and ordered eggs in the buffet. Alma gave what remained of their roubles to an old Jewish beggar selling matches. But the train was barely out of the station before she discovered a gold coin in a pocket of her purse; they could have visited the Polish capital in style!

Back in Vienna on Easter Sunday, 31 March, Gustav and Alma settled into the Auenbruggergasse flat, Justi having already moved out. During his first few months in that block of flats, Mahler had had an ill-tempered neighbour, an army officer who used to order his servant to play the gramophone every day at precisely the hour Mahler returned from the Opera and sat down to work. He too had now moved out, and Mahler took over the two rooms he had occupied as well.[77] Now he had three large rooms and three small ones. Unfortunately, his financial situation was precarious because there were still debts from the building of the Maiernigg house. According to Alma, they had not yet been repaid because Justi had proved incapable of reducing the household budget sufficiently for that purpose. Thus, 50,000 crowns were still owed, not counting the dowry for Mahler's sisters,[78] part of which he had borrowed. Alma was thus

[76] Mahler returned to Vienna on Easter Sunday, which fell on 30 Mar. It seems that the night in Warsaw was that of Easter Saturday, so it is surprising that all the shops were still shut (KMI). As usual, Mahler had chosen to be away during Easter Week, the Vienna Opera having gone into recess from the Tuesday, 25 Mar. Strangely enough, AMM claims it was Advent.

[77] Fortunately Mahler saw through the neighbour's stratagem and bribed the servant not to start the gramophone until he heard his master returning. See the plan of the Auenbruggergasse apartment. Mahler's apartment now had nine instead of six windows overlooking the Strohgasse. The officer's two rooms were nos. 10 and 2 on the plan. He had probably sublet them until then from the tenants of the next apartment (no. 27). Mahler's flat (no. 28) was situated on the third and top floor of the Otto Wagner apartment house, which was comprised of a parterre (ground floor), a mezzanine, and three floors. Immediately after the war, when he was forced to leave his own house by the allied forces of Occupation because of his connections with the Nazis, Karl Böhm became a tenant of apartments 48–54 in the same house.

[78] The sum due to the two sisters from their parents' estate had, it seems, been long since set aside for their dowries. None the less, Mahler later borrowed a part of this money to pay for the new house in Maiernigg. Ernst Rosé, son of Emma and Eduard, informed me that Mahler had to pay 100 marks a year to his mother Emma for a number of years. The figure given by Alma was much inflated. As Knud Martner noted, Mahler's salary at the Opera was 12,000 kronen a year (before tax) and she could never have repaid such an amount

obliged to assume a role as careful housekeeper for which she was ill prepared, since she had always lived on a grand scale with her father and then with Moll. Nevertheless she claims to have succeeded in paying off all Mahler's debts within five years.

On his return to Vienna Mahler found a letter from Angelo Neumann inviting him to conduct *Das Rheingold* and *Die Walküre* at a Wagner festival to be held in Prague in May[79] (he had conducted the premières of these works in Prague seventeen years earlier). However attractive this proposition, he had to refuse it, for he had only just arrived back from Russia[80] and intended to leave soon for Krefeld, where rehearsals for his Third Symphony, whose première he was to conduct at the festival of the Allgemeiner Deutscher Musikverein, would keep him away for ten days. In the meantime, much of his energy was taken up with the Hofoper, where a serious row had developed between him and the Philharmonic Orchestra. In engaging musicians for the Opera it was his custom to promise them, in addition to their salaries, the supplementary income they would derive from Philharmonic Concerts.[81] In principle he did not have the right to make such promises since, even if the two orchestras were in fact made up of the same musicians, the Philharmonic was an autonomous association which appointed its own members. Certainly the committee had never, up to that time, refused to admit newly hired musicians. Yet, in May 1902, it did precisely that. Mahler was bringing too many foreign elements into the orchestra[82] and the engagement of eight new wind players, in particular, however justifiable at the Opera for Wagner's works, was quite unnecessary for concerts, since the orchestra already comprised the 108 players provided for in the statutes, this being a kind of guarantee of the level of individual members' shares in the orchestra's earnings.

As early as June 1902 the *Österreichisch-Ungarische Musiker-Zeitung* had accused Mahler of arbitrarily hiring and firing musicians at the Opera, thus creating a 'climate of insecurity'. 'Human material is handled like inanimate objects,' it averred. On 27 June, the same magazine attacked again: 'Amid his

---

in the course of five years as well as paying rent for the flat in Vienna, a mortgage for the house in Maiernigg, wages for the two or three servants, not to mention buying food and clothes, etc. for a family of four (AMM3. 367).

[79] Neumann had offered Mahler 1,000 kronen for each performance (18 and 19 May). He also asked him to allow Leo Slezak and Selma Kurz to participate, a request which was granted (HOA, no. 277/1902). In May the two directors exchanged further telegrams on the subject of Edyth Walker. Mahler apologized for not allowing her to take part in the festival since 'there was never any question of her before, only of Slezak and Kurz'. In fact, since Walker had just cancelled a performance of *Lohengrin* because she was ill, he could hardly give her permission to sing elsewhere.

[80] Some time after his return, Mahler hurt his foot in a fall on the staircase at the Auenbruggergasse and had to keep to his room for several days.

[81] Cf. *Österreichisch-Ungarische Musiker-Zeitung* (12 Sept. 1902). This paper accuses Mahler, not without justification, of a certain 'fickleness' in his promises.

[82] According to Wilhelm Beetz (*Das Wiener Opernhaus 1869 bis 1945*, Central European Times, Zurich, 1949), Mahler engaged, during his 10-year tenure, about 80 new musicians, of whom no fewer than 33 were wind players.

compositional dreams, as his soul lingers far away in the realm of his imagination, it happens that Direktor Mahler appends his signature to a decree
depriving several musicians of their right to exist. Then he continues to follow
the thread of his soulful Adagio, creating the most celestrial harmonies . . .'. On
7 July Mahler wrote an official letter to the Philharmonic committee warning
that, in the future, his verbal consent would no longer suffice for the concerts,
but that it would have to be backed by an annual permission to be given in
writing, and this would be granted only if the Opera's new players had already
been admitted to the orchestra. For this he obtained the Intendant's agreement.[83] Theoretically, he had the right to do this, since, as we have seen, the
musicians were obliged each year to obtain the Opera Director's permission to
take part in the concerts. But the players now felt they were being submitted to
a kind of blackmail, and reacted accordingly.

At the beginning of the new season, on 3 September, the plenum voted
unanimously against the admission of the new wind instrumentalists. Mahler
thought he would placate the musicians by proposing to increase the number of
Philharmonic concerts to nine, but they found his proposal 'impudent' since
that would mean that 'we should work more to compensate for our smaller
shares'. Ludwig Karpath's account agrees on every point with the reports of the
contemporary press.[84] On 10 September, the *Deutsche Zeitung* bitterly censured Mahler for his attitude in this dispute: the liberal press had distorted the
facts and turned the Philharmonic's refusal into a mere 'question of money'. By
threatening to forbid the concerts, the Intendant had exceeded his powers,
which had only been granted to him to ensure that the musicians did not engage
in activities unworthy of them or contrary to the interests of the Opera. In a way
that was 'downright scandalous', Mahler had tried to introduce musicians
devoted to his cause into an orchestra whose majority opposed him.[85] He had,
moreover, achieved his aim, the article continued, for 'in order to curry favour
with him' the committee had proposed that every year, in addition to the Nicolai
Concerts, he conduct a 'supplementary concert' which would include one of his

[83] The letter is dated 7 July 1902: see Richard von Perger, *Fünfzig Jahre Wiener Philharmoniker, 1860–1910* (Fromme, Vienna, 1910), 44.

[84] BMG 170. Karpath, Clemens Hellsberg, and the contemporary press mention 'eight wind players'. However 6 wind players were engaged on 1 Oct. 1901, and one on 15 July 1902. The critic does not date the incident, which occurred at the end of the 1901–2 season. In an interview in the *Neues Wiener Tagblatt* (28 Sept. 1902), after the two general meetings of the Philharmonic had brought matters to a head, Richter defended the musicians of the Opera, claimed that they could not be reproached for wishing their statutes to be respected, and suggested that Vienna adopt the same system as Berlin, where the Opera players did not automatically became members of the Philharmonic, but only gradually as places became available. The Vienna statistics show that, of all the players engaged in 1901, 7 immediately became members of the Philharmonic while 3 never did. *Neue Freie Presse* (12 Sept. 1902), claimed that 7 of the 8 wind players had 'already been fired' by Mahler, who had similarly engaged and straightway fired several harpists. In Jan. and Nov. 1902, Mahler had corresponded with Alfred Holy, a virtuoso harpist who, though of Austrian origin, was a member of the Berlin Opera (HOA, Z.70/1902 and Nov. 1902). Holy became a member of the Opera orchestra in 1903.

[85] *Österreichisch-Ungarische Musiker-Zeitung* (12 Sept. 1902) even suggests that he hired the extra winds with a view to performances of his symphonies!

own works.[86] Thanks to this cunning move, he had deprived the orchestra of the liberty it had regained with great difficulty the previous year and had once more imposed an 'intolerable' yoke. It seems that a compromise solution was eventually found in 1903, in the form of a supplementary paragraph introduced into the Philharmonic statutes, whereby new members of the Opera orchestra would immediately become titular members of the Philharmonic but would not participate in concerts except when needed. They would at first be treated as 'postulants' and would receive no regular income from concerts.[87] In exchange for this clause, the Intendant agreed to raise the salaries of the Opera players.

An article in the Berlin newspaper *Der Tag* summed up the story with exemplary fairness:

In all the time the Hofoperntheater has existed, no director has done as much for the orchestra as Gustav Mahler. . . . We would also, in truth, report that the orchestra has missed no opportunity . . . to slander its exacting conductor. Nevertheless, Mahler's recent behaviour should equally be condemned, for he has obstructed and harassed the orchestra in the same measure as he has showered it with benefits.[88]

Clemens Hellsberg, in his series of articles on the Philharmonic, considers the whole conflict as typical of 'the tragic element which characterizes Mahler's relationship with the Philharmonic, for, strictly speaking, the enlargement of the orchestra was necessary and, in the final analysis, an advantage for the ensemble, although the Director's course of action initially gave rise to irreconcilable conflicts before a practical solution could be found'.

The 1902 conflict left scars, especially since another, simultaneous 'Affär' further poisoned Mahler's relationship with the orchestra.[89] Nevertheless it is obvious that Mahler's prestige remained high. The same general assembly which, in May 1902, refused to admit the new musicians, was called on to elect a conductor for the following season. At this time, 29 members voted for Mahler, who did not stand as candidate, although everyone knew he would refuse the post, 52 votes (less than the preceding year) went to Hellmesberger, who was re-elected, and 2 to Schalk. Mahler no doubt meditated once more on human ingratitude, for no one had fought more strenuously than he had to improve the players' living and working conditions. Indeed, he had increased their salaries at the Opera[90] and later on, in 1900, had obtained for them the title of Hofmusiker.

At the Hofoper, conflicts and petty jealousies broke out as usual among the star singers. Once again, in January 1902 Theodor Reichmann complained to

---

[86] In fact, this 'supplementary concert' was given only in 1902 and 1904. Moreover, Mahler never again conducted a Nicolai Concert.

[87] Perger, *Fünfzig Jahre*, 44.   [88] *Der Tag*, 425 (11 Sept. 1902).

[89] At the time of the Secession's Beethoven Exhibition (see below, this Chap.).

[90] This had cost the Opera an extra 40,000 gulden a year. *Österreichisch-Ungarische Musiker-Zeitung* (12 Sept. 1902) goes so far as to call this increase an attempt to 'buy' the Philharmonic players.

Mahler that he was not being allowed to sing his most successful roles often enough—Don Juan, Renato (in *Ballo in maschera*), the Templar, and the Vampire in Marschner's opera—and that this was alienating his public and undermining his image. A 'fiery spirit' like Mahler should nevertheless make an effort to understand other people's feelings, and should not oblige him to sing Luna in *Trovatore*, 'one of the few roles which evokes no enthusiasm in me at all'.[91] In April, when Reichmann was making guest appearances at the Berlin Opera, he telegraphed Mahler: 'At least let me sing the Vampire here on Friday. The management will be very displeased if I refuse. I might not be invited back. Please. Please'. Mahler's laconic reply was dismissive: 'Unfortunately impossible. *Tell* here on Saturday.'[92] Reichmann's eagerness to make the best of the last years of his career is just as understandable as the director's refusal to let him devote his time and now limited energy to other institutions than the Hofoper, which he was apt to do whenever the occasion arose. In July 1902, the singer was taking a cure at Marienbad when he agreed at the last moment to step in for Karl Perron and appear as Amfortas in Bayreuth, where he had not sung for several years. Later on, he participated in another Wagner festival, at the Prinzregenttheater in Munich, and suffered more 'heart pains' which forced him to cancel his first Hofoper appearances of the season. The fact is that Reichmann was now gravely ill. His last Viennese performance was in *Tannhäuser*, on 22 March 1903. Two days later, he suffered a bad attack of asthma. As it happened, his contract was then about to expire. On several occasions, Mahler had hinted that he would only renew it if the baritone were prepared to accept a lower salary. However, upon learning that Reichmann was terminally ill, he signed a new contract, presumably on the old terms, on 7 May 1903. Reichmann died on 25 May.[93]

In the same month, Reichmann's much feared younger rival, Leopold Demuth, threatened to leave the Opera after a disagreement,[94] and Franz Naval also tendered his resignation which was accepted. Mahler had warned him that in the forthcoming revival of Halévy's *La Juive* he would sing, not the leading role, but that of Prince Leopold, and had reminded him that this role, despite its brevity, was almost always taken by an important singer. Naval refused to accept that argument, and this time Mahler induced the Obersthofmeisteramt

[91] Reichmann's letter is dated 19 Jan. 1902 (HOA).

[92] Reichmann, who was born in 1849, was then reaching the end not only of his career, but of his life.

[93] In his much embroidered biography of Theodor Reichmann, subtitled 'novel' (*Amfortas*, Westermann, Brunswick, 1932), T. Elbertshagen constantly mixes fact and fiction, quoting authentic documents in full (such as Mahler's two long letters to Reichmann). According to Elbertshagen, Reichmann defied his doctor's orders by singing in Bayreuth in 1902 and died suddenly, from over-exertion, two weeks after the Festival ended. An even more far-fetched story is told by Norman Lebrecht in *The Maestro Myth* (Simon & Schuster, London, 1991): that Reichmann was dismissed by Mahler, who had caught him in the midst of a homosexual encounter with a male chorister, backstage at the Opera, and Reichmann died broken-hearted. There are many doubtful stories in Lebrecht's book, which often seems to prefer scandalous rumour to prosaic matters of fact, but this story is certainly fictitious. Reichmann was already critically ill in a sanatorium when he received the welcome news of his extended contract.

[94] *Neue Freie Presse* (19 and 21 Apr.).

to let him go.[95] Naval later admitted that he had been more concerned at that time with his career, and his success, than with his duties as a member of the Hofoper. According to him, the main reason for his departure was Mahler's refusal to grant him a long leave of absence because 'the members hired by him were supposed to remain at all times at his disposal'. He decided therefore to leave the Hofoper in order to be free to accept an invitation from the United States.[96]

In May the bass, Moritz Frauscher, whom Mahler had engaged three years earlier, complained in a letter to the management, that the director had 'rudely called him to order' backstage for having failed during a performance to cut a particular aria as instructed. He claimed that Mahler had never properly informed him that it was to be omitted, and that nobody had been able to confirm anything about it before he went on stage:

I have long wished to request you, and am now taking the opportunity of doing so, not to correct me so rudely on stage and in the corridors, like a lord addressing a bootblack. After all, I was not picked up off the streets, either as a man or as an artist. I have always observed the proprieties in my dealings with you. To return to what I was saying earlier, i.e. your reproach of my supposedly importuning you with continual visits, I can assure you that I shall no longer give you the displeasure of seeing and hearing me in any but the most exceptional circumstances. I am not in the habit of forcing myself on people, particularly when I fail to meet with the slightest warmth.[97]

In all likehood, Frauscher was no great singer, but Mahler had evidently sorely offended him. Nevertheless, he remained with the Opera for a further two years.

Shortly after this, Marie Gutheil-Schoder, one of the singers Mahler admired most, asked for leave in the middle of the season because she was pregnant. Since her financial situation was far from satisfactory, she begged him to make an exception to the rule and allow her to receive her full salary while she was gone. Having met with a refusal, she threatened to resign. Although Mahler had always been on the best of terms with her,[98] and perhaps precisely because he had already been accused of favouring her, he felt obliged to refuse her request. When she threatened to resign, he wrote her a friendly but firm letter explaining that the same rules applied in theatres everywhere[99] and that they had recently been broken all too frequently. Walker, Grengg, and Reichmann had

[95] Naval made his last appearance on the Viennese stage in *Ballo in maschera* on 11 Apr. 1902 (*Wiener Theateralmanach* (1903), 80).

[96] Karl Marilaun, 'Gespräch mit Franz Naval', *Neues Wiener Journal* (30 Oct. 1924). Naval was later to seek re-engagement at the Hofoper (see below, Vol. iii, Chap. 6).

[97] Letter from Moritz Frauscher of 22 May 1902 (HOA).

[98] Various letters show that Mahler had tried several times to extend her vacation. On 22 June 1901, she wrote asking him for permission to stay away from Vienna until Sept., in order to be there only 'under your protection', for 'you cannot imagine what it is like when you are away'.

[99] Mahler referred to the case of Wilhelm Hesch, operated on for cancer at the beginning of the summer. At first he had made an exception in his favour, but subsequently was forced to apply the rule.

been unable to sing for several months,[100] but nevertheless demanded their full salaries because Mildenburg, Hesch, and Gutheil-Schoder herself had previously received the same preferential treatment. Thus Mahler's own leniency was constantly being turned against him, and he had come to realize why the Intendant now demanded strict application of the rules. Although he deeply regretted having to apply them in the present case, to 'the most conscientious and reliable' of all the Opera's members, he was nevertheless obliged to recognize that 'the Intendant is right' and admit that:

I have previously acted impractically and foolishly and deserve to pay dearly for my unshakeable faith in people and belief in their corrigibility [*Corrigibilität*] since, in this case, even the member whom I perhaps value most highly, on whose fairness I count with implicit confidence, demands the waiving of a normal administrative rule common to all theatres, and threatens to resign.

He therefore asked her to reconsider and to write him 'one of her dear, good letters'.[101]

Gutheil-Schoder replied that she was so worried and anxious about making ends meet that she simply could not write a 'dear good letter'. The rule in question did *not* apply in all theatres, and the one thing she bitterly regretted was that she, 'the most conscientious and reliable of all members', had to suffer like the rest. Despite her disappointment, she would nevertheless refrain from handing in her resignation, since she felt she had 'forfeited the right' to do so. With great dignity, she ended her letter as follows: 'May the waves that beat and the storms that rage about your person subside, and may the hideous rumours (spread by envy, jealousy and inartistic self-seeking), which cause your supporters, admirers and friends much grief and concern, be stifled.'[102] These lines show that Gutheil-Schoder was made of different stuff from the majority of her colleagues, who were too often motivated by vanity, envy, and the spirit of intrigue. The unfortunate incident in no way affected her relations with Mahler, and she continued as a member of the Opera to the end of her life.[103] It is possible that Mahler had to take particular care, at that time, not to favour her, for his rather too passionate affection and admiration for her during the year 1900 had not passed unnoticed and it seems that, in 1902, malicious rumours were circulating that he was the father of the child she was about to have.

Fortunately, the era of his bitter disputes with the administration was now a thing of the past, although barely concealed differences of opinion still occurred every year when the time came round for the preparation and approval

[100] Mahler's feeling was that Reichmann behaved particularly badly by spending his vacations singing in Munich and Bayreuth instead of resting his voice.

[101] Only the signature is autograph in Mahler's letter (HOA, letter of 15 Sept. 1902).

[102] Letter dated 20 Nov. (HOA, Z.619/1902).

[103] She sang there until 1926, then became a stage-director and 'honorary member'. Having accepted Mahler's decision and agreed to a reduction in her salary, she wrote to him again on 11 Oct. at the end of her leave, to request an explanation for a further reduction in her salary, which had been promised her in full up to that date (HOA, Z.619/1902).

of the budget forecast for the following year.[104] The Intendant had the final say in this matter, something he never failed to bring home to the director, especially after the departure of Wlassack who, it seems, had remained favourable to Mahler and had helped him in his big battle with the Intendant in 1898–9 on the matter of the Dienst-Instruktion.[105] Each year, in the autumn, Mahler had to produce a forecast for the following year, including a 'provisional' estimate of income and expenditure. In the spring, the 'real' position (*Gebarungsabschluss*), based on existing income and expenditure, was calculated for the rest of the year. This was usually the time when Mahler had to face up to reprimands from the Intendant. Mahler's 'third period' as director, which started in 1904 and included all Roller's large-scale productions, was naturally going to involve greater expenditure. During those years, the subsidies necessary to balance the Opera's accounts were constantly in excess of forecasts.[106]

Mahler's own conducting activities had already slowed down considerably; in 1901–2 he conducted not more than 36 performances. The figure rose to 53 the following season, but then fell again. The full balance-sheet for the 1901–2 season shows that Wagner once again dominated the repertoire with 56 performances, among them four *Ring* cycles, and that Mozart was programmed only 10 times.[107] The only point on which Mahler was quite sharply criticized by the management was the invitation he extended to Lilli Lehmann to give six performances during October at a fee of 1,000 kronen for each appearance.[108] He was reprimanded for employing 'such an expensive guest artist' for 'a Wagner cycle which has absolutely no need for such supplementary attractions'. Far from giving in, Mahler invited the famous soprano for a larger number of guest appearances than planned, and gave her the role of Brünnhilde in a complete *Ring* cycle.[109]

In April 1902, artistic life in Vienna was wholly dominated by the fourteenth exhibition of contemporary art organized by the Vereinigung Bildender Künstler Österreichs (Association of Austrian Fine Artists), better known as

[104] At the Opera the financial year coincided with the calendar year, without reference to the theatrical 'season'.			[105] WMW 294.

[106] WMW 208. Franz Willnauer puts the real depreciation of the krone at 20% during these ten years (2% per year).

[107] *Figaro* and the *Flute* (4 performances each), *Don Giovanni* (2). The following works received 5 or more performances: *Les Contes d'Hoffmann* (39 performances, a success unprecedented in the annals of the Hofoper); *Pagliacci* (15); *Lohengrin* (13); *Die lustigen Weiber* (12); *Tannhäuser* (11); *Faust, Carmen, Mignon*, and *Trovatore* (10); *Meistersinger* (9); *Dot Mon* and *Manon* (8); *Feuersnot* and *Die Königin von Saba* (7); *Ballo* and *William Tell* (7); *The Flying Dutchman* (6); *Freischütz, Tristan, Aida*, and *Hänsel und Gretel* (5).

[108] What is more, Mahler had agreed that she should receive the whole amount without deduction of the statutory 5% for the pension fund.

[109] Letters from Mahler to Lilli Lehmann during the summer (Staatsbibliothek, Berlin, no. 55.354). In Dec. 1902 and Jan. 1903, the great soprano sang *Norma* (2 performances), *Don Giovanni, Fidelio, Tristan*, and the *Ring*. During the 1901–2 season Mahler performed cycles of the complete works of Wagner four times. On 24 Mar., during Mahler's trip to Russia, Massenet came on the occasion of Vienna's 100th performance of *Manon* and conducted the St-Sulpice act. He and the director exchanged telegrams of congratulation and thanks.

the Secession. At first sight it may seem surprising to speak of this exhibition as an important event in Mahler's life, since he had never shown any particular interest in the fine arts. But his marriage to Alma had opened up new horizons for him. The founding of the Secession on 3 April 1897,[110] only five days before Mahler was appointed Kapellmeister at the Hofoper, was without doubt the major event in the history of the arts in Vienna at the turn of the twentieth century. It was not the only movement of its kind, since the Munich Secession was launched in 1898 by Franz von Stuck, and its Berlin counterpart the following year, by Max Liebermann, but the Viennese Secession quickly became the most active and best known of the three. A glance at the posters and catalogues, or at any issue of the magazine *Ver Sacrum*, immediately shows the scope of the enterprise. No other European movement took so clearly as its goal the revolutionizing of the whole range of fine and applied arts—not only painting and sculpture, but also design, book illustration, engraving, typography, and so on.

The idea of the Secession originated in the minds of three Viennese painters, Gustav Klimt,[111] Josef Engelhart,[112] and Carl Moll,[113] who used to meet regularly at Berta Zuckerkandl's house.[114] One of the key ideas of the movement was 'to establish permanent contacts between the artistic life of Vienna and the latest developments of the avant-garde abroad, and also to organize exhibitions on the basis of purely artistic considerations, independently of any commercial motive' (according to the first manifesto produced by Klimt for the members of the Vereinigung). Because the existing galleries, especially the Künstlerhaus, remained closed to modern art in any form, it was decided to appeal for funds for the construction of a new building. The necessary money was collected in a matter of weeks, thanks to Engelhart's many contacts, to Carl Moll's organ-

[110] See Vol. i, Chap. 24.

[111] Gustav Klimt (1862–1918), son of an artisan, studied at the Kunstgewerbeschule (School of Applied Arts) in Vienna with Ferdinand Julius Laufberger, Julius Victor Berger, and Christian Griepenkerl. He began his career by decorating several theatres, notably the Burgtheater, in collaboration with his brother Ernst (d. 1892) who was also a painter. In 1890, he broke with Austrian academicism and turned to a style inspired by the Pre-Raphaelites and the Impressionists. He was elected president of the Secession when it was founded in 1897, but resigned from it in 1905, by which time he had moved on to his 'Byzantine' or 'gilt' period, inspired by the mosaics in Ravenna which he first saw in 1903. He was henceforth to use marble, copper, enamel, and precious stones as decorative elements.

[112] Josef Engelhart (1864–1941), painter and sculptor. Born in Vienna, he was a student at the Technische Hochschule of the Academy, and then completed his studies in Paris in 1890. He established contact between the Secession and the most important foreign artists. His landscapes, inspired by Impressionism, his scenes of Viennese life, and his portraits are still very much appreciated.

[113] Carl Moll (23 Apr. 1861–13 Apr. 1945), student of Christian Griepenkerl and of Emil Jakob Schindler. One of the Secession's principal members, he turned, after leaving it, towards a decorative neo-naturalism rather like Klimt's, and finally associated himself with painters like Kokoschka and Kolig. Moll painted numerous indoor scenes, landscapes, and still lifes. Recent exhibitions have shown that he had formerly been seriously underestimated. He wrote a short biography of *Schindler* (Österreichische Staatsdruckerei, Vienna, 1930). After the Anschluss, he fell under the influence of his daughter Maria Eberstaller, and became a convinced Nazi. He committed suicide at the age of 85 in 1945, as the Russians were entering Vienna.

[114] According to Berta, the idea of the Secession was first debated in her salon: Berta Zuckerkandl, *Ich erlebte fünfzig Jahre Weltgeschichte* (Bermann, Stockholm, 1939).

izational talent, and the prestige of Klimt, unanimously regarded as the greatest Austrian painter. Karl Wittgenstein, the celebrated millionaire businessman, is said to have contributed a large sum because his daughter Hermine was a great admirer of Klimt and collected his paintings.

The forty founding members of the Secession were recruited not only from among the artists of the Genossenschaft Künstler Wiens or Künstlerhaus, but also from the Hagengesellschaft[115] and the Siebener Club.[116] Gustav Klimt, who had just celebrated his thirty-fifth birthday, was not only the Secession's first president,[117] but also its predominant personality. He had reached the end of his first period and had just embarked on his second.[118] The younger members had 'great confidence in this taciturn man of sincere and well-known convictions. . . . With sure instinct they recognized in him the artist who could best help them escape the shackles of academicism. Klimt and the Secession thus became completely identified with each other during seven fertile years.'[119] Despite his fame, and the admiration his society portraits inspired, Klimt ran up against total incomprehension when the three big panels commissioned by the Ministry of Culture for the University were at last completed. In fact the three works, entitled *Philosophy* (1900), *Medicine* (1901), and *Jurisprudence* (1903) created such a scandal when the Secession exhibited them in 1903 that Klimt decided not to hand them over to the Ministry of Culture. Two of his supporters, August Lederer and Kolo Moser, helped him to refund all the money he had received as commission.

Thanks to the enormous energy of its founders, the generosity of a number of rich collectors, and the support of numerous political figures,[120] the Secession's New Exhibition Hall was built in record time. Even before the building was completed, the group had prepared and published the first issue of its magazine, *Ver Sacrum*,[121] whose editor in chief was Alfred Roller. The first issue, dated January 1898, contained an article by Hermann Bahr[122] entitled 'Secession' in which he declared that:

---

[115] When the Secessionists left the Künstlerhaus, they at first formed a Hagenbund. It was named after Herr Hagen, the proprietor of the restaurant Zum blauen Freihaus on the Gumpendorfstrasse.

[116] Founded in 1895, this group also originally met at Hagen's restaurant, before moving to the Café Sperl nearby.

[117] The second president was Carl Moll (1899–1901) and the third Alfred Roller (1902–5).

[118] Of which the *Portrait of Sonja Knips*, 1898, is the first important work.

[119] Christian Nebehay (ed.), *Eine Klimt Dokumentation* (Nebehay, Vienna, 1969), 126.

[120] Among them was the anti-Semitic burgomaster of Vienna, Karl Lueger, whose support for the Secession was a purely political gesture, an attempt to prove to the Kaiser, who had opposed his candidacy, that he was not 'an enemy of art'.

[121] *Ver Sacrum* (Sacred Spring). The title comes from a poem by Ludwig Uhland, 'Weihefrühling', about the sacred springtime of Rome, which carries within it 'the seeds of a new world'. *Ver Sacrum* was issued regularly, 1898–1903, by three successive publishers. The two 'literary advisers' to the publication, Hermann Bahr and Max Burckhard (Alma's friend and admirer), recruited a galaxy of distinguished contributors to the magazine, including Rainer Maria Rilke, Hugo von Hofmannsthal, Peter Altenberg, Franz Servaes, Richard Dehmel, Otto Julius Bierbaum, Detlev von Liliencron, Maurice Maeterlinck, and Emile Verhaeren.

[122] Hermann Bahr (1863–1934), born in Linz, art and drama critic, poet and novelist, began his career as

I have come to understand the task of our young Viennese painters, and know that their 'Secession' must be quite different from that of Munich or Paris. There, the Secession is intended to build a new art alongside the old. . . . For us it is different. It is not a battle for or against tradition, for we do not possess a tradition. It is not a struggle between a nonexistent old art and a new . . . but a struggle for art itself . . . and for the right of artistic creation. Our Secession expresses the revulsion of the artist towards pedlars who pass themselves off as artists and whose interest lies precisely in preventing the triumph of art.

The desire for renewal must have been immensely strong in the Austrian capital, a city steeped with pride in its past, for though this revolutionary programme demanded nothing less than a complete break with tradition, the ideas of the Secession quickly gained ground and were soon influencing every sphere of the arts and crafts in Vienna. The Secession's war on *Schlendrian* (the humdrum) and the Philistines soon brought its first victories. At first, under the influence of the Pre-Raphaelites and the Impressionists, the Secessionists developed a new style of decoration based mostly on plant motifs, but this soon evolved towards simple and increasingly geometric forms. At the same time they invented new techniques for working with utilitarian materials like concrete and iron, endowing them with new architectural and decorative forms.

The first official exhibition took place early in 1898 at the Gartenbausäulen, the old covered market on the Parkring. It included sculptures by Rodin (who had not previously exhibited in Vienna), and paintings by Besnard, Böcklin, Crane, Khnopff, Klinger, Liebermann, Puvis de Chavannes, Segantini, Stuck, and Thoma, as well as works by the Secessionists themselves. The Emperor came in person to open the exhibition, which attracted more than 56,000 visitors. More than half the works and objects were sold by the closing date. The Secession immediately became a force to be reckoned with. One of its members, the illustrator Felician Freiherr von Myrbach-Rheinfeld,[123] was shortly afterwards appointed director of the Kunstgewerbeschule (Institute of

'Dramaturg' at the Deutsche freie Bühne in Berlin in 1890, working with realist writers. In 1891 he announced, with surprising clairvoyance, that this movement would not last much longer. After a short Marxist period and much travel (notably in Russia), Bahr spent some time in Paris before moving back to Vienna in 1894. With friends, he then founded the newspaper *Die Zeit*, began writing articles about painting, and became friendly with Hofmannsthal and Schnitzler. In 1899 he also joined the *Neues Wiener Tagblatt*. In the course of his long literary career he frequently changed his aesthetic standpoint, from naturalism to neo-romanticism, from symbolism to expressionism. Closely bound up with the Secession from the beginning, he remained loyal to Klimt and his group when they left it, and supported the Kunstschau. A close friend of 'the prince of painters', Bahr purchased in 1900 one of Klimt's most famous pictures, *Nuda Veritas*. In the early years of the Secession he organized special visits for workers to the exhibitions, giving the commentaries himself. For many years he occupied an essential place in Viennese artistic life as an originator of ideas and an essayist. He also wrote many plays (*Die Mutter* 1891; *Das Tschapperl* 1898; *Der Meister* 1904; *Josephine*; *Das Konzert* 1909; *Das Prinzip* 1912; *Die Wienerinnen*, etc.), and many books, the most important without doubt being *Zur Kritik der Moderne* (Towards a Critique of the Moderns) publ. in 1890. In 1909, Bahr married Anna von Mildenburg. In the closing years of his life he became mentally deranged.

[123] Myrbach had made a name for himself in Paris as illustrator of Alphonse Daudet.

Applied Arts), which had hitherto been steeped in ultra-conservatism. The 'official canons of beauty' were transformed overnight and academicism was soon discarded in favour of the new trends. The famous 'Kunsttempel'[124] of the Secession, built in six months, was inaugurated together with the second exhibition, on the 12 November 1898. The architect, Josef Maria Olbrich,[125] only 33 years old, took his inspiration from a sketch by Klimt[126] for a building whose very conception was revolutionary: it rested entirely on six pillars, and its interior partitions could be moved, Japanese-fashion, in accordance with the needs of each exhibition.

Besides Klimt, Moll, and Engelhart, the founding members of the Secession included the architects Josef Hoffmann[127] (who had designed the Molls' house on the Hohe Warte, and the colony of villas around it) and Josef Olbrich, and the painters Koloman Moser,[128] Rudolf Bacher, Eugen Jettel, Hans Tichy, Josef Maria Auchentaller, Max Kurzweil, Maximilian Lenz, Alfred Roller, Felician von Myrbach, and Anton Nowak. The water-colourist and painter Rudolf von Alt (born in 1812), being the doyen of the group, became its honorary president and the first signatory of the initial manifesto. In October 1899 Otto Wagner,[129]

[124] 'Temple of Art'. The building still exists, but it was severely damaged by bombing in 1945. The interior no longer resembles Olbrich's original.

[125] Josef Maria Olbrich (1867–1908), architect and painter, was a pupil of Karl von Hasenauer and Otto Wagner. He and Josef Hoffmann were the leading architects of the Secession. They were outstanding innovators, in both architecture and the applied arts. Olbrich exercised considerable influence on the evolution of taste and aesthetic criteria in Austria and Germany. His principal works were the Artists' Colony in Darmstadt (1899); the Villa Friedmann in Hinterbrühl (1899); Hermann Bahr's villa at Ober-Skt Veit (1900); the Gallery for New Art on the Mathildehöhe in Darmstadt; and the Leonard Tietz Shop in Dusseldorf (1907–8), on which he was engaged at the time of his death.

[126] Reproduced in *Die Welt der Symphonie* (Polydor, Westermann, Hamburg, 1972), 189.

[127] Josef Hoffmann (1870–1956), born in Pirnitz in Moravia, pupil of Otto Wagner, taught at the Kunstgewerbeschule, 1899–1937. He is regarded not only as a great architect but also as the father of the Viennese school of applied arts. In 1903 he founded, with Kolo Moser, the famous Wiener Werkstätte. He left the Secession with Klimt in 1905 and in 1912 founded the Österreichische Werkbund (The Austrian Guild). In all his constructions the interior furnishings (furniture, carpets, silver, and even curtains and upholstery) were designed by him. From 1903 Hoffmann abandoned the curving lines of the *Jugendstil* (which still predominate in his first illustrations for *Ver Sacrum*) and turned to a purity of line and a simplicity of form that foreshadowed Cubism. His principal works were the Purkersdorf Sanatorium (1903–5), the Palais Stoclet in Brussels (1906), the Fledermaus Cabaret in the Johannesgasse (1907), the Palais Primavesi on the Gloriettegassel near Schönbrunn (1913–15), and the Wohnhausbauten der Gemeinde Wien (Viennese Municipal Houses) (1952). Hoffmann not only designed the Molls' house and its interior decoration, on the Steinfeldgasse, but also their second house on the Wollergasse, as well as Haus Ast (1909–10), the house which Alma Mahler bought in 1931 and where she lived until the death of her daughter Manon Gropius.

[128] Koloman Moser (1868–1918), painter, illustrator, maker of mosaics and woodcuts, designer of interiors and furniture. Son of the caretaker of the Theresianum Academy, Moser entered the Vienna Academy at 17 and later studied at the Kunstgewerbeschule (1892). In 1894 he became a member of the Hagenbund and in 1896 of the Künstlerhaus. He had met Klimt the previous year, and had attracted notice with a series of allegorical illustrations commissioned by a Viennese publisher. In 1900 Moser was appointed professor at the Kunstgewerbeschule and, in 1903, he founded with Josef Hoffmann the Wiener Werkstätte. In 1905 he left the Secession with Klimt's group and married a former pupil, Edytha Mautner-Markhof, daughter of a wealthy businessman. Moser designed the interior of the Fledermaus Cabaret in 1907 and, the following year designed the well-known stamps for the Emperor Franz Joseph's jubilee.

[129] Otto Wagner (1841–1918), student at the Wiener Polytechnische Institut and at the Königliche Bauakademie in Berlin, had also studied with Eduard von der Null and August von Siccardsburg, the two architects of the Hofoper. He was one of the first in his profession to invent a new and truly modern style,

the most famous architect in Vienna, also joined the Secession. During the next few years the Secession's exhibitions often coincided with those at the Künstlerhaus, but when that happened it was obvious that the Secession artists were getting the lion's share of the public's attention.[130] All the artists in the Secession collaborated in decorating the splendid 'Kunsttempel'.[131] The initial floral period, the *Jugendstil*, now being over, the façade was decorated in the new 'geometric' style with its aspirations towards a new form of classicism, using basic forms like the cube, the globe, and the square. A trace of 'Egyptian influence' was visible in the columns and pillars, which tended to narrow towards the top. A white façade, rectilinear, but delicately offset with gold laurel motifs adorning its upper corners, surmounted a splendid monumental doorway fitted with bronze doors by Georg Klimt, the painter's brother. The approach consisted of a flight of dark red marble steps edged with laurel bushes. The Secession's motto, 'Der Zeit Ihre Kunst: Der Kunst Ihre Freiheit',[132] stood proudly in letters of gold over the entrance. A great wrought-iron sphere, 5 metres in diameter, fashioned like a vast laurel arbour, surmounted the entrance hall between four truncated pillars narrowing towards the top.[133] This arbour was soon to earn the building its first Viennese nickname: 'the gilded cabbage'.

The disposition of the central roof, in the form of a tent, its windows inclined at an angle of 45 degrees, provided natural light for the interior and all the exhibits.

The interior of the hall in the shape of a Greek cross, is adorned with two enormous stucco reliefs representing gnarled tree-trunks decked with spring foliage. The entrance lobby, faintly lit from the exhibition halls and the main entrance, is intended

without any reference to the recent or distant past. Urbanist, and an ardent proponent of art nouveau, he designed the headquarters of the Wiener Gemeingebiet (Viennese Area Administration). His most important works, such as the *Postsparkassengebäude*/Post Office Bank (1904–6), the first Austrian building in modern, functional style, the Länderbank (1890), and the Steinhofkirche (1905–7), belong to history, but a great many of his projects never left the drawing-board. He was the architect of the big block of flats in which Mahler lived, in the Auenbruggergasse.

[130] No less than 23 exhibitions were organized by the Secession in Vienna, 1897–1905. Most of the information given here was taken from two collections of articles by Ludwig Hevesi (1842–1910), *Acht Jahre Secession: Kritik-Polemik-Chronik* (1906) and *Altkunst-Neukunst* (1909), first publ. in the contemporary press of Vienna and Budapest. Born in Heves, Hungary, the son of a doctor, Hevesi himself studied medicine before becoming a humorist and later an art critic, first in the *Pester Lloyd* (1866), then in the Viennese *Fremden-Blatt*. An indefatigable apologist of the Secession and chronicler of all its activities, Hevesi wrote articles and essays which are indispensable to an understanding of Viennese art at the turn of the 20th century. Several other books contain useful information about the 8 years of the Secession: Peter Vergo, *Art in Vienna 1898–1918* (Phaidon, London, 1975); Nicholas Powell, *The Sacred Spring* (New York Graphic Society, New York, 1974); Fritz Novotny and Johannes Dobai, *Gustav Klimt* (Thames & Hudson, London, 1968); Christian Nebehay, *Ver Sacrum 1898–1903* (Tusch, Vienna, 1975), and *Eine Klimt Dokumentation*.

[131] They all gave their services free, so that the entire decoration cost only 60,000 gulden.

[132] 'To each epoch its art; to Art its freedom.' Hevesi's motto being regarded as the property of the original members of the Secession, it was removed when the majority of them left the movement in 1905. Three years later, it was inscribed on the Kunstschau building.

[133] The contemporary press informed its readers that this arbour, through which one could see the sky, was made of 3,000 leaves, each 30 cm. long, and that there were 700 laurel berries.

to give the visitor a moment's repose before he encounters the bright colours of the main hall.

A triple door opened on to this central section, above which glittered a brilliantly coloured stained-glass window by Kolo Moser, depicting a woman, symbol of Art, in a flowery field, with another inscription, this time by Hermann Bahr: 'The artist unveils his own world, the beauty born with him, which has never yet been and never will be again.'[134] The 'gilded cabbage' quickly acquired new nicknames—'The Tomb of the Mahdi' and 'The Assyrian toilet' (this from a well-known Viennese humorist, Eduard Pötzl).

   One of the principal aims of the Secession was, as has been indicated, to introduce major foreign artists to the Viennese public. Thus Auguste Rodin, Puvis de Chavannes, Seurat, Signac, Besnard, Whistler, Hans Thoma, Max Klinger, Charles Rennie Mackintosh, Ferdinand Hodler, Edward Munch, Jan Toorop, and many others were presented during the first few years. The artists of the Secession, notably Roller, Hoffmann, and Olbrich, reacting strongly against the outdated techniques of the Künstlerhaus, conceived a manner of exhibiting works of art, itself a form of art, that was both beautiful and functional. In 1899, the third exhibition centred on an immense canvas by Max Klinger, *Christ on Olympus*. At the end of the same year the fifth exhibition, consisting entirely of sketches, watercolours, and engravings, introduced French artists like Carrière, Renoir, Pissarro, and Vallotton. In 1900 the Secession successfully exhibited works by its members at the International Exhibition in Paris. In the same year in Vienna the seventh exhibition, devoted to Khnopff, Toorop, and Stuck, together with pointillist works by Signac and others, was followed by a Japanese exhibition which was a relative failure with the public but which greatly influenced the Secessionists themselves. Apart from three new works by Degas, the eighth exhibition was devoted to the applied arts which, thanks to the influence of the Belgian designer and theoretician Henry van de Velde, had ceased to be regarded as secondary. It was on this occasion that Charles Rennie Mackintosh, his wife Margaret Macdonald, and Charles Robert Ashbee created a sensation with their first Viennese showing of furniture and objects. Hugo von Hennenberg (the Molls' neighbour on the Hohe Warte) and Wilhelm von Hartel, the government minister, bought and ordered furniture on the spot. The way was open for the Wiener Werkstätte (Viennese Workshops), founded three years later.

   The exhibition of January 1901 was dedicated to the memory of Giovanni Segantini, but incorporated thirteen drawings and some sculptures by Rodin, notably the plaster cast of the *Burghers of Calais*, the bust of Balzac, and *The Bronze Age*. The general scheme and the presentation of the works were by Alfred Roller. The next two exhibitions were exclusively Austrian, after which two more were devoted to Scandinavian, Russian, and Swiss artists. But the

[134] See Robert Waissenberger, *Die Wiener Secession 1897–1985* (Böhlhaus, Vienna, 1986), 43.

fourteenth (April–June 1902) differed radically from all its predecessors, being concerned solely with the provision of a suitable context for one new sculpture, Max Klinger's *Beethoven Denkmal* (Beethoven Monument).[135] Although he lived and worked in Leipzig, where he had been born, Klinger had been associated with the Secession from the beginning. An amateur musician, he was one of the few painters or sculptors of the period to take a serious interest in music. The music of Brahms, and his friendship with the composer, had inspired *Brahms-Phantasien* (1894), one of his series of engravings that heralded surrealism. Brahms, by then a very sick man, had responded by dedicating to Klinger his penultimate work, the *Vier ernste Gesänge*, Op. 120.

Following the example of ancient Greece, Klinger decided to use for his *Beethoven*, still today regarded as his most important sculpture, a gamut of multicoloured materials. The idea of the work came to him as early as 1885, when he was playing a Beethoven piano piece. The first model, in plaster, was made the following year. Klinger subsequently scoured Europe from the Pyrenees to Greece, spending more than 150,000 marks, for the black and coloured marble and the alabasters and ebony he needed. In 1900 he took up residence in Paris in order to supervise the casting of the huge throne, the back of which was sumptuously sculpted in bas-relief. The furnace burnt four days and nights to liquefy a ton of bronze and tin. News that the monument was approaching completion reached Vienna, where it aroused intense curiosity. Klinger was much admired there, which is why the Secessionists made the tremendous effort of preparing an entire exhibition simply to serve as a foil to what promised to be a major work of art.

From Hevesi we have a full description listing and explaining all the details of the great sculpture. According to him, Klinger's *Beethoven* faithfully reflects all the efforts, all the painful struggles of its creator towards a form of expression that would unite the ancient world with Christianity. It also reflects his ideal: a synthesis of his classical aspirations, his ardently romantic nature, his philosophical conceptions, and his innate mysticism. The massive bronze throne seems to rise on the summit of a distant and mythical mountain. The Spirit, in the form of an eagle, symbol of Prometheus, attribute of Zeus, and

---

[135] Max Klinger (1857–1920), painter, engraver, and sculptor, was the son of a soap manufacturer from Leipzig. He studied painting with Karl Gussow in Karlsruhe (1874–5), then at the Berlin Academy (1875–6). He was scarcely 21 when his first exhibition of paintings and ink drawings created a sensation, and something of a scandal, in Berlin, because of their strength and originality. In 1879 Klinger studied in Brussels with Emil Charles Wouters, and later lived in Paris (1883, 1885, and 1886) and Rome (1888, 1889, and 1891), studying classical and contemporary art. He finally settled in Leipzig in 1884 and worked relentlessly on an output as original as it is small: paintings, often of monumental proportions (*The Judgment of Paris*, 1887; *The Twilight Hour, Crucifixion, Pietà*, 1890; *Spring on the Beach*, 1892; *Christ on Olympus*, 1897); sculptures (*The New Salome*, 1893; *Cassandra*, 1895; *Brahms Monument*, 1905–9, etc.); and a large number of etchings (*Engraved Sketches*, Op. 1, and *Deliverance of the Victims of Ovid*, Op. 2, 1879; *Eve and the Future*, Op. 3; *Intermezzi*, Op. 4; *Amor and Psyche*, Op. 5, 1880; *Paraphrases on a Lost Glove*, Op. 6, 1881; *Landscapes*, Op. 7; *A Life*, Op. 8; *Dramas*, Op. 9; *A Love*, Op. 10, 1887; *Of Death I*, Op. 11, 1889; *Brahms-Phantasien*, Op. 12, 1885–94; *Of Death II*, Op. 13, 1901; *Time*, Op. 14, 1916). Klinger also collected his ideas on art in a theoretical work entitled *Painting and Design* (1891).

messenger of divine inspiration, has battled mightily to reach these vertiginous heights. His half-extended wings, and the clinging of his claws on the bare rock, suggest effort and exhaustion. Beethoven, the Titan of German music, sits naked to the waist. The body is made from a single block of Greek marble, while the 'mantle of genius' draped around his loins and legs is carved out of stratified onyx from Laaser. The will and the suffering of the master are symbolized by the imperiously clenched right fist resting on the right knee. Klinger considered that only the whiteness of marble could suit this mythical face, this 'god among artists'. The same 'colour of immortality' is used for the faces of the angels (or Spirits of Music?) which adorn the back of the throne. One of the four cherubs points toward Beethoven with his right index finger. The immaculate white of these medallions stands out from a mosaic of multi-coloured stone and glass, set with gold. Klinger's paintings had long betrayed his love for antiquity, but never in so striking a manner as in the back of the throne. There is a bas-relief—a naked Aphrodite and another voluptuous female figure occupy the foreground, between two palm-trees. Above them, a crucifixion scene supposedly confronts 'earthly' with 'heavenly' love, but its principal image seems rather to evoke a dying religion.[136] This is probably the reason why the *Beethoven Denkmal* aroused so much controversy in Viennese salons and cafés, and why the Court authorities eventually refused to acquire the work for the Vienna Museum, despite the efforts of the Secessionists and supporters of the new art.[137] Ludwig Hevesi lists in wonderment the colours and materials used by Klinger:

Dark, almost serpentine Pyrenean marble for the eagle, . . . the stratifications of the Laaser onyx that drapes Beethoven . . . against the horizontal banding of the plinth which supports the throne. . . . The white Greek marble from which he has 'conjured forth' the figure looks like chiselled flesh. . . . In this luxuriant symphony of coloured materials there are still deep resonances of real bronze. . . . The ivory heads stand like giant cameos along the edge of the throne's back, linked by magically sparkling pairs of wings which form a mosaic of opal, labradorite, jasper and other semi-precious stones. . . . This is the work of a sculptor who is also a painter . . .[138]

The layout and décor of the exhibition were works of art in themselves by Josef Hoffmann to enhance the effect of Klinger's monument. The main hall was turned into a sort of sanctuary with three naves. Since the visitor was not to 'enter the sanctuary without preparation' he first went into the hall on the left, whence he caught his first glimpse of the great statue through an opening made in the wall. The overall decoration utilized a whole range of new materials and

---

[136] Alexander Dücker, *Max Klinger* (Rembrandt, Berlin, 1976) and Max Klinger, *Leben und Werk in Daten und Bildern*, ed. Stella Wega Mathieu (Insel Taschenbuch, Suhrkamp, Frankfurt, 1976).

[137] Unwilling to allow such an important work by a local artist to leave Germany, the city of Leipzig bought the *Beethoven Denkmal* for the sum of 250,000 marks. Today it stands in the entrance to the chamber-music hall in the Neues Gewandhaus.

[138] Hevesi, *Acht Jahre Secession* (1906), 385.

processes, from concrete blocks to gilded plaster, from moulded lead to engravings and stencil painting. Abstract geometric forms dominated, in very soft colours which set off the polychromy of the sculpture. The hall on the left was lined with large pale uniform panels, with only a few prismatic reliefs for decoration. The upper parts of three walls bore decorative panels by Klimt, the three double panels of the famous *Beethovenfries*, painted with casein, its flat gold-leafed surfaces picked out with semi-precious stones. 'Slender dividing strips broke the continuity just enough to indicate an antithetical interplay of different areas, the intention being a succession of scenes, with different themes, which would symbolize the basic ethical idea of Beethoven's Ninth— the defeat of "the forces of Evil".'[139]

Now that so many of Klimt's canvases have been destroyed, this 30 metres long fresco remains as one of the last examples of his epic style. But it is also one of the first examples of his new creative period where, inspired by Byzantine mosaics and medieval miniatures, he abandoned attempts at volume and perspective and emphasized the empty spaces around the faces with greyish or pastel tones, using compositional procedures close to those of music.[140] Like most of Klimt's major works, it horrified the Viennese conservatives. While Klimt was still at work, in the exhibition itself, a Viennese collector, Count Karl Lanckoronski,[141] muttered in his presence, loud enough to be heard by all, 'Scheusslich! Scheusslich!' (Hideous! Hideous!) Klimt's fresco, like Klinger's monument, 'expresses in symbolic and naturalistic terms a grand philosophical idea'. One may wonder whether Mahler, as yet ill-prepared for modern painting, can have appreciated its power, originality, and subtlety. On the other hand, he may well have been moved by Klimt's love of music, and by the Beethovenian theme: man liberated from darkness, suffering, temptation, and doubt, slowly ascending towards happiness. Mahler, like Beethoven, illustrated all these themes in his symphonies. What is more, it is generally accepted that the figure of the hero, or solitary knight, in the first panel, guiding man's battle toward final victory, is Mahler himself, with his angular face and austere radiance.[142] Moreover, although it is always difficult

---

[139] Fritz Novotny and Johannes Dobai, *Gustav Klimt* (Galerie Welz, Salzburg, 1967), 29. The details of the themes of the three double panels were as follows: (1) The wish for happiness; The sufferings of weak humanity; The hero in his armour; Pity; Ambition. (2) The adverse powers; The giant Typhoeus and the Gorgons; Sickness; Madness; Death; Sensuality; Lewdness; Excess; Grief; The desires and longings of men fly above. (3) The wish for happiness appeased by poetry; The Arts lead us into the Ideal Kingdom; Choir of Angels in Paradise. *Freude schöner Götterfunke, diesen Kuss der ganzen Welt.* (See U. Jung-Kaiser, 'Gustav Klimts Beethovenfries', *Neue Zeitschrift für Musik*, 2 (1988), 9.)

[140] Ibid.

[141] Karl Graf von Lanckoronski (1848–1933) was one of the most influential personalities in Viennese artistic life. Thanks to his considerable fortune, he was free to follow his artistic and archaeological tastes, and became the friend of several painters and poets such as Hofmannsthal and Rilke. His art collection was famous.

[142] Klimt's knight was reproduced in the little book published as homage to Mahler on the occasion of his 50th birthday (BSP 94). When he authorized this reproduction, Klimt implicitly acknowledged that he had taken his inspiration for the knight's face from Mahler (see Alessandra Comini, *Gustav Klimt* (Le Seuil, Paris, 1975), 24). The decoration for the Beethoven Exhibition, having been conceived and realized specially for

and dangerous to draw parallels between music and the plastic arts, one finds in Mahler a deliberate rejection, similar to Klimt's, of the Impressionistic haze; a predominance of clear, firmly drawn forms; a pronounced taste for vast compositions, worthy of a fresco painter; the stylization of themes; and perhaps even the voluntary abolition of perspective effects. One can even see in Mahler's frequent use of the chorus, in Finales modelled on that of Beethoven's Ninth, a source of the painter's own inspiration, as he, too, added scenes inspired by the work in a series of images whose programme corresponded to the view of Beethoven current at the time.[143]

In the central room, behind Klinger's statue, Alfred Roller painted a decorative fresco *Die sinkende Nacht* (Nightfall) in which he attempted to 'humanize decorative art'. A young girl, her head lowered, and wearing a stylized transparent robe, holds in her hand a white disc in which she is reflected to infinity.[144] On the opposite wall, facing the entrance, above the principal doors which were closed for the occasion, was a fresco by Adolf Böhm, *Der werdende Tag* (Day Dawning). The exhibition also comprised sculptures and bas-reliefs;[145] other frescos and paintings;[146] engravings;[147] decorative plaques using diverse techniques like graffito, sculptured cement, mosaic, beaten metal, and marquetry;[148] mosaics;[149] stained glass;[150] and decorative objects.[151] The catalogue, published under the direction of Alfred Roller, was particularly luxurious, containing numerous original woodcuts. It is still today regarded as a masterpiece of its genre.

For the opening ceremony, on 15 April, Mahler was asked to conduct a Beethoven concert. He proposed the work which had inspired Klimt's frieze, the Ninth Symphony, to be performed by the Philharmonic Orchestra and the Opera chorus. The fee was to be paid into the Hofoper pension fund, which was sadly depleted. The chorus immediately offered to take part in the concert free of charge, but the orchestra flatly refused, declaring itself 'overworked'. Five months later, a controversy was to break out in the press on the subject of this refusal. The *Neue Freie Presse* reported, on 12 September, that the Secession's

the occasion, was subsequently destroyed. Thus the big frescos by Roller and Böhm are only known today through contemporary photographs. By chance Klimt's *Fries* escaped destruction at the last minute. It was exhibited again by the Secession the following year, after which it was bought by the collector Karl Reminghaus. Coming later into the possession of August Lederer, it was to escape by a further miracle the sad fate suffered by almost the whole of his collection at the end of the war. Bought by the Austrian state in 1972, the frieze has since been restored, and has just been returned to the Secession building where it is now on permanent display in the basement.

[143] See U. Jung-Kaiser, 'Gustav Klimts Beethovenfries'.
[144] Roller also used this figure for the posters of the exhibition.
[145] By Max Klinger, Leopold Stolba, Othmar Schimkovitz, and Georg Minne.
[146] By Josef Maria Auchentaller, Ferdinand Andri, Rudolf Jettmar, Max Kurzweil, Ernst Stöhr, Josef Engelhart, Rudolf von Alt, Felician von Myrbach, Elena Luksch-Makovsky, Wilhelm List, Anton Nowak, Hans Tichy, and Carl Moll.
[147] By Emil Orlik and Ferdinand Schmutzer.   [148] By Rudolf Bacher and others.
[149] By Maximilian Lenz, Richard Loksech, Kolo Moser, and Felician von Myrbach.
[150] By Kolo Moser.
[151] By Friedrich König, Emil Orlik, Wilhelm List, Ferdinand Andri, and Kolo Moser.

committee, on learning of the orchestra's refusal, had offered to finance the concert, and that they at that point had agreed to play, but that Mahler had then not only refused to conduct but had vetoed the concert altogether. The very next day, the *Illustrirtes Wiener Extrablatt* published an interview with Mahler in which he explained why he had made this decision. The reason given by the musicians to refuse to participate in the concert—overwork—had only been a pretext. No better proof of this was needed than their sudden acceptance when they heard that they would receive a fee. This new conflict broke out while Mahler's relationship with the orchestra was already at a low point because of the tension caused by the engagement of the new wind players in the orchestra. After the publication of Mahler's interview, the musicians held a special meeting on 14 September after a performance of *Götterdämmerung*, to discuss 'Director Mahler's behaviour *vis-à-vis* the orchestra'. Alois Markl, a flautist and later chairman of the committee, was also a member of the pension fund committee. He announced that the only reason for the orchestra's refusal had been his colleagues' 'fatigue' which would, in any case, have made the performance impossible. The committee deplored the fact that Mahler had 'publicly described the members of the orchestra as rogues' and decided that, since it would be useless to ask him to rectify his statement, the newspaper should be approached directly.[152] Statements duly appeared in the press claiming that the Philharmonic musicians had never been informed that the concert was intended for their benefit.[153] However, the excuses they presented are totally unconvincing, and the incident can only be seen as a further episode in the war being waged by the musicians against the director of the Opera, whose authority they were resolved to challenge wherever possible, that is to say everywhere outside the Opera itself.

Plans for a complete performance of Beethoven's Ninth at the opening ceremony of the Secession's Beethoven Exhibition having thus been foiled, Mahler had to content himself with a brass arrangement of a single passage from the Finale, which he conducted in the Klimt room.[154] A private viewing took place, very unusually, late in the afternoon on 14 April. When Klinger came through the bronze doors before entering the main hall, he suddenly heard six trombones from the Philharmonic Orchestra playing an extract from the Ninth transcribed by Mahler for the occasion:

> Ihr stürtzt nieder, Millionen?
> Ahnest Du den Schöpfer, Welt?[155]

---

[152] The meeting continued until 2.30 a.m.

[153] *Neue Freie Presse* (12, 13, 15, and 16 Sept. 1902), and *Österreichisch-Ungarische Musiker-Zeitung* (12 Sept. 1902).

[154] This performance, described by Alma in AMM, scarcely received a mention in the press, which nevertheless publ. numerous accounts of the opening. Some of the reviews claim that the musicians were placed in a 'higher gallery' but photographs show that this exhibition did not have an upper storey.

[155] Knud Martner has suggested that the passage Mahler must have selected in the Finale of Beethoven's Ninth was 'Seid umschlungen, Millionen, diesem Kuss der ganzen Welt'.

Alma was later to describe the sculptor's tear-drenched face, as he stood transfixed by the strains of this sublime music.

The evening concluded with a banquet at the Grand Hotel in Klinger's honour:

The two masters Klimt and Klinger sat next to each other. Two wonderful faces, bearing the stamp of powerful personalities in their expressive features. Klinger's, with white hair and beard shining around it, glowed with youthful fire, and his small narrow eyes sparkled. Gustav Klimt, brown-skinned, with a dark beard and somewhat lighter curly hair, was a picture of glowing health and exuberant strength. Simple contentment and peace seemed to radiate from him, the peace of a man who works hard and is for once allowing himself to rest from his labours. . . . There were numerous speeches, and Emil Orlik, recently returned from Japan, gave a toast in spoof Japanese. Klinger spoke just a few words, expressing his thanks for the gratifying comprehension he had met with from the Viennese artistic world. Real understanding and harmony were in the room.[156]

It was no doubt on this evening that Mahler and Alma made the acquaintance of Klinger and his mistress, Elsa Asenijeff,[157] described by some contemporaries as 'passionate and capricious' and by others as 'a cold dialectician'. Alma, seldom pleased to encounter women of intelligence and character, describes Elsa as 'a hysterical woman' and declares that 'she leads Klinger by the nose, sadistically'. No deep or lasting relationship was therefore to be established between the two couples, despite Klinger's passionate love of music.

At the beginning of June 1902, Auguste Rodin came to Vienna from Prague, where there had been a retrospective exhibition of his works, in order to see the famous Beethoven Exhibition.[158] He paid a long visit to it, being shown around by Klimt, Berta Zuckerkandl, and a group of Secessionists. Standing before Klinger's monument he said he was disappointed: he thought it was 'the opposite of sculpture', being rather 'a magnificent etching'.[159] Nevertheless, according to Berta, Klimt's fresco touched him deeply and he 'marvelled at the spirit of adventure' of the Secession and at its aim of producing 'anonymous and collective' art. Berta also relates that she took Rodin to the Opera. According to her, Mahler was conducting *Figaro* and Rodin was dazzled by his interpretation: 'What a dream! What a magical city! I am truly hearing Mozart for the

---

[156] Felix Salten, 'Erinnerungen an Klimt', *Neue Freie Presse* (18 Oct. 1936), 1.

[157] Elsa Asenijeff, née Packeny (1868–1941) had met Klinger in Leipzig in 1898. She had a child by him and lived with him until 1916. The cause of their separation appears to have been the increasing 'oddness' of her character.

[158] The Apr. 1902 Beethoven Exhibition atracted 58,000 visitors, thus making it the most successful of all the exhibitions organized by the Secession. Berta Zuckerkandl implicitly dates Rodin's visit by claiming she attended a performance of *Le nozze di Figaro* with him (see below). However his hotel bill, preserved in the archives of the Musée Rodin, proves that the sculptor did not arrive in Vienna until 3 June, after spending 3 days in Prague, 28–31 May, and 3 more in Moravia (according to Danièle Gutmann's thesis on Rodin and Mahler).

[159] It seems that Klinger was struck by the resemblance between the attitude of his *Beethoven* and that of Rodin's *Thinker*, which did not exist in 1886, when he finished the plaster model for his monument.

first time! A magician of the orchestra reveals him to me . . . No! This is Mozart himself, reincarnated—I see Mozart in Mahler's noble face!'[160]

Unfortunately, a number of established facts contradict Berta's story, much as one would wish it to be authentic, given posterity's fondness for summit meetings between great artists. For one thing, Rodin was not in Vienna on the only evening when Mahler conducted *Figaro* before the summer, but was on his way from London to Prague. Further, Paul Clemenceau, who in 1909 was to serve as intermediary between the Mahler family and Rodin in the commissioning of the famous bronze bust, makes it quite clear that Mahler was at that time unknown to the sculptor, and that Rodin was anyway not particularly interested in music.[161] The incident in question must therefore have been a figment of Berta's imagination.

Carl Moll and his wife regularly invited members of the Secession to their home, and most of the decisions concerning the policy of the movement were doubtless taken in their drawing-room. Kolo Moser, a tall, pale young man with large black eyes and Slav features, was always present, as was Alfred Roller, a man of strong convictions and few words, an ardent idealist who quickly caught Mahler's attention and sympathy. Indeed, Mahler could hardly have failed to respond to the young painter's passion for the theatre or to the way he discussed it, not only from an aesthetic but also from a technical point of view, expressing original ideas about scenery and lighting. Roller 'could evoke actions and scenes on the stage by visual image and by word', a gift which Mahler had recognized in him at an early stage. He also admired Roller's 'unemotional, uncompromising search for the often hidden truth in each work of art'. An added attraction for Mahler was the fact that Roller had joined the Secession as a realist, not as an out-and-out modern. He sought to produce simple direct effects and abhorred any kind of mannerism.[162]

Conflicting accounts make it impossible to establish the date of Mahler's first meeting with Roller. Berta Zuckerkandl claims that Mahler visited one of the Secession's exhibitions containing a design for the first act of *Tristan*. However, no contemporary article mentions any such design in any exhibition prior to 1902. The version given by Max Mell, Roller's biographer, is more likely to be accurate since Mell undoubtedly had it from the painter himself. According to him, the two artists met at Carl Moll's house, and it was there that Roller immediately started discussing theatre design with Mahler, and in particular stage designs for Wagnerian music-dramas.[163] It is not surprising that Mahler's

---

[160] Were it not for the insoluble problem of the dates, one would be tempted to see here the reason why Rodin whimsically entitled 'Mozart' the big marble bust of Mahler which he made in 1910 or 1911.

[161] See Paul Clemenceau, 'Mahler und Rodin', *Die Kunstauktion* (Berlin, 13 July 1930) and *Deutsche La Plata Zeitung* (13 July 1929): archives of the Musée Rodin.

[162] See Wolfgang Greisenegger, 'Alfred Roller: Neubedeutung des szenischen Raumes', in *Gustav Mahler und die Oper*, Symposium, Budapest, 1988, *Studia Musicologica Academiae Scientiarium Hungaricae*, 31 (Budapest, 1988), 271 ff.

[163] Ernst Decsey also recalls Mahler's meeting with Roller in EDS2. It could have taken place before Mahler left for Russia, in which case Mahler's first letter to Roller (MBR1, no. 295; MBR2, no. 304) would

interest should have been immediately aroused, for he had long complained of the eclecticism of the resident designer at the Opera, Anton Brioschi, and even of that of Heinrich Lefler whom he had subsequently engaged.[164] According to Hermann Bahr, Brioschi had 'painted bad designs to perfection'.

Certainly Lefler's appointment had been a step in the right direction. He was a talented painter, a former member of the Hagenbund who was later to be linked with the Wiener Werkstätte. However, his stage designs remained not only realistic, but also in other respects traditional. Roller, on the other hand, was soon to militate for a complete reform, and straightaway told Mahler how appalled he was at the style of design then current at the Hofoper. Such was his passion for *Tristan* that he had never missed a single performance, but he always preferred to listen with his eyes closed so as not to spoil his enjoyment. He already had ideas about designing new sets for it and had been working on them feverishly. In the heat of the discussion Roller began 'making sketches on the table', and promised to bring Mahler some models within a few days. Mahler was at once convinced that he had found the ideal man for the job, someone who could give the new *Tristan* the perfect setting required for this masterpiece among masterpieces.[165] 'I shall certainly take him on,' he said to Alma the same day, as they were leaving the Molls' house.[166]

At the end of May, Mahler left Vienna with Alma to prepare for his greatest venture to date as composer-conductor: the première of his Third Symphony, completed almost six years earlier and never performed in its entirety. A year after it was completed, the Berlin critics had called its composer a lunatic and a megalomaniac on hearing three movements only. Considering that it was mainly the length of the final Adagio (unique in symphonic literature) that upset them, one could not help wondering what the public's reaction would be to the first movement, which was nearly as long as the other movements put together. Come what may, Mahler was determined not to repeat the error of the Weimar Festival, where he had learnt that a bad performance was infinitely

date from Feb. 1902. An article in *Die Wiener Woche* (28 Mar. 1920) maintains that the first conversation took place in the Café Imperial and that Roller sketched his designs for *Tristan* on the tablecloth. Decsey also relates that 'Roller made his first sketches . . . on a café tablecloth.'

[164] Heinrich Lefler (1863–1919) (see above, Chap. 8) replaced Franz Gaul in 1900 as *Leiter des Ausstattungswesens*. A former pupil of Christian Griepenkerl at the Vienna Academy, he became a member of the Künstlerhaus in 1881 and later co-founder of the Hagenbund. He was one of the first stage-designers in Vienna to paint 'artistic' decors and to get rid of the customary canvas backdrop, replacing it as far as possible with 'practicable' items. It seems, nevertheless, that his innovatory zeal was less apparent in his work for the theatre than in his book illustrations. When Roller definitively replaced him at the Opera in 1903 Lefler was engaged by the Burgtheater. His last designs are said to have been influenced by Roller and Gordon Craig. Lefler was the brother-in-law of Josef Urban, who did most of the designs for the New York Metropolitan Opera (1917–33). Anton Brioschi had succeeded his father Carlo in 1886 as 'painter and designer' at the Hofoper.

[165] AMS. Early in summer 1902 Brioschi and Lefler were informed that the designs for the new *Tristan* were to be entrusted to Roller, but his definitive engagement dated from June 1903. During the summer which followed, Mahler wrote several letters to Roller congratulating him on sketches just received, and which 'greatly surpass my expectations'.

[166] AMM1. 72; AMM2. 80.

more dangerous for a new work than the most scathing reviews. The Third Symphony presented considerable difficulties which he made no attempt to minimize beforehand. In May, before the meeting of the Allgemeiner Deutscher Musikverein committee, he wrote to Strauss to demand two whole days of rehearsals with the full orchestra in Cologne, to be followed by two further three- and four-hour rehearsals in Krefeld before the final general rehearsal.[167] These were indispensable, he explained, because the symphony was 'difficult and unusual'. Moreover, his 'immediate future' depended on the première and he would prefer to put it off indefinitely rather than risk giving an imperfect performance which would add to the obstacles and pitfalls that might prevent the audience from grasping his intentions. The Symphony was already austere (*herb*) and difficult enough to understand.

'Believe me,' he added,

for this work I must have a faultless performance; otherwise, instead of helping to smooth my path as you most assuredly intend, you will be doing me great harm. It is therefore imperative that you make these rehearsals possible; I cannot give up a single hour. Otherwise, however sorry I might be, I simply could not participate. As far as the expenses are concerned, I'm delighted that you are so kindly prepared to take care of them this time. Nevertheless, I'm always ready to make necessary sacrifices and I know that you won't demand more than is absolutely necessary. I'm repeating this so that it can be your guideline in the event that difficulties arise during the Sunday meeting. Since your last letter, I am quite worried about the quality of the players brought in to increase the 30-man Krefeld Orchestra to 100?—From where? And how? A mediocre ensemble thrown together at random cannot play my work—I'm quite sure of that! Just take a look at the score! The first trombone must at all events be outstanding: he must have powerful lungs and and be able to produce an enormous volume of sound! Shouldn't you bring your first Berlin trombone, about whom people have spoken most highly to me? I leave all this in your hands, dear friend. Please reassure me as soon as you come to a decision on Sunday.[168]

That Strauss actually surmounted all these obstacles, and convinced his fellow committee members to make the financial effort needed for the performance, is greatly to his credit. To be sure, Mahler's symphonies had already caused quite a stir in Germany, but his style and aims were still sorely misunderstood by most audiences and musicians, and reactions had for the most part been hostile. Strauss's merit is therefore all the greater, especially in view of the failures of the Fourth Symphony in Munich and Berlin.

The weather was already very hot when the Mahlers set out for Cologne: the journey seemed interminable to Alma, since she was then in her fourth month of pregnancy. Mahler did his best to distract her with funny stories and constant

---

[167] Three hours on Friday morning; four hours on Sunday afternoon; and Monday's final rehearsal (MSB 83).

[168] Ibid. The preparation for the Krefeld Festival takes up a considerable amount of space in the correspondence between Strauss and Max von Schillings. The decisive meeting of the Verein Committee took place in Berlin on 9 Mar. (See Roswitha Schlötterer, *Richard Strauss–Max von Schillings: Ein Briefwechsel* (W. Ludwig, Pfaffenhofen, 1987), 65 ff.)

reassurances that they were nearly there. They stayed at the Disch, the best hotel in town. During the first rehearsals in the Gürzenich Hall, Mahler consulted Alma between each movement, and from time to time called to her from the podium to alter some detail of the score. After hearing the entire first movement for the first time, he came towards her and, paraphrasing the Bible, exclaimed happily: 'And He saw that it was good or rather, Herr Mahler saw'.[169] Thanks to the excellent, obedient orchestra, the Cologne rehearsals were a total success. The first time Mahler conducted the first, fourth, and fifth movements, he wrote to Justi: 'An effect of amazing grandeur. Not a single change to be made. I'm very pleased!'[170] He relaxed from the strain of the rehearsals by taking long carriage rides with Alma. During one of them he fell asleep with his head on her shoulder. But Alma was enjoying herself. For the first time, she found she liked one of his works, and discussed details of its orchestration with him after rehearsals.

In Krefeld, for lack of a good hotel, they had to endure the reluctant hospitality of a rich silk manufacturer. They occupied a vast and formal bridal chamber cluttered with hideous ornaments; on the mantelpiece stood a glass dome sheltering an old myrtle wreath, yellow with age. The entire family eyed Mahler with suspicion, regarding him as 'a well-known theatre director who, having composed a monstrous symphony for his own pleasure, now insisted, to everyone else's displeasure, upon having it performed'. Crushed by the weight of their host's disapproval, Mahler and Alma lived in permanent fear of disturbing someone or breaking something. One day indeed, Mahler came out of their room polishing his spectacles and kicked over a pail of water on the landing, sending it crashing and cascading down the stairs to the feet of his hostess. She wrung her hands and said plaintively: 'Really, Herr Mahler, the Graces were obviously not gathered round your cradle!'

In these pretentious bourgeois surroundings, Mahler one day received a visit from Hans Pfitzner,[171] who had already begun to make a name for himself with two neo-Wagnerian operas. The previous year Pfitzner, a close friend of Bruno Walter's, had sent Mahler the score and libretto of his new work, *Die Rose vom Liebesgarten*, together with a letter asking if he might play it for him one day.[172] Now, happening to be in Krefeld for a performance of his ballad for baritone

[169] AMM1. 52, AMM2. 67, and AML 227. Alma writes that a child sat behind her during the rehearsals in order to follow the score over her shoulder. Many years later, he was to introduce himself to her as Edwin Fischer (1886–1960). The famous pianist, however, subsequently declared that he met Mahler's wife not in Krefeld, but during a rehearsal of the Second Symphony the following summer in the cathedral at Basel. At that time Fischer was not a 'child' but a youth of 17.

[170] RWO.

[171] See below, Vol. iii, Chap. 3. Pfitzner was then considered to be most prominent member of the 'German neo-Romantic school'. *Die Rose vom Liebesgarten* had its first performance in Elberfeld in 1901. Under joint pressure from Alma and Bruno Walter, Mahler finally put on the work in Vienna in 1905. In a letter to Pfitzner of 6 Mar. 1902, Walter speaks of Mahler's 'surprising aversion' for Pfitzner's style and adds: 'You must not think that he treats it en passant. On the contrary he has been much preoccupied with it' (BWB 57).

[172] The letter is dated 30 Mar. 1901 in RWO.

and orchestra, *Herr Oluf*, he had come to press the matter further. Wishing to see him alone, Mahler asked Alma to wait in a curtained alcove in their room. He then proceeded 'coldly, calmly and curtly' to refuse to accept the opera: it was too long, and the obscurity of the libretto rendered it unfit for the stage.[173] Pfitzner begged him to reconsider his decision, for he thought that Mahler was the only person who could understand his work and this was his last chance. But Mahler was adamant. He said he thought highly of his music (indeed, shortly afterwards he was to advise Arnold Rosé 'that he could play Pfitzner's String Quartet without the slightest hesitation, on his recommendation') and he would 'have accepted *Die Rose*' if the libretto had been even halfway accept-able'.[174] Pfitzner was about to leave when Alma, feeling sorry for him, suddenly emerged from behind the curtain and shook him warmly by the hand. Mahler may have felt some remorse at his own hard-heartedness, for he was not angry at her impulsive gesture.[175]

Krefeld was a small provincial town and it wasn't long before everybody knew who Mahler was. Indeed, with his clean-shaven face, his habit of going out with his hat in his hand instead of on his head, and his odd, jerky stride, he immediately attracted attention. Moreover, although his suits were well cut, he always looked untidy, and Alma's dresses, cut 'reform-style' (*Reformkleider*) by Kolo Moser to conceal her pregnancy, were also extremely unusual for the time. As a result the Mahlers were often followed through the streets by bands of jeering urchins. On one occasion a boy came running up to Mahler to tell him he had left his hat in a shop; the noisy retinue escorted him and Alma back to the shop and then all the way back to their house. Later on, the couple had to open the window of their room (where they had joined the Rosés) and throw buckets of water over the ragamuffins to drive them away. According to the *Krefelder Zeitung*, the musicians did show a certain illwill during the early rehearsals[176] because they had read disparaging articles about Mahler and his music in the Viennese press. However, they very soon 'learnt to know their master'; many of them, 'during these long and painful working sessions, ex-perienced their conversion on the road to Damascus' and all joined in the applause on the night of the concert. After the performance, Mahler and Strauss both signed a letter of thanks addressed to the conductor of the Cologne Orchestra,[177] 'which this evening, thanks to its magnificent accomplishment, has won a complete victory for the Mahler Symphony'. It seems that Mahler was particularly delighted with the trombone soloist Franz Dreyer, a member of the

[173] The Vienna performance proved that Mahler's criticisms of *Die Rose vom Liebesgarten* were justified. Even Pfitzner's friends and admirers were soon forced to admit its theatrical weakness (see below, Vol. iii, Chap. 3).

[174] Letter from Bruno Walter to Pfitzner, 2 Dec. 1902: Catalogue of Mahler Centenary Exhibition, *Gustav Mahler und seine Zeit* (Vienna, 1960), 37.

[175] AMM1. 57, AMM2. 67, and AML 68.

[176] Apparently Mahler did not notice the musicians' hostility, for Alma asserts that the orchestra behaved irreproachably during the rehearsals.

[177] This letter, probably addressed to Fritz Steinbach, was sold during a Stargardt Auction in 1957.

Mannheim Orchestra. Dreyer played to perfection the difficult solos in the first movement of the symphony, and the composer, overwhelmed, promised immediately after the final rehearsal to engage him at the Vienna Opera.[178]

Dreyer himself left the following description of this encounter:

I was working in Cologne as first trombonist. Well then: Mahler came and made a short speech: 'Gentlemen, I have to make a confession to you, and it is this: every time one of my symphonies has been performed, people have hissed or made a noise, in other words they have disturbed it. Don't allow yourselves to be put off by this, we shall play our stuff to the end, as best we can; I hope you will help me in this, and then we'll see. All right, let's begin, let's just rehearse it . . .' There are a few notes of introduction, then comes a colossal note on the trombone, which I blew as hard as I could. I really bellowed into my instrument, and after a short silence Mahler called out: 'Bravo, trombone, bravo trombone, that's just the way I imagined it! Excellent!' When the rehearsal was over, Mahler came up and congratulated me: 'Yes, you see, that's what I call a trombone sound! Good God, why did it take me until now to find you . . .' After the preliminary rehearsals in Cologne we travelled to Krefeld. Mahler had a colossal success there. The Krefelders couldn't stop applauding. When the Festival was over, a colleague came up to me and said: 'Listen, Herr Mahler's waiting down there for you with Herr Rosé and Bruno Walter. They want to talk to you, you're supposed to go to Vienna with them'. I said 'Listen, you're joking.' We went down together and talked with them. But now my colleagues started saying, 'What, Herr Direktor, you're wanting to hire Dreyer here? He's nothing but trouble!' 'Oh, said Mahler, we get trouble every day in Vienna, we're used to it, and anyway I'm not engaging him to make trouble but to play the trombone and I'll never get another trombone-player like him. So I'm taking him to Vienna with me'. Mahler returned to Vienna, and for the next two years letters were exchanged. When I was 27 I signed the contract and went to Vienna. 'Now for the Third Symphony,' said Mahler as he greeted me. He gave me a cigar and added: 'Dreyer, you'll give yourself an excellent introduction, just make sure you play the solo the way you did in Krefeld, that was really wonderful, I'm still delighted about it'.[179]

But to return to Krefeld, in 1902: the star of the 38th Allgemeiner Deutscher Musikverein festival was undoubtedly Mahler, although works by other well-known composers, i.e. Strauss, Hugo Wolf, Reger, Eugen D'Albert, and Max von Schillings were performed, together with a number of scores by minor composers, renowned conductors such as Weingartner, Brecher, and Blech, or musicians nowadays totally forgotten, such as Eugen Lindner, Fritz Neff (1873–1904), Felix von Raths, Hermann Bischoff,[180] and Hans Sommer.[181] In

---

[178] The source of this information is the trombonist's daughter, Luise Dreyer-Seidler, harpist with the Vienna Philharmonic. Dreyer hesitated at first because the idea of living in Vienna did not please his fiancée. He finally joined the Hofoper orchestra in 1904. Bruno Walter, in a letter written in 1920, speaks of Dreyer as 'the greatest trombonist in the world' (BWB 181). In Dec. 1904, Mahler ordered two new instruments for Dreyer, an alto and a tenor trombone.

[179] Quoted in *Gürzenich-Orchester Köln 1888–1988* (Wienaud, Cologne, 1988), 53.

[180] Hermann Bischoff (1868–1936) studied at the Leipzig Conservatory, and lived for a time in Munich, where he was associated with Richard Strauss. He wrote symphonic poems and two symphonies of which the First (1906) was conducted twice in one season by Karl Muck with the Boston Symphony.

[181] Hans Sommer (1837–1922): two extracts from his opera entitled *Rübezahl* were performed at Krefeld.

such a context, the première of the Third Symphony could not but be an outstanding event. The whole concept of programme music now worried Mahler so much that he decided at the last moment not only to dispense with the original 'programme' of the Third but also to cut out the headings of the individual passages. According to the letter he wrote to the conductor Josef Krug-Waldsee shortly after the concert, these had merely been

an attempt to give non-musicians some point of reference or signpost to suggest the ideas, or rather the mood, of the individual movements and their relationship to each other and to the whole. I realized all too soon that my attempt had failed (and indeed, could never succeed) and had merely given rise to the worst kind of misinterpretation. The same misfortune has befallen me on previous occasions and I have since definitely rejected all commentaries, all analyses and every sort of guide!

In this same letter, Mahler nevertheless admitted that 'these titles . . . can certainly be very instructive once you know the score. They also give a hint as to how I conceived the increasingly articulate expression, which proceeds from the muffled, static and merely rudimentary existence (of the forces of nature), to the tender image of the human heart, which stands above it and reaches towards God.'[182]

For some years concert organizers had been begging Mahler to provide them with 'programmes' or at least commentaries or analyses of his work. But he was now more than ever convinced that music should not be accompanied by any sort of 'explanation'. That he published 'programmes' for his first three symphonies is well known, of course. But gradually the music of Strauss, and of all the *neudeutsch* school for that matter, turned him against all attempts at descriptive music. He had learnt to his cost that 'programmes' gave rise only to errors and misunderstandings. Nevertheless, with an inconsistency typical of artists, he did not always abide by his own principles. For instance, he had recently provided a Dresden audience with a detailed 'programme' for his Second Symphony, and though he had never produced anything as explicit for his Fourth Symphony, he probably dictated most of the text Bruno Walter sent to Ludwig Schiedermair in December 1901.[183] Although this text was now supposed simply to be made available to the audience rather than imposed on it, and although it was more general in tone than those for the first symphonies, it still looked strangely like a 'programme'. Yet, fourteen months earlier (on 20

---

[182] MBR1, no. 301; MBR2, no. 310 (summer 1902). Letter to Josef Krug-Waldsee, conductor of the Magdeburg Symphony Concerts, who was planning to perform the Third Symphony. Mahler thanked him for being 'brave enough to take on my monster'. On 19 Oct. Bruno Walter wrote a postcard to Arnold Berliner telling him that Mahler would be happy if he could attend the Magdeburg performance which took place on 22 Oct. 1902 (BMG). Krug-Waldsee (1858–1915), on leaving the Conservatory, had been the choral conductor of the Neuer Singverein in Stuttgart. Later he became a theatre Kapellmeister in Hamburg, Augsburg, and Nuremberg. In 1902 he had just been appointed chief conductor of the Magdeburg Symphony Concerts. Prior to the Krefeld Festival Nodnagel had quoted Mahler's original titles in an article in the *Musikalisches Wochenblatt*. At the last moment, Mahler forbade the magazine *Die Musik* to publish an analysis specially written for the Festival by Bruno Walter.

[183] See below, App.

October 1900), during a convivial supper at the Munich Park-Hotel, at the time
of the successful performance of his Second Symphony, Mahler had declared:

Down with programmes, which are always misinterpreted! The composer should stop
giving the public his own ideas about his work; he should no longer force listeners to
read during the performance and he should refrain from filling them with preconceptions. If he has succeeded in conveying the feelings that flow from him like a river,
then he has achieved his aim.[184]

Although Mahler felt incapable of explaining his musical intentions in
words, he was nevertheless conscious of expressing in his music powerful
truths which reached far beyond the realm of art. Well before 1900 the Prague
critic Richard Batka had addressed a questionnaire to creative artists asking
them about artistic creativity and the problem of what common cultural activity
the artist was contributing to. Mahler had answered as follows:

We are unfortunately living in a period when people ponder and write a great deal
'about' creative activity. That in itself is a sign that all is not well. But that you should
then go on to ask 'what is being contributed to' I find quite unacceptable. Only those
who come after us will be able to find an answer to that, and even then it will be
difficult, as the works of art historians and critics of all periods testify. You do me the
honour of counting me among the 'creative artists'; but in my opinion they are precisely
the people least able to answer such a question. I might just as well try to explain 'to
what I contribute' by living as 'to what I contribute' by creating. 'To weaving the living
garment of Divinity'[185]—that, at least, would be something! But then you would ask
further questions, wouldn't you? When I have composed a work, I like to know what
chords it strikes in 'others'. So far, however, I have not been able to explain it to myself,
let alone obtain an explanation from other people. This sounds mystical! But perhaps
the time has come when we and our works have again become somewhat un-'explain-
able' to us. Only if that is the case can I believe that we are indeed 'contributing to
something' by creating.[186]

Thus each new work of Mahler's not only expressed his whole self but, he
felt, went much further. None of them resembled its predecessor or announced
its successor, for he was fully aware of his own, constant development:

Just as my physical life is an organic development rather than an accumulation of bits
and pieces, so it is with the life expressed in my successive works. In each new
symphony, I pick up more or less where I left off in the preceding one; by that I don't
mean that I merely tie a new thread onto the old one I've finished spinning.[187]

[184] Ludwig Schiedermair, *Musikalische Begegnungen* (Staufen, Cologne, 1948), 46. Ernst Decsey, who was
also present, summed up this pronouncement in almost identical words.
    [185] Quotation from Goethe's *Faust, Part I*: 'So schaff' ich am sausenden Webstuhl der Zeit | Und wirke der
Gottheit lebendiges Kleid.' (Thus I work at the rushing loom of time | And weave the living garment of
Divinity.)
    [186] MBR1. no. 198; MBR2. no. 163, undated.
    [187] The passage is taken from the same letter Mahler wrote to Schiedermair, on 2 Nov. 1900 (quoted
at n. 184).

Thus, from 1902 onwards, he aspired increasingly to present himself to his audience as a composer of 'pure music'. 'I have been worrying for some time if I knew how to make myself understood when expressing myself in music,' he wrote to the Munich critic Richard Braungart.

You have reassured me by indicating that I am on the right path in letting each listener discover his own 'programme', finding in my music his own experiences and observations. Indeed in this regard music is something special, something which in all forms and all things is always the same and yet different (ἓν καὶ πᾶν) (one thing and everything). So again, ad infinitum, down with programmes! Let each man find his own road to salvation![188]

Already in 1900 Mahler had felt his works did not need to be 'explained' to the public in words:

On the whole, I have often been praised, and still more often censured; but what I yearn for, to be <u>understood</u>, has rarely been my lot. Least of all by people who have had no close connection with me and who have had to derive all their knowledge of me from those hieroglyphs called scores I have provided them with. . . . I have expressed myself sufficiently clearly in my works so that without verbal explanation people can assimilate the feelings and experiences they reflect simply by using their inner ear and eye. How relieved I would be to find just once someone who, by using his own intuition and the scores, would be able to see and hear.[189]

Yet only a year later, as we have seen, for the Dresden performance of the Second Symphony, Mahler had carefully devised a new, detailed programme[190] and thought enough of it to send it to his fiancée, though he did add a few qualifications:

Justi hasn't told you that this programme was written solely for a superficial and incompetent person (you know whom I mean). It only gives a superficial indication as does, in the final analysis, every programme of a musical work. And all the more so as regards this work, which is so much all of a piece and is as inexplicable as the universe.—For I am convinced that if God were called upon to produce a programme of the 'world' He created, He wouldn't be able to do so either. The most He could produce would be a sort of 'revelation' which would tell no more about the nature of God and life than my text does about my C minor Symphony. Indeed, this—like all religions based on revelation—leads to nothing but complete misunderstanding, incomprehension, simplification, debasement and finally to such distortion of the work and, above all, its composer, that both become unrecognizable.[191]

This, then, was Mahler's state of mind when he forbade the publication of a

---

[188] This letter, which belongs to Dr Lafrenz of Munich, was publ. by Richard Braungart in Mahler's lifetime in *Musikalische Rundschau*, 1: 6 (30 Nov. 1905). After the performance conducted by Bernard Stavenhagen in Feb. 1904, Braungart had sent Mahler a very far-fetched 'programme' of his own invention. At the beginning of his letter, Mahler thanks Braungart for his review of Schiedermair's monograph publ. in *Allgemeine Zeitung*, 51 (2 Mar. 1901).

[189] Letter to Schiedermair see n. 184.   [190] See Vol. i, App. 1.

[191] AMM1. 274; AMM2. 251, letter of 18 Dec. 1901.

'programme' for his Third Symphony. Several months earlier, in December 1901, Mahler asked Bruno Walter to reply to Ludwig Schiedermair who had enquired about the Fourth Symphony's 'programme':

Mahler most vehemently abhors all programmes. Is it really necessary, he asks, to have a programme in order to understand a movement with a first and second theme, a development and a restatement? Or a Scherzo with a Trio? Or an Andante with variations? The structure of the first three movements of the Fourth Symphony conforms so completely to this pattern that the clamour for a programme would seem to be justified solely by a desire to ascertain the relationship of the vocal fourth movement to the preceding ones; this desire is satisfied through the text of the final movement. Today, however, when musical forms seem complicated, people are accustomed to being enlightened by a programme as to the composer's every intention and it therefore does not occur to them that, even now, music can itself be at once kernel and hull; and this is indeed the case with Mahler. True, he has raised the expressiveness of music to the heights of perfection and effectively extended its frontiers. His emotional life, which is of unparalleled richness and complexity, has created its own musical language in which, however, like all pure musicians, he expresses only things that could never be clearly expressed in words, since they come from a realm outside time, space and the forms of individual appearances. Although the laws of musical progression resemble those which govern actual events (i.e. insofar as they have common roots), music can be considered as a symbol of reality only if it describes that which is typical or eternal about such an actual event. Since music has no special sounds to express the endless variety of forms and appearances, it has to leave this role to the other arts. For its own domain is closer to that of archetypes (*Mütter*).[192] It is precisely this difference between the symbolic capabilities of the different arts that makes it possible to put them together, so that the generality of musical representation, focussed through poetic or dramatic performance on specific incidents, brings greater precision, while again, perceptions expressed verbally or theatrically find the core of their being exposed with the most wonderful clarity by music. The deepest, most inexpressible things which, if we tried to clothe them in words, would at best attain merely the level of a poor translation, find in music their wholly perfect interpretation: against which, as already mentioned, music is never in a position to represent with the same clarity those things which can be exactly characterized in words. It therefore plays in programme music a doubly lamentable role, in that it not only abandons the essence of its expressiveness (which no other language possesses), but then stammers incomprehensibly, or at best half-comprehensibly, in a domain (that of specific incidents) which is foreign to it.[193]

Here Mahler makes it clear that his objection to programme music is the logical result of his conception of music, and of dramatic music. Opposed as he was to any verbal explanation, whether programme or analysis, he was never-

---

[192] This probably alludes to the well-known scene in *Faust*, I. ii.

[193] In another letter to Schiedermair, dated 6 Dec. 1901 (Staatsbibliothek, Munich) but probably sent with this one, Walter asked him on behalf of Mahler to publish the text of the first letter in full since Mahler's works had hitherto suffered considerably from 'classification in a category alien to them', that of the 'new programme symphonies'.

theless unable to prevent Ludwig Schiedermair from writing the thematic analysis commissioned from him by the Krefeld Festival. Later he acknowledged that the choice of music examples had seemed questionable to him, but as he attached no importance to the text he took care not to admit it. Ernst Otto Nodnagel, who was henceforth to consider himself Mahler's official commentator, attacked Schiedermair openly in the *Allgemeine Musik-Zeitung* and listed all his 'mistakes' *in extenso*.[194] However, Mahler did not hesitate to deflate Nodnagel's enthusiasm by asserting he had never specifically asked him to write an analysis:

I am and remain fundamentally opposed to all analyses . . . good or bad. No one can help the audience. They alone can help themselves by listening again and again and by studying [the score] again and again. That alone. If they cannot or will not, they should leave me in peace—as I am willing to leave them in peace. Kindly spare me from having to prove my 'thesis'! as you call it. Fortunately for me, my vocation is only to write music, not about music . . .[195]

These were harsh words which later on in the same letter Mahler tried to soften:

If in God's name my analyses must be printed, then, in the Devil's name, you write the damned things! In any case, rather you, since you understand the matter and treat it seriously and with affection, than others who perhaps only want to earn a fee or such like . . . I now realize that I ought to have stuck to my flat rejection of all analyses—at the risk of letting chance decide who should produce these things, for they now go forth as 'authorized' by me! And that is certainly not what I intended, but merely the result of your not understanding what I said . . . Since the legal protection I so impetuously demanded does not exist, I am now compelled to let things take their course. Yet I herewith solemnly declare that it is done against my will and that I don't want to have anything to do with it.

To this question, which had become vital for Mahler, and about which he frequently found himself adopting contradictory attitudes, he returned once again in a letter written, doubtless in 1902, the year after the Berlin review *Die Musik* was founded, to its founder and editor, Bernard Schuster:

While it is true that the composer creates without thinking of a future audience and whether it will be able to accept his way of expressing himself and share his feelings, it is, alas, even more true that in the long run he cannot do without understanding and sympathy for his efforts. I have felt for a long time that I lack a go-between, and that this function cannot be fulfilled by a 'programme' which the utterly degenerate and misdirected musical world of today clamours for with increasing insistence. I hope, and feel from what you have written, that you indeed are someone who understands this, because you have grasped the essential nature of my music, which can be apprehended

---

[194] *Allgemeine Zeitung*, 34–5 (22 Aug. 1902), 570. In a letter probably written after the Krefeld Festival, Mahler himself reproached Schiedermair for mistakenly regarding the Third Symphony as a representation of 'the struggle of an individual'.

[195] The text of this undated letter to Nodnagel is preserved in AMS.

only in and on its own terms and not by means of images or explanations. May you, dear Mr Schuster, be such a go-between.[196]

Such was and such remained Mahler's attitude to the very end. From his Fifth Symphony on, he no longer even contemplated providing his audience with an explanatory text.[197] The fact remains, however, that his first four symphonies did originally have 'programmes' and that, even though they were sometimes drawn up after the music had been composed, they should be known and quoted today for what they are, regardless of whether or not they are indispensable to a full understanding of the works. They provide an essential key to Mahler's creative imagination and to his own poetic world. Whenever he devised several different programmes for the same work, their dissimilarities are often instructive, while their similarities show the extent to which certain images remain indissolubly linked in his mind to certain pieces of music. However, there always came a point in the process of creation when a work began to exist on its own and to free itself from the motives that originally inspired it. Later on, when Mahler had acquired perspective and developed a more objective attitude towards his work, he admitted that the 'programmes' of his first works should not be dismissed. In fact, when he conducted his Third Symphony for the last time in 1907, he agreed to the publication of the original titles of the different movements. These often conflicting statements reveal both his obsession and his uneasiness when asked to explain the mystery of artistic creation. For him, as for most true creators, a work did not really begin to exist until he had succeeded in distancing himself from it. Its meaning only emerged after a lapse of time. It seemed to him, therefore, that the programmes of his first symphonies, far from 'explaining' them and making them more accessible to the public, failed to reflect the full scope of the works.

Donald Mitchell has suggested that one explanation for Mahler's change of mind about programmes was the development of his music, which from 1901 became more and more 'autobiographical', so that he himself 'becomes, increasingly, the programme of his own symphonies'.[198] Mahler himself did not encourage autobiographical interpretations of his works, but this dimension was nevertheless noticed very early, in particular by the Berlin critic Oskar

---

[196] Undated letter to Bernard Schuster (reproduced in the special Mahler issue of *Die Musik*, 10: 18 (June 1911), and, with a facsimile of the original, in RSM2. 24 (illustrations 59–60). On the subject of 'programmes' and Mahler's fundamental ambivalence in this respect, see Hermann Danuser, 'Zu den Programmen von Mahlers frühen Symphonien', *Melos* (Jan. 1975), 14 ff.

[197] It seems that Mahler expressed the same view to Richard Strauss. When Romain Rolland wrote to Strauss in May 1905, suggesting that he drop the programme for the performance of the *Symphonia Domestica* in Paris, Strauss replied: 'Perhaps you are right so far as the programme of the *Domestica* is concerned; you agree entirely with G. Mahler, who completely condemns the very principle of programme music. . . . Those who are interested in it can use it. Those who really know how to listen to music doubtless have no need for it.'

[198] Paul Banks and Donald Mitchell, 'Gustav Mahler', in *The New Grove: Turn of the Century Masters* (New York, 1985), 134.

Bie.[199] However that may be, Mahler always accepted that music has a 'lived (*erlebt*)' content and that 'since Beethoven, there has been no modern music without an inner programme', but he added: 'No music is worth anything if the listener first has to be told what the composer "lived" while composing it and what therefore he, the listener ought to "live". So, once again, down with all programmes!' People should bring to concerts their heart and their ears, and above all should give themselves over completely to the musician-rhapsodist. There will always be an element of mystery, even for the creator.[200] 'It cannot be denied that our music involves the "purely human" (all of it, including the "intellectual"),' he wrote two years later to Bruno Walter, announcing the completion of the Sixth Symphony:

As in all art, it is solely a matter of means of expression etc. etc. In making music, one should not try to depict, poetize and describe. Yet <u>what</u> one puts into music is one's whole (feeling, thinking, breathing and suffering) being. There would really be no objection to a programme (even though it's not exactly the highest rung of the ladder), except that the thoughts expressed in it must be those of a musician rather than of a writer, philosopher or painter (all of whom are part of the musician).

In short, he who lacks genius should abstain, and he who has it need fear nothing.— All this mulling over meanings reminds me of someone who, having begotten a child, racks his brain wondering whether it really is a child and whether he fathered it with the right intentions, etc. He simply loved and—was potent. Basta! And if one doesn't love and isn't potent, then there is no child! Again basta! And how you love, what you are like and how potent you are, that is what the child will be like! Once more: Basta![201]

To return to the summer of 1902: Mahler's 'child' was about to be baptized at Krefeld and everyone was awaiting the event with intense, though not always benevolent curiosity. On the evening of Monday, 9 June, long before the concert's[202] starting time of 8 o'clock, the hall was filled to overflowing. The local audience mingled with a large number of musicians who had come from all over Germany and elsewhere to attend the festival: Richard Strauss, Max von Schillings, Engelbert Humperdinck, Eugen d'Albert, the Dutch conductor Willem Mengelberg, and many others. Many of the listeners were strongly prejudiced against the 'gigantism' of the work, as shown by the following passage in a letter from Eugen d'Albert to Engelbert Humperdinck: 'The Krefeld public does not know me as a composer at all. . . . What effect can a

---

[199] Oskar Bie, *Die neuere Musik bis Richard Strauss* (Leipzig, n.d.), 4. Concerning this problem, Vera Micznik's study, 'Is Mahler's Music Autobiographical? A Reappraisal', *Mahler Review*, 1: 2 (1987), 48ff., should be also mentioned.

[200] MBR1, no. 274 (incomplete and wrongly dated); MBR2, no. 283 (complete text with date corrected) to Max Kalbeck.

[201] MBR1, no. 258: MBR2, no. 334 (1904, not 1906 as the book specifies). An examination of the original letter (LPA) shows that some changes were introduced for its publication in MBR.

[202] The final rehearsal had taken place at 9 a.m. The women's choir of the Oratorien-Verein participated with the St Anna-Knabenchor. The orchestra was made up of musicians from the Krefelder Städtische Kapelle and the Gürzenich Orchestra.

short inoffensive piece like my Overture[203] hope to produce? It would be smothered by Mahlerian cacophonies and other superhuman music.'

A breathless hush prevailed while the first movement was being played, followed by a burst of applause. The Swiss critic William Ritter has left another of his colourful descriptions of Mahler's conducting on this occasion:

This necromancer in his badly tailored coat, . . . this swarthy little man with his narrow lips and clean-shaven chin, looks like a defrocked priest but has the superhuman calm of a snake charmer facing his cobras; a tuft of stiff black hair crests his dolichocephalic skull as he hypnotizes his wild orchestra—staring up at him with pale faces—with a single glance from his jet-black eyes, as sharp as vipers' tongues, taming, rousing or subduing the unleashed dragons with the tip of a small hazelwood baton, the wand of those who conjure up the devil.[204]

The Dutch critic Sibmacher Zijnen[205] left a similar description of Mahler in Krefeld:

Small in stature, uncertain of gait and with a stoop, searching, short-sighted eyes behind big lenses, and the violent gestures of a nervous man,—but on the podium suddenly a different man, erect, his gestures now calm and assured, a conductor possessing great authority. Unforgettable his lovely phrasing, the care with which he prepares each climax, his iron command of rhythms, his sharp separation of the musical periods, his enthusiasm! . . . An energetic and original man, this conductor and composer from Vienna. Without the slightest scruple of any kind he exercises his right to follow his creative urge freely and without concern. Neither in his choice of means nor in the way he uses them does he pay the slightest attention to conventions.

Immediately after the first movement, Richard Strauss ostentatiously strode the entire length of the hall to shout his approval near the podium, a move which redoubled the audience's enthusiasm. After a ten-minute interval, the excitement steadily increased throughout each successive movement and the Finale was listened to from start to finish with rapt attention. 'Perhaps the greatest Adagio written since Beethoven,' wrote William Ritter.

After so many dazzling wonders, there was more to come! This man's inexhaustible verve never ceases to perform new miracles. Not one moment's boredom, not one second of fatigue! The great kaleidoscope of sound functioned all through this unique work. One was never, never tempted to slacken one's attention. The stunning impact of the first movement was followed by unending enchantment.[206]

At the end of the concert, the audience rose and cheered as one man. Many

---

[203] Letter from d'Albert to Humperdinck, dated 25 Apr. 1902, quoted by Wilhelm Raupp, *Eugen d'Albert* (Roehler und Amelang, Leipzig, 1930), 165. The d'Albert work performed at Krefeld was the Overture to the opera *Der Improvisator*, which was first performed on 20 Feb. 1902, by the Berlin Opera.

[204] WRE 263.

[205] In an article announcing the performance of the Third in Arnhem in Oct. 1903, he recalled the Krefeld concert which he attended: *Nieuwe Rotterdamsche Courant* (18 Oct. 1903). See below, Chap. 15, the biography of Sibmacher Zijnen.

[206] WRE 263.

people rushed towards the stage, while others stayed in their seats, waving handkerchiefs. Mahler was called back to the podium at least twelve times. According to the *Krefelder Zeitung*, the thunderous ovation lasted no less than fifteen minutes and the next day the *Niederrheinische Volkszeitung* stressed the unanimity of the audience's acclaim. That evening Alma, 'incredibly agitated', knew for certain that her husband was a 'great genius'. Feeling her child stir within her for the first time, she was deeply moved, wept tears of happiness. Realizing that so far she had merely 'submitted' to him, she 'vowed that from now on she would live for him alone'. Later the two of them went out to supper with Justi and Arnold, who had come from Vienna for the occasion. The only shadow to mar a triumph unprecedented in Mahler's life was, once again, Strauss's puzzling behaviour: despite his demonstrative approval of the first movement, he didn't even wait to speak to Mahler at the end of the concert. When they met in a small restaurant later that evening, Strauss merely shook his hand casually and said not a word. Upset and deeply hurt, Mahler sat in silence throughout the meal, quite incapable of joining in the conversation. Public enthusiasm suddenly paled into insignificance in the face of this disapproval by his greatest contemporary and colleague.

For once, however, there were no insults in the next day's press reports to detract from the memory of his triumph. The *Niederrheinische Volkszeitung*[207] acknowledged that, although he followed a path that was 'singular and new', Mahler had managed to touch and move the audience with an 'original genius' which expressed itself in 'clear and intelligible musical language'. Nevertheless the anonymous critic claimed that by refusing to publish his 'programme' and original titles, Mahler had prevented the majority of the audience from understanding him:

Music is not in itself a clear language . . . and if its more powerful effects are piled on one another, as is so frequently the case in the first movement, to the extent that they exceed the limits of music, then one is justified in asking what it is all about. . . . The first movement . . . is likely to bewilder and deter an audience. . . . Yet it is full of significance and it is worthwhile making the effort to follow its musical construction'.

As for the Finale, 'it is not easy to follow the profusion of its interwoven themes; motifs in various keys are often strung together without transition. The polyphony is magnificent and the colouring unusual and rich'. The *Volkszeitung*'s critic concluded by observing that the Third Symphony had shown that Herr Mahler had 'a quite exceptional talent, a wealth of inspiration and an admirable command of the orchestra'.

The *Krefelder Zeitung* also felt that this première would be of 'lasting importance in the history of modern music' and that it might well have 'ushered in a new stage in the development of German music'. 'Mahler himself admits

---

[207] According to this paper, the audience's enthusiasm was all the more remarkable since this was the penultimate concert of a festival at which a great number of new works had been presented.

that he has just experienced the happiest day of his life', the reviewer added. 'It was decisive for his entire creative life and brought him, after bitter struggle, a glorious victory.' The enthusiasm of public and critics alike was a fitting reply to the invariably hostile comments of the Viennese press. Mahler had been quite right not to offer any analysis of his work, the critic went on, for 'it is indeed so simple that you need glance only once at the score to see how modest, clear and naïve this composer is'. The march-like rhythm and thrilling and colourful exuberance of the first movement showed his 'phenomenal artistry', and although its melodies might have sounded like 'banalities', the next move- ment silenced the grumblers. This 'naïveté' could possibly conceal a 'lack of inventiveness', but the work was unquestionably a 'brilliant achievement'. Moreover, the quality of performance was admirable and the orchestra played 'with totally unstinting devotion'.

Even Rudolf Louis,[208] composer and critic of the *Münchner Neueste Nachrichten*, recognized that the performance of the Third had been the great event of the festival. 'Despite the lack of originality of his thematic invention,' he wrote, 'Mahler is most certainly a highly original musical personality. He is a serious artist, a master of compositional technique.' 'Whether or not one likes his music is quite another question.' Without wanting to pass judgement on the whole or on particulars, Louis declared that on this hearing he had not been convinced that this was 'music born of an inner necessity'. He admired 'the prodigious knowledge and very original character' of the composer who, de- spite the eclecticism of his inspiration, 'managed to combine utterly hetero- geneous foreign elements . . . into a new, strange and characteristic entity'. The too obvious 'desire for effect' reminded him of Meyerbeer, even though Mahler was 'a much more honest and authentic artist than the inventor of "grand historical opera"'. Louis concluded by admitting that the Third had made a better impression on him than the Fourth, despite the fact that it too contained 'an incomprehensible amalgam of the bizarre and cheap (*Triviales*)'.

This article, one of the first Rudolf Louis was to devote to Mahler, was a foretaste of the attitude that the whole German 'nationalist' school was to take towards him. Louis was known as much for his trenchant opinions as for his steadfast allegiance to Bruckner and Pfitzner, which was accompanied by a solid dislike of Brahms and Reger. This time, however, his article reveals the true extent of the Krefeld triumph. What is more, most of the critics who had been present sent to the German periodicals reviews as enthusiastic as those in

---

[208] Rudolf Louis (1870–1914), born in Schwetzingen, was a student in Geneva and Vienna, then studied composition with the Swiss composer Friedrich Klose and conducting with Felix Mottl. He held posts as Kapellmeister in Landshut and Lübeck and then moved to Munich in 1897. On the death of Heinrich Porges, in 1900, he became the chief music critic of the Bavarian capital's main newspaper, the *Münchner Neueste Nachrichten*. Influenced by the philosophy of Bahnsen, he wrote books about a number of composers (Wagner, Liszt, Berlioz, and Bruckner), and went on to produce a German nationalistic and anti-Semitic pamphlet *Die Deutsche Musik der Gegenwart* (Munich, 1901), as well as monographs of Pfitzner and Klose and an important treatise on harmony in collaboration with Ludwig Thuille. As composer he left a symphonic poem, *Proteus* (1903).

the Rhenish press. In the *Allgemeine Musik-Zeitung*, an anonymous correspondent (probably Otto Lessmann) declared that he had always disliked
Mahler's works because the huge means they required had always appeared to
be in inverse ratio to the thoughts and feelings they contained. While acknowledging Mahler's technical and orchestral mastery, he deplored his lack of
melodic invention, the vast accumulation of 'partly grotesque, partly trivial and
frivolous' details, and the 'atrocious cacophonies'. The first movement of the
Third Symphony merely confirmed this impression, he wrote. 'The composer's
imagination does occasionally soar', but it also sinks into 'the most incomprehensible platitudes'. In the absence of a programme, one is unable to discover
any image corresponding to 'the terrifying chaos of notes, the ear-splitting
dissonance and the bizarre instrumental effects that attain the ultimate in
repellent ugliness'. However, the subsequent movements, particularly the imposing and powerful Adagio, which ennobles the whole symphony and 'rises to
heights which situate this movement among the most sublime in all symphonic
literature', compelled the critic's admiration. 'Only a genius', he wrote, 'could
have created such a movement, in which powerful and fervent emotions are
expressed with incomparable nobility'. Conducting with imperturbable outward calm but correspondingly intense internal emotion, Mahler had conveyed
his will to both chorus and orchestra: the concert would leave a deep impression on everyone there, whether friend or foe of Mahler. It had truly given
the Krefeld Festival an importance that 'reached far beyond the present'.

The *Neue Zeitschrift für Musik* described the atmosphere that prevailed
before the concert. Mahler's supporters were expecting a 'major event in the
history of music', the others a 'comic turn'. Regarded by most people with
mistrust when he arrived in Krefeld, Mahler was acclaimed after the concert 'as
a victor and a conquering hero'. Admittedly, the work was novel, disconcerting,
both exalting and bizarre. Its dimensions were gigantic but so was its content!
Nor had Mahler made it any easier for the audience to understand by refusing
to provide a 'programme'. Yet the first movement, clearly a vast celebration of
nature, left listeners totally enraptured and it was difficult to imagine anything
more enchanting than the second. The 'mysterious and sublime atmosphere' of
the fourth 'grips our hearts, . . . as though a voice from eternity were speaking
to us', while the sudden transition to a naïve and childlike folk melody in the
choral movement was 'surprising, indeed bizarre. . . . Only a bungler or a
genius would do a thing like that'. As for the final Adagio, 'intoxicating,
overwhelming, shattering in its sublime splendour', it was 'perhaps the most
beautiful (movement) of all'. Mahler was unquestionably 'a great man', a man
possessed of 'primal strength' (*Urkraft*). His 'ingenious and often dazzling
orchestration' and 'the clarity with which he superimposed his motifs rather
than interlacing or contrasting them, as Strauss does', compelled admiration.
His 'soul, filled with the freshness of nature . . . speaks to us with all the charm
of the inherent wholesomeness that has more than once proved distressingly

absent during these past few days'. The roar of applause that greeted the end of the symphony 'was far more than acclamation, it was true homage'.[209]

Even the Berlin journalist who reported to *Die Musik*, Wilhelm Klatte, condemned the 'arbitrary' order of the movements and the work's 'commonplaces' and 'harsh and crude' sonorities, but found the whole work rich in 'interesting detail'. He praised the 'atmosphere' of the fourth movement, but to his mind, the Finale towered above all the rest.[210] The Dutch critic Siebmacher Zijnen's comment, although short, is also well worth quoting since it shows an exceptional understanding of Mahler's style:

In his invention of themes he often proves amazingly skilful. In his juxtaposition of materials made up of very diverse elements, in connecting and developing them he shows a rare originality which the public likes him for. Even those who would rather not say whether the obviously exciting orchestral means employed correspond to the inner content of the composition and can therefore be considered 'genuine',—even they find themselves roused by the tremendous sound effects and then captivated by the naïvety and folk inspiration (*Popularität*) which come at them as different pages of the score are turned.

The Krefeld triumph marked the beginning of a new era in Mahler's career as a composer. It won him the admiration of numerous critics, composers like Humperdinck[211] and conductors like Fritz Steinbach, Martin Heuckeroth,[212] and Willem Mengelberg (who promptly invited him to conduct the Concertgebouw Orchestra in Amsterdam the following year). Henceforth, all the German towns[213] vied for the honour of performing the Third Symphony. And instead of having to beg publishers to print his compositions, Mahler was now in a position to choose the highest bidder. Thus it was that, after mature consideration, he entrusted Peters with the task of publishing his Fifth Symphony, and signed a contract on far more favourable terms than any he had previously obtained.

---

[209] According to *Neue Zeitschrift für Musik*, the soloist, Frau Luise Geller-Wolter, sang somewhat off-key in the fourth movement. There were 114 musicians in the orchestra.

[210] *Die Musik*, 1: 19, 1764. A letter from Mahler to Strauss dated the previous summer reveals that the original plan had been to perform Liszt's symphonic poem *Tasso* and an orchestral excerpt from *Feuersnot* before the Third Symphony (MSB 67). William Ritter, whose description of Mahler on the podium suggests that he attended the Krefeld performance, although his report does not specifically say so, records that the first movement lasted 42 minutes, and the Finale 22 minutes.

[211] Orchestral excerpts from Humperdinck's fairy-tale opera (*Märchenspiel*) *Dornröschen* were on the Krefeld Festival programme. In a letter dated 6 July 1902 and preserved in RWO, Humperdinck warmly congratulated Mahler, told him again how deeply his Third Symphony had impressed him, and asked if he would send him the score so that he could study it during his holidays.

[212] See below, Chap. 15.

[213] Notably Elberfeld, Magdeburg, Nuremberg, and Dresden, where the Finale was encored.

14

Concerts in the Rhineland—first marital storms—
the first Roller collaboration: Roller's *Tristan*—
première of *Louise*

(June 1902–April 1903)

How long will it be before people will be capable of hearing <u>this</u>?

ON his return from Krefeld, Mahler spent a week and a half settling affairs at the Opera before leaving for Maiernigg around 20 June. As Alma describes it, his summer life as a newly married man differed little from his previous bachelor existence. Inspired by his recent triumph, he devoted all his energy to completing the Fifth Symphony. He would get up at his usual hour of 6 or so, and ring for his breakfast of *café au lait*, diet bread, butter, and jam, which he ate in the *Häuschen*. According to Alma, the cook had to carry the tray in all weathers up a steep, narrow path, well away from the main one, for Mahler didn't want to see or speak to anyone before settling down to work. He heated his milk on a small spirit stove, often burning his fingers in the process. If the weather was fine, he breakfasted out of doors. Alma's job, previously carried out by Justi, was to see to it that no sound got through to the *Häuschen* during his working hours, so she did her best to charm the next-door neighbours into keeping their dogs locked up by promising them Opera tickets.

Delighted as Alma was with the garden and the villa's setting, she was less happy with its 'old-fashioned and philistine' interiors.[1] Returning from the *Häuschen* one day, Mahler found her perched on a stool busily tearing all the fretwork off the cupboard cornices. The house was roomy and solidly built, but it faced north, since Mahler had chosen the lake's southern and least frequented shore. In a room next to his own he installed a work table, for the days when he was writing letters and did not need to climb to the *Häuschen*. Alma

---

[1] Mahler himself at first had also been disappointed 'by the ordinariness of the house, both inside and outside' (letter from Justi to Henriette Manckiewicz, 5 June 1901, LCW; see above, Chap. 10).

took Justi's bedroom on the floor below, giving on to a covered veranda. The guest room was soon to become the nursery.

On 31 July Mahler wrote to Nanna Spiegler:

I'm up to my ears in work with scarcely time to breathe . . . Fortunately my news is all good. You know that all I desire and demand of life is to feel an urge to work! This indeed is the case at present, more than ever. From which you can conclude that all is well. Once I can catch my breath after this mad race and have a little time, I'll write again.[2]

Mahler's long working hours worried Alma because the *Häuschen*, built in the middle of the forest on a natural terrace about 200 feet above the house, had no foundations and was very damp. Like the Steinbach *Häuschen*, it now contained a piano, a large work table, and two or three pieces of furniture, as well as a few books, including a complete edition of Goethe. The only scores were the complete Bachgesellschaft collection. Around midday, when Mahler had finished working, he would go back down to the lake for a swim. Once in the water, some distance from the bank, he would whistle for Alma to join him. She sat near him while he sunbathed, and told him the events of the morning.[3] Refreshed and relaxed, the two of them would walk slowly back up to the house through the garden, where Mahler took delight in every plant and flower. The soup had to be on the table when he got there. He insisted on light meals, 'simple, almost frugal, but thoroughly cooked', and with a minimum of seasoning. Alma, undoubtedly used to richer fare, despised this menu with its neglect of gastronomic refinement. She called it 'an invalid's diet'. Like her friend Burckhard, Alma was convinced that such unsubstantial fare was bad for the stomach.

After the meal they would chat for half an hour and then, rain or shine, Mahler would 'drag' Alma out for long walks, along the near shore, or on the far side of the lake, which they reached by boat. Alma did not share her husband's urge to exercise and complained later on that he walked too fast. Her theory was that the food in his stomach put pressure on his heart and prevented him from lying down after meals. This was why, she later wrote, he usually preferred a three- or four-hour outing to a nap.[4] Alma was already five months pregnant and the walks exhausted her. When she grew too tired, he clasped her tenderly in his arms and murmured: 'I love you, I love you', before they moved on. Sometimes he would stop, pull out his notebook, and jot down ideas, beating time with his pencil in between. If the pause grew too protracted, Alma would sit down on a tree-trunk, not daring to look at him for fear he would be distracted. When his idea pleased him, he would smile at her, 'for he knew that

[2] Letter to Nanna Spiegler (PML).

[3] Mahler had already adopted the modern custom, barbaric in Alma's view, of sunbathing and then taking a dip to cool off.

[4] Yet only a few pages later, describing Mahler's life in Vienna, she writes: 'As at Maiernigg, he took a short siesta.'

nothing in the world would make me happier'. Alma found this life of exercise and relentless work in the midst of nature, this 'Splendid Isolation', 'almost inhumanly pure'. At Pörtschach am Wörthersee,[5] the elegantly dressed holiday-makers would gather on the pier when the boats were coming in. 'We're not on the pier and they don't forgive us for that,' Alma quotes Mahler as saying, and adds: 'Because we were a centre of attention, rumours were continually being invented about us, but, thank God, we weren't even aware of them! It was as if, in our *Splendid Isolation*, we were protected by a glass dome.'[6]

As always in Maiernigg, Mahler's sole preoccupation was composing. Nothing was allowed to distract him. 'I tried to play the piano softly', Alma wrote,

but when I asked him, he said he had heard me although his *Häuschen* was a long way off in the woods. So I switched to copying all that he had so far completed of the Fifth Symphony. I always liked to keep up with him so that my manuscript was ready only a few days after he had finished his.[7]

When he was composing, Mahler tried to forget about the Opera and its worries. Now and again, however, a letter or a visit reminded him of his responsibilities. His secretary at the Opera, Alois Przistaupinsky, came as usual to Krumpendorf at the end of July to deal with matters requiring attention.[8] This year's principal concern was the engagement of new singers, especially a bass, sorely needed as both Karl Grengg and Willi Hesch were ill. The first two candidates Mahler tried out, Paul Bender and Hans Keller, had not proved successful.[9] But the problem was shortly to be solved by the engagement of the great Austrian bass Richard Mayr.

At the end of July Mahler took a break from work to visit Toblach in the Southern Tyrol once more.[10] From there he went, probably by bicycle, to Lake Misurina, at an altitude of 1,700 metres, and one of the loveliest places in the whole Dolomite range. He walked around the shore of the little lake looking up at the rugged peaks of the Cristallino, the Cadini, and the legendary Drei Zinnen. The beauty of the landscape moved him so much that he decided to return to it each summer, whenever he felt he needed a few days rest from composing.

Before she married him, Alma had promised Mahler that she would stop

---

[5] Alma, mistakenly, wrote 'Unterach am Attersee'. She probably meant Pörtschach, which is situated on the other side of the lake opposite Maiernigg, and where the Mahler family would usually get off the train and proceed by rowing-boat to Maiernigg. Sometimes Mahler was met by his servant, Anton, at Maria Loretto at the eastern end of the lake.

[6] AMM1. 70; AMM2. 79; AMM3. 369.

[7] In fact Alma's copy of the MS is dated (by another hand) 24 Oct. 1903. It was used by the publishers for the printed copy. Originally the property of the firm of C. F. Peters, it has belonged since Mar. 1985 to LPA. (See below, App. on the Fifth Symphony.)

[8] Four letters sent by Przistaupinsky to Carl Sageder and Ferdinand Graf (see above), have survived (HOA, Z.164/1902).

[9] Mahler also considered three other singers, Lohfing, Van Duinen, and de Rapp, and also his old friend from Leipzig days, Johannes Elmblad.

[10] This trip is mentioned in a letter Przistaupinsky wrote to Ferdinand Graf on 4 Aug. 1902.

composing and devote herself to 'his' music. But she continued to play the piano, as she would all her life. Alma claims she had to give up her favourite pastime for fear of disturbing Mahler when he was working in the *Häuschen*. But the ban must have been far from total, because a few pages further on in her memoirs she says that he slipped a Lied he had composed for her into a Wagner score which she 'often played on the piano'.[11]

As soon as the Fifth Symphony was finished, Mahler took Alma's arm one morning and led her 'almost solemnly' up to the *Häuschen* to play it for her. From the beginning, she appears to have appreciated it far more than the Fourth, except for the Chorale in the Finale, which she found 'ecclesiastical and boring'. Mahler reminded her that Bruckner had also introduced Chorales into his symphonies, but in reply she merely pointed out how different he was from the older composer. She felt aware of the 'underlying conflict between the Judaism of Mahler's forebears and youth and his strong attraction to Catholic mysticism'. This of course proves how little she understood of her husband's music. 'The chorale was one of Mahler's constants' from the First Symphony on, as John Williamson has pointed out.[12]

During her long periods alone—these could last for anything up to eight hours a day[13]—Alma again fell prey to 'doubts' and 'uncertainties'. Mahler, she felt, played the 'role' of a 'relentless, severe and unjust mentor'. 'Being young and frivolous', she deeply resented his contempt for every pleasure he did not share with her. 'Money, travel, clothes, beauty, everything worldly was despicable', for they only enhanced the youth and beauty he was afraid of. She particularly resented the fact that he had never given her a piece of jewellery, indeed a present of any kind—not even an engagement ring, since he considered the custom 'totally absurd'.[14] He wanted, she felt, to 'deprive her of all life but the life of the spirit'. A number of passages in Alma's private diary bring out in sharp relief the inner conflicts she was experiencing. The following entries were written on 10, 12, and 13 July:

I don't know what to do. There's such a struggle going on in me! And a miserable longing for someone who thinks OF ME, who helps me to find MYSELF! I've sunk to the level of a housekeeper! I've just come from Gustav's room. There was a heavy tome on philosophy lying on his desk—and I thought to myself—why can't he share it with me—let me join in—instead of devouring it all alone! I sit down at the piano—I'm

[11] See below and AMM1. 79; AMM2. 87. AML makes it clear that it was *Siegfried* which she 'often played on the piano' and confirms the correct date of the love-song Mahler wrote for his wife, 'Liebst du um Schönheit', as being 1902, not 1903 as AMM claims.

[12] See John Williamson, 'Liszt, Mahler and the Chorale', in *Proceedings of the Royal Musical Association*, 108 (1981–2), 123.

[13] According to a letter Mahler wrote to Lilli Lehmann in Aug. (Berlin Staatsbibliothek, no. 55.354), he noted that during his seven weeks' holiday he had had to 'toil without respite in order to finish at least part of my new work'.

[14] AMM1. 226; AMM2. 206. In 1910, when Mahler left Toblach for Munich, he asked Alma to give him her wedding ring to wear. Alma also complains that he did not give her a wedding present, contrary to the Austrian custom at the time.

dying to play—but I can't find my way any more. Someone has seized me roughly by the arm and dragged me far away—from myself. And I long to be back—where I was. The winter without work—this hectic life without time for reflection—having to give up 'LOOKING INTO MYSELF'—finally the loss of all my friends . . . The winning of a friend who doesn't even know me.

12 July. Today I think differently. The day before yesterday, in the afternoon, we had a bitter discussion. I told him everything. And he—with infinite kindness—pondered over how he could help me! And I do understand . . . he <u>can't</u> just now! He lives entirely for his composing. I will use this summer to improve myself in every way. I will try to learn—in so far as it's permitted me—to fulfil, to realize myself! Gustav was happy yesterday—because of the peace of mind I've given him. He kept on thanking me and said I wouldn't regret it . . . so I feel better, too. And I now have a goal. An ultimate purpose—to sacrifice my happiness for that of another—and in so doing find happiness myself.

13 July. I was alone the whole morning and afternoon, and when Gustav came down— still so wrapped up in and happy about his work—I couldn't share his happiness; I burst into tears again. He grew serious—terribly serious. And now he has doubts about my love! . . . How frequently I've doubted it myself. One moment I'm dying of love for him—and the next I feel nothing—nothing! When I'm filled with love, I can endure anything with the greatest of ease—when I'm not—it's an impossibility. Yet I know all the while that no human being has ever been so close to me. If only I could find my inner balance! I'm torturing myself and him. He said yesterday that he's NEVER WORKED SO EASILY AND CONTINUOUSLY AS NOW and I took heart. Knowing that through my suffering I'm giving him joy, how can I falter for a single moment! From now on I shall keep my inner struggle to myself.[15] I want to sow the ground on which he walks with peace, contentment, equanimity. But my face and my eyes betray me! And always these tears![16] I've never cried so much as now when I have everything a woman can aspire to . . .[17]

Mildenburg's presence in Maiernigg helped to create tensions between Mahler and Alma. She sometimes arrived at the villa without warning, accompanied by a 'wretched mongrel' which, she smugly explained, she had bought from a beggar 'out of the kindness of her heart'. Mahler loathed the animal but felt obliged to accompany his former mistress and her dog home after each visit. Finally he passed the chore on to his servant, whereupon Mildenburg's visits, Alma noted, became less frequent. One day during a violent storm she entered unannounced, 'playing the double role of Ortrud and Brünnhilde'. Her hair dishevelled and windblown, she dragged Mahler outside and ridiculed Alma's fear of thunder and lightning: 'She's a real coward!' (*die ist ja feig*), she said with a cruel smile.

Another day, changing her tactics, she called on Alma and regaled her with stories of Mahler's past, revealing secrets about her own former intimacy with

---

[15] This sentence is crossed out in the typed copy.   [16] Phrase crossed out.

[17] The original MS of these pages of AMT no longer exists. They are only known from an incomplete typed copy, which today is in UPL.

him and about the private lives of his sisters. Alma, however, suspecting
that Mildenburg was merely trying to gain her as an ally 'against' Mahler,
promptly told him all about it. He wanted to tell Mildenburg not to come again,
but Alma favoured diplomacy. The next time she appeared, he steered the
conversation onto the subject of Wagner and then sat down to play the last
scene of *Siegfried*. Mildenburg sang the whole of it 'better than she had ever
done on stage'. As the night was calm, her powerful voice carried far over the
lake—and was greeted with wild applause by the holiday-makers in the flotilla
of boats that had gradually gathered in front of the villa. Mildenburg eventually
tired of trying to win back Mahler. Yet she must have felt that she had found a
new ally in Alma, for later, when she met her in the corridors of the Opera, she
approached her in front of everyone with outstretched arms. Alma simply
nodded and passed on. 'I never stopped being afraid of her and her intrigues,'
she admitted later.[18]

During this first summer of their married life, Mahler was well aware of the
conflicts in Alma's heart. As proof of his love for her, he composed one of his
shortest, simplest and most moving Lieder, 'Liebst Du um Schönheit'.[19] Hoping
she would find it by chance in his absence, he slipped it into the score of
Siegfried, which she kept by the piano and often played from. As it happened
she did not open it that particular week. He waited until 10 August and then,
unable to contain himself any longer, handed her the score. When she opened
it, his 'first love song . . . a *Privatissimum* for you', fell out onto the floor. They
immediately played it together and the words of the last line, 'Liebe mich
immer, dich lieb' ich immer, immerdar' (Love me always, I'll love you always
and forever), stirred her deeply. She played it over and over again and later the
same day wrote in her diary: 'I almost wept. The tenderness of such a man! And
my lack of sensibility! I often realize how little I am and possess—compared
with his infinite riches!'[20]

Sometimes, Alma's journal, instead of describing her inner conflicts and
frustrations, records her vision of a higher and purer life, a sort of ascent
towards the absolute. Thus on 27 September 1903:

[18] AMS.
[19] According to Willem Mengelberg, the Adagietto of the Fifth Symphony composed during this same
summer was another declaration of love. Apparently both Mahler and Alma told him that he sent it to her
'without a word' and that she immediately understood what it meant and 'wrote asking him to come'. Mahler's
memory, or Mengelberg's, may have slightly altered the incident, for such an exchange of messages between
a husband and wife living in the same house seems fairly unlikely. It is even more unlikely that Alma would
fail to mention the incident in her book. (Cf. Karel Philippus Bernet-Kempers, 'Mahler und Willem
Mengelberg', *Bericht über Internationalen Musikwissenschaftlichen Kongress, Vienna 1956* (Hermann
Böhlaus, Graz, 1958).) Mengelberg adds the following note, and a poem (by himself or Mahler, but he does
not specify), whose words fit the principal theme of the Adagietto: 'NB: If music is a language, it says
everything in music, with sounds: *Wie ich Dich liebe* (How I love thee) | *Du meine Sonne* (Thou, my sun) | *Ich
kann mit Worten Dir's nicht sagen* (I can't tell thee in words.) | *Nur meine Sehnsucht* (Only my longing) | *Kann
ich Dir klagen* (Can I pour out to thee) | *Und meine Liebe* (And my love) | *Meine Wonne* (My rapture!)'
[20] AML 28. This passage from Alma's diary leaves no doubt as to when the Lied was actually composed,
i.e. 1902, and not 1903 as she writes in AMM.

I was walking along a broad, sunny path. Suddenly I came to a wooden fence, and I could see the sun shining through the cracks. A steep, stony, wearisome track lay before me. I climbed to the top—and behold—I could see beyond the fence and over the whole world. I stood there at the top, drunk with joy. My way leads ever higher. MY GUSTAV!

On 23 August 1902 Mahler wrote to Nanna Spiegler: 'At last I have finished! The Fifth is with us! Am very fit despite prolonged exertion. Now back into harness again.'[21] The next day, the same news was dispatched to Guido Adler: 'V! Affectionately, M . . . You know what this jubilant message means! (and with it my greetings. Freund.)'[22] Thus, at the end of August, Mahler left for Vienna and visited Justi and Arnold in Edlach near Reichenau, at the foot of the Raxalpe, before joining Alma on the train at the nearby station of Payerbach.[23] He returned to Vienna[24] with the draft score of the Fifth Symphony. As usual, all that remained to be done was to make a clean copy during the winter.

Alma's account of his daily routine in the capital is almost identical with Natalie's. As in Maiernigg, Mahler got up early and went to his work table, where his breakfast was served to him. He arrived at the Opera around 9 and stayed until 1. When his work was done, he would get someone to telephone to his home to make certain lunch would be ready on time. On arrival at their block of flats, he rang the bell at the main entrance, as a signal to the cook that the soup should be brought in, raced up four flights of stairs, hurried through the flat, slamming doors all the way, washed his hands in the bathroom, and went straight into the dining-room.[25] After lunch he took a short nap and then went for a walk with Alma, either in the Belvedere Park, not far from the Auenbruggergasse, or right round the Ring. As in Maiernigg, Alma found these long walks too strenuous. At 5 he had tea and returned to the Opera. Even when he wasn't conducting, he was always present for part of each performance. If he still had work to finish when Alma came to pick him up, she was sent off to the director's box to sit in on a few scenes. On the way home he would tell her how the opera ended. After dinner, he sometimes asked her to read to him.

At the beginning of November, as their child's birth approached, Alma's physician, Doctor Carl Fleischmann,[26] warned her that the baby was awkwardly

---

[21] Card to Nanna Spiegler (PML).

[22] Emil Freund's signature on the card shows that he was in Maiernigg at this time (RMA 38).

[23] According to a letter from Justi to Guido Adler (26 Aug. 1902). The same letter mentions the coming performance in Cologne of the Third Symphony, which was in fact postponed because of Franz Wüllner's death (see below). The Raxalpe is part of the Semmering mountains and a popular summer resort for the Viennese.

[24] According to *Neue Freie Presse* and HOA, Mahler returned on 27 Aug. For once, he did not start conducting that season until 22 Sept. (*The Magic Flute*). The season had opened on 18 Aug. with a performance of *Fidelio* conducted by Schalk.

[25] Alma drew a plan of the apartment in AMS.

[26] Alma's physician, Dr Carl Fleischmann, was born 30 Mar. 1859 in Bukowa, Bohemia. He had studied medicine at the Prague German Univ. and moved to Vienna in 1887. He was chief physician at the Rothschild Hospital, 1902–29, and wrote many books on gynaecology.

placed in her womb and that the birth would be difficult. He even told her that the long walks of the previous summer had caused this, which she was only too willing to believe. Though Mahler was not told, he sensed something was wrong, and as he had no one to confide in he tried to calm his nerves by taking longer and longer walks. Questions about Alma's health infuriated him. When Guido Adler showed his concern he cut him off sharply and called him an idiot. While Alma was in labour at Auenbruggergasse, he found it impossible to relax and paced restlessly up and down in the flat. After hours of mounting distress, Alma finally gave birth to a baby daughter. Mahler came to Alma's bedside, his eyes full of tears: 'How can men go on conceiving children,' he said, 'knowing that they will cause such suffering?' When he later was told the reason for the difficult breech birth, he burst out laughing: 'This is certainly my child, the part she straightaway presents to the world is the part it deserves!'

Born on 3 November, the little girl was named Maria in memory of Mahler's mother, and Anna after Alma's. Alma reveals in her diary that Maria's birth did not improve her emotional balance. 'I don't love her yet as much as I should. Everything in me belongs to Gustav. I love him so much that everything appears lifeless compared to him. And I cannot tell him so.'[27] For the moment, Alma's maternal instinct seemed dormant. When the child fell seriously ill a few weeks later, Mahler carried her about in his arms murmuring endearments as if the mere sound of his voice could heal her. Alma, on the other hand, nursed and massaged her but found no satisfaction in her motherly duties:

13 December. I feel as though my wings had been clipped. Gustav, why did you bind to you this splendid bird so happy in flight, when a heavy, grey one would have suited you better? There are so many heavy ducks and geese who cannot fly at all!' . . .

[15 December.] ˙. . . I've been sick for a long time. Gallstones. The cause, or perhaps the result, of my intense unrest. For eight days and nights now, I have been inventing music deep in my mind; it is so loud and insistent that I hear it between every word I speak and I cannot sleep at night! Yesterday I told Gustav that I was upset by his lack of interest in what was happening inside me, that he had not even asked me to play any of my works for him, and that I am tormented by his total indifference to my feelings. My knowledge of music suited him only insofar as it served his purposes. He didn't take me seriously.[28] He said: 'Because your golden dreams (Blütentraüme) have not been fulfilled. . . . You only have yourself to blame.'

My God, how hard it is to be deprived so mercilessly of <u>everything</u>, to be mocked about things closest to one's heart. Gustav lives <u>his</u> life. My child has no need of me. I <u>cannot</u> occupy myself <u>only with her</u>! Now I'm learning Greek. But my God, what has become of my goal, <u>my magnificent goal</u>! My bitterness is intense! I am constantly choking with tears! no one understands this. Everyone thinks I am happy, and yet one thing is missing, the one thing which is more important to me than all the rest. God help me! . . .

---

[27] AMT, 25 Nov.   [28] Sentence crossed out in the typed copy.

16 December: Again, a bitter resentment! I told him I needed someone to talk to. Gustav is so solitary, so distant! Everything in him is so deeply buried . . . that it cannot surface! Even his love; everything is muted. I need warmth! I am alone! Before, when I felt lonely, there were so many people there to protect me . . . To learn? To what purpose? Without a goal and without end? Oh, if only he were younger, younger to enjoy life!

At the beginning of the new year rehearsals for *Euryanthe* provoked her to a fit of jealousy. 'I've just come back from the Opera. First dress rehearsal of *Euryanthe*,' she writes on 8 January.

A nice rehearsal! Gustav let those whores drink out of his glass! He disgusts me <u>so much</u> that I dread his coming home. Playful, charming, cooing, like a young man he danced around Mildenburg and Weidt. My God! If only he <u>never</u> came home again. Not to live with him any more! I'm so agitated that I can scarcely write.[29] What an idiot I was to stay at home languishing for him! The thought of him nauseates me, I can hardly express it.

Difficult and beautiful times! [she writes a little later][30] Just as I finished writing the above, Gustav came home. He wanted to caress me and I repulsed him. At dinner, he asked me gravely, angrily what was the matter with me. I answered: 'You disgust me.' I did not get any further, we didn't talk to each other. The next day we had it out in the Stadtpark. He said he felt clearly that I did not love him. He was right. After what happened, everything in me was cold. But suddenly my feelings were all there again. Once more, I know how much I love him. I am determined to be calm. But then he says something like: 'As for that' . . . about <u>our</u> love life and everything in me goes to pieces! The day before yesterday, I began to speak about K[urz].[31] Furious, he left the room. That drove me crazy. I felt like jumping out of the window. But something held me back. I cried until I almost fainted, Gustav was still awake. He came over from his room. He was kind and calmed me. Often when I'm unhappy, it's not his fault, it is <u>only</u> mine.

Now that I am supposed to live only for someone else, I do not feel happy, although I truly love this man. Nothing really touches me. I cry, I rage, I rant, but all on the surface. Deep down, there is an indestructible, frightening calm. No pain affects me! No joy either! Recently Klimt and Burckhard were here! Burckhard made bold advances. I was neither shocked nor happy! Nothing! Yes, absolutely nothing, nothing, nothing! Wretched creature![32]

'I'm so weary,' writes Alma on 17 March.

I am quieter. I have decided to keep silent when I'm hurt. But then to whom could I talk? I'm so exhausted. I was playing the piano just now. But for what and for whom? I can't any more. My joie de vivre has fled! Yesterday evening, as there was no one else around, I played for Justi. She listened but she couldn't understand a thing. I played 'Siegfried'. She asked, 'By Gustav?' There is no one to whom I could pour out my heart! Gustav! he does not need me! I am so tired. If only the <u>one</u> thing was left to me—<u>my</u> music! If only I could still learn. Nothing can be changed! I vegetate. I'm so tired!

---

[29] Sentence crossed out in the typed copy.   [30] 29 Jan.
[31] 'A woman singer with whom he had had an affair,' adds Alma, no doubt on rereading that entry.
[32] Phrase crossed out.

The complaints, the reproaches, the outbursts of fury on every page of Alma's diary seem to indicate that the beginning of her married life was a nightmare. But as she wrote only in moments of crisis, the diary is mainly a record of their quarrels and her moments of rebellion. Clashes were inevitable between two such strong and different personalities. As for Mahler, the fact that he never complained or confided in anyone but his wife does not mean that he suffered or worried less. No doubt he also blamed himself for having listened to his heart rather than his head when he married Alma. Daily life for these two could only spark off supreme elation or utter despair. They were always either on the heights or in the depths.

At the Opera, things were not going smoothly either. The recent conflict between Mahler and the orchestra had left scars. In a long attack on Mahler published at the start of the season, Hirschfeld thought that prospects for a durable peace were slight, since the director 'had demanded resignations and premature retirements'. Also, because his recent illness had made him irritable, he didn't 'know how to make work easy or agreeable' for his colleagues. The Opera's ensemble had to be supplemented by last-minute invitations to guest artists.[33] Mahler's ill humour, Hirschfeld continued, taxed his energy— 'the essential element of his artistic nature!'—to such an extent that he now rarely conducted. In the *Neues Wiener Tagblatt*, Kalbeck, whose attitude to Mahler was usually more objective, this time agreed with Hirschfeld.[34] 'Mahler's nervous hand' could not always 'carry out the will of his fevered brain'. 'Too often this same hand was tightly clenched, thereby missing many masterpieces that should be in the repertory.' According to Kalbeck, the orchestra's hostility had even spread to the singers, some of whom had declined to perform for health reasons. Mildenburg, for instance, had abandoned her Wagnerian roles for several months because she was 'nervous and over-wrought'.[35]

Actually Mildenburg's plight was not only due to nerves. Her voice and her constitution had always tired easily, and her position as the Vienna Opera's first dramatic soprano often daunted her. Sometimes Mahler accused her of not taking enough care of her health. During the summer of the previous year she had caught a bad cold at the end of her vacation in Berchtesgaden and had returned to Vienna with 'catarrh'. 'I am sure you will understand, dear Frau Nina,' she wrote to Frau Spiegler,

---

[33] For instance, Mildenburg was absent from the stage for several weeks during the 1901–2 season. Sophie Sedlmair replaced her, but her smaller voice was inadequate for the great moments in *Tristan*, let alone the role of Brünnhilde (THE 309). In the article quoted above, Hirschfeld draws up a full list of his reproaches and of the *Affären* undermining the Vienna Opera ('Wiener Musik Brief', *Zeitschrift der Internationalen Musikgesellschaft*, 4 (1902), 187 and 180).

[34] The article was publ. at the time of the première of *Zaide*.

[35] Mahler wrote to Mildenburg at the beginning of the summer to warn her that he could not allow her to appear as a guest at the Munich Opera. She had been absent so long from Vienna that such an appearance would cause her, and him, serious problems.

how much I suffer from the consequences of this catarrh just now, at the beginning of the season. I am causing a lot of trouble for Direktor Mahler since this is the time of the big Wagner cycle in which all the most important parts were assigned to me. The effort would in any case have been too much for me at the beginning of the season: on the 1st, Irene;[36] 5th, Venus; 7th, Ortrud; 11th, Walkyrie; 15th, Götterdämmerung and 19th, Isolde. I might almost call it a blessing that I was unable to perform. This constant work with Wagnerian roles is bound to destroy an artist. I clearly feel that I must not, at any cost, again overtax my strength as I did last season! I can hardly tell you how depressed I feel at the thought of having to go on like this. Working exclusively in Wagner roles does not allow me to cultivate *bel canto* (*Kunstgesang*), the only kind of singing to preserve the voice. For a long time after singing roles like Isolde, Brünnhilde, Ortrud, etc., the condition of the vocal organs makes the study of refinements in singing technically impossible. This explains the current frightening vocal decline. It may be gratifying that in the realm of opera musical taste has tended towards greater depth but the consequences of this new tendency are very sad indeed. To my mind it spells ruin for the art of singing in general and for singers' voices. And yet, although I am fully aware of all this, I remain the interpreter of the biggest and most important of these punishing roles![37]

Mildenburg's letter clearly demonstrates the cruel dilemma of the Wagnerian singer who has been schooled in the best traditions of Italian opera and feels that the 'new' works she admires more than any other are ruining her voice. It suggests that many of Mildenburg's illnesses and last-minute cancellations were feigned and that she was perhaps wisely trying to preserve her voice. Mahler had endured too many of these incidents to accept them easily. Of course his point of view had changed considerably since he had become director of the Vienna Opera, and had put an end to his affair with Mildenburg. In Hamburg, she said, he had constantly urged her not to overstrain her resources. 'When I complained that it was too much to have to sing *Götterdämmerung*, *Brünnhilde* and *Isolde* in five days,' she wrote in the same letter, 'he told me that as director he could not agree. It is remarkable how far he has now stretched the limits nature imposes on an artist!'

The problem for Mahler was therefore to find as soon as possible another dramatic soprano beside Sophie Sedlmair who could replace Mildenburg at a moment's notice. Again, it was from among Rosa Papier's trainees that he found the singer he needed. In fact, Mildenburg herself had discovered Lucy Weidt at the Vienna Conservatory and brought her to her former teacher. Unfortunately, the young soprano was already engaged by the Leipzig Opera when she auditioned for Mahler early in 1902. Later, she was to describe this memorable audition, at which she sang the Nile aria from *Aida*. While she was singing, he remained 'as still as a bronze statue', fixing his eyes on her as if 'he wanted to

---

[36] In *Rienzi*.

[37] This letter from Mildenburg to Nanna Spiegler is not dated but the dates of the performances mentioned proved that it was written at the end of the summer 1901. Mildenburg wonders whether she would not be wise to give up singing and to take up acting instead (ÖNB, Handschriften).

penetrate her innermost thoughts'. Hardly had she finished when he offered her a contract. Weidt had to turn it down, as she had already accepted the offer from Leipzig. When she told him this, Mahler stamped the floor and cried furiously:

How could you be so out of your mind, Fräulein, as to want to leave Vienna? . . . Your place is here . . . Promise me that you will return as soon as possible and, when you are back, please let me know immediately . . . Forgive me for having spoken so harshly, but I am always angry when I cannot bring new talents to the Hofoper.[38]

Weidt finally made her début as a guest artist on 10 October 1902 and as a member on 13 November, both times as Elisabeth in *Tannhäuser*.

Good bass singers were in even shorter supply. Grengg had suffered a stroke on stage and Reichenberg was dying—which left only Wilhelm Hesch, also in bad health, and the mediocre Moritz Frauscher. Mahler then heard reports about Richard Mayr, a 25-year-old from near Salzburg, who was reported to have a splendid voice.[39] Mayr had at first hesitated between medicine and music. Even before finishing his studies, he made a brilliant début at Bayreuth in the role of Hagen in the summer of 1902. Back in Salzburg at the end of August, he received a telegram from Mahler asking him to come to Vienna. Two days later, at 11 in the morning, he presented himself at the Opera, where he sang 'without a trace of nervousness' Hagen's Wake from *Götterdämmerung* and the King's prayer from *Lohengrin*. Like Weidt, Mayr later gave a brief account of this audition. 'Agitated and nervous but not unfriendly,' Mahler had led him into his office where the following exchange took place: 'So, you want to join the Opera company?' 'No, Herr Direktor, it is you who wish to engage me.' Mahler went over to the window, tapped absently on the pane and asked the young basso what salary he expected. When Mayr didn't answer, he proposed 4,800 kronen. This was no more than the pocket money Mayr used to receive from his family during his student days. After a brief discussion, they finally agreed upon 8,000 kronen a year, with the possibility of increases in instalments to 20,000 kronen, and a six-year contract which could be revoked by either party at the end of three years. 'One more thing, Herr Mayr,' added Mahler, before taking leave of the young man. 'I've been told you drink too much.' 'Certainly not, Herr Director,' replied Mayr in his deep, reassuring voice. 'That was before; now alcohol doesn't agree with me.'[40]

On 4 October, Mayr made his début at the Vienna Opera in *Ernani*. During rehearsals the astounded chorus began to applaud. Mahler signalled them to stop, saying: 'You're going to turn him into a megalomaniac'. About to make his first entrance, Mayr tripped over a rail in the wings: a good omen, the stage-

[38] *Illustrirtes Wiener Extrablatt* (19 May 1911). Lucie Weidt (1879–1940), born in Troppau, Bohemia, remained a member of the company until 1927.

[39] Mayr's father, a brewer at Henndorf near Salzburg, was nicknamed 'Gablermayr' because he made a well-known beer called 'Gablerbräu' and ran a restaurant of the same name. His grandfather had a restaurant at the Hotel Schiff in Salzburg, and his grandmother owned the Henndorf brewery (GWO 40).

[40] Otto Kurz, *Richard Mayr* (Bergland, Vienna, 1933), 77 ff.

manager August Stoll assured him. And indeed it proved to be the beginning of one of the longest and most successful careers of any singer at the Vienna Opera. After his first performance, several critics (notably Max Graf and Julius Korngold) thought that his vocal technique needed improving. Nevertheless, he achieved outstanding successes in no fewer than nine different roles during his first season.[41]

To complete his 'ensemble', Mahler had for some months been exchanging an unusually large number of letters and telegrams with various German impresarios. He was looking for a lyric soprano to replace Frances Saville, who was leaving the Opera because he had decided to reduce her salary when renewing her contract.[42] Mahler considered as possibles a Breslau soprano named Sedlmaier (a name almost identical with that of the dramatic soprano already at the Opera) and two others, Fanchette Verhunck and Rosa MacGrew.[43] He finally engaged Grete Forst, and she, in spite of her rather passive temperament, successfully undertook lyric roles alongside Berta Förster-Lauterer and, later, Berta Kiurina. He also investigated several dramatic sopranos when it seemed that Lucy Weidt would not be available. Other singers he considered for possible recruitment were a Dresden baritone called Kiess (Bertram's sudden departure in 1901 having forced him to look also for baritones) and a Dresden basso called Leon Rains. None of these tentative approaches came to anything, either because of the artists' previous commitments or because they failed in their guest appearances.

The Opera archives contain an enormous number of telegrams, many of them in autograph, sent by Mahler to various agents and singers at this time. But none of them brought any results, apparently, and Mahler finally had to send Bruno Walter on a long tour of the principal German-speaking cities at the beginning of 1903. Walter visited Mannheim, Karlsruhe, Wiesbaden, Essen, Cologne, Strasbourg, Metz, Stuttgart, Zurich, Brunswick, Hanover, Aachen, Frankfurt, and Koburg, and heard hosts of new singers without making any sensational discoveries, except the lyric-coloratura Bella Alten[44] in Cologne

---

[41] Mayr's most celebrated roles were Gurnemanz, Sarastro, Baron Ochs, Rocco, the King in *Lohengrin*, St. Bris and Marcel in *Les Huguenots*, the Landgraf in *Tannhäuser*, Stadinger in *Der Waffenschmied*, the Hermit in *Der Freischütz*, the Cardinal in *La Juive*, Calchas in *Iphigénie en Aulide*, the Pope in *Palestrina*, Barak in *Die Frau ohne Schatten*, Leporello, Figaro, but he sang many others. He remained one of the most popular singers in Vienna until his death in 1935, at the age of 68.

[42] Letter from Frances Saville to Mahler dated 15 Dec. 1902 (HOA, Z.371/1902).

[43] Autograph letter to the Nuremberg agent Eugen Frankfurter, dated 14 Nov. 1902. Fanchette Verhunck later sang *Salome* at the Viennese première of the Strauss opera at the Deutsches Theater. She was invited for two guest performances at the Vienna Opera on 5 Apr. and 19 May 1903 but never returned there. Rosa MacGrew appeared as a guest in the Hofoper in 1907.

[44] Bella Alten (1877–1962), born in Zaxaczewo, in Poland, student of Gustav Engel in Berlin and Aglaia von Orgeni in Dresden, made her début in 1897 in Leipzig, where she spent the next three years. Engaged at Brunswick (1900–3) and Cologne (1903–4), she was twice invited to the Hofoper during Mahler's tenure, in 1903 and 1904. Alten then went to Berlin (1904–5) and subsequently sang every season until 1913 at the Metropolitan Opera, New York, where she created the role of Adele in the *Fledermaus* in 1905. In 1908 she was the Marzelline in Mahler's New York production of *Fidelio* (see Vol. iii, Chap. 2). The rest of her career was spent at the Vienna Opera (1917–23). After leaving it, she taught singing in Vienna until 1936, when she

and the lyric tenor Georg Maikl[45] in Mannheim. The latter was invited to the Vienna Opera in 1903, and was subsequently engaged, despite his failure to make a strong impression. Mahler wrote to the famous Berlin teacher Johannes Ress asking him to take the tenor in hand, for he had imposed as a condition of his engagement a preliminary period with this renowned teacher, who had taught Selma Kurz and several other famous artists.[46] One of Mahler's main problems was to discover artists with complete operatic personalities, not just beautiful or powerful voices. This is illustrated by his answer to the following telegram from the Intendant of the Dresden Opera: 'What is Fräulein Korb like? Does she have a vibrato (*Tremolo*)? What about top register, appearance and acting?' Mahler replied: 'Korb has a very big brilliant voice, particularly at the top, and is musical. Appearance without charm and lacks personality. Mahler.'[47]

Although the season began under favourable auspices with Weidt's début as a guest and the hiring of Mayr, it was marked, as usual, by a number of disputes. During the final rehearsals of *The Huguenots*, which was to have its première on 29 October, the members of the chorus were supposed, as usual, to appear in costume. One day, however, because the soloists were allowed to appear in normal dress, the chorus decided to do the same. One of the chorus masters berated them and threatened some of them with dismissal. As a gesture of solidarity, the choristers decided to go on strike, and to demand an increase in salary at the same time. Mahler himself had to intervene and smooth things out.[48] Two months later, on 4 December, Mahler stopped a rehearsal of *Pique Dame* to correct the violins. One of the players made an 'insulting' remark, which Mahler overheard. He lost his temper and demanded who it was. But once again the musicians closed ranks. After the rehearsal they all agreed to keep silent and Mahler finally had to give in.[49] Once again, such incidents did not improve Mahler's relations with the Opera's orchestra, which were in any case under strain, since he was still trying to engage the best musicians he could find to improve the orchestra's quality. After his negotiations with the trombonist Franz Dreyer, he exchanged a considerable number of letters and telegrams with a harpist at the Prague Opera, Alfred

moved to London. Bruno Walter's letters to Mahler are dated 6, 7, and 8 (Danzig), 16 (Brunswick) and 17 Feb. (Cologne) (HOA Z.142 and Z.938/1902). Walter took advantage of the journey to conduct some concerts in Danzig, his former place of employment (HOA, letter of 16 Dec. 1902, Z.VIII.4/1903).

[45] Here is Walter's evaluation of the tenor after hearing him for the first time: 'The voice is warm, slightly veiled, personality very attractive, young and full of fire, passionate and sensitive, though he is still something of a beginner.' Georg Maikl (1872–1951), born in Aippach near Zell an der Ziller, made his début at the Mannheim Opera in 1899 and remained there until his Vienna engagement on 1 Sept. 1904. He remained at the Vienna Opera until 1942.

[46] Undated MS letter (BGM, Halban-Kurz Collection). Maikl sang as a 'guest' at Vienna on 4 Nov. 1903.

[47] Reply to telegram from Graf Seebach dated 28 Jan. 1902 (HOA, Z.99/1902). Jenny Korb sang 9 times as guest at the Vienna Opera. Four of her appearances were during Mahler's directorship.

[48] *Neues Wiener Tagblatt* (30 Oct.) and *Neue Freie Presse* (28 and 30 Oct. 1902).

[49] *Neue Freie Presse* (5 Dec.) reported that the musician finally confessed of his own accord, and that he was a wind player.

Holy,[50] who had unfortunately just signed a lifetime contract with the Berlin Opera. Before he agreed to hand in his resignation, he demanded a place as teacher in the Vienna Conservatory and a contract for a minimum of ten years. Nearly twelve months of effort were required to fulfil these conditions.[51]

The 1902/3 season was one of Mahler's most brilliant at the Hofoper. It included two important premières, Charpentier's *Louise* and Tchaikovsky's *Pique Dame*, and four new productions, *Tristan*, *Les Huguenots*, *Ernani*, and *Euryanthe*. The Emperor's name-day was celebrated on 4 October with the first performance of Mozart's *Zaide*. This work, which dates from the end of the 1770s, is incomplete, Mozart having been interrupted by an urgent request from the Munich Opera for what was to become his first *opera seria* master-piece, *Idomeneo*. The manuscript had been bought, along with some others, around 1800 by Johann Anton André, who published it in 1838 with an Overture and Finale of his own. All the original prose text, except for that of the arias, had disappeared.[52] Thus, for the world première in Frankfurt in 1866, a text laboriously reconstructed by Carl Gollmick from published fragments was used. Not satisfied with this 'original' version, Mahler asked Robert Hirschfeld, already one of his harshest critics in the Viennese press, to produce a new text, and a new musical version of the work, doubtless because he had appreciated Hirschfeld's work on Haydn's *Lo speziale*, which he had conducted in Hamburg and Vienna.[53] In his memoirs, Korngold expresses the opinion that the juxtapo-sition of the light-hearted *Singspiel* music of *Zaide* with the dramatic and even tragic excerpts from *Thamos, König in Ägypten*, which Hirschfeld had drawn on to complete the unfinished work, was a grave error of judgement.[54]

The première of *Zaide* was conducted by Bruno Walter on 4 October. A second item on the evening's programme was a revival of Bizet's *Djamileh*, with

---

[50] Mahler's first undated and autograph letter to Alfred Holy was written in Hamburg during the 1893–4 season, since it bears the Fröbelstrasse address. It now belongs to the Männergesangverein Archives in Vienna, together with a correspondence card written at the end of 1902 and Mahler's final letter of confirmation, dated 17 Jan. 1903.

[51] Holy's letter of 13 and 23 Jan. 1902 and Mahler's letters of 17 and 29 Jan., as well as his telegrams of 1, 3, 4, 5 Nov. 1902, belong to HOA, Z.70/1902. Holy was engaged on 1 June 1903 and stayed on in Vienna until 1913.

[52] The author was Andreas Schachtner, a friend of Mozart and author of the German trans. of the French text of *Bastien et Bastienne*.

[53] In his version, Hirschfeld uses as the Overture the 'Symphony' No. 32 in G, K. 318, even though it requires four horns instead of two in *Zaide*'s. The Finale repeats the opening chorus, but with new words. Hirschfeld kept André's title, but changed all the names of the other characters, probably to avoid obvious similarities with the *Entführung* (despite the fact that, in 1902, this was not in the Hofoper's repertoire). Gomatz, the hero, becomes Timon; Allazim, Agathon; Osmin, Dodok; and the sultan Saladin, Pharases. Hirschfeld also transposes this last role, including its one surviving aria, down a fifth, giving it to a bass instead of Mozart's tenor, thus changing the original balance (and sonority) of the ensembles. Three arias were cut in this version: the sultan's in E flat (no. 11 in the Bärenreiter score), the heroine's in G minor (no. 13) and Allazim's in B flat (no. 14). Hirschfeld also inserts an entr'acte in the middle of the work, a storm scene, and a final scene for the high priest, all three borrowed from Mozart's *Thamos, König in Ägypten*, K. 345 fragments. In his new text, Hirschfeld tries to overcome the 'hollow pathos' of Schachtner's original. See Robert Werba, 'Mahlers Mozart-Bild: Am Beispiel der Zaide', *Mitteilungsblatt der Mozartgemeinde Wien*, 43 (May 1976), 31. Hirschfeld's version was publ. in Vienna by Weinberger.

[54] KIW 67 ff.

548 *Gustav Mahler*

Hermine Kittel replacing Marie Renard in the principal role, and Mahler conducting.[55] Unfortunately the critics were still prejudiced against Walter. The best they could find to say about him was that he worked hard. Only Liebstöckl recognized that 'this attention to detail can unreservedly be called talent'. In his opinion, Brioschi's costumes for *Zaide* fitted perfectly into the single abstract stage design composed exclusively of columns. The Hofoper's best singers had been assembled for the occasion, notably Ellen Forster-Brandt, who sang the title-role with great charm (but not without 'passivity') and Leo Slezak, who continued to triumph in Mozart despite his budding career as a Heldentenor. The dark voice of Hans Melms was, it seems, too powerful for Osmin/Dodok, while that of Moritz Frauschner, on the other hand, lacked character for the sultan Allazim (now the barbarian prince Agathon). Hans Breuer, a buffo tenor with a big range, triumphed as Saladin (Pharases), especially in his 'laughing' aria.

Despite all the care lavished on the production, it ran for only three performances.[56] As we have seen, Richard Specht and Paul Stefan considered that Hirschfeld's disappointment at the failure of *Zaide* accounted for his increasingly hostile attitude to Mahler from 1902 onwards.[57] From then on, 'his hatred of Mahler became an obsession'. It seems, according to Julius Korngold's memoirs, that he believed that Mahler had only put on *Zaide* in order to have the pleasure of taking it off again.[58] Korngold describes Hirschfeld as an embittered man who could never get over the fact that Hanslick had written a hostile review of one of his concerts of Renaissance music, and had entrusted Korngold with the task of reviewing the *Zaide* première instead of writing it himself. He resented even more Hanslick's refusal to consider him as his successor on the staff of the *NFP*. Hirschfeld's physical appearance (he was chubby and round-faced) (*breiten Bonhomme-Gesicht*) belied his real temperament: he was a bitter, sarcastic man who delighted only in negative criticism. Korngold compared him to 'the Englishman who used to follow a reckless tight-rope walker everywhere around in order to be sure to be there on the night when he would finally fall off'.

In an anonymous article in the *Wiener Zeitung*,[59] purporting to be a letter sent by Mozart from the other world, and undoubtedly written by Hirschfeld, Mozart takes issue with Mahler for not conducting *Zaide* himself[60] and 'advises' him to revive *Don Giovanni*. However, the day after the première, Hirschfeld wrote in the *Abendpost* that *Zaide* had been performed 'with love and enthusiasm'. Loath to 'judge a work to which he had contributed himself', he praised

---

[55] Cast for *Djamileh*, 4 Oct. 1902: Kittel (Djamileh), Schrödter (Haroun), Breuer (Splendiano).
[56] With *Djamileh* and Hellmesberger's ballet *Harlekin als Elektriker* on 4 and 10 Oct., and with *Pagliacci* and Franz Skofitz's ballet *Pan* on 17 Oct.
[57] See above, Chap. 7.   [58] KIW 67 ff.
[59] *Wiener Zeitung* regularly publ., under the pseudonym L. A. Terne, articles by Hirschfeld on artistic policy generally and on the theatre (see Werba, 'Mahlers Mozart-Bild').
[60] He also reproaches Mahler for giving the hero's role (Gomatz/Timon) to Slezak rather than to Schrödter.

the 'artistic achievements' of all the performers. Other critics, such as Kalbeck, reproached Mahler for not keeping the solemn promise he had made on arriving in Vienna that he would produce all the major works of Mozart. Mahler's reply to this accusation came four years later, when he discovered in Roller an ideal collaborator for the works of both Mozart and Wagner.

There is on record another eulogistic description of the performance of *Zaide*, all the more trustworthy because its author always showed himself to be particularly hostile to Mahler.

If I am not mistaken, it was on 4 October that I saw with my wife a almost unknown work of Mozart, *Zaide*, where in the very first bars, I was so struck by the immediate presence of this genius that, as always at such moments, I also felt your presence and passionately wished to share this experience with you . . . This is undoubtedly one of Mozart's least precious works, a youthful essay of which he never heard a performance and the text of which has even been lost! . . . Despite the icy coldness of the surrounding audience, which is used to mechanical 'ear massage', and at best capable of getting a little drunk on *Tristan* or *Götterdämmerung*, I tasted that evening one of the most delicate and finest pleasures in my whole life. Obviously Mozart was still a child when he wrote it. There is no forced tone (*gewaltiger Ton*), no sadness either, and sensuality is only a dream, not desire. But at the same time, there is no trace of the pastoral, idyllic quality—à la Watteau with panniers—which spoils one's enjoyment of his early compositions . . . There is instead a lot of pantomime and melodrama, the latter so incredibly delicate that I was enchanted.

One might expect someone who had experienced this Mozartian revelation to attribute at least part of his admiration to the interpreters of the work, that is to say the conductor (Bruno Walter) and the stage-director (Mahler). But that would be to misjudge Houston Chamberlain, the author of the letter, and Cosima Wagner, his close friend, to whom it was addressed. For the one as for the other, no artistic revelation of any kind could come from a Jew. Thus Chamberlain continues: 'although, as you may imagine, it was all played with the most brutal, and even monumental, lack of understanding. *Vous voyez d'ici*,[61] the barely suggested nuances of a still chaste, shy Mozart, interpreted by the art of a Mahler!' No doubt at a loss to explain his own enthusiasm, Chamberlain gallantly attributes it to none other than—Cosima herself. The performance by the Bayreuth tenor Hans Breuer, who sang the part of the villain (Pharases), was 'lively, natural, just right . . . so bursting with verve, fire and virtuosity, and so varied that even his poor, listless and soulless fellow artists were carried away and filled with admiration. I can hardly believe that the man could have performed this way without some kind of assistance from Bayreuth.'[62]

For Chamberlain and Cosima there was no truth, no life, no fire on the operatic stage except at Bayreuth. Another letter written to Cosima by

[61] In French in the text.   [62] Cosima Wagner and Houston Chamberlain, *Briefwechsel*, 646 ff.

Chamberlain from Vienna a few weeks later concerning a Liszt-Beethoven-Wagner concert by the Vienna Philharmonic conducted by Siegfried Wagner[63] expresses the same view:

Physicists ascribe to matter two properties: inertia and impenetrability. The Philharmonic possesses quite a lot of both. I had already noticed it at the rehearsal. When I remember the Eighth of a few years ago, I believe I can clearly recognize the influence of the Mahler era. From Hans Richter to Siegfried Wagner was a smooth and easy transition. Now for quite a few years Mahler has performed Beethoven—at times improving the instrumentation—and audiences have lost all purity of perception (*Reinheit des Empfindens*).[64]

One shudders to think of all that would have been lost if the world had been forced to accept the Bayreuth criteria for 'purity of perception' and had subscribed to one of the 'Green Hill's' articles of faith: Judaism = materialism = impurity = corruption of authentic, that is to say 'Germanic', values!

Two days before the première of *Zaide*, on 2 October, the revival of Verdi's *Ernani*,[65] also conducted by Walter, had met with equal reserve. Mahler had taken a bold initiative in selecting Selma Kurz, who was starting to specialize in the coloratura repertory, for the dramatic part of Elvira. Schönaich considered that the casting was chiefly responsible for the failure of the evening, since only the 'Mediterranean temperament' of the Italians could succeed in 'singing such banalities'. Hirschfeld failed to find 'a serious word to say' about this music, of which 'not one note belongs to the realm of art'. But if, in addition to the casting, the choice of *Ernani* itself was debatable at a time when the Opera's repertory had been steadily contracting, Mahler's idea of preparing a *Neueinstudierung* of *Les Huguenots* turned out to be successful. He continued to defend this work against the wholesale derision of the Wagner disciples and often quoted a passage written by Wagner himself in which he acknowledged the exceptional beauty of the E flat melody of the love-duet in Act IV.[66] Despite criticism that it was a 'dated' work, it enjoyed unfailing popularity with audiences. Its financial success moved Wlassak to comment that 'that, too, is a critical judgement, signed by a thousand hands!'[67] Mahler's ambition was not to tie himself down to any particular aesthetic preferences, but to be a 'universal' theatre director. For this early and most spectacular of the French grand operas, he wanted to produce a model performance, and chose for the seven principal roles the most brilliant 'seven stars' of the Hofoper.[68] Alongside Kurz

[63] The concert took place on 21 Nov. 1902.   [64] *Wagner-Chamberlain*, 654.
[65] Cast for *Ernani*, 2 Oct. 1902: Kurz (Elvira), Slezak (Ernani), Demuth (Don Carlos), Mayr (Ruy Gomez).
[66] He no doubt meant the famous phrase 'Tu l'as dit, oui, tu m'aimes!' in the Act IV duet, which starts in G flat then moves into E flat minor.
[67] Julius Stern, 'Wiener Theaterwoche', *Volkszeitung Wien* (21 Apr. 1929). The first five performances of the new production of *Les Huguenots* brought the Hofoper 32,000 kronen.
[68] *Les Huguenots* acquired its famous nickname 'the night of the seven stars' when sung at the Metropolitan Opera in New York, by Nordica, Melba, Scalchi, Jean and Edouard de Reszke, Plançon, and Maurel during the 1895–6 season (see below, Vol. iii, Chap. 1).

(page), Sedlmair (Valentine), Slezak (Raoul), Saville (Marguerite de Valois), Demuth (Nevers), and Hesch (Marcel), the new bass Richard Mayr appeared as Saint-Bris. Even the minor roles were allotted to excellent singers such as Stehmann, Marian, Breuer, Preuss, and Felix.[69]

Les Huguenots is pre-eminently a singers' opera and the production owed its triumph above all to the individual exploits of the 'stars'. Selma Kurz, in particular, always surpassed herself in the role of the page, for which she had developed some new and specially acrobatic cadences. 'This Kurz! I am convinced I can make another Patti of her!' exclaimed Mahler during one rehearsal. When she made her appearance at the top of the castle staircase in the Finale of the first act, her beauty made a powerful impression. At the dress rehearsal, the first cadenza of her aria 'Nobles seigneurs' made everyone hold their breath and Mahler interrupted the rehearsal to say, with a trace of sarcasm: 'You have all given me your word of honour that you would not hire private claques. *If*, through some miracle, a claque attends this new pro-duction, I ask you to instruct those hand-beating gentlemen with a score at hand. Tell them that with Meyerbeer a cadenza is always followed by an even more beautiful final cadenza.' The trick worked. Kurz was able to launch with incomparable brio into the second cadenza. Her final trill caused a stir of admiration and surprise in the hall, for nothing like it had ever been heard at this point in the score. She started pianissimo, then swelled very slowly to a superb forte. 'There were listeners who jumped up in fright, thinking that this young, fragile singer would suddenly collapse, because her lungs could not possibly hold a fraction of the breath required. But Kurz put ever more power into the trill. She did not wish as yet to decrescendo it until it finally breathed into a perfect pianissimo.'[70] All the preparatory work of the production was undertaken and carried out with enthusiasm but also, as always, with the greatest attention to detail. 'And how well he knew how to inspire each artist and indeed the chorus, with enthusiasm for the old, neglected, despised Mas-ter', reminisced the *Fremden-Blatt* just after Mahler's death.[71]

How wonderfully he managed to bring out the powerful ensemble, the blessing of the daggers in the fourth act. Enthusiasm reigned on stage and in the hall. Mahler had understood how to enlist his collaborators' zeal for Meyerbeer: 'I draw your attention,' he said during a pause in a rehearsal, 'to the fact that we will meet with opposition from some of the critics. Strange! Richard Wagner, who has created immortal, eternal works, Richard Wagner, who with his unrivalled authority belongs among the greatest of the great of this Earth; this Wagner has nevertheless not succeeded in killing off Meyerbeer. And what Richard Wagner has not accomplished, I do not believe that the critics of our day will succeed in doing. I have warned you, ladies and gentlemen, about the critics' opposition only because it compels us to perform the opera with even greater brilliance and perfection! So let's get to work!' And their efforts were repaid. As

[69] For the première on 29 Oct. 1902.   [70] Stern, 'Wiener Theaterwoche'.
[71] 21 May 1911.

if by miracle, Meyerbeer was suddenly playing to full houses. The first five performances brought in 32,000 kronen. Naturally, attacks from the critics were not wanting. A real salvo was let loose at Mahler, the 'Wagnerian artist'. But they did not influence the public.

In fact, the success of the première on 29 October was such that the work received a further eight performances before the year was out, followed by thirteen the next year. The morning after the première, Hirschfeld vainly scattered gems of sarcasm. He pretended to admire Mahler's 'solemn tempo' with which he had attempted to turn Meyerbeer into 'a thinker and a prophet of musical drama', a composer who, by divesting himself of the more old-fashioned choruses, such as the bathers' chorus, had clad himself in 'modern, dramatic costumes'. Hirschfeld went into feigned ecstasies over Mahler's 'marvellous talent' for concealing the work's weakness and 'lifting papier-mâché weights with the gestures and grimaces of an athlete'! Neck-craning, muscle-flexing, nothing was missing to make the audience believe, against all evidence, in Meyerbeer's 'aesthetic weight'. Only the connoisseurs, including perhaps Mahler himself, wrote Hirschfeld, were privately amused at the 'emptiness', the 'fabricated eloquence', of the music and the incredible unevenness of its inspiration. The Hofoper ensemble, although by nature not particularly well attuned to Meyerbeer, had managed, through hard work, to achieve a semblance of perfection'.

Only the anti-Wagnerian critics like Kalbeck felt that *Les Huguenots* 'deserved, after long neglect, the amends now being made'. Mahler had revived 'the grand historical painter of Romantic music, had given his score and characters "vigour and passion" such that individual weaknesses and triumphs were of minor importance within the success of the whole.'[72] Mahler was delighted with the production's success, not because he had any illusions as to the quality of the work, but because it allowed him to embark on more ambitious projects, not necessarily aimed at a broad public. 'Perhaps these gentlemen are right,' he said after reading the critics' vituperations, 'but they forget that I am an Opera director.' After the première, Mahler gave Slezak, who surpassed himself and achieved one of the greatest successes of his career in *Les Huguenots*, a photograph with the following dedication: 'To my dear Slezak, the irresistible Stolzing, the captivating Raoul etc., etc. (see repertoire). In memory of his triumph on 29 October 1902.'[73]

Having devoted so much effort to an ultimately not very rewarding task, Mahler turned to another area not much exploited in the German-speaking countries, namely Slav opera. He thought first of Dvořák's *Rusalka*, and even

---

[72] Instead of cutting Act V, as he had in Budapest, Mahler revived the choral episode in the execution scene. According to Kalbeck, he was quite right to eliminate some of the work's most flagrantly vulgar musical numbers, like Bois-Rosé's aria, the Huguenot soldiers' 'Rataplan' and the notorious Bathers' Chorus.

[73] Walter Slezak collection. 'Meinem lieben Slezak, dem unwiderstehlichen Stolzing, dem Hinreissenden Raoul, etc., etc. (siehe Repertoire), in Erinnerung an den Triumph des 29 Oktober 1902.'

got as far as devising a cast for it.[74] Dvořák himself came to Vienna to sign a contract with the Opera, but on learning that he would receive only 5 per cent of the takings instead of the 10 per cent he got in Prague, refused to accept it. Mahler pointed out that the 5 per cent the Hofoper offered would be worth much more to him then the 10 per cent he got in Prague, in view of higher ticket prices and a larger attendance. In vain he assured him that, with such a cast, his opera was bound to be a triumph, and that, in any case, the Hofoper was unable to change its rules on his account. Dvořák refused at the last moment to sign the document and declared that he wanted more time to think and talk things over with his wife.[75]

In the end, instead of *Rusalka*, Mahler put on Tchaikovsky's penultimate opera, *Pique Dame*, which he had already conducted in Hamburg. He found it the most 'mature and artistically solid' of the composer's works. Alma was present at most of the rehearsals and 'lived for several weeks with this opera and its lovely melodies'. A simple card, sent to the critic Max Kalbeck, author of the German translation of the libretto, gives a glimpse of Mahler's pleasure in bringing back Tchaikovsky's operatic masterpiece, and of the effort involved: 'If only you knew how difficult it is, this return to an old love. . . . But patience! A few days more and I'll be her devoted husband again . . . *Pique Dame* is nearly there. It's becoming excellent, and perhaps we can make the work as much alive as *Onegin*. Thank you with all my heart for your collaboration.'[76]

After the Vienna production, some of the critics questioned Mahler's penchant for Slav music. Gustav Schönaich, for one, deplored the 'dramatic weakness' of *Pique Dame*, and the hybrid character of its musical style, which he described as 'melodic syrup'. On the other hand, Kalbeck agreed with Mahler that it was Tchaikovsky's stage masterpiece, a 'cleverly conceived libretto' adorned with 'beautiful, refined music'.[77] Hirschfeld shared his opinion, congratulating Mahler for the time and care he had put into the production and for casting 'broad rays of white light on Tchaikovsky's sombre Slav work'. In a later magazine article,[78] Hirschfeld underlined the coolness of the audience's response to the work, due he thought to the fact that 'the most beautiful passages have only a secondary role in the action'. For him, Tchaikovsky's temperament was too lyrical, which robbed his dramatic line of firmness. The

[74] Förster-Lauterer (Rusalka), Gutheil-Schoder (the Foreign Princess), Slezak (the Prince), Hesch (Vodnik), according to Josef Bohuslav Förster (see below).

[75] JFP 715. The encounter was described to J. B. Förster by Willy Hesch, who was present. A performance contract for *Rusalka* had been signed by Mahler on 30 Apr. 1902. A letter from Mahler to Antonin Dvořák, dated 4 May 1901 and carrying the number Z.313/1901, was found among Dvořák's papers after his death. A second letter, dated 30 Sept. 1905, accompanied the score of *Rusalka* that Mahler returned in 1905 to Dvořák's widow.

[76] Undated letter to Kalbeck (Dec. 1902). Copies of these letters from Mahler were given to me by Anna Mahler.

[77] Kalbeck also congratulated Mahler for having 'cut out the tedious sections' and achieved 'dynamic progressions'. His 'peerless production' had nevertheless not met with the success it deserved.

[78] *Zeitschrift der Internationalen Musikgesellschaft*, 4 (Jan. 1903), 187.

melodies lingered and sighed plaintively without ever really expressing the uncontrollable obsession of the inveterate gambler. Mahler by no means shared the critics' opinions, and always considered *Pique Dame* to be a masterpiece of Russian opera in which Tchaikovsky's infinitely eloquent music expressed his fellow-feeling with a character who like himself was condemned to suffer on the margins of society.[79] Hanslick, on the other hand, had nothing but praise for the libretto, though he too regretted that the music employed only the 'soft hues of a watercolour'. The success predicted by the doyen of the Viennese critics was soon confirmed: *Pique Dame* was performed seven times in December 1902 and sixteen times the following year.[80] It is still to this day a favourite in the Vienna Opera repertory.

With two such successful productions, the Hofoper's new season was well launched. Meanwhile, since his Krefeld triumph Mahler's position as a composer had begun to change. Many German cities, including even the smaller ones, were now endeavouring to mobilize the resources required to perform his Third Symphony. The critics, however, were still not impressed. The correspondent of the *Neue Zeitschrift für Musik*, reviewing a performance conducted by Josef Krug-Waldsee on 22 October in Magdeburg, described the work as a strange 'pseudo-symphony', a 'coarse motley of musical ideas of little value or originality, written with the brain rather than the heart, at times ridiculous and in the long run unbearable to a sensitive ear'. Once again the conductor's lack of understanding or talent and the admittedly mediocre orchestra were probably most to blame for the poor reception accorded the work. As usual, Mahler had had strong misgivings from the outset. He had asked Bruno Walter to write to his old friend Arnold Berliner and ask him to attend the performance: 'Mahler would be happy to have a friend present who could report to him in detail about the quality of the performance, the audience's reaction, etc.'[81]

The Third Symphony was also performed, on 22 October, in Elberfeld, on 8 November at Barmen, and on 2 December in Nuremberg, where the *Generalanzeiger* again confessed itself incapable of 'solving the riddles of the first movement'. The work as a whole was 'alien to pure music' and impossible to follow without a programme. The Nuremberg *Fränkischer Kurier* condemned the first movement's 'dreadful cacophonies' and 'crude arbitrariness' (*rohe Willkür*), which defied musical logic and aesthetics. According to this review, Mahler had no true originality. Not one bar of the work bore his personal imprint. He was interested only in 'deafening and blinding himself as well as the audience'.[82] The Krefeld triumph may have led to a sudden increase in the

[79] The work's New York première at the Metropolitan Opera took place under Mahler's direction in 1910, and largely on his initiative. It proved to be the last opera he conducted.

[80] Cast for the première of 9 Dec.: Förster-Lauterer (Lisa), Kittel (Paulina), Petru (Countess), Schmedes (Hermann), Demuth (Tomsky), Mantler. As was his custom then, Mahler rehearsed two sets of principals and the major roles were performed two days later by Slezak and Lucy Weidt.

[81] Card from Bruno Walter to Arnold Berliner, dated 1 Oct. 1902 (BGM).

[82] The second concert of the Nuremberg Orchesterverein, conducted by Wilhelm Bruch, was given on 2

number of performances, but it did not change the attitudes of most critics, particularly when Mahler himself was conducting.

A projected performance of the Third Symphony placed Mahler in a difficult situation with the management of the Cologne Opera. Franz Wüllner,[83] director of the Gürzenich Concerts, had invited him in the summer of 1902 to conduct the Third on 19 November. The orchestra was to be the same as the previous season in Krefeld. But Mahler had doubts: he felt the acoustics and atmosphere of the Cologne Opera were unsuitable. When a planned visit to Vienna by the Cologne Opera Director, Julius Hofmann, failed to materialize, Mahler thought the project had been dropped, since Franz Wüllner had died on 7 September. In early November, three weeks before the scheduled performance, he received a letter urgently asking for the score. The wording of the letter gave Mahler the impression that its author felt obliged to fulfil an unwanted commitment, or in any case to make Mahler take the responsibility for a last-minute cancellation. Julius Hofmann having given a less than objective version of the incident to the press, Mahler was obliged to justify his refusal in a long letter in which he offered to conduct the symphony later in Cologne, but in the Gürzenich Hall rather than at the Opera.[84]

Several other scheduled performances of the Third failed to materialize, one of them in Berlin.[85] In Wiesbaden the management of the Kurhaus Concerts changed its mind at the last moment, and chose to perform the Fourth Symphony instead of the Third. Mahler was invited to conduct, and made the long trip from Vienna to Wiesbaden by train. To save expenses, Alma stayed behind. Alone in his compartment, Mahler looked out of the window at snow-covered fields shining in the January sun, and thought of her with tenderness and longing. During a long stop in Nuremberg, he strolled up and down the platform only to learn on his return to his carriage that the local conductor, Wilhelm Bruch, who had also recently conducted the Third Symphony, had come to visit him in his compartment in his absence.[86] He arrived in Frankfurt at one o'clock in the morning and spent the night there. The next day he woke with a migraine caused by the heating in his room. Before taking the train to Wiesbaden, he telegraphed Alma[87] and then took a long walk which he described to her in a very disillusioned way:

Dec. with the Frankfurt alto, Paula Jensen, the women's 'Classical Song Chorus', and the children's choir from the new Gymnasium. The Prelude to *Parsifal* preceded the Third Symphony.

[83] Franz Wüllner (1832–1902), a Munich pianist, conductor, and composer of considerable contemporary renown.

[84] Mahler's letter, dated 28 Nov. 1902, is addressed to an unknown person (*Sehr geehrter Herr*) (BGM). Mahler did conduct the Third Symphony in Cologne, but not until 1904.

[85] This is implied in a letter Mahler wrote to Humperdinck on 14 July 1902: it refers to the latter's request for a score. Mahler asked him in another letter to send him the libretto and score of his new opera, probably *Die Heirat wider Willen* (The Forced Marriage).

[86] Unpubl. letter to Alma, 21 Jan.

[87] The first of two letters (written in the train to Wiesbaden), along with the text of two telegrams, one sent from Frankfurt on 21 Jan. and from Wiesbaden on 23 Jan., are unpubl.

The people, the shops, the houses, all look alike, enormously reassuring, orderly, depressingly uniform. I stopped in front of a shop with a promising sign: 'Works of Art for sale'. I had a good laugh (but I was also a bit disgusted). That's what it is! What better description is there for what these philistines are looking for in theatres, concert halls or museums! And what will they think of the 'work of art' I will present them with the day after tomorrow, on Friday? . . . Brr! If only this cup could be taken from my lips.

Mahler arrived at Wiesbaden station on the morning of 21 January to be greeted by a delegation from the management of the orchestra. 'I nearly said . . . by young girls dressed in white,' he adds. Rehearsals began immediately. If only Alma could have been with him! She still disliked the Fourth, but he felt sure that this time she would have 'felt quite differently' about it: 'Oh Lord,' he complained once more,

how long will it be before people will be capable of hearing this . . . I wish I could run away. And yet there is so much contentment (*Behagen*) in this work, so much pleasure in lingering! And abundance of Love! During the Adagio, I saw you gazing at me with your blue eyes and that sweet expression they have when you love me and when you are sure that I love you just as much. If only you were here, my Almschi, if only I had with me a being, my being, who henceforth is everything to me, everything that belongs to me and that I belong to. It is so sweet to have a home (*Heimat*), and for me this home can be only one person, you my dearest. I must go out now and walk about as I always do, except when my disgust at everything vulgar (*ordinär*) forces me to retreat to my room.[88]

While in Wiesbaden, Mahler revived 'an old habit' and sent a greeting to Justi: 'Today I'm dreadfully bored . . . The orchestra is quite passable, but (as I have already noticed) the audience, terrible—à la Marienbad. Why did I ever come to this hole?'[89] The letter subsequently takes a more personal line:

But now I have a bone to pick with you. I've realized for some time that something's up with you—whether you're irritated with me or with Alma I can't tell. I think I can sense the same thing with Arnold, and probably you've been setting each other on. I want to say to you first, that this is stupid, second, that it is bad. You really ought to leave such hypersensitivity to 'people of Jewish temperament' (*jüdischen Gemüthern*)—and even if there were some proper grounds for offence, you should remember that everyone has his load to carry and no one has the right to make one's own or other people's any heavier. . . .

After all, you know that what I've always detested more than anything are these personal grudges, and I would hate to think that the way I see things has become a matter of indifference to you. I've been used to Arnold doing it for years, although in the end he always managed to resume the right attitude and the right tone towards me. So don't throw out the baby with the bathwater by working each other up. But I'm not

88 AMM1. 284; AMM2. 258.
89 Mahler was fond of using this slight variation of a quote from Molière's *Fourberies de Scapin*: 'Mais qu'allait-il donc faire dans cette galère?' ('But how did he come to be on this prison galley', i.e. how did he get himself into this mess?)

writing to you because of that. When I began I truly just intended to send you a greeting. The idea occurred to me as I was writing.[90]

This letter shows that Mahler's feelings for his sister were as affectionate as ever, and that he wanted to clear up without delay any misunderstandings. Typically, it is couched in the slightly bullying tone of the well-intentioned elder brother, the strict mentor, a tone which he had so often used in the past with Justi and which he was often to adopt with Alma.

The first item on the programme of the Wiesbaden concert of 23 January was Mahler's Fourth Symphony. It was much better received by the Wiesbaden audience than any previous performance. The next day the *Generalanzeiger* reported that Mahler seemed surprised by its friendly reception, that he some- what reluctantly took several bows,[91] and that he refused the traditional laurel wreath presented to him by the Kurhaus with a 'sarcastic expression' on his face. This time, even the critics were unusually broadminded. In articles in the *Wiesbadener Tagblatt* and the magazines *Die Musik* and *Musikalisches Wochenblatt*, Otto Dohrn[92] praised the taut energy and 'almost uncanny calm' of Mahler's conducting and wondered why 'the Fourth Symphony had ever been hissed'. The symphony was in fact 'anything but boring'; it was full of 'bizarre ultra-modernisms', harmonies which were even bolder than Strauss's. Cer- tainly, Mahler's music did not come from the heart, and it contained 'jokes', a cold, cutting humour, biting mockery and 'constant changes of colour rather than real spiritual depth'. Nevertheless, the instrumentation was so superb, so limpid, so noble and refined that even the most grating dissonances were softened. Though less original than Strauss, Mahler unquestionably surpassed him as an orchestral composer. The *Rheinische Kurier* was even more favour- able: Mahler was an 'unbelievably clever composer', a 'solid talent' from whom 'important new developments in the evolution of music could be expected'. Only the *Wiesbadener Anzeiger* adopted a more familiar attitude: it recalled to its readers the battle over a work usually considered the 'bizarre fruit of a deranged mind'. A missionary, an apostle visited by a transcendental vision, Mahler was a 'philosophical thinker' who despised the conventional values of life and art, and was for the moment 'devoted to exploration rather than discovery'.[93]

[90] Undated letter to Justi, sent from Wiesbaden on 21 or 22 Jan. 1903 (RWO).

[91] According to Otto Dohrn, he took his bows hesitantly, and with bad grace, because of 'unpleasant memories of former performances of this Fourth Symphony'.

[92] Otto Dohrn, son of the conductor Heinrich Dohrn, studied at the Stern'schen Conservatory in Berlin. In 1884, he settled in Wiesbaden, and became the music critic of the *Tageblatt* there, as well as Königlische Musikdirektor. As a composer, he left a number or orchestral works, some piano music, and also Lieder.

[93] The same newspaper praised Eugen d'Albert's 'phenomenally powerful playing' in Liszt's Concerto in E flat and Mahler's 'very Lisztian' accompaniment. In Jan. 1903 d'Albert visited Mahler at the Opera to play *Tiefland* for him and in 1905 he sent him the score of the same opera with a letter praising the Fourth Symphony and congratulating him for 'solving the problems of the modern symphony' (HOA). The eighth subscription concert began on 23 Jan. 1903 at 7.30 p.m. and the soloist in the symphony, Grace Fobes, a 'phenomenal coloratura' but devoid, it seems, of any interpretative ability, sang some Lieder at the end of the

At the Vienna Opera, which he never left for more than three or four days to conduct his own works, Mahler had started on the *Neueinstudierung* of a much maligned work which he felt deserved rehabilitation. This was Weber's *Euryanthe*, a work composed for the Vienna Opera which had fallen into obscurity because of its absurd libretto. In both the score and the libretto, Mahler made a few changes. A year later, he made further changes and sent the revised score to Max Kalbeck, with the following note: 'I should be happy if I were able in this manner to help poor *Euryanthe*, whom I love exceedingly, and ensure for her a comfortable, though perhaps not princely, stage existence. She certainly has a right to it, even if only on the grounds of her respectable descendants.'[94]

Mahler knew better than anyone the weaknesses of the libretto and the absurdities of the plot, in particular, in the third act, the ludicrously implausible meeting of all the characters in the middle of a rocky waste, a scene which he always alluded to as 'the merry country folk reunited'. However, as always happened when he was rehearsing a work which he cared about, he ended up by identifying himself with it and defending even its weaknesses. On the evening of the première, he had supper with Alma, Roller, the Rosés, and the Molls and, doubtless sensing their reservations, put up a defence of *Euryanthe*'s libretto as the model and precursor of *Lohengrin*'s.

After the première, Helm wrote that if Mahler's labour of love was unsuccessful (in fact there were only five performances in 1903), it was because of the casting: Slezak did not have the heroic voice required for the part of Adolar, and Demuth lacked the necessary fire and temperament for Lysiart.[95] The Vienna press, however, welcomed the event with unusual enthusiasm. Even the *Deutsche Zeitung* and the *Deutsches Volksblatt* congratulated Mahler on his conducting: 'One has rarely enjoyed such perfect pleasure at the Vienna Opera.' Hirschfeld praised Mahler for 'resolving the most formidable difficulties', for endowing each measure with 'freshness and life', and 'blending all elements of modern and classical styles in a new and superior way'. Richard Wallaschek, critic of *Die Zeit*, saw *Euryanthe* as 'a middle-aged lady, respected but unloved'. Though the present generation of Viennese singers lacked the technique of their predecessors, their dramatic superiority made their performance unsurpassable. The only hostile comment came from Kauders, who condemned 'poor *Euryanthe* to a new grave'. He accused Mahler of 'over-faithful

concert and an aria by Nicolo Jomelli (with variations by Pauline Viardot-Garcia), 'La calandrina', accompanied by the Musikdirektor, Louis Lüstner. The Fourth Symphony was followed by Liszt's First Concerto, after which d'Albert played Tausig's *Fantasy on Moniuszko's Halka*. To end this eighth and last concert in the Kurhaus series, Mahler conducted Berlioz's *Carnaval romain* Overture.

[94] MBR1, no. 275; MBR2, no. 327ff. Mahler added, in a postscript, that he had restored a passage which appeared as an appendix to the score and which Weber had cut at the time of the Viennese première.

[95] Schönaich agreed with Helm about Demuth and Slezak. In *Die Musik*, he wrote that Mildenburg had been a superb Eglantine, better than Förster-Lauterer (Euryanthe) whose vocal technique was unable to cope with the coloratura passages in the role.

obedience' to an unredeemable libretto that needed total revision.[96] Mahler eventually agreed and altered the text, written by Wilhelmina von Chézy, a poetess 'with a full heart and empty head'.[97]

With the new production of *Tristan and Isolde* on 13 February 1903, timed to mark the twentieth anniversary of Wagner's death, Mahler tackled one of the works he loved most. For the new staging of this, arguably Wagner's greatest work, no effort was to be spared. As a result the opening was postponed at the last moment until the 21st. During the preceding weeks of painstaking preparation, two events occurred which undoubtedly affected Mahler, if only because of the memories they must have aroused. On 11 February Bruckner's last and posthumous symphony, the Ninth, received its world première at the Musikvereinsaal by the Concertverein orchestra, under Ferdinand Löwe. The Vienna Akademischer Wagnerverein sponsored the event and also organized four days beforehand, in a small hall, a lecture by Rudolf Louis,[98] followed by a complete performance of the piano version of the work, which Löwe played, as he was later to conduct the work itself, entirely from memory. 'In accordance with the composer's wishes' the Te Deum[99] dating from 1884 was given as a Finale. During the concert, each movement was enthusiastically applauded. At the end, the work received a long ovation and the conductor was presented with two laurel wreaths. Vienna seemed to have set its heart on making amends for the unjust way it had treated the lonely old artist who had suffered so much from the indifference of his contemporaries. But in spite of the enthusiastic applause and the unanimous praise of the critics, this triumph remained a *succès d'estime*. That evening Mahler conducted at the Opera and did not, therefore, attend the concert, but he knew the score well, and described it in 1906 as 'the peak of absurdity' (*Gipfelpunkt des Unsinns*).[100] His revered friend's swan-song, one of his most profound works, still failed to convince him that, as an artist, Bruckner was anything but a 'colossus with feet of clay'.

Then, the day after the première of the new production of *Tristan*, that is to say on 22 February, Vienna learnt of the death of Hugo Wolf in the insane asylum to which he had been committed in 1898. Although he had long lived remote from the world and from musical life, he had retained many friends and admirers. To satisfy them, and perhaps also to blot out the memory of their quarrel in 1897 which had precipitated Wolf's first committal, Mahler put on the

---

[96] Kauders also criticized Mahler for his hurried tempo in the Overture, and for the 'stiffness' of some other passages, especially the recitatives.

[97] The cast for 19 Jan.: Förster-Lauterer (Euryanthe), Mildenburg (Eglantine), Kittel (Bertha), Slezak (Adolar), Demuth (Lysiart), Mayr (King). According to WMW, the sets were designed by Alfred Roller.

[98] See above, Chap. 13, a biography of this Munich critic and composer.

[99] Soloists: Agnes Bricht-Pyllemann, sop., Gisela Körner, alto, Hermann Winkelmann, tenor, Richard Mayr, bass. The choirs of the Singverein and the Akademischer Wagnerverein were combined for the occasion. The first performance of Bruckner's Ninth by the Vienna Philharmonic took place under Carl Muck on 4 Mar. 1906 (without the Te Deum).

[100] Unpubl. passage from a letter sent to Alma from Salzburg on 18 Aug. 1906 (AMM1. 365; AMM2. 318).

following year Wolf's only finished opera, *Der Corregidor*.[101] Mahler's name appears among the list of celebrities attending Wolf's funeral, which took place at the Votivkirche on 24 February 1903.[102] A piece by Wolf for mixed choir, and the Adagio of Bruckner's Ninth, with Ferdinand Löwe conducting, were performed in the church in his memory.

The historic production of *Tristan* in February 1903 was the result of Mahler's encounter, a year before, with the Secession painter Alfred Roller, who was henceforth to be a crucial figure in his life and career. Roller was born in Brünn (Brno) in Moravia on 2 October 1864, the eldest son of Josef Roller, a professor at the Vienna Technical University who came from Franconia. The family had strong artistic leanings. Roller's maternal grandmother loved painting and poetry and translated Spanish novels into German. His father drew and painted, and was the author of an excellent treatise on engraving. Roller's own artistic revelation occurred in 1892 when he visited Vienna's first big international exhibition with his parents, and saw a sketch of Puvis de Chavannes's famous painting of Liberty clasping hands with the City of Paris against a backdrop of fireworks. At that time Josef Roller was still trying to persuade his son to become a civil servant and study law, but the young man soon followed his true vocation by studying painting at the Vienna Academy of Fine Arts with Eduard Lichtenfels and Christian Griepenkerl. He was powerfully influenced during his formative years by visits to Venice and to Ravenna.

Josef Roller died in 1893, leaving young Alfred the head of a family of five brothers and sisters forced to survive on their mother's very modest pension. He nevertheless carried on with his studies and before long founded the Hagengesellschaft, a group of young artists who met regularly at the 'Blaues Freihaus' restaurant[103] in the Gumpendorfstrasse. It was from this group that the Secession sprang in April 1897. In 1900 the illustrator Felician Freiherr von Myrbach returned from Paris and assumed the directorship of the Kunstgewerbeschule (School for Applied Arts). He promptly engaged two Secessionists,[104] Josef Hoffmann and Alfred Roller, and their revolutionary teaching methods quickly became famous throughout Europe and even spread to America. Thus Roller soon exerted a considerable influence on many young painters, insisting particularly on life classes during their training. He published a great number of illustrations, woodcuts, and decorative 'cartouches' in *Ver Sacrum*, becoming its editor-in-chief in 1898, and designed the cover of the first issue: a young, symbolic tree, carrying in its foliage the three shields symbolizing the Secession, and whose powerful roots have broken the staves of

[101] See below, Vol. iii, Chap. 1.
[102] See below, Vol. iii, Chap. 1. Previously, on 3 Feb., the Prill Quartet had given the première of the Quartet Wolf had composed in 1879 at the age of 19. 'Left in a tram by the composer', the MS had just been found (THE 314).
[103] See above, Chap. 13.
[104] Roller was engaged on the recommendation of the famous architect Otto Wagner.

its barrel-shaped receptacle and plunged into the ground. In 1902 he replaced Carl Moll as Secession president.[105]

When he met Mahler, as we have seen, Roller had just discovered *Tristan und Isolde*; he was so overwhelmed by the work that he attended several performances at the Hofoper, 'avoiding looking at the stage', so intensely did he dislike the designs.[106] On returning home he made some preliminary sketches for new sets; it was these which he showed Mahler on their first meeting. Mahler immediately recognized the 'true visual expression' of the Wagnerian drama. The production had been planned to celebrate the 20th anniversary of Wagner's death. On 19 November, Mahler applied for permission to order completely new sets and costumes, which was unusual, even for a new production. Roller's estimated cost of 33,790 kronen was submitted on 31 May 1902. It was 25 per cent higher than a previous estimate which had been prepared by Heinrich Lefler and Anton Brioschi. This shows the importance Mahler attached to the new production and the risk he was taking in case of failure.

The first few notes Mahler sent to Roller, brief as they are, reveal the atmosphere of friendly musical and professional collaboration which was to characterize their relationship.[107] 'I am absolutely enchanted with your colour sketches, which I have just received,' Mahler wrote before leaving for Maiernigg. 'They far exceed my highest expectations. I am sending (them) immediately, as you requested, to Herr Lefler, and look forward with joyful eagerness to our collaboration next season, and I hope on other occasions, too . . .'. Mahler entered this new phase of activity with youthful enthusiasm. For the first time, he glimpsed the possibility of fulfilling his dream of a total art, an art that would both unify and transcend all the elements of the musical theatre. For Roller was a highly talented and versatile artist as well as a man of exceptional intelligence. Although he had never worked for the theatre, he had long pondered the problems of stage design for operas.[108] If ever there was an event in Mahler's life that today appears to us essential, inevitable, even preordained, it was this encounter. For it was thanks to Roller that he was able

---

[105] In order to take the job of director of Ausstattungswesen (scenery dept.) at the Hofoper in 1903, he obtained leave of absence from the Kunstgewerbeschule. During his years at the Opera, he designed the sets for Reinhardt's production of Hofmannsthal's *Oedipus und die Sphinx* (Deutsches Theater, Berlin, 1905) and three other Reinhardt productions: *Julius Caesar* (1905), *Faust, Parts I and II* (1909 and 1911), and Hofmannsthal's *Jedermann* in Salzburg.

[106] MMR 20. See above, Chap. 13.

[107] The first three notes publ. in MBR1 and MBR2 are wrongly dated; the first was probably written before Mahler's departure for Krefeld at the end of May 1902 and the second, later on, since Mahler must have seen the 'Modelle' before telling Brioschi and Lefler that the new production was to be entrusted to a new set designer. In this case, MBR1, no. 296; MBR2, no. 305. would date from Apr. and the journey which Mahler mentions would be his Russian trip: he might conceivably have met Roller before his marriage. The friendship between the two men 'survived' Mahler, as is shown by this little note that Roller wrote in his copy of *Die Bildnisse von Gustav Mahler*: 'His memory is forever fresh in my mind! A.R.'

[108] When asked as a child what he wanted to do when he grew up, Roller replied: 'To be one of those people who are allowed to go backstage' (MMR 20).

to do something he had been striving for since his Budapest days, that is to say to eliminate all that was merely 'decorative' in order to attain the supreme ideal, the Wagnerian *Gesamtkunstwerk*: total harmony between music and stage, score and text, word and gesture. The achievement of a synthesis of all the arts was not only the ideal of Wagner and his disciples: it was the essential aim of the whole *Jugenstil* movement at the beginning of the twentieth century. Theoreticians like Van de Velde not only wanted to break down the barriers between the 'pure' and applied arts, between the 'higher' and 'lower' forms of art; they also wanted to train polyvalent, universal artists like those of the Renaissance. In the theatre, forward-looking people were starting to think of the nineteenth century as a period of decline; the set-designer had become an uninspired craftsman simply turning out flats and backdrops in period style, with no influence over the costume designer or stage director. Worse, the introduction of electric lighting between 1885 and 1890 had revealed the limitations of such old-fashioned painted settings and their inability to blend with living, three-dimensional actors.[109]

At the turn of the century, revolutionary developments occurred in the theatre which were soon to affect the major artistic centres in Europe. As early as 1890, Paul Fort started his 'Théâtre d'Art' in Paris as a reaction to Antoine's realistic and naturalistic 'Théâtre Libre'. Two writers expressed the new aesthetics in energetic terms: 'Theatre is the paradise of the factitious, the arbitrary and the improvised. . . . While it is at home in the world of ornamental fantasy, the world of truth remains closed to it, for the theatre is not made for truth,' wrote Camille Mauclair in 1890. A year later Pierre Quillard wrote: 'The décor must be a purely ornamental fiction which completes the illusion by analogies of colour and rhythm with the drama.' One of Paul Fort's favourite slogans was 'the theatre, a pretext for the dream'. To create this dream, he enlisted the help of such outstanding painters as Odilon Redon, Paul Gauguin, Edouard Vuillard, Pierre Bonnard, Maurice Denis, Paul Sérusier, Henri de Toulouse-Lautrec, and Edvard Munch. He even used slide projections and shadow-theatre effects. The most daring of his efforts was a dramatic adaptation of the Song of Songs put on in 1891, and which combined the effects of words, music, and colours, and even included the spraying of expensive perfumes into the auditorium. Such lavish productions brought the Théâtre d'Art to bankruptcy in less than two years. However, Fort's experiments were continued and further developed by Aurélien Lugné-Poe, Antoine's former director, who founded the Théâtre de l'Œuvre in 1893, following the sensational success of his production of Maeterlinck's *Pelléas et Mélisande* earlier the same year. His professed aim was to suggest the atmosphere of the play by using simple, neutral, and carefully blended colours for both sets and costumes. Like Paul Fort, he collaborated with painters (the 'Nabi' group) in landmark perform-

[109] It was around 1898 that German and Austrian theatres began to install electrical control boards.

ances of Claudel, Ibsen, Wilde, and Jarry (*Ubu Roi* had its first performance at the Œuvre in 1896).

Thus, in the Paris of 1900, the idea of 'suggesting' an atmosphere rather than creating an 'illusion' was already taking root. In Germany, the experiments were less radical. In 1899 the Freie Bühne in Berlin, modelled more or less on the Théâtre Libre, put on realist plays by Ibsen, Hauptmann, Strindberg, Tolstoy, and Zola, and symbolist plays by Maeterlinck, d'Annunzio, and Hofmannsthal. In Munich, the way to progress opened with Ernst von Wolzogen's *Intimes Theater*. It was in Munich in 1900 that Peter Behrens (who, together with Georg Fuchs, was to create the Künstlertheater and then the Reliefbühne)[110] wrote: 'Stage design should be so stylized, so completely reduced to a few ornamental elements, that the whole atmosphere of the act is created simply by line and colour. The décor must not imitate nature, but should simply provide a framework for the action, a background that is both beautiful and characteristic.' George Fuchs claimed to be creating a totally new art form, 'the art of the stage'. With his friend and principal collaborator, the painter Fritz Erler,[111] he set about creating a modern theatre with neutral colours, simple lines, and few decorative elements. A stage lit mainly from below and above, a stage barely suggesting the place of the action, would 'do away with the fake universe of papier mâché, wire, burlap and tinfoil' and simply provide a framework to suit the actor.

Some time later, Hermann Bahr reflected on the meaning of the keyword 'stylization', now on everyone's lips:

It is a strange thing: when an idea is ripe, it suddenly turns up everywhere at once, as if by magic. People who do not even know each other all seem to be obeying the same word of command . . . To begin with a new catchword appears: 'stylized'. It means something different to everyone. But they all agree on one point, namely that stage-design should no longer pretend to *be* this thing or that, a castle or a forest, but that it should contribute towards creating a dramatic mood. It should achieve with line and colour what the playwright does with words, that is to say, make the spectator feel what the creator and director (*Leiter*) of the drama have felt. . . . All drama is—and never has been anything but—suggestion. . . . When the word 'forest' or 'castle' is uttered in a drama, the playwright never has a real castle or forest in mind but only the suggestive or connotative power of the word. And it is up to the stage-designer to express the same suggestion or connotation by means of line and colour. This was the meaning of 'stylisation' at the time . . .[112]

---

[110] Fuchs's and Behrens's 'Reliefbühne' took its inspiration from ancient Greece and the Japanese theatre. The actors performed in the middle part of a shallow stage, half-way between the proscenium arch and the backdrop, where they executed a kind of pantomime against a neutral background. This was the most radical of all the attempts at stylization and as such it was short-lived. Fuchs worked with several painters of the Munich Secession and contributed to its magazine *Jugend*. He wrote two theoretical books, *Die Schaukunst der Zukunft* (The Stage Art of the Future) and *Die Revolution des Theaters* (1909) which profoundly influenced his contemporaries, as did the lectures he gave from 1899 onwards.

[111] Fritz Erler later painted a portrait of Mahler (see below, Vol. iii, Chap. 4, the biography of this painter).

[112] Hermann Bahr, *Tagebuch* (Berlin, 1919), 35, quoted by LKR 65.

When Roller was engaged by the Hofoper in 1903, Max Reinhardt, arguably the most famous stage-director of all time,[113] had begun his career, not in his native Vienna, but in Berlin, where he was already a leading figure. A practical man of the theatre rather than a theoretician, and at the same time a baroque and eclectic artist whose taste was by no means infallible, Reinhardt advanced few theories. In 1903, however, he advocated 'a complete transposition of the reality of nature into the realm of abstract significance' and attempted to turn stagecraft into a *Gesamtkunst*, with the help of lighting and incidental music. His productions amply demonstrated that the scenery (*Ausstattung*) and the staging (*Inszenierung*) could be as important as the text and that only they could ensure the artistic unity of the overall performance. He had successfully collaborated with members of the Berlin Secession in working towards a new kind of symbolism of colour and form, particularly in his productions of Wilde's *Salomé* in 1902 (with sets by Lovis Corinth and Max Kruse), *Pelléas et Mélisande* (which used scrim and intricate lighting effects), and Hofmannsthal's *Elektra* in 1903. But the first major production of his maturity, Ibsen's *Ghosts* with sets by Edvard Munch (1906), was still to come. However, Reinhardt was very much of an autocrat, and as such he found it difficult to work with painters: they often lacked practical stage experience, or refused to conform to his demands. Later on he was to collaborate on several occasions with Roller, but his ideal remained not to work with known artists but to train a new race of painters, specialists who would work only for the theatre, men like Ernst Stöhr.

At the time, Georg Fuchs's idea of 'retheatrizing the theatre', as he put it, was discussed all over Europe. It was inconceivable that it would not one day extend to operatic productions, but this called for an opera director who would be bold enough to undertake the experiment and at the same time was endowed with sufficient authority and the necessary financial means. He also needed to find, as a collaborator, a painter of great talent and with a sense of theatre. Roller exactly answered to this description: he was both artist and artisan, professional and visionary, a man of imagination who was also in the most down-to-earth and concrete sense a showman. His avowed aim from the start was to banish from the stage all purely decorative or anecdotal elements, which are unrelated to the essence of the drama, to 'represent the inner meaning by a visible symbol', and to create by a symbolic use of colour and form an atmosphere suited to the psychological content of each scene. For him, colour was expressive, and thus an essential element of the drama; the choice of forms and their disposition in space was determined by the atmosphere of the drama and its central theme.

---

[113] Max Reinhardt (1873–1943), born Goldmann, came from a Viennese family. As an actor in Salzburg, he was discovered by Otto Brahm, the founder of the naturalistic Freie Bühne in Berlin, who hired him for the Deutsches Theater in 1894. Reinhardt remained there until 1903, by which time he had already become a well-known stage director, having founded the Kleines Theater the previous year.

Strong affinities existed between Mahler and Roller, not only in their ideas but also in their characters. Like Mahler, Roller was both artisan and idealist: a man of conviction, totally dedicated to one cause, the cause of art. In this respect he was not a typical Viennese, any more than Mahler himself.

He was never prone to making the amiable concessions so typical of the Viennese. Grey-haired, with a serious gaze, tall and somewhat powerfully built, he showed even by his appearance—artisan rather than official artist—that he was not a conformer. There was something of the old-fashioned guild-master about him; he could be both rude and exceptionally reserved. What seemed sometimes like churlishness was simply his obsessive matter-of-factness (*Sachlichkeit*), and the utter seriousness of his intense and powerful artistic will.[114]

But the likeness does not end there: the modesty with which Roller viewed his own work was similar to Mahler's. He used to say that 'to become an artist means ninety per cent hard work (*Fleiss*) and the rest God-given talent (*Zuwendung*)'. Like Mahler, he was essentially a solitary artist who avoided publicity and never went back on his convictions. He thought of himself merely as the servant of the work, and shared Mahler's reluctance to take curtain-calls, even when the audience clamoured for him. 'I am not here to be looked at,' he would say, 'only my work is!'[115]

As we have seen, Roller's concepts were not in themselves particularly revolutionary. They were in the air at the time and owed much to the ideas of Adolphe Appia,[116] a lonely and original genius who has justly been called the father of modern stage production, above all in the sphere of opera. A trained musician and passionate theatre fan since childhood, full of enthusiasm for the work of Wagner, he arrived in Bayreuth shortly before the master's death, and was bitterly disappointed by the narrow and outdated realism of the productions he saw. Later, when he became a close friend of Wagner's fervent admirer and future son-in-law Houston Chamberlain, he tried in vain to influence the Bayreuth productions, succeeding only in arousing the wrath of Frau Cosima, for whom every one of her husband's staging instructions, however trivial, was gospel and who considered it essential to preserve every minor detail of his original productions. Appia's ideas as expressed in *La Mise en scène du drame wagnérien* (1895) were as radical as they were revolutionary, and in 1899 he published in Munich his major work, *Die Musik und die*

---

[114] Karl Marilaun: 'Alfred Roller zum sechzigsten Geburtstag', *Neues Wiener Journal* (9 Oct. 1924), quoted in LKR 32.

[115] LKR 34.

[116] Son of a Genevan doctor, Adolphe Appia (1862–1928) studied music in his home town, then in Paris, Leipzig, and Dresden. There is no concrete evidence that Roller was ever acquainted with his writings, but Roller's own articles make it obvious that he was. On the other hand, a short letter from Mahler dated 10 July 1899, written to an unknown person who was probably Appia, seems to show that at the time Mahler also knew his writings and put some of his ideas into use in his own theatrical work (Jewish Univ. and National Library, Jerusalem).

Inszenierung (Music and Stage Design),[117] which deals for the most part with the *mise-en-scène* of Wagner's music-dramas.

Mahler's greatest productions, prepared in collaboration with Roller, certainly owed much to these pioneering books, so it is worth summarizing Appia's main ideas. Above all, he wanted the theatre to be 'a living art', a 'total art', to create a close relationship between 'the content (of the drama), its message and the means of communicating it'. This 'technical fusion of all the dramatic elements' was to 'draw its inspiration from the original idea of dramatic art' and would 'depend as much on the author's attitude' as on his subject. Appia believed that the 'inner meaning of a work could not be directly, positively communicated to the audience' unless the staging 'sprang from *the drama itself*'. This necessitated 'simplifying the décors' to the point where they ceased to have specific functions. Appia recommended a new approach in order to free the dramatist from 'the slavery of conventional staging' and allow him to 'win his spurs' and become an independent artist. For too long, he wrote, 'the bride (the stage) has been dressed without concern for the tastes of her bridegroom (the drama), who has been bullied, offended, and even mutilated until he ended up half-concealed beneath her gaudy skirts'. In opera, and particularly in Wagner, there could be no harmony between the music and realistic sets. In Wagnerian drama, 'musical gestures must be perceived with the help of the drama'. They had never been achieved, even in Bayreuth, where set-designers had decided that most of Wagner's ideas could not be realized. Wagner himself, towards the end of his life, recognized his failure in this area. Appia considered stage design all the more important in that the dramatic writer was confined to a time-scale limited by performance length. 'Realism' had therefore to be discarded in favour of a mere 'suggestion' of reality (*Andeutung*). The designer had to try to 'summon forth those dimensions and proportions which hover latent in all music, longing to take shape', as well as to 'reflect, within the framework of the poet's chosen content, the profundities revealed by timeless music in the fleeting image of the moment'.

Appia was one of the few theorists to emphasize the essential difference between the static easel picture and the stage picture, which had to conform to other laws because 'movement, the actor, change everything'. For Appia, the elements of a stage performance were: (1) the actors; (2) space; (3) lighting; (4) (and last) the set. He felt that the 'perfection of a static set' must at all costs be discarded, and the 'very conception of painting must be sacrificed'. New laws must be established and 'a living space' created. 'The design, the choice of

---

[117] F. Bruckmann, Munich, 1899. The original French version, *La Musique et la mise en scène*, was publ. only in 1963. An English trans., *Music and the Art of the Theatre* was issued in 1962 (Univ. of Miami, Coral Gables, Fla.). Nearly thirty years after *Die Musik und die Inszenierung* Appia publ. another book in French, expressing the same ideas in condensed form and likewise illustrated with sketches, most of them of Wagnerian set designs: *L'Œuvre d'art vivant* (Atar, Paris-Geneva, 1921; English trans. as *The Work of Living Art* (rather than 'The Living Work of Art'), Univ. of Miami Press, 1960).

lines,[118] must be determined with reference to the human body, which was 'the theatre's only fixed and immutable reality'. For him the palette of the theatre director and of the stage-designer had to be a living thing. It had to create for the actor an atmosphere, a content, a graphic and constantly shifting image.

A last essential point: in place of the unchanging colours of painted flats, colours could be made fluid and changeable by means of 'creative' (*gestaltende*) lighting. For light is no more synonymous with 'the ability to see than music is with sound'. 'Who has ever created on stage an equivalent to the infinity of music?' wrote Appia. Light would henceforth be responsible for 'achieving the necessary union of the actor with painted, cut-out canvas'; it would 'draw the stage towards the music', it would suggest what the music suggested and would 'bring everything together in order to heighten the dramatic expression'. Even darkness could serve the drama. Two of Appia's aphorisms are particularly relevant in this context: 'Without lighting, there is no expression' and 'Light creates the actor'. Thus the designer must always keep in mind the effect lighting would have on his sets. For Appia the two cardinal elements in the theatre of the future were the layout of the set, and the lighting.

Appia's new theatrical concepts were exposed in memorable language and accompanied by simple, functional sketches, showing their application to the Wagnerian dramas.[119] Appia no longer felt the need to separate the stage from the audience; he got rid of the curtain and presented the play on inclined surfaces, staircases, and platforms which created a special geometry, a 'vast, free and transformable' theatrical space. Appia was particularly interested in *Tristan*, where the lighting played a primary role: day, the symbol of suffering and separation; night, happiness and fulfilment. Appia's concepts were too bold and radical for his time; he was able to realize only a few of his Wagner designs, and that was many years later.[120] It was largely thanks to his influence on his close friend Jacques Copeau that his message reached the leading directors of his time.

Appia's contemporary, Edward Gordon Craig,[121] was far better known, both as a stage-director and as a theoretician. He too had published a great deal on

---

[118] More than those of any other designer's, Appia's sets were based on linear design.

[119] There are about 20 set designs at the back of Appia's two books, but very few have ever been carried out.

[120] Appia's first designs were for a private performance of *Astarte*, adapted from Byron's *Manfred*; for Act II of *Carmen* (Paris: 1903); for *Echo et Narcisse* by Jacques-Dalcroze and for *Orphée et Eurydice* by Gluck (Hellerau, near Dresden, 1912). They caused little stir. The designs for *Tristan und Isolde* (La Scala, Milan, under Toscanini in 1923) and the last two parts of the *Ring* (Basel: 1924–5) met with complete indifference and were not revived.

[121] Edward Gordon Craig (1872–1966), actor, draughtsman, engraver, stage director, set-designer, theoretician, and historian of the theatre, was the son of the famous English actress Ellen Terry and an architect who was also a theatre buff. He made his stage début at the age of 13 and became a noted Shakespearian actor. In 1893, Craig made a first and successful attempt at stage direction in Musset's *On ne badine pas avec l'amour*. He had already begun, completely self-taught, to paint and draw. He later formed his own company and produced *Hamlet* and *Romeo and Juliet*. In 1899 he exhibited engravings of his ultra-modern sets for *Hamlet*, Act II and between 1900 and 1902 he staged Purcell's *Dido and Aeneas* and *Mask of Love*, and Handel's *Acis and Galatea*. In 1905 he produced Otway's *Venice Preserv'd* (in Hofmannsthal's adaptation) at

such subjects as the functions of the stage-designer and the stage-director, the only authentic 'men of the theatre' and co-authors of the play with the actor; replacing stage painting with architecture; using lighting to 'create an imaginary space'; the unity of style and purpose which must be achieved not only by colour and line, but also by the rhythm of the dialogue and the gestures and movements of the actors. Craig was one of the first to introduce the notion of 'pure theatricality' and to try to build a totality out of décor, action, and gesture based on 'the meaning and essence of music'. He took from Appia terms like *Andeutungsbühne* (*Andeutung* = suggestion: *Bühne* = stage) as against the *Illusionsbühne* of former times.

Unlike the shy and retiring Appia, whose stutter kept him out of society and who led a solitary life while thinking out new methods of theatrical communication, Craig was able to put his ideas into practice, not only in England but also in Germany and even Russia, where Stanislavski invited him in 1912. Yet his main theoretical work (*The Art of the Theatre*) was not published until 1905, long after Appia's. Furthermore, he was often criticized for his monumental approach, which sometimes drew attention to lighting at the expense of the text and the actor. Although he was extraordinarily preoccupied with the smallest details of costuming, his professed aim was to reach the soul and the subconscious of the spectator. But it was also said of him that his ultimate ideal was 'theatre without authors or actors'.[122] There can be no doubt that Appia and Craig together led the way towards revolutionizing the theatre and infusing it with new life. But of the two Appia was certainly to have a greater impact on future developments.[123] He was not only the precursor of Roller and of Copeau's Vieux Colombier (1913), but also of Baty and Pitoeff in France, and of Wieland Wagner's new Bayreuth.[124] A glance at Appia's sketches suggest that Wieland Wagner owed some essential features of his stage productions to him. 'He was a musician and an architect,' wrote Copeau when Appia died. 'He taught us that the musical time-span, which envelops, commands and regulates the dramatic action, also creates the space in which that action develops.'

According to Paul Stefan, Mahler was familiar with Appia's *Die Musik und die Inszenierung*. Without subscribing to a stage conception as radical as the

---

the Lessing Theater in Berlin. He exhibited his set designs and engravings on various occasions (notably in Vienna: Hevesi gives an interesting account of this exhibition in *Altkunst, Neukunst*, 274). In 1908 Craig started the lavish theatrical magazine *The Mask*, which he continued to publish until 1929. His liaison with the famous American dancer Isadora Duncan was well-known and played an important part in her memoirs. Although he designed most of his sets himself, Craig also worked with painters like Emil Prichau and Cesar Klein.

[122] Hevesi, *Altkunst, Neukunst*.

[123] However, it has been claimed that in practice all these new tendencies were brought together not by Roller in Vienna, nor by Reinhardt in Berlin, nor even by Stanislavski in Moscow, but a few years later by Diaghilev in his 'Ballets Russes'.

[124] According to Walter B. Volbach, *Adolphe Appia, Prophet of the Modern Theatre* (Wesleyan Univ. Press, Middletown, Conn., 1968), Wieland Wagner remained faithful to the family tradition and was reluctant to acknowledge his debt to Appia, though he admitted having read his writings and studied his drawings.

'non-functional décor', Roller was also familiar with Appia's writings and borrowed some of his key ideas: to fire the imagination rather than fool the eye; to create the atmosphere of the drama by subtle means rather than imitating reality. Roller agreed with Appia that dramatic masterpieces, like precious stones, do not need to be 'decorated':

The décor (*Dekoration*) should never become an end in itself. Neither should it ever give the impression of a self-sufficient reality existing alongside or even above the work. It is there merely to set a mood at the rise of the curtain, the mood which the dramatist or the composer wishes to communicate to his audience. Everything concerned with the stage sets plays a secondary role. The designer is only the servant of the work. He does not 'decorate', does not illustrate the stage happenings, but instead creates with the utmost self-restraint (*Selbstlosigkeit*) the indispensable frame for the work of art.[125]

The designer who refuses to construct a glittering shell around the work, thereby concealing it wholly or partially, who prefers to build a solid foundation beneath it which will make its hidden architecture visible, cannot be helped by any theory, any cleverly devised system, any quasi-intellectual attitude. Inherent in each work are the principles governing its own stage production and whoever manages to bring them to the surface has won. Only a profound experience (*tiefes Erleben*) of the work can show the way. But to experience (*erleben*) a work means to feel (*empfinden*) it as though one had created it oneself.[126]

Elsewhere in his writings, Roller explained more precisely his general conception of 'décor':

The term 'stage picture' (*Bühnenbild*) is only a poor stopgap. The stage does not provide a 'picture'; it provides spaces, appropriate to the playwright's work and to the actors' words and gestures, vibrating with the rhythm of the play and the performance, not hindering but helping expression to become impression. The aim should be an identity of purpose with all the other forces mobilized in the performance. These are the essential requirements of the stage and its décor (*Ausstattung*). They do not possess a life of their own.[127]

Stage design is nothing but the art of framing (*Rahmenkunst*), never an end in itself; it is definitely a secondary element which can derive its principles and rules only from a particular work and which cannot obey any laws other than the very specific, often unique requirements of that work. What is the point, therefore, of searching for a new method of stage design? 'Do you favour stylization or illusion?' one is asked continually; 'three-dimensional sets (*plastische Dekorationen*) or painted backdrops (*Vorhänge*)?' as though one were asked at dinner: 'Do you prefer red or white wine?' We have no choice, for the replies to these questions can only be found within the work to be staged. One must know how to read and hear the answer. Each work of art carries within itself the key to its own production. If you create rules and methods today, then

[125] LKR 43 and Alfred Roller, 'Mahler und die Inszenierung', *Moderne Welt*, 3 (1922–3), 4 ff.
[126] Alfred Roller, 'Bühne und Bühnenhandwerk', *Thesis Theaterbuch* (1930), 145, quoted by LKR 75.
[127] Ibid. 137 (LKR 73).

tomorrow a playwright will come along and create something which will make them all seem absurd . . .[128]

Thus Roller felt that stage works deserved 'not a stage tableau, but a setting born of the essence of the work'. His anti-naturalistic reform was (of course) parallel to that of the Jung Wien writers who searched for a 'truth beyond reality' (*Metareale Wirklichkeit*), with the help of symbols, meant to awaken 'feelings', or the psychoanalysts who attempted to unravel the mysteries of a personality through the all-important key of dreams.[129] In Roller's sets, the architecture, colours, and even the decorative details were all to have a meaning, to serve the work by catching the imagination of those watching and listening, to correspond to a 'unity of intention' justifying every detail of the setting. Less daring than Appia, Roller wanted the stage image to seem real at first, 'and to reveal its sensual and emotional content only when the spectator begins to identify himself with the action'.[130] At first he would see the real thing, a ship, a street, a prison. Later, under the spell of the music and the drama, once he had penetrated to the heart of the work and suspended disbelief, he should be aware only of light and shadow, lines and colours. Roller's ideal, according to Hermann Bahr, was as follows: 'stage design which evolves with the spectator in accordance with that dramatic mutation which causes an onlooker (*Zusehender*) to become emotionally involved (*Mitfühlender*)'. Hermann Bahr summed up the basic concept underlying Roller's work in the phrase, 'Décor as expression'.[131]

Not the representational type of décor, which merely imitates the outword aspect of the place where the play is located, nor the abstract type of décor, which uses colours and lines to produce a mood that is the outcome of the play: the universally human, typically tragic or happy mood which we can only participate in when the particular events recounted in the play have been acted out. But this mood is an end-result, and the abstract décor, which we already have before us at the beginning of the play (i.e. when we are about to have the opening situation explained, and do not yet know how it connects up with the eternal scheme of things) anticipates instead of summing up. But Roller had the ability to combine the two.[132]

Most of Roller's ideas now seem familiar, even routine, to us, but in those days they were revolutionary, especially at the Opera, which is why Hermann Bahr took such trouble to explain and comment on them. Unlike Appia, Roller was primarily a painter. As such, he had assimilated the discoveries of the Impressionists, particularly in matters of light and colour. Light was for him an essential factor in the creation of atmosphere. He also attached great im-

[128] Alfred Roller, 'Bühnenreform?', *Der Merker*, 1: 5 (Dec. 1909), 193, quoted by LKR 50.
[129] See Moritz Csàky, 'Der Wissenssoziologische Kontext der musikalischer Gedankenwelt Gustav Mahlers. Wien um 1900' in Bruckner Symposium, 1986, *Bruckner, Liszt, Mahler* (Linz, 1989), 46.
[130] Hermann Bahr, 'Fidelio', Dec. 1904, in *Buch der Jugend* (Heller, Vienna, 1908), 24.
[131] Ibid. 19.
[132] Richard Specht, 'Rollers Scheiden', *Die Schaubühne*, Vienna, 5: 3 (21 Jan. 1909).

portance to architecture, sculpture, and linear design. His main concern was to unify all these elements in order to create a higher order of 'reality'.

The new production of *Tristan und Isolde* in February 1903 marked the start of a new epoch in the history of opera and brought together all aspects of the new aesthetics. For the first time, stage and music formed a homogeneous whole, and lighting was used to obtain totally new expressive effects.[133] 'Roller knew all the secrets of light,' wrote Liselotte Kitzwegerer.[134] 'He knew how light could intensify forms, how it could exalt them, dissolve them, bewitch them into something magical.' A contemporary account records how striking Roller's light effects could be:

Suddenly all was transformed. The wings vanished, the footlights were no more, there was a wonderful flood of light unlike anything seen on a stage before. Roller invented completely new methods of stage lighting: he built his ideal stage out of light and gushing colours. He was tireless in everything, wandering from stage to stalls, from stalls to gallery, trying out filters, coloured lenses, light intensities, changing, improving, discovering nuances imperceptible to a layman.[135]

The Berlin critic Oscar Bie[136] went so far as to speak of '*Lichtmusik*' ('light-music').

Roller's ideas about stylization appealed to Mahler, but it was only after thinking them over that he coined his own definition of them: 'A stage on which everything should only indicate and nothing should be.' (*Eine Bühne, auf der alles bloss bedeuten, nichts sein soll.*)[137] The stage-designer was to be 'the link between the director and the conductor,' wrote Roller. Their collaboration was to be similar to that of librettist and composer. Whereas, before Roller, the sets, costumes, and lighting were always the work of three different men, Mahler was the first to entrust all three to the *Leiter des Ausstattungswesen*.[138]

Influenced by the French Impressionists, Claude Monet in particular, Roller was well aware of the limits and constraints of realism in art. In his painting he had already gone beyond everyday reality in search of new means of expression and a new poetic universe. Rather than following Appia's insistence on abstraction and his rejection of painted flats as outdated, Roller took advantage of all

---

[133] RSM 131. The following description is taken principally from this work, from BSP 31, from EDS2. 148; also from GWO 163.

[134] LKR 43. In WMW 212, Franz Willnauer discloses that the complexity of Roller's effects necessitated the renewal of part of the Hofoper's electrical system, which was 16 years old at the time.

[135] Emil Lucka, 'Erinnerungen an Alfred Roller', *Deutsche Zukunft* (17 Dec. 1933), 15, quoted by LKR 44.

[136] Oskar Bie (1864–1938), German critic and writer on music, was born in Breslau. He studied philology and history of art in Leipzig and Berlin, taking his doctorate in 1886. At the same time he studied music with Xaver Scharwenka. From 1901 he taught history of art in Berlin and wrote for the *Berliner Börsencourier* and *Die Freie Bühne*. Later he founded and edited the *Neue Rundschau*, which became the foremost literary periodical of its time and to which he contributed articles on music. Among his many books are *Die moderne Musik und Richard Strauss* (1906), *Die Oper* (1913), *Im Konzert* (1920), *Franz Schubert* (1925), *Das deutsche Lied* (1926), and *Richard Wagner und Bayreuth* (1931).

[137] Egon Wellesz, 'Gustav Mahler und die Wiener Oper', *Neue Deutsche Rundschau*, 71 (1960), 2, and Roller, 'Mahler und die Inszenierung' (quoted n. 125), 5.

[138] Literally 'director of [stage] design and equipment'. This was Roller's official title at the Opera.

the painter's most subtle artifices, so much so that the writer Hermann Bahr described his work as 'Beseelung der Dekoration' (breathing soul into décors). When the curtain rose on the first act of the new *Tristan*, 'menacing' yellow-orange draperies around the shipboard pavilion suggested Isolde's secret fury and Tristan's still unconscious passion. 'Roller's colours for Tristan are not just realistic: they also make an immediate appeal to the senses (*unmittelbare sinnliche Reize*) which in turn arouses emotions,' wrote Hermann Bahr. The objects strewn about the deck looked superfluous, out of context: sumptuous pieces of furniture, heavy chests, brocaded cushions. All of them were decorated with gold, mother-of-pearl, or opal, even the brooch that fastened Isolde's robe or Tristan's scabbard. Brangäne's chest was in gold, fashioned like a reliquary, set with semi-precious stones and filled with gold and silver flasks. Isolde's couch, at stage right, was decorated with gold and black pagan Celtic carvings, and there were similar patterns on the great carpet in front of it.[139] Every detail evoked the luxury of a medieval princess's life as well as Isolde's inconsolable grief and her painful isolation on a ship of war which was taking her towards a destiny she had not chosen. The ship was far more realistically represented than in the original Munich production. Thick, massive beams, slightly curved, supported the upper deck above Isolde's cabin, which was surmounted by a rough, massive wooden rail. The rigging stretched out towards the audience and an invisible mast. A single wooden post supporting the stern deck was carved with simple motifs inspired by medieval Nordic art. The ship itself was placed diagonally, the stern turned slightly to stage right. In the semi-darkness, upstage, the audience could dimly make out a kind of narrow hold, lit only by an evil greenish light that seeped in through two square portholes. One felt the stifling atmosphere there, like the characters themselves caught in the stifling grip of fate. A new symbolic dimension brought another meaning to the seemingly realistic décor. The dark, narrow space gave a premonition of the lovers' tragic fate. Glimpses of blue sky and bright sunlight through openings in the awning served only to underline the feeling of claustrophobia until the audience could no longer 'distinguish between the visual image and the music'.

At stage left, a companionway, concealed part of the time behind a curtain, led from Isolde's cabin to the upper deck, at the back of which Tristan stood near the helm. In the middle of the first act, Kurwenal left Tristan's side to sing his ironic solo standing on the deck just above Isolde. When the ship reached Cornwall, the awning flaps opened wide and the scene changed completely. At stage left was the open sea, with a large red banner flapping in the wind, ship's rigging against a blue sky, a reddish-brown sail pierced by rays from a blinding sun and sailors spreading a long red carpet on the deck.

The entire act was dominated by the Junoesque figure of Mildenburg,

<hr />

[139] Roller had recently been sent on a tour of Germany, England, and France by the Kunstgewerbeschule, to study the various styles of furniture, jewellery and decorative objects.

dressed from head to foot in silver-grey. Her collar piece was encrusted with semi-precious stones arranged geometrically. A long stole touched the ground on each side at the front, its ends decorated with the same brocade as the cuffs of her robe. Every detail of the staging reflected the same concern for psychological truth. Instead of holding his sword out to Isolde as in earlier productions, Tristan placed its point against his chest and waited for her to plunge it in. After the love-potion scene, the sailors gathered at the front of the deck just above the couple who, in the first ecstasy of a love finally revealed to them, were utterly oblivious of being watched.[140]

The deep violet and velvety darkness of the second act provided a striking contrast to the bright orange-red of the first. Roller conjured up, with an astonishing power of suggestion, the splendour of a hot summer's night. Thousands of stars glittered on a black velvet sky.[141] This vast sky gave an intimation of infinity which lent a cosmic dimension to the love-duet. 'Out of the Prelude to the second act the blue night rose mysterious and this night was not the hitherto invariable, obvious, inward turning (*in sich suchendes*) picture, but breathed and trembled like the orchestra, the garden came alive around the lovers, getting darker or lighter with straying moonbeams and drifting shadows.'[142] At stage right stood a fairy-tale castle partly hidden by trees, with a plain, semicircular-arched doorway and a steep marble staircase leading to the keep. At the centre of the stage was a slightly raised octagonal terrace, decorated with black and white squares, a decorative motif much in favour with the Secession.

There were benches at the corners of the terrace on either side of the stairs leading up to it. The castle's white walls shone in the darkness with a soft, pink, almost supernatural light. Despite the magical effect of this suffused light, many critics reproached Roller for 'his orgies of darkness'. Behind a low wall decked with lilac, violets, and white roses, the garden, bathed in the moon's bluish light, sloped gently down to the sea. Towards the end of the act, at the moment of betrayal, the violet sky turned slowly grey, and the 'sickly' pallor of dawn filled the stage. Thick yellow clouds gathered above the blue hills and dark foliage, while a ray of sunlight spread its cruel gleams over the sea: an affirmation of the opera's basic contrast between night and day.[143]

Roller's set for the third act was generally considered to be his masterpiece. When the curtain rose, the scene 'with the wounded Tristan lying in the courtyard of his derelict castle was so gripping that the audience responded

---

[140] Even the critic of the anti-Semitic *Deutsches Volksblatt*, Hans Puchstein, described this scene as 'one of the most vivid ever seen on the Viennese stage'.

[141] Some critics complained that there were far too many stars and that they were too bright.

[142] Emil Lucka, article quoted in LKR 44.

[143] According to Ernst Decsey, this was one of the most striking examples of the new role lighting could play as a vital element in the dramatic action. One look at the glacial light, he wrote, sent shivers down his spine. Roller was interested in different lighting possibilities for the same scenery well before he took up with the theatre. As early as 1900 he exhibited at the Secession a series of paintings of the same landscape at different times of the day and seasons.

with a half-surprised "ah!"'.[144] A dull autumnal grey suffused the scene. Upstage was a massive square tower in the form of a truncated pyramid.[145] Right of centre stage Tristan, clothed in white from head to foot, lying on animal skins, seemed already buried in his ancestral ground-symbolized by two immense tree roots which encircled and hemmed him in. A giant lime tree, its branches almost bare, laden with ivy and mistletoe, loomed against the surrounding wall. Lit by the silvery rays of the autumn sun, it hung over the stage and cast huge shadows over the prostrate hero. Everything suggested ruin and neglect: the greyish moss and dead leaves carpeting the ground, the rough slopes over which sheep grazed in the distance, the thick, rugged walls, the grey deserted shore, with its distant white cliffs, a small stretch of pale and empty sea. Once again, the contrast between the loneliness and misery brought on by sin and the eternal renewal of nature was sharply emphasized. At the end of the act, Isolde appeared from the castle gate and came up an incline to Tristan. The battle took place in the background near the gate, as befitted the minor role it played in relation to the deeper meaning of what went on in the foreground. In their last moments of life Tristan and Isolde recognized the inevitability of their downfall and succumbed in an atmosphere of suffering and sin, and the day's delirium at last became quiet. Freed of illusion and pretence, the lovers entered the Kingdom of Night. Their final metamorphosis and apotheosis were suggested by light effects which transformed even the neutral colours of the costumes.[146]

Just as the sets and staging served to illustrate a central theme, Mahler's musical interpretation was built around crucial moments which he was at pains to underline. According to Erwin Stein:

There was certainly something feverish, and even delirious, in Mahler's performance. Unrelieved yearning, white-hot passion and violent suffering were the central moods which dominated the three acts. On the other hand, the vast form of the music became clear-cut by exact disposition of its component sections. Contrasts were carefully worked out; climaxes served as the pivots of the form. And Mahler's climaxes could be shattering indeed. To him they were not only a means of expression but also a means of architecture. There was in every piece of music he performed, in every act of every opera, one point at which the music's dynamics or tension culminated, with lesser climaxes in between; one main centre of gravity, as it were, and other subsidiary ones. In *Tristan* the first act culminated in Isolde's drinking of the potion; the second, not in Tristan's arrival, but in the last crescendo of the duet before the anticlimax of Marke's entry; in the third it was the fortissimo accompanying Isolde's appearance which towered above the earlier climaxes of Tristan's monologues.[147]

---

[144] ESM 301.

[145] As mentioned above, Olbrich flanked the laurel globe which surrounded his Secession Kunsttempel with four pillars in the shape of truncated pyramids.

[146] These costumes had absorbed much of Roller's attention. He often visited the costume dept. several times a day to ensure that they conformed to his instructions.

[147] ESM.

It seems that some of the most powerful effects were obtained through the calm which was henceforth to characterize Mahler's conducting. 'In this *Tristan*' writes another witness,

which even today is extraordinarily effective, there was something ineffably tortured, torturing, unresolved (*nicht befreiendes*). The physical aspect of his conducting had evolved towards immobility. Perhaps, consciously, shamefacedly, he withdrew into himself. The utmost suggestive power radiated from the marble—like immobility of his body. Yet this was the calm of a volcano. For mysterious reasons one was always expecting it to erupt. And this did sometimes happen, although very rarely. But the immobility would return immediately.[148]

Contemporary witnesses agreed that the originality of Roller's sets, the inspired stage-direction, and Mahler's musical interpretation made it one of the greatest operatic events of its time. The cast brought together three of the Hofoper's greatest singers, all engaged by Mahler. Despite a slight hoarseness on the night of the première which prevented him from giving his best, Erik Schmedes was a superb Tristan. '[He was] one of those giants from the north,' wrote Erwin Stein.

His voice was beautiful but heavy (he had been a baritone), and his singing and acting sensitive and intelligent. He had no difficulty in presenting a hero, but Tristan is largely a lyrical part. By sheer musicianship he forced from his rather unwieldy voice tender *piano* notes and *cantilena* of fine expression and phrasing. The self-imposed restraint of the singer, which one could still feel, corresponded aptly to the hero's inner conflicts. Schmedes was therefore a splendid and most convincing Tristan, and greatest in the tortured monologues of the third act.[149]

Since her Hamburg days, Mildenburg too had come to surpass herself in the role of Isolde. The chief merit of her interpretation was the tremendous wealth of shadings she managed to impart in her voice. According to Erwin Stein,

she had a very big voice, one of the biggest I have met, but with her this was not the main point, though it gave her an enormous range of expression. Her piano yielded as much variety of tone as her forte, and she could colour or swell the notes at will. Yet whatever her voice was capable of doing, it served the dramatic expression of the music. For she was not only a singer and a fine musician but—even more important with her—a great tragic actress. Her appearance and movements had the same grandeur of style as her singing. Among the many parts I heard her sing, Isolde was the most outstanding. True, the very top was not her best register and the C's in the second act caused her discomfort. That was the only flaw. The scope of the part was just the right one for her personality and I have experienced no other singer who could as movingly convey Isolde's tragic figure and the wide range of her conflicting emotions—her love and hate, gloom and rage, tenderness and spite, passion and despair, jubilation and sorrow.[150]

[148] *Musikalischer Kurier* (28 May 1922). See also below, Vol. iii, Chap. 6, Ernst Decsey's description of Mahler conducting *Tristan*.
[149] ESM.   [150] ESM.

Even though Mildenburg had lost, as we have seen, most of her agility in the upper register,[151] she was more telling than ever. Every gesture and every movement gave her vocal performance an extra dimension: 'Her bearing, her voice and her gestures struck one immediately by their calm nobility. They made her supreme as an actress, comparable only perhaps with Duse,' wrote another contemporary.

I shall never forget her monumental calm in the *Todesverkündigung*[152] or, in *Tristan*, her economy of gesture when, at *Befehlen liess dem Eigenholde*,[153] she slowly lowered the index finger of her partially closed right hand, a movement of inimitable expressivity. She never did anything stereotyped or calculated. Every detail fitted into the whole and accorded, in an absolutely masterly fashion, with the general conception.[154]

In *Tristan* her greatest achievements were in the first act, as a deeply hurt woman enraged at finding herself scorned and mocked.

Richard Mayr's King Mark managed to shed the traditional image of the ageing and slightly ridiculous cuckold. He moved the spectator by the nobility of his suffering, victim of a destiny both human and royal. According to Erwin Stein, he 'sustained the interest during his scene by the great variety of his expression and the impressive climax he built up'. His body was perhaps heavy and awkward but his voice had the 'depth and warmth of a trombone'. Its magnificence gave the role a rare authenticity, with no trace of pomposity. His finest moment was always during the long monologue at the end of the second act when, dressed like a fairy-tale king in hunting clothes and a crown, he stood on the terrace with the other characters gathered at his feet like a group in classical sculpture. Weidemann, who later on was to take on the part of Kurwenal, which he interpreted magnificently, 'represented very movingly Kurwenal's dog-like affection and faithfulness to his master'. This, then, was the basic casting. With the exception of a few performances, notably those with Lilli Lehmann, it remained unchanged for the duration of Mahler's directorship.

From the opening night onwards, the audience warmly applauded not only the musical interpretation but Roller's sets and lighting as well, particularly the effects of daybreak at the end of the second act and nightfall at the end of the third. None the less, even Roller's most ardent admirers saw signs of a lack of theatrical experience, and felt that at times he overindulged in painted flats and papier-mâché props which detracted from the general effect. These sets, the first he had ever made, also failed to take into account the sight lines of the

---

[151] According to Kauders, Mildenburg, exhausted by the rehearsals, was also not in good voice for the première. The passage 'Er konnte mich und sich verschmähen' had to be transposed down for her.

[152] In Act II of *Die Walküre*.   [153] Act I. i.

[154] Leonie Gombrich-Kock, 'Einige persönliche Erinnerungen an Anna Bahr-Mildenburg', unpubl, dictated in Aug. 1948, LPA.

various parts of the opera-house.[155] During the following summer, therefore, Roller insisted on having a ground-plan of the auditorium and stage, as well as longitudinal and cross-sections which helped him to plan his next productions.[156] He was also accused of disregarding one of Appia's basic precepts, that of integrating the actors carefully into the design of each scene.[157] Yet Roller soon became a craftsman as versed in the techniques of the stage as he was a great artist. He was one of the few stage designers ever to make a complete series of drawings, gouache paintings, and models of his sets before having them built. However well-founded the criticisms, they were of little importance in a production which excelled in so many respects. Roller's essential achievement was to prove that the abandonment of convention and of all purely decorative elements could reveal *Tristan und Isolde* for the first time in all its mythical grandeur.[158]

In any case, it would have been a miracle if this first attempt at a synthesis between stylization and realism had immediately achieved perfection. Far from being shocked or angry, as its reactionary tendencies might have led us to expect, the Viennese public gave a prolonged demonstration of its enthusiasm on the first night. In accordance with tradition, Roller's name did not appear on the playbill, but he had to take a curtain-call with the singers because everyone knew how much he had contributed to the evening's success. Erwin Stein remarked upon the effect this newborn *Tristan* had on the 'progressive' element in Vienna. Surprising as it may seem, the work itself, forty years after its world première in Munich but only twenty years after its Vienna première, was still considered by Austrians to be modern and even revolutionary. During rehearsals everyone had the feeling of participating in a major event, and there was a succession of crises and conflicts. At first, Mildenburg violently opposed every initiative Roller took. Thus she threatened to tear down with her own hands a certain 'ramp' that she found 'far too anti-artistic', and even refused to wear Roller's costumes. Every rehearsal provoked a new outcry; she contested every detail of the sets and props. According to Alma, Mahler finally advised Roller to try and mollify her by paying her an informal visit at home. The visit achieved its purpose: she was eventually won over to the point

---

[155] Hirschfeld noted that a section of the stage remained hidden from spectators sitting on the left. Later Roller started building cardboard models of the theatre and sets. Through holes in the walls, he could put himself in the place of each spectator. He studied the general effect of masses with little blocks of wood that he moved about the miniature stage (cf. Hevesi, *Altkunst, Neukunst*, 264). It seems in particular that the papier-mâché rocks commissioned for *Tristan*'s Act III were too big. The cost of changing them was high (WMW 212).

[156] Letter to the Intendant of 21 Aug. 1903. See Greisenegger, 'Alfred Roller', 276.

[157] He was criticized for putting the castle gate below stage level in the last act, so that few of the spectators could follow the battle scene. As for the lighting, it should be remembered that if some of the effects Roller called for were not altogether successful, this was due to the fact that the Hofoper's electrical equipment was still rather rudimentary despite certain improvements made 'on grounds of safety' during the rehearsals of *Tristan*.

[158] Vienna remembered Roller's first sets so well that in 1942, nearly 40 years after the 1903 production, they were reconstructed with the greatest care for a revival conducted by Wilhelm Furtwängler.

of becoming Roller's mistress. From then on she was his most stalwart defender in any dispute which arose over his work.[159]

With all previous cuts restored, the new production of *Tristan und Isolde* began at 7 p.m. and lasted until shortly before midnight. At the première Mahler, exhausted from rehearsals, suffered one of his worst migraine attacks. After the second act he collapsed on the sofa in his dressing-room and groaned: 'If only someone could take my place!' Alma recalls that Justi remarked tartly from the other end of the room: 'One thing pleases me, I had him young and you have him old!' It should be remembered once again, however, that whatever Alma says about Justi should be taken with a pinch of salt. For instance, Mahler had written to his sister from St Petersburg: 'I can give you the best possible news of Alma. You will be happy to see how she has blossomed out in every way.'[160] In this same letter, according to Alma, Mahler had also written: 'I am happy and desire nothing more from the world than what I have'—words which had made Justi faint when she received the letter in the doorman's lodge at the Opera. In fact, Justi was undoubtedly jealous of her sister-in-law, but Alma herself later acknowledged that this was not surprising: 'I had to forgive her . . . because she had lived with him for nine[161] years and was now completely obliterated from his life.'[162] In any case, Justi was now happily married to the man she had long loved. And Alma herself was subject to violent fits of jealousy, as is borne out by a passage in her private diary of 1903: 'Justi is reappearing like a ghost in Gustav's heart. I thought she was dead to him.' According to the first draft of Alma's memoirs, Mahler for several years had no idea of the true nature of Justi's relationship to Arnold Rosé, and it was Natalie who, apparently, opened his eyes. Again according to Alma, he was deeply hurt at the thought that he had been misled by someone as close as his sister. And, finally, Justi, when questioned directly, had denied the truth for fear of hurting him. Mahler felt all the more humiliated when he discovered that the entire orchestra knew of his sister's affair.

One of his letters to Justi which has recently come to light shows how much Mahler took for granted that she and Rosé were no more than old friends.[163] It was written in September 1901, just after Mahler's return from Maiernigg. Justi was still in Carinthia, and he tells her how he tried to persuade Arnold to come and keep her company. Arnold seems to have hesitated for 'form's sake', then to have allowed himself to be persuaded. Mahler says in the letter how pleased he is that Arnold had accepted his invitation. In her first book, written around

---

[159] According to Alma, Mildenburg was as possessive of Roller as she had been of Mahler. She went so far as to send one of the theatre employees to summon him to a performance in which she sang, threatening not to go on if he refused to come at once.

[160] See above, Chap. 13.

[161] In AMM, Alma speaks of 9 years (AMM1. 73; AMM2. 83). In fact, Justi arrived in Hamburg at the beginning of the 1895–6 season, which means she had spent 6½ years with her brother.

[162] AMS.

[163] The letter dated 5 Sept. 1901 formerly belonged to Mr David Stivender of New York. See above, Chap. 11.

1921, Alma wrote, in a passage she later decided to suppress,[164] that Natalie told Mahler the truth (presumably in September 1901) just before he went to meet his sister at the station. He ran into Arnold on the platform, and Justi got out of the train without suspecting anything. But the first glances and words she and Arnold exchanged confirmed what Natalie had told him. Alma claims this revelation destroyed Mahler's love for his sister (which is untrue), that he presented her with an ultimatum telling her that she must either break with Rosé or marry him (which is unlikely), and that finally he told her that he now considered himself free to marry too (which is even more unlikely).

Obviously Alma's statements about Justi are always strongly coloured by her own dislike of her sister-in-law. Conflicts and misunderstandings did now and again arise between the two couples, but Mahler's love for his sister remained intact.[165] In addition, there was the gratitude he felt for her years of devotion and self-sacrifice. Elsewhere in her memoirs, Alma accuses her sister-in-law of having spied on her and Mahler, spending many hours watching their door in the Auenbruggergasse to see who went in and out, and making scenes when she had not been invited to a party there. Alma claims that Arnold followed her one day all over Vienna, fearing, or rather hoping, she might disappear into a 'love nest' (*Absteigequartier*), but that she disappointed him by going straight home. In her published memoirs, Alma tells another unpleasant story to show that Mahler no longer loved his sister. One day Justi said to her brother, when he had been particularly angry with her: 'But Gustav, after all I am flesh of your flesh!' To which he replied: 'Filth of my filth, you mean!' (*Dreck von meinem Dreck*). Here is one case in which the unbiased reader must find it hard to give any credence to Alma's reporting. This idea of 'flesh' and 'blood' seems however to have obsessed Alma. She wrote on more than one occasion in her private diary, notably in the entry for 24 December 1901: 'Justi, whom I love because she is of his blood!'

To return to the *Tristan* première, when Mahler finally overcame his migraine attack and returned to the podium, he was greeted, before the third act, with loud and persistent applause, one of the most spontaneous demonstrations of admiration and respect he had ever received in Vienna. Some of the audience rose from their seats and, according to newspaper reports, would not stop clapping until he finally consented to turn and bow. Given the revolutionary character of the new *Tristan* production, the Viennese press might have been expected to react with indignant condemnations; but in fact the critics showed surprising moderation and open-mindedness. Even Max Kalbeck, one of Vienna's arch-conservatives, found the new sets 'appropriate to the music', 'carefully nuanced', possessing 'great graphic harmony', and felt that Roller had taken his inspiration, with exemplary fidelity, from the Nordic Middle Ages. Roller, while respecting Wagner's own precepts, had elevated opera to

---

[164] The two relevant pages of the first MS were later pasted together to prevent their being read.

[165] See below, Vol. iiii, Chap. 3.

the status of 'Gesamtkunstwerk', and so successfully that one could 'see and touch the music'. A relentless enemy of Wagner's aesthetics, Kalbeck added that the sets made the singers 'more expendable than ever'. The orchestra, with actors to mime the actions on stage, would have been enough to create the illusion. He looked on Mahler, far more than Roller, as the hero of the evening.

The convinced Wagnerian Theodor Helm shared Kalbeck's admiration for Mahler's 'inspired and inspiring' musical interpretation. However, he wondered whether it was a good thing thus to monopolize the spectator's attention at the music's expense, even though Roller had undoubtedly succeeded in creating 'stage pictures full of atmosphere', and deployed all his impressionist virtuosity in 'unusual effects of light and colour'. Rather than remaining the reserve of a coterie of Wagnerians, *Tristan* might well now become an 'attraction' for a public which would come specifically to see the famous sets.[166] Julius Korngold,[167] who was about to take over from Hanslick in the *Neue Freie Presse*, also recognized the physical beauty and symbolic value of Roller's sets and costumes, but he too wondered whether Wagner himself would ever have agreed to allow the staging to take on such a life of its own. To be sure, Roller's only aim was to reinforce dramatic and musical expression and he succeeded, particularly in his designs for the last act, which Korngold called 'painted *Tristan* music', the colours suggesting weariness, illness, ruin, and imminent death.[168]

Hirschfeld, on the other hand, would have been untrue to himself had he approved of Roller's *Neuinszenierung*. He did admire the 'magnificent nocturnal poetry of the second act', but he criticized the production's 'excessive subjectivity', which threatened to distract the spectator's attention from the music. Roller, he thought, had obliterated the work. In order to create a 'scenic atmosphere' out of his imagination he had dominated every aspect of costuming, props, even the grouping of the actors on stage,[169] which had previously

---

[166] In the *Musikalisches Wochenblatt*, Helm wrote that the new sets had cost about 80,000 kronen. His opinion of the cast was unfavourable: Schmedes was inferior to Winkelmann, while Mildenburg was not on a par with Lilli Lehmann or even with Sedlmair.

[167] Julius Korngold (1860–1945), born in Brno in Moravia, studied law and music. At the Vienna Conservatory he was, like Mahler, a pupil of Franz Krenn. He was engaged in 1902 by the *Neue Freie Presse* as Hanslick's assistant. He was later to publish collections of his articles: *Deutsches Opernschaffen der Gegenwart* (1920) and *Die romantische Oper der Gegenwart* (1922). After the Anschluss, he emigrated to the USA with his son Erich Wolfgang, the famous composer of operas and later film music (see below, Vol. iii, Chap. 6). Korngold's memoirs were recently published as part of the book *Die Korngolds in Wien* (Musik und Theater, Zurich, 1991: KIW).

[168] Later, in his memoirs, Korngold recalled the day, long before the première, when Mahler showed him the models of the sets: 'Vienna was just about to experience Mahler's epoch-making collaboration with Roller, the alliance of the musical stage with the plastic arts, which stressed the space factor (*der Raum*) in the stage picture, and put stylization in place of the prevailing 'illusion' principle. I was in a position from then on to enlist in a struggle on the side of reform which had been more than skeptically received' (KIW 106). Korngold admired Mildenburg but regretted her 'forcing her voice in the second act'. He praised all the other members of the cast, and above all Mahler's inspired conducting.

[169] According to Hirschfeld, Mayr was 'not a true King Mark'; Kittel was a 'solid and trustworthy' rather than 'truly moving' Brangäne; and Schmedes did not have the makings of a Tristan. Hermine Kittel (1879–1948) was born in Vienna, and started her career as an actress. She studied singing with Amalie Materna and

been the director's job. Mahler and Roller had worked in complete agreement, so that the visual and the dramatic elements joined hands. 'However,' Hirschfeld went on, 'the production is not harmonious'. It reflected a 'relentless struggle and an unparalleled clamour for the eye as well as the ear'. Each movement was 'beautiful, and appropriate to the dramatic effect'; even the slightest nuance in the score was meticulously executed by the singers; but the whole performance was 'over-refined'. Mildenburg shaded every word, pose, and expression, 'as if she were repeating a lesson, and wanted to give everything a logical or philosophical meaning'. As a result, the greatness of her interpretation was entirely 'synthetic'. Her 'subtle pantomime' was entirely lost on the spectator because of the darkness on stage.

As for the influential socialist newspaper *Die Zeit*,[170] on the subject of the new *Tristan* it published a short musical review by Richard Wallaschek,[171] in which he had nothing but praise for Schmedes's performance and 'a completely rethought and, down to the smallest detail, reworked' production, and another article devoted entirely to the staging. Its author, Josef Lutz, was a fervent supporter of the Secession. Surely 'Wagner dreamt of such a stage picture', he wrote. Whereas routine and tradition had previously ruled the Vienna stage, Roller was a pioneer, the first to attempt 'to render unto Wagner what was Wagner's'. The neutral tones of his costumes gave the characters a hieratic quality that recalled primitive paintings, and his sets had 'the beauty of old frescos'. Even the anti-Semitic press found many merits in the new production. Maximilian Muntz called the first- and third-act sets irreproachable, though the latter was so superb it 'diverted attention from the plot to itself'. Indignant, like some of his colleagues, at the very idea that people should go to a performance of *Tristan* simply for the new cast and designs, he took care to discover 'some dangerously arbitrary details' in Mahler's interpretation.[172] On the other hand, Puchstein, in the *Deutsches Volksblatt*, found it 'matchless', and warmly praised Roller. Even though the production was not perfect, he said, it was a 'colossal

in 1900 became a member of the Vienna Opera where she remained for 30 years. She also sang at the Bayreuth and Salzburg Festivals. Mahler must have admired her particularly since he engaged her a number of times to sing the solos in his Second and Third Symphonies.

[170] *Die Zeit* had been founded in 1894 as a magazine, with Hermann Bahr, Arthur Schnitzler, Hugo von Hofmannsthal, Felix Salten, Felix Dörmann, and Karl Kraus among its contributors. It became a daily newspaper in 1903, with important sections on politics and economics as well as the world of letters.

[171] Richard Wallaschek (1860–1917), born in Brno, studied law and philosophy in Vienna, Heidelberg, and Tübingen, then at the Univ. of Freiburg in Breisgau. In 1886, having publ. an *Ästhetik der Tonkunst* (Aesthetics of Music), he began studying the psychology of sounds, then spent 1890–5 in London studying the treasures of the British Museum. He became a professor at the Univ. of Vienna's Institute of Musicology, wrote for *Die Zeit*, and was joint president of the Society of Experimental Phonetics. In 1900–2 he taught aesthetics at the Vienna Conservatory. His many publications included: *Das musikalische Gedächtnis* (Musical Memory) (1892); *On the Origin of Music* (London, 1893); *Primitive Music* (London, 1893); *Urgeschichte der Saiteninstrumente* (History of the Origins of Stringed Instruments); *Geschichte der Wiener Hofoper* (A History of the Vienna Opera) (1907–8); see below, Vol. iii, Chap. 6, the story of Mahler's quarrel with Wallaschek.

[172] For Muntz, Schmedes was the 'only tenor capable of replacing Winkelmann'. As to Mildenburg, despite the progress she had made, 'she still fell short of the ideal grandeur' that one would wish.

step forward.' The sets were 'true miracles' and each detail revealed the 'skilful hand of an authentic artist'.

Two Viennese critics refused to join in the chorus of praise but took a resolutely hostile stance. According to Kauders, *Tristan*'s success was based only on a misunderstanding because sumptuous sets added nothing to such a work. 'Mahler,' he wrote, 'muffled' the orchestra to enable the audience to turn its attention from the music to the stage spectacle, which, admittedly, was attractive to the eye. As for Gustav Schönaich, the Viennese custodian of the Bayreuth tradition, he went so far as to side with earlier stage-designers, who had never had the privilege of 'starting from scratch'. Roller's palette was undoubtedly harmonious: admittedly his settings and costumes were closely linked to the plot, and his 'attempt to blend décor, poetry and music' was 'the most successful ever made'.[173] But *Tristan*, the most 'inward' work in the whole repertoire, was not a good choice for such an experiment. Needless to say, the Wagner family shared the same point of view. Siegfried, who attended the première on 21 February, later said that 'his father had staged *Tristan* himself in Munich' and that 'one should stick once and for all to his instructions'.[174] Again Mahler was aware of the gap that separated him from the direct descendants of a master whom he felt he loved and understood better than they did.

Among those present at this historic première was one of the leading figures of twentieth-century music, a Wagnerian of passion and conviction. Anton Webern had developed the admirable habit of recording all the important events of his life in a private diary. This was his entry for 21 February 1903:

Tristan und Isolde, new production. Schmedes took the role of Tristan for the first time. Unfortunately he was not very successful. His voice is not high enough and his acting leaves something to be desired. It was quite an exploit in itself, but it had many flaws compared with Winkelmann's, which is still vivid in my mind. As Isolde, Mildenburg overwhelmed me.

The new designs are something marvellous. The orange-yellow of Isolde's tent creates a lightness which contrasts wonderfully with the bright blue light shining on the sea in the distance. The second act décor is fascinating. A warm summer night, very dark blue, lit by the moon, breathes its magic onto your face. Violet shadows slip over the terrace and the house walls. The stone parapets of the terrace are entwined with superb flowers which surround the bench where the lovers are to sit. All the burning and captivating magic of an irresistible voluptuousness makes your heart beat faster.

The whole setting of the last act is full of endless sadness and despair. Under the great, knotted lime tree the hero lies suffering. The ground slopes, with the castle gate

---

[173] Cast for the performance of 21 Feb. 1903: Mildenburg (Isolde), Kittel (Brangäne), Schmedes (Tristan), Preuss (shepherd), Stehmann (sailor), Breuer (Melot), Melms (Kurwenal), Mayr (König Marke). It varied little in the course of the 27 performances that Mahler conducted before leaving Vienna, except for Lilli Lehmann's guest appearances and the role of Kurwenal, soon taken over by Friedrich Weidemann. Winkelmann also occasionally replaced Schmedes in the title-role.

[174] EDS2. 148. Wagner's son said this in Graz in front of Ernst Decsey. In view of his steadfast refusal to consider any changes in the staging of his father's works, one wonders what Siegfried Wagner would have thought of his own son Wieland's productions in Bayreuth in the 1950s.

lower down at the back. Scattered stones and the debris of crumbling walls lie about. Gustav Mahler conducted, and he brought out all the orchestral beauties superbly. Even the crescendo in the Overture was thrilling. All the merit of this new *Tristan* is due to him.[175]

Many other contemporaries shared Webern's enthusiasm and fully understood the significance and the implications of the event: 'It was not a piece of theatre, it was the revelation of a mystery,' wrote the Prague critic Felix Adler nine years later.

In *Tristan*, a drama of souls and emotions (*Seelen- und Gefühlsdrama*), everything relating to the concrete action seemed somewhat blurred (*verwischt*), the scenic design as a whole and its detail deviated from the composer's indications, and yet it was so Wagnerian through and through that later anyone who had heard the original *Tristan* in Bayreuth had to concede that the Wagnerian ideal had been fulfilled here in Vienna, not in the tradition-steeped *Festspiel*-town on the Roter Main, where one saw and heard only a tale of chivalry (*Ritterstück*) with music.[176]

For Hermann Bahr, the new *Tristan* production was without doubt the most successful attempt ever made to achieve the *Gesamtkunstwerk*, which had been Wagner's ideal but which he had never realized:

Reinhardt's aim, the same that Richard Wagner and later Appia, the young Fortuny, Olbrich and Kolo Moser cherished, has now been fulfilled for the first time by Mahler and Roller in *Tristan* and *Fidelio*. That aim is to remedy the insufficiencies of a single art, which no longer satisfies our increased dramatic demands, with resources from the other arts. In other words, what the poet or the composer tries to express in words and sounds is complemented by resorting to other media—gesture, light, colour. The desire to do this has been maturing in minds over the last hundred years, and is irresistible. It is only when it has prevailed that Germanic art will reach fruition, in an impulse which, from Shakespeare to Goethe and Schiller, from Goethe and Schiller to Wagner, propels us with increasing force towards the union of all the arts.[177]

'Gesamtkunst' (total art) was also the main theme of an article by Max Graf, the youngest of the Viennese critics, whom Mahler had treated so badly the previous year.[178] A month after the première, in a Hamburg newspaper, he wrote:

The nervous colour-romanticism of the moderns now prevails in the new *Tristan* sets by Alfred Roller. Light and air are called upon to make music along with the Wagner orchestra. The basic chords of each act are now brilliant light. For the first time Impressionist painting techniques (*Künste*) appear on the operatic stage. Richard Wagner's genius and his theatrical imagination have powerfully aroused the artist. His *Gesamtkunstwerk* will unite music and painting into a highly effective harmony. The

---

[175] Unpubl. passage from Webern's diary (Moldenhauer Archives in Spokane, Washington, DC).

[176] Felix Adler, 'Gustav Mahler', in *Programme des Musik-Fests Mannheim* (11 and 12 May 1912). 'Dem Andenken Gustav Mahlers', *Veranstalter der Philharmonische Verein, Mannheim*.

[177] Hermann Bahr, *Glossen zum Wiener Theater (1903–1906)* (Fischer, Berlin, 1907).

[178] See above, Chap. 13.

composer extends his hand to the painter. What would the master himself have said of
the art of light and colour displayed in this Impressionistic *Tristan*? Perhaps he would
have recognized with astonishment that the poetic force of his vision has transformed
the painter into a poet; but he may also have been shocked to find a liberated visual art
no longer serving the poet, but attempting to prevail in its own right.[179]

Adolf Loos, prophet of 'Ornamentlosigkeit' (ornamentlessness), an architect,
a leading figure of the avant-garde, had already embarked on his campaign
against the Secession, condemning it both for its tyranny and for its refusal of
austerity which was for him an article of faith. He took the modernist cause for
granted and considered that Roller had pushed things much too far:[180]

Wherever I chance to be, I have never yet missed a performance of *Tristan*. For me,
Tristan is the greatest work known to us. I should like to thank the gracious providence
that brought me into this world *after Tristan* was created.

I am no cry-baby. At those very moving plays where handkerchiefs are coming out
of pockets all over the place and the stalls are awash with tears I find myself thinking,
'What's wrong with everyone? Nothing will happen to Reinhold. And as for Reimers, an
hour from now he'll be eating Königsberg knödel at the Löwenbräu restaurant.'

But in *Tristan* I forget the name of the artists playing the parts. And the hour and a
quarter of music in Act I sends me completely off the rails; when the curtain falls there
are tears in my eyes at the frightful tragedy of Isolde's being torn from Tristan's side and
put in the royal strait-jacket. I feel afraid that someone will notice me. I'm ashamed.
Always.

Tristan has a new stage production. Professor Roller did the job. The curtain goes up.
But I fail to hear the voice of the young sailor. My eyes are just too busy. What kind of
a ship is that? It's in cross-section. Lengthways or across? Mildenburg is in good voice.
Across or lengthways?? Well, we'll see soon enough. The awnings will soon open. 'Luft,
Luft'. At last: they're drawn! Thank God! I couldn't have stuck it any longer. But what's
this? Tristan is handling the sails and steering both at once. Roller must have seen it

---

[179] Max Graf, 'Der Sezessionistische Tristan', *Hamburger Nachrichten* (15 Mar. 1903).

[180] Adolf Loos (1870–1933) was born in Brno, Moldavia, in the same year as Josef Hoffmann. Having read
at the Dresden Technical Univ. (1890–3), he spent 3 years in the USA studying architecture, in particular
with Louis H. Sullivan, who greatly influenced his development. From 1896 onwards he became famous first
as a designer, then as an architect, and also as a writer and theoretician. Loos grew friendly with Altenberg
and Karl Kraus, then with Kokoschka and Trakl, as well as with Wedekind, whom he profoundly admired.
He was an early contributor to *Ver Sacrum*, notably with a pamphlet criticizing the architecture of the
Ringstrasse entitled *The Potemkin City*. Loos afterwards gradually distanced himself from the Secession. In
1903 he founded the magazine *Der Andere* of which he was the sole contributor, like Karl Kraus in *Die
Fackel*. Before 1914 he was known principally as a decorator (Café Museum, 1899; the Steiner stationer's
and the Kärtner Bar, 1907) but he was also responsible for several buildings (the world-famous Goldman und
Salath shop and building on the Michaelerplatz, opposite the Hofburg, 1910–2; the Steiner House, 1912; the
Scheu House, 1912; the tailor Knitze's shop, 1913; the Lothargasse House, 1913). In 1906 Loos set up his
own school of architecture in Vienna, quite near Mahler's appartment on the Rennweg. In 1922 he left
Austria for France, following attacks in the press on his morality, and lived in Paris where he built the Maison
Tzara (1928). He returned to Vienna, designing several more houses there and in Prague. A fervent believer
in 'Ornamentlosigkeit' (total absence of ornament) and the 'Neue Sachlichkeit' (new functional design), Loos
was one of the great precursors of modern architecture. His most famous pamphlet was entitled *Ornament
and Crime* (1908). In it he condemned 'the serene eurhythmy of form', and 'aesthetic and moral consonances'
which pretend to be 'messages of felicity', proclaiming that intimate experience was the only source of truth,
and urged recourse to 'instincts until now repressed'.

done on the Attersee. 'Befehlen liess dem Eigenholde' (Sent summons to that stubborn man). . . . Or on the Gmundnersee. Gmunden. Altenberg's there. I wonder when he's coming back to Vienna? 'Wie lenkt' ich sicher den Kahn' . . . (How could I safely steer the ship). . . . That's Schmedes. Why not Winkelmann? Winkelmann won't like it. But it's none of my business. 'Heil unser Held Tristan'. . . . Brangäne closes the hangings. She is wearing a pretty costume. It would look good on my wife. For an art ball or something. 'Wie lenkt er sicher den Kahn' . . . Mildenburg must have got that from Klaus-Fränkel in Prague. Nearly time for the love potion. Where is it? There are too many coffers around. Nicely arranged. The carpet is Rudniker (Prague). I've used them too. For the entrance hall. All those cushions look nice. Sandor Jaray himself couldn't do better. 'Ich sah ihm in die Augen'. . . . He'll be furious that Roller beat him to it: 'Lady's bedroom in Norman style'. But which coffer has the love potion in it? Aha, that one. I thought it was. But then what's the other one there for? . . .

At the end of the act my curiosity was satisfied. The women rushed at the coffer in question, opened it—*the crown*!! Very good. I wouldn't have guessed it.

The curtain fell. People applauded. I suddenly jumped up. So this, this is how you listened to *Tristan*. I began to be ashamed, ashamed.

I hurried out. No, you can't sit through *Tristan* like that. I went home.

They have deprived me of something sacrosanct.

I don't know if others felt like that.[181]

A polemicist of outstanding talent, a mortal foe of any 'decoration', Loos was irritated by all the visual beauty that Roller created on stage, so troubled that he didn't hear the music. No doubt he would have preferred the old-fashioned simplicity of former productions. Here the extreme avant-garde joined forces with the most die-hard traditionalism; thus the enemies of the new aesthetics were not recruited solely from the ranks of the conservatives. But in spite of them all Mahler himself was aware that in *Tristan* he had realized his life's dream, a production as physically beautiful as it was rich in meaning and expression. 'You make me feel ashamed,' he wrote to Roller two days after the première.

I have spent days wondering how to thank you for all the greatness and beauty for which the Opera and I are indebted to you! I have come to the conclusion that since I don't know what to say, it's better to say nothing. In one respect, I know we are alike: in our completely disinterested commitment to art, even if we strive in different ways. And I knew too that you would not think me ungrateful or unperceptive if I did not try to find words for what you have accomplished and what you have become for me. I would be very sad to be exchanging such words with you now, as though I was saying goodbye, had I not arrived at the happy certainty that this collaboration of ours so far is only a beginning, a pointer towards the future.[182]

---

[181] Adolf Loos, *Trotzdem* (Nevertheless) (1900–30) (Brennerverlag, Innsbruck, 1931).

[182] MBR1, no. 298; MBR2, no. 314. Roller was officially appointed at the Vienna Opera on 19 May 1903. One of the conditions he had stipulated was that his 3-year contract could be terminated during the first year after nine months. In fact he had not resigned from his teaching post at the Kunstgewerbeschule but merely asked for a leave of absence.

The following month, with the Vienna première of Gustave Charpentier's *Louise*, no one could possibly have accused Mahler of failing to respect the composer's intentions. Not only did he send his principal stage director to France to study Charpentier's original staging, but he invited the composer himself to the final rehearsals. When he had visited Paris three years earlier with the Vienna Philharmonic Orchestra, everyone had been talking about the recent success of *Louise*,[183] and about the scandal it had provoked. He had looked at the score, and probably decided that it was unworthy of his attention. He had therefore resisted all those who tried to drag him to the Opéra-Comique. Yet, early in the preceding year, he had told Alma: 'I have received [the score of] a very remarkable opera. It does not seem very promising in piano reduction, but in orchestra score it must be splendid and dramatic. It is the high point of the Paris season.'[184] *Louise* had recently experienced a series of failures all over Germany—except in Hamburg. Did Mahler change his original opinion on re-reading the score? Or did he decide that, given the poor quality of the few new operas available, *Louise* seemed like a masterpiece by comparison?

Charpentier was delayed in Berlin, where another production of *Louise* had just opened,[185] and arrived in Vienna only four days before the date set for the première. On 26 February he cabled Mahler: 'Happy to come, but shall not conduct because impossible to equal you. Greetings.' During the rehearsals, Mahler showed his usual attention to detail. This did not prevent Charpentier from taking exception to the sets and costumes as soon as he arrived.[186] The whole thing seemed to him both 'too splendid' and 'too realistic', and he felt it had been too closely modelled on the Paris performance. Mahler immediately postponed the première to make the changes he asked for.[187] 'When the author speaks, we must obey,' he told his startled collaborators. When Gutheil-Schoder balked at the additional work, Mahler replied (according to Alma who never had much sympathy for the Opera prima donnas): 'Enough! A German voice should remain silent in the presence of a French master.' Thus Charpentier was able to make all the changes he wanted. He insisted, for instance, that the sleep-walker in the second act should wear a red light under his coat over his heart, and during the episode of 'the

[183] The première of *Louise* had been given at the Opéra-Comique on 2 Feb. 1900.

[184] AMM1. 74; AMM2. 82. This must have occurred in Jan. 1902 for Mahler signed the contract with Heugel, the publisher of *Louise*, on 27 Jan. 1902.

[185] This performance took place on 4 Mar. Mahler cabled to the Berlin Intendant on the 5th to ask where he had found the bells for *Louise*. The Vienna Opera paid Charpentier's publisher Heugel 3,000 kronen for the score and parts, plus 5% of the box-office receipts, including subscription evenings.

[186] In 1909, in the *New York Times*, Richard Aldrich published an account of the whole episode which he undoubtedly got from Mahler himself. Charpentier had also criticized his tempos. When Mahler visited Paris in Apr. 1910, his young disciple and friend Alfredo Casella published another account more or less identical to those of Aldrich and Alma.

[187] Probably not 'six weeks' as Richard Aldrich tells us, but several days. Concerning the costumes, it is likely that Mahler did not 'have new ones made' as Aldrich suggests, but only altered the old ones.

crowning of the muse' he called for a twirling ballerina in a tutu, with a violet follow-spot.

On the first day, Alma glimpsed Gustave Charpentier on the Ring, draped in a vast black cape. His unusual bearing and slightly comical gait made a strong impression on her. She marvelled at his 'light-heartedness, the way he never takes himself seriously, his Bohemian informality and his extreme gallantry'. Even 'his crude manners, when he spat under the table and bit his nails', delighted rather than shocked her. One evening in her box, he squeezed her knee to call her attention to the beauties of *Tristan*, but she was still not offended. Certainly she was unused to such unconventional behaviour, but she took it as a mark of his genius. Every day he sent her a lavish bouquet of flowers with a ribbon bearing this dedication: 'To Madame Mahler, gracious Muse of Vienna, from the grateful Muse of Montmartre.' He was attentive, told her stories about his difficult beginnings in life, and even tried to convert her to his socialist convictions. He also praised her highly to Mahler: 'How lucky you are to have such a *gamin!*' She is 'light, gaiety, the springtime that we artists all need'. He treated Alma and Mahler 'like two children' with whom he enjoyed conversing 'because they spoke their minds honestly'.

Although infatuated with the charms of his own music, 'as if it were a mistress,' Charpentier showed unshakeable respect and admiration for Mahler. Only once did his free-wheeling ways go too far: he brought a young woman he had doubtless met on the street into the director's box, and Rosé had to warn his sister-in-law to stay away. Despite this incident, Charpentier's stay in Vienna was unclouded. The letter and the two cards which he sent to Alma bear witness to the warmth of their relationship. In the letter he thanked Alma for her present, though 'he did not need it to retain a very warm and grateful memory of Vienna', and added that 'the beautiful smile of our Master, gracious and eager to fulfil my slightest wish, the gentle sympathy with which you honoured me, have encrusted in my memory a firmament of joy'. In a postcard written on 28 March, just before he left Vienna, he thanked Alma for the 'delicious but very heavy cake', and in a final card, sent much later from New York, he sent a 'brotherly greeting to the good Master, faithful to *Louise*'.[188]

Later, Erwin Stein was to recall the deep impression *Louise* had made on Alban Berg and himself. It was the first 'modern' opera they had heard and Charpentier's 'new and direct approach . . . fascinated us. . . . The milieu of common town people was a new thing in opera and very different from the "verismo" then in vogue.'[189] As usual, Mahler rehearsed two sopranos and two tenors for the main parts (Gutheil-Schoder and Förster-Lauterer as Louise and Schrödter and Slezak as Julien) and cast first-rank singers in the many second-

---

[188] UPL.
[189] ESM. The young musicians had also heard a new instrument in *Louise*: the celesta, which Mahler was soon to use in the last of the *Kindertotenlieder* and in his symphonies.

ary roles.[190] Gustave Charpentier himself recalled the Vienna rehearsals with Mahler conducting:

When Gustav Mahler mounts the podium, his cool and calm demeanour is striking. Apparently indifferent to his surroundings, his face shows no emotion. His will seems to control his nerves and to rule, to command, to dominate him before affecting the others. He sits down without affectation. As soon as he begins to conduct, his body is no longer his. Though one knows he is conducting the musicians, it is the ardent breathing of the instruments that sways, buffets and lifts him. His whole being follows the rise and fall of the sounds unleashed. He soars, as if suspended above this harmonious and vibrant ether. He is the embodiment of Baudelaire's verse: 'Music often sweeps me away like the sea!' And the results he achieves make you realize that what is true for authors also applies to conductors: in order to move, one must be moved; to inflame, to electrify, to raise the performers to paroxysms of passion, to bring out in vibrant sound the treasure of inner vibrations latent in those subject to his baton, he must himself participate in the divine exaltation. Still to love passionately an object, a person, an art form after years and years of living in close contact with it—do you realize that this is the most extraordinary thing in the world?[191]

Charpentier goes on to say that he had never understood *Tristan* better than in Vienna because Mahler conducted like 'a lover, as though he were hearing it for the first time'. Charpentier's earlier conception of the work was transformed by the spirit Mahler radiated. He returned to Vienna for the eighth performance of *Louise*, and still found 'the admirable orchestra of the early performances', 'the same eloquence, the same faith, the same enthusiasm'. He was moved by the way Mahler, on returning to the podium after each intermission, directed a long look 'towards the white figure leaning towards him in the box opposite, discreetly adorned with creamy white flowers', and 'shared his emotion for a vision so closely akin to the one in the opera'. Charpentier's account is all the more valuable because Alma, in her memoirs, seems often to forget, or to want to forget, the deep love Mahler had shown for her for so many years.

The first performance of *Louise* was a considerable success. Charpentier took several curtain-calls after each act. He tried to persuade Mahler to share the applause, but as always Mahler refused to take a bow. Charpentier, however, would not take no for an answer, and lifted him up to carry him on to stage. Mahler waved his arms and legs so violently that Charpentier had to put him down again. Shortly afterwards, to forestall any recurrence, he sent Charpentier a note saying he hoped this would be 'the first and last time I fight you'.

The Viennese critics who reacted favourably to the new opera were few in number. Theodore Helm praised it above all as a visual and theatrical feat, 'a

[190] At the première on 24 Mar. 1903, the following artists performed small parts: Pohlner, Michalek, Kittel, Kaulich (the dressmaker), Preuss, Breuer, Schittenhelm, Pacal, Stoll, Stehmann, and Felix, most of whom usually sang important roles. Willy Hesch even played the rag-picker. Charpentier himself preferred the 'naïve simplicity' of Förster-Lauterer to the 'refinement' of Gutheil Schoder in the title part.
[191] Gustave Charpentier, 'Souvenir de Vienne, 1903'. (Text given to the author in the 1960s by Philippe Heugel, the grandson of the publisher of *Louise*.)

true miracle of modern staging'. If the Viennese audience had been somewhat surprised by the work's musical 'oddities' it was nevertheless won over by its cleverness and originality. Max Kalbeck, feeling more 'modern' than usual, considered the production a 'victory on all fronts', and gave it credit for winning the audience's approval for this 'musical novel'. Schönaich recognized in Charpentier a composer who had really 'felt, experienced and lived' his work, and whose realism was genuine. Even though the banality of the story was not always compatible with the music, his 'authentic style' was to be preferred to the 'perfumed' language of Massenet.

The remainder of the critics condemned Charpentier's opera. Hirschfeld called the success 'superficial' and claimed that the applause had been mixed with catcalls. In his opinion, *Louise*'s music was only a 'caricature of Wagner', a 'succession of proclamations, appeals, and fanfares seasoned with a sentimental sauce'. Far from being the first 'atmospheric painter' in music, Charpentier 'perversely plays on the nerves and exaggerates all his musical effects'. Twenty-four hours later, the same critic ridiculed the work's socialist preachings,[192] its clumsy symbolism (the red light bulb), as well as its vocal writing and lack of melodic invention. With equal virulence, Wallaschek criticized the libretto for the incompatibility of its socialist realism with the elegant music. For him, Charpentier was nothing more than a 'clever arranger'.[193] The anti-Semitic *Deutsches Volksblatt*'s Hans Puchstein attacked the 'noisy and scandalous' pre-production publicity,[194] and Kauders also considered that the work was 'as tiring to the ear as it is to the nerves'. Only the 'perfect functioning of the immense machine in the second act,' he wrote, 'a masterpiece of Mahler's rehearsing and staging', did honour to the Opera and the thirty-eight soloists. *Louise* was performed a total of twenty-four times in Vienna,[195] and its success was all the more noteworthy since it was premièred during a traditionally difficult period for the theatre. Eleonora Duse, for instance, was playing in Vienna to half-empty houses, and had to cancel some of her performances. However, the popularity of Charpentier's work in Vienna was only a flash in the pan, for after 1904 it was never put on again. Still, this much applauded première was undoubtedly one of the outstanding successes at the Hofoper during Mahler's tenure. He eventually got tired of conducting it, and after two months finally handed it over to Franz Schalk.

Three weeks before the première of *Louise*, Strauss had come from Berlin with his own Tonkünstler Orchestra to give a concert,[196] and his stay brought a

---

[192] Despite 30 rehearsals, Mahler did not succeed, according to Hirschfeld, in making sense of an absurd and prosaic text lacking in form and feeling. Hirschfeld made fun particularly of the manner in which Charpentier restated his themes in the Finale of each act in a 'noisy thematic review'.

[193] Yet the 'Cries of Paris' carried the audience into a 'more exalted sphere', Wallaschek thought, as did the little orchestral Prelude to Act III and the brief love scene in Act IV.

[194] Puchstein takes Mahler to task for ignoring several 'German masterpieces', such as Schillings's *Ingwelde*, Wilhelm Kienzl's *Heilmar der Narr*, and Karl von Kaskel's *Der Dusle und das Babeli*.

[195] There were 21 performances in 1903, 8 of which were conducted by Mahler, and 3 in 1904.

[196] The programme on 4 Mar. was as follows: Tchaikovsky, Overture to *The Voyevoda*; Strauss, *Tod und*

little added excitement into Mahler's and Alma's lives. This time, the principal subject of conversation between the two musicians was the defence of the rights of composers, a cause to which Strauss was to devote a great deal of energy throughout his life. At the beginning of 1903, he was about to found in Berlin, with several other German composers, a society for the protection of orchestral composers' copyright. The idea of this society had been conceived around 1900 because orchestral composers hitherto received no royalties at all on performances of their works (unlike composers of opera who had been protected in Germany since 1870). France had given the lead in this field by establishing, in 1851, the Société des Auteurs, Compositeurs et Éditeurs de Musique. In Germany, symphonic works were utterly unprotected, and anyone who chose to do so could copy the orchestral parts of any work, without permission from the composer or the publisher.[197]

On 1 January 1902 a new law was finally passed in Germany, specifying that all musical works would henceforth remain under copyright protection for thirty years after the composer's death. The protection was to cover all his previous works as well. But in order to apply the law it was necessary to create a new organization which would list all performances of copyrighted works. This was Strauss's aim in founding, on 14 January 1903, with Friedrich Rösch and Hans Sommer, the Genossenschaft Deutscher Komponisten (Association of German Composers), whose first members were Humperdinck, Philip Rufer, Max von Schillings, Ludwig Thuille, Eugen d'Albert, Jean Louis Nikodé, Siegmund von Hausegger, and several others. The task of the Anstalt für Musikalisches Aufführungsrecht (AFMA or Agency for Performing Rights), a subsidiary of the Genossenschaft, was to keep records of performances and collect royalties. A small commission was to be charged to cover the agency's overheads. As could be expected, there was strong and immediate opposition by some of the impresarios[198] and symphonic societies,[199] supported by a number of conductors such as Georg Göhler in Leipzig. A few composers, Weingartner and Reinecke among them, also refused to join the Association, fearing that the imposition of additional royalties would discourage the various organizations from performing their works.

The matter was the subject of bitter controversy in the press throughout 1903 and 1904. The Berlin magazine *Die Musik* published correspondence between

Verklärung and *Aus Italien*, Liszt, *Tasso*; Alfred Bruneau, *Messidor* (Entr'acte). According to the *Neue Freie Presse*, a large audience came to applaud the famous visitor, so it cannot possibly be the concert to which Alma refers as unsuccessful (AMM1. 67; AMM2. 76).

[197] Works were only protected if it was explicitly stated at the beginning of all the copies of the score that the performance rights were reserved. However, most publishers were loath to reserve these rights because they feared that such a clause would limit the sales of the scores. In Feb. 1899 the Genossenschaft Deutscher Tonsetzer decided to insert such a clause in the scores of all its members (see Kurt Blaukopf, 'Mahler's materielle Existenz als Komponist', in Matthias Theodor Vogt, ed., *Das gustav-Mahler-Fest Hamburg 1989* (Bärenreiter, Kassel, 1991), 80).

[198] e.g. Louise Stargardt-Wolff.

[199] e.g. the Kaim Concerts, the Leipzig Gewandhaus and the Cologne Gürzenich.

supporters and enemies of the new Genossenschaft.[200] The opposition claimed it was unrealistic to try to keep track of all performances of protected works in every city in Europe, and that the cost of keeping such records would be too high. They even claimed that the Genossenschaft threatened the 'freedom' of performing musicians and would prevent the performance of contemporary music. To this the Genossenschaft members replied that the percentage paid on each performance was too small to discourage would-be performers, adding that their aim was to improve the status and living conditions of composers. Why should opera composers be paid royalties on each performance while the composers of symphonic or choral works drew no benefit at all from perform- ances?[201] It was obviously essential for the society's survival that the most frequently performed composers such as Strauss and Mahler should join it, for their royalties were required, especially at the beginning, to sustain it. Their contribution was in fact to be larger than the benefit they would derive, but the path of justice and progress obviously lay in that direction. It is to Mahler and Strauss's credit that they were among the society's first members. 'Dear Friend,' Mahler wrote to Strauss in January 1903,

My contract with my present publisher is so intricate (I, at any rate, can't quite understand it) that I do not know whether I am entitled to join the <u>Genossenschaft deutscher Tonsetzer</u>. For I have put myself under an obligation to join the <u>Society of Authors</u> here. (At the time, in order to be published I would not have minded joining a Society for the Preservation of Purgatory.) Shall I send you my contract? And could you or your experts find out whatever they need from it?—If it is all right, I should be most glad to be a member of your society and, of course, to sit on the committee. Would it not be best for us to discuss it all when <u>you are here</u>, and for you to keep open my right to membership until then?[202]

A few months later, Mahler found that he could not belong to both societies simultaneously and he decided to leave the Austrian society[203] as soon as his membership expired, namely at the end of 1903, in order to join the Berlin Genossenschaft.[204] Strauss must have been particularly eager for him to join for

---

[200] *Die Musik* (1904), 2: 342; 3: 42.

[201] In the *Süddeutsche Monatshefte*, 4 (1904), Siegmund von Hausegger spoke for the Genossenschaft in reply to Georg Göhler. His letter was publ. in several German magazines. He pointed out, e.g., that though Beethoven's contemporaries had failed to understand the 'Eroica', it had none the less filled the pockets of numerous concert promoters without having earned a penny either for its composer or his heirs. Did the composer not have the right to enjoy the fruits of his work? Was it not unthinkable that he should live on public charity, as Göhler suggested, when official criteria were far too vague and uncertain for help to be given to talented artists and those who most needed it?

[202] Undated letter from Mahler to Strauss, (early 1903, MSB 86).

[203] As early as 1900 Strauss had warned Mahler against the Austrian society, the AKM: 'the Directors of the Vienna Society for performance rights . . . are a fine bunch! Don't let the publishers get the better of you!' (Strauss's letter to Mahler dated 22 Apr. 1900: MSB 53).

[204] To be precise, on 21 Nov. 1903, according to the letter which Mahler sent to the founder-president of the Genossenschaft (Frankfurter Stadt- und Universitätsbibliothek, no. 1668). Mahler had belonged to the AKM since 1897. The new Berlin society soon prospered. During the first year the running costs took up 40% of the revenue. In 1907 this had already fallen to 25%. Up to 1907 the total revenue was 252,000 marks,

he wrote to him in mid-February: 'Why don't you sign your application for membership? It is most important that you do so before 1 March! Did you finally accept your election to the advisory board? Please, dear friend, stop dawdling, after all, it is your money you will lose if your name is not among the founder members.'[205] For many months, battle raged between the members and the opponents of the Genossenschaft. For a time Mahler regretted having joined it,[206] since his membership threatened to prevent the Cologne première of the Fifth Symphony and did in fact prevent its second performance in Leipzig, where Ernst Eulenburg, promoter of the Neue Abonnementskonzerte, was an opponent of the Genossenschaft.[207] In the autumn of 1903, Mahler still hadn't officially joined the Berlin Society. To a letter from Friedrich Rösch reminding him of the promise he had made to Strauss, he answered:

Because I am dreadfully busy and quite helpless and ignorant in these matters, I have asked my friend and counsellor Dr Emil Freund in Vienna . . . to get in touch with you. He has all power to act on my behalf in this affair and I would be grateful if you would address your kind messages (*Mitteilungen*) to him. For your information, I want you to know that the contract with the Vienna Authors Society must be terminated on 31 [*sic*] November, which is very advantageous in this case since today is 30 October.[208]

Alma's *Erinnerungen* do not mention the Genossenschaft affair, but they do tell of a particular episode, the first visit she made to Pauline Strauss in her Viennese hotel on the day of Strauss's concert. She was surprised to find the young singer still in bed, although she was supposed to sing that night, and still more surprised when Strauss came in a few minutes later with a diamond ring which he gave her, saying: 'Now will you get up?' At the concert, the hall was 'almost empty', according to Alma. While conducting, Strauss carried on a loud conversation with Mahler, who was sitting in the first row. He later referred to 'that stupid audience which deserves only bad music'. Again Alma's account gives rise to doubts, for Strauss was much too diplomatic to behave so outrageously before an audience in a foreign city. Furthermore, Pauline did not sing in the 1903 orchestral concert and the ring episode probably took place a year

whereas for 1907 alone it was 100,000 marks; 295 composers and 70 publishers belonged to it by 1907, in addition to the French composers and publishers that the Society represented in Germany. Strauss was still president in 1907 (*Beilage zur Neuen Musik-Zeitung*, 19: 17).

[205] Undated letter written by Strauss in mid-Feb. 1903. Its main purpose was to ask Mahler to send him a horn player and an oboist for the tour Strauss was about to undertake with the Tonkünstler Orchestra. Mahler found the musicians and cabled his acceptance in a telegram on 20 Feb. Its text is written out on the last page of his colleague's letter (HOA).

[206] See below Chap. 15 and Vol. iii, Chap. 1.

[207] Ernst Eulenburg (1847–1926), German music publisher, studied at the Leipzig Conservatory and founded his firm in 1874. In 1891 and 1894 he took over two different collections of pocket scores, that of Payne in Leipzig and Donajowski in London, combining the two series. More than 1,000 works have appeared in the 'Eulenburg kleine Partitur-Ausgabe'.

[208] Letter from Mahler to Friedrich Rösch, 31 Oct. 1903 (Stadt- und Universitätsbibliothek, Frankfurt am Main, Musiksammlung).

earlier, after the première of *Feuersnot* and before the Lieder recital Pauline gave with her husband at the piano.

While in Vienna on his way to Graz where he was to conduct two concerts, Strauss came with his wife to the Auenbruggergasse for a family dinner.[209] Pauline dominated the conversation with a constant stream of frivolous chatter. Strauss finally took Mahler into the next room. Left alone with Alma, Pauline poured out her woes and complained at length about the difficulties of living with an 'unappreciated genius'. They had no money, Strauss 'never talked to her', and when he finished working, he went out to play skat.[210] She was so overcome by her own story that she broke down in tears. Deeply embarrassed, Alma went to get the two men, only to find them engaged in an argument about Mommsen's *History of Rome*, a work much admired by Mahler but which Strauss did not like. It is obvious from the tone of this passage in Alma's book that Pauline's attitude shocked her deeply, even though her own diary reveals how little she herself was suited to life with a genius. As soon as the couples were together again, the atmosphere became more relaxed and Pauline questioned Alma about the relative merits of Viennese hairdressers. The two composers were discussing Beethoven: Strauss admired his earlier works most, considering them 'Mozartian', whereas the later ones 'lacked invention'. Aware of Strauss's delight in paradoxes, Mahler kept his temper, and while at the other end of the room Pauline was questioning Alma about the best shops in town for lingerie, he replied simply that 'the work of a genius like Beethoven could only grow deeper and purer as he grew older'. When they touched on opera, Strauss reproached Mahler for preferring singing actresses like Mildenburg and Gutheil-Schoder, whom he considered enemies of bel canto. He himself favoured such singers as Selma Kurz or Leopold Demuth with their perfect technique and flawless voices.[211] Strauss shocked Mahler by insisting that he was prepared to conduct 'no matter where, no matter what', as long as he had to earn a living as a conductor. Obviously Strauss delighted in saying whatever he thought might shock Mahler, yet there is no doubt that he was determined to live comfortably on the income he felt he deserved as a highly industrious and successful composer-conductor. As usual, this long conversation about material gain depressed Mahler who, alone with Alma, sadly commented: 'But it will degrade his soul!'

The record of a particularly busy Vienna season would be incomplete if no

[209] This postcard addressed by Strauss to Alma and dated 5 Feb. 1903, belongs to Dr Alois Kühnen, of Vienna, who kindly sent me a photocopy. 'I am arriving in Vienna on 4 Mar. (not before) 1.10 p.m. If 2.30 p.m. is all right with you for lunch, I'll come with the greatest pleasure. But perhaps it would be better in the evening after the concert, for I must hold a short rehearsal that afternoon. Is *Feuersnot* still thriving?' (MSB 87). Strauss's Graz concert took place on 5 and 6 Mar. 1903.

[210] *Skat*: a German card game, Strauss's favourite, similar to pinochle.

[211] Alma noted that their preferences in this respect were later to be reversed. In New York, Mahler was to conduct such international stars as Fremstad, Gadski, Sembrich, Destinn, Farrar, Bonci, Scotti, and Chaliapin, and Strauss was to rely on the two singing actresses he had previously disparaged, Mildenburg and Gutheil-Schoder, for the Vienna and Dresden premières of *Elektra* (1909).

mention were made of an important artistic event unrelated to music, the plans
and details of which were undoubtedly discussed in Mahler's presence during
the Secession meetings, many of which took place at the Molls' house on the
Hohe Warte. In May 1903, shortly after the big Klimt one-man show at the
Secession, which displayed for the first time the three panels commissioned for
the University (and which the painter soon withdrew in the face of bitter
criticism), the famous Wiener Werkstätte (Viennese Craft Workshops) were
founded on the model of a similar organization created by Charles Rennie
Mackintosh in Britain.[212] Fritz Wärndorfer, a rich Viennese patron of the arts,
who had recently visited London, had long worked with Josef Hoffmann and
Kolo Moser on the project which he had decided to subsidize. Thus the three
of them became the co-founders of the Wiener Werkstätte (WW, as they were
henceforth called in the Austrian capital). For the next decade Wärndorfer
spent a small fortune enabling Hoffmann and Moser, and the other artists who
soon joined them, to put their often expensive ideas into practice. The avowed
aim of the WW was 'to counteract badly designed mass-production and the
empty imitation of old styles . . . and to ensure that objects for everyday use
should be artistically designed'. The original manifesto also mentioned their
desire to 'establish a close relationship between the public, the designer and
the craftsman, and to create good, simple and at the same time attractive
household articles. Our starting point is the function of the object: our first
requirement is suitability for use. Our strength should lie in sound proportions
and appropriate treatment of the materials'.

Although WW products always remained beyond the means of the general
public, and were thus only purchased by the top stratum of Viennese society,
they did eventually succeed in 'awakening among the masses an interest in a
modern, refined style, without imitation of the past'. Soon they were turning out
not only jewellery, glasses, ceramics, cutlery, furniture, and small metal objects, but also fabrics, wallpapers, wickerwork, leather goods, bookbindings,
trimmings, and pearl embroidery. By 1905 they had engaged about 100
workers and 35 master craftsmen, who signed each object with their own
monograms.[213] Moser confined the WW designs to strict geometrical forms until
1906. The founding of the organization was marked by a big exhibition, and
the same autumn the Werkstätte opened an architecture division which co-
ordinated entire building and interior decoration projects.[214] Hevesi noted in

---

[212] The origins of the Werkstätte can be traced back to Klimt's assertion in 1897 that 'no sphere of human
existence is too small and too unimportant for artistic endeavour'.

[213] The Werkstätte first occupied a small warehouse at Heumühlgasse, in the Wieden district. In the
autumn they moved to Neustiftgasse 32. Wärndorfer remained their commercial manager until 1913, when
his place was taken by the banker Otto Primavesi. Later, the Werkstätte opened a shop for fabrics and textiles
on the Kärntnerstrasse, and WW branches opened in Zurich, Breslau, Marienbad, and Berlin.

[214] Two outstanding examples of this collaboration were Hoffmann's Sanatorium Purkersdorf (1905) and
the Palais Stoclet in Brussels (1905–11). The WW also organized many exhibitions, in Vienna and
elsewhere: in 1905 it held a display of art bindings, and in 1906 an exhibition of silver and table ware,
including a priceless silver box made in Pilsen to commemorate the Kaiser's visit. In 1908 the interior

1906 that 'Moser has designed new shapes of bread roll and found a sufficiently intelligent baker to shape and bake them'.[215]

The WW are without doubt the direct ancestors of modern design. That their reaction against machine-age standardization was a success is obvious from their record. It seems however that their influence eventually acquired a somewhat authoritarian flavour. A satirical article by Adolf Loos, called 'The Poor Rich Man', caricatures the rich Viennese patron whose entire house was designed and decorated by Secession artists:

Sometimes he had to summon the architect and unroll the blueprints to remind himself where [something] belonged. . . . Once it happened that the rich man celebrated his birthday. His wife and children had given him wonderful presents. The presents gave him exceptional pleasure and made him really happy. Then the architect came to put things right and make decisions on difficult matters. He entered the room. The master of the house welcomed him eagerly; he had so much to tell him. But the architect failed to notice his host's happiness. He noticed something quite different, and grew pale. 'What on earth are those slippers you're wearing?', he managed to blurt out. The rich man glanced at his embroidered slippers and heaved a sigh of relief: this time he was entirely innocent. The slippers had been made after an original design by the architect himself. So he reminded him: 'My dear architect! Surely you can't have forgotten? You designed these slippers yourself!' 'I certainly did,' thundered the architect, 'but I designed them for the bedroom. In this room you ruin the whole atmosphere with those two ghastly patches of colour. Can't you see?'

The rich man could indeed see. He quickly took them off, and was thrilled to death to discover that the architect seemed to have no objection to his socks. They went into the bedroom, where the rich man was allowed to put his slippers on again. 'Yesterday,' he began tentatively, 'was my birthday. My family literally showered me with presents. I asked you to come, my dear architect, so that you could tell me the best places to put them.' The architect's jaw dropped visibly. Then he exploded: 'What! How can you have allowed yourself to be given presents? Haven't I designed *everything* for you? Haven't I thought of *everything*? You don't need anything else! You are complete!' . . .

The rich man was annihilated. And yet, he still didn't give up. An idea: yes, he had an idea! 'And what,' he asked in triumph, 'if I buy myself a picture from the Secession?'—'Then just try and find somewhere to hang it. Can't you see I've designed a frame on the wall for every single picture here? You can't even *move* a picture! Just try and find room for a new one!'[216]

Loos's parable demonstrates above all the profound influence the members of the Secession and the Wiener Werkstätte exerted on the daily lives of the Viennese aristocracy and bourgeoisie. We have no concrete evidence to show how much Mahler had to do with the WW. But a letter dating from 1910 thanks Josef Hoffmann for designing a piece of jewellery for Alma.[217] And the note-

decoration of the Fledermaus cabaret on the Johannagasse was undertaken jointly by Kolo Moser and Hoffmann, and carried out exclusively by the WW.

[215] Peter Vergo, *Art in Vienna*, 140 (see above, Chap. 13).
[216] Adolf Loos: 'Von einem armen reichen manne', *Neues Wiener Tagblatt* (26 Apr. 1900).
[217] Undated letter from Mahler to Josef Hoffmann (Sept. 1910). See below, Vol. iii, Chap. 6.

paper he often used during the latter part of his life was designed for Alma by a member of the Secession, and probably printed by the WW.

The 1902–3 season at the Hofoper, one of the most brilliant, successful— and costly—which Mahler had ever organized, ended in a blaze of glory. Wagner had been performed 58 times, including three complete *Ring* cycles, Mozart 14 times (*Figaro* 5 times, *Don Giovanni*, *Zaide*, and *The Magic Flute* 3 times). The most performed works were as follows: *Contes d'Hoffmann* (20 performances), *Pique Dame* (19), *Pagliacci* and *Louise* (16), *Les Huguenots* (15), *Aida* (12), *Tannhäuser* and *Die Meistersinger* (11), *Tristan* (7), *Lohengrin* and *Ernani* (6), *Fidelio*, *The Flying Dutchman*, *Trovatore*, *Figaro*, and *Die lustigen Weiber von Windsor* (5). The last important event of the season was a new production of *Aida*, the second act of which was performed before the rest of the work, complete with March and Ballet, on 28 April on the occasion of a visit by the King of Saxony.[218] The sumptuous sets and costumes were this time designed by Heinrich Lefler[219] and painted by Anton Brioschi,[220] a conciliatory gesture on Mahler's part to make up for having 'appointed' Roller as set-designer for *Tristan*. Although he usually avoided conducting at galas, this time Mahler made an exception because he had been promised the funds for a complete new production and had always been particularly fond of this Verdi opera. Many extras[221] were hired for the triumphal scene and the deep stage, opened for the first time to its full dimensions (approximately 750 square yards), was filled with almost a thousand performers and extras.

On 11 May the first complete performance was greeted with enthusiasm. At the beginning of the third and fourth acts, there was prolonged applause.[222] Mahler put an abrupt stop to it by starting to conduct. The critics agreed that they had never seen the triumphal scene staged with such regal pomp or in such exquisite colors: pink, violet, pale green, and golden yellow. This was probably an indirect criticism of the 'impressionistic' sets. Hirschfeld again attacked Mahler's new policy which tried to hide weaknesses in a musical performance with lavish sets and refined staging. He and several other critics attacked the two female leads, Lucy Weidt (Aida) and Josie Petru (Amneris). In their opinion the latter was inferior by far to Edyth Walker, 'shamefully expelled' from the Hofoper by Mahler. Only Slezak, Demuth, and Mayr were unanimously praised. Korngold admired the 'unfailing rightness' of Mahler's interpretation and his gift for revealing to the full each dramatic detail. Muntz,

---

[218] On that occasion, Act II of *Aida* was preceded by the Overture to Nicolai's *Die lustigen Weiber*. As usual in such circumstances, the King awarded Mahler a medal, the Albrechtsorden, 2. Klasse.

[219] Lefler was primarily a costume designer. He only spent 3 years at the Hofoper and left it to direct a masterclass at the Vienna Akademie der bildenden Künste. At the same time he became Ausstattungschef (director of [stage] design and equipment) of the Hofburgtheater.

[220] Kauders thought that Lucie Weidt's new costume disfigured her and that the red ribbon wound into Mayr's (the Pharaoh's) false beard wagged in a ridiculous way when he sang.

[221] According to the *Fremden-Blatt* (12 May), 600 soldiers marched in Act II.

[222] In Hirschfeld's view, the claque was boisterous to the point of indecency and Mahler had been untrue to himself by giving them free rein.

on the other hand, condemned his 'small instrumental grimaces' and 'unnatural rallentandos' while Karpath took him to task for speeding up the tempos too often, 'overemphasizing dynamic effects', and making the brass section play so loudly that the singers had to shout.

Years later, Erwin Stein lovingly recalled Mahler's conducting of *Aida*: 'I know no music that could convey "the pangs of rejected love" as movingly as the theme of Amneris's jealousy; its breathless, stubborn insistence on the narrow semitone interval always suggested to me heartache's physical pain— always, until years later I heard it rushed through in a tempo which left no time for phrasing, rhythmic accentuation, or any kind of expression.'[223] Shortly after, Mahler gave the part of Amneris to Mildenburg, a dramatic soprano, in Stein's view one of his best pieces of casting: 'unorthodox but highly successful'.[224] 'I well remember the intense beauty of Mildenburg's phrase *Oh vieni, vieni, amor mio* in the second act and, in the fourth, the white-hot passion of her great duet with Slezak, whose magnificent singing equalled hers.'[225] Surprising as it may seem, since he so rarely conducted any Italian operas, Mahler appears to have had a particular fondness for *Aida*. Together with *Falstaff* and *The Barber of Seville*, it is one of the three Italian operas he conducted during his last years at the Vienna Opera.

[223] ESM.

[224] Mildenburg had been replaced by Petru because she was ill the night of the première, as was often the case. Cast for the 11 May 1903 performance: Weidt (Aida), Petru (Amneris), Slezak (Radames), Demuth (Amonasro), Mayr (King), Hesch (Ramfis). The gala performance of Act II had taken place on 28 Apr. with the same cast, except for Amneris, who was sung by Laura Hilgermann. It was followed by the first two acts from Nedbal's ballet, *Der faule Hans*, conducted by the composer. According to Korngold, Lefler's new costumes were obviously 'influenced by the Secession'.

[225] ESM.

15

Triumph in Basel—contract with Peters—the Sixth
Symphony completed—first trip to Holland

(April–December 1903)

Oh dear! What misery, having to chew it over
and over again right from the beginning!

A LETTER Mahler wrote to the impresario Norbert Salter early in 1903
shows how much Mahler's Krefeld triumph had transformed his career as
composer-conductor. He declared himself ready to conduct anywhere so long
as one of his own works was included in the programme: his fee would be 1,000
marks in Germany, and 1,000 florins (2,000 kronen) elsewhere.[1] Instead of
having to solicit engagements, he now considered himself able to set his own
terms. He would in any case have to be very selective in his acceptance of
offers because of the onerous nature of his post, which compelled him to
restrict his absences to a minimum.

The 1903 season was particularly busy, and after his trip to Wiesbaden in
January, Mahler stayed in Vienna until the spring. On 30 March, several days
after the première of *Louise*, he left for the Polish city of Lemberg (today Lvov),[2]
which in those days was part of Austrian Galicia. The Philharmonic Orchestra
there had invited him to conduct the last two subscription concerts of the
season, one of which was to include his First Symphony. As usual, the thirteen-
hour train journey was torture for him:[3] 'It is really terrible to remain cooped up

---

[1] *Bayrische Staatsbibliothek*, undated. In the same letter, Mahler asked Salter to convey his apologies to
the American impresario Wolfsohn. When Salter introduced Wolfsohn to Mahler in Krefeld, Mahler had
brushed him aside, mistaking him for an autograph-hunter. Mahler said that he was willing to accept an offer
from Wolfsohn.

[2] Lemberg (Lvov) had belonged to Poland for four centuries. In 1907 it had 180,000 inhabitants; the
fourth-largest Polish city in 1939, it is now the fourth-largest city in Ukraine. The University, founded in
1661, is the oldest in the ex-Soviet Union after Vilnius. The Lyczakowski Cemetery is one of the most
beautiful in Europe: *Frankfurter Allgemeine Zeitung* (19 May 1990).

[3] Mahler left Vienna on 30 Mar. at 7.50 a.m. and arrived at 8.45 p.m. (KMI).

hour after hour amid this horrible stench of coal smoke! If only we had reached the stage when I should no longer have to travel all the time for my work! . . . <u>Seven more hours</u> to go! I feel like jumping out of the window and throwing myself under the wheels.'[4] The last part of the journey was even worse. Mahler had an 'indescribably' severe attack of migraine followed by nausea. On arriving in Lemberg, his sole desire was to get to his hotel and shut himself up in a darkened room. He was dismayed to find a delegation of the principal members of the Philharmonic committee waiting for him on the platform: the conductor, director, concert-master, and secretary. In honour of his arrival they had hired a superb landau, but Mahler, 'eyes rolling in pain' and scarcely able to speak, stubbornly refused to climb inside. With hardly a word, he set off on foot as quickly as possible, the four astonished Poles trailing behind him. The station was a long way out, and it took the strange procession three-quarters of an hour to reach the Hotel George, in the very centre of the town. Mahler took abrupt leave of his entourage and went straight to bed after searching for the aspirin tablets which his 'clever' chambermaid, Poldi, had packed away so carefully that he couldn't find them.

The next morning he woke refreshed, and with a ravenous appetite. When he arrived at the rehearsal and mounted the podium, he was surprised to be greeted by a fanfare of trumpets and kettledrums. During the first session, in which he conducted his First Symphony, he found the orchestra eager, 'well-prepared', and better than he expected, although at times he found himself wondering, 'in a cold sweat': 'Where do people keep their ears and their hearts if they can't understand this?' Afterwards, he went on a tour of the city, which he found full of character. But he was highly amused by the Polish Jews 'who run around here like the dogs elsewhere' and in a letter to Alma he exclaimed: 'My God! So I am supposed to be related to these people! I can't tell you how absurd racial theories seem to me in the face of such evidence!'[5]

Several passages (deleted by Alma in the version published by her much later) show that she was going through a new period of uncertainty about herself and her husband. She must have alluded to these doubts in one of her letters to him, for on 2 April, he replied: 'What are these mysterious hints of yours? . . . What depresses you so? What are these "minor matters" that have become "major matters"? Will you never leave yourself in peace?' He went on to mention two of his favourite authors, the philosopher Theodor Fechner, whose *Zend-Avesta* he was rereading[6] and 'who brings back to my mind, like a dear

---

[4] From an undated and unpubl. letter to Alma written on 30 Mar. (AMS).

[5] This statement has aroused many comments. It has been taken as evidence of hidden 'anti-Semitic' feelings in Mahler. However, it must be remembered that the vast majority of Viennese Jews at this time favoured assimilation and furthermore that, as someone whose childhood had been spent as a member of a small German-speaking Jewish minority in Czech territory, Mahler could have little in common with the Yiddish-speaking East European Jews (*Ostjuden*). Theodor Herzl himself expressed similar views in the 1890s.

[6] Concerning Gustav Theodor Fechner (1801–87), see above Vol. i, Chap. 7. Fechner was a scientist as well as an idealistic philosopher and pioneer in psychophysics. He conceived of a highly animistic universe,

familiar face, things I knew, saw, and experienced myself long ago', and the poet Friedrich Rückert.

Strange how Fechner feels and sees things in a Rückertish way; they are two very similar people and one aspect of myself makes a third to go with them. How few people know anything about either of <u>those</u> two! . . . For you it will mean a <u>great deal</u> once you understand it. Then you will be able to rid yourself of many futile concerns which prevent you from seeing clearly. One senses in your letter how bottled up you feel, and hence tormented and frustrated. How little my example seems to have taught you! What is the use of Paulsen[7] and all the prophets if you always get involved in such rubbish (*Quark*)? . . . Independence is an empty word if you haven't achieved <u>inner freedom</u>. But that is something you can only do for yourself. So help me, and make a little effort to educate yourself.

Such was the tone Mahler took when he wanted to calm Alma by affecting not to take her distress too seriously.
   'You find my letters too cheerful?' he wrote the following day.

Must I pull as long a face as you? Shame on you, you cheeky thing (*Fratz*)! One must make the most of what one has and save one's grieving (*Weltschmerz*) for the real suffering of this world. If I didn't do that myself, I would mope and moan all day long and come home as thin as a rake! Instead I go about cheerfully, do my work, look forward to next Sunday—and so on. It's no pleasure to travel all over the place just for the sake of money, without even knowing where I can keep warm. It is so cold here, even in the inns and cafés, even in the hotel restaurant. Let my example teach you to bear up under the inevitable, Luxi.[8]

   In Lemberg, everything was going well, and Mahler found nothing at first to complain of apart from the cold and the incessant rain. The Philharmonic had already given over a hundred concerts, and Mahler was amazed to find himself famous so far away from Vienna. Everyone called him 'Herr Direktor' and 'put themselves at my disposal, to such an extent that I am embarrassed'.

his animism including even plants and stars. He rejected the notion of an a priori concept of God and sought to replace it by a pragmatic notion of God as we sense him in the world and within us. His special contribution to psychology lies in his renewed investigation into the relationship of body and soul. His influence on Mahler was tremendous and it endured until the end of his life. Fechner's main works are *Über das höchste Gut* (1848), *Elemente der Psychophysic* (1860), and *Vorschule der Ästhetik* (1876). In 1835, Fechner reviewed Rückert's *Gesammelte Gedichte* in the *Blättern für literarische Unterhaltung* and called his poetry 'the poetry of the colourful, changing present, of living, surging existence in all its rich and enriching relationships and symbols around us and within us'. Fechner undoubtedly appreciated Rückert's mystic pantheism, which was closely related to his own, as already defined by Gustav Pfizer, who, as early as 1837, wrote: 'The basic perspective of that system being the life-permeatedness, soul-inspiredness, indeed godliness of the universe, or: the omnipresence of God, not merely posited theoretically as a dogma, but perceived as something living, reconciling and soul-endowing.' (See Stefan Bodo Würffel, 'Und Lieb und Leid! Und Traum und Welt! Gustav Mahlers Textwahl und Textbehandlung', in M. T. Vogt, ed., *Das Gustav-Mahler-Fest Hamburg 1989* (Bärenreiter, Kassel, 1991).)

   [7] Friedrich Paulsen (1848–1908), a German philosopher who wrote *System der Ethik* (1889), *Schopenhauer, Hamlet, Mephistopheles* (1900), etc.

   [8] Undated letter, written from Lvov on 3 Apr. The second unpubl. half of this letter mentions Max Staegemann, the director of the Leipzig Theatre, who was then in Vienna for a visit (AMS).

The public was clearly 'music-hungry', and more serious in their approach than the Viennese. After the second rehearsal, Mahler went to the Opera, where he saw Puccini's *Tosca* for the first time, 'admirably performed for a provincial city', under the baton of Francesco Spetrino.[9] 'But the work itself!' he wrote to Alma.

In the first act, papal procession with continuous clanging of bells (which had to be specially ordered from Italy). Second act: one man screams horribly under torture, while another is stabbed with a pointed breadknife. Third act: again a deafening clanging of bells, ding! dong!, with a view from a citadel over all Rome while somebody is shot by a firing squad. I got up and left before the guns went off. Need I say that the whole thing is once again very much a skilful showpiece (*Meistermacherwerk*); these days, every shoemaker's apprentice is good at orchestration.[10]

In the same letter, Mahler said some hard things about some of the 'ideas' that Alma had liked to talk about with him before their marriage: in particular about Nietzsche, Maeterlinck, and occultism.

I enclose a cutting from the *Berliner Tageblatt* showing what Helmholtz thinks on a question that greatly bothers Miss Perrin[11] (who used to have much more sense). It is impossible to comment more concisely and more to the point on all this rubbish and related matters (Maeterlinck etc.) than he does. All these idiots, every one of them, are busy looking for strange happenings ('There are more things in heaven and earth than are dreamt of in your philosophy', etc.) as if hunting fleas. 'Occultism': what a lovely word they've invented. But what is there which, in the metaphysical sense, is not obscure, occult, secret? Muddle-headed. I'm sure they gulp down Nietzsche for breakfast and Maeterlinck for dinner, and never read a word of sense written by anyone else![12]

Rehearsals continued, but the atmosphere was no longer so good. Conditions were 'primitive', and the orchestra 'undisciplined in spite of its good will', but he was still quite cheerful. However, 'one needs the stomach of an ostrich (*Straussenmagen*)[13] to be a guest conductor and the menu here is drawn up to win applause (*applaustreibend*).' Judging by the rehearsals the *Leonore* Overture was being played for the first time in Lemberg. How could he have dreamt of proposing his Symphony? But it was too late to withdraw it, he had to do his best. 'Moreover, who can say where a lost seed may fall?' Further, his

---

[9] Spetrino was then the conductor at the Lemberg Opera. Mahler soon engaged him for the Vienna Opera.

[10] This explains why Mahler, who fully appreciated Puccini's *La Bohème*, could never bring himself to produce *Tosca* at the Hofoper. The work was not given there until 26 Jan. 1910, some two years after he left Vienna.

[11] This refers to Jenny Perrin, Mahler's former pupil (see above Vol. i, Chap. 7, and App. 1, on Mahler's First Symphony). Concerning the physicist Hermann von Helmholtz, see above, Vol. i, Chap. 7.

[12] Mahler was obviously moving further and further away from any materialist philosophy, and especially from Nietzsche's *Herrenmoral* (superman morality).

[13] Probably a play on words by Mahler to indicate Richard Strauss's readiness to swallow anything when guest-conducting, especially since the word 'applaustreibend', often used by Strauss, had become a part of Mahler's own vocabulary.

fee of 1,000 florins was one more step on the road to independence.[14] Otherwise his life was divided between the loftiest contemplation and the worldliest turmoil (at the rehearsals).

Mahler's impression of Lemberg worsened with the daily walks he persisted in taking in driving rain. He found the city 'repulsive'. 'Today I took a marvellous stroll during which I had some strange experiences (from the point of view of landscape and human psychology, I hasten to add, for God knows what you will imagine otherwise!). I shall tell you about it when we're together.' The idea of eating elsewhere than in his hotel was unthinkable, so grimy were the general conditions. None the less, on the day of the second concert he dined at the home of the local theatre director, 'the prototype of the provincial theatre director who tried to conceal his poverty under ostentatious display'. The man lived in a former theatre whose foyer he had made his living-room:

Everywhere, there were columns and niches decorated with fans, photographs, laurel wreaths, and other trophies of every hue, piled up as I've never seen. . . . His wife had to sing for me; I think he has hopes of future business relations. I suppose this is why I had to accept the invitation, and the public award of a laurel wreath (was it silver or gold? I don't know). You can imagine the face I made!

The programme of the first concert on 2 April started with Beethoven's *Leonore* Overture No. 3, followed by Mahler's own First Symphony, Berlioz's *Carnaval romain*, and Wagner's *Tannhäuser* Overture. A religious hush prevailed during the performance of Mahler's symphony. The audience's attention never wandered, and initial reserve turned to enthusiasm by the end of the performance.[15] Mahler received an unprecedented request to repeat his symphony at the start of the next concert on the 4th,[16] after which came Beethoven's Seventh and two Wagner Preludes, to *Tristan* and *Meistersinger*. Mahler's triumph was soon confirmed by the press: in the *Gazetta Lwowska*, Seweryn Berson[17] noted that the hall was far from full, but added that Mahler had won over 'the entire audience' and established himself as 'one of the most celebrated of living conductors, an artist capable of interpreting with equal perfection the depth of Beethoven, the finesse of Berlioz or the fire of Wagner'. With no programme, the 'hypermodernism' of his symphony was disconcerting in spite of 'marvellous passages' and Mahler's striking orchestral mastery. As a conductor, Mahler had shown what the Lemberg orchestra was capable of after a single week of rehearsal. His 'masterly' interpretations had deeply impressed

[14] This sentence confirms Alma Mahler's references to her husband's debts. However, Knud Martner suggests that Mahler might also have been saving money so as to retire from the Opera.

[15] According to the *Musikalisches Wochenblatt*, Mahler was called back 6 times to acknowledge applause after the First Symphony.

[16] The originally planned programme included Mahler's Fourth Symphony.

[17] Seweryn Berson (1858–1917), a lawyer and music critic, had been a pupil of Heinrich Urban in Berlin. A lawyer in Cracow and Lemberg, he was also the composer of an operetta, incidental theatre music and several orchestral works.

the Lemberg public and the second concert had been the high point of the entire season.[18]

Likewise, the correspondent from the *Musikalisches Wochenblatt* felt Mahler had 'performed miracles', particularly in the breakneck tempo at which he took the Finale of Beethoven's Seventh. But he scarcely mentioned Mahler's First, so that Adolf Chybimsky, correspondent of the Berlin magazine *Die Musik*, accused the local critics of 'arrogance and narrowmindedness' in more or less ignoring Mahler the composer (as they had done with Strauss two months earlier). Thus Mahler must have wondered once again whether his magnetism as a conductor was not responsible for a victory that his own works could never achieve on their own. However, other conductors were ready to perform his symphonies in his absence.[19] Julius Buths[20] conducted the Second Symphony on 2 April in Düsseldorf. Mahler wrote to him shortly before the performance with some advice on how to interpret it. Buths felt there should be a short pause between the fourth and fifth movements, and Mahler 'marvelled at the soundness of his intuition'. For he, too, thought the second pause necessary[21] (although it was not indicated in the score) in addition to the one prescribed at the beginning, following the opening Allegro, to avoid too abrupt a contrast.[22]

After the concert, the Düsseldorf press was unusually favourable, even though the *Volksblatt* called Mahler 'a powerfully and emotionally stimulated interpreter (*Nachempfinder*)'[23] of what others have felt rather than an 'inventor or someone who creates and builds on his own feelings'. For once, Mahler was not accused of eclecticism, although the anonymous critic thought he had discovered many 'reminiscences'.[24] 'Mahler,' he wrote, 'is a master at appropriating other people's means of expression'. The *Düsseldorfer Zeitung*, on the other hand, despite certain reservations, called the symphony 'the work of a great master'[25] and the *Generalanzeiger* went even further. Its critic felt that he could not 'do justice, in the space of a concert review, to this inspired, gigantic

[18] Berson admitted that Mahler had been granted more rehearsals than was customary for local directors. Mahler left Lemberg immediately after the second concert (0.45 a.m.) and reached Vienna the next day at 3.37 p.m., in time to conduct *Louise* that evening (KMI).

[19] e.g. during 1903 in Magdeburg, Elberfeld, Nuremberg, and Bremen.

[20] Julius Buths (1851–1920), conductor, composer, and director of the Düsseldorf Conservatory, conducted several of Mahler's symphonies during the Niederrheinische Musikfeste regularly held in Düsseldorf.

[21] Possibly to emphasize the link between the first movement and the Finale. It should however be noted that an overwhelming majority of conductors today rule out the pause between the last two movements.

[22] The Andante, an 'intermezzo', a 'remembrance of things past', seemed to him to interrupt 'the course of events'. In the same letter, he advises Buths not to have the chorus stand up when it begins to sing in the Finale, but only when the basses sing 'Mit Flügeln'. He advised him to place the horns and kettledrums backstage for the 'Last Trump', and the trumpets even further back. Mahler considered this passage 'the most difficult in the entire work'. He apologized for not attending the concert, due to take place on 3 Apr., when he would still be in Lemberg (MBR1, no. 293; MBR2, no. 315). In Sept., Mahler sent Buths his Fourth Symphony for a performance in Nov.

[23] Someone who has empathy for the feelings of others.

[24] In particular from *Parsifal*, *Siegfried*, and Liszt's *Héroïde funèbre*.

[25] The 2 Apr. concert, conducted by Julius Buths in the Kaisersaale der Städtischen Tonhalle, was performed with two soloists, the Berlin soprano Elfriede Götte and the Hamburg contralto Else Bengell.

work of genius'. Like Beethoven, and more than Strauss, Mahler put 'lived experience into music'. 'Mahler, therefore, seems more impulsive and satisfies the layman more quickly than the reflective Strauss, especially since by comparison he shows a striking preference for the melodic element: symphony and rhapsody (symphonic poetry) meet in both composers'. But 'Mahler's greatness lies elsewhere':

Since the death of Brahms the symphony has seemed to be orphaned. But Mahler's talent has independently found a new path. The artist, child of his time, trusting perhaps unconsciously to his own individuality and strength, has felt an inner necessity to take the symphony down into the warm, pulsating life of the people. Drawing on his own, rich emotions he has forced the old, aristocratic form to ally itself with the spirit, inherent in modern art, that bridges all kinds of class differences. Mahler uses all those things that music lovers of all social classes have always prized—enchanting melodies, insinuating rhythms, lively harmonic sequences, dance, song, the mixture of instruments and voices—to breathe new life into the traditionally accepted symphony, though taking considerable liberties with its basic structure. If Brahms is an academic, and Strauss a philosopher, Mahler deserves the honorary title of modern symphonist for the people. His achievement in bringing artistic expression into accord with the contemporary view of life, in striving for greater intimacy between the artist and the layman, like a new Stolzing or, even better, a Hans Sachs; in revealing the essence of all music-making, which is human experience translated into sound; surely this achievement in itself is great enough to commend his symphonies to public favour.

Thus as early as 1903, there were a few enlightened listeners brave enough to express an admiration which was far from being shared by the majority. Without changing one word, this article could have been written today. Seven months later, in the same city, the Fourth Symphony met with far greater reservations. The *Volksblatt* called it an 'imperfect and unsatisfactory' work, a 'cynical cacophony' of 'grimaces and gimmicks', composed by an 'hysterical romanticist,' 'a mosaic by an eclectic, an Icarus whose wings fail to carry him up into the sunlit realms of divine music'. The reluctant applause was 'clear proof' of the audience's distaste for the work.[26]

Mahler's letters to Alma during his stay in Lemberg indicate that they were planning to spend the Easter holidays together in Abbazia on the Adriatic coast, as they were henceforth to do each year until 1906.[27] A brief reference in Alma's private diary shows that they made the trip: 'Abbazia. A happy, free time. One small disturbance brought about by one of my attacks of moodiness!'[28] The five days on the Adriatic Sea brought Mahler only a short respite.

[26] The rest of the programme for the 5 Nov. concert under Julius Buths included Schubert's 'Unfinished' Symphony and six Lieder from Hugo Wolf's *Italienisches Liederbuch* performed by Marcella Pregi, who was also soloist for the Fourth Symphony.

[27] The Vienna Opera was closed every year at Easter from Tuesday to Saturday; in 1903, from 7 to 11 Apr., Easter Sunday falling on 12 Apr.

[28] AMT, TS 9. The date given is 1904, but 7 and 8 Apr. correspond only to the Easter of 1903. Alma adds: 'Consciousness could be represented within the mind like a hemisphere. The more profoundly a man comes to know his inner self, the wider spread the rays of his thought. And the deeper he goes, the more his inner

However, towards the end of May he and Alma were able to get away from Vienna to nearby Göding (Hodonin) near the border between Moravia and Austria, where their friends Fritz and Emmy Redlich[29] had a sugar factory and a small château. After a few days Mahler returned to Vienna and wrote to Alma that he had once again been racked by an attack of migraine which he had cured, in typical Mahler fashion, by walking furiously for an hour in the Schwarzenberg garden. 'I am now much better. I was beginning to be afraid that I would not be able to write to you, so that to-morrow, in the course of the day, you would have been convinced that I no longer love you and that you were born only to be unhappy.' Mahler's main task in Vienna during those days was to prepare the new Lefler and Brioschi production of *Aida*, the second act of which, as seen above, was performed on 27 April for a royal gala.[30]

The Opera season was practically over when Mahler the composer-conductor left Vienna again in response to a new invitation. His triumph in Krefeld at the preceding festival had induced Richard Strauss and the Allgemeiner Deutscher Musikverein Committee of which Strauss was now president to include the Second Symphony in the programme of the 1903 Festival, which was to take place in Basel between 12 and 15 June.[31] The venue for the final concert was quite exceptional: it was to be held in the Swiss city's famous Gothic Cathedral. Pleased and at the same time perplexed when he learnt this, Mahler had immediately written to Strauss:

I was flabbergasted by your news. Thank you very much for your really friendly concern for me. I really think that you will make a famous composer out of me too. I have already given instructions that the score and all the orchestra parts should be sent to the Basel address mentioned. But I would now like to know in greater detail about the particular circumstances of the performance—who are going to be in the orchestra and the chorus—nature and duration of the rehearsals—on the venue (what does Cathedral (*Münster*) mean? I hope it is not a church with dull, resonant acoustics)? To whom must I turn in these matters? Now you must be kind enough (now that you've got involved in this) to go on helping your tormentor. . . . In any case will there be time, in the middle of so much else, to rehearse the chorus in my Symphony?[32]

The Basel Festival was to last four days (12 to 15 June) and to include six concerts. On the 14th, Liszt's *Graner Mass* was to be performed, also in the Cathedral, but as usual few works of lasting interest were included in the programme. The only well-known composers besides Mahler were Richard Strauss (*Hymne* Op. 16 No. 2, for 16-part unaccompanied chorus), Max von

life is lit up. Oh! If only I could talk, talk (*reden*) in a comprehensible way!' (The last sentence was later crossed out.)

[29] Concerning the Redlichs, see Vol. iii, Chap. 4.   [30] AMM1. 295; AMM2. 264.

[31] Several letters were exchanged between Strauss and Max von Schillings during the preparation of the 1903 festival (see Roswitha Schlatterer, *Richard Strauss—Max von Schillings: Ein Briefwechsel* (W. Ludwig, Pfaffenhofen, 1987), 84 and 88–96).

[32] Recently discovered letter to Strauss, in spring 1903, Collection of Dr Jubert, Paris, *Bulletin de l'Association Gustav Mahler* (Nov. 1983, Paris) and MSB (ed. 1988), 233.

Schillings (*Hexenlied* Op. 15, for narrator and orchestra), Frederick Delius (*Nachtlied Zarathustras*), Emile Jaques-Dalcroze (Overture to *Sancho*) and Ernest Bloch.[33] Mahler very much wanted Alma to attend the Basel concert, as she had the previous year. Consequently, it was arranged that she would join him during the rehearsals. On the way to Basel, Mahler had planned to stop in Frankfurt, to audition some singers who had been recommended for the Vienna Opera.[34] His main object had been to attend the performance, on 6 June, of Goldmark's fifth opera, *Götz von Berlichingen*, which Bruno Walter had warmly recommended several months before. Mahler had read the score and did not share his disciple's enthusiasm, so he had planned to come and hear for himself. However, his trip was cancelled because he was anxious to attend the guest appearances in Vienna of the bass Otto Goritz. Goldmark had then reached the age of 73 and he could not endure being thought of solely as the composer of *Die Königin von Saba*. In a letter written in the middle of June, he told Mahler he was sorry that he had missed the Frankfurt performances and accused him of having 'changed his mind' concerning the new opera. He acknowledged that the performances it had received so far had not been particularly successful, but claimed that the quality of the Frankfurt performance had been absolutely lamentable. Besides, he was revising the score, 'correcting certain faults' and adding 'some passages full of atmosphere' which were bound, in his opinion, to have a 'tremendous effect'. He begged Mahler not to put off his consent, saying: 'I'm no longer young, I no longer have the time to wait.'[35]

As usual, Mahler took no notice either of the old composer's pleas or of his supporters' reproaches in the press, and certainly not of those of Ludwig Karpath, who was Goldmark's nephew and who wrote in 1904, in the magazine *Bühne und Welt*:

The man who expects the highest esteem from others for his works has the audacity to refuse a new Goldmark opera! One might perhaps hold it less against another opera director, but the composer Gustav Mahler could never be excused for such an offence were it not that a great artist must be forgiven for a good many things.[36]

The truth was that Mahler was rejecting the opera on purely artistic grounds. He himself had never liked Goldmark's music or considered him as an impor-

---

[33] Delius's work, *Nachtlied Zarathustras*, for baritone, chorus, and orchestra, was based on the same Nietzsche poem that Mahler had used in the fourth movement of his Third Symphony. It was later to be inserted in *A Mass of Life*. The festival also included works by the Berlin composer Friedrich Koch (1862–1923) (movements 1, 3, and 4 from *Das Sonnenlied*, for soli, chorus, organ, and orchestra), Hans Schilling-Ziemssen (*Ew'ges Licht*), Hans Huber (*Caenis* for alto solo, organ, and orchestra), Fritz Volbach (*Raffael*, *Stimmungsbilder*, Op. 26 for Chorus, Orchestra and Organ), Rudolf Louis (*Proteus*, Symphonic Fantasy for Orchestra and Organ), Hans Rössler, Ernst Boehe (*Aus Odysseus Fahrten*, Op. 6, for large orchestra).

[34] Eventually, Mahler went straight from Vienna to Basel. The singers he had planned to hear in Frankfurt were a coloratura named A. Schirocky, a baritone called Richard Breitenfeld (who had sung as a guest in Vienna in 1899), and a married couple named Hensel. The wife, Elsa Hensel-Schweitzer, was to sing as a guest at the Hofoper in 1904 (HOA, Z.1647, letters of 14, 15, and 26 May, and of 2 June 1903).

[35] HOA, Z.636/1903.   [36] 'Gustav Mahler und die Wiener Oper', *Bühne und Welt*, 6 (June 1904).

tant composer, and there were many who agreed with him. As early as 1911, the *Bilder-Atlas zur Musikgeschichte*[37] found Goldmark's style 'lacking in originality' and 'greatness of conception', despite his exceptional 'gift for colour'. Julius Korngold, in his memoirs, writes that Goldmark himself had at first had misgivings about setting Goethe's play to music, and called his opera *Szenen aus Götz von Berlichingen*. Mahler, it seems, objected both to the libretto and the *Homophonie* of the score and wanted to spare Goldmark a disappointment.[38] The future proved him right when his successor, Felix Weingartner, failed spectacularly with his Vienna production of the opera in 1910. Goldmark was so hurt by Mahler's refusal that he would not send him his new opera *Das Wintermärchen*. Julius Korngold agreed to act as intermediary and gave Mahler the score. Mahler finally consented to produce the work but it was only performed shortly after his departure for New York. For Goldmark it was no doubt only small compensation that Mahler decided to revive the *Königin*, with a new and particularly brilliant cast,[39] also restoring a duet at the end of Act IV which had previously always been cut.[40]

In Basel, the local conductor Hermann Suter[41] had offered to conduct as many orchestral and even choral rehearsals as Mahler thought necessary before his arrival. Mahler wrote back that a single brief rehearsal would be enough for the chorus, but that he would need, immediately on arrival, a separate full working session for the 'backstage' instrumental group required for the Finale:

In the concert hall, the positioning of the brass instruments in the separate group for the 'Last Trump' is usually hard to achieve for they have to be 'backstage' on different sides. How will it be in a church? I think this sort of thing could be set up with great effect. In any case, at some point or other, perhaps during a break, I must hold a brief preliminary rehearsal with the extra instruments in question in order to avoid losing time with the full orchestra present. In this passage, the rhythm is very difficult, and so is the ensemble playing. The desired sound can be achieved only by a long process of trial and error.[42]

---

[37] Schuster & Leffler, Berlin, 1911.   [38] KIW 97.

[39] Including Leo Slezak, who had finally agreed to learn the leading role.

[40] MBR1, no. 291 and 292; MBR2, no. 325 and 326, 2 and 6 Dec. 1903. The revival opened on 25 May 1904. In one of his letters Mahler advised Goldmark to accept the Frankfurt Opera's proposals for the performance of his *Merlin*, which implies that he himself had no intention of reviving this work, whose libretto was by Siegfried Lipiner.

[41] Hermann Suter (1870–1926), organist, composer, and conductor, was the son of a Basel organist. He studied in his native city (under Hans Huber) and later in Stuttgart and Leipzig (under Carl Reinecke) and returned to Basel where he became choral conductor and organist in 1894. In 1902 he was appointed conductor of the Symphony Concerts of the Allgemeine Musikgesellschaft and was appointed principal conductor for the 1903 Contemporary Festival of the Allgemeiner Deutscher Musikverein. From 1918 to 1921, he directed the Basel Conservatory. He wrote music of all kinds, including a Violin Concerto which is still occasionally performed.

[42] A typed copy of Mahler's letter to Suter dated 27 May 1903 was sent to Bruno Walter in 1956 by Richard Menzel, who received it as a gift from Suter's widow. Mahler also gives precious advice as to the performance of the string passages marked *Hälfte* (one half) and *getheilt* (divided). In the first case, the notes are to be played by the front stands, with the other players joining in at the 'tutti'. In the second, the left and right stands must each play a separate part.

Upon his arrival, Mahler was delighted with the 'attentive and eager' orchestra and the 'excellent' chorus, both carefully prepared by Suter.[43] His old friend Arnold Berliner had arrived from Berlin and a group of family and friends, comprised of Alma, Anna and Carl Moll, and Kolo Moser arrived for the last rehearsal.[44] Moll and Moser[45] had planned their trip to Basel to hear the performance and, at the same time, to meet Ferdinand Hodler[46] and Cuno Amiet, two Swiss painters who were to be exhibited at the Secession the following year. Thus Mahler had expert company for his visit to the famous Basel Museum: the letter he wrote to Justi about it mentions not only the world-famous Holbeins but also the Boecklins.

All the members of the Allgemeiner Deutscher Musikverein were gathered in the Swiss city for the festival when Mahler arrived. According to Wilhelm Raupp, Max von Schillings's biographer, the two composers met in Basel on this occasion, though they must have encountered each other previously, if only because both were friends of Richard Strauss, who did not attend the 1903 Festival.[47] Hans Pfitzner, the hero of the German nationalistic and post-romantic conservative school, also attended the festival, but left the day Mahler's symphony was performed, fearing no doubt that he would dislike it, a surprising breach of manners since he was then still hoping that Mahler would put on his *Rose vom Liebesgarten* in Vienna, but he was as well-known for his lack of tact as for his music. His excuse, as stated in a letter to Alma, with whom he henceforth corresponded regularly, was that he had to see his aged parents before taking up his new post at the Theater des Westens in Berlin.[48]

Max von Schillings[49] also cherished the hope that Mahler would perform one

---

[43] Letter to Justi, 14 June 1903 (RWO).

[44] An unpubl. card sent by Mahler to Alma from the Drei König Hotel in Basel asks her to meet him there. It is also signed by Arnold Berliner.

[45] A Weinberger score of the Second Symphony in the Stanford Library, Calif., carries the following dedication in Mahler's handwriting: 'To my dear friend Kolo Moser, in memory of the sunny days in Basel. Vienna, Christmas 1903. G.M.'

[46] Ferdinand Hodler (1853–1918), born in Berne, was a famous landscape and portrait painter and lithographer who had many friends among the French Impressionists. An indefatigable draughtsman, he started as a symbolist, under the influence of Corot, Puvis de Chavannes, and Degas. He later became one of the leaders of the expressionist movement and helped revive monumental painting.

[47] The long report which Schillings sent Strauss on 25 June concerning the Basel Festival leaves no doubt as to Strauss's absence (see below, the Strauss–Schillings correspondence in which this letter is included). Schillings informs Strauss that the performance of his *Hymnus* for a cappella chorus had been 'unforgettable' in the cathedral and had to be repeated.

[48] Letter to Alma, 30 June 1903. A typewritten copy of these letters is among Alma's papers (UPL). Pfitzner also refused Alma's invitation to Maiernigg on the grounds that it was too far from Berlin.

[49] Born in Düren, in the Rhineland, in 1868, Max (von) Schillings was influenced by Wagner in his youth, but also considered himself the direct heir to the 'classic German tradition of Beethoven and Hummel', having studied with Joseph Braumbach, himself a former student of Ferdinand Hiller. Schillings later completed his education in Munich, where he studied law, philosophy, and art history until Richard Strauss persuaded him to start a musical career. He left Bavaria in 1908 and became Generalmusikdirektor in Stuttgart. In 1918 he moved to Berlin, where he was appointed Intendant of the Staatsoper and then the Städtische Oper from 1932 until he died the following year. Schillings was a close friend of Pfitzner to whom he had been introduced in 1896 in Bayreuth by Humperdinck. He became a fervent supporter of Pfitzner's music and convinced Ernst von Possart to put on *Palestrina* in Berlin (1919). Both composers thought of

of his operas, *Ingwelde* or *Der Pfeifertag*, at the Hofoper. He was nevertheless an ardent anti-Semite and no admirer of Mahler as a composer, as witness the letter he had written some years before to Hermann Behn, whose enthusiasm for Mahler's music had survived the cooling of their relations after the latter's departure from Hamburg. 'I remain a stranger to Mahler's work, perhaps I am too much of a sentimental fool (*Gemütsduseler*) and not enough a man of reason (*Verstandsmensch*) to approach this gigantically conceived work from within.' Schillings's biographer, Wilhelm Raupp, promptly ascribed his hero's lack of understanding to Mahler's Jewishness, but it should be remembered that his biography was published in 1935, during the early and perhaps ideologically most virulent years of Nazism. In 1900, probably in Munich, Schillings first heard Mahler's Second Symphony, 'for which in many respects I cannot withhold my admiration, even if it affected me deeply only at certain moments'.[50] Raupp notes that

the works of the Jew Gustav Mahler were for Max Schillings the centre of a new musical wave whose everwidening circles will finally engulf pure German musical feeling (*Empfinden*). The far-sighted German had by then already realized what German scholars were to establish several decades later. [Rudolf] Louis reached the fully justified conclusion that 'Mahler's nine symphonies have not succeeded in convincing the world of Mahler's creative calling, while the creativity of Strauss and Reger are unquestioned by their most adamant opponents! . . .' Moser[51] sums up the result of his critical enquiry by labelling Mahler 'A worthy and ultimately incomprehensible guest (in the world of German art), but by no means a great German musician!' The insight which these distinguished connoisseurs managed to gain only through long experience, Max von Schillings had already acquired by 1902, thanks to the trustworthy instinct of his essentially German conception of the world and of art. To his utterly sincere sensibility, the craving for grandiose effect in these works was offensive, as was their lack of deep and real feeling, their pompous emptiness.

Even making allowance for the biographer's deliberate expressions of anti-Semitism, these remarks undoubtedly reflect Schillings's basic attitude towards Mahler. He was obviously furious, as many others were, to see the Vienna Opera in Mahler's hands and to find that Mahler was completely indifferent to his operas. 'Who is *imperator omnipotentissimus et absolutus*?' he wrote to Behn some time later, once again concerning the Second Symphony.

themselves as the true heirs to the German romantic tradition. Schillings wrote many orchestral works and four operas, the last of which, *Mona Lisa*, was frequently performed in Germany before the Second World War. His style and language always remained firmly conservative, with some post-romantic tendencies, so that he is often grouped with the second rank of pre-First World War composers like Ludwig Thuille, Siegmund von Hausegger, and Siegfried Wagner. In his day he was considered by many to be a leading figure. At the première of *Feuersnot*, Pauline Strauss went so far as to accuse her husband of having 'stolen it all from Maxi' (see above, Chap. 13).

[50] Wilhelm Raupp, *Max von Schillings* (Hanseatischer Verlag, Hamburg, 1935), 69.
[51] Hans Joachim Moser (1889–1967), a well-known musicologist and teacher, composer and singer, spent most of his life in his native city, Berlin. The best-known of his numerous publications, *Geschichte der deutschen Musik*, was completed and published in 1920 when he was 30.

Who cast us to the ground, shattered our bones, rent our hearts? You know very well! Your Mahler! It is impossible to sum up in two words a work which appears so serious and has all the attributes of the most exalted nobility. Only one thing: if I could be convinced that what I heard were honest and heartfelt, then I would cry out: 'Let all peoples go unto him, stand in awe and offer up their prayers!' Despite sincere efforts to convince myself I was wrong, I felt I was confronting a huge modern Meyerbeer of the symphony. If I am mistaken and if the wildly jubilant audiences are right, then one thing is certain. The twilight of all Germanic art is descending, and our Valhalla is already in flames, for against this Semite, a Strauss hasn't a chance![52]

Such were Schillings's pre-Nazi prejudices. They were undoubtedly shared by many musical conservatives in Germany and were exacerbated if anything by the fact that the public had at last obviously begun to appreciate Mahler's music. Under these circumstances, it is no surprise that Schillings's encounter with Mahler was anything but cordial. In another letter to Behn, the German composer tells of their first meeting in Basel in 1903:

Friend Mahler's C minor Symphony—you know what I think and feel about him. The way Mahler edged around me was highly comical! What can he possibly think of me? After the *Hexenlied*, he spoke to me warmly and sincerely. He had obviously been truly impressed. Later on he kept running away from me, avoided introducing his wife to me, etc. However, let's wait and see; an important fellow (*ein ganzer Kerl*) like him has the right to be unfair to others.[53]

Such is human nature. Any composer whose work has been rejected feels that he has been unjustly treated and can never believe that the unfavourable artistic judgement of others could possibly be objective. For Schillings, Mahler's short-sightedness and malevolence was simply further evidence of Jewish hostility to German art ('Aryan' art as it soon became).

The 1903 programme in Basel included works by twenty-five composers, a good third of whom—Max Schillings, Ernest Boehe, Guido Peters, Klaus Pringsheim, Max Reger, Rudolf Louis, Ermanno Wolf-Ferrari—belonged to the so called 'Munich School'. Felix Draeseke's new String Quintet, Paul Scheinpflug's Piano Quartet, Hans Huber's Trio, Josef Lauber's Violin Sonata were among the new chamber works performed. The larger works included Fritz Volbach's *Stimmungsbilder*, Hans Schilling-Zeimssen's *Ew'ges Licht*, Friedrich Koch's *Sonnenlied*, Hans Huber's *Caenis*, all with solo voice or chorus. None of these works earned anything like the acclaim which greeted Mahler's Second Symphony, and it is easy to imagine the disappointment and frustration of the fellow composers who witnessed Mahler's triumph in the Cathedral. The anti-Semite Rudolf Louis, who had had his *Proteus*, a Fantasy for Organ and Orchestra, performed, wrote two different reviews in the *Münchner Neueste Nachrichten*. In the first he questioned Mahler's right to have

[52] Raupp, *Schillings*, 84.
[53] Ibid. 63 ff., 69, 83 ff., 91, 104 ff. Schillings did at least conduct one Mahler symphony, the Second, on 9 Mar. 1910.

had his symphony included in the programme at all, since it had meant that there was no room for such a great contemporary masterpiece as the Symphony *Das Leben ein Traum* by Friedrich Klose. In his second, Louis reluctantly conceded that Mahler had towered head and shoulders above the whole festival, but as a conductor, not as a composer! His praise went not to the symphony itself but to the two Basel choruses, which 'had surpassed themselves'.[54] Fortunately there were other witnesses to Mahler's triumph. One of them was the Swiss composer Ernest Bloch, who had two movements from one of his own First Symphony performed that year.[55] A Jew himself, he could not be suspected of prejudice against Mahler on those grounds. However, Mahler had been described to him as 'a musical Voltaire', a 'sceptic', and an 'ironist', especially after the world première of the Fourth in Munich.

'I knew nothing about his work then,' wrote Bloch the following year,

except the thousand stories it had given rise to, and it was in this frame of mind that I heard the Second Symphony for the first time last June in Basel, during the annual festival of German composers. It was in the picturesque setting of the ancient cathedral jutting up from a hilltop on the banks of the Rhine that this titanic work was revealed to me, a work that can be counted among the greatest offspring of the human genius.

For me, the impression will never be effaced, nor will it be for anyone fortunate enough to have shared in it. The excited audience, transported and oblivious of its surroundings, gave the composer an enthusiastic ovation; it sensed the presence of an independent work, a work coming from the heart which spoke directly to their hearts. Since then I've studied Herr Mahler's symphony closely, and analysis only confirms my first spontaneous outbursts.

I've pointed out that Herr Mahler is not a member of any sect. Nevertheless he is a dedicated enemy of the 'explanatory programme', and rightly so, since at the moment this is a plague throughout Germany! You can't hear a Beethoven symphony any more without being handed leaflets that classify and dissect the most minor thematic idea. But if Mahler can be considered in this regard—and in a good many others—as the antithesis of Richard Strauss, he must not be looked on as the apostle of some other doctrine. His totally expressive music is a way of creating life, of crystallizing joy, suffering, all the human sentiments in which it excels, and when it needs to be more explicit, it has recourse to words sung by a solo voice or a chorus.

Herr Mahler is accused of lacking originality. This comment, which at first glance seems to have some truth in it, quickly evaporates under closer scrutiny. Melodically, his work owes something to Schubert, Wagner, and especially Bruckner; yet its general line is incontestably personal. I would say the same of his counterpoint, of his original way of juxtaposing themes, of his rich, robust and vibrant harmony. An interesting and completely new aspect is the effect he obtains by the graduated contrast of dynamic intensities. Moreover, Mahler's orchestration is prodigious. Everything sounds, everything is clear, nothing is written for the eye. It would take a treatise to analyze his methods and the immense effects he gets from the kettledrums and trumpets in particular.

[54] *Münchner Neueste Nachrichten*, 198 (24 June 1903).
[55] This is undoubtedly Bloch's Symphony in C sharp minor of 1901–2.

The most immediately striking aspect of his work from a technical viewpoint is the clarity and simplicity of his means. Herr Mahler is like a philosopher-poet who employs a very simple vocabulary, ordinary words that everyone can understand immediately; no specialist's jargon! And from this language, with its classical clarity, its impeccably structured logic, which throughout gives an impression of imperious necessity, Mahler's powerful thought emerges all the more easily because there is no barrier between it and the audience; the emotions are immediately touched; form is vanquished by thought, it disappears, one no longer thinks in terms of words—of notes—but directly experiences the composer's ideas. It's like being in the presence of a gifted actor; he makes us forget his talent but can bring tears to our eyes.

While Herr Mahler could not care less about astounding the experts or scandalising respectable people, while he does not waste time trying to achieve childish effects with outlandish accents or tricks of orchestration, his armoury is none the poorer for that! He is familiar with every modern resource, but he does not feel obliged to use them; he does not tie himself to any tyrannical system, but he can make them do what he wants and uses them at the appropriate moment whenever the internal sense demands it; for in his work everything is subordinated to that thought, everything must contribute to that aim; during the two hours his symphony lasts, there is never a single moment of boredom or lassitude.

From the first notes, its tragic grandeur seizes and penetrates us: it is as though we were face to face with the great problems of life or death . . . What he paints for us is not a struggle, but a portrait of implacable and savage Destiny. Now and then a glimmer of hope can be perceived, vague bliss seen through a veil of suffering . . . But the heavy bass rhythms persist obstinately, turning into a slow, muffled funeral march, with intermittent blasts on distant trumpets, *pp*, answered by the dull, muted roll of the kettledrums . . .

The prodigious finale which ends this gigantic work defies description; nothing can convey an idea of its power. Everything culminates in an impression of supernatural grandeur that glorifies the philosophical idea which inspired Mahler: the Resurrection . . .

While Mahler's work made an enormous impression on me, I will not forget the demeanour of the audience as it emerged from the cathedral: it wasn't arguing, it wasn't theorizing, it wasn't analysing! No, it had just lived life itself, relived its joys, its sorrows, its weariness and its hopes. And, without worrying whether Monsieur Mahler's philosophy was Christian or pantheist, it went on its way touched, stronger, happier, more powerful![56]

All witnesses concur with Bloch that the Basel concert was one of the greatest triumphs in Mahler's career, and that the immense vaults of the illuminated cathedral enhanced the work's majesty and grandeur. According to Alma, feelings ran so high and the applause was so thunderous that no one was surprised when the Czech composer-conductor Oscar Nedbal[57] knelt before

[56] *Le Courrier musical* (1 July 1904).

[57] Oscar Nedbal (1874–1930) was born in Tabor, Bohemia, and studied composition at the Prague Conservatory and with Josef Bohuslav Förster and Dvořák. He began his career as the viola player in the Bohemian Quartet, and toured in 1905 with the Czech Philharmonic, accompanying the violinist Jan Kubelik. Conductor of the Vienna Tonkünstler Orchestra and of the Volksoper between 1907 and 1918, he

Mahler, kissed his hand, and promised him that he would perform the work in Prague before the year was out.[58] Instead of putting a damper on the occasion, as it had done so many times before, the press universally echoed Mahler's triumph. The *Basler Nachrichten* congratulated him and his 'divine simplicity' for reviving the audience's interest in music after five more or less mediocre concerts. Though the anonymous critic admitted that he had trouble grasping the 'inspirational links' between the different movements of the work, he wholeheartedly applauded its 'harmonic clarity', its 'architectural transparence', its 'unaffected sentiment', and, in spite of the abruptness of contrasts its 'economy of sound colour'. The *National Zeitung* critic also praised Mahler's 'inspired' conducting, though he preferred the luminous simplicity of the middle movements to the grandiose style and titanic proportions of the first and last movements. He wondered whether music could really cope with subjects as vast as those of the Finale.

Mahler had often been accused of eclecticism, but this time the monthly *Schweizerische Musik-Zeitung* showed rare insight in pointing out that, while originality had never been considered a virtue in the eighteenth century, people had now become obsessed with it. What mattered most, it said, was that Mahler 'felt his music deeply' and composed with 'remarkable sureness, particularly in his instrumentation', that 'his art defied all description', and that the effect of the Finale, an 'architectural masterpiece', was overwhelming. In *Die Musik* and the *Musikalisches Wochenblatt*, the Munich critic Arthur Seidl,[59] a convinced Mahlerian, lavishly praised the cathedral concert. Although he had already heard the Second Symphony five times elsewhere, this 'peerless, inspired, ideal work', this 'epic in the form of a symphony', now in Basel he had appreciated for the first time its 'inexhaustible richness' and 'incomparable grandeur'. His joy was 'indescribable'. If only, Seidl wrote, those who regarded Mahler as no more than a 'sorcerer' and a 'skilful stage director' could possess, as he did, 'an expressiveness that goes straight to the heart' and 'authentic, true feeling'. This symphony, he went on, reflected a 'struggle for a universal vision', it was an 'inner experience', music composed with 'his heart blood and spiritual fervour'. Its sacred character found a perfect setting in the cathedral since it expressed profound religious feeling, an 'ardent yearning toward light, purity and truth, an ideal Christian culture'. 'One's soul vibrated with the music, and, stirred to the depths, one could only thank its creator for such an overwhelming impression

directed the National Theatre of Bratislava from 1929 until his suicide in 1930. Nedbal wrote one opera, six operettas, and six ballets, as well as concert works.

[58] Alma went to Prague for the concert. See below.

[59] See above Vol. i, Chap. 8, the biography of this writer and music critic from Leipzig who had sided with Mahler and defended his compositions since the Hamburg years. In July 1903 Schillings attempted to persuade Strauss to break with Seidl, who had tried to slander him as belonging to a 'clique' of Munich composers in the magazine *Freistadt* (see below and also Schlötterer, *Richard Strauss–Max von Schillings*, 93 ff.). Seidl also attacked Rudolf Louis concerning the article mentioned above in which Louis blamed the Allgemeiner Musikverein for including Mahler's Second Symphony in the programme of the Festival. Strauss flatly turned down Schillings' request.

and such a gripping artistic revelation after hearing much that was dubious in previous [programme items].'[60]

In his account of the Basel Festival, Seidl began by attacking those Munich conservatives who had written about the 'débâcle', the 'threatening collapse', the 'decadence' of German music. He also observed that he himself had heard the furious protests made openly against the loud ovations accorded to Mahler, 'whereas applause in the Cathedral was normally strictly frowned upon, and accordingly(?)[61] withheld from the others!' But Seidl's main target was Rudolf Louis.

When someone . . . who had every reason to be pleased with the faultless performance his own 'Protean' work has received before an august assembly, gets a swollen head and dares to allege that G. Mahler's monumental creation, the shining beacon of the whole Festival and its crowning conclusion, was an 'unjustified' choice which could have been done without, then we can only say that . . . this is a case of a pygmy taking on a giant. . . . And we must and can reject any responsibility for such discreditable reflexions, for we didn't start this quarrel. Indeed, the day after the memorable experience we heard important voices ranging from Switzerland right up to Finland who expressed utter indignation—thus confirming our own feelings in this matter—that it could ever have been considered possible to insult Mahler publicly in the press by hanging a warning label 'Cacophony!' round his neck.

To conclude, Seidl points out the manner in which Strauss himself had steadfastly supported Mahler 'often against the obstinate opposition of some of his closest friends and comrades in arms' and had from the beginning 'honestly admired him', and also ceaselessly defended a 'by no means harmless rival'.[62] For years Mahler had fought for recognition. Now that success had come, jealousy and envy were trying by every possible means to prove that it had been achieved by false pretences and by the lavishness of the orchestral and vocal resources used.

Mahler's Basel triumph, coming on the heels of his Krefeld success, made his star shine even brighter in the galaxy of German music. For some time he had been dissatisfied with his former publishers, the printer Waldheim Eberle, and the firms Joseph Weinberger and Doblinger, who distributed his works. So he decided to break with them. He asked his old friend and lawyer, Emil

---

[60] In the *Musikalisches Wochenblatt* Seidl also praised the verses Mahler added to Klopstock's ode. The concert took place on Monday, 15 June, at 7.00 p.m. with the soprano Marie Knüpfer-Egli and the alto Hermine Kittel as soloists, with the Basel choirs, the Gesangverein and the Liedertafel, and a 110-musician orchestra, that of Basel supplemented with musicians from Meiningen and Lausanne. The Basel concertmaster fell ill and was replaced at the last moment by another from Berlin, Karl Klinger. The Festival issue of *Die Musik* mentions Ernestine Schumann-Heink as soloist, but its version of the programme was completely different from the one actually given. The Second Symphony was in fact preceded by Friedrich Koch's *Das Sonnenlied* for chorus and orchestra and Hans Schilling-Ziemssen's *Ew'ges Licht*, Op. 7, for tenor and orchestra, both conducted by Hermann Suter.

[61] The ironic question mark is in the original German version.

[62] Arthur Seidl, 'Die "Münchner Schule" im *Allgemeinen Deutschen Musik-Verein*', *Freistatt, Kritische Wochenschrift für Politik, Literatur und Kunst*, 5: 27 (July 1903), 526 ff.

Freund for advice on the legal problems involved,[63] and on Strauss's recommendation, since he had joined the Society of German Composers, he
decided to try his luck with a German publisher. It was Gustav Brecher, the
conductor who had been engaged for a short while at the Hofoper,[64] who
brought the Fifth Symphony to the attention of the big Leipzig firm, C. F. Peters.
Brecher also encouraged Mahler at the end of the 1902–3 season to get advice
about the possibility of breaking with Waldheim Eberle and Weinberger.[65] The
earliest documents in Mahler's file in Peters's archives show that there had
been an initial contact some years before. One of them is a short draft in
Mahler's own hand listing his compositions, i.e. his first three symphonies,[66] the
Lieder eines fahrenden Gesellen and 'numerous *Humoresken*'. Mahler requested
'no fee, but only a share in the profits'. He also explained that the Second
Symphony had been printed but that the rights were still available. Nothing
came of this initial exchange of letters.

In 1903 it was very flattering for Mahler to receive an offer from Peters, who
were not only one of the world's largest and best known music publishing firms
but one of the oldest in Germany. The name dated back to 1814, when Carl
Friedrich Peters bought the Leipzig 'Bureau de Musique' firm Hoffmeister &
Kühnel (founded in 1800) which included an engraving works and a shop
selling printed music and instruments. Since then it had published a great
number of classical works, expanding its activities in 1863 when Max
Abraham, a doctor at law, became first partner and in 1880 sole owner. It was
Abraham who added the first contemporary name to the Peters catalogue:
Edvard Grieg, whose complete works were published by 'Edition Peters'. Soon
Grieg was joined by others: Brahms, Bruch, Liszt, Moszkowski, Sinding, and
Wagner. After Abraham's death in 1900, his nephew, Henri Hinrichsen (1868–
1942), the firm's sales manager for nine years, took over as director. He
expanded the catalogue with contemporary scores by Bruckner, Strauss, Hugo
Wolf, Reger, Pfitzner, and later Arnold Schoenberg.[67] So it was Hinrichsen who,

[63] See the undated letter (probably written in Maiernigg in Aug. 1903) where Mahler asks Emil Freund
for advice about the tactical position he should adopt (MBR1, no. 235; MBR2, no. 317 and Sotheby's
catalogue of 29 Nov. 1985, no. 147).

[64] See above, Chap. 10. The following pages owe a great deal to Eberhardt Klemm's article 'Zur
Geschichte der Fünften Symphonie von Gustav Mahler', *Jahrbuch Peters 1979* (Peters, Leipzig, 1980).

[65] Letters from Gustav Brecher to Henri Hinrichsen of 23 July and 23 Aug. 1903. Brecher had a long-
standing family friendship with Hinrichsen, who valued him as an adviser and colleague (Klemm, 'Zur
Geschichte', 52). In the first letter, Brecher passed on Bruno Walter's judgement of the new work, which he
considered to be 'tremendously powerful and attractive'. On 22 Oct. Brecher wrote a third letter to
Hinrichsen 'congratulating him on the success of his new business baby (*Verlagskind*)' after the Cologne
première. On the whole, he added, it emerged clearly from the reviews that 'despite an apparently cautious
reception, this was a success achieved by an original and profoundly important work'.

[66] The Third is referred to as being in F. As mentioned before, Mahler hesitated for a long time over its
tonality. The list probably dates from 1896–7, since it does not include the Fourth Symphony. Fritz
Ollendorf's reply, in Peters's name, dates from 29 Apr. 1897. It said that the firm could not, for the time being,
take on any new composers (Klemm, 'Zur Geschichte', 21).

[67] Peters was confiscated by the Nazi government after the Kristallnacht in 1938. Hinrichsen, a Jew,
died in the gaschambers of Auschwitz in Sept. 1942. His sons, Max (1901–65) and Walter (1909–69)

on Gustav Brecher's suggestion, approached Mahler to discuss publication of the Fifth Symphony. On the very day when he received Gustav Brecher's letter, he wrote to Mahler offering to publish the new symphony and asking what the conditions would be.

Mahler's first letters to the firm are simply answers to Hinrichsen, who wanted to meet him to discuss the financial terms of the contract. On 30 September 1903, after discussing the matter with Freund, Mahler finally set a price: 10,000 gulden or florins (that is 20,000 kronen or 16,000 marks) for the publishing rights[68]—a considerable sum since until recently he had been a relatively little known composer and his basic annual salary at the Opera now (without taking the generous allowances into account) amounted to 7,000 gulden. The amount he asked shows how his reputation had grown during the previous fourteen months.[69] On 2 October, Hinrichsen accepted, though declaring himself 'surprised by the amount',[70] especially as the contract covered only publication and distribution rights, the performance rights remaining with the composer in accordance with the rules of the Genossenschaft Deutscher Tonsetzer, of which both Mahler and Hinrichsen were now members. As seen above, the Genossenschaft was under fierce attack from other publishing firms as well as from impresarios and from the big German symphonic concert societies. In one of his first letters to the director of Peters, Mahler testified to the confidence he placed in him and wrote that he was highly honoured 'to entrust the fate of one of my works to a publishing house of your importance'. Hinrichsen answered immediately that it was an honour for him too: otherwise he would not have agreed to pay such an unusually high fee. Mahler signed the definitive contract on 4 October, giving Peters exclusive rights 'to publish, reproduce and distribute' the Fifth Symphony. He ended by thanking Hinrichsen for conducting and concluding the negotiations so rapidly, expressing the hope that the expectations placed in himself and his work would not be disappointed.

In early November Peters sent Mahler two pages of preliminary proofs which he approved and returned, also giving his assent to the simultaneous publication of two different piano transcriptions by Otto Singer,[71] for two hands and

founded publishing firms in London and New York. The original firm moved from Leipzig to Frankfurt in 1950.

[68] Mahler ceded to Peters, in exchange for the 10,000 gulden, the 'right to publish, reproduce and market (*Recht der Veröffentlichung, der Vervielfältigung und des Vertriebs*) the Fifth Symphony'.

[69] Mahler's undated letter to Freund was written in Aug. 1903 (MBR1, no. 235; MBR2, no. 317); he wrote to Hinrichsen on 30 Sept.

[70] Yet Strauss had just refused 30,000 marks (*c*.37,000 kronen) from Peters for his *Symphonia Domestica*, obtaining 35,000 for it from Bote & Bock. It seems an enormous sum, but he was then the most famous German composer, and the work, first performed in New York, had had considerable and immediate success. Two years later, Mahler asked for, and got, 15,000 gulden (30,000 kronen or 24,000 marks) from Kahnt for the Sixth. In 1912 Schoenberg was only paid 600 marks by Peters for his *Five Pieces for Orchestra*, Op. 15.

[71] Eberhardt Klemm ('Zur Geschichte', 53) has publ. the correspondence exchanged early in 1904 between Peters and Otto Singer concerning the piano-duet transcription. Singer (1863–1931) did all the piano reductions in the Peters catalogue. His four-hand transcription came out in Aug. 1904, the pocket

for four hands. He insisted on postponing the printing of the orchestral parts until after the première, to allow him, if necessary, to correct minor details of orchestration after rehearsals and performance. 'Concerning the première,' he added,

I would like to ask your advice (as where it should take place). I am afraid of big-city newspapers because on occasions like these they usually dream up some catchword which is then unthinkingly repeated a thousand times over. It took me years, for instance, to recover from the misunderstandings circulated by the Berlin papers. What do you think would be most in your and my interest under the present circumstances?[72]

In a letter written around this time to Arthur Seidl, Mahler mentioned Nikisch's offer to première the work in Berlin but added that he had unpleasant memories of the Prussian capital because the Berlin press had so severely ridiculed his symphonies that they 'were never played anywhere else in Germany'.[73] But in spite of his views about the critics, Mahler was aware that the essential thing was that his music should be heard and talked about. One day when talking with his old friend Josef Bohuslav Förster he summarized his thoughts on the subject: 'Let them tear me to pieces, but at least let them play me.'[74] That same day he showed Förster the instrument he had ordered from Paris for the rehearsals of *Louise*, the celesta, and played him several chords so that he could admire 'the exquisite sound of the middle register and the velvety softness of the bottom octave', adding: 'In my new piece, there will be a celesta!'[75]

Mahler had exerted himself to the utmost in Basel, as usual when he rehearsed and conducted one of his works, particularly before an audience of professionals. Thus he was now looking forward to several weeks of peace in which he could compose. Now that the world was beginning at last to take notice of him, and that he had become one of the leading figures in contemporary music, he was becoming more than ever aware of the limited size of his output as a composer. He knew he could only maintain the impetus of his growing reputation if he added more works to his oeuvre. No personal circumstances seem to explain the sinister mood of most of the music he wrote during

---

score in Sept. 1904, and the orchestral parts in Nov. and Dec. The transcription for two pianos was eventually made by August Stradal in 1914. See below, Vol. iii, Chap. 1 and App. 1, the long and involved story of the different versions of the Fifth Symphony.

[72] There are altogether 53 letters from Mahler, dating from 1896 to 1907, in Peters's archives. I obtained copies of them in 1976 thanks to the former director of the Leipzig firm, Bernard Pachnicke. All are numbered and most have been dated by an employee of the firm. The draft mentioned above is no. 2. The letters which I have quoted from or summarized date from 30 July (no. 3), 19 Sept. (no. 4), 30 Sept. (no. 5), 4 Oct. (no. 6), 15 Oct. (no. 7), Nov. (no. 8). Hinrichsen's letters of 23 Apr., 30 July, 2 Oct., 12 and 14 Oct. 1903 were also first publ. by Klemm, 'Zur Geschichte'.

[73] MBR1, no. 211; MBR2, no. 211, Sept. 1903.   [74] JFP 695.

[75] Ibid. Mahler kept his word, using a celesta not only in the Sixth Symphony but also in the Eighth, *Das Lied von der Erde*, the *Rückert-Lieder*, and the last of the *Kindertotenlieder*. However, the 1901 *Rückert-Lied* 'Ich atmet' einen linden duft' introduced a celesta. Mahler might have first heard the instrument during his trip to Paris in 1900. Or could it have been inserted later in the orchestration of the song?

the summer of 1903. However, when he wrote his happiest music at Alt-Aussee in 1899, he was in fact living in constant dread of having to tear himself away and return to the capital and the "hard labour" of the Vienna Opera, thus demonstrating that the current circumstances of his daily life seldom exerted a direct influence on the nature and mood of his music.

Anyone hoping to find in Alma's diary a detailed record of Mahler's summers, such as Natalie kept in her 'Mahleriana', will be severely disappointed. Alma's accounts are laconic and unsystematic. Although Mahler devoted most of his energy that summer to his Sixth Symphony, Alma unfortunately left practically no details about its composition. Thus, the chronology of the various movements is not easy to ascertain. According to Alma 'two movements . . . were finished in the summer and the schema of the others had taken final shape in his head'. The Andante in E flat, which was perhaps intended at this time as the second movement, is an island of peace amid the storms of the other movements. It reflects the tranquillity of Maiernigg and the woods surrounding the *Häuschen*. On the other hand, the first movement, with its relentless march rhythm, is a powerful statement of man's defiance of his destiny. The whole symphony is imbued with this same pessimistic yet assertive spirit, the very antithesis of the wistful resignation of the Funeral March in the Fifth. Here is a merciless struggle against fate, with death the only possible outcome. An unpublished card which Mahler wrote to Alma asking her to bring along the second and third movements seems to imply that the initial Allegro was also probably composed, at least in part, in 1903.[76] Thus it was probably in the summer of 1903 that Mahler one day came down from the *Häuschen*, as Alma reports, and said to her: 'I've tried to personify you in a theme. I don't know if I've succeeded, but you will have to be content with it!' Thus, in the battle he was to launch in the symphony, Alma was to be his ally, as she was to be involved consciously as well as unconsciously in all Mahler's struggles. In this particular instance she appears in the form of an ascending F major theme, impetuous and wilful, giving the opening Allegro an element of vigorous optimism found nowhere else in the work.

Mahler was not wrong in seeing Alma as his ally in their common struggle against fate. But they were also struggling against each other in the predicament they had created for themselves when they chose each other as partners for life. It is not enough to say that they were in love; they were indispensable to each other, but they were also aware of what separated them, when it did not actually set them at loggerheads. Alma openly despised her role as mother and housewife, in Vienna as well as in Maiernigg. 'We were terribly jealous of each other,' she writes in one of the early versions of her *Erinnerungen*. 'I was jealous of his past, which I naïvely imagined full of guilty pleasures. And he was jealous of my future. . .'. While Gustav wanted silence when he returned from the Opera, she longed for music. Other members of the family, such as

---

[76] This card is dated 11 July 1904 (see App. 1). To Bruno Walter, Mahler spoke of summer 1903 as 'the most productive summer in my life' (see below).

Anna Moll and Justi, often watched performances from Mahler's box, but Alma had to stay at home to take care of their child and play the role of 'wife of Gustav Mahler, the despised, sick and debt-ridden musician'. Her obsession deepened until it troubled her sleep. She described seeing Mahler in her dreams:

I'm waiting for my Gustav. Before me I see an endless succession of rooms. The last door opens suddenly and he comes towards me with his white face, black hair and black eyes, in his dressing gown. I see him open all the doors and walk across the long rooms, and as he is opening one door, I see him still by the previous door, making the same turning movement . . . as if he were his own double . . . he approaches . . . panic! I wake up!

I am brought some drawings to choose from. Without anyone noticing, Gustav punctures them one after the other with his pen. Horrified at the damage, I ask him why he is doing it. He doesn't hear me and thoughtfully whistles a melody. Suddenly he draws one of his legs up until his knee is touching his stomach, then the other leg, and so struts around the room. The doors open and little men appear from everywhere. The room is alive with them. I want to go to my own room: I open the door, but they come out of there too. I want to scream, I wake up.

A large green snake with long legs suddenly forces its way up inside me. I pull at its tail. It won't come out. I ring for the chambermaid. She pulls with all her strength. Suddenly she gets hold of it. It slides out with all my inner organs in its mouth. Now I am hollow and empty like a wrecked ship.[77]

The significance of these nightmares seems clear enough. Alma's deepest nature continually rebelled against Mahler's physical and mental domination. All achievement, all personal fulfilment were prohibited by the permanent and obsessive presence of a husband whose real or phantom image pursued her everywhere, even into her most secret self. The last nightmare appears to express Alma's frustration even more clearly. It seemed to her that the maternity resulting from sex with Mahler had mutilated her and deprived her of one of her basic needs: not only musical creation, but steady contacts and relationships with a group of close friends, and especially with men whom she usually bewitched with her wit and seductive feminity. But these interpretations can only be partial. The images strike the imagination, but in the absence of the person who is having the dreams (the dreamer), their meaning cannot be interpreted, in the Freudian sense of the term, as in an analysis. After ten years of hard work and research Freud came to the following conclusion:

Every dream reveals itself as psychical structure which has a meaning. . . . [It] has to be treated backward in the memory from the pathological idea to treating the dream itself as a symptom. . . . [Our] procedure for interpreting enables us to disclose a latent content in them which is of far greater significance than their manifest one. . . . It employs interpretation *en détail* and not *en masse*. [The dreamer should be] reporting

[77] AMT, 29 May 1903.

whatever comes into his head and not being misled, for instance, into suppressing an idea because it strikes him as unimportant or irrelevant or because it seems to him meaningless.[78]

Only then can one attempt to understand how and why the dream has transformed or transferred the latent content into manifest content.

Further analysis of Alma's dreams would surely yield rich dividends as to her real state of mind at that time, but the fact remains that, since she had received Mahler's long letter during their engagement, she had not dared to compose again. On 15 June (or July) she wrote:[79]

I've played over my compositions. I always feel THAT, THAT, THAT! I long to produce something again at last! The role I impose on myself is only an illusion. I love MY art! Everything I played today is so utterly familiar! If only I had Zemlinsky to work with! BUT THERE IS JEALOUSY! I have no one! These last days, tears. Justi reappears like a ghost in Gustav's heart! I thought she was dead to him. In my deepest self, I don't feel unhappy! Not at all! It's just that . . . something is missing . . . I could also stand more visible love from Gustav!

Towards the end of July, Mahler took a 'lightning trip' to Toblach, Schluderbach, and Dölsach. But it rained a lot, and he sat in cafés plagued by flies,[80] reading Helmoltz and cursing his bad luck. In Maiernigg, Alma was bored as usual by her 'splendid isolation' and the monotony of her summer routine. Not only did Mahler spend most of his time composing, but she did not share his enthusiasm for hiking, swimming, bicycling, and rowing. They often played duets on the piano, notably Brahms's chamber works. At other times Mahler romped with his baby daughter Maria (nicknamed Putzi), sang songs to her, and carried her in his arms, running and dancing about as if he himself were a child again. Almost every day he still took Alma on walks in the forest around the Wörthersee. One day, Alma received the first printed copy of Pfitzner's First Quartet. It was dedicated to her and had been given its first performance six months earlier in Vienna by the Rosé Quartet.[81] She hurried to

[78] Sigmund Freud, *The Interpretation of Dreams*, trans. James Strachey (Avon Books, New York, 1965), 35, 133, 196, 136, 133. This passage was called to my attention by the French psychoanalyst, Dr Jacqueline Duchêne.
[79] The date at the beginning of this passage in Alma's diary (15 June), of which the original seems to have vanished, is inaccurate because she was then with Mahler at the Festival in Basel for the performance of his Second Symphony. It was probably written a month later in Maiernigg, while Mahler was working up in the *Häuschen*, since 'Juni' and 'Juli' differ in German by only one letter.
[80] Unpubl. postcards of 21 and 24 July to Alma from Toblach and Dölsach near Lienz.
[81] BWB 66. Pfitzner's First Quartet was publ. by Max Brockhaus in Wiesbaden in autumn 1903. As regards Pfitzner, Mahler was no doubt coming under the combined influence of Alma and Walter, whose enthusiasm for Pfitzner was undiminished. Together with Alma and Arnold Rosé, he had heard Walter play the Quartet in a piano transcription on 18 Dec. 1902. Rosé had immediately decided to give the Viennese first performance on 13 Jan. 1903 (see BWB 66). Earlier, on 2 Dec. Walter wrote to Pfitzner about a long talk he had had with Mahler who could now be considered his 'keenest supporter *(dein eifrigster Freund)*'. Mahler himself had recommended the Quartet to Rosé, saying: 'You can accept a work by Pfitzner unseen, on my recommendation alone.' As for *Die Rose*, Mahler would have put it on if the libretto had been even halfway acceptable (letters from Bruno Walter to Pfitzner, ÖNB).

41. Anna von Mildenburg

42. Selma Kurz

43. Laura Hilgermann as Venus

44. Marie Gutheil-Schoder as Carmen   45. Marie Gutheil-Schoder as Louise

46 (*left*). Rita Michalek

47 (*above*). Berta Förster-Lauterer as Carmen

48. Erik Schmedes as Tristan (costume by Roller)

49. Herman Winkelmann as Siegmund

50 (*above*). Theodor Reichmann as Hans Sachs

51 (*right*). Richard Mayr as Pogner

52. Wilhelm Hesch

53. Leo Slezak (1911)

54. Leopold Demuth

55. Alfred Roller (portrait in oils by Walter Hempel) (© Direktion der Museen der Stadt Wien)

56 (*left*). Alfred, Fürst von Montenuovo

57 (*above*). Alois Przistaupinsky, Mahler's secretary at the Hofoper

58. Mahler in action (caricature by Fritz Gareis, *Luzifer*, 6)

59. 'Urgently needed invention by Kikeriki' (*Kikeriki*, 8 February 1900)

60. 'Start of the season at the Hofoper: it's perfectly all right,
Jahn's holding the reins, but it's better that Mahler should be
holding the whip' (Der Floh, 35 (1897))

61. Mahler taking over from the prostrate Jahn (caricature by
Theo Zasche, 1897)

62. 'Epidemic among Hofoper singers: they are probably suffering from Mahleria' (*Kikeriki*, 5 May 1904). 'Boorish behaviour' blows in from the sky while 'Jewish arrogance' clambers out of the water

63. 'Latest progress in naturalistic art: modern painters paint as they see. Why shouldn't modern musicians compose as they hear?' (*Kikeriki*, 17 April 1902)

64. Theo Zasche, 'The modern orchestra: much ado about nothing' (*Illustrirtes Wiener Extrablatt*, 88 (31 March 1907), 24)

65. 'Change of Manage-
    ment at the Opera:
    Director Mahler at
    work' (*Humoristische
    Blätter*, 17 October
    1897)

66 (*below left*). 'The new
    broom in Viennese
    artistic life' (*Kikeriki*,
    21 October 1897)

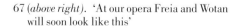

67 (*above right*). 'At our opera Freia and Wotan
    will soon look like this'

68 (*right*). 'Director Mahler on the podium and
    at the altar' (*Der Floh*, 12 (1902), 4)

69. Max Kalbeck, music critic of the *Neues Wiener Tagblatt* (Bildarchiv des Österreichischen Nationalbibliotheks)

70. Robert Hirschfeld (1867-1914), music critic of the *Wiener Abendpost*, with his wife and son

71. Richard Heuberger (1850-1914), music critic of the *Neue Freie Presse* (Bildarchiv des Österreichischen Nationalbibliotheks)

72. Ludwig Karpath, music critic of the *Neues Wiener Tagblatt* (Bildarchiv des Österreichischen Nationalbibliotheks)

73. The young Richard
    Strauss (*c.*1898)

74. The Musikverein; Mahler conducted the Philharmonic concerts here (1898-1901)

75. Max Oppenheimer, *The Symphony* (oil painting, 1923):
Mahler conducting the Vienna Philharmonic

76. Mahler (silhouette
by Hans Schliessmann)

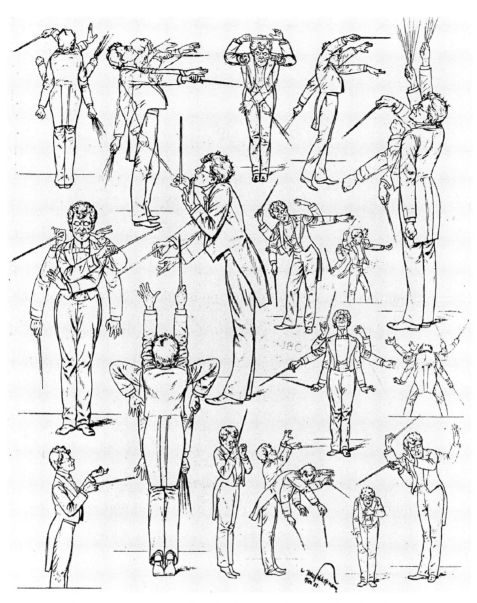

77. 'A hypermodern conductor: Kapellmeister Kappelmann conducts his *Sinfonia diabolica*' (caricature by Hans Schliessmann; *Fliegende Blätter*, March 1901)

78. Roller's sketches for *Tristan*, Act I (opening)

79. Roller's sketches for *Tristan*, Act I (end)

80. Roller's sketches for *Tristan*, Act II (opening)

81. Roller's sketches for *Tristan*, Act II (end)

82. Four sketches of Mahler by
    Emil Orlik (?Prague, 1903)

83. 'Megalomania: soon it won't just be a question of "improving" Beethoven's symphonies, but of
    making suitable changes to his monument' (*Kikeriki*, 4 March 1900)

the *Häuschen* to show it to Mahler, and later recorded that he came down two hours later proclaiming: 'It's a masterpiece'.[82]

As usual, Mahler's creative work had to be interrupted at the end of August. He brought back to Vienna the finished movements of his Sixth Symphony, partly copied in Alma's hand.[83] 'I suppose you know that Mahler has finished a Fifth?' Bruno Walter wrote to Pfitzner. 'The summer has already resulted in half a Sixth and lots more too; in his own words it has been the most productive summer of his life.'[84] Back in Vienna on Friday the 28th after a long uncomfortable journey in an antiquated carriage (the train was held up for several hours), Mahler went straight to the Opera to make his presence felt. Immediately after his arrival he saw Arnold Rosé, Alfred Roller, and Bruno Walter; he lunched with two members of the Secession, Kolo Moser and Josef Hoffmann, and went for a walk with Alfred Roller on the Leopoldsberg, where they drank tea and ate peaches while enjoying the wonderful view of Vienna.[85] The two friends came back to the Hohe Warte on foot and took a tram back to the Opera. As the apartment on the Auenbruggergasse was still closed, Theobald Pollak begged him to stay with him. However, Mahler decided to spend a few more days in the country and reserved a room at the Kahlenberg Hotel. It was an easy trip from there to the Opera. With Alma's birthday in prospect,[86] he combed Vienna in vain for a store open on a Sunday afternoon, and subsequently wrote to her: 'I hope that instead of an expensive gift you will welcome my most heartfelt greetings for tomorrow . . . What more can one give when he has already given all of himself? When you come we will take one of those lovely afternoon strolls in the Kärntnerstrasse and find something pretty for you!'

At the Kahlenberg Hotel, Mahler's two rooms were full of broken-down furniture upholstered in dirty velvet, but at least they afforded him splendid views of the Wienerwald and, at night, the city lights. On Sunday afternoon, he went to Vienna on foot and by tram and was greeted 'very affectionately' at the Opera by the Lord Chamberlain. After lunch with Pollak, followed by a long walk, he heard the first act of *Die Meistersinger* with a 'guest' soloist recommended by Bruno Walter[87] and then returned to Kahlenberg. 'You won't be

---

[82] In AMS, Alma claims that Pfitzner sent her the only copy of his MS, asking her to take good care of it, but she is mistaken. In fact Pfitzner, in a letter of 12 Mar. 1903 (ULP), asked her to accept the dedication of the work, and to return the MS, in exchange for which she would receive the first published score, which had just left the presses. Furthermore, in a letter written in 1946 to Alma, Pfitzner answers her request for a MS music page of his. He promises to send her one from his First Quartet, dedicated to her (letter dated 13 Oct. 1946, in *Pfitzner Briefe* (Hans Schneider, Tutzing, 1991), 1025).

[83] In a card sent from Vienna on the 28th which reached Klagenfurt on the 29th, Mahler wrote to Alma that he had been 'touched by the perfection of the copy when he saw it clean and finished before him'.

[84] BWB 66.

[85] Mahler was stung by a wasp and Roller bandaged his finger. This detail is important inasmuch as it helps date certain letters (see footnote below). In one of the first unpubl. cards Mahler sent Alma, he announced that he had found to his wonder and amazement that he weighed 70 kilos.

[86] 31 Aug.

[87] This refers to a performance on 30 Aug. with Peter Lordmann as Walther. On 1 Sept. a gala performance was given in honour of King Edward VII of England who was on an official visit to Vienna.

astonished, I hope, to learn that I feel your absence everywhere I go,' he wrote that evening to Alma, 'and that I think of you constantly. If only I had a word from you!' Although he had planned to move to Pollak's on Monday 31 August, so that he could stay until the final curtain every evening, Mahler spent several more days at the Kahlenberg because the hotel proprietor provided him with transportation to and from the Opera. He thus continued to enjoy the country air and the night-time silence. Every morning, he awoke before the other guests and breakfasted alone on the terrace, enjoying the splendid view. One day he lunched with Justi and Arnold, later commenting with affectionate irony in a letter to Alma on their parental enthusiasm over their infant son, Fredi.[88]

When Mahler left the Kahlenberg, he settled in nearby Hietzing instead of returning to Vienna. Alma threw a jealous tantrum that amused him: 'How could you imagine that I would stay at Hietzingerhof with Mildenburg! You know very well that she's lived for a year now across the street from Lipiner on the Gumpendorferstrasse! It was pointless to get so worked up.'[89] On 4 September Mahler returned to the capital to settle in the Auenbruggergasse apartment. He then left with Roller for the Semmering to meet Alma's train from Maiernigg.

The first public controversy of the Opera season concerned the lowering of the level of the orchestra pit, a project Mahler had ordered at the beginning of the summer, following the example of Bayreuth. His aim was twofold, to moderate slightly the volume of sound of the orchestra, thus allowing the singers to make themselves heard more easily, and to conceal the musicians' lamps from the audience.[90] Several years earlier, Mahler had fitted the lamps in the stage boxes, reserved for the Emperor and members of the court, with green silk shades, and later also those of the orchestra, but it soon became obvious that the pit floor would have to be lowered. A first step in that direction was taken early in January 1903: Mahler's original plan was to lower it by a metre and a half, but to install machinery to make it adjustable. In Mozart, for instance, the orchestra would be raised to the usual level, but he felt that in most of Wagner's late works the orchestra should be heard as though 'from a

---

[88] Alfred Rosé had been born on 11 Dec. 1902.

[89] This last letter, unpubl. and undated, was written on 4 Sept. 1903. Together with two earlier cards, it is now in the Moldenhauer archive at Spokane, Washington. Copies of the others have survived in AMS, but some of them are incomplete or incorrectly dated. The following is the proper chronology which Knud Martner helped me ascertain: card no. 1 (just before departure from Klagenfurt, 28 Aug., unpubl.); no. 2 (in the train from Klagenfurt to Vienna, 28 Aug., unpubl.); no. 3 (Kahlenberg, 29 Aug., wrongly dated 28; AMM1. 291; AMM2. 265); no. 4 (Vienna, 30 Aug.; AMM1. 386; AMM2. 334, wrongly dated 1907); no. 5 (undated: Vienna, 31 Aug./morning; AMM1. 291; AMM2. 266); no. 6 (31 Aug./evening: postmark Vienna, 1 Sept.; AMM1. 294; AMM2. 268); no. 7 (undated, Kahlenberg, 1 Sept.; AMM1. 388; AMM2. 329, wrongly dated 1907); no. 8 (unpubl., postmark Vienna, 1 Sept.); no. 9 (undated, Kahlenberg, 2 Sept.; AMM1. 292; AMM2. 267); no. 10 (unpubl., undated, Vienna, 4 Sept.).

[90] With the new opera-house the only miscalculation on the part of the architects was apparently the shallowness of the pit, which made the musicians visible to the audience, and made it difficult for the singers to make themselves heard above the orchestra. The pit had already been lowered shortly after the opening for both visual and acoustic reasons.

twilight distance' (*dämmeriger Ferne*) or 'from the lower depths'.[91] Work had started at the beginning of the summer but was interrupted because of a 'plinth' (*Gurte*) which no one wanted to take the responsibility of moving in case it was part of the foundation of a sustaining wall. Later it was discovered that the masonry in question had no structural function because of a previous architectural alteration.

Mahler gave animated explanations of what was going on to the critic of the *Fremden-Blatt* at the beginning of September:

As a matter of fact, I forgot to give you another reason for lowering the pit which has nothing to do with the acoustics for the artists. And it is an important reason! I am thinking of *Tristan und Isolde* and of the serious interference the electric lamps on the orchestra's music-stands inevitably cause for the stage lighting. However much we tried to create the right colour and intensity of lighting to match the atmosphere on the stage, the bright neutral beams from the orchestra lamps threatened to spoil it all.[92]

After the opening performance of the season on 18 August,[93] Karpath felt that the initial alterations had not affected the sound, but feared that a further lowering of the pit would be incompatible with the basic concept of the hall. Several other critics found all this an excellent excuse to renew their attacks on Mahler. They declared that the acoustics of the hall were 'muffled' and even 'distorted'. Even before returning to Vienna, Mahler had received several letters warning him of this press campaign, and as soon as he arrived he angrily accused Schalk and Wondra of being largely responsible for the affair, in which the musicians had also taken part because they were afraid that the deepened pit would be unsafe in case of fire. 'All the rumours about bad acoustics are nothing but stupid newspaper gossip,'[94] he wrote to Alma; a slight change in the seating of the players would put things right. He took advantage of a day off on 9 September to carry that out, and also to lower the pit still further.[95] A few days earlier, he had explained, again to the *Fremden-Blatt* critic:

I don't know what people find wrong with the orchestra . . . One person finds the sound too soft, another too loud, every so-called 'connoisseur' has some extremely 'sensitive', personal reaction. If I were to consult all these 'connoisseurs'! But I judge solely on the basis of my own impressions. Let me tell you, the orchestra is *excellently* placed; because the balance of the instruments has considerably improved, . . . so much so that I have wondered whether I should follow my original plan of lowering the orchestra

[91] However, Mahler felt that *Lohengrin*, and particularly the Prelude to Act III, required an orchestra raised to a normal level.

[92] *Fremden-Blatt* (6 Sept. 1903).

[93] *Lohengrin*, conducted by Bruno Walter with Förster-Lauterer, Hilgermann, Schmedes, Melms, Mayr, and Stehmann. In a letter written to Franz Schalk in summer 1903, Mahler says that he is going to ask Walter to conduct this performance, thus gaining a few days' extra holiday for Schalk and himself (MBRS 166). Since Mahler felt that *Lohengrin* should be performed with the orchestra at its normal level, the question remains as to whether the pit had been only partly deepened for this performance.

[94] AMM1. 387; AMM2. 334, where this letter is wrongly dated 1907.

[95] According to Karpath, the pit had temporarily been deepened by only a metre (BMG 166).

even further or leave it for the time being as it is now. The instrumental ensemble pleases me so much the way it is![96]

On 10 September, when the musicians arrived for a performance of *Tannhäuser*,[97] they were surprised to find that the new changes had been made without their knowledge. They complained the following day to the director. According to the *Neues Wiener Abendblatt* of 11 September, Mahler 'refused to discuss the issue' and the orchestra committee met that same evening to protest against the measures which, they felt, posed a danger because the orchestra was now unable to move around when at full strength. Mahler replied that lowering the pit floor had in fact given them fourteen square metres of additional space. For once, the disagreement did not degenerate into yet another Viennese *Affär*:[98] the orchestra capitulated. It was the music critics with their widely divergent views who prolonged the debate. Kauders complained that he could scarcely hear the harp[99] and that the violins were lifeless, especially when played softly. Wallaschek, on the other hand, found that the acoustics had improved. He also saw an additional advantage: now that the conductor's desk was in approximately the same position as that of the concert-master in Jahn's time, he was almost hidden from the audience and would be less tempted to show off. Korngold also praised the change, but advised Mahler not to go too far in following the example of Bayreuth, where the orchestra was concealed by a scrim. However, Mahler's opponents were not placated. After a performance of *Tristan*, on 14 September, the first time Mahler had conducted since the opening of the season,[100] Karpath attacked the brass section's 'deplorable' tone from the Prelude onwards; it 'seriously upset' the balance of the sound. He felt that despite Mahler's unprecedented increase in the number of strings, the cellos sounded blurred. In any case, only Wagnerian dramas might possibly benefit from the changes. Similarly, Maximilian Muntz, after attending a revival of *La Juive*, wrote that the singers were bothered by the lower level of the pit as it had created 'an unexpected and novel combination of sounds'. For once, Karpath's account, later included in *Begegnungen mit dem Genius*, lacks objectivity, no doubt because he was one of the leaders of the press campaign against the project. He claimed that Mahler gave up the idea of deepening the pit because it 'did not produce the desired results', when in fact, according to the *Neues Wiener Journal*,[101] Mahler further deepened it in March 1905. Work began in January 1904 in the wings and basement of the Opera for the

[96] *Fremden-Blatt* (6 Sept. 1903).   [97] Conducted by Bruno Walter.
[98] In the same article, the *Neues Abendblatt* added that the conflict 'had been denied later by both parties'.
[99] This he found particularly objectionable in Wolfram's aria in *Tannhäuser*, where he could hear only the harp's bass notes.
[100] The first *Tristan* of the season had the usual cast except for Moritz Frauscher in the role of King Mark. Karpath claimed that Mahler had gone back to the old placing of the musicians, and admitted that the conductor had surpassed himself in 'subtlety of feeling'.
[101] The article appeared 5 Mar. 1905. It referred to the double première of Leo Blech's *Das war Ich* and Eugen d'Albert's *Die Abreise* which took place on 28 Feb. The unsigned article said that the woodwind sound was now 'deadened, as if it came from another room, while that of the strings was strengthened'.

installation of hydraulic machinery to lower and raise the orchestra pit easily and quickly. This costly solution solved all the problems; thus the squabbles of summer 1903 had after all been useful.[102]

In September 1903 Mahler gave the complete cycle of Wagner's works, now an annual event.[103] It began on the 6th with *Rienzi* and ended on the 30th with *Die Meistersinger*. On the 13th, a young baritone named Friedrich Weidemann made a brilliant début in the part of Telramund in *Lohengrin*.[104] His voice, in Korngold's opinion, was occasionally weak and his high notes sometimes lacking in brilliance, but his 'controlled passion', his 'quiet warmth', and his 'noble sorrow', were admirable and he was the ideal successor to Reichmann. Weidemann was indeed the kind of artist Mahler enjoyed working with and wanted in the company. After the *Flying Dutchman* on the 20th, Korngold noted that Weidemann's Dutchman was more noble than diabolical, but added that his height, his noble presence, and his powerful voice, especially in the lower register, made him an ideal interpreter of heroic roles. Some days later, after a performance of *Aida* in which Weidemann sang Amonasro, the same critic felt that the part was even better suited to his temperament but that his high notes had 'breadth' (*Breite*) rather than 'bite' (*Spitze*). However that may be, his initial 'guest appearance' was so successful that he was immediately engaged and soon became one of the Hofoper's star singers. Although a tragedian rather than a seducer, he was a remarkable Count (in *Le nozze*), a superb Wotan (the first who embodied 'the full tragic dimension' of the part), a grave and thoughtful Hans Sachs, and a malevolent Pizarro.[105] He was also the ideal interpreter of Mahler's Lieder. Another important engagement at the beginning of the new season was that of the young Austrian conductor Artur Bodanzky, who subsequently made a brilliant career in Mannheim, and later at the Metropolitan Opera in New York, where he became one of the most fervent supporters of Mahler's work.[106]

---

[102] In 1907, Roller asked the Lord Chamberlain for permission to raise the lighting batten 7 cm. higher. He demonstrated in a sketch that light was not reaching the feet and ankles of the singers and stated that the work could be completed in a single night at a cost of no more than 200 kronen. Mahler added a two-word note: 'Urgently recommended'. The management's acceptance, attached to the letter, is dated 18 Jan. 1908 (HOA, Z.1024/1907, Roller's handwritten letter of 18 Oct.).

[103] With the usual exception of *Parsifal*.

[104] Cast for the 13 Sept. performance, conducted by Franz Schalk: Förster-Lauterer (Elsa), Hilgermann (Ortrud), Slezak (Lohengrin), Weidemann (Telramund), Mayr (King). In June 1902, Weidemann had asked Mahler if he could sing as a guest at the end of Aug., but Mahler insisted on his first appearance taking place 'when our regular public will be present' and had proposed either Sept. 1902 or May/June 1903 (letters of 19 and 21 June 1902, HOA, Z.287/1902).

[105] *Don Giovanni* was Weidemann's only failure. He apparently lacked the necessary 'elegance and frivolity' (RSM2, see below, Vol. iii, Chap. 5). Fredrich Weidemann (1871–1919) was born in Ratzeburg in Holstein. He was a pupil of Wilhelm Vilmar in Hamburg and Conrad Muschler in Vienna and he made his début with the Brieg Opera Company in Silesia in 1896. He sang in Essen, Hamburg, and Riga before joining the Hofoper, where he remained until his death.

[106] Artur Bodanzky (1877–1939) studied the violin at the Vienna Conservatory and joined the Opera orchestra at the age of 18. He was also a pupil of Alexander Zemlinsky, whose assistant he became at the Carl-Theater, after making his début as an operetta conductor in Budweis in 1900. He was engaged by Mahler at the Hofoper three years later, and subsequently conducted in Berlin (1905) and Prague (1906–9).

In planning his seasonal programme of new works and revivals, Mahler had to take account of the taste of Viennese audiences for spectacular French grand opera. In this section of the repertory he preferred, like Wagner before him, the warmer style of Jacques Fromental Halévy to the monumental shallowness of Meyerbeer. *La Juive* had not been sung since his arrival in Vienna six years earlier, and he started work on a new production at the end of September 1903. The Czech composer, Josef Bohuslav Förster, left a vivid account of one of the final rehearsals. In the third act, when Brogni pronounces his anathema against the two Jews and Prince Leopold,[107] the chorus received the news calmly and approached the Cardinal 'with a ceremonious dignity' completely at odds with the dramatic situation. At once Mahler stopped the rehearsal and climbed on stage. Standing near the prompter's box, he pointed out to the chorus the terrible meaning of the word 'anathema' at the time when *La Juive* was supposed to have taken place. He ordered the Cardinal and the Prince to stand motionless down stage right and left, while the chorus fled and huddled up stage left, 'as if stung by a viper', to 'gather in a confused huddle of terrified courtiers':

The entire episode of the anathema was repeated but Mahler was still not satisfied. He jumped on to the stage again, and the horror he expressed by face and gestures long remained in Förster's memory. This was no longer a member of the chorus acting a frightened courtier out of professional duty. This was someone seized by extreme terror, who had lost his senses and dignity despite the Prince and Princess's presence, and who had only one thought left: to escape the death ray [of anathema]![108]

The première of the new production of *La Juive* took place on 13 October. Though the cast was excellent, the opera's success did not match that obtained in the previous year by *Les Huguenots*. According to the *Neue Freie Presse*, the audience received it 'quite warmly, but not enthusiastically', while the *Deutsche Zeitung* noted that the house emptied gradually towards the end, and that the third act was greeted by a mixture of applause and catcalls. Once again, most of the critics disputed the choice of *La Juive* at a time when so many great works had been omitted for so long from the repertory. Kalbeck credited Mahler with bringing out *La Juive*'s 'vivid colours'. Hirschfeld said Mahler had 'fought for each note as though it was the most precious of treasures', that he had ennobled the work's melodies, 'corrected its features, improved the harmony of its body and limbs' and achieved a masterpiece of 'musical orthopedic virtuosity'. Thanks to the 'sparkle' he imparted to the performance, even mediocre actors like Slezak and Förster-Lauterer seemed imbued with fresh

---

In 1909 he was appointed Musikdirektor in Mannheim and organized the first Mahler festival there in 1912. After introducing *Parsifal* to London in 1914, he moved to New York in 1915. There he conducted the German repertory at the Metropolitan Opera until his death. He also led the New Symphony Orchestra (1919–22) and succeeded Stokowski as director of the Society of the Friends of Music (1921–31).

[107] In the famous bass aria: 'Vous qui du Dieu vivant'.   [108] JFP 520.

dramatic force.[109] For Wallaschek, the Finale of the first act was a 'masterpiece of musical and dramatic construction'.[110] However, Maximilian Muntz considered that 'even Mahler's genius was unable to resurrect the defunct corpse of "Grand Opéra"!' Despite the reviewers' disapproval, the revival of *La Juive* proved to be a worthwhile initiative. It was performed eight times during the last months of 1903 and remained in the repertory for the next eight years. Mahler could thus count it among his successes. That month Intendant Plappart informed him that 'the fine artistic and financial results which rewarded your unstinting efforts have been appreciated in the highest places' and that he would be awarded the Order of the Iron Crown, third class, 'for having undertaken the artistic direction of the Hofoper under difficult circumstances and restoring in comparatively short time, thanks to your tireless zeal and creative power, its traditional reputation and prestige'.[111]

On the other hand, of all the years Mahler spent as director, 1903 showed the biggest financial deficit. On 30 September the Obersthofmeisteramt issued a strict warning to the management after learning that the year's expenditure to date had exceeded the estimates in all items. It required the Opera's finances to be put in order forthwith and a new round of economies to be introduced.[112] Mahler gave the reasons for the increased expenditures in a letter to the Intendant on 9 October. The new productions of *Euryanthe*, *Tristan*, *Louise*, and *Aida*, and the première of the ballet *Der faule Hans*, had been particularly expensive. The last-minute changes to *Louise* that Charpentier had demanded; the renewal of some of the electrical equipment for *Tristan*; the extra rehearsals indispensable for the second act of *Aida*, the overtime worked by the stagehands, and the hire of walk-ons, had all occasioned considerable additional expenditure. Whilst acknowledging some of these considerations, the Lord Chamberlain recommended the strictest economy regarding overtime. As we shall soon see, Mahler made strenuous efforts to implement these instructions. The results for 1904 were much improved as regards both receipts and expenditures.[113]

[109] Mahler conducted only the first two performances. Cast for the 13 Oct. première: Elizza (Eudoxie), Förster-Lauterer (Rachel), Slezak (Eléazar), Preuss (Prince). As usual, Mahler prepared a second cast: Forst (Eudoxie), Schubert (Rachel), Winkelmann (Eléazar), Pacal (Prince) Hesch (Cardinal), Linder, Stehmann, Neidl, Marian, Felix. Several critics, Muntz in particular, felt that the depth of the orchestra pit created insurmountable difficulties of pitch for the singers.

[110] Wallaschek added that Hesch, who was in poor health, sang too softly in Act I and that the ovation would have lasted longer at the beginning of Act IV if Mahler had not interrupted it by beginning to conduct. He praised the chorus's precision as well as Slezak's diction, whereas Muntz thought that Slezak had failed to muster even 'the modest amount of dramatic strength required by the work'.

[111] HOA, 17 Oct. 1903. According to *Neue Freie Presse* (29 Oct.), Mahler had a personal audience with the Emperor Franz Joseph that day to thank him for his award. Mahler had already been decorated by the Kings of Sweden and Saxony. On 1 May 1902, von Possart, the Intendant of the Munich Opera, informed him that the King of Bavaria had awarded him the Order of Saint Michael, third rank, by decree of 22 Apr. (HOA, Z.370/1902).

[112] The total expenditure for 1903 amounted to 3,126,725 kronen, with a net deficit of 264,750 kronen (WMW 210).

[113] WMW 210.

Despite the temporary difficulty over finances, the award of the Iron Crown to Mahler showed that his 'untiring zeal' and 'unlimited energy' had not gone unnoticed, and that people in high places wanted to encourage him, although his appearances on the podium were dwindling, as he began to be increasingly in demand, in Germany and elswhere, as a composer-conductor. Once again, a shortage of Kapellmeister made itself felt at the Hofoper, especially since Hellmesberger had been forced to resign because of a personal scandal.[114] One of the pillars of the Hofoper, Franz Schalk, was 'threatening to leave' in response to a tempting offer from the Karlsruhe Opera. At the end of 1903, Mahler exchanged letters with Hugo Reichenberger,[115] who was the principal conductor at the Frankfurt Opera but wanted very much to come to Vienna. Mahler advised him to accept another post, since he would be unable to make him an offer for the time being. Mahler had in fact just engaged a new Opera Kapellmeister, but he had selected an Italian rather than a German, since he felt that only the Mediterranean temperament could do justice to the basically melodic style of Italian opera. He had heard Francesco Spetrino[116] conduct in Lemberg the previous season.

Spetrino made his début in Vienna on 31 October in *Lucia di Lammermoor*, which had been revived largely to show off the talents of Selma Kurz, who was gradually giving up lyric-dramatic roles[117] in favour of the coloratura parts more suited to her voice and temperament. In 1903 romantic Italian operas were deemed to be 'old-fashioned and outmoded'. Thus Hirschfeld and most other Viennese critics were indignant at the 'absurdity' and 'bad taste' of *Lucia*. Schönaich felt the production was a mistake because no Viennese singer was capable of 'turning into an Italian'. Yet Korngold, like Wallaschek, believed Kurz had found in *Lucia* one of her best roles. 'Her splendid voice sounded like a clarinet rather than a flute', he wrote, and her art surpassed the vocal pirouettes and usual acrobatics, turning the evening into her 'crowning glory' as a singer. Although Kalbeck considered that technically Kurz had 'a long way to go' before she would acquire the necessary assurance in 'her trills and vocalizing' and Muntz maintained that 'she possessed all the necessary qualities except soul', Selma Kurz was then on her way to becoming the darling of the

---

[114] See below.

[115] MBR1, no. 314 and 315; MBR2, no. 323 and 324; 8 and 18 Nov. 1903. Hugo Reichenberger (1873–1938), born in Munich, had studied music under Hermann Levi and Ludwig Thuille. He began his conducting career at Kissingen in 1894 and pursued it in Breslau, Aachen, Bremen, and Stuttgard. In 1903, he was Kapellmeister at the Frankfurt Opera. Mahler met him there in Dec. In the end, he engaged him just before his own departure from the Hofoper, where Reichenberger stayed until 1935.

[116] Francesco Spetrino (1857–1948) was born in Palermo. A pupil of Pietro Platania at the Conservatory in his native city and author of an opera, *Filippo II*, performed in 1876, Spetrino subsequently devoted himself to conducting, first in Italy, then in Spain and Poland (Grand Theatre, Warsaw: 1894–9; Civic Theatre, Lemberg: 1901–3). He remained with the Vienna Opera until 1908, when he was engaged at the same time as Toscanini by the Metropolitan Opera Company in New York (see below, Vol. iv, Chap. 3). He returned to Italy at the outbreak of the First World War, and gave up conducting to devote himself to composing.

[117] None the less, she was the first in Vienna to sing the title-role in *Madama Butterfly* on 31 Oct. 1907.

Viennese public in the coloratura repertory. The many recordings she made prove that her reputation was well deserved.[118] It was thanks to her that *Lucia* regained favour with audiences, but most contemporaries gave Spetrino credit as well. Schönaich conceded that Spetrino had a typically Italian 'sense of rhythm and tempo', while Hirschfeld felt he had overrefined the opera in order to give it a semblance of spirit and depth. Wallaschek's view was that his main virtue was his ability to 'muffle shrill colours, soften harsh rhythms and moderate tempo in order to give the singing its due'.[119]

A month later Spetrino was an obvious choice to conduct the first performance at the Hofoper of an Italian verismo work, first produced six years earlier at the Theater an der Wien. In 1897 Mahler had urged Jahn to produce Puccini's *La Bohème* rather than Leoncavallo's, but his advice was not followed, as the decision had already been made and the contract signed by his predecessor. According to the *Neue Freie Presse*, Mahler then expressed his real opinion in very vivid terms: 'Mich will's bedünken, dass sie alle beide stinken' ('To my mind, they both stink').[120] The same article conceded, however, that the discriminating musician was also a prudent Opera Director wise enough to cater to his subscribers' taste for novelty. Although in March Mahler had implicitly pronounced *Tosca* unworthy of Vienna,[121] this did not affect his plans concerning *La Bohème*. He invited Puccini to attend the final rehearsals and the première, but the composer refused 'because of urgent work which has to be finished for next season'. It is no surprise to learn from the *Neue Freie Presse* that during rehearsals Mahler showed 'selfless and unstinting devotion' and that he 'bestowed the same fatherly care on the little milliner as on the most imposing of the iron-clad Valkyries'. Having heard from Spetrino 'all the trouble Mahler had gone to for the production of *La Bohème*', Puccini wrote another letter assuring Mahler that 'he was certain it would be a first-rate performance!'[122] The double casting of the roles of Mimi and Rodolfo (Fritz Schrödter and Selma Kurz; Leo Slezak and Marie Gutheil-Schoder), as well as Spetrino's conducting guaranteed the success of the new opera, despite the bitter hostility of the press.

In his memoirs, Egon Wellesz later spoke of the impression which Puccini's orchestration had made on his friend Anton Webern and himself.[123] In one of

[118] Hirschfeld, however, felt she was not a 'genuine coloratura' and Schönaich that she had 'neither the style nor the vocal genius of a Patti or a Sembrich', but their views were too partisan to be completely convincing.

[119] Cast for the performance on 31 Oct. 1903: Kurz (Lucia), Pohlner (Alisa), Schrödter (Edgardo), Demuth (Ashton), Preuss (Arturo), Mayr (Raimondo).

[120] A quotation from Heinrich Heine.   [121] During his visit to Lemberg: see above.

[122] Puccini's letter, along with the one he wrote to Mahler after the success of *La Bohème*, is in HOA (Z.949/1903).

[123] They were particularly impressed by the chamber-music effects at the end of Act I and Act III. Wellesz speaks of the flute and harp triple pianissimo against a diminuendo violin chord (see p. 120 of the Ricordi orchestral score). In the last act (p. 402 of the score), Wellesz similarly notes, during Mimi's death scene, 'two flutes and harp triple *pianissimo*, with almost inaudible muted string chords' (EWL 27).

his last *Feuilleton* articles in the *Neue Freie Presse*, written shortly before his death in 1904, Eduard Hanslick condemned Puccini's opera as 'an endless gabble', embellished with a few brief and unnatural melodies, a jumble of 'nervous touches', and 'incessant changes of rhythm and modulations'. Outraged by the 'harmonic atrocities' of *La Bohème* and especially by the famous parallel fifths at the beginning of the third act, Hanslick denounced 'this vulgar musical insult' and 'refined cult of ugliness'. Distressing as it is to read such nonsense coming from one of the most famous critics in the history of music, the fact remains that most of Hanslick's colleagues were just as short-sighted. Hirschfeld rejected *La Bohème* as another 'musical excess from a school that already seems outdated'. 'Not one theme is developed according to musical laws', he wrote, instead we find 'little splashes of colour, pointillism, printwork, spatterings; a music of accent, exclamation and explosion'. Kalbeck was profoundly shocked by a libretto he considered to be no more than the banal odyssey 'of two prostitutes'. Despite the composer's 'prodigious technique', he doubted if the opera would survive another six years. The Viennese critics all sang the same tune: the opera was 'too flawed to last' (Wallaschek); it was much inferior to Charpentier's *Louise* (Schönaich); it had no quality, either musical or dramatic (Muntz). Only Max Graf appreciated the charm of its sequence of 'pleasant watercolours, graceful and sentimental, perfumed with tears and coloured with the tragic hues of Parma violets'. But he accused Mahler as director of the Opera of having 'lost his energy', of 'wavering' too often, of pandering to the public with works 'full of trills' or spectacle by Halévy, Meyerbeer, or Verdi, instead of giving them the masterpieces of Mozart, Weber, or Lortzing. As for Josef Scheu, who had been the first critic not belonging to the anti-Semitic lobby to come out against Mahler, right from the beginning of his tenure, he considered it unpardonable to have delayed so long before putting on this *Bohème*, concluding that Mahler did not 'know what worked' (*was wirksam ist*). Fortunately, the public was not swayed by these 'infernal judges', and *La Bohème* was performed eight times before the end of the year and eighteen times in 1904. Later on it was never absent from the Hofoper repertory for any length of time.[124]

The 1903–4 season at the Hofoper produced the usual crop of personnel disputes. In January, Leopold Demuth threatened to leave when he learnt that Mahler had called him 'shameless' for requesting additional leave. In a long letter betraying his sorely offended dignity, he reminded the director that he had never caused the slightest trouble and had always carried out his duties to the letter. And now, he went on, when for the first time he 'expressed a wish', Mahler 'wanted to have nothing to do with me, not even paying me the respect due to an artist!' When *La Juive* had its première, the tenor Franz Naval handed in his resignation because Mahler had cast his rival Leo Slezak in the main

---

[124] Cast for the première on 25 Nov.: Kurz (Mimi), Gutheil-Schoder (Musetta), Schrödter (Rodolfo), Stehmann (Marcello), Moser (Schaunard), Ritter (Alcindoro), Mayr (Colline), Marian (Bernard).

role, giving him the supporting part of the Prince. Towards the end of November, another dispute broke out between Mahler and the mezzo Laura Hilgermann, who until then had always been one of the most dutiful members of the company. She had asked to be allowed to sing outside Vienna, and for once Mahler seems to have given in, but he had also insisted on her singing Ortrud in *Lohengrin*, a role she felt was too dramatic and would harm her voice. The autumn had been chilly and Hilgermann came down with a cold. Her coughing was so bad one Sunday morning that she called in a doctor to find out whether she might possibly sing that evening: she knew that the performance would have to be cancelled if she couldn't. The doctor reluctantly agreed to give her sedatives which would enable her to go on.

Hilgermann felt that Mahler should have been grateful. But it appears that he flew into a temper with her two days later, when she reminded him of his promise to let her sing elsewhere.[125] 'In any case,' she wrote,

> I have the right to protest against the tone of voice in which Herr Direktor chose to address me. It is a tone unsuitable for speaking to a servant, let alone an artist. That is what irritates me the most, as it has others before me, and I allowed myself to call it 'inconsiderate' (*rücksichtlos*). Nor do I think Herr Direktor has any right to protest against the expression. Such behaviour is harmful not only to a member's health but to his profession and I am the living proof of that. My cough has now become so bad, as a result of the state of permanent upset I live in, that much to my regret I must cancel not only today's rehearsal, but also the performance. As far as the leave of absence goes, I could not care less at this stage, but I clearly see now how much trust I can place in my Direktor's promises!

The only other surviving record of this particularly unpleasant affair is an icy letter which Hilgermann's physician addressed to Mahler to defend his patient and confirm that she had run a serious risk by singing under sedation.[126] The main source of dispute was, as usual, Mahler's refusal, always supported by the Opera authorities, to grant the singers leave of absence to sing elsewhere remained an endless source of conflict. Some months earlier, when the Munich Opera invited Gutheil-Schoder to sing Despina in *Così*, Mahler agreed before realizing that she had already been granted permission to appear as a guest in Prague. A month later, another request from the same singer was turned down 'because the planned repertory makes her presence necessary in Vienna until the end of the season'.[127] It was no doubt to limit the possibility of such conflicts that Mahler convinced the Obersthofmeister to introduce a new regulation aimed at discouraging Opera members from asking for leave of absence. It had

---

[125] Why he changed his mind is unclear from the available documents; only Hilgermann's letters have survived.

[126] Hilgermann's letters are dated 23, 24, and 27 Nov., and that of Dr Schinkel 29 Nov. (HOA, Z.1032/1903).

[127] Intendant Possart's telegrams, 22 Apr. 1903; Mahler's telegram, 23 Apr. and Possart's answer of the 25th (HOA, Z.VIII.77/1903). Gutheil-Schoder's letter to Mahler is dated 20 May and Mahler's answer 22 May (HOA, Z.VIII.108/1903).

already been decided in 1902 that, in case of prolonged illness, the members' 'Funktionszulage' (activity allowance) would be withheld. From 1904 onwards, this sanction was also applied whenever a singer left Vienna for more than three days to sing elsewhere as a guest.[128]

Early in December 1903, a dispute of another kind broke out, the details of which were to fill many columns in the Austrian left-wing press of the time. In this case the protesting party was a whole group of people—the stage-hands of the two court theatres. Social and political implications gave the case a wider resonance than the personal disputes with individual singers so far mentioned. It seems that the stage-hands had begun to find their working conditions intolerable and wanted to improve them. With the aid of a lawyer they drew up a list of demands which they presented to the directors of both theatres, asking them to pass them on to the Obersthofmeisteramt:

1. Working hours will be as follows: 8 a.m. to 13 p.m. and 17 p.m. to 20 p.m.
2. All work done outside these hours will be paid at overtime rates of 60 heller per hour or, in the case of night work, after 22 p.m. at the rate of 1 krone per hour. Any part of an hour is to be counted as a full hour and paid in full. Work done on Sunday will be paid at overtime rates, except for work between 17 and 22 p.m.
3. Each stage-hand permanently employed at the Opera will receive a basic wage of 100 kronen a month and an activity allowance allowance (*Funktionszulage*) of 50 kronen a month. After 8 years of service, a seniority bonus will be granted of 10 kronen to a maximum of 30 kronen.
4. At the Burgtheater, there will be a breakfast break.
5. At the Opera, pension conditions and rights to be stipulated in employment contract.
6. A joint disciplinary board of 6 or 12 members, made up of equal numbers of employees and management.
7. 3 days off per month.
8. In case of illness, temporary replacement workers shall be hired immediately.
9. The following disciplinary measures will be instituted: warning, reprimand, transfer (*Rüge*, *Verweis*, *Versetzung*). Dismissal of an employee will be possible only in case of a court sentence for a criminal act.

A delegation of stage-hands presented the document to Mahler, who after hasty perusal allegedly threw it to the floor, saying that 'whoever had written it was an idiot'.[129] On 8 December, in the course of an interview published in the *Neues Wiener Abendblatt*, Mahler denied either using an 'offensive' word or throwing the document on the floor. He had told the delegation on their third visit:

I speak to you as a friend. It will not do you any good if I write a few meaningless words on your petition. I am quite willing to discuss the situation with you but I must warn you that you are getting poor advice. The person who counselled you is no friend of yours.

---

[128] Mahler's letter to the Intendant dated 19 Feb. 1904 (HOA, Z.351.1/1904).
[129] The actual word he used is not mentioned in the article.

You know me and you know that it was on my initiative that your wages were raised two years ago. I am always ready to help when there is something to be done but do not ask me to make promises that can't be kept. Keep your demands reasonable. With the goodwill of the higher authorities it can be assumed that you will obtain what is obtainable. Purely material questions are always open to discussion. I have shown you many times that I am your true friend.[130]

What Mahler found particularly unreasonable was the idea of setting up a joint disciplinary commission to include both workers and their superiors:

Why didn't the stage-hands turn to me at once? The idea of setting up a disciplinary commission composed of workers and management could have occurred only to someone who knows nothing about the theatre, where everything depends on strict obedience and absolute precision. In a theatre the safety of many thousands of people is at stake. Everything must run like clockwork and interference from the outside simply cannot be tolerated. The Director alone must have the authority to punish when orders have not been carried out.[131]

Mahler having rejected their petition, the stage-hands organized a meeting at Gasthaus Strohmeyer. Several hundreds attended. A Socialist member of Parliament named Julius Prochaska[132] was there to address the meeting. He launched at once into an attack on Mahler, declaring that the stage-hands were firmly resolved not to put up with maltreatment, since 'it was easier to replace a director than a well-trained body of workers', Loud applause broke out at this point. If Mahler did not agree to consider the memorandum, Prochaska said, they would find a way of going over his head to the Intendant or the Emperor himself, who after all owned both the theatres. If Mahler did not listen to the stage-hands and went on acting like their enemy, then the curtain would fail to rise on some gala evening (renewed applause). 'If Director Mahler wants a fight, then he will have it.' (Applause.) A resolution was unanimously adopted at the close of the meeting: 'The assembled stage-hands express their thanks to the Director of the Burgtheater for his goodwill and hope that the Director of the Opera will change his mind and support his employees.'[133]

Once again Mahler had been guilty of lack of diplomacy, but certainly not of goodwill. In the past he had always fought for the lowest paid Opera staff, taking personal risks in their defence, as in 1902. However, his long experience as Opera conductor had also taught him how necessary it was to maintain strict discipline, not only in the pit but also onstage and backstage. The very idea of a joint disciplinary commission, commonplace today, must have seemed utterly absurd at a time when the working class was just beginning to campaign for improved working conditions. Mahler had grounds for believing that the stage-hands were being manipulated by a small group of extremists. This is

---

[130] *Neues Wiener Tagblatt* (9 Dec. 1903).   [131] Ibid.

[132] Prochaska was a colleague of Victor Adler in the Socialist Party. He was also, at least in the early days of his career, an anti-Semite.

[133] *Neues Wiener Tagblatt* and *Abendblatt* (9 Dec. 1903).

confirmed by the text of a petition dated 11 August 1905, a copy of which is in the Opera archives. It is signed by seven stage-hands who had been dismissed three months earlier. They ask to be reinstated because 'they have families', because 'they have committed no breach of discipline', and because they are not 'troublemakers' or 'radical elements', but 'have always attempted to contain the radical movement which tried to penetrate our ranks, so far always success-fully'. Mahler forwarded the petition to his superiors with the following note:

The reasons for these measures were discussed orally in full detail and the decision was made only after careful investigation of the case. In the interest of the discipline of stage personnel, which seems now to have been reinforced by this decision. . . . the Director cannot support this request (for reinstatement) but urgently recommends that the decision be upheld.[134]

Mahler's 'tyrannical' nature, his dictatorial style as director, and above all the way he treated his colleagues when he was angry, were resented not only by the singers but also by the orchestra. As Philharmonic musicians they had elected and re-elected Josef Hellmesberger, junior, a Viennese conductor well-known for his agreeable disposition and mediocre talent, rather than run the risk that Mahler might be tempted to resume the conductorship of the Philhar-monic. Hellmesberger's final election, in May 1903, elicited words of steel and vitriol from Karl Kraus's pen:

Once more the 'Musikanten'[135] have prevailed over the musicians. Herr Hellmesberger has been reelected conductor of the Vienna Philharmonic. On the surface, everything went smoothly. The committee responsible for organizing the proceedings had invited Herr Hellmesberger to attend the meeting at which the choice was first to be discussed and then voted on. And because the proposals directed against Herr Hellmesberger would therefore have had to be justified and debated in his presence, they were not even put forward by the intimidated opposition. In his well cared-for corporeality the candidate of the many sat there, and the few did not dare say a word to recall his rival's ghost. Thus the problem which the election was supposed to solve wasn't even men-tioned. Instead, the Philharmonic's tradition was praised, its golden age under Hans Richter recalled and the present hard times lamented.

In fact, the times have not become harder since we now have a couple of dozen Philharmonic Concerts every year instead of the eight we used to have. The public's interest in philharmonic concerts has grown while its interest in concerts by the Philharmonic has declined. And in the face of the competition offered by the Konzertverein, it is useless to react merely by adopting a superior attitude and trying to pass off laziness (*Lässigkeit*) as composure (*Gelassenheit*), and inadequacy (*Unzulänglichkeit*) as reserve (*Unzugänglichkeit*). In no time at all this competitor, by dint of hard work and a conductor who has contrived to put himself at the head of both the Brahms and the Bruckner factions, has established its dominance over the whole

---

[134] HOA, Z.854/1905. The petition is dated 11 Aug. and Mahler's note to the Intendant 18 Aug. 1905.

[135] 'Musikant' in German means hired provider of music, a street musician, or a popular or village musician.

field of the symphony concert in Vienna.[136] Meanwhile the Philharmonic has remained true to its old habit of taking a single great work, a 'hit'—and whenever possible the same one, so as to avoid too much trouble with rehearsals—around which it puts together a programme of all sorts of musical tinsel (*Flitterkram*). Programmes which might cause violent controversy among critics of different tendencies, programmes based on historical or didactic considerations—nothing of that kind has ever been attempted by the Philharmonic. A body to which quite a number of dedicated musicians belong has been infected by the attitudes of those of its members who, because they also receive an income—at present reduced but still satisfactory—from their Hofkapelle jobs, are able to refrain from work which they have no inner urge to undertake. And the Hofkapellmeister, who is the Hofkapelle members' candidate for the Philharmonic conductorship, is also quite acceptable to the great mass of 'Musikanten', who speak of their obligations to a 'nice kind man' when they should be thinking of artistic ability. These easy-going and comfort-loving men would rather trot along under a 'Kapellmeister' than let themselves be carried away by a real conductor. Liszt once said that the conductor's job was not to keep the oarsmen rowing in time, but to be the helmsman. Herr Hellmesberger knows how to steer the ship. He simply cheerfully splashes his soft little hand in the water while the ship goes sailing on.

This is in no way to question Herr Hellmesberger's craftsmanlike competence. He is capable of doing—and he does—everything that requires no more than ability and industry. The word 'Kunst' (art) is derived from 'können' (to be able), but ability is still not art. What one *does* doesn't matter: the only thing that matters is what one *is*. Herr Hellmesberger is one of those people who are always going to be something but never are. One cannot justify his election as Philharmonic conductor on the grounds of his proficiency. It was a decision based on purely personal, not artistic considerations. But if personal antipathies are brought to bear against Gustav Mahler's election, if the 'Musikanten', despite hypocritical acknowledgement of his musical pre-eminence, justify their rejection of him on the grounds of his personality, they are using the personality issue to hide their real motives, that is to say the deep antagonism that exists between non-artists and the strong artist, the fear of having their comfort disturbed, of having their philistinism shaken up by the creative drive of a true musician. Mahler is certainly not the only man who could conduct the Philharmonic but today there is no one else in Vienna who could. And because he will not be its conductor, Vienna's musical life will suffer in two ways: Mahler will be restricted in his activity as a conductor and a professional musician capable of great things on which he should concentrate; and he will *not* be restricted in, or relieved of, his other area of activity, i.e. the management of the Opera, through increased activity as a conductor. Certain personal qualities which are irrelevant to the job of conductor are decisive when it comes to running an Opera. It is obvious by now to all his supporters that the diplomatic talents required for managing a theatre are not an organic part of Mahler's

[136] The Concertverein conductor was of course Ferdinand Löwe (see above, Chap. 7). Löwe was active as orchestral and choral director, chiefly in Vienna and Munich, later also appearing frequently in Budapest and Berlin. A pupil of Bruckner, he collaborated with Franz Schalk in a spurious score of the Fourth Symphony. Later on, he drew up on his own an even more obviously spurious score of the Ninth for the 1st edn. (1903). Löwe was certainly no great conductor, except perhaps in comparison to Hellmesberger. But he was undoubtedly a man of great energy and ability. See above, Chap. 6, for an account of Löwe's short engagement by the Hofoper.

nature, and even those who have so far been reluctant to go along with partisan music criticism which colours its attacks on a strong artistic personality with stupid religious prejudices have had to admit it. They have silently been watching the man's administrative shortcomings for quite some time, but they finally condemned him on the day when Mahler's bad temper had managed to embitter a truly distinguished artist and threaten the Hofoper with the loss of Fräulein Walker. No perceptive assessor of a temperament which currently wastes its energy in wrong-headed explosions, can have any more doubts—with all due respect to Herr Hellmesberger's proficiency—as to where Mahler's place should be in Vienna's musical life.[137]

Karl Kraus himself showed little interest in music; indeed *Die Fackel* devotes much less space to music than its importance in the daily life of the Viennese would justify. Nevertheless, his article shows that he was in touch with well-informed critics and musicians and was fully aware of Mahler's outstanding achievements. The about-turn at the end of the article is typical of the great satirist. He begins by ridiculing the Philharmonic and its 'Musikanten' spirit and ends with an attack on Mahler's 'lack of diplomacy'. Yet it could easily be argued that it was Mahler's very intractability, his basic artistic honesty, his total devotion to art, and his inability to compromise which made him a great Opera Director, even if these qualities were the cause of many 'scandals'. It was precisely these qualities which earned him lasting respect and support in the highest court circles. Despite the vast amount of ink spilt in discussing Mahler's 'tyranny' and his displays of temper, it must be remembered that no *Affär* ever ended with a major artist's resignation, except perhaps in the case of Edyth Walker. Apparently, for what reason we do not know, Mahler had decided that Walker no longer belonged in the company he had taken such pains to put together. That she had the support of several influential critics was certainly not going to make him change his mind. It was a deliberate decision, not a 'whim' or a fit of temper. For a director of the Opera such obstinacy was arguably a virtue rather than a vice.

The Philharmonic's choice of Hellmesberger over Mahler three years running[138] has often been cited as a typical example of the Viennese love of mediocrity, so long as it was home-grown. Yet it is most unlikely that Mahler would have accepted his former post, even if he had been offered it by a large majority of the members. The players were well aware of this and it suited them. However, an unexpected event was soon to result in the Philharmonic finding itself without a conductor. One morning, at the end of September, the gossip-loving Viennese were treated to one of those succulent newspaper scandals which nourished conversation in the city's drawing-rooms and cafés

---

[137] *Die Fackel* (June 1903).

[138] At the annual election of conductor for the 1903–4 season, taking place on 26 May, Hellmesberger received 70 votes to Mahler's 13. This, the lowest vote Mahler ever obtained, was a consequence of the dispute over the admission of the new Opera instrumentalists to the ranks of the Philharmonic and the dispute concerning the performance of Beethoven's Ninth Symphony planned for the opening of the Secession exhibition in Apr. 1902.

for weeks on end, filling Viennese hostesses with hypocritical horror. It must have raised many a laugh as well. It was common knowledge that 'der fesche Pepi' (the elegant Josef Hellmesberger, junior)[139] had a taste for very young girls and had for some time been carrying on with a young member of the Opera *corps de ballet* named Thekla Braun. The affair apparently attracted too much attention, particularly since such liaisons were thoroughly disapproved of by the authorities. Thekla Braun was dismissed from the Opera by an order dated 25 September. As soon as her father, the cardboard manufacturer Anton Braun, heard the news he rushed out of his house to track down the girl's lover, whom he considered responsible. He finally found him strolling casually in a street near the Opera, rushed up to him, and began to belabour him with his walking-stick, to the amazement of passers-by. Hellmesberger fled as fast as his legs would carry him, pursued by Anton Braun who had by now broken his walking-stick but was still shouting insults. The wretched conductor eventually had to seek refuge in a police station. The following day Anton Braun sent a furious letter to the director of the Opera, who had no choice but to pass it on to his superiors.[140]

Hellmesberger did nothing for several days, hoping the incident would blow over. But things had gone too far. Early in October he was obliged to yield to pressure, and resigned from the Philharmonic. Then, on 9 October, the Obersthofmeister requested him to resign from the Opera, which, after a fortnight of delays and vain hopes, he did.[141] Thus on 5 October the Philharmonic found itself without a conductor for the season which was just about to open. The musicians met to elect a replacement and one of the names put forward (without his consent, of course) was Mahler. For form's sake they cabled Hans Richter in England but he immediately refused. The options were then, in essence, either Mahler or a series of guest conductors. They voted twice; in the first ballot 53 votes were cast in favour of the second solution; 47 were cast for a permanent conductor (Mahler). Again the pro-Mahler members reminded the committee that each member of the Philharmonic had lost money since his departure two years earlier,[142] but the second ballot

[139] See above, Chap. 13.
[140] Cf. Jodok Freyenfels, 'Mahler und der fesche Pepi', *Neue Zeitschrift für Musik*, 4 (1971), 178. According to this author, Braun's letter was subsequently destroyed, which explains its absence from HOA.
[141] Hellmesberger's request for compensation on being obliged to quit his post after thirty years of loyal service was refused. But his wife was awarded moving costs of 30,000 kronen. Six months later, the success of his new operetta, *Das Veilchenmädchen*, at the Carl-Theater, brought Hellmesberger some consolation, especially when it was taken up in other European capitals. In 1904–5 he accepted a post at the Stuttgart Theatre, but soon returned to his beloved Vienna, and died shortly thereafter, without having had time to restore his reputation or financial position. As soon as Hellmesberger's departure from the Opera was known Bernard Stavenhagen, the pianist-conductor who had studied with Liszt, wrote to Mahler asking for his job. Mahler replied that he could take no decision until after Francesco Spetrino's first guest appearances (HOA, Stavenhagen's letter dated 10 Oct., Z.900/1903, and Mahler's reply, 28 Oct.). In fact Mahler had a low opinion of Stavenhagen's abilities and certainly had no intention of engaging him (see below, Vol. iii, Chap. 1).
[142] According to the *Neue Freie Presse* (10 Oct., 1903), plenty of seats were now available at the box-office before each concert whereas, when Mahler was conducting, they were sold out ahead of time. Under Mahler's

finally tipped the scales in favour of the guest conductors, 58 to 42. The candidates chosen as guest conductors were Schuch, Mottl, Muck, and Strauss.[143] The *Neue Freie Presse* attacked the committee's decision, claiming that two rehearsals were not enough to accustom the orchestra to a conductor and that the general level of performance would decline. If more musicians did not vote for Mahler, it said, that was because they knew he would not accept the appointment 'unless the vote was unanimous'. Mahler's name was eventually added, along with that of the Russian conductor Safonoff,[144] to the list of 'guest' conductors.

After returning from Maiernigg, Mahler continued to work each day putting the finishing touches to and copying the score of his Fifth Symphony, which he was due soon to conduct for the first time. The definitive score is dated 'October 1903' and bears an inscription: 'To my dear Almscherl, my faithful and brave companion on all paths'.[145] As soon as the score was finished, Mahler again became active as an itinerant composer-conductor. His first English perform-ance was to take place at Queen's Hall in London under Henry Wood, on 21 October, with the First Symphony. Far more important was the first tour he undertook, since it was to take him to a country he did not know, Holland, to conduct two of his symphonies, one of them the Third. To understand the unusual honour which the Amsterdam Concertgebouw was thus bestrowing upon him, it is necessary to look back to the première of the Third Symphony in Krefeld the previous year. The performance had been attended by three major Dutch musicians: Willem Mengelberg, who, at 31, was already famous as conductor of the Amsterdam Concertgebouw,[146] Martin Heuckeroth, chief con-ductor in Arnhem,[147] and Henri Viotta, director of the Conservatory of The Hague, editor of the magazine *Caecilia*, a conductor whose preference was for Wagner, and founder of the Residence Orchestra of The Hague.[148] It was thanks

leadership each musician's yearly income from the concerts had increased from 300 kronen (under Richter) to 350 kronen. In Hellmesberger's final season, this income had shrunk to 200 kronen.

[143] The first concert (8 Nov.) was conducted by Schuch; the second (22 Nov.) by Safonoff; the third and fourth (6 and 20 Dec.) by Nikisch; the fifth (10 Jan.) by Muck; the sixth (24 Jan.) by Schuch; the seventh (7 Jan.) by Muck; and the eighth (21 Feb.) by Schuch.

[144] Wassili Safonoff (1852–1918), conductor of the Russian Imperial Music Society and director of the Moscow Conservatory, was succeeded by Mahler in 1909 as head of the New York Philharmonic Orchestra (see below, Vol. iv, Chap. 4).

[145] PML, Robert Lehman deposit.

[146] Josef Willem Mengelberg (1871–1951), born in Utrecht of a German father, studied at the Conserva-tory of his native city, then at the one in Cologne. Music director in Lucerne from 1891, he replaced Willem Kes in 1895, at the age of 24, as chief conductor of the Concertgebouw, a post he held until 1945, giving his last concert in 1944. He was also conductor of the Amsterdam Toonkunst Chorus, with which he gave annual concerts of great choral works. In 1899 Mengelberg's international reputation was already such that Strauss dedicated to him his symphonic poem *Ein Heldenleben*.

[147] Martin Heuckeroth (1853–1936) began his conducting career in Arnhem in 1893. In 1901 he organized the first Arnhem music festival, with Beethoven's Ninth Symphony and Bruckner's Te Deum on the programme. When he met Heuckeroth after his Arnhem performance of the Third, Mahler said to him: 'So you're Heuckeroth! It all seems to have gone very well, but how did you ever have the courage to do it?'

[148] Henri Viotta (1848–1933), son of the singer and composer Johannes Viotta, studied under Richard Hal in Amsterdam and Ferdinand Hiller at the Cologne Conservatory, led parallel careers as lawyer, cellist, and

to the enthusiasm of this new trio of admirers that the Third Symphony received its first hearing outside the German-speaking countries, when it was performed at the Arnhem Festival on 17 October 1903, an event very well received by the critics, as we shall see.[149] The Arnhem performance had originally been announced in May as part of a two-day festival planned for July, but unforeseen difficulties held back the première until October, so that Heuckeroth must have been somewhat annoyed to find, shortly afterwards, that Mengelberg had invited Mahler himself to conduct the work with the Concertgebouw, and that the concert would take place only five days after the Arnhem one. But the simple fact that these two performances could be given in such a short space of time again shows what a sensation the first performance of the symphony in Krefeld had created.

So, for the first time since the Liège concert in 1899, Mahler set off on 18 October to discover a new country. As soon as he arrived in Amsterdam, he wrote to Alma to tell her about his journey, starting with his departure from Vienna:

The Crowned Head of the Belgians was travelling with me!—As I got on the train, I noticed to my surprise a great scurrying to and fro among the railway staff, carpets laid out and a whole crowd of uniforms and shakos. We passengers were hustled aboard like draught-cattle, and inspected and processed with particular rudeness. . . . The rumour spread with the speed of wind and everyone rushed excitedly to the carriage windows. I remained seated, of course, but I noticed from a sudden increase in the noise (which doubtless came from the beating hearts of the delighted, loyal subjects) that the world-shattering event was taking place. But then it happened to me! A few moments later, just when I thought I was safe, and looking innocently ahead of me, an imposing figure passed by the window of my compartment and gave me a piercing look: and then I realized it was our noble monarch [King Leopold II of Belgium was returning home after an official visit].[150] That was the first time on my journey that I regretted my Almscherl was not with me. I am sure she would have been enormously interested. Since then I've regretted it anew at least every half hour.

musicologist. Having played in the Bayreuth orchestra at the time of the première of *Parsifal*, he founded a Wagner Society and produced *Parsifal* in Holland, one of its first performances outside Bayreuth. Later, he expanded the repertoire of his society to include early composers like Lully and ultra-modern ones like Alban Berg and Hindemith. Conductor of the Caecilia Concerts in Amsterdam, and occasionally also of the Concertgebouw, from 1896 he was director of the Royal Conservatory in The Hague, where he founded the Residence Orchestra. Viotta's first account of the Third Symphony, after the Krefeld concert, was full of reservations, but the influence of his friend, the conductor Joan Adrian Van Zuylen van Njevelt, greatly helped to change his mind. In fact Van Zuylen had heard the Second Symphony in Basel and had written an enthusiastic review for the magazine *Caecilia*. He himself had decided to schedule the Second for the Residence Orchestra during the autumn, but in the end the performance was postponed. (See RMH and Eduard Reeser's collection of letters and documents relating to Diepenbrock: *Brieven en Documenten* (Nijhoff, The Hague, 1974).)

[149] The orchestra for the performance was that of the Arnhem Orkest-Vereeniging, augmented by the Utrecht Stedelijk Orkest. The last named orchestra participated in the première of Mahler's Sixth Symphony at Essen in 1906. The contralto solo was sung by Pauline de Haan-Manifarges.

[150] A gala performance of Nedbal's ballet *Der faule Hans* had been given in his honour at the Vienna Opera on 17 Oct.

As always the journey was 'incredibly long', but Mahler endured it better than usual. Every two hours he took out his 'food parcel and ate hungrily'. But he was 'so cold' that his 'teeth chattered'. The train finally arrived in Amsterdam at 10.00 in the morning, and well-meaning people 'began to compete for possession of my corpse'. Half an hour later he found himself seated by the fire 'munching Edam cheese' in the Mengelbergs' house near the Concertgebouw, 'one of the most beautiful parts of Amsterdam'. Immediately after lunch he conducted his first rehearsal. 'When my Third began,' he wrote, 'I was quite stunned! It's really breathtaking! The orchestra is excellent and has been very well prepared!' The next morning was free and Mahler walked around the town with the Mengelbergs. The streets and canals reminded him of Hamburg, 'although here everything is on a larger scale, more spacious'. The third day, he took a boat around the port as far as Zaandam, where he visited the house of Peter the Great, and also Berlage's brand-new stock exchange building,[151] considered by the Secessionists to be one of the masterpieces of contemporary architecture. He congratulated himself on having 'learnt to see' thanks to Carl Moll, and let himself go in his letter with unusually long and detailed descriptions:

One understands why painters feel at home in this county! Colourful houses, meadows, cows, windmills, water wherever you look, seagulls in the air or on the water, ships and forests full of masts, and the wonderful floating reflections of all that! One could wander here for weeks on end! . . .

These Dutch pastures, crossed by charming roads (paved and lined with trees) and these long, straight canals shining in the silvery light coming from all sides, those little green houses and over it all a grey-blue sky with innumerable flocks of birds! It's so beautiful! How I rejoice to think of the pleasure it will give you when you come here with me next year!

Later Mahler went to the Rijksmuseum to view the Rembrandts, which made a deep impression on him. He also visited The Hague, Scheveningen, and Haarlem. Alma had asked him to bring back some cheese and ham, but Mahler, knowing his 'clumsiness' in such matters, did not carry out the errand, nor did he mention it to his hosts for fear they would feel obliged to rush off to do his shopping for him.

For the moment Mahler was in two minds about the Dutch. Referring to a favourite book of his, Multatuli's *Max Havelaar*,[152] he confessed that he had 'looked everywhere for Havelaar and found mainly Droogstoppels' [the novel's anti-hero]. He found the people he met 'highly original', with 'a peculiar mixture of phlegm and resolve'. The Mengelbergs did their best 'to make life . . . even the world . . . easier for me'. His hosts' discretion was exemplary: they

---

[151] Hendrick Berlage, see below Vol. iii, Chap. 1.

[152] For further comments on Multatuli's book and the conversations Mahler had about it with his Dutch friends, see below, Vol. iii, Chap. 1.

even left him alone on the evening of his arrival, giving him an opportunity to look over a pile of scores by Dutch, Belgian, and French composers. 'My God, how tremendously imaginative and yet how sterile!' he wrote afterwards. But he decided, once again, never to accept such invitations again; he felt hampered by his responsibilities as a guest and had to make daily excuses to get off by himself to write to Alma. He preferred to spend most of his time alone as he had in Lemberg. Also, he had become an enthusiastic disciple of art nouveau and of the economy of line practised and preached by the Secessionists. Therefore, the *fin de siècle* decoration of the Mengelbergs' apartment distressed him. In fact Friedrich Wilhelm, the conductor's father, a German born in Cologne, was a sculptor by profession. With the help of his sons Otto and Joseph, he founded in Utrecht a studio which produced countless neo-classical statues which still today adorn many neo-Gothic churches in Holland. He made frequent visits to Amsterdam to stay with his son, whose apartment was profusely adorned in a similar style: the walls were covered with pictures as mediocre as they were conventional. They irritated Mahler so much that on one occasion he could not resist saying to a Dutch friend: 'The father's small-talk is hanging on the son's walls.'[153]

However, Mahler eventually came to be very glad of the Mengelbergs' invitation and to appreciate Dutch hospitality in all its aspects. Chief of the new friends he was to make on this first stay in Amsterdam was a gifted composer he met at the Mengelbergs, Alphons Diepenbrock,[154] whose loyal friendship and enlightened admiration he immediately began to appreciate. Diepenbrock, a distinguished Hellenist and Latinist, was above all the composer of a Te Deum for soloists, chorus, and orchestra which had been much applauded the previous year in its première under Mengelberg, and twice repeated in the same year. His passion for Wagner had led him to Nietzsche, who had become one of his favourite writers. In 1896 he decided that Strauss's symphonic poem *Also sprach Zarathustra* was a distortion of the great poet-philosopher's ideas. It had even turned him away from Strauss and from the *neudeutsch* movement, which he accused of a materialistic, militarist, and chauvinist orientation radically opposed, in his view, to the 'Greater Germany' of Goethe, Brentano, Novalis, and his favourite poet Hölderlin. For the same

[153] Hendrik de Booy, 'Menschen die ik ontmoette', TS, private collection, Amsterdam, quoted in RMH 18.

[154] Alphons Diepenbrock (1862–1921), born in Amsterdam to a Westphalian Catholic family, studied music at home before commencing his university studies. He began his professional life teaching classics and philology at Herzogenbosch, where his *Missa in die Festo* (1891) for solo tenor, choir, and organ attracted public attention in 1896. In 1897 he moved to Amsterdam, where he became a private tutor in Greek and Latin and composed notably *Hymnen an die Nacht* (on texts by Novalis) for soprano and orchestra, a *Stabat Mater* (1896), and a Te Deum (1897). His determining influences were the music of Wagner, which explains why he wrote only for the voice, and Gregorian plainsong, principal source of his polymelodic style (RMH 8). He later composed five operas. Eveline Nikkels has pointed out that Diepenbrock's choice of texts can be used as evidence of his affinity with Mahler's spiritual world. He composed an *Auferstehungshymne, Christus is opgestanden*; 2 *Hymnen an die Nacht*; a Veni Creator Spiritus; and set to music a text by Nietzsche, whom he fervently admired ('Alphons Diepenbrock, Mahler-Freund und Mahler-Forscher der ersten Stunde', in *Das Gustav-Mahler-Fest Hamburg 1989* (Bärenreiter, Kassel, 1991), 186).

reason, Diepenbrock was shocked to read in the Arnhem Festival programme note that Mahler had associated a *Wunderhorn* text with Zarathustra's famous 'Night Song' in the Third Symphony. Prior to Mahler's arrival, in correspondence with a Germanist friend in Utrecht, Willem Gijsbert Hondius van den Brock, he had made some sarcastic remarks about the composer of the Second Symphony and in particular about his long search for a text for the Finale.[155] Hondius was surprised therefore to receive from Diepenbrock, on the day of the Amsterdam performance, a telegram urging him to come at once for this 'very important' concert. The telegram arrived too late for its recipient to catch the Amsterdam train, but a letter from Diepenbrock to his former pupil Johannes Cornelis Hol shows how and why he had changed his mind:

Last week I met Gustav Mahler. This man has made a profound impression on me. I have heard and admired his Third Symphony. There is much that is ugly in the first movement, but on the second and third hearing, when you know what he is intending to say, it all seems quite different. Mahler is very straightforward, doesn't pose as a celebrity, is just what he appears to be. I have the greatest admiration for him. . . . A naive bon enfant, sometimes childlike, he looks out with wondering eyes from behind big spectacles. He is modern in every respect. He believes in the future: he made me feel like a mourning Romantic. I can tell you that his presence has done me good. I've told him that too, in a rather fulsome little letter. That his music seems to have the power of 'changing people', of inducing 'catharsis'. That is no small thing. Strauss's *Heldenleben* and *Don Quixote* make a sad showing beside his Third Symphony. Not only is neo-Prussianism and nickel-plating reduced to a minimum in the Third but the work as a whole, with its many folksongs (also a wonderful chorus for women's voices from *Des Knaben Wunderhorn*) stands in direct contradiction to the aforesaid nickel-plating. This music is not inspired by what the Prussians call 'Gründerthum' (speculative promoterism), unlike Don Quixote and the hero of *Heldenleben*, who both end up as Philistines, their only connection to heaven being by interurban telephone. With Mahler it is different. I'll tell you more about him another time, for I have lots more to say on the subject.[156]

For his part, Mahler was so delighted to have found such a distinguished companion, who moreover saw in his music all the virtues the Germans and Austrians were determined to deny to it, that he asked for Diepenbrock to be seated next to him every time he was invited out to dinner.[157] He thus saw him every day of his stay in Holland, and took the time to look through his new friend's scores. 'I've met here a very interesting Dutch musician called

---

[155] Diepenbrock had read the famous passage in Mahler's 1897 letter to Arthur Seidl (MBR1, no. 209; MBR2, no. 216) about the composition of the Second Symphony.

[156] Letter to Johannes Holl, RMH 10.

[157] Letter from Ludgardis Diepenbrock, the composer's youngest sister (1872–1944), to her sister Maria, 30 Oct. (Reeser, 'Alphons Diepenbrock', *Brieven* (see n. 148), 141). Ludgardis Diepenbrock relates that Mahler and her brother dined together in this way on 24 Oct. with one of the founders of the Concertgebouw, the banker Henrik Johan de Marez-Oyens, and the following evening with the editor of the *Algemeen Handelsblad*, Charles Boissevain, a member of the Concertgebouw's board.

Diepenbrock, who writes very interesting and singular church music,' he wrote to Alma.[158]

In Amsterdam as elsewhere, Mahler had been preceded by stories and rumours about his 'inhuman' and 'tyrannical' behaviour towards orchestral musicians. In June 1902 the Dutch periodical *Weekblad voor Musiek* had even reproduced a particularly virulent article on this subject from the magazine *Österreichisch-Ungarische Musiker-Zeitung*.[159] It dealt mainly with Mahler's allegedly scandalous treatment of Viennese musicians. Despite this, the atmosphere during the rehearsals of the Third Symphony seems to have remained euphoric throughout. The musicians were completely won over, not only by the conductor, but also by the work. Mahler was walking on air: 'It's incredibly beautiful. I can't find words to describe what I experience over and over again on hearing it.' All he needed to complete his happiness was Alma's presence, particularly since the Amsterdam performance would much surpass the one in Krefeld.[160] At the dress rehearsal, 200 school-children and their teachers 'roared' the *bimm-bamm* in the fifth movement and a choir of 330 female voices sang to perfection. As for the orchestra, the quality of the strings was as superb as that of the Vienna Philharmonic. He added: 'The performers never stopped applauding and waving. . . . Musical culture in this country is stupendous. These people really know how to listen!'[161] The promise of the rehearsals was fulfilled by the concert. At first the audience was somewhat cold, but from movement to movement they grew warmer, and in the fourth movement, where the contralto solo comes in (Mahler had brought Hermine Kittel from Vienna at short notice),[162] 'there was a general stir and tension and then the well-known progression to the end'. So as not to break the spell, Mahler kept the chorus standing until the end of the Finale. 'After the last chord, an outburst of jubilation that had something

[158] AMM1. 317; AMM2. 289.

[159] The article accompanied an account of a meeting of the committee of the Amsterdamsche Toonkunstenaars-Vereenigung on 31 May 1902. A text of rare ferocity, it had obviously been based on the reports of a member of the Opera orchestra. It claimed that instrumental players were systematically 'underestimated', were constantly being sacked for no good reason and replaced 'like pocket handkerchiefs', in a 'frighteningly arbitrary' fashion. Prudent musicians now hesitated to accept a post at the Opera for 'the work is difficult, the responsibility enormous and the pay small'. Further, 'the most outstanding work is scarcely noticed, while small faults receive punishment and humiliations'. Musicians had even been sacked after less than a year's service. In the second half of the article, publ. in a later issue of the same Dutch magazine, Schalk was taken to task 'for the manner in which he returned Diepenbrock's Te Deum without a word to its composer' and for the 'rudeness' of his behaviour towards the musicians.

[160] Letters from Holland written in 1903 are in AMM1, but mixed up with those from the following year. Those on pp. 319, 321, 322, and 324 were written in Oct. 1903.

[161] AMM1. 321; AMM2. 289. These are not excerpts from letters but from a series of postcards, the last of which has disappeared. It is possible Alma threw it away, for the interrupted sentence in the original text begins 'Aber Almschi . . .': Mahler was probably taking her to task.

[162] In a letter to the composer-conductor Wouter Hutschenruyter at the end of July, Mahler 'accepted with pleasure' the American-German alto Adrienne von Kraus-Osborne as soloist. 'I have never met her personally, but according to all reports, she is the performer best suited to my work,' he wrote (Gemeende Museum, The Hague). Kraus-Osborne having fallen ill, Pauline de Haan-Manifarges, soloist in the Arnhem concert, was approached, but she too fell ill (RMH 50).

impressive about it. Everyone tells me that there has been nothing like it in human memory. Strauss is very much in vogue here, but I'm now head and shoulders above him.' The concert was repeated with equal success to a packed hall on the following evening, 23 October.[163] Mahler had already begun rehearsals for the First Symphony, which he was also to interpret on two consecutive evenings as the first part of a classical programme conducted by Mengelberg.

The reviews in the various Amsterdam papers showed a degree of open-mindedness and objectivity rare for their time. The high quality of Dutch music criticism was not surprising, since, unlike their Viennese counterparts, most reviewers were musicologists, teachers, composers, and choir masters, some of whom had international reputations. Most were already acquainted with Mahler's Third Symphony, having travelled to the Arnhem Festival to hear it. The Arnhem orchestra, augmented for the occasion by the orchestra from nearby Utrecht, spared no pains to make it a great success. In his review in the *Nieuwe Rotterdamsche Courant*, Sibmacher Zijnen explained that only on this second hearing (after Krefeld) had he gained an intelligent insight into the work, notably into the gigantic first movement which the other critics, who were hearing it for the first time, greeted coolly. Barend Kwast, in *De Nieuwe Courant*, confined his appreciations to the second movement, the only one which he was able to regard as 'pure music' in conformity with Mahler's definition. The critic of the *Amsterdammer Weekblad*, Anton Averkamp,[164] heartily congratulated the little town of Arnhem 'for having introduced one of the most famous modern composers to Holland', and discussed at length the meaning of the Third Symphony and the 'programme' which Mahler subsequently refused to allow to be published in Amsterdam.[165] Averkamp objected mainly to the length of the first movement and to the posthorn solo in the third, but he nevertheless admitted that the symphony was 'written from the composer's heart', that it expressed the 'naïveté of his faith' and the 'innermost life of his soul'.

---

[163] The Third Symphony was performed twice in Amsterdam, on 22 and 23 Oct., with the participation of Hermine Kittel and choruses from the Amsterdam Society for the Encouragement of Music (*Bevordering der Toonkunst*) and the Society for Improvement of Folk Singing (*Verbetering van den Volkszang*). Mengelberg later conducted the Third in The Hague on 3 Feb. 1904.

[164] Anton Averkamp (1861–1934), who reviewed Mahler's concert for the *Weekblad 'De Amsterdammer'*, was born near Willinge Langerak, and studied musicology and choral conducting in Berlin and Amsterdam, where he was a pupil of Daniel de Lange. Later he studied composition in Munich with Josef Rheinberger and singing with Johannes Messchaert. After de Lange's chorus was dissolved, Averkamp formed a new one which he directed himself and which won a vast international audience thanks to the exceptional quality of the voices. Later he became singing teacher, then director, of the Toonkunst School in Utrecht, and wrote many books on music, as well as arrangements of Renaissance music and some original works which are today completely forgotten.

[165] The brochure distributed in Arnhem contained an excellent analysis of the symphony (24 pp. with 27 music examples) by Pieter Anne van Westrheene (RMH 9), a classics teacher and conductor of the local choir who had played a major part in preparing the concert. This writer reproduced Mahler's 'programmatic titles', while noting that the composer had forbidden their publication in Krefeld. (See Eduard Reeser, 'Die Mahler-Rezeption in Holland 1903–1911', in *Mahler-Interpretation* (Schott, Mainz, 1985), 81.)

A week later, after the Amsterdam concert, Simon van Milligen,[166] in the *Allgemeen Handelsblad* wrote with delight that thanks to Mahler's brilliant conducting he had finally succeeded in following the 'stream' of the first movement 'through all its capricious twists and turns'. This time, both Mahler's folk themes, used in the fashion of the Slav composers, and his 'Schubertian melodies and rhythms' had completely conquered him, all the more since the 'capriciousness' of the work was softened in the 'profound, quiet ecstasy' of the Finale. Milligen advised his readers to follow his example and hear the work twice. He considered Mahler a truly original composer in whom the 'childlike, trusting spirit that hopes and believes' was joined to 'that of the modern superman'; he was a conductor of 'genuine temperament' and 'absolute calm' whose 'power within tranquillity' made him seem 'a giant' on the podium.

In *Het Nieuws van den Dag*, Daniel de Lange's[167] opinion of Mahler was equally high. He placed him neither 'in the second or first rank' but rather 'beyond classification', because he was a composer to whom 'no rules apply'. Mahler's orchestral skills were so great, he wrote, that he wondered whether his music was 'art or pure sound', and whether Mahler's enormous cleverness did not conceal a certain 'superficiality'. Whether it was ugly or beautiful, de Lange had no doubts about the work's 'significance'. After the Amsterdam concert, Averkamp called him an 'interesting personality' and a 'master of orchestral technique' who was 'not content to walk the paths which others have trod before him' and who aspired above all to 'create atmospheres'. In his opinion, Mahler had a great sense of 'simple and childlike poetry' and had 'done violence to his nature for the sake of artistic modernism'.[168] But the anonymous critic on the musical review *Caecilia Maandblad*[169] found Mahler's art 'authentic and real', with such 'markedly individual qualities' that it could not but 'invite the most contradictory judgements'. In the *Weekblad voor Muziek*, J. H. Garms, junior, nevertheless had to confess that the work had made a profound impression on him, even approached as 'pure music'.

Thus the majority of the Dutch critics gave Mahler a welcome that was open-

[166] Simon van Milligen (1849–1929) was born in Rotterdam. He was a pupil of Samuel de Lange and Woldemar Bargiel, and studied musicology and composition in Holland and Paris before becoming a conductor, a specialist in French contemporary music, and a critic for *De Amsterdammer* and *Allgemeen Handelsblad*. In 1902, he became editor-in-chief of the magazine *Caecilia* and in 1913 he was named professor at the Amsterdam Conservatory. Author of a history of music, he also composed an opera and some Lieder.

[167] Member of a dynasty of musicians, Daniel de Lange (1841–1918) was the brother of the conductor, composer, and teacher Samuel de Lange, junior. Born in Rotterdam, he studied with his father, Samuel senior, whom he later joined in Paris. He was organist for the Reformed Church of Montrouge from 1860 until he left France at the start of the war of 1870. Pianist, cellist, and conductor as well as organist, he founded several Dutch choral and vocal groups with whom he made many international tours. He directed the Amsterdam Conservatory, 1895–1913, and composed a large number of instrumental and choral works.

[168] Averkamp points out in his *Amsterdammer Weekblad* article of 1 Nov. that, for the Amsterdam concert, Mahler varied the volume of the posthorn in the third movement by opening and closing a door, behind which the posthorn player was sitting.

[169] Eduard Reeser, in the article quoted above, claims that the author was the conductor and musicologist Henri Viotta (see above).

minded and respectful even if not always warm. The only really adverse review of the kind Mahler was used to was Otto Knaap's in *De Telegraaf*. The 'atrocious dissonances' of the Third had made his hair stand on end and caused him 'physical pain'—even 'unbearable torment'. He found some new epithets for the Third: 'the worst Chinese music', 'a parody of ultra-modern music' in which only snobs pretended to be interested! Fortunately, the weekly supplement of *De Telegraaf* subsequently published another article by Henri Viotta who admitted finding certain passages of the Third puzzling, but refused to pass final judgement for the time being. The work as a whole seemed to show 'great mastery'; its form was 'clear and transparent' and its instrumental colouring 'glorious'. Viotta persisted, however, in the attitude he had adopted after the Krefeld concert, according to which this music could not be regarded as 'pure', since the programme was just as indispensable for understanding it as in the case of Berlioz's *Symphonie fantastique*. This did not prevent him from seeing Mahler as 'a musician of great genius' or from praising the excellence of the Concertgebouw Orchestra. Mahler himself said after the concert that he had never heard his music performed so well.

A few days later, the second Mahler programme, with the Dutch première of the First Symphony,[170] evoked a much less favourable critical reaction. Although the audience remained 'enthusiastic and grateful', the symphony's merits and faults were hotly disputed by the press. It was judged by many critics unintelligible without a 'programme'. Averkamp found it bizarre rather than original, 'melodically naive, often cheap, even banal', and regretted that Mahler had not chosen his more mature Fourth, 'which would have met with no opposition', whereas the First had invariably provoked hostility since its 'Weimar première'.[171] In *De Nieuwe Courant* Barend Kwast found it 'unnatural, empty, untrue, unhealthy'. Daniel de Lange, on the other hand, felt that the First was accessible in spite of its complexities, and considered its Finale one of the most beautiful symphonic movements in contemporary music. Mahler, he went on, was a virtuoso, clever but superficial, a 'brilliant prestidigitator' who 'tried to capture the heart' with his intelligence. While listeners may have admired the perfection and superficial splendour of his art, few of them, thought de Lange, had been swept away by the composer's 'lofty ideal'.[172] Despite the reservations of the press concerning the First Symphony, Mahler

---

[170] The second half of the concert, conducted by Mengelberg, comprised Weber's *Oberon* Overture, Mozart's *Eine kleine Nachtmusik*, and the Overture to *Tannhäuser*.

[171] It is clear that Averkamp had read none of the articles on the Fourth Symphony publ. in Munich and Berlin. He was also unaware that the First Symphony had been performed twice before the Weimar Festival.

[172] At the beginning of Feb. 1904, Mengelberg conducted the First in The Hague, where the critics called Mahler a 'gifted charlatan', and deplored the banality of his themes. Only Jan de Jong, in *Het Vaderland*, conceded that he had found the work 'interesting, very interesting' and, at the end of the third movement, 'exquisite'. The critic of the *Residentiebode* claimed that listeners had left the hall in whole groups at the end of each movement. A short time before, after Mengelberg's performance of the same symphony in The Hague, the reviews had been even more unfavourable. Willem Landré called Mahler a 'charlatan of genius' in the *Nieuwe Courant*.

had won in Holland one of the greatest triumphs of his career as a composer. The general reaction was so positive that Mengelberg immediately invited him for the following year. Back in Vienna, Mahler wrote him a thank-you note and added: 'Thanks to your friendly care and profound artistic understanding, I feel that I have discovered a second home in Amsterdam.'[173]

While Holland was the first non-Germanic country to discover the Third Symphony, the list of German cities wanting to hear it continued to lengthen. Performances planned for 1904, in Heidelberg, Mannheim, Prague, and Cologne,[174] ensured that the Third would continue its already brilliant career. Meanwhile, on 7 December, the First Symphony was performed in Darmstadt under the local conductor, Willem de Haan,[175] with 'genuine success', although there were the usual 'conflicting opinions'. The *Darmstädter Zeitung* called Mahler 'a true master,' a symphonist with 'powerful and profound thoughts and a wealth of ideas', who 'blazed his own trail' with 'impressive self-assurance'. The *Tagblatt* found genius even in its eccentricities but found the work too 'full of contrasting moods' to merit the title of symphony.

During the Darmstadt performance, Mahler was in Vienna. He had just returned from Frankfurt where Ludwig Rottenberg[176] had asked him to conduct the Third Symphony at the Frankfurt Opera's third subscription concert. At the station, as he was leaving Vienna for Frankfurt, Mahler had met the composer Friedrich Rösch who was taking the same train as far as Munich, and they had had a long and 'very agreeable' conversation, probably concerning the Berlin Genossenschaft der Deutschen Tonsetzer, of which Rösch was President and which Mahler had decided to join.[177] After a fairly comfortable journey during which he managed to sleep until 9 o'clock in the morning, Mahler was interviewed over breakfast in the train by a journalist called Lothar.[178] Mahler later joked to Alma: 'I gave him the most exact information on my intentions concerning Marienbad pills and liquorice powder, and some interesting explanations about the nature of haemorrhoids.' Arriving in Frankfurt at midday, Mahler was met on the platform by Ludwig Rottenberg. Having taken a comfortable room at the Imperial Hotel he went, 'hungry as a horse', to dine with his colleague.[179] He then wrote to Alma about the journey before going

---

[173] MBR1, no. 302; MBR2, no. 322, undated (1 Nov. 1903). The tone and content of most of the articles Diepenbrock translated and sent him reinforced his impression of having conquered a new country and a new audience.

[174] Even small provincial orchestras now wanted to present the work. For instance Mahler wrote to the conductor of the military band in Szeged, Hungary, on 23 Nov. 1903, thanking him for wanting to perform his work, but reminding him that it 'required a first-class orchestra'. (Letter copied by Fritz Löhr in 1903, BGM.)

[175] Willem de Haan, born in Rotterdam in 1848, was named Hofkapellmeister in Darmstadt in 1878. The performance was part of the third Hofmusikkonzert held at the Hoftheater. Programme for 7 Dec.: Berlioz, Overture to *Benvenuto Cellini*; Mahler, First Symphony; Saint-Saëns, *Phaeton*; arias and songs (Angèle Bidron, soprano); and Berlioz, *Carnival romain* Overture.

[176] See above, Chap. 6, the biography of this conductor.   [177] See above, Chap. 14.

[178] This was probably Rudolf Lothar (1865–1943), the author of the libretto of Eugen d'Albert's *Tiefland*. In 1898 he had founded the Viennese magazine *Die Waage* and edited it until 1902.

[179] It was during this stay in the hotel that Mahler must have written his letter to Dr Richard Horn,

to the first rehearsal, with the first trombone (whose solos in the first movement are particularly taxing) and the flügelhorn (which was to play the posthorn solos).[180] Mahler insisted on arranging for a general rehearsal two days before the concert to decide on the positioning of the bells which he had brought with him from Vienna, 'since this will require complicated experimentation'.[181]

At the first rehearsal on 1 December, Mahler found the orchestra 'pretty rough, rather like the Vienna Konzertverein'. 'Oh dear! What misery having to chew it over and over again right from the beginning! I shall soon be fed-up with my Third if this continues!' he wrote to Alma. Furthermore, the contralto soloist, Clara Weber, was 'insensitive and devoid of any sense of poetry'.[182] Fortunately, the second rehearsal the following day was less discouraging. The orchestra appeared genuinely captivated by the work, and the chorus was excellent. Even the contralto solo now satisfied him. Mahler as usual spent his spare time exploring the streets of the city, in spite of the driving rain. He searched everywhere for traces of Goethe, Frankfurt's illustrious son, but found none except for 'a few café signs'. In the evening he attended the Opera, but without much interest: the singers he wanted to hear, because they had been hired for Vienna, were only 'pale stars'. At the dress rehearsal, the quality of the orchestra in the first movement of the Third Symphony seemed to him 'far too mediocre', but it improved in the subsequent movements. There was timid applause at the end, but Mahler paid no attention, and immediately set to work again with the orchestra.[183]

As often happened when he was away from Vienna, Mahler received almost every day a telegram from the Opera, telling him of the previous night's takings or of the success of this or that 'guest' singer. This time, his assistant Wondra telegraphed a gloomy assessment of the début of a tenor named Alois Penarini in *Tannhäuser* on 1 December. Also, Bruno Walter had fallen ill the same evening, in the middle of the performance, and had had to be replaced by Schalk at a moment's notice.[184]

enclosing an article from the *Kölnische Zeitung* (29 Nov. 1903), concerning the problems of contemporary physics, a letter which Alma dated 1907 in MBR1, no. 341, and MBR2, no. 369. See below, Vol. iii, Chap. 6.

[180] Unpubl. letter to Alma, 30 Nov. 1903. This was mistakenly filed with an envelope bearing the postmark 16 Jan. 1907. The mention of a rehearsal for the first trombone and flügelhorn indicates the performance of the Third in Dec. 1903. In 1907, Mahler conducted the Fourth at the seventh Museumskonzert, 18 Jan.

[181] Undated letter (Nov. 1903), no doubt to Ludwig Rottenberg (Stargardt Auction, May 1960, lot 548).

[182] Letter to Philip Wolfrum dated 10 Jan. 1904 (Collection A. Nogler, Zurich).

[183] The three letters written to Alma from Frankfurt in 1903 have been wrongly inserted with those of 1904. They were written on 30 Nov. and 1 and 2 Dec. 1903 (AMM1. 313 ff.; AMM2. 281 ff.). AMS also contains a copy of a postcard written to Alma on 29 Nov. from the Vienna station, just before Mahler took the train for Frankfurt.

[184] Walter had to keep to his room until 9 Dec. This lapse was an advance symptom of a psychosomatic paralysis of the right arm which was to affect the conductor for almost two years. Having consulted all the leading Viennese doctors, Walter went at the beginning of 1906 to consult Sigmund Freud, see below, Vol. iii, Chap. 5, and George H. Pollock, 'On Freud's Psychotherapy of Bruno Walter', in *The Annual of Psychoanalysis*, 3 (New York, 1975), 292.

On the evening of the public performance, the Third was greeted with less enthusiasm than in Krefeld or Amsterdam, and as usual reviews the following day were conflicting. The *Frankfurter Zeitung* found that in some passages the 'powerful means of expression employed' were out of all proportion to the 'thoughts and sentiments' expressed. The anonymous critic was amazed to find, in the midst of such a serious work, something that sounded like 'the changing of the guard', a combination of the 'grotesque' and the 'trivial', and 'witty orchestral jokes'. Nevertheless, the 'profound earnestness and fervour' of the Finale made one forget all that and ensured the work's success. The *Musikalisches Wochenblatt* correspondent found the Third 'confusing' and of an 'incomprehensible complexity'. Only 'orchestral effects' saved it from becoming wearisome. In *Die Musik*, the anonymous review attributed its success solely to Mahler's 'magnetism' and 'captivating' personality as a conductor.[185]

Oskar Nedbal's performance in Prague of the Second Symphony with the Czech Philharmonic on 18 December 1903, in the Rudolfinum Hall, was the direct consequence of Mahler's triumph in Basel Cathedral the previous June. Alma went from Vienna with her mother, since Mahler could not leave the Opera. There was such overwhelming acclaim that Nedbal immediately decided to repeat the concert ten days later.[186] As it was a purely Czech affair, it was reviewed only in the Czech press, with fulsome but vague praise for the performers and the work. *Čas* (the Prague *Times*) detected the influence of Czech folk music, particularly in the second and third movements. According to the same anonymous reviewer, Mahler surpassed even Berlioz as an orchestrator. His music expressed 'a great variety of moods and impressions' and clearly revealed a man 'fresh, youthful and filled with a strong love of life', in contrast to the 'titanesque old age' of a Bruckner. After the second concert on the 28th, the same critic pointed out the work's 'quotations from familiar sources' and Mahler's deliberate 'combination of styles', German, French, and Slav, into an 'international' idiom, strongly contrasting with the prevailing 'national' tendencies. 'The reasons for this lie much deeper than superficial imitation', the same perspicacious critic added. 'Mahler's music looks to the future and consequently cannot be judged by traditional musical standards.'

Finally, the newspaper *Národní Politika* praised the quality of the performance, but came to the surprising conclusion that, in addition to Schubert, the major influences on Mahler were Bizet and the French (an error of judgement also quite frequent in the contemporary German press, as exemplified by the Berlin critic who, in 1897, had described the minuet of the Third as

---

[185] The same critic marvelled that Mahler was able to 'create the illusion that he had held a dozen rehearsals'. The concert took place on 2 Dec. 1903 with the participation of the solo contralto Clara Weber and the Frankfurt Opera chorus and orchestra.

[186] Two unpubl. letters from Mahler to Alma which, though undated, were undoubtedly sent to Prague at the time of this performance, since they mention Nedbal and the Blauer Stern Hotel. They contain little beyond news of Putzi and the Auenbruggergasse household. Alma noted 'Prague 1903' on the typed copies (AMS).

französische Pikanterie).[187] In the periodical *Dalibor*, the Second was described as 'somewhat fragmentary' in effect, at least at the beginning, but also as 'invariably powerful'. The work's novelty was also emphasized, together with its originality and the possibilities it opened up for the symphony of the future. According to this reviewer, the second and third movements were better received by the audience than the rest. Yet there existed among all the elements of style and language a true harmony, an unmistakable coherence. The critic also insisted upon the Slav features of the Second, in addition to the many other influences it displayed.[188] Finally, the critic in the German-language magazine *Neue Musik-Zeitung*, the Czech composer Rudolf Freiherr Prochaska, whose opera Mahler had refused to put on at the Hofoper, hinted strongly that Nedbal was conducting the Second in Prague in payment for services rendered (his ballet *Der faule Hans* having been premièred in Vienna on 3 October).[189] For him, the Third was a 'monster work' (*Monsterwerk*) and the effect of its many beautiful, though rather theatrical features had been sensational: 'In the final apotheosis, which outdoes anything previously composed, one is faced with a "super-Beethoven" who elicits more exasperation than admiration.'[190]

The public was slowly becoming more receptive and discerning than the critics, and was beginning to show genuine appreciation of the two big symphonies on which Mahler's reputation was now mainly based. Many professionals continued to poke fun at their 'gigantism', and sometimes put their author's sincerity in doubt (if only people would stop raising the false issue of 'sincerity' in art!). Some people still found them 'bizarre' and 'enigmatic'. But they could no longer be ignored. Mahler now had several 'popular' triumphs to his credit, and even though the average listener was not always immediately won over, and was often puzzled at his own reactions to this strange art, it had come to be regarded as essential, if only for reasons of snobbery, to know about this composer's work, which was now frequently being described as providing some of the most characteristic examples of modernism and the avant-garde in music.

---

[187] This can be trans. only as 'French piquantry'.

[188] *Dalibor* (9 Jan. 1904), quoted by Arnošt Mahler in 'Gustav Mahler und seine Heimat', unpubl.

[189] The première of this ballet in five scenes, after a tale by F. K. Hejda, was conducted by the composer and directed by the choreographer Josef Hassreiter, ballet-master at the Hofoper.

[190] *Neue Musikzeitung*, 1 (1904), 181. The first concert, given on 18 Dec., began with Mozart's Piano Concerto No. 23, K.488, with Marie Bettelheimova-Timon at the piano. The second consisted solely of Mahler's symphony. For both performances the soloists were Gabriela Horvátová, contralto, and Božena Důrasová, soprano.

16

Der Waffenschmied, Euryanthe, Der Corregidor, Falstaff—Mannheim, Heidelberg, Prague, Mainz, Cologne—encounters with Hauptmann, Bahr, Hofmannsthal—Schoenberg, Zemlinsky, and the Vereinigung—birth of Anna—completion of the Sixth Symphony and the *Kindertotenlieder*

(January–September 1904)

> My Sixth will pose puzzles which only a generation which has already
> absorbed and digested my previous five can dare to solve.

AT the Hofoper the year 1904 began modestly enough with a revival of Lortzing's *Der Waffenschmied*, which Mahler often referred to as 'the little *Meistersinger*'.[1] The music's utter simplicity delighted him and he rehearsed it with tender care. He restored all previous cuts and, as usual, paid as much attention to the staging as to the music. Before the dress rehearsal, Mahler called the cast together and explained why he felt the *Waffenschmied* was far more than the light-hearted farce it appeared at first sight:

I would like to tell you of some of my ideas about *Der Waffenschmied*. I believe Lortzing attached a deeper meaning to it. He wanted to show—as it were—a kind of 'twilight of the knights' (*Ritterdämmerung*), the decadence of the medieval nobility which would throw into sharp relief the vigorous upward striving of the bourgeoisie. A world in decline, rich in poetic memories, was to light up with its dying rays a new kind of man. I don't know whether I'm expressing myself clearly. What I mean is that Lortzing's intention was to bid farewell to the medieval nobility and at the same time welcome the advent of the German bourgeoisie.[2]

---

[1] According to Natalie Bauer-Lechner, he 'built his entire interpretation around the humble and poetic aria' of the gunsmith Stadinger, 'Auch ich war ein Jüngling', at the end of the opera.

[2] *Illustrirtes Wiener Extrablatt* (30 Jan. 1904), 7. The tone of this article suggests that this incident was reported in order to embarrass Mahler.

Mahler then turned to the singer interpreting the innkeeper and suggested that he give his role a 'Mephistophelian' quality. According to the *Illustrirtes Wiener Extrablatt*, which reported the incident, the singer was dumbfounded. He had 'never heard anybody call Lortzing mystical before'.

At the première on 4 January, the chorus and the soloists performed splendidly, but the audience's reaction was cool, and the critics were harsh. Hirschfeld felt that Mahler had overrefined the performance and had provided yet another example of the 'fussy style which is now the rule at the Hofoper'. His interpretation had wavered between 'mystical obscurity and noisy brilliance'. But the humour, 'refusing to be domesticated', had taken flight. Muntz found that Mahler had contributed to the failure of Lortzing's music by 'analysing, commenting and stylizing'. His detrimental influence was evident throughout. The singers had been miscast, particularly Marie Gutheil-Schoder, whose 'mannerisms' (*Künsteleien*) and 'contrived posturing' merely resulted in a 'refined misinterpretation' (*Missdeutung*) of Lortzing's music. Even Schönaich accused Mahler of wandering 'like a "distinguished foreigner" into a land of innocence, naïveté and simplicity', where by 'his very presence and exaggerated courtesy' he paralysed Lortzing's merry characters. The same critic even claimed that a certain 'awkwardness and untidiness' were necessary in a performance of *Der Waffenschmied*, an unassuming work meant from the start to be performed by 'singing actors' rather than 'acting singers'. Max Kalbeck was the only Viennese critic who did not find the production 'overrefined'. He felt that Lortzing's Singspiel had been 'reborn', 'ennobled and transfigured', and that for once the singers actually sang instead of shouting. Wallaschek agreed with Kalbeck that Mahler had no peer in expressing 'the subtle and witty tone of comedy' and that he had given the opera 'the soft scent of dried flowers and old, faded books'.[3]

Two weeks later another event created a minor sensation at the Hofoper, the first performance of a 'white' ballet on a Chinese subject, *Die kleine Welt* (The Little World). The music had been composed by the official supplier of ballet music to the Opera, Josef Bayer, and the choreography was by the ballet-master Josef Hassreiter.[4] Two small girls, 11 and 12 years old, took the leading roles and the main attraction was a 'three-legged dance', in which they were draped in one large Chinese dress, the left leg of one tied to the right of the other, representing one single three-legged person. Hassreiter must have had a free hand in preparing this typically Viennese 'divertissement', since Mahler continued to look down on ballet which he considered a necessary evil, a pleasant entertainment for dilettantes, of whom there were many in Vienna.

On 19 January, the new production of *Euryanthe* again provoked conflicting

[3] Cast of 4 Jan. 1904 performance: Gutheil-Schoder (Marie), Petru (Irmentraut), Schrödter (Georg), Weidemann (Konrad), Ritter (Adelhof), Hesch (Stadinger).

[4] Josef Hassreiter (1845–1940) had had considerable success with his choreography of Josef Bayer's ballet *Die Braut von Korea* (see above, Chap. 12).

reactions from the critics. Disappointed by the near failure of the previous year, Mahler himself altered the libretto to eliminate 'the most flagrant implausibilities' and 'provide the plot with a minimum of coherence'.[5] However, he scrupulously avoided making any important changes in Weber's 'divine music'. His chief contribution was to get rid of the absurd story of the two ghosts, which, in the original libretto, is supposed to have happened long before the opera opens. In Mahler's version, the ring has been stolen from Euryanthe while she slept. As a result, the beautiful largo passage in the Overture (the 'ghosts' music) no longer referred to a mystery extraneous to the plot, but to Adolar's faith in his beloved.

The preparation of this 'new' version of an opera, which Robert Schumann called 'a string of glittering and precious jewels', 'filled with the noblest heart-blood', as usual absorbed all Mahler's 're-creative' energy, for he was totally, if not blindly, devoted to the work. The highly implausible meeting of all the principal characters in the 'wilderness' of the third act, however, still seemed to him absurd, even comic, and his affectionate nickname for it (a reference to Boieldieu's *La Dame blanche*), was 'the merry country folk all happily reunited' (*die munteren Landbewohner wieder alle vereint*). Sometimes, nevertheless, his re-creative fervour led him to defend Helmine von Chézy's libretto. On the evening of the première, Alma witnessed a typical instance of the incredible powers of conviction her husband possessed. After the performance he met his friends for supper at the Hartmann Restaurant, and arrived still immersed in Weber's splendid score, and radiant with happiness. 'When I've just re-staged and conducted such a work,' he would say on such occasions, 'I have to let the vibrations in me die down (*ausschwingen*). People must talk to me and I to them until I've regained my calm . . .'. At Hartmann's he began to defend Chézy's much-maligned poem, pointing out once again its kinship with *Lohengrin*. Alma couldn't believe her ears when she heard Bruno Walter agree with him, though shortly before Mahler arrived he had deplored the stupidity of the libretto, declaring that not even Weber's music could ever bring it to life on the stage.

The previous year a number of Viennese critics had been clamouring for a 'new version' and Mahler therefore informed them in advance of the revival. That he had put his whole heart into his revised version is confirmed by the letters he wrote in January to Hermann Stephani[6] and Max Kalbeck. He sent Kalbeck, together with the letter quoted above, the revised score to study, expressing the hope that *Euryanthe*, which he loved 'infinitely' (*unendlich*), would now have a respectable, if not pre-eminent existence on the stage.[7] However, he confessed that he had himself been uncertain whether his project

[5] Letter from Mahler to Hermann Stephani, Musikdirektor at the Univ. of Marburg, written in Jan. 1904 and reproduced later in the *Oberhessische Presse* in Marburg. Stephani had just published an article on *Euryanthe* in *Die Musik*, 3 (1903), 15, following a performance in Dresden under Ernst von Schuch. (See Vol. iv, App. 1.)   [6] See n. 5.

[7] MBR1, no. 275; MBR2, no. 327 see above, p. 558. Mahler went to the trouble of marking all his changes in a piano score for Kalbeck 'so that he would not waste time looking for them'.

would succeed, and feared that the work's 'slightly faded romanticism no longer held any appeal for a dear public gorged on *verismo* and other "isms"'.[8] He had devoted so much time and affection to *Euryanthe* that he considered having the score published and wrote to Henri Hinrichsen at his new publisher's, C. F. Peters:

Perhaps you might be interested to see my new arrangement of *Euryanthe*. I am therefore enclosing a libretto which will give you an idea of the work in its present form. Since several theatres have shown interest in my version, the thought occurred to me that a new edition of the score would be of use to them. Thus, this version which has proved to be effective in a number of performances, would become more accessible to the German theatre.[9]

Despite Mahler's efforts, the audience was rather small on opening night. However, the work was warmly received, and the following evening the theatre was full, probably for the first time since *Euryanthe*'s première at the Kärntnertortheater, seventy-nine years before.[10]

Although the new version failed to make *Euryanthe* a popular success, several critics, including Maximilian Muntz, praised Mahler's new version: the changes were 'clever and virtually imperceptible', and finally revealed the beauties of the score. If *Euryanthe* was to survive on the operatic stage, wrote Muntz, it must certainly be in this form. On the other hand, Richard Wallaschek, in *Die Zeit*, found the story so absurd and the plot and characters so impossible that the work was doomed to perpetual failure.[11] An unsigned article in the *Neue Freie Presse* also praised Mahler's changes, both textual and musical, for they 'speeded up the plot' and made the music far more effective. Once more, Hirschfeld emphasized Mahler's 'nervousness'—which by now was a theme running through all his articles. He thought this made the atmosphere of the performance 'oppressive', although 'with supreme skill, [Mahler] had imbued each note with dramatic expression'. One of the most virulent opponents of the new version was Gustav Schönaich, who felt that, far from attenuating the implausibilities of the libretto, it added to them, and that there was no point in trying to bestow the slightest appearance of logic on a plot which was utterly devoid of it. For Weber had used the libretto simply as a vehicle for the most wonderful musical inventions he had at all costs to

[8] Letter to Hermann Stephani quoted at n. 5.
[9] Letter to Henri Hinrichsen (undated; written at the beginning of 1904). Only the libretto was publ., as 'the Vienna Opera version' (Adolph W. Künast, Vienna, 1904).
[10] The new version was eventually performed in 12 German-language opera-houses; the most famous of these revivals was conducted by Hans Pfitzner at the Stuttgart Opera in 1911. Guido Adler publ. a long article on Mahler's version '"Euryanthe" in neuer Einrichtung', in *Zeitschrift der Internationalen Musikgesellschaft*, 5: 7 (Leipzig, 1904), 267.
[11] Wallaschek approved of certain changes Mahler made in the score, such as the deletion of the battle with the snake at the beginning of Act III and the replacement of the Act III Finale by a reprise of the Finale from Act I. But Schönaich thought that, in getting rid of the snake, Mahler had deprived *Euryanthe* of one of its finest musical episodes.

express. The libretto should be left in its original state; in any case, it was beyond saving.[12]

After *Euryanthe*, another opera with an unfortunate history absorbed Mahler's energy. In this case he undertook a much more ungrateful task for reasons which had more to do with personal sentiment than with aesthetic appreciation. The previous year, on the day after the new production of *Tristan* opened, Mahler's former fellow-student and friend, Hugo Wolf had died in the mental home in which he had been a permanent inmate, since 1898. Since their quarrel about *Der Corregidor*, no one had been able to persuade Mahler to produce the work, despite many pleas by Wolf's friends and the Verein that bore his name.[13] When pushed, he generally ended by confessing that the work had too many weaknesses for stage representation. However, he was honest and clear-sighted enough to recognize that Wolf was a major composer. So it was natural that Wolf's death (and perhaps the painful memory of their quarrel) should finally make him decide to add *Der Corregidor* to the Opera's repertory, despite the failure of its first performance in Mannheim in 1896 and of subsequent performances in Strasbourg, Prague, Graz, and Munich. Wolf's failure was all the more distressing in that, like many nineteenth-century composers, his life-long ambition was to compose a full-scale opera. He had considered setting Kleist's *Penthesilea* and *Der Prinz von Homburg* to music, and also Shakespeare's *The Tempest* and *The Midsummer Night's Dream*—not to mention the memorable *Rübezahl* project. He finally made the worst possible choice of subject, Alarcón's satirical novel *El sombrero de los tres picos* (The Three Cornered Hat), and in 1894 commissioned Franz Schaumann, Obmann of the Akademischer Wagner Gesangverein, to draft a libretto. Schaumann's text was apparently skilful enough, but Wolf turned it down and the following year asked another of his friends, Rosa Mayreder, to undertake the same task, doubtless forgetting that he had disliked a former effort of hers a few years before. Rosa Mayreder was a kind, generous patron, and had founded the Austrian League of Women,[14] but as a part-time poetess she had little talent, and in accepting her libretto Wolf showed just how little flair he had for the stage. The poem probably attracted him by its very weaknesses, by its lyrical rather than dramatic character. Everything in it should have made him wary: its lack of action, its literary and dramatic awkwardness, its superfluous episodes and unnecessary characters, not to mention the monotony of the trochaic tetrameters that were employed throughout.

Thus, during the summer of 1895, Wolf produced in the space of four months

[12] Cast 19 Jan. 1904: Förster-Lauterer (Euryanthe), Mildenburg (Eglantine), Kittel (Bertha), Winkelmann (Adolar), Weidemann (Lysiart), Mayr (King). The evening of the première Slezak fell ill and Winkelmann took over the main role at the last minute. But Korngold wrote that its tessitura was too high for him.

[13] Two exchanges of letters between Mahler and the Hugo Wolf-Verein survive in HOA. Mahler refused to attend the Prague performance of *Der Corregidor* (8 Apr. 1899). Then, in Aug. 1902, he wrote that, before putting on the work, he must 'wait for a certain circumstance that would make it possible to produce it'.

[14] Rosa Mayreder, née Obermayer, had married Karl Mayreder, an architect connected with Otto Wagner.

(although the orchestration subsequently was to take five more) a hybrid work, a Spanish comedy which in effect was nothing but a string of very German Lieder, interspersed with duets and trios, many of which sounded as if they were borrowed from *Die Meistersinger* because of the overweighted orchestra. No doubt Mahler recognized the greatness of his Conservatory friend's music, but he had no real feeling for it, even when it came to Wolf's undisputed masterpieces, his Lieder.[15] The rehearsals must have been a daily torture for him. Would he be able to correct some of the work's most glaring inadequacies without being accused by Wolf's admirers of sacrilege? Finally he went no further than to lighten the orchestration and rearrange the original four acts into three, for which he had the approval of some of Wolf's friends, including Michael Haberlandt, the president of the Wolf-Verein.[16] Mahler considered, that, in the original version, the act endings lacked dramatic impact. He therefore joined the silent scene at the end of the first act (the bishop's procession) to the opening scene of the second (the Corregidor's aria).[17] The Interlude which originally connected the two scenes of the original second act now became the prelude to the new one, which ended with the only dramatically effective scene in the whole opera: the Miller's jealousy aria.[18] The one slight disadvantage of the new version was that it linked scenes which originally were meant to occur a quarter or a half hour apart. But Wolf's friends gave way before Mahler's experience and authority, hoping that *Der Corregidor* would at last achieve recognition. All of them came to both the dress rehearsal and the première, which took place four days before the anniversary of Wolf's death. That evening, Rosa Mayreder's box, Alma recalled, looked like a 'veritable arbour of flowers'. The members of the Wolf-Verein did their best to stir up enthusiasm with loud bravos and strenuous applause, but failed to carry the rest of the audience along with them.

Wolf was much admired by several Viennese critics, and some of them, like Richard Wallaschek, claimed that *Der Corregidor* would have been better received if Mahler had respected the original and 'if he had not waited so long to perform it'. Wallaschek did however admit that the score was 'essentially undramatic', despite its 'genuine treasures'. Max Vancsa, the Wolf-Verein deputy spokesman, attacked what he considered to be a badly chosen cast.[19]

[15] EDS1.

[16] The Wolf-Verein had been founded on 13 May 1897. According to Heinrich Werner's book, *Der Hugo Wolf-Verein* (Regensburg, 1922), 169, Mahler had become a 'performing member' although he never performed at any of the Society's concerts. However, the same book notes that he offered his services as accompanist for Lieder-Abende (p. 40). Haberlandt told Mahler in a letter dated 25 Jan. 1904, that he 'and several other friends' of Wolf fully approved his intention to modify the layout of the acts (HOA, Z.1008/1904).

[17] The Corregidor undresses and climbs into the bed of the Miller's Wife—who has just fled from it.

[18] Tio Lucas, having found the old man's clothes at his house and seen him in the bed, believes that his wife has been unfaithful. The libretto of Mahler's version was publ. in Mannheim: *Mahlers Wiener Bearbeitung in drei Akten* (*Textbuch*) (F. Heckel, Mannheim, n.d.).

[19] *Neue Musikalische Presse*, 13 (1904), 6, 110 ff. Vancsa felt the role of the Miller's Wife should have been given to a 'Junoesque beauty', not to a 'small woman, bereft of temperament, like Förster-Lauterer'. Helm

He accused Mahler of 'substituting new weaknesses for those already inherent in the work' and claimed that, as a master of witty details, he had no understanding for the broad, carefree flow of Wolf's music. In the *Deutsche Zeitung* on the other hand, Muntz approved of the changes, while Helm thought otherwise but still called Mahler's conducting 'admirable and incomparable'. It comes as no surprise that Hirschfeld should have held Mahler entirely responsible for the work's failure. He accused him of 'toning down everything' and plunging the stage into semi-darkness with fatal results. Only three critics pointed to the opera's intrinsic weaknesses as the cause of the failure. Korngold regretted the orchestral accompaniment and the 'leaden polyphony' with which Wolf burdened the voices. Schönaich went further still, declaring *Der Corregidor* to be 'a stranger in the world of dramatic music', an opinion shared by Kalbeck, who found it of 'only historical and biographical interest'.

To convince his detractors that the opera could not work on the stage in any version, Mahler decided to return to the original version, on 10 March, for the last three performances, to which he devoted several additional rehearsals. He even reinstated the silent scene at the end of the first act, as well as the last chorus.[20] As expected, the result only convinced him that his modifications had been justified, but the critics stood firm. Muntz again blamed Mahler for the audience's cool reception and re-emphasized his 'errors in casting' and his 'indifference towards a work which he conducted only out of a sense of duty'. Wallaschek approved of the return to the original version, while Kauders and Schönaich felt that it would have been better not to restore the final ensemble, which prolonged a work already far too lengthy for the scant action it contained.[21]

The most sarcastic review by far was as usual that published by Hans Liebstöckl in the *Illustrirtes Wiener Extrablatt*. He ridiculed the Hugo Wolf-Verein and its efforts, and compared the triumvirate that led it to Wagner's three Rhinemaidens, who swam around the gold of the Verein and whose innumerable vows, warnings, and entreaties had convinced Mahler, 'the most independent of directors', to perform Wolf's original version and restore all the cuts:

also criticized her lack of freshness in the middle register and took Demuth to task for his 'lack of temperament'.

[20] The first performance of the original version (10 Mar.) was conducted by Bruno Walter. The part of Repela was now sung by Anton Moser (instead of Wilhelm Hesch) and the original orchestration was restored. Mahler's Act I included scene i of the original Act II. His Act II combined Wolf's Act II. ii with Act III. i to iv. The new Act III began with Act III. v and closed with the original Act IV, slightly shortened. On 18 Mar. Mahler conducted the sixth performance himself.

[21] Kauders conceded that it was in the Finale that Wolf had best exploited the refinements of his craft by combining all the main themes. Cast of the première of 18 Mar.: Förster-Lauterer (Frasquita), Hilgermann (Corregidora), Kittel (Manuela), Kaulich (Duenna), Breuer (Corregidor), Demuth (Tio Lukas), Preuss (Pedro), Pacal (Neighbour), Felix (Nightwatchman), Hesch (Repela), Marian (Tonuelo), Mayr (Alcade). The work was performed again at the Hofoper in 1914 (3 performances), 1926–8 (6 performances), and 1937 (4 performances).

Thus the poor 'Corregidor' stood yesterday before all eyes as Wolf had composed it, thin, undramatic, melodically undernourished, and once again it failed. The gallery was empty, the free seats were well occupied in the stalls. . . . Herr Mahler should have stood fast and have trusted more fully to his own good taste, ear, and musical good sense. . . . Was it necessary thus to underline the effect of the inner weaknesses by a shrill superficiality? The original orchestration in any case sounds bewildering. The sung parts of which, even in Mahler's version, only fragments could be heard, are now literally buried alive under the rain of stones and ashes of this eruptive, endlessly stubborn jumble of instruments. The motives, above all that of the Corregidor, ride in heavy armour. The last vestiges of Spanish humour are massacred by the brass. The thread, the melodic line is constantly interrupted, strings and brass snatch scraps of music from each other. The middle parts increase in volume, the Cantilene, insofar as this word is at all appropriate, fades into the background so that at times one is under the impression that Wolf could only think of the subsidiary part. Now we understand why Herr Mahler turned this orchestra off, why he only wanted to work on a low flame; it was a nice vestige of politeness which saved the singers from the worst. Hugo Wolf's memory has been poorly served by this revised version . . .[22]

A comparison of the 1904 *Spielplan* of the Vienna Opera with those of previous years shows it to have been richer than ever. But Mahler was beginning to be criticized for his frequent absences from Vienna in order to conduct abroad. Replying to the Lord Chamberlain's reproaches, he argued that, far from being harmful to the Hofoper, his successes as a conductor increased its prestige. He was nevertheless persuaded to limit the number and length of his guest performances. In 1904, for instance, he had to abandon several projects, including the première of the Fifth Symphony at the Cologne Festival in May, a trip to Russia,[23] and a tour of Southern Germany with the Kaim Orchestra, which had offered to include one of his works in its programme.[24] Mahler was now determined that his works should be 'performed in conformity with my intentions' and therefore made it a condition that he should conduct them himself.[25] He found that when they were performed in his absence by others, the results were far from encouraging. For example, when Bernhard Stavenhagen conducted the Third Symphony in Munich on 24 February, the *Allgemeine Zeitung* once again called Mahler an 'impotent, presumptuous' composer, a 'frog trying to imitate an ox'.[26] The anonymous critic denounced the

---

[22] *Illustrirtes Wiener Extrablatt* (19 Mar. 1904).

[23] Mahler made a point of asking Luise Wolff, the impresario, to demand a very high fee which was bound to be refused because 'his Viennese activity would probably not permit him to accept' the offer. Wolff did not obtain the 700 roubles (1,500 marks) he asked for and advised Mahler to reduce his demands to 1,000 marks (letter from Luise Wolff, 9 Apr. 1904 and Mahler's answer on 13 Apr., HOA).

[24] Letter from Kaim, and Mahler's reply dated 7 and 10 Apr. (HOA). The tour was planned for either Nov. 1904, or Jan. or Mar. 1905.

[25] Letter to Luise Wolff, quoted n. 23.

[26] In 1900, when Stavenhagen conducted the Second Symphony in Munich one week after Mahler's own performance, his interpretation had been execrable (see above, Chap. 9, Ludwig Thuille's letter to Mahler). The performance of the Third Symphony under Stavenhagen took place on 24 Feb. 1904, in the Kaimsaal, with the Leipzig contralto Harry van der Harst as soloist.

work for not containing 'a single personal idea'. 'Mahler', he wrote, 'flirts with religion, folk-art, sentiment'; he was 'a churner-out (*Macher*) of symphonies' and 'the most eclectic composer since Meyerbeer'. 'May the holy spirit of music keep such symphonic excrement from surviving and, even worse, from having any imitators', he concluded in a final burst of rhetoric. The review in the *Neueste Nachrichten* was kinder, acknowledging Mahler's 'exceptionally strong talent', 'incredible craftsmanship', and 'rare imagination and inventiveness', despite a desire to 'cause a sensation'. But the *Zeitschrift der Internationalen Musikgesellschaft*, or rather its reviewer, Edgar Istel,[27] listed the 'ingredients without which Mahler's symphonic "recipe" would be unthinkable: a dash of the revolt of the Titans (*Himmelstürmerei*), a dash of the sentimental, a poem from the *Wunderhorn* and a minuet'. Far from being an original artist, he wrote, Mahler was no more than 'a technician', 'who merely fabricates a homuncule— a work of art in an alembic—with stupendous refinement'.[28]

Thus, for the first time since his Krefeld triumph, his Third Symphony had had a very bad reception, this time in Munich, just as the première of the Fourth had had there in 1901. Mahler felt that his absence from the podium was largely responsible. The Third had also been performed in Zurich on 19 January under the Swiss conductor Volkmar Andreae.[29] In the *Neue Zürcher Zeitung*, an anonymous critic objected to the fact that Mahler had forbidden publication of the original 'programme', for the work could not be listened to as 'pure music'. The writer did not hesitate to invent one of his own. In his opinion the Third was a 'popular symphony' (*Volkssymphonie*), an image of 'the life of the present generation' and of the 'social movement', with its 'almost threatening demands for justice' and its 'fierce battle against the State and its military forces, its victorious jubilation on winning freedom'. The second movement described the family life of the people, the third their merry-making with some poetic interludes. In the fourth, Mahler reverted to the subjective, expressing the feelings of man alone in the depths of night, trying to find God, then the simple faith of a child, then happiness regained through divine love. Turning to the musical aspects of the work, the critic thought that Mahler had retained the classical form for the individual movements, 'though at times with wonderful

---

[27] *Zeitschrift der Internationalen Musikgesellschaft*, 5 (1904), 7. Edgar Istel (1880–1948), born in Mainz and a student at the city's Conservatory, was the composer of several operas and several books on opera. He edited and contributed to the monograph on Mahler's symphonies published by Schlesinger in Berlin in 1910. He emigrated to the USA, where his book on *The Art of Writing Opera Librettos* appeared in 1922.

[28] Later, Istel was to change his views completely, becoming one of the few Munich critics to defend Mahler (see below, Vol. iii, Chap. 3).

[29] The concert took place at 7.30 in the Tonhalle, for the benefit of the orchestra's pension fund, with the women's voices of the Zurich Mixed Choir, the Children's Choir of the First District Secondary Schools, and the contralto soloist Minna Weidele. Volkmar Andreae (1879–1962) studied at the Cologne Conservatory, then became successively Solorepetitor at the Munich Opera (1900), choirmaster at Winterthur, then conductor of the Zurich Mixed Choir (1902–43). He held the post of permanent conductor of the Tonhalle Orchestra, 1906–49, and was also director of the city's Conservatory (1914–39). Principally known for his work as a Bruckner conductor, Andreae was quite a prolific composer of works in all genres, including two operas.

extensions (*grossartiger Erweiterung*)'. Much of his work was of great beauty and his ideas so generously conceived that, despite his occasional extravaganzas, he could not be dismissed with a few words, as was so often the case. His mastery of instrumentation was without precedent. He decorated the iron framework of his symphonies with instrumental details in so brilliant a manner that they did not overshadow the greatness of the whole. His taste for popular song could easily be explained by the fellow-feeling he demonstrated for the people. Without doubt, even greater things could be expected of him. However far-fetched and unnecessarily specific the 'programme' invented by the critic of the *Neue Zürcher Zeitung* appears today, he must be given credit for discerning the genuineness of Mahler's preoccupation with 'folk' themes, and for anticipating some of the ideas which Adorno was later to explore, when he wrote: 'it sounds the death knell for the established concept of musical culture';[30] 'Mahler picked out the elements of the revolt against bourgeois music from that music itself';[31] and (referring to Mahler's great Marches) 'one can hear the persistent rumble of something collective—the movement of the masses'.[32] But in Zurich, few listeners went as far in their comprehension as the critic of the *Neue Zürcher Zeitung*, and an article in the *Neue Musikzeitung* probably reflected the general public's opinion more accurately. The Third Symphony, it claimed, 'cruelly tried' the listeners' nerves and the very 'spontaneous' applause was in the main a tribute to the 'young and gifted conductor and his gallant troops'.

Thus the poor quality of performances of his works when he himself did not conduct them, and the misunderstandings or lack of understanding this gave rise to, convinced Mahler that, for the time being at least, it was essential to conduct them himself: 'However I see how <u>important</u> it is at the moment for me always to be on hand, because what people do to my works in my absence is really absurd. Strauss is quite right always to conduct in person . . . I find this damned nomadic existence (*Herumvagieren*) terribly unpleasant, but it is necessary! I'm fully aware of this.'[33] So he was more than ready to accept an invitation to conduct two performances of the Third Symphony in the Rhineland, one in Mannheim, the other in the nearby university city of Heidelberg. This ambitious project had been put forward by Willibald Kähler, chief conductor of the Mannheim Grossherzogliches Theater, who suggested that Philip Wolfrum, head of the Bachverein Chorus and the Heidelberg Orchestra, join forces with him. Mahler wrote to Kähler to insist on conducting two rehearsals himself before the final one, adding:

The women's choir must be up to strength. It is better if their first entry, *Es sungen drei*

[30] Theodor Adorno, *Wiener Rede*, RWM 195: 'Dem etablierten Begriff von musikalischer Kultur geht es ans Leben'.

[31] TAM 50: 'Mahler hat die Revolte wider die bürgerliche Music aus dieser selbst hinausgelesen'.

[32] TAM 50: 'In Mahler dröhnt ein Kollectives, die Bewegung der Massen'.

[33] AMM1. 300; AMM2. 271 (letter dated 1 Feb. 1904).

Engel, which is allocated to the sopranos (who always sound too faint here), is sung by the whole of the choir. The entry of the boys' choir is very difficult to pitch correctly. It must be very well rehearsed. So far it has been bungled almost everywhere (the boys never hit the first F).[34]

Mahler also wrote to Wolfrum promising to bring the bells from Vienna (they had been used for the Frankfurt performance a month earlier). He asked him not to hire the Frankfurt soloist, Clara Weber, who was 'cold and unpoetic'. 'Anyone else,' he wrote, 'would be better'. He also suggested that Wolfrum get in touch with the Frankfurt conductor, Ludwig Rottenberg, since he had the score on which Mahler had made some important revisions.[35]

Since Alma was once again pregnant, Mahler made the trip alone. Just before boarding the train in Vienna on the evening of 27 January, he ran into his brother Alois, the 'writer and chief accountant', whom he had not seen for years. 'The poor boy looked at me out of the corner of his eye, half shy, half curious. We were more moved than I would have believed possible. My only fear was that he would end up travelling in the same coach with me. I even imagined him settled in the same sleeping compartment. Fortunately, I was spared that . . .'. As the train was full, Mahler was after all forced to share his compartment—with a stranger 'who didn't snore too much, wasn't noisy and didn't smell too bad'. Even so, 'to breathe the same air as a stranger in a closed compartment did not please me very much'.

As usual, Mahler complained in his first letter to Alma about the endless journey, during which he took walks on the platforms of every station at which they halted. In the afternoon, Willibald Kähler came to meet him in Mannheim and later wrote the following account of their first encounter:

I saw on the platform a small and obviously very nervous little man who was engaged in heated conversation with a very tall railway attendant to whom the small man was

---

[34] Mahler also suggested to Kähler that the flügelhorn be replaced by a trumpet, unless a 'real virtuoso' was available (undated letter from Mahler to Willibald Kähler, Jan. 1904). Cf Willibald Kähler, 'Gustav Mahler in Mannheim', in *150 Jahre Musikalische Akademie des Nationaltheater-Orchesters Mannheim 1779–1929* (Mannheim, 1929), 63. Willibald Kähler (1866–1938), grandson of the religious composer Moritz Friedrich, studied at the Königliche Hochschule in Berlin. In 1887 he began his career as orchestral conductor, and had posts successively in Hanover, Freiburg, Basel, Ratisbon, and Rostock. Succeeding Reznicek in Mannheim in 1891, he became Hofkapellmeister in Schwerin in 1911. He was assistant conductor at the Bayreuth Festival, 1899–1901. He composed Lieder, men's choral songs, piano pieces, an orchestral Prelude for Kleist's *Prince of Homburg* and incidental music for Goethe's *Faust*. Later, he revised the scores of Wolf's orchestral Lieder and worked on two Weber operas for a complete edn. He wrote analyses of Bruckner's Eighth Symphony and the Te Deum. Another letter, written in Maiernigg presumably during summer 1903, was probably addressed to Wolfrum. In it, Mahler accepts the modest fee of 500 marks to conduct the performance. However, 'so as not to create a precedent', he demands a reimbursment of his travel and accommodation expenses. He also asks for an assurance that the orchestra, the choruses, and the soloists will be identical in both cities (Hebrew Univ. and National Library, Jerusalem).

[35] Letter of 9 Jan. 1904 (G. A. Nogler Collection, Zurich). Mahler wrote Rotenberg instead of Rottenberg. The four letters to Alma mentioned below were written in Mannheim and Heidelberg (AMM1. 290; AMM2. 269). They all contain unpubl. phrases and passages. Five postcards are also unpubl. As was his habit, Mahler sent one from the Vienna station which Alma would receive still in bed the following morning and another the next day from Munich 'after a fair night'.

Gustav Mahler

giving a terrific dressing down, from low down in an upwards direction, angrily stamping his foot at every third word. The man was so surprised and shaken that he could not think of a single word in reply. I realised immediately: this can only be Mahler! And I was right. The cause of the excitement was his suitcase, which had been left behind somewhere. I came up, introduced myself and all traces of anger immediately vanished. The master greeted me in the warmest and friendliest way . . .

No doubt to avoid worrying Alma, Mahler did not mention the loss of his suitcase in his letters. He informed her instead that Kähler tried to persuade him to attend a rehearsal of the Third that evening but that he went instead to a performance of Shakespeare's *Romeo and Juliet*.

In spite of its amateurishness, I fell under the spell of the greatest of all poets—almost of all mankind—and once more much was revealed to me. In a certain sense, I prefer a <u>bad</u> performance of such a work to a half-good one. My imagination then starts to work and the 'unconvincing simulacrum' (*Unzulänglichkeit*) 'becomes a significant happening' (*wird zum Ereignis*)[36] and everything is transformed into archetype and symbol.

After the theatre, Mahler had supper with Kähler and Philip Wolfrum. Mahler had chosen to stay in Mannheim, but since the rehearsals took place in Heidelberg, he had to get up every morning at 6, and came home late in the evening. The first rehearsal on the 29th was 'acceptable'. 'It's curious that at first people always seem to find my music so strange. I experience this everywhere,' he wrote. The Rhineland was renowned for choral singing, but on this occasion the boys' choir proved far superior to the women's.

According to Kähler, the general nervousness reached such a pitch in the first half-hour that no one could relax while playing. But before long the orchestra grew accustomed to Mahler's individual style of conducting. Kähler writes of his 'incredible precision' and the way

he fascinated one and all with a glance. . . . He could not rest until every phrase was performed exactly as he wished it. He often made the following recommendation to the winds: 'In long-held notes, breathe wherever you wish, but never, at any cost, at the bar line.' (A golden rule for that matter.) Even in rehearsals, he insisted that everyone gave of his best. On the other hand he was always prepared to be considerate. For instance, when a horn player told him that he must keep something back for the evening performance. Mahler said to him: 'If you want to hold yourself back, just give me a hint, like this'—and he tapped his lips quickly several times with his left index finger. He warmly congratulated 'die Herren Buben' ('the young gentlemen') who had brilliantly succeeded with their difficult entry.

A little interlude occurred with the excellent first oboist. Mahler wanted him to play a certain passage with the bell of his instrument lifted into the air but he claimed it was impossible. 'And I tell you that in ten years no one will play such passages any other way! Just try!' Mahler retorted. And it worked! Like many

[36] 'Das Unzulängliche hier wird's Ereignis,' a famous line from the final passage of Goethe's *Faust* Part 2, which Mahler was soon to set to music in his Eighth Symphony.

before him, Kähler noticed a strong contrast between Mahler's 'rather vigorous and temperamental' gestures at rehearsals and his calm and controlled manner during the actual performance, when he almost always grasped the lapel of his coat with his left hand. When Kähler asked him why, he explained that 'this was how he forced himself to be outwardly calm'.

As usual, he spent his free time between rehearsals taking long walks. To his delight, he discovered Heidelberg's old quarter, 'a wonderful little place' (*herrliches Nest*) and its famous castle, and dined with Alma's sister Grete and her husband Wilhelm Legler. But he found Mannheim a 'ghastly hole' (*greuliches Nest*). 'In both cities, I've aroused enormous interest in all circles and the concert is fully sold out in advance (which has never happened before, even for Strauss).' Besides a performance of Maillart's *Les Dragons de Villars* in which he heard Georg Maikl, a tenor he engaged shortly afterwards for Vienna, Mahler went to see Pfitzner's *Die Rose vom Liebesgarten* on the evening of 31 January at the Mannheim Opera:

The performance was very good, and on the whole it confirmed the impressions I formed on reading the score. I've not changed my point of view. Powerful atmosphere and very interesting colourings. But too unstructured and blurred (*verschwommen*). Jelly and primeval slime constantly striving towards life but inhibited in their development. Creation proceeds at best only as far as the mollusc stage. The vertebrates never come into being. One can but exclaim like Calchas in *La Belle Hélène:* 'Flowers, nothing but flowers.' The public came with the best of intentions, but drooped in the stifling miasma of this stagnant fog and mysticizing (*mysticierende*) atmosphere.

For Alma, who was using every means at her disposal to persuade Mahler to introduce Pfitzner's new opera to Vienna, this must have seemed excessively severe. She later claimed that she had never tried to exercise the slightest artistic influence over her husband, except in the case of *Die Rose vom Liebesgarten*.

After the performance of Pfitzner's opera, Mahler dined again with Willibald Kähler and Philip Wolfrum.[37] They soon found themselves talking shop, Kähler reports. Mahler spoke of Strauss 'with respectful but somewhat prudent reserve'. He said little about his own compositions, although Kähler wanted to know the meaning of the major–minor motif in the first movement of the Third Symphony. Mahler thought for a moment, and then referred him to Greek mythology and 'the Tritons who play conches during the classical Walpurgisnacht'.[38] After dinner, Mahler and Wolfrum took the train once more back to Heidelberg, where Mahler had decided to spend the night. The atmos-

[37] Philip Wolfrum (1854–1919), born in Schwarzenbach in Franconia, was the son of a church organist. A pupil of Josef Rheinberger in Munich, he had himself been an organist and since 1885 occupied the post of Universitätsmusikdirektor and director of the Bachverein in Heidelberg. He was also professor of musicology at the Univ., a composer, and the author of a 2-vol. study of Bach.

[38] Willibald Kähler, article quoted in n. 34. The Mannheim Stadtarchiv contains two letters from Wolfrum to the Mannheim conductor Alfred Wernicke about the planned performance of the Third. They are dated 6 July and 14 Oct. 1903 (Nachlass Wernicke, no. 77).

phere at rehearsals remained excellent. The 'inevitable Nodnagel, as enthusiastic as a young girl' ('you don't have to be jealous' Mahler joked to Alma in his letter), had already made his appearance with a 'ghastly analysis' of the Third Symphony. Like all passionate admirers, he was sometimes a bore. Mahler was more at ease in the company of Albert Neisser, the famous dermatologist who had arranged to give a lecture in Heidelberg at that time in order to attend the two performances.[39] 'I like him now much better than before,' Mahler wrote of him. 'He is tremendously interested in my art and has exceptional understanding. He knows my Third by heart.'[40] Moreover, Neisser promised to invite him to conduct in Breslau the following year.

According to Guido Adler, who also attended the Heidelberg concert,[41] Wolfrum, like several other concert organizers of the period, was eager to conceal conductor, singers, and musicians from the audience 'in order to increase musical enjoyment'.[42] This arrangement had been tried out the year before in the Heidelberg Stadthalle, where the stage consisted of a series of platforms which could be raised or lowered as much as 3 metres either way. A painted cloth screen (*Schallwand*) extended across the front of the stage to conceal the performers, including the conductor, and the entire hall was then darkened. The choir was sometimes visible, placed on a separate raised platform at the back of the stage, and sometimes hidden behind another curtain. According to a young Heidelberg musicologist, who wrote a thesis on Philip Wolfrum, in the 1904 performance of the Third Symphony the chorus was positioned on an upper balcony, so that they could not be seen by the audience but could nevertheless see the conductor. Adler does not say whether or not Mahler approved of this unusual arrangement, but he probably accepted it with good grace, even though he had often said that the 'music in itself should be of such a quality that it could be listened to with open eyes and open mind'.

The Heidelberg performance of the Third Symphony, like the previous one in Mannheim, seems to have been of the highest quality, and was very well received. According to the two music magazines, the *Allgemeine Musik-Zeitung* and *Die Musik*, Mahler was acclaimed as seldom before. 'This time, I hope, I've taken a new step forward. I've gained new ground for myself in these parts. Both cities have decided to perform my work again this year, and next

[39] Albert Neisser (1855–1916), a world-renowned professor of dermatology at the Univ. of Breslau, discovered in 1879 the gonorrhoea bacterium subsequently named after him, and devised a new method using colours to confirm Hansen's discovery of the leprosy bacillus. Neisser was a second cousin of Arnold Berliner. Mahler had written to Neisser some weeks earlier giving him the programme of the Vienna Opera and suggesting that he visit the Rhineland at the time of the concerts (BGM). Neisser was the President of the Breslau Music Society and he later invited Mahler twice to conduct his own symphonies.

[40] Letter to Alma dated 1 Feb. 1904 (AMM1. 290; AMM2. 270).

[41] Adler speaks incorrectly of the Heidelberg 'Festival' and dates the concert for the autumn of 1903. The concert conducted by Mahler was in fact the fourth in a subscription series of the Bachverein (Guido Adler, *Wollen und Wirken* (Universal Edition, Vienna, 1935), 115).

[42] *Die Musik*, 3 (1903–4), 9, *Kunstbeilagen*.

year I myself will conduct the Second.'[43] The brief notice of the Mannheim concert published in *Die Musik* states that the first movement of the Third once again amazed and shocked the audience because of its 'lack of unity', but the final Adagio once more tipped the scales and was greeted with triumphant applause. The newspaper collections in the Mannheim library were destroyed during Allied bombings in 1943, and only the *Generalanzeiger* remains to bear witness to critical opinion. It states that the single work played in the 'Sixth Musical Academy' revealed 'one of the most interesting musical phenomena in the history of the last twenty years ... the most important symphonist since Brahms and Bruckner, ... combining a language which speaks directly to the heart with a strong will and tremendous technical ability'. Unlike the majority of his contemporary colleagues, the anonymous critic claims that, in Mahler's music, 'it is pointless to try and find reminiscences or imitations of others. His themes, even when they border on the trivial, are exquisitely melodious and spell-binding, thanks to their unusual and always interesting harmonic and instrumental treatment (*Verarbeitung*).' The same critic comments on Mahler's incredible command of the considerable orchestral and choral resources at his disposal, and which he controlled as much with his eyes as with his baton, and mentions the 'rare love and zeal' (*Liebe und Hingebung*) with which the orchestra fulfilled its difficult task.

In Heidelberg, the 'inevitable' Ernst Otto Nodnagel indulged in yet another lengthy paean of praise in the *Heidelberger Zeitung*. He enthused over the 'symphony's many wonders', among them the 'piquant harmonies' of the Minuet, the 'incredible melodic richness' of the Scherzo—and Mahler's superb conducting, his admirable orchestra, fine soloist, and magnificent choir. The *Heidelberger Tagblatt* reviewer was as enthusiastic as Nodnagel, but his praise gains credibility by also including some reservations. Mahler, he says, was 'a reactionary', in the sense that, although himself 'armed with the most modern of weaponry', he had been able to refurbish 'the old dogma of melody'. 'The public acclaims him because, accustomed as it has been to wrestling intellectually with the serious, demanding musical conundrums' of the moderns, 'it has suddenly found in Mahler's Symphony a melodious, transparent, immediately understandable work'. In the first movement, 'the March dominates in every form—serious, tragic (funeral march), carefree'. The work was a masterpiece of 'refined instrumentation', using a 'monstrous agglomeration of resources to overwhelm us with an inexhaustible variety of sound effects'. But one could not

---

[43] AMM1. 301; AMM2. 272. The planned performance of the Second Symphony was not realized. The Mannheim concert took place on 2 Feb. at 7.30 at the opera-house. The programme is reproduced in Knud Martner's *Gustav Mahler im Konzertsaal: Eine Dokumentation seiner Konzerttätigkeit* (Copenhagen, 1985), 80. The orchestra included 60 strings, 44 wind and percussion instruments, and 2 harps. The players were recruited from the orchestras of Mannheim and Heidelberg. The women's choir of the Bachverein and the children's choir of the Grand Ducal Gymnasium also participated in the two concerts of 1 and 2 Feb. The soloist, Betty Kofler, came from the Mannheim Theatre. According to the *Heidelberger Zeitung*, the orchestra had 32 violins, 10 violas, 10 cellos, 8 trumpets, and quadruple woodwinds. The choirs were made up of 130 women's and 50 children's voices.

perceive 'any unity of style, one which embraces (see Beethoven) all the contrasts. I could find no transition from the first movement to the others'. 'The thematic invention is for my taste too unscrupulous, too much inclined to cheap triviality. Much of it seems inspired less by an inner necessity than by a desire to produce an effect at all costs and by any means.'[44] The Minuet 'might have been written by Mendelssohn' and the trumpet solo in the Scherzo was so poetic and seductive 'that one forgives its allusions to well-known themes'. As for the Finale, it was the 'pearl' of the work, 'music of the purest and noblest gold, one of the most beautiful instrumental pieces written in recent decades'.

A tangible proof of the Third Symphony's immense popularity at the beginning of 1904 is the fact that even Angelo Neumann, whose actions were rarely inspired by pure idealism, invited Mahler to come to Prague to conduct it at the end of February. Some days before the concert Mahler wrote offering to bring with him the by now famous bells for the fifth movement. He asked that the contralto soloist, Ottilie Fellwock, be allowed to come to Vienna for an afternoon or evening to rehearse the fourth movement with him, to avoid losing precious time during an orchestral rehearsal.[45]

The Czech conductor Josef Stransky later recalled sitting in the Café Continental with Mahler during his brief stay in Prague. A local painter connected with the Vienna Secession, Emil Orlik,[46] proceeded to sketch Mahler's portrait on a postcard. For a long time this sketch was thought to have preceded his famous drawings and engravings of Mahler. But it is now known that Orlik's famous charcoal drawing is dated 6 March 1902, and that the big engraving dates from the same year. Thus Mahler was already acquainted with Orlik, and Stransky is undoubtedly mistaken in this respect. As usual, Mahler had to limit the time he spent away from Vienna, and Leo Blech, a young Czech composer-conductor, later to become famous, took charge of the preliminary Prague rehearsals.[47] The *Signale für die musikalische Welt* reports that the young man

---

[44] The critic from the *Heidelberger Zeitung* gives the duration of the first movement on that particular evening as 40 minutes, while the *Tagblatt* gives the timing as 42 minutes.

[45] This letter belongs to Mr Michael Schulman of Toronto, who kindly sent me a photocopy.

[46] *New York Herald Tribune* (22 Mar. 1931). Emil Orlik (1870–1932), born in Prague, a pupil of H. Knirr, W. Lindenschmitt, and J. L. Raab in Munich, spent a year in England (1898) and two years in Japan (1900–1). He was present at the Secession supper organized in honour of Klinger in 1902. A well-known painter, etcher, and lithographer, he designed the sets for several of Max Reinhardt's productions. He also specialized in musicians' portraits as well as genre pictures of Bohemian life, and led a renaissance of coloured woodcut prints, a technique he had studied in Japan.

[47] Leo Blech (1871–1958), born in Aachen, studied composition with Woldemar Bargiel and piano with Ernst Rudorff in Berlin. He became the conductor at the theatre in his home town, and studied for four years during his summer holidays with Engelbert Humperdinck. In 1899, Angelo Neumann appointed him conductor at the Neues Deutsches Theater in Prague, and in 1906 he went to the Berlin Royal Opera, where he eventually became Generalmusikdirector (1913–29). In 1925 he was engaged for a year by the Vienna Opera, but he returned to Berlin and the Staatsoper. Forced to leave Germany in 1937, he spent some time in Prague and then moved to Sweden, where he directed the Royal Stockholm Opera, 1941–9. Returning to Berlin after the war, he wound up his conducting career at the Städtische Oper, which he left in 1953. Blech wrote six operas, one operetta, and also songs, chamber music, and several symphonic poems. Of his dramatic works only *Versiegelt* has been really successful. On 6 Mar. 1902, Blech had conducted the Prague première of the second movement of the Third Symphony as part of the season's fourth Philharmonic concert.

did his job so well that when Mahler arrived on the morning of 25 February, there was 'nothing to change' and Mahler 'could find no words adequate to thank' Blech. When he appeared on the podium, on the evening of the concert, Mahler was greeted with applause which as usual he ignored, 'so coldly as to hurt his admirers' feelings' (according to Richard Batka in *Bohemia*). As before, the first movement surprised and disconcerted the audience, but by the final Adagio the work's success was assured. Mahler was obliged to return many times to acknowledge the applause.

William Ritter, faithful chronicler of a number of Mahler performances, was then living in Prague and attended the performance. Seated in the front row, he examined in close-up 'the man who was to become my hero':

He was obviously a man of total simplicity and naturalness. Once more, one's main feeling was that he inspired confidence. . . . The first thing one noticed was his manner of conducting: he was the man in charge, he knew all the tricks of the trade, he was not going to waste an ounce of his energies, in complete contrast to Weingartner's gesticulations at that time. He conducted with elbows tucked in, not waving his arms imperiously above his head, but simply like a metronome. He made no attempt to be anything but a time-keeping baton, at the performance and even at the dress rehearsal. I had seen this in Munich and also later on: all the effort had gone into the earlier rehearsals, and now the machine had to run on its own. On the day of the concert, this impeccable and almost mechanical beat never went higher than his shoulder. That was how it was when he conducted a concert standing up. But at the Opera, where he was sitting down, and his gestures had to be seen above the footlights, it was a different matter. In any case, the fascination of his glance could be almost diabolical, . . . as was his power of magnetism and sometimes the strange impression of lightning flashing from behind the lenses of his glasses. But on this occasion my last picture of the Master was when the audience was applauding him at the end; he looked like a disciplined Austrian schoolboy standing stiffly to attention, heels together, in the presence of his teacher. I had a clear vision then of how the young Mahler might have appeared, in front of the examiner at the Gymnasium in Iglau, on the final examination day.[48]

The Prague newspapers devoted a great deal of space to the event. *Dalibor*, the Czech daily, thought the immense work had made a 'fragmentary' impression, less powerful than that made by the Second, conducted by Oscar Nedbal two months before. Mahler, in trying to illustrate such a grandiose subject, which was beyond the scope of his musical invention, had attempted the impossible. The 'intellectual' effect was the strongest. The 'ideological' content was slight in comparison with the length of the piece and the vast musical resources involved. The whole 'excited admiration', certainly, but did not enthral the listener. In any case, it proved that composers would still have

The day after the 1904 concert, Angelo Neumann sent him a congratulatory letter referring to Mahler's praise, 'which must have given you great artistic satisfaction, coming from such a famous conductor and composer' (Arnošt Mahler, 'Mahler und seine Heimat', unpubl., 49e).

[48] *Schweizerische Musikzeitung*, 101: I (Jan.–Feb. 1961), 32 ff.

to struggle long and hard before they achieved the 'music of the future' they hoped for. Only a genius would be able to achieve 'what a modern virtuoso of orchestration never will'. Prague's German-language newspapers were also far from unanimous in their praise. The *Prager Tagblatt* recalled Mahler's Czech origin and his arrival at the city's German opera-house in 1885. It claimed that the First Symphony had been received in the Czech capital 'with open arms', but this time the Third was a disappointment because it was too ambitious. Mahler was evidently trying to draw closer to nature, but the path he had chosen was that of 'non-nature' (*Un-natur*). Rather than an 'abundance of motives' and 'attractive sound pictures', all he offered his listeners were 'melodic fragments, contrived and banal sound effects, and harmonic and contrapuntal puzzles without proper solutions'. This symphony had been created with 'borrowed capital' rather than his 'own resources'. The Finale, however, with its 'real musical feeling and orchestral colours', produced the desired effect, though in the critic's view it was a triumph of technique rather than of concept.

In *Bohemia*, Richard Batka[49] took the opposite point of view. He was one of the first critics to justify, with great insight, 'quotations' and 'banality' in Mahler's music. Declaring himself incapable of judging so vast a work after a single hearing, Batka reminded his readers that Beethoven's symphonies also appeared baffling in their time. He thought a fair-minded listener should have no serious problem with the Third Symphony, which, except for the first movement, was 'self-explanatory':

The lovely goes hand in hand with the joyous; the poetry of everyday life with profundity; the commonplace with the hymnic. Yes, Mahler has the courage to be commonplace. He uses this element as a means of expression and as a foil to set off the rest, that which is essential. My heartiest congratulations to him for this. Thus concert music leaves the path of allegory (*Allegorie*), and draws new forces and new impulses from life itself. 'Die Post im Walde' was normally the province of open-air bands. Mahler makes it concert-worthy. The effect is perhaps facile, but enchanting nonetheless. Why should every pleasure necessarily be paid for at a high price? Didn't Bach, Haydn and Beethoven draw upon the realities and banalities of everyday life for their symphonies?

The 'hymnic splendour' of the Finale 'should win over even the bitterest enemies of the new music', Batka adds. 'An artist touched by grace', Mahler had in this case 'very obviously obeyed his own inner must' (*Müssen*), even if he sometimes 'sought to impress by sheer wealth of technique'. Instead of

---

[49] A native of Prague, Richard Batka (1868–1922) studied both German and music at the Univ. Editor of the *Neue Musikalische Rundschau* (1896–8), then music critic of the *Neue Revue* and the *Kunstwart*, he founded the historical and modern concerts of the Dürerbund. In 1908 he moved to Vienna, where he worked for the *Fremden-Blatt* (1908–19) and, with Specht, for the review *Der Merker*. He also taught history of music at the Akademie der Tonkunst. Batka published a large number of books—*Die Musik der Griechen* (1900), *Die mehrstimmige Kunstmusik des Mittelalters* (1901), *Studien zur Geschichte der Musik in Böhmen* (1902), *Die Musik in Böhmen* (Berlin, 1906), *Allgemeine Geschichte der Musik* (2 vols., Stuttgart, 1909–11), *Richard Wagner* (1912), *Die Altitalienische Opernarie* (1912), etc.

wasting time in arguing over the relative greatness of Strauss or Mahler, he thought it would be better to rejoice at possessing 'two such fine fellows (*zwei solche 'Kerle'*) in our own times'.[50]

In his whole career, Mahler had rarely received such enlightened praise. Prague's *Deutsches Abendblatt* also took a firmly favourable stand. It judged the Third Symphony 'imposing', despite tedious passages, 'dissonances', and 'shifts of style'. Predictably, the paper's critic preferred the 'superb and majestic' Finale, which stood head and shoulders above the rest of the work. In *Signale für die musikalische Welt*, Victor Lederer stated that in few compositions did such extraordinary beauty and such strange aberrations stand side by side. He also reproached Mahler with an uneconomical use of means, but recognized that 'all serious musicians had been profoundly moved' by the Finale; he was saddened by the thought that a genius blessed with 'wings that would take him straight to heaven was rolling in the dust'.[51]

Another chapter was added to the success story of the Third Symphony, this time in the provincial Hungarian town of Szeged. It was performed there a few days before the Prague concert, by the local orchestra under the direction of Kapellmeister Ottokar Wöber, and was given the (by now) usual rapturous reception. 'You must really have accomplished miracles to have conveyed so much understanding of this colossus of a symphony to a public surely not very familiar with modern music,' Mahler wrote in thanks to the conductor.[52]

At the end of March, Mahler made another trip to the Rhineland, where he was to conduct two more concerts in the neighbouring towns of Mainz and Cologne. For the concert on 21 March, the conductor of the Stadt-Kapelle, Emil Steinbach,[53] had for once selected the Fourth Symphony instead of the Third. The two musicians had been corresponding with each other since the beginning of the year, and knowing he could only conduct the last two rehearsals, Mahler had asked Steinbach to hold at least four others beforehand. After the interminable train journey which he always so dreaded, Mahler settled into the hotel Holländischer Hof, where he was welcomed by a call from Steinbach, after

---

[50] In the same article, Batka compared the 'severe efficiency' and the 'surprising apparent calm' of Mahler's current conducting with his former 'nervous and agitated' manner. He adds that the audience warmly welcomed him on the podium and then 'applauded him long and loud'.

[51] Mahler's 25 Feb. performance of the Third Symphony in the Neues Deutsches Theater Prague, filled the whole programme of the fourth Philharmonic Concert in the 1903–4 season. The contralto soloist was Ottilie Fellwock, and the women's choir came from the 'Deutsches Landestheater' with a few extra soloists. According to Richard Batka, the orchestra numbered 120, including supplementary players. The organization of the concert cost Angelo Neumann 4,500 kronen in all.

[52] Letters from Mahler to Ottokar Wöber of 23 and 26 Feb. 1904, BGM.

[53] Undated and unpubl. letter to Alma (21 Mar. 1904). Emil Steinbach (1849–1919), native of the Grand Duchy of Baden, studied at the Leipzig Conservatory and later with Hermann Levi in Karlsruhe. His first engagements were in Mannheim, Hamburg, and Darmstadt. Later he moved to Mainz where, in 1877, he took over the direction of the Stadtkapelle. Subsequently he was appointed conductor at the Stadt-Theater. In 1893, he had been in charge of the Wagner season in London, which Mahler had conducted the previous year. Before the Mainz concert, Mahler sent four cards to him (PML: three of them are publ. in MBRS, 199 ff.). The first accompanied a score which was probably that of his *Jugendlieder*, since the publisher Schott is mentioned.

which he took a walk along the Rhine. 'The sun shines so agreeably and the air smells so sweet, that I'm upset not to have you here with me,' he wrote to Alma. 'I am thinking of the lovely days we spent on the banks of the Rhine in Basel and how happy you would be here. It's so warm that I can carry my overcoat over my arm.'[54]

Long letters written to Alma during the Mainz rehearsals discuss the plan she had just made to spend Easter in Abbazia as usual. Mahler was afraid that, at so late a date, she would be unable to book a room at the small inn they had discovered the year before, and a comfortable sleeping-car in which to travel, and advised her to spend the holidays at Edlach instead, in the Vienna suburbs. In view of all the trouble he took to advise her about the type of carriage and compartment she should choose, and the telegrams he sent to Pollak, his friend in the Ministry of Transportation, and Przistaupinski, his secretary at the Opera, concerning the booking, Alma's recollections of this trip to Abbazia sound unnecessarily ironic: 'He travelled as usual in a sleeping-car, while I myself took an ordinary compartment'.[55]

Mahler was no doubt worried as usual about this performance of the Fourth, for experience had led him to fear the reaction of public and critics to 'this persecuted stepchild, which has so far met with so little happiness in the world'.[56] 'In general I have found,' he continued, 'that humour of this kind (to be clearly distinguished from wit or gaiety) is often misunderstood even by the best people.' At his first rehearsal, Mahler found 'a fairly good and very willing orchestra, . . . admirably prepared by Steinbach'. As for the excellent soloist, Stefanie Becker, she had 'a fresh voice and a very unpretentious presentation (*schlichter Vortrag*)'—just what was required for the Finale of the Fourth. Mahler spent his first evening there at the Opera, which was giving Lortzing's *Undine*, but found the performance so dreadful (*hundsmiserabel*) that he left in the middle of the second act. The next day he lunched at the Steinbachs' and afterwards took a long two-hour walk through the city. After the evening rehearsal, he attended a performance of Shakespeare's *Twelfth Night*. The next morning's dress rehearsal proved entirely satisfactory, and Mahler wrote to Alma complaining at the absence of news from her. 'But', he added, 'it is a pleasure to see the orchestra's enthusiasm increase with each rehearsal. Even Steinbach, who was so reserved in the beginning, has now thawed and is so warm and sincere that it is a joy. I think I have gained another very estimable and important supporter.' Mahler increasingly regretted that Alma and her mother had not accompanied him, for 'you would understand and enjoy my work quite differently now'.[57]

[54] Unpubl. letter to Alma (21 Mar. 1904). Two others that Mahler sent from Mainz are wrongly dated 1905 in AMM1. 337; AMM2. 298.

[55] AMM1. 88; AMM2. 93.

[56] MBR1, no. 294; MBR2, no. 319, to Julius Buths, dated 12 Sept. 1903.

[57] AMM1. 337; AMM2. 298.

On the evening of the concert, the audience was disconcerted by the Fourth ('which is not surprising', remarked Mahler), but the final applause was warm. As always, the critics were shocked by the 'naïveté' of the work. The critic of *Mainzer Journal* confessed that, despite all his goodwill, he had not been able to form an opinion. The themes seemed to him merely strung together 'without any contrapuntal elaboration', 'without form or style', in a manner sometimes diverting, sometimes musically offensive. 'In turning his back on all the rules, Mahler has lost himself in a thicket.' His music was 'overrefined, anti-natural', and 'aimed only at superficial effect'. The *Anzeiger* saw only 'vulgarities', 'unnecessary repetitions, dissonances, an endless proliferation of details', and 'no well-defined perspective, structure or development'. The *Tagblatt* found just one detail of interest in the work, the 'contrast between the grotesque and the naïve'. Only the critic from the *Neuester Anzeiger* found anything in the Fourth worth praising: its 'flowing, melodious themes'. He did, however, condemn its overabundance of 'effects' and the 'insipid' text of the Finale.[58]

After the Mainz concert, Mahler had supper at Emil Steinbach's. The following morning he took the train for Cologne, where Emil's brother Fritz, who was the conductor of the Gürzenich Concerts, was waiting to take him to rehearse the brass for a performance of the Third Symphony.[59] The town was deluged with driving rain during the three days of final rehearsals in the Gürzenich Hall,[60] but this time Mahler was completely satisfied. The orchestra and chorus were first-rate, far better than at Krefeld, although many of the performers were the same. Mahler was so favourably impressed that he finally decided to accept Steinbach's proposals concerning the première of his Fifth Symphony. Although Fritz Steinbach wanted to schedule it during the Cologne Festival, on 20 May, Mahler decided to postpone it until October because Alma's confinement was approaching and he wanted her to be present at the première.[61] Furthermore, he had been travelling too much since the start of the season.

[58] The programme of the Mainz Städtische Kapelle's tenth symphonic concert, on 23 Mar., included: Mahler's Fourth Symphony (soloist, Stefanie Becker); Rubinstein's Concerto in D minor, Op. 70; Chopin's Nocturne in D flat, Op. 27 No. 2, Étude in G flat, Op. 10 No. 5, and Scherzo in B minor, Op. 20 (sol. Joseph Hofmann); three Lieder sung by Stefanie Becker: Schubert's *Die Forelle* D. 550; Schumann's *Mondnacht*; and Mendelssohn's *Auf Flügeln*; Beethoven's *Leonore* Overture No. 3. Steinbach conducted and accompanied the whole concert, except for Mahler's symphony.

[59] Fritz Steinbach (1855–1916) was taught by his brother before he studied at the Leipzig Conservatory and then with Gustav Nottebohm in Vienna. After conducting orchestras in Mainz and Meiningen, he settled in Cologne, where he became Städtischer Kapellmeister, and director of the Conservatory. In 1902, he undertook several tours with the Meiningen Hofkapelle orchestra founded by Bülow.

[60] Mahler had written the previous year to Steinbach advising him about the chorus and the flügelhorn player and insisting that the concert take place in the Gürzenich Hall and not at the Opera, where the acoustics were unsuitable. Steinbach complied with all his instructions (MBRS 86). In Feb., Mahler wrote to him again about the bells for the fifth movement and the trombone solo in the first, and asked for a separate rehearsal with the first trombone, the first trumpet, and the singer (letters to Fritz Steinbach of Feb./Mar. 1904, BGM). A few days before the concert Steinbach received another card from Mahler asking him to get a copyist to insert a few alterations in the orchestral parts and suggesting that the posthorn solo in the third movement be played by the first trumpet (LCW: MBRS 209).

[61] Undated letter to Alma (29 Mar. 1904), AMM1. 303; AMM2. 273 ff.

Steinbach would thus have plenty of time to study the score and rehearse the orchestra during the summer. His friendliness and hospitality equalled that of his brother in Mainz. Mahler took all his meals with him, and was convinced he had gained another supporter. 'Perhaps I have found an artistic homeland (*künstlerische Heimat*) here in Cologne. "On the Rhine, the vineyard for German wine!" Hurrah, if only for today! I am dead tired,' he wrote to Alma.[62]

At the dress rehearsal, the orchestra was excellent. The strings were 'almost as good' as Vienna's and the Berlin contralto, Marie Hertzer-Deppe, though a trifle theatrical, was a first-rate musician. The choruses were 'less good than I had hoped for from the banks of the Rhine', but nevertheless adequate. As usual, the applause was tentative after the first movement, but warmer at the end of the work. Although less enthusiastic than in Krefeld, the audience's approval was amply sufficient to prompt the announcement of a first performance of the Fifth Symphony in Cologne in October. The next day, however, Hermann Kipper complained in the *Volkszeitung* that since no explicit titles had been provided for this 'programme music', he had not been able to discover the 'unifying idea' in the first movement, despite the fact that he had taken the trouble to attend all the rehearsals.[63] He had praise only for the subsequent movements[64] but nevertheless felt certain that Cologne had discovered a 'new and considerable personality', 'a genius from whom much can be expected'.

Otto Neitzel's[65] article in the *Kölnische Zeitung* was so flattering that Mahler enclosed it in one of his letters to Alma. Neitzel regretted the tendency of an increasing number of modern composers to write programme music, that is to say a series of musical images based on the story of a legend, a piece of imaginative writing, an observation of nature, and so on. Mahler on the other hand, he felt, wrote music without a programme, 'straight from the darkroom of his bosom'. True, his four symphonies usually broke into song towards the end, and the words were mostly from the *Wunderhorn* anthology but these could be regarded as 'an essential factor basic to the music'. He used the new means of expression invented by the programme musicians (*Programmatiker*) to create sound colour and combinations—some of them strident and bizarre—which nevertheless observed 'the universal laws of beauty'. In this Symphony it was easy to discern not a programme, but the underlying mood and changes of mood, *joie de vivre* and despair, the 'scornful, satanic laughing' and the 'cynical gnashing of teeth'. Mahler's titanic will knew how to 'transpose the inspiration

[62] Undated letter to Alma (26 Mar. 1904).

[63] The first theme of the symphony reminded him of the student song 'Ich habe mich ergeben', also called 'Wir hatten gebaut ein städtisches Haus' (see above Vol. i, App. 1).

[64] Since there was no flügelhorn, the solo in the Scherzo was played by a trumpet, as Mahler had suggested. Kipper observed that Mahler appeared 'very nervous' during rehearsals, but displayed 'Olympian calm' at the concert.

[65] See above, Vol. i, Chap. 23, for this critic's biography.

of an hour or of a moment into art'. His handling of the themes and his masterful sense of tone colour 'uplifted and ennobled everything'.[66]

The Cologne concert had taken place on the evening of Palm Sunday. Immediately afterwards Mahler returned to Vienna. Since the planned holiday in Abbazia had now materialized, he travelled on to Mattuglie, in Istria, the next day, with Alma, Putzi, Anna Moll, and her daughter Maria.[67] As he was reading in his sleeping-car compartment, two young boys in the corridor kept peeping at him through the gaps in the curtains. He quickly recognized them as the sons of Archduke Otto of Habsburg.[68] When he got off the train, their mother, the Archduchess Maria Josefa, deliberately led the two boys up to Mahler and told them to 'take a good look at this gentleman' and never to forget him. Then she rejoined her entourage, who had been watching these goings-on with amazement.[69]

Mahler spent most of the few days in Abbazia working, since Peters was waiting for the final version of the score of the Fifth Symphony. Seeking quiet, the Mahlers had rooms in an annex at the bottom of the garden of the pension Wiener Heim. They usually had their meals served in their rooms, but to please the proprietress they ate once or twice in the main dining-room: on each occasion there was an embarrassed hush when Mahler appeared. One guest, however, was bold enough to ply him at once with the sauciest questions. He was none other than the operetta tenor Louis Treumann from the Carl-Theater.[70] Mahler, far from being offended, was very grateful to him for having broken the awkward silence.

On 3 or 4 April[71] Mahler returned to Vienna, and found that a 'veritable

[66] The concert, the eleventh in the Gürzenich Concert Series, took place on Palm Sunday, 27 Mar. 1904, at 7 p.m., with Marie Hertzer-Deppe as soloist. The general rehearsal had taken place the day before at the same time. In Cologne, Mahler heard a set of chromatic bells, the sound of which reminded him of a carillon. He obtained permission from the Intendant in Vienna to order a set for the Opera from the firm of Scheel in Kassel.

[67] Knud Martner has brought to my attention the fact that Mahler would hardly have had time to stop in Vienna on the way from Cologne to Abbazia. He could only have reached Vienna on the evening of the 28th. If he had spent two days in Vienna, he could have arrived at Abbazia on the evening of 31 Mar. (after a 13-hour train journey), only to return three days later to Vienna (on Sunday 3 Apr.). Furthermore, in one of the two letters he wrote to Alma after returning from Abbazia to Vienna, he writes: 'In the last 14 days a mountain of work has accumulated.' (Unpubl. letter, 5 Apr. 1904.)

[68] Archduke Otto (1865–1906) of Habsburg, brother of the Crown Prince Archduke Franz-Ferdinand, was married to the daughter of King George of Saxony. After the death of his grand-uncle Franz Joseph, his elder son, born in 1887, became Charles I, last emperor of Austria. Franz-Ferdinand had renounced his rights of succession by a morganatic marriage in 1900. Charles I's brother, Maxim Eugen Ludwig, was born in 1895.

[69] AMM1. 88; AMM2. 94. According to Alma, the Archduchess was particularly well disposed toward Mahler because he had pensioned off her husband's somewhat tactless mistress, the dancer Marie Schleinzer, stating that he did 'not need an Archduchess at the Opera'. Schleinzer was a member of the Vienna Opera from Sept. 1895 until Feb. 1901. She danced in Bayer's ballet *Die Braut von Korea*.

[70] Mizzi Günther and Louis Treumann both took part in the first performance of Lehar's *Die lustige Witwe* in 1905. Mahler and Alma later attended another performance.

[71] Mahler arrived in Vienna on Easter Sunday (3 Apr.) or Monday. As always, the Opera was closed for Easter Week from Tuesday 29 Mar. to Sunday 2 Apr. inclusive. His first appearance in the Opera pit was for *Tristan* on 8 Apr. As his first (unpubl.) letter sent to Alma in Abbazia was written the morning after a performance of *Les Contes d'Hoffmann*, a work not given again before the end of the month, it must be dated

mountain of work' was waiting for him. Hubert Wondra, his assistant at the Opera, had been the victim of an unsuccessful murder attempt by a madman some days previously, and he was still in hospital.[72] Franz Schalk was in Portofino convalescing from a serious illness.[73] In Alma's absence, Mahler took his meals with Carl Moll and Theobald Pollak, and saw two of his old friends of whom Alma disapproved, Fritz Löhr and Guido Adler. Over their lunches together, his brother-in-law Arnold Rosé told him of the latest exploits of his baby boy, and also brought him up to date on all the latest plans of the Vereinigung Schaffender Tonkünstler, recently founded by Schoenberg and Zemlinsky.[74] It was during this interlude that Mahler added the finishing touches to the score of the Fifth Symphony and sent it to Hinrichsen who planned to publish it before the October première.

Among the singers he had been able to call on at the Hamburg Opera, Mahler had for several years had a first rate 'vocal quartet', and he once told Josef Förster that he hoped to reunite its members in Vienna. Now he had almost achieved his aim, since Förster-Lauterer, Mildenburg, and Demuth had joined him. Only the tenor, Willi Birrenkoven, was missing. Mahler had tried to lure him away from Hamburg as early as 1897, offering him 'the highest starting salary ever offered to a tenor' and a contract made to measure for him.[75] Mahler had written to him privately assuring him that life in Vienna was certainly no more expensive than in Hamburg, and adding:

The [Vienna] public worships its artists and your kind of singing will be enthusiastically received here. I flatter myself that I can also contribute personally a great deal to your well-being (particularly in the artistic realm). Just imagine what an advantage it will be not to be overworked any longer (that will never happen here), to let all roles (*Aufgaben*) truly mature, and to be able to work them out to the smallest detail. And finally, living in an environment which is worthy of you and which appreciates your worth, you will be able to go on singing here ten years longer than anywhere else in the world. Just ask Mildenburg, who has recently been here, or Demuth, who has just signed a contract and knows exactly what things are like in Vienna![76]

5 Apr. Half of this long letter deals with Mahler's efforts to obtain first-class reservations of a sleeper or compartment from Mattuglie for Alma, Anna Moll, Maria, Putzi, and the maid.

[72] The date of the attempt, at the beginning of Apr., allows definitive dating of two previously unpubl. letters Mahler wrote to Alma before her return. The second mentions rehearsals for *Falstaff* as well as the murder attempt.

[73] In a recently publ. letter, Mahler urges Schalk 'not to worry, as the Opera can manage without you until the autumn' (MBRS 167).

[74] See below.

[75] Autograph telegrams from Mahler to Birrenkoven, Dec. 1897 (HOA, Z.659/1897).

[76] Mahler's letters to Birrenkoven were published by Irmgard Scharberth in her article 'Gustav Mahlers Wirken am Hamburg Stadttheater' (*Musikforschung*, 22 (1969), 4, 443). They belong to the archivist of the Hamburg Opera, Joachim Wenzel. The letter quoted above is wrongly dated (16 Feb. 1904), probably because it was coupled with an envelope belonging to a later letter. It clearly dates from 1897 because it mentions Mildenburg's 'recent' arrival and Demuth's contract. It also mentions Pollini, who died at the end of 1897. Mahler offers Birrenkoven a salary of 24,000 gulden from the third year and an annual winter break of four weeks. Mahler also sent Birrenkoven a telegram around the same time (HOA, Z.659/1897).

In the same letter, Mahler promised Birrenkoven that he would occasionally grant him leave of absence to sing elsewhere and added: 'So you will have to admit that conditions will be much more favourable here than anywhere else. I beg you now, dear friend, to accept, and to confirm your acceptance quickly by telegram, so that I can send you a contract at once.' Now that Winkelmann was about to retire, and Alois Penarini had failed with the public at the end of 1903,[77] Mahler again made an offer to Birrenkoven, since he urgently needed a new Heldentenor. On a handwritten card he asked him to keep his proposal secret until the beginning of 1905, but made clear to him that any *contractual* right to winter leave was out of question for the first two years.[78] Birrenkoven finally yielded, but the reason for his fears and hesitations became sadly apparent at the very beginning of his series of guest appearances: his once superb voice had now lost most of its former brilliance.

The tenor's début as a guest singer at the Hofoper took place on 11 April 1904. Birrenkoven must have suffered fresh anxieties at the last moment, for Mahler wrote him a final letter in January, assuring him that engagements at the Opera were free of favouritism and that he would be judged solely on his 'artistic accomplishment'. Mahler was hoping that Birrenkoven would take Winkelmann's place, and share the dramatic tenor roles with Slezak and Schmedes, both of his own high standard. Unfortunately, Birrenkoven's début dashed Mahler's hopes. There was general disappointment among public and critics: Korngold found that his voice was 'dry and tired' in the treble register, and even as far down as the G. He added that, without technique, only 'routine' kept Birrenkoven going. Muntz's verdict was equally unfavourable: he found that Birrenkoven's voice was 'completely inadequate to take on the Heldentenor roles in Vienna'. Graf was of the same opinion, commenting regretfully that this guest appearance had 'taken place ten years too late'.[79] Three days later, the *Abendpost* announced that, having sung 'despite a serious indisposition' and 'bronchial catarrh', Birrenkoven had had to postpone the rest of his guest appearances until late autumn and 'leave for the South to rest'. In fact, he never again sang in Vienna.

Abandoning his hopes that Birrenkoven could take Winkelmann's place, Mahler made strenuous efforts to retain the services of the two young tenors who were now indispensable to the Hofoper, Erik Schmedes and Leo Slezak. Schmedes's problem appears to have been a taste for high living and a consequent tendency to run into debt. By June 1904, he owed at least 12,000 kronen,

---

[77] See above, Chap. 15. Penarini's guest performances had taken place on 1, 5, and 7 Dec. 1903. According to the two telegrams addressed by Mahler to Willi Birrenkoven and Heinrich Chevalley (10 and 12 Dec. 1903), the Hamburg press was in error in publishing the news of Penarini's Vienna engagement.

[78] HOA, Z.78/1904.

[79] Birrenkoven made his début in Vienna on 11 Apr. 1904 in *Pagliacci* with Gutheil-Schoder (Nedda), Moser (Tonio), and Stehmann (Silvio), under the direction of Spetrino. According to J. B. Förster, the immediate cause of Birrenkoven's failure was 'a small mishap that produced a comic effect in a tragic role' (JFP 515).

or almost as much as he could earn in six months if he was in good health and did not cancel any performances.[80] At the end of 1903, he received an advance of an additional 6,000 kronen to pay off half his debts, and which had to be repaid at the rate of 1,000 kronen a month from January 1904 onwards. Unfortunately, Schmedes had to pay allowances to his divorced wife and to a former mistress by whom he had had a child. Also, illness had forced him to cancel several performances, thus further reducing his earnings. On the strength of a letter from Schmedes's lawyer, Mahler granted him more time to repay his debts, but also an additional loan of 300 kronen per month.[81]

The other star tenor, Leo Slezak, was also in difficult financial straits because of an illness which had kept him off the stage for sixteen days, thus reducing his earnings. As soon as he recovered, he requested leave to make outside guest appearances and 'make up the financial loss he had suffered'. Mahler was bound to refuse, given the singer's failure to carry out his duty within the company of which he was a member. Furthermore, Slezak had agreed some time earlier to learn the role of Assad in *Die Königin von Saba*[82] and had not yet kept his promise. Stoll and Przistaupinski were therefore instructed to inform him that his request had been refused. Slezak appealed directly to Mahler, who explained to him once more why his request could not be granted. Shortly afterwards, backstage at the Opera, Slezak irritated Mahler by making a third approach in person. This time, Mahler reminded him of the four occasions on which he had already been granted leave of absence that season, and called this new attempt 'impudent'. When the tenor refuted the charge, Mahler told him 'in an improper tone' (according to Slezak) that he 'ought not to have to concern himself with the reasons why members of the Opera could not fulfil their obligations toward the institution'. Their exchange grew so heated that several singers came out of the rehearsal-rooms to listen. Slezak felt that Mahler had offended and humiliated him in front of his colleagues. He turned on his heel, declaring that 'anybody who let himself be treated this way was a fool' and that 'he would never again set foot on the stage of the Opera as long as Mahler was director'. This was the damaging, but no doubt accurate, version of the 'Slezak affair' as reported in the contemporary press. A humorous version of the dispute was published just after Mahler died. The quarrel, it seems, had reached such a pitch that it seemed as though the two adversaries must come to blows. Willy Hesch, the Czech bass, was in the corridor pretending not to hear the furious voices. Suddenly there was a terrible crash in the director's office, followed by deathly silence. A few seconds later

---

[80] Schmedes's yearly salary then amounted to 34,000 kronen, a fixed amount of 12,000 plus 22,000 kronen in 'performance allowances' for actual appearances. Thus his monthly salary amounted to 2,833 kronen, of which 232 kronen were deducted for taxes, the Opera's pension fund, and so on.

[81] Letters from Dr Herzberg-Fränkel, Schmedes's lawyer, to Mahler and Mahler's answer of 16 June.

[82] According to MBR1, no. 291 and 292 (MBR2, no. 325 ff.), Mahler had indeed done his best to induce Slezak to learn the main tenor role in *Die Königin von Saba*. The opera was given with a whole new cast (including Slezak as Assad) on 21 May 1904.

Slezak burst out of the office, crimson with rage. Hesch calmly greeted him with the words: 'Slezak, tell me . . . is he dead?'[83] The day after the dispute, Slezak was due to sing the role of Tamino in *The Magic Flute*, but he cancelled at the last minute, giving 'nervous agitation' as his excuse.[84] That same day, he sent Mahler a letter of resignation complaining that he had been treated 'in such a humiliating and insulting way'. He also wrote a letter to the Lord Chamberlain, accusing Mahler of 'being too conscious of his superiority', and 'making the members of the Opera suffer because of his own nervousness and moodiness'. Most of his colleagues had been subjected to this kind of treatment and Mahler 'had been amazed to find that there was at least one person who refused to put up with it'.[85]

Prince Montenuovo already knew about the incident: Mahler had written him a letter the previous evening, putting his side of the case. In his view, as director he had done nothing but 'exercise his rights and carry out his duty' in rebuking the tenor, and Slezak had no reason whatever to resign. The singer wrote another letter some days later to the Prince to 'demand at least some redress', but finally calmed down. Mahler had certainly gone too far in calling him to order; on the other hand, like most of his colleagues, the now famous tenor was obviously far more concerned with his own affairs than with those of the Opera.[86] He was nevertheless one of the Hofoper's stalwarts, and despite their many conflicts, Mahler was fully aware of this. Besides, he was always ready to try to understand his colleagues' human problems, and proved this, shortly after the 'Slezak affair' had subsided, when the tenor wrote asking for a salary increase because of the high cost of living in Vienna, and the fact that he had just taken out an expensive life insurance. He reminded Mahler that until now he had done his best to sing both lyric and dramatic roles at the Opera, and that he was a favourite with the public. Mahler granted the 4,000 gulden a year increase even though Slezak refused to sign a four-year extension of his contract beyond its expiry date in 1908.[87]

During the summer Mahler sent Slezak two further handwritten personal letters which confirm that the quarrel had been no more than a temporary interruption to the cordial relationship between them. In the first, Mahler tells Slezak that in order to please him, his first appearance in the new season would be in *Aida* on 20 August. He adds: 'Much fine and interesting work awaits you, and will surely bring you yet more success'. In the second letter, he agrees to

[83] *Illustrirtes Wiener Extrablatt* (19 May 1911) and *Die Musik* 10: 18 (June 1911).

[84] This is undoubtedly the 13 Apr. performance sung by Alfred Boruttau. The most detailed account of the Mahler–Slezak conflict is to be found in the *Neues Wiener Tagblatt*.

[85] As evidence of Mahler's injustice, Slezak in the same letter gave the Obersthofmeister a list of the new roles he had learnt. He claimed that each time he had taken a leave of absence (Mahler had already given him 4), it had been arranged so as not to upset the Opera's repertory. In any case his contract could never oblige him to sing two days in a row.

[86] Slezak's letter of resignation is dated 13 Apr., as is Mahler's to the Lord Chamberlain (HOA, Z.1411/1904, G. 2413). Slezak wrote again to the Intendant on 15, 18, and 25 Apr.

[87] HOA, Z.530/1904. Slezak's letters are dated 11 May and 14 June.

Slezak taking on the leading role in *La Juive*, although he would have to learn it quickly, as the date of the revival had already been announced. Moreover, this must not prevent him from learning the tenor role in Puccini's *La Bohème*. But he warns: 'In any case I would like to ask you once again, when you are learning this new part to pay a little more attention to my directions than you did last time.'[88] No better proof is needed of Mahler's high opinion of Slezak than these two letters written in the middle of summer, at a time when Mahler usually devoted all his thoughts and energies to composing during the few weeks of grace the Opera accorded him.

At the end of the 1903–4 season, Mahler tried again to get rid of the organized claque, his first attempt made soon after his arrival having been only partially successful. The claque's leader had died soon after Mahler's first offensive, but another had soon emerged and the group was still active, much to the annoyance of genuine music lovers. Furthermore, the singers themselves complained of the exorbitant rates the claque charged. Mahler suggested to the Intendant a new series of countermeasures, including the hiring of detectives to sit among the audience in the top galleries. This was, however, one of the few battles in which Mahler never gained a complete and lasting victory.[89]

While the 'Slezak affair' was still in the news, Mahler and Roller were preparing the Hofoper's first production of *Falstaff*. Mahler had conducted the opera ten years earlier in Hamburg.[90] His enthusiasm for the work and its composer was as great as ever. And since Verdi had died three years earlier, the première of his last opera was a fitting tribute to the greatest Italian composer of the nineteenth century. Mahler felt that in Verdi's last two operas 'the old master had finally learnt how to concentrate the overflowing riches of his invention, instead of merely squandering his individual ideas, one after another, without ever thinking about them, giving them a logical sequence, working them out or developing them'.[91] *Falstaff*'s instrumentation had always fascinated Mahler; it 'opened new artistic paths'.[92] He decided to conduct and stage the work himself instead of entrusting it to Spetrino, as he did with other Italian operas. Spetrino nevertheless attended the rehearsals, and later praised the extraordinary quality of the production and the beauty of Roller's sets. The Italian conductor recorded how Mahler, at the beginning of the first full rehearsal, said to the company: 'I am entrusting this glorious Italian masterpiece not just to your intelligence but to your hearts',[93] thereby reaffirming the love for Verdi's music he had shown the previous year, when he had made the *Aida*

---

[88] Letter from Mahler to Slezak (summer 1903, MBRS 194). The first letter contradicts itself as to date and place: Maiernigg, 30 Aug. (therefore after the *Aida* performance). In it, Mahler tells the tenor that the season will begin for him with a performance of *Aida* on 20 Aug. No doubt Mahler wrote the wrong month, and the letter dates from 30 July. The second letter is undated.

[89] *Bohemia* (Prague, 14 Feb. 1904).

[90] The work had previously been heard in Italian by a small section of the Viennese public at a festival performance in May 1893, when Victor Maurel sang the title-role.

[91] NBL1. 128; NBL2. 146.   [92] NBL1. 172; NBL2. 199.

[93] Francesco Spetrino, Mahler obituary, *Il mondo artistico* (Milan, 1 June 1911).

revival 'one of the most beautiful and impressive productions imaginable'.[94] The German translation was full of terrifying hurdles for the Viennese singers because of the rapid tempos which made articulation difficult. The morning after the first performance, Max Kalbeck, the author of the translation, claimed in the *Neues Wiener Tagblatt* that this was the main reason why the Vienna Opera had postponed the opera's première so long. Kalbeck felt that Mahler had fully succeeded in bringing this German *Falstaff* to life, 'solving all its difficulties' and creating out of the actor-singers and the musicians in the pit 'a harmonious whole, both supple and coherent'. Even Hirschfeld conceded that Mahler had 'freed the tongues' of his singers and 'that the orchestra showed such eloquence and individual colourings' that at times the listener could not tell whether the music's witty asides 'came from the singers or the instruments'.[95]

Korngold felt that it was a 'masterly' performance that had 'brought out the spirit of the work and given it life on the stage as well as in the orchestra'. Schönaich also found that, thanks to Mahler's unique talent, the work 'had been tuned and unified into a single miraculous whole'. In the *Musikalisches Wochenblatt*, Theodore Helm[96] rebuked the audience for leaving the hall during the last act, before the final fugue. He hoped this 'Italian *Meistersinger*' would remain in the repertory for a long time, because the production itself was a masterly achievement.[97] For Max Vancsa, the learned correspondent of the *Neue Musikalische Presse*, *Falstaff* was one of the outstanding masterpieces in the history of opera, a 'pure gem', and it was scandalous that it had had to wait so long before being taken into the Hofoper's repertory. With sovereign mastery Mahler had brought out all the bewitching 'gold filigree' of Verdi's orchestration. He marvelled at the apparent ease with which Mahler had resolved the crucial problem of the German translation and sustained the 'comic tone'.

Falstaff is not an amusement for the crowd, it is an exciting and beautiful entertainment for connoisseurs. A distinguished opera house, pursuing higher artistic goals, must maintain a solid stock of such refined, exquisite delights, which can be offered at certain times during the season to the more adventurous, more musically cultured sections of the audience. For the broader public, works like Nicolai's *Die lustigen Weiber* will obviously remain as staples of the repertoire.

The critics were almost unanimous in praising the exceptional quality of the work, the production, and the cast. Only Demuth was criticized, as having the voice but not the temperament of the *Pancione*. Richard Wallaschek, on the

[94] Francesco Spetrino, ibid. See above, Chap. 14.

[95] Hirschfeld was shocked that the audience had seemed to be getting bored in spite of the cut made in the last act. He expressed 'great doubts as to its taste'.

[96] Helm had been replaced at the *Deutsche Zeitung* by Maximilian Muntz, but he continued to write longer articles in the *Wochenblatt*.

[97] Helm recalled that Victor Maurel had had to encore 'Quando ero paggio' twice in the 1893 performance while this time the monologue passed unnoticed, no doubt because Demuth lacked personality and humour.

other hand, claimed that *Falstaff* could never supplant Nicolai's *Lustigen Weiber*: the 'constant parlando' being 'monotonous and tiring'. He was alone in his opinion, but with hindsight it is possible today to understand why *Falstaff* has never remained for long in any repertory: the individual and collective effort required to put it on can hardly be sustained for more than a few exceptional performances. Ten performances in 1904, two the following year, and one in 1906 nevertheless constitute a considerable run for a *Falstaff* production,[98] and few other opera-houses have beaten that record.

At the time of the *Falstaff* première, Lilli Lehmann had begun one of her guest appearances in Vienna with performances of *Norma, Traviata,* and *Fidelio*.[99] On 7 May, a *Traviata* performance sung in Italian without a single Italian in the cast, except the conductor Francesco Spetrino, elicited a very caustic article in the *Illustrirtes Wiener Tagblatt*.[100] The anonymous critic claimed that Italian was another of Mahler's 'whims' and wondered whether *The Bartered Bride* would soon be sung in Czech, a prospect he obviously felt was preposterous, or *Die Königin von Saba* in 'the language of Solomon'. Not only did he think Frau Lehmann looked too old for the part of Violetta, but she 'listened to herself like a wealthy lady from Dresden who has sacrificed her all to learn and speak that tongue'. Nevertheless, he praised her singing as 'great art' and admired the ease with which she hit her high Cs and D flats.[101]

The records for the 1903–4 season show that Wagner was performed 36 times, with 3 complete *Ring* cycles and 8 performances of *Lohengrin, Tannhäuser*, and *Die Meistersinger*. Mozart was put on only 8 times, probably because Mahler was planning a series of new productions for his 150th anniversary. *Les Contes d'Hoffmann*, which had lost nothing of its popularity, was given nine times, as were *Aida* and *La Juive*. As for individual operas, Puccini's *La Bohème* and *Pagliacci* topped the list with thirteen performances each, and were followed by *Cavalleria* (10); *Lohengrin, Tannhäuser* and *Die Meistersinger* (8); *Der Corregidor* (7); *Figaro, Faust, Carmen, Les Huguenots, Mignon,* and *Louise* (6); and *Fidelio* and *Die Fledermaus* (5). As mentioned before, Mahler was called sharply to order in autumn 1903 for having exceeded budget estimates of expenditure for the year. In 1904 box-office receipts were higher than at any time during his directorship,[102] until the increase in ticket prices

[98] Cast on 3 May: Michalek (Ann), Gutheil-Schoder (Alice Ford), Hilgermann (Meg), Petru (Quickly), Boruttau (Fenton), Breuer (Bardolf), Demuth (Falstaff), Weidemann (Ford), Preuss (Dr Cajus), Mayr (Pistol). A letter from Mahler written in 1902 to the conductor Emil Paur shows the importance he attached to this production. Paur had asked for tickets for the Wagner cycle and Mahler replied: 'Would *Falstaff* interest you too?' (Buffalo and Erie County Library, Buffalo, NY)

[99] As noted previously, Mahler invited the German soprano regularly.

[100] The cast included Fritz Schrödter (Alfredo) and Anton Moser (Germont).

[101] The dates of the Lehmann performances were: *Norma* (1, 10, and 17 May); *Traviata* (7 and 15 May); *Fidelio* (4 and 13 May). Again, Lehmann received a 'fee' of 1,000 kronen for each performance, with no deductions for taxes or the pension fund.

[102] 2,891,571.65 kronen.

which came into force in autumn 1906. Thus, at the end of 1904, the deficit was very much smaller than that of the previous year.[103]

In March 1904, the contract of Ferdinand Löwe, who had succeeded Richard von Perger in 1900, expired, and the venerable Gesellschaft der Musikfreunde Concerts[104] found themselves without a conductor. Doubtless through lack of rehearsal, the quality of playing at its concerts was generally poor, and Mahler probably did not feel particularly honoured when the committee, at the instigation of Karl Goldmark, one of its members, decided on 15 March 1904, to offer him the post of conductor of the Gesellschafts-Konzerte. True, several years earlier he had dreamt of conducting a Bach *Passion* at one of these concerts.[105] And in the past famous conductors like Herbeck, Richter, Rubinstein, and Brahms had held this post. None the less, the orchestra's prestige had waned under second-rate conductors like Perger and Löwe, and Mahler knew he was being called upon to restore brilliance to a tarnished image. Several years earlier, when he was still in Hamburg and trying desperately to return to Vienna, the Gesellschaft had turned him down as Richter's successor solely because he was Jewish.[106] Apart from that, it would have been absurd, after abandoning the conductorship of the Philharmonic Concerts for reasons of health, to accept another inglorious post at a time when cities all over Germany were vying with each other for the honour of having him conduct one of his symphonies. After his unofficial refusal on 15 March, the Gesellschaft decided to form a delegation of well-known personalities solemnly to renew the offer of the post to Mahler. Their determination is all the more remarkable in that it shows how much support there was for Mahler within the Gesellschaft, where even his usual enemies now voted in his favour. They went so far as to plan the engagement of an assistant conductor who could relieve him of routine rehearsals.[107] It was a bitter disappointment, therefore, when Mahler, on his return from the Rhineland, once more refused. He recommended first Mengelberg and then Emil Paur[108] for the post which they both refused. It was Franz Schalk who was finally chosen. A happy consequence of this choice was that relations between Mahler and the Gesellschaft improved considerably, so much so that

---

[103] 149,456.45 kronen instead of 264,750.82; that is to say 115,000 kronen less (WMW 214).

[104] Founded in 1812, the society set up the Vienna Conservatory and the Singverein chorus in the same year. The latter participated in all its concerts, which numbered four a year, plus one or two 'extraordinary' concerts.

[105] See above, Chap. 10.   [106] See above Vol. i, Chap. 19.

[107] Letter from Karpath to Theobald Pollak dated 19 Mar. 1904, Schweizerische Nationalbibliothek, Berne.

[108] In 1904 Mahler wrote to Emil Paur: 'I was very sorry that you didn't accept the Musikverein's offer. I had been hoping Vienna would be able to keep you. I would have gained a comrade in arms!' (letter quoted in n. 98). Emil Paur (1855–1932), born in Austrian Bukowina, studied at the Conservatory in Vienna. Having started his career as a violinist, in 1880 he was appointed first kapellmeister of the Mannheim Opera, and then resident conductor of the subscription concert series. He was conductor at the Leipzig Theatre from 1891 to 1893, in due course succeeding Nikisch as musical director of the Boston Symphony Orchestra and then Seidl at the New York Philharmonic. In 1904, after virtually deciding to return to Europe for good, he eventually accepted the conductorship of the Pittsburgh Symphony Orchestra, which he held until 1910. From 1912 to 1913 he directed the Royal Opera in Berlin.

the Vienna premières of his Third and Fifth Symphonies in 1904 and 1905 took place under his baton at 'extraordinary' Gesellschafts-Konzerte.

The affair is related in detail in Ludwig Karpath's memoirs.[109] He does not, however, mention Mahler's dealings with the Gesellschaft over a much more important matter. At that time, Guido Adler had just drawn up an ambitious project for the complete reorganization of the Conservatory with a view to transforming it into a National School, and the creation of a new 'General Inspectorate of Pedagogical Institutions' with Mahler at its head. Adler presented his plan to the Minister of Culture, Wilhelm Ritter von Hartel, together with a memorandum praising Mahler's 'artistic qualities, energy, intelligence' and 'character', and pointing out that he was capable of making the Conservatory an 'exemplary institution'. Mahler himself was very interested in his friend's plan, and refers to it in several letters.[110] According to Adler, Mahler was even willing to accept the position, for administrative reasons, without a salary as long as he remained director of the Opera. Unfortunately, owing to a change of ministers, the reorganization project, which also included the appointment of Zemlinsky to teach conducting[111] and Schoenberg to teach theory and composition, ended up in some obscure bureaucrat's desk-drawer.[112] Later, when the Conservatory was finally transformed into the Kaiserliche Königliche Akademie für Musik und darstellende Kunst (the Imperial and Royal Conservatory of Music and Dramatic Art), Mahler held what was only an honorary post on its boards.[113]

The 'splendid isolation'[114] of Alma's life with Mahler depressed her more and more. She wrote in her diary on 25 February 1904:

I must begin another life, for I can't bear this one any longer. My dissatisfaction grows hour by hour! I'm growing shallow (*Ich verflache*)! I must start reading again, learn more! I've just had music sent from the music shop. I want to practise again. I want to lead an intellectual inner life again, as I used to do. What a misfortune no longer to have any friends, but Gustav won't see anyone.[115] Yesterday I spent all afternoon reading my old diaries. In those days my life was full of new experiences. How monotonous and calm it has now become! I must have some stimulus. If only Pfitzner lived in Vienna. If only I had the right to see Zemlinsky! Schoenberg interests me too. I've been thinking a lot . . . It must all change . . .

---

[109] BMG 138 ff. Karpath claims that one of the Gesellschaft committee members, the lawyer Heinrich von Billings, was Mahler's principal opponent in 1895, and that Brahms, despite his lack of racial prejudice and his admiration for Mahler, had failed to exert his full authority in Mahler's support on that occasion.

[110] AMM1. 338 (from Mainz) (AMM2. 299) and unpubl. letters to Alma.

[111] Zemlinsky was then, as we shall see, chief conductor of the Volksoper.

[112] Adler also proposed Karl Luze and Eugen Thomas to teach choral singing, Arnold Rosé to teach violin and chamber music, and Eusebius Mandyczewski to teach counterpoint.

[113] Guido Adler, *Wollen und Wirken*, 97, and RAM 42. Adler's memorandum is dated Christmas 1904 (Univ. of Georgia Library). At the same time that Adler was working on his reorganization project, he sent Mahler one of the first copies of the Wagner lectures he was publishing (*Vorlesungen, gehalten an der Universität Wien*, Leipzig, 1904).

[114] See above, Chap. 15.   [115] This last phrase was added later in Alma's handwriting to the TS.

Many things indeed were on the brink of change in Alma's life, and happily Gustav would profit from the transformation as well. Mahler's daily encounters with Secession painters and artists had opened his eyes to a world which he knew little of before meeting Alma. Carl Moll and Alfred Roller had of course exerted their influence and he now showed all the fervour of a neophyte for painting: Rembrandt, Holbein, and Franz Hals took their places on his personal Parnassus alongside Shakespeare, Goethe, and Beethoven. To keep up with new developments he must have visited every Secession Exhibition until its dissolution in 1905, following Klimt's withdrawal from the group. In January–February 1904, a big 'European' exhibition brought together artists from Germany (Hans von Marées, Ludwig Hoffmann, Wilhelm Laage, and Emil Rudolf Weiss); Switzerland (Ferdinand Hodler and Cuno Amiet, whom Moll and Moser had visited after they left Basel in June 1903); Holland (Thorn Prikker); Norway (Edvard Munch); and Finland (Axel Gallen). Cuno Amiet was in Vienna for the occasion with his friend Hodler and recorded in his memoirs several informal musical get-togethers at the Moll's Hohe Warte villa at which Mahler was present.[116] The Austrian composer Wilhelm Kienzl also visited the exhibition with the conductor Karl Muck and his wife. In his private diary he recalls meeting Mahler, Alma, and Carl Moll there on 6 February.[117]

When she first met Mahler, Alma had been studying composition with Alexander Zemlinsky, and would no doubt have pursued her studies if Mahler hadn't forced her to give them up. Nevertheless, in the spring of 1904 Zemlinsky again found himself a member of Mahler's circle of friends. In 1900, the year of the première of *Es war einmal*, he had been engaged as Kapellmeister at the Carl-Theater and had conducted a number of operettas there, several of which in world-premières.[118] He had also been active as a composer and published a number of new works.[119] The ill-fated *Triumph der Zeit* ballet remained unfinished, except for the complete second act.[120] In 1903, an opera project, *Malva*, had likewise been abandoned, largely on Mahler's

[116] Cuno Amiet, 'Hodler und Wien', *Neujahrsblatt der Zürcher Kunst Gesellschaft* (1950), 22. Alma's *Erinnerungen* alludes to Hodler's Viennese visit and to his Don Juan temperament (AMM1. 81; AMM2. 88).

[117] Kienzl's MS is at the Stadtsbibliothek, Vienna. 'Mahler behaved in a very superior, overbearing way, passed contemptuous judgements, and spoke with painful Jewish smugness about symphonic music,' Kienzl writes. 'I had to contradict him, which he treated with disdain.' It would be fascinating to know just what the conversation was about and why their points of view differed. The chances are that Kienzl's traditional 'German' outlook provoked Mahler into making scathing and paradoxical remarks, as he often did in the face of unenlightened opposition.

[118] One of these was Heinrich Reinhardt's *Das süsse Mädel*, another Heuberger's *Ein Opernball*, which had a triumphant reception in 1901.

[119] *Fantasien über Gedichte von Richard Dehmel*, Op. 9 (1901), and *Irmelin Rose und andere Gesänge*, Op. 7, dedicated to Alma Schindler (id.).

[120] See above, Chap. 12. Zemlinsky conducted excerpts from the second and third acts of the ballet at the Konzertverein in 1903, under the title *Drei Balletstücke*. In Mar. 1904 Hofmannsthal wrote to Alfred Roller in the hope that he might persuade Mahler to produce the new version of the ballet, but Mahler would not be swayed. See Antony Beaumont, 'Alexander Zemlinsky: Der Triumph der Zeit—Drei Balletstücke—Ein Tanzpoem', in Stefan G. Harpner and Birgit Gotzes (eds.), *Über Musiktheater: Ein Festschrift* (Ricordi, Munich, 1992), 13 ff.

advice,[121] but Zemlinsky's career as a conductor prospered. The same year he was engaged, again as an operetta conductor, at the Theater an der Wien and stayed there for one season. At this time he decided to leave the Tonkünstlerverein, of which he had become vice-president four years earlier[122] and became active in the Ansorge Verein, for which he wrote some of his finest Lieder.[123] However, Zemlinsky soon became dissatisfied with both Vereine, and this is why he decided to create a contemporary music society, together with Arnold Schoenberg, who was not only his intimate friend, but also the most powerful, gifted, and, controversial musical personality in the Austrian capital.

The Viennese-born Schoenberg was then nearly 30. Although his musical gifts had been evident since early childhood, until he was 17 his compositions lacked originality. At the age of 21, as we have seen, he played the cello in the Polyhymnia orchestra which was conducted by Zemlinsky.[124] The two young men immediately struck up a close friendship and began frequenting the Café Griensteidl and its literary and musical circle, together with Artur Bodansky and Karl Weigl, both of whom studied with Zemlinsky. In 1896 Schoenberg helped make the piano transcription of Zemlinsky's first opera *Sarema*. At the time, he was earning his living in a bank. Zemlinsky started giving him lessons in counterpoint, the only formal teaching he ever had in his life. '[I owe him] nearly everything I know about the technique and the problems of composition', Schoenberg wrote later. In 1897, he finished his early Quartet in D major[125] which, thanks to Zemlinsky, was performed semi-privately on 20 December 1896 by the Fitzner Quartet at the Tonkünstlerverein in Vienna. He then composed his Lieder, Op. 1, 2, and 3, and then at last *Verklärte Nacht* (Transfigured Night), the first of his works to be published. However, at that time he had no income (in the mean time he had married Zemlinsky's sister Mathilde) other than from transcribing and copying music. In 1901 he went to

[121] The libretto was by Ernst Hutschenreiter, to whom Zemlinsky wrote on 21 Apr. 1903: 'I have not given you any news for a long time because I am truly very busy and because I have been waiting for Mahler's answer. I received it two days ago. He is dead against [our project]. He thinks not only that such a subject would be impossible to dramatize but that it does not suit me. So! I have no more interest [in the project], not because his criticism has destroyed my courage but because it confirms our doubts.' (Otto Biba, *Alexander Zemlinsky: Bin ich kein Wiener?* (Catalog der Ausstellung im Archiv der Gesellschaft der Musikfreunde, Vienna, 1992), 53.)

[122] The Wiener Tonkünstlerverein had been founded and supported by Brahms. Zemlinsky became a member in 1894, a committee member in 1897, and vice-president in 1899. The president was Richard Heuberger, and the secretary Hugo Botstiber. Two of Zemlinsky's closest friends also belonged to this Verein, Friedrich Buxbaum, the cellist of the Fitzner Quartet, and Arnold Schoenberg.

[123] See below.

[124] See above, Chap. 7. The President of the Polyhymnia association was the dentist Alois Botsiber, whose son, Hugo, was an intimate friend of Schoenberg and Zemlinsky and was Eusebius Mandyczewski's assistant in the Musikverein Archives. The facts of Alexander von Zemlinsky's life are now better known thanks to Arnošt Mahler's work (publ. in *Die Musikforschung*, 24 (1971), 3, 251), to the Universal Edition vol. of contributions to the 1974 Zemlinsky Symposium held in Graz, and to Otto Biba's catalogue of the Zemlinsky Exhibition held at the Musikverein in 1992.

[125] This Quartet was long thought to have been lost, but it was discovered and published in 1966 by Faber Music. It has been recorded several times since then. The programme of the Fitzner Quartet concert also included Beethoven's 13th Quartet.

Berlin, where he took a job as conductor of the orchestra in Ernst von Wolzogen's famous cabaret, the Überbrettl. At that time he completed the first score of the *Gurre-Lieder*, and his symphonic poem, Op. 5, *Pelleas und Melisande*.

Max Graf later claimed to have been the first to mention Schoenberg to Mahler in 1902. Zemlinsky had introduced the young man to Graf, who had 'immediately noticed the "sparkle" in his eye', and recognized that behind his flamboyance and contradictions was a powerful mind and forceful personality. Graf listened to the D major Quartet and told the readers of a small newspaper for which he was then writing: 'His name is worth remembering. He is called Arnold Schoenberg'. Later Schoenberg brought Graf his new Sextet *Verklärte Nacht* and Graf was so impressed by its 'novelty' and the boldness of the harmonies that he showed it to Mahler. Graf felt that Mahler

who composed unusual music must understand unusual music. But Mahler's judgment was just as hesitant as mine. Yet in this music which he claimed not to understand, there was something which interested him and he asked Rosé to play it one afternoon in his office at the Opera. He invited me to this private performance and we were both fascinated by the lively sound of this poetic and expressive music. Mahler told Rosé several times: 'You must play this at your next concert'.[126]

The fact that Graf had become one of Mahler's bitterest enemies after their conflict in 1902 casts some doubt on many of his statements, but this story seems too detailed to have been invented. Where Graf is wrong, however, is in his claim that Rosé's first performance of *Verklärte Nacht* was loudly hissed, not only by the audience, but by the Viennese critics. In fact it was greeted with much warmth at the first performance. In a glowing article in the *Allgemeine Zeitung*, Schönaich said that the Sextet was 'rich in invention, powerful in inspiration, genuine in feeling and captivating in its sonorities, despite the wrong notes'. Heuberger saluted the birth of 'an authentic and admirably gifted musician', someone who was 'serious and profound', even if he sometimes wrote 'deliberately confused and ugly' music. Mahler was in St Petersburg at the time, but his sister wrote to him about it. He replied that the performance 'would have been of great interest to me', though this does not necessarily imply that he already knew the score.

This initial success in Vienna did not prevent Schoenberg from leaving for Berlin, where he succeeded in attracting the attention of Richard Strauss. Thanks to his help, he obtained the annual Allgemeiner Deutscher Musikverein Prize (the 'Liszt Stipendium') and was later appointed to teach composition at the Stern'sches Konservatorium.[127] But Schoenberg remained

---

[126] Max Graf, *Legende einer Musikstadt*, 329 (and GWO 351). Willy Reich (*Schoenberg*, 29) speaks of 'several rehearsals at the Opera' but H. H. Stuckenschmidt claims that Mahler first heard the work at the time of its second performance, in 1904 (HHS 73).

[127] At that time Strauss obviously had not the remotest idea of what was in store. Later, after Mahler's death, when as a member of the Mahler Stiftung he agreed to give Schoenberg a grant, he added: 'Though I

Viennese at heart and was happy to return to his native city in September 1903. He spent the summer in Payerbach, near Vienna, continued with the orchestration of the *Gurre-Lieder* (a task he was soon to interrupt once more), and, with the help of his friend the architect Adolf Loos, obtained a teaching post at the school headed by Eugenie Schwarzwald. This headstrong and energetic woman, a pioneer in the field of education who had entrusted the designing of her school to Adolf Loos, felt that it was wrong that a composer who had already acquired a certain renown should spend all year waiting for hypothetical pupils. She decided to put her school at Schoenberg's disposal on the days when her pupils had no classes, so that he could teach in a sort of free conservatory. It was there that, until 1905, Schoenberg gave his harmony and counterpoint course with his two chosen assistants, Zemlinsky and Elsa Bienenfeld, a student of Guido Adler's.[128]

That was the beginning of Schoenberg's great career as a teacher: Alban Berg and Anton Webern were among his first pupils in autumn 1904. Earlier that year, on 11 February, a group of his Lieder were premiered at the Ansorge Verein,[129] a small society of musicians closely linked to the Hagenbund,[130] founded for the purpose of 'cultivating great art, old and new, preferably little-known'. An angry audience booed Schoenberg furiously. A few supporters dared to applaud, but this caused the booers to redouble their efforts. The conflict grew into a true Viennese 'scandal', one 'which has still not died down', as Schoenberg later remarked half-ruefully, half-humorously. Nevertheless few

believe it would be better for him to shovel snow than blacken music paper'. He nevertheless admitted he could not foretell what opinion future generations might form of Schoenberg's music (Walter Thomas, *Richard Strauss und seine Zeitgenossen*, 127).

[128] Elsa Bienenfeld (born 1877, died in a concentration camp at an unknown date) studied music history with Guido Adler and music theory with Schoenberg. In 1904 she completed her Univ. studies with a thesis on 'Quodlibets at the end of the Renaissance' and for several years she contributed articles to the *Neues Wiener Journal*, notably on Schoenberg's 1907 premières.

[129] The Viennese 'Ansorge Verein für Kunst und Kultur' was founded in 1903 by Zemlinsky, the critic Paul Stefan, and the stage director Wilhelm von Wymetal. The critic Franz Servaes and the opera bass Moritz Frauscher were also members. The Society owed its name to the Berlin composer-pianist Konrad Ansorge (1862–1930), who studied at the Leipzig Conservatory, then with Liszt in Weimar and Rome, and taught first at the Klindworth-Scharwenka Conservatory in Berlin (1898–1903) then at the Prague Academy of Music. Famous as a pianist playing the classical repertoire, Ansorge also wrote Lieder as sombre and introspective as they were original, earning the nickname 'The Maeterlinck of Music'. Thus the Ansorge Verein performed mainly Lieder and chamber music. The opening concert took place on 29 Nov. 1903. In 1904 jointly with the Künstlerbund it put on two concerts, the first of which was held on 12 Jan. in the Festsaal of the Continental Hotel. It offered exclusively contemporary Lieder, including several by Zemlinsky. The second, on 11 Feb., took place at the Festsaal of the Nieder-Österreichischer Gewerbeverein. Accompanied by Zemlinsky, the Viennese tenor Walter Pieau, a close friend of Schoenberg's and Zemlinsky's, sang the world première of three Schoenberg Lieder from Op. 2 and Op. 3. It was this concert which ended in the 'scandal which has still not died down' referred to by Schoenberg (HHS 74). The Ansorge Verein concerts were usually centred on a single composer or poet. In 1904 there was a 'Dehmel evening' on 6 Mar., to which the Hamburg poet had been invited, with songs by Pfitzner, Zemlinsky, Ansorge, Strauss, etc. (attended by Gustav and Alma Mahler), an Ansorge-Reger-Marschalk concert on 23 Mar., two Lieder concerts of poems by Liliencron (set to music by Brahms, Ansorge, Strauss, d'Albert, Zemlinsky, and Reger, sung by Marie Gutheil-Schoder) on 10 and 14 Apr. Later there was a Hebbel evening, a Stefan George evening, and a Nietzsche celebration. The Ansorge Verein was short-lived for lack of financial assistance.

[130] See above, Chap. 14.

people in the Austrian capital even then would have denied that he had 'a strong and original musical talent', or that he possessed a 'wealth of musical ideas and a powerful technique'.[131]

However, the overwhelming majority of Viennese were utterly unaware of the fact that the Austrian capital was about to become the centre of the musical avant-garde in Europe. Zemlinsky and Schoenberg were destined to become historic figures, not only because they were, besides Mahler, the two most important composers then active in Vienna, but as a living link between the past and the future, and also between the two factions, the two parties, which had divided musical life in the capital at the end of the nineteenth century. Zemlinsky had not forgotten all he had learnt from Brahms in his early years, and he had convinced Schoenberg that much still remained to be gained from the technical refinements of his music, while Schoenberg had opened his friend's eyes to the tremendous resources of Wagnerian harmony and the new path Wagner had opened towards the future.[132] To achieve a successful synthesis between the two different trends became the implicit aim of the new school. The first step towards what was soon to lead to the founding of the 'Viennese school',[133] was taken in 1904. All too aware of the neglect and contempt in which official institutions and impresarios held their music, on 23 April 1904 Schoenberg and Zemlinsky, with a group of other composers—including Karl Weigl,[134] Oscar Posa,[135] Josef von Wöss,[136] Bruno Walter,[137] Robert Gound,[138] Oscar Noe,[139] Erich J. Wolff,[140] Gerhard

[131] *Bilder-Atlas zum Musikgeschichte* (Schoeffler & Leffler, Berlin, 1911).

[132] Wagner's influence, particularly that of *Tristan*, was already discernible in Zemlinsky's early opera *Sarema*.

[133] Here I deliberately avoid the use of the term 'Second Viennese school' since no such thing as a 'First Viennese school' ever existed. Mozart, Haydn, Beethoven, and Schubert were all great masters and powerful personalities. Each one of them would have been astounded to hear that the 20th-cent. considered them as members of a 'School'.

[134] Karl Weigl (1881–1949), born in Vienna, studied with Zemlinsky and at the Vienna Conservatory, then with Guido Adler at the Univ. In 1904 Mahler engaged him as Solorepetitor for the Vienna Opera. Author of numerous works belonging to all genres, he was appointed teacher at the New Conservatory of Vienna in 1918, and at the Univ. in 1930. Later he emigrated to the USA and pursued his teaching career in Boston and Philadelphia. PML owns a postcard addressed by Mahler to Karl Weigl, asking him to come and see him 'during his office hours', no doubt at the Opera.

[135] Oscar Posa (1873–1951), born in Vienna, studied law before devoting himself to composition and conducting. He wrote mainly chamber works and Lieder.

[136] Josef Venantius von Wöss (1863–1943), made many four-hand piano transcriptions of works by Bruckner and Mahler (see above, Chap. 11 and 13).

[137] Bruno Walter had at that time composed a number of chamber and orchestral works (including two symphonies and a choral work) but Mahler was never able to take him seriously as a composer.

[138] Alma's counterpoint teacher (see above, Chap. 12).

[139] Oscar Noe (1872–1910) a pupil of the Hochschule für Musik in Berlin, where he studied violin and singing (under Julius Stockhausen). He latter settled in Leipzig, where he taught singing. He also composed numerous Lieder.

[140] Erich J. Wolff (1874–1913) was born in Vienna. He studied at the Conservatory under the Fuchs brothers but was largely self-taught as a pianist and composer. He studied for some time with Zemlinsky whose close friend he became at the turn of the century. Later he became well-known in Berlin as an accompanist and composer of chamber and orchestral music as well as Lieder. Wolff was touring the USA as an accompanist when he died in New York on 12 Mar. 1913, at the age of 38.

Keussler,[141]   Franz   Schmidt,[142]   Gustav   Gutheil,[143]   and   Rudolf   Stefan
Hoffmann[144]—decided to found the 'Vereinigung Schaffender Tonkünstler in
Wien' (Association of Creative Musicians in Vienna: a variation on the Se-
cession's 'Vereinigung Bildender Künstler'). Its aims were to

set up a permanent institution for the encouragement (*ständige Pflegestätte*) of contemporary music in the capital, and create direct contact between its musicians and the
public; keep the latter informed of current developments in musical creation; cultivate
and promote contemporary musical works and the development of artistic personality
by arranging public performances of important new compositions which have not yet
been adequately appreciated; support the professional interests of its members.[145]

For such a daring enterprise, however noble its aim, the young musicians'
first task was to enlist the material and moral support of their elders. Although,
as a musicologist, Guido Adler was mostly concerned with music of the past,[146]
he clearly did not fear the new. Hanslick, who had been instrumental in having
him appointed head of the Musicological Institute in the Vienna University,
never ceased to wonder how Adler 'could possibly love both Josquin Desprez
and Bruckner'.[147] It was Adler who announced the formation of the Vereinigung
and introduced it in a long article published on 1 April in the *Neue Freie
Presse*, and in which he courageously defended ultra-modern tendencies in
music. With astonishing lucidity and open-mindedness, Adler commented on
the situation of Viennese music and the unshakeable respect of the Austrians
for their classic tradition, and thus for their past. He pointed out that the
greatest musicians in history had always had to make superhuman efforts in
order to break down the barriers of the city's conservatism, and added that 'the
greater the artist, the more he had to suffer'. Thus the conservative spirit of the
capital forced contemporary composers to follow the example of Vienna's
painters and create a kind of 'musical Secession'. Social changes meant that

[141] Gerhard Keussler: see biography below, Vol. iv, Chap. 3.
[142] Franz Schmidt (see below, Vol. iii, Chap. 1) played the cello in the Opera orchestra (see above, Chap.
1). None of his works were performed at the Vereinigung concerts.
[143] Gustav Gutheil (1868–1914), born in Blankenheim near Vienna, conducted in Strasbourg and Weimar
before moving to Vienna in 1900. He was known there chiefly as conductor of the popular Konzertverein
concerts and as husband of Marie Gutheil-Schoder, whom he married in 1902. Among his compositions are
a Cello Concerto and some Lieder.
[144] Rudolf Stefan Hoffmann (1878–1939), born in Vienna, a writer and physician as well as composer,
studied music under Zemlinsky before conducting the Philharmonic Choir and the Singakademie. He
composed chamber music and wrote librettos, as well as two small booklets on Franz Schreker and Erich
Wolfgang Korngold.
[145] Practically the whole of this passage from the manifesto of the Vereinigung is quoted by Guido Adler
in his article in the *Neue Freie Presse*. According to Adler, the Vereinigung brought together 19 composers
of widely different tendencies.
[146] On 7 Feb. 1904 Hanslick published a long article in the *Neue Freie Presse* which warmly praised Guido
Adler's activity as founder and director of the Musikhistorisches Institut at Vienna Univ. and as editor of the
Denkmäler der Tonkunst. Vols. xxi and xxii of this series had just been issued, including the *Trienter Codex*
and the Muffat Concerti Grossi. Hanslick also noted that a group of scores by Mahler and Bruckner had just
been donated to the Institut.
[147] KMI 90. Korngold also points out that Adler was Webern's teacher at the Univ.

musical creation no longer depended, as it once did, on princes or patrons. It arose from a deep, private impulse within the artists themselves, who for the moment were compelled to work in complete isolation. It was therefore hardly surprising that they should form an association in order to obtain what a musician wants above all else: performances, and good ones at that. It was common knowledge, Adler went on, that the historic Viennese institutions, i.e. the Philharmonic Orchestra and the Gesellschaft der Musikfreunde, were generally speaking hostile to innovation. But the composers of the Vereinigung refused to submit to their judgement. For the moment they desired only the 'rights of the living' and to find an audience for their works. Adler also hoped that government support, which was being extended to all forms of culture, would also be granted to the Vereinigung, which needed its aid to survive. Adler called Mahler the 'spiritual leader' of the 'young' generation and announced that he would conduct at least one of the concerts (three orchestral evenings, three of chamber music, and one 'special' concert) to be organized by the new group.

Indeed it was Adler who re-established a link between Zemlinsky and Mahler and who convinced his old friend to accept the honorary presidency of the Vereinigung. Guido Adler, as one of the few musicians in Vienna who held Schoenberg (and Zemlinsky) in high regard, cannot have been the narrow-minded conservative that Alma described. Early in 1904, he sent two of his students to Berlin to study under Hans Pfitzner at the Stern'sches Konservatorium. Pfitzner's scathing remarks about Gustav Mahler, whom the young men admired both as a man and as a musician, so infuriated them that they immediately returned to Vienna, whereupon Adler sent them to Schoenberg.[148] This incident acquires historical significance when it transpires that one of the two young composers was Anton Webern, who began studying with Schoenberg in the autumn of 1904, together with Alban Berg, Egon Wellesz, Erwin Stein, and Heinrich Jalowetz (who was Webern's companion when he called on Pfitzner).

Guido Adler's interest in the extreme avant-garde of his day was ill-regarded by many. Ludwig Karpath tells of lunching one day with Mahler, Hans Kössler, his old friend from Budapest,[149] and Guido Adler, after the first Viennese performance of one of Mahler's symphonies.[150] Adler said that he had detected in the work a tune by the French troubadour Adam de la Halle, and Mahler, good-humouredly, asked 'whether his de la Halle had also muted French horns'. Adler said he hadn't, but insisted that there was a resemblance in the themes. 'In this case I am going to have an apple,' said Mahler and proceeded nonchalantly to eat it, while Kössler and Adler began a dispute about music under his amused and somewhat caustic gaze. The next day, he told Karpath

---

[148] HHS 74; HMW 71.   [149] See above, Vol. i, Chap. 13.
[150] The conversation undoubtedly took place after the first Vienna performance of the Third Symphony in Dec. 1904, a time when the Vereinigung was the main subject of conversation in Vienna musical circles.

that Kössler had remarked to him that he would never have imagined that Adler, a solid musician in the classical tradition, could have supported 'the crazy young composers' in the way he did. 'So you see,' Mahler said, 'you can't please everyone. Adler is not as super-modern as Kössler thinks and Kössler isn't as reactionary as Adler thinks. Anyway, I had fun watching them argue. I think highly of both of them'.[151] Posterity can be grateful that Mahler had not broken with Adler, as he had, under Alma's influence, with some of his early friends; for the musicologist, quite unexpectedly, served as a link with the main representatives of the musical avant-garde. According to Alma, until 1904, Schoenberg had been anything but an admirer of Mahler. When she had first met him at Frau Ida Conrat's[152] in November 1900, at the Vienna première of the First Symphony, they had both been bitterly critical about Mahler. Later, in January 1902, without admitting to Schoenberg that she had meanwhile made Mahler's acquaintance, Alma asked him if he planned to attend the performance of the Fourth Symphony. The young man replied: 'Mahler already showed he was incapable of anything in his First and I suppose the Fourth is the same, only more so!'[153] Thus in 1904 Zemlinsky had a hard job persuading his brother-in-law to accept Mahler's invitation to visit him, and their first meeting in the Auenbruggergasse apartment was stormy. Mahler had sent Zemlinsky the following message: 'Dear Herr von Zemlinsky! Wouldn't you be kind enough to pay me a visit one of these days? We need to discuss the matters which concern us face-to-face. Would you like to come and have coffee with us this afternoon? If so, please come at about two. Cordially, Mahler. Perhaps with Schoenberg.'[154]

According to Alma, Zemlinsky himself was uneasy about the meeting, because he felt that everyone paid court to Mahler in order to get something out of him. Alma informed her husband of his qualms and as a result Mahler begged the young composer not to confuse the issue and to trust him. Despite all his efforts, the atmosphere was tense. An unpublished passage in Alma's *Erinnerungen* states that Schoenberg was at that time outwardly unattractive, even unkempt (*unappetitlich*: 'but he was soon to undergo a complete transformation', Alma immediately adds). Yet Mahler was already saying of Schoenberg: 'Take a good look at him for the world is going to have much to say about him'.[155] That first evening, Mahler, Zemlinsky, and Schoenberg gathered round the piano talking shop. Soon Schoenberg began peremptorily to expound some particularly bold and controversial ideas. Mahler, who did not like to be contradicted, replied in a sardonic and professorial manner, but Schoenberg persisted and went 'from paradox to paradox' until the inevitable explosion

[151] BMG 177.   [152] See below.
[153] AMM1. 101; AMM2. 105. Alma's reference to the Fourth is of course erroneous since Schoenberg was in Berlin in Jan. 1902. He returned to Vienna only in 1903 and Alma is probably referring to the première of the First (18 Nov. 1900) which followed that of the Second (9 Apr. 1899).
[154] MBR1, no. 317; MBR2, no. 340 (PML).   [155] AMM1. 100; AMM2. 104.

occurred. He then stood up and left with hardly a goodbye, followed shortly afterwards by his extremely embarrassed brother-in-law. No sooner had the door closed than Mahler asked Alma 'never again to invite those two boors', while Schoenberg, going down the stairs, swore 'that I will never again set foot in that house'. However, this superficial conflict between the generations left no scars. A few days later, Mahler asked Alma 'why Eisele and Beisele[156] don't come any more'. Alma, astonished, reminded him of his own words and then, without pursuing the matter, promptly reinvited the two composers.[157]

A pupil of Schoenberg's, Dika Newlin, tells of another less stormy encounter between the two men which Schoenberg himself had described to her:

At one time, Schoenberg was living in an attic in Vienna and was much disturbed while composing by the constant pealing of church bells which dinned into his ears from all sides. He complained about this in Mahler's presence, but Mahler commented, airily (*sehr von oben herab*): 'Oh, that doesn't matter; just put the church bells into your next symphony!'[158]

Newlin also recalls that Schoenberg, who had heard every one of Wagner's operas twenty to thirty times by the time he was 25, knew them so well that he invented a new game to play with his disciples during performances of *Tristan*: 'The winner was the one who would find the most "new melodies" in Wagner's highly plastic inner voices.' Newlin adds: 'Does this not also tell us something important about Mahler's technique of conducting . . . his concern with ab- solute clarity, with giving each inner part its own life, its own plastic form.'[159]

It was in discussing Wagner that the two composers first began to understand each other. Schoenberg found Mahler's ideas about Wagner so captivating that he was happy to listen, leaving in abeyance his usual tendency to assert himself against the older man, the established artist:

In one conversation about Wagner I admitted that *Lohengrin* was the work I could least come to grips with. Mahler did not feel the same way about it, and he gave me an interpretation, personal perhaps, but wonderful precisely because of that, because it shows that a work of art always has in it what a creative artist thinks it has. He said that Elsa was a doubting woman, unable to trust the man who had given her an example of trust by believing her fully, without ever wondering whether she was guilty. The capacity to trust is masculine, mistrust is feminine. That is really one of the main traits that give a deeper meaning to *Lohengrin*. But even if it weren't: whoever is able to see something in it is right; he who does not see anything is wrong. Mahler saw something, everywhere. And above all, he respected the truly great men and knew we have a duty to understand or to admire when they speak.[160]

---

[156] During the 19th cent., the two humorous figures of Dr Eisele and Baron Beisele were extremely popular in Vienna. They first appeared in the Munich paper *Fliegende Blätter*, but were soon seen on stage as well. In fact, even dolls of these characters were being sold. Johann Strauss, senior, composed a polka named 'Eisele-und-Beisele-Sprünge' (1847).

[157] AMM1. 100; AMM2. 104.

[158] Dika Newlin, 'Arnold Schoenberg's Debt to Mahler' (*Chord and Discord* (1948), 21).   [159] Ibid.

[160] Arnold Schoenberg, 'Rede auf Gustav Mahler' 1913, *Finale und Auftakt* (Otto Müller Press, Vienna

Episodes like these give an idea of the admiration the younger man was beginning to acquire for the older. Mahler, on the other hand, was obviously prepared from the outset to forgive a good deal, for he perceived behind Schoenberg's touchy character and fondness for contradictions an unusual intelligence, an exceptional creative gift, and a passionate idealism and hatred of compromise that equalled his own. He found an occasion to commit himself publicly to the young composer's cause on 1 March 1904, by attending the Rosé Quartet's second public performance of *Verklärte Nacht* at the Musikvereinsaal. This was originally to have been included in the Ansorge Verein series, but was cancelled because of the uproar provoked by the recital of Schoenberg's Lieder in February. However, Rosé, obviously no coward, firmly believed in the young composer's genius and played the work at a semi-private concert of the Tonkünstlerverein. It seems that its reception, unlike that at the première in 1902, was rather mixed. Rosé's answer was simply to repeat the performance, this time in public, on 1 March 1904, at the Musikvereinsaal.[161] This time the audience's reaction was intensely hostile. According to Paul Stefan, Mahler was present and applauded vigorously. Bruno Walter reports hearing him say after the performance: 'A very bold, interesting and significant work! But most important of all, there's a great deal of heartfelt warmth in it!' (*Ein sehr kühnes, interessantes, bedeutendes Werk. aber vor allem ist echte Herzenswärme* [darin]!)[162] Again according to Bruno Walter, who attended this second public hearing, Mahler advised Schoenberg to make a string orchestra version of the piece because 'six players are not enough. It sounds like a first idea for a piece, but now it needs to become real. It needs power, flesh and blood'.[163]

We have seen that it was thanks to Guido Adler's intercession that Mahler accepted the honorary presidency of the Vienna Vereinigung Schaffender Tonkünstler, of which Zemlinsky was president and Schoenberg vice-president. During a meeting of the constituent assembly chaired by both composers on 23 April 1904, it was decided to approach Mahler, who reacted favourably and promptly: 'Dear Mr Zemlinsky, It was a joy to express by word of mouth my participation in your efforts and my full sympathy for your aims. Since you consider it advisable or appropriate that I should acknowledge my faith in the future by officially (!) accepting such a title, then appoint me to whatever

---

1898–1914). This version of the exchange with Mahler about *Lohengrin* is less elaborate, and probably much older, than the one usually quoted (RWM 45) and which is given below in Vol. iii, Chap 5.

[161] Paul Stefan, *Das Grab in Wien*, 33. The programme also included Ernst Jokl's Quintet for Strings and Brahms Sextet No. 2. According to Paul Stefan, this concert occasioned the first meeting between Mahler and Schoenberg, but we have seen that they had probably met before.

[162] Bruno Walter, 'Erinnerungen an Gustav Mahler', in *Neue Freie Presse* (16 Nov. 1935). Surprisingly enough, Bruno Walter never inserted this important recollection in any of his later books or articles, presumably because he himself never had any sympathy for Schoenberg's music.

[163] Unpubl. memoirs of George Sebastian. In the same text the conductor recalls that one day in New York before the War, Bruno Walter conducted *Verklärte Nacht*. Schoenberg allegedly reproached him for having revived this 'sin of his youth', which is surprising since he never rejected any of his early works.

position you think fit.'[164] Several letters from Schoenberg to Adler have survived,[165] but they are of no help in dating the first meeting between Mahler, Adler, Schoenberg, and Zemlinsky, though it probably took place early in 1904, at the time of the second performance of *Verklärte Nacht* and shortly after Alma complained in her diary of the monotony of her life. This is all the more likely since the dates of the first Vereinigung concerts had already been set for November 1904 and January 1905, and the programmes certainly had to be decided on well before the summer if they were to include first performances of recognized masters. A letter from Schoenberg to Guido Adler dated 1 June refers to his conversation with Mahler about rehearsal schedules and the huge fee demanded by the Philharmonic musicians.[166] Another letter from Schoenberg to Adler on 11 November mentions a meeting planned for the same day at Mahler's to discuss both the plans of the Vereinigung and a request to the famous banker Baron Albert von Rothschild for financial aid. Mahler visited the Baron and put the request personally in January 1905, but obtained a disappointing response. Mahler broke the news to Schoenberg:

Dear Schoenberg, our hopes have been quickly and finally dashed! Rothschild has just had his secretary telephone me to say that he is putting 1,000 kronen at your Verein's disposal, in view of the fact that he has no interest in—and therefore no money for—music. Faced with this polite but quite definite attitude, against which there can be no appeal, I pass on to you this Job's message without more delay, and regret having nothing more agreeable to report. The 1,000 kronen are at your disposal until you need them. What now?[167]

Rothschild's refusal caused alarm and despondency in the headquarters of the Vereinigung, for the new society could only have carried on with his help, and had thus been sentenced to death. During the few months of its existence, however, it had caused quite a stir: between October 1904 and January 1905, press reports show that a veritable mountain of scores had been submitted to the committee by composers hoping to be performed.[168] As an indirect consequence of the formation of the society, Zemlinsky and Alma resumed in 1904

[164] Otto Biba, catalogue of the Zemlinsky Exhibition held at the Gesellschaft der Musikfreunde, Vienna, 1992, 54 (see above).

[165] They are among Adler's papers in the Univ. of Georgia Library. The first is dated 16 Nov. 1903; the others cover 17 Feb. to 1 June 1903; and there are two others from 11 Nov. 1904 and 7 Jan. 1905.

[166] Stadtbibliothek, Vienna. The first concrete evidence of contacts between Mahler and Schoenberg consists of two letters addressed by Alma to the young composer, dated (no doubt by him) Apr. 1904. In the first (two dates were written by a later hand on the autograph, 5 Apr. or 4 May) Alma thanks him for a book of songs he sent her and adds: 'I am drawn more and more to your Lieder Op.2'. She had found the ones she had just received so difficult that she had had to go through them several times. In the second letter (of 26 Apr.?), Alma invited Schoenberg to 'spend Wednesday evening' at the Auenbruggergasse and added: 'We are immersed in your six Lieder which have just appeared.' (LCW). She must be referring to Op.3, the only one among Schoenberg's first collections to consist of six Lieder.

[167] Undated letter from Mahler to Schoenberg, LCW (MBRS 82). In another undated letter, Zemlinsky asks Alma to persuade Countess Wydenbruck to put pressure on Baron Rothschild (UPL).

[168] 858 scores by 127 composers, according to the press of the time: 69 orchestral works, 73 chamber-music works, and 709 Lieder.

a correspondence which had been interrupted by the abrupt termination of their liaison when Mahler appeared on the scene. One of four letters from him that year congratulated Alma on the birth of her second daughter[169] and informed her of the progress of the opera *Der Traumgörge*.[170] In December Zemlinsky sent Alma a long letter mainly intended for Mahler, expressing the deepest admiration for the Third Symphony, which had been a revelation to him. With the founding of the Society, Schoenberg and Zemlinsky became frequent visitors of the Auenbruggergasse apartment.

Mahler's favourite disciple Bruno Walter was also a frequent caller, and his close relationship with her husband occasionally aroused Alma's jealousy. 'Bruno Walter is here,' she wrote in her diary.

Gustav is playing the Fifth Symphony for him. He is letting him look into the depths of his soul. Up to now, the work belonged only to me! I copied it and we have often sung the themes for ourselves . . . And now it belongs to others. Bruno Walter is the only one whose connivance I do not grudge to admit . . . And yet—I had to go out of the room . . .[171]

When Alma decided to widen the circle of Mahler's acquaintances, she could have chosen one or other of her former admirers, notably Klimt, who was then Vienna's most famous painter. But Alma must have known that Mahler, even though she had almost certainly never given him a full account of her early and unconsummated love affair with the 'prince of painters', would not willingly accept him as a friend. She had, in the past, 'cursed the stupidity of her family who had broken so strong a bond'. Klimt always admitted that whenever they met, he was still 'greatly affected by her charm'. She, for her part, 'trembled each time he approached'. Hinting that Klimt's unrequited love had led him astray, she claimed that the painter surrounded himself with empty-headed females 'and that is why he was searching for me, because he felt I could have helped him'. This nostalgic longing for each other, sweeter no doubt because quite without hope, haunted them all their lives (or at least all his life, for Klimt died in 1918), but Alma frequently recalled the memory of it in the almost forty years that remained to her after his death. 'Klimt was the first great love in my life,' she wrote, 'but I had been an innocent child, drowned in music and remote from life.'[172]

An extraordinary and hitherto unpublished document has recently come to

[169] Undated letter written on a Sat. (18 or 25 June), UPL.
[170] The work, although not mentioned by name, was most likely this one, the only opera Zemlinsky composed between *Es war Einmal* (1899) and *Kleider machen Leute* (1908–9). It was in part inspired by the composer's unhappy love affair with Alma (see below, Vol. iii, Chap. 7). Alma for her part recommended him to read the correspondence between Wagner and Mathilde Wesendonk, which had fascinated Mahler at the beginning of the summer. She also sent him a score of Pfitzner's Quartet (see below).
[171] AML 37. The MS score of the Fifth, copied by Alma, is now in LPA. The last three sentences but one do not appear in the original TS of Alma's diary. They were perhaps written much later, before the diary excerpts were publ. in AML.
[172] AML 27 and 29.

light concerning relations between Alma, her parents, and Klimt. This is the letter which Klimt sent to Carl Moll in 1899 on their return from Italy, after Moll, recognizing the danger of the increasing attentions Klimt was paying to a Alma, had taken the precaution of temporarily denying him access to his house:

Dear Moll,
Your letter hurts me deeply. What makes things worse is the thought that I am causing trouble and sorrow to one of my dearest friends. Dear Moll, are you not painting things too black? I think that both you and your dear wife are unduly disturbed by a number of various other things/[173] and that now, in your fatherly concern, you are seeing the picture darker than it is. In sincere friendship I propose to give a rough outline of events/between us there should be no secrets.

For years I have been an indescribably unhappy man/though people don't see it/they think the opposite/they even envy me. In all my undertakings over the last 7 or 8 years/ misfortune and misery have been my constant companions. Obviously I yearn for moments of happiness/of genuine pleasure/I snatch at them like a starving stray dog snapping at a morsel of food. In this state of inner conflict your clear mind refreshed me and I felt drawn to you in sincere friendship, more than to almost anyone else/I felt happy in your family circle/you seem to live a model life and I envy people who have a clear understanding of what they should do, what they want/I don't think I shall ever achieve this.

I came to your house in all innocence. I already knew Alma, that is to say I had seen her briefly at the unveiling of the Schindler monument, and she pleased me, as a beautiful child does please us painters/I saw her again in the Moll home/and found her more beautiful than ever/I was surprised that you had never painted her nor anybody else. She barely noticed me. In your kind way you frequently invited me when you had company/I am no great lover of large gatherings/but to your house I came gladly.

I think everyone liked coming.

Alma was often seated next to me and we spoke about harmless things together, she told me about her adoration for Wagner, for *Tristan*, for music/for dancing, I thought of her as a blessed creature and delighted in her. I never courted her in the real sense of the word/and even if I had, I would never have expected to succeed/many men come to the house and they all admired her/quite wrongly I mentally paired her off with some of them and I drew wrong conclusions.

This winter the young lady and I, who had frequently been neighbours at table, were given places a long way apart by means of a pre-arranged, written seating order. This struck me/perplexed me. I began to think. I thought it must be the girl's wish/that I bored her/also I found it natural enough not always to be allowed to sit next to her/on account of the company and on account of gossip. I no longer came often to your house/even before I only came when you invited me or when there was something important to discuss/but when we all met at the Spitzer's, the Henneberg's or at an exhibition and so on and she and I were always separated in the order of seating/I was

[173] This letter, with its lack of order, repetitions, unusual punctuation, words omitted, and occasional incoherence, reveals by its form as much as by its content the mental anguish Klimt was suffering as he wrote it. No attempt has been made to polish the text in the trans.

vexed by this form of mistrust, but as I have said, I found it natural—because of society and gossip.

Only very recently/when the journey to Florence had already been decided on, several things occurred to me/notably that the girl must have found out a good deal about my affairs (*Verhältnisse*)[174]/much that is true and much that is wrong/I am not quite sure about them myself, nor do I want to be—all I know for sure is that I'm a poor fool—in short, I gleaned from certain pointed questions and remarks that these things were not, as I had at first imagined, a matter of indifference to the girl. Then I became rather anxious/for I fear and respect genuine love/I was to some extent in conflict with myself/in conflict with my true feelings of friendship for you/but I reassured myself with the thought that on her side it must be all a lighthearted game, a passing mood/. Alma is beautiful, clever, witty/she has in abundance all that a discerning man could look for in a woman/I am sure that wherever she sets foot in the world of men/she is mistress, sovereign/perhaps she was getting bored by it all, perhaps she wanted a little romance/perhaps I did not behave as I would have done under other circumstances, and as all the others did, and perhaps that is what interested her/but even as a game I thought it was dangerous, and now it was up to me, with my experience, to be sensible/ and there began my weakness.

I had all kinds of thoughts, some confused, some clear—all mixed up.

One thing was quite clear—It could not be allowed to happen—.—

Everything still depended on conjectures, inferences/I had nothing definite to go on of course. And it seemed too stupid and conceited that an old duffer like me was afraid of making a conquest—that an old ass like me should even imagine that he could arouse the stirrings of genuine first love in this beautiful, blossoming young child! Was I to use counter-measures against a danger I could not believe in? How could I imagine that she, who moves so much in society, should think of me of all people, of a wretched creature like me! When Spitzer pays court to her and says many flattering things to her, does this seem dangerous to you? No/it would be laughable, and how much younger than him am I?

Wasn't I bound to expect that one fine [day][175] she would have a good laugh at me/ that one fine day, if I behaved like that, she would say/'Are you really so vain and silly as to believe that I feel something for you?'

My word! That was something I would have dreaded. And on the other hand/is it really so easy to feel indifferent towards her/doesn't everyone love her? Isn't everybody bound to care for her? Do you not find it understandable that in her presence there are moments/when one's thinking become erratic, confused? Are we human beings perfect? Then came your trip to Italy. I was working quite hard. The time for my trip to Florence was approaching. I was afraid. A vague something—my conscience perhaps—held me back. It told me: 'you shouldn't,' I became irresolute. This would have been the moment to show true friendship. I had a faint feeling of doing something wrong—I wanted to write then and there saying I won't come, I can't come. But the longing to get out of my gloomy hole, away from my daily routine/to see new things/new works of art/to have new stimulating experiences/the prospect of taking a beautiful trip

---

[174] Here Klimt seems to be playing on the double meaning of *Verhältnisse*, which can mean 'way of life' as well as 'liaisons'.
[175] The word 'day' is missing.

in most pleasant company/all of this helped to make me irresolute again/then your telegram came/I set off, hardly knowing what I was doing.

At the beginning everything went very well/I didn't feel quite comfortable, but it was alright. Strange surroundings inevitably bring people closer. I saw more of your family than I had in the whole of the previous two years. I noticed your dear wife's very understandable and natural efforts to keep Fräulein Alma and myself apart. How things stood between us required clarification. I had many serious conversations with Fräulein Alma/some general, some particular. These talks were friendly and confidential, but in any case mostly far from what might be called courting. <u>Both</u> of us came to know clearly, <u>very clearly</u>, what is meant by: 'Thus far and no further.' So draw back! The path of unrighteousness was not to be trodden.

Then came that evening in Venice. I am a bitter man, and that sometimes makes me say quite spiteful things which I deeply regret afterwards. And that's what happened there. I had been drinking rather more than I should/I don't want to use that as an excuse, I was more careless than usual in what I said/and that was what you heard, probably/after which you drew your own/too extreme/too sinister/conclusions. Your intervention made us both fully conscious/that one cannot live one's life as a dream, one has to live it with one's eyes open. The situation was made absolutely plain, there could be no doubt.

I believe I can safely assume that our painful discussion, and the letter which so upset both you and me, were no longer necessary. Forgive me dear Moll/if I caused you sorrow/I beg your wife's generous forgiveness, and as for Fräulein Alma/I think she won't find it difficult to forget it all. Let us hope time will heal this wound. When I turn these things over in my mind, I fear for myself what I have feared for a long time/my father died from a brain disease/my . . .[176] was in a asylum/my elder sister went mad a few years ago/perhaps there are the first signs in me—then, dear Moll, I am probably one of . . .[177]/the madness that will kill me will not be a happy one. I hope it's not yet come to that. I am going to keep out of people's way—I don't know how to behave.

I beg for your friendship. Your punishment is hard, I don't know if it is necessary in this form—I'll do whatever you say—because you are cleverer than I.

I have made you a full confession in the foregoing, because I prize your friendship/ and I want to keep you as a friend/I have told you many things that must remain between us/and I am counting on your discretion/I have written at length and would have liked to write even more, not to excuse or whitewash myself, but to reassure you as to the future/I have given you certain undertakings concerning myself, word of honour and shake hands on it, you can count on me.

I hope that the time will come when I can again come to your house without causing trouble, as I used to.

It makes me terribly sad that this had to happen. As far as my relatives' stay in the country is concerned, you needn't worry. I think, I'll do my best to see that it is not near Goisern/I myself shall only go to the country for a month, and not before the end of July. I shall let you know the place.

Warmest greetings from your unhappy friend

Gustav Klimt.[178]

[176] Another word seems to be missing here.　[177] An illegible word.
[178] Letter from Gustav Klimt to Carl Moll, 19 May 1899, Stargardt Auction of 25 Nov. 1981.

A rambling letter written by an unhappy man, its pathos often bordering on despair, its sentiment sometimes rising to nobility. But its final message was clear. Klimt valued his friendship with Moll more than his love for Alma, Alma's first reaction, confided to her diary, was that she had been thrown overboard in the storm to save the ship. On 7 November 1901, the day Mahler first met Alma at the Zuckerkandls' house, she was seated next to the 'prince of painters', which shows that the Molls considered all danger to have passed. And yet Klimt's name continued to rouse poignant memories in Alma's mind, as this entry in her diary, dated 10 September 1904, shows: 'Klimt is getting married! My youth is over. Mama told me yesterday. He was very close to me.' But further on, on the same page, Alma scribbled, certainly much later: 'Klimt never married'.[179] The woman Klimt was reported to be about to marry was no doubt his mistress Emilie Flöge, a dressmaker from a rich and respectable bourgeois family. She and her sister ran a fashionable dress-shop on the Kärntnerstrasse, which had been designed and decorated by Secession artists and the Wiener Werkstätte.

Though Mahler was by no means the rigid puritan she often made him out to be, Alma must have felt that, quite apart from his awareness that there had been something in the past between her and Klimt, he would not have taken kindly to the painter's manner of living, his peasant nature, his monk's robes, his complete disregard for conventions, and his well-known erotic obsessions expressed in countless drawings. A few notes from Klimt in Alma's papers suggest that their meetings were brief and infrequent, except for the Secession gatherings at the Molls'.[180] Thus Alma turned to another old friend and admirer whom Mahler had probably come to accept, even though their relationship remained somewhat distant: Max Burckhard. As director of the Burgtheater he had launched Ibsen and Hauptmann in Vienna, and was associated with the leading personalities of the contemporary theatre. Formerly his staunchly Nietzschean ideas had deeply influenced Alma who had adopted some of his more provocative sayings: 'A man who is falling should be pushed, not caught', or, 'Whoever needs help does not deserve to receive it.'[181] Yet Mahler's influence prevailed, and Alma did not listen when Burckhard, who was not above being anti-Semitic, advised her against marrying Mahler.

In 1904 Burckhard was already a sick man. He finally decided to leave Vienna and retire with his books to the Salzkammergut, the Northern Tyrol or Northern Italy, where he could write at leisure, commune with nature, and, he

---

[179] AMT.

[180] In one of these undated notes, a masterpiece of calligraphy that verges on pure design, Klimt refuses (after accepting by telephone) to attend a dinner party at the Mahlers' to which Anna Moll and Josef Hoffmann were invited. The Mahlers insisted on his arriving early but he had long promised his 'landlady' he would 'keep the whole day free for her'. For this late refusal he begs Alma not to bear a grudge nor 'seek revenge'.

[181] These remarks by Max Burckhard (or Alma) were told to me by Anna Mahler.

secretly hoped, die one day far from the noise of cities.[182] In the first surviving letter from Burckhard to Alma, dated September 1903, he promised to teach her Greek and to come back to Vienna every now and again to see her. The next two letters were written in January and February 1904[183] from Ospedaletti, on the Italian Riviera. The longest and most interesting is the second, in which Burckhard refers mysteriously to conversations with Alma concerning marriage and the union of two personalities: 'So many couples consist of two noughts, so why shouldn't there be some consisting of two real numbers. And even if one of them is higher, this does not make the other one lower. And if each retains its own free space, they can still be added together . . .'. Could this be a subtle allusion to the fact that Mahler made Alma give up composing when he married her? Or an answer to a letter in which she told him all she was sacrificing, and denying herself, so as not to risk a clash of personalities? In the same letter, Burckhard does his best to persuade Alma to join him in Florence with Mahler and the Molls instead of going to Abbazia for Easter. Later on, in June, Burckhard writes again suggesting a visit to Maiernigg.

Although Burckhard was now away from Vienna most of the time, he still kept an apartment there, in which he organized dinner parties at which Gustav and Alma would be able to meet various prominent authors. His first attempt with Hermann Bahr,[184] whom Mahler had probably already met in connection with the Secession movement, was not a success. Yet Bahr was a brilliant essayist and a very prolific playwright whose plays, social satires of incisive objectivity and subtle humour, were almost every year a topic of conversation in the Austrian capital.[185] His lively intelligence, his friendships with the Jung-Wien school and numerous other writers such as Schnitzler, Hofmannsthal, Zweig, Rilke, and Altenberg, his activities as a journalist and as co-founder of *Die Zeit*, the prophet's beard he wore in homage to Walt Whitmann—all this made him one of the most conspicuous personalities of the capital. Perhaps it was precisely his lively mind, his brilliant and abundant conversation, and his predominantly critical turn of mind that disturbed Mahler, who liked to live on lofty heights and who believed in eternal values rather than those of his time. Could he really be expected to have a meaningful exchange of ideas with a man who had formulated his own aesthetic thus: 'The critic must be a master of rapid changes of mind, a rubber man, a mental acrobat, a snake continually casting off its skin in order to penetrate into the skins of others so as to be able to offer information from the inside'.

Whatever the reason, Mahler and Bahr did not take to each other. Mahler

---

[182] AML 22; Alma writes that his wish was not granted and that Burckhard died in Vienna 'as a result of negligence by his doctors'.

[183] The typewritten copies that have survived among Alma's papers (UPL) give one of the letters the date 26 Feb. but the contents show that it was written before the other, which has the date 7 Feb.

[184] See above, Chap. 13, Hermann Bahr's biography.

[185] In 1980, *Der Unmensch* (The Brute) (1919) was one of the major successes of the Festival and the theatrical season in Vienna.

could not work up much interest in him, and as always when ill at ease, he communicated an unbearable awkwardness, an 'oppressive atmosphere' (*Beklemmung*).[186] Another of Burckhard's attempts was far more successful. Probably in February 1904, at the time of the Viennese première of *Rose Bernd*, he invited the Mahlers together with Gerhart Hauptmann,[187] the most famous German playwright of the day, and the celebrated actor Josef Kainz.[188] Hauptmann had come to Vienna on 2 February to rehearse his new play at the Burgtheater, and in his honour the Deutsches Volkstheater arranged a perform- ance of one of his earlier plays, *Die versunkene Glocke* (The Sunken Bell).[189] Much later, in her memoirs, Alma recalled this evening with emotion. The discussion had immediately centred on *Die versunkene Glocke*. It was the first symbolist work from a playwright then considered a champion of naturalism, and it had caused quite a stir. According to Alma, Kainz claimed that evening that he possessed a 'first version' of the play in which the heroine, the elf Rautendelein, returns to the spring from which she was born; in the final version, she is unfaithful to her true nature by 'returning to life',[190] in other words by choosing the world of human beings. The lively discussion continued as Mahler and Hauptmann left Burckhard's apartment and walked most of the way from the Frankgasse to the Rennweg. Time passed rather slowly for Alma and Margarete Marschalk, the poet's companion, as they followed some dis- tance behind, particularly as the two men constantly stopped under street lamps, gesticulating or holding on to each other's coat buttons. Finally, Alma and Margarethe sat down on a bench to wait until a pause in the conversation would allow them to remind the men of their existence and the late hour. At the

[186] See Vol. iv, Chap. 5, the conversation Mahler had with Ernst Decsey in summer 1900 about Bahr.

[187] Wilhelm Kienzl's diary mentions that, on 5 Feb. after the *Euryanthe* performance, Mahler had supper with the Hauptmanns at the Hotel Sacher before meeting Kienzl at the Hotel Kaiserin Elisabeth. Gerhart Hauptmann (1868–1946) was born in Silesia. Originally a sculptor, he turned to literature at the age of 23. From his first play in 1889 to his last novel (publ. posthumously), Hauptmann espoused in turn naturalism, symbolism, materialism, and mysticism. He also wrote a number of poems. In all these styles, Hauptmann showed a creative power unique for his time. It is impossible to mistake the 'social' character of Hauptmann's first plays: they contain sharp criticism of bourgeois society and its outworn values. Above all, he brought on to the stage the Silesian proletariat, and socialist workers in *The Weavers* (1892), the tragedy of an exploited class. He was awarded the Nobel Prize for literature in 1912. Hauptmann gave a new lease of life to the German theatre, which had been dormant since Hebbel, and thus occupies a significant place in the literary history of his country. Although some of his works, perhaps those most prized by his contemporaries, today seem dated, many of his writings retain all their original impact. Hauptmann's principal plays, up to 1904, were: *Vor Sonnenaufgang* (1889), *Einsame Menschen* (1890), *Die Weber* (1892), *Florian Geyer* (1895), *Die Versunkene Glocke* (1896), *Fuhrmann Henschel* (1898), *Michael Kramer* (1900), *Der rote Hahn* (1901), *Der arme Heinrich* (1902), *Rose Bernd* (1903). The Viennese première of the last-named play had been at the Burgtheater on 11 Feb. 1904.

[188] Josef Kainz (1858–1910), a famous Austrian actor born in Hungary, was enormously successful at the Deutsches Theater in Berlin, and from 1899 at the Burgtheater in Vienna. Early in his career, he attracted the attention of King Ludwig II of Bavaria. He was as successful in classical roles (Shakespeare, Goethe, Schiller) as in the modern repertory (Ibsen, Hauptmann). His most famous role was Hamlet.

[189] With music by Margarete Marschalk's brother, Max, an old acquaintance of Mahler's from Hamburg times. Hauptmann and Margarete were married on 18 Sept. 1904.

[190] In the play as we know it today, Rautendelein returns to the lake after giving Heinrich the 'kiss of death'.

Michaelerplatz, Alma persuaded Mahler to take a horse-drawn cab. The couple parted from their new friends after promising to visit them the next day at the Hotel Sacher. The following day Hauptmann noted in his diary: 'Yesterday met Gustav Mahler. Outstanding mind. Demonic force of nature. Stamp of great genius unmistakable.' On this occasion Alma went for a long walk in the town with Margarete and later described the young woman's strange and whimsical personality, her satin trousers, and her long black shoulder-length ringlets. She seemed to Alma to be the very incarnation and possibly the model for Rautendelein, the heroine of *Die versunkene Glocke*, 'as if Hauptmann himself had brought forth from his imagination a living being'.

Mahler and Hauptmann saw each other practically every day during these two weeks. On 8 February, Hauptmann wrote in his diary: 'Yesterday evening, tête-à-tête with Mahler and his wife. Affinity and similarities in all respects. Strength. Nothing forced in our relationship, as still with Hofmannsthal.' Hauptmann came to performances of *Euryanthe* and *Tristan* at the Opera,[191] while Mahler watched the première of *Rose Bernd* from Hauptmann's box at the Burgtheater. Again, on 13 February: 'Evening: Mahler: with Klimt, Moll, Moser etc. Mahler full of the grace of genius. The child. No false dignity as director of the Opera. Not a trace of it,' wrote Hauptmann in his diary, adding the following day after the performance of *Tristan*: 'Powerful impression. Mahler incomparable man.'

Some time after their first meeting, Hauptmann wrote a letter which shows how close he already felt to Mahler, both intellectually and emotionally:

I think of you every day and all the stimulating strength I have derived from it is still very much alive in me and after all the greatest gift for the children of this earth is personality,[192] and not necessarily their own. Although you are not in any way responsible for the greatness, goodness and potent beauty which live in you, I shall always be grateful to you for the lasting share in these you allowed me to have. People like you make it possible for long stretches of our journey on earth to be illuminated by a happy and divine light. What reason could I possibly have for not telling you that?[193]

Later, when Hauptmann was recovering from pneumonia in the Italian lake district, he proposed to Mahler that they use the familiar *Du* form when addressing each other, 'so that we may meet in the near future as two healthy and vigorous old friends. Since we did not have the good fortune to know each other when we were young, why should our riper years suffer the consequences, for our inner journeys are the same?'[194] Hauptmann also wrote of his desire to hear Mahler's music and spend an entire summer with him. 'Your husband

[191] On 5 and 13 Feb. 1904.
[192] A reference to a famous line from Goethe. 'Das grösste Glück der Menschenkinder sei nur die Persönlichkeit' (The greatest good of the children of this earth must only be personality), for it is in the individual that 'the spiritual and the creative' reside.
[193] Undated letter (AMM1. 332), not included in AMM2.
[194] Letter dated 28 Feb. 1904 (AMM1. 332 ff., not included in AMM2).

really has an enthusiastic admirer in Hauptmann,' Burckhard wrote to Alma early in 1904. 'It is touching how he worships him. He told me today that, even if *Rose Bernd* had failed, his Viennese trip would have been worthwhile because he had got to know him!'[195]

With Arthur Schnitzler, another of the outstanding Viennese literary personalities of the time, Mahler had a relatively superficial but sustained relationship. He had been told of the writer's admiration for him, and that, as an opera enthusiast, he tried never to miss any performance conducted by Mahler.[196] The two men talked to each other only once, at Arnold Rosé's, in autumn 1905.[197] Yet Mahler played an essential role in the life of the music-loving Schnitzler. Every time he 'appeared on the podium, our hearts beat faster,' writes Olga Schnitzler, 'we knew that an ecstatic experience, an unforgettably powerful stimulus, awaited us. After such hours of total rapture, we would walk home late at night through the empty streets'. What is more, Schnitzler had been an early admirer of Mahler's symphonies, which he played four-handed with his mother, and he attended all his Viennese premières, at the back of a box where he could 'see and hear well while remaining invisible'. The two men had not yet met when, one day, the secretary of the Gesellschaft der Musikfreunde came to Schnitzler in his box and asked him for some cigarettes for Mahler, who had left his at home.

Some time afterwards, the first meeting took place at the Rosés' house. Mahler's personality captivated Schnitzler. Henceforth 'it was obvious to him that this was one of the few great men he had met, and he always felt for him a profound yet almost timid love.' They were never to become close friends, no doubt because of Schnitzler's 'timidity'. In December 1904, he attended the Viennese première of the Third and his wife wrote later:

The first movement seemed to him to symbolize Mahler's fundamental mood with its vision of a crowd surging past in the most brutal and unreflecting high spirits, while he, the sole spectator by the roadside, heard from within the promptings of a profound knowledge of the world and of a demonic and turbulent (*aufgewühlter*) melancholy. Schnitzler felt very close to this state of mind, and the same longing (*Sehnsucht*) appears frequently in his work, the same consciousness and the same affliction.[198]

One day, when someone was telling him how much Schnitzler admired him, Mahler is said to have exclaimed naïvely: 'But what a wonderful man Schnitzler must be!'[199] Indeed Schnitzler considered him 'the greatest living composer' and wrote in his diary, when Mahler left Vienna:

[195] Letter quoted above, dated 7 Feb. in the typed copy.

[196] A letter to Hermann Bahr dated 14 Dec. 1904 shows that Schnitzler went to hear the Third Symphony that evening, the tickets having been sent to him by Mahler (Arthur Schnitzler, *Briefe, 1875–1912* (Fischer, Frankfurt, 1981), 506 and 909).

[197] Ibid. 968; extract from Schnitzler's diary, 19 May 1911.

[198] Olga Schnitzler, *Spiegelbild der Freundschaft* (Residenz, Salzburg, 1962), 21 and 113.

[199] RSM2. 25. Much later, after Mahler's death, Schnitzler wrote in his diary (14 Apr. 1912) of a walk on the Semmering with Professor Heitler, who spoke to him of a walk he had taken with Mahler along these same

How can it be explained that Mahler for me is one of those utterly strange, rich personalities who express their very essence in music (unlike Bruckner who simply lets beautiful music pour out of him) gripping, communicative, autobiographical to the highest degree—while others find him tortured, torturing, untrue? Others who perhaps have just as strong relationships to the essence of music as I do.

Considering the great success of his first poems, published under the pen-name Loris in 1890, it is surprising that Hugo von Hofmannsthal never interested Mahler, although he had met him in 1896 at the house of Ignaz Brüll by the Attersee.[200] The two men were in contact again during the spring and summer of 1901, when Hofmannsthal wrote to the director of the Opera about his new ballet scenario, the score of which was being composed by Zemlinsky. This was of course the ill-fated *Triumph der Zeit*, the subject of Mahler's lively exchange with Alma when they first met at the Zuckerkandls. Mahler answered briefly from Maiernigg, in summer 1901. He apologized for not having replied earlier; wholly absorbed in composition, he was at present unable to answer letters; however, he asked Hofmannsthal to send his manuscript to the Vienna Opera so that he could read it there on his return at the end of August.[201]

In Vienna, Mahler fulfilled his promise, read the ballet scenario, and discussed it with Hofmannsthal in his office at the Opera. On 18 September, Hofmannsthal wrote to Zemlinsky to tell him of his disappointment:

Dear sir, I am very sorry to have to inform you that Mahler, who has had the libretto[202] for some weeks, seems not to like it very much. This upsets me, but also surprises me, for this Spring, after the stage designer Leffler had spoken to him about the first two acts, Mahler talked to me about it in such a way that I was completely unprepared for his present negative attitude. Unfortunately he does not criticize particular details or sections over which I would have been very willing to make concessions in the interest of work together. No, the truth of the matter is that there is nothing in it that he likes,

heights, discussing Beethoven and Mozart. Two days later, Schnitzler played the first movement of Mahler's Second Symphony on the piano (four hands), and then the opening of Bruckner's Third.

[200] See above, Vol. i, Chap. 18 and 22. Born in Vienna, of an Austro-German mother and Jewish father, grandson of a merchant ennobled for services to the army, Hugo von Hofmannsthal (1874–1929) showed his poetic gift at an early age and became part of the literary circle at the Café Griensteidl. Stefan George and Hermann Bahr, deeply impressed by the incomparable refinement of his poems (1890) under the pseudonym Loris, made a special trip to see him and were stupefied to find a schoolboy in short trousers. After publishing under the pseudonym Theophil Morren a first play on a Renaissance subject, *Gestern* (Yesterday) (1890), Hofmannsthal became a brilliant student at the Univ. of Vienna (writing theses on 'The Poets of La Pléiade', 1899 and Victor Hugo, 1901), did his military service and also had several plays performed. By 1904 he already had a long list of works to his credit. For the theatre: *Der Tod des Tizians* (1892); *Der Tor und der Tod* (1893); *Der Kaiser und die Hexe*, *Die Frau im Fenster*, *Der weisse Fächer*, *Das kleine Welttheater* (1897); *Die Hochzeit der Sobeide*, *Der Abenteurer und die Sängerin* (1899), then *Das gerettete Venedig* (after Thomas Otway, Venice Preserv'd) (1904: put on in Berlin by Gordon Craig), *Alceste*, and *Elektra* (1903). In prose: *Das Märchen der 672. Nacht* (1895); *Reitergeschichte* (1899); *Das Erlebnis des Marschalls von Bassompierre* and *Brief des Lord Chandos* (1902).

[201] Antony Beaumont, 'Alexander Zemlinsky', 21 (see above, n. 120).

[202] The work was the three-act ballet *Der Triumph der Zeit*, refused by Strauss first of all. Zemlinsky's drafts and MS score are in the LCW. See above, Chap. 12, and Horst Weber, 'Stil, Allegorie und Secession, zu Zemlinskys Ballet Musik nach Hofmannsthal "Der Triumph der Zeit"', in *Art Nouveau, Jugendstil und Musik* (Atlantis, Zurich 1980).

neither the pantomimic nor the more decorative parts. I am afraid that he just does not have the one quality required for this: visual imagination. He thinks poorly of that whole branch of art, and told me bluntly that the way a thing looks, the effects that can be produced with lighting and so on, 'all that is of no importance'.[203] It is a stupid kind of criticism, though, to reproach someone in the context of one particular work with the deficiencies or limitations of the art form in which he works. He also criticized the relationship of my poetry to the music, said in one breath that I had introduced too much subtlety, and in the next that I had not shaped distinct characters (*gestaltet*), but had confined myself to generalities, which is the opposite of his previous remark. He harped on this lack of characterisation which seems to mean lack of individualisation, and I couldn't make him understand that this idea of characterisation, a Wagnerian notion that obviously dominates his whole theoretical approach, was quite irrelevant in this case, because one couldn't expect our mimers to portray anything that went beyond the typical.—Well, since I am no good at arguing with people about my work, our conversation, which incidentally remained friendly throughout, soon came to an end, though I at least got him to say: 'I'll have to see, I wonder what the composer has been able to make of it'. He also promised me he would take his time and read it through again; he must have read it very carelessly the first time. Another instance of the fiendish unreliability of everyone and everything to do with the theatre . . .

As far as Mahler is concerned, everything now depends on your music and with the way you talk to him about the text: as the composer, you're in quite a different position from me as the author. There seemed to be a thought in the back of his mind: 'Perhaps I am wrong'.[204]

This unfortunate encounter over the *Triumph der Zeit* certainly did not help in establishing a dialogue between Mahler and the young writer. No evidence survives to throw light on subsequent relations between them, except for a letter of Hofmannsthal to Alma written in the late spring of 1908, from which it emerges that she had invited the poet and his wife to the Auenbruggergasse: Hofmannsthal excuses himself, since he is to leave the next morning for a fortnight in the Tyrol.[205] Nothing has emerged so far about Mahler's opinion of the poems of 'Loris' or indeed of any other contemporary poet. Nor does Alma divulge what he thought of the libretto of *Elektra*, which he saw at the Hammerstein Opera in New York in 1910. Obviously it is regrettable that the first professional relationship between the two men should have related to a ballet, an art form in which Mahler was never interested, and not to one of

---

[203] One can see from this how great a change was shortly to come over Mahler under the influence of Roller, who put a great deal of effort into lighting.

[204] Letter from Hofmannsthal to Zemlinsky, *Freier Deutscher Hochstift*, Frankfurt am Main, publ. in the *Frankfurter Allgemeine Zeitung* on the occasion of Hofmannsthal's centenary, 2 Feb. 1974. It will be recalled that, when Mahler and Alma first met at the Zuckerkandls', one of their first subjects of conversation was Zemlinsky and his ballet (see above, Chap. 12). Mahler's opinion of the libretto was in fact much lower than he led its author to understand.

[205] 'We have been putting off our departure for the last ten days,' he writes, 'and now we really are going. We shall be back on the 18th or 19th of June. Could you not come and see us down there [in Rodaun]? Or could we come and see you?' (Undated letter from Hofmannsthal to Alma, probably written in June 1908, for Hofmannsthal adds: 'How sad it was this winter to have anything whatsoever to do with the Opera and to have to move in its depressing, poisonous atmosphere').

Hofmannsthal's opera librettos for which Strauss was to write the music from 1906 on. A Strauss-Hofmannsthal work, produced and performed by Roller and Mahler—such a doubles match between four men of genius—would have been an historic event, and could have happened at the Vienna Opera during the space of the next two short years, but the opportunity ended abruptly with Mahler's departure in 1907. Before he got to know Roller, a stage performance as a *Gesamtkunstwerk* capable of transcending the merely anecdotal by a dynamic synthesis of all art forms was only a remote dream for Mahler. As for Hofmannsthal, he was then still a poet who had not yet mastered the stylization necessary to transpose his art to the theatre; and a ballet plot was further from his grasp than an opera libretto.

In June 1904, Alma was in an advanced stage of pregnancy and had difficulties in walking. So Mahler one day took her in a carriage to the Prater. 'As long as my wife is still up,' he wrote to Guido Adler, 'I want to devote all my time to her. When she takes to her bed I'll write to you. Meanwhile, I'm reading your paper (*Elaborat*).'[206] On the evening of the 14th, they came home to find the Rosés in the entrance hall of their building, and were persuaded to go with them to the Burgtheater where Hauptmann's *Der arme Heinrich* was playing, with Kainz in the title-role. Alma was profoundly moved and began to reread the play that night in bed. She fell asleep, and woke at daybreak with the poet's lines still running through her head. Then, as she felt the first labour pains, she opened the window and watched the slow awakening of nature. When her pains increased, she woke Mahler and asked him to fetch the midwife.[207] He tried to comfort her during her labour by reading Kant aloud, but the monotonous sound of his voice and the nature of the text, which she would in the best of circumstances have found uncongenial, so exasperated her that she begged him to stop.

That Anna was born at midday on 15 June—the middle of the day, of the month, and of the year—seemed a good omen to the parents. The baby was soon looking at the world with such bright blue eyes that her official names (Anna, after Anna Moll, and Justine, after Mahler's sister), were put into cold storage, and the family called her Gucki,[208] a nickname which stuck to her until adolescence. The evening of the day the baby was born, Alma fell asleep, and awoke with a start to see a large cockchafer dangling a few inches from her face. Mahler was holding it by one leg: 'I know you love animals,' he said, 'so I caught this for you!' Several days later Alma had a sudden appetite for cheese, and Mahler rushed into town to buy her a piece of delicious but pungent Schwarzenberg. Since he hated carrying even the smallest package, he tied the

---

[206] RAM 42. It certainly concerned plans for the reorganization of the Vienna Conservatory (see above).

[207] In her memoirs, Alma says that Gucki was born before the doctor and the midwife arrived, and that all the doctor had to do was to tend the minor lesions she suffered because of the unusually brief labour (AML 230).

[208] From *gucken*: to look, peep.

bag containing the cheese to a buttonhole of his overcoat and, lost in thought, forgot it completely as he walked home. He was mystified by an increasingly unpleasant odour. True, they were repairing gas pipes in the Walfischgasse, but in the next street the air was equally foul! When he reached Alma's room, he was completely baffled to find the same awful smell there. When Alma pointed to the cheese he laughed heartily at his own forgetfulness. Alma tells of another similar incident. One day he had an acute attack of toothache. She had no trouble in persuading him to see a dentist and agreed to accompany him. She was sitting in the waiting-room, when the door of the dentist's surgery suddenly burst open. Mahler stood there, asking: 'Alma, which tooth was it that hurt?' The burst of laughter provoked by his question surprised him, but he ended up, as usual, by joining in.

After Anna's birth, the doctor prescribed three weeks of rest in bed for Alma, particularly as she intended to breast-feed the child. Knowing that he had only two more months of the summer vacation to devote to composing, Mahler decided leave Alma in her mother's care, and go alone on 21 June to Maiernigg, where she would join him later.[209] But the feverish activity of the Opera's summer season, the frequent journeys to guest performances, and the emotional strain of the birth of his second child had taken their toll of his reserves of creative energy. He spent several days trying 'to collect the scattered pieces of his inner self' and wondering if he would ever succeed. A whole week passed before he could bring himself to write a note of music. His daily letters to Alma provide a detailed record of this agonizing period of waiting for the urge to compose to return.[210] These letters of course do not reveal explicitly the full extent of his despair and frustration in the face of this composer's block, for Alma was still in bed convalescing, and he was always careful not to worry her. The morning after his arrival he wrote:

Yesterday I went to bed dead tired at nine-thirty, and slept right through until eight and then had my breakfast in the *Häuschen*. But it's strange: every time I come here, the climate invariably makes me profoundly depressed. As soon as I'm in Maiernigg, I lose all my energy and vitality and it always takes me two or three weeks to get myself back into some sort of shape. You remember what it was like the last two summers. This time it's exactly the same except that you are not here, so that I have to drag myself around alone all day. God knows when I'll be able to pull myself together. It's been a long time since I've felt so low (*sordiniert*)! For the time being my only consolation is that the climate here is so excellent for the children, so they at least will benefit from it. Nevertheless, I would very much like to get rid of this villa . . .[211]

The weather was dreadful and Mahler spent the greater part of his time in Alma's rooms, for his own room had been repainted and the smell of 'sour size'

[209] MBR1, no. 281; MBR2, no. 330 (undated, to Arnold Berliner; postmark 19 June 1904).

[210] Among the 25 letters and cards Mahler sent Alma between 21 June and 11 July, only 6 are repr. in AMM1.

[211] AMM1. 306 ff.; AMM2. 275 ff.

forced him to sleep upstairs. In an effort to put himself in a creative state of mind, he read books and played scores on Alma's piano. For the moment, the newly published correspondence between Wagner and Mathilde Wesendonk, which he had brought from Vienna and read all day long, filled him with elation.[212]

I learned a great deal from it because it gave me a new insight into an important, perhaps the most important, part of the life of this dear and unique great man. The great attraction in such reading lies in the analogies one continually discovers, on one level or another, with one's own life. This allows us on the one hand to follow the arguments with understanding and sympathy, and on the other, we feel wonderfully gratified to find in these lofty regions companions in sorrow whose destinies are so similar to ours. You will always encounter this whatever life you may read about. Beyond time and space, there exists a select society of lonely people who, for that very reason, live together all the more intensely . . .[213]

Mahler at the same time read Tolstoy's *Confessions*,[214] but in small doses, because he found them 'horribly sad, full of barbarous self-laceration and distorted questioning that result in unlimited destruction of all possible good-ness acquired by heart or mind'.[215] He went on to read Oscar Wilde's *Picture of Dorian Gray*. Soon, this 'very exciting' book seemed to him 'an empty shell . . . a good enough idea, but spoiled by dilettantism and a taste for the arbi-trary'.[216] He advised Alma not to read it.

At the piano, he played most of Brahms's chamber works and found them 'unfortunately often sterile and contrived . . . If I hadn't suddenly discovered a marvellous Sextet in B flat,[217] I would have lost all hope in Brahms, as I do in myself these days.' Several days later, he added:

I've now been through most of the Brahms. I must say he's a tiny little fellow with a rather puny chest. Lord! When you think of the absolute gale that blew from Richard Wagner's lungs! How carefully Brahms has to husband his scarce resources in order to make ends meet! I don't mean any offence to him! But where he really falls down—and you won't believe me when I tell you, is in his so-called 'developments' (*Durchführungen*). His themes are often beautiful, but only very rarely does he know what to do with them. In any case, Beethoven and Wagner are the only ones who knew how to go about it.[218]

---

[212] AMM1. 304; AMM2. 277. Edited by Wolfgang Golther, the Wagner–Wesendonk correspondence had just been publ. in Berlin.

[213] AMM1. 309; AMM2. 280, undated letter (9 July).

[214] The *Confessions* (1879), written as the Russian writer was going through a crisis of depression and pessimism, were originally intended as a preface to an exposé of his religious doctrine. Faced with the giddying thought of nothingness, Tolstoy painfully experienced the impossibility of living without faith, which he found to be intact only among the ordinary people. Henceforth he tried to free himself from the parasitic life of the wealthy and for two years he kept to very strict religious practices.

[215] AMM1. 304; AMM2. 277.   [216] AMM1. 308; AMM2. 278.

[217] The First Sextet, Op. 18. (AMM1. 305; AMM2. 277).

[218] AMM1. 308; AMM2. 278. In a substantial article, Rosamund McGuiness subtly underlines the ambiguity of Mahler's relationship to Brahms and lists quotations or 'reminiscences' of Brahms in various

After Brahms, Mahler turned to Bach for relaxation before tackling the Bruckner symphonies, which did not please him any more than Brahms. Both composers were in his eyes 'mediocre'. 'Now I am playing Beethoven. There are only <u>he</u> and Richard, and apart from them, <u>no one</u>.'[219] Returning to Brahms a bit later, he found the Piano Quartet in G minor, 'which I liked from beginning to end',[220] and a week later, the 'marvellous first movement of the one in C minor that I played four-hands with you last year. The first two parts are wonderful. So far, only the G minor satisfies me completely. What a shame that the last two movements are so uninspiring (*so verflachen*).'[221]

Not having expected to remain inactive so long because of his composer's block, Mahler had brought no other books with him. He began to be afraid that, without anything to read, he would be entirely at the mercy of his darkest moods. 'I am slowly beginning to get used to my solitude', he wrote on 25 June, three days after his arrival, 'to situations which can't be helped. But in all my life I've never been so lonely'. At the beginning of July, long walks and excursions were made impossible by constant thunderstorms that raised the lake to record levels. 'Sometimes I try to go a few steps in the rain; I had coffee in Maiernigg. But the sight of the petits bourgeois all around me, old, unappetising women knitting, and bald fat men wolfing down cheese, quickly drove me away.' Other outings were no more successful. One day, as he was walking home from Klagenfurt, a thunderstorm broke out and drenched him to the skin. On another occasion he took a rowing-boat to Krumpendorf, where the sight of the locals and holiday-makers depressed him once more: 'Now that I wander about alone, I take a closer look at the people here. I am sure that in the whole of Europe you can't find a more hopelessly stupid type of person (*Menschenschlag*)!'[222]

Even the few people he had contact with bored him to death. When he visited his nearest neighbour, the architect Alfred Theuer, he was treated to a long demonstration of his newest toy, a sort of immobile motorcycle whose engine 'roared and vibrated and emitted a fearful stink'. Then the architect described all his friends' and acquaintances' misfortunes, including the prolonged and painful 40-hour birth pains undergone by a relative.[223] Mahler's Maiernigg gardener, Anton, who always came to fetch him in a boat at Krumpendorf when he returned from Klagenfurt, recited 'all the catastrophes that had befallen Carinthia during the previous year'. The cook Elise imagined herself a 'milkmaid in a mountain pasture' and fed him nothing but salads. But Mahler bore his trials with detachment and a sense of humour. As a diversion, he had planned one of his 'lightning trips' to the

Mahler works ('Mahler und Brahms. Gedanken zu "Reminiszenzen" in Mahlers Sinfonien', *Melos* (May 1977), 215).

[219] AMM1. 309; AMM2. 278.   [220] Unpubl. letter, 28 June.

[221] PS from an undated letter (written 4 or 5 July) inserted in the book at the end of a letter written on 6 June 1905 (AMM1. 311; AMM2. 275).

[222] Unpubl. postcard dated 25 June 1904.   [223] Unpubl. and undated letter (*c.*27 June).

Dolomites, but the weather for the time being was as unstable as his digestion and morale.

I am always unwell despite my frugal life. It's only today that I've begun to work a little. . . .[224]

I'm going out now. Another difficulty here is that on this side (of the lake) all the places are difficult to reach. In company even the worst paths are easier, and you don't even notice how often you have taken them in the past.[225]

He could of course remember other summers when he had been similarly plagued by composer's block, but he was also obsessed by a persistent fear that one day he might have nothing left to say and be obliged to give up composing altogether. To complete his misery, the doctor refused to allow Alma to leave her bed and join him as planned. She would have to stay in Vienna for another week: her nipples were inflamed as a result of breast-feeding Anna, and the lesions she had suffered during her labour were slow in healing. At one time the doctor thought that an operation might be required and, to comfort Alma, Mahler offered to return to Vienna. Luckily her condition soon began to improve. Mahler sent her affectionate advice on treatments she should follow, and also told her all about the purchases and preparations he was making for her and the children: furniture for Putzi—a bed, table, and chair—the clearing of an enclosure near the lake destined to make a play-pit for the children. Alma worried about the water snakes that frequently came out of the lake, but 'water snakes are never poisonous', he assured her. 'It's a well known fact!' For his daily exercise, Mahler took up a new sport: carrying sand from the road to the new play-pit.

A few days before Alma was due to arrive with her mother and the children, Mahler went to Klagenfurt to reserve two carriages, one of which was 'the most beautiful one in town, with rubber wheels and excellent springs. (It had been bought for the Kaiser.) In it, if the doctor permits, you will enter your castle like a princess . . .'. This was decidedly a very different Mahler from the thoughtless and insensitive husband Alma so often depicted in her diary and memoirs, who showed so little concern for her comfort, who allowed her so little spending money that she could not buy the clothes she needed while he bought his at the best tailors.[226]

At the beginning of July the weather at Maiernigg grew even worse. Storm followed storm. 'Outside, it never stops pouring,' wrote Mahler,

thunder, lightning, crashes, one joy after another! For the moment I have to make the best of what the lake can offer! Outside, the storm, and inside me comfortably installed in your drawing room, with lamps, books, scores, a piano, paper! . . . How long will it

---

[224] Unpubl. and undated letter (*c*.24 June).   [225] Unpubl. and undated letter (*c*.25 June).

[226] She even complained in her *Erinnerungen* that she had to refuse a dinner invitation at the Rothschilds because she had nothing but old dresses which she had to let out when she was pregnant and take in again once her confinements were over.

last? If only something more were possible, something more energetic, and the paths more passable! So, I spend my time in my own way, looking at myself and the world, half blissful, half expectant. Unfortunately, I've run out of books already! And as I'm not able, like Quintus Fixlein[227] gradually to write my own library I'll have to go and buy something when I get to Klagenfurt. Today is Sunday, and all this vermin on the lake and roads can't seem to make enough noise! As soon as one bubble of well-being rises in their muddy brains it must immediately burst as a salvo for the world: whoopee! etc., etc. as if we all had to know that Hans Whosit or Peter Whatsit is having a good time![228]

Mahler had not known a comparable period of composer's block since 1900, when he had gone through a similar crisis in Maiernigg as he tried to complete the Fourth Symphony. On 29 June, he wrote to Alma that at least he had 'done a bit of work', but on 11 July in an unpublished card sent from Schluderbach, he asked her to bring him the two middle movements of the Sixth Symphony, left by mistake in the drawer of his desk in Vienna. What then did he compose in the last days of June and early in July? The answer is fortunately provided in an unpublished letter to Willem Mengelberg, for once dated by Mahler himself, '29 June: I'm making an effort here to take up an old work and, if possible, to finish it'. Alma's *Erinnerungen* and diaries confirm that during this summer, in addition to the Sixth Symphony, Mahler completed the *Kindertotenlieder* cycle, which had remained unfinished since 1901. It is thus between 29 June and 11 July that he composed the second and last songs (and not the last *three* as Alma incorrectly claims, since three out of five songs date from 1901).[229] Mahler's reasons for deciding to finish the cycle that particular summer can be traced to a promise he made to Zemlinsky and Schoenberg when he became honorary president of the Vereinigung Schaffender Tonkünstler. He told them that he would conduct a first performance of one of his own works during the coming season. As the Fifth Symphony would be too costly and had in any case already been promised to Steinbach in Cologne, there remained only one other possibility: a Lieder concert, which would be of special interest because most of his Lieder with orchestral accompaniment had never been performed. Thus he completed the cycle by composing two more songs, for which he had no doubt already chosen the poems, particularly the last, which provided the serene conclusion he needed.

Surprising as it may seem, Mahler did not mention the *Kindertotenlieder* in any of his many letters to Alma that summer. It is true that he never spoke of his works in his correspondence until they were completed. But he must at some time have given her a hint of his intention to finish the cycle. In her

---

[227] Principal character of a novel by Jean-Paul: 'As soon as he saw a new title announced, he wrote his own book around it.' Mahler adds in an unpubl. passage of this letter.

[228] AMM1. 308 ff., AMM2. 278 and AMS (undated, Sun., 3 July 1904).

[229] As mentioned above (Chap. 11), a study of the MS in PML indicates that the 2nd and 5th songs in the cycle date from 1904, see below, App. 1.

Erinnerungen she writes that she had at once objected that, now he had become a father himself, it would be 'tempting the devil' to set to music these poems in which Rückert mourned the death of his own children. However that may be, all the indications are that the *Partitur-Entwurf* or at least the *Particell* of the two new *Kindertotenlieder* was ready when Mahler left on 11 July for the Tyrol. His custom was to make such a trip only when he had reached a natural break in his work. No doubt he also worked on them after his return, at least on the orchestration, for Alma writes: 'I was unable to understand how anyone could sing of the death of children when he had just kissed and hugged his own, hale and hearty, half an hour earlier.' Much later, Alma called the two works composed that summer the most 'lived' and 'personal' that Mahler had ever written. In retrospect they became for her a premonition of the tragic events to come.

No doubt because the first score of the new *Kindertotenlieder* was finished, Mahler wrote to Alma on 9 July:[230]

I can't bear this stifling heat any longer. I am going to take my courage in both hands and make one of those lightning visits I love so much into the Dolomites. I travel tomorrow, Sunday, (at 6.30) to Toblach, then go by way of Schluderbach to Misurina; I'll do some walks and spend the night there, and return by the same route the next day (Monday), so that I'll be in Maiernigg by evening. I'll do your shopping for you, and Wednesday, God willing, I'll be waiting for you in Klagenfurt.

The heat wave partly spoilt not only Mahler's excursion but also the convalescent Alma's train journey to join him.[231] But at Lake Misurina, 1,700 metres up, beneath the still grandeur of the rugged Drei Zinnen, whose three massive blocks towered majestically skyward, Mahler experienced as before an almost mystical emotion, which sent him to his desk to finish his interrupted symphony in one final burst of work. Though the first sketches for the Sixth's huge Finale, like those of the opening Allegro, most likely date from the preceding year, the movement in its final form took shape during the summer of 1904. Hitherto, *both* of the last movements were attributed to 1904, but an unpublished card from Mahler to Alma, dated 11 July, sent from Schluderbach, now shows that the Andante was written, as was the Scherzo, in 1903.[232] Why then did Alma insist in the section of her *Erinnerungen* concerning the summer of 1904, that this movement was inspired by the 'unrhythmical games' of the children in the Maiernigg garden? Did Mahler expand or alter it that summer? Or did he merely draw a parallel in conversation with his wife between Putzi's

---

[230] This 'Saturday' letter can only have been written on 9 July, as it is followed by only two cards, one sent the 11th from Schluderbach, the other from Villach. Alma arrived in Klagenfurt with her mother and the children on Wed. the 14th.

[231] In AMS, Alma recalls that she suffered so much from the heat that on arriving she fainted in Mahler's arms.

[232] 'I especially need the second and third movements of the Sixth, which I have forgotten to bring along.'

games[233] and the Scherzo's fluctuating rhythms, the 'infant voices which gradually grow tragic'?

However that may be, it is obvious that a true creative fever seized Mahler in Maiernigg after Alma's arrival. In the short space of six weeks, from 15 July to the end of August, he not only corrected the final proofs of the Fifth and completed the Finale of the Sixth, one of the longest and most complex movements in all his symphonic output, but also completed the two Andantes entitled by him 'Nachtmusiken' and destined for the Seventh.[234] Once more it is to be regretted that he told Alma so little about his work, in contrast to the way he had formerly talked to Natalie as the music was taking shape in his mind. While composing the Finale of the Sixth, he did however speak to her of the three blows of fate that strike the symphonic hero, 'of which the last fells him like a tree'. If, by chance, he had not written to Alma later on that: 'the preceding summer [in 1905], I decided to finish the Seventh, whose two Andantes were already in existence', no one would ever have imagined that these Nocturnes had been written at the same time as the nightmarish Finale of the Sixth and one year before the rest of the Symphony.

Mahler himself later told his Dutch friends that the first 'Nachtmusik' from the Seventh was inspired by Rembrandt's famous *Nightwatch*, which he had admired for the first time in the Amsterdam Rijksmuseum the previous autumn.[235] Composing these relatively brief and cheerful pieces was probably his way of relaxing after the grim and tragic music he had just written. The following scene, reported by Alma, might well have taken place while he was writing the Sixth's Finale, since the composer of so frightening a piece of music could well have experienced mysterious, almost visceral, attacks of overwhelming terror. One day, Mahler came running down from the *Häuschen*. He was gasping for breath, perspiring profusely, incoherent in word and gesture. Eventually he explained what had happened. He told Alma he had been working alone under the trees in the heavy summer heat. Not a sound to be heard! Suddenly a terrible feeling of danger swept over him. Terror and panic! This feeling of being watched by the smouldering, terrible eye of the god Pan often came to him, Alma commented. When it happened he was so frightened that he left his work and ran down the hill through the forest to seek for the reassuring warmth of human contact. He would then not return to the *Häuschen*, but worked instead at his desk on the top floor of the villa. 'I had to run all over the three-storey-high house telling everyone to keep quiet,' wrote Alma.

---

[233] Alma speaks of 'two' children, but Anna was then only a month old. Perhaps she meant Putzi and the Moll's daughter Maria who was then still a small child.

[234] AMM1. 451; AMM2. 328. Donald Mitchell has pointed out two thematic relationships which seem to confirm the simultaneous composition, not only of the last *Kindertotenlied* and the Finale of the Sixth, but also that of the same Finale and the second 'Nachtmusik' in the Seventh (DMM2. 40).

[235] Alphons Diepenbrock explains in one of his letters that Mahler 'did not want to describe the Nightwatch' but had offered it as a point of comparison (see RMH 31, and below, Vol. iv, Chap. 5).

The cook was not allowed to make the slightest noise. The children were shut up in their rooms. I stopped playing the piano, didn't sing, didn't dare move around. And things stayed that way until he reached a 'break' in his work and surfaced radiant with joy, as always after he had finished working and wanted to reestablish contact with our life. Such were <u>my</u> experiences at that time. I no longer had any of my own. He didn't even notice that I had given up my own life. His work was so relentless, he was so utterly occupied with himself that every interruption, whatever it might be, was unbearable. Work, work, a noble existence, the renouncement of all personal joy—reaching towards the infinite . . . this was his life for ever. I myself had completely obliterated my own existence and my own will, but I kept my self-control with great difficulty. He realized nothing of all this. He was unbelievably egocentric, but not for himself, always for his work. Inwardly I withdrew from him—with tremendous respect—and awaited some kind of miracle. That was stupid. I had it within reach—though in a purely abstract sense. For at his side I remained a young girl despite children and the endless pregnancies. He only saw the friend, the mother of his children, the housewife, and learned only too late what he had lost! These carnivorous geniuses who think they are vegetarians! I've encountered this all my life: it is easy to preach morality but almost impossible to put it into practice.[236]

As always, Alma was torn between two incompatible states of mind: on the one hand, her respect for Mahler, her passionate admiration, her possessive affection for him (one hesitates to call it love), and on the other her intense need to live for and by herself as well as having someone to possess and dominate. For the time being she was outwardly the devoted and submissive wife that Mahler had always wanted, but rebellion was never far off, and as usual she confided it to her diary.[237] Despite the tragic character of the Sixth and the *Kindertotenlieder*, the diary nevertheless acknowledges that the summer of 1904 was exceptionally peaceful and happy, and that Mahler had never been 'more human and more communicative'. He spent long hours playing with little Putzi, for a 'strange' and powerful bond seemed to unite father and daughter. He kept on making up new faces, invented strange stories, or read fairy-tales to her. A favourite was Brentano's *Gockel, Hinkel und Gackeleia*.

Unfortunately, only one of the three letters mentioning the completion of the Sixth[238] can be dated with any certainty and it was written after Mahler returned to Vienna. However, as he always considered his excursions into the Dolomites as relaxation, a reward for work accomplished, it is almost certain that the *Particell* of the Finale was already completed when he returned there in the middle of August, as shown by a card sent to Alma on the 18th from Dölsach (near Lienz), on the way, this time, to Heiligenblut and the Gross Glockner rather than to the Dolomites. He was to conduct in Vienna for the first time in

---

[236] AMM1. 146; AMM2. 144 and AMS.

[237] In the typed copy of Alma's diary now in UPL, all pages referring to 1905–11 have been torn out. Very likely they contained intimate passages concerning the crises and conflicts of those years. There remains only the expurgated version of *Mein Leben*. It is to be hoped that these pages may one day be found.

[238] MBR1, nos. 238, 258, and 282; MBR2, nos. 336, 334 and 335. The latter merely states 'My Sixth is finished. I am too!' (BGM).

the season on 6 September. On the last day of August, Mahler left for the capital,[239] but this time with Alma; for if he had gone on ahead and left her to follow later with the children he would have sent, as always, daily letters, and no letters have survived that were written in early September of that year.

Before leaving Carinthia, Mahler wrote to Guido Adler: 'My Sixth is finished and I am gradually getting ready to come back to Vienna with wife and children. Pity! Still, I look forward to seeing you soon!'[240] To Bruno Walter he broke the news in a letter in which he once more attacks the idea of 'programmes':

> Apart from that there is no other reason for objecting to a 'programme' . . . but it is the musician who must be expressing himself in it, not a writer, philosopher, painter (all of whom are part of the musician), in a word, those without genius should abstain and those with genius have nothing to fear. All the sophisticated argument on this subject reminds me of someone who begets a child and afterwards starts worrying whether it really is a child, whether he engendered it with the right intentions, etc. He just wanted to make love—and managed it. Basta! If you don't want to make love and can't manage it, then there will be no child. Again basta! The way you love and the way you are— that's what the child will be like! Yet again basta! My Sixth is finished. I believe I've managed it! A thousand times Basta![241]

Happy as he was, Mahler had no illusions about how his new symphony would be received: 'My Sixth will pose puzzles that only a generation which has already taken in and digested my previous five can dare to solve.'[242] As always, he considered it 'unchaste' to play a single note of his new work to anyone before it was completely finished. But now that the work was ready, he asked Alma to accompany him and they walked up to the *Häuschen* arm in arm—as they had done two years earlier for the Fifth—'with great solemnity'. As he played, Alma was deeply moved by the most 'profoundly personal' music he had ever written, music that 'flowed straight from the heart', and they both shed 'tears of emotion'.

On 1 May Mahler had heard the news of Dvořák's death. The first time he had met him was in Vienna, when he conducted the première of two of the composer's last symphonic poems. He had seen him again in 1901, when he had planned to put on *Rusalka* at the Vienna Opera. At the beginning of August, news reached him in Maiernigg of the death of Hanslick, the 'Bismarck of musical criticism' as Verdi called him, the most highly reputed of the Viennese critics, or at least the most widely read, the most influential—and the most hated. The last articles he had written—a condemnation of *Der Corregidor*

[239] See BWB 73.

[240] Card to Guido Adler (RAM 44). Mahler also expresses the hope 'that the clean copy of your "opus" [presumably the *Wagner Vorlesungen*] is also ready, so that I can now have the whole of it conveniently in front of me'.

[241] MBR1, no. 250; MBR2, no. 334. Another passage from the same letter concerning 'programmes' is quoted above (Chap. 13).

[242] MBR1, no. 238; MBR2, no. 336.

in February, then a paean of praise for *Falstaff* in May—were favourable to
Mahler, whom he thus supported to his last breath despite their differences of
opinion, notably concerning Wagner.[243] In an obituary whose tone alternated
between the strongest criticism (notably concerning Hanslick's hostility towards Wagner) and respectful admiration, Schönaich acknowledged that
Hanslick 'never wrote a boring article' during his sixty-year career. Although
critics as a rule meant little to Mahler, he undoubtedly remembered the whole-
hearted support which Wagner's bitterest enemy had given him when he needed
it most, i.e. when he was applying for the post of director of the Vienna Opera.
Nor would he have forgotten Hanslick's loyalty during his first years as director.

During the summer of 1904, while Mahler spent the greater part of his time
in the *Häuschen* composing, a number of visitors relieved Alma's solitude. This
may be one reason why she was happier in that summer than in previous ones.
The Molls came first with their youngest daughter Maria, Alma's half-sister who
was three years older than Putzi. According to Moll's unpublished memoirs[244]
they rented for two consecutive years a neighbouring villa. Moll was later to
recall the long walks with his son-in-law, in the course of which he came to
understand the latter's intimate and deep feeling for nature, 'not a feeling that
stopped at details, as with us painters, but which on the contrary included
distance (*Weite*) and height (*Höhe*)'. After the Molls came the faithful Theobald
Pollak, then Alfred Roller to discuss plans for the new season, and the *Fidelio*
which was to cause as much of a stir as *Tristan* the previous year. Then came
Burckhard, and even Zemlinsky, who probably wanted to discuss the latest
plans for the Vereinigung.[245] In August, Erica Conrat, a young friend of Alma's,
introduced a cheerful note. She was the youngest daughter of a rich Viennese
businessman, Hugo Conrat, who had been a close friend of Brahms.[246] Conrat

---

[243] Born in Prague, 11 Sept. 1825, Eduard Hanslick was the son of a bibliographer of Jewish Bohemian
origin. Having studied law and music in Prague and Vienna, he sat for his Doctorate of Law in 1849 and then
spent some time in a government office. He began writing about music in 1846, first in the *Wiener
Musikzeitung*, then in the *Wiener Zeitung* (1848–64), and the *Presse* (1855–64), and finally the *Neue Freie
Presse* (founded in 1864). To the end of his life, his articles 'played a decisive role in the musical life of the
capital'. With his graceful, refined style and his encyclopaedic knowledge, Hanslick in a sense typified
Viennese public taste, or at least the taste of the conservative élite. A very talented polemicist, he fought all
his life for purity of form and discipline in writing, and against romantic excess. He thus came to be thought
of as a reactionary, enemy of Wagner and Bruckner and friend of Brahms (see above, Vol. i, Chap. 4). Yet
Hanslick was a pioneer in musicography: it was for him that the Univ. of Vienna created the first Chair of
History of Music and Aesthetics, which he occupied 1870–95. Hanslick died on 6 Aug. 1904 and left many
works, most of them collections of his articles and *Feuilletons* in the *Neue Freie Presse* in addition to the
famous essay *Vom Musikalisch-Schönen* (The Beautiful in Music) (Leipzig, 1854).

[244] Memoirs already cited (BGM).

[245] Zemlinsky's presence at Mahler's summer retreat is surprising. They had only recently begun to see
each other again, and Mahler had probably hesitated to renew the acquaintance. But his visit is confirmed
by the unpubl. TS of Alma's *Erinnerungen*. Although the visit was brief, Mahler undoubtedly confirmed his
intention to do his utmost for the new Vereinigung and to conduct (no doubt without fee) a whole evening of
his Lieder. A letter Zemlinsky sent to Alma from Gmunden on the Traunsee, where he was spending the
summer, mentions his visit to Maiernigg (UPL). He asks if Mahler has 'finished his work'.

[246] Hugo Conrat's two brothers had different names. The elder, Ferdinand Cohn, a scientist, was named
after his father, a merchant in Breslau. The second, Oscar Justinius, was a humorist and poet.

had translated twenty-five Hungarian 'national poems' into German and shown them to Brahms, who liked them so much that he used eleven for the *Zigeunerlieder*, Op. 103 and four others for vocal quartets. Erica's mother, Ida Conrat, was a woman with intellectual interests whose salon on the Walfischgasse was open once a week to intellectuals and artists from Vienna and elsewhere. Brahms came there regularly until the end of his life. The eldest daughter, Ilse, was a talented sculptress who had studied under the Belgian Charles van der Stappen. Brahms had one of her sculptures in his bedroom and, after his death, it was Ilse who, at the age of 24, was commissioned to produce a monument for his tomb in the Vienna Zentralfriedhof.[247] As for Erica, she was an enthusiastic student of art history.

Whereas in the summer of 1900 Mahler had composed his happiest, most optimistic work while in the throes of uncertainty and anxiety, in this summer of 1904 which was 'beautiful, happy, devoid of conflict',[248] he now had written the darkest, most pessimistic music of his entire career. Erica Conrat later wrote an account of her stay in Maiernigg based on letters she had written to her family. Her idyllic picture is in complete agreement with Alma's. One evening Mahler described one of his most frequent childhood dreams[249] and Alma 'listened to him intently, with lowered eyes, so that I could barely see the admiration and enthusiasm that shone in them. He broke off, laughed to himself, and there they were all alone.'[250] Erica described the evenings on the terrace overlooking the lake

with nothing before us but water and mountains like shadows on the horizon . . .

We hardly say a word, for we have the feeling that Gustav Mahler is getting ready to work. Suddenly he gets up and mentions a book he has just read, by Lichtenberg,[251] for instance, or talks about Goethe in his old age, and I often have a truly biblical sensation of scales falling from my eyes.

One afternoon Alma and Erica were relaxing in hammocks on the shore of the lake. A sailing boat approached, then moved away. Alma announced 'in a plaintive but nonetheless satisfied tone':

Gustav would never do that—sail on the lake lying on his back, hands beneath his head, content to look up at the sky. He doesn't know how to *enjoy* anything. If he decides to go boating, he rows, and does it with all his might. I think that if he went sailing, he would want to take along a volume of Kant!' . . . And it's true! Yesterday we had to have four roosters slaughtered because their crowing disturbed him while he was sunbathing.

---

[247] The monument had been unveiled on 7 May 1903.

[248] AMM1. 92; AMM2. 97.   [249] See above, Vol. i, Chap. 5.

[250] Excerpts from Erica Conrat's Maiernigg letters, Aug. 1904 (AMS).

[251] Georg Christoph Lichtenberg (1742–99), a German physicist and satirist, campaigned against Lavater's theories of physiognomy and the literary school of *Sturm und Drang*. He also did research into electricity, a branch of science then in its infancy.

One evening they had a long conversation about Napoleon, a figure who fascinated Mahler. 'It's only after their downfall,' he explained,

that one realizes whether men were really great or whether it was only that circumstances made them appear so. Shakespeare gave us a wonderful example of this in Wolsey (Henry VIII). But Napoleon was not a great man. At Saint Helena, he gnawed at the bars of his cage like a lion and wasn't happy until he had set up a puppet version of an imperial state on that barren island.

Mahler reminded everyone of the famous anecdote about Beethoven tearing up the dedication page of the 'Eroica' Symphony, and recited the first lines of Goethe's poem in which the Devil reads out the list of Napoleon's sins to God. 'God replies: "That's enough, stop! If you have the courage to get hold of him, you may drag him down into your hell!" '[252] Then they spoke of Goethe, one of Mahler's heroes. Goethe had accepted a position as minister in order to 'help'. 'No man can "help" another,' Mahler declared, 'neither from the throne, nor as a minister, nor as a fine lady doing "good works". The only thing to do is to work on one's self, to improve one's self. The highest egotism is in fact altruism. (You would say: When one has fulfilled one's self, then only . . .)' No thought of Mahler illustrates more perfectly what his contemporaries often considered to be a veritable 'lust for power'. It was in fact a pressing need for personal expression in which he was conscious of obeying a will other than his own. That is why his 'supreme egotism' (Alma's term) was really placing himself at the service of a higher cause.

On the evening of Mahler's discourse on Goethe and Napoleon, Alma brought the conversation to an abrupt halt by declaring that Mahler went too far and that she had learnt that very day through personal experience that someone else's help could be precious. That morning, the chambermaid, Josefine, had done her a great favour by killing a flea in her bed, so that now she could finally enjoy some peace at night! On another occasion, as Erica helped Alma with some heavy task, Alma said: 'Look Gustav, how strong she is!' 'I see,' he replied, 'but even if she weren't it wouldn't matter! She has the will, the strong will. That counts as much as strength. That's why she's managed it.' Erica recalls several other interesting statements by Mahler, such as the following:

I don't believe in supermen (*Übermenschen*), but almost all people are sub-men (*Untermenschen*). They walk upright, with their bodies yes. But who dares really to walk upright, facing the sun? I tell you, Erica, the little joy that you can only have on a fine day—or do you sometimes feel joy about the sun itself? Imponderable though it may be, the sun is doing its bit to keep you going!

'I don't know how to describe my relationship with Gustav Mahler,' wrote Erica.

---

[252] 'Am jüngsten Tag, vor Gottes Thron | Stand endlich Herr Napoleon . . .' (Goethe: *Sämtliche* Werke (Musculus Verlag, Gotha, 1827–33), xlvii. 226).

I love him like a father, or rather like a great teacher, as there is not the slightest feeling of tenderness between us of the sort I think is usual with a father. In his presence, I am so terribly conscious of my intellectual insignificance (*e d'ogni suo difetto allor sentiva*). It is impossible to make any sort of insincere remark (*eine Phrase*) to him. Not that he would see through it. Oh no! he is as gullible and naive as a child, and believes the most exaggerated lies. But precisely because he is so trusting, and has eliminated any imposture in himself, any half-decent person finds it impossible to be other than absolutely honest with him. I couldn't possibly say anything to him I'm not absolutely convinced of . . .

One afternoon, the Mahlers took Erica to Krumpendorf by boat. Alma was at the tiller, Erica took one oar and Mahler the other. 'It was he who called the stroke, and as if I were the whole Opera orchestra, I trembled for fear of not keeping time,' wrote Erica.

The arrival there, the afternoon tea, were real torture for me! This lovely woman, this famous man, known to everyone. On the way back, I sat opposite Alma. Her hair was flaming red in the light of the sunset. She looked like a superb beast of prey. What a splendid thing that these two beings are married! As though, to crown his happiness, this man who always aims for the highest had to be chained to the miraculously beautiful earth!

Another evening Erica took Alma and Putzi in the rowing-boat as far as Loretto to pick up Mahler who was returning from Klagenfurt. On the way home he took the oars. Seated on Erica's knees, Putzi snuggled up to her, her cheek against Erica's, and slowly fell asleep. Not a word was spoken during the ride, and the young Erica never forgot the cool cheek and the calm breathing of the sleeping child. On another occasion, Erica remembers:

It was a fine night. I was sitting alone on the terrace. . . . At half past ten, G.M. joined me, and quoted the lines from the *Westöstlicher Divan*, 'Das Lebendige will ich singen . . .', and then he spoke of Goethe's life, that it is really fragmentary, since he is a beginner, a beginner in a higher sense, a beginner in a sphere which we can never come to understand. And then he talked a lot about how it does not really matter whether 'it's a rocket that soars up and then falls without a sound into the lake or the course of a sun lasting billions of years, we must strive just the same to create for beyond our own time and beyond ourselves, to become better—just the same.' He also spoke of the miracle, the intoxicating wonder a musician feels when he hears his work for the first time: it would never have been possible for him to imagine it would be like this. Then Mahler went into the living room and played a lot of short pieces by Bach, so clear and simple that one could have believed oneself in ancient Greece.

And I stayed on outside, sitting gazing at the starry sky and watching the fireworks far away falling into the water, and listened . . .[253]

With this picture of a quiet Maiernigg evening, Erica Conrat's recollections come to a close, but Alma tells of other conversations with Mahler which

[253] AMS.

probably date from the same period, since they appear in her diary at this time. One day, during a walk, she admitted to him that 'what I love in a man is only his achievement', that 'the greater his achievement, the more I must love him'. 'That really poses a danger for me,' answered Mahler, 'for what if someone else came along who is better than I?' 'Then I would have to love him,' said Alma. Mahler smiled and concluded: 'I'm not worried for the moment, because I don't know anyone who is better than I (*der mehr ist als ich*) . . .'.[254]

At times, when Alma reproached him with not showing his love for her enough, he would say: 'If only you were suddenly disfigured by illness, for instance by smallpox. Only then, when you were no longer attractive to anyone else, could I show you how much I love you!' Here Mahler was expressing the uneasiness he felt at his young wife's radiant beauty and the powerful attraction she held for other men. He may also have been aware of the uneasiness which she herself felt over the power of seduction she exercised, wondering—who knows?—about the possible consequences of infidelity? Mahler undoubtedly realized that Alma's determination to let him raise her 'to a higher level', thereby denying an integral part of her own nature, was neither very deep nor very strong, that one day she might well weaken, and that he would then need superhuman strength to face the storm.

[254] AMM1. 93; AMM2. 98.

APPENDIX 1

Catalogue of Mahler's Works

Autograph Sources (the source is undated if no date is mentioned)

APD   Autograph preliminary draft (for full movement or substantial part of one): orchestral works are mostly in *Particell*; Lieder mostly v(oice) and p(iano)

AOD   Autograph orchestral draft

AFC   Autograph fair copies

CFC   Copyist's fair copy (included only when necessary)

Libraries

ACA   Amsterdam Concertgebouw Archive

ASI   Arnold Schoenberg Institute, Los Angeles, California

BBC   Biblioteca Bodmeriana, Cologny, Switzerland

BGM   Bibliothèque musicale Gustav Mahler, Paris

BLL   British Library, London

BSB   Berlin, Staatsbibliothek Preussischer Kulturbesitz

BSM   Bayerische Staatsbibliothek, Munich

CPA   Czech Philharmonic Archive, Prague

GMF   Gesellschaft der Musikfreunde Library, Vienna

HLH   Houghton Library, Harvard University, Cambridge

HMS   The Hague, Gemeente Museum, Mengelberg Stichting

IMG   Internationale Gustav Mahler Gesellschaft, Vienna

JNJ   Jerusalem, Jewish National and University Library

LCW   Library of Congress, Washington, DC

LPA   Library of the Performing Arts, Lincoln Center, New York

MAS   Moldenhauer Archive, Spokane, Washington, DC

NLC   Newberry Library, Chicago

NUE   Northwestern University, Evanston, Ill., USA

ÖNB   Österreichische Nationalbibliothek, Vienna

PML   Pierpont Morgan Library, New York City

RWO   University of Western Ontario, Rosé room, London, Canada

SBW   Stadts- und Landesbibliothek, Vienna

SOU   Southampton University Library, Great Britain

SSB   Paul Sacher Foundation, Basel, Switzerland

SUL   Stanford University Library, Stanford, Calif.

UEA   Universal Edition Archive, Vienna

VPA   Vienna Philharmonic Archive

YUL   Yale University Library, New Haven, Conn.

COMPLETED WORKS

0. **Piano Quartet movement** in A minor: *Nicht zu schnell. Entschlossen.* AFC (1876), PML (Rosé bequest). Published Sikorsky, Hamburg, 1973. 1st public perf.(?) New York, 12 Jan. 1964, Peter Serkin and Galimir Quartet.

1. **3 Lieder** for tenor and piano (1880), poems by Mahler, dedicated to Josephine Poisl. AFC, RWO. 1st perf. Radio Brno, 30 Sept. 1934: Zdeněk Knittl, tenor; Alfred Rosé, piano. AFC, RWO. 1st publ. critical edn. IGMG/UE 1990.

   (*a*) 'Im Lenz' (19 Feb. 1880)
   (*b*) 'Winterlied' (27 Feb. 1880)
   (*c*) 'Maitanz im Grünen' (5 Mar. 1880), cf. 3*c*

2. **Das klagende Lied**, poem by Mahler. Original vers. (1880), in three parts, for soprano, alto, tenor, baritone, bass solos, chorus, and orchestra. CPC (with auto. corrections), YUL (Osborn col.). 1st rev. (Dec. 1893). AFC, PML (Heineman col.); 2nd rev. (May 1899) (without *a*), for soprano, alto, tenor solos. 1st perf. Vienna, 17 Feb. 1901. Publ. Sept. 1902, Weinberger. Critical edn. IGMG/UE 1978.

   (*a*) ['Waldmärchen' (omitted in 1899), for soprano, alto, tenor, bass solos. 1st perf. radio Brno 26 Nov. 1934/Alfred Rosé. Publ. 1973, Belwin-Mills.]
   (*b*) 'Der Spielmann'. APD (21 Mar. 1880), SBW; AOD, SBW.
   (*c*) 'Hochzeitsstück' (Beg. of APD, Oct.–Nov. [1880], J. Bruck col., NYC).

3. **5 Lieder** for voice and piano (1880–7), forming Part I of *Lieder und Gesänge*, entitled after Mahler's death: *Lieder aus der Jugendzeit*, poems by Richard Leander, Mahler, and Tirso de Molina; entitled, in the only known manuscript, '5 Gedichte komponiert von Gustav Mahler'. AFC, RWO. Publ. Feb. 1892, Schott. Critical edn. IGMG/Schott 1990.

   (*a*) 'Frühlingsmorgen' (Richard Leander). 1st perf. Prague, 18 Apr. 1886
   (*b*) 'Erinnerung' (Leander). 1st perf. Budapest, 13 Nov. 1889
   (*c*) 'Hans und Grete' (Mahler), practically identical with 1*c*. 1st perf. Prague, 18 Apr. 1886
   (*d*) 'Serenade aus Don Juan' (Tirso da Molina) (1887)
   (*e*) 'Phantasie aus Don Juan' (Tirso da Molina) (1887)

4. **4 Lieder eines fahrenden Gesellen** for voice and orchestra (1884–5), poems by Mahler. 1st surviving AFC, v & p, RWO (1884–5?); 1st surviving AFC, v & o (1893?) and 1896, SSB. 1st perf. Berlin, 16 Mar. 1896. Publ. Dec. 1897, v & p and v & o, Weinberger. Critical edn., v & p and v & o, IGMG/Weinberger 1982.

   (*a*) 'Wenn mein Schatz Hochzeit macht'

   (*b*) 'Ging heut' morgens übers Feld'

   (*c*) 'Ich hab' ein glühend' Messer'

   (*d*) 'Die zwei blauen Augen'

5. **First Symphony**, D major (1885–8) [sketched as 'Symphony I' (1885) (GAM 99)]. 1st perf. 'Symphonic poem in two parts', Budapest, 20 Nov. 1889. 1st rev. without (*b*) (Jan. 1893); 2nd rev. with (*b*) (16 Dec. 1893): 'Symphony (Titan) in 5 movements (2 parts)'. AFC, YUL (Osborn col.). 2nd perf. 'Titan, symphonic poem in the form of a symphony', Hamburg, 27 Oct. 1893: CFC, LPA (Walter col.). 3rd perf. Weimar, 3 June 1894. Final rev. without (*b*) (1896). CFC, ÖNB. 4th perf. 'Symphony in D major', Berlin, 16 Mar. 1896. Publ. Dec. 1898, Weinberger; May 1906, UE. 1st critical edn. IGMG/UE 1967; 2nd critical edn. 1992.

   (*a*) *Langsam, schleppend; Immer sehr gemächlich.*

   [(*b*) *Andante alegretto* [*sic*], *Blumine*. AFC (16 Aug. 1893 renovatum), subsequently omitted. Publ. 1968, Presser.]

   (*b*) *Kräftig bewegt, doch nicht zu schnell*. AFC (27 Jan. 1893 renovatum).

   (*c*) *Feierlich und gemessen, ohne zu schleppen.*

   (*d*) *Stürmisch bewegt. Energisch.* AFC (19 Jan. 1893 umgearbeitet).

6. **9 Wunderhorn-Lieder** for voice and piano (1887–90), forming Parts II & III of *Lieder und Gesänge*, entitled after Mahler's death: *Lieder aus der Jugendzeit*. AFC, RWO. Publ. Feb. 1892, Schott. Critical edn. IGMG/Schott 1991.

   (*a*) 'Um schlimme Kinder artig zu machen': 1st perf. Berlin, 14 Dec. 1907

   (*b*) 'Ich ging mit Lust'

   (*c*) 'Aus! Aus!': 1st perf. Hamburg, 29 Apr. 1892

   (*d*) 'Starke Einbildungskraft'

   (*e*) 'Zu Strassburg auf der Schanz': AOD, unfinished, BGM

   (*f*) 'Ablösung im Sommer': 1st perf. Berlin, 14 Dec. 1907

   (*g*) 'Scheiden und Meiden': 1st perf. Budapest 13 Nov. 1889

   (*h*) 'Nicht Wiedersehen!': 1st perf. Hamburg, 29 June 1892

   (*i*) 'Selbstgefühl': 1st perf. Vienna, 15 Feb. 1900

7. **Second Symphony**, C minor (1888–94), with soprano, alto solos, and mixed chorus. AFC (18 Dec. 1894), PML (Kaplan dep.). 1st perf. (*a*), (*b*), and (*c*) Berlin, 4 Mar. 1895. 1st complete perf. Berlin, 13 Dec. 1895. Publ. 1895, 2 pianos (Hermann Behn), Hofmeister; orch., 1897, Hofmeister & Weinberger; April 1906, U.E. Critical edn. IGMG/UE 1970. FS edn. Kaplan Found., New York, 1986.

   (*a*) *Allegro maestoso* (*mit durchaus ernstem und feierlichem Ausdruck*). 1st vers. AOD (8 July 1888), JNJ; AFC (as *Todtenfeier*: 10 Sept. 1888), SSB. Final vers. (29 June 1894 renovatum).

(b) *Andante moderato* (*Sehr gemächlich*) (begun 1888). AOD (30 July 1893), location unknown.

(c) *In ruhig fliessender Bewegung.* AOD (16 July 1893), PML (Lehman dep.).

(d) *Urlicht* (*Sehr feierlich aber schlicht*), alto solo, from *Des Knaben Wunderhorn* (c.1892). AFC (19 July 1893), BLL (Zweig col.).

(e) *Tempo des Scherzo. Wild herausfahrend; Kräftig; Langsam; Misterioso*, poem by Friedrich Klopstock and Mahler. AOD (28 June 1894); AFC (18 Dec. 1894).

8. **Third Symphony,** D minor (1895–6), with alto solo, women and children's chorus. AFC (22 Nov. 1896), PML (Lehman dep.). 1st perf. (b), (c), (f) Berlin, 9 Mar. 1897. 1st complete perf. Krefeld, 9 June 1902. Rev. May 1899. Publ. 1899, Weinberger; Jan. 1906, UE. Critical edn. IGMG/UE 1974.

(a) *Kräftig, Entschieden.* AOD (28 June 1896), AFC (17 Oct. 1896).

(b) *Tempo di Menuetto* (*sehr mässig*). AOD (June 1895), former Ernst Rosé collection; AFC (11 Apr. 1896). 1st perf.: Berlin, 9 Nov. 1896/Nikisch. 4th perf.: Budapest, 31 Feb. 1897.

(c) *Comodo, Scherzando, Ohne Hast.* AOD (June 1895), PML (Cary coll.); AFC (25 [29?] June 1896).

(d) *Sehr langsam, Misterioso*, alto solo 'O Mensch!', poem by Nietzsche (summer 1895). AOD, PML (Cary col.); v & p (summer 1896), LCW.

(e) *Lustig im Tempo und keck im Ausdruck*, alto solo, women and children's chorus: 'Es sungen drei Engel', from *Des Knaben Wunderhorn.* APD, v & o (Aug. 1895), PML (Cary col.); AFC (8 May 1896), PML (Lehman dep.).

(f) *Langsam, Ruhevoll. Empfunden.* AFC (11 Nov. 1896).

Analyses of the above works will be included in Volume i.

9. **10 Wunderhorn-Lieder** for voice and orchestra (1892–8) (a), (b), (c), (d) and (10d) entitled in 1892: *5 Humoresken*. Publ. 1899–1900, Weinberger.

(a) 'Der Schildwache Nachtlied' (1888?): APD, LCW; AFC, v & o (28 Jan. 1892), BSB; AFC, v & o (26 Apr. 1892), GMF. 1st perf. Berlin, 12 Dec. 1892.

(b) 'Verlorne Müh': AFC, v & p (1 Feb. 1892), BSB; AFC, v & o, GMF. 1st perf. Berlin, 12 Dec. 1892.

(c) 'Trost im Unglück': APD, v & p, MAS; AFC, v & p (22 Feb. [1892]), BSB; AFC, v & o (26 Apr. 1892), GMF. 1st perf. Hamburg, 27 Oct. 1893.

(d) 'Wer hat dies Liedlein erdacht?': AFC, v & p (6 Feb. 1892); AFC, v & o, GMF. 1st perf. Hamburg, 27 Oct. 1893.

(e) 'Das irdische Leben' (1893: NBL1. 10; NBL2.27): APD, priv. col. (Newlin), USA; AFC, v & o, PML (Cary col.). 1st perf. 14 Jan. 1900, Vienna.

(f) 'Des Antonius von Padua Fischpredigt': AFC, v & p (8 July 1893), PML (Lehman dep.); AFC, v & o (1 Aug. 93), HLH. 1st perf. Vienna, 29 Jan. 1905.

(g) 'Rheinlegendchen': AFC, v & p (9 Aug. 1893), BSB; AFC, v & o (10 Aug. 1893), PML (Lehman dep.). 1st perf. Hamburg, 27 Oct. 1893.

(*h*) 'Lied des Verfolgten im Turm': AFC, v & p (July 1898), PML (Lehman dep.). 1st perf. Vienna, 29 Jan. 1905.

(*i*) 'Wo die schönen Trompeten blasen': AFC, v & p (July 1898), PML (Lehman dep.). 1st perf. Vienna, 14 Jan. 1900.

(*j*) 'Lob des hohen Verstandes': APD in E, entitled 'Lob der Kritik' (14 June 1896); APD (21 June 1896), MAS. 1st perf. Vienna, 3 Feb. 1905.

(*k*) 'Es sungen drei Engel' (summer 1895, cf. 8*e*): No known autograph of song version.

(*l*) 'Urlicht', AFC, v & o (19 July 1893): BLL (Zweig col.). Cf. 7*d*.

10. **Fourth Symphony**, G major (1899–1900), with soprano solo. AFC, GMF. Complete preliminary drafts and orchestral drafts of (*a*), (*b*), and (*c*) broken up and dispersed, now in ÖNB, PML, BGM, MAS, SUL. 1st perf. Munich, 25 Nov. 1901. Last rev. July 1910. Publ. Jan. 1902, Doblinger; Jan. 1906, UE. Critical edn. IGMG/UE 1963.

(*a*) *Bedächtig, nicht eilen* (1899–1900).

(*b*) *In gemächlicher Bewegung, ohne Hast.* AFC (5 Jan. 1901).

(*c*) *Ruhevoll (Poco Adagio).* Partial AOD (6 [5] Aug. 1900), MAS & BGM; AFC (5 Jan. 1901).

(*d*) *Sehr behaglich,* soprano solo: 'Wir geniessen die himmlischen Freuden', from *Des Knaben Wunderhorn.* AFC/orig. song, v & p (10 Feb. 1892), BSB; AFC/id., v & o (12 Mar. 1892), GMF. 1st separate perf. Hamburg, 27 Oct. 1893. Orch. rev. 1900.

11. **7 Lieder** entitled, after Mahler's death, *Aus letzter Zeit.*

(A) **2 Wunderhorn-Lieder** for voice and orchestra (1899–1901). Publ. Aug. 1905, Kahnt. Critical edn., v & p and v & o, IGMG/Kahnt, 1984.

(*a*) 'Revelge' (June/July 1899): CFC, v & o, LPA (Walter col.) (NBL2. 135). 1st perf. Vienna, 29 Jan. 1905.

(*b*) 'Der Tamboursg'sell': APD, PML (Lehman dep.); AFC, v & p (12 July 1901); AFC, v & o, MAS. 1st perf. Vienna, 29 Jan. 1905.

(B) **4 Rückert-Lieder** for voice and orchestra (1901). 1st perf. Vienna, 29 Jan. 1905. Publ. Aug. 1905, Kahnt. Critical edn., v & p and v & o, IGMG/Kahnt 1984.

(*a*) 'Blicke mir nicht in die Lieder!': APD, v & p (14 June 1901), ÖNB; AFC, v & p, Vienna (priv. col.).

(*b*) 'Ich atmet' einen linden Duft' (summer 1901) (NBL1. 166; NBL2. 193 ff.): AFC, v & p, BSM; AFC, v & o, priv. col. USA; AFC, v & o, PML (Lehman dep.).

(*c*) 'Ich bin der Welt abhanden gekommen': APD (3) (one: 16 Aug. 1901), PML (Cary col.); AFC, v & p, BGM.

(*d*) 'Um Mitternacht' (summer 1901): APD, SBW; AFC, v & p, BGM; AFC, v & o, ASI.

(C) **1 Rückert-Lied** for voice and piano (Aug. 1902) (AML 33).
'Liebst du um Schönheit': AFC, BGM. Publ., p & o, 1905, Kahnt; orch. Max Puttmann (1910?). Critical edn., v & p, IGMG/1984.

12. **Fifth Symphony** (1901–2). Orch. 1903. Rev. 1904, etc. AFC, PML (Lehman dep.); FC by Alma Mahler, LPA. 1st perf. Cologne, 19 Oct. 1904. Publ. Sept. 1904, Peters. Rev. 1905, 1911. 1st critical edn. IGMG/Peters, 1964; 2nd critical edn. 1988.

    1st part

    (a) *Trauermarsch* (*In gemessenem Schritt. Streng. Wie ein Kondukt*) (prob. 1901)
    (b) *Stürmisch bewegt mit grösster Vehemenz* (prob. 1901)

    2nd part

    (c) *Scherzo* (*Kräftig, nicht zu schnell*) (summer 1901).

    3rd part

    (d) *Adagietto* (*Sehr langsam*) (prob. 1902). FS edition, Kaplan Found., 1992.
    (e) *Rondo-Finale* (*Allegro*) (1902).

13. **5 Kindertotenlieder** (1901–4), poems by Friedrich Rückert. AFC, v & p, songs (b) to (d); and v & o, complete, PML (Lehman dep.). 1st perf. Vienna, 29 Jan. 1905. Publ. Aug. 1905, Kahnt. 1st critical edn. IGMG Kahnt, v & p and v & o, 1979; 2nd crit. edn. 1992.

    (a) 'Nun will die Sonn' so hell aufgeh'n' (summer 1901) (NBL1. 166; NBL2. 193). APD, v & p, GMF
    (b) 'Nun seh' ich wohl, warum so dunkle Flammen' (summer 1904) (AMM1. 91; AMM2. 97)
    (c) 'Wenn dein Mütterlein' (summer 1901)
    (d) 'Oft denk' ich, sie sind nur ausgegangen' (summer 1901)
    (e) 'In diesem Wetter' (summer 1904)

Analyses of the following works will be included in Volume iii:

14. **Sixth Symphony**, A minor (1903–5). AFC (1 June 1905), GMF. 1st perf. Essen, 27 May 1906. Rev. 1906 and 1907. Publ. Mar. 1906, Kahnt. Critical edn. IGMG Kahnt 1963. 1st edn. (b) Scherzo, (c) Andante; 2nd edn. (b) Andante, (c) Scherzo. Mahler's final perf. (b) Scherzo; (c) Andante.

    (a) *Allegro energico, ma non troppo* (summer 1903?)
    (b) *Scherzo* (*Wuchtig*) (summer 1903)
    (c) *Andante moderato* (summer 1903)
    (d) *Finale* (*Allegro moderato*) (summer 1904)

15. **Seventh Symphony**, B minor (1904–5). AFC, ACA. 1st perf. Prague, 19 Sept. 1908. Publ. Dec. 1909, Bote und Bock. Critical edn. IGMG/Bote & Bock 1960.

    (a) *Langsam; Allegro risoluto ma non troppo.*
    (b) *Nachtmusik* (AFC: *Nachtstück*) (*Allegro moderato*) (summer 1904)
    (c) *Schattenhaft* (*Fliessend, aber nicht zu schnell*) (summer 1905). Incomplete APD (15 Aug. 1905), LPA (Walter col.)
    (d) *Nachtmusik* (*Andante amoroso*) (summer 1904)
    (e) *Rondo-Finale* (*Allegro ordinario*) (summer 1905)

16. **Eighth Symphony**, E flat major (1906), with 3 sopranos, 2 altos, tenor, baritone, bass solos, children's chorus, and mixed double chorus. AFC, BSM.

1st perf. Munich, 12 Sept. 1910. Publ. Feb. 1911, UE. Critical edn. IGMG/UE 1977.

(*a*) Hymnus: 'Veni Creator Spiritus' (Part I) (drafted: July/Aug. 1906)
(*b*) Final scene of Goethe's *Faust* (Part II) (drafted: July/Aug. 1906)

Analyses of the following works will be included in Volume iv.

17. **Das Lied von der Erde** (1908), 'Symphony for tenor and alto (or baritone) and orchestra', poems adapted from the Chinese by Hans Bethge. AD, complete, v & p, priv. col., Kallir, Scarsdale, NY. AFC, v & o, PML (Lehman dep.). 1st perf. Munich, 20 Nov. 1911/B. Walter. Publ. 1912, UE. Critical edn. v & p, IGMG/UE 1989; v & o, IGMG/UE 1964.

   (*a*) 'Das Trinklied vom Jammer der Erde': AOD, v & o (14 Aug. 1908), missing.
   (*b*) 'Der Einsame im Herbst': AD, v & p (July 1908), see above, Kallir col.
   (*c*) 'Von der Jugend': APD, v & p, and AOD (in folder dated 1 Aug. 1908), GMF.
   (*d*) 'Von der Schönheit': AD, v & p (21 Aug. 1908), see above, Kallir col.; APD, v & o, PML (Lehman dep.).
   (*e*) 'Der Trunkene im Frühling': AOD, SBW.
   (*f*) 'Der Abschied'. APD, v & p (1 Sept. 1908), HMS; AOD (1 Sept. 1908), HMS.

18. **Ninth Symphony**, D major (1909). AFC, PML (Lehman dep.) 1st perf. Vienna, 26 June 1912/B. Walter. Publ. July 1912, UE. Critical edn. IGMG/UE 1969. FS ed. (*a*) to (*c*), UE, 1971.

   (*a*) *Andante comodo*: AOD, ÖNB.
   (*b*) *Im Tempo eines gemächlichen Ländlers*: AOD, ÖNB.
   (*c*) *Rondo-Burleske* (*Allegro assai. Sehr trotzig*): AOD, ÖNB.
   (*d*) *Adagio* (*Sehr langsam; molto adagio*): AOD (2 Sept. 1909), BGM.

19. **Tenth Symphony**, F sharp (1910), unfinished. Sketches, AOD and AFC, ÖNB. 1st perf. (*a*) and (*c*) Vienna, 12 Oct. 1924/F. Schalk. FS edn. 1924, Zsolnay. Publ. (*a*) and (*c*) 1951, AMP. 2nd FS edn. Ricke, Munich, 1967. Performing vers. by Deryck Cooke, 1963. 1st incomplete perf. BBC London, 19 Dec. 1960/ Berthold Goldschmidt; 1st complete perf. BBC London, 13 Aug. 1964/Berthold Goldschmidt. Publ. Faber, 1976.

   (*a*) *Andante. Adagio*
   (*b*) *Scherzo* (*Schnelle Viertel*)
   (*c*) *Purgatorio* (*Allegretto moderato. Nicht zu schnell*)
   (*d*) (*Scherzo II*) 'Der Teufel tanzt es mit mir'
   (*e*) *Finale* (*Einleitung; Allegro moderato*)

Fragmentary and unfinished works will be listed in Volume i.

UNFINISHED WORK, COMPLETED BY MAHLER

Weber, Die Drei Pintos, opera in three acts (libretto rev. by Karl von Weber and Mahler, 1887–8). 1st perf. Leipzig, 20 Jan. 1888. Publ. 1888(?), Kahnt.

TRANSCRIPTIONS AND ARRANGEMENTS

Bruckner, Symphony No. 3 (Transcribed for piano duet, supposedly in collaboration with Rudolf Krzyzanowski, whose name, however, does not appear on the title-page (see Vol. i, Chap. 4). Publ. Bussjäger & Rättig, 1878.

J. S. Bach, Suite aus seinen Orchesterwerken (1909). Bach-Gesellschaft score with aut. corrections sold at auction in 1992. Publ. Feb. 1911, Schirmer.

    (*a*) Ouverture (from Suite No. 2)
    (*b*) Rondeau (from Suite No. 2)
    (*c*) Badinerie (from Suite No. 2)
    (*d*) Air (from Suite No. 3)
    (*e*) Gavottes 1 and 2 (from Suite No. 3)

WORKS REVISED BY MAHLER

1. Orchestration

Mahler left several different versions of many works. The location of the various scores is briefly listed here.

Bach, Cantatas Nos. 19, 65, 78: SOU
Beethoven, Quartet No. 11, in F minor, Op. 95 (version for string orchestra): VPA; publ. 1990, Weinberger
—— Symphonies Nos. 1 and 2: SOU
  No. 3: SOU, UEA
  No. 4: SOU
  Nos. 5 and 6: UEA
  No. 7: UEA, CPA
  No. 8: UEA
  No. 9: SOU, UEA
—— Overtures: Coriolan: SOU, UEA, CPA
  Egmont: UEA, HMS
  Die Weihe des Hauses: SOU, UEA, SBW
  König Stephan: SOU
  Leonore Nos. 2 and 3: UEA
—— Piano Concerto No. 5: SOU
Bruckner, Symphonies No. 4 and 5 (with substantial cuts): UEA
Mozart, Symphonies Nos. 40 and 41: UEA
Schubert, Quartet No. 14, in D minor, 'Der Tod und das Mädchen' (version for string orchestra): D. Mitchell col.; publ. 1894, Weinberger.
—— Symphony No. 9, in C major: SOU, BSM, UEA
Schumann, Symphonies No. 1: YUL, Osborn col., UEA
  No. 2: SOU

No. 3: Copyist's score, IGMG
No. 4: YUL, Osborn col., UEA
—— Overture to **Manfred**: UEA
Smetana, Overture to The Bartered Bride: UEA
Wagner, Overture to Die Meistersinger: UEA
Weber, Overture to Oberon

2. Stage Versions

Mozart, Le nozze di Figaro (new accompanied recitative for the trial scene); publ. Peters, 1906
Weber, Euryanthe (changes to the libretto and several passages in the score), libretto publ. Künast, 1904?
—— **Oberon** 'Neue Bühneneinrichtung' (added 'melodramas'), publ. UE

APPENDIX 2

Detailed History and Analysis of Works Composed between 1898 and 1904

TEN WUNDERHORN-LIEDER FOR VOICE AND ORCHESTRA
(1892–1898)

Composition

The first four Lieder of this group, and 'Das himmlische Leben', which later became the Finale of the Fourth Symphony, were composed and orchestrated in a very short time (January–April 1892). Mahler looked for an original descriptive title for these unusual compositions and his first choice was *Humoresken*. The following year he renamed the still incomplete collection *Balladen und Humoresken aus 'Des Knaben Wunderhorn'*. In the concert programme of 27 October 1893 (six Lieder, of which four were first performances), only 'Das himmlische Leben', 'Verlorene Müh'' (*sic*), and 'Wer hat dies Liedlein erdacht?' were entitled *Humoresken*. Thus 'Der Schildwache Nachtlied', 'Trost im Unglück', and 'Rheinlegendchen' were presumably *Balladen*, but were presented merely as 'aus "Des Knaben Wunderhorn"'. One month later, in Wiesbaden, these last three songs bore the title *Drei Gesänge aus 'Des Knaben Wunderhorn'*. In the autograph piano version now in BSB,[1] and which includes six songs (the five 1892 *Humoresken* and the 1893 'Rheinlegendchen'), the title reads *Des Knaben Wunderhorn*. Thus, Mahler had already abandoned the term *Humoresken*, and never used it again after 1893. As a matter of fact, these songs were not performed again with orchestra until Selma Kurz sang three of them with the Vienna Philharmonic in 1900,[2] and on that occasion they were merely called *Gesänge*.

In her study of Mahler's *Orchesterlieder*, Elisabeth Schmierer says that the word *Gesang* appeared early in the nineteenth century, but that it was only after 1850 that the term was more widely adopted. It came increasingly to be applied to songs which did not conform to Goethe's ideal of simplicity, but in which the accompaniment was given a more independent role, and simply repetitive strophic arrangements were replaced by *durchkomponiert* techniques.[3] Many critics and musicologists considered that this 'widening of the genre' was 'a sign of . . . the decadence of the spirit of the Lied'[4] and a dangerous intrusion of dramatic procedures into an essentially lyrical form.

Should the original subtitle, *Humoresken*, be regarded as defining a new musical

---

[1] See above, the keys to the various Libraries preceding the catalogue of Mahler's works.

[2] See above, Chap. 7.

[3] Elisabeth Schmierer, *Die Orchesterlieder Gustav Mahlers* (Bärenreiter, Kassel, 1991), 11 ff.

[4] See Hermann Kretschmar, 'Das deutsche Lied seit dem Tode Richard Wagners' (1898), in *Gesammelte Aufsätze über Musik und Anderes aus den Grenzboten* (Heuss, Leipzig, 1911), 289.

genre? Mahler himself referred to Aristotle's *eironeia* in explaining the defensive, desperate, and tragic character of his irony, which was not the aggressive irony of cynicism or sarcasm.[5] This explains the meaning of the indication 'Mit Humor' frequently used to indicate tempo or mood at the beginning of the songs. The romantic novelist Jean Paul,[6] in his *Vorschule der Ästhetik* (Elementary Aesthetics), defines humour in literature and music as the effect of a destructive idea (*vernichtende Idee*) which expresses contempt for the world. He speaks in this context of *Keckheit* (cheek, effrontery), and the indication *keck* (cheekily) is often found at the beginning of Mahler's Lieder, or sometimes even over particular passages.

It seems highly unlikely that Mahler was harking back to Schumann's *Humoreske*, Op. 20, although he had played it in his youth, or Humperdinck's composition bearing the same title, which dates from 1878. He later considered using the same title, *Humoreske*, for the Fourth Symphony, and it seems clear that he was not thinking of a new vocal genre, but meant rather to define the character, the contents of these songs, and that his idea of 'humour' came very close to Jean Paul's definition.[7]

Mahler and Des Knaben Wunderhorn

For the literary history of the *Wunderhorn*, Mahler's discovery of the famous anthology, the editions he used, his choice of poems, see above, Vol. i, Appendix 1, section 9 on the *Wunderhorn-Lieder* with piano accompaniment.

Cycle or collection?

The orchestral *Wunderhorn-Lieder* are symphonic songs composed in the same vein as the contemporaneous Second and Third Symphonies. In fact, they are so thoroughly orchestral in conception that they lose a great deal when accompanied on the piano. They do not, properly speaking, make up a cycle—a logically ordered whole—and their sequence corresponds more or less to the chronological order of their composition. In an undated letter, written in December 1906 to the Dutch baritone Johannes Messchaert, Mahler asks him to make up his own mind about the sequence. Because they have so much in common (poems, themes, atmosphere, musical language) they are often performed together, but not in any particular order. Their epic style and dimensions bring them close to the tradition of the great ballads of Schubert and Loewe. As in the earlier, shorter, simpler songs with piano accompaniment, Mahler proves in this unique collection how much at home he felt in the colourful, naïve world of the Arnim-Brentano anthology. In it he found striking glimpses of man and his earthly destiny, both humorous and tragic, and reflections on the human condition which are often more vivid and profound than those conveyed by literary poetry.

The numbering of the Lieder

As mentioned above, this conforms only in part to the order of composition. It has already been noted that the first four songs were composed in 1892. When Mahler later decided to withdraw 'Das himmlische Leben' in order to insert it in the Fourth Symphony, 'Das irdische Leben' became number 5 (though the orchestral score bears

[5] MBR1, no. 177; MBR2, no. 165.   [6] See Vol. i, App. on the 1st Symphony.
[7] Renate Hilmar-Voit, *Im Wunderhorn-Ton. Gustav Mahlers sprachliches Kompositionsmaterial bis 1900* (Schneider, Tutzing, 1988), 33 ff.

the number 6). The 'Fischpredigt' (1893) became number 6 (instead of 8, as in the manuscript), and 'Rheinlegendchen', written the same year, number 7 (instead of 9). The two Lieder which date from 1898, 'Lied des Verfolgten' and 'Wo die schönen', were given the numbers 8 and 9, and the collection was completed by 'Lob des hohen Verstandes', composed in 1896, as number 10.

Solos or duets?

Ever since an English recording of the complete collection appeared in 1966, with the 'dialogue' Lieder sung as duets for male and female voices, this has become the custom, both in concerts and on records. The performance obviously gains in liveliness and diversity, but the effect is highly artificial, since Mahler never intended the songs to be performed in this way. Most of the dialogue excerpts[8] are so short that the change of voice is not only unconvincing, but often detrimental to the unity of the music. Mahler himself wrote in a letter around 1904: 'My songs are all conceived for male voices.'[9] Elisabeth Schmierer points out that the two main sections resemble those in exposition in a sonata-form movement and that they are also, in many cases, closely related thematically to each other. Furthermore, most of the 'dialogues' (for instance in 'Schildwache Nachtlied' and 'Lied des Verfolgten') are of an imaginary nature—they take place in the imagination of one of the protagonists—and the texts of the poems make this abundantly clear.[10]

Nevertheless, for the Hamburg performance of Lieder (*a*) to (*d*) and (*g*),[11] Mahler did use two singers, a man and a woman, but never to sing in one and the same song. In the 1893 performance, 'Wer hat dies Liedlein erdacht?' and 'Verlorene Müh'' (*sic*) were sung by Clementine Prosska, and in 1900 Selma Kurz sang 'Verlor'ne Müh'', 'Das irdische Leben', and 'Wo die schönen Trompeten blasen'. At the Vienna and Graz concerts in 1905 all the songs were sung by men, with one exception: on 3 February that year, at the second Viennese performance, 'Verlor'ne Müh'' (*sic*), 'Lob des hohen Verstandes', and 'Wer hat dies Liedlein erdacht' were entrusted to a soprano, Marie Gutheil-Schoder. However, Mahler's own concert programmes confirm that he preferred a male voice. The only works for which he wanted—and expressly called for—a contralto voice were the Second and Third Symphonies and movements 2, 4, and 6 of *Das Lied von der Erde*. Although it is perfectly legitimate to entrust some of the *Wunderhorn-Lieder* to female voices, in particular 'Wer hat dies Liedlein erdacht' and 'Rheinlegendchen', it is none the less certain that Mahler would have strongly objected to the current practice of turning the 'dialogue' songs into duets. Who would dream of having Schubert's 'Erlkönig', to cite only the most celebrated 'dialogue' Lied in the repertoire, sung by three (or four) different voices?

In a letter of 2 March 1905, addressed to Karpath, Mahler describes the *Wunderhorn* poems as 'fundamentally different from any "literary" poetry . . . Rather than art, they are about nature and life (the source of all poetry).'[12] When he wrote that, it was four years since he had set a text from the anthology to music, but he was as convinced

[8] The proportion is still bigger if the 24 *Wunderhorn-Lieder* are taken as a whole, for 17 of them (nearly three-quarters), contain dialogues. This is a peculiarity in Mahler's output, considering that the corresponding proportion in Schumann is one-fifteenth, and in Brahms about one-fifth. See Hilmar-Voit, *Im Wunderhorn-Ton*, 28.

[9] Card to Oskar Fried (c.1904), presented by me to Dietrich Fischer-Dieskau.

[10] Schmierer, *Orchesterlieder Mahlers*, 120ff. and 136ff.

[11] See Catalogue of works.   [12] MBR1, no. 230; MBR2, no. 341.

as ever that it was a splendid source of inspiration, and continued to accord his settings from it an important place in his oeuvre. Posterity has certainly not proved him wrong.

The orchestral Lied

It may seem at first sight surprising to devote a section of this study to the orchestral Lied as a genre, since the *Lieder eines fahrenden Gesellen*, which were completed in 1884–5, are usually thought of as the first known example of a cycle (or collection) written specifically for voice and orchestra. However, although the earliest known autographs of these songs show that Mahler had the orchestra in mind when he composed them, no evidence has been found of an early orchestral version. The songs were most probably orchestrated in 1893 or perhaps even as late as 1896, as stated by Natalie Bauer-Lechner.[13] Thus, the 1892 *Humoresken* were in fact the first Lieder written by Mahler directly for voice and orchestra. In a pioneering article published over fifteen years ago, Edward Kravitt has sketched the history of the orchestral Lied or *Gesang*.[14] He refers to 'its unexpected flowering around 1900'. The concept was of course not new in 1900. In 1856 Berlioz had orchestrated his *Nuits d'été*, composed several years earlier, with results so successful that the original piano versions are nowadays practically forgotten. Like Liszt, Ferdinand Hiller, and Brahms, Berlioz also orchestrated Schubert Lieder. Nevertheless, only Liszt, the eternal innovator, felt completely at ease writing orchestral songs, and this as early as 1860. He thus became the pioneer of a new genre which was soon to flourish, as the Lied broke away from its earlier home, the salon, to establish itself firmly in the concert hall. There it acquired an existence in its own right, quite apart from the former concert Scena or the Aria, which Mendelssohn, Max Bruch, Carl Reinecke, and others continued to compose until about 1870.

Another author, Hermann Danuser[15] has drawn a parallel between the sudden success of the orchestral Lied and the blossoming of the Lieder-Abend in the years 1870–80, which coincided with a corresponding decline in the custom of including piano Lieder recitals in orchestral concert programmes. Felix Mottl's transcriptions of Wagner's *Wesendonk-Lieder* achieved such success that audiences soon forgot that Wagner himself had only orchestrated one of them ('Träume'). But the first genuine orchestral Lieder were composed by conductors such as Felix Weingartner (*Die Wallfahrt nach Kevlaar*, Op. 12: 1887) and Pfitzner (*Herr Oluf*, Op. 12: 1891).[16] Frederic Delius, in *Sakuntala* (1889) and *Maud* (1891) was another pioneer of the orchestral Lied, while Hugo Wolf orchestrated (rather clumsily) eight of his songs in 1890, in the hope that Weingartner would include them in one of his symphonic programmes. In the early 1890s Richard Strauss also began orchestrating some of his songs so that his wife Pauline could appear as soloist at the numerous concerts where he was invited to conduct.[17]

---

[13] NBL1. 30; NBL2. 46.

[14] Edward Kravitt, 'The Orchestral *Lied*: An Inquiry into its Style and Unexpected Flowering around 1900', *Music Review*, 37: 3 (1976), 209 ff.

[15] Hermann Danuser, 'Der Orchestergesang des Fin de siècle: Eine historische und ästhetische Skizze', *Die Musikforschung*, 30 (1977), 425 ff.

[16] Pfitzner wrote 100 piano Lieder, orchestrated 3, and wrote 15 orchestral songs.

[17] Altogether, Strauss orchestrated 27 of his piano Lieder and wrote 15 others (including 4 complete opera) for voice and orchestra.

The reasons for writing orchestral Lieder are clear: as the century came to a close, composers hoped to reach a larger public than the more intimate recitals of songs with piano accompaniment could reach. They also sought to achieve greater intensity and subtlety of colour and expression. The reasons why so many critics opposed them are just as clear. There seemed to be a complete incompatibility between the intimacy of the Lied and its new orchestral garb. Rudolf Louis, the reactionary Munich composer-critic, a virulent anti-Semite and opponent of the *neudeutsch* school, wrote as late as 1909:

An orchestral accompaniment represents a danger for a purely lyrical text. . . . There arises all too easily a disturbing incongruity between the intimate content of the text and demands for intensity made today upon [orchestral] media. Furthermore, the temptation now is to lay more stress upon superficialities such as illustrative tone-painting, pure sound effects and the like . . . than is consistent with the nature of lyrical texts.[18]

Mahler was in any case taking an ever greater risk by choosing traditional folk-texts for his first Orchesterlieder and by deliberately refusing in his musical settings to make any concessions to the folk-like nature of the poems, using instead symphonic variation procedures and the most sophisticated orchestral techniques. Although there was a precedent in Loewe's epic ballads for the use of art-song procedures in setting folk- or folk-like texts, the overwhelming majority of music critics of his time never forgave him for the 'modern' musical refinement of his settings.

Autographs and editions

As seen above, the autograph piano version, most likely dating from 1893, is now at BSB. It includes Lieder (*a*) to (*d*), and (*g*), as well as 'Das himmlische Leben' (see below). It was probably used for the rehearsals of the 1893 Hamburg concert, which included precisely these songs. Other autographs will be mentioned below, in the sections devoted to the individual songs. The piano version of the complete collection was first published by Weinberger in March 1900 in two separate volumes. They include 'Urlicht' and 'Es sungen drei Engel'. The orchestral scores were printed at the same time. The first Universal Edition appeared in 1914.

A modern voice and piano edition of the fourteen *Wunderhorn-Lieder* (including those from the Second and Third Symphonies and the last two, originally included in the *Sieben Lieder aus letzter Zeit*, published by Kahnt in 1905) was issued by Universal Edition as part of the IGMG critical edition in 1993. Hitherto the importance of these voice and piano versions had undoubtedly been underestimated. For a long time, they were considered as less than adequate transcriptions, whereas Mahler obviously intended them to be alternative originals. In several instances, they were composed before the orchestral versions. It was essential therefore to prepare a reliable critical edition, particularly since the piano versions differ in many details from the orchestral versions. However, there can be no denying that Mahler wrote these great songs with the orchestra in mind, and that the piano will always remain a poor substitute. In my opinion, these piano versions were meant not only for rehearsal purposes, but for Lieder-Abende, at a time when Mahler considered it unlikely, if not impossible, that he could have them performed in orchestral concerts.

---

[18] Rudolf Louis, *Die Musik der Gegenwart* (Müller, Munich, 1909), 237, quoted by Kravitt, *Orchestral Lied*, 211.

In her detailed introductory text, Renate Hilmar-Voit, who prepared the new edition, makes a number of interesting points. For instance, several of the autograph piano versions have no indications meant to be used as a guide to later orchestration, which would seem to prove that Mahler intended then to exist on their own. Furthermore, study of these autographs shows that the piano and the orchestral versions in many cases developed independently of each other. Some other details are also significant. For instance, the tempos for all the Lieder composed in 1892 and 1893 were indicated by metronome markings which were preserved in the edition only for 'Das irdische Leben' and 'Des Antonius'. Frau Hilmar-Voit also compared the C minor version of 'Revelge' with the earlier D minor version and found that it contained a number of improvements. The printer's proofs of this song, corrected by Mahler himself (now in IGMG), are apparently dated 6 June 1902, although the first edition was only published by C. F. Kahnt three years later.

After Mahler signed a new contract for the publication of the *Wunderhorn-Lieder* with Universal Edition on 11 August 1910, the firm reissued the original Eberle edition. As mentioned above, a new, two-volume, edition followed in 1914, in two alternative versions for high and middle voice. In this edition, the original text had been altered in many instances, undoubtedly to bring the piano and orchestral versions closer to each other. Needless to say, these changes were made without Mahler's consent. The last two songs, 'Revelge' and 'Der Tamboursg'sell', were then added to the Universal Edition catalogue, together with the *Rückert-Lieder*, which Universal Edition must at some time have bought from Kahnt, although no trace of a contract has been found.

The 1993 edition includes Mahler's own, original, versions of the fourteen *Wunderhorn-Lieder* published partly by Eberle and partly by Kahnt, as well as Mahler's original, unpublished, piano version of 'Das himmlische Leben'. Until then, Doblinger had only issued 'a piano score of the soprano solo from the Fourth Symphony'. This was republished by Universal in 1910.

Texts

Renate Hilmar-Voit has compared the various editions of the Arnim and Brentano anthology with Mahler's texts.[19] Thanks to small details such as the spelling of words, she has identified the particular editions which Mahler used. According to her, his main source was the 1883 Robert Boxberger edition.[20] However, from 1896 on, he turned (except for 'Revelge') to the original three-volume edition of the anthology,[21] which Anna von Mildenburg had given him in 1895.

Orchestration

This aspect will be dealt with in the sections devoted to the individual Lieder. However, it is perhaps worth reminding contemporary conductors and orchestra managers that the first performance after publication of songs (*a*), (*c*), (*d*), (*g*), and the world-premières of songs (*f*), (*h*), and (*j*) took place, by Mahler's own choice, in the Kleiner

---

[19] See Renate Hilmar-Voit, 'Vorwort' and 'Revisionsbericht' in 1993 edn. of voice and piano versions of 15 *Wunderhorn-Lieder* (Universal Edition, Vienna, 1993), p. xxxi, 133.

[20] Hempel, Berlin, 1883, 2 vols. All the page-references for the poems below refer to this edn. See also Vol. i, App. 1, on the early *Wunderhorn-Lieder*.

[21] Vol. i (Mohr & Zimmer, Heidelberg, 1806); Vols. ii–iii (Mohr & Zimmer, Heidelberg, 1808).

Musikvereinsaal, a hall which can only house an orchestra of approximately 40 to 50 musicians.[22] Four months later, Mahler conducted performances of (*e*) and (*i*) the small Stephanien-Saal in Graz. The size of the orchestra varies considerably from one song to the other. 'Rheinlegendchen' is scored for chamber orchestra, whereas 'Der Schildwache Nachtlied', 'Trost im Unglück', and 'Lied der Verfolgten im Turm' are scored for a full symphony orchestra, including four horns and two trumpets.

(*a*) 'Der Schildwache Nachtlied' (The Sentinel's Night Song)

In a conversation reported by Natalie Bauer-Lechner,[23] Mahler describes this song as the only remaining fragment, dating from 1888, of an opera on which he was working with Karl von Weber, in which case it would be one of the earliest results of his discovery of *Des Knaben Wunderhorn*. A three-page preliminary sketch, which used to belong to Natalie Bauer-Lechner, is now in the LCW. Donald Mitchell has seriously questioned the statement attributed to Mahler by Natalie[24] that the Lied in question was begun in Leipzig. He argues that, if the song had been composed as early as 1888, it would have been included among the early Lieder published by Schott in 1892. He also rightly doubts that the song could ever have been inserted in an opera. However, even if the sketched pages in LCW were found, on closer inspection, to date from the Hamburg period, I would hesitate to question Mahler's own dating, for the song could have remained unfinished until 1892. Furthermore, its length and large-scale accompaniment would make it too unlike the early *Wunderhorn-Lieder* to be included in this collection. For the Wiesbaden concert of November 1893, Mahler gave this Lied a new subtitle: 'Eine Szene aus dem Lagerleben' (A scene from army life).

Autographs: APD: v & p (composed of two separate sheets, the first one named as the song, and a further one bearing the title 'Verlorene Feldwacht' and containing the last episode): LCW;[25] AFC, v & p (28 Jan. 1892): BSB; v & o (12 Mar. 1892): GMF.

Key: B♭, ending on the dominant (as in low voice edn.). 1st perf.: Paul Bulss, baritone, 1893.

Time signature: 4/4, changing to 6/4 (mixed with 3/4 and 4/4).

Rhythm: Quick march.

Tempo: *Marschartig* (like a march); *Etwas gemessener* (somewhat slower); *Langsamer* (slower).

Orchestration: 3 flutes (including piccolo), 3 oboes (including cor anglais), 2 clarinets, 2 bassoons, 4 horns, 2 trumpets, timpani, triangle, side-drum, big drum, cymbals, harp, and strings.

Text: Vol. i. 235.[26] Mahler's alterations are very slight (*Lieb' Knabe* instead of

---

[22] See below, in the sections devoted to Lieder (*b*), (*c*), (*d*), (*g*), (*h*), and (*j*), the exact number of strings used for each song during the Vienna and Graz performances, in 1905.

[23] NBL1. 162; NBL2. 190.

[24] DMM2. 252 ff. The MS sheet from LCW was reproduced by Emanuel Winternitz in *Musical Autographs: From Monteverdi to Hindemith* (Princeton, NJ, 1955), pl. 163.

[25] See above the alphabetical list of keys to autograph sources and libraries.

[26] The p. nos. refer to Robert Boxberger's edn. of *Des Knaben Wunderhorn* (Hempel, Berlin, n.d. [1883]). Three previous edns. had appeared, besides the original (1805–8): one in Arnim's *Sämtlichen Werken*, xiv–xvii (1845–6), another ed. Anton Birlinger and Wilhelm Crecalius (Killinger, Wiesbaden, 1874–6), and one by Friedrich Bremer (Reclam, Leipzig, 1879).

Ach Knabe, musst instead of *sollst* in the second stanza, first line; *geh'* instead of *komm* in the third stanza, first line). Several groups of words are repeated. As Fritz Egon Pamer[27] has pointed out, one of Mahler's alterations is more important than it would seem at first sight. Between Stanzas 4 and 5, the *Wunderhorn* reads:

An Gottes Segen	On God's blessing
Ist Alles gelegen,	Everything depends,
Wer's glauben thut.	[For] the one who believes it.

By changing the comma after 'gelegen' into an exclamation mark, Mahler gave the next line an ironic implication, and the following stanza says that those who believe it are far away from the battle line: they are the kings and emperors who cause the wars to be made. Mahler's changes to the last stanza undoubtedly make it more 'musical'. The original reads:

Halt! Wer da?—Rund	Halt! Who goes there? Patrol!
Wer sang zur Stund	Who sang just then?
Verlorene Feldwacht	The lost sentry
Sang es um Mitternacht	Sang it at midnight.
Bleib mir vom Leib!	Stand back!

Mahler replaced this with:

Wer sang es hier?	Who sang it here?
Wer sang zur Stund'?	Who sang just then?
Verlor'ne Feldwacht	The lost sentry
Sang es um Mitternacht,	Sang it at midnight,
Mitternacht! Mitternacht!	Midnight! Midnight!
Feldwacht!	Sentry!

Form: The poem is in dialogue form, yet Elisabeth Schmierer has made a pertinent comment about all of the *Wunderhorn* dialogue songs. To her mind the two contrasting sections evoke those of a sonata-form movement rather than the words exchanged by two characters in a play. Such a contrast is to be found in all the *Wunderhorn-Lieder*, except 'Rheinlegendchen', 'Wer hat dies Liedlein', and the four Lieder included in the symphonies, i.e. 'Fischpredigt', 'Urlicht', 'Es sungen drei Engel', and 'Das himmlische Leben'.[28] In 'Schildwache Nachtlied', the dialogue in the last stanza proves to have been imaginary, the dream vision of the soldier which the title suggests.

Like all those in dialogue form, this song is a rondo: the structure can be summed up as ABABAB, yet this simple pattern cannot suggest any of Mahler's subtle touches, such as apparent restatements which retain from the original passage the characteristic rhythms, motifs, accompaniment figures, or dynamics, but nothing else. Short orchestral interludes connect the various sections, and the last episode, conceived in symphonic terms, heightens the effect of 'Wer da! Rund! Bleib' mir vom Leib'.

[27] In 'Gustav Mahlers Lieder: Eine stilkritische Studie', Ph.D. thesis, Vienna University, 1922.
[28] Schmierer, *Orchesterlieder Mahlers*, 121.

738 Appendix 2: History and analysis

Together with 'Trost im Unglück', 'Lied des Verfolgten', and 'Revelge', this is one of Mahler's war songs. The soldier's stanzas are written almost exclusively in 'military' idiom, with drum rolls, trumpet calls, buoyant march rhythms, and rising fourth intervals in the bass.[29] The sentinel's challenge, in the vocal part, imitates a trumpet call, a motif which plays an essential part in the structure of the song as a whole. The voice's melody which follows, in the relative minor key, is later restated in major. The 'girl's' stanza is preceded by a caressing, lilting semiquaver triplet ostinato figure,[30] which turns out to be a diminished version of her melody and persists throughout this section. The triplet motive in the accompaniment unifies the two sections, while the melodic and harmonic sixths add to the feminine charm of the subsidiary episodes. As Fritz Egon Pamer has pointed out, the frequent changes in rhythm suggest a folk-singer gasping for breath between the phrases of his song, as in the first of the *Gesellen-Lieder*. The last lyrical section is extended into a short, serene coda based on material borrowed from the soldier's stanza, including the opening arpeggio motif, twice repeated pianissimo. The whole song fades away into silence and midnight darkness with an inconclusive dominant chord.

Edward Kravitt has noted an interesting dissimilarity in the dynamic markings at the end of the song. The piano version has *Verklingend* (dying away) while the orchestral score has *bis zur gänzlichen Unhörbarkeit* (diminish until completely inaudible).[31] Mahler, he feels, 'aims to utilize, often to the utmost, the great expressive potential of the orchestra'. Mahler intensely disliked any commentary or analysis of his music. When, in 1906, Ernst Decsey pointed out this ending to him and emphasized the tension generated by the dominant pedal and the changing harmonies, he merely answered, 'Oh! Dominant! Consider these things simply, as they were conceived!'[32] Was he perhaps not entirely conscious of the unlimited complexity of his compositional techniques?

Several known folk-songs are based on this poem. One of them, of Westphalian origin, bears a certain likeness to Mahler's (see Ex. 2):[33]

Ex. 2. Westphalian song

Ich kann und mag nicht trau-rig sein, wenn an dre schla-fen, so muss ich wa-chen, muss den ken dein.

[29] Schmierer, *Orchesterlieder Mahlers*, 121. 124 ff.

[30] The same motif occurs in Act III of Verdi's *Otello* (in the hero's monologue 'Dio! Mi potevi scagliar'). Mahler was particularly fond of Verdi's late operas. He had probably seen the score of *Otello* and possibly heard a performance when he visited Italy for the Budapest Opera in 1890. Elisabeth Schmierer points out the resemblance between the flute motif in bars 41–3 and the opening of the first *Gesellen-Lied*. (*Orchesterlieder Mahlers*, 125)

[31] Kravitt, 'Orchestral Lied', 219.   [32] *Die Musik*, 10: 21, 144.

[33] Ludwig Erk and Franz M. Böhme, *Deutscher Liederhort* (3 vols., Leipzig, 1893–4), ii. 568 (mentioned from here on as *DLH*).

(*b*) 'Verlorne Müh' (Labour Lost)

Autographs: AFC, v & p (1 Feb. 1892), entitled 'Verlorene Müh'', as in *Knaben Wunderhorn*: BSB; v & o (subtitled 'Eine Humoreske'): GMF.

Key: A major (and minor), as in high voice edn. (1st perf.: Amalie Joachim, alto, 1892; 2nd: Clementine Prosska, coloratura soprano, 1893).

Time Signature: 3/8.

Rhythm: Slow ländler.

Tempo: *Gemächlich, heiter* (moderate, gay) (on piano MS: ♪ = 132).

Text: Vol. i. 400, under the title: 'Verlor'ne Müh''. The poem had been published in Arnim's 1790 collection: *Fünf weltliche schöne neue Lieder*. Mahler kept only the first and last stanzas of the poem, in which he made few changes, other than repeating lines and groups of words, and adding interrogation and exclamation marks.

Orchestration: 2 flutes (changing to piccolos), 2 oboes, 2 clarinets, 2 bassoons, 2 horns, triangle, and strings. For the Vienna performance of 3 Feb. 1905, Mahler used a string section composed of 10 first violins, 8 second violins, 8 violas, 6 cellos, and 3 double-basses (?).[34]

Form: Strophic *Tanzlied*. Like all Mahler's other dialogue songs, this one has two separate musical sections. Here the contrast is less striking than usual. The boy's replies are short and abrupt, and there is a short semiquaver ritornello separating them from the girl's pleadings. Fritz Pamer has analysed the means which Mahler used near the end to achieve a crescendo effect: unexpected modulations and a rising vocal line. In bar 17 (*Unsere Lämmer*), Guido Adler noted the presence of Mahler's private 'signal', which he borrowed from Beethoven's Eighth Symphony and often used in daily life.[35] This is probably a deliberate quotation, connected in some way with the humour of the poem. Jon Finson has pointed out that 'the musical material for the characters remains basically the same in each strophe, as does the sequence of events and phrases, but nothing repeats exactly'. Thus, Mahler merely 'alludes' to strophic form, a procedure which is characteristic of his compositional methods.[36] The alternation of the major and minor modes is another typical Mahlerian feature. There is no known original folk melody for this text.

(*c*) 'Trost im Unglück' (Comfort in Misfortune)

This is the fifth of the 1892 *Humoresken*. Mahler's original title was 'Wir wissen uns zu trösten' (v & o autograph, GMF). Like 'Der Schildwache Nachtlied', it was subtitled for the Hamburg première in 1893: 'eine Szene aus dem Lagerleben der Landsknechte' (a scene from the army life of the mercenaries).

---

[34] Part of the orchestra material used for the Vienna and Graz performances of seven *Wunderhorn-Lieder* has been preserved in SBW (UE Archiv) and IMG. The number of string-players quoted here is of course based on the number of parts, each of them serving for two players. See Renate Hilmar-Voit, 'Symphonischer Klang oder Kammermusikton?', in *Nachrichten zur Mahler Forschung*, 28 (IGMG, Vienna, Oct. 1992), 8 ff. She includes in her list the parts which were not used during the performance. The figures quoted above take into account only those which were used. The number of double-basses seems surprisingly high, unless each player had his own part, which is more likely.

[35] See NBL1. 58; NBL2. 74.

[36] See Jon W. Finson, 'The Reception of Gustav Mahler's *Wunderhorn* Lieder', *Journal of Musicology*, 5 (Winter 1987): 91 ff and 98 ff.

Autògraphs: APD (one sheet recto-verso): MAS; v & p (22 Feb. 1892): BSB; v & o (26 Apr. 1892): GMF.

Key: A major (as in high voice edn.: the contrasting section is mostly in G major). (1st and 2nd perfs.: Paul Bulss, baritone, 1893; 3rd: Anton Moser, baritone, 1905).

Time signature: 6/8, 2/4 (in the piano and voice edn.). In the orchestral score, the initial time signature is 6/8, with frequent, not always simultaneous changes into 2/4 in the voice and the instrumental parts. Indeed, one of the salient features of this song is the constant alternation of binary and ternary rhythms, which are often used simultaneously.

Tempo: *Verwegen. Durchaus mit prägnantestem Rhythmus* (Bold. Throughout with strongly emphasized rhythm). (On piano MS: ♩ = 100.)

Text: Vol. i. 399, under the title 'Geh' Du nur hin, ich hab mein Theil'. The poem is another dialogue between a hussar and his girl, the last stanza being sung by both. The subject-matter is similar to that of the preceding song, and the two poems follow each other in the anthology. The *Wunderhorn* poem remains practically unchanged in the song. One word is suppressed and two are repeated. The four-line refrain 'Geh' Du nur hin', etc., returns five times in the poem but only three times in the song, and to different music.

Orchestration: 3 flutes (including piccolo), 2 oboes, 2 clarinets, 2 bassoons, 4 horns, 2 trumpets, timpani, triangle, side drum, strings. At the Vienna performances, 8 first violins, 6 second violins, 6 violas, 6 cellos, and 3 double-basses (?) participated.[37]

Form: There is a rondo feeling, due to the recurrence of the original ritornello, but the form can be roughly summarized as AABA. B is the girl's stanza; the rhythm is the same as in the beginning, but the almost conjunct intervals give her remarks a 'feminine' character. The last stanza combines A with elements of B. Although the lively dispute between a hussar and his fiancée has little to do with army life, the song is full of quick triplet upbeats, horn and trumpet calls (even in the vocal line), military drums, and triangle. In this song Mahler unmistakably quotes from a well-known Silesian folk-setting of the same text: 'Husarenliebe' (see Ex. 3).[38]

(*d*) 'Wer hat dies Liedlein erdacht?!' (Who thought up this little song?)
This is the third of the 1892 *Humoresken*.

Autographs: AFC, v & p (6 Feb. 1892): BSB; v & o, entitled 'Eine Humoreske', no. 5: GMF.

Key: F major (as in high voice edn.: 1st perf.: Clementine Prosska, coloratura soprano, 1893; 2nd: Selma Kurz, coloratura soprano, 1900).

Title: Mahler could not make up his mind about the diminutive form of 'Lied': the Berlin v & o autograph has 'Wer hat dies Liedlein'; in Hamburg, in October 1893, Mahler changed this to 'Wer hat dies Liedchen'; in the v & p 1st edn. (Weinberger, 1900), he changed back to 'Liedlein', but the Philharmonia miniature score retains 'Wer hat dies Liedel' (as in the GMF MS). The original *Wunderhorn* text uses the word 'Liedchen'.

Time signature: 3/8.

Rhythm: Ländler.

---

[37] See Hilmar-Voit, 'Symphonischer Klang', 10. [38] *DLH* iii. 281.

Ex. 3. 'Husarenliebe'

Wohl - an die Zeit ist kom - men, mein Pferd das muss ge -
sat - telt sein: ich hab mir's vor - ge - nom - men, ge -
rit - ten muss es sein. Geh du nur hin, ich
hab' mein Theil, ich führ dich nur am Nar - ren - seil; oh - ne
dich kann ich schon le - ben, oh - ne dich kann ich schon sein.

Tempo: *Mit heiterem Behagen* (With easy gaiety); *Gemächlich* (Moderate) for the middle
  stanza (in the Berlin MS: ♪ = 160; at bar no. 47 ♪ = 152).
Text: The text is derived from two *Wunderhorn* poems, 'Wer hat dies Liedlein erdacht?!'
  and 'Wer Lieben erdacht' (Vol. i. 243 and 198). Both the piano manuscript and the
  first piano edition retain the original title of the poem. Mahler used the first and last
  stanzas of this poem but replaced the middle one with a stanza from the second (from
  'Mein Herzle ist wund' to 'macht Kranke gesund'). In the second stanza of the first
  poem, a sum of money ('Tausend Thaler') is mentioned as necessary to conquer the
  lady. Always the true romantic idealist, Mahler replaced it with another which extols
  the sovereign power of the lips of the loved one. In addition to this major alteration,
  he made two smaller ones: 'wacker Mädel' is changed into 'fein's lieb's Mädel
  heraus', and 'am Berg' is added in the first line. John Williamson[39] defines the
  musical outline of the three verses as follows: epic objectivity gives way to lyrical
  subjectivity, and then to ironic banter—a truly original use of the tripartite Lied
  form! Elisabeth Schmierer, on the other hand, lays emphasis on the song's 'irritating'
  flavour, resulting from the two long coloratura vocalises, which are completely out of
  context in a *Tanzlied* such as this one, and also from the many dissonant harmonies
  which accompany a folk-like vocal line of diatonic character.
Orchestration: 2 flutes, 2 oboes, 2 clarinets, 2 bassoons, 2 horns, triangle, and strings.
  For the second Vienna concert, 10 first violins, 8 second violins, 8 violas, 6 cellos,
  and 3 double-basses (?) took part.[40]
Form: Strophic *Tanzlied*. The construction is far more subtle than at first appears, as is

[39] John Williamson, 'Harmonic and Orchestral Rhetoric in Mahler's "Wunderhorn" Songs', author's
communication, 13.
[40] See Hilmar-Voit, 'Symphonischer Klang', 10.

always the case with Mahler's seemingly naïve and innocent Lieder. The many different thematic fragments are unified by a nearly continuous sixteenth-note motion and by the first motif's return as a kind of refrain. Starting in D minor and modulating from there, the second stanza provides an element of contrast, while the last one restates only the conclusion of the first, but with many variants. Such techniques anticipate those Mahler was to use so brilliantly in the Fourth Symphony, and which originated in the *Gemächlich* movement of the First. The first and last stanzas end with a long sixteenth-note vocalise in which the influence of the Tyrolian yodel has been detected. It is often quoted as an example of Mahler's 'instrumental' use of the voice. Constantin Floros and Hans Heinrich Eggebrecht both point out a striking resemblance between the opening bars of the song and the Trio of the Scherzo of Bruckner's Fourth Symphony.[41]

(e) 'Das irdische Leben' (Earthly Life)

Composition: From Natalie's reference to this song in her *Mahleriana* we can deduce that it was composed before the 'Fischpredigt'.[42] The undated orchestral autograph bears the number '7', while that of the piano version of the 'Fischpredigt' is dated 8 July 1893 and bears the number '8'. Mahler's aim, in changing the title, was obviously to create a parallel with 'Das himmlische Leben', which at that time still belonged to the collection. But he had another thought in mind, which he expressed in Natalie's presence:

> The text only suggests the deeper meaning, the treasure that must be searched for. Thus, I picture as a symbol of human life the child's cry for bread and the mother's attempt to console him with promises. I named the song 'Das irdische Leben' for precisely that reason. What I wished to express is that the necessities for one's physical and spiritual growth are long delayed, and finally come too late, as they do for the dead child. I believe I have expressed this in a characteristic and frightening way, through the eerie sonorities of the accompaniment, which roars and whistles like a storm, and also through the tortured and anguished cries of the child and the uniform, monotonous reply of the mother, Destiny, who does not always answer promptly enough our anguished request for bread . . .[43]

Mahler, a composer scorned and misunderstood like few others by his contemporaries, was no doubt thinking also of his own deprivation, and subconsciously expressing his longing to be recognized and appreciated.

Autographs: APD: private collection, Dika Newlin, USA; AFC, v & o: PML (Cary col.).

Key: B♭ minor (Phrygian mode, with flattened supertonic) (as in high voice edn.): 1st perf.: Selma Kurz, coloratura soprano, 1900; 2nd and 3rd: Fritz Weidemann, baritone, 1905).

Time signature: 2/4.

Tempo: *Unheimlich bewegt* (uncannily agitated); ♩ = 104 (orchestral MS). *Nicht zu schnell, doch in stetig gleicher Bewegung* (not too fast, but always in the some tempo) in piano version.

Text: Vol. i. 452, under the title 'Verspätung' (Too late). Two folk-songs, at least, are

[41] Constantin Floros, *Gustav Mahler* (3 vols., Breitkopf & Härtel, Wiesbaden, 1985), ii. 170, and Hans Heinrich Eggebrecht, *Die Musik Gustav Mahlers* (Piper, Munich, 1982), 201.
[42] NBL1. 10 ff; NBL2. 27 ff.   [43] Ibid.

based on this text,[44] but neither bears any resemblance to this setting. Mahler made no alterations, except to suppress two stanzas: the first, in which the mother announces that the wheat will be sown, and the penultimate one, in which she promises to grind the grain. He thus shortened the poem and intensified the drama. In the last line, he replaced 'schon auf der Bahr' with 'auf der Totenbahr'.

Orchestration: 2 flutes, 2 oboes and cor anglais, 2 clarinets, 2 bassoons, 1 trumpet, cymbals, and strings (divided).

Form: Strophic song. The expressive intensity grows relentlessly until the tragic end. While the mother's 'warte nur' symbolically remains the same, the child's cry, 'Gib mir Brot', continually changes key (Eb minor, Ab minor, Eb minor, Cb minor, and Fb minor) until the final climactic high Gb. The melodic interval of a rising minor ninth symbolizes with astonishing realism the anguish of the starving child, whose pleas go unheard and who will die before the bread is baked. The continuous sixteenth-note ostinato of the accompaniment gives the feeling of feverish urgency but at the same time evokes the slow, harsh grind of daily life (the *Weltlauf*, to use Adorno's famous term borrowed from Hegel) which forever drives on, untroubled by human suffering, until it is interrupted by the final muffled cymbal clash. Despite the economy of means employed, this is one of the most gripping of all Mahler's songs, because of the unyielding monotony of the accompaniment and the contrast between the child's plea, continually modulating as it grows ever more pressing, and the stubbornly repetitive replies of the mother.

John Williamson[45] has drawn attention to the accompaniment to the 'narrator's' lines: Mahler reduces his accompanying semiquavers to a single line, pulsing gently on Bb and Cb. Above this, the voice part is filled out in parallel six-three chords which acquire strange chromatic inflections at 'rief das Kind noch immerdar'. The clashes generated here are such as to imply a loss in the narrator's impartiality, a sudden declaration of sympathy with the suffering child. This is intensified by the seeming neutrality with which the narrator had begun: it is he who revolts against fate, rather than the indifferent mother.

(*f*) 'Des Antonius von Padua Fischpredigt' (St Anthony of Padua's Sermon to the Fishes)

Composition: I have already related[46] the curious history of this Lied's composition. It was one of the most unusual episodes in Mahler's creative life since, rather than borrowing the substance of a symphonic movement from an earlier song, as he did several times, he worked on the Lied and the symphonic Scherzo simultaneously. Mahler explained the song's symbolic meaning to Natalie in the following terms:

A somewhat sweet-sour humour reigns in the *Fischpredigt*. The blessed Anthony preaches to the fishes, but his speech sounds completely drunken, slurred (in the clarinet) and confused. And what a glittering multitude! The eels and carps and the sharp-nosed pikes, with their stupid expressions as they look at Antonius, stretching their stiff, unbending necks out of the water: I practically saw them in the music and burst out laughing. Then, the sermon over, the assembly swims away in all directions:

---

[44] *DLH* i. 580.   [45] See Williamson, 'Rhetoric', 3.   [46] See Vol. i, Chap. 18.

The Sermon has pleased
They remain as ever!

not an atom the wiser, although the saint has performed for them! Only very few people will understand the satire on humanity in this story![47]

Autographs: AFC, v & p (8 July 1893), with dedication to Arnold Rosé and an added note: 'A preliminary study for the Scherzo of the Second': PML (Lehman dep.); AFC, v & o (Steinbach, 1 Aug. 1893): HLH.

Key: C minor (as in low voice edn., with one F major section) (1st and 2nd perfs.: Anton Moser, baritone, 1905; 3rd: Fritz Weidemann, baritone, 1905).

Time signature: 3/8.

Rhythm: Slow ländler.

Tempo: *Behäbig. Mit Humor* (Comfortable. With humour). ♪ = 152 (MS piano/PHL; ♪ = 138; orchestra/HLH).

Text: Vol. i. 375, reproduced with many changes, inversions, cuts, etc., in the *Wunderhorn* from Abraham a Sancta Clara's *Judas, der Erzschelm*.[48] (Mahler made no changes apart from omitting the second and fourth refrain 'Kein Predigt niemalen', altering three insignificant words and repeating the penultimate line).

Orchestration: 2 flutes, 2 oboes, 3 clarinets, 3 bassoons, 2 horns, timpani, triangle, rute, tamtam, big drum, and cymbals, and strings.

Form: Strophic, rondo form, but, as usual, with considerable freedom of treatment: the phrase that opens the first stanza is repeated at the beginning of the next, but, as usual, the continuation is always slightly different. Thus, 'Mahler once again alludes to strophic form by means of two gestures repeated sporadically in the vocal line, and he has reminded his listener that the text is indeed strophic, though his setting is really ternary'.[49] In the overall AABA structure, each section is made up of two poetic stanzas. The contracting B episode has a Trio character, and indeed plays that role in the symphonic Scherzo. As in 'Rheinlegendchen' and 'Wer hat dies Liedlein erdacht?', there is a continuous sixteenth-note motion, in ternary rhythm and sometimes in thirds. As usual, Mahler thinks mainly in terms of polyphony, and the figuration in thirds often runs on with complete disregard for the harmonies they engender. The parallel fifths in the bass produce an odd, archaic effect. Mahler's annotations in the autograph score of the Scherzo show that he was thus deliberately violating the sacrosanct 'laws' of composition (see above, Vol. i, Appendix 1, on the Scherzo of the Second Symphony).

An interesting feature of this song has been described by Jon Finson:

. . . in a melody like that for 'Antonius', he adopts the conventional folk manner of dealing with an unaccented initiation. . . . But the fifth measure . . . begins a melodic process very different from that found in German folk song. Here a new motive appears, and the line descends by means of immediate sequential repetition to the dominant. Mahler returns to the tonic by means of a similar falling sequence which entails, moreover, fragmentation and a touch of chromaticism. The melody . . . is extremely teleological: it uses motivic material in an intensely redundant fashion to promote a strong sense of direction. And though the motives themselves resemble fragments of diatonic folk melody, manipulation often leads them into

[47] NBL1. 10; NBL2. 28.
[48] Abraham a Sancta Clara, *Sämtliche Werke*, ed. Friedrich Winckler (Passau, 1895), ii. 47 ff.
[49] See Finson, 'Reception', 91 ff.

chromatic realms, explaining why Mahler's lines can sound at once both somewhat familiar and also exotic.[50]

The initial eighth-note motif (G-C-E♭-D-C), with its typical Mahlerian fourth on the upbeat, returns at the beginning of each poetic stanza like a refrain. The composition is full of subtle and interesting details, such as the anticipation of the vocal motif of B in the second A stanza, and the statement, in the middle of B, of a new short melody ('cantabile'), which plays an important part in the Scherzo of the Second. Mahler himself recognized in the 'Fischpredigt' the 'Bohemian music of his birthplace . . . The national feeling shows up in its crudest basic features, borrowed from the piping (*Gedudel*) of the itinerant Bohemian musicians.'[51] Vladimir Karbusicky has pointed out the similarity between the clarinet's quaver ostinatos and a Bohemian folk dance, the *Rejdovák* or *Rejdovačky* (or *Redowa*), the region's commonest dance with the polka.[52]

(g) 'Rheinlegendchen' (Little Rhine Legend)

Composition: Mahler told Natalie that the main musical theme for this song emerged first in his mind and that he had then looked through the anthology to find words to suit it:

consequently the result differs greatly from the *Wunderhorn-Lieder* composed earlier in Leipzig: it is much more direct, that is, at once childish, mischievous and heartfelt; you have never heard anything like it! And the instrumentation is both gentle and sunny, like the pure colours of a butterfly. But, despite its folklike simplicity, it is also highly unusual, especially as regards the harmony, so that people will not understand it and will call it far-fetched. Nevertheless, the harmonies are the most natural imaginable, simply those which the melody required.[53]

Autographs: AFC, v & p (9 Aug. 1893), entitled 'Tanzreime für hohe Stimmlage': BSB; AFC, v & o (10 Aug. 1893): PML (Lehman dep.).

Key: A major (high voice) (1st and 2nd perfs.: Paul Bulss, baritone, 1893; 3rd: Anton Moser 1905) (on the piano MS: ♪ = 132).

Text: Vol. i. 458, under the title 'Rheinischer Bundesring'. Mahler's original title was 'Tanzreime', and later 'Tanzlegendchen'. He made practically no changes in the text, two stanzas of which are of Bavarian or Tyrolian folk origin, and the rest art poetry (no doubt by Arnim or Brentano).

Orchestration: flute, oboe, clarinet, bassoon, horn, and strings. Edward Kravitt points out the unusually large number of dynamic markings in this song (nevertheless scored for small orchestra): sometimes 'the composer calls for a special nuance not only for each beat but even for each half-beat.'[54] In the Vienna and Graz performances, 8 first violins, 6 second violins, 6 altos, 6 cellos, and 2 double-basses (?) took part.[55]

Form: *Tanzlied* in Mahler's most characteristically Austrian vein. Instead of retaining the strophic construction of the poem, Mahler divides the song into two 16-bar

---

[50] Ibid. 113 ff. [51] NBL2. 28. [52] VKM 52.
[53] NBL1. 11; NBL2. 29. [54] Kravitt, 'Orchestral Lied', 219.
[55] See Hilmar-Voit, 'Symphonischer Klang'.

sections. Elisabeth Schmierer calls this structure 'ambiguous', if only because the last two stanzas are separated by a two-bar Interlude which destroys the symmetry. The first notes of the vocal theme recur at the beginning of each musical stanza, as do several other melodic fragments, but what follows is always different. Beneath the usual appearance of folk-like innocence and spontaneity, the vocal line links a whole series of distinct melodic strains which are unified only by the ländler rhythm and the continuous semiquaver movement. Not only is the atmosphere similar to that of the Fourth Symphony, but so is the technique. Even the ritenuto upbeat (in the second bar), an effect characteristic of ternary dance music, and found in many Strauss waltzes, is present at the very beginning of the Symphony.

Fritz Egon Pamer's detailed enumeration[56] of the purely 'folk music' features in the song's principal melody is worth quoting: they include the structure of the first phrase, its eight-bar periods, the dance rhythms, the sequential appoggiaturas, and, in the accompaniment, the succession of simple chords and the 'Nachsatz' (second part of the first phrase), modulating to the dominant. But Pamer also points out many other features that are quite foreign to the folk-song idiom, such as the highest note in the first vocal phrase appearing on an unaccented beat, and the end of the same phrase, 'Was hilft mir', with its sudden return from the key of F♯ major to E minor. Most of the harmonies are, as Mahler himself noted, far from obvious.[57] Once again, Jon Finson makes an interesting point:

The technique of motivic usage is drawn, of course, from the classical tradition of German instrumental music. . . . Mahler's melodies are brilliant studies in variation, repetition and fragmentation, the hallmarks of German developmental art music. Mahler's referential structure, then, alludes by citation or imitation to the conventions and vocabulary of folk music, but he manipulates these elements using the ultimate refinements of art music. Mahler's critics were quite correct in perceiving a dichotomy in his *Wunderhorn* settings. . . . what reviewers saw as contradiction was a source of interest in his time and remains so today: what contemporary reviewers saw as a contradiction we view as fascinating tension. The dichotomy is at once disquieting and compelling.[58]

The well-known folk melody, 'Das Märchen vom Ringlein', quoted by Pamer[59] has much in common with Mahler's (see Ex. 4). Pamer has also quoted the Trio in ländler rhythm from Schubert's 1826 G major Sonata, D. 894, which is closely related to one of Mahler's melodic fragments (see Exx. 5 and 6).

Ex. 4. 'Das Märchen vom Ringlein'

[56] Pamer, 'Gustav Mahlers Lieder', 221. [57] NBL1. 11; NBL2. 29.
[58] Finson, 'Reception', 114 ff. [59] Pamer, 'Gustav Mahlers Lieder', 221.

Ex. 5. 'Rheinlegendchen'

Ex. 6. Schubert, Sonata in G, D. 894 (trio)

(h) **'Lied des Verfolgten in Turm'** (Song of the Prisoner in the Tower)

Composition: This Lied and the following one were composed during the summer of
   1898, in Vahrn.
Autographs: AFC, v & p, numbered '8' (Vahrn, July 1898): PML (Lehman col.).
Key: D minor (as in high voice edn.: 1st perf.: Anton Moser, baritone, 1905).
Time signature: 12/8 (changing to 6/8 for the girl's stanza).
Tempo: *Leidenschaftlich, eigenwillig* (passionate, wilfully obstinate), alternating with
   verzagt, schmeichlerisch (despondent, flattering).
Text: Vol. ii. 338. In the original poem, of Swiss-German origin, quoted by Fritz Egon
   Pamer, there is no dialogue. The girl's stanzas were added by Arnim and Brentano.
   Mahler has made no changes other than to repeat two lines and cut out another ('und
   was mich erquicket', in the penultimate stanza. In the orchestral MS in PML, each
   dialogue intercept is preceded by 'Der Gefangene' (The Prisoner) or 'Das Mädchen'
   (The Girl).
Orchestration: 2 flutes, 2 oboes, 2 clarinets, 2 bassoons, 4 horns, 2 trumpets, timpani,
   and strings. In the Vienna and Graz concerts of 1905, 10 first violins, 8 second
   violins, 6 violas, 6 cellos, and 3 double-basses (?) took part.[60]

   [60] See Hilmar-Voit, 'Symphonischer Klang'. Only one trumpet was used, although two parts had been
prepared.

Form: Like most of the dialogue songs, it can be summarized as ABABABA, a rondo form made up of two strongly contrasted episodes. However this is only a very rough approximation of what occurs in this song, which Elisabeth Schmierer analyses in great detail, listing the innumerable subtleties and asymmetries which Mahler has introduced within a traditional frame.[61]

The stanzas proceed through a succession of different keys: D minor, G major, G minor, B♭ major, C major, F major, D minor: Mahler returns to the opening key only at the end. Although the short A sections, in minor, remain nearly identical despite their change of key, there are considerable differences between the girl's lyrical stanzas, all in major. The second, which is the longest, displays Mahler's most ingenious development and counterpoint techniques. The portamento upbeats are inspired by the yodel singing style. The third A stanza is brilliantly accompanied by trumpets and horn. Another striking and archaic succession of 'crude' fifths can be detected here in the bass, followed by a motif borrowed from the accompaniment of B. Given the subject-matter, it is not surprising to find a host of military effects such as march rhythm, fast triplet upbeats, and trumpet calls in arpeggio form (even in the vocal part). At the same time the descending chromatic fragments and relentless rhythm express the same bitterness and despair as the text, a feeling rarely found with such intensity in Mahler's Lieder. The contrast between the odd stanzas (1, 3, 5, and 7) and the 'feminine' stanzas in the major mode is so sudden and so startling that it becomes an effect in itself. Although the thematic contents of the two groups are more clearly linked than, say, in 'Schildwache Nachtlied', Mahler needed all his word skill to unify such totally dissimilar elements.[62]

(i) 'Wo die schönen Trompeten blasen' (Where the Proud Trumpets Blow)

Composition: Like the preceding song, this one was composed in Vahrn in 1898. It is therefore, by date, the last in the collection. Mahler mentioned it only once, in the presence of Natalie, who records his words in an unpublished passage of her *Mahleriana* (January 1900),[63] just before the song's first performance. It seems that Siegfried Lipiner and Albert Spiegler both believed the poem's male figure to be dead, appearing before his sweetheart as a ghost, while Mahler himself saw him alive but imagining his death on the battlefield.

Autographs: AFC, v & p, numbered '9' (July 1898): PML (Lehman dep.).

Key: D minor (as high voice edn.) (1st perf.: Selma Kurz, soprano, 1900; 2nd: Anton Moser, baritone, 1905).

Time signature: 2/4 alternating with 3/4 in secondary sections.

Tempo: *Verträumt. leise* (dreamily, softly), *sehr gehalten* (very restrained). In the PML MS: *Geheimnisvoll zart, durchaus leise* (tender and mysterious, quiet throughout).

Text: Passages chosen from two poems in Vol. ii (406, 'Unbeschreibliche Freude'; 378, 'Bildchen'), which have about ten lines in common. In fact, Mahler practically invented a new poem. Stanzas 1, 2, and 3 of the first poem are quoted verbatim, while

---

[61] Schmierer, *Orchesterlieder Mahlers*, 133 ff.

[62] Elisabeth Schmierer's book contains a detailed analysis of the harmonic scheme of this song. It brings out the sharpness of contrast between the complex harmonies and the simplicity of the vocal line. (Ibid. 140 ff.)

[63] NBLS.

5, 6, and 8 of the second are altered, particularly by the addition of the girl's lines ('Willkommen lieber Knabe mein!'). According to Pamer, the last stanzas of 'Bildchen' are not true folk poetry, and Mahler replaced them with verses from another poem because of their somewhat artificial character. The words and lines added by him are more naïve than the originals and therefore closer to the folk style. Pamer calls his work a 'philological restoration'.

Orchestration: 2 flutes, 2 oboes, 2 clarinets, 2 bassoons, 4 horns, 2 trumpets, and strings. In the Vienna and Graz performances of 1905, 8 first violins, 6 second violins, 6 violas, 4 cellos, and 1 double-bass (?) took part.[64]

Form: The dialogue is once again of an 'imaginary nature'. According to Elisabeth Schmierer the role of the instrumental prelude, a distant echo of military music, is to create this 'imaginary' atmosphere. Its expressive content resembles that of the first two original stanzas of the poem, which Mahler suppressed. Schmierer points out that the 'dialogue' in the music does not adhere exactly to that of the text. The number of the lines awarded to the male figure (3/4, in major, with string accompaniment) varies considerably, while, for once, elements of military music accompany the girl's lines. The roles of the two partners are, as it were, inverted and this occurs in no other dialogue Lied by Mahler. Schmierer summarizes the (rondo) form as A, B, A', C, A", B', A", i.e. a much more complex structure than that of the other dialogue songs. Stanzas A' and A" do not belong to either of the protagonists but to a 'narrator'. Schmierer's harmonic résumé reveals important features such as the dissonances resulting from the pedal-note (or suspension). Sequences of fifths occur once again.[65] Only in the last stanza, when imagination gives way to reality, do the trumpet and horns play for the first time without mutes.

Each episode is in a different key: D minor to D major, back to D minor, G♭, B minor, D major, and D minor. Only the last one returns to the original key. The whole song, a genuine tone poem in Mahler's most evocative vein, is based on the sounds of the trumpet and the horn and their 'signals'. Nothing in the text suggests that the soldier is a ghost, yet the very character of the nocturnal and distant music seems to imply it (contrary to what Mahler himself stated): the feelings expressed are or seem to be those of someone who has lost all contact with life's vanities.

The mastery of form and technique attained by Mahler at the time of the Fourth Symphony is evident throughout this song, in which the stylized military 'signals' are endlessly transformed. Just before the voice enters, distant, ghostly drum rolls echo from the low strings, with characteristic triplets on the upbeats. Mahler's use of rhythm here achieves new heights. After the end of the instrumental prelude, the three bars in 3/4 are both a written-out allargando and a suggestion of the later B section. The brass signals' arpeggios, on which the beginning of the vocal A section is based, contrast with the conjunct degrees of the B melody, accompanied by muted pianissimo strings playing in sixths. The emotional climax of the song, indeed one of the finest passages in all of Mahler's music, is the melting G♭ lullaby episode (C) with its muted string accompaniment. An amazing intensity of expression is achieved throughout, although the dynamics never exceed forte. Pamer draws a parallel between the initial oboe theme and Luigi Denza's, 'Funiculi, funicula',

---

[64] See Hilmar-Voit, 'Symphonischer Klang', 10.   [65] Schmierer, *Orchesterlieder Mahlers*, 133 ff.

which Mahler particularly liked,[66] and an even more striking parallel between the main vocal melody and a *mitteldeutsch* folk-song, 'Die Freundenlose' (see Ex. 7).[67]

Ex. 7. 'Die Freudenlose'

For Hans Heinrich Eggebrecht this song exemplifies an expressive principle inherent in the whole of Mahler's music, the illustration of an edge-situation, in which day-to-day normality includes the horror of war in a mutual dialectic of ambivalence; there is no escape because the human subject, personified by the soldier, consciously identifies with it. Mahler's composition transposes this unity of opposites into purely musical terms: the trumpet, a 'beautiful' instrument, symbolizes beauty (popular theme in triplets and thirds) as well as war and death, just as the green turf is both the place for love and the place for war.[68] Both Eggebrecht and John Williamson[69] mention the importance of the sforzato dissonance on an augmented fourth resolving in a melismatic figure, whose status, initially ornamental, only acquires full affective weight in the passage 'Das Mädchen fing zu weinen an'.

(*j*) 'Lob des hohen Verstandes' (In praise of high intelligence)

Composition: The last song, no. 10 in the orchestral *Wunderhorn* collection, was composed before those numbered 8 and 9, in mid-June 1896, while Mahler was awaiting the arrival of the sketches for the first movement of the Third Symphony, which had been mailed to him from Hamburg. Like the other songs, 'Lob des hohen Verstandes' was certainly orchestrated immediately. Mahler's original title was 'Lob der Kritik'. He called it 'a humorous mockery of the critics'. 'You'll laugh when you hear it,' he wrote to Mildenburg.[70] He was delighted by the poem: 'In this case, my problem was not to spoil anything, and to reproduce faithfully all that it contained, whereas elsewhere one can often add a great deal, deepen and enrich the poetic substance with music.'[71]

---

[66] See above, Chap. 7.   [67] *DLH* ii. 396.

[68] Hans Heinrich Eggebrecht, '"Wo die schönen Trompeten blasen": Über die Musik Gustav Mahlers', author's communication, 1990.

[69] Williamson, 'Rhetoric' (see n. 36), 7

[70] See above, Vol. i, Chap. 22, and undated letter to Anna von Mildenburg (Tuesday [16 June 1896]), not included in MBR2.

[71] NBL1. 40; NBL2. 56.

Autographs: APD in E major, entitled 'Lob der Kritik', originally belonging to Anton Webern (14 June 1896): NUE; APD (21 June 1896): MAS.

Key: D major (same as high voice).

Time signature: 2/4.

Rhythm: Binary dance ('bourrée').

Tempo: *Keck* (cheekily).

Text: Vol. i. 476, under the title 'Wettstreit des Kuckuks mit der Nachtigall' (The Contest between the Cuckoo and the Nightingale). The sixteenth-century five-voice setting of the poem by a Nuremberg Mastersinger was published as no. 14 in Jacob Regnart's anthology, *Neue kurtzweilige Teutsche Lieder*, and it includes an extra stanza, not in the *Wunderhorn* version. A nearly identical version of the same poem was included by Goethe's friend, Johann Gottfried Herder, in an anthology named *Volkslieder*, which appeared in the late 1770s and was republished in 1809 under the title *Stimmen der Völker in Liedern*.[72] Mahler made many small alterations, cutting out some words, adding or altering others, deleting two whole lines from the fourth stanza. At the end of the third stanza the call 'Ija' is his, as is the 'Kuckuk, Kuckuk, Ija!' at the end, a comic combination of the two 'languages', that of the victor and that of the judge.

Orchestration: 2 flutes, 2 oboes, 3 clarinets, 2 bassoons, 4 horns, trumpet, trombone, tuba, timpani, triangle, and strings. At the Vienna and Graz performances, 12 first violins, 10 second violins, 8 violas, 6 cellos, and 2 double-basses (?) took part.[73]

Form: Simple strophic structure: AAABA. The third A section starts in minor, to a grotesque accompaniment of horns, bassoons, and trombones, but is abruptly cut off at the end of the first phrase. The orchestra takes up and pursues the main line, and the voice enters only a few bars later for a single bar, in unison with the strings. The length of the interludes somewhat upsets the natural balance of the stanzas: these elaborate tutti give to the simple Lied a strong 'art song' flavour. The last stanza is a restatement of the first. The voice soon restates, in octaves with the woodwind, the instrumental prelude. To this is added a tiny coda in which the cuckoo sings in thirds, like the real bird, rather than in fourths as in the Introduction to the First Symphony. The dotted rhythms with their rapid triple quavers give the whole song an archaic, parodic flavour.

Mahler himself quoted from this song in the beginning of the final Rondo of the Fifth Symphony. Pamer notes two interesting similarities, the first between the main theme of the Lied and a fragment from a Tübingen folk-song, itself similar to the *Quodlibet* from Bach's *Goldberg Variations* (see Ex. 8). The second is between a fragment from the last movement of the Schubert G major Sonata, D. 894 (bars 21 and 22), and one of the orchestral interludes in 'Lob des hohen Verstandes' (bars 70 and 71): see Exx. 9 and 10.

Mahler conducted 'Lob des hohen Verstandes' only once, on 3 February 1905, with Marie Gutheil Schoder as soloist, in the repeat of his Lieder concert of 29 January, which had included many world premières of *Wunderhorn-Lieder*. Why had he left out this Lied in the first concert (and why did he do so again later in the Graz

---

[72] See Herta Blaukopf, 'Die deutsche Romantik und Mahler', in James L. Zychowicz, ed., *The Seventh Symphony of Gustav Mahler* (University of Cincinnati, 1990), 3.

[73] See Hilmar-Voit, 'Symphonischer Klang'.

Ex. 8. 'Lob des hohen Verstandes'

"Es wohnte eine Müllerin", Folk-song from Tübingen

Lob des hohen Verstandes

Quodlibet from Bach's *Goldberg Variations*

Ich   bin   so   lang   nit   bei   dir__   gwest.

Ex. 9. 'Lob des hohen Verstandes'

Ex. 10. Schubert, Sonata in G, D. 894

concert)?[74] Did he perhaps fear that the critics would understand only too well that they were the object of the satire and that this would increase their hostility towards his music?

Two further Lieder were included in the original voice and piano edition of the orchestral *Wunderhorn-Lieder.*

(k) 'Es sungen drei Engel einen süssen Gesang' (Three Angels Sang a Sweet Song)

The song version is called 'women's chorus from the Third Symphony. Transcription for one voice.' The first three bars, i.e. the children's chorus 'Bim, Bam', are of course

---

[74] According to Renate Hilmar-Voit, a note written on the instrumental parts of this song by the hornist Alois Schantl, proves that it was indeed performed at the Graz concert, although it was not included in the printed programme.

eliminated, as are the last ten decrescendo bars. The published versions are in E♭ (low voice); or F (high voice, as in the symphony).

When Donald Mitchell examined the various versions of this transcription,[75] he made a curious discovery. Mahler's solo voice version was published with the rest of the collection in 1900, in a version with piano. Strange as it may seem, when Universal Edition reissued the voice and piano version of all the *Wunderhorn-Lieder* around 1913, the arrangement of 'Es sungen drei Engel' was no longer Mahler's, but a different, anonymous one, much closer to the symphonic movement than to the composer's own arrangement, although an inscription on it claims that it was done by Mahler. Donald Mitchell supposes that the anonymous arranger was none other than Josef Venantius von Wöss, author of numerous piano transcriptions of Mahler. He must have known Mahler's own version, since he suppresses a modification of the *Wunderhorn* text which figures in the symphonic movement ('Liebe zu Gott nur alle Zeit' instead of 'Bete zu Gott' in the original), but which Mahler abandoned in his transcription. Donald Mitchell thinks that Mahler's version for piano deserves to be known and sung today, since it is different from the symphonic movement, preserves the integral text from the anthology, and thus constitutes an authentic *Wunderhorn-Lied* rather than a transcription.[76] Unfortunately Mahler never took the time to orchestrate this version for solo voice. Thus the only existing orchestral score is that by Josef von Wöss of his own version, published in the 1920s.

(*l*) 'Urlicht' (Primeval Light)

This is the piano original of the orchestral song that Mahler inserted in the Second Symphony as a slow introduction to the Finale (see Vol. i, App. 1). The key is the same (D♭). The whereabouts of the original version, for voice and piano, is not known. Thus the first available source is Hermann Behn's two-piano version, which is part of the early transcription he made of the Second Symphony. In a letter to Behn, Mahler mentions the now missing voice and piano version, 'the original version of the composition . . . before I knew I would orchestrate it and insert it in the symphony'. The orchestration was filled out when the song was inserted in the Symphony. The version for voice and piano published in 1900 by Weinberger and in 1914 by Universal Edition is probably the original version with piano (1893). The orchestral manuscript of this Lied is in the British Library, London. It bears the title: 'Urlicht aus dem Knaben Wunderhorn. No. 7 für eine Singstimme mit Orchester von Gustav Mahler'. It is dated Steinbach, 19 July 1893.

FOURTH SYMPHONY
(1899–1900)

Composition

Mahler had spent four entire summers (1893–6) composing two symphonies of vast dimensions, the Second and the Third. Then came the most important event in his

---

[75] *DLH* ii. 396. See below.   [76] DMM2. 129 ff.

professional career, his appointment as director of the Vienna Opera. The directorship involved an enormous increase in administrative and artistic responsibilities, and this, combined with a period of ill health, prevented him from engaging in creative activity for the next two summers. When the urge to compose came upon him again, in Alt-Aussee at the end of June 1899, he did not embark immediately on a new symphonic project, but spent the first weeks of his holidays revising the Third Symphony and correcting the proofs of *Das klagende Lied*. Then one day without warning he drafted the complete sketch for 'Revelge', and the mood for composition was upon him. Work on the Fourth Symphony started in mid-July and lasted until the end of the month, when his duties as director compelled him to return to Vienna and the Opera. I have described above[1] how his frustration mounted at the thought that he would have to tear himself away with the new work far from completed and a stream of new ideas constantly surging into his mind.

Remembering the descriptive title he had originally given to his first orchestral *Wunderhorn-Lieder*, he decided that it suited the light-hearted character of the new work, and accordingly named it 'Symphony No. 4 *(Humoreske)*'. The original plan contained three songs (Nos. 2, 4, and 6), instead of the one in the final version:

No. 1: 'Die Welt als ewige Jetztzeit' (The World as Eternal Now), G major
No. 2: 'Das irdische Leben' (The Earthly Life), Eb minor
No. 3: 'Caritas' (Adagio), B major
No. 4: 'Morgenglocken' (Morning Bells), F major
No. 5: 'Die Welt ohne Schwere' (The World Without Gravity), D Major (Scherzo)
No. 6: 'Das himmlische Leben'[2] (The Heavenly Life), G major

This plan was undoubtedly drawn up several years earlier, contemporaneously with that of the Third Symphony, since it can be seen that Mahler was still considering using 'Morgenglocken' (which he finally used as the fifth movement in the Third) and also 'Das irdische Leben', which now forms part of the *Wunderhorn* collection of orchestral songs. The Fourth's C minor Scherzo is not to be found in this early draft, and the D major Scherzo mentioned is undoubtedly the one which eventually became part of the Fifth Symphony. The other movements are those of the present symphony. Can the planned B major 'Caritas' movement be identified with the Fourth's Adagio? It is of course as close in spirit to the Finale of the Third, as 'Caritas' is to 'Love', but it is rare indeed to see Mahler change the key of a projected movement. The title 'Caritas' reappeared in 1906 in the first sketched 'synopsis' of the Eighth Symphony.

Between the summer during which the Fourth was begun, and the next summer when it was completed, there occurred another important event in Mahler's life: the purchase of the Maiernigg plot of land and the building of the *Häuschen*. Mahler arrived there at the end of June 1900 exhausted by his visit to Paris, and took some time to settle down to work again. When he finally succeeded (at the time of his birthday, i.e. around 7 July), he realized that the symphony had developed and progressed in his mind, although he had never consciously thought about it. He put this down to the activity of a mysterious 'second self'. Later on, he stated that three of

---

[1] See above Chap. 6.

[2] BMS 145. The page on which this plan is noted in very careful writing belonged to Paul Bekker, the author of the first major work on the Mahler symphonies (BMS). Alma Mahler gave it to him as a present in 1919. It now belongs to the Public Library of Cincinnati and Hamilton County.

the movements had been left uncompleted in Aussee. However, the first two had probably been close to completion and his main task, during the second summer, was to compose the Adagio. It was interrupted by a few days' trip to the Dolomites, after which he completed the slow movement, which is dated 'Sunday 6 August [1900]' in the first orchestral score.[3]

Contrary to his earlier habit at Steinbach, Mahler did not speak to Natalie about his new symphony until 1 August, when the *Partiturentwurf*[4] was nearly completed. At this time he estimated its duration as about forty-five minutes. During the following winter he managed to spend some time each day working on the new work. According to Natalie, the Scherzo was then 'restored in its first version', 'as he had originally sketched it' (although its first ending had been a 'tarentella' that is not to be found in the final version). In January, while in bed with the flu, he worked on the first theme of the first movement[5] and, in April, barely recovered from the haemorrhage that had almost cost him his life, he received the score fresh from the copyist's hand. He was then amazed to discover that the Scherzo had been placed third instead of second and that two versions of the same passage in the Adagio had been included whereas he had meant them as alternative versions. Thus, he reflected, if he had not recovered from the haemorrhage these errors would probably never have been detected.

In Abbazia, where he spent several weeks of convalescence after his operation in April 1901, he revised the orchestration of the Finale, which was until then identical with that of the earlier *Wunderhorn-Lied*. Back in Vienna, he continued retouching and correcting the copied score, explaining that he was only able to see what changes were needed when the handwriting was no longer his own. He also confessed that he would only be able to straighten out the last details when he had the printer's proofs in front of him. And in fact he finally corrected the proofs only after reading the work through with the Philharmonic Orchestra, at the end of October, shortly before the Munich première.[6]

Although the Fourth Symphony resembles no other work by Mahler, in that it breathes happiness, *joie de vivre*, and serenity, it was, as seen above, written during a period of ill health and anxiety. Furthermore, this happy work invariably aroused hostile reactions from the public and the press, at least during Mahler's lifetime. The main reason for its early failure is easy to discern: the musical public expected from Mahler more 'large' symphonies like the Second and the Third. The Fourth's 'humour', its references to a classical past, seemed just as artificial and lacking in authenticity as the folk style of the earlier *Wunderhorn-Lieder*.

Autographs, Different Versions, Editions

In the introduction to the first critical edition of the work, published in 1963 by Universal Edition in the Internationale Gustav Mahler Gesellschaft series, Erwin Ratz prepared a first list of autograph sources for this symphony. It has now been completed and implemented by James L. Zychowicz, in a scholarly and comprehensive disserta-

[3] The real date, as seen above in Chap. 8, was undoubtedly 5 Aug., which was a Sunday. An error in date seems more likely than a wrong day of the week.

[4] This is the name usually given today to the first orchestral score (AOD) Mahler wrote after his three- or four-stave *Particell* (APD). He always revised it extensively later on.

[5] NBLS.   [6] NBL1. 170; NBL2. 197 ff. and NBLS.

tion on the Fourth and its autograph sources.[7] From the preliminary sketches of the first movement, a single page of part of the exposition is in SUL,[8] another, for the development section is in BBC. There are two two-page sketches for the same section, one in NLC and the other privately owned. A photocopy of a single-page sketch for the recapitulation is in IMG. ÖNB owns a group of sketches of the Scherzo. PML (Lehman deposit) has a single-page sketch for the second theme of the Adagio and ÖNB a single-page sketch for the 'Presto' variation in the same movement.[9]

A complete set (sixteen pages) belonging to the *Particell* (APD) of the Adagio (up to the Presto variation) is in PML, while a *Particell* of the exposition of the first movement is in private hands. The first page of the APD of the first movement was sold at Stargardt in 1977. The AOD which used to belong to Alma Mahler is now in MAS, minus the last bifolio (BGM). IMG owns partial photocopies. The AOD does not include the Finale, which Mahler must have copied later. It concludes with the mention: *Dritter Satz und somit die ganze Symphonie Sonntag 6 August* [actually 5 August 1900] *zu Maiernigg beendet* (third movement and with it the whole symphony finished in Maiernigg Sunday 6 August). Two *Einlagen* (insertions) for bifolio 10 of the first movement, and for bifolio 5 of the third are in ÖNB. Finally, a four-page scored fragment of the opening of the Scherzo, with seventeen bars of the violin solo noted on a separate sheet, dated 29 December 1900 and dedicated by Mahler to Arnold Rosé on 11 January 1902, the day before the Viennese première, belongs to RWO.[10] It is clear that the composer worked with his brother-in-law on the solo for tuned-up violin.

Both the first edition and the orchestral parts for the work's first performance were published by Doblinger in 1902. They were based on the complete autograph orchestral score, copied by Mahler during the winter 1900–1 (GMF). It bears only one date, at the end of the Scherzo: 5 January 1901. After the first performance, the score was revised and retouched more often even than in the case of the other symphonies. The first proofs carry interesting metronome markings. Mahler made many further corrections in the summer of 1905, in view of the Graz première which was to take place on 3 November under Richard Wickenhauser.[11] They were included in 1906 in the first Universal Edition score of the symphony.[12] Others, made in the summer of 1910, were also incorporated into the later published version. However, Mahler's final version, prepared in New York after he conducted the work there in January 1911, was only

[7] James L. Zychowicz, 'Sketches and Drafts of Gustav Mahler 1892–1901: The Sources of the Fourth Symphony', Ph.D. thesis, Univ. of Cincinnati, 1988.

[8] See, above, the list of keys preceding the catalogue of works.

[9] All these sketches have been studied in detail by Stephen Hefling in 'Variations "in nuce": A Study of Mahler Sketches, and a Comment on Sketch Studies', in *Beiträge der Österreichischen Gesellschaft für Musik, 1979–81* (Bärenreiter, Kassel, 1981), 102 ff. It emerges from Hefling's study that Mahler in 1899–1900 had adopted certain work practices which did not change thereafter, such as the habit of circling passages destined for further revision, the use of different colours (pencil, blue ink, blue pencil) for the various stages of correction, etc.

[10] Now in RWO. The dedication is as follows: *Erinnere Dich bei diesem Blatte an unsere gemeinschaftliche Appretur dieses Solos! Zur Zeit meiner Reconvaleszenz* (this page will remind you of our work together on this solo! when I was convalescing).

[11] See below, Vol. iii, Chap. 4.

[12] See Gösta Neuwirth, 'Zur Geschichte der 4. Symphonie', in Rudolf Stephan (ed.), *Mahler-Interpretation* (Schott, Mainz, 1985). Since Universal Edition was not an independent firm at this time, the name of the original publisher, Doblinger, was mentioned on the title-page. A pocket score and a piano-duet arrangement by Josef Venantius von Wöss were publ. at the same time.

discovered in 1929 by Erwin Stein in the archives of Universal Edition. Stein immediately wrote an article about it in the magazine *Pult und Taktstock*. However, the changes, numerous and substantial, were ignored in editions by Boosey & Hawkes (London, 1943), International Music Publishers (New York, 1951), and Universal Edition (Vienna, 1952). They were finally incorporated into the 1963 Mahler-Gesellschaft edition.[13]

A precious document for the interpretation of the Fourth Symphony is the score annotated by Mahler and sent to Willem Mengelberg before the first Amsterdam performance on 23 October 1904. It contains corrections and explanatory notes in red ink and pencil, in Mahler's own hand, as well as a great number of annotations, metronome markings, etc., made by Mengelberg during rehearsals conducted by the composer, and later.[14]

A Programme?

Although by 1899 Mahler firmly refused to prepare explanatory programmes for his works, some of the remarks he made to Natalie come very close to providing one.[15] He defined the basic mood (*Grundstimmung*) of the Symphony as the

uniform blue of the sky which is harder to suggest than any changing and contrasting tints. But sometimes the atmosphere darkens and grows strangely terrifying. Not that the sky itself clouds over: it goes on shining with its everlasting blue. But we suddenly become afraid of it, just as on a brilliant day in the sun-dappled forest one is often overcome by a panic terror.[16]

(As with the flower movement in the Third Symphony, it is hard to identify the passages which Mahler wrote to indicate this 'panic terror'.) Later on, in 1901, he speaks of 'an unheard-of gaiety, a supraterrestrial joy, which attracts and repels at the same time; an incredible light, an incredible air, in which very touching human sounds are also present',[17] and also a gaiety 'coming from another sphere, and hence terrifying for humans: only a child can understand and explain it, and a child does explain it in the end: a child who, if only at the chrysalis stage (*Puppenstand*), already belongs to this superior world'.[18] Mahler compared the whole symphony to a primitive picture, painted on a gold background, and added that every small element and detail within it was varied, as happens with the human body and mind, 'which from birth to the grave remains always identical and yet is always different'.[19]

In August 1900, Mahler admitted that he had thought up the most beautiful titles for each movement, in the manner of those of the Third, but that he had decided not to disclose them, 'so as to avoid giving rise to further absurd misunderstandings'. He

[13] In 1966, Eulenburg (London) publ. a score based on that of 1951, with a long preface by Hans Ferdinand Redlich attacking Erwin Ratz's 1963 edn. Although he does expose some errors in the earlier editor's text, some of his arguments are unconvincing.

[14] These annotations have been listed and commentated upon at length by Klaus Kropfinger, 'Gerettete Herausforderung: Mahler 4. Symphonie—Mengelbergs Interpretation', in Stephan (ed.), *Mahler-Interpretation*, 111 ff.

[15] See above, Chap. 8.   [16] NBL1. 143; NBL2. 162 ff.

[17] Letter from Bruno Walter to Ludwig Schiedermair, 5 Dec. 1901 (BSB). The text was plainly dictated by Mahler himself.

[18] NBL1. 171; NBL2. 198. The expression *Im Puppenstand* (in the chrysalis stage) comes from the last scene of Part II of Goethe's *Faust*, which Mahler was later to set to music in the Eighth.

[19] NBLS, Oct. 1901.

never ceased to emphasize the polyphonic complexity of the work, which he envisaged as the close of a great tetralogy of symphonies.[20] (It is still generally considered nowadays as the last of the '*Wunderhorn* Symphonies'.) Mahler was aware that the new work reflected his full technical mastery at the time. In January 1901 he told Natalie of the trouble he had with the crystal-clear opening theme, whose complete beauty is only later revealed ('like a dewdrop on a flower that, suddenly illuminated by the sun, bursts into a thousand lights and colours').[21] According to the Dutch composer Alphons Diepenbrock, who wrote an analysis of the Fourth after having discussed it many times with the composer,[22] Mahler sometimes described the first movement as expressing the same 'heavenly gaiety' (*überirdische Fröhlichkeit*) as he had achieved in the Third Symphony.

The second movement originally bore the subtitle *Freund Hein spielt zum Tanz auf; der Tod streicht recht absonderlich die Fiedel und geigt uns in den Himmel hinauf* (Death strikes up the dance for us; he strokes the fiddle most strangely and plays us up to heaven).[23] The Scherzo is 'mysterious, confused (*verworren*), uncanny', Mahler said when composing this movement in 1900. 'It will make your hair stand on end. But in the Adagio which follows everything will be unravelled, and you will understand that no harm was meant after all.'[24] In October 1901, Mahler spoke of its terrifying humour again, comparing it to the Scherzo of the Second Symphony and the opening Allegro of the First. He was particularly proud of having created, with the Adagio, his first real variations (although they are of a very unconventional type: see below). A melody both 'divinely gay and deeply sad'[25] pervaded the whole movement. To this melody he lent the features of one of the saints in the Finale:

St Ursula herself, the most serious of all the saints, laughs, so gay is this higher sphere: that is to say, she smiles, and her smile resembles those on the faces of the prone statues of old knights or prelates one sees lying in churches, their hands joined on their bosoms and with the peaceful gentle expression of men who have gained access to a higher bliss; solemn, blessed peace; serious, gentle gaiety, such is the character of this movement, which also has deeply sad moments, comparable, if you wish, to reminiscences of earthly life, and other moments when the gaiety becomes very lively (*Steigerung der Heiterkeit ins Lebhafte*).[26]

Mahler also confided to Natalie that, while composing the Adagio, he could sometimes see his mother's face, as she smiled through her tears, she who had suffered so terribly, but could always resolve and pardon everything through love.[27] In the radiant final tutti of the movement, the opening of the gates of heaven, the atmosphere becomes catholic, almost churchlike.[28] For the Finale, Mahler gave no programme other than the text itself: 'When man, now full of wonder, asks what all this means, the child answers him with the fourth movement: "This is the Heavenly Life"'.[29]

[20] NBL1. 144 ff.; NBL2. 163 ff.   [21] NBL1. 154; NBL2. 180.

[22] This analysis was originally publ. in a programme of the Concertgebouw Orchestra in Amsterdam for a concert on 14 Apr. 1910, and was later included in Diepenbrock's *Verzamelde Schriften* (Spectrum, Utrecht, 1950).

[23] Extract from Bruno Walter's letter to Schiedermair, quoted from above.

[24] NBL1. 143; NBL2. 162 ff.   [25] NBL1. 144; NBL2. 163.

[26] Bruno Walter's letter to Schiedermair, quoted above.

[27] NBL1. 144; NBL2. 163.   [28] NBL2. 163.

[29] Bruno Walter's letter, quoted above.

Using Mahler's unpublished early 'titles' for the movement, Paul Bekker has suggested the following programme as being that originally conceived by Mahler:

A dreamlike journey up to the heavenly fields of Paradise, starting in the first movement with the gay tinkling of sleigh bells and proceeding through the sometimes smiling sometimes melancholy landscapes of this 'World as everlasting Now' to *Freund Hein* (Death), who is represented here in the friendly, legendary guise of the fiddler tempting his flock to follow him out of this world into the next. In the Adagio variations, which start peacefully and gather speed in a gradual crescendo, the new world spreads out ever wider and clearer before the pilgrims, who progress through a series of metamorphoses, until they reach their last abode where all their wishes are fulfilled and where spirits dance and sing in blissful play.[30]

Cyclic Procedure

In the Fourth, as in the earlier symphonies, Mahler deliberately attempted to make the work a unified whole by establishing links between the various movements, and took enormous trouble to achieve this. When the Leipzig conductor Georg Göhler failed to mention these links in the notes he drew up for the first performance in that city, in 1911, Mahler wrote to him a few days before he fell fatally ill:

Did you overlook the thematic relationships that are of such importance for the conception of the work? Or did you only feel that you must spare the public any technical explanations? In any case, I beg you to discover them in my work. Each of the first three movements has the most profound and significant thematic links with the last.[31]

Some of these thematic recurrences are obvious, like that of the opening wind ritornello in the Finale, and the anticipation of the main theme of 'Das himmlische Leben in the first movement exposition (bar 96, oboe) and development (bars 134 ff.) and at the end of the Adagio. Others are infinitely more subtle: for instance, within the first movement, the small wind fragment in bar 20, which later recurs in the coda and becomes part of the new theme in the development and which also anticipates one of the main sections of 'Das himmlische Leben'; or the fragment of Bar 22 (A"), which, augmented, becomes one of the main features of the development section and is proclaimed by the trumpets at the end of the Adagio, in the big tutti introducing the Finale (it is also found in the third bar of the main vocal theme of the Lied). Klaus Kropfinger considers that the beginning of the tuned-up violin solo in the Scherzo is a transformation of the cello and bass motif starting in bar 7 of the first movement,[32] and Paul Bekker believes the first theme (cello) of the Adagio to be derived from the opening theme of the symphony.[33]

The thematic links in the other movements, are more subtle. Some authors (Paul Bekker, Alphons Diepenbrock, and Fritz Stiedry) have noticed a resemblance between the Trio of the Scherzo and the main theme of the Finale (particularly the G♯ minor middle section of the E major coda: bar 159 ff.).[34] In the Adagio, there exists a certain affinity between the second theme (B, bar 63 ff.) and the passage 'Sankt Ursula selbst dazu lacht' in the Finale (bars 150–3), and also a link between the bass motif in bars 290–5 of the last variation of theme A and the chorale-refrain (bars 36–8) in the Finale.

[30] BMS 146.   [31] MBR1, no. 420; MBR2, no. 463.
[32] Kropfinger, 'Gerettete Herausforderung' (see n. 14), 160.   [33] BMS 143.
[34] This resemblance becomes particularly obvious in bars 78 and 79, and also in bars 212 ff. of the Scherzo.

In his study of the sketches of the work, Stephen Hefling has observed that the overall key structure of the symphony is based on intervals of a third surrounding E: first movement in G major, second movement in C minor, third and fourth movements in G major and E major.

James L. Zychowicz sets out these thematic links in a table in his thesis.[35] He draws attention among other things to the presence, in the Adagio (bars 45–7; 326–37; 344–50), of the rising *Ewigkeits-Motiv*, used for the first time in the Second Symphony and recurring in virtually all of Mahler's works (see Ex. 13). It occurs right at the beginning of the Fourth Symphony, in the wind ritornello in the Finale, in the anticipation of the principal theme of 'Das himmlische Leben' in the development of the first movement (bar 126 ff.) and at the end of the Adagio (bars 321–3). Similarly, it is clear that the periodic recurrences in the first movement of the sleigh-bell motif that opens the symphony, are recalled once more in bars 40–7 of the Finale, thus creating a link that spans the whole work from beginning to end.

Adolf Nowak, in a recent article, has shown how the 'story' of the whole symphony can be retold in terms of the transformations of the Finale motive.[36] A fragment of it appears in the winds at bar 20 of the first movement but another anticipation, in the clarinets, stands out even more at bar 32. Another anticipation comes at bar 126 ff.: this is the passage György Ligeti refers to when he points out the effect of the four flutes playing in unison. Towards the end of the development, it reappears in the trumpets (bar 221–2), after the 'childish' theme of bar 32, with which it is associated, has served as climax to the whole section. Finally, at bar 240, it replaces the main theme at the beginning of the re-exposition. Its apotheosis is of course its appearance in the trumpets ('Pesante') at the end of the Adagio, which anticipates the main theme of the Finale (bars 320–3). All the previous variations can be seen as pointing to this climactic moment. The gradual transformation of this theme

is the opposite of regression to the infantile stage! . . . The eternal now-time, which recalls in a new way the past and the classical theme-type, the sonata form, is . . . broken open by a new theme of great importance for the future course of the symphony, and which finally proves to have to do with the religious imaginings of childhood.

Analyses

Besides those included in the familiar books by Richard Specht (RSM2), Paul Bekker (BMS), and Karl Weigl (in Edgar Istel's little guide), there is a monograph by Rudolf Stephan[37] and a detailed analysis in Constantin Floros's third volume.[38] The first theme of the Adagio movement has been analysed at length by Theodor Schmitt[39] and the Finale by Bernd Sponheuer.[40]

---

[35] See 'Sketches and Drafts', 67.

[36] Adolf Nowak, 'Zur Deutung der Dritten und Vierten Sinfonie Gustav Mahlers', in Hermann Danuser (ed.), *Wege der Forschung: Gustav Mahler* (Wiss. Buchges., Darmstadt, 1992), 203 ff.

[37] In *Gustav Mahler. IV. Symphonie in G-dur* (Fink, Munich, 1966). See also, by the same author, 'Betrachtungen zu Form and Thematik in Mahlers Vierter Symphonie', in *Neue Wege der Musikalischen Analyse* (Merseburger, Berlin, 1967), 23 ff.

[38] In *Gustav Mahler*, iii, *Die Symphonien* (Breitkopf & Härtel, Wiesbaden, 1985), 102 ff.

[39] In *Der langsame Symphoniesatz Gustav Mahlers* (Fink, Munich, 1983), 106 ff.

[40] In *Logik des Zerfalls: Untersuchungen zum Finalproblem in den Symphonien Gustav Mahlers* (Schneider, Tutzing, 1978), 183 ff.

Orchestration

4 flutes (including piccolos), 3 oboes (including cor anglais), 3 clarinets (including bass and E flat clarinet), 3 bassoons (including contrabassoon), 4 horns, 3 trumpets, timpani, percussion (big drum, triangle, sleigh-bells, glockenspiel, tamtam), harp, and strings. Adorno notes that the wind instruments repeatedly challenge the strings for their dominant role even at the end of the first theme, which is played by a horn in its highest register (bars 10–11).[41]

(*a*) **Bedächtig.** *Nicht eilen* (Deliberate, unhurried). *Recht gemächlich* (very leisurely) (*Haupttempo*) (main tempo). Mengelberg's note: <u>*Der erste Satz in Ruh[ig] gemessenem Tempo* etwa! *80–92-manchesmal 96 (aber immer wieder in selbes zurck) und fliessend flottes Tempo*</u> (The first movement in calm, steady tempo! about 80–92—sometimes 96 (but always slowing down to the same again) and flowing, brisk tempo.) Over the beginning of the main theme, Mengelberg quotes a remark Mahler made to the orchestra: *Bitte spielen Sie das rall.[entando] so, als wir in Wien einen '<u>Wienerwalzer' anfangen</u>!* (Please play the rallentando in the same way as we begin a 'Viennese waltz' in Vienna.) Erwin Ratz notes that a first set of printed proofs changes the first tempo marking to *Heiter, behaglich* (gay, comfortable) (♩ = 88) and the main tempo ♩ = 76. The first edition (Doblinger) has at the beginning *Heiter, bedächtig* (gay, deliberate) with the metronome markings crossed out. The present tempo marking was introduced only in the 1905 edition.

Key: G major.
Time signature: 4/4 with a few 3/4 and 2/4 bars.
Tempo: Few movements in Mahler's *œuvre* have so many tempo changes, each one corresponding to a new musical thought. During the rehearsals before the performance conducted by Mahler in Amsterdam on 22 October 1904, Mengelberg made markings in his score which make it clear that the tempo of the introduction, *bedächtig* (deliberate): ♩ = 69 is slower than the main tempo, *gemächlich* (leisurely): ♩ = 80. In his detailed study of the Dutch conductor's score and tempo markings, Klaus Kropfinger concludes that Mengelberg's 'analytical' view of the score, his sharper and more numerous changes of tempo, emphasize the symphony's ambiguity (*Doppelbodigkeit*) and probably reflect Mahler's intentions more faithfully than Walter's more stable interpretation.[42]
Duration: 20 minutes (Amsterdam, 1904).
Form: This is one of Mahler's shortest first movements, but its conciseness only emphasizes the richness of its invention and the density of its writing. Here the composer carries the experiments of the initial Allegro in the First several steps further. None of the analyses that have so far appeared really gives an idea of its abundance and complexity. Having opted for the most concentrated style possible, and reached a point when his mature mind and polished technique constantly produced new variations (or 'variants', as Adorno calls them), Mahler never ceased to invert, augment, and combine the original motifs and even to transfer them from one theme or group of themes to another. Erwin Stein describes this procedure in the following way: 'Sometimes, he [Mahler] shuffles the motifs like a pack of cards, as it

[41] TAM 82. [42] Kropfinger, 'Gerettete Herausforderung' (see n. 14), 174ff.

were, and makes them yield new melodies. The motifs of the theme reappear, but in a different arrangement.'[43] Adorno interprets the *symphoniefremde* sleigh-bells in the Introduction in the following way: 'It is really the tinkling of a jester's bells, which, without saying it, says: What you are now hearing is completely untrue'.[44] In the first movement of this 'classical symphony', Mahler has adhered closely to the traditional criteria of sonata form.

Exposition

1–3	*Bedächtig* (deliberate). Introduction (I): composed of three motifs (flutes and clarinet): E minor (or B minor?). On Mengelberg's score, Mahler added in his own hand: *Ruhig* (calm).
4–31	*Recht gemächlich* (very leisurely). Theme A in 3 parts (A: 4 to 7; A': 8 to 17; A in imitations with leading motif of the future coda and development theme: 18 to 21; A'': 22 to 31) G major
32–7	*Frisch* (fresh). Bridge modulating from G to D major
38–57	*Breit gesungen* (broadly sung). Theme B in 3 parts: D major
58–71	*Plötzlich langsam und bedächtig* (suddenly slow and deliberate). Theme C (transition): D major. The original tempo marking was *Sehr gemächlich (langsam)* (very leisurely, slow). Mahler replaced it in Mengelberg's score with *Plötzlich langsam und bedächtig* (suddenly slow and deliberate) (*Molto meno mosso*).
72–6	Theme I: E minor (false recapitulation, introducing a rondo character to the movement)
77–90	*Tempo primo*: Theme A much varied: G major
91–101	Coda: *Wieder sehr ruhig* (very calm again)

Development

102–8	*Tempo primo*: Theme I: E minor
109–15	Theme A': E minor
116–24	Theme A: A minor
125–54	*Fliessend aber ohne Hast* (flowing, but unhurried). New theme[45] (using a motif already introduced in the middle of A (bar 20) and anticipating the main theme of Finale)
155–66	Theme I and new motif derived from bar 22 of A'', etc.: A♭ minor
167–208	Theme I, motif from A'', C, A, etc.: F minor, C minor, D minor
209–20	Fortissimo climax: Motif from A'' and bridge: C major.[46]
221–38	Motif from A'', I, trumpet call which Mahler himself entitled 'Der kleine Appel' (The little summons) return of beginning of A: F♯ major. C major.

[43] Erwin Stein, *Orpheus in New Guises* (Rockliffe, London, 1953), 7.   [44] TAM 81.

[45] György Ligeti has pointed out a chracteristic trait of Mahler's contrapuntal procedure in this symphony. The example given is bars 125–9 of the first movement, where the four flutes anticipating the theme in the Finale sound like one gigantic single flute (or like a dream ocarina, in Adorno's terms), while the bass clarinet motif in bar 127 belongs to another world and another space, as do also the cello trills and their figurations (bars 125 ff.). All events occurring at once are clearly discernible thanks to the transparent scoring, the differences in register, and Mahler's uncanny sense of timbre. (See 'Gustav Mahler und die musikalische Utopie: Musik und Raum—ein Gespräch zwischen György Ligeti und Clytus Gottwald', *Neue Zeitschrift für Musik* (Jan. 1974), 7 ff.).

[46] Adorno compares this tutti to 'the noise children make banging on pots and pans and hoping to break them' and notes that this noisy tutti returns in the recapitulation where it takes the place of the first bridge passage (bar 251 ff.) (TAM 79).

Hans Swarowsky, in his analysis of this movement, rightly claims that the 'veiled' recapitulation begins at bar 225.[47]

Recapitulation

239–52 *Wieder wie zum Anfang* (as at the beginning again): restatement of A (with augmented motif from A") starting one bar before A" itself: G major
253–62 Bridge: G major
263–82 *Schwungvoll* (racy). Theme B in strings alone: G major
283–97 *Wieder plötzlich langsam* (Suddenly slow again): Theme C
298–322 Motif I, fragments from A", A, A'

Coda

323–40 *Ruhig und immer ruhiger werden* (calm, and steadily getting calmer still): A and new development motif
341–9 *Sehr langsam* (very slow), *poco a poco stringendo*: A and bridge.

The apparent simplicity of the overall structure is of course totally deceptive, for Mahler has pushed the motivic development techniques invented by the eighteenth-century Viennese classical composers, and perfected by Beethoven, further than perhaps anyone before him—so far indeed that he creates a mosaic of constantly varied motives of dazzling complexity, comparable only to the endlessly changing patterns in a kaleidoscope. One of the most striking features is the evolutive character of the developments, the various new versions of the themes 'resulting' from earlier ones.

Theodor Adorno shows how the succession of variants is never fortuitous, but logically, or rather teleologically, organized. As an example of this procedure, he uses a 'joker' motif from the first movement (bars 5–6), whose highest note (F#) is at first lowered (F♮, E), only to rise later (A), until it reaches its highest point (D, and finally F *in alt*) in the recapitulation.[48] Adorno also quotes the anticipation of the Finale theme, improvised so to speak during the restatement of the first theme (bar 20) to show how it gradually gains in importance at the end of the false recapitulation (bars 91 ff.), until it becomes a fully-fledged theme in the development (bars 127 ff.).[49] Such means are used by Mahler to create tension spanning many groups in a movement (*Spannung über viele Gruppen eines Satzes*).

Another typical example is that of the augmented version of the motif from bar 22 (A"), which has played an essential role in the development (starting in the basses at bar 148). It appears as a counterpoint in the trumpet over the original form of theme A" in the third bar of the recapitulation (bar 241). Thus, as in a novel where the characters evolve in accordance with events in the plot, the transformations of themes and motifs are shown to be irreversible. One of a vast number of observations that could be made about this exceptional movement is that neither nature nor Mahler's beloved military music are absent from it. There are bird-calls (in bars 186 and 187 of the development) derived from the flute motifs in the second and third bars of the introduction, and, before the recapitulation, a trumpet-call which will become the opening theme of the following symphony, the Fifth. Mahler called this last passage 'Der kleiner Appell' (the little summons), as opposed to the 'Grosser Appell' (the big summons) of the Second

---

[47] In Manfred Huss (ed.), *Wahrung der Gestalt: Schriften über Werk und Wiedergabe, Stil und Interpretation in der Musik* (Universal Edition, Vienna, 1979), 52 ff.
[48] TAM 121 ff.   [49] TAM 78 ff. See above, Cyclic Procedures.

Symphony (bar 229 ff., see Chapter 8). 'When the confusion and bunching of the previously well-deployed troops gets out of hand, a peremptory order from the commander brings them at once back into the old formation under his standard.'[50]

From the point of view of the classical sonata form, the only unusual features in this movement are the recurrence of the main theme in its original key just before the end of the exposition, a 'false recapitulation'; the uncertain tonality of the introduction (it is later revealed to be in E minor); and its rondo-like recurrence several times in the same opening key (except for the A♭ minor episode—bars 155 ff.—where it is combined with A'). Mahler himself was conscious of the richness of his first theme, which, despite its air of 'old-fashioned simplicity', later 'created six or even seven further themes', all of which he played for Natalie on the piano.[51] Exx. 11 and 12 show the striking resemblance between this theme and a few bars in the exposition of the first movement of Schubert's E flat Sonata, D. 568 (bars 53–6).[52]

Ex. 11. Schubert, Sonata in E flat, D. 568

Ex. 12. Fourth Symphony, first movement

(*b*) **In gemächlicher Bewegung.** *Ohne Hast* (in measured tempo, unhurried). Trio: *Etwas gemächlicher* (a little more moderate). Mengelberg's note: *Walzer, nicht zu schnell*, and further, *Totentanz Holbein. Der Tod führt uns* (Death leads us).[53]

Key: C minor (with F major Trio).
Time signature: 3/8.
Rhythm: Slow ländler.
Duration: 8 minutes (Amsterdam, 1904).
Instrumentation: To suggest the crude sound of the fiddle, Mahler requires the leader of the orchestra to play a number of passages on a violin that is tuned a whole tone higher than usual. During the preliminary rehearsal, which he organized with the Vienna Philharmonic on 12 October 1901, he decided that the sound was not

---

[50] NBL1. 145; NBL2. 164.   [51] NBL1. 171; NBL2. 198. See above Chap. 11.

[52] It should here be recalled that Mahler was a pupil of Julius Epstein who edited Schubert's piano sonatas for the complete edn. of his works and that Mahler was probably aware of sonatas which were virtually unknown in his time. The rising motif that opens the principal theme is also an echo of the Finale of the Sonata in D, D.850, by Schubert (cf. the passage marked 'un poco più lento').

[53] According to Klaus Kropfinger, Mahler was thinking of a series of 51 woodcuts by Holbein named *Bilder des Todes*.

characteristic enough and planned to entrust the 'fiddle passages' to a solo viola played by the same leader, thinking that it would sound even shriller. Before the Amsterdam performance of 23 October 1904, he reversed his decision and decided to 'try' a violin with normal tuning, which apparently was used for the Dutch première.[54] However, the score in its present form calls for a tuned-up violin. György Ligeti emphasizes the manner in which Mahler contrasts the crudeness of the tuned-up violin's sonority and the softness (*Weichheit*) of the orchestral violins. He also quotes the sudden break of the solo violin line at bar 144, where its last note is taken up and held by other instruments. Over this C, the muted tutti violin melody sounds as if played from far away (*in Riesenentfernung*).[55]

Form: The movement is composed in a sequence of short alternating sections, as befits a Scherzo.

Scherzo

1–33	Introduction (on horn: four bars, later serving as a transition between each episode) and A: C minor
34–45	B: C major
46–63	A: C minor

Trio

64–109	Five-bar transitional horn passage (as postlude to Scherzo or introduction to Trio) and C: F major

Scherzo

110–44	Transition (horn: six bars) and A: C minor
145–56	B: C major
157–84	A: C minor (with one-bar introduction)
185–200	B: C major

Trio

201–53	Two-bar transition and C (varied): F major
254–75	Development of C: D major. Klaus Kropfinger sees in the sphärenhaft (music of the spheres) character of this episode an anticipation of the Adagio movement.

Scherzo

276–313	Five-bar transition and A: C minor
314–29	B: C major
330–64	Six-bar transition and Coda derived from A (chromatically modulating) and introductory motif.

This is the only true ländler movement since the Scherzo of the First Symphony (1888), and other ländlers were to follow in the Fifth and Ninth Symphonies. Several authors have found a similarity between one of the Trio themes and 'Das himmlische Leben' (see above, Cyclic Procedures). However, rather than the *Totentanz* which Mahler seems to have had in mind, this movement sounds more like a debonair ländler. The

---

[54] In a letter to Mengelberg dated 13 Oct. 1904 and accompanying a revised and corrected score (RMH 50).

[55] Ligeti-Gottwald, 'Musik und Raum', 10.

contrast of its style within the work as a whole is not so pronounced as in the Second (Andante) and Third Symphonies ('Animal', binary Scherzo), because the outer movements are not so grandiose and heaven-storming.

(c) **Ruhevoll** (calm) (*Poco Adagio*) Mengelberg's notes: <u>*Nicht zu langsam*</u> (Not too slow). *fliessend ruhiges Tempo* (flowing, calm tempo); further, *Wir sehen hier wo der Tod uns hingeführt hat* (we now see where Death has led us).

Key: G major (second theme in E minor).
Tempo: Changing to *Viel langsamer* (much slower) for the second theme and speeding up to Allegro molto in the variations.
Duration: 19 minutes (Amsterdam, 1904).
Time signature: 4/4 changing to *alla breve*, 3/4, 3/8, 2/4 in the variations.
Form: The variation belongs to one of the most time-honoured genres inherited by the classical composers from the Renaissance and the Baroque. Mahler proudly called this movement 'my first real variations', but the truth is that such an independent and innovative mind and a perpetual innovator could not adhere blindly to a traditional form. Consequently, this movement, so crystal clear at first glance, is actually one of the hardest to analyse in Mahler's œuvre. Many authors have attempted to break down its structure; it is so complex that no one yet has wholly succeeded. The essential facts are the following.

1. This is a variation movement, but on two contrasting themes, in the manner of the slow movement of Beethoven's Ninth Symphony. The two themes have several motifs in common, both in the melody and the accompaniment. The first creates a mood of serene meditation, while the second, in the relative minor key, introduces a note of unrest and yearning. But the diagnosis 'variations on two themes' already proves inaccurate, since the second theme is not genuinely 'varied', but only amplified when restated.

2. There is a strong passacaglia feeling throughout the main section, because of the ostinato bass motif, which is always present in some form or other. Matters are further complicated by the fact that the theme and its bass seem to be constructed in sixteen-bar periods, whereas other features point occasionally to an eight-bar construction. (The bass design of bars 1–4 resembles that of bars 9–12, and Mahler uses the same counter-melody in bars 25–8 as in 17–20). Thus there are three themes, A, B, and the bass motif, which are sometimes simultaneously varied; for instance, bars 151–6 are a variation in the treble of bars 45–50, while a variation of the bass theme starts two bars *before* the end of the same period (at bar 155) and continues after it has reached its conclusion.

3. The bass 'passacaglia' theme itself is often melodically varied.

4. Bars 107–78 are a fairly strict variation of bars 1–61.

5. The variations follow an evolutive process recognizable in all Mahler's music from now on (except perhaps in some of the Scherzos). They are often variations of a previous variation, rather than of the theme.

In my view, the periodic structure of the theme is as in Fig. 4. The symmetry between theme and variations ends a few bars after 144, when the bass theme becomes a new subject for variation and is treated in imitations by the various

	First period			Second period			Final period
1–8	9–16	17–24	25–36	37–44	45–51	51–61
107–114	115–122	123–130	131–142	143–150		

Fig. 4. Periodic structure of the theme, Fourth Symphony, Adagio

orchestral groups. The first part of the second period (bars 25–36) is twelve rather than eight bars long, and the same extension is found in the varied restatement (bars 131–42). It can be attributed to the horn interlude (bar 31–6), which reappears after bar 137 (on clarinets and bassoons). One last detail should be noted: at bar 123, while the cellos vary and ornament their opening melody (A, from bar 25 ff.), the oboe starts to vary on the original bass motif in the treble, although the same motif is already present in the pizzicato basses—a situation so complex that it makes one's mind whirl!

The bass theme has been called a 'bell motif' by Paul Bekker because of its intervals and because it is played on pizzicato strings. In the first sixty-one-bar statement of the theme, many elements are already elaborated in variation form. Here is a complete synopsis of the movement.

1–24	A (first period in three parts, see above): G major
25–50	A' (second period), with horn and bassoon interlude
51–61	A'' (closing period)
62–75	B, *Viel langsamer* (much slower), with fragments of initial bass motifs, diminished: E minor
76–92	B' varied (on same bass); bar 80 anticipates the motif: 'Warum so dunkle Flammen, in the second *Kindertotenlied*
93–106	B'': third section based on bass of theme (coda): D minor
107–30	A, *Anmuthig bewegt* (gracefully animated): variation of first period of A (with variation of bass motif appearing in the treble)[56]
131–50	Variation of beginning of second period (A'), with horn and bassoon interlude now in clarinets and bassoons: G major
151–78	*Sehr fliessend* (very flowing) free variation of the end of A
179–91	B, *Wieder wie vorher* (again as before): B (without ostinato bass): G minor
192–204	*Fliessend* (flowing): B' second period, (fortissimo climax): C# minor
205–21	*Leidenschaftlich und etwas drängend* (passionate and somewhat pressing): B'' last period (coda): F# minor/major
222–37	A, *Andante* 3/4: first variation proper of A: G major
238–62	*Allegro subito* 3/8: second variation: G major
263–77	*Allegro subito* 2/4: third variation: E major
278–86	*Allegro molto* 2/4: fourth variation cut short (*Andante subito*) by horn interlude from first section: G major

[56] Vladimir Karbusicky has found a quotation from a Czech folk melody called 'Andulko, mé dítě', at bar 107 ff. of the Adagio, in the variation *Anmuthig bewegt* (VKM 54).

287–314   *Poco Adagio*: variation of the end of A (bars 37–61): G major
315–25   *Poco più mosso*: triple fortissimo: anticipation in the brass of main theme
          of Finale (*Pesante*), part of which was heard in development theme of first
          movement: E major
326–53   Coda: ascending theme (based on motifs from both A and B): E major, C
          major, G major (ending on the dominant)

Although different in many other respects, this movement is closely related in
feeling to the Finale of the Third Symphony. Both are based on two contrasting
elements: a serene melody,[57] and another, gently mournful, in the minor mode. In a
work dedicated to the classical spirit, it is understandable that Mahler should have
used the most classical of all forms, the variation. Nevertheless his use of it, as
briefly summarized above, is as far removed from its famous models as Beethoven's
fugal movements in sonata form are from the traditional fugue. The variations keep
moving further and further away from the theme, each one being a logical result of
the preceding one. In the third A section, the 'senseless bustle' (Adorno's *Weltlauf*
again, a term he borrowed from Hegel) of everyday life gradually disperses the
pensive mood of the opening, and the tempo accelerates, like a spinning wheel
gaining speed. The opening theme is gradually destroyed and distorted, but the
nightmarish vision is cut short before the end of the last variation by a sudden
modulation (recalling that between bars 374 and 375 in the Finale of the First
Symphony, for, like it, it is a sudden change of key rather than a modulation). Mahler
then creates a state of static bliss and takes his listeners through the wide open gates
of the only heaven accessible to humans, that of childhood and popular imagery, in
a glorious tutti passage which anticipates (bars 320–2) the main theme of the Lied-
Finale. Once again, to represent the final ascent into Heaven, Mahler appropriately
uses the Ewigkeit motive (see Ex. 13).

Ex. 13. Fourth Symphony, last movement, Ewigkeit motive

(*d*) **Sehr behaglich** (at ease), soprano solo, 'Wir geniessen die Himmlischen
Freuden' from *Des Knaben Wunderhorn*. Mengelberg's note: *Das ganze himmlisch,
lustig. Ein <u>Kind</u> erzählt*! (Heavenly, joyous throughout. A child tells a story.)

It was indeed an original and daring idea, in 1899–1900, to close a symphony with
a simple Lied, yet the 1892 song was the seed from which the whole work grew. As
Mahler later remarked, 'Das himmlische Leben' had long been one of his favorite
Lieder, and it was one of the richest in substance, 'having given birth to no less than
five symphonic movements' (Mahler probably means the whole of the Fourth Symphony

---

[57] A striking similarity has often been noted between the beginning of this Adagio and the introduction
to the Quartet 'Mir ist so wunderbar' in Act I of Beethoven's *Fidelio*, especially the characteristic bass
line. A conscious allusion or an unconscious reminiscence? Here as in many other cases, one will
never know.

and the choral movement of the Third).[58] In August 1900 he called his Finale the 'tapering apex' (*verjüngende Spitze*) of the symphony.[59] From the song that was the very source from which the whole work sprang, Mahler borrowed its initial refrain (bar 40) to start the first movement.

Autographs: AFC/original song, v & p (10 Feb. 1892): BSB; AFC/original song, v & o (12 Mar. 1892): GMF; AOC for the symphony (Mar. 1901): GMF; CFC, with many corrections in Mahler's hand (sold at Stargardt anction, June 1984).

Key: G major, ending in E major.

Time signature: 4/4, changing here and there to 2/4.

Tempo: The metronome markings on the BSB piano manuscript are as follows:[60]

bar 25 (number 2)	$\downarrow$ = 108
bar 36 (four before 3)	$\downarrow$ = 92
bar 40 (number 3)	$\downarrow$ = 116
bar 57 (number 5)	$\downarrow$ = 104
bar 76 (number 7)	$\downarrow$ = 116
bar 80 (tempo primo)	$\downarrow$ = 96
bar 95	$\downarrow$ = 126
bar 106 (number 10)	$\downarrow$ = 92
bar 115 (number 11)	$\downarrow$ = 116
bar 112 (number 12)	$\downarrow$ = 96

Orchestration: The original *Besetzung* called for 3 flutes (including piccolo), cor anglais, 2 clarinets, 2 bassoons, 4 horns, 2 trumpets, timpani, triangle, cymbals, harp, and strings. Mahler later added a tambourine.[61]

Duration: $9\frac{1}{2}$ minutes to 10 minutes (Amsterdam, 1904).

Text: *Des Knaben Wunderhorn*, i. 335, under the title 'Der Himmel hängt voll Geigen'. Its origin is a folk-song, well-known throughout Bavaria and Bohemia, which can be traced to a late eighteenth-century Lied by Peter Marcellin Sturm, 'Nach Kreuz und ausgestandenen Leiden'. Mahler's only alteration was to suppress four lines from the fourth stanza. Thus the original poem has five ten-line stanzas, while Mahler's version has three ten-line stanzas and two of eight lines. Sturm himself set this poem to a melody which has nothing in common with Mahler's. While revising the orchestration of this Lied in Abbazia in April 1901 Mahler expressed his delight at the 'roguishness and deep mysticism' of the poem.

Form: Strophic *durchkomponiert*. There are three main sections, with a contrasting middle episode (in minor) and a long coda that varies and develops the initial motifs.

---

[58] NBL2. 172. Donald Mitchell has also found the principal theme of 'Das himmlische Leben', in the form of a refrain in chords, recurring throughout the first movement of the Third Symphony and, in a scale motif from the same source in the second movement (DMM2. 313, 315 and 364: see above, Vol. i, App. 1), the section concerning the Third Symphony.　　[59] NBLS.

[60] It is interesting to compare these markings with those on Mengelberg's score, probably noted under Mahler's eyes, with the Dutch conductor's tempos in his 1939 recorded performance, and also with Mahler's own tempos in the Welte-Mignon roll of 1905 (see Kropfinger, *Gerettete Herausforderung*, 152 ff.). The tempo of 'Das himmlische Leben' seems surprisingly rapid in the only studio recording, made by Bruno Walter in 1946. The soloist, Desi Halban, informed me that she was following instructions from the recording engineers, who had to keep in mind the duration of an 78 rpm side.

[61] Zychowicz, 'Sketches and Drafts', 114 ff.

Two different 'refrains' separate the various sections: the fast ritornello used by Mahler in the first movement, and the slow chorale common to this song and to the fifth movement of the Third Symphony.

1–11	Orchestral introduction presenting the first theme
12–35	Main section A in two parts (A and A')
36–9	*Plötzlich zurückhaltend* (suddenly slower): chorale: E minor
40–56	*Plötzlich frisch bewegt* (suddenly sprightly and animated): refrain (from the first movement),[62] developed: E minor
57–71	*Etwas zurückhaltend* (somewhat slower again): contrasting section (B): E minor
72–5	*Wieder zurückhaltend* (slower again): chorale: E minor
76–9	*Wieder lebhaft* (lively again): refrain: E minor
80–105	*Tempo primo*: sections A (abridged) and A' (developed): G major
106–14	*Wieder plötzlich zurückhaltend* (once again suddenly slower): chorale: D minor
115–21	*Wieder lebhaft* (lively once again): refrain: B minor

Coda

122–41	*Tempo primo: Sehr zart und geheimnisvoll bis zum Schluss* (very tender and mysterious until the end): orchestral introduction stating new theme based on A
142–68	Theme A in E major (varied)
169–74	Chorale (without harmonization in parallel chords): E major
175–84	Pianissimo orchestral conclusion (fragments of A)

There is a striking similarity between bars 32 and 33 of the Finale of Schubert's D major Sonata, D. 850, and bar 128 of the E major theme from the coda of 'Das himmlische Leben'—undoubtedly a subconscious reminiscence, Mahler being guilty for once of one of those 'memory lapses' which he censored in composers such as Goldmark or Zemlinsky (see Exx. 14 and 15). Again, this shows how well he knew

Ex. 14. Schubert, Sonata in D, D. 850, Finale, bars 32–3

Ex. 15. Fourth Symphony, last movement, bar 128

---

[62] Since the Finale was written long before the other movements, the truth is of course that the beginning of the first movement was borrowed from the Lied-Finale.

Schubert's sonatas. Although they were seldom performed at this time, he had played them at the Vienna Conservatory, under Julius Epstein.[63]

Viewed in the context of an overall survey of Mahler's *œuvre*, the Fourth Symphony may appear as a diversion, an innocent intermezzo, non-essential to the whole. But closer examination shows that it cannot be thus dismissed as an untypical accident in his career as a composer. Mahler perhaps expended more energy and time, and at least as much care and attention, on its forty-five minutes as on the ninety minutes of each of the two preceding works, and achieved in the Fourth a higher degree of technical mastery than in either of the longer works. Musicologists, historians of musical forms, and analysts are still far from having analysed and explained all its intricacies. Adorno also points out that none of Mahler's works is so self-sufficiently unique as to be a 'monad in relation to the others'.[64]

Although Mahler explicitly required the soprano soloist in the Finale to 'adopt a joyous, childish tone, without the slightest hint of parody', his contemporaries considered his naivety, his imitation of folk style and traditional spirit as something false, affected, and even shocking. But the neo-classicism *avant la lettre* of the Fourth is neither nostalgic for the past nor wilful parody, such as some neo-classical composers were to practise later in the twentieth century. In the context of its time, the Fourth was a bold, avant-garde work, an important step forward in Mahler's development as a composer. It represents a new discovery by Mahler of himself, the revelation of a stricter, more disciplined style, a tighter polyphonic web, a new economy of means, a more concentrated musical language, an unprecedented complexity of expression. In his alleged 'return to Haydn', to music's 'age of innocence', i.e. the golden age of Viennese classicism, Mahler borrows classical 'clichés' from traditional figures, but enriches and transforms them endlessly, gives them an elaborately contrapuntal treatment and places them in a wholly new and original harmonic context. In fact, he gives this inherited material the same freedom and the same artistic refinements as he gives to the folk idiom of the earlier *Wunderhorn-Lieder*. Hermann Danuser's analysis of a passage in ternary rhythm from the Scherzo proves how far removed Mahler's music is from the folk- and entertainment music in which he found his inspiration. Rather than superposing different voices, he here intermingles three different levels of composition (*Resultat eines komplexen Ineinandergreifens dreier kompositorischer Schichten*), and his harmonization defies all the rules (*regelwidrige*).[65]

Mahler himself stated that the scoring of the Fourth closely resembled that of a string quartet. Turning his back on the colossal proportions of his earlier symphonies and the large orchestral resources he had called on for them, he even left out the trombones which he was strongly tempted to use at least for two bars at the end of the Adagio. Clarity, economy, and transparency were obviously demanded by the 'subject-matter' of the work. He predicted that orchestras would have the greatest difficulty in playing the Fourth, and he was not mistaken. Its chamber-music

---

[63] Max Steinitzer later recalled having heard Mahler play Schubert's Sonata in D in Leipzig (BSP 13). Laurent Riou, a Mahlerian scholar from Lyons, has pointed out another reminiscence deriving from this sonata: bars 165 ff. of the Finale of the Fourth have the same melodic line and the same harmonic progression as bars 58 ff. of the Scherzo from the Sonata in D.

[64] TAM 77 ff.

[65] Hermann Danuser, *Gustav Mahler und seine Zeit* (Laaber, Laaber, 1981), 87 ff.

character gives each musician in the orchestra the role of a soloist. Thus the symphony as a whole is a redoubtable virtuoso piece for a modern orchestra. As already mentioned, Mahler continued to perfect the orchestration until the end of his life, thus showing the importance he attached to even the smallest detail of writing and balance.

It is difficult, today, to understand why the Fourth Symphony was so badly received by virtually all its early audiences, particularly the Lied-Finale, so fresh, so spontaneous, and so rich in melodic invention. Like that of the preceding movement, the lovely E major coda, 'heavenly' music if ever anything was, leaves us entirely convinced that 'no terrestrial music can compare' with that of the higher spheres. It teaches us that even a 'modern' spirit such as Mahler, a man often tormented by doubt and determined not to ignore any of the frustrations, the heartbreaks, and the tragedies of the human condition, could also claim to have entered the Kingdom of Heaven. It matters little that this paradise, 'depicted with the features of a peasant-like anthropomorphism', appears here too concrete, too reassuring for one really to believe in it, as one believes in the mystic resignation of the Finales of the Ninth and of *Das Lied von der Erde*. To quote David Schiff,

In Beethoven's Ninth, joy is attainable; in Mahler's Fourth it is always there—yet it is irretrievable. The child's vision is untouchable, outside experience. Mahler's use of *Des Knaben Wunderhorn* underscores this irony. Is the naïve world of these German folk poems a metaphor for Mahler's childhood, or is it the opposite? . . . In setting the naïvely Christian poems . . . , Mahler was, in one sense returning to a world that was never his—though in another sense he was creating an appropriate metaphor for his own childhood, or for anyone's, a metaphor which reveals and conceals. Here is the childhood everyone had and no one had, a naïvely sentimental mask covering primal anxieties—and the very forms and gestures of the symphonic tradition are shown to be in complicity with this deception. . . . The child gives us the child's inevitable, unchangeable answer—is it correct, or absurd?[66]

As usual, Adorno takes a wholly pessimistic view of the work's seemingly optimistic 'message':

Mahler's theology, again like Kafka's, is gnostic: his fairy-tale symphony is as sad as his late works. When it dies away after the promising words 'that everything awakens for joy', no one knows whether it has not fallen asleep for ever. The phantasmagoria of the transcendental landscape is both posited and negated by it. Joy is still unattainable; and all that remains of transcendence is nostalgia.[67]

Recently, Adolf Nowak has presented another view of the 'message' delivered by the Fourth.[68] He considers it to be a reflection of Nietzsche's philosophy. He is convinced that the irony which is symbolized in the Finale of the Fourth by the sleigh-bells refrain gives 'Das himmlische Leben' the character of a *Wunschtraum*, one in which the hungry child of 'Das irdische Leben' is at last saved from his hopeless 'earthly' predicament. Thus the child projects into the other world every pleasure

---

[66] See 'Jewish and Musical Tradition in the Music of Mahler and Schoenberg', *Journal of the A. Schoenberg Institute*, 9: 2 (Nov. 1986), 217 ff.

[67] TAM 83.

[68] Adolf Nowak, 'Zur Deutung der Dritten und Vierten Sinfonie Gustav Mahlers', in Danuser (ed.), *Wege der Forschung: Gustav Mahler*, 191 ff.

and enjoyment that has been denied him in this one. According to Nietzsche, the vision of heaven 'belongs to children; the belief expressed here is not a hard-won belief . . . it is as it were the childlike taking refuge in the spiritual'.[69] At the time when Mahler intended to include the Lied-Finale in the Third Symphony, he gave it the title: 'What the child tells me' (*Was mir das Kind erzählt*).

The concept of religion offering in the hereafter a place where human desires and longings are fulfilled, a heaven as solace for earthly suffering, was of course derived by Nietzsche from post-Hegelian critics of Christianity like Ludwig Feuerbach.[70] The fact that Mahler also set to music what is perhaps Nietzsche's essential 'credo', the 'Mitternachtslied', in the Third Symphony just before a *Wunderhorn* vocal movement which is both literarily and musically connected with 'Das himmlische Leben', gives credence to this view of Mahler's Finale.

But Mahler's outlook was even more influenced by Fechner's and Lotze's 'Allbeseelungslehre', the belief that everything that exists – minerals, plants, animals, even the earth itself – has a soul. This belief underlies the 'programme' of the Third Symphony, to which Mahler had originally planned to give a Nietzschean title, 'Die fröhliche Wissenschaft'. Adolf Nowak is of course quite right to point out 'that to say that the last word belongs to the child contradicts the doctrine of the animist philosophers no less than that of Nietzsche', a remark which once more underlines the ambiguity of Mahler's *Weltanschauung*. Nowak goes on to show how this ambiguity is musically expressed in 'Das himmlische Leben', not by strains reminiscent of Kinderlieder, but by musical topoi, 'clichés traditionally associated with childlike things', like the arpeggio intervals of the 'bucolic' clarinet motif, which symbolize innocence. Similarly the chorale of the second refrain justifies 'the statement that the promise of the Kingdom of Heaven is indeed a case of "the childlike taking refuge in the spiritual" '. Adolf Nowak also underlines the irony present in the *Wunderhorn* poem itself, in the 'd'rum' in the second line as in the 'dennoch' in the fourth. Both seem to express 'an awareness of the projection' (*ein Bewusstsein von der Projektion aus*). According to him, the contrast between the two 'refrains' (the sleigh-bells and the chorale) casts doubt on the earnestness of the vision and expresses irony as much as faith, while the use of the 'modern' technique of progressive variation also contradicts the infantile, regressive, wishful-thinking (*Wunschdenken*) element.

Theodor Adorno's and Adolf Nowak's attempt to examine and interpret the ambiguity of Mahler's vision of 'heaven' invite reflection, if only because the same remarks can be made about the 'optimistic' Finales of the Fifth and Seventh Symphonies. Undeniably, music is the only art which can simultaneously affirm and deny, ask and answer questions, express the most contradictory sensations, the most contrasting moods, the most disconcerting ambiguities. The very fact that Mahler's music gives rise to such speculation is proof of its depths of meaning. The Finales of Symphonies 4, 5, and 7 are of course ambiguous, but no more and no less than life itself. For who can draw a firm line between faith and doubt, truth and illusion, revelation and reality?

---

[69] Friedrich Nietzsche, *Der Antichrist*, critical edn. by G. Golli and M. Montinari (Berlin, 1968), vi. 3, 201.

[70] Ludwig Feuerbach (1804–72) taught at the Univ. of Erlangen but finally had to resign because of his unorthodox views on religion. His most influential work was *Das Wesen des Christentums* (1841).

SEVEN LIEDER
entitled, after Mahler's death, *Aus letzter Zeit* (1899–1901)

A. 2 **Wunderhorn-Lieder** with orchestra

(a) 'Revelge' (Reveille)

Composition: I have already mentioned[1] the somewhat unusual circumstances in which this Lied was written. Mahler enjoyed confiding to his friends that, after long wanting to set the poem to music, the right melodic inspiration had only come to him one day in June 1899 in Alt-Aussee[2] while he was sitting on the toilet, and that he had emerged with the completed sketch for the setting in his hand. In her *Mahleriana*, Natalie states that three *Wunderhorn-Lieder* had been composed in Vahrn the previous year. However, only two songs are known which date from that year: 'Lied des Verfolgten im Turm' and 'Wo die schönen Trompeten blasen'. Could 'Revelge' have been the Lied he referred to as the one 'which achieved the strongest expression of anger and frustration . . . feelings which, for several reasons, have continuously affected me this year'?[3] In that case, the musical inspiration that came to Mahler on that memorable day in Alt-Aussee may have concerned only compositional details he had so far been unable to solve. Good story though it is, it is difficult to believe he could have composed under such circumstances the complete sketch for a Lied of such unusual length as 'Revelge'.

The day he finished the orchestration of 'Revelge', Mahler announced that this was the most successful and beautiful of his *Wunderhorn-Lieder*, even 'the most important of all his Lieder'. He said that the first movement of the Third Symphony had been just a 'study in rhythm' for 'Revelge'. He also commented interestingly on the text and recalled that Goethe, in his review of the Arnim-Brentano anthology, had said that it was 'priceless for someone with enough imagination to follow it', and that 'the vivid poetical picture of a limited situation reveals a particular happening to be part of an infinite whole, so that we believe that in that small space we are looking at the whole world'. He also added, prophetically, 'God willing, it may tempt composers to write new meaningful melodies for it.'[4]

Autograph: No autograph manuscript has yet been found. The Bruno Walter collection (LPA) has a CFC.[5] The title-page carries the words: *'Revelge', aus 'Des Knaben Wunderhorn' von Gustav Mahler*. The composer added in his own hand: *für Singstimme mit Orchesterbegleitung* (for voice with orchestral accompaniment). IMG has a set of proofs of the v & p version with numerous autograph corrections in Mahler's hand.

Key: D minor and major (with numerous modulations to G minor, B♭ major, G♭ major, E♭ major, F♭ minor, etc.). First and second performances: Fritz Schrödter, tenor. Of the Lieder first performed in 1905 in Vienna, this was the only one for which Mahler

---

[1] See above, Chap. 6.

[2] Some years ago (1983) I searched for the house Mahler stayed in during the summer of 1899 in Aussee and found the Villa Kerry (not Seri) in Alt-Aussee (not Ausee), situated on the edge of the forest, on the hill overlooking the lake.

[3] NBL2. 119.   [4] See Vol. i, Chap. 6.

[5] Copyist's MS of the v & o version (see above, the keys preceding the catalogue of works).

used a tenor.[6] A transposed version for v & p in C minor was published in 1905 by Kahnt. It had been undoubtedly revised by Mahler.

Time signature: 4/4.

Rhythm: A quick march. The most striking feature is the 'military' rhythmic figure which asserts itself from the start (see Ex. 16).

Ex. 16.

(Rhythm): $\left(\frac{4}{4}\right)$ 𝄽 ♩♩♩ ♪ 𝄾

Tempo: *Marschierend. In einem fort* (marching, from start to finish). When the phantom soldiers return (bar 140 ff.): *etwas gemessener als zu Anfang* (somewhat more measured than at the beginning).

Text: i. 113. The original name of the *Wunderhorn* poem is 'Rewelge' (the modern German form is 'Reveille'), meaning the military bugle-call used to awaken the soldiers. According to Susanne Vill, the first three verses were transcribed by Bettina Brentano and the rest probably added by her brother Clemens.[7] In the *Wunderhorn* original, the order of the verses is different (2–3–1). Mahler repeats various lines and fragments. In bar 61, in the second refrain 'Ach Brüder', he replaces 'als wär's mit mir schon vorüber' with 'als wär's mit mir schon vorbei', and suppresses a rhyme. Immediately afterwards he skips a line, 'Ihr Lumpenfeind seid da' (You enemy scum are there).[8] Further on, he changes the first line of the last verse, 'Da stehen morgen die Gebeine' into 'Des Morgens stehen da die Gebeine'. There are no further changes to the original text beyond a few elisions and inversions, and the replacing of the word 'Schätzel' (bar 125) by 'Schätzelein'. The tune of the folk-song in Ex. 17 resembles Mahler's 'Revelge'.

Ex. 17. 'Revelge'

Des_ Mor-gens zwis-chen drein und vier-en, da__

*müss-en wir Sol-da-ten mar-chie-ren die_ Gäss-lein auf_ und_*

ab mein Schätz-lein sieht_ her_ ab. Tra la

la la la, tra li la la la, mein Schätz-lein sieht_ her_ ab.

[6] In a letter written in 1905, Mahler also advised Oskar Fried to use a tenor for this song. Fried engaged Ludwig Hess for the concert on 19 Dec. 1905 (see below, Vol. iii, Chap. 4).

[7] In *Vermittlungsformen verbalisierter und musikalischer Inhalte in der Musik Gustav Mahlers* (Schneider, Tutzing, 1979), 97, Susanne Vill gives Heinz Rölleke's 1975–8 edn. of *Des Knaben Wunderhorn* as a source.

[8] Susanne Vill explains this omission by suggesting that the line is too pugnacious to suit the 'sad, bitter but resigned' atmosphere of the 'Trio' and that, in Mahler's version of the song, friends and enemies are brothers in misfortune.

Orchestration: The most striking characteristic is the use of military instruments, brass (4 horns and 4 trumpets), and percussion (triangle, 2 sets of cymbals, snare drum, bass drum, and tam-tam in addition to kettledrums). In the ghost episode Mahler has the strings play *col legno* and the brass with mutes. The piano can give only a poor idea of the rich instrumental colours of this, the most 'symphonic' of all Mahler's Lieder. A number of instrumental parts, often essential to the music, have to be left out to make the piano part playable. Thus it will always sound like an inadequate transcription rather than an alternative original.

Form: 'Strophic durchkomponiert', according to Pamer. Mahler's comments about Carl Loewe and the composition of Lieder in general, have been quoted above, and also his advocacy of the 'durchkomponiert' form, which he nevertheless hardly ever used himself.[9] The obsessive march rhythm, the apparent simplicity of the melodic material, dominant-tonic upbeats, military signals, conceal one of the most complex structures Mahler ever devised for a Lied. The scheme AA'-BB'-CD-A"A sums it up only very approximately, for Mahler ceaselessly transforms his material and uses cells taken from earlier elements to construct new melodies.

STANZAS		BARS	KEYS
POETIC	MUSICAL		
PRELUDE		1–7	Dm
1. Des Morgens zwischen . . .	A	8–17	Dm-Cm
2. Ach Bruder, jetzt bin ich . . .	A'	18–27	Gm-Dm
INTERLUDE		28–31	Dm-B♭
3. Ach Bruder, ich kann dich . . .	B	32–47	B♭-G
INTERLUDE		48–56	G
4. Ach Brüder, ihr geht ja . . .	B'	57–72	G-D
INTERLUDE		73–5	D
5. Ich muss wohl meine . . .	C	76–89	D-Dm
INTERLUDE		90–6	D-Dm-B♭-E♭m
6. Er schlägt . . .	D	97–108	E♭m
INTERLUDE		109	
7. Er schlägt die Trommel . . .	D'	110–27	E♭m-F♯m
INTERLUDE		128–53	F♯m-D♯m
8. Da stehen morgens . . .	A"	154–69	Dm-D
POSTLUDE		170–1	

The table will perhaps give a better approximation of the overall form, in which 8 poetic stanzas have been turned into four musical ones. However, the length of each musical stanza varies considerably: 19 bars for the first; 40 for the second; 32 for the third; 59 for the last. The longest interlude is the one which separates the two halves

---

[9] See above, Chap. 6.

of the last stanza. Elisabeth Schmierer has shown that the asymmetries are carried much further than the length of the musical stanzas. The comparison she makes between the various versions of the refrain (*trallali-trallaley*) reveals much about Mahler's compositional methods at this stage in his career. Each stanza uses the refrain in a different way and the refrain itself is varied and becomes the melodic substance of Stanza 3 (sections C–D). Sometimes it assumes its normal role of indicating the end of a verse, sometimes it becomes part of it. In (poetic) stanzas nos. 5, 6, and 7, it is repeated twice. The same author points out that, contrary to the other dialogue Lieder, most of which are in the same 'military' idiom, the main contrasts are here provided, within each stanza, by the march episodes, usually accompanied mainly by strings, with a stable harmonic background, while the refrain nearly always has a rich wind and brass accompaniment, and changing harmonies. Unlike the dialogue songs, the contrasts in 'Revelge' are not between the world of reality and that of dreams. The initial contrast between the bitter 'military' reality of stanza A and the more lyrical style of stanza B is not carried further—and only reappears at the end. Schmierer also shows that the harmonies engendered by the vocal part do not always coincide with those of the accompaniment (in measures 8 and 10 for instance, where the voice's dominant arpeggio is supported by tonic harmonies). She also notes the presence of augmented chords (end of bar 9) which she interprets as symbolizing death, as in 'Wo die schönen Trompeten blasen'.

The D–D' section, in E♭ minor, develops the refrain (*Trallali*). The unity of the whole is ensured by the march rhythm and the obsessive dactylic figure of the trumpets, and also by a highly original compositional logic: each variation follows as a consequence of the preceding one until the melody itself appears to give birth to its own transformations. At the restatement of A (A"), the second phrase is shortened and enriched with borrowings from C. Each section is followed by the refrain *Trallali, trallaley*, which itself undergoes considerable modification. Thus this Lied is not only 'symphonic' in scope and in its orchestration, it also shows the hand of a symphonist in a totally different way from the earlier *Wunderhorn-Lieder*, and is also quite unlike the intimate *Rückert-Lieder*, in which the techniques are also symphonic.

Susanne Vill, in her analysis, notes the similarity of subject and atmosphere between this and previous *Wunderhorn-Lieder* in which the sad fate of poor soldiers is also suggested by brass fanfares and melodic elements borrowed from military music. She observes that 'the more life slips away' the louder the soldier's voice grows, as if the soldier, like a frightened child, speaks more and more loudly as he becomes aware of being alone and abandoned. Finally she stresses that, in the battle episode (beginning at the fifth verse, 'Ich muss wohl'), 'all the elements are concentrated, the combining of motifs, the modulating harmonies, the orchestration picked out in dynamic relief', while the refrain becomes almost a 'battle song'. The sound of the drum 'grows real' and the fourth interlude prepares the entrance into the kingdom of the dead. In the bar which introduces the ghostly stanza (string chords *col legno*, muted brass), the previous fanfares and brass trills are echoed in the unearthly sound of high pianissimo woodwinds. With a blow on the tam-tam ('a ghostly metallic transformation of the drum') and a triple fortissimo-pianissimo final chord, the closing bars give the ending an expressionist character well suited to the whole Lied. Susanne Vill justifiably regards it as foreshadowing the sinister marches and savage combats in the Sixth Symphony rather than harking back to the grotesque march episodes in the first movement of the Third.

This visionary song, to which Mahler added two years later the sombre postlude of 'Der Tamboursg'sell', brings to a worthy conclusion the large collection of *Wunderhorn-Lieder* written by him between 1888 and 1901. Its musical language, ceaselessly combining and alternating major and minor, is full of idiomatic borrowings from military music, fanfares, dotted rhythms, drum rolls, and woodwind trills. The crude colours, hard rhythms, and almost literal realism of the military music[10] provide a particularly striking example of what Adorno described as Mahler's challenge to the laws of musical 'propriety', an exorbitant breach of the 'purity of style' that had been the ideal of the entire nineteenth century. Not until the 1920s, in particular with Kurt Weill's settings for Brecht's plays, does one encounter music as hard, cruelly realistic, and violently plebeian, in fact so anti-romantic, as this.

(b) 'Der Tamboursg'sell' (The Little Drummer Boy)

As seen above,[11] the tune for this Lied came to Mahler one day in Maiernigg after a meal, and he then finished the whole of it sitting by the spring. He subsequently remembered the poem, and found that it exactly fitted his musical sketch. The Lied was finished by 10 August, since Mahler played it to Natalie on that day. So it is an exact contemporary of the first *Kindertotenlieder*, the *Rückert-Lieder*, and the first movements of the Fifth Symphony. I have noted above the mournful character of much of the music written that summer, and have attributed it to Mahler's shock on learning, after his haemorrhage, that he had narrowly escaped death.[12] The inevitable end that awaits all life had become far more concrete to him than before. 'Der Tamboursg'sell' is the gloomiest of all the *Wunderhorn-Lieder*. Mahler was alluding to it, just as much as to the *Kindertotenlieder*, when he made the following comment to Natalie: 'It hurt one to write them and I grieve for the world which will one day have to hear them, so sad is their content.'[13]

Autographs: APD, v & p (2 pages): PML (Lehman dep.). Donald Mitchell notes that the second page, written in pencil, is very incomplete, so that the Lied took on its final dimensions only when written for orchestra; AOD (16 pages): PML (Lehman dep.). IMG has a set of proofs of the v & p version with many pencilled corrections and inserts by Mahler. A Particell of the v & o version was sold at auction by Stargardt in June 1984.

Key: D minor (ending in C minor) with modulations to G minor and A minor, and a constant alternation of major and minor. The stability of the key creates a deliberately monotonous effect, well-suited to the desperate character of the text. The

---

[10] On this subject see, in addition to Vladimir Karbusicky's book (VKM); Ernest Klusen, 'Gustav Mahler und das böhmisch-mährische Volkslied', in *Bericht über den internationalen musikwissenschaftlichen Kongress Kassel*, 1962 (Bärenreiter, Kassel, 1963); and 'Gustav Mahler und das Volkslied seiner Heimat', *Journal of the International Folk Music Council*, ed. L. Picken, (Unesco, Cambridge, 1963), 29. See also Edward Kravitt's substantial article on the 'vogue' of the folk-song in 1900–10: 'The Trend towards the Folklike, Nationalism and their Expression by Mahler and his Contemporaries in the Lied', *Chord and Discord* (1963), 40.

[11] See above, Chap. 10.

[12] Feder, 'Gustav Mahler um Mitternacht', *International Review of Psycho-analysis*, 7 (1980), 11.

[13] NBL1. 166; NBL2. 193.

ending in C minor, a key far removed from that of the opening, can be seen as symbolizing the drummer's 'farewell'. Mahler entrusted the first and second performances to the baritone Friedrich Weidemann, the same singer as for the *Kindertotenlieder*.

Time signature: 2/2 (alla breve).

Rhythm: Funeral march.

Tempo: *Gemessen, dumpf (nicht schleppen)* (measured, muffled without dragging); *Bedeutend langsamer* (perceptibly slower) at bar 91.

Text: i. 631. The *Wunderhorn* poem is entitled simply 'Tambursgesell'. It dates from the end of the eighteenth century and is closely linked with 'Zu Strassburg auf der Schanz'.[14] Mahler kept the peculiarities of the Bavarian dialect ('i' for 'ich') but they are not used systematically. He also lengthened the verses by repeating some lines. Goethe also praised this poem as: 'a brilliant rendering of an anguished state of soul. The connoisseur would have difficulty in finding another poem to compare with it.'

Form: Strophic *durchkomponiert*, according to Pamer, with several recurrences of the opening theme, followed each time by different material. The overall structure is retained but the symmetry is only apparent, as was now usual with Mahler. The first bars of the song return, as in a rondo, but the thematic material evolves continuously, each variation arising, in the same manner as in 'Revelge', as a consequence of the previous one. After a fairly extended interlude, finishing with a snare drum solo recalling the opening, the two final verses appear in C minor, constantly oscillating between the major and the minor, and in a slower tempo. The drummer's farewell to the world introduces new thematic material.

Susanne Vill notes that the expressive and dynamic climax of this Lied is in the third verse, which is followed by the only real interlude (bars 13 to 20). (This is where the thematic link with the Funeral March in the Fifth is most obvious.) The same author notes that the repetition of the last two *Gute Nacht* (Goodnight) is Mahler's only important addition to the original text. From beginning to end, no single ray of light relieves the darkness, which, if anything, intensifies towards the end. In relation to the previous Lieder, there is a tendency, new in Mahler, towards a spareness of texture and an economy of means that also characterizes the four *Rückert-Lieder* written during the same summer of 1901. The last two verses, in the new key of C minor, are the ones in which the condemned drummer takes his leave of all those he has known. Here the theme of farewell inspires, as in *Das Lied von der Erde*, some of Mahler's most deeply felt music. The austere two-part counterpoint and the melodic ideas themselves constantly recall the *Kindertotenlieder* and the Funeral March from the Fifth. The bleakness and despair of the final bars, in which the vocal line descends from the major to the minor third and thence chromatically to the tonic, achieves an intensity of emotion all the more poignant for being contained.

Orchestration: Mahler's exclusion of all strings, except the cellos and double-basses, and the use of the lowest registers of the woodwinds, contributes to the dark mood of the song. The 'military' instruments once again predominate, i.e. the snare drum and bass drum, horns, tuba, and bass clarinets. Mahler deliberately avoids the brilliant

[14] See Vol. i, App. 1.

sound of the trumpets, which would be out of place in a funeral dirge. Towards the end, the melancholy sonority of the cor anglais comes to the fore.

Markings: Susanne Vill observes that the voice part carries a great many indications that give it an almost expressionist character, such as *mit naïvem Vortrag, ohne Sentimentalität* (with naïve delivery, without sentimentality); *mit Grausen* (with horror); *mit sehr erhobener Stimme* (in a very loud voice), followed by *schreiend* (shrieking) and then *kläglich* (plaintively); and finally, in the coda, *mit Gefühl* (with feeling) and *mit gebrochener Stimme* (in a broken voice). Here Mahler approaches an operatic style generally very far removed from his Lieder.

The leitmotif of the Sixth Symphony, the major chord turning to minor, appears twice in this Lied (bars 153–4 and 155–6). Donald Mitchell notes that, in these last two *Wunderhorn-Lieder*, 'the songs are no longer prime sources for the symphonies but, on the contrary, derive their unique characteristics from the nature and process of Mahler's symphonic art'.[15] Pamer also observes that the Lied makes a quotation in the minor from a popular song, 'Der gute Kamerad' (bar 14 and onward: 'man führt mich aus dem G'wölb!'). see Exx. 18 and 19.

Ex. 18. 'Der Tamboursg'sell'

Man führt mich aus dem G'wölb __ man _ führt mich aus dem G'wölb!

Ex. 19. 'Der gute Kamerad'

Die _ Trom-mel schlug zum Strei - te, es _ ging- en mein-er Sei - te

In an article about the Lied 'Um Mitternacht', the psychoanalyst Stuart Feder makes some pertinent observations about 'Der Tamboursg'sell'.[16] He claims that Mahler's guilt complex, linked to the deaths of his brothers, Isidor and Ernst, and voiced in what he said to Natalie on arriving in Maiernigg in 1901: 'Es ist zu schön, man vergönnt es sich nicht!',[17] appears here in the form of guilt occasioned 'by his success, and by the fate of his rivals'. But the last part of the Lied, the farewell to the world in the form of a funeral march, can also be taken in a more general sense, especially since the key is different. As already noted, the 'pessimistic' leitmotif of the Sixth Symphony—the major chord becoming minor by the lowering of the third—is twice heard. For Stuart Feder, the whole of this ending symbolizes Mahler's farewell both to his youth and to the world of the *Wunderhorn*.

After 'Der Tamboursg'sell', Mahler put aside the Arnim and Brentano anthology which had inspired so many of his works over the previous thirteen years, giving rise to four symphonies and twenty-four Lieder.[18] For the next three years he turned to

[15] DMM2, 139.   [16] See Feder, 'Gustav Mahler', 11.
[17] NBL. 159; NBL2. 187.
[18] 'Hans und Grete', the four *Lieder eines fahrenden Gesellen*, the nine *Wunderhorn-Lieder* with piano, and the ten *Wunderhorn-Lieder* with orchestra.

Rückert. The change could be seen as a symbolical farewell to childhood, and as the beginning of a new creative period in which he wrote three instrumental symphonies and ten new songs. The criticisms levelled for so long at Mahler the 'folklorist', that he was Jewish and therefore 'a stranger to the German soul', seem utterly absurd to us today. Posterity has all but forgotten the *deutsch-national* composers who regarded themselves as the true heirs of the German tradition and considered Mahler as an intruder and 'usurper'. Indeed, if the soul of German folklore, and the romantic nostalgia for the distant past which *Des Knaben Wunderhorn* so eloquently expressed, are still very much alive in our concert halls today, this is due not to the few Lieder that Schumann, Brahms, and others wrote on these texts but to Mahler, who incorporated their essence into his settings with such art, vigour, and conviction, creating new forms, new developmental procedures, and a new method of using 'folk' material. In Mahler, the folk-musician (*Musikant*) was never entirely submerged by the art-music composer (*Kunstmusiker*). He never ceased to be closely identified with the people, and especially with the people of the country of his birth.[19] And yet, as Theodor Adorno has rightly observed, his name and his music were, in a sense, 'a catalyst for anti-Semitic instincts'. For this reason, many Germans saw his art as 'not genuine' (*unecht*). Today, his settings of folk poems appear in many ways closer to the 'realism' of Janáček or Bartók than to the popular sentiment idealized by musicians such as Schumann or Brahms, or by the neo-romantics, Mahler's contemporaries, who so painstakingly attempted to rediscover the soul of the people as expressed in their music.[20] What finally occurred is the reverse of the prophecies of Pfitzner and Schillings and their spokesman Rudolf Louis. Perhaps, indeed, there exists no better proof of the absurdity of racist theories in art than the freshness and apparent simplicity that characterize Mahler's *Wunderhorn-Lieder*. Despite the sophistication of their compositional techniques, they ring true. That is what has enabled them to survive, that is what will always make them sound 'modern'.

B. Four Rückert-Lieder with orchestral accompaniment

Alongside the great symphonies and the cycles and collections of orchestral Lieder, the *Rückert-Lieder* could, at first sight, be considered minor works, particularly because their brevity and intimate character contradict the traditional image of Mahler and his music. They represent a short interlude of pure lyricism in his work, far removed from the titanic struggles and searing questions which form the stuff of his middle-period symphonies. With the *Kindertotenlieder*, they also mark the supreme consummation and perfection of the Mahler Lied.[21] In fact, these songs express not only Mahler's awareness of having reached artistic maturity, but also the sudden improvement in the material conditions in which he had to compose. He was now the owner of a comfortable house, beautifully situated between forest and water, on one of the most picturesque Austrian lakes, and he had at his disposal a *Komponierhäuschen*, a little hut with a piano, set among the trees, at a safe distance from noise and the bustle of everyday life. This of course did not mean that his mind could not dwell on sombre themes, as

---

[19] See VKM.   [20] In this context, see Kravitt, 'Trend' (n. 10).

[21] Donald Mitchell writes that the Lieder of 1901 'are establishing, staking out, the sources and resources that he [Mahler] was to call on and further develop . . . to the composition of *Das Lied von der Erde* and the Ninth' (see DMM3. 56).

witness the *Kindertotenlieder*, 'Um Mitternacht', and the funeral marches, 'Der Tamboursg'sell' and the opening movement of the Fifth.[22] Nor did it completely exclude a certain humour ('Blicke mir nicht'), nor the metaphysical questions that constantly preoccupied him ('Um Mitternacht'). The fact remains that these Lieder express a relatively little-known but essential aspect of his personality.

Mahler and Rückert

At first sight it may seem surprising that Mahler should turn his back on such a rich and varied world as the *Wunderhorn*, and should devote his attention instead to the works of such a 'literary' poet as Rückert. Yet he remained faithful to him for three years, composed ten masterpieces based on his poems, and even, much later, copied out in his own hand one of Rückert's translations from the Persian, doubtless with the intention of using it in one of his compositions.[23] As it happens, Rückert does not rank highly in the Parnassus of the German literary historians, who generally classify him as a minor poet.[24] But in this context it should be recalled that Mahler had long maintained that accomplished poetic masterpieces should not be set to music.[25] In any case, there were many features of Rückert's poetry that appealed strongly to him.

Born in Schweinfurt, near Coburg in Bavaria, on 15 May 1788, the son of a lawyer, Friedrich Rückert spent his childhood in a village in Franconia, showing a gift for poetry at an early age. On returning to the town of his birth, he refused to follow his father into an administrative career, and began a classical education which he completed at the Universities of Würzburg, Heidelberg, and Jena. When he took up his first job as a teacher in Hanau, he was already writing poetry, in particular sonnets with a pastoral inspiration. Then came the Napoleonic Wars. In 1814 he published, under a pseudonym, a collection of poems entitled *Deutsche Gedichte* (German Poems). These included the martial *Geharnischte Sonette* (Armoured Sonnets), a stirring appeal to Prussians to join in the Wars of Liberation (1813–15) from Napoleonic domination. Rückert stayed home during the war at his parents' request. In 1816 he moved to Stuttgart, and edited the magazine *Morgenblatt für gebildete Stände* there. After spending a year in Italy, he moved on to Vienna where he met the orientalist Joseph von Hammer-Purgstall, who had earlier awakened Goethe's interest in the Persian poet Hafiz. Rückert learnt Persian from him and in 1822 published his first collection of pseudo-oriental poems, *Ghaselen*, some of them translated from the Persian after the fashion started by Goethe with his *West-Östlicher Divan*. He continued in the same vein with *Östliche Rosen* (Eastern Roses) (1822) and the six volumes of *Die Weisheit des Brahmanen* (The Wisdom of the Brahmin) (1836–9). Meanwhile he had settled in Coburg, married the daughter of an archivist, and published a volume of more intimate lyrical poems, *Liebesfrühling* (Springtime of Love) (1822) which were dedicated to his young wife. The collection met with immediate success and inspired several great

---

[22] As we shall see below, there is no proof that this March was composed in summer 1901, but there are strong indications that it was.

[23] See Vol. iii, Chap. 7.

[24] Concerning the varying attitude of several generations of German literary scholars towards Rückert, see Peter Russell, *Light in Battle with Darkness: Mahler's Kindertotenlieder* (Peter Lang, Berne, 1991), 29ff.

[25] See below Vol. iii, Chap. 3, and also AMM1. 120 and AMM2. 121, the remarks Mahler made in the presence of Ida Dehmel. It always seemed to him to be an act of barbarism, when composers set to music poems whose beauty was (already) perfect.

composers, Schubert and Schumann in particular.[26] While teaching oriental philology at Coburg and Erlangen, Rückert translated Sanskrit, Arabic, Persian, Hebrew, and even Chinese texts into German. He was so steeped in oriental culture that he felt himself to be an Asian speaking German as if it were a foreign language.[27] He was living and teaching in Erlangen, in 1833, when two of his children died and when he wrote the *Kindertotenlieder* in their memory. In Erlangen, Rückert also wrote the *Haus- und Jahreslieder*, as well as further translations from the Persian and Chinese, and several historical plays now forgotten. From 1841 to 1848 he settled in Berlin, where he taught at the University. His last poems were increasingly mystic. From 1848 until his death, Rückert lived in retirement at Neuses, near Coburg, in an estate he had inherited from his father-in-law, devoting himself to scholarship, poetry, and his family. He died at Neuses on 31 January 1866.

Rückert's poems were widely read in his lifetime. A twelve-volume edition appeared immediately after his death, followed by another in 1881–2. Later on, his reputation became the subject of controversy. However, as Peter Russell has pointed out,[28] interest in his poems revived between 1895 and 1900, when a new biography and a large number of popular editions of selected poems appeared. Rückert's popularity subsequently declined and reached its lowest point after the Second World War. His detractors criticized him for the Biedermeier content of some of his poems, for his reactionary sentimentalism, and his tendency to indulge in gratuitous puns and overrefined play on words. He was called a maniériste, an indefatigable verbal experimenter, a virtuoso of language, a graceful and refined, but at times precious, poet, for whom the sounds of words mattered as much, and sometimes even more, than their meaning. However, in this respect he seems to some extent to have anticipated Mallarmé and other modern poets. His subtle, distilled poetry draws its originality, its charm, and its atmosphere of serene resignation, from the versified epigrams of the Orient, notably China and Japan. Mahler always felt close, in heart and mind, to this subtle and delicate lyricism.[29] Furthermore, he, like Rückert, admired folk-art, as the living source of all poetry, but a source which both of them subjected to infinite refinements.

Mahler's *Rückert-Lieder* are of course composed in a style utterly different from that of his previous Lieder and symphonies. 'Gone are the fanfares, the military signals, the dance and march rhythms and the quasi-folk style of the *Wunderhorn* songs. Gone are those songs' satirical excursions, with their accompanying instrumental pungencies and sarcasms,' writes Donald Mitchell.[30] Admittedly the orchestra for the *Rückert-Lieder* is of normal size,[31] but their transparent scoring is devised with chamber-music delicacy. These songs have a poignancy that arises from their delicate, intimate character. No trace of post-Wagnerian declamation can be detected in their purely

---

[26] Schumann's *Lieder*, Op. 37; *Myrthen*, Op. 25 No. 1, 'Widmung'; *Minnespiel*, Op. 101; *Ritornelle in canonischen Weisen*, Op. 65 for men's choir; and *Adventlied*, Op. 71, are set to poems by Rückert, as are two of Schubert's most famous songs, 'Du bist die Ruh' and 'Sei mir gegrüsst'. Others were later set by Brahms, Robert Franz, Reger, Pfitzner, Wolf, and Richard Strauss.

[27] According to Donald Mitchell, the orientalist element in Rückert undoubtedly prepared and 'conditioned' Mahler's reaction to Bethge's collection of Chinese poems in 1907 (DMM3. 128).

[28] Russell, *Light*, 30 ff.

[29] See above, Chap. 15, Mahler's letter to Alma written from Lvov (Lemberg) in Apr. 1903.

[30] DMM3. 68.

[31] Each song uses only part of the resources of the full orchestra. Mitchell has underlined the influence of this Mahlerian 'chamber music' on works like Schoenberg's *Herzgewächse*, Op. 20 (see DMM3. 68).

lyrical style. Melody reigns throughout, melody which, at this time in Mahler's life, ceaselessly renews itself, passing from the voice to the instruments and from the instruments to the voice, the voice being treated here as an instrument among the others, *primus inter pares*. In 'Ich atmet' einen linden Duft', in particular, Adorno draws attention to this characteristic, 'which lifts Mahler's Lieder composition as a whole far above those of his time, even from the point of view of technique: the motivic/thematic synthesis of voice and accompaniment. The two media blend into one another perfectly, so that emotional intensity finds an outlet in extreme tenderness.'[32] Elisabeth Schmierer considers that in these songs Mahler has achieved a successful synthesis of two different traditions, the Lied and the Gesang, resulting in a new and original form.[33]

The briefness of most of the *Rückert-Lieder*, their subjectivity, refinement, the subtlety of their moods, their transparent orchestration, make them appear at first sight the very antithesis of Mahler's huge symphonies. Admittedly, the relationship between them and the three 'instrumental' symphonies written immediately after is much more subtle than that between the *Wunderhorn-Lieder* and the *Wunderhorn-Symphonien*.[34] These three symphonies contain apparently fortuitous quotations from the Lieder.[35] Yet there is also a much deeper link in the way the instrumental sonorities and the thematic material are treated, which makes the total fusion of genres which Mahler later achieved in *Das Lied von der Erde* not only foreseeable but also logical.[36] This essential link operates at the level of 'motivic' composition, to use Adorno's neologism, and of 'evolving' themes. The Lieder use the same compositional procedures as the symphonies—variations, inversions, augmentations, etc.—they also avoid literal recapitulations, and above all display the same architectural sense. It is none the less true, as Fritz Egon Pamer notes, that the form of each Lied, its crescendos, its climaxes, and its general structure, are initially determined by the content of the poem, if not by the words themselves. The obvious use of symphonic techniques in such miniatures as 'Ich atmet' and 'Blicke mir nicht' is not the only apparent paradox in the *Rückert-Lieder*. The influence of the *Volkslied*, for example, is also evident, although they are among the most accomplished examples of the genre of the *Kunstlied*. Mahler shared with Rückert a love of nature and of the life of the people, but both are strikingly absent from these songs, the subjects of which are man's loneliness in the world ('Ich bin der Welt' and 'Um Mitternacht'), the shyness of the artist who protects his unfinished works from prying eyes ('Blicke mir nicht'), the emotion aroused by the sweet smell of a sprig of lime-tree leaves given to the poet by his sweetheart ('Ich atmet''), and the anguished sadness of a father at the deaths of his children (*Kindertotenlieder*). Yet folklore is always close at hand, in the simplicity of the rhythms, the constant predominance of the

---

[32] Theodor Wiesengrund Adorno, 'Zu einer imaginären Auswahl von Liedern Gustav Mahlers', in *Impromptus, Gesammelte Schriften* (Suhrkamp, Frankfurt, 1982), xvii. 189.

[33] Schmierer, *Orchesterlieder*, 170.

[34] On this topic, see Kurt von Fischer's article, 'Zu Gustav Mahlers Liedern', *Neue Zürcher Zeitung*, 153 (16 July 1975), reproduced in *Musik und Bildung* (July 1977), 400.

[35] Monika Tibbe, *Lieder und Liederelemente in instrumentalen Symphoniesätzen Gustav Mahlers* (Katzbichler, Berlin, 1977), also mentions a striking parallel which had not previously been made, between the Finale of the Ninth Symphony (bars 573–6, first violins) and a passage from the fourth *Kindertotenlied* ('mit inniger Empfindung', on the words 'Im Sonnenschein! Der Tag ist schön auf jenen Höh'n!'). (See below, the section devoted to the *Kindertotenlieder*.)

[36] The similarity of mood between the end of the *Kindertotenlieder* and that of *Das Lied* has often been noted.

melodic, or simply musical, element over the words,[37] and, in the language itself, the diatonicism characteristic of all Mahler's music.

Mahler has been accused of thinking in terms of music rather than of words, of committing errors of accentuation and declamation in his word-setting. He has also been blamed occasionally for his 'poor taste' in his choice of poems.[38] His choice of Rückert, an allegedly minor romantic poet, has also been criticized. The author of this indictment, Hans Mayer, nevertheless acknowledges that Mahler in fact created a new genre, or rather a new relationship between music and literature. The previously existing link, notably in Wagner and the Wagnerian Hugo Wolf, had been essentially psychological. But Mahler used his musical settings to suggest or express (*deuten*) the general mood or sentiment underlying the substance of the text, which meant that he devoted relatively little attention to details of the words, and never illustrated them literally. Initially, the structure of the poem determines the musical architecture,[39] which then takes charge. If Mahler deliberately avoided setting literary masterpieces, it is because he could alter the words without being accused of sacrilege. And Adorno adds:

In the choice of his texts Mahler had a way of looking at the past more akin to the discoveries of Karl Kraus than to quaint 'olde worlde' (*Butzenscheiben*) romanticism. It is too easy to pass summary judgment on the lyric poetry of the lean years of the nineteenth century. Now that such poetry has receded so far into the past that no one is tempted to imitate it, we should take another look at it. And, in a poet like Rückert, an experimenter in words and rhymes who for a long time had a poor reputation on the grounds that his procedures were pretentiously artificial, we might find a surprising amount of common ground with the most recent trends. That Mahler the composer had an ear for such links, and took no notice of official value categorizations, is to his credit, not something to be ashamed of. And it should not be forgotten that the best Lieder compositions have by no means always been based on the best poems. In many cases the text has such an independent life of its own that it cannot be taken over into music. Even Schubert could not manage it with Goethe's 'Über allen Gipfeln ist Ruh'.[40]

Mahler certainly showed great perspicacity in his choice of poems, each of which offered him a pre-eminently 'musical' situation, a point of departure from which to create not only a structure, but also an atmosphere. He created 'poetico-musical organisms', or 'revealed the music inherent in the poem'.[41] He accomplished exactly the task he set himself, which naturally led him, in the course of composition, to depart from the text neither more nor less than happens in folk-songs, in which the poems are similarly manipulated.[42]

[37] Hugo Wolf, in whose Lieder Mahler censured the predominance of 'Deklamation', recognized that a large number of his songs were actually 'dramatic scenes'.

[38] On this topic, see Hans Mayer's article, 'Musik und Literatur', RWM 142. He observes that Mahler's additions to Klopstock's poem, in the Finale of the Second, completely change its meaning and 'shift its religious position', proclaiming that man can redeem himself, something quite contrary to the religious thinking of the 18th cent.

[39] Mayer claims that, with Mahler, the text simply serves to 'fix the emotional attitude and suggest a musical architecture'.

[40] Theodor Wiesengrund Adorno, 'Zu einem Streitgespräch über Mahler', in *Gesammelte Schriften* (Suhrkamp, Frankfurt, 1984), xviii. 255 ff.

[41] See Egon Lustgarten, 'Mahlers lyrisches Schaffen', *Musikblätter des Anbruch*, 2: 7/8 (Apr. 1920), 269.

[42] It might even be argued that the only instance where Mahler chooses to set a text recognized as great in its entirety, and where he adopts an attitude of scrupulous respect, the second movement of the Eighth, is not his most successful.

Form: Because of the technical mastery Mahler attained in his maturity, formal analysis proves very difficult in the *Rückert-Lieder*, whose symmetries are almost always
illusory. Mahler often recapitulates by taking the melody in the same direction, but
without reproducing the same intervals, just as he does in the symphonies. Yet
Zoltan Roman has shown[43] that one of the last of the *Rückert-Lieder*, 'Liebst du um
Schönheit', is one of the few Mahler songs using a fairly simple strophic form,
whereas the post-Wagnerian *durchkomponiert* form, hardly ever used by Mahler,
occurs in one of his first Lieder, 'Frühlingsmorgen'. Furthermore, all of them end
with cadences of which 'each one is individually shaped, each one of a different
character, and each one an emphatic compositional gesture'.[44]

Orchestration: Each *Rückert-Lied* calls for a specific body of instruments. It has become
the usual practice to include them in orchestral concert-programmes, and therefore
to perform them in large halls. It should be remembered, however, that for the first
performance in Vienna in 1905, Mahler insisted on a small hall and reduced
orchestral resources.[45] As with most of Mahler's Lieder, the piano and the orchestral
versions were composed simultaneously. He sometimes accompanied them at the
piano himself, and the piano version should be regarded as a viable alternative, not
as a transcription or a reduction.

Order of the Lieder: Richard Specht, in his early booklet on Mahler published in 1905,
speaks of a 'cycle of five Lieder'. No one would today claim that the *Rückert-Lieder*
form a cycle rather than a collection, especially since different sources present them
in a different order. The order I have chosen below is that of the orchestral scores.
It corresponds, more or less, with the chronology of their composition (except for 'Ich
bin der Welt', which was completed last). But the piano score gives the following
order: (1) 'Ich atmet', (2) 'Liebst du', (3) 'Blicke mir nicht', (4) 'Ich bin der Welt', (5)
'Um Mitternacht'. On a sheet of music paper which must have served as title-page
and cover for the manuscripts of 1901,[46] Mahler drew up a list (most likely for his
publisher, C. F. Kahnt) with the *Kindertotenlieder* first, and then (1) 'Blicke mir
nicht', (2) 'Um Mitternacht', (3) 'Der Tamboursg'sell', (4) 'Ich atmet', and (5) 'Ich bin
der Welt'. On 29 January 1905, in his Vienna programme, Mahler placed the
Rückert-Lieder after the *Kindertotenlieder* in the following order: (1) 'Ich atmet', (2)
'Blicke mir nicht', (3) 'Ich bin der Welt', and (4) 'Um Mitternacht'. Three days later,
he performed them as follows: (1) 'Ich bin der Welt', (2) 'Blicke mir nicht', (3) 'Ich
atmet', and (4) 'Um Mitternacht'.

   In the Graz programme on 1 June, 1905 Mahler only included 'Ich bin der Welt'
and 'Um Mitternacht', each sandwiched between two *Wunderhorn-Lieder*. When he
accompanied Johannes Messchaert's Berlin recital, on 14 February 1907, the order
was as follows: (1) 'Blicke mir nicht', (2) 'Ich atmet'', (3) 'Um Mitternacht', and (4)
'Ich bin der Welt'. Evidently Mahler frequently changed his mind according to
circumstances, singers, and the nature of the programmes as a whole. He generally
finished orchestral performances with 'Um Mitternacht', whose major-key fortissimo
coda provides a suitable ending to the group. But in a concert in which the piano

[43] See 'Structure as a Factor in the Genesis of Mahler's Songs', in Hermann Danuser (ed.), *Gustav Mahler*
(Wissenschaftliche Buchgesellschaft, Darmstadt, 1992), 84 ff.
[44] DMM3. 74.   [45] See Vol. iii, Chap. 3 and 4.
[46] This sheet, which formerly belonged to Alma Mahler, is presumably now in MAS. It contains a sketch
for piano and voice of the first 12 bars of the last of the *Kindertotenlieder* (see above).

provided the accompaniment, and with one of the greatest Lieder singers of his time, he was prepared to end the evening with the slowest and least spectacular song, 'Ich bin der Welt', just as he was to end *Das Lied von der Erde* and the Ninth Symphony with long Adagios ending pianissimo.

(*a*) **'Blicke mir nicht in die Lieder'** (Don't look at my songs)

Composition: Maiernigg, June–July 1901.

Autographs: APD, v & p (14 June 1890, with numerous corrections and variants): ÖNB (cod. s. m. 4.365). There are several crossed-out versions of the ending. Mahler has also written two big question marks after the double bar, above and below the date; AFC, v & p: private col. (Vienna); AOD (8 pages): PML (Lehman dep.). The autograph and printed sources, and also Mahler's compositional process, have been studied in detail by Hermann Danuser.[47]

Key: APD, v & p; and AFC, v & o: F major. The second and last verses are in minor. For the first performance on 29 January 1905, and the second on 3 February, this Lied was interpreted by the baritone Anton Moser.

Time signature: 2/2.

Rhythm: Perpetual quaver motion (almost, but not quite continuous).

Tempo: *Sehr lebhaft* (very lively); in ÖNB sketch, *Heiter* (cheerful)

Orchestration: 4 woodwinds, horn, harp, and muted strings (without basses). The cover used for the orchestra material of the *Wunderhorn-Lieder* (see above, the section devoted to these songs) has an autograph list written by Mahler himself of instrumental parts for this Lied, 22 in all. It shows that he planned to include in the string section 10 first violins, 8 second violins, 6 violas, 6 cellos, as well as 1 flute, 1 oboe, 1 clarinet, 1 bassoon and 2 harps—37 players altogether.[48]

Text: The poem was published in the fourth book of *Haus- und Jahreslieder*, autumn 1833, under the title 'Verbotener Blick' (Forbidden glimpse), as part of the collection entitled *Eigener Herd* (Home). Mahler has made no alterations, except to turn the two six-line poetic stanzas into six (twice three) musical phrases or sections. The first includes lines 1 to 3, the second lines 4 and 5, while the last combines line 6 with a repetition of line 1.[49] At bar 45, he replaces *reifen Honigwaben* (ripe honeycombs) with *reichen* (rich). This is probably just a misreading.

Form: Although Pamer sees it as a simple strophic form, it fits better into the scheme AA'; AA', the A' episodes being in the minor. A seven-bar introduction and a coda of the same length begin and end the song, and one- or two-bar interludes connect the various sections. There are numerous variants in the reprises, with exchanges of notes between the vocal and instrumental parts, and even changes in the harmony. Examining the ÖNB APD, Hermann Danuser found interesting evidence that Mahler always gave pre-eminence to the musical structure over the meaning of the words.[50]

Both Alma and Natalie have reported Mahler's reluctance to show his works to anyone before they were completely finished. This was undoubtedly the reason for

[47] Hermann Danuser, *Gustav Mahler und seine Zeit* (Laaber, Laaber, 1991), 60 ff.

[48] See Hilmar-Voit, 'Symphonischer Klang oder Kammermusikton', in *Nachrichten zur Mahler-Forschung*, 28 (IMG, Vienna, Oct. 1992), 11.

[49] See Danuser, *Mahler und seine Zeit*, 62 ff.   [50] Ibid.

choosing this poem which, Mahler told Natalie, he 'could have written himself'.[51] The perpetual motion form was probably suggested to Mahler by the second verse, about bees. Some recent commentators on this song[52] fail to mention an important feature of the poem, the typically Rückertian play on words between 'Lieder' and 'Lider' (eyelids). Although 'Lieder' is spelt throughout with an 'e', it is impossible not to be aware of the homonym 'Lider', especially because of the second line, 'meine Augen schlag' ich nieder' (I close my eyes).

'Blicke mir nicht' can be seen as another *Humoreske* belonging to the long line of perpetual-motion pieces composed by Mahler. It begins with 'Das irdische Leben', continues with the Scherzo of the Second Symphony (and its model, the Lied 'Des Antonius von Padua'), includes the Lied 'Wer hat dies Liedlein', and concludes with the *Purgatorio* in the Tenth Symphony. However, the mischievous animation of this song does not have the same dark undertones as most of the other pieces mentioned above. Here the atmosphere is fleeting, bitter-sweet, and the whole song is so brief that it seems over almost before it has begun. Deryck Cooke regards it as the least inspired of all Mahler's mature Lieder,[53] but does not substantiate his categorical judgement. More recently, Elisabeth Mary Dargie has suggested that the poem's comparison between artistic creation and the work of bees is as unflattering to the one as to the other, because the activity of creation is hardly a matter of routine repetition and the instinctive perfection of the bees' work can never be equalled by art. The same writer criticizes the use of the prosaic word *nasche* (to nibble or munch, usually sweets), especially as it is emphasized by the prosody. Yet the word seems quite in keeping with the song's capricious mood. Here, as elsewhere, Mahler attained the goal he set himself, and created with the most subtle and sophisticated means a delightful miniature which retains the appearance of simplicity and provides a refreshing contrast to the slow and serious Lieder in the same collection.

(b) 'Ich atmet' einen linden Duft' (I breathed a sweet scent)

Composition: Maiernigg, June–July 1901.

Autographs: AFC, v & p, from Natalie Bauer-Lechner's collection: now in BSB (no. Mus. MSS 5656, cim 450). AFC, v & o, given by Alma Mahler to Artur Bodanzky, is also in BSB (3 pages folio, undated, 8 staves per page, black ink). It bears a marking for the conductor (Conductor: slow fourths) as well as a few corrections.[54] There are also a number of phrasing indications in the vocal part which were not included later in the published version. Another AFC, v & o, is in PML (Lehman dep.). There are also two copies made for the printers, one by a copyist and the other by Alma, with corrections in various hands, including Mahler's (IMG).

Key: D major, modulating to E♭ in the last stanza. There were three original editions of the orchestral score (1905), for high voice (F major), middle voice (D), and low

---

[51] See above, Chap. 10.

[52] Vill, *Vermittlungsformen*, 128, and Elisabeth Mary Dargie, *Music and Poetry in the Songs of Gustav Mahler* (Peter Lang, Berne, 1981), 270.

[53] Deryck Cooke, *Gustav Mahler 1860–1911*, 32.

[54] See Zoltan Roman, 'Die autographe Partitur zu "Ich atmet' einen linden Duft"', *Nachrichten zur Mahler-Forschung*, 25 (Mar. 1991), 5. In the first 2 bars, Mahler originally planned to use a piccolo flute. A celesta is also mentioned in the copy prepared by Alma Mahler for the publisher. Several other discrepancies between the publ. version and the autograph apparently originated in Alma's not too careful copy.

voice (C). In its first and second performances, this Lied was interpreted by the baritone Anton Moser.

Time signature: 6/4, with six bars of 3/4.

Rhythm: A slow and almost continuous quaver ostinato is woven around the crotchets of the vocal line, anticipating that of the second movement of *Das Lied von der Erde*. Elisabeth Mary Dargie compares the gentle rocking rhythm with that of a lullaby.

Tempo: *Sehr zart und innig* (very tender and intimate). *Langsam* (slow).

Orchestration: A miracle of transparency, refinement, and economy, it is comparable only to a spider's web, at the heart of which an uninterrupted arabesque gently unfurls in the muted first violins' medium and high registers, over sustained bassoon notes and open fifths on the harp and low horns, always pianissimo. In the Munich orchestral manuscript, Mahler used a piccolo in the first two bars. The low strings are silent throughout this Lied, as is the flute, which enters only in the last four bars to take up the counter-melody previously played by the oboes. In the last bar it holds the B, which remains unresolved (see below). Donald Mitchell has noted small differences in the scoring between the orchestra score of the high voice edition (in F) and middle voice (in D).[55] Elisabeth Schmierer considers Mahler's use of a small orchestra and his whole method of orchestration the most original feature of the *Rückert-Lieder*. In her words, 'the structure owes more to the colours than to the shape of the composition'. Comparing the accompaniment of Strauss's and Mahler's orchestral Lieder, she concludes: 'With Strauss it is clear that the full polyphonic multiplicity of parts cannot be rendered by the piano, and therefore requires instrumentation. Whereas with Mahler it is precisely the composition's structure which, because there is no compact set of accompanying chords, is inadequate.'[56]

Text: Published in May–June 1833, in *Haus- und Jahreslieder*, it belongs to a group of poems entitled *Lenz* (Spring). In a later edition of Rückert, the title is changed to: 'Dank für den Lindenzweig' (Thanks for the linden branch). The repetition of the last line of the first stanza at the beginning of the second is inspired by oriental models. Of all the poems Mahler set, this is the one which perhaps best embodies Rückert's alchemy of words, with the basic ambiguity between *linden* (gentle) and *Linden* (lime) and the numerous alliterations on liquid sonorities such as *linden, lieber, Linde, lieblich, leis, gelinde*. Independently of their meaning, they create what Adorno calls 'musical situations'. Mahler makes two important changes to the original text. The first is a seemingly insignificant transposition that moves the fourth line into second place. This is more important than it seems for

> Im Zimmer stand
> Ein Angenbinde
> Von lieber Hand
> Ein Zweig der Linde

becomes

> Im Zimmer stand
> Ein Zweig der Linde
> Ein Angebinde
> Von lieber Hand

---

[55] DMM3. 69 ff.   [56] Schmierer, *Orchesterlieder*, 185 ff.

'In the room was a linden branch, a present from the loved one's hand' replaces: 'In the room was a present...'. In the last line, Mahler replaces the rather heavy *Herzensfreundschaft* (friendship of the heart) with *Liebe* (love), thus shortening the line from eight feet to six (Mahler compensates for the resulting asymmetry by lengthening the note values, so that the verse lasts longer).

Form: With the exception of the singer's first phrase (which picks up the opening chord of the fifth and sixth, and which can be regarded as an introduction), the two parts of the Lied are practically symmetrical, like the stanzas of the poem. But further study reveals innumerable changes of detail, the principal one being the exquisite modulation to the most distant key of all, E♭, creating an effect of pure magic.[57] For all its brevity, 'Ich atmet' einen linden Duft' once again displays the exquisite subtlety of Mahler's art. Elisabeth Schmierer's book contains a detailed analysis of this song: once again, the musical stanzas do not coincide with those of the poem, which has in fact been 'adapted to the syntax of the music', so that the first line of each poetic stanza is separated from the others. Thus the first musical stanza starts only with the second line of the poem. The resulting asymmetry turns out to be complete. Schmierer's chart of the parallel phrases and their musical setting is revealing.[58] This song also demonstrates Mahler's original use of polyphony and timbre. The orchestration is 'substantial' because the accompaniment is not polyphonic in the traditional sense, but consists of superimposed layers, each of which has a different function.

To Natalie, Mahler spoke of this song as describing 'the feeling one experiences in the presence of a person one loves and of whom one is quite sure, two minds communicating without any word needing to be spoken'.[59] Adorno wrote of Mahler's setting that the poem had been 'in truly heart-rending fashion, not so much composed as re-portrayed in musical colour and line'.[60] The music here is as light and ethereal as the perfume of the lime-tree in the spring air, with a rarefied, disembodied sonority.

In the second part, the instrumental soli (oboe, horn and flute) introduce a note of melancholy into this idyllic tableau, so brief that it is virtually cruel, as often happens with Webern. Hovering on the brink of silence, this Lied, with its strictly tonal relationships, is reminiscent of a Webern gesture. The ribbon of melody soars high above harmonic depths; when it finally comes down to them again, they are integrated with the form, that is to say, reconciled.[61]

A feature of this song affirms Mahler's new style, which was to find its fullest expression in *Das Lied von der Erde*: the omnipresence, not only of an instrumental figuration (of pentatonic character), but also of the 'Mahlerian' augmented sixth. This reinforces the feeling of immateriality by weakening almost all the cadences and the other tonal functions (as in 'Ich bin der Welt'). In the final chord, the flute holds a B over the tonic chord (D, F♯, A) of the other instruments. As with the last chord of *Das Lied von der Erde*, this augmented sixth opens to eternity the brief instant of pure lyricism provided by the thirty-six bars of the song.

[57] Elisabeth Mary Dargie's book contains a detailed analysis of this Lied, as does Reinhard Gerlach's article 'Mahler, Rückert und das Ende des Liedes, Essay über lyrisch-musikalische Form', in Dagmar Droysen (ed.), *Jahrbuch des staatlichen Instituts für Musikforschung Preussischer Kulturbesitz* (Merseburger, Berlin, 1975), 37. In this article, the author analyses the E♭ modulation in the second stanza.
[58] Schmierer, *Orchesterlieder*, 177 ff.   [59] NBL1. 166; NBL2. 193 ff.
[60] Adorno, 'Streitgespräch' (see n. 40).   [61] Adorno, 'Auswahl' (see n. 32), 36.

(c) 'Ich bin der Welt abhanden gekommen' (I have become lost to the world)

Composition: More information is available about the genesis of this Lied than for the other *Rückert-Lieder*. A special paragraph is devoted to it in Natalie Bauer-Lechner's *Mahleriana*.[62] As seen above, it was probably not yet finished on 10 August 1901, when Mahler played for Natalie the 'Seven Lieder' written at the beginning of the summer. One of the three manuscript sketches[63] is dated 16 August, which means that this Lied must have been the last to be composed in the summer of 1901.

Autographs: Several sketches and APDs, v & p, bearing the initials 'M.W.', are in PML (Lehman deposit), one including a fragment from the second of the *Kindertotenlieder*.[64] Two are incomplete and deal with the middle section of the Lied only. In the third, which is complete and dated 16 August 1901, the accompaniment is sketched on two staves more in the manner of an orchestral reduction than a piano version. An AFC, v & p, from Justine Rosé's collection, is in BGM. The whereabouts of the AFC, v & o, presented by Mahler to his friend Guido Adler, on 1 November 1905, are at present unknown.[65] Mahler's dedication refers to the title of the song: 'With a hug, a kiss and a dedication to my dear friend Guido Adler (who I hope will never be lost to me) as a souvenir for his 50th birthday.'

Key: F major in all the sketches and in the piano manuscript. This however bears the words: 'transpose into E♭'. The orchestral score is in the latter key. The middle passage modulates first into A♭ (in the orchestral version) then into C and C minor. In its first and second Viennese performances this Lied was sung by the baritone Friedrich Weidemann.

Time signature: 4/4 (with one 2/4 bar resulting from an elision which is crossed out in the piano manuscript).

Tempo: *Äusserst langsam und zurückhaltend* (extremely slow and restrained); *zögernd* (hesitant) at 'mit der ich sonst'; *nicht eilen* (unhurried) at 'gestorben'; then *etwas fliessender, aber nicht eilen* (a little more fluent, but still unhurried) at 'es ist mir auch gar nicht'; *nicht schleppen* (do not drag) at 'denn wirklich'; *wieder zurückhaltend* (again restrained) before 'ich bin gestorben' and finally *ohne Steigerung* (no crescendo) up to 'in meinem Himmel'.

Orchestration: The strings are here complete, but they play with mutes until the middle section. Besides the four woodwind parts (2 clarinets, 2 bassoons, oboe/cor anglais) there are two horns in E♭ and a harp. Note the essential roles played by the cor anglais, which begins and ends the Lied, and by the harp which plays all the triplet arpeggios. Here again, the orchestration is strikingly sparse, notably in the bass-line, played on the harp and the pizzicato basses. Such effects are to be found more and more frequently in Mahler's late works. Elisabeth Schmierer points out differences of scoring between the orchestra scores in E♭ and F.[66]

Text: Taken from the early collection *Liebesfrühling*. It is the twenty-ninth poem in the Fünfter Strauss (Fifth Bouquet), which bears the general title 'Wiedergenommen' (Reprise). Most of the changes are minimal: OR: *von mir nicht*, Mahler: *nichts von*

[62] See above, Chap. 10.   [63] See below.

[64] See Schmierer, *Orchesterlieder*, 271. On the composition and autographs of this song, see also Stephen E. Hefling, 'The Composition of "Ich bin der Welt abhanden gekommen"', in Danuser (ed.), *Gustav Mahler*, 96 ff.

[65] See RMA 46.   [66] *Orchesterlieder*, 259.

mir; OR. *Ich leb' in mir*, M: *Ich leb' allein*; OR: *dem Weltgewimmel*, M: *dem Weltgetümmel*. This last change has been universally approved by scholars of German, *Getümmel* (tumult, turmoil) being much preferable to *Gewimmel* (swarm, throng). It will be recalled that this Lied was composed in the little Maiernigg *Häuschen*,[67] which Mahler had just had built. The blissful seclusion in the woods in Carinthia probably influenced his choice of poem.[68] Recent commentators have noted that two different interpretations can be given of the poem, according to the relative importance given to the last two lines, 'Ich leb' allein in meinem Himmel, | In meinem Lieben, in meinem Lied.' Is the 'Ich' a happy artist isolated from the world in his art or a happy lover isolated in his love?[69]

Form: According to Egon Pamer, this is one of the few Mahler Lieder that can be regarded as 'durchkomponiert'. However, it contains three clearly separated sections, the second of which produces a mild effect of contrast (at 'Sie mag wohl glauben'), with a faster tempo which gradually accelerates. The recapitulation, which soon takes on the character of a long coda, is followed by an instrumental epilogue in which the ascending melodic gestures of the prelude now descend. It ends, in the penultimate bar, with a long suspended fifth (C in the cor anglais) which recalls the augmented sixth which concludes 'Ich atmet''.[70]

As for the previous Lied, an effect of timelessness is achieved by a sixth added to the tonic chord. It gives the song a strong pentatonic flavour, anticipating that of *Das Lied von der Erde*.[71] All the melodic fragments start on a weak beat of the bar. In the introduction, the main theme hesitates three times before rising to the fifth;[72] the voice's final descent (already heard in the seventh and eighth bars of the introduction) is, in a sense, inversely symmetrical with the opening rise, so that the short instrumental prelude in itself sums up the whole Lied. Schmierer notes that the vocal line uses mostly intervals of seconds, or more rarely arpeggios.[73] This song is, with 'Um Mitternacht',[74] the longest of all the *Rückert-Lieder* and the most deeply felt. It also appears to be the most autobiographical,[75] and is perhaps the high point of Mahler's Lieder output as a whole.

[67] Ernst Decsey heard Mahler say that this Lied expressed the feeling of peace he experienced in the *Häuschen* (EDS1, 44).

[68] Alma Mahler relates that, while composing this song, Mahler had in mind a reclining effigy like those seen in Italian churches, 'a cardinal with his hands folded and his eyes closed' (AML 32). The slow movement of the Fourth Symphony inspired a similar image.

[69] Hans Heinrich Eggebrecht (*Die Musik Gustav Mahlers*, 275 ff.) believes that the first interpretation is the right one. See also Schmierer, *Orchesterlieder*, 198.

[70] Vill, *Vermittlungsformen*, 124, and Dargie, *Music and Poetry*, contain detailed formal analyses of this Lied.

[71] Donald Mitchell also finds in this song an anticipation of the 'heterophonic' technique which Mahler later used in *Das Lied*. It is described by Adorno as *unscharfes Unison* (unfocused unison) 'in which identical parts are rhythmically a little out of step with one another . . . as a kind of improvised counterbalance to the excessive "finish" characteristic of art songs' (DMM3. 62).

[72] To my knowledge, no one has yet pointed out the similarity between these first bars and a passage from the Adagio of the Fourth Symphony (bars 333 ff.).

[73] *Orchesterlieder*, 199.

[74] James L. Zychowicz has shown the constant recurrence, in the vocal line as well as in the accompaniment, of what he calls the 'Ewigkeit motive'. (See above, on the Fourth Symphony, and Zychowicz, 'Quotation and Assimilation', 14.)

[75] The criticisms levelled by Dargie against this Rückert poem, as prosaic and lacking in rhythm, have not generally been made by German musicologists. On this occasion, Mahler's choice was surely governed more by the content of the poem than by its literary quality.

Schmierer shows that, as usual, the basic structure is musical rather than poetic, but that Mahler has for once made a few concessions to the 'Deklamation' he so violently disapproved of in Wolf's Lieder. Most of the time, the musical and poetic accents do not coincide. However, the climax of the first stanza comes with the word 'gestorben' which reaches F, the highest note in the whole song, and is followed by a descending melisma.[76] The same author makes interesting comments on Mahler's thematic procedures in this song: the first bars resemble a symphonic introduction, the principal motif being developed gradually from the first interval of an ascending second, the harmony constantly alternating between F and D minor. The voice then takes up the theme, which has thus been anticipated in the introduction. In fact, the whole first stanza can be considered to be an introduction. These procedures, as Schmierer shows, are closer to those of symphonic than to those of Lieder composition, especially because of the constant interplay of material between the voice and the instruments. For instance, the vocal line for 'in meinem Lieben' and 'in meinem Lied' is drawn from the instrumental accompaniment to the first stanza. The closing character of the last stanza comes from its being a new version of the closing section of the instrumental prelude. Unlike Adorno, who speaks of 'small elements . . . unfocussed to the point of irrelevance', Schmierer finds each one of the transformations significant, as they are in a symphony.[77]

The resemblance of this Lied to the Adagietto of the Fifth Symphony (emphasized by the use of harp triplets) has often been pointed out. It is indeed obvious. The expressive content is also very similar, even though Willem Mengelberg claimed to have heard, from both Mahler and Alma, that this movement was another secret love message addressed to Alma (during the summer of 1902), like 'Liebst du um Schönheit'. Susanne Vill has suggested that the 'isolation' could be a death symbol, and it seems likely that the idea of death was consciously or unconsciously present when Mahler composed this song, if only because it was written during the summer of his near-fatal haemorrhage.

Mahler himself claimed that he had simply wanted to describe the sensation of being alone in the midst of nature. Natalie writes: 'He himself said of the unusually fulfilled and controlled nature of this Lied: "It is a feeling that surges right up to the lips, but does not go beyond them. And that is precisely me!"'.[78] Few composers have been able to attain such intensity of expression without a single forte, and to give such a feeling of quiet and timelessness. Thanks to harmonic and tonal as well as rhythmic immobility, the whole song resembles the calm surface of a lake reflecting the sky, or the repose of a Zen garden.

(d) 'Um Mitternacht' (At midnight)

Composition: Maiernigg, June–July 1901.
Autographs: They include a complete 2-page APD (in B♭ minor), with accompaniment on two staves and corrections in pencil in SBW (MH 11380/C); an AFC, v & p, dedicated to William Ritter (Vienna, 1908) and with a wrong date of composition: *componirt entstanden 1899—oder 1900* (BGM); an AOD in B♭ minor, dedicated by Alma Mahler to Arnold Schoenberg on 13 June 1920 (ASI).

---

[76] Schmierer, *Orchesterlieder*, 201.   [77] Ibid. 202 ff.   [78] NBL1. 166 ff.; NBL2. 194.

Key: APD: B♭ minor; AFC, v & p: B minor; v & o: B♭ minor (with the comment: 'transpose to B minor');[79] orchestral edition: A minor. The second and last verses are in major. Elisabeth Schmierer points out that the key of this song inclines towards the Phrygian mode, to which the first descending scale of the E♭ horn belongs. In its first and second Viennese performances, this Lied was sung by the baritone Friedrich Weidemann, but Mahler chose a Heldentenor, Erik Schmedes, for the Graz concert of 1 June 1905.

Time signature: 3/2, alternating for single bars with 2/2, 4/2, 6/2.

Tempo: Ruhig. Gleichmässig (quiet, even). *Fliessend* (flowing) for the second verse and the end of the fourth. *Mit mächtigem Aufschwung* (with powerful impetus) for the fifth.

Orchestration: Although—or perhaps because—Mahler does not employ any strings, the winds are exceptionally numerous: 2 flutes, oboe d'amore[80] and normal oboe, 2 clarinets, 2 bassoons, and contrabassoon, 4 horns, 2 trumpets, 3 trombones, tuba, timpani, harp, and piano.

Text: In the *Liebesfrühling* collection, 'Mitternacht' (this is the poem's original title) is part of the 'Fünfte Reihe' (fifth series), which is entitled *Sommer* (Summer). Mahler changed nothing in the poem. Once again, Dargie finds the Rückert poem weak.[81]

Form: The musical structure reflects that of the poem, which has five verses. At first glance, the symmetry between the first two stanzas and between the fourth and fifth (ABAAB) is the essential feature, but there are as always countless variants. Actually the third verse imitates the first more closely than the fourth does, where the anguish of the lonely poet breaks forth in a long melisma in the form of a descending scale on the word 'entscheiden'. The melodic cells are stated in the introduction.[82] They include a descending and ascending motif of a third, with its 'answer' high in the treble; long descending scales; the refrain 'Um Mitternacht' followed by the rising vocal phrase 'hab' ich gewacht'. As in the first movement of the Fourth Symphony, the different elements are constantly altered, augmented, diminished, and variously joined. Thus, in the second verse, the refrain 'Um Mitternacht' takes the form of a descending scale, while the final 'apotheosis' uses the same descending scales, augmented and in the major. Schmierer is 'amazed' at Mahler's transformation of Rückert's modest closing lines into a resplendent apotheosis, completely unlike anything that has happened before in the song. The closing episode, with its prolonged note-values, its chorale character, and rich orchestration, is obviously a 'Durchbruch', in the Adornian sense of the word. However, it looks back to the

---

[79] Elisabeth Schmierer notes that this is the only song for which the key of the autograph differs from that of all the edns. (*Orchesterlieder*, 271).

[80] The AFC, v & o, in ASI replaces the oboe d'amore with two normal oboes. Mahler's attention was probably drawn to this rare instrument by the first performance of Strauss's *Symphonia Domestica*, which he conducted in Vienna on 23 Nov. 1904. Mahler also decided upon horns and trumpets in E♭, whereas they are in F in the Schoenberg Institute autograph. Similarly, the two clarinets in B♭ are replaced by clarinets in A. The original scoring does not include a piano.

[81] *Music and Poetry*, 286.

[82] They are identified and classified, in the different forms they adopt throughout the Lied, in 2½ pp. of Reinhard Gerlach's article, 'Mahler, Rückert und das Ende des Liedes, Essay über lyrisch-musikalische Form', in Droysen (ed.), *Jahrbuch*, 37. See also Dargie's analysis in *Music and Poetry*, 285, and the shorter one by Vill (*Vermittlungsformen*, 125).

second stanza, which is also in the major mode and in strong contrast with the bare lines of verse 1. The fifth stanza can thus be considered as a recapitulation of the second rather than a true 'Durchbruch'. Schmierer also draws attention to the contrast between the first two stanzas, which has no parallel in the poem, where the first two verses are in exactly the same mood.

Adorno has cast doubt on the 'triumphant' character of Mahler's optimistic Finales. Likewise, Schmierer finds the triumphant ending of 'Um Mitternacht' ambivalent, like a 'forced reinstatement of an already abandoned idea'. To support this idea, she quotes the dissonances in the climactic passage (trumpet notes which do not belong to the chords), and the final cadence which has a plagal colouration and unusual dynamic markings (crescendos and diminuendos) in the wind parts. In her opinion, these features reveal 'some vestiges of critical reserve'.[83]

Numerous commentators have been intrigued by the song's sparseness, its expressive intensity, the *Angst*-ridden regularity of the rhythm, and the quite unusual orchestration with its rare and exceptionally deep sonorities. Stuart Feder[84] suggests that it reflects feelings of anxiety aroused in Mahler by his recent haemorrhage: night and solitude (and also sleep and awakening from sleep, already present in the Finale of the Second Symphony and the Nietzsche setting in the Third) symbolized by the low instrumental register, and by the stark and unadorned melodic material; death (Finale of the Second, 'Tamboursg'sell', *Kindertotenlieder* of the same period, and the Funeral March in the Fifth) appearing in the initial refrain, where Feder hears the tick-tock of a pendulum clock 'slowed down to the point of absurdity', or the beating of the heart which one becomes aware of in the silence of the night;[85] pain, sadness, depression, despair suggested by the long scale motifs which plunge to the abyss of the deep pitches;[86] the God depicted in the last verse who is the God of armies, the all-powerful God who never sleeps, the Eternal to whom man in a sense delegates the responsibility for his fate and whose power is manifested in the calls of the brass, a strident sound reminiscent of a military band.[87] Feder also observes that Mahler had just turned 40 and entered middle-age, and that the decision he was about to take to change his life by marrying was to be put into effect within a few months.[88] To Feder, the fundamental rhythmic instability, with thirty-six bar changes in a piece only ninety-four bars long, along with the hasty, feverish writing in the APD now held in SBW, shows with what haste and under what emotional stress Mahler composed this song.[89] At least once, in the instrumental interlude connecting the first two verses, the anguished mood prevailing in the song breaks out into a cry, the oboe d'amore's high G. (On the piano score, Mahler wrote

[83] *Orchesterlieder*, 237.

[84] Article mentioned in n. 12, 'Gustav Mahler um Mitternacht', 11.

[85] 'Die Schläge meines Herzens' (the beating of my heart), says the poem. Stuart Feder draws attention to the long note-value given to the word *Puls* (bar 43), which in his opinion reveals the anguish provoked by the thought of death.

[86] Feder recalls that the motif symbolizing pain in *Das klagende Lied* is also a descending scale.

[87] In the same passage, Feder mentions the Hebrew hymn 'Piyyutim', written for days of penance, where the first and last lines of each verse, as in the poem 'Mitternacht', begin with the same refrain.

[88] Feder points out a parallel between certain lines in the first love poem Mahler sent anonymously to Alma, 'Das kam so über Nacht' (see above, Chap. 12) and 'Um Mitternacht', which it in a sense 'parodies'.

[89] The same author finds the mistake Mahler made about the date of this Lied's composition when sending the MS to William Ritter (BGM), 1899 or 1900 instead of 1901, significant. He was unconsciously setting the song back to a time before his 40th birthday and his haemorrhage of Feb. 1901.

grell (shrill) here.)[90] It is followed by a melodic plunge of almost two octaves down to a low A, fortissimo.[91] The brevity of the melodic phrases, broken by rests, also evokes anguish, and the melisma mentioned above (at 'entscheiden': bars 57 to 70) marks another paroxysm of despair. The blackest mood is maintained right to the beginning of the final verse, despite a few bars of apparent optimism when the second stanza moves into the major key.[92]

The change from deepest night to brightest day comes suddenly, at the beginning of the fourth bar in the last verse, just when the tuba has taken the descending scales down into the abyss of a low A. Without the slightest warning, the mood changes to major, the sun shines through in triumphal peals of brass, the rhythm broadens, the voice takes on a liturgical solemnity, and the piano and the harp join in the final apotheosis with rising scales and arpeggios over the continuous roll of the timpani. Mahler himself drew a parallel between this triumphant affirmation of faith and the one which concludes the Second Symphony. This time, however, the proclamation is perhaps a little too loud to be as convincing as the luminous resignation at the end of the *Lieder eines fahrenden Gesellen*, the *Kindertotenlieder*, or *Das Lied von der Erde*. The final 'triumph' in 'Um Mitternacht' recalls the resplendent altars in Austrian baroque churches, with an optimism that is decorative rather than deeply felt. As Adorno has aptly observed, 'the power which now appears has powerlessness too close at its heels; were its promised power a reality, and not still simply a promise, it would not need to protest its power so loudly.'[93]

C. *Rückert-Lied with piano*

'Liebst du um Schönheit' (If you love for beauty's sake)

Composition: As seen above,[94] Alma's private diary makes it possible to correct the chronological error she made in her *Erinnerungen*, which ascribe this song to the summer of 1903. In fact, this Lied was composed in Maiernigg between the beginning of the holiday and 10 August 1902. For it was on 10 August that Alma opened the piano score of *Siegfried*, into which Mahler had slipped the manuscript of the Lied.

Autograph: The only known one was written specifically for Alma, now in BGM. It contains only one important correction: portions of two bars in the instrumental interlude separating the second and third verses are crossed out, so that it lasts for two four-beat bars and not, as previously, two four-beat and one three-beat bars. The marking 'espr(essivo)' that went with the 'piano' of the first bar is also crossed out, as is the 'ritenuto' of the next one. Mahler has added *nicht rit.* in pencil at 'der jung ist' and has written *rit.* above the last two bars of the interlude (there is an a *tempo* above 'um Schätze). On the other hand, the *steigernd* found on the orchestral score

[90] Donald Mitchell detects a striking resemblance between the oboe d'amore's 'cry of pain' (bars 65–6), and a passage in the Adagio of the Fourth Symphony (bars 211–12). (See DMM3, 57 ff.)
[91] Edward F. Kravitt, 'Mahler's Dirges for his Death', *Musical Quarterly*, 64: 3 (July 1978), 329 ff., recalls the Nietzsche setting in the Third Symphony (bars 73–5), in which the oboe is given a passage closely related to this one (in the episode Mahler entitled 'The Night Bird').
[92] Donald Mitchell has noted that, rhythmically ('Um Mitternacht') and ('Der Einsame') are identical, like certain heterophonic passages in 'Um Mitternacht' which anticipate the opening movement of the Ninth Symphony (DMM3. 64).
[93] TAM 20.   [94] See Chap. 14.

at 'Liebst du um Liebe'[95] is not in the original autograph. Mahler undoubtedly copied this Lied again, or had it copied, before submitting it in 1905 to C. F. Kahnt, his publisher, and this was when he introduced these additional markings.[96]

Key: C major (MS and spurious orchestral score) without any modulations to speak of. The second stanza opens in the minor. Apparently this Lied, a *Privatissimum* written expressly for Alma, was not sung in public in Mahler's lifetime.

Time signature: 3/4, with seventeen changes (in thirty-four bars!).

Tempo: Innig, fliessend (tender, flowing). The orchestra score bears only the first of these indications.

Orchestration: The orchestral score, published in large format by C. F. Kahnt, apparently in 1910,[97] reads 'Orch. Max Puttmann'.[98] A former director of the firm informed me that Puttmann was at the time employed by C. F. Kahnt, that he did orchestration for them, and that in 1905, before the publication of the Sixth Symphony, he wrote a biographical article about Mahler.[99] Before it was known that the publisher had identified the orchestrator of the Lied in the early scores, I once discussed the matter with two eminent Mahlerians. Harold Byrns was the more critical of Puttmann's work, pointing out a few unfortunate details which would certainly not have escaped Mahler's eye.[100] Deryck Cooke, without objecting so much to the whole, made a number of severe criticisms: unpardonable doublings;[101] the harp arpeggios in bars 25 and 26, inserted at a point where Mahler would certainly have wanted absolute stillness; and above all an arbitrary change to the harmony in bar 24.[102] However, in other respects, he found certain virtues in Puttmann's work, especially since it was

[95] Strangely, the piano score has *allargando* here.

[96] For instance accents, brief crescendos and decrescendos, etc. In v & p version, some of the *piano* indications are in parentheses, which seems to imply that they were added by the editor.

[97] This is the date on the score. However, it is hard to believe that Mahler, in his lifetime, would have allowed his publisher to entrust the scoring of a song to a mere employee of the firm. It would be more logical for him to have done it himself, or else to have vetoed it and insisted that he wanted the Lied sung only with piano accompaniment. Mahler handed over the four *Rückert-Lieder* with orchestra in a contract dated 15 Apr. 1905, but did not decide to do the same with 'Liebst du um Schönheit' until 8 Dec. (see below, Vol. iii, Chap. 4). For obvious reasons, the publisher preferred to have five songs with orchestra in his catalogue, rather than four orchestral songs plus one with piano accompaniment.

[98] In his thesis written in 1922, Fritz Egon Pamer claims that all the Lieder dating from Mahler's maturity were for voice and orchestra, which suggests that he regarded the orchestration of 'Liebst du um Schönheit' as original. Even Edward Kravitt, 'The Orchestral Lied', *Music Review* (Aug. 1976), 215, offers the same hypothesis, declaring that Mahler 'wrote no Lied with piano accompaniment in his maturity'. Elisabeth Mary Dargie, without making any particular comment on the nature of the accompaniment, speaks of the 'change of character' in the accompaniment at bar 25, which means she believes the harp triplets added by Puttmann in these two bars (and indeed the whole orchestration) to be Mahler's. Only Reinhard Gerlach writes that the orchestration is not original, giving as his source the musicologist Rudolf Stephan (see 'Mahler, Rückert', 29).

[99] The article was publ. in the magazine *Haus- und Kirchenmusik*. Max Puttmann (1864–1935), born in Berlin, was critic on the *Erfurter Allgemeiner Anzeiger* and was later engaged by the *Leipziger Volkszeitung*. He also taught music, and lived in Panitzsch, near Leipzig.

[100] Particularly the *pianissimo subito* at bars 7 and 25, in which Mahler would certainly have suppressed some of the instruments. Harold Byrns was particularly shocked by Puttmann's doubling of the first oboe by the first clarinet and the first violins at bar 25. Furthermore, he considered the scoring at bar 20 ('Liebe die Meerfrau') far too heavy in the bass-line.

[101] Particularly the addition of two notes in the first clarinet and bassoon at bar 9; doubling at the octave between the violas and the horns at bar 12; and the frequent doubling of the cellos with double basses.

[102] Here Puttmann adds a descending scale motif, played by the horns in thirds. In the last bar, the notes B♭ and D do not appear in the original piano accompaniment.

done at a time when no close study of Mahler's methods of orchestration had been made.[103]

Text: This, like 'Ich bin der Welt', is taken from the Fünfter Strauss (Fifth Bouquet), entitled 'Wiedergenommen' (Reprise). Mahler makes only one change, adding the word 'immer' before the poem's final 'immerdar'. He also changes 'die' (who), the first word of the last line in the third verse, to 'sie' (they). Clara Schumann set the same text to music in her *Drei Lieder von Rückert*, Op. 12, and the poem was later used by Robert Schumann in No. 4 of *Zwölf Gedichte aus Liebesfrühling* (Rückert), Op. 37, by Robert and Clara Schumann.

Form: Zoltan Roman[104] singles out this song as the only mature one by Mahler that uses simple strophic form. The structure is, in effect, more rudimentary and symmetrical than in the other *Rückert-Lieder*, with three musical verses of six bars each and a fourth which lasts nine bars because the key notes are lengthened.[105] But it should be recognized that this symmetry is, as usual, more apparent than real, each verse being subtly varied in relation to the preceding one, and the second verse being in the minor. Each verse is made up of three ascending phrases, one for each line, followed by a fourth phrase which descends. In the last verse, the order of the phrases is changed, the third descending and the fourth, now ascending, followed by an ecstatic melisma on an arpeggio that falls back to A (the added sixth on the tonic chord, which already played an essential role in the final cadence of 'Ich atmet'' and 'Ich bin der Welt'). In the final bars, the melody is taken up by the piano and gradually descends to the tonic, C, which is reached only in the very last bar. Also striking (as in 'Ich bin der Welt') are the pauses on strong beats in the second and fourth lines of each verse: this is no longer true of the last verse where, as we have seen, the phrases are rearranged. Each verse is made up of twice times three bars, but the durations are unequal because of the changes of metre, which are far more frequent than usual since, for once, Mahler faithfully observes the metrics of the poem. These changes give the vocal line a freedom and an air of spontaneity which successfully counteract the symmetry of the structure. Erwin Stein has aptly called this procedure a 'rubato obligato'. Each verse culminates musically in a high F, from which, in the last verse, it descends in a long, ecstatic, melisma.[106]

Many commentators have been critical of this little song, which they have found too simple, too respectful of the poem's metre, and less refined in technique than the other *Rückert-Lieder*. But it should be remembered that this is Mahler's only 'love-song',[107] that it was probably written very quickly, and that its main aim was to convey a message. In the hands of a composer like Mahler, it was nevertheless bound to become a accomplished work of art. Its economy of means is as admirable as the many subtleties which make of it a masterpiece no less refined, if more spontaneous, than the other pieces in the collection. Every detail shows the hand of the master, for instance the introductory bars, which anticipate the last phrase of the first verse, or

---

[103] Letter from Deryck Cooke to the author, 25 June 1975.   [104] 'Structure', 84.

[105] This lengthening corresponds to an essential development in the poem, where three negative sentences are followed by a fourth affirmative one.

[106] 'Liebst du um Schönheit' has been analysed in detail by Zoltan Roman (in 'Structure', 84 ff.), Reinhard Gerlach (in 'Mahler, Rückert', 27), Elisabeth Mary Dargie (*Music and Poetry*, 291), and Susanne Vill (*Vermittlungsformen*, 129).

[107] As seen above, Willem Mengelberg regarded the Adagietto of the Fifth Symphony as another.

the postlude, with its succession of chromatic chords over a dominant pedal, or even the final cadence, where the leading note goes down to the sixth and then to the dominant rather than moving straight to the tonic. Rising melodic gestures, so plentiful in Mahler's work, from the Resurrection theme in the Second to the 'Accende Lumen' of the Eighth, by way of the famous Adagietto of the Fifth, constantly recur here like a veritable signature. It has been noted that the minor key of the second verse is justified only in terms of the music, for it does not correspond to anything in the text (unless Mahler felt a moment of sadness at the thought of his own 'lost youth' and of Alma's radiant youth).[108]

Further on in the same verse there is an eloquent example of the 'rubato obligato' mentioned above, when Mahler prolongs the high F of 'Frühling' by moving from binary to ternary rhythm. 'Liebst du um Schönheit', Adorno writes, 'carries us to the brink of the documentary, like the private diary pages of *Das Lied von der Erde*. The minor inflection of *Jugend*, the last muffled note that does not even resolve, suddenly and involuntarily reveals, at the very core of inherited language, the aesthetic image (*Gebilde*), calmly hermetic (*in sich ruhende*).'[109]

All the feeling of the Lied culminates in the final melisma 'immer, immerdar', which delays the ending of the phrase and, so to speak, leaves it hanging, ecstatically, in mid-air. As Adorno puts it, it is 'as if the feeling could not get out, but was suffocating in its own excess. What is expressed is so overwhelming that the act of doing it renders the language of the music irrelevant. It can't finish what it is saying, all it can do is sob.'[110] The phrase indeed remains as if suspended on an A, while the accompaniment has already introduced the dominant chord. Finally, one wonders whether it was not the intense emotion generated by this short song that deterred Mahler from orchestrating it himself before death overtook him.

FIFTH SYMPHONY
(1901–1902)

Composition

As already pointed out,[1] several of the works composed in the summer of 1901 ('Der Tamboursg'sell' and the *Kindertotenlieder* were among them) were concerned with mourning and death. Mahler's brother-in-law, Arnold Rosé, like Bruno Walter, clearly remembered the poignant remark Mahler made just after his haemorrhage in February of that year: 'I lost a third of my blood that night. I shall certainly recover, but the illness will still have cost ten years of my life.'[2] Alma states that two movements of the Fifth Symphony were completed during that summer. Since the Funeral March is so

---

[108] The instrumental ritornello of this Lied was anticipated by bars 112–13 of the contralto solo (*Mitternachtslied*) in the Third Symphony.

[109] Adorno, 'Zu einer imaginären', 37. [110] TAM 189.

[1] See above, Chap. 10, and the section in the Appendix dealing with 'Der Tamboursg'sell'.

[2] Mahler's remark, made in the presence of Arnold Rosé, was quoted by Julius Stern in the 'Wiener Theaterwoche' column of the *Wiener Volkszeitung* after the performance of the Eighth Symphony on 11 and 12 Apr. 1933.

closely linked thematically to the Allegro which follows, it seems likely that it was written in the same year, together with the Scherzo and 'Der Tamboursg'sell', which it so much resembles in atmosphere and even thematically. According to Natalie's reminiscences, Mahler completed the Scherzo first. It can thus be seen as a *Dankgesang eines Genesenen* (song of thanks of one restored to health) like the third movement of Beethoven's Fifteenth Quartet. It is one of Mahler's most optimistic compositions, breathing happiness and *joie de vivre*.[3] The idea of the Scherzo seems to have been in his mind for several years, however. The early plan of the Fourth Symphony, put together some time before that symphony was composed (it still included the choral movement of the Third), contained a 'Scherzo in D major' entitled 'Die Welt ohne Schwere' (The world without gravity). But the actual composition of the Scherzo was undoubtedly started, and probably completed, in Maiernigg at the end of July and beginning of August 1901.[4]

When he spoke for the first time to Natalie of his new symphony, Mahler told her that the movement he was then writing was 'terribly difficult to work on because of its structure and the high degree of artistic mastery it requires in all relationships and details. As with a Gothic cathedral the apparent chaos must resolve itself into the highest order and harmony.'[5] A few days later, Mahler told her that the movement was a Scherzo which would express 'incredible power' and 'man in the full light of day, having reached the peak of his existence'. Mahler, with a perceptiveness not often found among composers judging their own works, realized that this Scherzo was 'completely unlike anything I have written before', all the elements in it were so well 'kneaded' that 'no crumb remains unmixed or unaltered. Every note is fully alive, and it all spins round like a whirlwind or like the tail of a comet.' He was still hard at work on this movement when he formulated one of the fundamental ideas of his mature creative years: 'The harmonic progression (*Akkordführung*) is particularly difficult, especially because of my principle that nothing must be repeated, everything must develop further from within itself . . .'. The first movement of the Fourth showed the same concern with continuously enriching and developing the material, in accordance with what Adorno calls *Nichtumkehrbarkeit*, that is to say, the impossibility of going back over a path aheady trodden. But in the Fifth the principle is applied with a new vigour. Mahler's creative imagination leads him into newer and richer pastures: a new orchestral opulence compensates for the deliberate abandonment of the human voice and its resources, while the polyphonic web is tighter, more complicated in its weave.[6] It is probably no coincidence that Mahler, at this time, was studying Bach's Motets.

[3] Yet two writers at least have apparently found in the Scherzo traces of ambiguity and of that conflict, always present in Mahler's music, between exuberance and the underlying 'deep movements of the soul'. One of them is Vladimir Karbusicky (VKM 2), and the other Bernd Sponheuer, who stresses the mixture of irony and nostalgia revealed by the music's reference to the past and to its 'quotations' of waltzes and ländler (see below). However, Karbusicky still regards this movement as the 'constructive force' of the work as a whole and 'the kernel of its message'.

[4] Gustav Brecher, who was then assistant conductor at the Hofoper, and acted as intermediary between Mahler and C. F. Peters, confirms that the Scherzo was composed before the other movements (see Sander Wilkens, Gustav *Mahlers Fünfte Symphonie: Quellen und Instrumentationsprozess* (Peters, Frankfurt, 1989), 27).

[5] NBL2. 192

[6] A Ph.D. thesis has been written on this subject: Thomas F. Bibl, 'A Study of the Contrapuntal Style in the Fifth Symphony of Mahler', Indiana Univ., July 1971.

Manuscripts

According to Edward R. Reilly, a sketch of the first eleven bars of the Scherzo is now in the possession of the widow of the Viennese tenor Anton Dermota.[7] Another, more extensive draft, may have survived. It is mentioned in a telegram, dated 2 Nov. 1949, from the New York dealer Pierre Berès, catalogued by Nathan van Patten at Stanford University, California. Unfortunately the autograph itself was not purchased and its present owner is unknown. The full draft (*Particell*), which was completed by 23 Aug. 1902, has disappeared. Mahler's fair copy of the score, inscribed to Alma, is dated October 1903.[8] The format is 34 by 26.5 cm. The number of pages per movement are 48 (1); 66 (2); 80 (3); 17 (4); and 88 (5). Alma's undated copy of the manuscript, most likely made in spring or summer 1903, was used by the engravers in October of the same year. Corrections to it were made by Mahler.

Various revisions and editions

As seen above, Mahler became aware of the defects in his orchestration after the two run-throughs with the Vienna Philharmonic, on 17 and 26 September 1904. He was somewhat surprised to find that his orchestration technique, over which he felt he had acquired full mastery by then, had not fully adjusted to the evolution of his style and the requirements of a polyphonic texture that was more intricate than before. On 27 September he wrote to Henri Hinrichsen, his publisher: 'I have had to do some retouching. The percussion in particular was somewhat too heavy and would certainly have spoiled the impression.' A day later he added: 'In such a very poly-phonic work it is not possible beforehand to get everything right down to the last detail.'[9] Alma's statement that Mahler 'had the percussion instruments and sidedrum constantly making such a din that little beyond the rhythm was recognizable', and that he later, on her advice, 'crossed out in red pencil nearly the whole sidedrum part and half the percussion instruments as well',[10] had always appeared to me exag-gerated. Colin Matthews, who studied the manuscripts and the various printed scores, writes that

the first edition of the score (published before the reading rehearsals) actually has very slightly more percussion in the first movement (to which Alma is surely referring) than the manu-script; while the second edition merely omits a mezzo-forte cymbal and two pianissimo bass drum strokes. The orchestral revisions are, however, all concerned with lightening and clarifying the texture—the first version was heavily scored, in places almost clumsily so, as if Mahler was unsure of how to deal with the middle-period change of style ushered in by this Symphony.[11]

This first revision was in fact followed by several more. Bruno Walter claimed that most

[7] See Gilbert E. Kaplan (ed.), *Adagietto: Facsimile, Documentation, Recording* (The Kaplan Foundation, New York, 1992), 39.

[8] PML, Mary Flagler Cary Collection. See above, Chaps. 14 and 15. According to Edward R. Reilly, the titles and inscription were probably added after the copy was completed (see Kaplan, (ed.), *Adagietto*, 40).

[9] See Eberhardt Klemm, 'Zur Geschichte der Fünften Sinfonie von Gustav Mahler', in *Jahrbuch Peters 1979* (Aufsätze zur Musik, Leipzig, 1980), 41 ff.

[10] AMM1. 95; AMM2. 100.

[11] See 'Mahler at Work: Aspects of the Creative Process', D.Phil. thesis, Sussex Univ., 1977, 59. Alma's copy of the MS is now in LPA. As seen above, it was used by the engravers and contains some corrections and additions in Mahler's hand but is otherwise identical with Mahler's fair copy.

of the fee paid to Mahler by Peters was used to pay for further changes to the plates after the first performance.[12] To the end of his life Mahler continued to improve on the orchestration of the Fifth: the final revision was one of his last acts as a composer, just before his last illness, in 1911.[13] A fortnight before he was forced to cancel a concert and take to his bed, he wrote to Georg Göhler:

I have finished the Fifth. I had in fact to re-instrumentate the whole of it. I simply cannot understand how I could have fallen back into such beginner's errors at that time. (Evidently the routine I had developed in the first four symphonies let me down completely on this occasion— when a completely new style required a new technique.)[14]

The late musicologist Eberhardt Klemm put together a full account of the revisions and editions of the Fifth,[15] and Sander Wilkens has studied and analysed the changes down to the smallest detail.[16] The full orchestral score, published by Peters in November 1904, contained numerous alterations made by Mahler to the pocket score, including a reduction in the numbers of brass instruments, decided upon after the Vienna Philharmonic rehearsals. Klemm confirms that nearly all the plates had corrections in ink made to them. After this run-through and the first performance of 18 October, the orchestral parts were also altered, and Mahler's corrections copied by hand into the pocket scores henceforth sent to conductors. The orchestral parts were engraved in accordance with this first revision in November–December 1904.

The fact remained that the study score had been printed before the revision. No correction was made to it before Mahler's death, even though Hinrichsen promised a new edition in a letter written on 2 June 1910.[17] Furthermore, when in the spring of 1913 Georg Göhler decided to give the first performance of the final version, Hinrichsen declared that the work had already cost him a great deal of money, that it had been only rarely performed, and that he refused to contemplate spending any more on it.[18] Mahler had in fact offered to pay part of the cost of the new edition out of his own pocket, but, when his death intervened, Hinrichsen was content to have the orchestral parts corrected by hand,[19] and then only on condition that Alma Mahler hand over to him the revised score, which he intended to keep.[20] Meanwhile, Peters had decided to publish Schoenberg's *Five Pieces for Orchestra*, Op. 16, and Hinrichsen informed the young composer that he was planning to melt down the plates of the Fifth Symphony, since it was falling into obscurity.[21] Schoenberg

---

[12] However, Klemm ('Geschichte', 94 n. 47) confirms that Bruno Walter was exaggerating when he claimed, in his memoirs, that the symphony had had 'quite simply to be reorchestrated after the Cologne première' and that 'the work took months'.

[13] See below, Vol. iv, Chap. 8.

[14] MBR1, No. 420, 8 Feb. 1911; MBR2, No. 463. The letter is in the Ratschulbibliothek in Zwickau.

[15] In 'Geschichte', 13. Otto Singer's four-hand piano reduction had already appeared by Aug. 1904.

[16] In *Fünfte Symphonie*.

[17] Klemm, 'Geschichte', 51. See also below, Vol. iv, Chaps. 6 and 7.

[18] Letter from Henri Hinrichsen to Georg Göhler, 13 Apr. 1913 (in Klemm, 'Geschichte', 61).

[19] 'He can't decide whether to have the orchestra material altered according to Mahler's directions', wrote Schoenberg to Berg on 16 July 1913, 'he doesn't think it would be worth it. . . . That's when I realized the importance of performing the Fifth and told him so. Consequently he has now decided to have the parts prepared.' (*The Berg-Schoenberg Correspondence*, ed. Brand, Hailey, and Harris: Norton, New York, 1987, 183).

[20] Alma Mahler's response to this request is unknown, but Mahler's printed score with autograph corrections probably remained the property of Peters.

[21] Hans Heinz Stuckenschmidt, *Schoenberg* (Atlantis, Zurich, 1974), 148.

was so shocked by this threat that he started at once to draft a lecture on Mahler, the lecture which gave rise to his famous article quoted on a number of occasions in this book.[22]

The rest of the correspondence between Hinrichsen and Göhler proves that the score and orchestral parts of the Fifth were corrected by hand at the end of autumn 1913.[23] The first performance of the final version eventually took place on 9 January 1914, in the Albert Hall in Leipzig, as part of the third subscription concert of the Musikalische Gesellschaft, with the augmented Winderstein Orchestra conducted by Georg Göhler.[24] However, the story does not end there. In April 1913 Hinrichsen, at the very time when he was having the orchestral parts copied in conformity with Mahler's last score, was reprinting 250 copies of the old pocket score,[25] knowing full well that two successive revisions had rendered it doubly obsolete. In 1919, Peters Edition was still offering Fritz Busch the early orchestral material as being 'the most often used', and went on to recommend it to performers with a zeal perhaps connected with the fact that there were only two copies, corrected by hand, of the final version. That same year, Hinrichsen tried to minimize the importance of the alterations in his correspondence with Rudolf Mengelberg, much to the disgust of Willem Mengelberg in whose score Mahler had, as far back as 1906, made many of the changes that were later to appear in the final version, for performance by the Concertgebouw.[26] Mengelberg having strongly recommended a new edition of the full score, Hinrichsen finally gave way and republished a hastily and perfunctorily corrected full score in November 1919.[27] Just before the Amsterdam Mahler Festival, in April 1920, Peters also issued a new pocket score, but without the mention *Neue Ausgabe* (new edition). Worse still, however, this was not identical with the full score. Corrections had been made only in the original 1904 pocket score and many of Mahler's later alterations had been left out. However, the resulting amalgam of two different versions remained the only pocket score available until the Ratz IGMG edition of 1964.[28] The list in

---

[22] This lecture was later extended into an article of which the definitive German version was included by Ivan Vojtech in *Stil und Gedanke: Aufsätze über Musik* (Fischer, Frankfurt, 1976), 7 ff.

[23] Hinrichsen complained, in a letter written on 1 Dec., that the amount of work had been 'enormous' (Klemm, 'Geschichte', 63).

[24] Ibid. 95. The programme also included some of Mahler's Lieder and Wagner's *Siegfried-Idyll*.

[25] Klemm notes that the only difference between the first and second pocket scores lies in the colour of the lettering on the cover, the name of Mahler being printed in red letters on a pink background in the 1st edn. of 1904, and in black in the 2nd of 1913.

[26] Klemm's article quotes from the 1919 correspondence between Peters and Rudolf Mengelberg. Recently, the Netherlands musicologist Robert Becqué discovered in Antwerp the score used by Mahler for the concert of 5 Mar. 1906 (see below, Vol iii, Chap. 5, and Becqué, 'Mahlers Antwerpener Partitur der Fünften', *Nachrichten zur Mahler Forschung*, 25 (May 1991), 8 ff.) containing numerous corrections in red ink in the composer's hand, significantly different from those in Mengelberg's score.

[27] 43 pp. out of 250 were re-engraved, and the new score had 246 pp. instead of 251, Mahler having suppressed numerous brass and other passages.

[28] Klemm, 'Geschichte', 16. Among the scores left by Bruno Walter in his will to the library of the Vienna Conservatory (Hochschule für Musik) are two, a pocket score and a full score (Catalogue nos. 38389 and 38390). The former must have been one of the four original copies Mahler received at the beginning of Sept. 1904, before the reading rehearsals. It has many corrections in Mahler's hand, one of which is the list of instruments, the note at the bottom of the first page of music (p. 3 in the score), and the note on p. 13, etc. This also seems to be the last score corrected by Mahler before his death. All the corrections were incorporated in the IGMG critical edn. of 1964. Walter's full score seems to be older. It was apparently bought by Mahler in Strasbourg in May 1905 and used by him for performances. It includes many corrections in red ink, definitely in Mahler's hand, and markings by Walter. All the autograph corrections are likewise

chronological order of the various printed versions of the Fifth Symphony reads as follows:[29]

1. Pocket edition (19.5 × 28 cm.), impression number 9015, publication number 3087.251 pages. Date of issue: Sept 1904. Described in Peters's 1917 catalogue as 'first version', it was the small format version of a full score which was never printed.

2a. Full score (26.5 × 33 cm.), impression number 8951, publication number 3082. 251 pages. Date of issue: November 1904. Contains a number of alterations not included in 1.

2b. Orchestral parts (engraved), impression number 8952, publication number 3082. Date of issue: November 1904. Identical with 2a.

3a. Orchestral parts (manuscript), impression number 8952, publication number 3082. Date of issue: December 1913. It bears the notice: 'Second edition, re-orchestrated by the composer during the last year of his life.'

3b. Full score (26.5 × 33 cm.), impression number 8951, publication number 3082. 246 pp. Date of issue: November 1919. Wording: 'new edition'. Identical with 3a.

4. Pocket score (19.5 × 28 cm.), impression number 9015, publication number 3087. 246 pp. Date of issue: April 1920. Does not bear the notice 'new edition'; pp. 3 to 24 and 26 to 39 correspond to the corrected plates of 1; all the other pages are identical with 3b.[30]

5. First critical edition: IGMG-Peters, Erwin Ratz, ed., 1964, 246 pp.

6. Second critical edition: IGMG-Peters, Karl-Heinz Füssl, ed., 1989.

Thus Eberhardt Klemm's 1979 article shows that the 1964 score cannot be regarded as definitive, firstly because, as Erwin Ratz admitted in his introduction, the much discussed score corrected by Mahler in 1910–11, which alone can offer a solution to certain editorial problems, has (temporarily, it is hoped) disappeared,[31] and secondly because Erwin Ratz clearly did not grasp why so many discrepancies existed between the various printed scores.

---

in the Mahler Gesellschaft edn. It also contains markings by Bruno Walter in pencil. Besides the two Walter scores, several others have survived with markings by Mahler: a full score used and corrected by him for the Trieste performance on 1 Dec. 1905; another, also corrected, used for the Antwerp performance on 5 Mar. 1906 (see above); and yet another, annotated by Mahler and Mengelberg and probably used for the Amsterdam performance on 8 Mar. 1906. Two different sets of parts, likewise corrected by Mahler, have survived, one for the Strasbourg performance of 21 May 1905 (Stadtbibliothek, Vienna), and the other for that of St Petersburg on 9 May 1907. The corrections are not always identical with those in the scores published during Mahler's lifetime.

[29] Sander Wilkens, *Fünften Symphonie*, originally a Ph.D. thesis, is devoted to the sources, different versions, and orchestration of the Fifth. It lists every difference or discrepancy between the various scores and versions.

[30] The 1964 issue of the 'definitive version' in critical study score, as part of the IGMG edition, gave rise to a debate between Erwin Ratz, who made the revision, and Hans Ferdinand Redlich (see his article 'Mahler' in the encyclopaedia *Musik und Gesellschaft*, and also his book *Bruckner und Mahler* (Dent, London, 1955), 202, and especially 'Gustav Mahler, Probleme einer kritischer Gesamtausgabe', *Musikforschung*, 19 (1966), 390). Eberhardt Klemm was the first to notice that most commentators and revisers had not realized that the first full score and the first pocket score were not identical. The staff of the firm of Peters were themselves for a long time unaware of this, which explains why the 1920 pocket score was so inadequately corrected.

[31] Fortunately, Egon Wellesz copied all Mahler's corrections into his own score.

A programme?

After the Fourth Symphony,[32] that is to say after 1900, Mahler decided once and for all to abstain from providing, in writing or by word of mouth, even the briefest descriptive title or comment which might be used to interpret the inspirational content of his works. He had become aware of the aesthetic gulf separating him from composers of 'programme music' like Richard Strauss. Thus the intimate moods, memories, and associations which inspired the Fifth Symphony can only be guessed at from the music itself, and from what we know of the circumstances in which it was written. Mahler, now fully mature both as man and as an artist, wanted to write 'absolute' music as a musician, without a programme, as he explained to Bruno Walter.[33] He was inevitably influenced by the circumstances under which he now composed: he had just moved into his new house in Maiernigg; in February he had come close to death, and was now recovered. To say that the Fifth was the beginning of a new creative period, a demonstration of the victory he had won over death, is therefore as much a statement of fact as an interpretation of the spirit that underlies the music.

Two attempts have nevertheless been made to provide the Fifth with a 'hidden' or 'inner' programme. James L. Zychowicz interprets as programmatic the various self-quotations from songs 'Tambourg'sell' and 'Nun will die Sonn'' in the Funeral March; 'Ich bin der Welt' in the Adagietto; 'Lob des hohen Verstandes' and 'Wer hat dies Liedlein' in the Rondo-Finale.[34] Barbara R. Barry attempts to draw a parallel between Mahler's Fifth and Beethoven's, which she considers a 'structural blueprint for the later work'.[35] Neither attempt can be considered wholly convincing.

Key

As often in Mahler's symphonies and Lieder cycles, the Fifth Symphony uses a 'progressive' tonal scheme. An A minor Allegro follows the C sharp minor Funeral March. Then comes a Scherzo in D major, an Adagietto in F, and the Rondo-Finale in D. Within each movement, unusual key relationships prevail between the different thematic complexes, such as the diminished fifth relationship (A minor, E♭ minor) in the second movement, or the non-diatonic submediant (D major, B♭ major) in the Scherzo and the Finale.

A Neapolitan relationship even spans the entire symphony: D major, a tonality of varying weight in each of the last four movements, is, of course, in that relationship to the C sharp of the opening movement. This latter technique is very close to and was most probably borrowed from Beethoven's C sharp minor String Quartet, with its second movement in D major.[36]

Nadine Sine, in her 1983 thesis,[37] detects a firm and deliberate logic in the suc-

---

[32] As seen above, Mahler, while continually declaring after 1900 that he was utterly opposed to all 'programme music', nevertheless allowed the occasional publication of comments strangely reminiscent of a 'programme'.

[33] BWM 84.

[34] Zychowicz's view that the figuration in the Rondo-Finale, just before rehearsal no. 30, is a quotation of the *Wunderhorn-Lied*, is to my mind unconvincing. See 'Reciprocity and Reconstruction: The "Hidden" Program in the Fifth Symphony of Gustav Mahler', unpubl. article (1986) given to the author.

[35] Ibid.

[36] See Edward Murphy, 'Unusual Forms in Mahler's Fifth Symphony', *Music Review*, 47: 2 (1986–7), 109.

[37] See 'The Evolution of Symphonic Worlds: Tonality in the Symphonies of Gustav Mahler, with Emphasis on the First, Third, and Fifth', Ph.D. thesis, New York Univ., 1983, 242 ff.

cession of keys: C♯ minor and A minor, 'taken together, create a dominant preparation for the third movement in D'. She points out that, in the Funeral March, Mahler 'withheld all his devices for confirming a key' and that the tonic D emerges in the ensuing Allegro, but only finds full affirmation in the Finale.[38] Another important feature pointed out by the same author is that the main contrasting key of each movement is that of the submediant: 'The fourth movement holds a crucial position in the tonal plan: it stands a minor third *above* the tonic of the work: the climax in F sharp (G flat), a major third above the tonic, resolves by steps into D$^6_4$, which in turn dissolves into F. Thus in the course of the Symphony, Mahler approached the tonic D from the dominant and then contrasts it with the subdominant, as well as the minor thirds above and below it.'

Sine also says that the overall plan may seem fairly simple at first glance, yet the development of the polyphonic style in Mahler's middle period 'generates large segments in which the tonality cannot be pinpointed', with the music 'often thrust into very transitory keys', with 'few extended pedals', and a scarcity of 'extended dominant chords'. As an example of this tonal instability she cites the ending of the Funeral March which is 'deflected towards A' and has 'no cadential progression'. However the A quite naturally prepares the way for the Finale, being the dominant of the last movement's main key.

General outline

The division into 'parts' is familiar from the First and Third Symphonies. The general outline was determined in 1901 but it was only in the following year that Mahler added to the Scherzo and the other movement(s) he had completed[39] (probably the March and the Allegro), a final 'section' comprising the famous Adagietto and the Rondo-Finale. Thus the outline becomes symmetrical: slow, fast; Scherzo; slow, fast. Mahler was experimenting with a hitherto unexplored architecture which he was to use again in a very similar way in the Seventh and the Tenth Symphonies. But in no other work did he write a Scherzo so extensive and so complex in form and compositional technique, and make it the nub, the centre of gravity, of the work.

The Fifth Symphony displays the mastery of a fully mature composer at the peak of his powers who also felt the need to renew himself. Paul Bekker describes it as 'his first attempt to reshape the world in the light of the changes he felt within himself',[40] that is to say, a move towards abstraction, towards the abandonment of all references to the past (the *Knaben Wunderhorn*), childhood and paradise (the Fourth), philosophical-religious themes (the Second), and pantheism (the Third); an attempt to achieve a tighter polyphonic web and a new orchestral style, an enriched and broader variety of sound and a denser, more coherent symphonic structure (numerous thematic recurrences,[41] interdependence of the first two and last two movements). Despite the thematic links which the Fifth still has to his Lieder of that period, it represents a decisive move on his part towards the purely orchestral works which he was to continue to compose throughout the few years that remained to him, with the exception of the Eighth Symphony and *Das Lied von der Erde*.

---

[38] See 'The Evolution of Symphonic Worlds': 244 ff.

[39] In my opinion, the Funeral March must have been completed at the same time as the Allegro, in summer 1901. The two movements are thematically linked, indeed almost of a piece, and he might not have made this clear to Alma (see above, Chap. 10).

[40] BMS 178.　　　　[41] See below 'Cyclic Procedures'.

Like the Second Symphony written nine years before, the Fifth opens with a powerful Funeral March. The symphonic hero is being laid to rest. Death is accepted as a painful but inescapable reality. We hear a proud resignation, an almost impersonal sorrow, even amid the violence of the first episode (or Trio) or the gentle acceptance of the second. The absence of protest is underlined by the abandonment of the sonata form. The thematic material develops continuously from a group of basic cells or motifs, in a procedure characteristic of Mahler's style. Theodor Adorno analysed and described this 'variant' technique as Mahler's principal innovation. He compared his method to that of a novelist who pursues his narrative and keeps adding new episodes without a preconceived plan. In Adorno's words, Mahler's narration constantly brings in 'the unexpected, the seemingly accidental but nevertheless inevitable; the detours which prove all the same to be the only road'.[42] His 'narrative' should be listened to 'from one chapter to the next . . . like a story of which one does not know the ending'. Unity is ensured by Mahler's use of the 'variant'. In the Funeral March of the Fifth, the two episodes, which one hesitates to call 'Trios', even though they are obviously meant to create the contrast to be expected within a march as within a dance, use some themes derived from previous material. This method of drawing upon a common supply of motifs helps to free the composer from the constraints of formal, predetermined patterns. In this respect it was a decisive step towards a new concept of musical architectonics.

Cyclic procedures

These are infinitely more numerous, subtle, and deliberate in the Fifth than in the *Wunderhorn* Symphonies, and would merit a study to themselves.[43] They will often be alluded to in the following pages and I shall only mention the main ones here. There are links between the March and the Allegro; the theme of the second Trio of the March becomes the subsidiary theme of the Allegro; the triplet crotchet theme (violins, bar 165 ff.) reappears in bar 117 of the Allegro; the sighing melodic ninths and repeated semi-quaver thirds in the second Trio (bar 74 ff.) keep on recurring throughout the following movement; and the *Abgesang* episode of the March (bar 120 ff.) is quoted at the end of the development in the Allegro (bar 266). Linking the fourth and fifth movements, the central episode of the Adagietto reappears in the Rondo as a contrasting theme. In the first and last movements, the two chorale themes are closely related. And the fugato sections in the Scherzo and Rondo are thematically akin and often in the same tonality.

Orchestration

Four flutes (including piccolo); 3 oboes (including cor anglais); 3 clarinets (including bass clarinet); 6 horns, 4 trumpets, 3 trombones, 1 tuba, percussion (4 timpani, cymbals, bass drum with cymbals, snare drum, triangle, glockenspiel, tamtam, whip), harp, and strings.

Analyses

From the Fifth Symphony onwards, Mahler's compositional techniques became increasingly subtle and complex. Numerous articles and even whole books or mono-

---

[42] *Gesammelte Schriften*, ii. *Quasi una Fantasia* (Suhrkamp, Frankfurt, 1978), xvi. 328 ff.
[43] See Sponheuer, *Logik*, 221.

graphs have been written about them. Thus it becomes more and more difficult, within the scope of a short survey of the works, to give a precise and faithful picture of this formal complexity. I shall therefore limit myself from now on to giving a brief summary of essential characteristics, referring the reader to analyses and articles that have already been published for each work. As regards the Fifth, there are, in addition to the detailed analyses by Richard Specht and Paul Bekker,[44] other studies by Ernst Otto Nodnagel (38 pp.),[45] Karl Weigl (18 pp.),[46] Hermann Kretzschmar (3 pp.),[47] Neville Cardus (38 pp.),[48] Edward Murphy,[49] and also the more recent book by Bernd Sponheuer,[50] who devotes sixty pages to the Finale alone. Allen Forte devoted 18 columns, in small print, and 8 graphs to a Schenkerian analysis of the Adagietto.[51] Carolyn Baxendale writes 23 pages about Mahler's 'long-range musical thought' in the Rondo-Finale.[52] Vladimir Karbusicky's book[53] also contains a long and interesting discussion of the Scherzo of the Fifth.

Erste Abteilung (First Part)

(a) **Trauermarsch** (Funeral March): *Im gemessenen Schritt. Streng. Wie ein Kondukt* (with measured tread, austere, like a funeral cortège).

Key: C sharp minor, modulating to A flat (dominant key), to B flat minor (1st Trio), D flat, A minor (2nd Trio), etc.

Time signature: 2/2.

Rhythm: Funeral March.

Tempo: see above; *Pesante* (bar 59). *Etwas gehaltener* (somewhat more restrained) (bar 35), etc. *Plötzlich schnell. Leidenschaftlich. Wild* (suddenly rapid, passionate, wild) (Trio 1: bar 155). *Allmählich sich beruhigend* (gradually getting calmer) (bar 233). *Unmerklich zu Tempo 1 zurückkehrend* (gradually going back to Tempo 1) (bar 242). *Immer dasselbe Tempo* (same tempo throughout) (Trio 2: bar 323).[54]

---

[44] BMS 173 ff. and RSM2. 279 ff.   [45] Peters, 1905.

[46] E. Istel (ed.), *Mahler's Symphonien* (Meisterführer No. 10; Schlesinger, Vienna, n.d. [1913–14?]), 85.

[47] *Führer durch den Konzertsaal* (Breitkopf, Leipzig, 1913), 804.

[48] *Gustav Mahler, his Mind and his Music*, i (Gollancz, London, 1965), 152.

[49] Murphy, 'Unusual Forms', 101.

[50] *Logik des Zerfalls: Untersuchungen zum Finalproblem in den Symphonien Gustav Mahlers* (Hans Schneider, Tutzing, 1978), 219.

[51] See 'Middle Ground Motives in the Adagietto of Mahler's Fifth Symphony', *19th Century Music*, 8: 2 (Autumn 1984), 153 ff.

[52] 'The Finale of Mahler's Fifth Symphony: Long-Range Musical Thought', *Journal of the Royal Musical Association*, 112: 2 (1986–7), 450.

[53] VKM 1 and 83.

[54] In 'Aspects of Mahler's Fifth Symphony: Performance Practice and Interpretation', *The Musical Times*, 130: 1755 (May 1989), 260, Paul Banks lists approximate metronome tempos in Mahler's Welte-Mignon piano-rolls: bar 1: ♩ = 76; 35 ♩ = 58; 61 ♩ = 72/76; 89 ♩ = 63; 103 ♩ = 58; 125 ♩ = 69; 133 ♩ = 60/58; 155 ♩ = 92; 233 ♩ = 69; 254 ♩ = 76; 262 ♩ = 58; 323 ♩ = 60; 345 ♩ = 69. These tempos are taken from the 1985 Intercord record. What is interesting is that, sometimes (bars 103, 125, and 133), Mahler modifies the previous tempo although the score contains no marking at this point. It should be pointed out that, because of the problem of establishing the correct speed for a reproduction apparatus, these tempos have relative rather than absolute value. All in all, they are close to those noted by Mengelberg (except for Trio 1 in which they are markedly slower, probably because of the limits of Mahler's keyboard technique). The total duration of Mengelberg's performance was 11 minutes, while that of the Intercord transfer of Mahler's piano roll is 12 minutes, 51 seconds.

Duration: 12 minutes (Bruno Walter pocket score and general rehearsal under Mahler, Hamburg Philharmonic, 12 March 1905).[55]

Form: Most analysts have called the two contrasting sections (or episodes) Trios 1 and 2, a logical choice since, contrary to the initial movement of the Second Symphony, the March does not contain any development sections.[56] However, Nadine Sine discerns in this movement 'the large divisions of Sonata-form', with exposition (bars 1–152), development (153–232), and recapitulation (233–415). Thus she calls the movement 'a unique fusion of song and sonata-form elements',[57] with the second 'Trio' (or B section), in A minor, anticipating the key of the ensuing Allegro.

Edward Murphy considers that the A section of the March is composed of two separate Marches, one (bars 1–33) 'severe in mood and "brassy" in tone', the second (bars 34–60) 'much calmer', with 'softer timbres'.[58] He gives the following schema for the first movement: ABABA, and considers the B sections 'too heavy in nature and too frantic in quality' to be called 'Trios', particularly since the climax of the whole movement occurs in the second B section (bar 369: *klagend*). To him, the A section's calmer and more melodious second March (in A flat: bar 20 ff.) is more in the manner of a Trio. Murphy also points out the very unusual key relationships of the various sections.

Analysis: The grim trumpet fanfare in C sharp minor is clearly another reminiscence of Mahler's childhood. The list of signals and drumbeats of the Austrian army includes the signal *Generalmarsch* (see Ex. 20).[59] An almost identical fanfare occurred in the first movement of the Fourth, at the end of the development when, in Mahler's own words, 'on a sharp order by the commanding officer the troops suddenly get back into line'.[60] But here the key of C sharp minor gives it a sombre and fateful character, especially when the phrase, remorselessly hammered out by trombone chords, kettle and bass drums, plunges to the depths and dies in the lowest notes of the tuba. Sometimes varied, sometimes transposed, sometimes reduced to its first few bars, passing from the trumpets to the horns and even to the timpani, it continually reappears like a refrain, linking different episodes or couplets. The second element (violins and cellos pianissimo, bar 34) belongs to the same world as the last of the

Ex. 20. Fifth Symphony, first movement, 'Generalmarsch'

Etwas langsamer als im Marschtempo

etc.

[55] Hermann Behn attended this rehearsal and noted the tempos in a score which Mahler had inscribed to him (Stanford Univ. Library, Calif.). On that occasion, the total duration of the symphony, excluding three short pauses, was 76 minutes.

[56] See Bernd Sponheuer, 'Durch Nacht zum Licht: Zur Interpretation des Chorals in Gustav Mahlers Fünfte Symphonie', in *Musik, Deutung, Bedeutung* (Plane, Dortmund, 1986), 91.

[57] Sine, 'Evolution', 249. The same author points out, as a sonata-form feature, the first appearance of the 'consolatory' *Abgesang* in the dominant key (A♭ = G♯) and the second in the tonic major (D♭ = C♯).

[58] Murphy, 'Unusual forms', 101 ff.

[59] See Emil Rameis, *Die Oesterreichische Militärmusik von ihren Anfangen bis zum Jahre 1918* (Hans Schneider, Tutzing, 1976), 186.

[60] NBL1. 145; NBL2. 164.

Wunderhorn-Lieder, 'Der Tamboursg'sell'.[61] At its second exposition (violins and woodwinds) it is followed by a new 'consolatory' element (*Abgesang*) (A♭, bar 120) in sixths, based on the same trochaic rhythm.

The third repetition of the trumpet fanfare is brutally cut short at the third bar (bar 155) by an outburst of grief and passion in feverish quaver figurations accompanied by syncopated horn chords. Here the principal melody is again played on the trumpet, with a counter-melody in the strings. Several familiar motifs recur, in particular the opening fanfare. The excitement increases with a more optimistic rising motif, in crotchet triplets, played first on the horns and then on the violins (bar 189 ff.). It reaches a brief climax, which mixes triplets and feverish semiquavers, and which is repeated almost note for note in the next movement. The opening fanfare restores the previous mood of resignation, with the march theme, pianissimo, in the winds (bar 262 ff.). A restatement of the *Abgesang*, transposed into D flat (as mentioned above: bar 294), ends in the woodwinds with a quote from the first of the *Kindertotenlieder*[62] (bars 313–14). The timpani then takes over the fanfare motif, preparing the arrival of the second 'Trio' (pianissimo strings, A minor: bar 322 ff.). Its breathless and syncopated accompaniment motif, in the second violins, is actually a rhythmic variant of the fanfare itself. Although the atmosphere is still one of gentleness and resignation, as far removed as possible from the revolt in Trio 1, the principal subject is in fact a variant of the same gesture of defiance, interspersed with other familiar fragments. From here onwards the violas' sighing ninth and seventh appoggiatura motifs play an important role right to the end of the symphony. The A minor episode also announces the tonality of the following movement, where it is quoted several times. A long crescendo gradually builds up to a new climax in big triple fortissimo chords, the upper voices descending chromatically over a long dominant pedal (*Klagend*, bar 369).

Almost immediately the opening trumpet fanfare reappears on long string tremolos, and ushers in the coda. Its descent to the bass register brings about a lengthening of the note-values, expressing discouragement, exhaustion. The concluding bars combine simplicity and economy of means with overwhelming eloquence. The initial fanfare gradually dissolves as it rises and passes from pianissimo trumpet to pianissimo flute, as if receding into the distance.

(*b*) **Stürmisch bewegt**. *Mit grosser Vehemenz* (violently agitated, with much vehemence).

Tempo: See above, then *Bedeutend langsamer* (significantly slower) (restatement of the March: bar 74 ff.), etc.
Duration: 15 minutes (Hamburg 1905); 13½–14 minutes (Walter miniature score).
Key: A minor, F minor (2nd theme). The development traverses a considerable number of transitory keys, G minor, B flat minor, B major, A flat major, etc. In the recapitu-

---

[61] Sine, 'Evolution', 250, quotes five different versions of the theme, bars 35–43, 89–97, 132–7, 153–61, 263–9, and 322–9.

[62] The passage quoted here (bars 313–16) is borrowed from the first Lied in the cycle (bar 14/15: 'die Nacht geschehen'; 34/5: 'scheinet allgemein'; and 76/7: 'dem Freudenlicht der Welt'). Paul Bekker sees a gleam of hope in the tragic darkness of the March, based on the optimistic words of the third verse. But Sponheuer (*Logik*, 271) points out that the same melodic phrase is used also at the end of the two preceding verses, where no gleam of hope can be discerned in the text.

lation the second theme is transposed to E minor. Nadine Sine notes that 'much of the movement remains tonally vague', with a number of chords having several possible resolutions (augmented dominants, diminished sevenths, etc.). The appearance of the chorale, in D, foreshadowing that of the Finale, obscures the tonality further. According to Sine, Mahler wanted the D major of the Scherzo 'to sound even more decisive'.[63]

Time signature: 2/2.

Form: Sonata. Edward Murphy interprets the form as 'a large five-part ABABA structure comparable to that of the Funeral March' (A: bars 1–254; B: 254–322; A: 322–91; B: 392–519; A: 520–76). Murphy points out the very unusual key relationships between the various sections (A minor, E♭ minor in the A section; E♭ minor–A major in section B, F minor, etc.)[64]

At first, the recall of episodes and motifs from the March makes the second movement seem like a rapid, more fevered development of the first. However, Mahler's letters to his publisher[65]—and the fact that he kept faithfully to the sonata form—show that this was for him the true first movement, the March being simply a long introduction.[66] After the contained and resigned sorrow of the preceding movement, violent emotion bursts forth irresistibly in the Allegro (one is reminded of the initial outburst of the Finale in the First Symphony, in connection with which Mahler spoke of 'violent emotions too long contained'). In this respect, it is but a continuation of the angry mood of Trio 1 of the March. The brief ostinato in the basses is one of those motifs which keep on returning to their point of departure, and which occur everywhere in Mahler's music, from the first of the *Lieder eines fahrenden Gesellen* to the *Rondo Burleske* in the Ninth. Each of its successive appearances is punctuated by fierce diminished seventh chords, played at startlingly irregular intervals, on violins and trumpets. The sighing appoggiatura ninths of the March's second Trio here become cries of anguish in the high woodwinds. They set off a new element, again in the violins, rising and descending scales (with the inverse as a counterpoint in the basses), imbued with a kind of despairing frenzy. The true first subject appears only at bar 32, still in the violins. Several familiar elements recur in turn, particularly the basses' feverish scales and opening ostinato (played by 6 stopped horns), giving this exposition its hasty and fragmentary character. The first climax, achieved almost immediately, disintegrates in an Adornian *Einsturz*, chromatic descending scales on winds, accompanied by two more sighs from the strings. An ominous silence over a quiet timpani roll creates the expectation of some new event, but the two motifs which then appear are both familiar: they are the breathless repeated thirds (in the high winds) and the ninth appoggiatura sighs (bar 74: violas, then clarinets, then flutes) of the March's second Trio. The principal theme of this section soon reappears in the cellos, but in a mostly new form (*Bedeutend langsamer. Im Tempo des ersten Satzes*, bar 74) and followed by Trio 1's ascending theme (violins and cellos, bars 116 ff.). After this long backward glance, the rapid tempo is abruptly reinstated[67] (bar 141) with the frantic descending-scale motifs. This is the

---

[63] Sine, 'Evolution', 253.   [64] Murphy, 'Unusual Forms', 104 ff.

[65] See below, Vol. iii, Chap. 1.

[66] Adorno treats the Allegro simply as a *Durchführung* of the March (TAM 130).

[67] The French pianist Claude Helffer has pointed out a striking similarity between the four bars which precede the 'Tempo 1 subito' and a passage in Chopin's First Ballade (see TAM 106).

beginning of the development which, in early scores, was preceded by a double bar and a repeat sign.

The first section of the *Durchführung* (bar 141 ff.) begins, in the depths of darkness and despair, with persistent repetitions of the ostinato (A minor, then G minor). Light rekindles first in the form of an upward thrust of crotchet triplets, taken from the March, and then with a new motif, this time resolutely optimistic (bar 168). This first surge is almost immediately crushed by a new *Einsturz*, a chromatic wind motif which sinks to the bass register with two sighs from the strings. Over a timpani roll, the cellos, at first hesitant and plaintive, and then growing more and more confident, improvise a long recitative based on the main March theme (bar 191 ff.). Soon the theme of Trio 2 of the March returns (horns in octaves) with its two satellite motifs, the sighs and the repeated staccato chords. Suddenly, the atmosphere grows feverish again (bar 154 ff.), especially with a return of the basses' tumultuous scale motifs which are soon to serve as a counterpoint to the optimistic violin theme (bar 254). At the very moment when victory seems at hand, the consolatory *Abgesang* from the Funeral March (woodwinds) is unexpectedly interposed (*Plötzlich wieder langsam*, B major: bar 266). This fleeting return to the resigned mood of the March is interrupted by the return of the optimistic motif, which gradually makes its way to the violins' high register, while leaps of a ninth (the sighs, this time in the melody) take on an increasingly forced and fragmented character (*più mosso subito*, A♭: bar 288). Preparation for the recapitulation none the less takes on a triumphal air, with much arpeggio activity in the strings, and the first notes of an ascending chorale in the brass, but the triumphant tone is immediately cut short by a new *Einsturz*, after which the fevered anguish of the opening episode returns with its chromatic motif and its sighs (bar 322).

There are many surprises in the recapitulation. Certainly the stormy and tormented atmosphere remains the same. But when the first theme should appear the high strings only allude to it, and the satellite motifs gradually bring in the second instead, in the violins, over the low string arpeggios that accompanied the first theme in the exposition (bar 355 ff.). Just as one begins to suspect that the first theme will not return at all, its principal motifs entwine with those of the second, so that these strongly differentiated elements are finally blended together. The furious tutti that follows, with its whirlwind of quavers and triplets, brings back an explosion of grief comparable to that of Trio 1 of the March (*nicht schleppen*: bar 392). However, rising, optimistic elements begin to prevail among the scale motifs, sighs, and augmented fragments of the first theme. Against a background of string arpeggios and scales, the brasses proclaim the victorious chorale which had been cut short at the end of the exposition (D major: bar 464). However, despite its air of triumph, this first appearance of a symbolic chorale has, as Adorno observes, 'the fantastic character of a celestial apparition'.[68] The tension and the fever are not to be so easily overcome and the splendid edifice collapses within an instant in a new *Einsturz* under the back-and-forth battering effect of the opening motif, in the midst of the melodic sighs and chromatic scales. In the Coda (bar 526: *Pesante*) the storm reaches its paroxysm, after which everything swiftly subsides into darkness and mystery. A last reminiscence of the frantic scale motif, punctuated by mysterious repeated thirds on

[68] TAM 27.

woodwinds and harp, passes like a fleeting ghost in the low strings. Soon nothing is left of it but the first bar of sighing ninths. The last of the three notes of the final descending scale (pizzicato, low strings), is a single timpani stroke, pianissimo. In Adorno's words, 'the old storm becomes a feeble echo of itself'.[69]

Zweite Abteilung (Second Part).

(c) **Scherzo**: *Kräftig, nicht zu schnell* (energetic, not too fast).[70]

Key: D major, with many transitory modulations. Nadine Sine remarks in her thesis that, although the key of the whole movement is clearly D, the passages in which that main key is reached are not as decisive as those of the Finale. Furthermore, there are sections, like the Trio, in which 'the key remains ambiguous'. The main contrasting key is B flat.[71]

Time signature: 3/4.

Rhythm: Ländler (and Waltz).

Tempo: See above. *Etwas ruhiger* (a little quieter: Trio 1, bar 136); molto moderato (Trio 2: bar 308), etc.

Duration: 17 minutes (Hamburg 1905); 15 to $15\frac{1}{2}$ minutes (Bruno Walter pocket score).

Orchestration: A unique feature in Mahler's *œuvre*, it includes a solo horn called 'corno obbligato'. There are no instructions as to its positioning, but Willem Mengelberg's conducting score recommends placing it at the front of the stage near the leader of the orchestra. Whether Mahler himself used this seating arrangement is not known.

Form: It is exceptionally irregular and asymmetrical, especially for a movement of such large proportions, so that it is difficult to sort out the different episodes which mix and blend thematic elements from others: fragments of the B and C sections keep intruding in the development of A. Edward Murphy discerns two appearances of the Trio section and two long developmental areas. His summary is the following: A (Ländler: bars 1–135); B (Waltz: bars 136–73); A (174–217 + trans.: 218–69); C (Trio: 270–307); D (development: 308–489); A (490–579); D (579–695); C (696–763); trans. (745–763); A (764–819).[72] My view of the form is somewhat different. I have tried to summarize it below.

> *Scherzo*
>
> 1 to 39: A, A' (yodel), D major.
> 40 to 47: B (fugato), B', B".
> 48 to 82: A, A', A", B minor, B♭ major.
> 83 to 92: B, B', D minor.
> 93 to 135: A, A'.
>
> *Trio 1*
>
> 136 to 150: Trio 1, B♭, D♭ etc.
> 151 to 173: Trio 1, with Trio 1' and Trio 1".
>
> *Scherzo*
>
> 174 to 200: A
> 201 to 240: B (fugato), B', B", D major, F minor etc.

---

[69] TAM 20.   [70] See Banks, 'Aspects' (n. 54), 259.
[71] Sine, 'Evolution', 260.   [72] 'Unusual Forms', 107.

Trio 2

241 to 307: Trio 2, with B" and A', C minor, G minor.
308 to 336: Trio 2 (dev.), with B" (pizz.), D minor.
337 to 428: Trio 2 (dev.), with B" and A, Trio 1
and Trio 1", F minor
429 to 461: Trio 1 (dev.) with B, Trio 1' and Trio 2".
462 to 489: Stretto, A, A', B'.

Scherzo

490 to 526: Repeat: A, A' (with Trio 1, B"), D major.
527 to 531: B, B', B".
532 to 562: A, A'.

Trios 1 and 2

563 to 578: Trio 1 (triple *fortissimo*)
579 to 632: B, B" (with Trio 2), D major, F minor, A minor
633 to 647: Scherzo, Trio 1, A, G major
648 to 661: Stretto, A, B, G minor
662 to 699: Trio 1 (with B and A'), D major

Coda

700 to 744: Trio 2 and B alternating, A minor, F major
745 to 763: Trio 2 in pizz., D minor.
764 to 819: Stretto, B', B, then A, B", Trio 1", Trio 2, A.

The change of mood from the Allegro, one of the stormiest and most desperate Mahler ever wrote, to the radiant good humour of the Scherzo, is startling, and meant to be so. This is the longest of all Mahlerian Scherzos (819 bars) but also one of the few where no conscious element of parody or caricature creeps in. Paul Bekker calls it 'the most straight-lined (*gradlinigste*) [Scherzo] Mahler ever wrote' and Hans Ferdinand Redlich 'perhaps the most Austrian of all Mahler's movements'.[73] The alternation between country and city dances (ländler and waltz) has drawn many comments. Deryck Cooke has pointed out the many compositional subtleties of the main theme and thus shown how different it is from a folk dance: Mahler omits certain bars which the ear expects, disrupting the traditional schemes in a way that instantly nullifies the charge of banality so often laid against him. Cooke also observes that the main theme undergoes important changes each time it appears, often through the elision of one or two bars of each section, or through a different accentuation of the phrases.[74] The most remarkable thing about the Scherzo is not its huge proportions but the complexity of its thematic elaboration and developmental

[73] RBM 201. But Sponheuer nevertheless discerns a 'deep ambivalence' (*Logik*, 235) within this movement, if only because the counterpoints destroy the appearance of naïvety. The discrepancy between the folk-like ländler spirit and the polyphonic treatment of the themes is certainly much more striking than the 'return to Haydn' first movement of the Fourth, in which Mahler truly rediscovered the innocence of childhood and invented a 'neo-classical' style in which parody plays little or no part. However, the ambiguity of the Fifth's Scherzo was to be carried still further in the Scherzo movements Mahler later composed, from the Rondo-Finale of the Fifth to that of the Seventh and on to the Scherzo and demonic *Rondo Burleske* of the Ninth.
[74] 'Mahler's Melodic Thinking', in *Vindications: Essays on Romantic Music* (Faber, London, 1982), 100. Cooke also emphasizes the fact that elision is one of Mahler's most frequent procedures. Thus the ländler theme and its first two variants are respectively 12, 11, and 13 bars long, and make up 36 bars instead of the 48 which would result from symmetry between the sections. As seen above (Chap. 10), Mahler stated that he

areas, which rival those of a movement in sonata form. The Trios are preceded and followed by extensive transitions, a rare feature in Mahler's Scherzos. The summary above is of course not an analysis of this hugely complex piece but simply an attempt to identify the principal themes and episodes.

The marking *Kräftig, nicht zu schnell* first appeared at the beginning of the Scherzo of the First Symphony. The key is also identical but the style and atmosphere are quite different. Four horns open with a three-bar 'signature tune', whose highest and lowest notes again form the interval of a minor ninth (absolutely inconceivable in authentic folk music). The opening rhythm (see Ex. 21) predominates in the various stretti which come later.

Ex. 21.

Immediately, the true first subject (A) is played by the 'obbligato' first horn, which acts as soloist throughout the movement. As seen above, folk music is only the inspiration, the original impulse, behind this immensely sophisticated composition. A is quickly taken up by the woodwinds. The dance rhythm is constantly contradicted by syncopations and displacements of the strong beat, in a manner typical of refined 'art music'. The first important counter-melody belongs to the woodwinds, playing in thirds, but, on its second appearance (bar 15), the theme is accompanied by a rustic yodel from the violins (A").

Before the second full statement of A, a second element has made a brief appearance (bar 39), a quaver figuration soon to be developed in fugal style (B: violas), with an ostinato motif laid over it (B': clarinets in the opening rhythm of the horns). This is to play an essential role in all the fugal episodes. A first climax soon occurs with the final statement of A (horn, trumpets, and woodwind) accompanied by rapid scales in the strings. The original horn 'signal' prepares the entrance of the first Trio (bar 136, *etwas ruhiger*, B♭ major, in the violins), an idealized Viennese waltz which is characterized by a slight rhythmic hesitation, but has a simpler texture since it lacks the syncopations and countermelodies of the opening *ländler*. This is only an 'invitation to the waltz'—a brief anticipation of what is to come—and the horn call soon brings back the Scherzo (bar 174), completely transformed and followed by a fugal development of the second subject, with its short ostinato countersubject (trumpets, woodwinds, then violins: bar 201). Just as one is expecting the fugal episode to be extended, its principal motif becomes a simple yodel, first in the strings and then in the woodwinds. This is soon to become the background for a dreamy melody, exchanged by the horns and the woodwinds and again characterized by its large yodel-style intervals (bar 241).[75] The nostalgic melody soon proves to be that of the seond Trio, in a role analogous to that of the posthorn solo in the Scherzo of the Third, and which is to undergo a whole

had borrowed one of the themes in the Scherzo from the Carinthian composer Thomas Koschat (1845–1914). I have not been able to find the Koschat waltz *An dem blauen See* of which Mahler spoke. However, as seen above, a *Liederspiel* by Koschat, entitled *Am Wörthersee*, was in the repertoire at the Hofoper.

[75] The resemblance between this episode and a theme in the first movement of Brahms's Second Symphony is obvious.

series of reincarnations and metamorphoses. It is exchanged in dialogue, in the form of an 'improvised' recitative, between the obbligato horn and the cellos (bar 286), then taken up by the pizzicato strings (molto moderato), which transform it into a Viennese waltz and link it with the Trio 1, whose first bars soon reappear in their original form on the oboe (bar 329). The lyrical atmosphere is prolonged throughout another development of the second Trio, mingled with elements of the Scherzo and of the first Trio, so closely joined and intertwined that it subsequently becomes impossible to distinguish them one from another. A first rhythmic and dynamic stretto (on the Scherzo motifs: bar 462) leads to a genuine reprise into which innumerable modifications soon creep (bar 490 ff.). The first Trio, not to be heard again in its original form, now becomes an ecstatic waltz (violins, triple fortissimo: bar 563). Combined with the second (trumpets and horns) and with the string fugato, it gives rise to a second development.

At the final repeat of the Scherzo (Tempo 1: bar 633), the first Trio (in the basses) serves as a counterpoint to a variant of motif A (first violins). The kaleidoscope of themes and motifs attains a dizzying complexity that fully justifies Mahler's proud words, as reported in Natalie's memoirs and expressed in a letter he sent Alma during the Cologne rehearsals.[76] After a new climax, the horns attempt to restore peace with the Trio 1 melody (horns, then cellos: bar 662), but before long there is renewed turmoil (Scherzo motifs A and B). The horn tries a further three times to revert to Trio 2 (bars 700 ff.), but the fugato motif inexorably returns. Ultimately the nostalgic song prevails (bar 751) but this is the last moment of calm before the final tumult of the Coda. This opens with the bass drum stubbornly repeating the opening rhythm of the movement, after which all the elements, even that of the dreamy second Trio, are artfully entwined in a dizzying waltz that grows faster and faster until it is brutally cut short, with quasi-Beethovenian rage, by a twice repeated angry three-note motif derived from the opening signal. Nowhere does Mahler more fully reveal his genius for constructing long-range structures, or the inexhaustible wealth of his musical imagination, nowhere is he more sure of himself and his art. This movement represents a unique moment in his output, an unparalleled burst of imagination, energy, and optimism.

Dritte Abteilung (Third Part)

(d) Adagietto[77]

Composition: As seen above, Willem Mengelberg claimed that this movement was a declaration of love composed by Mahler for Alma. The Dutch conductor even wrote on his copy of the score a few lines of poetry which fit the music, but are probably his own.[78] He states that he had been told the same story on different occasions by

---

[76] See below, Vol. iii, Chap. 1: 'And the public—heavens!—what kind of face will they make when they are confronted with this chaos out of which a world keeps being born, only to fall apart again at once, these primeval jungle sounds, this rushing, roaring, raging sea, these dancing stars, these breathtaking, scintillating, flashing waves?' Vladimir Karbusicky has found the original of these images in Jean Paul, notably the stars and the sea (VKM 93). He has also analysed the above sentences (VKM 94).

[77] In his introduction to the facsimile score, Gilbert E. Kaplan describes an 'Adagietto' as 'faster, shorter, lighter in texture than an Adagio' (see *Adagietto*, 12).

[78] See above, Chap. 14. The score is now the property of the Amsterdam Concertgebouw Orchestra.

both Mahler and Alma: Mahler had sent Alma the Adagietto as soon as it was finished, and she, understanding its message, immediately came to see him. We cannot take such a circumstantial account lightly, coming as it does from a devoted friend of Mahler and one of his most ardent admirers and defenders. But if he is right, then the Adagietto and 'Ich bin der Welt abhanden gekommen', two pieces so closely akin in atmosphere and thematic material, were written in response to quite different feelings. To my mind, however, some doubt remains about Mengelberg's story. It seems to me improbable that Mahler could have written two pieces so related in every way with such different meanings. I also find it highly improbable, if Mengelberg's story is true, that Alma should have failed to mention the true meaning of the Adagietto at some time during the half-century in which she survived Mahler. She was always very careful to record and preserve each one of her *Trophäen*[79] and kept the autograph of 'Liebst du um Schönheit' on her living-room wall in New York. We are indebted to Gilbert E. Kaplan for comprehensibly assembling all the relevant information about the composition and performance of the Adagietto which have been long-standing preoccupations of Mahler scholars.[80] Mengelberg's statement outlines the three possible dates of composition: the summer of 1901, at the same time as 'Ich bin der Welt', in which case Mahler would have changed the basic meaning of the piece when he sent it to Alma (practically out of the question in my opinion since Natalie would have certainly mentioned it); the weeks following Mahler's meeting with Alma (unlikely too, since after 1892 Mahler had never composed during the Opera season); or the summer of 1902, when its role in the symphony was finally defined, to serve both as an introduction to and source of materials for the Finale.

Manuscript: A facsimile of Mahler's autograph fair copy and Alma's copy have recently been published by Gilbert E. Kaplan. As seen above, Mahler's copy is the earlier of the two. Edward R. Reilly observes[81] that the number 4 at the beginning of the movement has been written in over another number that had been scratched out. An interesting correction can be seen in bar 2 of Alma's copy: a G has been scratched out and replaced by a B♭, without which no one today would probably be able to identify the familiar melody.[82]

Key: F major (with a series of modulations in the middle section, to C minor, G♭ major, E major, D major, etc.).

Time signature: 4/4.

Tempo: *Sehr langsam* (very slow); *Fliessender* (more flowing) (bar 39); *Nicht schleppen* (do not drag); *Etwas flüssiger als zu Anfang* (somewhat more fluid than at the beginning); *Etwas drängend* (somewhat more urgently) (bar 43); Tempo 1. Molto Adagio (bar 78); *Noch langsamer* (still slower); *Drängend* (urgently) (bar 96). Mahler certainly did not anticipate, nor would he have wished for, the excessive sentimentality which most conductors today indulge in when playing this short piece. The slowed-down tempo at which they take it completely distorts its tender, contemplative character and changes it into a syrupy elegy. Donald Mitchell rightly observes that the movement is really an orchestral song and that no singer in the world could

---

[79] See Elias Canetti, *Das Augenspiel: Lebensgeschichte 1931–37* (Hanser, Munich, 1985), 59 ff.
[80] See Kaplan (ed.), *Adagietto* (n. 7), 35 ff.
[81] Reilly, 'Manuscripts and Printed Copies', ibid. 41
[82] However, the third bar of the reprise (bar 75) retains Mahler's original version.

possibly sustain such an absurdly slow pace. Gilbert Kaplan has rightly given emphasis to this important issue of interpretation.

Admittedly, Bruno Walter's tempo (total duration 7 minutes, 38 seconds) seems almost too fast, yet Mengelberg, who was just as close to Mahler, clocked up similar times (7 minutes on his first recording, 8 minutes, 20 seconds, on his second). Among more recent versions, however, Kubelik and Solti have the shortest times (9 minutes, 44 seconds, and 9 minutes, 40 seconds) while Tennstedt, Abbado, Farbermann, and Scherchen are much slower (respectively 11 minutes, 52, 53 and 58 seconds, and 13 minutes, 7 seconds). The present world record for slowness is held by Haitink: his second recording (1988) lasts 13 minutes, 55 seconds.[83]

Duration: 9 minutes (Hamburg 1905); $7\frac{1}{2}$ minutes (Walter's miniature score); 7 minutes (St Petersburg 1907); 7 minutes (Mengelberg's 1926 recording); 7 minutes, 58 seconds (Walter's 1938 recording); 7 minutes, 38 seconds (Walter's 1947 record).[84]

Form: Although the recapitulation is abridged and considerably modified, the form can be summed up as ABA, section B being a modulating extension of the main melody.

Analysis: After the Scherzo's great burst of vitality, it would have been inconceivable to end this symphony in a tragic vein and even more inconceivable to follow it with another lively, boisterous movement. A contrast was needed at this point, and this is the main justification for the Adagietto, a simple 'song without words' played by strings alone, with a discreet accompaniment of harp arpeggios. Despite Mengelberg's statement that it was meant as a love message, it seems to express the same feeling as 'Ich bin der Welt', lonely and blissful contemplation, away from the turmoil of the world and above all the city life which Mahler knew so well. The first phrase is whispered pianissimo by the first violins while the second, more declamatory, exploits the warm sonority of the cellos. The melody proper belongs to the large family of Mahlerian themes which rise by conjunct degrees, a family which includes the Resurrection theme in the Second, that of the Allegro in the Fourth, and the 'Accende Lumen' in the Eighth.[85] It is a masterpiece of emotion intensely felt and yet restrained in expression. There are those who consider its charm too facile, its appeal too immediate (especially since it was used as an accompaniment to Luchino Visconti's film *Death in Venice*).

It is interesting and instructive, in this respect, to compare two articles which have appeared in the last ten years. One, by Victor Ravizza, sets out to 'prove' that the Adagietto is 'one-dimensional, indulgent, sentimental', 'entering areas dangerously close to the point where art becomes a cheap imitation of itself'.[86] Ravizza thinks that Mahler 'failed' because he intended the Adagietto to be a message of love and 'the heartfelt singing of love was not his forte'; nor did he have at his disposal 'any appropriate musical vocabulary'. A very different verdict is reached in a

[83] Gilbert Kaplan recalls the performances conducted by Leonard Bernstein in memory of Serge Koussevitzky and Robert F. Kennedy, and later those performed in his own memory by numerous conductors around the world.

[84] One might be inclined to think that Walter's and Mengelberg's tempos were quicker because of the maximum length of a 78 rpm record, but even in 1926 it was possible to record more than 9 minutes of music on two sides.

[85] This is the family of rising themes that James L. Zychowicz has analysed under the name of 'Ewigkeit Motive' (see 'Quotation and Assimilation: The Ewigkeit Motive in the Music of Mahler', unpubl. article, 16 ff.).

[86] See 'Emanzipation einer Episode: Zu Gustav Mahlers Adagietto', *Zürcher Zeitung* (16 Nov. 1991).

detailed and scholarly study published in 1984 by the Schenkerian analyst Allen Forte. He analysed the 'middleground motives' of the Adagietto, using no less than seven different charts, and described Mahler's compositional method as 'motivic counterpoint'. After examining every detail of the score, Forte ends his ten closely printed columns of analysis with a comment on the 'extraordinary and perhaps unexpected conclusion to this splendid composition'.[87] Those who are perhaps blinded by the popularity of the Adagietto should try to distance themselves from the hackneyed outpourings of sentiment it has given rise to in the hands of irresponsible conductors and take a fresh objective approach. They should for instance study the way Mahler creates an effect of weightlessness by avoiding the tonic in the first two bars; how he varies the sonority in the middle section with more elaborate string parts and by dispensing with the harp arpeggios; or creates an effect of timelessness in the final bars by a series of retardations, as if each note were loath to regain its place within the common chord. But these are only a few of the innumerable refinements of this short movement. In the first section, A minor and C minor play an important part, besides the tonic key of F, but these short modulatory sections are omitted in the reprise. In the central section (bar 47), the upper register of the violins develops and amplifies the opening melody in a slightly faster tempo, at first in G flat (the 'Neapolitan' tonality),[88] then in D major, before returning suddenly to the home key in one of those melting Mahlerian modulations, whose magic lies in their very unexpectedness. The opening is then recapitulated (bar 73) in a shortened and simplified form. The last phrase of the wonderful melody 'which has constantly been seeking but always been denied a resolution'[89] descends little by little from the vertiginous heights to which it has climbed, and dies pianissimo low down in the violins.[90]

5. Rondo-Finale

Key: D major (with a great many contrasting major keys in the development sections).
Time signature: 2/2.
Tempo: Allegro (for the Introduction); Allegro giocoso. *Frisch* (fresh); *Grazioso* (bar 100); a tempo, grazioso (bar 191), etc.
Duration: 15 minutes (Hamburg 1905); 14 minutes (Walter's pocket score).
Form: This is the first occasion that Mahler employed the term 'rondo' to describe one of the movements he had composed, but the form he actually adopts has little to do with classical models of the rondo.[91]

---

[87] See 'Middleground Motives in the Adagietto of the Fifth Symphony', *19th Century Music*, 8: 2 (Autumn 1984), 153 ff.

[88] The second verse of 'Ich atmet' einen linden Duft' also modulates to the key of the flattened supertonic.

[89] Sine, 'Evolution', 266. The author makes many interesting comments on the harmonic structure of the movement.

[90] Sine rightly claims that the resolution of the final note, A, comes only with the tonic, D, of the Rondo-Finale.

[91] Another outline, different in several ways from Sponheuer's, is given by Edward Murphy, 'Unusual Forms', 108: A (bars 1–166); trans. (167–90); B (190–272); A (273–89); C (development: 280–372); B (372–415); trans (415–23); C (423–96); 4 (497–525); C (526–622); B (623–86); A (711–91). This brings to three the number of developmental areas and, like the Scherzo's, the total design is asymmetrical. Murphy points out the unusual key relationships which occur in each of the movements (especially tonic-submediant: C#–A in 1; D–Bb in 2; F–D in 4, etc.). Such experiments, he points out, are new in Mahler's music. Carolyn

Outline[92]

1–23   Introduction, in five fragments (bassoon, oboe, bassoon, horn, and clarinet).

24–55   *Allegro grazioso*: Principal theme (A), D major.

56–135   *Sempre l'istesso tempo*, then *grazioso*; 1st fugal episode (B).

136–66   *A tempo subito*: A.

167–90   *Sempre l'istesso tempo*, then *nicht eilen* (do not hurry): 2nd fugal episode (B') B flat major, D major.

191–252 *Grazioso*: Theme C (from middle section of the Adagietto), B major, B flat major.

253–372 2nd fugal episode (B'), prolonged (with march episode at 307), G, D, A, C, A flat major, G sharp minor, D.

373–422 *Grazioso*: new version of C (C'), D major.

423–96   3rd fugal episode (B"), B flat major, D minor, D, C, D.

497–525 *Plötzlich wie zu Anfang* (suddenly as at the beginning): A in D major.

526–80   4th fugal episode (B'''), B flat major, C minor, C major.

581–622 *Unmerklich etwas einhaltend* (very slightly slower): A varied (A'), A flat, A major.

623–710 Theme C varied (C"), G, E flat major, D minor, etc.

711–48   *Drängend* (urgently); *Sehr drängend* (with great urgency); *Pesante*: Coda (B""), chorale: D major.

749–91   *Allegro molto und bis Schluss beschleunigend* (and accelerating to the end). Elements of the chorale and of the other Rondo themes.

The first thing to be said in the light of the above outline is that the title 'Rondo' is hardly appropriate, since theme A appears less frequently than the fugal episodes. However, the heading 'sonata' would be equally inappropriate because of the independence of the various episodes, the abruptness of the transitions (even though the contrapuntal writing here is less rigorous and dissonant than in the Scherzo). However, some commentators have been tempted to discern in this rondo a disguised sonata whose outline would be as follows:

Exposition: bars 1 to 166 (A, B, A).
Development: bars 167 to 496 (B', C, B', C', C").
Recapitulation: bars 497 to 710 (A', B''', A", C").[93]

There are very strong arguments against adopting this hypothesis. The true contrasting theme (C) does not appear until the development and nevertheless becomes more and more important within it (just as the lyrical theme of the second Trio steadily became more important towards the end of the Scherzo). The most striking feature of the movement is undoubtedly the alternation of homophonic and contrapuntal episodes, the former principally appearing as melodic episodes in

Baxendale, who has also published an extensive analysis of the Finale, mainly based on key relationships (see 'Finale', 265), disagrees with Murphy's proposed schema and calls the labelling of the C section 'development' 'highly suspect'. The plan she gives is far more complex.

[92] I here reproduce Bernd Sponheuer's outline. Once again it is impossible, in a limited space, to give a complete picture of the enormous complexities of this movement.

[93] Sponheuer, *Logik*, 252.

strings and woodwinds, the latter that of persistent non legato figures in the low strings.[94]

A single A, from the horn, is echoed pianissimo by the first violins which seem loath to abandon the contemplative mood of the previous movement. But the horns are anxious to start anew and they play a summons in fourths (A–D–A)[95] to which the woodwinds reply with an improvised and playful divertissement in four sections. The first, for the bassoon, is a note-for-note quote from a *Wunderhorn-Lied*, 'Lob des hohen Verstandes', a humorous account, as already described above, of a singing contest between the cuckoo and the nightingale. Appointed judge, the ass pronounces the more conservative of the two, that is to say the cuckoo, to be the winner.[96] The original title of the song was 'Lob der Kritik' (In Praise of Criticism); Mahler might have had in mind the 'infernal judges' who were soon to condemn his symphony, as the ass did the song of the nightingale. Another little tune is hesitantly put forward by the oboe, to which the bassoon replies in a more assured manner. The clarinet then links the preceding question and answer in one, after the horn has tossed out another fragment with the same air of detachment. Is another mischievous singing contest thus starting between the woodwinds? For the time being, uninformed listeners could hardly imagine that, within these few bars, the whole thematic content of the Rondo has already been stated. The oboe picks up, more insistently, the clarinet's last three notes, which the horn then seizes, for they are the first three notes of the main theme (A). The theme is soon expanded and developed by the strings, then by the woodwinds. Some have found in it a late echo of the second theme from the Finale of Beethoven's Second Symphony, and the similarity is indeed striking. Furthermore, Mahler is in fact following Beethoven's example in combining rondo and sonata form, with numerous additional fugal elements. A brief, playful wind motif, whose diatonic freshness suggests the *Wunderhorn-Lieder*, closes the first theme proper and sets off, at first in the cellos, a long fugato (B) on a subject closely related to that of the Scherzo and to the main theme (A) of the Rondo.[97] At the eighth bar the basses bring back the clarinet refrain from the Introduction as a counter-subject. One after another, the motifs in the introduction return.

Scarcely has this first fugato ended when its principal motif (in the basses), combined with that of 'Lob des hohen Verstandes', furnishes the material for a *Grazioso* episode (bar 100) which is twice cut short by fortissimo horn octaves. The final bars of the Introduction now bring in the principal refrain (A) (bar 136). The following interlude, in B flat, begins like the previous one as a fugato. In the third bar, the horn introduces a motif already sketched in the first Grazioso episode, where it seemed to be derived from 'Lob des hohen Verstandes'. This new Grazioso section is much longer than the previous one, and soon reveals its true origin: the central

[94] See Arno Forchert, 'Zur Auflösung traditioneller Formkategorien in der Musik um 1900: Probleme formaler Organisation bei Mahler und Strauss', *Archiv für Musikwissenschaft*, 32 (1975), 2, 85. The writer observes that Mahler constantly varies the 'refrain', whereas the 'episodes' remain more or less alike.

[95] 'A summons to the "real world" after the composer has been "lost to it" in introspection (*der Welt abhanden*)', according to James L. Zychowicz (see 'Inner Program', 12).

[96] See above, in the App., on the orchestral *Wunderhorn-Lieder*.

[97] Baxendale, 'Finale', 265, observes that, just 'as Mahler's Finale secularizes the traditional function of the chorale, so does he divest the fugue of the monumentality with which it was frequently associated in the nineteenth century'. 'He invests it with a "breathless and impatient quality" . . . contributing to a sense of enthusiastic accumulation.'

section of the Adagietto, which is quoted almost complete, but in a fast tempo which lends to it a humorous, whimsical character (C).[98] The ensuing development (bar 253 ff.) combines it with two other previous motifs. The contrapuntal web grows steadily more dense, with melodic fragments intertwining and changing through numerous modulations, until a vigorous tutti leads to a third Grazioso episode (bar 373). The strings then take up the Adagietto melody, to which the woodwinds add counter-melodies. The fugato section (bar 423) gradually broadens to a furious tutti, after which the main theme (A) returns (at last) in a new triplet crotchet rhythm (bar 497). It takes on a new character and announces the climactic chorale to come (trumpet: bar 510 ff.).

After the fugato has modulated to C major we expect the refrain (A) to return in the home key, but in fact it reappears in A flat and in a startlingly new guise, in the bassoons, low strings, and tuba (bar 581). Following the principle that a change of key has the maximum effect when there is no modulation, Mahler moves on without transition to the most distant key, A major, for an episode whose lyricism is emphasized by several *espressivo* markings and by a transparent orchestration. In the final Grazioso section (bar 606 ff.), the Adagietto melody takes on an obsessive character. Its intervals are ceaselessly repeated and gradually enlarged, accelerando, amid a whirlwind of scales derived from the fugato. The same scales become the background for a triumphant brass chorale, which is related to that of the second movement, but is in fact an augmented version of the clarinet motif from the Introduction (see below). The whirlwind gains momentum throughout the coda, which intricately entwines all the previous thematic fragments and motifs. After a deceptive cadence on a B flat held by the brasses, whole tone scales rush down to the final chord.

This Rondo, with its absolute mastery of technical means and compositional procedures inspired by the classical tradition, but enriched by his inexhaustible musical imagination, marks a new high point in Mahler's output. The chorale merely confirms the carefree mood of the opening bars and seems the logical outcome of the previous, kaleidoscopic swirl of melodic fragments, always familiar, always recognizable, yet always new. In this joyous exuberance, Theodor Adorno thought he could detect something forced and unspontaneous, a 'flaw' which made this affirmation a confession of weakness rather than a display of strength, and few of his statements have been so extensively quoted and provoked so much comment. Taking an overall view of Mahler's work, one sees that with this Rondo he is inaugurating a new type of movement. From then on these brilliant Rondos demand virtuoso performances and a virtuoso orchestra. They confirm his mastery of classical composition, but in an increasingly peremptory, even strained manner right up to the *Rondo Burleske* of the Ninth Symphony[99] (via the Rondo-Finale of the Seventh). In the early symphonies, the lively, optimistic, sometimes triumphant Finale, regarded as a necessity by romantic and post-romantic composers, had in a sense been avoided by Mahler. After the partial success of the First, whose tragic Finale terminates in a somewhat artificial apotheosis, the ending of the Second attains,

---

[98] 'Why the Adagietto should return at all is difficult to explain since the breathless, almost frivolous, character of the Rondo does not lend itself to the idea of a final, summarizing statement of the work, in which previous elements may be synthesized.' (See Baxendale, 'Finale', 271.)

[99] Adorno also noted the thematic relationship between the Burleske in the Ninth and the second movement in the Fifth (TAM 212).

thanks to the chorus, a sumptuous theatricality which is, so to speak, extra-symphonic. In the Adagio-Finale of the Third, Mahler again scales the heights, but in a tempo that is opposed to tradition. In the Fourth, he brilliantly resuscitates the innocent, childish vision of heaven and concludes the symphony in a completely new way with a Lied. With the Fifth, therefore, Mahler finds himself for the first time facing the 'Finale problem', on which so many romantics and post-romantics, and even Bruckner, so often came to grief. And the need for a catharsis, for a fast and carefree last movement, is felt all the more in the Fifth because the symphony started in a deeply tragic mood.

The feeling of uneasiness which prevents us from taking Mahler's optimism altogether seriously, in the Finales of both the Fifth and Seventh Symphonies, may be caused in part by his return to the past (here to the fugal style), to learned, 'old-fashioned' forms of composition, to which Wagner gave new vitality in *Die Meistersinger* while yet linking it to the comic nature of the work. In Mahler, it has retained the same kind of ambiguity. He himself acknowledged it by using, in his fugati, the satirical theme from 'Lob des hohen Verstandes'. If the gaiety of the Rondo-Finale often seems to verge on caricature, it is because, as Adorno says, 'Mahler, in line with musical classicism and certainly with *Die Meistersinger*, still often associates counterpoint with humour and play.'[100] He also betrays himself by accelerating the lovely melody of the Adagietto, which, like 'Ich bin der Welt', had symbolized the sacred isolation of the artist: it finds itself desecrated and brutally dragged into the bustle of everyday life.[101] How could the chorale 'apotheosis' be taken at face value when it is nothing but an augmented variant of the whimsical clarinet figure in the opening bars (see Ex. 22).

Ex. 22. Fifth Symphony, Rondo-Finale

Yet Bruno Walter and Richard Specht have both spoken of the 'will to live' and even of the 'will to power',[102] Heinrich von Kralik of a 'manifestation of musical joy',[103] and Paul Bekker of a 'Hymn to Life' (*Lebenshymnus*), of the 'happiness and solitude of artistic creation', and finally of 'a masterpiece of skillful condensation in brilliant style'.[104] Certainly Mahler wished the whole work to reach *per aspera ad*

---

[100] TAM 151.

[101] Sponheuer compares this rapid transformation of the theme of the Adagietto with the speeding up of a film (*Logik*, 250). Mahler uses the same procedure in the Ninth Symphony, this time caricaturing in advance in the *Rondo Burleske* a thematic element from the final Adagio.

[102] BWM 84; RSM2. 239.

[103] Heinrich von Kralik, *Gustav Mahler*, ed. Friedrich Heller (Lafite, Vienna, 1968), 51.

[104] BMS 202 and 226.

astra, but for Adorno, 'the image, which holds out its arms towards the breakthrough (*Durchbruch*),[105] remains defective, since the breakthrough, like the Messiah, doesn't come. To realize the breakthrough musically means to bear witness to its actual miscarriage.'[106] 'Powerlessness shows through the display of power: if it were the fulfilment of the promise, and not still only the promise, it would not need to vaunt itself as power.'[107]

Mahler was an unconvincing yea-sayer (*war ein schlechter Jasager*). His voice falters, like Nietzsche's, when he upholds values and speaks solely out of sentiment; when he himself practises that dreadful concept of overcoming, which the thematic analyses then dismember, and composes as if joy were already present in the world. His vainly jubilant movements unmask jubilation, his subjective incapacity for the *happy end*[108] itself denounces it. It was still built into the traditional forms, and could just about get by so long as convention relieved it of specific responsibility; but it fails when the joke becomes serious.[109]

Bernd Sponheuer, who wrote the first detailed analysis of this movement, has observed that the triumph in the Finale is as equivocal as the *joie de vivre* in the Scherzo. It is in no way a *Durchbruch*, since the movement as a whole is affirmative. On the contrary, this conclusion has something predictable and deliberate about it[110] and is no longer an 'allegory of the absolute', to use Adorno's expression.[111] Furthermore, says Sponheuer, this chorale, made up (as seen above) of thoroughly profane (*weltlich*) everyday musical fragments taken from the Rondo's introduction, lacks any genuinely transcendental character. In the optimistic context in which it is set, it does not have the same 'Deus ex machina' or *Durchbruch* effect as in the second movement, and 'has to do essentially with itself'. It is 'a chorale without chorale character' or a 'change-of-fortune celebration where no change of fortune has taken place'. It only speaks aloud all that is implicit in the rest of the movement.[112]

Sponheuer uses the word 'secularization' (or 'laicization') to describe this process, similar to that of the 'sacred' melody of the Adagietto which is rendered *weltlich* (profane) in the Finale. Here the affirmatory gesture reflects 'the logic of effect rather than of the thing itself'; it is an 'illusion', a 'phantasm' (*Phantasmagorie*), a 'semblance as vision' (*Schein als Vision*). What is more, it does not have the last word, for it is followed by a stretto which denies the affirmatory gesture by using the same material, again broken up and accelerated.[113] Carolyn Baxendale takes the ambiguity of the 'affirmation' for granted but attributes the effect of the chorale to the many interruptions, uncertainties, ambiguities, unexpected developments, and distant thematic connections which delay its appearance, as if the music were 'striving for a solution which is as yet beyond its grasp'. Like Sponheuer, she finds the chorale 'blended with secular, even pagan traits, conveying expressions of personal mastery as opposed to complete confidence in some higher order'.[114]

No one today would try to claim that the 'optimistic' conclusions to the Fifth and

[105] The meaning of this Adornian concept, which continually recurs in Adorno's writings on Mahler, is explained in the first chapter of his *Mahler* (TAM 9). See also TAM 60.
[106] TAM 13.   [107] TAM 20.   [108] In English in the text.
[109] TAM 180.   [110] *Logik*, 260.   [111] TAM 63.
[112] See Sponheuer, 'Interpretation', 92.
[113] *Logik*, 267. Dika Newlin also called the chorale simply 'an isometrically harmonized diatonic melody preferably intoned by the heavy brass' (DNM 178).
[114] Baxendale, 'Finale', 277 ff.

Seventh Symphonies are as clear and convincing as the apotheosis of the Eighth or the visionary ending of *Das Lied von der Erde*. To take up Adorno's idea, the image of joy goes through too many deviations, too many of those increasingly cruel distortions which will later lead to the aggressive parody of the *Rondo Burleske*. And these cannot be fully explained by the traditional romantic association of humour with grief, pleasure with pain: Mahler, heir of the great German poets, builds his whole discourse on this alchemy of opposites. But he goes much further in instinctively assuming the uncertainty, the doubts, the secret anguish, the fundamental ambiguity, that marked his time and still weigh so heavily on ours. Ambiguity is indeed an underground stream feeding his art, the thing that makes it both inexhaustibly rich and perpetually fresh, and opens up the most unexpected and the most fertile perspectives. If Mahler had composed a traditional apotheosis for the Fifth and presented it as a proclamation of faith comparable to that of the Eighth, he would not continue to puzzle and challenge us as he does, ever more searchingly with the passage of time.

FIVE KINDERTOTENLIEDER (1901–1904)

The Poems

In 1872, six years after Friedrich Rückert's death, the Frankfurt firm of J. J. Sauerländer published the first edition[1] of the *Kindertodtenlieder* collection.[2] It was a small volume of 408 pages, cloth-bound and gold-engraved,[3] and contained 425 poems. Eighteen further poems on the same tragic theme, and grouped under the titles 'Vorahnungen' and 'Nachträge zu den *Kindertodtenliedern*' (Premonition and Additions to the *Kindertotenlieder*), were added later.[4] The preface to the 1872 edition, for which the poet's son, Heinrich, acted as editor, explains that these poems were circulated in manuscript by Rückert among his friends at the time of writing, but that he had never been able to bring himself to hand them over to a publisher for them to be read by a wider public.

Friedrich Rückert was living in Erlangen with his wife and six children when, in 1833, the youngest, Luise (born 25 June 1830), contracted scarlet fever the day after Christmas. She died on New Year's Eve. Her 5-year-old brother, Ernst (born 4 January 1829), contracted the same illness and died on 16 January.[5] Three other children in the house also caught this infection, but fortunately survived. But the father long remained inconsolable. For the rest of his life he kept close to him a pastel portrait of his two

---

[1] According to Peter Russell, *Light in Battle with Darkness: Mahler's Kindertotenlieder* (Peter Lang, Berne, 1991), 37, Edward's Kravitt's statement (in 'Mahler's Dirges for his Death', *Musical Quarterly*, 64: 3 (July 1978), 347) that some of the *Kindertotenlieder* had appeared in Rückert's lifetime is mistaken.

[2] This is Rückert's own spelling, which Mahler used in his MSS. The modernization of German spelling led to the suppression of the second 'd'.

[3] The allegorical figure on the cover was a young boy scantily clad in drapes, holding an extinguished torch dipped toward the earth and still smoking.

[4] Russell, *Light*. These 18 poems were not included in the 1872 volume.

[5] Peter Russell notes that the poems used for Mahler's first two songs were written about Luise Rückert's death, as is explicitly the third. Only the fourth and fifth songs refer to both children (*Light*, 6).

youngest children done in the autumn of 1833, a few months before their death. During the first six months of 1834, he wrote the 425 poems included in the first edition, pouring them forth at the rate of two or three a day. The eighteen further poems on this theme were written later and express his reconciliation to his loss.[6]

For the 1872 edition, his son Heinrich grouped the poems into four sections: (1) 'Lied und Leid' (Song and Suffering), 25 poems; (2) 'Krankheit und Tod' (Sickness and Death), 168 poems; (3) 'Winter und Frühling' (Winter and Spring), 66 poems; (4) 'Trost und Erhebung' (Solace and Exaltation), 166 poems.[7] The poems Mahler chose are from the second (56: (i) 'Wenn zur Thür' and (ii) 'Wenn dein Mütterlein'; 69: 'Nun seh' ich wohl') and fourth sections (47: 'Oft denk' ich'; 83: 'In diesem Wetter', and 115: 'Nun will die Sonne'). After her brother's death, in 1881, Marie Rückert brought out a new edition named *Lied und Leid*, containing 241 of the poems in an entirely different order, based on the poet's private diary. The sections were now called: (1) 'Leid' (Suffering); (2) 'Trost und Erhebung' (Solace and Exaltation); (3) 'Zeit und Ewigkeit' (Time and Eternity); (4) 'Ritornelle'. Although Susanne Vill believes that Mahler used the second edition,[8] Peter Russell shows that the sequence of poems in both volumes is actually very different from Mahler's. In his opinion, the 1872 edition was certainly available to him and had a wider circulation than the later one.[9]

Many commentators have criticized Rückert's poems on literary grounds. Most of them were written in great haste and were probably never intended for publication. Edward Kravitt[10] writes of a somewhat 'sentimental' treatment of the subject but praises their 'unusual syntax, diction and spellings . . . used to solely evocative purpose, several decades before the French symbolists',[11] while several other writers have commented on the far greater simplicity, vigour, and naturalness of Eichendorff's ten poems on the same subject, *Auf meines Kindes Tod*.[12] Peter Russell, the author of the most recent and detailed study of the cycle, concedes that few of these poems are 'wholly successful in an artistic sense',[13] but rightly points out that 'in the furnace of Mahler's genius a tremendous alchemy has taken place, transmuting baser metals to gold'. 'Mahler was not merely looking into Rückert's soul', he adds, 'but also into his own.' Russell believes that Mahler's selection of poems was made in the light of 'a common symbolism' of 'darkness and light'.[14]

Composition

There have long been doubts about the exact chronology of Mahler's *Kindertotenlieder*.[15] They first arose because the various manuscripts are undated, and

[6] Ibid. 33. The same author notes that 'the dominant attitude is not one of faith and surrender to God's higher wisdom but one of stoical resolve'.

[7] Russell finds the editor's success 'only partial', since the order corresponds neither to a sequence of events, nor to a 'progression of feeling' (ibid. 34).

[8] Vill, *Vermittlungsformen*, 108 ff.   [9] Russell, *Light*, 38.   [10] In 'Dirges' (n. 1), 353.

[11] In this context. Kravitt quotes Conrad Beyer, *Nachgelassene Gedichte Friedrich Rückerts* (Braumüller, Vienna, 1877, 345), which lists unusual details of syntax and spelling in the *Kindertotenlieder*, notably, in the second poem, *von wannen, verblendenden Geschicke* and *Ihr sprühtet*.

[12] The third of them is quoted in its entirety in E. Mary Dargie's book, *Music and Poetry in the Songs of Gustav Mahler* (Peter Lang, Berne, 1981), 229.   [13] Russell, *Light*, 46.

[14] Russell also observes that in *Das Lied* 'sunshine and hope' are associated with light, and suffering with darkness (see *Light*, 160 ff.).

[15] Cf. Christopher O. Lewis, 'On The Chronology of the Kindertotenlieder', *Revue Mahler Review*, 1 (BMGM, Paris, 1987), 21 ff.

because of the error Alma Mahler committed in her *Erinnerungen*.[16] A careful study of Natalie's report of summer of 1901 confirms what Alma later wrote in *Mein Leben*, i.e. that in June 1904 Mahler added two Lieder to the three he had written during the summer of 1901.[17] His letter to Mengelberg, quoted above,[18] fixes to within a few days the dates of composition of these last two Lieder, on which he was working by 27 or 28 June 1904. As for his reason for finishing the cycle that summer, that seems quite clear: he was fulfilling his promise to Schoenberg and Zemlinsky that he would provide them with a complete concert of Lieder for the Vereinigung series.

Nevertheless, one question long remained unsolved: which Lieder were written in 1901, which in 1904? To my mind, Christopher O. Lewis, in his study of the sketches and manuscripts, has found conclusive evidence confirming the hypothesis I had made in my French Volume ii (1983). Like me, he is convinced that Lieder 2 and 5 were added in 1904 to the three composed in 1901. He bases his argument on the evidence provided by the presence (or absence) of sketches, draft scores, fair copies, and autograph copies. Lewis's reasoning is hard to summarize in a few lines but totally convincing. According to him, the piano draft of Songs 3 and 4 are fair copies, yet fair copies of 2 and 5 are missing, no doubt because Mahler was pressed for time and orchestrated straight from the drafts. This would explain why the orchestral drafts of 2 and 5 are so heavily corrected, far more than the other three, and show signs of being 'works still in progress'. Further confirmation of this hypothesis is that Mahler also corrected the piano vocal drafts of songs 2 and 5 from the orchestral scores. Further-more, the orchestral drafts of 2 and 5 are written on the same 20-stave paper, although No. 2 uses only 13 staves. The figure corrected on the title-page of No. 3 could only have been a 3 (replacing a 2).[19] Thus, Nos. 3 and 4 were originally 2 and 3. All the evidence thus concurs to suggest that songs 2 and 5 were indeed the ones composed during the last days of June 1904.[20] The identical colour of the paper of the orchestral drafts provides further confirmation: for Lieder 2 and 5, the format is large (26.5 × 34 cm.) and the paper is yellowish, while the paper for the third and fourth Lieder is white and of a normal format as regards length (25.5 × 32 cm.). Songs 3 and 4 are on identical paper.[21]

---

[16] As seen above, Alma's *Erinnerungen* state that 2 Lieder were written in 1901 and 3 in 1904 (AMM1. 91 and AMM2. 97). However, the mistake is rectified in AML, which states that 3 Lieder date from 1901 and 2 from 1904 (AML 46). Natalie's MS leaves no doubt that 3 of the Lieder were composed in 1901 (see above, Chap. 10).

[17] See above, Chap. 16.

[18] RMH 47. Letter sent to Mengelberg from Maiernigg and bearing an Amsterdam postmark with the date 29 June 1904.

[19] Only the lower part of the figure has been erased and the only two figures sharing the same upper part are 2 and 3.

[20] See Lewis, 'Chronology' (n. 15) 23 ff.

[21] Kravitt, 'Dirges' (n. 1) 437, notes the difference in paper in the piano MSS but not that which exists in the orchestral version. He wrongly claims that the Stanford Univ. Library, Calif., possesses a series of corrected proofs (these are actually at IMG). The Californian library possesses only one of the first copies of the 1905 edn., with a dedication to Frau Edytha Moser. There are two or three handwritten markings, but not in Mahler's hand. Kravitt had seen a 'philosophical' link between the first, second, and fifth Lieder and also between the third and the fourth. He therefore suggests that 1, 2, and 5 dated from 1904. Mitchell also noted the difference in paper in the piano MSS between 3 and 4, and 2 and 5, without drawing our conclusions as to the chronology. The piano score publ. in 1979 by IMG lists the differences between the MSS but also fails to draw any conclusion. The *Revisionsbericht* goes so far as to claim that the order of composition of the different Lieder cannot be ascertained.

Title-page

A manuscript title-page, written on 20-stave paper (like the orchestral drafts of Lieder 2 and 5) had survived among Alma's papers.[22] It lists the four 1901 *Rückert-Lieder*, and *Kindertotenlieder* 2 to 5. However, the two figures have been scratched out and replaced with the title of another 1901 Lied, 'Der Tamboursg'sell'.[23] This cover obviously dates from 1904, and Mahler used it temporarily for the 'Kindertotenlieder 2 to 5'. Then, changing his mind, he erased 'No. 2 to No. 5' and added the titles of the four *Rückert-Lieder* of 1901 and that of the last *Wunderhorn-Lied*.[24]

Manuscripts

Sketches: No. 1: early and incomplete, in C# major (71 bars: GMF); No. 2: 2 pages (PML); No. 3: 1 page (whereabouts unknown); No. 5: first 11 bars (Alma Mahler, now most likely Moldenhauer).
Piano drafts: Nos. 2 to 5 (PML).
Fair copies (*of piano drafts*): Nos. 3 and 4 (PML).[25]
Orchestral drafts: complete (PML).
The sketch of 'Nun seh'ich wohl' (the second page of which only has writing on one and a half staves) has several versions of the phrase 'drängen eure ganze Macht zusammen' (bar 18), over which Mahler has written (in French!) 'meilleur' and 'le meilleur'.[26] The essential differences between the manuscripts and the published versions will be indicated below in the section concerning each of the Lieder. In the piano versions, the second Lied occupies one full page (format 26.5 × 34 cm., 24 staves) and less than a stave and a half of a second; the third occupies two and a half pages (25.5 × 36 cm.);[27] the fourth, two pages plus one stave (id.); and the last, three pages plus a stave and a half (26.5 × 34 cm.). The orchestral draft, which formerly belonged to Bruno Walter, contains in all 61 pages, format 34.5 × 26 cm., not counting the five title-pages (1st song: 12 pages; 2nd: 10; 3rd: 12; 4th: 9; 5th: 18). (As seen above, the paper for numbers 1, 3, and 4 has 18 staves, and that for numbers 2 and 5 has 20.) Several sets of proofs have survived in IMG.

Psychoanalytical Theories

Theodor Reik devotes several pages of his book, *The Haunting Melody*,[28] to the *Kindertotenlieder*. His thesis is substantially the following. After Putzi's death, Mahler told Guido Adler that he could never have written those songs if he had already lost his daughter at the time. By then it seemed to him that the works of the summer of 1904,

[22] The page is probably now part of the Moldenhauer Archive, the complete contents of which have never been disclosed.
[23] The numbers have been partially erased, but are still legible under the title of 'Der Tamboursg'sell'. The title-page also has an autograph of the first 11 bars of 'In diesem Wetter'.
[24] For some unknown reason, Mahler does not seem to have had the piano version of the first *Kindertotenlied* with him in Maiernigg in 1904, which perhaps explains why it is not in the PML with the other Lieder. Could Mahler have made a present of it to one of his friends?
[25] The disappearance of the piano-draft of song 1 has not been explained.
[26] However, the final version is slightly different from the one here marked 'le meilleur', the pianist's right hand making its entry at '(zu)sammen' after the third beat, rather than before the second.
[27] The two songs most probably composed in 1901 (Nos. 3 and 4) have titles at the beginning, whereas the two others (from 1904) have none.
[28] RHM 315.

the *Kindertotenlieder* and the Sixth Symphony, foreshadowed the catastrophes which were to befall him three years later. As with the Finale of the Second and the burial of Bülow,[29] Reik regards the choice of these texts as having been determined by an unconscious memory, a theory confirmed by what Mahler said to Guido Adler: 'I put myself in my thoughts into the situation of a man whose own child has died. When I really lost my daughter, I could not have written these songs any more.'[30] Reik believes that Mahler must have known, since the fact is mentioned in the first edition of the *Kindertotenlieder*, that one of Rückert's dead children had been named Ernst.[31] Before Mahler was born, his own parents lost a first child named Isidor, and later Mahler's younger brother Ernst died at the age of 14. Rückert's poems revived, without his knowing it, the memory of his parents' double bereavement. What Mahler said to Natalie about how sorry he felt 'for himself that he had to write these songs, and for the world which would one day have to listen to them', seems to indicate that he recalled the emotions he had shared with his father at the loss of the two children.[32] Such identifications are often reinforced, Reik adds, by the unconscious jealousy and envy children always feel when witnessing the sorrow of their parents at the death of one of their siblings. In 1904, when he completed the cycle, Mahler was married, and the father of a 2-year-old and a new-born baby. He was thus all the more able to relive his father's mourning in that he unconsciously feared that he might lose his own children. After Putzi's death he imagined that he had foretold the event in music rather than simply thinking: 'I was afraid one of my children might die.' But the real motivating force in the composition of the *Kindertotenlieder* had been memories from the distant past, from the time when he had identified with his father and with the grief caused him by the death of his children.

In attempting to explain Mahler's choice of poems, Suzanne Vill[33] recalls the macabre games Justi had played when she was a child[34] and the morbid visions Mahler himself had had while composing *Das klagende Lied*.[35] The psychoanalyst Stuart Feder also studies the *Kindertotenlieder* in his article 'Mahler Dying',[36] and his argument runs as follows: (1) Mahler's 'pseudo-death' in February 1901 shook him profoundly and awoke in him an unconscious desire to have children as a way of 'staking a claim to immortality'.[37] (2) This was one of the reasons, again unconscious, for his 'whirlwind' courtship of Alma. (3) He gained relief from the obsession with death that pervaded his thoughts, his art, and his life by seeking to overcome it through birth. (4) He symbolized his desire to have children by putting himself, in the *Kindertotenlieder*, in the position of a father mourning his children; death reflects the opposite concept of birth. Edward Kravitt elaborates on the principal points of Stuart Feder's analysis by recall-

---

[29] See above, Vol. i, Chap. 19.

[30] RMH 315. I have not been able to discover Reik's source for this quotation. Did he perhaps discuss this matter with Guido Adler whom he might well have known?

[31] As seen above, none of the poems selected by Mahler for his cycle is dedicated to Ernst alone. Luise's death seems to have affected Rückert more. She is the subject of 3 of the 5 poems used for the cycle, while the remaining 2 mention both children.

[32] NBL1. 166; NBL2. 193.   [33] *Vermittlungsformen*, 110.

[34] See above, Vol. i, Chap. 7.   [35] Ibid., Chap. 6.

[36] *International Review of Psycho-Analysis*, 5 (1978), 125. Stuart Feder's theories are summarized by Edward Kravitt, 'Dirges' (n. 1), 333.

[37] Edward Kravitt emphasizes that Mahler had always been obsessed with the idea of immortality and that, as we shall see below, he was influenced in this respect by Fechner and his 'pan-psychism'.

ing that the haste Mahler showed in his courtship of Alma proves that his desire to marry was very strong,[38] but that his obsession with death was equally strong, especially since his haemorrhage.[39] Kravitt draws attention to an interesting change made by Mahler on the original score of the *Kindertotenlieder*: in the last line of the cycle ('They are resting, they are resting in their mother's house'), he replaced *Haus* (house) by *Schoss* (lap or womb).[40] According to Kravitt, this reveals that the idea of birth and the idea of death were closely bound together deep in Mahler's being and that death for him was, in a sense, a new birth.

Given the circumstances in which Mahler started and later finished this cycle, it is easy to understand why psychoanalysts have asked themselves why Mahler, a confirmed bachelor, should have thought of setting to music these elegies that speak so subjectively of a father's grief; and why in 1904 the happy new husband and father that he had become should have returned to, and completed, the cycle and also composed his 'Tragic' Symphony. Edward Kravitt observes that, if this happy period was 'artistically expressed by its opposite',[41] it was perhaps because Mahler was now aware of how much he had to lose, accustomed as he was through his own childhood to bereavement. In this respect, what happened in 1904 is the exact reverse of events in 1899, when during a period of great torment he completed his happiest work, the Fourth Symphony. Peter Russell's recent book lays much emphasis on the symbolism of light and darkness in all five songs of the cycle, and makes the following comment on the nature of the 'light':

The reader familiar with the Christian tradition is struck by the fact that in all these poems the source of this 'light', and the nature of the afterlife it symbolizes, remain completely undefined. Nothing suggests that Rückert's imagery should necessarily be interpreted in a Christian sense; on the contrary, his avoidance of the obvious opportunities for Christian imagery ('the light that shineth in darkness', 'I am the light of the world', etc.) could be construed as suggesting that he did not wish to be understood in this sense. Equally, though, there is nothing to suggest an interpretation in terms of Eastern religion or philosophy. The generality of Rückert's imagery was doubtless one of the reasons Mahler found these poems attractive; for Mahler at this time, though he had become a Catholic, was dissatisfied with the conventional Christian view of the world and was struggling to arrive at a truth of his own. His evolving vision of human life clearly responds to Rückert's as expressed in the *Kindertotenlieder*.[42]

Russell's view of Mahler's deeper religious feelings coincides so exactly with mine that no further comment by me is necessary.

Outline of the Cycle

The *Kindertotenlieder*, like the *Lieder eines fahrenden Gesellen*, were conceived and composed as a true cycle whose coherence is ensured by the music and in particular the choice of keys. This cycle, unlike the previous one, begins and ends in the same

---

[38] Kravitt is mistaken, though ('Dirges' (n. 1), 334 n. 8), in claiming that Alma was 19 at the time of their marriage. She was actually 22.

[39] Kravitt recalls in this context the nightmare Mahler had in Abbazia two months afterwards, when death presented itself to him in the form of a merry-maker at a feast. He also notes that the marriage took place symbolically on a date close to the anniversary of his haemorrhage (24 Feb. 1901–9 Mar. 1902).

[40] Written 'Schoos' in the MS with piano and 'Schoss' in the autograph orchestral score. Only in the proofs of the piano score of 1905 (IMG) is 'Schoos' crossed out and replaced with 'Haus'.

[41] 'Dirges' (n. 1), 353.   [42] Russell, *Light*, 52.

key, D (minor and major). On the first page of the score, Mahler had the following warning printed: 'These five songs form a complete and indivisible whole, and for this reason their continuity must be preserved (by preventing interruptions, such as for example applause at the end of each song).' In this context, it has been observed that, from the textual point of view, the first Lied establishes a situation that the last one resolves, and that certain comforting symbols, like the rays of light glimpsed in 'Nun will die Sonn', look forward to the final solace at the end.[43] Edward Kravitt also stresses certain thematic relationships, notably between the first and second songs, but I do not find these sufficiently striking to dwell on here.[44] In his view, the essentials of the philosophical, stylistic, and musical content of the cycle are to be found in the first, second, and last songs, whereas the third and the fourth confine themselves more to the sphere of daily life.[45] Here the musical treatment is more lyrical, simple, sustained, whereas in the others it is far more fragmented. The cycle, in its unity of structure and atmosphere, looks forward unmistakably to *Das Lied von der Erde*, and the resemblance goes much further than the reconciliation shared by the two endings. In my opinion, Edward Kravitt rightly finds in the *Kindertotenlieder* the first sign of Mahler's new attitude towards the fundamental problem of existence, a vision of the world as eternally recurring, akin of course to what one finds in Nietzsche, but also in oriental philosophy and the 'pan-psychism' of Fechner, one of Mahler's favourite philosophers.[46] This belief was to find its fullest and most moving expression in *Das Lied von der Erde*. It is no coincidence that the poems for this work come from the Orient, whose influence is felt as much in Fechner's philosophy as in Rückert's poetry.

Orchestration

The five *Kindertotenlieder* are perhaps not so differentiated in their instrumentation as the *Rückert-Lieder*. However, most of the time Mahler uses only part of an orchestra made up of the following instruments: 3 flutes (with piccolo), 2 oboes and cor anglais, 2 clarinets and bass clarinet, 4 horns, harp, glockenspiel,[47]

---

[43] Dargie, *Music*, 330.

[44] Kravitt, 'Dirges' (n. 1), 345. Some commentators claim that, because of the absence of the narrative technique characterizing the *Gesellenlieder*, 'the cycle does not have the unity of the earlier cycle or of the later *Das Lied*, and that its unity derives from the common mood and topic of the five songs.' (DMM3. 75). The presence of the rising motif, called by James Zychowicz 'Ewigkeit Motive', has been noted in the second (bars 29–30) and the last of the *Kindertotenlieder* (bars 115–16; see 'Quotation and Assimilation: The Ewigkeit Motive in the Music of Mahler').

[45] Kravitt notes in this context the title 'Eigener Herd' (Hearth and Home) given to one section of the Rückert collection *Liebesfrühling*. Susanne Vill (*Vermittlungsformen*, 109) nevertheless considers that Mahler's musical treatment 'objectivises' the subjects of these Lieder and gives them universal validity.

[46] In 1903 Mahler read *Zend-Avesta, oder über die Dinge des Himmels und des Jenseits* (1851), and in 1905 *Vorschule der Aesthetik* (1876) (see AMM1. 288 and 345; AMM2. 262 and 304). Mahler wrote to Alma in 1903: 'Strange how Fechner feels and sees things in a Rückertish way. These are two very similar people and one aspect of myself makes a third to go with them. How few people know anything about either of these two!' (See above, Chap. 14.)

[47] Mitchell (DMM3. 135) points out that the bell strokes are mentioned in the sketch of song 1 as 'Glöcklein'. However, Mahler's later inclusion of the glockenspiel in the list of instruments for the whole cycle leaves no doubt as to the nature of the timbre he intended. The Eulenburg pocket score nevertheless lists 'Campanelli' in the Italian orchestral inventory. The Philharmonia miniature score, following the Kahnt original (and Mahler's MS), has Glöcklein instead of glockenspiel, an obvious lapse committed by Mahler, who couldn't possibly 'have imported a fresh instrumental colour . . . for these six bars'. The critical 1979 edn. absurdly lists both Glöcklein and Glockenspiel. Mitchell observes that the glockenspiel is related to childhood, as sleigh-bells are to fairy bells (DMM3. 378).

celesta,[48] timpani, tamtam, and strings. Donald Mitchell notes that the main orchestral impact in Song 1 is on austere wind sonorities in the odd stanzas, and strings and harp in the even, 'consolatory' stanzas; that that of Song 2 is mainly on strings and harp; Song 3 is coloured mainly by the cor anglais and the string section, of which Mahler retains only violas and basses. Song 5 is of course the only one which employs the full forces of the orchestra. Thus, says Mitchell, 'there is a conscious and fresh exploration of the orchestra in each song'. The orchestration is strikingly sparse, the instruments mainly being treated as soloists, as in the *Rückert-Lieder*. The third and fourth horns, the piccolo, the contrabassoon, the celesta, the timpani, and the tamtam appear only in the last Lied. Mitchell thus suggests that 'the 20th century chamber orchestra' might be considered to have been initiated by the *Kindertotenlieder*.[49]

Structure and Word-setting

While Peter Russell draws attention to Mahler's word-setting, his 'detailed awareness of his text', and the way his 'musical construction' 'duplicates the formal structure of the poem', Elisabeth Schmierer lays emphasis on his 'musical strophes' which include not only the vocal part, but also the instrumental preludes, interludes, and postludes. To her mind, there is in this cycle 'a radicalised tendency of the Lied towards instrumental music'. 'Thus, in spite of the briefness of the form, the essentials at least of the infrastructure for a symphonic strophe are provided'.[50] A strong case can and has been made to support either point of view, which proves once again the multi-faceted nature of Mahler's compositions.

Voice

In his lifetime, Mahler always chose a baritone (Friedrich Weidemann in Vienna and Graz; Gerhard Zalsman in Amsterdam replacing Weidemann, who was ill; Johannes Messchaert in Berlin with piano). Only in New York, on 26 January 1910, did he engage the German tenor Ludwig Wüllner. But Wüllner was a former actor, more famous as an interpreter than as a singer, and Mahler was probably thinking more of his artistic personality than of his tessitura. He never engaged a woman to sing this cycle. However, several women did sing it in his lifetime, notably the Dutch contralto Tilly Koehnen and the soprano Anna von Mildenburg.

Analyses

The lengthiest and most searching treatments are by Peter Russell[51] and Donald Mitchell.[52] Further detailed analyses are to be found in Elisabeth Mary Dargie,[53] Susanne Vill,[54] and Edward Kravitt.[55] Individual analyses of a particular song will be mentioned in the section devoted to that song.

(a) 'Nun will die Sonn' so hell aufgehn' (Now will the sun so brightly rise)

Manuscript: See above.

---

[48] Strange as it may seem, the celesta, which plays almost continuously in the major coda of the last Lied, is missing from the list of instruments at the front of the Philharmonia miniature score.

[49] DMM3. 96.   [50] Schmierer, *Orchesterlieder*, 216 ff.

[51] Russell, *Light*, 64 ff.   [52] In DMM3. 75 ff.   [53] *Music*, 299 ff.

[54] *Vermittlungsformen*, 108 ff.   [55] 'Dirges' (n. 1). 329 ff.

Key: D minor (and major) with only fleeting modulations.

Time signature: 4/4.

Tempo: *Langsam und schwermütig. Nicht schleppend* (slow and melancholic, do not drag); *heftiger* (more violent: bar 37) before the third verse, and *etwas bewegter* (with more movement: bar 59), *Mit leidenschaftlichem Ausdruck* (with passionate emphasis) before the final interlude. *Tempo primo* for the fourth (bar 73).

Text: The poem belongs to the fourth section ('Trost und Erhebung') of the 1872 edition and is numbered 115 (p. 369). The theme, the poet's grief set against the permanence of nature, is virtually the same as in the first of the *Lieder eines fahrenden Gesellen*. Mahler made only the following changes: OR: *Sonne*, M: *Sonn'*; OR: *auch mir allein*, M: *nur mir allein*; OR: *Du musst die Nacht nicht*, M: *Du musst nicht die Nacht*; OR: *Lämpchen*, M: *Lämplein*; OR: *Freudenlichte*, M: *Freudenlicht*. Mahler repeats, in the first stanza, the words *kein Unglück*; in the second, *die Sonne*; in the third, *ins ew'ge Licht* (OR: *ins ewige Licht*) and in the last, *Heil* and *dem Freudenlicht der Welt*.

Peter Russell finds this poem 'an inspired choice' to open the cycle 'because it so strikingly moves from the immediacy of loss and lament to emotional resolve and finally optimism, and in affirming 'the eternal light' juxtaposes personal loss and universal salvation in a way no other poem does'.[56]

Orchestration: Donald Mitchell has made interesting remarks on the subtle scoring of this first song.[57]

Analysis: This Lied has been analysed in detail by Elisabeth Mary Dargie (*Music*, 302); Susanne Vill (*Vermittlungsformen*, 11), Edward Kravitt ('Dirges', 342), and more recently by Elisabeth Schmierer.[58]

Form: The poem has four verses of two lines each. From the musical point of view, strophes 1, 2, and 4 are closely related; the third is faster, though it uses the same material.[59] The structure can be summed up in the scheme AABA, a *Reprisenbarform* in Zoltan Roman's classification.[60] After a four-bar introduction, the first two verses are separated by a nine-bar interlude. That preceding the third verse (which provides a contrasting middle section and a true development section)[61] is longer (eleven bars). After four bars in the main tempo, the interlude picks up speed. Throughout the next stanza and the next interlude, the pace continues to accelerate, and the original tempo returns only midway through the last verse. The chromatic last interlude is eight bars long while the last stanza is preceded, interspersed, and followed by a two-bar interlude and a postlude in which the orchestra takes up part of the earlier vocal part, and vice versa. Elisabeth Schmierer studies the means by which Mahler continuously increases the tension in each strophe, until the orchestral climax which follows the third.[62]

The despair in the poem is reflected in the sparse counterpoint, the mournful canons, the austere instrumental imitations, the insistently repeated intervals, the

[56] Russell, *Light*, 69.　　　[57] DMM3. 94 ff.　　　[58] See *Orchesterlieder*, 210 ff.

[59] Zoltan Roman (see 'Mahler's Songs and their Influence on his Symphonic Thought', Ph.D. thesis, Univ. of Toronto, 1970, 323 and 400) draws attention to a striking harmonic detail at the beginning of this verse: the passage in two-part counterpoint (solo voice and oboe) over a double pedal of thirds (flutes), interrupted by one bar's rest, on a note which is neither the tonic nor the dominant but the supertonic. This pedal suspension intensifies the effect of the resolution on to the tonic at bar 52.

[60] Ibid.　　　[61] DMM3. 105 ff.　　　[62] Schmierer, *Orchesterlieder*, 218.

sighs over a minor and major second, and then, further on, in the chromatic rise of
the melody, a procedure Mahler rarely uses in this form. The cadence figure in
stanzas 1, 2, and 4 has aroused much attention, not only because it is quoted twice,
note for note, in the initial Funeral March of the Fifth Symphony, but because the
words to which it is set emphasize the essential symbolism of the whole cycle:
'Nacht' (Night: bars 12–15); 'scheinet allgemein' (shines for all alike: 33–6):
'Freudenlicht der Welt' (gladdening light of the world: 74–7).[63] Zoltan Roman
and Peter Russell underline the way Mahler makes 'ins ew'ge Licht versenken' (sink
into the eternal light) the expressive (if not dynamic) climax of the Lied, with an
extended melisma on 'ew'ge', the longest of the piece, and the highest note
(E flat) in the whole voice part.[64] The F on *Licht* then rises to F sharp, and this
fleeting major mode 'brightens the harmonic palette' before the phrase falls again
with the word 'versenken' (sink) and relapses once more into the minor mode in
which the orchestra pursues the despairing mood with the last interlude. Its first five
bars (59–64) are the real emotional and dynamic climax, with the only forte in the
whole song. The passionate violin figure grows sinuous and chromatic, *mit grossem
Ausdruck* (with much expression).[65] It is interrupted by the 'death knell' of the
glockenspiel.

Everything else in this Lied is acutely felt but contained grief, with a deliberately
monochromatic sound, and the voice always in the middle register, as if the afflicted
father lacked the strength to raise his voice. Several details of the orchestration are
particularly striking: the melodic use of horn, the general predominance of the
winds—except in the second halves of the stanzas and in the last interlude—then
the horn octaves, like a knell, before the third verse; and finally the doubling of the
voice by the cellos, pianissimo in their highest register, on *als sei kein Unglück* (bar
11 ff.)[66] The glockenspiel[67] notes are heard in the three interludes and the postlude,

[63] Russell, *Light*, 70, and DMM3. 103. However, Susanne Vill (*Vermittlungsformen*, 111) points out the
contrast that Mahler creates within each stanza (with the second line of the text) using various means: major
instead of minor mode; chromaticism instead of diatonicism; muted strings and harp instead of winds,
playing *klangvoll* (sonorously) instead of *klagend* (plaintively); the melody rising instead of falling; a
periodicity of 5 bars instead of 4; the lengthening of the cadence; a postlude amplifying the theme where it
was previously shortened. Mitchell observes that 'in the poem, which starts from a low pitch of grief', the
'light' gradually increases in intensity . . . and indeed at *"ew'ge Licht"* begins to reach its highest pitch'
(DMM3. 93).

[64] Russell draws attention to the rising harp arpeggios that precede the word 'Licht' (bar 57). He quotes
several other instances of harp figures (e.g. 'Um Mitternacht': bar 77 ff.; Symphony 2: bar 680 ff.; *Lied von
der Erde*: bars 460 ff. and 486 ff., which consistently signal the coming of light (*Light*, 72).

[65] Elisabeth Schmierer observes that Mahler creates this climactic effect without ever filling in the inner
voices of the orchestra which has only two separate parts supported only by a pedal tone. The violin figure
increases in intensity until the climax proper (bar 63), while the harmonies in the accompaniment (low
strings, harp, and woodwinds) are foreign (*verfremdet*) to those suggested by the melody. Schmierer draws
attention to the great number of motifs and figures in this song which are derived from the baroque
vocabulary (see *Orchesterlieder*, 224).

[66] The same effect is used in the third song (bar 22 ff.).

[67] Edward Kravitt compares the thrice three Ds on the glockenspiel (in bars 44 ff., 64 ff., and 83 ff.) with
the three hammer blows in the Finale of the Sixth. For him they symbolize the eternal light that shines at the
end of the poem. Mitchell also comments on the bell strokes, whose 'placing . . . throughout the song is
characteristically irregular but also calculated with equally characteristic precision. . . . Each sequence is
related not so much to symmetry as to poetic context or dramatic need' (DMM3. 132 n. 25). Mitchell assigns
to these glockenspiel notes a cyclic function, their gloomy sound in the first Lied being metamorphosed into
consolation in the final one.

where it plays the Lied's last note. The instrument then remains silent until the coda of the last song. Some commentators have called these tinkling sounds a death knell, while others consider them as heralding the eternal light which will shine at the end of the cycle. The eloquent simplicity of the coda, a reprise of the first interlude, on which the voice sings a slightly modified form of the previous horn solo, must also be mentioned. Russell draws attention to Mahler's 'avoidance, at the end, of a fully articulated V-I cadence'.

(*b*) '**Nun seh' Ich wohl, warum so dunkle Flammen**' (Now I can see why such dark flames).

Manuscript: As seen above, this Lied was probably composed in 1904.

Key: OR (with piano): C sharp minor (but with only five sharps written on the stave, which shows that Mahler hesitated at first about the tonality of this piece); OR (orchestra) and final version: C minor. The key signature subsequently changes several times, suggesting modulations to C and D major; however, since all the cadences are imperfect or interrupted, or weakened by suspensions, the key remains ill-defined and unstable right to the end. Once again, the final cadence itself is more of a suspension than a conclusion. Zoltan Roman[68] remarks on the complete absence, in this Lied, of one of Mahler's most frequent and most striking stylistic features, pedal points, an absence which helps to account for the virtually permanent tonal ambiguity. Here is the key sequence as Roman sees it: C minor, C major, D major, G minor, B flat major, C major, C minor. The same writer observes that the two C major passages illustrate the 'rays' and 'stars' in the text, and that the one in D major goes with the word 'light', each time with a perfect triad—as opposed to the preceding seventh chords—but of a precarious character suggested by the six-four inversion. Roman also shows that the modulation to G minor (on 'Doch ist uns') illustrates in a similar way the meaning of the words. As a third example of musical symbolism, he gives the episode *Weil Nebel mich umschwammen, gewoben vom verblendenden Geschicke* (because mists shrouded me, woven by blinding destiny), where Mahler uses augmented chords to give the impression of modulating to F sharp minor, only to return immediately to C major.

Time signature: 4/4, with two bars of 3/2 and one of 2/4.

Tempo: OR (piano); *Andante* (crossed out). *Nicht schleppend. Innig aber zart. Durchaus ohne ritenuto* (do not drag, intense but tender, no ritenuto throughout). OR (orch.) and final version: *Ruhig, nicht schleppend* (peaceful, not dragging). *Etwas bewegter* (a little faster: bar 29); then *Tempo1* (bar 41).

Text: Rückert's sonnet belongs to the second section of the 1872 edition, 'Krankheit und Tod' (no. 70, p. 76). Mahler adds 'voll' after 'gleichsam um' in the first quatrain, and repeats 'O Augen!' and, in the last line of the second quatrain, 'Dorthin'. In the second line of the first tercet, he drops 'immer' from between 'dir' and 'gerne'. The most important changes are in the second tercet: OR: *Sieh' recht uns an!*, M: *Sieh' uns nur*[69] *an* and OR *dir noch Augen*, M: *dir nur Augen*.

[68] Roman, 'Songs', 404.

[69] Mahler having changed *noch* to *nur* and having added a *nur* after *uns*, the word *nur* is repeated three times in the last tercet, which tends to suggest simply errors in reading.

Analysis: Robert Schollum has written an interesting commentary on this song and V. Kofi Agawu has analysed it in a very perceptive article.[70]

Form: As Reinhard Gerlach observes,[71] Mahler lengthens the tercets to conform with the quatrains by bringing back, at the end of the first and after the first line of the second, melodic phrases taken from the voice part in the quatrains, but now given to instruments. The form more or less corresponds to the scheme ABCB, the final tercet being closely related to the second quatrain[72] whereas the first tercet uses almost entirely new material. Gerlach analyses the tonal suspensions in the introduction, suggesting an ellipsis of the dominant chord on D between the third and fourth bars. The instability of this opening shows the influence, extremely rare in Mahler,[73] of a Tristan-style *Sehnsucht*. But the rising melody[74] is related to those in 'Ich bin der Welt' and the Adagietto of the Fifth, two pieces quite unlike this one, because of their diatonic language. Mahler rarely diverged so far from his usual style. Gerlach emphasizes the role of the pauses in this Lied, describing them as 'allusive' (*die Andeutung gibt*), 'prophetic' (*ahnenden*), in music that is 'symbolic, metaphorical'. 'On the one hand', Gerlach continues, 'he writes music with sounds, on the other with pauses. In both instances he creates space through economy; and Rückert's writing also stemmed from the economical disposition of certain grammatical features. The stylistic procedure of ellipsis, so incomparably mastered by Webern, was bequeathed by Mahler to the new Viennese School.'[75]

Peter Russell observes that, in this song as indeed in the whole cycle, the musical divisions match those of the poem's stanzas. He also notes that the opening ascending fragment echoes the last vocal phrase of the preceding song ('-licht der Welt!'). He says that this fragment, the leitmotif of the Lied, is to be closely associated with eyes and seeing, the form assumed in this song by the main imagery of the cycle, light and dark. The more optimistic beginning of the first tercet gives rise to an ecstatic (Tristanesque!) D major passage (*mit eurem Leuchten sagen*: bar 41 ff.).[76] However, its fleeting, temporary nature is emphasized by the bass note, A instead of D, the dominant instead of the tonic. Yet the passage does at least bring contrast and relief from the dissonant appoggiaturas and tonal instability of the rest of the song.

Elsewhere, as seen above, none of the appoggiaturas is ever satisfactorily resolved. The *Sehnsucht*, the unsatisfied yearning in which the whole Lied is steeped, comes from the unstable and questing mood sustained by the harmonic ambiguity of

[70] See Robert Schollum, *Das Österreichische Lied des 20. Jahrhunderts* (Schneider, Tutzing, 1977), 35–6, and V. Kofi Agawu, 'The Musical Language of the Kindertotenlieder No. 2', *Journal of Musicology* (St Joseph, Mich., 1983), 83 ff.

[71] 'Mahler, Rückert', 33. See also the same writer's subsequent work, *Strophen von Leben, Traum und Tod: Ein Essay über Rückert-Lieder von Gustav Mahler* (Heinrichshofen, Wilhelmshaven, 1982). E. Mary Dargie (*Music*, 306) has made the most detailed analysis of this Lied.

[72] However, Dargie regards this Lied as *durchkomponiert*.

[73] Zoltan Roman finds 'Nun seh' ich wohl' 'overtly tristanesque'.

[74] Edward Kravitt observes that this melody appears each time on the word *Augen* or on one of its symbols, *Strahl* (ray) or *Leuchten* (beam), and that Mahler sketched 9 different versions of the phrase 'zu drängen eure ganze Macht' in the piano MS. (Donald Mitchell traces this phrase to the duo 'In questa tomba' from the last act of *Aida*, where the heroine uses the words 'e qui lontana da ogni umano sguardo').

[75] Gerlach, *Strophen*, 35.

[76] Russell here draws attention to the two-bar kettledrum roll which increases the tension (bar 39 ff.), 'an inspired device', and 'the light, high orchestral effects' (flutes, violins, clarinet, high bassoon) which 'bring a sudden great warm effulgence of light', a 'glimpse of heaven'.

retardations and chains of suspended dominants. A great deal of the melodic substance is furnished by the one motif, thanks to augmentations, diminutions, and variants. The last two lines 'summarize the poem's fundamental symbolic polarities' with the images *Augen, Tagen, Nächten, Sterne.*[77] Edward Kravitt and Jens Malte Fischer believe that Rückert's image of the child's eyes becoming stars in heaven was in complete accordance with Mahler's belief in pan-psychism, i.e. Fechner's theory that the whole cosmos has consciousness and that, after our death, we remain immortally present in it, in a higher spiritual form. Although the postlude recalls the introduction and gives the impression that the key of C minor is about to be reaffirmed at last, Mahler finishes the piece with as inconclusive a cadence as possible: a dominant-seventh chord on D flat (key of the 'Neapolitan sixth' chord) resolving on a tonic C minor chord without the leading note or the dominant being played. Thus the atmosphere of questing unease is maintained right to the end.[78]

(c) **'Wenn dein Mütterlein'** (When thy Mother dear).

Manuscript: In my opinion, substantiated by Christopher Lewis's study (see above), this is the second song written in 1901. It was originally prefaced by the number (2). Edward Reilly lists a sketch of this Lied among manuscripts belonging to Natalie Bauer-Lechner which have now disappeared.
Key: OR and orchestral draft: C minor (with an apparent modulation to G minor).
Time Signature: 4/4, alternating with 3/2.
Tempo: OR and definitive version: *Schwer, dumpf* (heavy, muffled); at the voice entry: *fliessender* (bar 8: more flowing); *Etwas fliessender* (somewhat more flowing) (bar 19); *Wie zu Anfang* (as at the beginning) (bar 33); *Etwas fliessender* (somewhat more flowing) (bar 40); *Etwas bewegter* (somewhat livelier) (bar 50); *Wieder wie zu Anfang* (again as at the beginning) (bar 64).
Text: In the original edition, two poems share the number 56 (p. 59) in the second section ('Krankheit und Tod'). The first begins 'Wenn zur Thür herein Tritt dein Mütterlein' and the second, like Mahler's Lied, 'Wenn dein Mütterlein Tritt zur Thür herein'. The first has two verses of fourteen lines (5 and 6 feet) and the second, a verse of thirteen lines and one of three. Mahler, by a process of collage, makes of these two a new poem of two verses, one of fourteen and one of eleven lines. He starts with the first thirteen lines of the second poem (which become fourteen by repetition of the penultimate line), omits its three last lines, then repeats the first two lines of the second poem and links them to lines 3 to 7 of the first poem. The conclusion is the last three previously missing lines of the second poem (made four by repeating the final one). On the other hand, the whole second stanza of the first poem (7 lines) is dropped. That completes the list of changes made by Mahler except for a few repetitions ('näher' and 'dort' in the first verse, 'O du' in the second and, as we have seen, two full lines of the poem) and some differences of punctuation. Both Dargie

[77] Russell, *Light*, 81. Russell underlines the harp arpeggios which, as in the preceding song, accompany the passage, and the crescendo with pianissimo subito which leads to the crucial word *Sterne* (bar 66).
[78] See also Christopher Lewis, 'Poetic and Musical Symbolism in Mahler's "Nun seh' ich wohl"', unpubl. article made available to the author.

and Russell feel that the omission of the first stanza was fortunate and that Mahler's version is an improvement on the original.[79]

Orchestration: The most striking feature is the absence of violins and the resulting dark colouring of the song. Russell points out the contrast between the two halves of each stanza, the first played in counterpoint by winds with pizzicato basses and the second by horns and lower strings, 'bringing more warmth to more plastic musical phrases'.[80]

Form: This is exceptionally symmetrical, and can be summed up as ABAB.[81] The seven-bar prelude, in counterpoint (bassoon and cor anglais on pizzicato basses), anticipates the opening bars of the song itself.[82] Each of the two verses has a second section more agitated than the first (and also homophonic as opposed to contrapuntal),[83] with the vocal part rising to a culminating point (on F) and slowly falling, in a long melisma that constitutes the expressive climax of the whole Lied, down to a low G whence it rises again to the tonic. By various and subtle means, Mahler virtually eliminates the difference in length between the two verses. The parallel passage to 'sondern auf die Stelle' from the first part is given to the orchestra in somewhat varied form in the second, in which there are quite a number of other changes: contrapuntal inversion of voice with accompaniment, changes of rhythm, elisions,[84] etc.

Ernst Klusen has drawn attention to a striking similarity between the opening phrase in the voice and a Moravian popular song (see Exx. 23 and 24).[85] The opening phrase for the voice, which starts on the lowest note of the baritone voice, 'schwermütig' (melancholic) takes up, in crotchets, the quaver motif played by the cor anglais (bars 1 and 2). The singer seems to lack impetus or energy. The pizzicato accompaniment in the basses (not unlike that of the beginning of the Adagio of the Fourth Symphony) suggests both the heaviness of the father's heart and the mother's

Ex. 23. Kindertotenlieder, No. 3

Wenn dein Mütt-er-lein   und den Kopf ich dre - he   fällt auf ihr Ge-sicht
tritt zur Tür her-ein   ihr ent-ge-gen se - he   erst der Blick mir nicht

[79] See Russell, *Light*, 84, and Dargie, *Music*, 313 ff. However, the two writers disagree in that Dargie questions Mahler's right to interfere with Rückert's poem, an odd statement to make for an author who never ceases to disparage Rückert's poetry.

[80] Russell, *Light*, 85.

[81] Zoltan Roman does not acknowledge the division of each part of the Lied, which seems to me quite clear, and sums up the form in the scheme AA'.

[82] Once again, Russell hears in the opening bars (C–D . . . E♭) an echo of the closing phrase of the preceding song (*Light*, 86). The pizzicato basses are, he thinks, 'a musical depiction of the mother's footsteps'.

[83] DMM3. 99.

[84] In the recapitulation, Dargie draws attention to the elision of bar 16, which passes almost unnoticed even though this bar then seemed indispensable to the musical continuity of the first part. Dargie notes that, in bar 50, the voice takes up the orchestral melody from bars 19–20.

[85] See 'Gustav Mahler und das Volkslied seiner Heimat', *Journal of the International Folk Music Council*, 15 (1963), 29. The song is numbered 25*b* in the František Bartoš collection *Narodní písně moravské* (Prague, 1899).

Ex. 24. Bartoš: No. 25b

U čach - či - ne   na do - li - ně
le - ží   Jan - ko vroz-ma - rý - ně le- ží le - ží

za - bi - tý   roz-ma-rý-nem při - kry - tý.

footsteps.[86] The bare counterpoint once again gives an impression of unbearable sadness, reinforced here by the gloomy sonority of the low wind instruments (the cellos and violas only play *arco*—with the bow—in the second half of each verse). Dargie compares this two-part counterpoint with eighteenth-century German figured chorales, where the melody is decorated by the instruments beforehand. The effect of contrast in the second part of the following section (bar 19 ff.: 'sondern auf die Stelle') is achieved by interrupting the quaver ostinato and introducing a more expansive melody with a recurrence of the appoggiaturas that characterized the preceding song. The melody is taken up by two horns with the bassoons as bass. The faster tempo and the long, climactic vocal melisma (reinforced by the high cellos) also contribute to the change of atmosphere. The short coda starts by repeating the introduction, gradually lengthening the note values in a 'rubato obligato'. The final passage remains suspended on a dominant chord, as if the father's grief had deprived him of the strength for even a final sigh.

(*d*) **'Oft denk' Ich, sie sind nur ausgegangen'** (Often I think they have just gone out for a walk).

Key: OR and final version: E flat (the first phrase of each verse is in the minor), with modulations to G flat at the middle of each verse[87] and with frequent tonic and dominant pedals.

Time signature: 2/2 (*alla breve*), with 6 bars of 3/2.

Tempo: OR (piano): *Ruhig* (calm); OR (orch. draft: *Ruhig bewegt, ohne zu eilen* (quietly moving on, without hurrying); *Nicht eilen* (do not hurry) (bar 46). The marking *mit Empfindung* (with feeling) that headed the accompaniment in the piano original has disappeared in the orchestra score, like the word *zart* (tender) above the vocal part in 'Der Tag ist schön'.

Text: From the last part of the original edition ('Trost und Erhebung'), No. 47, p. 311. The poem has three four-line strophes. Mahler changes small details only. 1st verse (2nd line): OR: *nach Haus*, M: *nach Hause*; 4th line: OR: *weitern Gang*, M: *weiten Gang*; 2nd verse (2nd line): OR: *nach Hause gelangen*, M: *nach Hause verlangen*; 4th line: OR: *Sie machen den Gang*, M: *Sie machen nur den Gang*; 4th verse (2nd line): OR: *werden nicht hier nach Haus*, M: *werden nicht wieder nach Haus*; 4th line: OR:

---

[86] Russell, *Light*, 87.

[87] Zoltan Roman notes that, in the first two verses, the modulations to G♭ accompany a burst of optimism, which, in the final verse, adds a new meaning to the text ('and they will never come home').

Im Sonnenschein, der Tag ist schön, M: *Im Sonnenschein! Der Tag ist schön auf jenen Höh'n!* Mahler alters the punctuation by adding ten exclamation marks.

Form: Zoltan Roman and Susanne Vill speak of a *Strophenbarform*[88] (ABABAB), in which the *Stollen* (A) retain the same length whereas the consolatory *Abgesang* (B) grows more protracted (as seen above). 'From the first moment', Russell writes, 'we realize we are in a different world from that of the first three songs': the pulse is quicker, 'the orchestral texture richer'. Yet, from the first moment too, 'we are aware of the ambivalence, the tensions which will permeate the song'.[89] Russell finds confirmation of the song's unstable mood in the syncopated rhythms of the basses, the irregular phrase lengths, the varying time signatures, and especially the 'unpredictable harmonic changes'. One of these is of course the entrance of the voice in the sixth bar with a minor inflexion (it soon returns to the major). Russell draws attention to the harp arpeggio heralding, as before, a passage 'suffused with light', in which the restless motion of the instrumental parts comes to a stop and the orchestral texture is lightened. Thus, he isolates the third line of each stanza 'as a moment of vision from the thematic and rhythmic material which pervades the rest of the song'.[90] The arrival of light in the second stanza ('O sei nicht bang') is even more striking, with two harp arpeggios instead of one, a sforzando in the oboes and clarinet, a pianissimo subito of melting effect, and the oboe playing an inverted replica of the vocal line, which is extended by one bar. In the third stanza, the 'light' episode takes on a new, completely triumphant, character, with an ecstatic extension of the vocal phrase 'reaching the highest pitch of visionary intensity' ('Der Tag ist schön': bars 66–9).[91] The flute and strings, in a very high register, evoke 'the radiance of the sunny heights'. However, as H. H. Eggebrecht points out, when the emotion reaches its climax, 'the liberating thought in Mahler's setting reveals its lack of foundation. It collapses, and the song returns to its beginnings'.[92]

Despite the gradual increase in length of the *Abgesang*, this is one of Mahler's simplest forms, with the A elements in minor (after a major introduction)[93] and the

[88] According to Zoltan Roman this is actually the only Lied Mahler wrote in this form. Because the first two phrases of each stanza begin in the same way, he describes the form in the following scheme: AA'B, AA'B, AA'B, but it should be noted that the end of the first verse, 'machen nur einen', is a variant of the second line, 'Bald werden sie wieder'.

[89] Russell, *Light*, 92. H. H. Eggebrecht's claim that he can perceive the song's 'four fundamental emotions' within the three bars of the instrumental prelude appears a little far-fetched, although the four moods are indeed present in the song (*Die Musik Gustav Mahlers* (Piper, Munich, 1982), 235 ff., quoted in Russell, *Light*). The moods are *ruhige Bewegtheit* or *Bewegte Ruhe* (emotion-filled calm); *Leiden* (suffering); *bohrendes Wollen* (gnawing insistence); *schmerzliche Vergeblichkeit* (painful frustration).

[90] Russell (*Light*, 100) again finds a musical connection between the first bars of this song and the last one of the preceding one, but it is much less apparent than in the other songs.

[91] DMM3. 100. This is the phrase (bars 64–7) to which Monika Tibbe had drawn attention because it is quoted at the end of the Finale of the Ninth Symphony. Tibbe ascribes an extra-musical significance to this quotation. The passage in the Lied, an extension of bars 20–1 and 41–3, is about the children's 'walk' and about *jenen Höh'n*, the sunny heights which symbolize paradise. Thus, the last visionary section of the symphonic Adagio is 'in a sense a paraphrase of the ending of the Lied' (see Tibbe, *Verwendung*, 121). Tibbe also detects a quotation of bars 65 and 66 ('schein! Der Tag ist') in the second part of the Eighth Symphony (bars 573–4). Bar 576 of the same symphony also reproduces the descending scale from bar 68 of the song, and the flute and violin parts in the song's bars 67–8 are present in the same movement of the Eighth (bars 698–9).

[92] Eggebrecht, *Gustav Mahler*, 246.

[93] In Mitchell's words, the minor inflexion 'is just sufficient to remind us that there is still a residue of conflict and pain to be dispersed' (DMM3. 100).

B elements in major.[94] The stanzas are tightly connected by interludes that sometimes even begin before the vocal phrase has ended (notably at 'nach Hause
gelangen'). In the piano version Mahler twice specifically indicates (bar 21 and bar
43) that the accompaniment is to conclude the vocal line. The concision of this piece
is particularly arresting, with its instrumental prelude of just five bars, the short
interludes separating the verses (two bars), and the scarcely longer ones within
verses (four bars between the two sections of the second and third verses).

The Lied is the first one in the cycle in which the 'consolatory' element gains the
upper hand, but, as Russell observes, it is a song 'of aspiration, not of fulfilment'.
The acceptance at the end of 'In diesem Wetter' is anticipated here in the last verse,
where the poet announces that he will find his children on those radiant 'heights'
which in fact are heaven. The whole of the orchestral accompaniment creates a
contrast with what has gone before, by means of the richness of the sound, due in
particular to the parallel sixths in the principal motif.[95] At the end of each verse a
rhythmic unease takes over with the instrumental introduction motif. In the second,
the parallel sixths are given to two clarinets (with bassoons as the bass) instead of
two horns. In the third, the parallel sixths are replaced by a new 'restless' dactylic
motif high in the clarinets. Mahler thus creates the effect of a progression right to the
voice's final cadence (perfect, this time). This is followed by an instrumental coda,
a last evocation of the parallel sixths which end the Lied with a final question by
merely coming to rest on the tonic, without any previous cadence.

(*e*) **'In diesem Wetter, in diesem Braus'** (In this weather, in this storm).

Composition: This final Lied was certainly composed during the summer of 1904 (see
above).

Manuscript: See above. A piano version of the first eleven bars was written on the
double page, written in 1904, which served as cover for the 1901–4 Lieder (former
Alma Mahler collection, now probably in the Moldenhauer archive).

Key: D minor, virtually without modulations, but with references to B flat and A major.
The last stanza, in D major, constitutes a separate song in itself, although thematically linked with the rest.

Time signature: 4/4.

Tempo: OR (piano): *Stürmisch* (stormy). *Mit ruhelos schmerzvollem Ausdruck* (with
unremittingly painful expressiveness). *Im Anfang nicht zu schnell* (not too fast to
begin with). The final version drops the first and last of these markings, keeping only
the second. Doubtless through an oversight, Mahler wrote no indication at the head
of the autograph orchestral score. In the last verse, *Allmählich langsamer* (gradually
slowing) (bar 94) and then *Wie ein Wiegenlied* (like a cradle song) (bar 101). The
definitive version keeps these two indications but adds *Langsam* before *Wie ein
Wiegenlied*.

Text: In 'Trost und Erhebung', the final section of the 1872 edition, this poem is
numbered 83 (p. 341). It has four verses of four lines each. Mahler hardly changed

---

[94] Roman notes that the three *Stollen* (A sections) finish on a B♭, while the first *Abgesang* finishes on a
(dissonant) E♭, the second on an F♮ and only the third on a B♭.

[95] Monika Tibbe observes a striking similarity between two passages in parallel sixths (bars 19–21) and
three bars in the second *Nachtmusik* of the Seventh Symphony (bars 32–4), composed of course during the
same summer (see *Verwendung*, 121).

the first three. In the third line: OR: *man hat sie hinaus getragen*; M: *man hat sie getragen, getragen hinaus!* 4th line: OR: *dazu nichts*; M: *nichts dazu*. Mahler repeats 'nie hätt' ich gelassen die Kinder hinaus' in the second line of the second verse but otherwise makes no changes in this stanza or the next.

However, he repeats the whole of the first strophe after the third (but with *Graus* instead of *Braus*), and extends the final stanza as follows:

ORIGINAL	MAHLER
In diesem Wetter, in diesem Braus,	In diesem Wetter, in diesem Saus, in diesem Braus,
Sie ruhn als wie in der Mutter Haus,	Sie ruh'n, sie ruh'n, als wie in der Mutter,
	der Mutter Haus,
Von keinem Sturme erschrecket,	Von keinem Sturm erschrecket,
Von Gottes Hand bedecket.	Von Gottes Hand bedecket,
	Sie ruh'n, sie ruh'n wie in der Mutter Haus,
	wie in der Mutter Haus!

   Peter Russell notes that 'Rückert's poem is not in itself tempestuous, but reflective' and that 'Mahler transforms it to his own ends'.[96] He felt a need for a climax and a release, and 'invested Rückert's poem with . . . much more force and character than the poem itself implies', giving the storm 'a role of central and psychological importance'.[97]

Orchestration: The effect of anguish and feverish agitation is reinforced by the smothered sound of the strings, which play with mutes throughout.[98]

Form: Freely strophic, according to Zoltan Roman. The first four verses are different from one another, but start in a similar manner and use the same basic material (a descending scale motif adorned with trills,[99] on lower woodwinds and lower strings,[100] and the same intervals of fourths and fifths) but the rest varies. In the first stanza, the initial D is obsessively repeated through three bars. In the second the voice rises by a second, soon to leap a minor seventh,[101] and then an octave. In the third, the D rises to E and then again to G, and this time the big leap that follows widens to a major seventh. Throughout all this it is the rhythm, the accompaniment, and the principal motifs that maintain the unity.

   Zoltan Roman has drawn attention to a fascinating feature of this song: after the first 59 bars, the rest of the Lied is played out over tonic or dominant pedals, sometimes even both at once. In his view, these pedals (or their absence) are justified by the text: they are not present during the storm's climax. The first calming pedal point appears at bar 60 with the words: 'Ich sorgte, sie stürben morgen; Das ist nun

---

[96] See *Light*, 45.   [97] Ibid. 103.

[98] The effect of mysterious tension thus produced prompts a comparison with Alfred Cortot's well-known interpretation of the Scherzo in Chopin's Sonata in B flat minor, which he played forte but with the soft pedal.

[99] Zoltan Roman observes that this implacable ostinato is interrupted in bars 20–7 of the first verse and that the harmonies are stretched out in a long II, V, I progression (supertonic, dominant, tonic) to underline the words 'Nie hätt' ich gesendet die Kinder hinaus. Man hat sie hinausgetragen.' (I would never have sent the children out. They have been carried out.)

[100] Peter Russell considers them an echo of the voice's last descending phrase, at the end of the preceding song.

[101] Walter Abendroth, 'Das Geheimnis der Gesangsmelodie bei Mahler', *Allgemeine Musikzeitung*, 55 (1928), 7, 163, shows that the most 'painful' intervals are in the penultimate verse, setting off the words most laden with emotion, that is to say 'nie hätt' ich die Kinder'. Russell quotes the beginnings of the four vocal stanzas, pointing out the differences (*Light*, 103).

nicht zu besorgen.' (I would worry they might die tomorrow; Now that is no cause for worry). 'The subsequent, virtually uninterrupted pedal point to the end of the song', writes Roman. 'reflects the irreversible nature of the event. Having reached their breaking point in the first part of the song, the emotions begin to subside.[102] The distress rises to a pitch in the penultimate verse, with its 'stetig steigernd', gong, kettledrum roll and fortissimo horn.' This is called by Russell 'the culmination of the storm's fury and the singer's agony'.[103] Later, the tonic pedal is joined by another, on the dominant. Roman notes that the dominant pedal alone remains during the transition episode leading to the ultimate consolation. In the last verse there is another double pedal at 'sie ruh'n' (they rest), and then the mediant is superimposed over the dominant and the tonic seven bars before the end, so that these three pedal points, which are those of the perfect tonic triad, are left sounding alone to conclude the Lied and the cycle as a whole.

Before the voice enters, a seventeen-bar prelude describes the storm, incidentally without a single fortissimo, but with instruments little used up to this point, i.e. the piccolo flute, the bass clarinet, the contrabassoon as well as two extra horns, timpani, side drum, and tamtam (these latter entering only just before the last verse). As Susanne Vill and Peter Russell have noted, the procedures used by Mahler to symbolize the storm (melodic fourths and fifths, chromatic scales, growling trills and tremolos, stopped horns, dynamic surges) have changed little since *The Flying Dutchman*. They 'create an effect of agitation, turbulence, and emotional uproar'.[104]

The general outline of this Lied can be summarized as follows:[105]

Prelude
lst verse: 10 + (1) + 3 = 14
Interlude (1)
2nd verse: 6 + (2) + 4 = 12
Interlude (7)
3rd verse: 6 + (2) + 2 + (2) + 2 = 14
Interlude (9)
4th verse: 2 + (3) + 4 + (2) + 2 + (1) + 3 = 17
Interlude (transition to the major mode) (7)
5th verse (2) + 12 + (2) + 10 = 26
Postlude 15[106]

Thus, the structure is unusually complex and asymmetrical, its most striking feature being the crescendo of anguish obtained towards the end through shorter and shorter phrases (separated by rests) in conjunction with the sole vocal fortissimo. The last verse, because of its slow tempo, is longer than all the others put together. Here, as seen above, the material for the accompaniment is borrowed from the prelude (cor

---

[102] Roman, 'Mahler's Songs', 421.   [103] Russell, *Light*, 107.   [104] Ibid. 105.

[105] Zoltan Roman uses the numbers in brackets to represent the instrumental bars, the others the vocal bars. Roman remarks that the beginning of the last vocal phrase in the 5th verse (*von keinem Sturm*) is in fact a variant of the last lines of the 1st, 3rd, and 4th verses ('Songs', 315).

[106] Edward C. Bass, 'Counterpoint and Medium in Mahler's "Kindertotenlieder"', *Music Review*, 50: 3/4 (Aug. 1989), 211 ff., compares the structure of this song to that of a baroque concerto-aria form, with tutti and solo sections and 3 ritornello sections (bars 1 ff., 45 ff., 67 ff.).

844   *Appendix 2: History and analysis*

anglais and horn, bar 14),[107] while the vocal melody also contains references to the opening verses.

Analysis: For this concluding song, the mood of mystical resignation which was that of the coda of 'Oft denk' ich' is suddenly dispelled by an explosion of violent despair and uncontrollable anguish, echoing the unleashed forces of nature, even though the predominating mood is still piano, with fortes followed always by diminuendos. The initial descending scale, in trills in the basses,[108] dominates the whole piece. The march theme recalls those in the previous symphonies.[109] Mitchell underlines its relationship to two important motifs from the Finale of the Sixth,[110] written during the same summer. As always with Mahler, the march tread is linked with the idea of fate and death. The first vocal phrase, in rapid quavers, with its characteristic alternation of conjunct and wide intervals, expresses the father's obsessive anxiety. As his frenzy increases, they grow, as seen above, to wider and wider melodic intervals. Mitchell notes that the initial theme is 'a typical self-developing Mahler melody, compounded of a mosaic of motives that are constantly reassembled in new patterns and in a new order'.[111] Its plaintive chromaticism, rare in Mahler (bars 5–12), becomes even more insistent at the end of the penultimate strophe (bar 73 ff.), before the transition leading to the major coda.

At the end of stanza 3, the fullest orchestra in the whole cycle is called for, with the addition of kettledrum and gong. Most of the orchestral parts are marked fortissimo. It is 'the culmination of the storm's fury and the singer's agony', as Peter Russell observes (bars 77–85). But 'the storm suddenly dwindles' during the last vocal line ('. . . nichts dazu sagen'!). Two notes on the glockenspiel (with harp octaves), a distant echo of the first Lied, interrupt the implacable progression, as if the sun were suddenly appearing after the storm. It is here that the chromatic accompaniment motif, taken from the prelude and from the fourth verse, transposed to the major and becoming increasingly diatonic, initiates the safe journey through the 'Lullaby' that serves as Finale to the cycle. Donald Mitchell makes interesting comments on the twelve glockenspiel As which precede the voice's entry in the coda. The first and third are reinforced by harp octaves and a high A played in harmonics by the cellos, and rapidly decreasing to piano at the end of the bar. Another high A is heard simultaneously on the piccolo flute, a note which Dargie compares to 'sunshine breaking through the clouds'[112] and Mitchell to a 'piercing ray of light', a 'laser beam'.[113] The last bell strokes 'have been divested of their funereal association and emerge as serene heralds of the concluding lullaby'. Mitchell rightly calls this whole episode 'a miniature exercise in *Klangfarbenmelodie*'. The muted string

---

[107] Edward Kravitt observes that the motifs which in the first Lied illustrated the words *Nacht* (night, i.e. death) and *Licht* (light) are used in the last to symbolize birth (bar 110: the mother) and rest (bars 119–20: *sie ruh'n*) ('Dirges' (n. 1), 345).

[108] Fritz Egon Pamer considers this chain of trills, as well as the 'Mannheim breaks' in the march theme (which echo those in the first Lied—on 'kein Unglück'), to be a deliberate archaism.

[109] In *The Art Song* (Univ. of Oklahoma Press, Norman, Okla., 1953), James Husst Hall points out a resemblance between this theme and that of the first Lied in *Liebestreu*, Op. 3 No. 1 of Brahms.

[110] Compare bars 24–7 of the Lied ('Man hat sie getragen'), where the voice is doubled by the horns in octaves, with bars 37–9 of the Finale (horn solo). The same fragment is later incorporated into the first theme of the Finale (bar 118 or bars 578–80). There is also a similarity of mood between the Andante of the Sixth Symphony, also a lullaby, and the coda of 'In diesem Wetter'. The opening theme of this same movement belongs to the melodic world of the *Kindertotenlieder*.

[111] DMM3. 81.   [112] Dargie, *Music*, 107.   [113] DMM3. 83.

sonority, with that of the celesta low in its range; the major key; the broad, lyrical, diatonic vocal melody; the chorale-like melody for the winds (bar 116: 'von Gottes Hand bedecket'), taken up by the horn which prolongs the voice's last phrase; the 'magical' transformation of one of the storm's anguished motifs into 'the gentle rocking accompaniment figure of the lullaby';[114] all this reinforces the calming effect of Rückert's words.[115]

Peace and hope reign in this conclusion, which recalls that of the *Lieder eines fahrenden Gesellen* and heralds the mystic, pianissimo coda in *Das Lied von der Erde*, in which the celesta also plays a leading role. Prior to the Sixth Symphony, the last *Kindertotenlied* is of course the second of Mahler's compositions to use a celesta.[116] Mahler had discovered the instrument a year before, when he was conducting *Louise*. The first violins superimpose over the vocal line an ethereal high descant[117] that reveals a hope, even a certainty, of immortality and of eternal bliss. This melody passes from the violin to the flute's highest register. It seems to float in mid-air above the voice's melody, to which it adds ethereal ornamentation.[118] The coda of the *Kindertotenlieder* conjures up a 'vision of calm and beauty' which 'breaks in from another world'.[119] It is an important step towards the codas of the Ninth and of *Das Lied von der Erde*, suffused with peace and resignation, unique moments of luminous stillness. After the voice has fallen silent, the horn takes up the melodic line and the cellos, unmuted this time, add a new expressive counter-melody lasting to the perfect cadence. This is followed by seven instrumental bars within which the accompaniment motif gradually dissolves in stillness and silence.

Because of the *Kindertotenlieder* and the final *Abschied* in *Das Lied*, Mahler was long regarded as a 'morbid' composer, concerned only with tragedy and eternal farewell. Admittedly there exists little music as subjective, as 'lived' as this, none in any case where suffering has more communicative force. Only a musical genius, who was at the same time a master craftsman could have achieved such accomplished form, subtle detail, and imaginative orchestration while expressing a universal truth by the most direct means, that of melody. Except perhaps for the storm in the last Lied, Mahler never tries to illustrate pictorially, but aims only at the most intimate and direct expression. He avoids all theatrical declamation, and relies on song in all its purity, song that always seems to flow from the heart of things, from necessity, as in a Volkslied. From the historical point of view, it seems that the *Kindertotenlieder* were the first true cycle ever to be *composed* with orchestral accompaniment.[120]

---

[114] Russell notes that this is not only a transformation of the motif at bar 14 (in the cor anglais and French horns), but also of another, from the first song (and the Fifth Symphony's Funeral March).

[115] Susanne Vill, *Vermittlungsformen*, 121, associates the concept of maternal protection with that of the Venusberg, with Goethe's *ewig Weibliche*, and the end of the Eighth Symphony (*Jungfrau, Mutter, Königin, Göttin*), and with the choice of the 'maternal' alto voice for *Das Lied von der Erde*, as for 'Urlicht' in the Second Symphony and Zarathustra's Midnight Song in the Third. One is reminded here of Mahler's slip, when he wrote *Schoss* (womb), instead of *Haus* in his MS (see above).

[116] The first was 'Ich atmet' einen linden Duft' (see above).   [117] Russell, *Light*, 109.

[118] Edward C. Bass points out in 'Wenn dein Mütterlein' (bar 11 ff.) another passage in which 'voice and instrument present simultaneously, both simple and elaborated versions of a line' (see 'Counterpoint and Medium' (n. 104), 209).

[119] Eggebrecht, quoted by Russell (*Light*, 111).

[120] See above, the section on the *Wunderhorn-Lieder*. The songs in *Nuits d'été* of Berlioz were not immediately orchestrated, like the *Lieder eines fahrenden Gesellen*, while the *Wunderhorn-Lieder* are not a cycle, but a collection.

Contrary to what might be feared, the orchestral accompaniment only heightens the emotions expressed without ever destroying the effect of intimacy. A soul is being laid bare in these transparent sounds, these simple melodic lines with ascetic counterpoint nearly always played by solo instruments. The total orchestral forces are more or less those used in the Fourth Symphony,[121] yet each piece is in fact accompanied by a chamber-music group. The refinement of sound is comparable with that of the most delicate passages of the symphonies, and is achieved by the same means: unusual combinations of timbre, and the use of instruments in other than their habitual registers. Timbre becomes a fundamental element of composition.

To ensure that the emotions expressed in the cycle remain those of a father, Mahler wanted the *Kindertotenlieder* always to be sung by a man. He wanted the grieving father to give an impression of suffering contained, and feared that the female voice might introduce a note of sentimentality. Schoenberg rebutted the accusation of sentimentality so often made against Mahler by pointing out that in his view a sentimental composer was one who wallowed in his own suffering without seeking to transcend it. He observed that in fact Mahler's two 'saddest' works (apart from the Sixth Symphony) both end with a radiant vision of eternal life, without which this deeply mystical, if not conventionally religious, man would not have been able to bear the reality of human suffering. The principal message of the cycle lies in the disembodied tenderness of its conclusion, where Mahler seems to find a new answer to the metaphysical questions that had always obsessed him. The belief in eternal renewal and in the union of man with nature was one of the great revelations in this mature phase. It was only one transcendental step from these songs to the luminous melancholy of the Adagios of the last symphonies.

---

[121] Yet Mahler insisted on the first performance taking place in a chamber-music hall, the Kleiner Musikvereinsaal, where there is room on the stage for no more than 50 players.

SELECT BIBLIOGRAPHY

Abendroth, Walter, *Vier Meister der Musik (Bruckner, Mahler, Reger, Pfitzner)* (Prestel, Munich, 1952).

Adler, Guido, *Wollen und Wirken: Aus dem Leben eines Musikhistorikers* (Universal Edition, Vienna, 1935).

Alf, Julius, 'Gustav Mahler—Hans Sachs und Bassa Selim im Sinfoniefinale', *Dialog mit der Musik, Von Leonin bis Bartok* (Wort und Welt, Innsbruck, 1984), 177–81.

Anbruch, Musikblätter des, Mahler issues, 2: 7–8 (Universal Edition, Vienna, Apr. 1920); 12: 3 (Universal Edition, Vienna, Mar. 1930).

Appia, Adolphe, *Die Musik und die Inscenierung* (Bruckmann, Munich, 1899).

Arc, L', Mahler issue, 67 (L'Arc, Aix-en-Provence, 1976).

Bahr, Hermann, *Meister und Meisterbriefe um . . .* , ed. Joseph Gregor (Bauer, Vienna, 1947).

Balan, George, *Gustav Mahler sau cum exprima muzica idei* (Editura Muzicala, Bucarest, 1964).

Barford, Philip, *Mahler: Symphonies and Songs* (Univ. of Washington, Seattle, 1971).

—— 'Mahler: A Thematic Archetype', *Music Review*, 21 (1960), 297–316.

Barsova, Inna (ed.), *Gustav Mahler, Pisma, Vospominania* (Mouzyka, Moscow, 1964).

—— 'Rouskaia Premiera Vosmoi Symphonii Mahlera', *Sovietskaia Mouzyka* (Apr. 1984), 55–60.

Bartoš, František (ed.), *Mahler, Paměti, Korespondence, Dokumenty* (Statní Hubední Vydavatelství, Prague, 1962).

Bass, Edward C., 'Counterpoint and Medium in Mahler's Kindertotenlieder', *Music Review*, 50: 3 and 4 (Aug. and Nov. 1989), 206–14.

Bauer-Lechner, Natalie, *Recollections of Gustav Mahler*, ed. Peter Franklin, trans. Dika Newlin (Faber, London, 1980).

Baxendale, Carolyn, 'The Finale of Mahler's Fifth Symphony: Long-Range Musical Thought', *Journal of the Royal Musical Association*, 112: 2 (1987), 257–89.

Beetz, Wilhelm, *Das Wiener Opernhaus 1869–1945* (Central European Times, Zurich, 1949).

Bekker, Paul, *Die Sinfonie von Beethoven bis Mahler* (Schuster & Loeffler, Berlin, 1922).

Bethge, Hans, *Die Chinesische Flöte* (Inselverlag, Leipzig, 1907).

Bie, Oskar, *Die moderne Musik und Richard Strauss* (Giegel, Leipzig, 1907).

Biebl, Thomas F., 'A Study of the Contrapuntal Style in the Fifth Symphony of Mahler', Ph.D. thesis (Indiana, 1971).

Blaukopf, Herta, 'Mahler und das Hofopernorchester', *Studia Musicologica Academiae Scientiarum Hungaricae*, 31 (Budapest, 1989), 245–52.

Blaukopf, Kurt, *Gustav Mahler oder der Zeitgenosse der Zukunft* (Molden, Vienna, 1969).

—— *Mahler: A Documentary Study* (Oxford University Press, New York, 1976).

Blaukopf, Kurt, 'Gustav Mahler und die Tschechische Oper', *Österreichische Musikzeitschrift,* 34 (1979), 285–8.

—— and **Herta,** *Mahler: His Life, Work and World* (Thames & Hudson, London, 1991).

—— *Die Wiener Philharmoniker* (Zsolnay, Vienna, 1986).

Blessinger, Karl, *Mendelssohn, Meyerbeer, Mahler: Drei Kapitel Judentum in der Musik als Schlüssel zur Musikgeschichte des 19. Jahrhunderts* (Hahnefeld, Berlin, 1939).

Böke, Henning, 'Gustav Mahler und das Judentum', *Archiv für Musikwissenschaft,* 49: 1 (1992), 1–21.

Brod, Max, *Gustav Mahler: Beispiel einer deutsch-jüdischen Symbiose* (Ner-Tamid-Verlag, Frankfurt, 1961).

Bruner, Ellen Carole, 'The Relationship of Text and Music in the Lieder of Hugo Wolf and Gustav Mahler', Ph.D. thesis (Syracuse, NY, 1974).

Busoni, Ferruccio, *Briefe an seine Frau,* ed. Friedrich Schnapp (Rotapfel, Erlenbach, 1935).

Cardus, Neville, *Gustav Mahler: His Mind and his Music,* i (Gollancz, London, 1965).

Carner, Mosco, *Of Men and Music* (Joseph Williams, London, 1944).

Chop, Max, *Emil Nikolaus von Reznicek: Sein Leben und seine Werke* (Universal Edition, Vienna, n.d.).

Chord and Discord, i, 10 issues (Bruckner Society of America, New York, 1932–9); ii, 10 issues (Bruckner Society of America, New York, 1940–63); iii/1 (Bruckner Society of America, New York, 1969).

Cooke, Deryck, *Gustav Mahler (1860–1911): An Introduction to his Music* (BBC, London, 1960).

—— *Gustav Mahler: An Introduction to his Music* (Faber, London, 1980).

—— *Vindications: Essays on Romantic Music* (Faber, London, 1982).

Csampai, Attila (ed.), *Toblacher Mahler Protokolle-I, 1991: Mahler und die Schallplatte* (Bosse, Regensburg, 1992).

Danuser, Hermann, 'Der Orchestergesang des Fin de Siècle: Eine historische und ästhetische Skizze', *Die Musikforschung,* 4 (Oct.–Dec. 1977), 425–52.

—— *Gustav Mahler und seine Zeit* (Laaber Verlag, Laaber, 1991).

—— (ed.), *Gustav Mahler: Wege der Forschung* (Wissenschaftliche Buchgesellschaft, Darmstadt, 1992).

Dargie, Elisabeth Mary, *Music and Poetry in the Songs of Gustav Mahler* (Peter Lang, Berne, 1981).

Davison, Peter, 'The Nachtmusiken from Mahler's Seventh Symphony: Analysis and Reappraisal', Ph.D. thesis (Univ. of Cambridge, 1985).

Decsey, Ernst, *Musik war sein Leben: Lebenserinnerungen* (Hans Deutsch, Vienna, 1962).

—— *Die Spieldose* (Tal, Leipzig, 1922).

Del Mar, Norman, *Mahler's Sixth Symphony* (Eulenburg Books, London, 1980).

Diepenbrock, Alphons, *Verzamelde Geschriften* (Het Spectrum, Utrecht, 1950).

—— *Brieven en Documenten IV,* ed. Eduard Reeser (Martinus Nijhoff, The Hague, 1974).

Durney, Daniel, 'Aspects du problème de la forme dans la musique instrumentale au tournant du siècle: Mahler, Schoenberg, Berg, Webern, Debussy 1890–1910', Ph.D.

thesis (2 vols., University Paris IV, 1981).

Duse, Ugo, *Studio sulla poetica liederistica di Gustav Mahler* (Istituto Veneto di Scienze, Lettere ed Arti, Venice, 1960–1).

—— *Gustav Mahler: Introduzione allo studio della vita e delle opere* (Marsilio, Padua., 1962).

Effenberger, Rudolf, *Fünfundzwanzig Jahre Dienstbarer Geist im Reiche der Frau Musika* (Gesellschaft der Musikfreunde, Vienna, n.d.).

Eggebrecht, Hans Heinrich, *Die Musik Gustav Mahlers* (Piper, Munich, 1982).

Ekman, Karl, *Jean Sibelius* (Kustannusosakeyhtiö, Helsinki, 2nd edn. 1935).

—— *Jean Sibelius: The Life and Personality,* trans. Edward Birse (Wilmer, London, 1936).

Engel, Gabriel, *Gustav Mahler: Song-Symphonist* (Bruckner Society of America, New York, 1932).

Farga, Franz, *Die Wiener Oper* (Franz Göth, Vienna, 1947).

Feder, Stuart, 'Gustav Mahler, Dying', *International Psycho-Analytical Review,* 5: 125 (1978), 125–48.

—— 'Gustav Mahler: The Music of Fratricide (Youth's Wondrous Horn)', *Psychoanalytic Explorations in Music* (International Universities, Madison, Conn., 1990), 341–90.

Filler, Susan, 'Editorial Problems in Symphonies of Gustav Mahler: A Study of the Sources of the Third and Tenth Symphonies', Ph.D. thesis (Northwestern Univ., 1977).

—— *Gustav and Alma Mahler: A Guide to Research* (Garland, New York, 1989).

Finson, Jon W., 'The Reception of Gustav Mahler's Wunderhorn Lieder', *Journal of Musicology,* 5 (1987), 91–116.

Floros, Constantin, *Gustav Mahler,* i. *Die geistige Welt Gustav Mahlers in systematischer Darstellung* (Breitkopf & Härtel, Wiesbaden, 1977); ii. *Mahler und die Symphonik des 19. Jahrhunderts in neuer Deutung* (1977); iii. *Die Symphonien* (1985).

Forte, Allen, 'Middleground Motives in the Adagietto of Mahler's Fifth Symphony', *19th Century Music,* 7: 2 (University of Calif., Fall 1984), 153–63.

Franklin, Peter, 'Music, the Will and Ideas', *The Idea of Music: Schoenberg and Others* (Macmillan, Houndmills, 1985), 1–17.

Fülöp, Peter, *Mahler's Discography* (Studia Musicologica Academiae Scientiarum Hungaricae, 26; Budapest, 1984).

Gartenberg, Egon, *Mahler: The Man and his Music* (Schirmer Books, New York, 1978).

Gerlach, Reinhard, *Strophen von Leben, Traum und Tod: Ein Essay über Rückert-Lieder von Gustav Mahler* (Heinrichshofen, Wilhelmshaven, 1983).

Gradenwitz, Peter, *The Music of Israel* (Norton, New York, 1949).

Graf, Max, *Wagner Probleme und andere Studien* (Wiener Verlag, Vienna, 1900).

—— *Geschichte und Geist der modernen Musik* (Humbold, Stuttgart, 1953).

—— *Jede Stunde war erfüllt: Ein halbes Jahrhundert Musik- und Theaterleben* (Forum, Vienna, 1957).

Grasberger, Franz, *Richard Strauss und die Wiener Oper* (Schneider, Tutzing, 1969).

—— (ed.), *Die Welt um Richard Strauss in Briefen* (Schneider, Tutzing, 1969).

Greene, David B., *Mahler, Consciousness and Temporality* (Gordon & Breach, New York, 1984).

Greisenegger, Evanthia, and Wolfgang, and Pausch, Oskar (eds.), Alfred Roller und seine Zeit (Böhlau, Vienna, 1991).

Greisenegger, Wolfgang, 'Alfred Roller: Neubedeutung des szenischen Raumes', *Studia Musicologica Academiae Scientiarum Hungaricae*, 31 (Budapest, 1988), 271–81.

Gutheil-Schoder, Marie, *Erlebtes und Erstrebtes, Rolle und Gestaltung* (Krey, Vienna, 1937).

Hadamovski, Franz, *Gustav Mahler und seine Zeit: Katalog der Austellung* (Wiener Festwochen, Wien, 1960).

Hahn, Reynaldo, *Thèmes variés* (Janin, Paris, 1946).

Hanslick, Eduard, *Am Ende des Jahrhunderts 1895–1899* (Allgemeiner Verein für Deutsche Literatur, Berlin, 1899).

—— *Aus Neuer und Neuester Zeit* (Allgemeiner Verein für Deutsche Literatur, Berlin, 1900).

Harcourt, Eugène d', *La Musique actuelle en Allemagne et en Autriche-Hongrie* (Durdilly, Paris, 1908).

Harten, Uwe (ed.), *Bruckner Symposion: Bruckner, Liszt, Mahler und die Moderne*, Internationales Brucknerfest Linz, Sept. 1986 (Anton Bruckner Institut, Linz, 1989).

Hartungen, Hartmut von, 'Der Dichter Siegfried Lipiner (1856–1911)', Ph.D. thesis (Munich, 1932).

Hauptmann, Gerhart, *Tagebücher 1897–1905* (Propyläen, Berlin, 1987).

Hellsberg, Clemens, *Demokratie der Könige* (Schweizer Verlaghaus, Zurich, 1992).

Hevesi, Ludwig, *Altkunst Neukunst, Wien 1894–1908* (Konegen, Vienna, 1909).

Heyworth, Peter, *Conversations with Klemperer* (Gollancz, London, 1973).

—— *Otto Klemperer: His Life and Times*, i. *1885–1933* (Cambridge University Press, Cambridge, 1983).

Hilmar-Voit, Renate, *Im Wunderhorn-Ton, Gustav Mahlers sprachliches Kompositionsmaterial bis 1900* (Schneider, Tutzing, 1988).

Hoffmann, Rudolf Stephan, *Erich Wolfgang Korngold* (Stephenson, Vienna, 1922).

Holbrook, David, *Gustav Mahler and the Courage to Be* (Vision, London, 1975).

Holde, Artur, *Jews in Music* (Owen, London, 1959).

Hopkins, Robert George, *Closure and Mahler's Music: The Role of Secondary Parameters* (Univ. of Pennsylvania, Philadelphia, 1990).

Hutschenruyter, Wouter, *Mahler* (Kruseman, The Hague, n.d.).

Istel, Edgar (ed.), *Mahlers Symphonien* (Meisterführer No. 10; Schlesingersche Buch- und Musikhandlung, Berlin, n.d.).

James, Burnett, *The Music of Gustav Mahler* (Fairleigh Dickinson Univ., Assoc. Univ. Presses, London, 1985).

Jolizza, W. K. von, *Das Lied und seine Geschichte* (Hartleben, Vienna, 1910).

Jülg, Hans-Peter, *Gustav Mahlers Sechste Symphonie* (Musikverlag Katzbichler, Munich, 1986).

Karpath, Ludwig, *Lachende Musiker* (Knorr & Hirth, Munich, 1929).

Keegan, Susanne, *The Bride of the Wind: The Life of Alma Mahler* (Secker & Warburg, London, 1991).

Kennedy, Michael, *Mahler* (Dent, London, 1974).

Klein, Rudolf (ed.), *Beiträge 79–81: Gustav Mahler Kolloquium 1979* (Bärenreiter, Kassel, 1981).

Klemm, Eberhardt, 'Zur Geschichte der Fünften Sinfonie von Gustav Mahler', *Jahrbuch Peters 1979* (Aufsätze zur Musik, Leipzig, 1980), 9–116.

Klemperer, Otto, *Klemperer Stories: Anecdotes, Sayings and Impressions of Otto Klemperer* (Robson Books, London, 1980).

Kloer, Gisela, 'Mahlers Sprachgestus im Instrumentalen und Vokalen: Vergleichen Sie den 1. Satz der IV. Symphonie mit seinen Liedern "Rheinlegendchen", "Wer hat dies Liedlein erdacht?", "Wo die schönen Trompeten blasen" und versuchen Sie, Mahlers Sprachgestus im 4. Satz der IV. Symphonie darzustellen', Ph.D. thesis (Dortmund, 1988).

Kolleritsch, Otto (ed.), *Gustav Mahler: Sinfonie und Wirklichkeit* (Universal Edition, Graz, 1977).

Korngold, Luzi, *Erich Wolfgang Korngold*, ed. Elisabeth Lafite (Österreichischer Bundesverlag, Vienna, 1967).

Kralik, Heinrich, *Die Wiener Philharmoniker* (Frick, Vienna, 1938).

—— *Das Buch der Musikfreunde* (Amalthea, Zurich, 1951).

—— *Gustav Mahler*, ed. Friedrich Heller (Lafite, Vienna, 1968).

Kraus, Hedwig, and **Schreinzer, Karl** (eds.), *Statistik der Wiener Philharmoniker 1842–1942* (Universal Edition, Vienna, 1942).

Krebs, Carl, *Meister des Taktstocks* (Schuster & Loeffler, Berlin, 1919).

Kühn, Helmut, 'Ohne Rücksicht auf das Tempo: Über Mahlers Verhältnis zur Tradition', *Über Symphonien* (Schneider, Tutzing, 1979), 157–71.

—— and **Quander, Georg** (eds.), *Gustav Mahler. Ein Lesebuch mit Bildern* (Ein Buch der Berliner Festwochen, Orell Füssli, Zurich, 1982).

Kunz, Otto, *Richard Mayr* (Bergland, Vienna, 1933).

La Grange, Henry-Louis de, 'Mahler Today', *The World of Music*, 11: 2 (Bärenreiter, Kassel, Mar. 1969), 6–17.

—— 'Mistakes about Mahler', *Music and Musicians*, 21: 2 (Oct. 1972), 16–22.

—— 'Mahler und Schönberg: Tradition und Revolution', *Bruckner Symposion* (Linz, 1986), 15–24.

—— (ed.), *Colloque International Gustav Mahler*, Jan. 1985 (Association Gustav Mahler, Paris, 1986).

—— 'Mahler and the Metropolitan Opera', *Studia Musicologica Academiae Scientiarum Hungaricae*, 31 (Budapest, 1989), 253–70.

—— 'Gustav Mahler auf der Suche nach der verlorenen Unendlichkeit,' *Gustav Mahler: Leben, Werk, Interpretation, Rezeption*, Int. Gewandhaus Symposium, 1985 (Peters, Leipzig, 1990).

—— 'Berlioz und Mahler: Vom musikalischen Roman zum Sphärengesang', in Peter Petersen (ed.), *Musikkulturgeschichte*, Festschrift für Constantin Floros (Breitkopf & Härtel, Wiesbaden, 1990).

—— 'Mahler and France', in Matthias Theodor Vogt (ed.), *Das Gustav-Mahler-Fest-Hamburg, 1989* (Bärenreiter, Kassel, 1991), 229–46.

—— *Vienne: Histoire musicale*, ii, *1848 à nos jours* (Coutaz, Arles, 1991).

—— 'Auf der Suche nach Gustav Mahler', in Hermann Danuser (ed.), *Gustav Mahler: Wege der Forschung* (Wiss. Buchges., Darmstadt, 1992), 30–68.

Lea, Henry A., *Gustav Mahler: Man on the Margin* (Bouvier, Bonn, 1985).

Lebrecht, Norman, *Mahler Remembered* (Faber, London, 1987).

Liberman, Arnoldo, *Gustav Mahler o el corazón abrumado* (Altalena, Madrid, 1st edn. 1982; 2nd edn. 1983).

—— *Gustav Mahler: Annäherung in vier Sätzen* (Europäische Verlagsanstalt, Hamburg, 1992).

—— *La fascinacion de la mentira* (Altalena, Madrid, 1986).

Lipman, Samuel, *Music after Modernism* (Basic Books, New York, 1979).

Loeser, Norbert, *Gustav Mahler* (Gottmer, Haarlem, 1968).

Louis, Rudolf, *Die Dcutsche Musik der Gegenwart* (Müller, Munich, 1909).

MacCaldin, Denis, *Mahler* (Novello, Sevenoaks, Kent, 1981).

Mahler, Alma (ed.), *Zehnte Symphonie: Facsimile of the Manuscript* (Zsolnay, Vienna, 1924).

—— *Gustav Mahler: Erinnerungen und Briefe* (1st edn. Allert de Lange, Amsterdam, 1940).

—— *Gustav Mahler: Memories and Letters*, trans. Basil Creighton (Murray, London, 1946).

Mahler, Gustav, *Ausstellung Gustav Mahler und seine Zeit*, exhibition catalogue (Wiener Festwochen, Vienna, 1960).

—— *Mahler Feestboek* (6 and 21 May 1920) (Concertgebouw, Amsterdam, 1920).

Martner, Knud, *Gustav Mahler im Konzertsaal: Eine Dokumentation seiner Konzerttätigkeit 1870–1911* (KM-Privatdruck, Copenhagen, 1985).

Marx, Joseph, *Betrachtungen eines romantischen Realisten* (Gerlach & Wiedling, Vienna, 1947).

Matter, Jean, *Mahler le démoniaque* (Foma, Lausanne, 1959).

—— *Connaissance de Mahler: Documents, analyses et synthèses* (L'Age d'Homme, Lausanne, 1974).

Mellers, Wilfrid, *Studies in Contemporary Music* (Dobson, London, 1947).

Mengelberg, Rudolf (ed.), Das Mahler-Fest. Amsterdam, May 1920 (Universal Edition, Vienna, 1920).

—— *Gustav Mahler: Vorträge und Berichte* (Breitkopf & Härtel, Leipzig, 1923).

Merker, Der: Mahler issue, 3: 5 (Vienna, Mar. 1912).

Lieberwirth, Steffen (ed.), *Gustav Mahler, Leben—Werk—Interpretation—Rezeption*, Gewandhaus-Symposium, Gewandhaus-Festtage 1985 (Peters, Leipzig, 1990).

Metzger, Heinz-Klaus and Riehn, Rainer (eds.), Musik-Konzepte Sonderband, *Gustav Mahler* (Pribil, Munich, 1989).

Meysels, Luciano O., *In meinem Salon ist Österreich: Berta Zuckerkandl und ihre Zeit* (Herold, Vienna, 1984).

Mittag, Erwin, *Aus der Geschichte der Wiener Philharmoniker* (Gerlach & Wiedling, Vienna, 1950).

Moderne Welt: Mahler issue, ed. Ludwig Hirschfeld, 3: 7 (Vienna, 1921–2).

Moll, Carl, *Emil Jakob Schindler (1842–92): Eine Bildnisstudie* (Österreichische Staatsdruckerei, Vienna, 1930).

Monson, Karen, *Alma Mahler, Muse to Genius* (Houghton Mifflin Company, Boston, Mass., 1983).

Morold, Max, *Wagners Kampf und Sieg* (2 vols., Amalthea, Zurich, 1930).

Müller, Karl Josef, *Mahler: Leben—Werke—Dokumente* (Piper-Schott, Mainz, 1988).

Murphy, Edward, 'Unusual Forms in Mahler's Fifth Symphony', *Music Review*, 47: 2 (1986–7), 101–9.

Musical, Revue du Châtelet, n. 9, 'Mahler et la France', H.L. de La Grange (ed.) (Paris, Feb. 1989), by Alain Surrans, Nathalie Brunet, Marc Vignal, Henry-Louis de La Grange, Gérard Pesson, William Ritter, Guilhem Tournier.

Musik, Die: Mahler issue, ed. Bernhard Schuster, 10: 18 (Schuster & Loeffler, Berlin, 1910–11).

Namenwirt, Simon Michael, *Gustav Mahler: A Critical Bibliography* (3 vols., Harrassowitz, Wiesbaden, 1987).

Nebehay, Christian M. (ed.), *Eine Klimt Dokumentation* (Galerie Nebehay, Vienna, 1969).

—— *Ver Sacrum 1898–1903* (Tusch, Vienna, 1975).

Nejedlý, Zdeněk, *Gustav Mahler* (Státní Nakladatelství Krásné Literatury, Hudby a Umění, Prague, 1958).

Nemeth, Amadé, *Gustav Mahler életének Krónikája* (Zenemükiado, Budapest, 1984).

Nemeth, Carl, *Franz Schmidt: Ein Meister nach Brahms und Bruckner* (Amalthea, Vienna, 1957).

Niemann, Walter, *Die Musik der Gegenwart* (Schuster & Loeffler, Berlin, 1913).

Nikkels, Eveline, *Mahler en Nietzsche: A Comparative Study with a Summary in English* (Rodopi, Amsterdam, 1984).

—— '*O Mensch! Gib Acht!*' *Friedrich Nietzsches Bedeutung für Gustav Mahler* (Rodopi, Amsterdam, 1989).

Nodnagel, Ernst Otto, *Mahler: Fünfte Symphonie. Technische Analyse* (Peters, Leipzig, 1905).

Novotny, Fritz, and **Dobai, Johannes**, *Gustav Klimt* (Galerie Welz, Salzburg, 1967).

Oltmann, Michael Johannes, '"Ich bin der Welt abhanden gekommen" und "Der Tamboursg'sell": Zwei Liedkonzeptionen Gustav Mahlers', *Archiv für Musikwissenschaft*, 1 (1986), 69–88.

Österreichische Musikzeitschrift: Mahler issue, 15: 6 (Vienna, 1960).

Osthoff, Wolfgang, 'Hans Pfitzners "Rose vom Liebesgarten": Gustav Mahler und die Wiener Schule', *Festschrift Martin Ruhnke* (Hänssler, Neuhausen-Stuttgart, 1986), 265–93.

Paumgartner, Bernhard, *Erinnerungen* (Residenz, Salzburg, 1969).

Pausch, Oskar, '"Mahlerisches", in den Rollerbeständen der Wiener Theatersammlung', *Studia Musicologica Academiae Scientiarum Hungaricae*, 31 (1989), 343–52.

Pedrell, Felipe, 'Gustavo Mahler', *Músicos contemporáneos y de otros tiempos* (Ollendorff, Paris, 1910), 235–48.

Perez de Arteaga, José, *Mahler* (Salvat, Barcelona, 1986).

Perger, Richard von, *Fünfzig Jahre Wiener Philharmoniker: 1860–1910* (Fromme, Vienna, 1910).

Pfitzner, Hans, *Reden, Schriften, Briefe* (Luchterhand, Berlin, 1955).

Pickett, David Anniss, 'Gustav Mahler as an Interpreter: A Study of his Textural Alterations and Performance Practice in the Symphonic Repertoire', 3 vols. Ph.D. thesis (Univ. of Surrey, 1988).

Pott, Gertrud, 'Die Spiegelung des Sezessionismus im Österreichischen Theater', Ph.D. thesis (Vienna, 1970).

Powell, Nicolas, *The Sacred Spring: The Arts in Vienna 1898–1918* (introduction by Adolf Opel) (New York Graphic Society, 1974).

Principe, Quirino, *Mahler* (Rusconi, Milan, 1983).

Rauchhaupt, Ursula von (ed.), *Die Welt der Symphonie* (Polydor International, Westermann Verlag, Hamburg, 1972).

Raupp, Wilhelm, *Max von Schillings* (Hanseatischer Verlag, Hamburg, 1935).

Raynor, Henry, *Mahler* (Macmillan, London, 1975).

Redl, Renata, 'Berta Zuckerkandl und die Wiener Gesellschaft. Ein Beitrag zur Österreichischen Kunst- und Gesellschaftskritik', Ph.D. thesis (Vienna, 1976).

Reeser, Eduard, *Gustav Mahler und Holland: Briefe* (IGMG, Universal Edition, Vienna, 1980).

Reich, Willi (ed.), *Gustav Mahler: Im eigenen Wort. Im Worte der Freunde* (Arche, Zurich, 1958).

Reznicek, Felicitas von, *Gegen den Strom* (Amalthea, Zurich, 1960).

Richolson-Sollitt, Edna, *Mengelberg spreekt* (Kruseman, The Hague, n.d.).

Rizzuti, Alberto, *Sognatori, utopisti e disertori nei Lieder 'Militari' di Gustav Mahler* (Passigli, Florence, 1990).

Robert, Gustave, *La Musique à Paris 1898–1900*, v–vi (Delagrave, Paris, 1901).

Rolland, Romain, *Musiciens d'aujourd'hui* (Hachette, Paris, 1922).

—— (ed.), *Richard Strauss et Romain Rolland: Correspondance, Fragments de Journal* (Albin Michel, Paris, 1951).

—— *Fräulein Elsa: Lettres de Romain Rolland à Elsa Wolff* (Albin Michel, Paris, 1964).

Rölleke, Heinz, 'Gustav Mahlers "Wunderhorn" Lieder', *Jahrbuch des Freien Deutschen Hochstifts* (Niemeyer, Tübingen, 1981), 370–8.

Roman, Zoltan, 'Mahler's Songs and their Influence on his Symphonic Thought', Ph.D. thesis (2 vols., Toronto, 1970).

—— *Prelude and Finale*: 'Musical Jugendstil in Selected Songs by Mahler and Webern', in Erick Nielsen (ed.), *Focus on Vienna 1900* (Fink, Munich, 1982), 113–21.

Russell, Peter, *Light in Battle with Darkness: Mahler's Kindertotenlieder* (Lang, Berne, 1991).

Rutters, Herman, *Gustav Mahler* (Baarn, Hollandia, 1919).

Ruzicka, Peter (ed.), *Mahler: Eine Herausforderung, ein Symposion* (Breitkopf & Härtel, Wiesbaden, 1977).

Salten, Felix, *Gestalten und Erscheinungen* (Fischer, Berlin, 1913).

Schaefer, Hans Joachim, Rölleke, Heinz, and **Linnebach, Andrea** (eds.), *Gustav Mahler, Jahre der Entscheidung in Kassel 1883–1885* (Stadtsparkasse, Kassel, 1990).

Schaeffers, Anton, 'Gustav Mahler Instrumentation', Ph.D. thesis (Bonn, Nolte, Düsseldorf, 1935).

Schalk, Franz, *Briefe und Betrachtungen* (Musikwissenschaftlicher Verlag, Vienna, 1935).

Schibler, Armin, *Zum Werk Gustav Mahlers* (Kahnt, Lindau, 1955).

Schiedermair, Ludwig, *Gustav Mahler* (Seemann, Leipzig, 1900).

—— *Musikalische Begegnungen* (Staufen, Cologne, 1948).

Schiff, David, 'Jewish and Musical Tradition in the Music of Mahler and Schoenberg',

Journal of the A. Schoenberg Institute, 9: 2 (Nov. 1986), 217–31.

Schlüter, Wolfgang, *Studien zur Rezeptionsgeschichte der Symphonik Gustav Mahlers*, Ph.D. thesis (Technische Universität, Berlin, 1983).

Schmidt, Leopold, *Aus dem Musikleben der Gegenwart* (Hofmann, Berlin, 1909).

—— *Erlebnisse und Betrachtungen* (Hofmann, Berlin, 1913).

Schmierer, Elisabeth, *Die Orchesterlieder Gustav Mahlers* (Bärenreiter, Kassel, 1991).

Schmitt, Theodor, *Der langsame Symphoniesatz Gustav Mahlers* (Fink, Munich, 1983).

Schneider, Gunter, 'Egon Wellesz über Gustav Mahler', *Österreichische Musikzeitschrift*, 12: 85 (Vienna, 1985), 637–47.

Schoenberg, Arnold, 'Gustav Mahler', 'Stil und Gedanke', *Gesammelte Schriften*, i, ed. Ivan Vojtěch (Fischer, Frankfurt, 1976). 'Gustav Mahler', *Style and Idea* (Philosophical Library, New York, 1950); in German, in Rainer Wunderlich (ed.), *Gustav Mahler* (Leins, Tübingen, 1966).

—— *Briefe*, ed. Erwin Stein (Schott, Mainz, 1958).

—— 'Banalität und Genie. Zum 100. Geburtstag Gustav Mahlers', *Forum*, 8: 79/80 (Vienna, 1960), 277–80.

Schollum, Robert, *Das Österreichische Lied des 20. Jahrhunderts* (Schneider, Tutzing, 1977).

Schorske, Carl E., *Fin de siècle Vienna: Politics and Culture* (Knopf, New York, 1980).

Schreiber, Wolfgang, *Gustav Mahler: in Selbstzeugnissen und Bilddokumenten* (Rowohlt, Reinbek bei Hamburg, 1971).

Schrott, Ludwig, *Die Persönlichkeit Hans Pfitzners* (Atlantis, Zurich, 1959).

Schuh, Willi (ed.), *Richard Strauss, Jahrbuch 1954* (Boosey & Hawkes, Bonn, 1953).

—— *Richard Strauss: Jugend und frühe Meisterjahre. Lebenschronik 1864–1898* (Atlantis, Zurich, 1976).

Schumann, Karl, *Das kleine Gustav Mahler Buch* (Residenz, Salzburg, 1972).

Schünemann, Georg, *Geschichte des Dirigierens* (Breitkopf & Härtel, Leipzig, 1913).

Schuschitz, Elisabeth Désirée, 'Die Wiener Musikkritik in der Ära Gustav Mahler 1897 bis 1907: Eine historisch-kritische Standortbestimmung', Ph.D. thesis (Vienna, 1978).

Seckerson, Edward, *Mahler* (Omnibus Press, London, 1984).

Seidl, Arthur, *Moderne Dirigenten* (Schuster & Loeffler, Berlin, 1902).

—— *Moderner Geist in der deutschen Tonkunst* (Bosse, Regensburg, 1912).

—— *Aufsätze, Studien und Skizzen* (2 vols., Bosse, Regensburg, 1926).

Silbermann, Alphons, *Lübbes Mahler-Lexikon* (Lübbe, Bergisch Gladbach, 1986).

Sine, Nadine, 'The Evolution of Symphonic Worlds: Tonality in the Symphonies of Gustav Mahler, with Emphasis on the First, Third, and Fifth', Ph.D. thesis (New York Univ., 1983).

Slezak, Leo, *Mein Lebensmärchen* (Piper, Munich, 1948).

Sopeña, Ibanez Federico, *Estudios sobre Mahler* (Rialp, Madrid, 1983).

Specht, Richard, *Mahler, Symphonie VI: Thematischer Führer* (Kahnt, Leipzig, 1906).

—— *Das Wiener Operntheater: Erinnerung aus 50 Jahren* (Knepler, Vienna, 1919).

—— *Mahler. Symphonies, I, II, III, IV, VII: Thematic Analyses* (Universal Edition, Vienna, n.d.).

Sponheuer, Bernd, *Logik des Zerfalls: Untersuchungen zum Finalproblem in den Symphonien Gustav Mahlers* (Schneider, Tutzing, 1978).

—— 'Durch Nacht zum Licht? Zur Interpretation des Chorals in Gustav Mahlers Fünfter Symphonie', *Musik: Deutung, Bedeutung* (Pläne, Dortmund, 1986), 91–3.

Stahmer, Klaus Hinrich (ed.), *Form und Idee in Gustav Mahlers Instrumentalmusik* (Heinrichshofen, Wilhelmshaven, 1980).

Stauber, Paul, *Das wahre Erbe Mahlers* (Huber & Lahme, Vienna, 1909).

Stefan, Paul, *Das neue Haus* (Strache, Vienna, 1919).

—— *Bruno Walter* (Reichner, Vienna, 1936).

—— and Heinsheimer, Hans (ed.), *25 Jahre Neue Musik: Jahrbuch 1926 der Universal Edition* (Universal Edition, Vienna, 1926).

Stein, Erwin, 'Mahler and the Vienna Opera', *Opera Bedside Book* (Gollancz, London, 1965), 296–317.

Steinert, Heinz, 'Der Skandal Gustav Mahler: Der Mythos von der Vertreibung Mahlers aus Wien', *Adorno in Wien* (Gesellschaftskritik, Vienna, 1989), 77–95.

Steinitzer, Max, *Richard Strauss* (Schuster & Loeffler, Berlin, 1911).

Stephan, Rudolf, *Mahler: II. Symphonie C-Moll* (Meisterwerke der Musik; Fink, Munich, 1979).

—— (ed.), *Gustav Mahler: Werk und Interpretation: Autographe, Partituren, Dokumente*, Catalogue of Exhibition held at the Heinrich Heine Institut, Oct. 1979 to Jan. 1980 (Volk Verlag, Cologne, 1979).

—— 'Zu Mahlers Komposition der Schlussszene von Goethes Faust', *Vom musikalischen Denken* (Schott, Mainz, 1985), 98–104.

—— 'Mahlers letztes Konzert in Berlin: unbekannte Briefe Mahlers', *Festschrift Rudolf Elvers zum 60. Geburtstag* (Schneider, Tutzing, 1985), 491–503.

—— (ed.), *Mahler-Interpretation: Aspekte zum Werk und Wirken von Gustav Mahler* (Schott, Mainz, 1985).

Storck, Karl, *Die Musik der Gegenwart* (Metzlersche Verlagsbuchhandlung, Stuttgart, 1922).

Storjohann, Helmut, 'Die formalen Eigenarten in den Sinfonien Gustav Mahlers', Ph.D. thesis (Hamburg, 1952).

Strauss, Richard, and Hofmannsthal, Hugo von, *Briefwechsel* (Atlantis, Zurich, 1952); English trans. Hans Hammelmann and Ewald Osers (Random House, New York, 1961).

—— and Rolland, Romain, *Correspondance: Fragments de Journal* (Albin Michel, Paris, 1951).

—— and Schalk, Franz, *Ein Briefwechsel*, ed. Günter Brosche (Schneider, Tutzing, 1983).

Stuppner, Hubert (ed.), *Mahler in Toblach, Mahler Festwoche 1981–1988* (Unicolpi, Milan, 1989).

Swarowsky, Hans, *Wahrung der Gestalt* (Universal Edition, Vienna, 1979).

Tarazona, Andres Ruiz, *Gustav Mahler: El cantor de la decadencia* (Real Musical, Madrid, 1974).

Thomas, Walter, *Richard Strauss und seine Zeitgenossen* (Langen-Müller, Munich, 1964).

Tibbe, Monika, *Über die Verwendung von Liedern und Liedelementen in instrumentalen Symphoniesätzen Gustav Mahlers* (Katzbichler, Munich, 1971).

Tischler, Hans, 'Die Harmonik in den Werken Gustav Mahlers', Ph.D. thesis (Vienna, 1937).

Trenner, Franz (ed.), *Richard Strauss: Dokumente seines Lebens und Schaffens* (Beck, Munich, 1954).

Unger, Anette, 'Zur Thematisierung von Welt, Leben und Kunst in der Musik: Gustav Mahlers III. Symphonie und Richard Strauss' Tondichtung "Also Sprach Zarathustra"', Ph.D. thesis (Rheinischen Friedrich-Wilhelms Universität, Bonn, 1990).

—— Welt, Leben und Kunst als Themen der 'Zarathustra-Kompositionen' von Richard Strauss and Gustav Mahler (Europäische Hochschulschrifter; Lang, Frankfurt, 1992).

Van Leeuwen, Jos (ed.), *Fragment Completion? Proceedings of the Mahler X Symposium, Utrecht 1986* (Universitaire Pers, Rotterdam, 1991).

—— *A 'Mass' for the Masses: Proceedings of the Mahler VIII Symposium, Amsterdam 1988* (Universitaire Pers, Rotterdam, 1992).

Vergo, Peter, *Art in Vienna 1898–1918: Klimt, Kokoschka, Schiele and their Contemporaries* (Phaidon, London, 1975).

Vestdijk, Simon, *Gustav Mahler: Over de Structuur van zijn symfonisch œuvre* (Bakker, The Hague, 1960).

Vignal, Marc, *Mahler* (Le Seuil, Paris, 1966; 2nd revised edn. 1977).

Vill, Suzanne, *Vermittlungsformen verbalisierter und musikalischer Inhalte in der Musik Gustav Mahlers* (Schneider, Tutzing, 1979).

Vogt, Matthias Theodor (ed.), *Das Gustav-Mahler-Fest Hamburg 1989, Bericht über den Internationalen Gustav-Mahler-Kongress* (Bärenreiter, Kassel, 1991).

Vondenhoff, Bruno, and Eleonore, *Gustav Mahler Dokumentation* (Schneider, Tutzing, 1978).

Vondenhoff, Eleonore, *Sammlung: Ergänzungsband zur Gustav Mahler Dokumentation* (Schneider, Tutzing, 1983).

Wagner, Cosima, *Briefwechsel mit Prinz Ernst zu Hohenlohe Langenburg* (Cotta, Stuttgart, 1937).

—— *Das zweite Leben: Briefe und Aufzeichnungen 1883–1930* (Piper, Munich, 1980).

Waissenberger, Robert, *Die Wiener Secession, 1897–1985* (Böhlhaus, Vienna, 1986).

Walker, Frank, *Hugo Wolf* (Knopf, New York, 1952).

Walter, Bruno, *Gustav Mahler* (1st edn. Reichner, Vienna, 1936; 2nd edn. Fischer, Berlin, 1957; 3rd edn., *Gustav Mahler: Ein Porträt*, Heinrichshofen, Wilhelmshaven, 1981; English trans. James Galston, with biographical essay by Ernst Krenek, Greystone, New York, 1941; revised, ed., and trans. by Lotte Walter Lindt, Knopf, New York, 1958).

—— *Thema und Variationen* (Fischer, Berlin, 1950; trans. James A. Galston, Knopf, New York, 1946).

—— *Briefe 1894–1962* (Fischer, Frankfurt, 1969).

Weber, Horst, *Alexander Zemlinsky* (Lafite, Vienna, 1977).

Weber, J. F., *Mahler: Discography Series* (Utica, New York, 1st edn. 1971; 2nd edn. 1974).

Weingartner, Felix, *Die Symphonie nach Beethoven* (Fischer, Berlin, 1898).

Wellesz, Egon, *Arnold Schoenberg* (Tal, Leipzig, 1921).

—— *Die neue Instrumentation* (2 vols., Hesse, Berlin, 1928).

Wellesz, Egon, and **Emmy,** 'Mahler', in Franz Endler (ed.), *Egon Wellesz, Leben und Werk* (Zsolnay, Vienna, 1981), 21–5.

Werba, Robert, 'Mahlers Mozart-Bild (I–VIII)', Mozartgemeinde, Wiener Figaro (Vienna, 1975–9).

—— 'Marginalien zum Theaterpraktiker Gustav Mahler: Aspekte seiner regielichen und dramaturgischen Tätigkeit an der Wiener Oper im Spiegel der Kritik', *Studia Musicologica Academiae Scientiarum Hungaricae*, 31 (Budapest, 1989), 371–88.

Wiesenthal, Grethe, *Der Aufstieg: Aus dem Leben einer Tänzerin* (Rowohlt, Berlin, 1919).

—— *Die ersten Schritte* (Rowohlt, Berlin, 1947), 181.

Wiesmann, Sigrid (ed.), *Gustav Mahler in Wien* (Belser, Stuttgart, 1976).

Williamson, John G., 'The Development of Mahler's Symphonic Technique with Special Reference to the Compositions of the Period 1899 to 1905', Ph.D. thesis (Liverpool, 1975).

Wilkens, Sander, *Gustav Mahlers Fünfte Symphonie: Quellen und Instrumentationprozess* (Peters, Frankfurt, 1989).

Williamson, John, 'Liszt, Mahler and the Chorale', *Proceedings of the Royal Musical Association*, 108 (1981–2), 115–25.

—— 'Deceptive Cadences in the last movement of Mahler's Seventh Symphony', *Sounding*, 9 (1982), 87–96.

—— 'The Structural Premises of Mahler's Introductions: Prolegomena to an Analysis of the First Movement of the Seventh Symphony', *Music Analysis*, 5: 1 (Mar. 1986), 29–57.

—— 'Mahler and Veni Creator Spiritus', *Music Review*, 44: 1 (Feb. 1983), 25–35.

Willnauer, Franz, *Gustav Mahler und die Wiener Oper. Wiener Themen* (Jugend und Volk, Vienna, 1979).

Wolf, Hugo, *Familienbriefe*, ed. Edmund Hellmer (Breitkopf & Härtel, Leipzig, 1912).

—— *Briefe an Heinrich Potpeschnigg*, ed. Heinz Nonveiller (Union Deutsche Verlagsgesellschaft, Stuttgart, 1912).

—— *Briefe an Melanie Köchert*, ed. Franz Grasberger (Schneider, Tutzing, 1964).

Worbs, Hans Christian, *Gustav Mahler* (Hesse, Berlin Halensee, 1960).

Zaccaro, Gianfranco, *Gustav Mahler: Studio per un'interpretazione* (Sansoni-Accademia, Milan, 1971).

Zuckerkandl, Bertha, *Ich erlebte fünfzig Jahre Weltgeschichte* (Bermann, Stockholm, 1939).

—— *Österreich intim* (Propyläen-Ullstein, Frankfurt, 1970).

Zweig, Stefan, *The World of Yesterday* (Viking Press, New York, 1943).

—— *Die Welt von Gestern* (Fischer, Berlin, 1977).

Zychowicz, James, 'Sketches and Drafts of Gustav Mahler 1892–1901: The Sources of the Fourth Symphony', Ph.D. thesis (3 vols., Univ. of Cincinnati, 1988).

—— (ed.), *The Seventh Symphony of Gustav Mahler: A Symposium* (Univ. of Cincinnati, 1990).

INDEX

Compiled by Frederick Smyth

An asterisk (*) denotes that the opera or other work concerned is described in the text as having been *conducted* by Mahler himself. Unless otherwise identified, it may be taken that a titled work listed under a composer's name is an opera. Page numbers in **bold type** indicate the more important references; 'q.' stands for 'quoted'.